D0842939

ENCYCLOPEDIA OF
POLITICS

The Left and The Right

ENCYCLOPEDIA OF
POLITICS

The Left and The Right

VOLUME 2: *The Right*

GENERAL EDITOR
Rodney P. Carlisle, Ph.D.
RUTGERS UNIVERSITY

SETON HALL UNIVERSITY
niversity Libraries So. Orange, NJ 07079-26

A SAGE Reference Publication

SAGE Publications
Thousand Oaks ■ London ■ New Delhi

OVERSIZE
JA
61
.E54
2005
v.2

Copyright © 2005 by Sage Publications, Inc.

All rights reserved. No part of this book may be reproduced or utilized in any form or by any means, electronic or mechanical, including photocopying, recording, or by any information storage and retrieval system, without permission in writing from the publisher.

Volume 1 Cover Photo: President Lyndon B. Johnson signs the Civil Rights Act of 1964 on July 2, 1964, as Martin Luther King, Jr. looks on. Credit: LBJ Library Photo by Cecil Stoughton.

Volume 2 Cover Photo: President Gerald Ford (center, right) and former presidential candidate Ronald Reagan (center, left) show solidarity at the Republican National Convention, August 19, 1976. Credit: Courtesy Gerald R. Ford Library.

For information:

 Sage Publications, Inc.
2455 Teller Road
Thousand Oaks, California 91320
E-mail: order@sagepub.com

Sage Publications Ltd.
1 Oliver's Yard
55 City Road
London EC1Y 1SP
United Kingdom

Sage Publications India Pvt. Ltd.
B-42, Panchsheel Enclave
Post Box 4109
New Delhi 110 017 India

Printed in the United States of America

Library of Congress Cataloging-in-Publication Data

Encyclopedia of politics: The left and the right / Rodney P. Carlisle, general editor.
    p. cm.
Includes bibliographical references and index.
ISBN 1-4129-0409-9 (cloth)
   1. Right and left (Political science)—Encyclopedias. 2. Political science—Encyclopedias.
I. Carlisle, Rodney P.
JA61.E54 2005
320'.03—dc22

                                                            2005002334

This book is printed on acid-free paper.

05 06 07 08 10 9 8 7 6 5 4 3 2 1

GOLSON BOOKS, LTD. STAFF:		SAGE PUBLICATIONS STAFF:	
President and Editor:	Geoff Golson	*Acquiring Editor:*	Rolf Janke
Managing Editor:	Laura Laurie	*Editorial Assistant:*	Sara Tauber
Design Director:	Kevin Hanek	*Production Editor:*	Denise Santoyo
Copy Editor and Proofreader:	Martha Whitt,	*Proofreader:*	Doris Hus
	Lori Kranz	*Production Artist:*	Michelle Lee Kenny
Indexer:	Gail Liss		

ENCYCLOPEDIA OF
POLITICS

VOLUME 2 CONTENTS
The Right

ALSO SEE VOLUME 1: *The Left*

The Right

Africa

IN A CONTINENT where conservative empires like Germany, which originally held today's Namibia and Tanzania (except for Zanzibar), Belgium, England, and France, it is interesting to note how two of the most important African countries clung to conservative ideologies after independence: Kenya and South Africa. Both are effective case studies of how assuming power can bring about extensive change in the tactics and ideology of a national independence movement.

Although the Mau Mau of Kenya, led by Jomo Kenyatta, committed many atrocities during the struggle for independence, it was not motivated by any real political ideology, like the communists who later fought the Portuguese in Angola and Mozambique, or would overthrow and kill Emperor Haile Selassie in Ethiopia. Kenyatta's struggle for independence was a purely pragmatic one, and did not embrace communism or any other leftist ideology. Though constitutionally a one-party state, Kenya conservatively planned its post-independence future under Kenyatta and his successor, Daniel arap Moi. According to the Kenyan government, "Kenya welcomed both private and government investment. Every farmer needed to be sure of his land rights, land consolidation, and land registration for title deeds. The government wanted to ensure that property was used in the mutual interest of the society and its mem-

bers. Varying forms of ownership were introduced to avoid concentration of economic power and a progressive system of taxation introduced to ensure an equitable distribution of wealth and income."

Politically, however, Kenya sided clearly with the democracies against regional terrorism, which began after the Arab defeat in the Middle East war of 1967. As Gordon Thomas writes, it was the Israeli Mossad that enlisted Kenya in the battle against the attempt by the Chinese communists to subvert Africa. The Chinese communists formed a direct threat to the moderate Kenyan government, and the Mossad gave the Kenyans vital information. It was in gratitude for this that arap Moi let the Israelis use Nairobi, the capital of Kenya, as a refueling stop in the epic Operation Thunderbolt in July 1976, the rescue of the Jewish hostages held by Arab terrorists in Idi Amin's anarchic Uganda.

After its declaration as the Union of South Africa in 1961, the Boer government entered into a bloody struggle against the left-leaning African National Congress (ANC), in which its BOSS intelligence service would become the most rightist and feared organization on the continent. Anti-terrorism brought South Africa and Israel into a natural alliance, fostered by Israel's Prime Minister Golda Meir. Both the ANC and the Palestine Liberation Organization (Israel's enemy) were ideological kinsmen, and a further diplomatic demarche would occur between South Africa's Prime

Minister P.W. Botha and Ezer Weizman that, according to Thomas, amounted to a mutual defense pact.

In September 1981, South Africa's Minister of Defense Magnus Malan asserted that "the onslaught here is communist-inspired, communist-planned, and communist-supported." Israel gave South Africa much aid in return for uranium destined for the Israeli nuclear research facility at Dimona in the Negev Desert. However, once the ANC assumed power in 1994 under Nelson Mandela, its political coloration significantly changed.

Executive Outcomes (EO) had been formed as a highly sophisticated rightist military organization by Eeben Barlow in 1989. This Outcomes group was recruited from former members of the South African Defense Force, or army, which was committed to battling the ANC. When Mandela became president in 1994, he did not disband Executive Outcomes. Instead, he used its soldiers to help bring stability to West Africa. With the help of EO, the Angolan government was able to defeat Jonas Savimbi's UNITA force in 1993. Only two years later, EO seriously mauled the terrorist forces of Foday Sankoh in Sierra Leone. However, due to diplomatic confusion, Sankoh would still remain in power for years, to die in United Nations custody in 2003 after his fall from power in 2000.

Mandela, rather than attempt to hold on to power as with many other African heads of state, voluntarily resigned from office in 1999 to be replaced as South African president by Thabo Mbeki. When widespread publicity focused on EO, it disbanded in 1999, but informed speculation holds that it has continued its mission under similar corporate entities like the Saracen or Lifeguard firms, and still is attempting to restore stability to post-independence Africa.

RIGHTIST REACTIONS

Much of the history of the right in Africa has to do with rightist reactions to leftist movements, whether legitimate (but Soviet-backed) independence movements or terrorist organizations. Moreover, during the 1960s, the newly emerging African states became increasingly embroiled in the Cold War between the United States and the Soviet Union. This was no more evident than in the Belgian Congo, which emerged as a free nation in June 1960. In October 1958, Patrice Lumumba had founded the Congolese National Movement (MNC), and became its first prime minister in June 1960. However, Lumumba began a flirtation with the Soviet Union, which threatened to bring the influence of the Soviet Premier Nikita Khrushchev directly into the

strategic heart of Africa. Lumumba was captured in a coup led by Colonel Sese Seko Mobutu. Under circumstances still unclear, Lumumba was assassinated in Elizabethville in January 1961. Although CIA complicity has been alleged by leftists, no evidence has come to light except through the prism of communist propaganda. Lumumba's death initiated a civil war that can stand as a microcosm of Africa's experience in the 1960s.

As a result of Lumumba's Marxist flirtation, Moishe Tshombe and the diamond-rich Katanga province seceded from the Congo. Backed by the Belgian Union Miniere company, Tshombe was able to hire white mercenaries, whose fighting skills were superior to the Congolese Army, really an armed police force. Forced into exile, Tshombe returned to serve as prime minister in July 1964. General Mobutu staged another military coup in November 1965. In July 1967 Tshombe was kidnapped and taken to Algeria, and died in prison of a heart attack two years later. Mobutu brought stability to a country ravaged by war and, except for an insurrection in 1978, governed for nearly three decades.

At the other end of the continent, another struggle became aggravated in South Africa. While it was the Union of South Africa, the dominant Afrikaans, or Boer, population, descended from 17th-century Dutch colonists, began to press for strict segregation of the races. The racism of the Boers had been the factor that set into motion one of the world's great independence movements. When Mahatma Gandhi lived in South Africa during the early years of the 20th century, the effect so traumatized him that he went home to free his India from the British rule that had tolerated such racism in South Africa.

As a result of apartheid segregation, the ANC was formed, with a strong communist coloration. Thus, the intense racist feeling of the Boers had brought into being a destabilizing communist movement in South Africa. The extreme right-wing National Party won in 1948, making apartheid the official policy of the country. The Union of South Africa became the Republic of South Africa on May 31, 1961, and left the British Commonwealth in the face of condemnation of its apartheid policies. For over 30 years, the struggle between the ANC and the apartheid regime would dominate South African life. The conflict was resolved relatively peacefully when apartheid was finally abolished when the ANC came to power in 1994.

South Africa was not alone in its rightist apartheid regimes. When Tanzania was formed in the 1960s,

Southern Rhodesia became the state of Rhodesia under Ian Smith, who followed the precedent of South Africa in creating a white-dominated African country. The *History of Rhodesia* recorded that Britain pushed for a constitutional reform of its colony that would grant the African population majority political representation. Ian Smith and the Southern Rhodesian parliament were unwilling to accept this and in 1965 unilaterally declared independence, the state now being called Rhodesia. Britain opposed this measure and negotiations continued; the Smith government drew support from South Africa's apartheid regime.

The negotiations with Britain failed in 1969, and the British Commonwealth decided to boycott Rhodesia; the country's athletes could not participate in Olympic Games, and many nations refused to trade with Rhodesia. In 1970, Rhodesia proclaimed the republic. The ZANU (Shona, led by Robert Mugabe) and ZAPU (Ndebele, led by Joshua Nkomo) organizations began to hurt Rhodesia by guerrilla raids from bases in Mozambique (which became independent in 1975, under a socialist regime). The situation became more and more difficult. In 1980, the Rhodesian administration agreed to general elections with African participation; Robert Mugabe's Zanu emerged victorious. The country was renamed Zimbabwe.

Yet the 1960s also saw the rupture of the most promising country in West Africa, Nigeria. In May 1967, the secessionist Republic of Biafra was proclaimed, largely to protect the Igbos, many of whom were Christians. By the time the war ended, according to the U.S. Library of Congress, "Estimates in the former Eastern Region of the number of dead from hostilities, disease, and starvation during the 30-month civil war are estimated at between 1 million and 3 million. The end of the fighting found more than 3 million Igbo refugees crowded into a 2,500-square-kilometer enclave. Prospects for the survival of many of them and for the future of the region were dim."

While the Cold War served to be the dominant factor affecting African nationalism in the 1970s, the continuing struggle in the Middle East reached out as well. In 1971, President Milton Obote of Uganda was toppled by Idi Amin Dada, who had begun his military career in the colonial British King's African Rifles (KAR), which had fought in the Mau Mau Emergency in Kenya. As the U.S. Library of Congress states, "presidents Julius Nyerere of Tanzania, Kenneth Kaunda of Zambia, Jomo Kenyatta of Kenya, and the Organization of African Unity (OAU) initially refused to accept the legitimacy of the new military government. Nyerere, in

particular, opposed Amin's regime, and he offered hospitality to the exiled Obote, facilitating his attempts to raise a force and return to power." The Amin regime, a return to the days when Ugandan (then Bugandan) kings persecuted Christians in the 19th century, would lead a reign of terror with his State Research Bureau (SRB) in which some 50,000 to 120,000 of his citizens may have perished. At the same time, he allied himself with the Palestinians, who had been fighting a war of terror against Israel since it defeated the Arab states in the Middle East war of June 1967. In this, he became allied with Colonel Muammar Quaddafi, who had seized power in Libya in 1962.

On June 24, 1976, the Palestinian and German terrorists hijacked an Air France jet to Entebbe airport in Uganda, with Israeli citizens aboard, apparently with the help of Amin. Negotiations were begun, including talks directly with Amin by Israeli Colonel Baruch Bar-Lev, who once had been a military adviser in Uganda. When the lives of the hostages seemed threatened, Israel launched Operation Thunderbolt, a daring rescue mission to save them. The success of the historic mission was helped by Kenya. Eventually, Amin's rule became a barbaric embarrassment for the neighboring African countries, especially Tanzania. When Amin used Libyan troops to attack Tanzania, Nyerere launched a counterstrike in April 1979 which drove Amin out of Uganda. Amin died in exile in Saudi Arabia in August 2003.

The Cold War, never far from the surface in Africa, became especially pointed in Somalia during the 1980s. Mohammed Siad Barre, dictator of Somalia, had launched in 1977 an invasion of the Ogaden Province in neighboring Ethiopia. The invasion would exacerbate a growing famine that plunged Somalia and Ethiopia into turmoil. Both the Soviet Union and the United States desired the Horn of Africa at Somalia because the nation that controlled the narrow Red Sea there would control the entire maritime traffic through the Red Sea to the Arabian Sea and beyond.

Barre remained in power by carefully balancing Soviet and American aid, but fell in a coup in 1991. The coup led to an internecine war among the powerful clans of Somalis, in which Mohammed Aidid eventually emerged as the paramount warlord.

DEMOCRACY OVER MARXISM

A major turn to democracy and the end of Marxist influence in East Africa came in October 1992 when Mozambique celebrated its first democratic elections in its history. With political stability came the hope of a free market economy to stimulate the hope of capitalist investment not only in Mozambique, but in the entire East African region.

As the millennium dawned in 2000, it brought mixed hope for stability in the African continent. Tragically, the Christian and Muslim strife in Nigeria only grew worse. Yet, in the area of the worst slaughter, Rwanda in the 1990s, there had already been signs of the rule of law. In 1996, the United Nations International Criminal Tribunal in Rwanda began hearing from conspirators in the massive bloodshed. At the same time, intervention by the British Paratroop Regiment finally brought peace to Sierra Leone. Edward Harris reported in *The Philadelphia Inquirer* that "prosecutors opened the first UN-backed war-crimes trial yesterday in Sierra Leone's vicious civil war, calling for a just accounting for the agony of 10 long years."

SEE ALSO

Volume 1 Left: Africa; Egypt; Socialism; Uganda.
Volume 2 Right: Capitalism; Globalization.

BIBLIOGRAPHY

"The Mau-Mau and the End of the Colony," www.kenyalogy.com (July 2004). Patrice Lumumba, www.sci.pfu.edu.ru (July 2004); Christopher Adams, "Sands of Time See Libya Join War on Terror," *Financial Times* (March 26, 2004); Joseph S. Nye, *Peace in Parts* (Rowman and Littlefield, 1987); Library of Congress Country Studies, www.lcweb2.loc.gov (July 2004); Obituary Foday Sankoh, July 31, 2003, www.guardian.co (July 2004); "Mobutu Sese Seko Dies at 66," Associated Press (September 1997); Edward Harris, "War-Crimes Trial in Sierra Leone Starts with Surprise," *Philadelphia Inquirer* (June 4, 2004); Bill Berkeley, *The Graves Are Not Yet Full* (Perseus, 2001); Karl Maier, *Into the House of the Ancestors: Inside the New Africa* (Wiley, 1998); Jimmy Carter, *Keeping the Faith* (Bantam, 1982).

JOHN F. MURPHY, JR.
AMERICAN MILITARY UNIVERSITY

Agrarianism

AGRARIANISM IS THE belief that true freedom belongs to the independent farmer who owns his or her own land. Only the yeoman farmer who can provide his own food from his own land remains truly independent and virtuous. Only the yeoman farmer truly has a stake in the land to defend it against attack in times of danger. Honest and incorruptible, independent farmers enjoy true freedom according to the agrarian view.

Agrarianism also harkens back to a more stable, settled social order of reciprocal social bonds that existed before the rise of cities and machines. Sir Roger de Coverley, a character from *The Spectator* by Joseph Addison and Richard Steele, exemplifies the best kind of paternalistic and rural values envisioned by many agrarians. James Everett Kibler's study of a South Carolina plantation, *Our Fathers' Fields*, offers a historical portrait of a similar society and its devastating encounter with modernity in the Civil War.

Thomas Jefferson is the foremost American exponent of agrarian ideals. Although Jefferson himself remained mired in debt for much of his adult life and relied upon slave labor, he wrote eloquently of the life of the yeoman farmer. In "Query XIX" of *Notes on the State of Virginia*, Jefferson wrote: "Those who labor in the earth are the chosen people of God ... whose breasts he has made his peculiar deposit for substantial and genuine virtue. Corruption of morals in the mass of cultivators is a phenomenon of which no age nor nation has furnished an example ... Dependence begets subservience and venality, suffocates the germ of virtue, and prepares fit tools for the designs of ambition." Many of Jefferson's political ideas grew from his agrarian views: in particular, his opposition to the commercial and political views of Alexander Hamilton. Hamiltonian attitudes would triumph in America with the defeat of the Confederacy in the Civil War.

In the 1920s and 1930s, a group of southern writers and academics attempted to revive the agrarian ideal. Allen Tate, Andrew Nelson Lytle, Donald Davidson, and nine other southerners contributed to *I'll Take My Stand*, which they termed an agrarian manifesto. They constructed an elegant appeal to America to return to a traditional economic and moral order, and wrote with a deeply felt love of history and tradition. Southern agrarians also harkened back to an idealized version of antebellum southern life. *I'll Take My Stand* condemned both industrialism and socialism as soulless and equally destructive of freedom and Western civilization. In particular, *I'll Take My Stand* attacked the idea of progress, especially the American idea of progress not toward a goal, but for its own sake. The kind of conservatism espoused by southern agrarians differs sharply from the conservatism of the Republican Party with its closeness to big business. Seven years after the publication of *I'll Take My Stand*, some of the same authors reunited for

Agrarian ideals harkened back to the days unspoiled by progress and were especially espoused by Thomas Jefferson. Southern agrarians in the United States conservatively reacted against modernity's social ills, such as poverty and alienation.

Who Owns America?, a volume of essays that condemned both communism and capitalism as threats to freedom. At its core, southern agrarianism was a reaction against modernity and all of modernity's attendant societal ills.

In the last decade of the 20th century, Victor Davis Hanson emerged as a leading defender of agrarian values. Hanson, a classics professor in California and a successful popular military historian, became a leading agrarian writer. Unlike the southern agrarians, Hanson wrote from the perspective of one born and reared on a farm, who witnessed the decline of small farming in America. Hanson also differs from the southern agrarians in his distaste for the Confederate States of America, an attitude in full flower in some of his writings on military history.

By the beginning of the 21st century, aspects of agrarianism appealed to elements on both the right and left of the American political spectrum. Although it shares with environmentalism a reverence for land, agrarianism differs from that movement in its reverence for a traditional political and moral order, and in its conservatism. Nowhere has it appeared as a practical political program with genuine support, nor is it likely to in a nation so comfortably wedded to machines and big government. Yet the agrarian life can still be appreciated through books, preferably read out-of-doors with a hound at one's side, and lived by those untroubled by fighting for a lost cause.

SEE ALSO
Volume 1 Left: Alienation; Communism; American Civil War; Jefferson, Thomas.
Volume 2 Right: American Civil War; Autarchy.

BIBLIOGRAPHY
Herbert Agar and Allen Tate, eds., *Who Owns America? A New Declaration of Independence* (Houghton Mifflin, 1936);

Eugene D. Genovese, *The Southern Tradition: The Achievement and Limitations of an American Conservatism* (Harvard University Press, 1994); Victor Davis Hanson, *Fields Without Dreams: Defending the Agrarian Idea* (The Free Press, 1996); Victor Davis Hanson, *The Land Was Everything: Letters From an American Farmer* (The Free Press, 2000); Thomas Jefferson, *Writings*, Merrill D. Peterson, ed. (Literary Classics of the United States, Inc., 1984); James Kibler and James Everett, *Our Father's Fields: A Southern Story* (Pelican Publishing Company, 2003); Mark G. Malvasi, *The Unregenerate South: The Agrarian Thought of John Crowe Ransom, Allen Tate, and Donald Davidson* (Louisiana State University Press, 1997); Paul V. Murphy, *The Rebuke of History: The Southern Agrarians and American Conservative Thought* (University of North Carolina Press, 2001); William A. Percy, *Lanterns on the Levee: Recollections of a Planter's Son* (Alfred A. Knopf, 1941); Ben Robertson, *Red Hills and Cotton: An Upcountry Memory* (University of South Carolina Press, 1960); Twelve Southerners, *I'll Take My Stand: The South and the Agrarian Tradition* (Harper, 1930).

MITCHELL MCNAYLOR
OUR LADY OF THE LAKE COLLEGE

Ali, Noble Drew (1886–1929)

NOBLE DREW ALI (born Timothy Drew), founder of the Moorish American Science Temple, was born in North Carolina. During the first decade of the 20th century, Ali migrated to Newark, New Jersey, where he preached the principles of a new black nationalism in homes and on the streets. Ali, a contemporary of Marcus Garvey, did not call for emigration to Africa by black Americans. Instead, he urged African Americans to become knowledgeable about their African heritage and to become Muslims to overcome racial oppression in the early 20th-century United States.

According to the teachings of the Moorish Science Temple, Drew, before changing his name, embarked on a pilgrimage to North Africa where he was given a mission by the King of Morocco to bring the teaching of Islam to African Americans. In order to prove he was the prophet of Allah, Drew had to pass a test. Drew was dropped inside the pyramids of Egypt and had to find his way out, which he did successfully, proving that he was indeed the prophet of Allah, or God. In 1913, Drew organized the Moorish Science Temple in Newark as the prophet of Allah, Nobel Drew Ali.

Ali taught his followers that African Americans were Asiatics, and specifically Moors who came from Morocco. According to Drew Ali, African Americans were "descendents of the ancient Moabites who inhabited the northwestern and southwestern shores of Africa." He believed that Islam was for people of African descent and Christianity was only for Europeans. He believed peace on earth would only come when each racial group had its own religion. Ali published his philosophy in a 64-page *Holy Koran*.

The Moorish Science Temple Holy Koran combined Ali's teachings with those of the Christian Bible, Garvey's African nationalism, and the Islamic Quran. He taught that North America was an extension of the African continent because Africans were enslaved and brought to North America. African Americans, he said, must refuse to be called Negro, black, colored, or Ethiopian. Instead, they must call themselves Asiatics, Moors, or Moorish Americans.

Members of the Moorish Science Temple pray facing the east three times a day, at sunset, noon, and sunrise. Members take the name El or Bey as their "free national name," much the same way that members of the Nation of Islam replace their Christian name with "X." They are also given a membership card, containing their name, which proclaims their honor for "the divine prophets, Jesus, Mohammad, Buddha, and Confucius," and which concludes with the declaration: "I am a citizen of the USA." Male members wear a red fez with a black tassel and are permitted to dress casually when not attending official functions. Female members wear long skirts or pants and a turban. The fez and turban are symbolic protection for the knowledge embodied by the membership. Marriages are monogamous and divorce is rarely permitted.

In addition to organizing temples throughout the northern and eastern United States, most prominently in Chicago, Illinois, and Detroit, Michigan, Ali established collectively owned small businesses. Some of Ali's subordinates exploited these businesses for financial gain. When Ali attempted to intervene, a power struggle ensued. In 1929, a splinter faction leader, Sheik Claude Greene, was shot to death in Chicago. Although Ali was not in Chicago at the time of the shooting, he was arrested and charged with Greene's murder. Ali was later released on bond. A few weeks after his release in 1929, Ali died of suspicious causes. Many believe he either died of injuries inflicted by the police or he was murdered by followers of Greene.

After Ali's death, John Givens El in Chicago, Illinois, and Master Fard Muhammad in Detroit, Michigan, claimed each to be Ali reincarnated. Those who followed John Givens El are present-day members of the Moorish American Science Temple. Those who followed Master Fard Muhammad, who disappeared in 1933, joined Elijah Muhammad, who founded the Nation of Islam in Chicago in 1934.

Ali, like many other black nationalists in the United States, rejected the liberal doctrine of racial integration and sought to build a separate black identity. To the extent that his movement was social and political rather than religious, it can be said to fall in the category of a nationalistic doctrine, generally regarded as conservative or right-wing in nature. Although hostile to the exploitation of black Americans by U.S. institutions, Ali never offered a radical or left-wing challenge to those institutions.

SEE ALSO

BIBLIOGRAPHY

Clifton E. Marsh, *From Black Muslims to Muslims: The Resurrection, Transformation, and Change of the Lost-Found Nation of Islam, 1930–95* (Scarecrow Press, 1996); E.U. Essien-Udom, *Black Nationalism: A Search for an Identity in America* (University of Chicago Press, 1962); Gilles Kepel, *Allah in the West: Islamic Movements in America and Europe* (Stanford University Press, 1997).

JAMES WERTZ
AMERICAN UNIVERSITY

American Civil War

THE POLITICAL RIGHT during the Civil War was generally (and derisively) known as Copperheads. The origins of this political group stem from a variety of sources. With the start of the Civil War in 1861 and the election of the Republican Abraham Lincoln, many former Democrats and some Republicans believed that civil war and violent confrontation were unnecessary. In the days leading up to Fort Sumter (April 1861), tensions had escalated within the political realm. Lincoln had discussed at his inaugural address maintaining the status quo on the issue of slavery while also criticizing the seceded states, those that had left the Union to protest the election of an abolitionist Republican, for having committed an unconstitutional act. Lincoln had no alternative but to engage in military confrontation to restore the Union. Clearly, Lincoln was stuck between a rock and a hard place. As Lincoln sent relief supplies to Fort Sumter on that fateful April morning, the Copperheads criticized the president for provoking this phase of the war. To many Copperheads like Clement Vallandigham, Lincoln's policies were leading the country to a violent war. Many believed that Lincoln should have done more in the early stages of the war.

Thus the conservatives within the political spectrum were from the outset extremely critical of Lincoln's provocatory policies. At the initiation of the war, their criticisms continued unabated. Vallandigham constantly derided the president as being an extreme radical who did not believe in peace. One of Lincoln's greatest debacles for the right was his suspension of the writ of habeas corpus. This writ essentially guaranteed those who are put in jail the opportunity to hear the charges against them within 48 hours. The goal of this writ was to limit the powers of the federal government in holding prisoners indefinitely. As a result of widespread political opposition, specifically, Maryland was the site in 1861 of pro-secessionist violence that had as its mark the president.

After a legislature defeated Maryland's secession, Lincoln suspended the writ to ensure the defeat of the anti-secessionist movement. In the fall of 1861, the pro-Confederate mayor of Baltimore and 19 state legislators were jailed and held indefinitely. This action angered many "peace Democrats" who believed that Lincoln had overstepped his political powers.

Another issue that many on the right criticized Lincoln about was his view on emancipation. Lincoln was essentially a moderate on the issue of slavery. Like many Republicans, he viewed slavery as an evil but he did not want to eliminate it from the states where it already existed. His desire was not to allow the incoming states to enter the Union as slave states. Lincoln's basic view was that the war was about maintaining the integrity of the Union. This view changed in 1862. Many slaves had escaped to the North. In March 1862, Congress passed a law that did not allow for the return of fugitive slaves. After the Battle of Antietam, Lincoln opted for emancipation, believing that this act would garner support in the North by putting the war on a moral footing. According to the Emancipation Proclamation, the states that did not return to the Union risked the emancipation of their slave labor force.

Southerners denounced the policy as hypocritical because Lincoln could not free property or individuals that were not in his control.

Copperheads viewed the Emancipation Proclamation as further proof that Lincoln's aim was to free the slaves and he was willing to risk military conflict to achieve these aims. In the election of 1864, Lincoln's popularity was extremely low, as many viewed the war at this point as unnecessary. The Democrats nominated former Union General George B. McClellan. McClellan, at the Democratic Convention in Chicago, pledged a peace platform that demanded the end of all hostilities and that the federal union be restored. McClellan, as a member of the Lincoln opposition, was out for revenge against the president, who had fired McClellan two years earlier. Democrats published specious cartoons, spreading rumors and semi-obscene poems suggesting that Lincoln possibly had black ancestry.

In the end, Lincoln won the election, winning 55 percent of the vote with a triumph in the Electoral College by winning 212 to 21 over McClellan. In Congress, the Democratic right lost positions, including in the Senate. It was clear that the messages of the right, anti-war, and anti-Lincoln position simply did not resonate among the American electorate. As the Civil War ended in 1865, the Copperheads had been politically defeated and discredited.

SEE ALSO

Volume 1 Left: American Civil War; Lincoln, Abraham. *Volume 2 Right:* Republican Party; Lincoln Abraham.

BIBLIOGRAPHY

Bruce Catton, *The Civil War* (Houghton Mifflin, 1985); James McPherson, *Abraham Lincoln and the Second American Revolution* (Oxford University Press, 1990); Mark Neely, *The Fate of Liberty: Abraham Lincoln and the Promise of America* (Oxford University Press, 1993).

JAIME RAMÓN OLIVARES, PH.D.
HOUSTON COMMUNITY COLLEGE, CENTRAL

American Conservative Union

THE AMERICAN Conservative Union (ACU) organization began its career as the conservative watchdog for the nation in 1964 in response to the conservatives' widespread loss of power in the national political arena.

Founded in December 1964 by such figures as Frank S. Meyer, William F. Buckley, Jr., and Robert E. Bauman (organizer of the first meeting), the ACU sought to create a vehicle for the ideas and concepts of the conservative right. The mission of the new organization was (and is) threefold: "Consolidate the overall strength of the American conservative movement through unified leadership and action, mold public opinion, and stimulate and direct responsible political action." During the first several meetings, the new group appointed a 50-member board of directors, including those from the first organizational meeting as well as Lammot Copeland, Peter O'Donnell, John A. Howard, Congressman Donald C. Bruce of Indiana (elected as the first chairman), and John Dos Passos.

Within the month, the group had raised $350,000 as operating capital, decided on its first political actions, and announced itself to the media. Within nine months, the membership reached 7,000, and the new lobby group removed itself from other, more militant conservative groups such as the John Birch Society. Wanting the support of the conservative majority, the ACU stipulated in its bylaws that it welcomed the support of those willing to participate in only "responsible political action."

Over the next seven years, membership in ACU fluctuated but finally reached 45,000 by the end of 1972, and its political activity and affiliations were often front-page news. Among its affiliations, the ACU began establishing a network of local groups under the program Action Now. These groups, or clubs, promoted conservative political action by the members and soon led to state affiliates. This program and the state clubs are still a strong part of the ACU. Another affiliation the organization undertook in its first years, the merger with Public Action Incorporated, provided the impetus for its registration with the government as a lobbyist.

Other landmark events at this time included the launch of the ACU's first publication, the *Republican Report*, which covered the internal affairs of the Republican Party. By 1971, the *Report* had changed its name to *Battleline*, published in 2004 in electronic format. Once it had established its basic foundation and garnered national support, the ACU started making forays in the national political picture: passing resolutions to reject federal government nominees who did not follow their conservative platforms, sending representatives to the national Republican conventions where they influenced the party votes, and endorsing those political nominees who proposed a conservative agenda. These types of activities firmly established the ACU's political influence and enabled it to create the Conservative Victory Fund, a fund used in contributing to the campaigns of many conservative electoral candidates.

From these successful beginnings, the American Conservative Union has grown into one of the the the most influential lobbying groups in the national government. ACU has worked diligently to fulfill its purpose to promote capitalism, educate the public on what it believes to be the founding fathers' intent in the Constitution and the Bill of Rights, instill confidence in the conservative ideal of moral values, and support a strong national defense. The ACU has worked to influence major national policy, including battling the Occupational Safety and Health Administration, opposing the Strategic Arms Limitation Treaties, supporting anti-Marxist revolutionaries in foreign countries, and promoting the need for American deployment of its strategic defenses.

As a lobbying organization, the ACU is known for its rating of members of Congress. Annually, the ACU publishes a list of all members of the U.S. Senate and House of Representatives, rating each on his or her adherence to the principles of the conservative philosophy based on votes on all major issues. These ratings find their way into political campaigns and are frequently quoted in the media.

Consistently upholding its original Statement of Principles, the American Conservative Union has taken a strong lead in American politics, supported by a nationwide membership and the strong financial backing of its members. With each new administration, the ACU establishes a relationship with the new president, either supporting or fighting presidential public policies. Presidents, senators, and representatives often find themselves caught in the scrutiny of this most conservative of organizations, and the ACU seems intent on maintaining that power.

SEE ALSO

Volume 1 Left: American Civil Liberties Union; Lobbying. *Volume 2 Right*: Buckley, William F., Jr.; Lobbying.

BIBLIOGRAPHY

"Battleline," www.conservative.org (v.11, 1977); "ACU Commercial Too 'Controversial' for TV," *Human Events* (v.50/31, 1994); Ralph Z. Hallow, "Parties Gravitate to Center during Bush Presidency: Lawmakers Lose Conservative Tag," *Washington Times* (January 20, 2004).

GLORIA J. HICKS
UNIVERSITY OF WYOMING

American Enterprise Institute

THE AMERICAN ENTERPRISE Institute for Public Policy Research is a very influential Washington, D.C.-based think tank. Founded in 1943, the American Enterprise Institute (AEI) defines itself as a "private, nonpartisan research institution dedicated to the principle that the competition of ideas is fundamental to a free society." Although the institute is nonpartisan in the sense that both Republicans and Democrats have served on its staff, participated in its programs, or used its resources, the institute consistently reflects a conservative perspective and proposes conservative solutions to policy questions.

From its beginnings as a center for economic studies, AEI has broadened its research to include many of the critical political and social issues confronting U.S. society. In 2004, AEI defined itself as an organization "dedicated to preserving and strengthening the foundations of freedom—limited government, private enterprise, vital cultural and political institutions, and a strong foreign policy and national defense—through scholarly research, open debate, and publications."

One important goal of AEI is to influence the formulation of U.S. government policies, both domestic and foreign. To that end, the AEI conducts research and provides analysis and publications on topics that affect the American people and the U.S. global position. The subjects studied and discussed by the AEI cover a wide range. For example, in the 1980s, fellows at AEI debated questions such as "With the trade deficit of the United States growing and the less-developed countries of the world facing unprecedented debt, how should U.S. policy respond?" or "How can public policy help to achieve a balance between an ensured level of quality in the nation's healthcare and an acceptable cost for providing it?" and "How has the increased power of the media influenced American society?"

Under the stewardship of AEI President William J. Baroody, the think tank grew exponentially in the 1970s. Thanks in part to increased financial donations from U.S. corporations, the number of AEI scholars grew from 12 "resident thinkers" to 145 well-funded resident scholars, 80 adjunct scholars, and a large support staff. The ability of the AEI to influence public and government opinion increased as well.

Over the years, AEI has established a variety of means to communicate its findings to the public and government officials. AEI research fellows publish their studies in books and pamphlets; they appear on talk shows; and they meet with and/or provide their analysis to members of Congress, government agencies, and the press. Between 1943 and 1983, AEI published roughly 1,000 titles; in 1983–84 alone, AEI published 78 titles. In 1972, 96 U.S. senators and 391 representatives received AEI publications. AEI has sponsored public debates on television, including the show *Rational Debate*, which began in 1966; 145 radio stations transmitted AEI debates in the 1970s. In the 1966–67 program, one debate was on "Law, Order and Civil Disobedience," and featured the Reverend William Sloane Coffin and former U.S. Supreme Court Justice Charles E. Whittaker. In the 1971–72 program, Senator James L. Buckley and Paul Warnke debated "Strategic Sufficiency: Fact or Fiction?" AEI's magazine, *The American Enterprise*, is available on the internet.

The relationship between conservative sectors and individuals within the U.S. government and AEI is a close one; in fact, some individuals shuttle between the two bodies. President Gerald Ford was a distinguished fellow at AEI, and maintained an office there in the 1970s and 1980s. AEI fellow Jeanne Kirkpatrick distinguished totalitarian governments (the Soviet Union) from authoritarian ones (apartheid South Africa and the Pinochet regime in Chile), the former being unacceptable to the United States and the latter two being acceptable since they opposed communism. Kirkpatrick became President Ronald Reagan's U.S. Permanent Representative to the United Nations in the 1980s. Richard Perle, former assistant secretary of defense for international security policy in the Reagan administration and a former member of the Defense Policy Board at the Department of Defense, became a resident fellow at AEI in 2004.

Distinguished members of the academic community serve as advisers or work as researchers at AEI. For example, Milton Friedman, the eminent professor of economics at the University of Chicago, was on AEI's Academic Advisory Board in the 1970s. AEI researchers possess expertise in their particular fields of research, publish prolifically, and frequently appear in public forums expressing their opinions.

One reason why the AEI is so visible, productive, and influential is that it is very well funded. The AEI Board of Trustees is composed primarily of corporate executives, and many U.S. corporations have generously donated millions of dollars to support the work of the institute. According to a media watchdog group, between 1992 and 1994 AEI received almost $7 million to finance its work.

By 2004 the number of scholars working at AEI had risen to close to 70. Among their numbers are Lynne Cheney, wife of Vice President Dick Cheney; Newt Gingrich, former Republican representative from Georgia and Speaker of the House from 1995 to 1999; Jeanne Kirkpatrick; Michael Novak, who is also a member of the Board of the National Endowment for Democracy; and Christina Hoff Sommers, the anti-feminist author of *Who Stole Feminism?* and *The War Against Boys*. Many of AEI's scholars are ideologically neoconservative and helped to develop the arguments that led to the George W. Bush administration's 2003 attack on Iraq.

SEE ALSO
Volume 1 Left: Think Tanks; Democratic Party.
Volume 2 Right: Think Tanks; Ideology; Bush, George W.

BIBLIOGRAPHY
American Enterprise Institute (AEI, 1976 and 1977 editions); American Enterprise Institute, *Annual Report 1983–84* (AEI, 1984); American Enterprise Institute, www.aei.org (May 2004); Media Transparency, www.mediatransparency.org (May 2004).

MARGARET POWER
ILLINOIS INSTITUTE OF TECHNOLOGY

American Liberty League

THE AMERICAN Liberty League (ALL) existed a short six years, from 1934 until 1940, but still managed to find a place in the history books. The national depression of the 1930s gave rise to many types of organized groups, for example lobbyists, labor unions, coalitions, and cooperatives, all with the same general goal: relief from the effects of the depressed economic situation following the market crash of 1929. ALL was the one conservative group that lobbied for less government interference, less legislation, and less federal funding. Chartered on August 15, 1934, ALL largely consisted of a group of successful businessmen, ones who might have had the most to fear from Franklin D. Roosevelt's New Deal policies.

Funded by the Du Pont family, Alfred P. Sloan (president of General Motors), and other powerful figures, the league could afford to offer no-fee memberships to the public and support activities often denied other groups whose membership lacked big-business support.

In a speech given by Jouett Shouse on September 7, 1934, over national radio, ALL presented its principles, aims, and reasoning for its existence. First and foremost among the themes touted by the league was an opposition to government interference in business and the protection of individual liberties. Its principles were threefold: to "defend and uphold the constitution of the United States ... to teach the necessity of respect for the rights of persons and property as fundamental to every successful form of government ... teach the duty of government to encourage and protect individual and group initiative and enterprise, to foster the right to work, earn, save, and acquire property, and to preserve the ownership and lawful use of property when acquired." ALL also proclaimed that it was not anti-Roosevelt, was nonpartisan, and was dedicated to helping the national administration guide the country back to economical stability.

From the beginning, the American Liberty League utilized the popular press and radio for its educational programs and to lobby for and against proposed legislation and policies. Although self-proclaimed as nonpartisan, the league's first officers were all opposed to the New Deal, and by the beginning of 1936, it was recognized as one of the most conservative groups in the nation. During the first two years of its existence, ALL became the spokesman for the floundering Republican Party, and the national press looked to it for a conservative and opposing view to New Deal policies.

These first two years of its existence were not only the league's most visual but also the most influential. Appealing to Congress numerous times to oppose those measures and policies that, in its estimation, threatened either the Constitution or property rights or both, ALL often provided the arguments that mitigated federal spending and New Deal legislation. In 1935, the league rallied around Al Smith when he decided to run against Roosevelt for the Democratic nomination. However, Smith refused the offer of such support, fearing that the reputation of ALL would hurt his chances, but his refusal didn't help him attain the nomination. Roosevelt was the Democrats' choice. The league turned to the Republican nominee for president, Alf Landon. However, ALL's fervent and antagonistic attacks on Roosevelt and the New Deal became such an embarrassment that the recovering Republican Party refused the organization's advocacy. But by this time, the American Liberty League had declared for Landon and publicized its anti-New Deal and anti-Roosevelt stance through propaganda, with claims of the unconstitutionality of much of the New Deal legislation. Many in the

Republican Party, including Landon, felt that their devastating loss in the November election was due in large part to the league.

In November 1936, Roosevelt carried all but two states, and the American Liberty League never recovered. Within four years, ALL disbanded. Many historians and analysts, searching for the reasons for the organization's inability to do more damage to Roosevelt and his New Deal policies, believe that the league's members and officers lacked a real understanding of the political and economic climate. Their belief in American rugged individualism and the platform of the "American dream" could not provide the relief or recovery the nation sorely needed.

SEE ALSO
Volume 1 Left: Roosevelt, Franklin D.; New Deal.
Volume 2 Right: Republican Party; *Laissez-Faire*.

BIBLIOGRAPHY
George Wolfskill, *The Revolt of the Conservatives: A History of the American Liberty League, 1934–40* (Houghton Mifflin, 1962); Frederick Rudolph, "The American Liberty League, 1934–1940," *The American Historical Review* (v.56/1, October 1950); Alan Brinkley, "The Problem of American Conservatism," *The American Historical Review* (v.99/2, April 1994):;"Liberty League," *The Reader's Companion to American History* (Houghton Mifflin, 1991).

GLORIA J. HICKS
UNIVERSITY OF WYOMING

American Party

THE AMERICAN PARTY, more commonly known as the Know-Nothings, was a nativist political party existing from 1853 to 1856. In that time, the party claimed 1.25 million members and was successful in electing many of its candidates to both state and national office. The party put forth Millard Fillmore as its presidential candidate in the election of 1856. Fillmore pulled in eight electoral votes and 874,534 popular votes.

The party began as a secret society in 1850, known as the Order of the Star Spangled Banner (OSSB), founded in New York City, a hub of immigration. The society's members took an oath of secrecy, agreeing to conceal the party's existence. Members pledged to use their votes to remove political power from immigrants and the politicians who courted them. By 1853, the society was no longer secret and became openly known as the Know-Nothings due to its members' legendary claim that they knew nothing of such an organization. In 1855, due to internal disputes, many Know-Nothings left the party and joined the newly organized Republicans. Those who remained reorganized and became known as the American Party.

At its inception, the original Know-Nothing Party organized against the boom of immigration. From 1845 to 1854, almost 3 million immigrants came into the United States, making up 14.5 percent of the total American population, the highest proportion in American history. Over 40 percent of these immigrants were Irish Catholic, a religion that many Americans considered at odds with the principles of liberty and equality. The Know-Nothings believed fiercely that Protestantism defined American society through its emphasis on individuality and democratic congregations. The system of hierarchy and autocracy within the Catholic Church seemed to challenge the very foundation of American government. Know-Nothings accused the Catholic Church of discouraging individuality and Bible reading, as well as the possibility of having a personal relationship with God, all of which were values they believed the founders held dear. They also believed that the Catholic system of intercession and hierarchy subverted the political system because priests held an enormous amount of power over their congregations in elections. This system, the Know-Nothings held, allowed a minority to wield disproportionate power.

The party is best known for its opposition to immigrant voting power. Its best-known slogan was "Americans Must Rule America." Know-Nothing ideology held that professional politicians actively pursued the votes of ignorant immigrants. These demagogues lacked the virtue of the founding fathers, putting party interests before those of the nation.

The party structure needed to be dismantled in order to reestablish traditional political values. Specifically, the party proposed an extension of the naturalization period from five to 21 years and a permanent prohibition on the appointment of any foreign-born individual to political office. Know-Nothings also embraced temperance legislation, blaming alcohol consumption for immigrant immorality.

Few Know-Nothings proposed a restriction or end to immigration. Most party leaders only wished to keep the immigrant population politically powerless until individuals were fully Americanized. Their fear was that the founders' vision was being perverted due to party

The American Party, or Know-Nothings, ran conservative Millard Fillmore for president in the 1856 election.

corruption and immigration. Their conservatism rested on a desire to return to the country's early days when political leaders valued virtue and true republicanism.

Practical interests also motivated the nativism in the Know-Nothing Party. Immigrants, party members argued, stole jobs from native-born Americans because they worked for very low wages and glutted the job market. This issue gave the party urban appeal. The party also appealed to rural Americans because of its anti-slavery platform.

Slavery, like Catholicism, was tyrannical and threatened the future of the United States. Both slaveholders and Catholics would never be satisfied with a stagnant existence. Both wished to expand until their interests dominated American society. Slavery, the party argued, disrupted the existence of individualism and economic opportunity. Because of this disruption, slavery could not be allowed to spread to new territories. Its anti-slavery platform allowed many members of the Know-Nothing Party to be quietly absorbed by the Republican Party after 1855.

SEE ALSO

Volume 1 Left: Progressive Party; Democratic Party.
Volume 2 Right: Republican Party; Conservatism; United States.

BIBLIOGRAPHY

Taylor Anbinder, *Nativism and Slavery: The Northern Know-Nothings and the Politics of the 1850s* (Oxford University Press, 1992); Stephen E. Maizlish, "The Meaning of Nativism and the Crisis of the Union: The Know-Nothing Movement in the Antebellum North," *Essays on American Antebellum Politics, 1840–60* (Texas A&M University Press, 1982).

STEPHANIE R. ROLPH
MISSISSIPPI STATE UNIVERSITY

American Revolution

THE AMERICAN REVOLUTION, as an intellectual, social, political, and military event, can be understood as having begun in 1763 and ended with the inauguration of George Washington as the first president under the federal Constitution in 1789. Although it had extensive democratizing effects, those were largely unanticipated and unintended; the Revolution should be understood as essentially conservative in nature.

In the main, the Revolution arose out of the British government's attempts to govern its enormous empire more rationally, and to spread its burdens more equitably, after the Seven Years' War. The British victory in that first world war, with the acquisition of an enormous amount of New World territory from France, came at a substantial price. From the point of view of cash-strapped Britons, one logical response loomed: to tax the colonists more. In addition, the newly won territories would be governed on liberal lines and an effort would be made to head off further difficulties with the American Indians.

Colonists in 13 of Britain's 26 New World colonies resisted and/or resented attempts to implement these new policies. Thus, for example, Pontiac's Rebellion in 1763 led to the establishment of a western boundary to colonial expansion at the peaks of the Appalachian Mountains. Members of elites in all the mainland colonies, who had invested in land titles in areas now closed to them indefinitely, lamented this policy. Beginning with the Sugar Act of 1764, Parliament attempted to tax the colonists.

From the beginning, colonists believed that the new vector of British policy deprived them of two of their most significant rights: the right to be taxed only by their own representatives and the right to trial by jury. In the same year, the Currency Act extended the prohibition on New England legislatures' printing of legal tender notes to all of the North American colonies. Protests against these measures tended to stress Britons' inherited rights, not to stake out some ideal argument for the perfection of society. James Otis's 1764 pamphlet, *The Rights of the British Colonies Asserted and Proved*, typified colonial answers to the new departure of the British government in insisting that the colonists had brought with them to North America all of the rights of Englishmen. Patrick Henry, in his first term as a burgess, sponsored resolutions making similar claims through the Virginia General Assembly in 1765. These arguments against British policy were conservative in that they attempted to preserve the colonial assemblies' traditional prerogatives.

The potential explosiveness of colonial resistance to British policy received its first illustration in the wake of the Stamp Act, which Parliament adopted March 22, 1765. In that law, Parliament undertook to tax various types of products in the colonies, including legal paper, newsprint, playing cards, dice, and a number of other items and types of documents. Parliament dispatched paper to all of the colonies and named stamp agents throughout its New World empire, but the Stamp Act proved to be a revenue loser. Through physical intimidation by groups such as Samuel Adams's Boston "Sons of Liberty," the colonists forced stamp agents to resign in most colonies without the distribution of any stamped paper; the act's costs far exceeded the revenue it yielded. In the end, Parliament saw the futility of its measure and repealed it.

By the time it did so, however, it had adopted the Quartering Act, which required the colonists to provide various types of material to support the armed forces quartered in them. More on this score would follow. The push to repeal the Stamp Act yielded strident debate within and outside the House of Commons. Outside Parliament, Thomas Whately asserted in 1765 that while the colonists might not actually be represented in Parliament, they benefited from "virtual representation." American colonists hooted this assertion down.

The first official congress of representatives from the American colonies issued its declaration October 19, 1765. This Stamp Act Congress, with delegates from nine colonies, assigned the task of drafting a statement of its position to Pennsylvanian John Dickinson, who would stake out a position as a conservative defender of colonial liberties. The Stamp Act Congress began by avowing that it loved the royal dynasty and conceding that colonists owed all the duties owed by subjects in Great Britain; it then said that colonists insisted on all the rights of subjects in Great Britain, and noted that because of the distance separating North America from the mother country, the right not to be taxed without representation amounted to the right of colonists to be taxed only by the colonial assemblies.

Within Parliament, opponents of repeal insisted that the principle of Parliament's power to tax the colonists must not be surrendered. Thus, the act's repeal came in tandem with adoption of the Declaratory Act of March 18, 1766, Parliament's assertion of a right to legislate for the colonies "in all cases whatsoever."

While this debate went on, Sir William Blackstone published his *Commentaries on the Laws of England*, which was destined to become the foremost book in English legal history. There, Blackstone asserted that since Parliament was sovereign, Parliament's decisions could not be appealed. In addition, he said that sovereignty was indivisible; this assertion would have great repercussions for America, because it meant that Parliament could not simultaneously adhere to Blackstone's theory of sovereignty and concede that only the colonial legislatures could tax the colonists.

BURGESS RICHARD BLAND

Partially in response to Blackstone, Burgess Richard Bland of Virginia published his masterwork "An Enquiry into the Rights of the British Colonies" in 1766. Here, for the first time, Bland laid out the theory of colonial history that would underlie the Declaration of Independence 10 years later.

According to Bland, the American colonists had come to North America in pursuit of their natural right to emigrate. Having done so, they had entered into a state of nature, and then had created new societies in the way described by John Locke in his *Second Treatise: On Civil Government*. Having created new societies, Bland said, the colonists were free to invite the English monarchs to be their monarchs too, which they did; having selected the English monarchs for their own purposes, the Americans then remained free to defy them anytime their performance of their role proved unsatisfactory.

Bland's account of colonial history, building on his and other Virginia pamphleteers' earlier writings concerning the Old Dominion's history, was by turns at variance with the standard British account, inconsistent with the actual histories of various of the British colonies, or both. It also provided a theoretical jumping-off point for independence.

At the end of his life, Thomas Jefferson noted that Bland, whom he called the foremost constitutional authority he had ever known, had been the first to see the true situation of the Americans and put it into print. Virtually no one wanted independence in 1766, but Jefferson ultimately would base his argument of 1776 on Bland's of a decade earlier. In 1765, New York's assembly refused to comply with the Quartering Act lest it establish a precedent for indirect taxation of the colonists by Parliament. In 1767, still intent on extracting revenue from its North American possessions, Parliament adopted the Townshend Acts. Named for the Chancellor of the Exchequer, these acts placed new taxes on glass, tea, painter's colors, various kinds of lead, and paper imported into the colonies. Colonial anger flared again.

From 1767 to 1768, John Dickinson published his *Letters from a Farmer in Pennsylvania*, in which he laid out a classic argument for American assemblies' rights. Accepting the rationale of the New York assembly's refusal to abide by the Quartering Act and finding that law's effect congruent to the effect of the Stamp Act, Dickinson cautioned that "a dreadful stroke is aimed at the liberty of these colonies." He insisted that all the colonies were affected, "for the cause of one is the cause of all." The point at which Parliament could tax colonists without their consent, he said, would be the day they were unfree. "We are taxed without our own consent," he argued. "We are therefore SLAVES." In 1768, Parliament tried stationing troops in Boston to cow that most resistant of American cities. Americans, for their part, responded with nonimportation and petitions. Everybody of any consequence in England, from the king to the House of Lords, the House of Commons to various bishops, received public protests from the Americans in these days. When, in 1770, a detachment of British soldiers harassed by a Boston mob finally fired upon them, American propagandists dubbed the shootings "the Boston Massacre," and word circulated that further outrages were contemplated.

The ungovernable Americans continued to insist on receiving the benefits of empire free; the British authorities persisted in wanting nothing of it. In 1773, Parliament adopted a Tea Act giving the East India Company trade privileges, and thus an enormous price advantage, in America. Massachusetts radicals said that Parliament's motive was to coax Americans into paying a tax on the tea by offering them tea at a lower price; their answer to the Tea Act was the Boston Tea Party (1773), in which a large quantity of the valuable leaf was dumped into Boston Harbor. Boston's radical leadership would not see any taxes paid to Britain, come hell or high water.

Parliament, in a fit of ill-considered anger, overreacted to the Tea Party by adopting the Intolerable Acts. Here was the fulfillment of the nightmare long at the back of Puritan New England's collective mind: the Massachusetts charter revised, the port of Boston closed, trials of British officials charged with murder to occur outside New England, and a new Quartering Act further burdening colonists with their own oppression.

Again, the point of the resistance was colonists' insistence on their inherited rights, coupled in the New England colonies with a sense that their societies' historic mission was imperiled. This feeling gained reinvigoration when the colonies received word of the Quebec Act, a very reasonable measure adopted by Parliament to provide for the government of Britain's French subjects in Québec. How could Catholics be allowed by a British king and Parliament to keep their Catholicism, and with tax support? How could the unrepublican political culture of Québec be left essentially intact? Solipsistic New England understood the Québec Act as part of Satan's mission to expunge the True Religion (read: New England's) from the earth.

FIRST CONTINENTAL CONGRESS

In 1774, resistance leaders organized the first Continental Congress. Its majority remained decidedly moderate and monarchist, but here was a first step along the road to some kind of continental government. Thomas Jefferson, a young Virginian, rose to prominence with his proposed set of instructions to Virginia's first congressmen, "A Summary View of the Rights of British America." There, in language far more confrontational, he told King George the story of America's founding first adumbrated by Bland in his "Enquiry" nearly a decade before.

Congress did not go that far, but it did adopt a new Continental Association as an economic weapon, with nonconsumption and nonimportation of British goods to be implemented in that order and nonexportation to

follow. There the matter lay when, on April 19, 1775, British forces and Massachusetts militiamen confronted each other at Lexington and Concord.

Radicals in Congress, seeing the political need for it, selected Virginia's George Washington to head what was at first a New England army, the Continental Army. That army and its commander became the symbols of American nationality, and they would remain so throughout the war; Congress, a mere assemblage of ambassadors, only coordinated policy.

General Washington early recognized that his chief task was simply to keep an army in the field. Britain, recall, had initiated its imperial reforms because of its difficult financial position after the Seven Years' War, and Washington judged it unlikely that Britain would be able to stomach an American war as long as Americans would. Still, it took over a year for the Americans to declare their independence. Many people, most notably Dickinson and New York's John Jay, clung to hopes of a negotiated settlement. While the Parliament was not their parliament, in Bland's argument, the king was their king.

Finally, however, George III's public refusal to consider their petitions, let alone intervene with Parliament, decided the matter for Americans; public opinion received a nudge, too, from Thomas Paine, whose "Common Sense" made independence seem inevitable. Why should an island 3,000 miles away govern a whole continent, he asked. What sense did monarchy make? Even if monarchy were sensible, why concede the majesty of that "royal brute," George III?

On July 2, 1776, Congress voted, on motion from Virginia's Richard Henry Lee, to adopt a revised version of a declaration of independence drafted by Thomas Jefferson. The chief difference between Jefferson's draft and the final declaration lay in the excision of Jefferson's accusations against King George concerning slavery in the United States; some congressmen recognized that George was not responsible for American slavery, while others denied that slavery required any apology.

The war effort received declining support from the civil population, and in the end it was only won through the substantial and timely financial, diplomatic, military, and naval assistance of Britain's mighty rival, France. Congress in the war years repeatedly claimed that the United States' cause was God's cause, that British war tactics offended Providence, and that Americans' duty to the almighty drove them to stand up in defense of rights God had given them. Their ministers supported them in their cause, and the colonial elites (with localized exceptions, particularly in upcountry South Carolina) fell into line behind the Revolution to a degree that shocked British leaders.

One of the first results of the Declaration of Independence was the elimination of the proclamation line of 1763, and thus the vindication of wealthy Americans' substantial western land claims. (Leading investors included George Washington, George Mason, John Hancock, Thomas Jefferson, Patrick Henry, the Morrises … a virtual who's who of American society.) Indian rights be damned.

The exigencies of the war, particularly the sudden creation of a slew of new offices in the state and federal governments, drew a new class of men into political life. Upset with the economic policies those men adopted and by their hesitance to provide adequate manpower and materiel to the Continental Army, reformers led by James Madison, Alexander Hamilton, and George Washington pushed for a new federal constitution. The Articles of Confederation, drafted by Congress in 1777 and ratified in 1781, dissatisfied them.

In 1787, then, continental reformers met at Philadelphia. While the states had been told that this conclave would produce amendments to the Articles, its organizers' actual goal was to substitute a new constitution for the old one. This new constitution, they believed, should create a congress dominated by the larger states and possessing power to tax and to raise armies without the states' concurrence. In addition, Madison and his coadjutors desired federal constitutional provisions preventing the democratic state legislatures from passing tax and other laws favoring debtors and common men over creditors and the wealthy.

The product of the Philadelphia Convention gave Federalists, as they called themselves, most of what they wanted. In place of highly democratic state legislatures dominated by men representing average farmers, a new, much smaller congress composed of far wealthier and better educated men who could "think continentally" would make America's most significant policies. In addition, the federal Constitution banned some of the revolutionary era's most popular forms of debtor relief. When Virginians George Mason and Edmund Randolph, joined by Massachusetts's Elbridge Gerry, insisted that the draft constitution include a bill of rights, they were ignored. Mason, father of the first American bill of rights and constitution in Virginia in 1776, took this as an ill omen and a personal affront, and he vowed to marshal opposition to ratification in Virginia.

Majorities in New York, North Carolina, and Rhode Island opposed the new constitution, but Federalists' skillful management of the ratification process led to those states' grudging adoption of the Constitution. In Virginia, a close vote for ratification came only after Federalists promised both that a bill of rights would be added to the Constitution by amendment as soon as the first federal Congress met and that Congress would have only those powers it was "expressly delegated." In other words, Federalists in the most populous, most prestigious state assured opponents led by Mason and Patrick Henry that the Constitution did not threaten home rule.

On balance, then, while intended to be counterrevolutionary, the Constitution proved less so than its advocates had hoped. It did remove substantial power from the democratic state governments, but it left more to them than Federalists would have preferred. If the two issues of the Revolution were, then, home rule and who should rule at home, the colonial elites had their way in both regards. The Constitution deprived state governments of power over some questions, but only in those areas in which the continental leadership judged that the Revolution had proven them untrustworthy. The new Congress's membership, as James Madison hopefully described it in *The Federalist #10*, would consist of men drawn from a more select group than the state legislatures, and thus more likely to make "wise" decisions. Lest the federal government run amok, however, its powers were narrowly limited.

The Revolution, then, began for conservative reasons. It concluded with a conservative measure to rein in its worst (that is, its most democratic) excesses. With the federal Constitution, any possibility of enduring state "agrarianism" was blasted in the name of defending that most defenseless of minorities: the wealthy. Whatever unmanageable social forces it may have unleashed, then, the Revolution thus concluded on a conservative note, too.

SEE ALSO

Volume 1 Left: American Revolution; Jefferson, Thomas; Washington, George; Liberalism.
Volume 2 Right: United Kingdom; Conservatism; Monarchism; Colonialism.

BIBLIOGRAPHY

John R. Alden, *A History of the American Revolution* (Alfred A. Knopf, 1969); Jack P. Greene, ed., *Colonies to Nation* (W.W. Norton, 1975); Kevin R.C. Gutzman, "Jefferson's Draft Declaration of Independence, Richard Bland, and the Revolutionary Legacy: Giving Credit Where Credit Is Due," *Journal of the Historical Society* (v.1, 2001); Woody Holton, *Forced*

Founders: Indians, Debtors, Slaves, & the Making of the American Revolution in Virginia (University of North Carolina Press, 1999); Edmund S. Morgan, *Inventing the People: The Rise of Popular Sovereignty in England and America* (W.W. Norton, 1988); Norman K. Risjord, *Jefferson's America* (Rowman & Littlefield, 2002); Charles Royster, *A Revolutionary People at War: The Continental Army and American Character* (W.W. Norton, 1979); Gordon S. Wood, *The Creation of the American Republic* (University of North Carolina Press, 1969); Gordon S. Wood, *The Radicalism of the American Revolution* (Alfred A. Knopf, 1992).

KEVIN R.C. GUTZMAN, J.D., PH.D.
WESTERN CONNECTICUT STATE UNIVERSITY

Anti-Abortion/Pro-Life

BOTH THE PRACTICE OF artificially terminating a pregnancy and the debate about its morality are as old as human civilization. Even the Hippocratic Oath, composed in ancient Greece, refers to abortifacents as one of the things doctors were not to administer. But the abortion question became a major political issue in the United States after the 1973 *Roe v. Wade* decision, in which the Supreme Court ruled that the state could not regulate first-trimester abortions, could only regulate for the woman's health in the second trimester, and could only regulate on behalf of both woman and fetus in the third, after the fetus reached viability. The Supreme Court based its reasoning upon the principle of the right of privacy, in particular, that a woman's body is her own business and that she alone should be the one to decide if she wishes to carry to term.

Almost immediately after that decision legalized abortion on demand, there was strong opposition from conservative religious groups. In particular, the Roman Catholic Church had a firmly stated position that life begins at conception and that artificially terminating a pregnancy is impermissible, even to save the life of the mother. Thus, it was not surprising that many of the earliest leaders in the opposition to abortion came from the Catholic clergy and laity.

Among these Catholic leaders were Joseph Scheidler and John O'Keefe. O'Keefe had been profoundly affected by his brother's death in combat in Vietnam. He came to oppose violence on the grounds of the harm that killing did to the killer, not the victim, and ultimately became a pacifist. While performing alternative service as a conscientious objector, he had a lengthy discussion with a woman who had had an abortion. Until that time, he had paid little attention to the question of abortion, beyond knowing that the Catholic Church opposed the procedure on moral grounds. Noticing how the woman seemed obsessed with the need to justify her decision to him, even a year after the event, he concluded that she was still haunted by her choice and was using her self-justification as a substitute for mourning her lost child.

This experience convinced O'Keefe that legalized abortion was a major social ill that needed to be dealt with. However, his experiences with existing anti-abortion organizations were unsatisfactory. He considered them little better than debating societies, reading and discussing existing arguments against abortion but never taking any greater action than writing letters to the editors of local newspapers. O'Keefe believed that a greater sacrifice was needed in response to a grave wrong, comparable to those of the civil rights movement and the protests against the Vietnam War. He organized nonviolent protests at abortion clinics in the late 1970s and early 1980s, and was one of the first to consider his activities not merely in a symbolic sense, but as actually rescuing the unborn from death. He argued that a woman who went home when confronted with a clinic protest might subsequently choose to keep her baby instead of going to another clinic, and that the life thus saved justified the disruption brought about by the demonstration.

By contrast, Scheidler led the movement's militant wing, forging the first links between peaceful protest and violence. A big man who liked to carry a bullhorn during clinic protests, he was often characterized as a bully by his opponents. He was the first to obtain dead fetuses from a pathology department and use them as visual aids in protests. He argued that such shock tactics were necessary to break through people's denial and force them to confront the reality of the fetus's essential humanity. However, his severe claustrophobia made it impossible for him to risk arrest and imprisonment for his beliefs, which undercut Scheidler's standing in the movement.

However, abortion really became a major, divisive issue in American culture when it was brought to the attention of evangelical Protestant denominations. The key event for this shift was Francis Schaeffer's 1979 book, *Whatever Happened to the Human Race?*, coauthored by future U.S. Surgeon General C. Everett Koop. In this book, Schaeffer and Koop laid out a detailed indictment of American culture for accepting abortion, and argued that it was not sufficient simply to abstain from having abortions oneself, since the mere acquiescence to the legality of abortion made one complicit in the problem.

MORAL MAJORITY

In that same year, Baptist minister Jerry Falwell, already well known for his *Old Time Gospel Hour* television program, created the Moral Majority. This organization was intended to mobilize a supposed silent majority of people in favor of traditional moral values who were being ignored by the media. The plan was to draw together various religious organizations who might not share particular theological views, but did share key moral values, in particular the sanctity of human life. Falwell made opposition to abortion a major part of the group's agenda, and used the organization's resources to reach out to other conservative Christian groups and mobilize them in the resistance to legalized abortion.

The election of Ronald Reagan to the presidency in 1980 gave abortion opponents hope that they would soon see favorable legislation. However, their hopes were quickly frustrated. Although Reagan did appoint Koop as Surgeon General, the desired legislation did not follow. Koop continued to hold his stated opposition to abortion, but he refused to distort facts to support the pro-life cause, particularly in relation to a study about post-abortion psychological problems that abortion opponents wanted to use to prove that abortion was in itself harmful to women's mental health. Although the Reagan administration proved to be a disappointment for the pro-life movement on the political front, the years of Reagan's presidency were years of growth for the pro-life movement. William Brennan's *Abortion Holocaust* began the practice of comparing abortion to the Nazi genocide of Jews, Gypsies, the disabled, and other so-called undesirables. This imagery became increasingly popular in pro-life literature through the 1980s, until some Jewish organizations began to complain that they were actually ending up undermining people's sense of the seriousness of the actual Holocaust.

Another important document of the pro-life movement from this period was *The Silent Scream*, a video of an ultrasound taken during an abortion. It was used to show the fetus as a sentient being, responding to its environment and trying futilely to protect itself from the abortion instruments, right to the moment in which it was torn apart and sucked from the womb. However,

abortion providers argued that the video footage had been heavily edited, and that the voice-over narration encouraged the projection of the viewer's own feelings upon the fetus when in fact one was only seeing random responses of a very primitive sort.

Protests at abortion clinics continued, with new tactics including John Ryan's 1985 move to recruit children for prayer vigils and other appearances in anti-abortion demonstrations. His intent was to lead viewers to mentally connect the fetus to the cute children, but opponents argued that he was exploiting the children and placing them in harm's way.

OPERATION RESCUE

It was only with the creation of Operation Rescue by Randall Terry that anti-abortion demonstrations became a mass movement. Terry originally organized Operation Rescue in 1986, but the group came to the forefront of public awareness in 1988 as Terry was able to mobilize thousands of protestors, flooding the entire area around an abortion clinic with human beings. His organization became so powerful that it was pushing the National Right to Life Committee (NRLC), one of the leading anti-abortion groups of the time, onto the sidelines. The NRLC chairman, Jack Willke, then retaliated by completely ignoring Operation Rescue, a strategic mistake that effectively divided their forces.

Operation Rescue's first big event was the New York City protest of May 1988, which involved moving 600 protestors, many of them from other locales and unfamiliar with the big city, through the subways to an Upper East Side clinic. To outwit potential opposition, only key personnel were given the full directions or objective. Ordinary protestors were led sheeplike through the lengthy and circuitous route to the targeted clinic. In the narrow confines of some New York City streets, even a few hundred demonstrators could create an overwhelming impasse and effectively block access to the clinic.

Buoyed by his success, Terry then organized a similar event in Atlanta, Georgia. However, things did not go so well, and the event was often referred to as the second siege of Atlanta. It was particularly noteworthy for the practice of arrested demonstrators refusing to properly identify themselves, instead giving their names only as "Baby Doe." By doing this, they were supposed to be identifying with aborted babies, but to many people not already firmly committed to opposing abortion, they only succeeded in making themselves look somewhat ridiculous.

Anti-abortion or pro-life activists often employ disarmingly cute or shockingly real images to drive home their point that a fetus is a bona fide human being. The above is a billboard produced by a Minnesota pro-life organization.

Following the disaster of the Atlanta demonstrations, Operation Rescue began to fragment, breaking off into several regional splinter groups. Terry lost overall control of the organization, although he remained one of its important guiding lights.

In 1991, the new leadership of Operation Rescue decided to organize another major event, this time in Wichita, Kansas. By moving away from the East Coast to the Midwest, they hoped to tap into a strong culture of traditional values. The targeted abortion clinics made one major tactical mistake in deciding to simply close during the week of the planned protest, then reopen for business as usual after riding out the storm. In doing so, they inadvertently gave encouragement to their opponents, and what had originally been intended as a relatively brief demonstration turned into a lengthy high-energy super-rally known as the Summer of Mercy. As the Operation Rescue demonstrators celebrated each additional day that passed with no abortions performed, the abortion providers grew steadily more desperate, since it was becoming clear that waiting them out indefinitely was not going to be an option. Finally, police were called to forcibly disperse the demonstrators.

Although Operation Rescue held several other demonstrations later, none of them ever equaled the Summer of Mercy. There was less interest in participating in mass demonstrations, particularly as a number of successive court cases were placing restrictions on abortion. To many abortion opponents, these cases looked like such significant progress that demonstration and the rescue movement no longer seemed necessary.

CRITICAL LAW CASES

One of the most critical of these cases was *Webster v. Reproductive Health Services*. In this 1989 case, the Supreme Court ruled that states may require viability testing after the 20th week of pregnancy, and allowed states to outlaw abortion in public hospitals and to forbid public employees from assisting in abortions. Since many poor women would not be able to afford the fees of private abortion clinics, this ruling was effectively a major restriction on the availability of abortion.

The following year saw *Rust v. Sullivan*, which upheld federal regulations forbidding abortion counseling at federally funded clinics. Critics of the case saw it as yet another strike against poor women's choices, since they often did not have the option of going to a private clinic that would not be constrained from including abortion among the options they would discuss for dealing with an unintended pregnancy. Another 1990 case required minors to obtain parental consent in order to obtain an abortion.

However, in 1992, *Planned Parenthood of Eastern Pennsylvania v. Casey* upheld *Roe v. Wade* by a margin of five to four. Although the Supreme Court did rule that states might require counseling or waiting periods before a woman could obtain an abortion, it left intact the principle that a woman should have the right to choose whether to terminate her pregnancy.

The rescue movement took a major blow in 1994 with *National Organization for Women v. Scheidler*, which opened the door for prosecuting people who block access to abortion clinics under racketeering laws. Suddenly getting arrested in a clinic demonstration was no longer a trivial matter of spending a few days in jail and paying a small fine for misdemeanor trespassing or disturbing the peace. Instead, protestors could now face felony convictions that would mean years in jail.

VIOLENT OPPOSITION

However, even as the mass demonstrations of the rescue movement were dying down, a new and darker side of the anti-abortion movement was becoming prominent, namely the violent opposition. Most of the groups organized to oppose abortion, including the National Right to Life Committee and the Christian Coalition, disapproved of illegal acts. Even organizations such as Operation Rescue, which encouraged acts of civil disobedience, drew the line at violent crime. However, the outer fringes of anti-abortion activism were growing steadily convinced that any action was justified if it saved unborn lives, even to the point of taking born lives. These fringe activists often argued that the abortionists' lives were already forfeit as shedders of innocent blood.

The violent undercurrent to the anti-abortion movement had been present from its earliest days. Supreme Court Justice Harry A. Blackmun, who wrote the *Roe v. Wade* decision, had been the recipient of hate mail and even death threats for years, reaching a peak in 1985 when an unknown assailant shot at him. This was not long after the bombing of three clinics in Pensacola, Florida, on Christmas Day, 1984. Fortunately, the clinics were not open at the time and no one was hurt, although thousands of dollars of damage was done to equipment and physical plant, closing the clinics for significant periods of time.

Michael Bray, an anti-abortion leader involved in these early abortion clinic bombings, developed theological arguments justifying violent action against abortion providers. Although he had argued that violent action was acceptable, even mandated by God, to save innocent unborn lives, he had always stopped short of saying that it was acceptable to kill in defense of the un-

born. With these justifications, the violent fringe began to coalesce into an amorphous organization calling itself the Army of God, and carried out a series of increasingly violent attacks on abortion clinics and even doctors and other employees.

While the earliest acts of violence were often carefully timed to ensure that the targeted clinics were empty and only property would be destroyed, later attacks abandoned Bray's caveat against the taking of lives and deliberately targeted clinic personnel. In one of the most notorious attacks, a sniper shot and killed abortion doctor David Gunn. The culprit, Michael Griffin, was later captured and ultimately sentenced to life in prison for his action. After Gunn was murdered, his job was taken over by Dr. John Bayard Britton, who was subsequently murdered by another anti-abortion activist, Paul Hill.

This sequence of violent murders led many mainstream churches and anti-abortion organizations, which had previously given tacit approval to the violent fringe, to instead firmly condemn anyone who resorted to violence in the fight against abortion. Griffin and Hill would not become folk heroes of the anti-abortion movement, unlike the way John Brown had become a folk hero of the abolitionists after being sentenced to death for leading the raid upon the federal armory at Harper's Ferry, Virginia.

Some pro-lifers, completely disgusted by what they perceived as a betrayal of the sanctity of life by the very people who claimed to be protecting it, began forging links with pro-choice groups to create an organization known as the Common Ground Network for Life and Choice. Many hoped to thus find a way to balance the interests of both the woman and the unborn child, instead of subjugating one to the other, but these people were often regarded as suspect by members of their own organizations for compromising with the hard-line stance.

During the second half of the 1990s, the tactics of mainstream anti-abortion organizations shifted away from trying to stop abortion altogether to nibbling away at one procedure after another. Their particular target was a technique they termed a "partial-birth abortion." This technique, used for very late-term abortions, involved dilating the cervix enough to pull the body of the fetus through the birth canal, then aspirating the brain to collapse the skull enough to get it out. Pro-life leaders argued that this procedure was being used as a method of convenience for women who had carelessly delayed until the last possible minute, while pro-choice medical personnel argued that the procedure was almost never used except in cases where a fetus with severe congenital defects could not be brought to term without undue risk to the mother. Even as anti-abortion activists were raising a furor about partial-birth abortions, the actual incidence of abortion in the United States was going down. Sociologists studying the phenomenon have concluded that this shift is not so much the result of anti-abortion activism but rather a function of contraception becoming more a part of mainstream life.

However, anti-abortion activism left a permanent mark on the American political landscape. Opposition to abortion brought fundamentalist Christians back into worldly politics, and facilitated the creation of the religious right as a political force to be reckoned with. Although they were not able to achieve a victory against abortion, the experience had shown them that they could make a difference in secular society, and they soon saw other causes worthy of their attention.

SEE ALSO
Volume 1 Left: Abortion/Pro-Choice; Feminism; Healthcare. Volume 2 Right: Family First; Feminism.

BIBLIOGRAPHY
Joan Andrews with John Cavanaugh-O'Keefe, *I Will Never Forget You: The Rescue Movement and the Life of Joan Andrews* (Ignatius Press, 1989); Patricia Baird-Windle and Eleanor J. Bader, *Targets of Hatred: Anti-Abortion Terrorism* (Palgrave, 2001); Marian Faux, *Crusaders: Voices from the Abortion Front* (Birch Lane Press, 1990); Jerry Reiter, *Live from the Gates of Hell: An Insider's Look at the Antiabortion Underground* (Prometheus Books, 2000); James Risen and Judy L. Thomas, *Wrath of Angels: The American Abortion War* (Basic Books, 1998); Francis A. Schaeffer and C. Everett Koop, *Whatever Happened to the Human Race?* (F.H. Revell, 1979); Joseph M. Scheidler, *Closed: 99 Ways to Stop Abortion* (Tan Books and Publishers, 1993).

LEIGH KIMMEL, PH.D.
INDEPENDENT SCHOLAR

Apartheid

IN A SPECIFIC SENSE, apartheid is a description of the political regime in South Africa from 1948 to 1990, in which there was state-sanctioned and enforced racial segregation. The word is an Afrikaner term that literally translated means "apartness." The policy of apartheid was designed to preserve the political and economic power of the Europeans in South Africa.

More generally, apartheid can be used to describe any polity in which there is compulsory and legally sanctioned segregation of the races. Such a situation was prevalent in many parts of the American south up until the 1960s.

The origins of apartheid in South Africa go back to the earliest European settlements. The early Dutch East Indian settlers, who settled Cape Town in 1652, classified their society according to race. Until 1834, Afrikaner society operated with slavery and almost all nonslave blacks were at the bottom of society. There was, in other words, an almost total overlap of race and social class in which those at the top were almost exclusively white. Despite this, as the 19th century progressed, there were gradually more egalitarian political developments. The nonracial franchise gave the right to vote to all moderate property holders. This included a few blacks as well as persons of mixed race. These developments were later reversed as the number of eligible blacks increased. Additionally, the late 19th century witnessed an increase in white supremacist laws and practices, including the introduction of poll taxes.

An early version of apartheid segregation existed in Natal under the Shepstone System. Shepstone was the colonial supervisor of "native affairs" in 1846. The system established an early form of homelands for blacks. Further developments toward racial segregation existed in the Mines and Works Act (1911), which established racial segregation in employment; the Native Land Act (1913), which divided land ownership on the basis of race; and the Native (Urban Areas) Act (1923), which set up a system of urban racial segregation. From the 19th century on, blacks were subject to a series of pass laws. These laws controlled the mobility of nonwhites.

THE PARTY SLOGAN

The first widespread use of the term *apartheid* emerged as a slogan of the Gesuiwerde Nasionale Party (later the Herenigde Nasionale Party or HNP) in the mid-1930s. In this era, the prime minister, J.B.M. Hertzog, espoused a philosophy of territorial segregation and racial preference for whites that was essentially an apartheid vision. The Afrikaner nationalism that bolstered such views borrowed ideological elements and a range of invented folk traditions, symbols, and rituals from the Nazi ideology of Hitler's Germany. While Afrikaner nationalism was uncomfortable with the violent excesses of the

Nazi persecutions, it was comfortable with its social Darwinist and eugenicist racist belief systems, and in sympathy with its conceits of Nordic *volk* (folk) greatness. A small group of Afrikaner intellectuals founded a Suid-Afrikaanse Bond vir Rassestudie (South African League for Racial Studies) in 1935. Prominent among the intellectuals was Professor Gert Cronje, who published *Regverdige Rasse-apartheid (Justifiable Racial Separation)* in 1947.

The HNP won the 1948 election and began systematically to implement the policy. In the 1940s and 1950s there were a series of new and important acts under the premierships of the Malan and H.F. Verwoerd National Party that established the framework of the apartheid state. The underlying principle was that of *aparte ontwikkeling* (separate development). The goal of Verwoerd was nothing less than the complete and unambiguous decoupling of white and black destinies in every sphere of existence. So determined was the government to achieve apartheid's goals that it stacked the courts and the senate in order to manipulate the defeat of constitutional provisions that would have guaranteed certain rights to the colored (mixed-race) population. The Prohibition of Mixed Marriages Act (1949) and the so-called Immorality Act (1950) prohibited marriage and even consensual sexual relations between the races. The Population Registration Act (1950) classified people according to four designated races, white, colored (mixed race), "Asiatic," and "Bantu" (black African). The Group Areas Act (1950) and other similar legislation compelled individuals of different races to be resident in distinct designated areas. The Reservation of Separate Amenities Act (1953) enforced apartheid in social and cultural settings, while the Bantu Education Act (1953) introduced a separate and distinctly unequal system of racialized educational provision. The Native Resettlement Act (1954) forcibly removed African residents from Johannesburg. Each of these acts was an ingenious contribution to the overall attempt to guarantee white minority dominance into the indefinite future.

In this time period, white European variants of support for apartheid came to be referred to through the use of two Afrikaner terms, *verligte* (enlightened) and *verkrampte* (unenlightened). From the 1950s until the end of the apartheid regime, these terms defined the principal options available to white South Africans as they reflected on the future and stability of their regime. While both tendencies supported the regime in principle, the *verkrampte* voices supported the more reactionary and hard-line stances against rebellion within and the international community beyond, while the

verligte tendency was prone to reform, accommodation, and adaptation. The *verkrampte* tendency was to lead ultimately to the breakaway conservative party of Treurnicht in the early 1980s, as the National Party regime moved toward moderate reformism and the apartheid movement split.

PROTESTS AGAINST APARTHEID

Opposition to apartheid began in earnest in the 1950s, with boycotts of so-called Bantu schools, and the refusal of women to obey the hated pass laws, which required them to carry state identification papers and to show them on demand. The African National Congress (ANC) coordinated most of the mass protests, including those based on workplace grievances. Events culminated in a fateful march to the police station in Sharpeville in March 1960. Panic-stricken police opened fire on unarmed black protestors, most of them women, shooting many in the back; 69 died and 178 were wounded. As a result of the Sharpeville massacre, international pressure increased on South Africa to abandon apartheid. Taking a contrary course, the regime instead cut itself off from the international community, introduced even more draconian regulations, and banned the principal black representative organization, the ANC.

The fateful decision of the Malan and Verwoerd governments to promote a rigid and fixed system of apartheid in South Africa came at the wrong historical time. The rest of the world had defeated the totalitarian order of Nazism and fascism, and was undergoing a process of decolonization, in which the emphasis was on anti-racist and pro-democratic reforms. The regime of apartheid flew in the face of such developments and to the extent that it did, the South African regime became an international pariah. The years 1960 to 1965 saw the international business community abandon South Africa as capital and other assets flooded out and investment sources dried up. British Prime Minister Harold Macmillan addressed the South African parliament in February 1960.

Having taken shrewd measure of the political culture of decolonization among the black African nations of the continent, Macmillan referred to a "wind of change" blowing across the continent. Making his implicit message explicit, he added that his government could not continue to support an apartheid regime. Having declared itself a "republic" in order to diminish the British connection, South Africa nonetheless applied to remain in the British Commonwealth in March

1961. It became clear that other members of the Commonwealth would leave should South Africa be admitted as a republic. Verwoerd formally withdrew South Africa's application and the country ceased to be a member until the fall of apartheid almost 30 years later.

In response to the intransigence of the apartheid regime and the declaration of states of emergency, the leader of the ANC, Nelson Mandela, announced a turn to greater militancy and an end to the peaceful approach toward conflict resolution. A new militant wing of the ANC was founded, called Umkhonto we Sizwe (Spear of the Nation). From this time forward, the ANC engaged in acts of sabotage and armed resistance. The General Law Amendment Act (1963) gave sweeping new powers of arrest and detention to the authorities. The government introduced strict censorship and began to dominate editorial decision making in the South African Broadcasting Corporation. Alarmed by increasing evidence of urban black protest, the South African state removed increasing numbers of blacks from urban areas, compelling them to resettle in tribal or Bantu "homelands," which were essentially designated holding areas for black South Africans with no jobs or prospects. Based on the "reserved areas" designated in the Native Lands Act of 1913, these so-called Bantustans were barren and limited in size. In order to appease the international community, certain of these areas, such as Transkei, Boputhatswana, Venda, and Ciskei, were designated as "sovereign" and independent lands, therefore removing South African citizenship from their citizens and nullifying any claim they had as victims of apartheid. These homelands were only recognized by South Africa itself and nearby Rhodesia. In reality, they were almost completely dependent on South Africa and independent in name only. Throughout the 1960s, millions of blacks were forcibly relocated to the homelands.

BLACK POWER

While the 1960s remained relatively quiescent in terms of overt protest, the exiled ANC and other groups were developing powerful new forms of black consciousness. Leaders such as Steve Biko—who was allegedly murdered by the apartheid regime in 1977—began to take notice of black consciousness, black power, and black theology movements that had been developing in other parts of the world, through the teachings of intellectuals such as Frantz Fanon and Martin Luther King, Jr. The South African Students Organization (SASO) formed in 1968, and the Black People's Convention,

founded in 1972, were manifestations of the new black consciousness. By the early 1970s, strikes by workers, protests by culturally assertive school children, and increasing repression on the part of the apartheid state culminated in the massacre of school children in Soweto in June 1976.

Following a protest against the Bantu schools in Soweto and a demand for an end to education in Afrikaans, teenage protestors faced down the police. Ordered to "advance no further," one by one they did. As they did so, the police shot them to death. The sight of hundreds of young black children, such as 13-year-old Hector Petersen, being shot dead in cold blood shook apartheid to the core. Soweto marked the point at which apartheid became untenable, even as it limped on for another 15 years. South Africans of all races and members of the international community alike were appalled.

A combination of harsh and damaging economic sanctions from the international community, continued repression and strife at home, and a black population increasingly alienated from Pretoria, the capital, was met with some partial and limited reforms to apartheid, such as the attempt in 1983 to create limited legislative representation for coloreds and Indians. As with so many other reforms in this era, the reform package was too little and too late. Each of the front-line states surrounding South Africa (Mozambique, Angola, Rhodesia, and Namibia) underwent an assertive process of decolonization and gained full independence in the 1970s. This removed the so-called *cordon sanitaire* of states sympathetic to apartheid. South Africa became increasingly isolated as the still-exiled leaders of the ANC moved their camps ever closer to the South African border.

South African capitalists had coexisted more or less willingly with apartheid and had been prepared to leave social and political matters to the regime. However, South African capitalism was changing, too, and apartheid was no longer an economically viable system. It simply did not permit sufficient numbers of talented people to get the jobs they deserved and the economy needed them to have. Gradually, in the 1980s, the most excessive of the apartheid laws were repealed—the pass laws and the prohibitions on mixed marriages—and some autonomy was given to black township councils.

The 1980s witnessed the ever-growing waves of what was essentially a civil war, with the exiled ANC leadership increasingly regarded as a government-in-waiting. Moreover, in the civil war, the South African army, increasingly starved of white recruits, was rapidly becoming an agency that questioned rather than supported the logic of apartheid. The most logical recruits were those very young blacks whom the army was supposed to be suppressing.

The writing was on the wall by the late 1980s, and the only question remaining in South Africa was how quickly and easily might the apartheid regime be undone. As with many dying authoritarian regimes, the final years were marked by bitter internal dissent and collapse as well as much violence. On the white side, neofascist Eugene Terreblanche and his supporters deserted the National Party in their bid to preserve apartheid. Other breakaway groups with similar ideals included the Blanke Bevrydigyngs Beweging (white liberation movement). Black protest, such as rallies, strikes, and rent boycotts, continued unabated; by 1984 most of South Africa was under a state of emergency declaration and would remain so until the end of apartheid some five years later.

In January 1989, Prime Minister P.W. Botha suffered a mild stroke and stepped down. He was replaced by F.W. de Klerk. Sensing the possibility of a serious and sustained move away from apartheid, the ANC drafted a declaration for the Organization of African Union, meeting in Harare on August 21, 1989, stating that it was prepared to consult with de Klerk on the basis of a declared intention to move toward a democratic and nonracist regime. In response de Klerk "unbanned" a series of protest organizations in 1989, including the ANC and the South African Communist Party. Some of the most egregious forms of apartheid were removed and Mandela, along with other political prisoners, was released unconditionally in 1990. Following a positive whites-only referendum result, apartheid was finally abolished in 1992. However, the death throes of apartheid were ugly and protracted. In the late 1980s, the death toll from civil strife was between 600 and 1,400 per year. By the early 1990s, that number had increased to between 2,700 and 3,800 per annum. To put matters further in perspective in 1994, when apartheid was officially over, deaths from political violence were triple those of 1976, the year of Soweto. Bringing together the various parties proved to be an act of monumental faith and trust and required great courage on the part of the principals.

The new post-apartheid South Africa was grounded in the constitutional elegance and balance of a new progressive and nonracist document, drafted for ratification in May 1996. The first black president, Mandela, offered people the hope of a massive and ambitious Reconstruction and Development Program (RDP). Under the stewardship of Archbishop Desmond Tutu, South Africans of all backgrounds came together to remember, confess, tell their stories, forgive, and be forgiven in the remarkable Truth and Reconciliation Commission.

SEE ALSO

Volume 1 Left: South Africa; King, Martin Luther, Jr.; Desegregation.
Volume 2 Right: South Africa; Segregation.

BIBLIOGRAPHY

Chris Alden, *Apartheid's Last Stand: The Rise and Fall of the South African Security State* (Macmillan, 1996); Rodney Davenport and Christopher Saunders, *South Africa: A Modern History* (Macmillan, 2000); Robert M. Price, *The Apartheid State in Crisis: Political Transformation in South Africa, 1975–90* (Oxford University Press, 1991); Patti Waldmeir, *Anatomy of a Miracle: The End of Apartheid and the Birth of the New South Africa* (Norton, 1997); Nigel Worden, *The Making of Modern South Africa* (Blackwell, 1994).

PAUL NESBITT-LARKING, PH.D.
HURON UNIVERSITY COLLEGE, CANADA

Argentina

THE ARGENTINEAN RIGHT is a form of opposition to democratization processes that has motivated reactionary political actions during the 20th century and continues to have an ongoing impact on the politics and social organization of the country. The right inherits key aspects of traditional colonial caudillismo, dwells on a peculiar totalitarian culture within the Catholic Church, and has been reinforced by militarism. It yields to the formation of several parties and gains newer cultural elements, especially in times of crisis.

The greater impact of the right in Argentina coincides with the cycles of military interventionism in the country, starting in 1880, passing through the crises in 1930 and 1953, and culminating in the military coup d'etat in 1976, before the return to democracy in 1983.

The role of conservatism in Argentina during the 19th century was defined by José Luis Romero in his book *El Orden Conservador.* He argued that conservatism can take different positions according to the need of the moment. Thus, conservatives could be provincial caudillos, who aimed at maintaining the old colonial order, or also liberal conservatives, who were

Right-wing dictatorships have put Argentina in harm's way, such as the ill-fated attempt to wrest control of Britain's colony, the Falkland Islands, which Argentina knows as the Malvinas. The road sign above emphasized the government's rightist point of view.

influenced by the so-called generation from the 1880s and incorporated modern and positivist ideas into their political thinking. Therefore, students of the Argentine right have centered their attention on the merging of an extreme right in Argentina with nationalism, Catholicism, and fascism after the 1920s.

The rise of the right in Argentina occurred after the election of Hypólito Yrigoyen in 1916. In opposition to Yrigoyen's social reforms and his party, the Unión Cívica Radical, the authoritarian right developed several lines of action. One was formed by the intellectuals Carlos Ibarguren, Leopoldo Lugones, and Manuel Gálvez, who published their ideas in *La Nueva República* and *Nueva Orden*, attacking democracy and defending fascism. Another line was represented by Catholic nationalism, which became popular between 1930 and 1943 through the movement called Catholic Action and the journal *Criterio*, which also defended nationalism.

A third line of action was provided by fascist groups such as the Argentinean Civic Legion (LCA), the Republican League, the Argentinean Nationalist Action (ANA), and other groups and parties such as the Fascist Party from Cordoba. Between 1930 and 1945, these groups tried to implement the ideas of Italian fascism, Spanish Francoism, and German national socialism in Argentina.

Nationalist populism is the most peculiar phenomenon in Argentinean political history, and cannot be related only to the political right, for it involved liberals, socialists, and the labor movement. However, right-wing elements of populism can be identified when they support oligarchism, integralism, fascism, and authoritarianism. This process cannot be understood without considering the multifarious role of Juan D. Peron.

Having participated in the Uriburu's revolution of 1930 as captain, by 1943 Peron had grown to the rank of colonel and was one of the most important officials in the army. He was able to use the military structure for his purposes. On the other hand, he had spent some time in Europe from 1938 to 1940, where he was influenced by the social changes in Spain, Italy, France, and Germany, and had traveled widely through Argentina, learning about the miserable conditions of the Argentinean "shirtless masses" (*descamisados*). Moreover, through his association with Eva Peron, he was able to appeal to the working classes. Evita, who died in 1952, became a legend due to her ascension from destitute woman to first lady. This sui generis combination was responsible for Peron's election in 1946. His program became known as a popular integral nationalism, which reunited distinct aspects such as corporate syndicalism, military bureaucracy, social-welfare reforms, and totalitarianism in a dictatorial regime.

A consistent support to the right has come from leaders of military interventions. From the 1970s until 1982, the military promoted a "dirty war" and murdered some 40,000 Argentines suspected of opposing the government, the so-called disappeared (*desaparecidos*), and imposed a rigid authoritarian regime but squandered international loans. They finally experienced a humiliating defeat by the British in a war over the possession of the Falkland/Malvinas Islands. This defeat forced a democratization process, with the election of President Raul Alfonsin, but militarism continued to be associated with the extreme right. Thus, between 1987 and 1990, armed "military with painted faces" (*carapintadas*) opposed the democratic government and questioned the judicial processes against past military leaders. As a result, Carlos Menem, who was president during the 1990s, acquitted them from the charges of abuses committed against the Argentinean civilian population.

The political right in Argentina has had the support of several elite parties. Already in 1874, the National Autonomist Party (PAN) was formed to oppose liberalism. Later, leagues were created to oppose the Radical Civic Union of Yrigoyen. After the 1950s, the legacy of Peron's dictatorship was perpetuated in the Peronist Party. Although these became mainline parties in Argentinean politics, other groups, such as the Argentinean Civic Union, the Alliance of the Nationalist Youth, the Argentinean Anti-Communist Alliance, and the Union del Centro Democratico (UCD) were created to defend specific interests of the right in Argentina.

Finally, right-wing ideologies have been defended also by the periodicals *La Fronda* (founded in 1919) and *Criterio*, as well as by organizations defending anti-Semitism and even terrorism. This explains why Argentina seemed to be the country of choice for sympathizers of German Nazi fascism after World War II.

SEE ALSO

Volume 1 Left: Argentina; South America; Socialism; Guevara, Che.
Volume 2 Right: Fascism; Totalitarianism; Peronism.

BIBLIOGRAPHY

José Luis B. Beired, *Sob o signo da nova ordem. Intelectuais autoritários no Brasil e na Argentina* (São Paulo, Ed. Loyola, 1999); Sandra McGee Deutsch, *Counterrevolution in Argentina, 1900–32: The Argentine Patriotic League* (University of Nebraska Press, 1986); Marvin Goldwert, *Democracy, Militarism and Nationalism in Argentina: 1930–66* (University of Texas Press, 1972); David Rock, *La Argentina Autoritaria. Los Nacionalistas, su historia y su influencia en la vida pública* (Buenos Aires, Ariel, 1993).

AMOS NASCIMENTO
METHODIST UNIVERSITY OF PIRACICABA, BRAZIL

Aristocracy

SEE VOLUME 2: Monarchism; Feudalism.

Aryan Nations

THE ARYAN NATIONS organization was founded in the 1970s by Richard Butler, a veteran of World War II. First involved with Wesley Swift's Christian Defense League, Butler then established the Aryan Nations white supremacy organization. Its headquarters was in Hayden Lake, Idaho. Butler's philosophy was strongly influenced by the Christian Identity movement, which views the white Aryan Nations as the true "Chosen People" of the Old Testament, not the Jews. According to Christian Identity, the Jewish People are in reality the "Children of Satan," and nonwhite races like African Americans, Mexicans, and Asian peoples are the "mud people." One of the marks of the true Chosen People—the Aryans—is that, being of fair skin, they can bring "blood in the face" if they are slapped and their cheek grows pink with the blood underneath.

The idea of building a white nation is much at the heart of the philosophy of Butler and his adherents. The largely white population of the American northwest was seen as desirable territory, with Idaho at its core. In 1996, Butler issued his "Declaration of Independence" for all Aryan peoples. In part it read: "all people are created equally subject to the laws of nature ... such is now the necessity which impels [Aryans] to alter their systems of government." A primary tenet of the Aryan Nations' beliefs is that the United States is now ruled by a largely hostile Zionist occupation government (ZOG) that perpetuates the alleged financial control of world Jewry, and whose purported design for world control was the subject of the Nineteenth Century Protocols of the Elders of Zion. The declaration goes on to say that the goal of ZOG is "the establishment of an absolute tyranny over these states; moreover, throughout the entire world." The heart of the document is a challenge that "we must secure the existence of our people and a future for white people."

As part of its goal of reaching out to as many whites as possible, in 1979 Aryan Nations began an intensive prison outreach program throughout the United States. There are now few state or federal penal institutions that do not have an Aryan Nations chapter among their white inmate population. In 1983, Louis Beam, Butler's close associate, wrote: "the ever increasing prison ministry of the Church of Jesus Christ Christian [Christian Identity Movement] has begun to be felt throughout the state prison system as a major force." Also, aided by Tom Metzger of the White Aryan Resistance movement (WAR), Aryan Nations has mounted a campaign to reach out to the white youth of America. An Aryan Nations Academy was established in 1982, but only some 15 members appear to have joined. Far more successful has been the effort to find common ground with the Skinhead movement, whose "oi" music has been played at youth concerts hosted by Aryan Nations.

The movement also served as a seed bed for the militia movement, which grew during the years of the Bill Clinton administration (1992–2000), a period when right-wing conservatives felt that Clinton was waging a war against the Christian right. In 1992, the focus of concern was Ruby Ridge in Idaho, where Christian survivalist Randy Weaver was besieged at his home by local and state law enforcement authorities and the Hostage Rescue Team (HRT) of the Federal Bureau of Investigation (FBI). FBI sniper Lon Horiuchi shot to death Weaver's wife. Weaver's son and a U.S. marshal also died. Many Skinheads descended on the siege to show their solidarity with the Weavers.

One of the leaders of the militia movement is John Trochmann, who founded the large Militia of Montana (MOM). In 1990, Trochmann, who has testified before the U.S. Congress, was a featured speaker at the Aryan Nations annual congress. Among other states that have had militias are Maine, California, Georgia, and Ohio. In order to fight the vast power of the ZOG, Louis Beam has emerged as the ideologue of Aryan Nations and has advocated a struggle of "leaderless resistance." Under this doctrine, the militias and other armed groups united with them would wage a guerrilla war against the forces of ZOG, strike their blows, and then fade away.

The 1990s was a time of great struggle for the Aryan Nations, in part because of a legal campaign waged against the group by Morris Dees of the Klanwatch association, part of the Southern Poverty Law Center. As a result of lawsuits filed against the movement, it appeared that Aryan Nations was headed toward dissolution. In 2001, Butler lost the traditional compound at Hayden Lake as the result of a court decision in a suit brought by Dees and Klanwatch. An ugly period of internecine squabbling broke out within the ranks of the movement. Butler, who was ill, had agreed to share power with Ray Redfeairn of Ohio and August Kreis of Pennsylvania. Pennsylvania newspapers wrote of a new Aryan Nations compound being established in central Pennsylvania, and of the concern such a development brought forth from liberal groups and the National Association for the Advancement of Colored People (NAACP). By 2002, the new agreement collapsed, and Redfeairn and Kreis continued to lead their own state movements. Although sickly, Butler announced his resolve to continue leading the Aryan Nations movement.

The Aryan Nations movement, with its strains of political paranoia, explicit racism, and its advocacy of armed force in politics, has echoes of European fascist movements, and as such, is properly seen as an extreme right-wing phenomenon in the late 20th and early 21st century in the United States.

SEE ALSO

Volume 1 Left: NAACP; Ideology; American Civil Liberties Union.
Volume 2 Right: Black Separatism; Shockley, William B.; Conservatism; Xenophobia.

BIBLIOGRAPHY

John F. Murphy Jr., *Day of Reckoning: The Massacre at Columbine High School* (Xlibris, 2001); Howard L. Bushart and John R. Craig, *Myra Barnes, Soldiers of God* (Pinnacle Books, 1998); Joel Dyer, *Harvest of Rage: How Oklahoma City Is Only the Beginning* (Westview Press, 1998); Alan M. Schwartz, ed., *Danger: Extremism* (Anti-Defamation League, 1996); James Ridgeway, *Blood in the Face* (Thunder's Mouth Press, 1995); "Richard Butler and Aryan Nations: Extremism in America," "The Militia Movement: Extremism in America," Anti-Defamation League, www.adl.org (May 2004).

JOHN F. MURPHY, JR.
AMERICAN MILITARY UNIVERSITY

Asia

WITH VERY FEW EXCEPTIONS, Asian inhabitants rarely regard themselves as Asians. The perception of Asian wholeness derives from the West's idea of itself, which was constructed largely by saying what others were not. It is connected with dividing the world in Occident (the West or Europe) and Orient (or the rest of the world which in the Middle Ages extended from the eastern Mediterranean to the Pacific).

The main geographic and cultural regions of Asia are North Asia, which comprises underpopulated Asian portions of the contemporary Russian Federation; East Asia: China (including Hong Kong, Macau, and Taiwan), Japan, North and South Korea; Southeast Asia: Brunei, Myanmar, Cambodia, East Timor, Indonesia, Laos, Malaysia, the Philippines, Singapore, Thailand, Vietnam; South Asia: Afghanistan, Bangladesh, Bhutan, India, Maldives, Nepal, Pakistan, Sri Lanka; and Central Asia: Kazakhstan, Kyrgyzstan, Mongolia, Tajikistan, Turkmenistan, Uzbekistan.

The Middle East (Near East or Southwest Asia) has its own subregions. Anatolia (Greek for "east"), also called by the Latin name of Asia Minor, is a region of continental Asia that is represented today by thge Asian part of Turkey. The Levant is an approximate geographical term referring to an area adjoining the Mediterranean Sea in the west, Israel, Palestine, Jordan, Syria, and Lebanon. Mesopotamia ("between the rivers" in Greek) is the alluvial plain between the Tigris and Euphrates rivers in contemporary Iraq. Arabia is a peninsula at the junction of Africa and Asia and includes Saudi Arabia, Yemen, Oman, the United Arab Emirates, and Qatar. About 50 states and bodies politic have an Asian location in whole or in part.

ORIGINS OF ORIENTAL DESPOTISM

Asia was the home of the three world's oldest civilizations, located in river valleys of the Indus and the Huang Ho and in Mesopotamia. A fourth one, on the Nile, bordered on Asia. The empires of Sumer, Babylonia, Assyria, Media, Persia, and Muslim civilizations of Arabs and Turks prospered in Southwest Asia, while in the South and Far East the ancient civilizations of India, China, and Japan thrived. The nomadic tribes of North and Central Asia (Huns, Mongols, etc.) induced the immense westward migration and established great empires in the Middle East.

Because of Asia's peculiar semiarid climate and territorial conditions, artificial irrigation by canals and waterworks had to be the basis of a flourishing agrarian economy. Only despotic state power resting on the mighty bureaucratic system could really become the principal organizer of such works. Oriental despotism was also founded on common property. But there was one more important cause for the formation of despotic rule in the East. Cultural relativists deduce the reason from the peculiarities of the commune's existence in the ancient East. The representatives of this approach rest on Karl Marx's (March 1881) observation about communes being isolated units disconnected from each other. He labeled a commune a localized microcosm.

While in solving internal problems each commune is really almighty, the complete helplessness of this archaic unit is revealed when facing outward. The outside world might appear as a foe in numerous forms. It could be nomadic *coup de main* or pirate inroad, locust attack, or floods. This danger of being devastated by the hostile outer world urges communication between agrarian microcosms. As a result of such a composition of the people (out of small communes), whose economic interests were the same, and precisely because of that they were not common, state power becomes the condition of the nation's existence. The absence of immediate (direct) ties between communes in the ancient East was compensated for by the emergence of state power as a whole-creating entity. But this uniting single entity by necessity turns to despotic rule. The insularity and negligibility of each element of the ancient Asian social edifice, the hostile estrangement of their like interests, and the same level of social relations around the country turn the social power into an omnipotent entity that intrudes into all spheres of physical and spiritual life and the property relations of its citizens.

The state power of ancient Eastern society was built hierarchically and the power of the despot attained a sacred character. In the society considered, the real social ties of which are embodied in the despot, takes place the transformation of his or her figure into a personality cult, into the only public personality, or the person-society. And the society itself turns into the means of the despotic personality's existence.

Individualism and rationalism of the West are on the one hand, and communitarianism and spirituality of the East are on the other hand. Westerners assert rights; Asians respond to duties. Westerners are governed by law and contract, Asians by customs and personal ties. In the West, decisions are made by voting; in Asia they are made by consensus. Those fundamental distinctions were always the cause of mutual misunderstanding and estrangement. "Oh, East is East, and West is West, and never the twain shall meet, Till Earth and Sky stand presently at God's great Judgement Seat," as Rudyard Kipling put it.

IMPERIALISM IN ASIA

In the first half of the 20th century, large areas of Asia, as well other areas of the world, were subjected to imperial control by European nations, the United States, and Japan. There are many reasons why this could happen so easily and to such an extent. Asian regions did not experience the Industrial Revolution, so the Europeans had better arms and warcraft.

Asiatic governments were unpopular. The survival of ethnic and tribal loyalties at the expense of nationalist feeling and the prevalence of mass illiteracy impeded the development of cohesive societies and strong administration. And the presence of valuable raw materials and abundant cheap labor exerted a powerful attraction. Colonial powers were moved by a variety of aims, including commercial penetration, military glory, and diplomatic advantage.

The largest empire in Asia was British India, and Britain always acted to protect its Indian interests. Following British-French colonial struggles that began in 1746, Robert Clive's victory at Plessey (1757) helped to establish informal British rule in India. The transition to formal imperialism was taking place in the Indian subcontinent, including Burma, today's Myanmar. The process found symbolic expression in crowning Queen Victoria Empress of India. Britain acquired Ceylon during the Napoleonic Wars. The British acquisition of Singapore (1818) and Aden (1839) placed British power across major trade routes and led to a protectorate over Malaya, Sarawak, Brunei, and Sabah.

Basically, British imperial ideology incorporated two contradicting principles. The first was the imperial philosophy of equality or the High Victorian concept of fair play, according to which all colonial peoples were subjects of the queen and therefore enjoyed her justice irrespective of color or faith. The second was the principle of racial superiority, connected mostly with Africa but also with Asia, and was embodied in Cecil Rhodes's "visionary project" of the world superiority of the Anglo-Saxons who had to reign over the rest of the peoples for their good.

The other two major empires in Asia were the French and the Dutch. France seized Saigon in 1859 and used it as a bridgehead to acquire almost all of Indochina by 1893. Like the English and the French, the Dutch started their Asian penetration via trading in the East India Company, and then the Dutch government took over political rights and benefits in 1799, gaining control over the huge archipelago that is now the country of Indonesia.

Britain and Russia were rivals in the theater of Central and West Asia. In the late 19th century, Russia took control of large areas of Central Asia. This brought a brief crisis with Britain over Afghanistan in 1885. In Persia (now Iran), both nations got concessions and set up banks to extend their economic control, having respectively Russian (in north Iran) and English (south and center) spheres of influence. Neighboring Iraq as well as Transjordan and Palestine were also under control of Britain as mandated territories since 1920.

In 1899, the United States obtained the Philippines from a defeated Spain, and used the islands to open up Chinese trade. China was subject to incursions by all great European powers, the United States, and Japan. The latter also had Taiwan (since 1895) and Korea (1910) as colonies, and spread its control over Manchuria (1931), Beijing, and major ports of China (1937). Though there was an Asian (Japan) power among the imperialist ones, the classic colonialism is associated with the Western presence, control, and influence in Asia.

For the enemies of imperialism, the term *empire* was among the dirtiest words in the modern political vocabulary and meant brutal exploitation and dehumanization, exhibiting some surprising links between English liberalism and Russian Marxism. But at its best, European imperialism brought new standards of administration and public health to subject countries. Asia was looked upon as a negative essence, a symbol of despotism and obedience alien to the European idea of human rights and freedoms. The very term *Asiatic* has acquired a disparaging shade of meaning. Such a view was combined with the negative appraisal of Asian peoples as passive, uncreative, and doomed to backwardness. At the end of the 19th century, the most inhumane forms of imperialist exploitation almost disappeared, the standards of colonial administration were improved, and a new justification of the rule of non-Europeans by the European powers was found in the idea of "the white man's burden" or "civilizing mission," which advanced the notion that the developed nations of Europe and the West in general had the duty to rule Asians and other "underdeveloped" peoples to lead them to a higher level of civilization and culture and prepare them for independence. In 1899, Kipling gave those sentiments poetic shape:

Take up the White Man's burden—
Send forth the best ye breed—
Go, bind your sons to exile
To serve your captives' need;
To wait, in heavy harness,
On fluttered folk and wild—
Your new-caught sullen peoples,
Half devil and half child.

The approbative approach in the appreciation of colonial empires of the past in Asia, moreover, has a new sense in the contemporary light of terrorist threats, which reportedly come from Asia, especially from the Middle East. The theory of "new (moral) imperialism" and the practice of preemptive intervention toward seedbeds of terrorism, such as Afghanistan in 2001, were taken by the United States and Great Britain as weapons against that hazard.

WORLD WAR II

The initial aggressor of World War II in Asia was Japan, which joined Germany and Italy in the Tripartite Alliance. The Japanese occupied large territories of Indochina in September 1940. On December 7, 1941, they attacked the main American Pacific naval base at Pearl Harbor and then moved on Hong Kong, Malaya, and the Philippines. On January 27, 1942, Japanese forces destroyed the Allied fleet in the Battle of the Java Sea, and seized the Dutch East Indies in March 1942. Huge areas of East and Southeast Asia as well as most of Oceania fell under Japanese control.

The "Asian spirit" rhetoric of pan-Asianism was set in motion. It was traced to the idea of the divine origin of the Japanese and the writings of Okawa Shumei (1886–1957) and Abdurresid Ibrahim (1854–1944), who were prominent pan-Asianists, influencing the Japanese leadership and advocating Japan's alliance with rising Muslim nationalism. In 1942, Japan's pan-Asian propaganda of the Greater East Asia Coprosperity Sphere under Japan leadership came to a boil. The Greater East Asia Ministry, which dealt with affairs within Greater East Asia, was separate from the Foreign Ministry of Japan, which handled "pure diplomacy." Prime Minister Tojo Hideki stated that there was "no need for foreign relations" within the Coprosperity Sphere of "blurred boundaries."

In the decisive battle at Midway (1942), U.S. forces protected the island. Midway was the turning point; thereafter the Allies began to drive the Japanese back and eventually accepted the surrender of the Japanese

The immensely tall Petronus Towers in Kuala Lumpur, Malaysia, symbolize the economic rise of East Asia.

empire in 1945. After the end of the war, imperial power in Asia fell apart. In 1945, the colonial empire of defeated Japan collapsed. The Japanese occupation brought a redrawing of certain territorial boundaries, but these changes were reversed immediately after the surrender in conformance with the idea that the peace should bring a return to the status quo ante. But very soon, British India acquired the status of dominion in 1947, being divided into the Indian Union and Pakistan. Burma became independent in 1948. Indonesia became free from Holland in 1949 and Malaya from Britain in 1957, and others followed.

DECOLONIZATION IN ASIA

Conservatives write about decolonization with disapproval. They depict chaotic and sometimes bloody processes as reactive fatuity and formless rivalry. "The colonial powers did not conspire against the natives," writes Paul Johnson. "They conspired against each other. Each colonial power hated all the rest, despised their methods, rejoiced in their misfortunes and happily aggravated them when convenient." One reason there was no alignment of policy for decolonization was that neither of the two biggest colonial powers, Britain and France, actually possessed one.

One thing decolonization did not lack was paper constitutions. When ex-colonial peoples gained independence, they thought they were being given justice. All they got was the right to elect politicians. While ordinary people saw the res publica in terms of justice, their nationalist leaders saw it in terms of votes. The beneficiaries of decolonization were therefore the vote manipulators, most of whom became dictators very soon. The former colonies thus became superlative prey for crops of new professional politicians.

PILLARS OF THE EAST'S SUCCESS

For half a century of postcolonial rule, the leading Asian countries gained appreciable success in developing their economies. Japan became an Asiatic leader in manufacturing and banking in the 1960s and 1970s, followed by the four "East Asian tigers" (Korea, Taiwan, Hong Kong, and Singapore) in the 1980s and mid-1990s, and the three "aspiring tigers" (Thailand, Indonesia, and Malaysia). China in the 1980s and 1990s and India in the 1990s gained remarkable economic accomplishments as well. All the above-mentioned countries and a number of others continued to grow.

The outgoing character of Asian economic development in the last decades is evident owing to four interlocked peculiarities that have become a source of Asia's new power.

They are: 1) the implementation of the long-term strategy of the export encouragement model of economic development when competitive price, high quality, and the offering of required goods were the keys to success in the international markets; 2) firm autocratic rule that secured the possibility for unpopular and painful but necessary restructuring monetarist reforms beyond parliamentary and media discussions as well as savings drive campaigns in the cause of the common good; 3) making favorable conditions (climate) for foreign direct investments and loans (it is calculated, for instance, that the economic growth in South Korea in 1980s without this factor would be 2.5 percent slower); 4) the traditions of Asian labor that have taught large masses of population to work hard for a long period of time for relatively low pay.

ASIATIC VALUES

All that is connected with the widely discussed issue of Asiatic values is a set of ideas, concepts, and statements formulated by the intellectuals and political leaders of Japan and the new industrial countries. Asiatic values reflect changes in the public consciousness of the Asian nations, changes that have occurred as a result of their economic and technological rise for the last decades.

No doubt the forces now dominating world politics and economy and intending to preserve their supremacy are hostile to the rising East. Thereby they are holding the conservative fort and to some extent are confirming the orthodoxy of portraying conservatism by its critics as an unprincipled apology by the ruling elite interests. Asiatic values are assumed to be pervasively shared among the dozen countries and 2.7 billion people in the Asian region (including India) and to be distinct from Western values. Because of the East's ambiguity, there is no consent on how to define the notion of Asiatic values precisely.

But on the whole, the basis of Asiatic values amounts to the following: collectivism and group interests instead of individuality; reliability concerning community instead of individual rights and freedoms; paternalistic, family-oriented, consensual, and clientelist political action instead of pluralism and democracy, that is, the family is regarded as an optimal model of power organizing and responsibility in the frames of the political system; and respect and acceptance of authority and social order. (That is, the organic understanding of the society in which the state is the main warrantor of its fundamental interests.)

Asiatic values also include power predominance over wealth. In the West, if the people who have made money at the market use it to buy political power and to influence it, in the East they seek power in order to make money with the help of politicians. Asian values have a higher rating of personal relations than personal qualities; harmony and consensus instead of discourse and confrontation, conflict and competition. That is, putting common interests before political rivalry on the priority scale and recognizing the mutual responsibility of an employer and an employee, of a governor and governed. High ratings in values also include ethics and morality before the law, and specific values of work ethics: diligence, hard effort, thrift and frugality, self-discipline, obedience, and patience.

The Asiatic values rhetoric may be explained as an attempt to overcome its peculiar inferiority complex concerning the West. Asians are capable of doing everything as well as the peoples of the West, and can equally compete with them in the most important spheres of life. The fact that such cities of the region as Tokyo, Singapore, and Hong Kong are replacing London, New York, and Paris as the world financial and economic centers is illustrative too. Economic advance assures the people of Asia of their future. The most active supporters of Asiatic values are representatives of local elites, many of whom were educated in the West and have played a key role in the modernization of their countries. The slogan "Asiatization of Asia" has become popular in their ranks. The Asian self-consciousness is being revived and the usage of the very notion of Asia in the positive sense indicates this. Many leaders and political scientists have been speaking of the advent of an Asian Age, a kind of Pax Asiana, which is coming to replace the Pax Americana or Atlantic Age.

According to Asiatic values supporters, just when Western values are devitalizing and losing their effectiveness, Asian education and outlook are strengthening actuality and significance. These values, which form the ideological basis for a number of East Asian regimes combining political conservatism with market economy, are increasingly promoted by many regional politicians as an alternative to Western liberalism and social-democratic values. The majority of Asian elites contravene the principle of universalism of human rights and freedoms, believing that they have to be appraised by taking into consideration national, historical, religious, and other traditions.

Western conservatism recognizes the economic successes of the East Asian model but focuses on its price as unacceptable. It also stresses the transience and changeability of Asian achievements in the light of the 1997 economic crisis. Ironically, the two types of conservatism contradict each other. The Asian one wants to preserve Asian customs by supporting distinctively conservative principles such as loyalty, duty, and hierarchy. It aims at using these traditional values for consolidating Asian societies and for strengthening Asian positions when competing with the West and in changing the world hierarchy of prosperous nations, a world hierarchy that is toughly defended by Western conservatism.

One product of the Asian values debate is a proposal that, in addition to liberalism and socialism, there is an ideological and cultural third force, labeled patriarchalism. "Patriarchalism both assumes the naturalness of inequalities in the social relations between people and justifies these by reference to the respect due to a benevolent father or father-figure who exercises a joint right," explain the supporters of such an approach. They suggest that "a revival of the human rights project on a more equal civilizational basis that, because it assumes the hybrid nature of all societies, is neither Occidentalist nor Orientalist, might yet become possible," according to Anthony Woodiwiss in *Globalisation, Human Rights and Labour Law in Pacific Asia*. One can also find a quite opposite approach, which would nevertheless remain in the right conservative framework. It argues that the "Asian" combination of capitalist economics and authoritarian rule is not exceptional, and Asian values are decidedly more similar to Western values than is usually presumed. For some dimensions of values, Asians diverge more from one another than they do from Americans and Western Europeans.

HUMAN RIGHTS

As for the interrelationship of Asian values and human rights, the problem is rather complicated. Asiatic values propaganda serves as a bulwark against a Western emphasis on human rights that is not "Asian," and which constitutes either meddling by outsiders or their use of discourse about human rights to further purposes that are inimical to Asian interests. Some Asian intellectuals charge their opponents in the West with assuming that any idea coming from them is perfect and must be accepted by the whole world.

Instead of Western human rights rhetoric, Asians rely on their own traditional values. The concept is welcomed by cultural relativists, cultural supremacists, and isolationists alike as fresh evidence for their various positions against a political liberalism that defends universal human rights and democracy. They claim that 1) rights are "culturally specific," and the circumstances that prompted the institutionalization of human rights in the West do not exist in Asia; 2) the importance of the community in Asian culture is incompatible with the primacy of the individual, upon which the Western notion of human rights rests; 3) social and economic rights take precedence over civil and political rights because the former are the spirit of people's life and the latter are not; 4) rights are a matter of national sovereignty, and the right of a nation to self-determination includes a government's domestic jurisdiction over human rights, and thus human rights are internal affairs, not to be interfered with by foreign states or multinational agencies.

But most conservatives in the West join liberals in viewing this assertion of "Asian values" simply as a cloak for arrogant regimes whose newly gained confidence from rapidly growing economic power makes them all the more resistant to outside criticism. However, the Asian crisis of 1997 forced a reconsideration and revision of their political and economic systems.

ASIAN CRISIS

Triggered by the collapse of Thailand's baht on July 2, 1997, four economies that had high positive gross domestic product growth for several years now experienced negative growth (between 5 and 12 percent) in late 1997 and 1998. Asset values in these "crisis" countries (Thailand, South Korea, Malaysia, and Indonesia) plummeted by about 75 percent owing to currency depreciation, deflated equity, and property valuations. Averaging over the four economies, an asset worth $100 in June 1997 was worth only $25 a year later. Because of the currency crisis, East Asia had lost some $500 billion of purchasing power. There was a general problem of overlending with huge pyramids of bad debts, overinvestment, and in some cases overproduction. When the baht collapsed, the international investors took fright and withdrew their money. When capital is pulled out, it can cause a country to collapse completely. Enormous wealth has gone from Eastern Asia as a result. The crisis countries became more in debt to the International Monetary Fund and Western banks. Even those countries that were not in quite the same position as these four faced enormous difficulties. The crisis seriously endangered the livelihoods of millions of people, causing untold misery and suffering.

As a result of the economic crisis, governments have fallen in Indonesia, Thailand, and South Korea or, as in Malaysia, have come perilously close to the precipice. For Western conservatives, it meant that liberal democracy has one huge advantage over authoritarian capitalism or communism: government authority does not crack as soon as the economy goes down. Liberal democracies "can weather almost any economic storm," it was said. The events at the end of the 1990s in Asia have shown the political fragility of government systems whose legitimacy is almost entirely based on the continued promise of riches.

Some Western right-wing viewers assert that Asiatic values provide little if any explanation for what happened in East Asia. Instead, they are looking for answers in the macroeconomic monetary and fiscal policies pursued by various Asian countries, in their foreign-debt policies, in their use of nonmarket-based rather than market-based modes of resource allocation, and in the impediments they place in the way of entrepreneurial activity, both domestic and foreign.

Asian conservatives blame globalization extremists from the rich countries of the West. Former Malaysian Premier Mahathir bin Mohamad equates contemporary capitalism with the new imperialism. Once Russian communism was defeated, Western capitalism was no longer constrained. In light of the Asian crisis, Mohamad is suspicious about unregulated markets because they are only about making profits.

According to such statist critique, there must be a balance between a free market and some regulations that are essential in order to safeguard the interests of consumers and of people in general. "It is not true at all that a free market will ensure a democracy. It doesn't," Mohamad says and goes on: "We believe in trade, but we didn't believe in just being a market for other people. When it comes to global economy, it should be a world consensus, not a Washington consensus which enriches the rich at the expense of the poor."

SEE ALSO

Volume 1 Left: Asia; Liberalism; Anti-Globalization.
Volume 2 Right: Capitalism; Orientalism; Imperialism.

BIBLIOGRAPHY

Hans Antlov and Tak-Wing Ngo, eds., *The Cultural Construction of Politics in Asia* (Palgrave Macmillan, 2000); Ian Barnes and Robert Hudson, *Historical Atlas of Asia* (Arcadia Editions Ltd., 1998); Daniel A. Bell, *East Meets West: Human Rights and Democracy in East Asia* (Princeton University Press, 2000); Beng Huat Chua, ed., *Communitarian Politics in Asia* (Routledge, 2004); Jorn Dosch, Remy Davison, and Michael Kelly Connors, *New Global Politics of the Asia Pacific* (Curzon Press, 2004); Niall Ferguson, *Empire: The Rise and Demise of the British World Order and the Lessons for Global Power* (Basic Books, 2003); Bernard Lewis, *What Went Wrong: Western Impact and Middle Eastern Response* (Oxford University Press, 2002); Richard Robison, "The Politics of Asian Values," *Pacific Review* (v.3, 1996); Edward W. Said, *Orientalism* (Vintage Books, 1979); Muzaffar Sivaraksa, Sulak Sivaraksa, and Chandra Muzaffar, *Alternative Politics for Asia: A Buddhist-Muslim Dialogue* (Lantern Books, 2003); Joseph E. Stiglitz, *Globalization and Its Discontents* (Norton, 2003); Han Sung-Joo, ed., *Changing Values in Asia* (Japan Center for International Exchange, Tokyo, 1999)

IGOR CHARSKYKH
DONETSK NATIONAL UNIVERSITY, UKRAINE

Associative State

THE TERM *associative state* describes a particular kind of partnership between firms and the government. In an associative state, the government promotes techniques of administrative management to rationalize production and distribution in industry. Firms and government cooperate to reshape the self-interest of industrialists to accord more closely with the public interest, in order to guarantee economic growth.

The idea of associationalism was first developed by Herbert Hoover as Secretary of Commerce in the 1920s. By rejecting the liberal model of *laissez-faire*, Hoover encouraged the formation of trade associations for the exchange of information about materials, production, and marketing that would have allowed corporations to contain prices while eliminating costly competition. As an engineer dedicated to efficiency, Hoover considered many aspects of competition among companies as wasteful, such as the inability of firms to create new technological developments, and the inability to take advantage of existing opportunities through simplification and standardization. Excessive economic individualism in the form of anarchic competition was in fact perceived by Hoover as the main cause of overproduction and unemployment. Nevertheless, the capitalistic economic system could have been reformed through voluntary association and cooperation, in which the government would have played a key role. In this regard, the role played by the state in an associative system was only a temporary one. The associative state was in fact needed only during the transitional phase. After having fulfilled its task as economic mediator, the associative state would have disappeared or been relegated to symbolic functions.

In order to establish an associative state, Hoover, as Secretary of Commerce, strategically used his department to reorganize the government to equip it with those tools necessary to improve government services for American businesses. This was achieved through a system of committees established to encourage organization and cooperation in the private business sector at different levels. Primarily, he encouraged the exchange of information regarding production and prices among American companies.

Second, Hoover promoted the establishment of industrial standards. This also included supplying companies with reports on opportunities in foreign trade and investment to enrich the informational climate so that the individual firm could become the main instrument of economic stabilization. Finally, Hoover used coercive regulatory power to rationalize "sick industries" such as coal and to stimulate new infrastructure industries such as aviation and radio broadcasting to promote consumption.

As president, Hoover retreated from the associative vision after many of his projects failed for lack of funding. However, the idea of associationalism did not fade away. Instead, it was ironically carried out by Hoover's successor, Franklin D. Roosevelt. Among the several initiatives promoted by the Roosevelt administration associated with the notion of associative state, the most important was the drafting of the National Industrial Recovery Act (NIRA) in 1933, with which the government empowered trade associations and private businesses to draft codes of fair competition under the supervision of a National Recovery Administration (NRA). The vagueness of its statute, however, sparked a huge debate among political and economic forces regarding the true nature of the NIRA. For the associationalists, it was a genuine attempt of self-government for the industry. For its detractors, it was an instrument in the government's hands to control the industry. The debate over the nature of the NIRA ended two years later, when the NIRA was declared unconstitutional in 1935.

Despite the failure of the NIRA, the notion of associative state did not totally disappear from the American political scene. It periodically reappeared, even if in a more subtle way. From the Office of Scientific Research and Development (OSRD), which supervised a set of committees composed by civilian and industrial scientists and military officers established to promote research in the military sector during World War II, to the Cooperative Research and Development Agreements (CRADAs) between government laboratories and private firms during the Reagan administration, the idea of associative state has proved its endurance on the American political and economic scene.

The similarity between the ideas of the associative state and the adoption of a similar method of industrial regulation and management by the Italian fascist state has led some to regard Hoover's associative state concept as a variant of that right-wing ideology. However, in the American context, Hoover's economic plan for state intervention through industrial associations has been seen as less conservative than a pure *laissez-faire* position.

SEE ALSO

Volume 1 Left: Roosevelt, Franklin D.; New Deal.
Volume 2 Right: Capitalism; *Laissez Faire.*

BIBLIOGRAPHY
Ellis W. Hawley, "Herbert Hoover, the Commerce Secretariat, and the Vision of an Associative State, 1921–28," *Journal of American History* (v.61/1, June 1974); David M. Hart, "Herbert Hoover's Last Laugh: The Enduring Significance of the Associative State in the United States," *Journal of Policy History* (v.10/4, 1998); David M. Hart, *Forged Consensus* (Princeton University Press, 1998); Mark A. Eisner, *From Warfare State to Welfare State* (Pennsylvania State University Press, 2000).

PIETRO PIRANI
UNIVERSITY OF WESTERN ONTARIO, CANADA

Australia

AUSTRALIA IS A FEDERAL system, which means there is both a national government and a second level of government, the state and territorial governments. It is a liberal democratic government and its government structure is a hybrid, reflecting the influence of both the British parliamentary model and the American presidential model. The queen is the head of state and the governor general represents the monarch in her absence (which is most of the time). The head of state is a mostly symbolic position. The national parliament is bicameral, with a House of Representatives and a Senate. Like a parliamentary system, there is a blending of the legislative and executive branches; there are cabinet solidarity and responsible government; and there is strict party discipline. Australia has a written constitution. The date of elections is not fixed, but there is a maximum length to a term (and different terms for both houses) and an election must be called before the end of the term. The individual states also have constitutions, and these documents may be amended in most parts by the state legislature without the express consent of the people.

The Australian party system in theory is a multiparty one. In actuality, it is a strong bipolar party system, essentially a two-party structure. The Liberal Party is a center-right party and the National Party is also a center-right party and together they act as a coalition to counter the center-left Labour Party. All of the main parties differ more with respect to social policy than to economic policy.

The Liberal Party of Australia formed in 1944 out of a concern with the Labour Party's postwar socialist plans. The Liberals brought together 18 nonlabor parties, which separately could do nothing against the dominant Labour Party. Robert Menzies, former prime minister (1939–41) and leader of the United Australia Party (a party that was defeated in the 1943 national election and never recovered), resigned following his party's division over World War II policy, and spearheaded the formation of the new Liberal Party. The name "Liberal" was chosen to associate the party with progressive 19th-century liberal ideas, including free enterprise and social equality.

In their first election in 1946, the Liberals presented a new choice for the people of Australia and garnered 17 out of 75 seats. This was followed with success in the state elections in 1947; in fact, the Liberals took power in Western Australia, Southern Australia, and Victoria. In the national election of 1949, the Liberals formed a coalition with the Country Party and began a 23-year winning streak (all in coalition). Menzies led the country as prime minister from the win in 1949 until 1966. The impact of his political legacy was duly recognized by his knighthood in 1963. Although the Liberals lost in 1972, they regained power in 1975 and held office for seven years (also in a coalition government). Again, in 1996, they entered a coalition with the National Party to dominate national politics in Australia, and this coalition has successfully continued through elections in 1998 and 2001. In the 2001 national election, the Liberal Party won 68 seats in the House of Representatives; the National Party won 13 votes; and the Country Liberal Party won 1 seat (all forming the Liberal/National coalition). The Australian Labour Party won 65 seats. In the sometimes bizarre breakdown of seats that can occur in single-member districts when there are multiple parties running for a plurality of the vote, the Labour Party garnered 37.84 percent of the popular vote, whereas the Liberal Party only won 37.08 percent of the popular vote and the National Party brought in a further 5.61 percent of the popular vote. The Liberal Party describes itself as the party of initiative and enterprise. The Liberals also promote several conservative principles, including individual initiative, private enterprise, traditional family values, the reduction of taxes, and the limitation of government intrusion into the private lives and choices of individuals.

NATIONAL PARTY

The National Party is over 80 years old and is a conservative party that stresses the preservation of traditional values. Originally named the Country Party, the party was renamed the National Country Party in 1975 and became the current National Party in 1982. This party advocates the promotion of private enterprise and self-initiative as well as a balanced, if not limited, role for government. The party tries to instill the interests of the citizens in rural and remote areas of Australia (that is, farmers) into national politics, to ensure that the interests of the people residing in the populous cities do not overwhelm these regional interests. The National Party presents three bedrock principles: the preservation of security for the nation, for local communities, and for families; the promotion of individual achievement; and the search for Members of Parliament who are strong local advocates and champions for their regions yet have the ability to come together as a team.

The National Party, despite its limited base of support, plays an often critical role in Australian politics, presenting the pivotal votes in a coalition government. The Liberal Party has never managed a majority national government, requiring the National Party's added seats to govern. It is a convention that the party leader of the smaller partner in the coalition government shall be the deputy prime minister.

SEE ALSO

Volume 1 Left: Australia.
Volume 2 Right: Conservatism; United Kingdom.

BIBLIOGRAPHY

National Party, www.nationals.org.au (May 2004); Liberal Party, www. liberal.org.au (May 2004); Brian Galligan, Francis G. Castles, and Geoffrey Brennan, eds., *Federal Republic* (Cambridge University Press, 1995).

AMANDA BURGESS
WAYNE STATE UNIVERSITY

Austria

LIKE THE REST OF central Europe, during the 20th century the people of Austria suffered a great deal from war and political conflict, the latter particularly rooted in right-left conflict. Five major cases in the last 100 years illustrate the power of the right wing in Austria. These are: 1) right-left conflict during the First Republic; 2) the 1938 *Anschluss* with Nazi Germany; 3) the post-World War II rehabilitation of Austrian Nazis and Nazi sympathizers, as well as Austrian reluctance in

restitution of stolen art, stolen property, seized bank accounts and gold, as well as life insurance policies; 4) controversy over the presidency of Kurt Waldheim; and 5) the participation of Jörg Haider in the Austrian government.

CONFLICT IN THE FIRST REPUBLIC

Austria's First Republic was established in November 1918, at the end of World War I, in the wake of the collapse of the Austro-Hungarian Empire. The empire was a long-standing multinational entity but it was on the losing side of the Great War and was, along with the German and Ottoman Empires, liquidated by the victors. Based on the theory that each nation should have a state of its own, the Republic of German Austria was created.

The majority of Austrians were and are German-speaking, but the victorious countries, particularly France and the United Kingdom, would not accept a large, single German state.

The entire history of the First Republic was conflict-ridden. In the early 1920s, Austria suffered under private armies controlled by right- and left-wing political movements. These armies, the Heimwehr (right) and the Schutzbund (left), were formed by officers and soldiers of the Austro-Hungarian army, who had never been properly demobilized or disarmed. In February 1934, Austria experienced civil war when fighting broke out between police and military and the left-wing Schutzbund in its strongholds of Linz and "Red Vienna." As a consequence, the Social Democratic Party and elements of the labor movement were outlawed. This represented the consolidation of an authoritarian state, inspired by the Italian model, under Dr. Engelbert Dollfuss and the "Christian Socials."

ANSCHLUSS WITH GERMANY

Hitler came to power in Germany in 1933, and he immediately proceeded to put pressure on his neighbors, in part through allied Nazi parties. There were three forces in Austria at this time: Social Democrats and Communists on the left, traditional conservatives such as the Christian Socials on the right, and the Nazis. In July 1935, the Austrian Nazis killed Dollfuss, and afterward they continued to destabilize the country. In March 1938, Hitler marched 100,000 troops into Austria, and in April the government agreed to hold a plebiscite on the question of a union between Germany and Austria (*Anschluss*), despite the fact that this move

bility for Nazi aggression and crimes against humanity, particularly the Holocaust, has caused significant problems for the Second Republic, founded by the Austria State Treaty in 1955. Before World War II, there were 190,000 Jews in Austria, and at least 65,000 were killed in the Holocaust and many others fled as refugees. But until the 1990s, there had been little willingness in Austria to restore bank balances, real property, and artworks to their rightful owners or to provide reparations for victims of the Holocaust.

Further, there were 500,000 members of the Nazi Party in Austria and yet, after the war, they were largely absolved of responsibility, both by the Allied powers that controlled Austria from 1945 to 1955 and by the Austrians themselves.

KURT WALDHEIM AND JÖRG HAIDER

This legacy of left-right conflict and the Austrian values and role in World War II continue to haunt the country. Waldheim served for two terms as secretary-general of the United Nations, and in 1986 he decided to run for the Austrian presidency. However, investigations revealed that Waldheim, who had served as an officer in the German army in World War II, had underplayed his role in that conflict. Rather than playing a minor role, he had, in fact, served in Yugoslavia, where Nazi military policy had been harsh.

Waldheim was elected to the presidency and the country's international relations and reputation suffered accordingly. After Waldheim's retirement, the world was again reminded of the strength of the right in Austrian life. In 1999, Haider, the leader of the ultra-right Freedom Party (FPO), made an electoral breakthrough in Austria, with 27 percent of the vote, and he was asked to join a conservative coalition government. The Freedom Party was anti-immigrant, anti-refugee, and against European Union. It called for an Austria First employment policy and has supported paying mothers to stay at home and care for their children. In 2002, the FPO vote collapsed to 10.2 percent but the party was still asked to continue in the new Austrian government.

SEE ALSO

Volume 1 Left: Austria; Socialism; Communism; Germany.
Volume 2 Right: Fascism; Germany.

BIBLIOGRAPHY

Elizabeth Barker, *Austria 1918–72* (Macmillan, 1973); Lothar Höbelt, *Defiant Populist: Jörg Haider and the Politics of Austria*

In 1999, Jörg Haider, the leader of the ultra-right Freedom Party, made an electoral breakthrough in Austria.

was illegal under the terms of the 1919 Treaty of Versailles. Austrian leaders, including Karl Renner, who would lead Austria after World War II, recommended a "yes" vote, and 90 percent of the voters did so.

NAZI REHABILITATION, RESTITUTION, AND THE AUSTRIAN HOLOCAUST

There is something of a myth, perpetuated by Austrians and by the victors of World War II, that Austria was the first victim of Nazi German aggression. There is some truth to this, but many Austrians were active supporters of the German nationalism represented by the Nazi Party and its Austrian-born leader, Adolf Hitler. This tendency to absolve the Austrian people of culpa-

(Purdue University Press, 2003); Anton Pelinka, *Austria: Out of the Shadow of the Past* (Westview Press, 1998); Hella Pick, *Guilty Victim: Austria from Holocaust to Haider* (I.B. Tauris Publishers, 2000).

GEOFFREY R. MARTIN
MOUNT ALLISON UNIVERSITY, CANADA

Autarchy

ANY STATE, REGION, OR community, or even a plantation or manor, which is entirely self-sufficient is an autarchy. When the term is used in a strictly economic sense of a state that seeks to limit foreign imported goods or to operate entirely with domestic products and manufactures, the policy goal is sometimes spelled as "autarky." In that economic policy usage of the term, a state that adopts high tariffs or other barriers to imports, or that seeks to develop domestic sources for previously imported goods or products, can be said to be moving towards autarky or autarchy. Although an economic concept of self-sufficiency, the term autarchy has also been applied more broadly in a cultural context, as an aspect of nationalism, with political and ideological overtones. A cultural autarchy is a state or region that rejects the importation or usage of alien ideas, cultural styles, mannerisms, and language.

In the 20th century, numerous states have adopted a policy of autarchy or self-sufficiency. Those that made the greatest efforts at autarchic economy and autarchic culture tended to be the most intensely nationalistic, or states in a period of nationalistic isolation. For the most part, those states have been found on the right side of the political spectrum, although from time to time, more democratic or socialist regimes have sought economic independence or economic nationalism and have been said to be moving in an autarchic direction. During the 1920s, the Soviet Union sought to structure its economy to be independent of foreign trade, and its policy in that period was regarded as tending toward autarchy. In the 1930s, when Benito Mussolini's Italy was under international sanctions for its invasion of Ethiopia, the nation sought to build economic independence. Adolf Hitler's Germany, in the same period, developed an official policy of self-sufficiency or autarchy. Mahatma Gandhi advocated Indian independence of reliance on imports in the 1940s, and his ideology had autarchic aspects. Spain was isolated from the international community in the period after World War II and had to rely on domestic products, adopting a policy of autarchy.

The term *autarchy* has been applied with another meaning to leaders and regimes who were so autocratic in their rule that they tended to exclude the advice and opinions of others. The term has been used in this fashion to describe rulers who isolate themselves within their government and seek to rule single-handedly or self-sufficiently. In modern states, the charge that a ruler sought autarchy in this sense has represented a severe criticism of his or her rule. Such a critique has sometimes been utilized as part of a program to remove the ruler from power. Thus, for example, when Tzar Nicholas II of Russia dismissed his minister of war in September 1915 and assumed control of the Russian army, critics charged Nicholas with autarchy. The reliance for advice by Nicholas and Tzarina Alexandra on the popularly hated monk Gregory Rasputin fed the image of an autarchic or autocratic leader refusing to share power with responsible administrators and advisors. That criticism, voiced by middle-class reformers, nobility, and the radical leaders of the revolutionary political parties in Russia, contributed to pressure leading to the tzar's abdication in February 1917.

In the early 21st century, economic autarchy has been regarded as a form of nationalism incompatible with globalization. Thus, those regimes that isolate themselves from the exchange of goods, products, information, culture, and services, such as the governments of North Korea and Iran, are regarded as contemporary autarchies.

SEE ALSO

Volume 1 Left: Russian Revolution.
Volume 2 Right: Germany; Fascism.

BIBLIOGRAPHY

William Carr, *Arms, Autarky and Aggression* (Norton, 1973); Gordon Alexander Craig, *Germany 1866–1945* (Oxford University Press, 1980); Nils Gilman, *Mandarins of the Future* (Johns Hopkins University Press, 2004); Amos Jordan et al., *American National Security* (Johns Hopkins University Press, 1998); Adrian Lyttleton, *Liberal and Fascist Italy* (Oxford University Press, 2002); Anthony D. Smith, *Nationalism and Modernism: A Critical Survey of Recent Theories of Nations and Nationalism* (Routledge, 1998).

RODNEY P. CARLISLE
GENERAL EDITOR

B

Ba'athism

MICHEL AFLAQ was a product of the French mandate in Syria after World War I. He was born in 1910 and raised in the French tradition of education introduced into Syria and Lebanon after France took political control in 1920. Philip K. Hitti wrote that the French "organized an educational system, encouraged archaeological researches, gave fellowships for study in France especially in such neglected fields as art, set up a department of public health and sanitation, and developed public security. Modern codes of law were promulgated."

Even the Druze tribes, who had lived with some independence under the Ottoman Turks, were made to feel the presence of French law, through the expeditions of the French Foreign Legion into their mountainous country, the Djebel Druze. However, the French colonial administrators encountered a paradoxical effect from their efforts at modernization. They realized, too late, that exposing the natives of Greater Lebanon to the ideas of the French Enlightenment would lead to them desiring *liberté*, *égalité*, and *fraternité*—from the rule of the French! Hitti recorded how "repressive measures were taken against nationalists. Future officials of the republic, including Shukri al-Quwatli, Faris al-Khuri, Salih al-Haffar, and other leaders of thought and action were, at some time or other, banished or jailed."

The French colonial authorities began a concerted effort to stamp out any independent tendencies in the Greater Lebanese region. However, an effective check existed on their excesses. News of the repression reached France and outraged voices were raised in the Chamber of Deputies, the French Parliament, and the independent press. The French Republic dispatched Henri de Jouvenel to become the new high commissioner. While Jouvenel was unsuccessful in stopping the nationalist agitation, he is considered the most liberal of the high commissioners to have ruled during the French mandate. Jouvenel's policies did not bring an end to nationalist agitation within Greater Lebanon. In January 1927, a nationalist congress was held in Beirut.

It was against this background that Aflaq went to study at the Sorbonne in Paris, clearly one of the highly educated Syrians the French would have coveted for their colonial administration. However, once exposed to French ideas, like his contemporary Ho Chi Minh, he became an ardent nationalist who desired the end of French rule in his country.

His idea was one of a secular nationalism, as befitting a student of the French Enlightenment. It was a basically socialist vision, but more in keeping with French social thought than the communism of Vladimir Lenin. Aflaq wrote poetically: "Nationalism is spiritual and all-embracing, in the sense that it opens its arms and spreads its wings over all those who have shared with the Arabs their history and have lived in the environment of their language and culture for generations, so that they have become Arab in thought and feeling."

Aflaq foresaw the clash that secular nationalism would have with the traditionalists in the Muslim world who still felt that the *sha'riah*, the Islamic law from the time of the Prophet Mohammed, should hold sway in Muslim countries. Indeed, he realized that in the old days of the Arabian caliphate in Baghdad, and in the more modern Ottoman Empire, which had ruled Syria and Lebanon until the end of World War I, church and nation were really synonymous in an Islamic state. "There is no fear," Aflaq assured, "that nationalism will clash with religion, for, like religion, it flows from the heart and issues from the will of God; they walk arm in arm, supporting each other." While Aflaq embraced Islam as the religion for the Arab peoples, it was ironic that he had been raised a Christian.

During World War II, he admired Adolf Hitler and saw in Nazism the type of national socialism he espoused for the Arab world. At the time of the 1941 fascist Rashid Ali coup in Iraq, he and Salah Bitar formed in Syria the Society to Help Iraq. The society would later form the nucleus of the Ba'ath, or "Renaissance" Party, which Aflaq and Bitar established in 1947.

The Ba'ath socialist party would grow in the Arab world as a response to the Arab nations' defeat by Israel in the 1948 Middle East war. However, Aflaq's nationalistic mysticism did not suit the hardheaded and power hungry military men who would adopt it as their philosophy. But his fascist, militarist leanings did.

According to *The Syrian Encyclopedia*, "The Iraqi branch of the Ba'ath party was established in 1954 after the merger of the Ba'ath with Akram al-Hurani's Arab Socialist Party in 1952, to form the Arab Ba'ath Socialist Party." In February 1963, General Abdul Karim Kassim was overthrown by Ba'ath army officers in Iraq and shot. Soon the Ba'athists were marginalized by the military men, as Abd al-Salam al-Arif became president of the new National Council of the Military Command (NCMC).

By 1969, Saddam Hussein began to co-opt the Ba'ath Party at the 7th Party Congress in 1969. It was here that he started to build the loyalty of members of the party to him, much as Josef Stalin, whose communism many Iraqi Ba'athists admired, had done after the death of Lenin in 1924. Charles Tripp would write of Hussein in this stage of his dictatorial career that he "ensured that the party lost any kind of existence independent of the direction which he himself was to give it."

In March 1963, the Ba'ath Party in Aflaq's native Syria came to power. *The Syrian Encyclopedia* notes: "on March 8, it came to power in Syria after the March Revolution. Inter-party disagreements were one of the major factors that led to the Correction Movement led by Hafez al-Assad, the movement ended years of conflict within the party. A new constitution, approved in 1973, stated that the Ba'ath Party is the 'leading party in the state and society.' In 1972, the Ba'ath also became the leader of the seven Syrian parties forming the National Progressive Front (NPF). The national committee of the Ba'ath is effectively the decision making body in Syria."

The Syrian Ba'ath rule under Assad, while based in the military, would not metamorphose into the dictatorship that evolved in Hussein's Iraq. Hussein would finally seize power in 1979. However, on June 25, 1980, when the rival Muslim Brotherhood of the Syrian branch attempted to assassinate Assad, he reacted viciously. In retaliation, he unleashed the Syrian Army on the Brotherhood stronghold of Hama; some 15,000 to 25,000 people were killed in an assault that began in February 1982. Assad would, however, follow a path of hegemony as he took control of Lebanon, which had been wracked by civil war between Muslims and Christians since April 1970. In that month, driven from Jordan by King Hussein's Bedouin army, Yassir Arafat's Palestine Liberation Organization (PLO) would establish itself in Beirut. In 1982, Israel would launch Operation Peace for Galilee against the PLO in Lebanon and heavily damage the Syrian forces in the Bekaa Valley. In June 2000, Hafez Assad died and was succeeded by his son Bashir, by training an ophthalmologist, but also the commander-in-chief of the armed forces. Finally, in July 2000, Prime Minister Ehud Barak began the withdrawal of Israeli forces from a security buffer zone in southern Lebanon. But, as Human Rights Watch noted, continued problems were posed by "the Syrian presence in Lebanon, and the ultimate fate of some 350,000 stateless Palestinian refugees, some of whom have lived as unwelcome residents in Lebanon for over 50 years."

Meanwhile, having seized power in 1979, Hussein used the Ba'ath Party to follow a path of repression as thuggish as the Nazi Party, which Aflaq had so admired. Like Assad, he also followed the path of expansion. In September 1980, he embarked on a war of aggression against the Iran of the Ayatollah Khomeini, whose theological regime was the antithesis of the Ba'ath state socialism. The war ended with a United Nations cease-fire in July 1988. One year later, in 1989, Aflaq, who had united Arab nationalism with fascism, was buried at a state funeral in Baghdad. Only one year later in August 1990, Saddam embarked on a another disastrous war when he invaded Kuwait. In February 1991, his troops were decisively defeated in a 100-hour ground war by a coalition of forces united to stem his aggression, led by the United States. Finally, with the fear that Saddam was harboring nuclear, biological, and chemical weapons of mass destruction, President George W. Bush announced the intention to intervene in Iraq militarily.

In December 2003, Hussein, the "Butcher of Baghdad," was captured hiding near his hometown of Tikrit. A massive effort was made to eradicate Ba'athist influence, even aborted plans to destroy the tomb of Aflaq. However, in the face of mounting difficulties in governing Iraq, the United States was reconsidering the banning of former Ba'ath Party members from public life. On April 20, 2004, Barry Schweid wrote for the website, www.findlaw.com, that "thousands of Iraqis who swore allegiance to Saddam Hussein's political party may be getting jobs under the U.S.-led coalition in Baghdad as the Bush administration—struggling to put down resistance—undertakes a major shift in policy."

SEE ALSO

Volume 1 Left: Socialism; Asia; Middle East.
Volume 2 Right: Fascism; Middle East; Iraq.

BIBLIOGRAPHY

Sylvia G. Haim, ed., *Arab Nationalism* (University of California Press, 1962); *The Syrian Encyclopedia*, www.damascus-online.com/se (July 2004); Human Rights Watch, "Israel's Withdrawal from Lebanon: The Human Rights Dimension, May 2000," www.hrw.org (July 2004); Judith Miller and Laurie Mylroie, *Saddam Hussein and the Crisis in the Gulf* (Random House, 1990); Charles Tripp, *A History of Iraq* (Cambridge University Press, 2000); John F. Murphy Jr., *Sword of Islam: Muslim Extremism from the Arab Conquest to the Attack on America* (Prometheus Books, 2002).

JOHN F. MURPHY, JR.
AMERICAN MILITARY UNIVERSITY

Balance of Power

THE BALANCE PROCESS: Two states compete with each other for influence in international relations. They aim to shape the international environment and dominate the interrelationship between states with their views and values. Put differently, they want to transfer their power to other states to become the lead nation followed by others. In this scenario, both states are relatively powerful; both enjoy vast economic power and military capabilities. However, the first state is more powerful and capable than the second. The weaker state, still a rising power, is trying to challenge the existing power order in international relations. It wants to be the dominant influence, or the next superpower that shapes the global atmosphere. The outcome of this struggle for world power is that the more powerful state exerts its military, political, and economic supremacy to limit the influence of the weaker state. In other words, it balances off its power and contains the rising state while ensuring stability in international relations. This stage, where two states finally settle their power struggle, can be called equilibrium, a balance of power.

Eugene R. Wittkopf and Charles W. Kegley believe the main aim of this theory "is the idea that peace will result when military power is distributed so that no state is strong enough to dominate the others." The more powerful state strives to create an equilibrium of power where other states are powerful or capable but not quite as powerful as itself. The existing superpower preserves the balance of power by limiting the chances of the rising and aspiring states that desire to become predominant in international relations.

The clearest example of the concept of the balance of power can be found in the Cold War. Both sides, the Soviet Union as well as the United States, were powerful nations that acquired military capabilities that would enable them to destroy each other. Their arms built up over the years and the engagement in military alliances deterred domination by the other. The United States used its atomic weapon to defeat an enemy during World War II. Shortly after that, the Soviet Union acquired its atomic weapon and surprised the Americans with the development of a thermonuclear bomb during the 1950s. This was the beginning of an arms race. By the end of the Cold War, both countries knew about the enemy's military capabilities, the number of their long-range missiles, nuclear weapons, and number of forces. During this time, governments sought to secure their territory through traditional military strength. During the 1970s and early 1980s, the United States and the Soviet Union negotiated various arms treaties to maintain a favorable military balance. This can be seen as a classical example of a balance of power theory. The United States was the superpower born after World War II, and the Soviet Union was the rising power that tried to challenge the United States for world dominance. Both countries balanced off their power and engaged in military alliances that deterred the competitor away.

THE BALANCE OF POWER THEORY

The balance of power theory is a classical realist theory of international relations and one of the oldest of its kind. By the same token, it is also one of the most controversial and most debated theories of international politics. Generally speaking, it is referred to as a theory that tries to explain: 1) the distribution of power, 2) international hegemony, 3) stability and instability, and 4) power politics. However, if we only think in terms of equilibrium rather than superiority or hegemony, then the theory of balance of power becomes less confusing. If states reach a stage of power equilibrium they are better off than before.

However, balance of power as a system, according to some viewpoints, refers to a multinational environment where all nations preserve their identity, integrity, and independence. The major supposition of the theory is that all states act rationally and only pursue policies that they consider being in their national interest. States are also seen as unitary actors in an international environment that is anarchic. It is assumed that states will make use of their power to gain influence over other states, regionally or even globally if it is in their national interest to do so. However, to reach this goal, they must prevent other states from dominating. Realist theory assumes that every state drives to expand its territory and therefore all countries are possible adversaries. Therefore, it must strengthen its military capabilities to protect itself. This assumption requires military superiority because others pursue it as well. Nevertheless, these military buildups are seen as necessary security measures. This ultimately creates a security dilemma where one state invests heavily in military capabilities, which gives other states the same incentive to build up as well in order to avoid aggression by the stronger state. However, this problem cannot be resolved completely. Every state is responsible for its own national security and each strives for survival in a hard competition with other states. This obviously creates conflicts that challenge the existing world order. In other words, the security dilemma is both the root and the outcome of the balance of power.

If a state is threatened, then it will balance against the threat. The notion of reaching equilibrium of power cannot only be found in political science literature. Biologists talk about the "balance of nature" and economists refer to the balance of international trade. States will balance internally as well as externally. They will push domestically for military buildups and investments in military forces. This process is not easy, because domestic legislators need to be convinced of the necessity of such a move and the external threat.

States tend to balance externally as well through building up or engaging in alliances. A classic example of this behavior is the engagement of the United States in the North Atlantic Treaty Organization (NATO) in 1949. Smaller and less powerful states such as Germany, France, and many others joined the alliance fearing a hegemonic Soviet Union that would leave them in a polarity vacuum between the United States and the Soviet Union. However, this does not mean that alliances have to remain stable for a long period of time; they might shift from time to time. However, in a situation of equilibrium of power it might occur that some states react languidly to any power that is trying to distress the balance. At this point, it might be useful for the system itself to possess a great power that is capable of restoring the balance quickly with military force. Historically, England played this role with its European partners.

The balance of power theory serves many functions and purposes. Its foremost purpose is to prevent war among great powers that could lead to vast destruction of people and land, as well as to preserve the system of the state itself. It also tries to prevent states from becoming a hegemonic power that will dominate the interrelationship with other states for a long period of time. The theory also tries to ensure stability and mutual security in the international system prolonging the peace and prosperity of the people.

TOOLS AND TECHNIQUES

The balance of power theory applies many techniques in order to prevent a major war or conflict among states that could lead to war. The balance of power theory possesses nine major techniques to reach a power equilibrium:

1) One of the most popular techniques is to influence and divide positions of other states diminishing their power in international relations.

2) Especially after a war, governments of weaker states could align with each other, creating a buffer state between them and the great power. This would limit the ability of the great power to expand outside its own territory. It would also give them time and options to react and prepare should this occur.

3) Territorial compensations could be negotiated, easing the hunger of states for more territory and influence. This negotiation would be settled in peace rather than after a war.

4) Smaller and weaker states could align with each other in confronting the great power. In this case, a great power would be deterred from aggression against one weaker state, because an attack on one single state could be interpreted by the alliance as an aggressive act against all of them. Therefore the great power has to consider not only the military strength of one single state but also of all member states of the alliance.

5) Great powers' influence can be diminished by a reduction of armaments in general.

6) The balance of power can also be restored by a race of armaments or armaments competition. This is the Cold War scenario where the United States and the Soviet Union started an arms race.

7) The balance could also be restored by intervening preemptively in a country. This requires superior military capabilities and detailed intelligence information about where to attack best.

8) Probably the weakest form of restoring an equilibrium of power is through traditional diplomacy and international negotiation. This is a time- and human resource-consuming bargaining situation, which not all states are in favor of.

9) The last resort of rebalancing hegemony is by war itself.

However, these tools and techniques sometimes collide with the rule of international law. Preemptive interventions cannot be justified under the charter of the United Nations without a cause. In other words, before a state may legitimately choose to use force against another state, there must first be a violation of legal rights, which can then be defended by using force.

THE NOTION OF POLARITY

There are basically three main concepts of polarity. In each of the cases we have a great power on the top of a triangle, with middle powers in the middle section and small powers in the lower section. In a unipolar world there exists only one superpower that enjoys great military capabilities and is unsurpassed. Today, the United States can be seen as the only remaining superpower that enjoys great power status.

Moreover, in the concept of a bipolar world the hegemony of the superpower is shared by another superpower that possesses equal strength. The best example for this form of polarity can be found during the Cold War when two superpowers, the United States as well as the Soviet Union, enjoyed the status of great powers with equal might.

In a multipolar world, many superpowers share equal strength and capability on the top of the pyramid. In this case, a balance of power takes place among more than two great powers trying to find an equilibrium. The best example for a multipolar world view was after World War I, the "Golden Age of the balance of power where a Eurocentric system existed for more than two hundred years. However, the record of the balance of power theory can be seen as rather modestly successful because it did not prevent two major and cataclymsic world wars.

The concept of polarity goes back to the political scientist Morton Kaplan. He identified three dissections of international power after World War II. They are unipolarity, multipolarity, and bipolarity. Polarity in general can be understood as a concentration of power among different states.

Multipolarity: Realist theory assumes that if the international system is multipolar, then international conflict among great powers will be much more likely. In this case, great powers might decide to threaten other great powers in order to reduce the risk of being attacked themselves. One of the greatest dangers of multipolarity is the difficulty of interpreting the other state's behavior. In other words, uncertainty, misperceptions, and misinterpretations are the greatest dangers of multipolarity. It is most likely in a multipolar world that cleavages will weaken the relationship between nation states.

Unipolarity: After World War II, most European countries were left destroyed. Their source of power, economic statecraft, military capabilities, and human resources were exhausted. Nevertheless, the war took place on European soil and left the United States with a powerful economy and a less exhausted military. America was the only remaining superpower after the war and globally unsurpassed. In addition, Washington was the only government in place that possessed nuclear capabilities, which it already had demonstrated during the war. "The United States was not just stronger than anybody else—it was stronger than everybody," note Wittkopf and Kegley; Washington was the only hegemon.

Bipolarity: If the international system is bipolar, the probability of risking a conflict is much smaller. This was the case during the Cold War when the Soviet Union gained strength and included a number of territories in its empire after World War II. In the following years Moscow grew to a second great power beside the

Americans. It developed and delivered its own atomic bomb a few years later in 1949 and exploded a thermonuclear device in 1953. In other words, bipolarity was shaped by an international setting where military capabilities became concentrated in the hands of two hegemonic powers. Therefore, it can be said that the balance of power provides a basis of control for states when dealing with each other. In this sense, the balance of power theory is a useful concept to explain the behavior of states in an anarchic international environment.

Superpowers are not reluctant to make use of their vast military force and fight rather than submit to subordination. A collaboration of power would deter rising states or would-be attackers from pursuing expansionism. One form of collaboration could be alliances that combine the power of various states denying the additional power to the enemy. These groups of realists are called structural realists, who traditionally focus on structural causes of alliances. In their view, neorealism is a structural theory and a formal extension of realism. Therefore, hostile aggression would be repelled and therefore unlikely. This form of alliances would deter and contain possible antagonists who might align themselves into a group, trying to avert the risk of detachment. In 1949 the United States formed and joined NATO. A few years later, in May 1955, the Soviet Union and Eastern bloc countries met in Warsaw and signed the Warsaw Pact, a military alliance of countries collaborating with Russia. "If they refused to ally, their own vulnerability would encourage the expansionist state to attack them at a later time," Morton Kaplan explains. According to Kaplan, to maintain a certain order of power the school of realist theory recommends that states should follow the following rules: "1) increase capabilities but negotiate rather than fight; 2) fight rather than fail to increase capabilities; 3) stop fighting rather than eliminate an essential actor; 4) oppose any coalition or single actor which tends to assume a position of preponderance within the system; 5) constrain actors who subscribe to supranational organization principles; and 6) permit defeated or constrained essential national actors to re-enter the system as acceptable role partners."

In this sense, competition for power and influence is desirable because it will lead to the equalization of capabilities of states. Even though the concept of power is debatable and difficult to measure, threat perception is an important characteristic of realist theory and also in the balance of power theory. Stephen Walt argues that states care less about the allocation of power than about the distribution of threats. Threats can be understood as perceived intentions that make states enhance their offensive military capabilities when entering an alliance. The United States, one of the most powerful countries after World War II, perceived the rise of communism in the 1950s and later during the Cold War as a threat to national security.

CONDITIONS OF BALANCE

Power is widely seen in this theory as military power, and therefore war is a functional tool to measure national powers. According to Wittkopf and Kegley, the following conditions must exist to maintain a balance of power: "States must possess accurate information about others' capabilities and motives and react rationally to this information. There must be a sufficient number of independent states to make alliance formation and dissolution readily possible. There must be a limited geographic area. National leaders must have freedom of action. States' capabilities must be relatively equal. States must share a common political culture in which the rules of the security regime are recognized and respected. States in the system must have similar types of government and ideologies. States must have a weapons technology that inhibits pre-emption-quick mobilizations for war, first-strike attacks that defeat the enemy before it can organize a retaliatory response- and war of annihilation."

These were the conditions of a balance of power during World War I and the interwar period. The international system was characterized by a multipolar system whereby almost equal capabilities were shared among a number of powerful states.

The outbreak of two world wars in 20 years discredited the balance of power concept and led the way to a search for alternatives. It was President Woodrow Wilson who thought to replace the theory with a new form of alliance, namely the concept of collective security, meaning that if one state is attacked, the aggression will be met by all other states of the collective security pact. Shortly after that, the concept of collective deterrence evolved into the League of Nations, the United Nations, and the North Atlantic Treaty Organization.

In conclusion, the balance of power has been tied to right and left ideology in many ways. For example, during the Cold War, those individuals within the United States who supported the Soviet Union as radical dissidents were on the left of American society; similarly, those who, in the Soviet Union, favored the American way of life were also dissidents, and within the Soviet context, their advocacy of personal liberty made them "radical," although some of them were conservative in religious ideology. There are other aspects of this issue as well: as the Soviets attempted to spread their doctrine, they used the Comintern and international communist parties around the world to attempt to win allegiance to their side of the multipolar world in the 1930s, and side during the more or less bipolar Cold War. The concept of pursuing a balance of power has been primarily a rightist policy from the Western ideological perspective.

SEE ALSO

Volume 1 Left: Soviet Union; Stalin and Stalinism; Cominform; Communism; United States.
Volume 2 Right: Cold War; Vietnam War; Soviet Union; United States; Hegemony.

BIBLIOGRAPHY

Morton A. Kaplan, *System and Process in International Politics* (Wiley, 1957); Charles W. Kegley Jr. and Eugene R. Wittkopf, *World Politics: Trends and Transformation* (St. Martin's Press, 1997); Stephen M. Walt, *Origins of Alliances* (Cornell University Press, 1987); Stephen M. Walt, "Revolution and War," *World Politics* (v.44/3, April 1992); Kenneth N. Waltz, *Theory of International Politics* (Addison-Wesley, 1979); Stephen M. Walt, "Structural Realism after the Cold War," *International Security* (v.25/1, Summer 2000); Christopher Layne, "The Unipolar Illusion: Why New Great Powers Will Rise," *International Security* (v.17/4, 1939); Hans J. Morgenthau, *Politics among Nations* (Alfred A. Knopf, 1973).

BENJAMIN ZYLA
ROYAL MILITARY COLLEGE OF CANADA

Basque and Catalan Separatism

SEPARATISM REFERS to a political movement that obtains sovereignty and so splits a territory or group of people from another. Motives for establishing separatist movements include religious commitment, nationalism, and inadequate economic or political sway (for example, the northern Italian separatists who saw the progress of the industrial north being hindered by the lack of development in the more traditional south of the country).

Separatist movements, significantly, can be both peaceful and violent. Spain, for example, arguably has one of the most well known and violent of all contemporary separatist movements. Spain is a country of strong regional differences. Historically, regions have developed with their own customs, flags, cultures, and in some instances, languages. For example, in Catalonia civilians speak not only Spanish but also Catalan. In the Basque region in the north of Spain, Spanish is widely spoken but so is Euskara (Basque). The separatists in this region of Spain have their modern origins dating from the start of the 20th century when the Spanish government revoked certain autonomous freedoms Basques had enjoyed.

However, their wider popularity was essentially established under the dictatorship of Francisco Franco (1939–75) when regional cultures, languages, and identities were sometimes forcefully suppressed. The Basque separatist movement is probably best known due to the activities of a Marxist group called ETA (Euskadi Ta Askatasuna, which means "Basque Country and Liberty"), founded in 1959. This group, part of the wider Basque National Liberation movement, seeks to form an independent Basque state, and in order to achieve this goal, frequently uses terrorist means. With its political movement, Batasuna (formed 1978), the separatist movement manages to attract about 10 percent of Basques who vote in elections, despite the attempts of the national government in Spain to suppress the movement's finances and operations. Despite ETA's illegal status, the terrorist group frequently targets politicians, military figures, and members of the police services to achieve their principal goal: an independent Basque nation. Assassinations by the group (more than 800 in total from 1969 to 2004) occur across Spain. However, it is foolhardy to judge all Basque separatist movements as being similar to ETA, although some other Basque groups have equally barbed views. For example, the Basque Nationalist Party (Eusko Alderdi Jeltzalea/Partido Nacionalista Vasco) was formed in 1895 as a racist (anti-Spanish) Catholic movement. Now it is a nationalist organization of moderate views and describes itself as democratic.

Separatism in Catalonia, located in the northeast of Spain, has in the 19th and 20th centuries largely been political, advocating political autonomy and not terrorist means to achieve an independent state. Separatism in Catalonia is evident in both the left and right of political fields, and has shown itself within the Generalitat de Catalunya (the official name of the autonomous system of government in Catalonia).

Despite being abolished in 1939 by Franco, the Generalitat's reintroduction in 1980, under the presidency

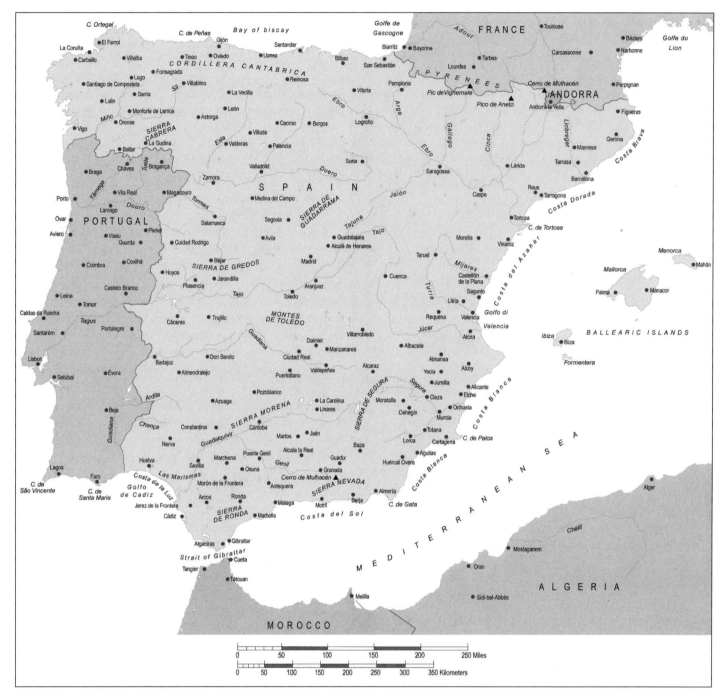

The Basque separatist region is in the north (Vitoria, Bilbao, above) of Spain, while the Catalonian separatist movement is located in the northeast (Barcelona, above) of the country. Both political agendas use nationalism in seeking separatism from the Spanish government.

of Jordi Puyol (1980–2003), has allowed Catalans of all political persuasions to air their opinions on matters ranging from taxation to the environment and, in some instances, has allowed greater political autonomy in Catalonia.

Today, there are three main political groups that may be described as Catalan separatists: the Convergència Democratica de Catalunya (Democratic Conver-gence of Catalonia, a nationalist group), the Unió Democratica de Catalunya (also a nationalist group), and Esquerra Republicana de Catalunya (Republican Left of Catalonia). Currently led by Josep-Lluís Carod-Rovira, the leftist Esquerra Republicana de Catalunya (formed in 1931) campaigns for Catalan independence. The Generalitat, led by Pasqual Maragall, a former mayor of Barcelona and current leader of the Socialist Party, is governed by a leftist coalition, and many political experts see this coalition as trying to ensure increasing autonomy for the Catalan region. Of course, such a policy will naturally bring the region into conflict with the largely centralist national government.

Though these separatist movements in Spain occur on both the left and right, their rightist nationalism groups them together merely for study purposes on the right.

SEE ALSO

Volume 1 Left: Spain.
Volume 2 Right: Spain; Nationalism; Fascism.

BIBLIOGRAPHY

Albert Balcells and Geoff Walker, *Catalan Nationalism: Past and Present* (Palgrave Macmillan, 1996); Robert Clark, *The Basques: The Franco Years and Beyond* (University of Nevada Press, 1980); Javier Corcuera Atienza, *The Origins of Basque Nationalism* (University of Nevada Press, 2004).

IAN MORLEY, PH.D.
MING CHUAN UNIVERSITY, TAIWAN

Bennett, William J. (1943–)

WILLIAM JOHN BENNETT was born in Brooklyn, New York. Strong academically, Bennett graduated from Williams College with a bachelor of arts degree and went on to study at the University of Texas, where he obtained a Ph.D. in political philosophy. Later, he studied at Harvard Law School and obtained a law degree as well.

In 1976, Bennett was the executive director of the National Humanities Center, an academic research center located in North Carolina. He was the director until 1981. At that time, President Ronald Reagan selected Bennett to become the director of the National Endowment for the Humanities. His tenure there lasted until 1985, when Reagan selected him to become the secretary of education.

As secretary of education, Bennett was unable to avoid controversy over many of his initiatives and beliefs. He put forward the conservative stance on the issues of affirmative action, school vouchers, curriculum reform, and religion in public education. His distaste for multicultural coursework in public schools was one of his most controversial positions. Instead, he preferred an education style that was steeped in the classics and Western culture. Schools that were not performing well were often unable to escape harsh criticism and funding cuts from Bennett as well. As a result of the controversies and a desire to go in another direction with his career, Bennett resigned from his position during the final days of Reagan's administration.

Bennett, however, was unable to avoid controversy. He was appointed by President George H.W. Bush to become the nation's first "drug czar," as director of the Office of National Drug Control Policy. Having established himself as one of the nation's most well-known moral crusaders, Bennett's selection wasn't a surprise to many on Capitol Hill, and he was confirmed in a 97-to-2 vote by the Senate. From the post, Bennett conducted the nation's War on Drugs, but soon after decided to leave the position in 1990.

Drawing upon his many experiences in Washington, D.C., and his long career with the Republican Party, Bennett became a conservative writer and public speaker after leaving government office. Through his work, he has continued his moral crusade, attacking what he perceives as the lack of virtue in American society, particularly among the nation's youth. He has continued his efforts to improve the nation's public and private schools, basing his plans on what he calls the most important "Three C's: Choice, Content, and Character." He meets with key political leaders and education experts and writes articles featured in the nation's leading newspapers and magazines. He has written and edited more than 10 books, including *The Book of Virtues*, *The Children's Book of Virtues*, and *The Death of Outrage: Bill Clinton and the Assault on American Ideals*, which was briefly number one on the *New York Times* bestseller list.

Even in his journalist and writing role, Bennett has been unable to escape criticism in his private career, similar to his public one. His vehement support of the War on Drugs and proposals in favor of lengthy incarcerations for first-time drug offenders who possess only minimal amounts of illegal drugs has led many critics to attack Bennett's own past as a rock fan during the 1960s and 1970s. Interestingly, during his years of graduate study at the University of Texas, Bennett was set up on a blind date by one of his friends with rock star Janis Joplin. When the story of this brief relationship hit the tabloids, *People* magazine labeled it "one of the least likely blind dates of all time."

In 2003, Bennett revealed that he was an extremely high-stakes gambler who had lost millions of dollars in Las Vegas and Atlantic City casinos. Clearly a contradiction with his public moral crusader image, Bennett's status as a conservative virtue and moral defender began to crumble and he was no longer as highly sought after on the lecture circuit. He admitted to losing more than $8 million within the period of a single year, but still claimed that he wasn't addicted to gambling. In addition, he has never labeled gambling a vice or problem in any of his speeches or writings. In defense, Bennett compared his behavior to responsible drinking, but at least acknowledged that his gambling was not a good example for him to set. Consequently, he stated repeatedly that he had complied with all laws on reporting wins and losses and that his "gambling days are over." More recently, Bennett has given most of his attention to a project known as Americans for Victory Over Terrorism (AVOT). Through AVOT, Bennett worked to address terrorist threats and the ideologies that produce them. The privately funded organization is dedicated to winning public opinion in favor of the ongoing War on Terrorism with a mixture of advertising, intellectual advocacy, and mass communications.

Bennett is also a director of Empower America and a Distinguished Fellow at the Heritage Foundation. He works alongside former Democratic Senator Sam Nunn as cochair of the National Commission on Civic Renewal. He continues his work in the War on Drugs with the Partnership for a Drug-Free America, collaborating with former New York Governor Mario Cuomo.

SEE ALSO

Volume 1 Left: Clinton, William J.; Liberalism.
Volume 2 Right: Reagan, Ronald; Republican Party; Education.

BIBLIOGRAPHY

"William Bennett," The Heritage Foundation, www.heritage.org (March 2004); "GOP Moralist Bennett Gives Up Gambling," CNN, www.cnn.com (May 5, 2003); William J. Bennett, *The Broken Hearth: Reversing the Moral Collapse of the American Family* (Doubleday, 2001).

ARTHUR HOLST, PH.D.
WIDENER UNIVERSITY

Bilbo, Theodore G. (1877–1947)

IN TWO TERMS as governor of Mississippi, followed by two terms in the U.S. Senate, Theodore Gilmore

Theodore Bilbo, though a progressive populist, was an unabashed white segregationist and racist.

Bilbo emerged as a national symbol of unapologetic southern white supremacy. He was vilified unmercifully in the pages of progressive publications and by leftist folksingers like Pete Seeger. Across the white south, however, he was hailed as a hero. Ironically, apart from his racial attitudes, Bilbo was very much a progressive populist. Upon taking political control of the Mississippi statehouse in 1916, he embarked on a campaign to modernize the state's road system and pressed the University of Mississippi to admit more poor white students, even threatening at one point to relocate the school unless it complied—a move that got him burned in effigy.

Bilbo was born on a farm near Poplarville and received his college education at both Vanderbilt University and the University of Michigan. After several years of teaching at Mississippi public schools, he began practicing law in 1908, the same year he was elected to the state senate. He became lieutenant governor in 1912 and was elected governor four years later; he served another term as the state's chief executive from 1928 to 1932.

In 1934, Bilbo was elected to the U.S. Senate and became a passionate advocate of Franklin D. Roosevelt's (FDR) New Deal—except where racial matters were concerned. In 1942, for example, Bilbo led a filibuster that effectively killed FDR's attempt to eliminate the racist poll tax. By then, the five-foot-two Bilbo had become a giant in the white supremacy movement. Two years earlier, he introduced a bill demanding that Congress appropriate $1 billion to deport all African Americans to Liberia, so that "the blessings of the white man's civilization shall forever remain the proud possession of Anglo-Saxons."

His venom was not restricted to African Americans: When students at Hunter College passed a resolution declaring him "unfit to hold public office," he replied in an official letter denouncing his young critics as a "communistic mongrel congregation." Critical letters from northerners were answered on his official Senate stationary accompanied by the crudest ethnic slurs: His reply to one woman with an obviously Italian name, for example, began, "Dear Dago." Antics like that earned him regular denunciations in the pages of leftist newspapers like *PM*. Folksingers Seeger and Lee Hays recorded a song, "Listen Mr. Bilbo," which included the chorus:

> Well, you don't like Negroes, you don't like Jews
> If there is anyone you do like, it sure is news.
> You don't like Poles, Italians, Catholics, too
> Is it any wonder, Bilbo, that we don't like you?

With the Senate election of 1946, Bilbo's racial rhetoric was fully unleashed. He called on "the red-blooded Anglo-Saxon men of Mississippi to use any means" to prevent blacks from voting, adding: "And if you don't know what that means, you are just not up on your persuasive measures." And he put his racial theories down on paper, in a self-published book called *Take Your Choice: Separation or Mongrelization*, which argued that it was better to see America "blotted out with the atom bomb than to see it slowly destroyed in the maelstrom of miscegenation, interbreeding, intermarriage and mongrelization." (The book remains wildly popular today on numerous white-supremacist internet websites.)

His overwhelming reelection victory, however, was met with opposition within the Senate, as conservative Republicans joined with northern liberals in a bid to deny Bilbo his seat. One investigation refused to uphold a charge that his campaign speeches had intimidated African Americans from voting. Another probe, into allegations that he had pocketed campaign contributions for personal use, was never resolved.

In the summer of 1947, following several operations for treatment of cancer of the mouth, Bilbo died suddenly of heart failure, without ever having taken his Senate seat for a third term. A few weeks before his death, he gave a remarkable interview to Leon Lewis, editor of *Negro South*, in which he insisted that despite his fervent opposition to black-white social mingling, "I hold nothing personal against the Negroes as a race."

SEE ALSO

Volume 1 Left: Desegregation; Civil Rights; Constitutional Amendments.
Volume 2 Right: Segregation.

BIBLIOGRAPHY

"Bilbo Dead at 69 of Heart Ailment," *New York Times* (August 22, 1947); Robert A. Caro, *The Years of Lyndon Johnson: Master of the Senate* (Knopf, 2002); "Member's Death Ends a Senate Predicament," www.senate.gov (April 2004); David G. Sansing, "Theodore G. Bilbo," www.mshistory.k12.ms.us (April 2004).

ERIC FETTMANN
INDEPENDENT SCHOLAR

Black Nationalism

AFRICAN AMERICANS who became famous for their confrontational style of leadership during the days of slavery and Jim Crow racism were generally called black nationalists. The term is nebulously defined, and it is used loosely to describe any African American who strives for something other than integration and equal rights within the traditional white society and political system. Black nationalism is often considered a conservative ideology, but it would be more accurately described as a type of counterconservativism.

Historically, black nationalists have refused to compromise with whites on political issues. During the era of slavery, they rejected gradual abolition, and thereafter rejected limited civil rights and slow, steady improvement, in favor of immediate and dramatic change. Their demands were often viewed by the mainstream as revolutionary, and their tactics were generally designed for maximum shock value; that is, to get the attention of white Americans and political leaders via the news media.

For their efforts, which most whites and many fellow blacks considered scary at best and almost terroristic at the very worst, they were labeled "bad" or "militant" or worse.

Examples of black nationalists throughout American history include David Walker, the radical abolitionist from Boston who, in 1829, published the most shocking challenge to the slave labor system ever written, in his pamphlet the *Appeal*. Walker's *Appeal* urged southern slaves to rise up and violently overthrow their oppressors. Martin Delany, Alexander Crummell, and Bishop Henry Turner were abolitionists-turned-colonizationists who led the pan-African movement in the late 1800s. Unlike contemporaries Booker T. Washington, Frederick Douglass, and John Mercer Langston, they found no hope for a better future for their race in the United States and looked for the black man's salvation in Africa. In the early 20th century, the most famous black nationalist was Marcus Garvey. A Jamaican by birth and a New Yorker by immigration, he founded the Universal Negro Improvement Association and the Black Star Line of steamships. He took on the honorary title of "Provisional President General of Africa" with the intention of founding a great black nation in Africa. Soon after, Garvey was displaced by black socialist A. Philip Randolph as the country's most visible black nationalist. As the foremost spokesman for black labor, he applied pressure to the Franklin Roosevelt administration, producing tangible gains for his race.

MALCOLM X

Undoubtedly the most famous black nationalist of the civil rights movement era was Malcolm X. A member of the radical black Muslim group the Nation of Islam (NOI) until 1964, Malcolm X became the spokesman for a generation of young African Americans who considered the pacifist rhetoric of Martin Luther King, Jr., to be an ineffective message. He preached deliberate separation from whites, black pride, and violent retaliation against acts of racism and discrimination. In 1964, he left the NOI and started the Organization for Afro-American Unity (OAAU), intending to compete with the NOI for membership and media attention. He also adopted a more conciliatory policy toward whites, ridding himself and the OAAU of the black separatist philosophy, although never dismissing the black nationalist ideology totally.

Meanwhile, the NOI survived without Malcolm X and has continued to be a minor player in the general population of black Americans under the leadership of Louis Farrakhan up to the present. Farrakhan's leader-

ship of the Million Man March in 1995 (which has been called the "golden event" and greatest "triumph" in the history of black nationalism) catapulted him to fame among the general population, while concomitantly reminding most Americans, black and white alike, why they never could embrace the radical NOI.

Malcolm X's assassination in 1965 by NOI rivals opened the door for imitators and would-be leaders to take his place as the most visible and vocal black nationalist in the late 1960s. In 1966, the Student Non-violent Coordinating Committee (SNCC), a previously integrated civil rights organization devoted to fulfilling Martin Luther King's plan of nonviolent integration, changed focus when new president Stokely Carmichael took over. Carmichael kicked out all white members from SNCC and began espousing "black power," which was little more than a catchy slogan that meant basically what Malcolm X had been preaching for years, although with a twist of socialism and communism added. Carmichael subsequently converted to Islam, changed his name to Kwame Ture, and moved to Africa, abandoning his quest to make America a better place for his people.

At about the same time that Carmichael came to power, another black nationalist group, the Black Panthers, was organizing in Oakland, California. After demonstrating in the California State Capitol, carrying shotguns and rifles, the Panthers left the building and peacefully entered police custody, having made their point that the right to bear arms extended to blacks. They, like Carmichael, presented their followers with a type of communism in which the black community would depend upon itself, under Black Panther leadership, for all its wants and needs. Although it did some good work for inner-city black youth, it was seen as a subversive organization by the FBI, which kept the group under surveillance and, working with local law enforcement agencies, raided their various headquarters. Some leaders of the Black Panthers were killed, some exiled, and others subsequently ended up in prison on miscellaneous charges. A national organization by that name still exists today, although it is a mere shadow of what the original group was in its glory days.

In 1969, after four straight years of race rioting in more than 150 American cities, new SNCC leader James Forman issued the "Black Manifesto," which was essentially a statement of what the various black nationalist sects of the past and present had long wanted: reparations for slavery and oppression. Ironically, the manifesto was aimed at white churches and synagogues rather than the U.S. government. At the time, whites generally dismissed it as ridiculous, although it did raise awareness of an issue that is still on the table politically today.

Black nationalists and their respective organizations have been few in number and of little consequence in influence since the 1970s. Because black nationalism automatically carries an element of black separatism in its ideology, readers should consult the following article on "black separatism" for further treatment of the black nationalist philosophy.

SEE ALSO

Volume 1 Left: Carmichael, Stokely; Malcolm X; Black Panthers.
Volume 2 Right: United States; Black Separatism; Segregation.

BIBLIOGRAPHY

Robert L. Jenkins and Mfanya D. Tryman, *The Malcolm X Encyclopedia* (Greenwood Press, 2002); John Hope Franklin and Alfred E. Moss, Jr., *From Slavery to Freedom: A History of African Americans* (McGraw-Hill, 2000); Stokely Carmichael and Charles V. Hamilton, *Black Power: The Politics of Liberation in America* (Vintage Press, 1992); Wilson J. Moses, *The Golden Age of Black Nationalism, 1850–1925* (Oxford University Press, 1988); Robert L. Jenkins, Mfanya D. Tryman, Curtis Austin, and Thomas Adams Upchurch, *The Greenwood Encyclopedia of Black Nationalism* (Greenwood Press, 2006); Rodney Carlisle, *The Roots of Black Nationalism* (Kennikat, 1975).

THOMAS ADAMS UPCHURCH, PH.D.
EAST GEORGIA COLLEGE

Black Separatism

THE ULTIMATE MANIFESTATION of black nationalism is black separatism. Black nationalism taken to its most extreme, or its logical conclusion, produces the ideology of racial separation chosen deliberately by African Americans. This ideology is, like black nationalism, a counterconservative approach to race relations in the sense that it is basically a reaction to racial discrimination perpetrated by whites.

Black separatism has most often been associated with pan-Africanism, but not necessarily. Separatism can take the form of internal separation or psychological "withdrawal" from the mainstream of American society and culture for the purpose of racial pride and the opportunity for self-determination. It can also take the more physical form of blacks' choosing geographic separation from whites inside the United States.

Black separatism has a long history, beginning in the colonial era when slaves and free blacks sought to establish as much control over their own destinies as possible under their difficult circumstances. The idea of returning to their African homeland was always a hope and dream of first-generation slaves. With passing time, however, the thought of such a return grew increasingly dim, and pan-Africanism thus reemerged in later generations as a plan not merely for individual aspirants but for the black population as a whole. Mitigating against such a plan of physical separatism, however, was the fact that, for any mass emigration to Africa to occur, black emigrants would have to depend upon the charity and logistical help of whites and, from about 1820 to 1890, the white-run American Colonization Society.

Although many black nationalists, such as Martin Delany, Bishop Henry Turner, Alexander Crummell, and Marcus Garvey, continued in the late 1800s and early 1900s to cling to the increasingly unlikely pan-Africanist dream of physical separation, eventually the idea of psychological separation and black self-determination emerged to replace it. Black-owned newspapers written especially for black readers arose, as did black-owned banks, life insurance companies, fraternal organizations, and various business enterprises. Madam C.J. Walker, for instance, made a fortune catering hair-care products exclusively to blacks. Such separatists, however, had to compete with accommodationists like Booker T. Washington and integrationists like Frederick Douglass and eventually the NAACP, for the allegiance of the black community in general, and thus were relegated to a secondary status, same as always.

By the time the civil rights movement ensued, there only one major black separatist organization was making any impact on the masses: the Nation of Islam (NOI). Founded in Detroit in 1930 as the "Lost-Found Nation of Islam in the Wilderness of North America," the NOI preached that blacks had always constituted a nation within a nation—a nation held captive by white devils (white Americans and Europeans) until Allah's plan of redeeming his chosen (black) people should be revealed. Then Allah would raise his people up and destroy the white oppressors. This religious mysticism, seemingly metaphysical in nature, was coupled with a quite physical plan for achieving separate nationhood within the confines of North America. The NOI demanded that the U.S. government surrender up to eight southern states for the establishment of Allah's "Black

Kingdom" on earth. Although the demand was immediately dismissed as quixotic because it would require the relocation not only of millions of blacks into the south but many more millions of whites out of the south, it started a movement for reparations in one form or another that has persisted to this day. Likewise, despite the fact that American political leaders have consistently rejected the NOI's demand for land for the past 40 years, the NOI holds fast to the plan even to this day.

Similar black separatist groups, such as the Republic of New Africa (RNA), tried to build upon the land-for-reparations ideology of the Nation of Islam. The RNA actually began the process of claiming the five deep south states of Louisiana, Mississippi, Alabama, Georgia, and South Carolina for building its separate black nation by starting a black communal society in central Mississippi in 1971. It was shut down, however, by the FBI, which viewed the RNA as a subversive organization, in a bloody shootout. Today, there is little attention paid to the land-for-reparations idea, although monetary reparations are still a topic of serious discussion.

The most important manifestations of black separatism in recent years have been the creation of all-black businesses, such as the FUBU clothing line, *Ebony* magazine, and the BET television network. The continued success of standard all-black organizations such as the Alpha Phi Alpha fraternity and the Prince Hall Masons also shows that black separatism is still alive and well, despite constituting only a fringe of the overall black community in America. Black separatism, as an expression of ethnic nationalism, has more in common with the politics of the right than it does with the left.

SEE ALSO

Volume 1 Left: Carmichael, Stokely; Malcolm X; Black Panthers.
Volume 2 Right: United States; Black Nationalism; Segregation.

BIBLIOGRAPHY

Robert Carr, *Black Nationalism in the New World* (Duke University Press, 2002); John Hope Franklin and Alfred E. Moss, Jr., *From Slavery to Freedom: A History of African Americans* (McGraw-Hill, 2000); James A. Geschwender, *The Black Revolt* (Prentice-Hall, 1971); Dexter B. Gordon, *Black Identity* (Southern Illinois University Press, 2003).

THOMAS ADAMS UPCHURCH, PH.D.
EAST GEORGIA COLLEGE

Borah, William E. (1865–1940)

BORN IN ILLINOIS the same year that the Civil War ended, Republican Senator William Borah spent much of his political life attempting to keep the United States out of foreign wars and to prevent American participation in what he saw as dangerous international entanglements. Borah opposed entering World War I on the grounds that it was based on protecting American corporations rather than serving the interests of democracy. After the war, Borah became an "irreconcilable" opponent of the League of Nations proposed by President Woodrow Wilson. Borah was convinced that the British were influencing Wilson in order to protect their own political and economic interests. Borah and his powerful colleague, Henry Cabot Lodge, were ultimately successful in blocking the Treaty of Versailles, which the Senate failed to ratify by seven votes. The frustration and disappointment over the failure of the League of Nations may have contributed to the stroke in the fall of 1919 that robbed Wilson of his ability to govern for the final year of his term.

As a young man, William Borah set out for California but ran out of money in Boise, Idaho. He remained in Boise, where he made a name for himself by prosecuting "Big Bill" Haywood and other union leaders accused of conspiring to murder ex-governor Frank Steurenberg. Borah represented Idaho in the Senate from 1907 until his death in 1940. From 1924 until 1933, Borah served as chair of the powerful and prestigious Senate Committee on Foreign Affairs.

The election of Franklin D. Roosevelt (FDR) in 1932 propelled the Democrats to majority status, demoting Borah to ranking minority member of the committee. He then devoted himself to blocking many of Roosevelt's New Deal policies. However, Roosevelt won Borah's support on 11 of 17 New Deal bills on which the Senate voted. Nonetheless, throughout his political career, Borah was well known for fighting liberal reforms such as the Federal Reserve Act of 1913 and the Federal Trade Commission Act of 1914. Borah provided the main obstacle to passage of the Industrial Recovery Act of 1933. Conversely, Borah was often able to bring factions together to pass legislation.

Well known as a progressive, Borah shared many common values with Democrats and considered himself a follower of classical liberals such as Thomas Jefferson and Adam Smith. Borah, who often identified himself as a Lincoln Republican, was conservative both by nature and by choice. As a result, he rejected many progressive-supported reforms, never totally comfort-

SEE ALSO
Volume 1 Left: Haywood, William D.; Roosevelt, Franklin D.; Democratic Party.
Volume 2 Right: Roosevelt; Theodore; Republican Party.

BIBLIOGRAPHY
Le Roy Ashby, *The Spearless Leader* (University of Illinois Press, 1972); David A. Horowitz, "Senator Borah's Crusade to Save Small Business from the New Deal," *Historian* (Summer 1993); Robert James Maddox, *William E. Borah and American Foreign Policy* (Louisiana State, 1969); Marion C. McKenna, *Borah* (University of Michigan Press, 1961); Karen A.J. Miller, *Populist Nationalism* (Greenwood, 1999).

ELIZABETH PURDY, PH.D.
INDEPENDENT SCHOLAR

Republican U.S. Senator William E. Borah attempted to block Democratic President Franklin D. Roosevelt's social policies.

able with legislation supported by both right- and left-wing progressives. Despite his loyalty to conservatism, Borah was dubbed "the great opposer" because he refused to adhere to strict Republican party lines.

Borah enjoyed the public life and relished making his positions known to the media at press conferences that he regularly initiated. His opinions were often varied. A supporter of Theodore Roosevelt, Borah hated monopolies and saw himself as an advocate for small businesses. Borah lobbied for recognizing the new government of the Soviet Union when most of his colleagues preferred to defer recognition. He believed that the United States had no right to interfere in Latin American politics. Borah was a strong advocate of disarmament, maintaining that stockpiling weapons made nations more likely to engage in wars.

Brazil

THE BRAZILIAN RIGHT is characterized by its opposition to democratic initiatives that represent a threat to traditional institutions, such as the agrarian elite, the church, the judiciary, and the military. Analysts have tried to trace the metamorphoses of the Brazilian right, but the main characteristic of the right is its authoritarian character, masked by an ideology of conciliation that is proper to Brazilian political culture.

The Brazilian right has its origins in the colonial institutions that were installed upon Portuguese colonization in 1500. The Portuguese monarchy never developed a strong army, but ruled through ideological tools. Different from the Spanish, the Portuguese did not create institutions for a middle class or intelligentsia. Education was centralized at the University of Coimbra, which trained bureaucrats to serve the Portuguese colonies. Brazilian colonial society was made up of powerful landlords (*senhores do engenho*), priests, lawyers, small landowners, poor workers, slaves, and natives. Despite the complexity of this society, it had a simple structure marked economically by landlords and the working masses, and politically by the monarchic bureaucracy, the church, and the juridical institutions.

In his book *A Ideologia do Colonialismo*, Nelson Werneck Sodré shows how the church and bureaucrats implemented a culture of colonial power and internalized submission. The judiciary was responsible for administrating the colony, and as Thomas Flory affirms, the Portuguese sent lawyers rather than military troops to enforce royal decisions. Through negotiations, a system of economic authority, tutelage, and *personalismo* was created. Thus, the right inherited the legacy of colonialism based on feudal authoritarianism that did not allow for democratic initiatives.

CONSERVATISM AND THE MONARCHY

Between 1644 and 1817 there were several rebellions against Portuguese rule, such as the Quilombo dos Palmares (1644–94), the War of the Barbarians (1683–1710), and the Inconfidência Mineira (1789). However, in 1822, Brazil declared its independence, and then became the only monarchy in the Americas. After independence, there were other revolts. The government received the support of conservative political groups that opposed these initiatives and proposed alternatives to a democratic regime, such as eclecticism, regressivism, a "transition process," and centrism. As a result, the ideology of conciliation became characteristic of Brazilian politics. But even this conciliatory proposal was an illusion, since through it the right has been able to maintain its hold on Brazilian politics.

Romantic conservatism was the expression for this political ideology in the 19th century. It criticized modernity, avoided revolution, and opposed the rationality of science and intellectual initiatives. Important conservatives were Gonçalves de Magalhães, José de Alencar, and Álvares de Azevedo. Alencar criticized the importation of foreign ideas—including liberal democracy and abolition. In order to diminish the African threat and negate the white colonizer, Alencar turned to a romanticized version of the "Indian" and the syncretic "Mestizo" as the ideal Brazilian identity. Therefore, the conservative ideology of syncretism represented an aesthetic complement to the political ideology of conciliation. Both brought the ideology of colonialism to newer standards, were incorporated by the masses, and became fundamental for the right.

POSITIVISM, INTEGRALISM, AND ESTADO NOVO

Abolition in 1888 was a condition for establishing a republic in 1889 without a civil war. This change occurred through a coup promoted by the military bourgeoisie, and led by the positivism of the military academy. Although the situation of the poor did not change, the middle class emerged, which favored science and questioned traditional power. A series of movements during the 1920s was initiated within the military, including the

most important popular communist movement led by Captain Luiz Carlos Prestes from 1924 to 1929.

During the 1930s, the nationalist Brazilian right represented by integralism emphasized the ideas of homeland and nation. Founded by Plinio Salgado in 1932, integralism was led by such conservative intellectuals and politicians as Oliveira Vianna, Miguel Reale, and Azevedo Amaral. They not only defined an ideology of nationalism, but also organized associations and paramilitary groups, involving the masses according to the fascist model in vogue in Europe at that time.

President Getulio Vargas, who took power through a military coup in 1930, adopted integralism to establish his dictatorship, the Estado Novo, which suppressed the left and opposing parties. Vargas, like Juan Peron in Argentina, cannot be completely reduced to the authoritarianism of the right, due to the complexity of his populism whereby he became "father of the poor." Nevertheless, his fascist sympathies and his questioning of democracy show the authoritarian character that is part of the right.

MILITARY DICTATORSHIP AND THE RIGHT

While the Proclamation of the Republic in 1889 was led by the military and other liberal movements, the army would later change its role. Between 1930 and 1950, the army backed attempts at overthrowing democratically elected politicians. Between 1964 and 1985, the military became the bastion of authoritarianism and support for the right during the military dictatorship, as in almost all other Latin American countries. The right, afraid of the growing mobilization of peasants and possible confiscation of their land, strongly supported the military. The military based its intervention on the doctrine of national security within a framework of the ideology of geopolitics, which called for total war against subversive elements that might threaten the security of the state, seen as an organism in and of itself. During this period, thousands of intellectuals, artists, and social activists were imprisoned, tortured, and murdered or disappeared, while others were forced into exile. The emergence of social movements, and particularly the steelworkers' unions, which later developed into the Workers Party (PT), were able to demand a return to democracy in the late 1980s.

Even after the return to democracy, the political right can be identified in Brazil. Traditional colonial institutions are present in the rural areas despite opposition by the Landless Movement (MST) and efforts toward agrarian reform. The judiciary, plagued with corruption, was able to maintain its traditional structure and avoid reforms.

Within the church, traditional and conservative groups have gained more visibility, including the Catholic Charismatic movement, while Liberation Theology, censored by Pope John Paul II, is restricted. Moreover, Pentecostals in Brazil control a party and are a powerful force in Congress. The heirs of conservative and integralist intellectuals can be found not only in universities and think tanks established during the military dictatorship, but also in authors such as Ubiratan Macedo, Vamireh Chacon, and Vicente Barreto. Especially powerful groups in the mass media can be included, as they received the support of the regime and continue to defend the interests of the right.

The origins of the Brazilian right can be traced to colonialism, but the arguments for its hegemony have changed. In colonial times, a metaphysical imposition by the monarchy was incorporated by an agrarian economy and blessed by the church and legal system. After independence and the establishment of the Brazilian monarchy, conservatism served as the basis for the partisan politics of the aristocracy according to the principle of conciliation.

After the installation of the republican regime and into the 20th century, the politics of the right were expressed by political parties and military governments. The most important expressions of this authoritarianism were the integralist movement of the 1930s and the military dictatorship of 1964 to 1985. The post-authoritarian right is represented by intellectuals, organizations, religious groups, parties, and politicians elected by democratic means and supported by traditional institutions. They continue to use the ideology of conciliation to be part of the system, while dismantling opposition and contradicting democratic ideals.

SEE ALSO
Volume 1 Left: Brazil; South America.
Volume 2 Right: South America; Monarchism.

BIBLIOGRAPHY
David Samuels, *Ambition, Federalism and Legislative Politics in Brazil* (Cambridge University Press, 2002); Eduardo Hoornaert, *Formação do Catolicismo Brasileiro: 1500–1800* (Vozes, 1974); Miguel Reale, *Imperativos da revolução de Março* (Martins, 1965); Nelson W. Sodré, *A ideologia do colonialismo* (Vozes, 1981).

AMOS NASCIMENTO
METHODIST UNIVERSITY OF PIRACICABA, BRAZIL

British National Party

THE BRITISH NATIONAL PARTY was formed in 1982, following serious splits in the National Front, largely over tactics and strategy, between those who wished to place the emphasis on direct action against ethnic minorities and immigrants and those who wished to imbue the party with a semblance of respectability in order to broaden its electoral appeal. Ironically, though, the British National Party (BNP) was to experience many of the schisms and intraparty conflicts—some ideological, some strategic, and others deriving from personality clashes and internal power struggles—that had split the National Front.

For the remainder of the 1980s, the BNP's leader, John Tyndall, sought to pursue a quasi-respectable electoral strategy, primarily intended to attract disillusioned conservatives (who would not have wanted to turn to the left-leaning Labour Party during this period). However, this strategy yielded very limited success, and thus refueled tensions between those who wished to persevere with electoralism in order to secure longer-term respectability and those who were quite content to rely on direct action and physical attacks against ethnic minority groups in inner-city districts as well as on organizations of the left. (For example, in 1992, the offices of the communist newspaper *The Morning Star* were attacked.)

IDEOLOGY AND POLITICS

The BNP sought to present an image of greater respectability in the 1990s, partly by formally placing more emphasis on electoral politics (at both national and local, grassroots, levels), and by electing in 1999 a Cambridge University graduate, Nick Griffin, as party leader. However, its core ideology continued to be based on conceptions of white racial supremacy and the need to halt all further immigration into Britain, while also repatriating (to their country of origin) non-whites already resident in Britain. Since the late 1990s, this core anti-immigrant stance of the BNP has been yoked to mounting public concern—driven by various anti-Labour newspapers—that Britain is being swamped by asylum seekers, many of whom are deemed to be economic migrants rather than genuinely fleeing political persecution. In accordance with its claim that ethnic minorities receive preferential treatment on various issues, partly because of political correctness and positive discrimination in the appointment to various jobs and the allocation of public housing, the BNP has various campaigns to promote rights for whites, alleging that in some districts, it is the indigenous white population that is now the discriminated-against minority.

On other issues, the BNP evinces a blend of right-wing authoritarianism, fervent nationalism, and populism. For example, it advocates a much tougher law-and-order policy, with more powers for the police and the courts, the restoration of the death penalty, a return to traditional standards and discipline in schools, and the reintroduction of national service for young people. Economically, the BNP's promotion of British interests and those of British workers leads it to call for withdrawal from the European Union and resistance to globalization via the introduction of import controls on foreign goods. The BNP also advocates boosting Britain's armed forces and military strength, while withdrawing from NATO and closing down foreign military bases on British soil. In the latter respect, the BNP criticizes what it terms Britain's "spineless subservience to the United States."

ELECTORAL PERFORMANCE

During the 1980s, the fledgling BNP received only a negligible number of votes in the national and local elections in which it participated, partly because it was competing against the remnants of the National Front. However, Margaret Thatcher's own pronouncements (as Conservative Party leader and prime minister) on curbing immigration and protecting British/national identity also played a part in limiting electoral support for the BNP.

It was not until the 1990s that the BNP began to make relatively significant electoral advances, albeit in specific districts and regions of Britain, most notably the East End of London, and in various former mill-towns of Lancashire and Yorkshire in northern England. These were areas in which there were relatively high proportions or concentrations of ethnic minority communities. These districts proved to be fertile ground for the BNP to exploit grievances and resentment among sections of the indigenous white working class, some of whom readily blamed their own unemployment, socioeconomic deprivation or poor housing conditions on the "takeover" of the area by immigrant communities. The BNP also reflected and reinforced a belief among sections of the local white working class that, due to a combination of well organized or vocal lobbying and "political correctness," ethnic minority communities and asylum seekers were being granted preferential treatment by local administrators over a range of deci-

sions and policies, including the allocation of financial resource and assistance.

Thus, in a 1993 local government by-election in Tower Hamlets (an impoverished East London district with a significant Bangladeshi community), a BNP candidate was elected, receiving 34 percent of votes cast. The same level of support was received in a local government by-election the following year by the BNP's candidate in the nearby district of Newham.

In the 1997 general election, the BNP fielded candidates in 13 constituencies, and secured enough votes in 3 of them to save their deposit (by winning more than 5 percent of votes cast). Two years later, in the 1999 elections to the European Parliament—for which a system of proportional representation was adopted—the BNP polled 100,000 votes, and in the 2000 election to the new Greater London Assembly, the BNP won a total of 47,000 votes.

These electoral advances were sustained in the 2001 general election, when the BNP contested 33 constituencies, secured an average level of support of 3.9 percent in these seats, and saved its deposit in five of them. The most notable result was in the Lancashire constituency of Oldham West, where the BNP leader, Nick Griffin, received 16 percent of the vote, and in neighboring Oldham East, where the BNP candidate secured 11 percent of votes cast. The BNP also won a number of local council seats in the nearby towns of Burnley (where it became the second largest party) and Blackburn in 2002 and 2003, and looked set to consolidate these electoral advances in the 2004 European Parliament elections.

SEE ALSO

Volume 1 Left: United Kingdom; Labour Party, UK; Immigration.
Volume 2 Right: Nationalism; Immigration Restriction; Thatcher, Margaret; United Kingdom.

BIBLIOGRAPHY

Roger Eatwell, "Britain, the BNP and the Problem of Legitimacy," *New Party Politics of the Right: Neo-Populist Parties and Movements in Established Democracies,* H.G. Betz and S. Immerfall, eds. (St. Martin's Press, 1998); Roger Eatwell, "The Extreme Right and British Exceptionalism: The Primacy of Politics," *The Politics of the Extreme Right: From the Margins to the Mainstream,* Paul Hainsworth, ed. (Pinter, 2000); Sophie Goodchild and Paul Lashmar, "On the Le Pen Menu: Roast Beef and Raw Bigotry," *The Independent on Sunday* (April 25, 2004); Roger Griffin, "British Fascism: The Ugly Duckling," *The Failure of British Fascism* M. Cronin, ed. (Palgrave

Macmillan, 1996); Piero Ignazi, *Extreme Right Parties in Europe* (Oxford University Press, 2003).

PETER DOREY
CARDIFF UNIVERSITY, UNITED KINGDOM

Bruder Schweigen

IN SEPTEMBER 1983, the Bruder Schweigen (also known as the Silent Brotherhood or The Order) was formed by Robert "Robbie" J. Matthews in Washington state. Matthews had been born in Marfa, Texas, but his family had been forced to move to Phoenix, Arizona, when the dry goods business owned by his father, John, collapsed. As a youth, Matthews became concerned with the threat of communism to the United States, especially in 1964 when conservative icon Senator Barry Goldwater from Arizona ran for the presidency on the Republican Party ticket. Matthews fell under the influence of the John Birch Society, founded in 1958. The society was named for U.S. Captain John Birch, who was shot by the Chinese communists while on a mission in Suchow, China, in August 1945. American far-right conservatives consider Birch to be the first casualty of the new Cold War.

As he matured, Matthews also came under the influence of Richard Butler and his Aryan Nations movement, with its headquarters in Hayden Lake, Idaho. By 1980, the movement, with its philosophy rooted in the Christian Identity faith, had become the magnet for many of those who felt their affairs were no longer controlled by a loyal administration in Washington, D.C., but by the Zionist Occupation Government (ZOG), a conspiratorial group that served as a thinly disguised front for what they considered to be world Jewry. Matthews attracted the attention of the leadership of the Aryan Nations and kindred groups when he vocally confronted opposing demonstrators at an Aryan Nations rally in Spokane, Washington, in 1983.

Matthews was an avid reader of *The Turner Diaries*, a novel by William Pierce that described the making of a white resistance movement against what he perceived to be the mixing of white blood with that of "inferior" races and against the increasingly anti-American government in Washington, D.C. An excerpt from *The Turner Diaries* shows the flavor of the book: "It is now a dark and dismal time in the history of our race. All about us lie the green graves of our sires, yet, in a land once ours,

we have become a people dispossessed." Inspired by the group in *The Turner Diaries* called The Order, formed by a fictional man called Earl Turner, Matthews decided in 1983 to form his own. The name Bruder Schweigen came from a history of the Nazi German SS of Heinrich Himmler, a group modeled after the Jesuits, the Society of Jesus, which has had a great influence on America's far right. The full title of the book, *When Alle Bruder Schweigen (When All the Brothers Are Silent)* came from a line in a poem by German soldier Max von Schenckendorf, who had fought in the 1813 German war of liberation against Napoleon. The full line, according to Kevin Flynn and Gary Gerhart, reads (translated): "When all our brothers keep silent, and worship false Gods, we will keep our faith." The influence of the first of the Old Testament Ten Commandments, something intrinsic to the Christian Identity faith, is also evident: "Thou shalt have no other gods before me," in the King James version of the Holy Bible. Matthews translated Bruder Schweigen as "the Silent Brotherhood." Among its more prominent members would be David Lane, Richard Scutari, Richard Kemp, and Gary Yarborough. As of December 2003, all were believed to be in prison.

Matthews and The Order decided to wage a campaign to fund the white resistance that had been prefigured in *The Turner Diaries*. To do so, they carried out a whirlwind series of robberies that netted some $4 million for their coffers. On June 18, 1984, The Order shot and killed Denver, Colorado, Radio Station KOA talk show host Alan Berg. Matthews and his men did so because Berg was Jewish and a vocal critic of the far right. During the same period, The Order member Thomas Martinez, from Philadelphia, Pennsylvania, began to act as a Federal Bureau of Investigation (FBI) informant on The Order's activities. The end for Matthews came when he was cornered in a house on Whidbey Island, Washington, on December 8, 1984. He died as the cabin he was in caught fire and burned in the siege by law enforcement authorities. Richard Scutari was one of the members of The Order to avoid apprehension the longest, until his arrest in Seattle, Washington, in 1986.

SEE ALSO

Volume 1 Left: United States.
Volume 2 Right: Christian Identity; Militia Movements; John Birch Society.

BIBLIOGRAPHY

William Norman Grigg, "John Birch: A Patriot Exemplar," John Birch Society, www.jbs.org (May 2004); "Martyrs, Heroes, and Prisoners: The Order Bruder Schweigen," www.eye-onhate.com (May 2004); "Inmate Loses Parole Bid in Berg Slaying [Richard Scutari]," *Rocky Mountain News* (November 22, 2003); John F. Murphy Jr., *Day of Reckoning: The Massacre at Columbine High School* (Xlibris, 2001); Howard L. Bushart, John R. Craig, and Myra Barnes, *Soldiers of God: White Supremacists and Their Holy War for America* (Pinnacle Books, 1998); Joel Dyer, *Harvest of Rage: How Oklahoma City Is Only the Beginning* (Westview Press, 1998); Alan M. Schwartz, ed., *Danger: Extremism: The Major Vehicles and Voices on America's Far-Right Fringe* (Anti-Defamation League, 1996); James Ridgeway, *Blood in the Face: The Ku Klux Klan, Aryan Nations, and the Rise of a New White Culture* (Thunder's Mouth Press, 1995); Kevin Flynn and Gary Gerhart, *The Silent Brotherhood* (Signet, 1989).

JOHN F. MURPHY, JR.
AMERICAN MILITARY UNIVERSITY

Buchanan, Patrick J. (1938–)

PATRICK J. BUCHANAN was born in Washington, D.C. Intelligent and strong academically, Buchanan attended Georgetown University and graduated in 1961 with a Bachelor of Arts in English and philosophy. Then he received a graduate M.S. degree from the Columbia School of Journalism in 1962. After completing his schooling, Buchanan accepted a post as an editorial writer for the *St. Louis Globe-Dispatch*, where he worked until 1966.

After leaving St. Louis, Missouri, Buchanan became a speechwriter for Richard Nixon. He worked for Nixon from 1966 to 1974 and escaped from Nixon's administration and the Watergate scandal relatively unharmed. Much later, it was revealed in a declassified 1972 White House memo that Buchanan had endorsed activities that aimed to harass Democratic campaigners, even though he had told the 1973 Senate Watergate committee that he didn't know of any proposed or enacted actions designed to covertly harass political opponents. As a result of being unscathed, he was able to return to the White House as an assistant to President Gerald Ford, who even later nominated Buchanan as the U.S. ambassador to South Africa, although he never took the post. After the Ford administration, Buchanan went on to become President Ronald Reagan's director of public communications, dealing with controversial issues including the Iran-Contra scandal.

Drawing upon his vast experience in the White House and his strong educational background, Buchanan was able to become a well-known conservative and political journalist. Outside of government positions, he has cohosted CNN's popular *Crossfire* talk show from 1987 to 1991, from 1992 to 1995, and from 1996 to 1999. He has worked as a widely syndicated newspaper columnist, even during his years in the White House, from 1975 to 1985 and from 1987 to 1999. Buchanan continues to spend most of his time writing and is the author of numerous political books.

Politically, Buchanan has sought but been unable to attain election to the White House, losing his bids for the presidential nomination of the Republican Party in 1992 and 1996. In the 2000 election, after leaving the Republican Party during the caucus circuit, he became the presidential nominee for the Reform Party. His main political proposals all focus on his America First platform, which is based upon highly protectionist trade policies and a pro-life social and moral stance. Going into the 2000 campaign, Buchanan did have the benefit of nationwide name recognition as a result of his government work and journalism background, but he had trouble making any significant progress beyond his core constituency. In the 2000 polls leading up to the election, Buchanan never had more than 6 percent of the projected vote.

Buchanan advocated his America First policies as well as pursued a conservative Stop Bush agenda. Unfortunately for Buchanan, two other social conservatives, Steve Forbes and Gary Bauer, entered the 2000 campaign, splitting Republican voters into three different campaign camps that wanted someone other than Bush. After taking fifth place in an Iowa Republican straw poll in 1999, behind Forbes and Bauer, Buchanan officially left the Republican Party and campaigned with the Reform Party, eventually accepting its presidential nomination.

However, Buchanan didn't receive the nomination until after the Reform Party was fragmented by his adamant pro-life (anti-abortion) and anti-homosexual rights views, which alienated many of the traditional Reform Party supporters swayed by the socially liberal yet economically conservative stance of Ross Perot. As the nominee for the Reform Party, Buchanan was able to obtain $12.6 million in federal election matching funds as a result of the party's somewhat surprising and strong showing in the 1996 election.

Around the same time as he received the nomination and the matching funding, one of Buchanan's most inflammatory books, *A Republic, Not an Empire*, which advocated a return to noninterventionist foreign policy and the end of support for Israel, was released in bookstores nationwide. As a result, prominent members of the Republican Party, including John McCain, Elizabeth Dole, and William Bennett, who were worried about Buchanan's potential "spoiler" role in the election, criticized Buchanan as "pro-Hitler." In return, Buchanan simply labeled his critics as adamant members of "the Israel lobby" that he believed held too much power on Capitol Hill. In order to escape criticisms of being a racist, he selected Ezola B. Foster, an African American political activist from California, to be his running mate. He was unable to escape from the controversy and took fourth place in the 2000 election with only 449,000 votes. As a result of his poor performance, the Reform Party did not achieve the necessary number of votes to receive federal matching campaign funds again in 2004.

After admitting that his foray into third-party politics may have been a mistake, Buchanan returned to journalism. In 2004, he was a frequent guest on various cable news programs, and continued to work with the foundation he established, The American Cause, to further his America First agenda.

SEE ALSO

BIBLIOGRAPHY

Patrick J. Buchanan, *A Republic, Not an Empire: Reclaiming America's Destiny* (Regnery, 2002); "Campaign 2000: Pat Buchanan," www.politics1.com (April 2004); "Pat Buchanan," *Washington Post*, www.washingtonpost.com (April 2004).

ARTHUR HOLST, PH.D.
WIDENER UNIVERSITY

Buckley, William F., Jr. (1925–)

A SELF-DESCRIBED libertarian journalist, William (Bill) Buckley has been one of the most influential and controversial figures in the recent history of conservative politics and thought in the United States. In 1955, Buckley, graduate of Yale University and member of the prestigious and secret Skull and Bones Society, founded the *National Review*. It came to be a key forum for the intellectual rebirth of American conservatism, fusing traditionalism, libertarianism, and anti-communism against the alleged complacency of President Dwight Eisenhower's "Modern Republicanism."

Buckley was born in Sharon, Connecticut. His family was Catholic and his father, who was making a fortune in the oil business, was an ardent anti-communist. Buckley made a name for himself as a right-wing firebrand in his years at Yale. As the chairman of the Yale *Daily News*, he challenged the university's tolerance of Keynesian economics and the New Deal with an agenda of individualism, free enterprise, and "active Christianity." His book, *God and Man at Yale* (1951), marketed with the help of his father, promoted a "counterrevolutionary" rather than status quo conservatism, and provoked a great deal of controversy.

In 1952, after a brief stint with the Central Intelligence Agency in Mexico City, Buckley was hired by the conservative publication *American Mercury* in New York City. Together with Brent Bozell, he defended the concept of McCarthyism, even after McCarthy's demise, as a principled anti-communist crusade against any policy not in the national interest. With the help of his father and other financial backers (including South Carolina textile magnate Roger Milliken), Buckley established the *National Review* in 1955. After overcoming initial anti-Catholicism, the message of uniting the various strands of conservatism against the liberal orthodoxy and Eisenhower's partial acceptance of it energized radical conservatives. "Fusionism," so named by Bozell, "sought to combine the libertarian defense of economic and political freedom with the traditional and Christian emphasis on virtue as the end of society." Nonisolationist anti-communism provided the glue. But there were other elements as well: In an early editorial ("Why the South Must Prevail," in August 1957), Buckley argued against integration and voting rights for African Americans, based on a constitutional argument for states' rights and, while avoiding overt racism, made a claim of a de facto "advanced [white] race" and civilization.

In his *National Review* editorials and in radio and TV appearances, Buckley described himself as an "intellectual revolutionary" against the New Deal. Buckley's book, *Up from Liberalism* (a play on Booker T. Washington's "Up from Slavery") targets liberal hegemony and Eisenhower's "Modern Republicanism," which he called "measured socialism." He argued that liberalism was preoccupied with democracy as its preferred method of politics, rather than focusing on the objective of politics: a virtuous society. In the end,

Buckley accepted some of the political realities of the administration, for example that an attack on Social Security was dangerous at the polls and that nuclear war could not be risked over an intervention in the Hungarian uprising against communism. But he stressed the importance of principled long-term strategies that involved, for example, convincing Americans that Social Security in the end limited economic freedom.

The 1960s counterculture and politics provided necessary visible enemies, and the *National Review* became the intellectual forum for the emerging movement. Buckley distanced himself from the anti-Semitic "irresponsible right," in particular the growing John Birch Society, because he feared that the conservatives would be marginalized. He was encouraged by Arizona Senator Barry Goldwater's emergence, but in the 1964 presidential election, Goldwater lost everywhere outside the deep south.

Buckley's failed mayoral campaign for the Conservative Party in New York City gained him nationwide attention. Kevin Phillips used his example in his important book, *The Emerging Republican Majority*. In fact, the vote for Buckley anticipated the future northern urban coalition of Ronald Reagan: White ethnic votes could be won based on fiscal conservatism and fear of African Americans. Buckley began to host the TV show *Firing Line*, where he sharply debated liberals as long as they would dare to appear on the stage with him.

President Lyndon Johnson's landslide election and Great Society seemed to cement the New Deal hegemony, but, in fact, the country was torn. Richard Nixon's southern strategy attempted to exploit the civil rights controversy. While Nixon was "not a *National Review* conservative," because he was centrist on economic and civil rights issues, Buckley, in the end, supported him because of his anti-communism and electability. Buckley thus became an "establishment conservative" after all, defending Nixon's Keynesian policies, which infuriated his fellow conservatives and editors, and endorsed him for reelection in 1972 despite disagreement over Nixon's détente policies with the Soviet Union.

After the Watergate scandal, Buckley temporarily came under attack from a group of younger, more populist conservatives who considered him too reformist and too elitist. Buckley withdrew to write spy novels, while the New Right was applying what they had learned from the *National Review* by building a network of foundations and think tanks. This included, for example, Paul Weyrich's Heritage Foundation, which would prove to be invaluable for the conservative cause

in the future. But Buckley's prime time in the center of conservative politics was yet to come. While not directly involved in the campaign, his support for his old friend Ronald Reagan was crucial. Using the *National Review* as well as personal relationships with Henry Kissinger and George H.W. Bush, he mediated between the Reaganites and more moderate Republicans, finally helping to get Bush the vice presidential slot.

With Reagan in the White House, Buckley became more of a national celebrity in the Republican Party. On many occasions, he disagreed with the president (for example, he advocated abrogating the 1972 anti-ballistic missile treaty to pursue the Strategic Defense Initiative), and he continued to be at the center of many political and social controversies, such as when he proposed to have people who had contracted HIV/AIDS be tattooed.

What is Buckley's legacy? While based on a more populist approach than Buckley ever envisioned, Reagan's success, as well as Newt Gingrich's success and George W. Bush's success, were also built on the foundations of a conservative movement that Buckley had helped to revive.

SEE ALSO

Volume 1 Left: Liberalism; Johnson, Lyndon B.
Volume 2 Right: New Right; Libertarianism; Bush, George H. W.; Conservatism.

BIBLIOGRAPHY

William F. Buckley, Jr., *Happy Days Were Here Again: Reflections of a Libertarian Journalist* (Random House, 1993); E.J. Dionne, *Why Americans Hate Politics* (Simon and Schuster, 1991); John B. Judis, *William F. Buckley, Jr. Patron Saint of the Conservatives* (Simon and Schuster, 1988).

THOMAS GREVEN
FREIE UNIVERSITÄT, GERMANY

Burke, Edmund (1729–1797)

ANGLO-IRISH STATESMAN and author Edmund Burke served a long career as a Whig member of the British Parliament. His fame endures for his blistering denunciations of the French Revolution, which he perceived as a direct threat to society, religion, and the rights of Englishmen. Born in Dublin, Ireland, on January 12, 1729, he grew up as a member of the Ascendancy, the ruling Protestant elite of Ireland. Burke studied at Trinity College for five years, trained for the law, then later turned to writing and politics. He wrote two early works, *A Vindication of Natural Society* (1756) and *A Philosophical Inquiry into the Origin of Our Ideas of the Sublime and Beautiful* (1757). He married Jane Nugent in 1757, and they had a son, Richard, the following year.

In the early 1760s, Burke and his good friend Samuel Johnson founded the Literary Club, a place where the stars of literary London could meet and exchange the kind of conversation that is so well represented in James Boswell's *The Life of Samuel Johnson*. It is a testament to Burke's extremely intense personality that he could actually exhaust Johnson in conversation. That decade also saw the launch of Burke's political career. He spent much of his career allied to the faction known as the Rockingham Whigs, which formed around the Marquis of Rockingham, whose secretary Burke became in 1765. That same year Rockingham assisted Burke's entry into politics by helping him become a member of Parliament for Wendover. During the course of his long career, his pronouncements on America, India, and the French Revolution would earn him a reputation as a leading conservative voice in Great Britain. Although known in the 20th century as a great conservative thinker, in his day Burke belonged to the Whig Party, and during that time the Tory Party was generally more conservative. Burke's conservatism is not that of a rustic like Henry Fielding's Squire Western but is rather based on a deep love for and understanding of the English constitution.

Nine years later, Burke was elected member for Bristol, around the same time that he began to deliver the speeches on the American question, for which he became famous. While sympathetic with the pleas of the colonists and believing that they only sought to defend traditional English rights, Burke did not support independence. Rather, Burke advocated conciliating the colonies in a famous speech delivered to the Commons on March 22, 1775. Since distance made sending Americans to Parliament impractical, Burke called on Parliament to allow the colonial assemblies to tax their citizens and send money to the Mother Country. To Burke, British conquest of America would push the limits of Britain's sovereignty over its colonies, an act that offended Burke's deep devotion to moderation and political prudence and his hatred of extremism. During the War for American Independence, Burke feared that if a large military force subjugated the American colonies, British liberty would soon come under threat as well.

Although he failed in his American endeavors, Burke would continue his efforts against arbitrary and oppressive government in the 1780s, scrutinizing British colonial rule in India. Burke led the impeachment of East India Company official and British Governor General of India Warren Hastings. Attacking Hastings, Burke would declare, "No man can lawfully govern himself according to his own will; much less can one person be governed by the will of another." Burke denounced the arbitrary power Hastings wielded in India, for he saw that no one could rightfully wield such power. For Burke, all power was justly limited by law, whether natural law ordained by God or by the English Common Law. Man was created to be ruled by law, not by will, a principle that applied equally to the government in England as it did to colonial administrators in India. The long trial of Hastings would be one of the most dramatic spectacles of late 18th-century London, and a showcase for some of the most eloquent oratory of the period. Nevertheless, Hastings would be acquitted in 1795.

In 1789, the French Revolution inaugurated all the modern trends of totalitarianism and despotism: the insistence on the rule of "the people," on social engineering, and on the complete and violent eradication of all opposition to the revolution. Burke recognized early on that the French Revolution differed sharply from the English revolution of 1688. French revolutionaries sought to overthrow completely the *ancien regime* of France and remake French society according to the most extreme principles of the European Enlightenment. Abandoning tradition, custom, and historical precedent in favor of a new order based on "Reason" as ordained by French *philosophes* ran counter to all of Burke's ideas about government. Schemes for the perfection of man through science and reason held no charms for a Christian like Burke, who understood that mankind is fallen and corrupt.

In November 1790, Burke published *Reflections on the Revolution in France*. That work began as a response to a sermon that praised the revolution, delivered by the Non-Conformist minister Richard Price; Burke expanded his response to probe and denounce the character of the French Revolution. With blistering rhetoric, he savaged the revolutionaries and argued that their methods were too harsh and would bring on problems far worse than those they set out to address. Burke also argued that the French enthusiasm for the unrestrained "rights of man" could never translate into a system that guaranteed practical liberty. Of the revolutionary order at hand in France and threatening at that time to metastasize throughout Europe Burke commented: "On this scheme of things, a king is but a man, a queen is but a woman, a woman is but an animal—and an animal not of the highest order. All homage paid to the sex in general as such, and without distinct views, is to be regarded as romance and folly. Regicide, parricide, and sacrilege, are but fictions of superstition, corrupting jurisprudence by destroying its simplicity." Passages such as this show both Burke's insight into the revolution and why *Reflections on the Revolution in France* would endear Burke to later generations of conservatives.

The French Revolution would break apart Burke's friendships as well, most notably that with Charles James Fox. Although a Whig, Burke did not embrace the radicalism of Fox or other Whig leaders such as Richard Brinsley Sheridan, who had fought alongside Burke in the Hastings trial. Burke himself defended the principles of the Glorious Revolution of 1688. Burke saw that revolution not as popular sovereignty run amok but as a last resort to restore the balance of the English constitution, which the absolutist ambitions of James II had upset. These thoughts were codified in his pamphlet *An Appeal from the New to the Old Whigs*.

In 1794, Burke retired from Parliament, but not from writing. Burke continued to rail against Jacobinism in his 1796 *Letters on a Regicide Peace*, denouncing it as "the revolt of the enterprising talents of a country against its property." Then he proceeded to argue that France had a kind of established Jacobinism, in which Jacobins had built their regime on the confiscation of property and on outlawing any attempts to defend the old monarchy. He likewise condemned Revolutionary France for its atheism, for Jacobin France sought not to offer religious toleration but to eradicate Christianity altogether. Burke died on July 9, 1797. He lies buried in Beaconsfield, in a spot he ordered concealed, so that if revolutionaries would triumph in England, they might not disinter and defame his remains.

In the second half of the 20th century, American conservatives discovered Burke and embraced him as a kind of father of American conservatism. Russell Kirk, in his books *The Conservative Mind* and *Edmund Burke: A Genius Reconsidered*, helped to popularize Burke with a new generation of American readers. *Reflections on the Revolution in France* appealed to readers during the Cold War because it denounced excesses of the French revolutionaries that were copied and exceeded by 20th-century communists.

Burke, in particular, appeals to American conservatives because so much American political writing from the 18th century is radical in tone, such as the writings of Thomas Paine and Thomas Jefferson. Burke spoke out in favor of conserving the edifices of the past and on the debt that the present owes to the past. These sentiments were not in harmony with the sentiments of many American revolutionaries. They were even less in sympathy with the 20th-century socialists and communists against whom modern conservatives were reacting. By an interesting twist of history, an Anglo-Irish statesman who had opposed American independence became the favorite author of 20th-century American conservatives. This development serves to highlight the vast gulf between liberals and conservatives in postmodern America: Conservatives have more common ground with one who supported the British government in the War for American Independence than they do with the political left.

SEE ALSO

Volume 1 Left: Liberalism; France; French Revolution.
Volume 2 Right: Conservatism; France; Monarchism.

BIBLIOGRAPHY

Stanley Ayling, *Edmund Burke: His Life and Opinions* (St. Martin's Press, 1988); Edmund Burke, *The Portable Edmund Burke*, Isaac Kramnick, ed. (Penguin Books, 1999); Edmund Burke, *Select Works of Edmund Burke: A New Imprint of the Payne Edition* (Liberty Fund, 1999); Russell Kirk, *The Conservative Mind from Burke to Eliot* (Regnery, 1994); Russell Kirk, *Edmund Burke: A Genius Reconsidered* (Intercollegiate Studies Institute, 1997); Isaac Kramnick, *The Rage of Edmund Burke: Portrait of an Ambivalent Conservative* (Basic Books, 1977); Harvey C. Mansfield, Jr., *Statesmanship and Party Government: A Study of Burke and Bolingbroke* (University of Chicago Press, 1965); Harvey C. Mansfield, Jr., ed., *Selected Letters of Edmund Burke* (University of Chicago Press, 1984); C.C. O'Brien, *The Great Melody: A Thematic Biography and Commented Anthology of Edmund Burke* (University of Chicago Press, 1992); Peter J. Stanlis, *Edmund Burke and the Natural Law* (University of Michigan Press, 1958).

MITCHELL MCNAYLOR
OUR LADY OF THE LAKE COLLEGE

Bush, George H.W. (1924–)

THE BUSH FAMILY is one of the preeminent political dynasties in the United States, matched in recent history perhaps only by the Kennedys. George Herbert

Walker Bush served as the country's 41st president from 1989 to 1993. While he never truly excited his party, the Republicans, or the American public, he did receive unprecedented approval ratings at the height of the 1991 Persian Gulf crisis. His presidency saw the fall of the Berlin Wall, the end of the Cold War, and also the first major armed conflict of the post-Cold War era. His lack of action in the face of a recession probably cost him a second term. But the Bush dynasty came back with sons George W. Bush, 43rd president, and Jeb Bush, governor of Florida.

The Bushes' roots include a distant link to England's royal family, but their relevance for American politics was not established until Bush's father, investment banker Prescott Bush, became Republican senator for Connecticut. Bush's background in the eastern establishment included Phillips Academy in Andover, Massachusetts, and, after a distinguished service as U.S. Navy pilot in World War II, Yale University. At Yale, he was inducted into the secret Skull and Bones society (to which his son, George W. Bush also belonged), allowing him to build his own political networks. Such connections—including controversial ones to Saudi Arabian families such as the bin Ladens and the energy and defense industries—would prove to be as valuable to Bush's political and business prospects as the wealth of his father and maternal grandfather, George Herbert Walker.

After Yale, Bush attempted to establish himself in the Texas oil business. His father's connections (which had also included controversial ones with wartime Germany) helped him land a job with Dresser Industries, an oil services company. His work there, as well as in other oil ventures, was largely related to the financial side of the business, for example using tax shelters and off-shore subsidiaries.

Bush decided to go into politics and, after a failed senatorial campaign, was elected to the U.S. House of Representatives in 1966, and again in 1968. This turned out to be his only elected office prior to the vice presidency, because he quickly achieved inner-circle status in the Richard Nixon and Gerald Ford administrations, again due to the family's connections. Bush served as U.S. ambassador to the United Nations from 1971 to 1973, as chairman of the Republican National Committee from 1973 to 1974, as U.S. envoy to the People's Republic of China from 1974 to 1975, and as director of the Central Intelligence Agency from 1976 to 1977.

In 1980, he lost in the Republican presidential primaries—in which he ran without both a record of election victories and a clear base outside his establishment connections (including, however, former President Ford)—to Ronald Reagan. Reagan reluctantly chose Bush as running mate, due, in great part, to Bush's place in the eastern Republican establishment and to his foreign policy experience and internationalist credentials as a member of the Trilateral Commission and Council on Foreign Relations.

The Reagan years were characterized by supply-side economics (Reaganomics), which Bush had lambasted as "voodoo economics" in the primaries; an arms race with the "evil empire," the Soviet Union, and then arms control treaties; and numerous scandals in which Bush was involved to some degree. First, during the campaign against President Jimmy Carter, it was alleged that Bush had helped work out a deal with the revolutionary Iranian government to prevent a so-called October Surprise, that is, the timely rescue of the American hostages in Iran. Nothing was ever proven, but the hostages were released within minutes of Reagan's inauguration, and two months after that, weapons were secretly delivered to Iran. Potentially linked to this episode was the Iran-Contra affair of 1986–87, when money was funneled to the Contras who were fighting the communist Sandinista government in Nicaragua, clearly in violation of the law. Bush was never directly implicated but the scandal haunted him somewhat in his own presidential campaign in 1988.

KINDER, GENTLER

Promising a "kinder, gentler" version of Reaganism, Bush initially trailed the Democratic challenger, Massachusetts Governor Michael Dukakis, in the polls. Among the factors that turned the Bush campaign around, the infamous Willie Horton television advertisements—although not run directly by the Bush campaign—deserve special mention. Horton, an African American prison inmate, was on a government-authorized furlough when he raped a white woman. Dukakis was successfully portrayed as "soft on crime," and the so-called Reagan Democrats once again voted for a Republican candidate.

Neither in the campaign nor during his term did Bush excite the Christian right. On the contrary, he angered this political base by refusing to commit to anti-abortion laws and right-wing Supreme Court appointments, yet he still appointed the ultraconservative Clarence Thomas to the bench. In contrast to his son, George W. Bush, who considers himself a born-again Christian, Bush always remained part of the eastern WASP establishment of the party and the country, despite his relocation to Texas. His administration was characterized by "prudence," a favorite Bush expression. Domestically, Bush deserves notable credit for the Americans with Disabilities Act and the Clean Air Act Amendments of 1990.

Having expressed no use for what he called the "vision thing," Bush came to be criticized for showing no leadership, for letting the country drift. He did propose a capital gains tax cut to please the libertarian wing of his party, but this proposal was frustrated by the Democratic Congress. In the end, he even angered the libertarians by reneging on his famous "read my lips: no new taxes" commitment, when his fiscal conservatism convinced him that something had to be done about the federal deficit. These decisions came back to haunt Bush in his 1992 reelection campaign, but initially it seemed as though he was unbeatable because of his foreign policy successes.

THIS WILL NOT STAND

Whether anything that Reagan or Bush had done, such as renewing the arms race, led to the demise of the Soviet Union is still hotly debated. But the communist bloc imploded quickly after the Berlin Wall fell in November 1989. Bush did exert leadership in orchestrating German unification but had to fight a "wimp" image until Saddam Hussein of Iraq, a former ally in the fight against the Islamic regime in Iran, invaded neighboring Kuwait in 1990. Bush declared, "this will not stand," and ordered U.S. troops to the Persian Gulf, first in Operation Desert Shield to protect Saudi Arabia, then in United Nations-authorized Desert Storm to liberate Kuwait. Both operations were controversial in the United States, even leading to a lawsuit against the president initiated by 40 members of Congress, but ultimately successful.

Bush's subsequent high approval ratings deterred Democratic challengers, but when he seemed incapable of dealing with a fairly mild recession (forgetting the lessons of Reagan's victory against Jimmy Carter: that a president had to do something in times of economic crisis), his reelection was suddenly in danger. Arkansas Governor Bill Clinton famously ran with a slogan that emphasized the president's inaction: "It's the economy, stupid." He came across as sharing people's concerns while Bush seemed out of touch; he was caught looking at his watch while debating the nation's domestic worries.

After fighting off a primary challenge from the far right wing of his party by television commentator Pat

George H.W. Bush (right) and George W. Bush have each brought their own brand of conservatism to the presidency.

Buchanan, Bush had to face Clinton and an independent candidate, Texas billionaire Ross Perot. Perot, who attracted fiscally conservative Republicans and protest voters, received 19 percent of the vote in November 1992, and probably split the conservative electorate enough to give the presidency to Clinton.

As president, Bush's continuation of Reagan's policies established him as a conservative Republican, but the discontent of the extreme right wing of the party and the Perot conservatives with Bush's presidency suggests that his political place was more in the tradition of Jeffersonian "disinterest" in the clash of social forces than it was an ideological commitment to right-wing values.

SEE ALSO

Volume 1 Left: Clinton, William J.; Carter, James E.; Democratic Party.
Volume 2 Right: Reagan, Ronald; Elitism; Bush, George W.; Republican Party; Buchanan, Patrick J.

BIBLIOGRAPHY

George H.W. Bush with Victor Gold, *Looking Forward: The George Bush Story* (Doubleday, 1987); John Robert Greene, *The Presidency of George Bush* (University Press of Kansas, 2000); Kevin Phillips, *American Dynasty: Aristocracy, Fortune, and the Politics of Deceit in the House of Bush* (Viking Publishers, 2004).

THOMAS GREVEN
FREIE UNIVERSITÄT, GERMANY

Bush, George W. (1946–)

REPUBLICAN GEORGE W. Bush, son of George H.W. Bush, 41st president of the United States, and brother of Jeb Bush, governor of Florida, has built his political career on a strategic linkage between the Bush family's eastern establishment political networks and nationwide business connections, and a Texas-style populism reminiscent of the log cabin myth. As much as he liked to appear this way, the 43rd president of the United States, controversially elected in 2000, is clearly not your next-door neighbor, but belongs to one of the preeminent American political families.

George W. Bush pursued a career remarkably similar to his father, albeit initially with much less success, and often surrounded by controversy. He grew up in Texas, where his father had established himself as an oil businessman, but also belonged to the eastern establishment. He attended Phillips Academy in Andover, Massachusetts, Yale University, and then Harvard University. At Yale, he was inducted into the prestigious secret Skull and Bones honor society (allegedly by his father, who is also a member).

Much has been written about the young Bush's "youthful indiscretions" (as he would later describe his reputation as a "frat brat"). He had problems with alcohol, including arrests, and perhaps with drugs. Even more controversy ensued about Bush's time in the Texas National Guard, in which he served from 1968 on to avoid the draft of the Vietnam War. His father's connections helped him to jump a long waiting list, and questions remain about whether he missed time during his commitment. Astonishingly, even though they were raised many times, neither these episodes nor suspicions of a dyslexic condition have hurt Bush's political career. One reason may be that Bush quit drinking after his 40th birthday, guided by evangelist Billy Graham, and became a born-again Christian, changing his denomination from Episcopalian to his wife Laura's Methodist.

After graduating from Harvard Business School in 1975, Bush was at first unsure of what he wanted to do with his life. Once again following in his father's footsteps, he finally decided to go into politics, but his campaign for a seat in the U.S. House of Representatives in 1978 failed.

In 1979, Bush attempted to establish himself in the Texas oil and gas business and started a company named Arbusto (Spanish for "Bush"). Once again, his father's connections proved helpful. Despite a rather dismal business performance and after renaming, restructuring, and eventually selling his company, Bush was able to come out with a profit.

While working on his father's presidential campaign in 1988, Bush met Karl Rove, a political consultant with a clear vision of where to take the Republican Party and the country: not only back to the pre-New Deal era but right back to the Gilded Age's Republican dominance. Rove was so impressed with Bush's charisma that he became his political adviser in his campaigns and in the White House.

In 1989, Bush joined some of his father's friends to buy the Texas Rangers. He became managing general partner of the baseball franchise, a position that gave him important Texas credentials, and later again faced allegations of wrongdoing regarding the specifics of the purchase of a stadium. Bush went on to challenge Texas Democratic Governor Ann Richards, who was the first of many political opponents to underestimate him, occasionally calling him "shrub." In the context of the Republican sweep of 1994, the "Gingrich revolution," Bush won, while his brother Jeb—widely regarded as the better heir to his father's political career—lost in Florida. The governorship in Texas is not a powerful position per se, but Bush was able to focus on key conservative issues, crime, tort law and welfare reform, and education. He worked with the Texas Democrats in a bipartisan fashion, and even appealed to the growing Latino population. Bush was reelected in 1998, already gearing up for a presidential bid.

In the buildup to the 2000 election, Bush quickly came to be regarded as the favorite in Republican Party establishment circles and among major donors, and was able to amass a huge campaign war chest. He established a system for classifying and honoring big donors, the Bush Pioneers, modeled after his father's Team 100. Bush then used his growing support among evangelicals and the religious right as well as the machinations of adviser Rove to overcome his main challenger, Senator John McCain of Arizona, who had beaten him in the New Hampshire primary in February 2000, and secured the nomination. He selected Richard Cheney, defense secretary in his father's administration, as his vice presidential candidate.

COMPASSIONATE CONSERVATISM

Promising a "compassionate conservatism" and a return of dignity to the White House after the Bill Clinton scandals, Bush was able to seriously challenge the Democratic nominee, even though Vice President Al Gore ran as an incumbent in a time of peace and prosperity. Bush did not win the majority of the national vote, and eventually needed a controversial five-to-four Supreme Court decision to discontinue a recount in Florida, where the results had been extremely close and voting rights had allegedly been impaired, to gain a majority in the Electoral College.

This extremely controversial election, which has continued to anger Democrats and in particular African Americans, did not kept Bush from acting as if he had won a clear mandate. The Republicans were able to hold on to paper-thin majorities in Congress, even though one of the few remaining moderates, Senator James Jeffords of Vermont, decided to quit the Republican conference and thus gave the Senate majority to the Democrats until the mid-term elections of 2002.

Cabinet and other federal positions were filled from his father's networks as well as from business circles and the ever-growing system of right-wing foundations and think tanks. Prior to the September 11, 2001, terrorist attacks, the Bush administration had signaled disengagement in foreign policy, for example withdrawing Clinton's commitment to the Kyoto Protocol on climate control, and focused on two rounds of major tax cuts, largely benefiting Republican constituencies. The Bush family's business connections in the oil and energy industry played themselves out in controversial oil drilling projects in Alaska. Later, the accounting scandals surrounding energy giant Enron Corporation and others forced Bush to temporarily disassociate himself from his friends in the industry. Bush's evangelical Christian backers were pleased about the appointment of John Ashcroft as attorney general and about the proposal on faith-based initiatives that would permit the use of federal funds for church efforts in social policy.

Critics, however, have argued that the "compassionate" part of compassionate conservatism has never received sufficient funding or presidential support, not even signature policies such as the Leave No Child Behind education program. Critics also feared that faith-based voluntarism was ill suited to substitute for government action, and violated the separation of church and state.

Aside from the legacy of tax cuts, which have resulted in record budget deficits and federal debt and have angered fiscal conservatives on both sides of the aisle, the Bush administration will undoubtedly be remembered mostly for its actions (and inactions) after the attacks of September 11, 2001, when the Islamic terrorist network al Qaeda flew hijacked passenger planes into the World Trade Center and the Pentagon, killing more than 3,000 people.

Initially, Bush's foreign policy catered to the isolationist impulses present in the Republican Party. The major project was to be a National Missile Defense (NMD) system, reminiscent of Reagan's Strategic Defense Initiative proposal, attempting to insulate the United States from foreign threats. Critics, however, were proved right about the changed nature of security threats. No system of missile defense would have been able to prevent the terrorist attacks. While Bush was able to work out an agreement with Russia regarding NMD, he irritated the international community over the nonparticipation in the Kyoto Protocol, the International Criminal Court, and the ban on landmines.

After September 11, active unilateralism became the guiding principle of U.S. foreign policy. Much has been written about the role of a group of mostly Jewish neoconservative intellectuals and hawks in the new policy making process. People like Paul Wolfowitz, Richard Perle, and Lewis Libby, who had worked with Donald Rumsfeld, Cheney, and others in previous Republican administrations, had weathered the Clinton years in a think tank called the Project for a New American Century. There, they had developed a blueprint for a national security strategy that included much of what became, after September 11, the Bush foreign policy of preemptive strikes, Israel-friendly actions (which found the support of millennialist evangelicals who are preparing for Armageddon) and, some argue, even resulted in the war against Saddam Hussein's Iraq.

There is, however, no question about the initial widespread support of the American public for almost all measures taken by the Bush administration, including military action in Afghanistan and then Iraq, and domestic security measures enacted in the so-called Patriot Act, and through the establishment of a mega-bureaucracy for a new Homeland Security Department. While critics in the media and in the streets raised questions about threats to civil liberties, the treatment of prisoners in Guantanamo (the U.S. military base in Cuba), the misplaced rhetoric of a "crusade" against an "axis of evil" (to be pursued by a "coalition of the willing" rather than backed by the United Nations), economic interests of Bush family friends in the oil-rich Middle East, and the dangers of the Bush doctrine of preemption in general, support for the president remained high through the spring of 2004, when news about widespread torture in U.S.-run prisons in Iraq raised doubts about the moral high ground the United States claimed to occupy.

Bush's combination of eastern establishment, business connections, and conservative populism in some ways places him in the tradition of Ronald Reagan, albeit in a more southern and religiously colored fashion. In some contrast to his father's WASPish "country club" Republicanism, Bush adopted much of the political style and policy preferences of west Texas. Those who consider the Bush family a political dynasty may point to the revenge theme regarding Hussein present in the second Bush presidency, to the favoritism toward the energy and defense industries shown by both, even to the concept of "permanent government." But only the future will show whether the Bush presidencies have to be considered as part of one conservative era, with only a brief Clinton interlude, or whether George W. Bush's two-term presidency is itself an interlude to a longer Democratic era.

SEE ALSO

Volume 1 Left: Clinton, William J.; Anti-Globalization; Church and State Separation; Democratic Party.

Volume 2 Right: Bush, George H.W.; Reagan, Ronald; Republican Party; Isolationism.

BIBLIOGRAPHY

Eric Alterman and Mark Green, *The Book on Bush: How George W. (Mis)leads America* (Viking, 2004); Lou Dubose, Jan Reid, and Carl M. Cannon, *Boy Genius: Karl Rove, the Brains Behind the Remarkable Political Triumph of George W. Bush* (Public Affairs, 2003); James Hatfield, *Fortunate Son: George W. Bush and the Making of an American President* (Vision, 2002); Michael Lind, *Made in Texas: George W. Bush and the Southern Takeover of American Politics* (Basic Books, 2003); Kevin Phillips, *American Dynasty: Aristocracy, Fortune, and the Politics of Deceit in the House of Bush* (Viking, 2004); Ron Suskind, *The Price of Loyalty* (Simon and Schuster, 2004); Bob Woodward, *Bush at War* (Simon and Schuster, 2002).

THOMAS GREVEN
FREIE UNIVERSITÄT, GERMANY

The Right

Canada

IN TERMS OF LANDMASS, Canada is the second-largest country in the world after Russia. It has vast wildernesses, huge expanses of farmland, enviable hydroelectric power potential that is just beginning to be tapped as an export industry, and rich mineral resources. From a right-wing perspective, the left is so entrenched in Canadian politics that truly right-wing candidates have little chance of being elected.

An irony is that Canada traditionally adheres to a broad spectrum of right-wing policies, including a weak central government with broad provincial autonomy, unfettered international trade, and free market economics. The Liberals have stayed in power and seem to dominate the broad middle of the Canadian spectrum by utilizing patronage effectively and keeping the budget balanced and maintaining a healthy economy—both of which ordinarily would be considered right-wing policies. Conversely, in terms of social policies such as universal healthcare, Canada's Conservative Party is considerably left of center by U.S. standards.

In 2004, after a series of scandals surrounding liberal politicians, the electorate seemed in the mood to throw the Liberals out of office. Canada's Conservative Party seemed to be putting together a viable coalition of Quebec separatists and splinter candidates from the far right. When it came time to go to the polls, however, the liberals remained in power, seemingly because far too many Canadians feared that Canada's conservatives, if put into power, would emulate Great Britain's Margaret Thatcher, swerving to the hard right. Despite public rhetoric, polls indicated there was actually little support for privatizing the national healthcare system, banning abortions, repealing gun control, or sending Canadian troops to intervene in the Middle East alongside their American cousins.

Unlike their American neighbor to the south, Canada remained a British colony until 1867 when it became self-governing, but retained ties to the British crown. Officially Canada's chief of state is the British monarch, represented by a governor general, who is appointed by England's king or queen on the advice of the prime minister for a five-year term. However, the true head of Canada's government is the prime minister, who takes office following nationwide legislative elections. The leader of whichever party gains or retains a clear majority in the House of Commons is prime minister. In the event that no party has a majority, a coalition is formed of minority parties. That coalition then elects a prime minister.

Economically and technologically, Canada has developed in parallel with the United States and is an equal member of the exclusive industrialized Group of Seven (G7) major powers with the United Kingdom, France, Germany, Italy, Japan, and the United States. In

Though dominated by leftist ideology, Canada also traditionally adheres to a broad spectrum of right-wing policies, including a provincial autonomy, unfettered international trade, and free-market economics (as in its logging industry, depicted on the nation's currency).

terms of economic philosophy, Canada is quite "right wing" in terms of its market-oriented economic system, local autonomy enjoyed by the provincial governments, and high living standards. Since World War II, the free market has empowered impressive growth in manufacturing, mining, and the service sectors, transforming Canada from a largely rural economy into an industrial world leader. Canada claims to be the second-most decentralized nation in the world after Switzerland. It is that very decentralization that poses Canada's greatest ongoing challenge: the possibility that the province of Québec with its French-speaking residents and unique culture might secede and form a separate nation, splitting Canada in two with the Atlantic provinces separated from the rest of the nation. However, it is the local autonomy afforded Québec that has kept it from pulling out of the national federation.

Canada, while considering itself liberal, is a signatory to the 1989 U.S.-Canada Free Trade Agreement (FTA) and the 1994 North American Free Trade Agreement (NAFTA), which eliminated many trade barriers between the United States, Canada, and Mexico—contrary to the traditionally leftist policy of protectionism. The trade agreements have sparked dramatic increases in trade and an economic integration with the United States. Another conservative position—open borders and relatively unrestricted emigration between America and Canada—have also resulted in a migration of pro-

fessionals to the United States, lured by higher pay, lower taxes, and opportunities in high tech, made easier by the fact that roughly 90 percent of the Canadian population lives within 160 kilometers (100 miles) of the American border.

In the weeks leading up to the 2004 elections, opinion polls suggested that Canadian voters were shifting away from their usual liberal leanings and had suffered lack of faith in liberal leadership. Conservative Party leader Stephen Harper repeatedly was seen as holding a narrow lead in what became a very tight race. One of Liberal Party Prime Minister Paul Martin's vulnerabilities seemed to be his perceived desire to erase any important differences between Washington's and Ottawa's policies regarding Haiti. Martin seemed anxious to repair the strained relations between Canada and the United States. He was also impacted by a patronage and money laundering scandal entailing allegedly inflated payments for services provided by Quebec public relations firms, which were major contributors to Liberal Party candidates.

However, in the end, the Conservative Party's campaign platform ran counter to long-standing Canadian opinion on many social issues, including the country's universal healthcare, gay rights, and legalized abortion. Harper also was criticized for proposing a budget that featured large tax cuts, which the Liberals charged would threaten a number of Canadian social programs.

SEE ALSO
Volume 1 Left: Canada; Liberal Party, Canada.
Volume 2 Right: Conservatism; United States.

BIBLIOGRAPHY
National Geographic Atlas of the World (National Geographic Society, 1999); John Chuckman, "Why Stephen Harper Lost: Reflections on an Interesting Canadian Election" (Canadian Democratic Movement, 2004); *World Almanac and Book of Facts* (World Almanac, 2004); *World Factbook* (CIA, 2003); Alison Villarivera and Tony Kolenic, "Canada's Martin Faces an Uncertain Fate in Upcoming National Elections," Council on Hemispheric Affairs, www.coha.org (June 2004).

Rob Kerby
Independent Scholar

Capitalism

REALISTICALLY, the phrase "conservative capitalism" is an oxymoron because, as defined separately, the two terms operate under opposite rules. Capitalism, concerned with the dynamic forces of the market must, by its very nature, continually move forward. Conservatism, on the other hand, concentrates on holding on to remnants of the tried and proven past. In an economic sense, capitalism from the perspective of the right is oriented toward a completely free market that furthers the interests of capitalists over the rights of the working class. The fact that the system results in inherent inequalities is taken for granted. The pure conservative believes in the "trickle down" theory of economics that, in the 1980s, formed the basis of Ronald Reagan's economic policy in the United States, as well as that of Margaret Thatcher in Great Britain.

Put simply, the theory stated that as rich capitalists amassed greater wealth, the profits would "trickle down" to those who were lower on the economic scale. Critics of the theory point out that rather than trickling down, money remained in the hands of a select few, while the poor became measurably poorer under conservative economic policies.

The rise of capitalism occurred during the early days of the Industrial Revolution as the wealthy learned that enormous profits were to be made from investing in new technologies and from offering goods to consumers both domestically and internationally. It immediately became clear that profits increased drastically when capitalists were able to control the costs of production, including workers' wages. It was this desire for increased profits that led to the rise of mercantilism in Europe. The mercantilists manipulated governments into developing policies that protected their interests, including monopolies and restrictions on foreign imports.

In the late 17th century, the rise of classical liberalism with its emphasis on individualism and limited government swept away the remnants of mercantilism. John Locke presented the novel ideas that each individual was given an inherent right to life, liberty, and property ownership and that individuals owned the result of their own labors. In 1776, Adam Smith's *An Inquiry into the Nature and Causes of the Wealth of Nations* completed what Locke and his fellow social contract theorists had begun by announcing that the governments could best serve the interests of the nation as a whole by leaving the market alone to seek its own equilibrium. Smith's ideas influenced new government policies around the world, particularly in the United States.

Ideological divisions occurred, with those on the left favoring the rights of workers and government interference, while those on the right promoted the interests of capitalists and limited government. As industrialization flourished, along with a rising interest in socialism, governments became increasingly concerned with providing a basic standard of living to citizens. This concern for the masses reached its height with the Great Depression during the 1930s, resulting in the introduction of the social welfare state in which governments initiated wage and price controls and offered public assistance, healthcare, unemployment subsidies, and disability and retirement pensions for the first time. Conservative economists reacted to the rise of the social welfare state, as personified by the theories of John Maynard Keynes and the policies of President Franklin Roosevelt, by turning to conservative economics.

Conservatives believed they had found their justification in the works of Friedrich von Hayek, who distrusted government implicitly and who argued as Smith had done two centuries before that the market should be free of government manipulation. In 1950, Hayek accepted a position at the prestigious, so-called Chicago School of Economics, joining conservative economist Milton Friedman and his colleagues in their fight to advance conservative capitalism.

In the 1970s, conservative intellectuals and writers spread the tenets of conservative capitalism to the public; but it was only after battling liberalism for some 30 years that conservative economic theories became poli-

Friedrich von Hayek's economic philosophy greatly influenced conservatives Ronald Reagan and Margaret Thatcher.

cies with the election of Reagan to the American presidency in 1980 and with the rise of Thatcher to prime minister of Great Britain a year earlier. Similar changes were taking place in other parts of the world.

Both Reagan and Thatcher were heavily influenced by Hayek, and instituted tax cuts, decreased social spending, and renewed an emphasis on individualism rather than equality. The election of Reagan swung the American right toward some extremist points, including and a solid disregard for individuals who found themselves at low points on the economic scale. Privatization, deregulation, and corporate mergers became the watchwords of Reagan's brand of conservative capitalism, resulting in recession, an increased deficit, and an ideologically divided population. While conservative capitalism did not end with the tenures of Reagan, Thatcher, and other adherents, the theory failed to maintain its popularity at 1980s levels.

SEE ALSO

Volume 1 Left: United States; Democratic Party.
Volume 2 Right: *Laissez Faire*; Reagan, Ronald; Thatcher, Margaret.

BIBLIOGRAPHY

James Fulcher, *Capitalism: A Very Short Introduction* (Oxford University Press, 2004); F.A. Hayek, "Why I Am Not A Conservative," *Conservatism in America Since 1930: A Reader*, Gregory Schneider, ed. (New York University Press, 2003); F.A. Hayek, *The Road to Serfdom* (University of Chicago Press, 1994); Kenneth Hoover, *Economics as Ideology: Keynes, Laski, Hayek, and the Creation of Contemporary Politics* (Rowman and Littlefield, 2003); Kenneth Hoover and Raymond Plant, *Conservative Capitalism in Britain and the United States: A Critical Appraisal* (Routledge, 1989); "John Maynard Keynes" http://cepa.newschool.edu (November 2004); John Locke, *Two Treatises of Government* (Cambridge University Press, 1967); Milton Friedman, *Capitalism and Freedom* (University of Chicago Press, 1962); David Reisman, *Conservative Capitalism: The Social Economy* (St. Martin's, 1999); David Schweickart, *After Capitalism* (Rowman and Littlefield, 2002); Adam Smith, *An Inquiry into the Nature and Causes of the Wealth of Nations* (Random House, 1985); David Stockman, The Triumph of Politics: How the Reagan Revolution Failed (Harper and Row, 1986); Benjamin Ward, *The Ideal World of Economics: Liberal, Radical, and Conservative Economic World Views* (Basic Books, 1979).

ELIZABETH PURDY, PH.D.
INDEPENDENT SCHOLAR

Cato Institute

THE CATO INSTITUTE, a nonprofit public policy, academic, and research foundation, more commonly known as a think tank, works to promote libertarian principles and is headquartered in Washington, D.C. Established by Edward H. Crane and David H. Koch in 1977, the two named the new foundation after *Cato's Letters*, libertarian pamphlets printed during the time leading up to and during the American Revolution that helped to lay the philosophical basis for the United States. The mission of the Cato Institute is "to broaden the parameters of public policy debate to allow consideration of the traditional American principles of limited government, individual liberty, free markets, and peace." In order to do so, the foundation seeks to advocate libertarian principles, like those detailed in *Cato's Letters*, by informing the public and proposing alternatives to certain government initiatives.

The Cato Institute works to achieve its aims by releasing numerous publications that deal with the entire realm of public policy issues. These publications include books, newspaper articles, monographs, and short studies on topics such as the federal budget, Social Security reforms, military spending, the War on Terrorism, and energy policy. In addition to publications, political scientists from the Cato Institute regularly appear on television debate programs, where they are often labeled nonpartisan experts as a result of their openly ideological agenda. Cato also holds major public policy conferences throughout the year, which determine the institute's stand on current issues and are then detailed and explained in the foundation's publication, the *Cato Journal*.

In order to maintain its nonpartisan status and ideological independence, the foundation does not receive or accept any government funding. Instead, it receives funding from other private foundations, corporations, and individuals. Donors include the Castle Rock Foundation, Charles G. Koch Charitable Foundation, JM Foundation, and ExxonMobil. Cato's publications are generating more and more income yearly, covering a larger percentage of the foundation's expenses each year. Legally, the Cato Institute is a nonprofit and tax-exempt educational foundation, formed under Section 501(C)3 of the Internal Revenue Code.

Media mogul Rupert Murdoch is one of the Cato Institute's most well known former board members. Even though Cato vehemently attempts to retain its ideological independence, many of the institute's board members have strong ties to the Republican Party; however, that does not guarantee that the foundation backs all of the Republican Party's decisions. In 2003, it released numerous publications and statements against President George W. Bush's decision to go to war in Iraq. Years earlier, it was against George H.W. Bush's decision to lead a coalition and to participate in the first Gulf War. Other actions criticized by Cato include the ongoing War on Drugs and the 1998 multibillion-dollar tobacco industry settlement.

Advocates at the foundation have, on some occasions, been willing to support positions or actions that are clearly in conflict with libertarian principles. Cato has supported the Bush administration's post-September 11, 2001, decision to restrict civil liberties; dissension within Cato on controversial positions is often visible.

Cato's research and publications concentrate on 10 major focus areas, which are each directed by a senior staff member. These areas include fiscal policy, energy, regulation, healthcare, foreign affairs, global economic liberty, the U.S. Constitution, education, environment, and monetary policy. The foundation's positions and publications in these main areas have evidently gained a sizeable fan base of avid readers; over 25,000 people visit the Cato Institute's website every day. Cato has one of the most popular political think-tank websites and

continues to work toward the reestablishment of libertarian principles in American governance.

SEE ALSO
Volume 1 Left: Think Tanks; Anarchism.
Volume 2 Right: Think Tanks; Republican Party; Libertarianism; Rand, Ayn.

BIBLIOGRAPHY
John Trenchard and Thomas Gordon, *Cato's Letters* (Da Capo Press, 1971); "About the Cato Institute," Libertarian Online, www.libertarian.org (April 2004); "Politics: The Cato Institute," *Washington Post* (August 21, 2003); "The Cato Institute," The Cato Institute, www.cato.org (april 2004).

ARTHUR HOLST, PH.D.
WIDENER UNIVERSITY

Censorship

CENSORSHIP IS THE practice of restraining or controlling communication on the basis of content. Because of the strong tradition of First Amendment rights to freedom of expression, censorship has negative connotations in the United States, but in many other parts of the world it is an accepted part of life. Censorship may be formal, in which it is part of official government policy and enforced by police and the courts, or informal, in which community organizations indicate their disapproval of objectionable content. There are four basic types of censorship: morals, military, political, and religious.

In the United States, the political right is most frequently associated with morals censorship, and in particular the suppression of sexual content in the arts. Conservatives have traditionally been very concerned about the possibility that such portrayals can erode the public morality, and as a result have rigorously supported legislation against obscenity and pornography. Conservatives have also objected to favorable portrayals of crime and disrespect for established authority on similar grounds of endangering good moral order.

Obscenity is defined as language or behavior that is lewd or indecent, whereas pornography involves written or pictorial content. However, in common parlance the terms are often used interchangeably. The first federal moral censorship law was passed in 1842 as part of the Tariff Act, and dealt with the importation of objectionable materials from abroad. However, the best-known decency legislation in the United States is the Comstock Law, passed in 1873 by controversial reformer Anthony Comstock. This law prohibits the mailing of indecent material or information on abortion and birth control. While it was probably intended to be used by police and the courts, in fact it was used to support postal officials' seizure of materials they found objectionable. For 80 years this administrative censorship continued, but social change in the 1960s brought an end to the practice, although the law was never repealed.

MORALS CENSORSHIP

The first blow against formal morals censorship by the American right was struck in 1957 with *Roth v. the United States*, in which the Supreme Court ruled that the First Amendment guarantee of free speech restricted prosecution to only those materials that a court had found obscene. The next critical judgment against broad applications of morals censorship came in 1973 with *Miller v. California*, which established the "contemporary community standards" rule for determining what constituted indecency. The court also added that a work could only be considered indecent if it lacked any literary, artistic, political, or scientific value, protecting such materials as classical nudes and gynecological texts.

Although the sexual revolution slowed formal morals censorship in the United States, informal censorship by conservative organizations remained strong. The motion picture and television industries have policed themselves as a result of concern that groups such as the Catholic Decency League and later the Moral Majority might otherwise press for legal measures. Restrictive protocols such as the Hayes Office have largely given way to ratings systems such as the Motion Picture Association of America (MPAA), which informs viewers of potentially objectionable content and permits parents to decide what they will allow their children to see while making adult material available to mature audiences.

Conservative organizations such as Focus on the Family have been in the forefront of the opposition to pornography. Dr. James Dobson has argued that exposure to pornography leads directly to sexual degeneracy by leaving the user jaded to normal sexual experience. He based his thesis upon interviews with notorious sexual serial killer Ted Bundy and other sex offenders, all of whom claimed to have begun with soft pornography depicting consensual intimacy and moved to progres-

sively harder materials depicting violence and degradation.

In the 1990s, the spread of access to the internet led to fresh calls for formal morals censorship. To conservatives, pornography on the internet was a threat not only to societal standards of acceptable sexual conduct, but also to parental authority over children. While it is reasonably easy to bar children's access to adult cinemas and bookstores, this new electronic medium made it easy for children to present themselves as adults. As a result, Republicans in Congress helped to pass a series of laws censoring the internet. When the Communications Decency Act of 1996 was struck down by the Supreme Court as being excessively broad and violating the rights of adults, Republican members of Congress responded with two more carefully written laws, the Children's Internet Protection Act (CIPA), which mandated that public libraries receiving federal funds had to install filtering software, and the Children's Online Protection Act (COPA). However, filtering systems posed problems of their own, including such embarrassing fiascoes as the blocking of lifesaving breast cancer information while almost 20 percent of objectionable content slipped through.

Morals censorship has been common in other countries when controlled by regimes on the right. The most notorious was Nazi Germany's exhibit of "degenerate art," which they accused of eroding the morals of the German people through images of sensuality and self-indulgence, painted in other than traditional realistic styles. In the 21st century, formal morals censorship on the right has been most frequently found in Middle Eastern countries such as Saudi Arabia and Iran in which Muslim clerics have a strong influence on the government, but morals censorship can also be found in the laws of strongly Catholic countries such as Italy and Ireland.

MILITARY CENSORSHIP

Military censorship in the United States has usually been associated with times of actual war. However, even during peacetime there has been some informal censorship, because the right has often perceived the military as being besieged by pacifists on the left whose calls for accountability look more like betrayals of vital information.

Even such apolitical publications as *Popular Science* have been the recipients of angry letters by self-proclaimed conservatives who accuse them of having stepped over the line by providing detailed coverage of cutting-edge military technology such as the aircraft tests at Groom Lake in New Mexico.

During periods of actual warfare, the U.S. government has a far greater scope for restricting the discussion of sensitive military topics, both to protect secrets from enemy intelligence forces and to maintain morale on the homefront. During the 1991 Gulf War, the Republican administration doled out cleared information to selected press pools in order to make sure that negative information would not appear on television at home, as had been the case during the Vietnam War. In the 2003 Iraq War, also under a Republican administration, Fox News reporter Geraldo Rivera was removed as an embedded journalist after he drew a crude map on the sand, a breach of rules intended to protect American forces from attacks based upon such information.

However, military censorship has also been used by conservative administrations to cover for their mistakes and shortcomings. When the *New York Times* published the Pentagon Papers, which revealed the depth of misjudgment by the top levels of America's military, the Nixon administration accused them of betraying sensitive information and endangering the war effort. The administration's injunction against the publication was blocked by the Supreme Court, although the court did allow that suppression of information actually critical to the war effort, such as deployment schedules, was acceptable, and such revelation could be punished. More sinisterly, many right-wing governments in other countries have covered up outright wrongdoing by declaring it a military secret, the most notorious example being the Third Reich's classifying all materials relating to the Final Solution (Holocaust) as a military secret.

POLITICAL CENSORSHIP

Political censorship by the right has generally involved the suppression of socialist and particularly Marxist views. It was particularly pronounced in America during the two Red Scares, the first following World War I and the second during the early 1950s. During the first Red Scare, numerous anarchist and Bolshevik publications were closed and their equipment seized. During the second Red Scare, led by Wisconsin's Senator Joseph R. McCarthy, intellectuals in universities and the media were accused of harboring pro-Soviet views, and many leading Hollywood figures fell under a blacklist that made it difficult or impossible to find employment in the entertainment industry. Anyone who spoke out against the witch hunt ran the risk of being accused of communist sympathies. So dangerous was dissent

that Arthur Miller had to frame his own rebuttal in the form of a historical play about the Salem witch trials, *The Crucible*.

After the fall of the Soviet Union and the end of the Cold War, political censorship subsided until the September 11, 2001, attacks. The War on Terrorism brought renewed formal and informal censorship of political communication. The Republican administration's Patriot Act included gag rules that prevented banks and other institutions from letting customers know they were being investigated by the government. Conservative individuals and groups also attacked people who publicly opposed or even criticized the War on Terrorism, the best known being the Dixie Chicks music band, who were vilified by saying they were embarrassed that President George W. Bush was from Texas.

In other countries, political censorship on the right side of the political spectrum has generally been focused upon suppressing socialist and communist organizations. The most notorious was the suppression of communists by Nazi Germany following the Reichstag fire, but many right-wing regimes have suppressed political oppositions with methods ranging from mild harassment to outright violence.

RELIGIOUS CENSORSHIP

In the United States, formal religious censorship has been precluded by the First Amendment's provisions of religious freedom. As a result, statements such as George W. Bush's comment during his 2000 presidential campaign that Wicca is not a real religion are regarded with grave concern. Even in the absence of formal religious censorship, conservative organizations have frequently urged the removal of materials that they consider disrespectful to Christianity, such as the film *The Last Temptation of Christ* (although this film was later embraced by the religious right).

In many other countries, right-wing groups and governments have far greater latitude to suppress speech and materials they consider offensive to their religion. In Saudi Arabia and many other Muslim countries of the Middle East, proselytization and public observance of any other religion are a criminal offense. Iran's 1989 *fatwa* declaring Salman Rushdie's novel *The Satanic Verses* a blasphemy against Islam sent the author into hiding in fear of his life. And although the Nazi persecution of Jews was primarily on racial rather than religious grounds, the Third Reich did pass laws making it difficult to practice Judaism, laws largely spurred by lurid stories in *Der Stürmer* about supposed perverse practices in Jewish ceremonies.

Groups and governments on the right of the political spectrum have regularly engaged in censorship. In democracies, they have described their policies and actions in terms of protecting society from the assaults of those who would undermine it, whether morally, militarily, politically, or spiritually.

SEE ALSO

Volume 1 Left: Censorship; United States; New Left.
Volume 2 Right: New Right.

BIBLIOGRAPHY

J.M. Coetze, *Giving Offense: Essays on Censorship* (University of Chicago Press, 1996); Carl Jensen, *Twenty Years of Censored News* (Seven Stories Press, 1997); David C. King, *The Right to Speak Out* (Millbrook Press, 1997); Jonathan Rose, *The Holocaust and the Book: Destruction and Preservation* (University of Massachusetts Press, 2001); Victoria Sherrow, *Censorship in Schools* (Enslow, 1996).

LEIGH KIMMEL, PH.D.
INDEPENDENT SCHOLAR

Central America

IN THE REGION of Central America, conservatism has facilitated the rise of a potent right wing. The right in Central America has generally been aligned with a tough military that on numerous occasions has determined the outcome of political contests. The right in Central America is politically composed and supported by members of the upper class, the landowning oligarchy, the Catholic Church, and other sectors of the elite. Recently, the right has witnessed the arrival in its coalition of the middle classes who have joined the movement to counter the guerrilla and working-class movements in Central America.

The historical origins of the right, dominated by the landed oligarchy, date to the colonial era when Central America formed a distinct region within the Spanish colonial empire. The major function of the southern section of the Viceroyalty of Nuevo Espana was to serve as the southern defensive boundaries of the Mexican viceroyalty. With the independence movement of Mexico in the early 19th century, the region underwent a substantial amount of political change as its role shifted from a dependency in a viceroyalty to a dependency within the Mexican empire.

In 1821, a congress of Central American Creoles declared their independence from Spain, to be effective on September 15 of that year. The Spanish captain general sympathized with the rebels. He decided that he would remain as interim leader until a new government could be formed. However, this initial independence was short-lived. On January 5, 1822, the Mexican leader Agustín Cosme Damián de Iturbide y Arámburu decided to annex Central America. Central American liberals, many members of the landed oligarchy, objected to the forced annexation, but an army from Mexico under General Vicente Filisola occupied Guatemala City and quelled any form of dissent and opposition to the annexation.

When Mexico became a republic the following year, it surprisingly acknowledged Central America's right to determine its own status. On July 1, 1823, the congress in Central America declared absolute independence from Spain, Mexico, and any other foreign nation, and established a republican system of government

In 1823, the nation of Central America was formed. It was known alternately as "The United States of Central America" or "The United Provinces of Central America," but most commonly simply as "Central America" (Centroamerica). The Central American nation consisted of the states of Guatemala, El Salvador, Honduras, Nicaragua, and Costa Rica. This alliance would be short-lived, however, as localism and provincialism among the oligarchy led to the alliance's dissolution.

Throughout the remainder of the 19th century, each country in the region was plagued by a political conflict between the liberal and conservative factions. There did not exist a profound difference between the groups except for the fact that the conservatives tended to be ideologically pro-clerical. By the early 20th century, it was apparent that the export-oriented growth, coupled with the increasing centralization of each of the Central American nations, would create a profound sense of political polarization. In the 20th century, the right within Central America tended to be ideologically conservative, traditional, reactionary, and nationalistic. They formed a close alliance between the oligarchs, members of the traditional landed families, and the military, the Church, and the conservative factions.

Throughout the 20th century, the right in Central America became politically dominant in governing their particular nations. Essentially, the increase in exports and the interests of the large landowners—espe-

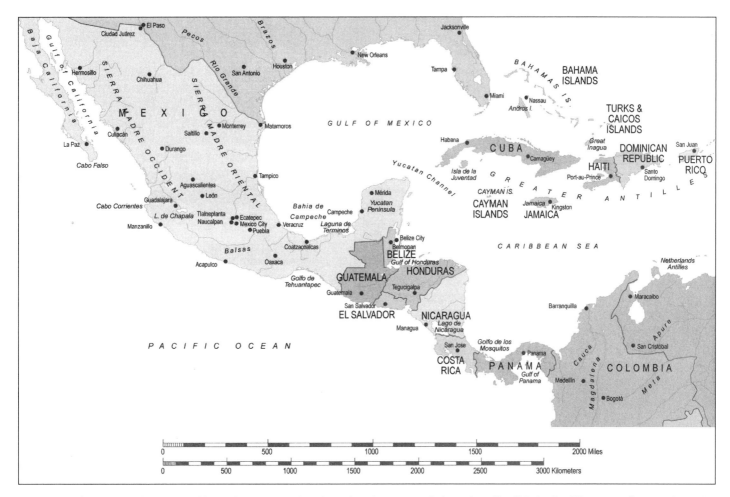

The right in Central America, spurred by native conservatism, has played a strong role in nations like El Salvador, Nicaragua, Guatemala, and others. The proximity and reach of Cuba's communism have also fueled reactionary conservative forces in the region.

cially coffee growers—established the economic and political boundaries of the right. An increase in profits from the export sector as well as international crises like the Great Depression, World War II, and the Cold War facilitated the rise of extremely powerful right-wing movements.

The onslaught of the Great Depression facilitated the rise of a right-wing political ideology throughout the Central American region. Led by a decrease in exports and a decrease in American interest in the region, many right-wing governments came to power during the 1930s. The types of governments varied from conservative oligarchical governments to military dictatorships. By far, the greatest example of a military dictatorship occurred in Nicaragua.

In the midst of the Great Depression, Nicaragua underwent a series of economic and social changes. The international Depression caused a decrease in the price of export commodities and the ensuing unemploy-

ment, and the conservative right in Nicaragua assumed political power. In 1933, an American educated military officer, General Anastasio Somoza, was named director of the national guard. Over the next few years, Somoza, with the aid of the right wing, centralized political power and modernized the nation. During his tenure as "president" of Nicaragua, Somoza, with the aid of the right-wing conservatives, was pro-American and favored foreign investment along with repressing any type of dissent from opposition groups. Somoza ruled Nicaragua until 1956, when he was assassinated by a member of the opposition. His son, Luis, assumed the presidency and ruled the country in a milder form. In the 1960s, the conservative wing of the Liberal Party, led by the Somozas, dominated the country. In 1972, an earthquake devastated the country and Anastasio Somoza Debayle was unable to effectively rule the country. Indeed, his inability, along with the seeming crassness of the conservative oligarchy, acted as a catalyst in the rise of a communist opposition known as the FSLN. In 1979, the conservative oligarchy was overthrown by the Sandinistas. With the end of the Cold War, the right in Nicaragua attempted another political stab at power and failed. In the 1990s, the right in Nicaragua—for that matter, any extremist groups—has been shunned by the electorate for their unabashed support of the United States as well as their exploitative historical past.

EL SALVADOR

Much like Nicaragua, El Salvador's historical past facilitated the rise of a prominent conservative movement. For the years prior to the 1970s, the oligarchy maintained strict control over the political system. Enmeshed in a country wrought with poverty and inequality, the oligarchy, in alliance with the political right, maintained hegemony over the masses. The system essentially starved the poor. The oligarchs were able to control the nation's wealth as the United States funneled an increasing amount of financial aid into the region to combat communist influence. With the escalation of the Cold War in the 1970s, El Salvador's right increasingly sought an alliance with the military. The result was an increasing social tension as the peasantry sought social change and the ruling military-oligarchal alliance refused to budge to relinquish political power. With the fall of the Somoza regime, many thought that the conservative regime, which was pro-American and pro-elite, would also collapse under its own weight and pressure. With the aid of the United States, a cadre of junior officers overthrew the regime. After the 1979 coup, many conservatives made an attempt to legitimize their actions by calling for "elections." The crisis was deepening.

In 1980, Colonel Medrano and Major Roberto D'Aubuisson assassinated Archbishop Oscar Romero, who had been critical of the government's use of right-wing death squads to curtail communist influence. The communist movement splintered into a political wing and a guerrilla, radicalized wing. The group, the FSLN, began a communist insurgency against the right-wing government. The result was the commencement of a 20-year civil war in which the right wing conservatives sought to maintain political power. As the civil war escalated, thousands of peasants and communist insurgents were killed by right-wing death squads in the name of national security.

The oligarchy, with its ties to the land and to foreign investment, used American financial aid to sustain its political power. The result was a chaotic and violent civil war—one of the bloodiest in Latin American history. By the 1990s, both sides had extinguished ideological defenses and sought a peace conference. By the mid-1990s, the oligarchy had maintained its hold on political power. Their power melded into an economic and a sort of behind-the-scenes hegemony.

GUATEMALA

Like the other Central American nations, Guatemala experienced an intense ideological conflict between left and right. Historically, the influence of foreign capitals (the United States) and the socioeconomic division inherent in Guatemalan society facilitated the rise of a prominent conservative movement. The conservatives within Guatemala, in alliance with the military industrial complex, dominated Guatemalan politics for many years. In the 20th century, the conservative wing has come to dominate the political scene. In 1931, a caudillo named Jorge Ubico, a conservative military chief, assumed power. Over the next 11 years, Ubico ruled with the tacit approval of the elites, and with an iron fist. Fearing communist influence, Ubico became increasingly repressive toward any subversive elements. He imprisoned many dissidents in harsh Guatemalan jails. Moreover, Ubico removed any vestiges of the local indigenous customs of self-rule and centralized local administrative power in an *intendente* (local governor), who most of the time was of European descent. In 1941, political pressure from an alliance of national elites, conservatives, and liberals forced Ubico from power.

Presidential elections were held and a liberal, Juan Jose Arevalo, was elected. A social democrat, Arevalo, with his plans of social and economic reform, alienated many within the conservative oligarchy. In the early 1950s, Jacobo Arbenz was elected as president. More radical than Arevalo, Arbenz sought not only reform of the economic and social system, but a complete and radical transformation of Guatemalan society. These policies alienated many military and conservative oligarchs. On June 18, 1954, Carlos Castillo Armas, a junior level officer, with the aid of the American Central Intelligence Agency, invaded Guatemala from Honduras to topple Arbenz and install himself as dictator. In the successful endeavor, Castillo assumed power and ruled over the next few months with conservative acceptance. The removal of Arbenz signaled the beginning of conservative, right-wing ideological hegemony. In other words, the conservative oligarchy had the tacit approval from the military and from the United States to rule as it saw fit.

With the escalation of the Cold War (Bay of Pigs, Cuban Missile Crisis, and Alliance for Progress) and the rise of a powerful indigenous guerrilla movement, the conservative right created an alliance with the military that proved quite formidable in the long run. In the 1960s and 1970s, the Guatemalan right strengthened its political power in the political system.

During the 1980s, President Ronald Reagan supported the Guatemalan military, who by this time had become large landholders and allied with the reactionary elements in society. In 1982, with the approval of Reagan and the United States, a conservative oligarch, Efrain Rioss Montt, assumed dictatorial powers over the country. He ruled for a year until he was toppled by the oligarchy and the military. Over the course of the 1980s, the military and the right governed the nation through authoritarianism and repressive measures. In the early 1990s, the military relinquished formal power and instituted a liberal democratic system. However, the conservatives continued to dominate the political system.

In 1996, the conservative mayor of Guatemala City, Alejandro Irigoyen, became president. He initiated policies of austerity and conservative social government. Within the context of the democratic system, an election was held in 2003. In this election, the right controlled the campaign trail. Three right-wing political parties, the Great National Alliance, National Unity of Hope, and Guatemalan Republican Front, dominated the electioneering and the vote. Clearly, the right in Guatemala experienced a profound historical and political development.

The right in the other Central American nations has had a more difficult time in achieving the control and hegemony that existed in the other nations. In Honduras, the right had control of the political system and did not have a guerrilla insurgency that strained the system. In the 1980s, the right wing truly controlled the system, despite attempts at liberal reform. Receiving aid from the United States, the large landowners association and the Council of Private Business condemned any attempts at social reform. In Costa Rica, also lacking a concentrated guerrilla movement, the right decided to work within the confines of the democratic political system.

Thus, the right did not see a need to seek an alliance with the military to combat any insurgency. To a certain extent, the right accepted any liberal reforms and did not submit to repressive measures and tactics.

SEE ALSO
Volume 1 Left: Central America; South America.
Volume 2 Right: Reagan, Ronald; United States.

BIBLIOGRAPHY

Cole Blasier, *The Hovering Giant* (University of Pittsburgh Press, 1976); Piero Gliejeses, *Tilting at Windmills: Reagan in Central America* (Simon & Schuster, 1982); Richard Immerman, *The CIA in Guatemala: The Foreign Policy of Intervention* (University of Texas Press, 1982); Henry Kissinger, *Report on the National Bipartisan Commission on Central America* (Diane, 1984); Walter LaFeber, *Inevitable Revolutions: The United States in Central America* (Norton, 1983); Ralph Lee Woodward, *Central America: A Nation Divided* (Oxford University Press, 1985).

JAIME RAMÓN OLIVARES, PH.D.
HOUSTON COMMUNITY COLLEGE, CENTRAL

Chile

FOR OVER 100 years (from the mid-1800s to 1966), the Conservative and Liberal parties represented the right in Chile. The Conservative Party formed in 1857, primarily to defend the Catholic Church from anticlerical attacks by the liberals. It remained a staunch supporter of the church and Spanish traditions, as well as the political expression of the large landowners who dominated agricultural production in Chile's Central Valley. The Liberal Party drew on key tenets of British liberal philosophy; it sought to modernize Chile by undermining the power and moral authority of the church and by promoting democratic freedoms and civil liberties.

Since the Liberal Party reflected the political perspective and economic demands of both urban industrialists and the commercial sector, it did not apply these liberal ideals to the majority of Chileans, many of whom were peasants or workers. During the 1870s and 1880s, the Liberal Party, along with the equally anticlerical Radical Party, controlled the government. They passed a series of laws that limited the church's power, such as making civil marriage compulsory. The Chilean right has proven itself to be an astute political actor; it simultaneously projects itself as upholding tradition and is adept at adopting innovative ideas and practices.

From the 1920s through the 1950s, the growing middle class and an increasingly assertive working class challenged the dominance of these two parties. Although the rightist parties failed to elect their candidates to the presidency, during the 1940s and 1950s they managed to maintain a plurality in Congress. The fact that the landowners controlled the votes of the *inquilinos* (tenant laborers) who worked for them and depended on them for a living is one reason why the right was able to obtain so many votes. However, the Chilean Congress passed laws in 1958 and 1962 that introduced secret balloting and ended the practice of purchasing votes, two measures that undercut the strength of the right.

The 1960s saw further challenges to the right. The Catholic Church switched its allegiance from the Conservative Party to the Christian Democratic Party and the left gained increased popularity. Fearing the electoral victory of Salvador Allende, in 1964 the right failed to field its own candidate, instead giving its support to Christian Democrat Eduardo Frei. Reeling from a substantial decline in their political support and realizing the need to project a less outmoded image, the two parties dissolved in 1966 and formed the National Party.

In 1970, Allende, a socialist, won the presidency and the National Party went into action against him. It mounted an ongoing and increasingly antagonistic campaign against the Allende government that ranged from fielding opposition candidates, to supporting damaging strikes, to sabotaging production, to promoting the overthrow of the democratically elected government. When the Chilean armed forces overthrew the Allende government on September 11, 1973, the National Party supported their takeover and the subsequent disbanding of Congress and the ending of political life.

AUGUSTO PINOCHET

The majority of the right lined up behind General Augusto Pinochet during his 17-year rule (1973 to 1990). Members of the right served in his cabinets, provided the military government with political support, helped to implement neoliberal (free-market) economic policies, and remained silent in the face of the human rights abuses committed by the dictatorship. They backed the military rule because they believed it was their best defense against the left and the threats the Allende government had posed to their status and position in Chilean society.

A large number of women played a key role in the right and were one of its key bases of support. In 1917, the Conservative Party first proposed giving the vote to women, since it understood that it was the party most likely to benefit from women's suffrage. Many women, often with leadership from female members of the National Party or independents, mobilized against the Allende government. Their December 1971 March of the Empty Pots demonstrated their willingness to transform their roles as wives and mothers into those of political activists in pursuit of a rightist agenda: opposition to the socialist government. They volunteered to work in projects sponsored by the Pinochet regime and eagerly campaigned for him when the 1988 plebiscite on his rule came to a vote. After Pinochet's arrest in London, England, in 1988, women rallied around their beloved general and staged weekly protests in Santiago demanding his return.

In the 1980s, as opposition to military rule mounted and the possibility of elections approached, the right created two political parties. National Renewal (RN, Renovación Nacional), which to a certain extent evolved out of the Liberal Party, called for political liberalization and worked to ensure that the coming political changes would not endanger the free-market model they enjoyed. The Independent Democratic Union, (UDI, Unión Demócrata Independiente), the other party, allied itself closely with Pinochet. Rejecting any criticisms of military rule, UDI has built a base among a cross section of Chileans, including the poor, and emerged in the 1990s as the stronger of the two rightist parties. In the 2000 presidential elections, its candidate, Joaquín Lavín (a member of Opus Dei), almost defeated Ricardo Lagos, the candidate of the ruling Concertación coalition.

SEE ALSO

Volume 1 Left: Chile; Socialism; Christian Democracy; South America.
Volume 2 Right: South America.

BIBLIOGRAPHY

Pamela Constable and Arturo Valenzuela, *A Nation of Enemies: Chile under Pinochet* (W.W. Norton, 1991); Sandra McGee Deutsch, *Las Derechas: The Extreme Right in Argentina, Brazil, and Chile 1890–1939* (Stanford University Press, 1999); Brian Loveman, *Chile: The Legacy of Hispanic Capitalism* (Oxford University Press, 2001); Margaret Power, *Right-Wing Women in Chile: Feminine Power and the Struggle against Allende, 1964–73* (Pennsylvania State University Press, 2002).

MARGARET POWER
ILLINOIS INSTITUTE OF TECHNOLOGY

China

THE MANCHU DYNASTY had continued to rule China since 1644, in spite of the cataclysmic Taiping rebellion of the middle years of the 19th century. The overthrow of the Manchu (Qing) Dynasty in 1911 in China began a period of instability that would last until the establishment of the Communist People's Republic in 1949. The revolution led to the establishment of the Chinese Republic in 1912 by Sun Yat-sen, who wrote in his autobiography, "in 1912 I assumed office, and ordered the proclamation of the Chinese Republic."

Actual power was soon wrested from Sun by General Yuan Shih-k'ai, who, as head of the Peiyang Army, led the only modern fighting force in China. Unfortunately, Yuan's militarist bid for power led to the era of the *tuchuns* (warlords), who would regard rational government as an impossibility. The period had a searing impact on Sun, to whose republic was paid scant attention by the Western powers or Japan, although China had supported the Western powers in World War I. At the Versailles Peace Conference in 1919 after World War I, Don Lawson wrote in *The Eagle and the Dragon: The History of U.S.-China Relations*, "the United States went so far as to sign an agreement with Japan that recognized Japan's 'special interests' in China while at the same time stating that China's territorial sovereignty ought to be maintained."

In 1919, the May Fourth movement marked the birth of strong, rightist Chinese nationalism—and as an unforeseen political development, communism. C.P. Fitzgerald wrote in *The Birth of Communist China* that "it was clear that the Western way was not the solution, and tacitly it was abandoned, even by the revolutionary element." The American abandonment of China led Sun to ardently embrace Russia, where in 1917, Vladimir I. Lenin had successfully led the Russian Communist, or Bolshevik, Party to victory. In July 1921, the first indigenous Chinese Communist Party was formed by Chinese Marxists aided by Russian Gregor Voitinsky. Sun accepted Soviet overtures for a united front or alliance. In 1923, a formal pact was made between the Communist International (Comintern), which had been set up by Moscow to subversively export communism, and the Kuomintang (the Chinese Nationalist Party).

However, in 1925, Sun died, leaving in power his chosen successor, the strongly anti-communist Chiang Kai-shek. In July 1926, Chiang was able to begin his Northern Expedition to unite the country by force. Within a year, he felt strong enough to strike at the communists, who had worked steadily to gain control of the united front. In April 1927 in Shanghai, Chiang struck at the Communist Party with his Kuomintang forces, shattering them completely. In 1928, Chiang's Soviet-trained army would successfully complete the Northern Expedition by entering Beijing, the capital. Now, he turned his energies to his extermination campaigns against the communists. In September 1930, Wang Ming replaced Li Lisan as head of the party, with Mao Zedong still waiting in the wings. Yet in January 1931, Wang's fear of assassination caused him to flee to Moscow. Mao had emerged as leader of those communists who remained behind in China. In October 1934, Mao, in the party sanctuary in Jiangxi, decided on a massive retreat from the blows of Chiang's extermination campaign and began the communists' Long March to faraway Shensi. Mao and his men arrived in Shensi (Pinyin: Shanxsi) exactly one year after their departure. Anne Freemantle wrote in *Mao Zedong: An Anthology of His Writings*, "of the army that had left Kiangsi on October 6, 1934, 100,000 strong, barely 20,000 remained." In December 1935, the Red Army was refreshed enough to march to Yenan where, for 11 years, Mao made his base.

While the war was going on between the communists and the Kuomintang, the Japanese Kwantung Army had successfully taken over the Chinese province of Manchuria in 1931 and 1932. The Japanese had renamed it Manchukuo, and put on its throne as a Japanese puppet, Pu Yi, who had been a child emperor at the time of the revolution in 1911. Chiang, however, still focused his energies on eliminating Mao. But Chiang, in December 1936, was kidnapped at Sian by the son of the *tuchun*, the "Old Marshal," Chang Tso-lin, the "Young Marshal," Chang Hseuh-liang. The Young Marshal's troops had fought bravely against the Japanese in Manchuria, without any Kuomintang support. He now forced Chiang to end the civil war against the Chinese communists and form a united front against the Japanese invaders. However, the Young Marshal's deed was an act of mutiny; yet instead of executing him, Chiang placed him under house arrest as an honored guest. In July 1937, in the skirmish at the Marco Polo Bridge outside Beijing, Japan initiated a full-scale attempt to conquer China. Faced by a severe threat, Chiang reluctantly joined forces with the communists. While Chiang fought a more traditional war against the Japanese, Mao embraced a style of war that embraced both conventional and guerrilla strategy.

When the Japanese were defeated in September 1945, the situation between the communists and the

A lone protestor, facing tanks, came to symbolize the pro-democracy movement crushed in Tiananmen Square in 1989.

Kuomintang had already begun to deteriorate. Mao pushed on with his efforts to conquer China. In spite of mediation efforts by American General George C. Marshall from 1945 to 1947, open war broke out between the two factions. In 1946, Mao formed his People's Liberation Army out of the Eighth Route Army and the New Fourth Army. With some one million soldiers, he defeated Chiang, who fled to the island of Taiwan, which had been regained from Japan. In October 1949, Mao proclaimed the one-party rule of the People's Republic of China.

Soon after the revolution, the communists forcibly occupied Tibet, ultimately forcing the ruling Dalai Lama to seek asylum in India in 1958. From the beginning, Soviet aid had been essential to the establishment of Mao's rule in China, but a rift between the two communist countries took place in the 1960s, which in 2004 was still not completely healed. By 1969, relations with the Soviet Union had deteriorated to the point that war almost erupted along the disputed Ussuri River frontier. Mao, in retaliation, began normalization of relations with the United States. In September 1972, President Richard M. Nixon visited the People's Republic and in the Shanghai Agreement recognized the People's Republic as the legitimate Chinese state. While this normalized relations with mainland China, it consigned Taiwan, where Chiang had sought refuge in 1949, to an uncomfortable political limbo where it languished into the 21st century.

After Mao died in 1976, ultimately power came to rest with Deng Xiaoping, who had accompanied Mao on the Long March. Under Deng, China followed what were known as the Four Modernizations: industry, agriculture, national defense, and science and technology. However, the government set its face against what reformist Chinese called the Fifth Modernization, democ-

racy. Although by 1989, Deng had relinquished most formal party posts, he authorized the brutal attack on the democracy demonstrators in Tiananmen Square on June 4, 1989, in which thousands may have been killed. Those who could fled to Hong Kong, but hundreds were sent to the Chinese gulag for "reeducation."

Deng died in February 1997, with power already safely transferred to President Jiang Zemin. In June 1997, Hong Kong was returned to China by the United Kingdom under the "one country, two systems" philosophy. Fears were rife of a creeping communization in the former Crown Colony, where memories of the Tiananmen massacre were kept alive by the refugees. Indeed, in March 1996, Taiwanese elections were intimidated by the People's Liberation Army firing dummy missiles into the seas around the island. By the sixth anniversary in 2003 of the communist takeover in Hong Kong, Agence France Press reported that "Hong Kong will mark its sixth anniversary under Chinese rule on July 1 with a huge protest march over proposed national security legislation which many fear will restrict fundamental freedoms."

"In June 2004," the *San Francisco Chronicle* reported, "the massacre of the democracy demonstrators in Tiananmen Square was marked by a demonstration in San Francisco, home to one of the largest Chinese-American communities in the United States." It remains to be seen how long it will be before the Fifth Modernization, democracy, comes to China, 75 years after it was first introduced as a political goal in the May Fourth Movement of 1919.

SEE ALSO

Volume 1 Left: China; Asia; Communism.
Volume 2 Right: Capitalism; Globalization.

BIBLIOGRAPHY

"The Life of Deng Xiaoping," www.cbw.com (July 2004); PBS, Online News Hour, "Deng's Legacy" (February 25, 1997); Richard Heller, "The Young Marshal," www.clarity4words.co.uk (July 2004); Library of Congress Country Studies, "China," lcweb2.loc.gov (July 2004); Stuart R. Schramm, ed., *Quotations from Chairman Mao Zedong* (Bantam Books, 1972); Franz Schurmann and Orville Schell, *Imperial China, Republican China, and Communist China* (Vintage, 1967); Herbert Feis, *The China Tangle: The American Effort in China from Pearl Harbor to the Marshall Mission* (Atheneum, 1966); Anne Freemantle, *Mao Zedong: An Anthology of His Writings* (Mentor Books, 1962); Winberg Chai, *Essential Works of Chinese Communism* (Bantam, 1972); C.P. Fitzgerald, *The Birth of Communist China* (Penguin Press,

1952); Don Lawson, *The Eagle and the Dragon: The History of U.S.-China Relations* (Crowell, 1985).

JOHN F. MURPHY, JR.
AMERICAN MILITARY UNIVERSITY

Christian Coalition

THE CHRISTIAN COALITION was founded by Marion Gordon (Pat) Robertson in 1989. Its professed goals are to strengthen families, protect innocent life, give local school boards and parents control of education, reduce taxes for families, punish criminals and restore the rights of victims, fight pornographic pollution, defend marriage as an institution, and safeguard religious freedom.

To accomplish those goals the Christian Coalition (now the Christian Coalition of America) commits itself to lobby for family values in whatever political arena, from local to national; to speak and write in the media on these issues; to train leaders to be effective social and political activists; to inform voters about issues and potential laws; and to protest "anti-Christian bigotry" while defending the rights of believers. The general statements are relatively innocuous, quite attractive to millions of Americans, but of great concern to millions of others, especially when rhetoric translates into specific demands for action.

The organization's Christianity is conservative both morally and politically. It is within the American tradition that traces itself to the early 20th-century fundamentalists, who rejected theological modernism. Early fundamentalist crusades helped to bring about Prohibition and to outlaw the teaching of evolution in public schools. The movement peaked in the 1925 Dayton, Tennessee, trial of a local schoolteacher for teaching evolution. The trial's adverse publicity for fundamentalism and the death of William Jennings Bryan (who prosecuted the teacher) seemed to put the movement into eclipse.

In the 1930s and 1940s, new leaders arose—men such as Gerald L.K. Smith who were anti-Semitic, anti-communist, and anti-integrationist. Other fundamentalists were Gerald B. Winrod and the Catholic priest Charles E. Coughlin, whose radio broadcasts reached millions until the church silenced him. Again, with the loss of Coughlin's voice, the movement faded to the fringes.

While conservative religious groups watched from the sidelines, mainstream America went through decades of what appeared to be moral decline. Flappers, Hollywood, the repeal of Prohibition, the increasing secularization of society—all these liberal ideas spread as fundamentalist and conservative Christians stood helplessly by. To make matters worse, World War II seemed to write the finish to political conservatism, which had emphasized isolationism and limited government, both of which had been under assault since the New Deal. Still, conservatism persisted, found its intellectual breath on the political side, and found its salvation on the religious side. For conservative religion, the 1950s and 1960s meant spreading its message by radio, then television. Because the free public service required by the Federal Communications Commission went to mainstream churches on Sunday mornings, the fringe right learned quickly how to raise funds to buy broadcast time. The radio and television evangelists mastered the art of the mass-appeal mass mailing.

Their mailing lists and the mailing lists of Richard Vigurie, veteran of the failed conservative Barry Goldwater campaign (which had re established the credibility of conservative ideas), brought the conservatives back from obscurity. And for two decades, the conservative politicians took advantage of the conservative religious believers. The religious right let it happen, not yet convinced of the propriety of mingling religion and politics.

Then came *Roe v. Wade* in 1973, which made abortion legal and galvanized conservative morality, as did the patriotic celebrations of the bicentennial in 1976. Jerry Falwell conducted "I Love America" rallies at each state capital. Later, he would found the Moral Majority in 1979. The right-leaning organizations were upset that President Jimmy Carter's administration was challenging their tax-exempt status because he regarded them as too political, not quite purely religious organizations. The right had supported Carter as a born-again southern Baptist, but he had failed to make political decisions based on religion—at least that's how they saw it. The right found that there was another way in 1980 when Robertson's Washington for Jesus campaign showed that politics might be an arena for leading, instead of just trying to steer politicians such as Carter in the appropriate direction. The 700 Club and the Christian Broadcasting Network (CBN) television venues were powerful resources.

In 1980 the Christian right supported the candidacy of Ronald Reagan. Robertson and half a million Pentecostals gathered on the Washington Mall for a Washington for Jesus rally, which also brought increased visibility for the Moral Majority, especially with the Reagan victory. Early in the 1980s, Falwell was the visible leader, but Robertson toiled in the background. He was creating a televangelical empire, the CBN, which would give him a springboard for a presidential run in 1988. Again, as with Carter, Reagan had proved to be a politician first, a moral rightist second. His eight years had done nothing to stem the moral decay the religious right saw in every sector of American life. The Supreme Court was still pro-abortion, and the National Abortion Rights Action League was still plaguing the anti-abortionists.

Burned and spurned by Reagan, the right had no truck with the even more liberal George H. W. Bush, the next president. Robertson decided that it was time to quit carrying water for the conservatives and getting nothing in return. He ran, lost badly, but firmed up the financial network, the mailing list, and the other lessons of a serious do-it-yourself political campaign. The candidacy was short-lived, but the organization was the precursor of the Christian Coalition. Under the leadership of Executive Director Ralph Reed, the grassroots political organization became a serious force in American politics.

The late 1980s was a time of clearing away the pretenders in conservative political religion and religion in general. The Moral Majority lost its luster, especially after the Praise The Lord (PTL) and other televangelist enterprises were accused of fraud, as one preacher after another was exposed as corrupt or a charlatan and a huckster.

The Christian Coalition first drew major national attention in June 1990 when it objected vehemently to the decision of the National Endowment for the Arts to fund tasteless art, specifically the "Christ in Urine" painting of Andres Serrano and the homoerotic photography of Robert Mapplethorpe. The next year, 1991, the coalition took some of the credit for Senate confirmation of the conservative Clarence Thomas for the U.S. Supreme Court.

In 1992, after only three years, the Christian Coalition membership was 250,000 and its budget was $8.5 million a year. A decade later, the group has over 1,400 chapters with 1.7 million members. The Christian Coalition has no consistent theology, being more a political organization. Its Christianity, the founders claim, underlies its political positions. Those positions were Robertson's as expressed on CBN's *700 Club*. Some of their claims include: Abortion is murder, "America's Holocaust"; the feminist movement is "fanatical and

ugly ... anti-God, anti-capitalism, anti-family, anti-birth, and heterosexual-heterosexual." Robertson advocates a "traditional" family structure, with the man working and the woman making the home and otherwise subordinating herself to him. The organization opposes homosexuality, the "liberal" media, and the liberal entertainers who are bringing on America's moral decline. Coalition members believe religion must return to public schools because its absence is leaving them bereft of moral and religious values, making them one great social science experiment, leaving them vulnerable to crime, drugs, alcohol, permissive sex, and violence. The message of moral decay crying out to be reversed by Christian America resonates with Americans concerned with the moral state of the nation, and who are willing to let religion solve the decay. The message of fundamentalist intrusion into secular areas of American life concerns others who see it as a threat to the separation of church and state.

Reed kept the coalition at a distance from Robertson's more radical religious views, creating instead an organization that could fit into the mainstream of right-wing politics. He stressed the coalition as a pro-family voice in Washington, D.C. It was tax-exempt, so it could not be overtly politically partisan in its lobbying or social welfare activities. The "neutrality" of the organization tended to align it with the Republican Party's positions, specifically when it supported House Majority Leader Newt Gingrich's Contract with America, by creating one of its own, a "Contract with the American Family" supported by virtually all conservative senators and congressmen. The coalition's contract called for preservation of the sanctity of the American family through opposition to abortion, the Equal Rights Amendment, and pornography. It also called for a religious equality amendment that would allow religious activities at voluntary public events when led by students or individuals. It also wanted the return of schools to local and parental control, school choice, parental rights legislation (deemphasizing the role of social institutions in rearing children), and privatizing the arts.

The coalition does not support candidates. It distributes political literature outlining candidates' positions on issues of concern to its members. Its 1.7 million members are a major electoral bloc, but it also has the capability of sending 30 to 50 million pieces of its literature through local churches just before any election. The record, for the 2000 election, was 70 million.

The coalition's success generated liberal opposition. Among the organizations established to stop it in the late 1990s were Fight the Right and The Interfaith Alliance. People for the American Way, established in 1980, was an organization set up to counter Falwell's Moral Majority. The American Civil Liberties Union objected to the religious right because it manipulated religion to bring about an extreme political agenda that infringes on civil liberties. Americans United for the Separation of Church and State began as a Baptist lobbying organization opposed to the coalition's efforts to breach the wall of separation and its attempts to impose its agenda in areas such as abortion, gay rights, and public education, an agenda the mainstream would oppose. Americans United publications opposed the coalition and its push for school vouchers.

Reed left the organization in 1997, moving into mainstream Republican political organizing. Without Reed, the organization lost momentum, and Robertson eventually proved unable to stem the decline. In the late 1990s, the group was operating on a shoestring budget of $3 million whereas in the early 1990s it had enjoyed $25 million budgets. In 2001, African American staffers in the Washington, D.C., office sued for racial discrimination. Robertson resigned in late 2001, citing a need to return to the ministry. The reorganized Christian Coalition of America took on new life under President Roberta Combs. Much of its agenda seemed to receive a sympathetic hearing from President George W. Bush.

SEE ALSO

BIBLIOGRAPHY

Americans United for Separation of Church and State, "Pat Robertson Resigns from Christian Coalition," www.au.org (December 2001); Michele Bidelspach, "Christian Coalition 1997," http://religiousmovements.lib.virginia.edu (May 2004); Rob Boston, *The Most Dangerous Man in America?: Pat Robertson and the Rise of the Christian Coalition* (Prometheus Books, 1996); Christian Coalition, www.cc.org (May 2004); Christian Coalition of Alabama, "Robertson to Focus on Ministry, Roberta Combs Becomes Next President of Christian Coalition of America, December 5, 2001," www.ccbama.org (May 2004); Frederick Clarkson, *Eternal Hostility: The Struggle between Theocracy and Democracy* (Common Courage, 1997); Joe Conn, "The Christian Coalition: Born Again?" *Church & State* (November 2002); Georgia First Amendment Coalition, "The Hijacking of the Christian Church, 1998," www.tylwytheg.com (May 2004); Ralph Reed, *Active Faith: How Christians Are Changing the Soul of American Politics* (The Free Press, 1996); Pat Robertson, *The Turning Tide: The Fall of Liberalism and the Rise of Common Sense* (Word Publishing, 1993); Justin Watson, *The Christian Coalition: Dreams of Restoration, Demands for Recognition* (Palgrave Macmillan, 1997).

JOHN BARNHILL, PH.D.
INDEPENDENT SCHOLAR

Christian Identity

ACCORDING TO an article in the St. Louis, Missouri, *Post-Dispatch* on March 5, 2000, the Christian Identity movement "began in England in the 1840s, [led] by Reverend John Wilson, who preached that Anglo-Saxons were God's 'chosen people' as the descendants of the 12 lost tribes of Israel. They migrated across the Caucasus (and were so called Caucasians). Thus, the Lost Tribes were the people who inhabited northern Europe and the British Isles. Wilson's teaching moved quickly to the United States because Caucasian followers surmised that if the English, and not the Jewish people, were the blood descendants of the ancient Israelites, then so were the white Americans." Wilson's main treatise on the subject is his *Lectures on Our Israelitish Origin.*

Christian Identity received a major infusion of new blood in the United States when it was adopted by the evangelist Gerald L.K. Smith. In 1933, he joined William Dudley Pelley's Silver Shirts, which have been dubbed a fascist group by the liberal press. A major change came with Smith when he moved to the First Christian Church in Shreveport, Louisiana. There, Smith became the national organizer for Louisiana Governor Huey Long's Share Our Wealth campaign. H.L. Mencken, the famed American muckraker, called Smith "the greatest rabble-rouser seen on Earth since Apostolic times." After Long was cut down by an assassin's bullet in 1935, Smith devoted himself fully to the development of Christian Identity thought within the United States. Among other accretions, Smith popularized the addition of the tribe of Mannasseh, the 13th tribe, to the Lost Twelve. He considered symbolic of their inclusion such "coincidences" as there being 13 original states and 13 letters in *E Pluribus Unum.*

It was through Smith's relationship with Henry Ford that anti-Semitism and its corollary in their belief system, anti-communism, merged with the original theory of Christian Identity. Smith later admitted, "the day came when I embraced the research of Mr. Ford and his associates and became courageous enough and honest enough and informed enough to use the words 'communism is Jewish.'" His religious bias embraced such ideas that American public figures as disparate as President Franklin D. Roosevelt and President Dwight D. Eisenhower were "closet Jews." In the late 1960s, his beliefs moderated somewhat and he admired the diplomacy of Henry Kissinger who, although a Jew, was "one of the greatest diplomats who ever lived." Significantly, Smith never abandoned his belief in the American democratic system.

By the 1970s, however, those championing Christian Identity moved past the religious-tinged populism of Smith. They began to feel that America was fast being betrayed by what they called the Zionist Occupation Government (ZOG), part of the conspiracy of world Jewry to control all the nations of the world. At the same time, the growth of the civil rights movement had brought about in Identity a profound distaste for America's nonwhite population. This extended to nonwhite immigrants as well. Louis Beam, one of the rising stars of the Christian far right, gained notoriety in 1981 when he attempted to stop Vietnamese immigrants from fishing. A common term for these nonwhites was "mud people."

One of the most dynamic figures in the history of Christian Identity is Robert Miles. As with many on the Christian right, the 1968 presidential candidacy of Alabama Governor George Wallace was a seminal event in his career. Miles served as the main Wallace campaigner in Michigan. In 1969, he became the grand dragon (leader) of the Michigan Ku Klux Klan. Four years later, as James Ridgeway relates in *Blood in the Face*, Miles was sentenced in court for being involved in a conspiracy to bomb empty school buses in a campaign against a forced busing program to achieve court-mandated integration of schools in Pontiac, Michigan. The campaign against school busing had echoes throughout the nation at the time, and served to strengthen Christian far right animosity toward the "mud people"—and the federal government, which seemed to be advancing their interests at the expense of the white majority. Affirmative action policies as well served as a lightning rod that attracted new followers to all groups on the Christian extreme right in this period.

After his release from prison in 1979, Miles's farm in Cohoctah, Michigan, became a magnet for like-minded individuals, as did the compound of Aryan Nations founder Richard Butler in Hayden Lake, Idaho.

Together, they provided a rallying point for figures from across the right-wing spectrum, from the Ku Klux Klan to the White Patriot Party of Glenn Miller. Christian Identity was the theological link that brought all these groups together. It was in Ridgeway's film of the April 1986 gathering at Cohoctah that a Christian Identity pastor made the statement that the white race could be recognized from all the others because the faces of its members became red when struck, the idea of "blood in the face."

Christian Identity was also the philosophy behind The Silent Brotherhood, or The Order, the extremist group that Robert J. Matthews founded as an offshoot of Butler's Aryan Nations. The Order was founded by Matthews in a frame building he called the "barracks" in September 1983. Determined to raise money for the coming white revolution, he and other members of The Order robbed a Brinks Company armored car of some $3.8 million in July 1984. Inadvertently, Matthews left behind a handgun at the scene of the robbery, which put authorities on his track.

However, it was the killing of Denver, Colorado, KOA radio station talk show host Alan Berg in June 1984 that brought sensational attention to The Order. Berg was killed in the garage of his apartment complex because he was Jewish and a vocal enemy of the extreme Christian right. Matthews was killed in a fiery gun battle with federal authorities in December 1984. Richard Scutari, the final member of The Order to be apprehended, was arrested in 1986. Most recently, Eric Rudolph, the bomber of the abortion clinics in 1998, and Burford Furrow, who went on a shooting spree the next year, have been associated with Christian Identity beliefs.

In the 2000s, perhaps the most visible Christian Identity spokesman is the Reverend Jim Wickstrom, leader of the Posse Comitatus. Another internet web site belonging to the movement is hosted by The Kingdom Identity Ministries. It describes the group as being "a Politically Incorrect outreach ministry to God's chosen race (true Israel, the White, European peoples)." Although violence has been committed by those who espouse Christian Identity beliefs, this is meant in no way to reflect on the large majority of believers in the creed.

SEE ALSO

Volume 1 Left: American Civil Liberties Union; Civil Liberties; Long, Huey.
Volume 2 Right: Posse Comitatus; Aryan Nations; Militia Movements; Bruder Schweigen.

BIBLIOGRAPHY

"Christian Identity," Anti-Defamation League, www.adl.org (May 2004); "Kingdom Identity Ministries," www.kingidentity.com (May 2004); "Heroes and Prisoners: The Order Bruder Schweigen," www.eyeonhate.com (May 2004); "Inmate Loses Parole Bid in Berg Slaying [Richard Scutari]," *Rocky Mountain News* (November 22, 2003); Howard L. Bushart, John R. Craig, and Myra Barnes, *Soldiers of God: White Supremacists and Their Holy War for America* (Pinnacle Books, 1998); Joel Dyer, *Harvest of Rage: How Oklahoma City Is Only the Beginning* (Westview Press, 1998); Alan M. Schwartz, ed., *Danger: Extremism: The Major Vehicles and Voices on America's Far-Right Fringe* (Anti-Defamation League, 1996); James Ridgeway, *Blood in the Face: The Ku Klux Klan, Aryan Nations, and the Rise of a New White Culture* (Thunder's Mouth Press, 1995); Kevin Flynn and Gary Gerhart, *The Silent Brotherhood* (Signet, 1989).

JOHN F. MURPHY, JR.
AMERICAN MILITARY UNIVERSITY

Because of his consistent opposition to both fascism and communism, Churchill's heritage is deeply conservative.

Churchill, Sir Winston (1874–1965)

WINSTON CHURCHILL earned his reputation as one of the greatest statesmen of the 20th century in a political career that lasted more than 50 years. During that time, he consistently opposed the aggression and totalitarianism of imperial Germany, Nazi Germany, and the Soviet Union. During his long career, he also frequently employed his impressive oratorical skills and wrote constantly throughout his public life. This impressive corpus of speeches, journalism, memoirs, and histories gives the student of Churchill a thorough map of the great man's mind.

Born into British and Tory aristocracy, he was the eldest son of Lord Randolph Churchill and an American heiress, Jennie Jerome. As a youth, Churchill attended Harrow and Sandhurst (military academy), and then served as a subaltern in a variety of postings across the British Empire. While serving on the frontier, Churchill read extensively to supplement his lack of a university education, fought in several sharp engagements, and launched his writing career.

In 1900, he was elected to Parliament; he first entered the cabinet as undersecretary for the colonies. In 1911, Prime Minister Herbert Asquith made Churchill first lord of the admiralty. While there, Churchill oversaw the Royal Navy in the early years of World War I.

He left the admiralty in 1916 as the scapegoat for the British failure in the Gallipoli campaign. During that offensive, Churchill had hoped to capture Constantinople, first by naval attack, then with a combined operation aimed at the Turkish capital. The campaign turned into a disaster, as British forces failed to advance up the Gallipoli peninsula. Churchill fell from power and then went to serve on the western front for several months. Late in the war, he returned to the cabinet as minister of munitions and attempted, unsuccessfully, to secure the necessary support to thwart the Bolshevik revolution in Russia.

POLITICAL WILDERNESS

Throughout the 1920s, Churchill continued to serve in a variety of cabinet posts, before being driven into the political "wilderness" for much of the 1930s. During that decade, Churchill focused on two projects that would help to ensure his lasting fame: his colossal biography of his great ancestor John Churchill, first Duke of Marlborough, and his warnings of the rise of Adolf

Hitler and Nazi Germany. Throughout the 1930s, Churchill denounced British military weakness and the appeasement of Nazi policy. His warnings went unheeded.

With the outbreak of World War II in September 1939, Prime Minister Neville Chamberlain recalled Churchill to serve as first lord of the admiralty. In May 1940, following British defeats in Scandinavia and the Nazi invasion of France, Churchill was called on by King George VI to form a national government; Churchill would continue as prime minister until shortly after the defeat of Germany in 1945. During the war, Churchill displayed the iron resolve necessary to keep Great Britain in the war, and his wartime speeches show that resolve in thrilling detail. Perhaps his greatest strategic decision of the war was to pay court to Franklin Roosevelt and to begin laying the groundwork necessary to secure American aid early in the war. Yet, once America and Russia entered the war, Britain and Churchill began to lose influence over the course of strategy. Churchill was ignored or overruled by Roosevelt and Russia's Josef Stalin late in the war, notably at the Yalta Conference. Churchill rightly perceived, far sooner than many in the West, the growing threat of Soviet communism to western Europe and the world, which he attempted to hinder at Yalta and later openly denounced in his "Iron Curtain" speech in 1946. Churchill served another term as prime minister from 1951 to 1955.

Due to his change from the Conservative Party to the Liberal Party and back again, and because of his extremely long political career, Churchill defies simple categorization. Because of his veneration of history, his consistent calls for military preparedness, his vision of a world in which great powers are inhibited not through goodwill but through the balance of power, and his consistent and vociferous opposition to both fascism and communism, Churchill's heritage and legacy are deeply conservative.

SEE ALSO

Volume 1 Left: Roosevelt, Franklin D.; Soviet Union; Liberal Party, UK; Labour Party, UK.
Volume 1 Right: Conservative Party, UK.

BIBLIOGRAPHY

Winston Churchill, *Never Give In!: The Best of Winston Churchill's Speeches* (Hyperion, 2003); Winston Churchill, *The Second World War* (Houghton Mifflin, 1948– 3, 6 vols.); Martin Gilbert, *Churchill: A Life* (Henry Holt, 1991); John Keegan, *Winston Churchill* (Viking, 2002); Jon Meacham, *Franklin and Winston: An Intimate Portrait of an Epic Friendship* (Random House, 2003).

MITCHELL MCNAYLOR
OUR LADY OF THE LAKE COLLEGE

Cold War

THE COLD WAR was a global political, military, ideological, and economic struggle between the communist world, led by the Soviet Union, and the capitalist world, led by United States. Throughout the Cold War, conservatives staunchly opposed communism and attacked it on moral, political, and economic grounds.

The far left in the Western world, socialists and communists, were aligned for better or worse with the Soviet Union via its Comintern policies of spreading international communism. Meanwhile, the far right in America saw spies and communists influencing government and entertainment. Thus, despite bipartisan anticommunism in the United States, it was the right that mainly fought the great ideological battle against the communists.

Communism and American conservatism are polar opposites. Indeed, American conservatism reevolved in the second half of the 20th century partially as a reaction to communism and to the socialist schemes promoted by the political left. Communism sought the end of private property and the government control of industry; conservatism recognized the efficiency and dynamism of the free market and proclaimed that property is an invaluable safeguard of liberty. Communism conceived of people not as individuals, but as members of groups, and that the group was more important than any individual. Conservatism cherished a tradition of individual rights and liberty that is well rooted in English and American history. Communism placed the state before all else; conservatives valued limited government and the rule of law. Communist leaders worked to deny the existence of God; most American conservatives viewed man through Christian eyes as fallen, but capable of redemption through God's grace.

Even though the Soviet Union was seen, in the words of conservative Ronald Reagan, as an "evil empire," America would be forced to confront it not over moral issues, but over the realities of world power and geopolitics. The two world powers increasingly clashed over Soviet attempts to extend Moscow's influence abroad, and conversely what the Soviets saw as American imperialism.

Several factors made the West perceive the Soviet Union as a threat during the years following World War II: the Soviet leader Josef Stalin himself (a ruthless dictator), the communist ideology, traditional Russian expansion, and a Soviet desire for border security following the German invasion of 1941. Equally important, the Soviet leaders sought to expand communist ideology wherever possible.

FIRST POLITICAL SALVOS

An unprecedented era of American peacetime involvement in the world began in 1947 when President Harry Truman ordered U.S. forces to fill the power vacuum left by British forces withdrawing from Greece and Turkey. Without an intervention, the Soviets would gain control of those countries. Such an acquisition would give Russia Constantinople, the prize it had sought for centuries, along with unrestricted access to the eastern Mediterranean and the Middle East. In late 1944, Britain and the Soviet Union agreed to give Britain primacy in Greece after the war, in return for Soviet control of other parts of the Balkans. But postwar Britain proved unable to maintain a military force in Greece. British withdrawal would mean that the Soviets would move in.

Getting the U.S. Congress and the American people to go along with such a policy took an enormous effort on the part of the Truman administration. That effort culminated in the Truman Doctrine. The Truman Doctrine asserted that the nations of the world faced a choice between a free representative government and totalitarian oppression. This was realpolitik sold to the American people under the label of a moral crusade. In that policy, Truman planted the public seed of what would later flower as the policy of containment. Whenever communist forces threatened the free peoples of the world, the United States would provide military, economic, political, and diplomatic aid to contain their influence.

More and more aid would be required to keep Europe safe from communism. Three years after the end of World War II, much of Europe still lay in ruins. A collapse of the frail European economy seemed imminent, so U.S. policy makers set about developing an aid package to resuscitate the European economy. An economic collapse would invite a communist takeover of the country by overt or covert means. Truman pre-

sented a multibillion-dollar aid package, which would become known as the Marshall Plan, although he experienced difficulty in Congress. Truman also approved formation of the Central Intelligence Agency to collect intelligence and conduct covert operations against communists around the world. In order to buttress Europe against Soviet aggression, America would help to form the North Atlantic Treaty Organization, a collective security organization designed to resist a potential invasion of Western Europe.

When Stalin attempted to challenge America by blockading the Western sectors of Berlin, deep within East Germany, an airlift by the United States achieved the delivery of the minimum number of tons of supplies needed to keep the city alive. This put Stalin on notice that America would not roll over at his tactics, and also that American willpower and industrial might could work to thwart his policies. The blockade lasted until May 1949 when Stalin finally backed down.

In its earliest exercises, the Truman Doctrine showed that while Americans would confront communism worldwide, the Truman administration saw Europe as the geopolitical center of gravity when confronting the Soviet Union. Faced with an alarmingly small budget, the Truman administration focused on the defense and recovery of Europe and the slow development of conventional military forces. In addition, men such as Secretary of State Dean Acheson had a lifelong interest in Europe. The Pacific, and specifically Korea, came low on the list of American foreign policy and defense priorities. Although tensions in Western Europe would remain throughout the end of the Cold War, violent conflict shifted to the periphery. Once the Truman Doctrine, the Marshall Plan, and NATO were in place, the price the Soviets would have to pay to march to the English Channel increased dramatically, particularly in light of America's nuclear deterrent. America would make sure, one war or another, that Europe, or at least Western Europe, would not fall to the Soviets. Thus, the focus of the development of communist societies shifted away from Western Europe.

REGIONAL PROXY WARS

In 1949, communist leader Mao Zedong founded the People's Republic of China, after winning a long civil war against the nationalist forces of Chiang Kai-shek. With the founding of that state, communist forces controlled much of mainland Asia: Mongolia, the Asian provinces of the Soviet Union, China, and North Korea. Shortly after the founding of the People's Re-

At the heart of the Cold War was the MAD doctrine, or mutually assured destruction through nuclear weapons. Though it helped maintain a balance of superpowers, nonnuclear surrogate wars proliferated in Southeast Asia and Central America.

public, Mao moved to form an alliance with Stalin, fearing that the United States would move to conquer China. Conservative critics in the United States would hammer the Truman administration for "losing" China.

From the 1950 outbreak of the Korean War to the end of the Cold War, America and the Soviet Union would confront each other around the world in proxy regional wars, where superpower forces would not confront each other directly, but rather through surrogate governments in smaller nations' pro- and anti-communist conflicts. Southeast Asia was the scene of protracted conflict between America and its allies and various communist entities.

America's most difficult Cold War conflict came during the Vietnam War. Conservatives heavily criticized American policy in Vietnam as lacking sufficient vigor to defeat communist forces there. Democratic President Lyndon Johnson sought to wage war under a strategy of "graduated pressure," which would communicate American resolve to communist leaders in North Vietnam, rather than win the war through a resolute application of American military power.

The Vietnam War also precipitated a sharp breach in American society, between those who supported American involvement in Vietnam and those who opposed it. The latter were often allied with the Democratic Party. Although America would not prevail in Vietnam, conservatives spoke up in favor of American efforts to preserve a free South Vietnam and praised American soldiers for brave efforts in a very difficult conflict.

At home, most Americans feared the spread of communism. Only a vocal and influential minority supported communist ideas. Some Western intellectuals felt that capitalism had failed during the 1930s and that communism would eventually triumph around the world. Some who embraced communism eventually fled the Communist Party at great personal cost and at the risk of their lives. Whittaker Chambers followed such a path and became one of the greatest conservative authors of the early 1950s by publishing his book *Witness*, about his break with the Communist Party. Excommunists such as Chambers were in a superb position to denounce the evils of a system that they knew firsthand.

Other conservative voices would reach a larger audience with the founding of the *National Review* by William F. Buckley, Jr. The 1964 presidential campaign of Barry Goldwater marked a watershed for the conservative movement in America; although he would lose in a landslide to liberal Democrat Lyndon Johnson, Goldwater had ideas of limited government and a strong line against the Soviets that would come to fruition in the presidency of Ronald Reagan.

Before conservatives took control of the Cold War, American foreign policy would take another turn. President Richard Nixon developed a new policy known as détente. Under this approach, America would treat the Soviet Union as a great power and seek to coexist with it. Nixon also played traditional balance-of-power politics by seeking open relations with China, and to benefit from a rift that had developed between the two largest communist countries. He hoped that such a move would help to wring concessions from the Soviets, especially on arms control. Conservatives such as Buckley and Reagan were uneasy with this approach, for it caused America to do business with Red China, which had just completed a brutal slaughter of its own people in the Cultural Revolution.

Even some Democrats began to view American policy, as advocated by both political parties, as too weak against the Soviet menace. These people, known as neoconservatives, or "Reagan Democrats," were Democrats who preferred a forceful and moral American foreign policy. Members of this group, such as Richard Perle and Jeanne Kirkpatrick, would play important roles in the Reagan administration.

THE REAGAN COLD WAR

American policy changed decisively in 1981 with the election of Ronald Reagan as president. Unlike earlier presidents, Reagan condemned the Soviets as an evil and tyrannical regime, brutal words in the normally soft language of diplomacy. Rather than accommodate the Soviet Union or seek a balance of global power, Reagan moved to win the Cold War. Reagan sought to meet the Soviets on ground favorable to America: forcing the Soviets into an expensive arms race in which they could not afford to keep up, developing more technologically sophisticated weapons systems, and aggressively supporting anti-communist groups in Poland, Latin America, and Afghanistan. In addition, Reagan pressed for the development of the Strategic Defense Initiative (SDI), a space-based missile defense system that could thwart a Soviet nuclear missile attack.

The Cold War reached a climax in October 1986 as the Soviet economy was finally imploding with defense costs, and Reagan stood firm against Soviet efforts to bargain away SDI at a summit with Soviet Premier Mikhail Gorbachev in Reykjavik, Iceland. Gorbachev unleashed liberal policies into the Soviet system, suffering from its own internal contradictions, which, coupled with the U.S. stance, precipitated a communist collapse. By 1989, East Germans threw off the shackles of Soviet rule and began to tear down the Berlin Wall, paving the way for German reunification. Poland and other Soviet satellites were equally and as successfully gaining independence from the Soviet bloc. President George H.W. Bush and Russian leader Boris Yeltsin presided over the end of the Cold War in 1992.

Throughout the Cold War, American conservatives consistently called for the strong defense of America and its allies against Soviet aggression. But it was with the formulation of Reagan conservatism that winning the Cold War became a focused top priority. Scholars continue to debate whether it was Reaganism or the inherent weakness of the system that finally did the Soviets in. Most would agree it was a combination of both and that the American right is quick to claim credit.

SEE ALSO

BIBLIOGRAPHY

Dean Acheson, *Present at the Creation: My Years in the State Department* (W.W. Norton, 1987); George Bush and Brent Scowcroft, *A World Transformed* (Knopf, 1998); Whittaker Chambers, *Witness* (Random House, 1952); Robert Conquest, *Reflections on a Ravaged Century* (W.W. Norton, 2000); John Lewis Gaddis, *We Now Know: Rethinking Cold War History* (Oxford University Press, 1997); *The Reagan Administration's Secret Strategy That Hastened the Collapse of the Soviet Union* (Atlantic Monthly Press, 1994); Joseph Shattan, *Architects of Victory: Six Heroes of the Cold War* (Heritage Foundation, 1999); Richard Nixon, *RN: The Memoirs of Richard Nixon* (Grosset and Dunlap, 1978).

MITCHELL MCNAYLOR
OUR LADY OF THE LAKE COLLEGE

Colonialism

WHILE COLONIALISM can date from the ancient world, and Rome's final vanquishing of its old rival Carthage in the Punic Wars, modern colonialism could be measured from the first voyage of Christopher Columbus for Spain in 1492. Columbus's voyage was intended to find a less expensive route to find the riches of the Orient after the Ottoman Turkish conquest of Constantinople in 1453 had made the cost of overland commerce prohibitive. In 1493, the 15th pope, Alexander VI, arbitrarily drew a line at the Treaty of Tordesillas to divide the world between Spain and Portugal. Immediately, the other European countries denounced this compact and began a heated competition for the riches of the world.

From this time on, there would be no European wars that would not have repercussions throughout the world. Asia was opened to European trade when the Portuguese Vasco da Gama reached India at the port of Calicut in 1494. Between 1519 and 1540, Spain had explored and conquered Central and South America, with the exception of Brazil, which became a colony of Portugal. In 1565, Pedro de Menendez had established Saint Augustine in today's Florida as the first permanent European settlement in the future United States. Within 60 years, driven both by the desire for exploration and economic success, the European nations had virtually spanned the globe with their commercial settlements, or "factories." The first British settlement in North America, on Roanoke Island, Virginia, failed in 1587; the second one at Jamestown succeeded in 1607. While sociologist Max Weber wrote that Protestantism as a new religion impelled the drive for commercial expansion, the aggressive colonialist policies pursued by traditionally Catholic nations like Portugal, France, and Spain disproves the thesis.

Gradually, a political philosophy arose that has been used to interpret the explosion of European interests across the world from the 15th to the 17th centuries: mercantilism. Mercantilism held that the European countries should acquire overseas "facto-ries"—and colonies—to provide them with raw materials for the growing manufacturing industries at home. From the beginning, with the acquisition of the Spanish colonies in the Americas, colonies were also seen as a way of using the indigenous inhabitants as slave labor, working at no wages for their colonial masters.

By the end of the 17th century, England and France had become embroiled in fierce commercial rivalry, which spread from the plains of Germany to the rich colonies that they coveted in India. Earlier, the Netherlands, after it had won freedom from Spain, had fought a series of spirited naval actions against England. In 1678, however, the old animosity was resolved in a joint treaty directed against the French of King Louis XIV, the Sun King. In 1688, allied thus with the Netherlands, William III of England, who had ruled the Netherlands as William of Orange, entered into a series of wars with France which that continue with brief interludes of uneasy peace until 1763. In that year, at the Treaty of Paris, the final conflict, the Seven Years War, came to a triumphant conclusion for the British. France was effectively removed as a colonial rival in the Americas and India as well. As an example of how mercantilism dominated French political thought, the French decided to keep their sugar-rich islands in the West Indies and relinquish their vast Canadian colony, New France, to British rule.

However, as part of the settlement of the North American colonies, or plantations, the colonists from Great Britain brought with them their conception of their political rights as Englishmen. Over time, the idea of self-government became well established in the thirteen British colonies. When the Mother Country attempted to establish tighter control after the defeat of the French in the Seven Years War, the colonies revolted. Armed conflict broke out in the colony of Massachusetts in April 1775 at Lexington and Concord. The American Revolution had begun. By the time the Americans, with the aid of France, had decisively defeated Great Britain at Yorktown, Virginia, in 1781, they had already declared their political independence from the Mother Country on July 4, 1776. Thus, ironically, the political ideal of democracy that the British colonists had brought with them to the New World ultimately led to the destruction of this first British empire, which had been called into existence to serve the needs of the other predominating political ideal: mercantilism.

Colonialism would continue to dominate European politics throughout the era of the French Revolution and the Napoleonic Wars (1789–1815). Indeed, it would be during the Napoleonic Wars that Great Britain seized what is now Cape Town in South Africa, opening the path for British domination of South Africa.

As the working classes and middle classes began to gain influence in government, the political regimes began to need their support for colonialism. In 1832, for example, the great Reform Bill extended the voting franchise in England, while the revolution in France in 1830 had reaffirmed the growing dominance of the bourgeoisie, or middle class. In Great Britain, the effect of colonialism on the electorate in terms of liberal and conservative political viewpoints is the more marked, if only because England had the earliest truly functioning conservative parliamentary system. The rise of literacy in both France and England made the general public more aware of the issue of colonialism, and newspapers vociferously supported views both for and against the policy.

CONSERVATIVE COLONIALISM

By the middle of the 19th century, strong support for colonialism became a hallmark of the Conservative, or Tory, Party in England, while the Liberal Party tended to be anti-colonialist. A term that gained popularity was *Little Englanders*, because they tended to be concerned mainly about political affairs in England and were against widening the empire, as happened in 1858 when India became a colony after the Great Indian Mutiny. It had previously been owned as a mercantile empire by the Honorable East India Company, operating with Crown support. Indeed, what was becoming an ideological clash over colonialism (which by the 1870s was considered synonymous with imperialism) was symbolized by the perennial rivalry between the Conservative Party's Benjamin Disraeli and William Gladstone of the Liberals. Indeed, it was one of the rare ironies of British history that, whereas Disraeli had acquired controlling interest for England in Egypt's Suez Canal in 1875, it was the Little Englander Gladstone who had to send British troops to protect it in 1882.

After Germany became unified in 1871 as the German empire, the same political dynamic operated there. Chancellor Otto von Bismarck astutely co-opted the concerns of the working class in Germany by beginning what remains one of the most innovative social welfare schemes in Europe. Politically, the most influential parties were the Conservatives and the Free Conservatives on the right, the Centre Party, and the National Liberals. Indeed, until the fall of the empire at the end of World War I, socialists and communists found themselves dumbfounded by the "house that Bismarck built." As early as 1869, a Marxist Party had been established in Germany. W.N. Medlicott wrote in *Bismarck and Modern Germany* how he had undercut the National Liberals in part "by giving a lead to more democratic political forces with the introduction of universal [voting] suffrage." A latecomer in the race for empires, Bismarck nevertheless secured for Germany colonies in West and East Africa and the Pacific islands.

When the European empires clashed in World War I (1914–18), the German, Austrian, and Russian empires were destroyed. The Ottoman Turkish empire, which had only really been driven out of Europe in the Balkan War of 1912, also was cast into history. Although the Bolsheviks (communists) under Vladimir I. Lenin fought until 1922 to hold on to the Russian empire they had gained through the revolution of 1917, they also promulgated anti-colonialism against their conservative European rivals, France and Great Britain. This was not done so much to free the peoples living in the empires, but to gain Russian influence among them to supplant that of the colonial masters. Thus, the struggle for anti-colonialism as advocated by Russia began during the 1920s, not in the Cold War era.

One of the most important successes that the Russian Communists had was in China, which had been severely mauled by the colonial powers since the British took Hong Kong in the Opium War of 1842. The first president of the Chinese Republic, Sun Yat-sen, was extremely pro-communist, after the declaration of the republic in 1912. His party the Kuomintang, or Nationalists, remained so until his successor, the conservative Chiang Kai-shek, asserted his power in the anti-communist coup of 1927.

After World War I, even the conservatives in France and England embraced a more liberal concept of empire, emphasizing the bringing of civilization and prosperity to their colonial peoples. Indeed, in what is now Syria and Lebanon, France's Henri de Jouvenel worked to install a progressive regime after a reactionary period immediately after the war.

When Benito Mussolini and his fascists seized power in Italy in 1922, the liberal empire that had existed before was replaced by a ruthless imperialism seen both in Libya (which the Italians had occupied in 1912) and in Ethiopia.

During World War II, the anti-colonialism of the Russian Comintern (Communist International) was muted by the need for support from the Western democracies by Soviet Russia's Premier Josef Stalin. In fact, Russia and Great Britain together occupied Iran (then Persia) after 1941 when the ruler Reza Shah threatened to interrupt deliveries of vital war materiel from British India to Russia from the south. However, after the war, and especially when Nikita Khrushchev became premier following Stalin's death in 1953, anti-colonialist "wars of national liberation" began to be warmly embraced in a Russian bear hug.

In Southeast Asia, Ho Chi Minh led the communist Viet Minh in the struggle against the restoration of the rule of the French in Indochina, especially in what is now Vietnam. In this effort he had the support of both Russia and China. Later, especially in Africa, Russia and China would be bitter rivals for leadership of the "anti-colonialist camp." Within the French Army, which had been badly split between Free French and the collaborationist Vichy French forces in the war, the struggle to re-colonize Indochina became in effect a way to redeem its honor through a right-wing crusade against communism.

After defeat in Indochina at Dien Bien Phu in May 1954, France was almost immediately embroiled in the war in Algeria, where the National Liberation Front (FLN) began its revolt in November 1954. When in 1958, Charles de Gaulle, who had led the Free French in the war, became the leader of the Fifth French Republic, he did so with the ultimate intention of relinquishing Algeria to the FLN so as to focus on restoring France's position in Europe. When news of his plans became public, in April 1961, elements of the French army in Algeria under General Maurice Challe staged a rightist coup. Although supported by units like the First Foreign Legion Paratroop Regiment, the coup failed because of the army's overall loyalty to de Gaulle.

By 1961, with the ending of the French and British colonial roles in Africa and Southeast Asia, the United States became embroiled in a bitter third world Cold War with Russia and, to a lesser extent, China. The assassination of the pro-communist premier of the Congo, Patrice Lumumba, after the Congo gained its independence from the Belgians in 1960, effectively marked the beginning of the superpower Cold War in Africa.

The war saw the introduction of unique surrogates on both sides, as Cuban mercenaries supported the communist "liberation" forces in the fighting in Angola and the Israeli Mossad carried on a bitter struggle against the Chinese in the Congo. Indeed, from 1961, when he took power from Lumumba, the United States saw President Mobutu Sese Seko of the Congo as a bulwark against communist expansion in Africa. Africa would remain a battlefield between the United States, which continued to back stable regimes like Mobutu's in the Congo, and the Soviet Union, which aided communist leaders like Robert Mugabe, in today's Zimbabwe, until the collapse of the Soviet federation in 1991.

Throughout its long history from the days of Columbus's first voyages, colonialism has been a rightist policy combining mercantilism and imperialism, and has provided surrogate third world stages for conflict between superpowers, whether they be the French and British of the 19th century, or the Americans and Soviets of the 20th.

SEE ALSO
Volume 1 Left: Socialism; Anti-Globalization.
Volume 2 Right: Monarchism; Imperialism; Cold War.

BIBLIOGRAPHY
Francis Parkman, *Montcalm and Wolfe* (Collier Books, 1962); W.M. Wallace, *Appeal to Arms: A Military History of the American Revolution* (Crown, 1964); Douglas Edward Leach, *Arms for Empire: A Military History of the British Colonies in North America, 1607–1763* (Macmillan, 1973); Philip Magnus, *Gladstone* (Dutton, 1964); T. Harry Williams, *Americans in Arms* (Collier Books, 1962).

JOHN F. MURPHY, JR.
AMERICAN MILITARY UNIVERSITY

Conservatism

CONSERVATISM IS A MODERN way of thinking that favors historical continuity and the establishment, proposes the maintenance of traditional institutions, and opposes changes in the status quo ante. It has become a major political force, exerted strong social impact, and disseminated reactionary values. Therefore, it can take the form of an ideology, a political organization, or a cultural movement.

Conservative ideas became aroused in the 18th century as an anti-intellectual initiative against liberalism. As a political group and a party in the 19th century, conservatives reacted against liberals in the British parliament and against modernists and revolutionaries in Europe. They gained force in the 20th century as an anti-revolutionary movement opposing the Soviet revolution and the spread of communism after World War II. Later on, they backed the opposition to civil rights, counterculture, welfare policies, and human-rights initiatives in several countries. At the beginning of the 21st century, conservatism had embraced the war against terrorism and established a new approach to international relations.

THE EUROPEAN ROOTS OF CONSERVATISM

Conservatism originated as a reaction to modern institutions promoted by the liberal industrial bourgeoisie. Its initial project was to defend the ancien regime (a term for the prerevolutionary French monarchy) and aristocracy, based on the principles that society has its own natural laws and history is the *magistra vitae*, which teaches about the future as it mirrors tradition. One auspicious moment for an assemblage of conservatives was the French Revolution, when conservatism became a counterrevolutionary ideology elaborated by several European political thinkers.

Edmund Burke was an important philosopher and politician who published *Reflections on the Feelings of the Beautiful and the Sublime* in 1753 and *A Vindication of Natural Society* in 1756. He emphasized tradition, morals, and religion, as well as pragmatism in dealing with the British colonies, arguing that popular customs—religious rituals, funeral ceremonies, and class divisions—should receive special deference. Even though he supported the revolutionary movement for the independence of English colonies in America, in *Reflections on the Revolution in France*, published in 1790, he criticized the French Revolution for being violent, nontraditional, and corrupt. The English poets Samuel Taylor Coleridge and William Wordsworth continued formulating conservative ideas for the British Tories, albeit in an aesthetic fashion.

In France, conservatism was developed by Joseph de Maistre, Louis de Bonald, and Hugues Felicité de La Mennais. De Maistre wrote *Considérations sur l'histoire de France* in 1797, criticizing the Constitutional Assembly for not including French traditional values in the constitution. He also opposed the republicans and made an apology of monarchy and the pope, going so far as to suggest the extermination of intellectuals, Jews, republicans, and others who were a threat to the sovereignty of his planned monarchic theocracy. De Bonald's major work was *Théorie du pouvoir politique et religieux dans la société civile*, published in 1796, while he was an anti-revolutionary emigré in Heidelberg, Germany. He valued categories such as order, monarchy, and theocracy, and developed a point-by-point refutation of the Enlightenment, arriving at the following conservative

formula: "A general will, a general love, and a general force achieve the aim which is the conservation of social beings." La Mennais contributed to François Chateaubriand's journal *Le Conservateur*, founded in 1818, before investing in what later became known as the Parti Conservateur in France.

These ideas were present also in Germany and reached the Americas in the 19th century. In Germany, Justus Möser and Adam Müller were the first to embrace conservatism as a philosophy of history. Later, Karl von Savigny applied conservatism to juridical thinking, founding the school of historical jurisprudence. In North America, conservatism arrived as both a British and a French heritage. In Canada, a Parti Conservateur was founded in Quebec. In the United States, conservative ideas were expressed in the organization of the American Founding Fathers, the Federalist Party of John Adams, and the initiatives of politicians such as Adams, Alexander Hamilton, John Roanoke, and John Caldwell Calhoun. Conservatives in Mexico supported the wars of independence from Spain, but then tried to establish a monarchy of the Bourbon family in Mexico City, while in Argentina and Brazil conservatism arrived later, directly from France, as both countries had their own Partido Conservador.

Conservative thinkers have reacted to several revolutions—the Industrial Revolution, French Revolution, American Revolution, the revolutions of 1830 and 1848 in Europe, and the independence of South American countries. They also reacted to liberalism, anarchism, socialism, communism, and other movements in different countries during the 20th century. This explains the meaning of the term *reactionary*, often inextricably linked, as in *reactionary conservatism*. However, conservatism is by no means a whole and uniform block, but rather the expression of several—and sometimes contradictory—tendencies in different contexts.

CONSERVATISM IN THE UNITED STATES

Even though there were traces of conservatism in the 18th century, conservatism in the United States actually started in the second half of the 20th century and has since then shaped American politics.

Authors such as Friedrich von Hayek and Russel Kirk represent an awakening process that took place after World War II. In 1944, Hayek published *Road to Serfdom* and in 1953 Russel Kirk published *The Conservative Mind: From Burke to Elliot*, establishing a line between 18th-century Britain and the contemporary United States. Both argued for the need for strong conservative values in order to guarantee the cement of society. Several shorter articles after these publications served as a political thermometer of that epoch. In "The Conservative Mood," published in *Dissent* in 1954, Wright Mills critically reviewed the ideas of Kirk. Bernard Crick raised questions about the meaning of conservatism in the United States in "The Strange Quest for an American Conservatism," which appeared in the *Review of Politics* in 1955. Following a similar path, Samuel Huntington suggested, in his article "Conservatism as an Ideology," published in *American Political Science Review* in 1957, that conservatism was an extemporaneous ideology that would arise as a reaction to any attack on given institutions but that still lacked an appropriate theory.

The development of conservatism as a political theory can be seen as an attempt to respond to these issues. First, conservatism was embraced by partisan politics and by organizations of the so-called right. Based on this articulation, the Republican Party tried to elect Douglas MacArthur to the presidency in 1944, 1948, and 1952; supported the presidential campaign of Barry Goldwater in 1964; and elected Ronald Reagan in the 1980s and George W. Bush in 2000.

Finally, conservative action through radical activism was promoted by the creation of associations, publication of newspapers and magazines, and the use of media such as telephone, radio, and television, among others. During the 1950s and 1960s, these strategies backed the anti-communist activities of McCarthyism, the opposition to civil rights by groups such as the Ku Klux Klan, the American Liberty League, the John Birch Society and others, as well as the anti-ecumenical propaganda against mainline churches by fundamentalist preachers. During the "culture wars" of the 1980s, there were similar initiatives by the Christian right and the Moral Majority, which opposed affirmative action, feminism, and liberal theology. By 2000, several groups had developed a culture of opposition to the welfare state, to the United Nations, and to foreign ideas.

The challenge, however, is how to connect these various positions to conservatism. Their links are assumed in times of need (in opposition to communism or to terrorism, for instance), but not easily established in a clear way—especially because they also seem to be rejected whenever these groups or associations go too far astray. Social scientists have then tried to explain and measure the impact of radical activism. Daniel Bell dedicated two books (*The New Right* in 1955 and *The Radical Right* in 1964) to the study of these movements. Allen Broyles published *The John Birch Society: Anatomy*

of a Protest in 1964 and David Chalmers presented statistics about the Ku Klux Klan in *Hooded Americanism: The History of the Ku Klux Klan* in 1965. In *The Politics of Unreason: Right-Wing Extremism in America* (1970), Seymour Martin Lipset attempted to show how the radical right was a form of extremism similar to the radical left, with belligerent and irrational strategies that soon separated the right wing from traditional conservatism.

It was only with the greater impact of the Christian right on American politics, first electing Jimmy Carter in 1976 and then supporting Ronald Reagan as president of the United States, that a new interest arose in the study of the relationship between conservatism and religion. The book *American Evangelicalism: Conservative Religion and the Quandary of Modernity*, written by James Davidson Hunter in 1983, and Sara Diamond's *Roads to Dominion: Right-Wing Movements and Political Power in the United States* (1995) are good examples of analyses of this trend.

TYPES OF CONSERVATISM

The different aspects mentioned above and the historical development of conservative ideas, organizations and social groups indicate that conservatism has not remained unchanged. First, the historical situation has changed since the 18th century. Second, conservatism was inserted in different countries and cultural contexts. And finally, it continuously adapts its strategies. Therefore, it is necessary to differentiate conservatism according to different issues that run parallel to the accounts above. For that purpose, the following categories can be applied:

Traditional conservatism is defined by Jürgen Habermas as a hermeneutic philosophy that emphasizes tradition and existing institutions in Europe. In the United States, this trend is represented by Kirk, who relied on traditional southern politics, well described by Paul Gottfried and Thomas Flemming in *The Conservative Movement* (1988), and by Eugene Genovese in *The Southern Tradition: The Achievement and Limitations of an American Conservatism* (1994). This form of conservative thinking continually gained more adherents, involving also politicians, journalists, lobbyists, and organizations.

New conservatism is a label applied to a turn that occurred in the 1940s under the influence of Hayek's *Road to Serfdom* and Peter Viereck's *Conservatism Revisited*. But its popularization occurred with William F. Buckley in the 1950s, as he published *God and Man at Yale* and *McCarthy and His Enemies* and launched the

National Review—which became the most important U.S. conservative journal. In Britain, Michael Oakeshott defended this new form of conservatism from 1947 until his death in 1990, while in Germany, Ernst Forsthoff and Arnold Gehlen were its main representatives.

Neoconservatism has sometimes been identified as the ideology of frustrated socialists who broke ranks with liberalism and joined the Reagan administration. The list includes sociologists such as Bell, Irving Kristol, Daniel Moynihan, and Nathan Glazer, among others. As trained sociologists influenced by the political theory of Leo Straus, they understood the rationality of distinct spheres of society, and integrated newer categories to political discourse, exerting considerable intellectual influence during the Reagan administration. This trend was represented in Germany by Hermann Lübbe and Robert Spaemann in France by Raymond Aron and Alain de Benoist, and in Brazil by José Guilherme Merquior and Vamireh Chacon.

Ethnic neoconservatism is a label than can be applied to a series of representatives from different minority groups, who became involved with neo-conservatism and brought their arguments to the public sphere. This was first identified with the term black neoconservatism applied to African American authors such as Thomas Sowell and Stephen Carter, who opposed affirmative action. However, this label was later dropped in order to include Asian and Latino writers such as Francis Fukuyama, Dinesh d'Souza, Linda Chavez, and many others.

Compassionate conservatism is a program based on the thinking of Marvin Olasky, a view that was embraced by George W. Bush when he was governor of Texas. Elected president of the United States, Bush followed Olasky's advice and combined it with the policies of the Republican Party, proposing a government administration that should be more sensitive to social issues. One part of this new policy was the Faith-based and Community Initiative; another was the inclusion of the issues of the poor within the government domestic agenda.

All things considered, there is a line uniting the several conservative ideas and groups outlined above. We can confirm that conservatism has ideological, organizational, and cultural aspects. It favors historical continuity and stability and defends traditional institutions, arguing for the preservation of the status quo. However, conservatism is not static. In order to defend these ideas, it embraces strategies of modernity, changes its form, and integrates new groups, always adapting to changing situations.

SEE ALSO

Volume 1 Left: Liberalism; New Left; Socialism.
Volume 2 Right: Bush, George W.; Buckley, William F., Jr.; *National Review.*

BIBLIOGRAPHY

Jürgen Habermas, D*ie neue Unübersichtlichkeit* (Suhrkamp, 1985); Paul Gottfried and Thomas Flemming, *The Conservative Movement* (Twayne, 1988); James Hunter, *American Evangelicalism: Conservative Religion and the Quandary of Modernity* (Rutgers University Press, 1983); Jerry Muller, *Conservatism: An Anthology of Social and Political Thought from David Hume to the Present* (Princeton University Press, 1997); George Nash, *The Conservative Intellectual Movement in America since 1945* (Basic Books, 1976); Marvin Olasky, "Compassionate Conservatism," *Veritas* (2000); Roger Scruton, *The Meaning of Conservatism* (Barnes & Noble, 1980); Peter Steinfels, *Neoconservatives: The Men Who Are Changing America's Politics* (Simon & Schuster, 1979).

AMOS NASCIMENTO
METHODIST UNIVERSITY OF PIRACICABA, BRAZIL

Conservative Party, UK

THE CONSERVATIVE Party is the oldest British political party and arguably the oldest political party in the world. It has given rise to some of Great Britain's greatest leaders, is unofficially referred to as the Tory Party, and its members are called Tories. Under a system favoring two dominant parties, this center-right party is the only party with a realistic prospect of providing a counterbalance to the Labour Party. Throughout its existence, the party has stood for stability and order. It was early identified with the lesser aristocracy, the church, the monarchy, property rights, and agricultural interests, but during the Industrial Revolution it strove to align itself with the urban working class and produced significant reforms. It would subsequently become the party most associated with empire, the middle class, and business.

Conservatives today advocate private enterprise, lower taxes, and government reduction and efficiency. The party is also less enthusiastic than the Labour Party about the movement toward European integration and includes elements known as "Euroskeptics" who object to a European currency and the surrendering of sovereignty to the European Union. Divisions over the European Union have caused internal party bickering, although Conservatives are suppressing these differences. The party is achieving new unity in opposing Labour's domestic policies and constitutional reforms. Even though usually advocating measures promoting social stability and traditional values, since the party's founding, it has demonstrated a determination to remain relevant to contemporary issues, while avoiding long-term doctrinal disputes or ideological rigidity. It has also shown agility in rebounding from serious splits and electoral defeats and a willingness to renew and democratize itself.

THE TORIES OF PITT AND PEEL

Party origins are traceable to the loose Tory faction appearing in the late 17th century. The Tories found permanent cohesion under William Pitt the Younger, who began his political career championing parliamentary reform and became prime minister in 1783. Pitt's reforming zeal cooled with concerns over the influence of the radicalism of the French Revolution, and he became the implacable builder of anti-French international coalitions. After Pitt, Lord Liverpool, who served as prime minister from 1812 to 1827, masterfully built the party.

Under the anti-reform leadership of the Duke of Wellington, the aristocratic victor over Napoleon at Waterloo and a reluctant politician, the Tory Party fractured and lost power because of the adoption of reform measures granting political rights to Catholics. The democratization of the Great Reform Act of 1832 further reduced Tory parliamentary representation. Its strength would not be rebuilt until Robert Peel, the father of the modern Conservative Party, assumed leadership of the Tories and attracted middle-class and business constituents. Under Peel, the "Conservative Party" name came into use, the Tamworth Manifesto of 1834 announced the tenets of conservatism, and in the same year Peel served briefly as a minority prime minister.

By 1841, the Conservatives were the majority in Parliament and Peel was firmly established as prime minister. In 1846, however, the party divided over the issue of repeal of the protectionist Corn Laws and Peel resigned. Eventually many of Peel's free trade supporters called "Peelites," most notably William Gladstone, joined the Whigs and formed the Liberal Party.

The 14th Earl of Derby, who led minority governments in the 1850s and 1860s because of Whig divisions, revived Conservative fortunes. But it was due to the creativity and political skill of Benjamin Disraeli

that Conservatives regained a majority in Parliament. The road to power was paved by Disraeli's achievement in securing enactment of the Reform Act of 1867, which extended the franchise. With significant support from industrial workers, Conservatives managed to form a majority government with Disraeli as prime minister in 1874. Disraeli devised a strong party organization, including the opening of the Conservative Central Office in 1870, and the party associated itself with far-flung imperial successes, business enterprise, patriotism, and progressive policies promoting inclusion of the working class called Tory Democracy. Nevertheless, a resurgent Liberal Party commanded by Gladstone, benefiting from an economic downturn, defeated the Conservatives in 1880, but the Tories returned to power under Disraeli in 1886 due to the Liberals' division over Irish Home Rule.

SALISBURY, UNIONISTS, AND DEFEAT

Even after Disraeli's departure, the Conservative Party enjoyed broad-based appeal and benefited from support of disgruntled Unionist Liberals who opposed their party's stance on Ireland. Accordingly, Conservatives regularly won elections under the 20-year leadership of the able Third Marquis of Salisbury. In 1895, the Conservative-Liberal Unionist coalition was active albeit unofficial, but by 1912 the coalition became official and the term *Unionist* was regularly used in the place of *Conservative* through the 1920s. The Conservatives in Scotland would be called Unionists until the 1960s. After Salisbury's retirement in 1902, the party declined under Salisbury's nephew, Arthur Balfour. Exacerbating Unionists' troubles was disagreement over proposed tariff reform, which encountered opposition from a small but determined free trade faction within the party and working-class worries about higher prices resulting from higher duties. In 1906, the party faced rejection at the polls.

COALITION, REBELLION, AND BALDWIN

While out of power, Unionists opposed Liberal reform proposals, which led to new party divisions and the resignation of Balfour. After a Unionist House of Lords defeated the government's budget in 1910, partisan battle ensued in the House of Lords, and the Liberals countered with measures to reduce the power of the lords. Within the party, the position of party chairman was established to manage the Central Office. Andrew Bonar Law became party leader and aggressively chal-

Election posters produced by the Conservative Party in the United Kingdom focused on anti-Labour Party messages. The posters are from the elections of, from left to right, 1929, 1929, 1951, and 1955.

lenged the disunited Liberals. Due to effective party leadership, restoration of morale, unpopularity of Liberal constitutional reforms, and perceived mismanagement of the early days of World War I, the Conservatives gradually returned to power, first in a coalition formed in 1915 with Liberal Prime Minister H.H. Asquith, and, commencing in 1916, as the dominate party in a coalition led by Liberal Prime Minister David Lloyd George.

The coalition would continue into the postwar period. With Bonar Law's departure in 1921, an unpopular Austen Chamberlain became party leader. Yet in a revolt led by Law, Chamberlain was removed, the coalition collapsed, and Law became prime minister. The reform-minded and popular Stanley Baldwin, who was viewed as the embodiment of English virtues and appealed to business and professional voters, became party leader and prime minister in 1923. Due to the world economic crisis, another coalition was forged, called the National Government, in 1931 under Liberal Prime Minister Ramsey MacDonald. Baldwin returned for his third premiership in 1935.

WORLD WAR II, CHURCHILL, AND POSTWAR DIFFICULTIES

On Baldwin's retirement in 1937, a popular Neville Chamberlain became party leader and prime minister, but resigned over failure of his German appeasement policy. In a time of war, Conservatives and the nation turned to the indomitable leadership of Winston Churchill. But at war's end, voters ousted Churchill and the Conservatives in 1945. The party nevertheless returned to office under an aging Churchill in 1951 and accepted much of Labour's social reforms. After Churchill's retirement in 1955, Conservatives held power until 1964 under Prime Ministers Anthony Eden, Harold Macmillan, and Sir Alec Douglas-Home. However, Conservative administrations of the 1960s and 1970s faced economic ills and a resurgent Labour Party. In 1965, Edward Heath was named party leader and became prime minister in 1970. Heath led Britain into the European Common Market, but after losing elections in 1974, was defeated as leader by Margaret Thatcher in 1975. She was the first leader since before the war not to come from the party's moderate mainstream.

THATCHER AND MAJOR

Thatcher was more ideological than her recent predecessors and moved the party to the right. She was elected Britain's first woman prime minister in 1979 and was reelected in 1983 and 1987. The "Iron Lady" achieved victory in the Falklands War, a close relationship with President Ronald Reagan, and greater European cooperation in foreign affairs, and she championed free enterprise. Although her domestic policies sometimes proved unpopular, she was successful in curbing the trade unions and privatizing many government-controlled industries. Despite achieving much of her domestic agenda, known as Thatcherism, many Conservatives in Parliament tired of her leadership and resistance to European integration and feared the next election. After failing to achieve victory on the first ballot of party members in Parliament, Thatcher resigned in 1990.

John Major, chancellor of the exchequer, won the race to replace Thatcher and went on to lead the party to a close victory in the 1992 general election, only to confront leadership challenges in the mid-1990s. Throughout his premiership, Major continued with much of Thatcher's agenda, but the Conservative majority declined to a tenuous level and party division over the European Union increased. Scandals, recession, hostile press coverage, and a reinvigorated and more moderate Labour Party resulted in an unsurprising Conservative defeat in 1997.

Back in opposition, the Conservatives turned to the youthful leadership of William Hague. He instituted changes in the leadership selection process to include the party's rank and file, but proved unable to dislodge Labour in the 2001 election and resigned. With the support of Thatcher loyalists, Ian Duncan Smith was selected as leader by a vote of the party membership. Smith was more moderate than expected and ended open party dissension over the European Union, but was seen by many as a lackluster challenger to Labour Prime Minister Tony Blair. After losing a confidence vote of parliamentary Conservatives, Smith resigned and the party swiftly unified behind Michael Howard in November 2003.

As a former home secretary and Conservatives' economic spokesman in Parliament, Howard offered experience, a statesmanlike image, and the hope of presenting a party ready to govern. To the delight of Conservatives, he proved to be an enthusiastic parliamentary debater against Blair, and mounted a television campaign and toured Britain attacking Labour's record on government services, crime, education, and taxation, and criticized proposed reform of the judiciary and a proposed European constitution. Howard has also reemphasized Conservative beliefs in limited and efficient government and streamlined party organization at the Central Office and in Parliament.

SEE ALSO

Volume 1 Left: Labour Party, UK; United Kingdom.
Volume 2 Right: United Kingdom; Conservatism; Thatcher, Margaret; Reagan, Ronald.

BIBLIOGRAPHY

Stuart Ball, *The Conservative Party since 1945* (St. Martin's Press, 1998); Robert Blake, *The Conservative Party: Peel to Major* (BRP Publishers, 1998); Neal R. McCrillis, *The British Conservative Party in the Age of Universal Suffrage* (Ohio State University Press, 1998); Philip Norton, *The Conservative Party* (Pearson Education, 1996); John Ramsden, *An Appetite for Power: A History of the Conservative Party since 1830* (Harper Collins, 1998); Earl A. Reitan and E.A. Reitan, *Tory Radicalism: Margaret Thatcher, John Major, and the Transformation of Modern Britain* (Rowman and Littlefield, 1997); Jeremy Smith, *The Taming of Democracy: The Conservative Party* (University of Wales Press, 1997); Robert Stewart, *Foundation of the Conservative Party* (Longman, 1978).

RUSSELL FOWLER, J.D.
UNIVERSITY OF TENNESSEE, CHATTANOOGA

Coolidge, Calvin (1872–1933)

THE 30TH PRESIDENT of the United States, Calvin Coolidge, was born on Independence Day, 1872, in Plymouth, Vermont, as John Calvin Coolidge. Later in his life he dropped the "John" from his name. He was the son of John Calvin Coolidge, a man of many trades (including storekeeper, teacher, politician, and farmer) and Victoria Josephine Moor Coolidge. His mother died at age 39 when Coolidge was 12. In 1895, he graduated from Amherst College with honors. Following his graduation, he studied law in Northampton, Massachusetts, in the offices of John Hammond and Henry Field. After being accepted to the bar in 1897, he opened his own practice where he did collection work for business houses, managed estates, performed title work for banks, and dealt with real estate issues.

Throughout his life, Coolidge was very involved in politics and was an active member of the Republican Party. On December 6, 1899, he was appointed city councilman, the beginning of his public service career. He continued to move up the political ladder, holding many government positions. Coolidge became governor of Massachusetts at the age of 47 on November 5, 1918.

During his service as governor, he became nationally known for his stand during the Boston Police Strike on September 11, 1919. He believed that the police should not be allowed to go on strike. Coolidge declared: "There is no right to strike against the public safety by anybody, anywhere, anytime." He dispatched the National Guard despite warnings by colleagues that it might destroy the Republican Party in Massachusetts and also his career. When the strike was over, Coolidge did not allow the strikers to return to work. He was re-elected that fall.

In 1920 he took a run at the presidency, but Warren G. Harding received the Republican nomination. Coolidge was selected vice president. That November, the Harding and Coolidge team won by a landslide. Harding died on August 2, 1923, and Coolidge became president. His father, who at the time was a notary public, swore him in. During the one year that was left of the term, he gained enough support within his party to receive the presidential nomination for the 1924 campaign, which he won easily. He received about 72 percent of the electoral votes. During his second term as president, he successfully achieved most of his goals. He was known for his conservative views, perhaps best summarized in his public statement: "We do not need more intellectual power, we need more moral power. We do not need more knowledge, we need more character. We do not need more government, we need more culture. We do not need more law, we need more religion."

His domestic economic policies successfully followed the conservative Republican line: He cut the national budget almost in half, he kept unemployment at 3.6 percent, and the nation's wealth increased by 17.5 percent. Educational spending increased and illiteracy was cut in half. On June 2, 1924, he signed a bill that made all Native Americans citizens of the United States.

Coolidge is known for supporting the Kellogg-Briand Pact, is a multilateral pact under which 62 countries renounced war as a means of international policy, which was later turned into international law. It was ratified by the U.S. Senate and signed by Coolidge on January 17, 1929. Throughout his presidency, he was one of the most popular presidents in American history. He was also known to be very quiet and always calm. Some historians point out that Coolidge's economic policies, especially his *laissez-faire* attitude toward American business, helped contribute to the causes and effects of the subsequent Great Depression of the 1930s.

SEE ALSO

Volume 1 Left: Roosevelt, Franklin D.; New Deal.
Volume 2 Right: Conservatism; Republican Party.

BIBLIOGRAPHY

Calvin Coolidge Memorial Foundation, "Calvin Coolidge Chronology," www.calvin-coolidge.org (April 2004); The White House, "Calvin Coolidge," www.whitehouse.gov (April 2004); Cal Thomas, *Silent Cal Speaks: Why Calvin Coolidge Is the Model for Conservative Leadership Today* (The Heritage Foundation, 1996); University of Kansas, "Calvin Coolidge Biography," American Presidency, www.grolier.com (April 2004).

ARTHUR HOLST, PH.D.
WIDENER UNIVERSITY

Corporatism

CORPORATISM, derived from the Latin word *corpus*, is a political or social system in which a government or society creates alliances with professional, social, and economic groups to promote an agenda. In general terms, a corporatist system usually refers to governmental systems. Essentially, corporatism alludes to the parts of a society contributing to the development of that particular entity. However, on the social level, it can refer to social systems in relation to the Catholic Church or other interest groups.

Historically, the idea of corporatism evolved in the medieval era, in the 1300s. Medieval society was centered around the Catholic Church or societal guilds. Thus, corporatism in the pre-Reformation era centered on social guidance, rather than on any political or economic goals. In more recent times, however, the idea of corporatism emerged in an increasingly political environment.

In the late 19th century, industrialization gripped Europe. In a previously rural and agrarian society, the onslaught of mechanization and technology signaled the end of a tranquil way of life. Industrialization led to migration to the cities in search of employment and more stable living conditions. Arriving in the crowded cities, many worked in crowded factories with long hours, earning low wages and subject to horrible working conditions. The result of the process of industrialization was an increasing sense of hostility and alienation.

Many joined syndicalist unions and conglomerates to protect against the exploitative practices of employers. Especially in the late 19th century, radical ideologies of communism, socialism, and anarchism permeated many of these unions. The unions, in turn, became radicalized as the groups promoted radical action against capitalism, specifically in the form of violence and protests. This pattern occurred in many European societies, from Spain to Germany.

In the mid-19th century, with radicalism and unionism threatening to tear European society in half, many observers began to look for alternatives to the radicalism of the communists or anarchists. The earliest known expression or reaction to corporatism surfaced from the writings of the ebullient Adam Müller. Müller professed his views in response to the egalitarianism of the French Revolution and as a critique of Adam Smith's *Wealth of Nations*. Müller argued that there existed a contradiction in 18th-century Europe between the notions of community and capitalist individualism.

Utilizing Müller's concepts of individualism, and in response to the economic chaos of 19th-century industrialization, the ideology of corporatism emerged. In 1884, in the German town of Freiburg, local church leaders met to discuss social ills and poverty, which were endemic throughout Europe. The church leadership demanded that the state solve society's social problems. The meeting essentially served as a base of operations for a rejuvenated Catholic Church. On May 15, 1891, Pope Leo XIII issued an encyclical named *Rerum Novarum*. With the subtitle, "Condition of Labour," the encyclical discussed the travails of the working class in the late 19th century. It proceeded to refute the ideological claims of the socialists and communists on the importance of private property and, indeed, promoted the capitalist notion of private property. Finally, the encyclical demanded that the state form an alliance with the worker, against capital, for both mutual protection and self-protection. As a result of the *Rerum*, the basic component of corporatism surfaced. That is, an alliance between the state and the workers, excluding the unions and syndicates, would alleviate the power of the communist unions and decrease political radicalism. Essentially, the *Rerum* provided an alternative route, or what later corporatist theorists would call the Third Way.

The impact on the ideological basis of corporatism by the Catholic Church must be looked at in relation to the influence of other philosophical stimuli. Most important was the impact of German philosopher W.F. Hegel. Hegel argued convincingly that the state is an expression of the community. The community's primary (sole) purpose is to attain a common good. The community is also composed of distinct components or corporations, and these corporations must manage private property and organizing the principles of the organizations so that the state can function efficiently. This idea would become an essential component of corporatism. A final source of corporatism emerged from the Italian corporatists of the early 20th century. Reconstituting the corporatism of the church with that of Hegel and Saint Simon, Constantine Panunzio argued that corporatism would be effective with the impetus of nationalism. The Italians promulgated a secular, nationalistic, authoritarian, and materialistic version of corporatism. It is this brand of corporatism that, in the 20th century, has emerged as the driving force behind the different forms of national corporatism.

In the early 20th century, it became quite evident that corporatism would emerge in societies that carried a long tradition of Catholicism and centralism. The first example would emerge in Italy. In the 1920s, the fascists promoted the ideals of the corporatist model. Led by Benito Mussolini, the fascists organized the employers in the country as "corporations," according to their particular industries. These corporations were given representation in a legislature known as the *camera dei fasci e delle corporazioni*. In the Italian example, corporatism assumed both a traditional corporatist as well as a personalist form.

Another corporatist brand, with less ideological and personalist forms, emerged in the Iberian peninsula. In the 1920s, the conservative governments of Spain and Portugal supported corporate organizations in competition with the radical unions and syndicates. Spain's Primo de Rivera, in his conservative dictatorship, attempted to co-opt the major union, the UGT, (Union general de trabajadores) into his alliance. In Portugal, Antonio de Oliveira Salazar created organizations like *Federacao Nacional para a Alegria no Trabalho* (FNAT) to organize cultural events in the country.

In Latin America, especially after the 1930s, corporatism assumed a new form. Whereas in Europe corporatism was closely aligned with the church, Latin American corporatism assumed a populist tinge. In Argentina, where Juan Peron initiated his own brand of corporatism, the working class was given freedom to react and was integrated into the particular political systems.

AMERICAN CORPORATISM

To a certain degree, corporatism hit the shores of the United States in the 1930s. In 1932, Democrat Franklin Roosevelt was elected president to alleviate the economic collapse caused by the Great Depression. Roosevelt's program, the New Deal, sought to placate certain economic and social sectors. For example, the National Industrial Recovery Act (NIRA) sought to bring the working class into the Roosevelt coalition. Under the New Deal's early experiment with the National Recovery Administration (NRA), the Code Authorities included representatives of industrial associations, labor unions, and the general public (usually represented by academics). In setting prices, standards, and labor conditions, the Code Authorities resembled the Italian *corporazioni*. However, when the Supreme Court declared the NIRA unconstitutional, the New Deal moved in the direction of control by regulatory body and by federal programs of direct employment.

SEE ALSO

Volume 1 Left: Unions; Italy; New Deal; Spain.
Volume 2 Right: Italy; Fascism; Capitalism; Associative State.

BIBLIOGRAPHY

Robert Himmelberg, *Survival of Corporatism during the New Deal Era, 1933–45* (Garland, 1994); Juan J. Linz and Alfred Stepan, eds., *The Breakdown of Democratic Regimes* (Johns Hopkins University Press, 1978); Sebastian Royo, *Corporatism in Southern Europe, Spain, and Portugal in Comparative Perspective* (Praeger, 2002); Phillippe Schmitter, *Corporatism and Public Policy in Authoritarian Portugal* (Sage Publications, 1975); Howard J. Wiarda, *Corporatism and Development: The Portuguese Experiment* (University of Massachusetts Press, 1977); Howard J. Wiarda, *Corporatism and National Development in Latin America* (Westview Press, 1981).

JAIME RAMÓN OLIVARES, PH.D.
HOUSTON COMMUNITY COLLEGE, CENTRAL

Corsican Separatism

THE STORY OF CORSICAN separatism rightfully begins in the history of France. In 1768, the island was acquired by King Louis XV from Italian Genoa. Under the dynastic politics of the era, it was only another transfer of territory, much as France had earlier ceded its colony of New France (Canada) to Great Britain by the Treaty of Paris in 1763.

However, to the Corsicans, they themselves were the citizens of a free republic. Pasquale Paoli declared that on "January 30, 1735, … Corsica is declared independent by Cunsulta of Orezza which voted the first Corsican constitution, the first modern democratic constitution. The legislative power is entrusted at an assembly made up of deputies selected by the people and the executive power is entrusted to a junta of six members elected by the assemblée [assembly]." Corsicans

thus rightfully consider themselves to have had one of the first republics in Western political history.

From the time of the meeting of the Cunsulta, Corsicans fought for their freedom against Genoese rule. But, to paraphrase the English historian Hillaire Belloc, the Genoese had the maxim gun, and the Corsicans did not. Giacintu Paoli became the leader of the Corsican resistance, and was forced to flee the island under persecution from Genoa in 1739. By 1768, Genoa had had enough of attempting to suppress the Corsican desire for freedom and representative government. Thus, the Genoese transferred authority to France.

King Louis sent large forces to suppress Corsican independence, and soon Paoli's forces were compelled to withdraw. As Emil Ludwig writes in *Napoleon*, "there was a terrible retreat through the dense forests and the rugged mountains." Paoli was forced to flee his beloved island in June. His adjutant, Carlo Buonaparte, made peace with the conquerors. In August 1769, his son Napolione was born. Carlo became a loyal servant of the French and was duly rewarded with the title of count. His son Napolione was sent to France for education in the military and studied artillery. The son now took on the name by which he is known to history: Napoleon Bonaparte.

The "Little Corsican," as he would always be known, seized power in France in November 1799, 30 years after his native Corsica had surrendered to the French. Ironically, the extreme centralization that Napoleon imposed on France made Corsican independence even more of an impossibility. It was now just one of the *départements* (provinces) of France, ruled from Paris, with none of the sense of respect for the institutions or traditions for the regions of France that still marked the old monarchy until it fell in the French Revolution of 1789. However, the Corsican people jealously kept alive memories of their independence and celebrated their own culture, writing in their own language, Corsu.

In the 1970s, however, the desire for Corsican independence—or separatism—took a dangerous turn. The Corsican National Liberation Front (CNLF) allied itself with terror organizations like the Palestine Liberation Organization (PLO) and the Popular Front for the Liberation of Palestine (PFLP). Thus, it became a target for French intelligence, the SDECE, the Service de Documentation Extérieure et de Contre-Espionage, and the DST, the Direction de la Surveillance du Territoire, which was concerned more with French internal security. Ironically, most of the members of the special Action Branch of the SDECE were Corsicans, and some would form the anti-independence movement Francia. Beginning as early as July 1960, Radio Corse had transmitted Corsican nationalist views. However, the identification of Corsican nationalism with anti-French terrorist acts caused the government in Paris to take drastic action against it.

According to Roger Falligot and Pascal Krop in *La Piscine: The French Secret service Since 1944*, "a team of frogmen from SDECE landed on the island on the morning of 14 August [1978] and blew up the station's transmitter." Since 1997, the Manca Naziunale has been the leftist organization dedicated to Corsican separatism. On its internet site, the Manca Naziunale declares: "Since the month of November 1997, patriots of the left decided to enter into a free, public, and plural process. A Manca Naziunale defines itself as a political guidance of the Left which fight[s] for the right of self-determination for Corsican People."

Two other Corsican political parties exist, the Corse Nouvelle (New Corsica) and Corsica Nazione (Corsican Nation). Corse Nouvelle states its position, in keeping with traditional Corsican emphasis, "we will always be faithful to our beliefs" for Corsican identity, yet it also states that it holds to "the close interrelationship of cultures, Corsican and French."

From 2000 to 2002, violence struck Corsica again, leading to the assassination of the governing French prefect. According to the *International Herald Tribune*, "for French governments, Corsica is a political issue that, like hot tar, sticks unpleasantly to anyone who dares touch it."

SEE ALSO

Volume 1 Left: France; French Revolution.
Volume 2 Right: France.

BIBLIOGRAPHY

Roger Falligot and Pascal Krop, *La Piscine: The French Secret Service since 1944*, W.D. Halls, trans. (Blackwell, 1989); Joseph Fitchett, "The Corsican Conundrum Ensnares French Politics Anew," *International Herald Tribune* (undated); Emil Ludwig, *Napoleon* (Pocket Books, 1961); "A Manca Naziunale," www.manca-naziunale.org (May 2004); "Pasquale Paoli, Father of the Corsican Nation," www.pasqualepaoli.com (May 2004); "Autonomist and Pro-Independence Political Parties," www.eurominority.org (May 2004); "Présentation du mouvement Corse Nouvelle," www.corsenouvelle.free.fr (May 2004).

JOHN F. MURPHY, JR.
AMERICAN MILITARY UNIVERSITY

Coughlin, Charles E. (1891–1979)

FATHER COUGHLIN was a Canadian-born Catholic priest noted as founder of the million-member National Union for Social Justice (Union Party), but more known for his weekly radio sermons from Birmingham, Michigan, that drew an audience of around 30 to 40 million. Those 40 million listeners were approximately one-third of Americans. Coughlin was one of the first to realize the potential of radio, and his message of sympathy for the distressed person, dislike for exploitive big business, and indifferent big government resonated with millions of listeners.

Coughlin was a natural public speaker, almost mesmerizing. With strong encouragement from his mother, he entered the priesthood in Toronto, Canada, in 1916. His first work was as professor at Assumption College, Windsor, Ontario. His ability to manipulate through words was such that he convinced his students to build him a house. He left Assumption in 1923 because the Basilican order required a vow of poverty. He became assistant pastor at St. Leo's Cathedral, Detroit, Michigan, and quickly became popular for his powerful fundamentalist sermons. He attracted the attention of Michael Gallagher, bishop of Detroit, who in 1926 made Coughlin head pastor of a small church in Royal Oak, a suburb of Detroit. The church, The Shrine of the Little Flower, had problems with the anti-Catholicism of the local Ku Klux Klan (KKK), whose fiery cross partially burned the church. It was also a poor parish in need of more money. Coughlin began broadcasting over the radio to bring the church money and to neutralize the KKK. Beginning on October 17, 1926, he preached on the Columbia Broadcasting System through the 1930s until the church silenced him in 1942. His voice was warm, emotional, almost ingratiating, and a natural attraction for millions.

Coughlin originally broadcast sermons and talks with children. He soon began expressing his political beliefs. After the stock market collapsed in 1929, he began calling for religion and leadership to get America through the crisis. His popularity continued growing, and in 1930, CBS began broadcasting his sermons nationwide. Coughlin established the Radio League of the Little Flower. A year later, he averaged 80,000 letters received each week. Many included money. Coughlin had the means to finance the improvement of his parish. More important, he had the funds to spread his political views.

Initially, Coughlin blamed the economic hard times on Herbert Hoover, president during the collapse.

Coughlin supported the presidential candidacy of Franklin D. Roosevelt in 1932. He campaigned for the Democrat on his broadcasts with slogans such as "Roosevelt or Ruin." Coughlin wanted a position in the Roosevelt administration, but he received nothing. He continued to speak against the evils of capitalism. His radio league continued to grow. One New York radio station poll in 1933 found 55 percent of those polled agreed that he was the most useful American other than the president.

Coughlin initially thought that Roosevelt was as radical a reformer as he was. Roosevelt's rhetoric about chasing the money changers from the temple resonated well with Coughlin's populist monetary reforms. When Roosevelt lost interest in reform, Coughlin felt betrayed and double-crossed by Roosevelt.

Coughlin established the National Union for Social Justice on November 11, 1934. The union advocated for private property, the Roosevelt administration (if it could be made to move faster on monetary reform), and easier money policy based on the silver standard. Roosevelt rejected the idea and arranged for publication of an article listing the largest holders of silver in the United States. Among the largest owners of silver were Father Charles Coughlin and the National Union for Social Justice.

Coughlin became disenchanted with the slow pace of New Deal reform, and he declared it to be a communist conspiracy. He began associating more closely with right-wing organizations, and his anti-Semitism became more pronounced. His radio talks became attacks on Roosevelt's policies and personal behavior.

Coughlin's National Union for Social Justice, as the Union Party, ran its own presidential candidate against Roosevelt in 1936. Congressman William Lemke of North Dakota received no electoral votes, although Coughlin spoke viciously of Roosevelt and the New Deal. Coughlin had rashly promised to give up broadcasting and campaigning if his man received fewer than 9 million votes. Because Lemke received just over 900,000, Coughlin retired from broadcasting, but only until 1937.

On his return, he was even harsher in his criticism. He persisted in calling the New Deal a communist conspiracy, and his sermons became more conspicuously anti-Semitic. After Kristallnacht, the Nazi-led anti-Semitic riot in Germany in 1938, his broadcast was so anti-Semitic that one radio station refused to carry his next one. The Nazis railed at Coughlin's censorship. Coughlin's publications included the anti-Roosevelt, anti-Semitic *Social Justice*, which also propagandized about an alleged government conspiracy. He also published a version of the *Protocols of the Elders of Zion*, the classic anti-Semitic forgery.

Coughlin's popularity faded quickly once the U.S. entry into World War II ended any American sympathy for the Axis or fascism. The Federal Bureau of Investigation wanted him off the air and his publications out of the mails, but his right to free speech was protected by the First Amendment. After a 1942 grand jury indictment for violating the Espionage Act, Coughlin lost his second-class mailing privilege, a mortal blow to mail solicitations and, thus, to fundraising. The bishop told Coughlin to leave the air, and he returned to the Little Flower congregation, serving as pastor until his retirement in 1966.

Coughlin wanted the silver standard, the end of private banking, and the establishment of a central bank to control prices. More money, to his thinking, would spread the wealth. He was on the side of the little people. There is a lot of the old populism in Coughlin's monetary thinking. Unfortunately, his legacy lives, if at all, in the efforts of extreme right-wing groups today, which make him an elder statesman of their racist movements.

SEE ALSO

Volume 1 Left: Lippmann, Walter; Media Bias, Left; Roosevelt, Franklin D.
Volume 2 Right: Limbaugh, Rush; Media Bias, Right.

BIBLIOGRAPHY

David H. Bennett, *Demagogues in the Depression: American Radicals and the Union Party* (Rutgers University Press, 1969); Alan Brinkley, *Voices of Protest: Huey Long, Father Coughlin, and the Great Depression* (Knopf, 1982); PBS *American Experience,* "Reverend Charles E. Coughlin," www.pbs.org (March 2004); Social Security Administration, "History: Father Charles E. Coughlin," www.ssa.gov/history (March 2004); Donald and David Warren, *Radio Priest* (Free Press, 1996).

JOHN BARNHILL, PH.D.
INDEPENDENT SCHOLAR

Coulter, Ann H. (1961–)

IN THE LATE 1990s, lawyer and author Ann Coulter established herself as one of the most aggressive conservative commentators in America. While other columnists prefer to moderate their criticisms for a politically correct age, Coulter wrote with an instinct for the jugular and the will to employ that instinct. Indeed, Coulter stands apart even from other staunch conservatives, such as Sean Hannity, in the unmitigated ferocity with which she carves into her opponents.

Born in Connecticut, Coulter attended Cornell University and later earned a J.D. degree from the University of Michigan. Coulter enjoyed a prestigious early legal career, serving as an editor of the University of Michigan law review and clerking for Eighth Circuit U.S. Court of Appeals Judge Pasco Bowman II, before entering the Department of Justice Honors Program. She later practiced law in New York City, and worked for the Senate Judiciary Committee, and for the Center For Individual Rights. During the Bill Clinton scandals involving extramarital affairs, Coulter performed pro bono work for the sexual harassment suit Paula Jones brought against Clinton.

Beginning in the late 1990s, Coulter began to establish herself as a television commentator and she appeared on a variety of television shows, including *Hannity and Colmes* and *Politically Incorrect*. She briefly wrote for the conservative *National Review* magazine, but left shortly after the September 11, 2001, terrorist attacks. In response to those attacks, she wrote a column arguing that the United States should invade Middle Eastern countries and convert their populations to Christianity, an idea that was not well received in many quarters.

Her first book, *High Crimes and Misdemeanors*, argued in favor of the impeachment and conviction of Clinton and offered a brief history of impeachment and historical examples of high crimes and misdemeanors. Coulter forcefully argued that "high crimes and misdemeanors" need not refer strictly to criminal acts, but that they could also refer to personal misbehavior. According to Coulter, Clinton's sexual relationship with an intern in the Oval Office, and then lying to cover up the offense, more than qualified as grounds for impeachment.

Her first book became a *New York Times* bestseller, as did her second book, *Slander*. In that book, Coulter introduced quotation after quotation of shrill and extreme liberal rhetoric. She also included a several-page-long list of people in the news media with extensive Democratic political ties, along with another list showing instance after instance of conservative books being described as "surprise bestsellers." One of the strengths of the book is Coulter's repeated demonstra-

tion of a liberal preference for engaging in ad hominem attacks on its conservative opponents, rather than actually arguing with them.

Coulter's third book, and third bestseller, *Treason*, argued that liberals have consistently supported enemies of America over the last 50 years. She included a spirited defense of Senator Joseph McCarthy (known for McCarthyism, strident anti-communism) and describes in precise detail the support for communism from the American left. She also cited numerous examples of liberal attempts to invoke the Vietnam War at every opportunity, a comparison that has continued with numbing regularity throughout America's War on Terro and Iraq War.

By arguing that big-government, statist liberals are the enemy of America's heritage of liberty, Coulter continues the work of a long line of conservative writers that traces at least as far back as F.A. Hayek's *The Road to Serfdom*. Coulter excels at the task of filleting her opponents by quoting their own words to demonstrate the ridiculousness of their ideas. In *Treason*, as in almost all of her writings Coulter lays out an aggressive case that liberalism undermines all aspects of American life and American values.

SEE ALSO

Volume 1 Left: Carville, James; Liberalism; United States; Media Bias, Left.
Volume 2 Right: Conservatism; McCarthyism; Media Bias, Right.

BIBLIOGRAPHY

Ann H. Coulter, *High Crimes and Misdemeanors: The Case against Bill Clinton* (Regnery Publishing, 1998); Ann H. Coulter, *Slander: Liberal Lies About the American Right* (Crown, 2002); Ann H. Coulter, *Treason: Liberal Treachery from the Cold War to the War on Terrorism* (Crown, 2003); Ann Coulter, www.anncoulter.org (April 2004).

MITCHELL MCNAYLOR
OUR LADY OF THE LAKE COLLEGE

Courts and Law

THE COURTS AND THE LAW together are integral parts of a complex system that regulates the lives of all people in a structured and organized society. Laws may be natural, which means that they are an inherent part of human nature. Natural laws are the foundation upon which acceptable human behavior in a society is based. Man-made laws, the jurisprudence of a society, encompass all the rules, regulations, and procedures that are written down, and they may certainly be derived from natural law. Jurisprudence also includes the history of legal decisions and precedents that structure subsequent legal decisions.

The court system is a component part of the legal system. Simply put, legislators write the laws, bureaucrats implement laws, the police enforce the laws, and the courts interpret the laws. All of these components of the legal system need to work in concert; of course, with so many different roles and multiple actors involved, this is a system that necessarily leads to disagreement, misinterpretation, and confusion. However, this is also a system that permits the members of society who are bound by the laws to have many avenues of input into the system. Also, changes in society's attitudes and new ideas can be introduced into this complicated, fragmented, and flexible system.

The United States is a federal system, which means that there is both a national government and a series of state governments. This further means that each level of government makes laws within its area of jurisdiction, and there necessarily needs to be a court system at each level to interpret these laws and deal with any conflicts that might arise. So in the United States, there are, in effect, two court systems, a national court system (called the federal court system) and a state court system. But it gets a bit more complicated, because each state may determine its own court structure, so there is variation among the state systems. Also, there is interaction between the court systems.

STATE COURT SYSTEM

Each state decides the structure of its courts as well as the method of judicial appointment. The court system is hierarchical: there are lower courts (referred to as minor trial courts), where cases originate, and then a case may be appealed to a higher court (first, a major trial court, then sometimes also an intermediate appellate court, and finally the state's highest court). The grounds for appeal also vary by state and according to the crimes or issues involved in the case. In some states, the highest court is called the court of appeal; in other states, there is a state supreme court. Ultimately, a case may be appealed to the country's highest court, the U.S. Supreme Court, but only if the case meets the requirement for appeal to the Supreme Court, that is, if the

case involves claims arising under federal law, which includes the Constitution.

Although there are five primary methods of judicial selection, each state has its own unique variation, and sometimes a state uses different selection methods for different levels of state court. It has been stated that there is perhaps no other office in the United States that offers such diversity in selection. Virginia is the only state that currently uses legislative appointment, whereby the state legislature has the sole appointment power. This used to be more widely used, but now executive appointment is a more common variant, whereby the state governor has sole appointment power. Some states require that the governor's appointment be confirmed by the legislature. The most common method requires that a judicial hopeful be elected. The election may be partisan or nonpartisan. In a partisan election, the judicial candidate usually runs in a party primary to gain nomination and then runs again in a general election where his or her party affiliation is listed on the ballot. In a nonpartisan election, there would be no party primary and the ballot at the general election would not have any party affiliation listed.

Last, there is the merit plan of selection (also called the Missouri Plan, as Missouri was the first state to institute this method, in 1940). This is a hybrid method. Typically, the governor nominates a judge for a short term of office. Then, in a "retention election," the voters are simply asked whether the judge should retain his or her office. If the people decide not to retain the judge, the process starts again with a gubernatorial nomination.

There is a "federal court myth" that holds that the federal court system is the most significant part of the American judicial system. However, state courts handle approximately 95 percent of all the legal cases that arise, and this belies the impact of the federal court system.

FEDERAL COURT SYSTEM

The jurisdictional limits of the federal court system are set by the Constitution (Article III) and Congress. Like the state court system, the federal court system is also hierarchical. At the base of the structure are the federal district courts, and there are currently 94 federal district courts in the United States. Each state has one to four federal district courts, and the District of Columbia, Puerto Rico, the territories of the Virgin Islands, Guam, and the Northern Mariana Islands also each have a district court. The district courts are the courts of original jurisdiction (the first court to hear a case) for the federal court system, except for cases that are heard in specialized federal courts.

The specialized courts include the Court of Appeals for Veterans' Claims, the Court of Appeals for the Armed Forces, the Tax Court, the Court of Federal Claims, and the Court of International Trade. The Court of Appeals for Veterans' Claims, for example, is composed of seven judges who are appointed for 15-year terms by the president, and these appointments are confirmed by the Senate. This court may review final decisions of the Board of Veterans' Affairs (although it is not connected to the BVA). Most of the cases the court hears concern the entitlement to and/or amount of disability or survivor benefits. There are 12 Courts of Appeal that hear appeals from the District Courts. The District Courts are assigned a "circuit," and courts from each circuit may appeal to their assigned Court of Appeal. For example, the Second Circuit includes the various District Courts in Connecticut, New York, and Vermont, and appeals from the District Courts in these states go to the Court of Appeal for the Second Circuit. The top of the federal court hierarchy is the Supreme Court. The Supreme Court has appellate jurisdiction over appeals from the 12 Courts of Appeal and the justices of the Supreme Court are assigned at least one circuit to oversee. The Supreme Court also has original jurisdiction over specific cases specified in the Constitution (this means these special cases may be brought directly to the Supreme Court, bypassing the previously explained hierarchical structure of the federal court system). These cases involve matters where a state is a party to the matter or an ambassador is involved. (This is not a frequent occurrence; in fact, there have been fewer than 200 cases of original jurisdiction brought before the justices in the Supreme Court's history.)

JUDICIAL INDEPENDENCE

The Constitution recognizes the need for a Supreme Court and puts its creation and existence in the hands of Congress. Article III, section 1 of the Constitution guarantees the principle of judicial indepen-dence: federal court judges are to be appointed, not elected, and they hold office for life (or more accurately, as long as they show "good behavior"; federal judges may be impeached if they commit crimes or accept bribes, but they are protected from removal just because the decisions they may make are unpopular). Further, federal judges are protected from Congress reducing their pay (the Founding Fathers anticipated that one branch of

government, Congress, might be tempted to interfere with the independence of federal judges by threatening their compensation).

There is also an "upper-court myth" that concerns the belief that the lower courts are guided strictly by decisions coming from the Supreme Court. Although the Supreme Court is the highest court in the land, it possesses considerable discretion in the cases it selects. There are more than 7,000 applications made to the Supreme Court every term, yet the court hears oral argument and releases its written opinion in fewer than 100 cases per term. This allows members of the Supreme Court considerable leeway in selecting a case with issues that attract the court, and in selecting cases with narrow facts (this means that the court is not interested in settling every conceivable aspect of an issue, but instead deals with an issue incrementally).

Further, Supreme Court decisions may be misunderstood, the facts of a case may be different from subsequent cases, and Supreme Court decisions are very broad in scope, leaving room for creativity on the part of trial judges. Thus, it is difficult for lower courts to be strictly guided by decisions from the Supreme Court.

The various courts and the laws the courts interpret are part of an amazingly complex and vibrant system that impacts all aspects of life in America. New court decisions, at all levels of court, are made every day. The ability to negotiate through this system, the internal procedures of this system, the decisions that courts reach, as well as questions of justice and fairness—all indicate the constant scrutiny this system endures. And yet the system does endure.

Courts and law in the United States are concepts associated with the right or conservatism. Though both the left and the right use the courts and law to effect change in American society, it is mainly the right that holds to judicial and legislative authority. Often, the left may disregard the concepts of courts and law in favor of more radical action to seek change.

SEE ALSO

Volume 1 Left: Supreme Court; United States; Liberalism; Constitutional Amendments.
Volume 2 Right: United States; Conservatism.

BIBLIOGRAPHY

U.S. Courts, www.uscourts.gov (May 2004); U.S. Supreme Court, www.supremecourtus.gov (May 2004); Lawrence Baum, *The Supreme Court* (Congressional Quarterly, 1995); John B. Gates and Charles A. Johnson, *The American Courts: A Critical Assessment* (Congressional Quarterly Press, 1991);

Thomas G. Walker and Lee Epstein, *The Supreme Court of the United States: An Introduction* (St. Martin's Press, 1993).

AMANDA BURGESS
WAYNE STATE UNIVERSITY

Czech Republic

THE LANDS THAT became the Czech Republic in 1993 were part of communist Czechoslovakia from 1948 to the collapse of totalitarianism in 1989. During that period all right-wing political activity was persecuted. During the 1950s, political opponents of the regime were killed and imprisoned. But the late communism of the 1970s and 1980s suppressed dissident initiatives more mildly. Dissidents lost their jobs and their children were barred from higher education. Some came under pressure to become informants or emigrate. But only a few were jailed for considerable periods of time. In that environment, the dissident human rights movement of Charter 77 came into being as a coalition of anti-communists from Hapsburg monarchists on the right to reform communists on the left.

The philosopher Jan Patocka, who was one of the first three spokespersons of the Charter 77 movement and died following a police interrogation in 1977, was particularly influential in dissident circles. Under the influence of his teacher, the phenomenologist Edmund Husserl, Patocka blamed the decline and self-destruction of Europe on the scientific-instrumental concept of politics, devoid of values and meaning. Following Martin Heidegger, he considered modern society to be alienating human beings from their essence. He considered sacrifice and the solidarity of those ready to sacrifice themselves (dissidents) as ways to overcome alienation and materialism. Vaclav Havel applied this philosophy to analyze communism as a form of alienation. Other right-wing dissidents were influenced by Catholicism or Hussite-Protestant theology and the natural law tradition.

Economists, who were neither dissidents nor communists at the Institute for Economic Prognostication of the Academy of Science in Prague, were in a privileged position in the communist system by having access to literature in "capitalist" economics. This group of economists, including Vaclav Klaus, was influenced in particular by free-market economists like Ludwig von Mises, Friedrich von Hayek, and Milton Friedman.

In November 1989, student demonstrations that won popular support brought down communism. Civic Forum, an umbrella movement led by Havel that included all anti-communists, replaced the communists. Civic Forum was an uneasy coalition between former dissidents, intellectuals, and professionals mostly from Prague who were concerned with human authenticity, ethics, and values, and others who were more concerned with economic reforms and personal advantages for themselves and their supporters. This tension dominated Czech right-wing politics.

Initially, the former Charter 77 dissidents led Civic Forum and the Czech half of Czechoslovakia. Playwright and philosopher Havel became president, and historian Petr Pithart (who translated Roger Scruton's book on conservatism) was prime minister. Of the economists, only Vaclav Klaus served in the Czech cabinet as minister of finance. In 1991, Klaus and his supporters advocated liberalization of price controls and reduction in subsidies. This led to the division of Civic Forum and the founding of two right-wing parties, the Civic Democratic Party, led by Klaus, and the Civic Democratic Alliance, led by another economist, Vladimir Dlouhy. The nonpolitical dissidents formed the Civic movement led by Pithart, Jiri Dienstbier, and Martin Palous (a follower of Eric Voegelin).

The 1992 elections resulted in a right-wing victory in the Czech lands. New Prime Minister Klaus formed a coalition with the Civic Democratic Alliance and the more centrist Christian Democrats that ruled the Czech Republic until 1997. Since the Slovak part of Czechoslovakia elected a nationalist government, tensions between the two halves of Czechoslovakia were resolved by the division of Czechoslovakia into independent Czech and Slovak Republics.

After the "Velvet Divorce," the Klaus government continued its policy of coupon privatization, the distribution of coupons to all adults that can be used only to buy shares in privatized industries. Coupon privatization was advertised as a method for privatization when ordinary citizens have no capital. It was politically wise because it made the Czechs a nation of shareholders with a small stake in capitalism; it prevented international corporations and foreign individuals from visibly owning Czech firms that would have been unpopular in the xenophobic culture that communist isolationism encouraged, while preventing the former communist elite with stolen funds from grabbing all legally. Additionally, some small businesses, shops, and houses were restored to their precommunist owners or purchased by their tenants. The government continued to own strategic properties, the banks, the insurance monopoly, and utilities.

Though small privatization was on the whole successful, coupon privatization proved an unmitigated disaster. Since it distributed ownership in society without a legal framework by which owners may control management, the "red" managers stole the properties they were entrusted to manage by stripping their assets, selling their products to family and friends. The government reacted by concentrating ownership through buying back the coupons through its banks that created privatization funds for this purpose. This led to even greater corruption when management continued to steal but spread their gains by bribing bankers, bureaucrats, and politicians for receiving more and more "loans" from the banks to cover mismanagement and theft. Despite the government's free-market rhetoric, industry was not restructured or privatized. The Czech Republic had the lowest employment in Europe and the economy collapsed.

President Havel and the former dissidents who were quite passive and weak during the mid-1990s were emboldened to bring down the government. For a few months, Havel managed to use the political stalemate to gain power, but after the 1998 elections, Klaus preferred to bring the Social Democrats, his ideological rivals, into power rather than go back into coalition with his ideological allies and political rivals from the Freedom Union Party. He made the smaller right-wing parties and President Havel politically irrelevant, ensured im-

munity from prosecution for his corrupt party leaders, and left a Social Democratic government in a situation where it was forced to undertake unpopular reforms.

The Social Democrats gradually privatized the banks and allowed some of the inefficient industries to collapse, leading to unemployment. Nevertheless, the Social Democrats won a second term in 2002, this time in coalition with four right-wing parties. They concluded the negotiations over accession to the European Union. Meanwhile, Klaus's rhetoric has become increasingly nationalistic and even xenophobic. He succeeded in replacing Havel as Czech president in 2003 by cutting a deal with the Communist Party. As ideological and personal feuds within the smaller right-wing parties multiplied, the Civic Democratic Party is the only surviving ideologically right-wing party.

SEE ALSO

Volume 1 Left: Czech Republic; Socialism; Communism.
Volume 2 Right: Capitalism; Laissez-Faire.

BIBLIOGRAPHY

Rick Fawn, *Czech Republic: A Nation of Velvet* (Harwood, 2000); Robin E.H. Shepherd, *Czechoslovakia: The Velvet Revolution and Beyond* (Palgrave, 2000); Aviezer Tucker, *The Philosophy and Politics of Czech Dissidence from Patocka to Havel* (Pittsburgh University Press, 2000).

AVIEZER TUCKER
AUSTRALIAN NATIONAL UNIVERSITY

The Right

D

Darwinism

CHARLES DARWIN (1809–1882) laid the foundation of a theory that sheds light on the "problem of adaptation" in the animals and plants by means of "natural selection." Tooby and Leda Cosmides have elaborated on Darwin's initial thought, which led to the whole new perspective, known as Darwinism, that extends Darwin's biological hypothesis to explain social behavior. Thus, a biological theory, which came into prominence by providing explanation of the human anatomical features and basic survival behaviors, became equally useful for understanding social behaviors as well. This innovation led to a new term, *social Darwinism*, which was coined in the late 19th century to describe the idea that humans, like animals and plants, compete in a struggle for existence in which natural selection results in survival of the fittest. Based on Darwin's basic hypothesis of adaptation in the species, social scientists established the modern version of evolutionary theory, which attempts to extend Darwin's logic and tries to analyze mental mechanisms that help us filter information from our environment and translate that into human behavior. However, the ability of evolutionary theory to explain and predict the complex of behaviors of everyday life and politics has been questioned.

However, some social Darwinists started to argue that governments should not interfere with human

Charles Darwin's "survival of the fittest" evolutionary theories were applied to politics with the advent of Darwinism.

competition by attempting to regulate the economy or cure social ills such as poverty. Instead, they advocate a *laissez-faire* political and economic system that favors competition and self-interest in social and business affairs. Social Darwinists typically deny that they advocate a "law of the jungle." But most propose arguments that justify imbalances of power among individuals, races, and nations because they consider some people more fit to survive than others.

Thus, the term *social Darwinist* is applied loosely to anyone who interprets human society primarily in terms of biology, struggle, competition, or natural law. Social Darwinism characterizes a variety of past and present social policies and theories, from attempts to reduce the power of government to theories exploring the biological causes of human behavior. Many people believe that the concept of social Darwinism explains the philosophical rationalization behind racism, imperialism, and capitalism. The term has negative implications for most people because they consider it a rejection of compassion and social responsibility.

DEVELOPMENT OF SOCIAL DARWINISM

Social Darwinism originated in Britain during the second half of the 19th century. Darwin did not address human evolution in his most famous study, *On the Origin of Species* (1859), which focused on the evolution of plants and animals. In his other book *The Descent of Man* (1871), Darwin directed his theory explicitly to the single species *homo sapiens*. Much of the book is devoted to developing the evolutionary significance of sexual selection—that is, the preferential choice of reproductive partner. Apart from that, the argument follows two main lines. The first is physical: The immediate evolutionary forebears of mankind are unknown. Darwin never represented man as deriving from apes. He did establish that man must in all probability be descendant from species that are classified among primates, and further that man and the higher apes resemble each other anatomically more closely than the latter resemble the lower primates.

The second line of argument is behavioristic. It maintains that intellectual and social faculties are themselves adaptive and in their variations make for the greater or lesser survival of the creatures that possess them. Other species besides man subsist with the aid of rudimentary or developed forms of social organization and communication, and Darwin could see only differences of degree between these and the characteristics of human community and moral awareness.

The last of Darwin's expressly evolutionary treatises carries behavioristic comparisons even further. Probably *The Expression of the Emotions in Men and Animals* (1872) is the most dated of Darwin's writings. Nevertheless, in comparing phenomena like the physi-

cal manifestation of hostility in dog and master—the similarity of the snarling jaw to the drawn lips—and many other states of temper, Darwin did carry biology into treatment of faculties traditionally reserved for moral studies.

The application of Darwin's theory of natural selection specifically to human behavior was interpreted as justifying cruel social policies at home and imperialism abroad. The Englishman most associated with early social Darwinism, however, was sociologist Herbert Spencer, a social philosopher, often regarded as one of the first sociologists. Spencer coined the phrase "survival of the fittest" to describe the outcome of competition between social groups. In *Social Statics* (1850) and other works, Spencer argued that through competition, social evolution would automatically produce prosperity and personal liberty unparalleled in human history.

In the United States, Spencer gained considerable support among intellectuals and some businessmen, including steel manufacturer Andrew Carnegie, who served as Spencer's host during his visit to the United States in 1883. The most prominent American social Darwinist of the 1880s was William Graham Sumner, who on several occasions told audiences that there was no alternative to the "survival of the fittest" theory. Critics of social Darwinism seized on these comments to argue that a "dog-eat-dog" philosophy of human behavior that justified oppressive social and political policies cannot be rationalized by the hypothesis of "natural selection."

HEREDITARIANISM

Studies of heredity contributed another variety of social Darwinism in the late 19th century. In *Hereditary Genius* (1869), Sir Francis Galton, a British scientist and Darwin's cousin, argued that biological inheritance is far more important than environment in determining character and intelligence. This theory, known as hereditarianism, met considerable resistance, especially in the United States. Sociologists and biologists who criticized hereditarianism believed that changes in the environment could produce physical changes in the individual that would be passed on to future generations, a theory proposed by French biologist Jean-Baptiste Lamarck in the early 19th century. After 1890, hereditarianism gained increasing support, due in part to the work of German biologist August Weismann. Weismann reemphasized the role of natural selection by arguing that a person's characteristics are determined genetically at conception.

THE STRUGGLE SCHOOL

Toward the end of the 19th century, another strain of social Darwinism was developed by supporters of the struggle school of sociology. English journalist Walter Bagehot expressed the fundamental ideas of the struggle school in *Physics and Politics* (1872), a book that describes the historical evolution of social groups into nations.

Bagehot argued that these nations evolved principally by succeeding in conflicts with other groups. For many political scientists, sociologists, and military strategists, this strain of social Darwinism justified overseas expansion by nations during the 1890s. In the United States, historian John Fiske and naval strategist Alfred Thayer Mahan drew from the principles of social Darwinism to advocate foreign expansion and the creation of a strong military.

REFORM DARWINISM

After 1890, social reformers used Darwinism to advocate a stronger role for government and the introduction of various social policies. This movement became known as reform Darwinism. Reform Darwinists argued that human beings need new ideas and institutions as they adapt to changing conditions. For example, U.S. Supreme Court Justice Oliver Wendell Holmes, Jr., reasoned that the Constitution of the United States should be reinterpreted in light of changing circumstances as American society progressed through the decades.

Some reformers used the principles of evolution to justify sexist and racist ideas that undercut their professed belief in equality. For example, the most extreme type of reform Darwinism was eugenics, a term coined by Sir Francis Galton in 1883 from the Greek word *eugenav*, meaning "well-born." Eugenists claimed that particular racial or social groups—usually wealthy Anglo-Saxons—were "naturally" superior to other groups. They proposed to control human heredity by passing laws that forbid marriage between races or that restrict breeding for various social "misfits" such as criminals or the mentally ill.

SOCIAL DARWINISM IN THE 20th CENTURY

Although social Darwinism was highly influential at the beginning of the 20th century, it rapidly lost popularity and support after World War I. During the 1920s and 1930s, many political observers blamed it for contribut-ing to German militarism and the rise of Nazism. During this same period, advances in anthropology also discredited social Darwinism. German American anthropologist Franz Boas and American anthropologists Margaret Mead and Ruth Benedict showed that human culture sets people apart from animals. By shifting the emphasis away from biology and onto culture, these anthropologists undermined social Darwinism's biological foundations. Eugenics was discredited by a better understanding of genetics and eventually disgraced by Nazi dictator Adolf Hitler's use of eugenic arguments to create a "master race." During World War II, the Nazis killed several million Jews, Roma (Gypsies), and members of other groups, believing them inferior to an idealized Aryan race.

Social theories based on biology gained renewed support after 1953, when American biologist James Watson and British biologist Francis Crick successfully described the structure of the DNA molecule, the building block of all life. During the 1960s, anthropologists interested in the influence of DNA on human behavior produced studies of the biological basis of aggression, territoriality, mate selection, and other behavior common to people and animals. Books on this theme, such as Desmond Morris's *Naked Ape* (1967) and Lionel Tiger's *Men in Groups* (1969), became bestsellers. In the early 1970s, American psychologist Richard J. Herrnstein revived the social Darwinist argument that intelligence is mostly determined by biology rather than by environmental influences.

During the 1960s, British biologist W.D. Hamilton and American biologist Robert L. Trivers produced separate studies showing that the self-sacrificing behavior of some members of a group serves the genetic well-being of the group as a whole. American biologist Edward O. Wilson drew on these theories in *Sociobiology: The New Synthesis* (1975), where he argued that genetics exerts a greater influence on human behavior than scientists had previously believed.

Wilson claimed that human behavior couldn't be understood without taking both biology and culture into account. Wilson's views became the foundations of a new science—sociobiology—and were later popularized in such studies as Richard Dawkins's *The Selfish Gene* (1976). Wilson's critics have alleged that sociobiology is simply another version of social Darwinism. They claim that it downplays the role of culture in human societies and justifies poverty and warfare in the name of natural selection. Such criticism has led to a decline in the influence of sociobiology and other forms of social Darwinism.

SEE ALSO
Volume 1 Left: Socialism; Liberalism.
Volume 2 Right: Capitalism; *Laissez Faire*; Conservatism.

BIBLIOGRAPHY
C. Darwin, *On the Origin of Species* (Harvard University Press, 1964 reprint); C. Darwin, *The Descent of Man and the Selection in Relation to Sex* (Appleton, 1930); Francis Galton, *Hereditary Genius: An Inquiry into Its Laws and Consequences* (Macmillan, 1892 reprint); Walter Bagehot, *Physics and Politics* (Batoche Books, 2001 reprint); Edward O. Wilson, *Sociobiology: The New Synthesis* (Harvard University Press, 1975); Richard Dawkins, *The Selfish Gene* (Oxford University Press, 1989); Herbert Spencer, *Social Statics: or, The Conditions Essential to Happiness Specified, and the First of Them Developed* (John Chapman, 1851).

JITENDRA UTTAM
JAWAHARLAL NEHRU UNIVERSITY, INDIA

Despotism

DESPOTISM CONNOTES autocracy, the absolute rule of one or a select group and exercise of power without imposed limits. The word is closely associated with a host of other concepts, including tyranny, domination, absolutism, dictatorship, oppression, and servitude. In politics, it refers to a specific model of governance regarding the ability to make others do what one wants them to do despite their possible opposition.

Despots come into a position of power in a number of different ways: seizing power through inheritance (the cases of Roman Emperors Caligula and Nero), through military means and then legitimizing their position once in power ex post facto (the case of Roman Emperor Augustus), and through revolution and bloodshed (Josef Stalin following after Vladimir Lenin in the new Soviet Union), through bids for power supported by the religious or other key establishments in the society (Alexander the Great of ancient Macedonia). It should be kept in mind that despotism was not always regarded as a dangerous political practice. Its dubious heritage is related to the fact that the word *demokratia* did not even exist before the 5th century.

Furthermore, the ambiguities around the meaning of the word *tyrant* were part and parcel of ancient Greek politics. In effect, tyranny practically meant a transitional government in the Greek *polis* that emerged in times of crisis, one that served to weaken an overbearing and exclusivist aristocratic government, one that can manage rapid economic change and enlarge the range of citizenship. According to Aristotle, for instance, tyrants were commonly champions of the many and the poor against the few and the rich. They were thus seen as the engines of transformation that initiated a shift from oligarchy to democracy. It is only later in history that tyranny and despotism began to be associated with evil and cruelty guarded by a narrow, unchecked, and more often than not class-based rule. Still, the ancient tyrants themselves also had class ties: many of them had aristocratic origins and sought after further fame, fortune, and power. Their main difference perhaps was that they wanted to weaken the rule of older, more traditional aristocracy. In other words, ancient forms of tyranny had a lot to do with internal class feuds within the aristocracy, although the tyrants opted for populism while the settled aristocrats tended to favor elitism. This characteristic was generally maintained by later instances of despotism in history.

Plato's tyrant is, by definition, a person governed solely by desire and hence totally out of balance, as he or she is indifferent to both reason and honor. Whereas the philosopher-ruler purposes rationality and prioritizes justice and well-being of the society, the tyrant is portrayed as someone chasing after narrowly defined satisfaction and as enslaved by pleasure. This characterization of tyranny is also present in the writings of Aristotle, Tacitus, and later Machiavelli. Neither Plato nor Aristotle defined despotism as the opposite of freedom. Their problems with despotism or a particular despot were related more to the issues of virtue, excellence, and justice.

Similarly, Charles de Montesquieu described despotism as part and parcel of the rule of French monarchs, that is, an integral part of the political system. It was only in the 19th century that despotism assumed a decidedly negative face. In particular, founding fathers of sociology were deeply troubled by what they identified as new forms of tyranny, despotism, and what they perceived as the iron hand of the burgeoning modern life, the city, bureaucracy, and technology. Alexis de Tocqueville, for instance, was worried about the invisible tyranny of modern life in society without the existence of an identifiable tyrant to blame. Others, on the other hand, were warning against the mechanisms of bureaucracy as an internalized system with which citizens tyrannize themselves.

The common ground among all these differing definitions is that the despot does not have to answer to anyone, and does not seem to have a moral compass that can legitimize this ultimate exercise of power. A derivation of this simplified formula for despotism is that it is a model of governance composed of unwilling subjects and run according to arbitrary rules. Hence, in observing a despotic system, there is marked concern about the well-being of the polity at large, as well as rulers' lack of consideration for general interest and absence of mechanisms of control over the actions of the government.

These concerns, in turn, are expected to be taken care of via democratic rule. In summary, although despotism may meet at least some of the basic physical needs of a society, from Plato to Hannah Arendt there is consensus among political thinkers that it is the least conducive form of human governance to fulfill what may be called higher human needs. Despotism forces the political aspirations of human nature to be shunned, to be kept away from the public realm by way of silencing opposition and refusing to provide a platform of interaction between the rulers and the ruled. As citizens are eliminated from the public sphere and as their active participation in politics is curtailed via mechanisms of fear and violence, city halls, streets, parks, theatres, and public auditoriums are isolated and forced to remain quiet.

Surrounded by a loyal army, police force, militia, secret police, spies, and informers, from ancient times onward, despots needed protection from their own people to sustain their rule. Interestingly, this need for protection from one's own also constitutes the very factor that makes despotism a highly fragile political model that can only be maintained for a limited period of time and at great cost.

Although despots have been found on both the right and left ends of the political spectrum, right-wing despots have tended to justify their hold on power by claiming to protect a nation from foreign domination or from disloyal groups within, while left-wing despots justify their rule on the grounds that they alone can implement the doctrine of the revolution or revolutionary party with which they associate themselves.

SEE ALSO

Volume 1 Left: Despotism; France; Stalin and Stalinism.
Volume 2 Right: Totalitarianism; Fascism.

BIBLIOGRAPHY

Hannah Arendt, *The Origins of Totalitarianism* (Meridian Books, 1958); Eric Carlton, *Faces of Despotism* (Scolar Press, 1995); Roger Boesche, *Theories of Tyranny from Plato to Arendt* (University of Pennsylvania Press, 1996); Sheldon Wolin, *Politics and Vision: Continuity and Innovation in Western Political Thought* (Little, Brown, 1960); Karl Wittfogel, *Oriental Despotism: A Comparative Study of Total Power* (Vintage Books, 1981).

NERGIS CANEFE
YORK UNIVERSITY, CANADA

Dewey, Thomas E. (1902–1971)

THOMAS E. DEWEY achieved prominence during three terms as governor of New York and twice as the Republican presidential nominee, in 1944 and 1948. Thomas Edward Dewey was born above his grandfather's general store in Owosso, Michigan, to George M. and Annie (Thomas) Dewey. The Deweys were distant relatives of Admiral George Dewey. Thomas's father, George Dewey, was the local newspaper publisher and active in Republican politics. Dewey had perfect attendance from kindergarten through high school. He graduated in 1923 from the University of Michigan with a degree in choral music and went on to law school at Columbia University. This brought him to New York City, where he would make his career as a lawyer and politician. One of Dewey's hobbies extending from his childhood was singing, and it was as a young lawyer in New York that he met his wife, the former Frances Hutt, at their vocal teacher's studio. She was a star of the musical theatre on Broadway. They were married in 1928. To this union were born two sons, Thomas E. Dewey, Jr., and John M. Dewey.

Dewey was in the private practice of law in New York City from 1925 until 1931, when he was appointed chief assistant to the U.S. attorney. Dewey briefly served as U.S. attorney after his superior resigned in 1933. In 1935, he was appointed special prosecutor by Governor Herbert Lehman to investigate organized crime. Dewey achieved much success with his prosecutions, and as a result of his newfound fame, he was drafted by Fiorello H. LaGuardia to run for district attorney of Manhattan (New York County). He then continued his prosecution of organized crime on the state level. During his first year in office, he made his first run for governor, against Lehman, to whom he lost narrowly.

In 1940, President Franklin D. Roosevelt was finishing his second term, and it was expected that he would not run again, as no president had sought a third term. Dewey, who was still only a county-level official, was nevertheless one of the best-known Republicans in the country, and he was urged by many to seek the presidency. Dewey was nominated at the national convention but lost to Wendell Willkie. It may have been just as well for Dewey, as Roosevelt indeed sought a third term and easily defeated Willkie in the election.

Dewey next turned his attentions to the buildup preceding World War II. He headed an effort by the United Service Organizations for National Defense (USO) to equip military bases with social facilities, raising more than $16 million for the cause. He did not seek reelection as district attorney. Instead, he ran again for governor in 1942. Lehman had decided to retire, and there was a split on the political left. This was one of the first electoral contests for a new party, the American Labor Party (ALP), which represented a left-wing break from the Democratic Party. (The ALP later merged into the Liberal Party of New York, which is still a factor in state and national politics in the Empire State.) Dewey won with a majority despite a three-way race. He made a thorough house-cleaning of the state government through a series of appointments, the Republicans not having held the governorship for 20 years. One of the hallmarks of his tenure as governor was the passage of the first state law barring religious and racial discrimination in employment.

Dewey was nominated nearly unanimously by the Republican Party in 1944 to challenge Roosevelt, who was running for an unprecedented fourth term. Dewey chose as his running mate John W. Bricker, governor of Ohio. Although the race was closer than Roosevelt's first three victories, he and Harry S Truman defeated Dewey and Bricker decisively. Roosevelt was aided by the country being at war, and there was a general feeling that it would be a bad time to change leaders. Dewey was reelected governor in 1946. He chose to run for president again in 1948, this time against Truman, who had succeeded to the office upon Roosevelt's death. The Republicans nominated California Governor Earl Warren as Dewey's running mate, giving the party a ticket consisting of the governors of the two largest states. The Democrats had stumbled badly in the 1946 congressional elections, losing control of both chambers, and polls throughout the year had suggested that Truman would lose. Dewey was perhaps too confident of his expected victory and did not campaign effectively enough. (There was also a suggestion that the polls had been influenced by the use of telephone polling at a time when affluent voters, who usually

voted Republican, were more likely to have telephones.) Truman turned the poor Democratic Party performance of 1946 into a plus for him by running against the "do-nothing" Republican Congress. It was a close election, and Truman and Alben W. Barkley won, but only after some newspapers had gone to press proclaiming Dewey the victor. Dewey was reelected governor again in 1950.

In each of his national races, Dewey had carried the banner of the internationalist, progressive, liberal wing of the Republican Party. He opposed the isolationism of the conservative wing of the party. By 1952, it was clear that Dewey was finished as a presidential contender. The party was ready to move on to others who had not suffered two losses. It was perhaps Dewey's greatest triumph that he was able to support to victory an internationalist candidate, Dwight D. Eisenhower. Eisenhower's triumph over Robert A. Taft served to bury isolationism, possibly forever.

Dewey declined to seek reelection as governor in 1954. He returned to private law practice. Dewey died in Bal Harbor, Florida, on March 16, 1971, and was buried in Pawling Cemetery in Pawling, New York.

SEE ALSO

Volume 1 Left: Roosevelt, Franklin D.; Democratic Party.
Volume 2 Right: Republican Party.

BIBLIOGRAPHY

Richard Norton Smith, *Thomas E. Dewey and His Times* (Simon and Schuster, 1982); Mary M. Stolberg, *Fighting Organized Crime: Politics, Justice, and the Legacy of Thomas E. Dewey* (Northeastern University Press, 1995); Stanley Walker, *Dewey: An American of this Century* (Whittlesey House, 1944).

TONY L. HILL
MASSACHUSETTS INSTITUTE OF TECHNOLOGY

Dos Passos, John (1896–1970)

JOHN DOS PASSOS found a unique place in the history of American literature and politics with his shift from the radical left of his early career to the conservative right that lasted until the end of his life, with both stances informing and structuring his writing. Born in the midst of worldwide social upheaval, Dos Passos had a youth that followed the template of the privileged: private schools, the European tour, and Harvard University. It was at Harvard that he began his exploration of perceived social injustices and Europe's various socialist uprisings. In 1917, Dos Passos joined many young Americans, including Ernest Hemingway and other literati, in Europe as a volunteer ambulance driver. As with most of the young and naive Americans, he was horrified by the brutality, the senselessness of the deaths, and the lies of the leaders. From his experiences during this time, Dos Passos formed the background for his novel, *Three Soldiers*, which signaled the beginning of his self-"declassing" and further explorations into social awareness.

From this early beginning until his disillusionment during the Spanish Civil War, the young author aligned himself with various socialistic enterprises. Dos Passos explored various methods of infusing his work with a social perspective, addressing the inequities of the American capitalist social structure. His interests in socialism and the dehumanizing effects of modern industrialization on the working class pervade his most famous works: *Manhattan Transfer* (1925) and the trilogy *U.S.A.* (1929–36).

Dos Passos also acted upon his interests in the plight of the modern worker. From the mid-1920s through the late 1930s, he wrote for the leftist publication *The New Masses* and for the radical theater group New Playwrights Theatre. Although his political stance was decisively leftist during this period, Dos Passos never joined the Communist Party. He explained this refusal to friends and political compatriots by denouncing the bloody violence of the communist revolutions in Europe, as well as claiming that the Communist Party was another bureaucratic machine trying to control the masses through lack of education and control of the wealth. Fascism was "a disease of sick capitalism," he wrote.

By the mid-1930s, his socialist ardor began to cool, but he continued to look for solutions to the condition of the working class both in America and abroad. In 1937, his work as a reporter eventually took him to Spain during the Spanish Civil War, where he found fascists and the Republican government in an alliance to suppress the newest social revolution. When he returned from Spain, the once angry and fervent socialist began exploring other options for reform instead of revolution. Demoralized and bitter, Dos Passos turned from Europe and its widespread anarchy and toward American tradition and democracy for the answers to his search for the freedom of the individual in the midst of the "bureaucratic industrial organization." His shift to the conservative right began. Convinced that only in American traditions and democracy would the country

solve its social problems, Dos Passos immersed himself in the lives and events of 17th- and 18th-century American history.

Through his reading, the now middle-aged author found a host of radicals working for noble ends, self-sacrificing and dedicated to democracy and individual freedom. This successful search provided a message of hope and a direction for Dos Passos. He continued an active involvement in politics, sponsoring and joining in groups and activities that focused on civil liberties and individual freedom. During the Second World War, he traveled across America and to England, reporting on the effects of the war at home and abroad. Again, war fueled political fervor in Dos Passos, but this time it also inspired a deep chauvinism in the previously pro-European.

Once an avid proponent for radical and far-reaching change, he now advocated the continued prosperity of postwar productivity and feared change and centralized, concentrated power. During the last two decades of his life, the radical-turned-conservative abhorred communism and, as always, any bureaucracy. In 1947, Dos Passos wrote about the failure of socialism, especially Marxism, in a complete about-face from his former beliefs in an article for *Life* magazine appropriately titled "The Failure of Marxism."

As with his earlier writings, Dos Passos wanted to include and illustrate his new political and philosophical views in his mature work. However, few of these later works ever achieved the power and innovation of his trilogy. The most successful of his later works, in terms of sound writing and innovation, is *The Grand Design* (1949), in which he continues his lifelong attack on bureaucracy and explores the dangers of social reform originating from the top and not from the workers themselves. Most critics agree that his work in the 1950s and 1960s never matched the creativity and power of his earlier works, but they never agree on whether or not the failure of these works is a reflection of his change in political perspective.

SEE ALSO

Volume 1 Left: Socialism; Spain; Communism.
Volume 2 Right: Conservatism; United States; Capitalism.

BIBLIOGRAPHY

Robert C. Rosen, *John Dos Passos: Politics and the Writer* (University of Nebraska Press, 1981); William Solomon, "Politics and Rhetoric in the Novel in the 1930s," *American Literature* (v.68/4, December 1996); Daniel Aaron, *Writers on the Left* (Octagon Books, 1974); Robert C. Rosen, "John Dos Passos

1896–1970," *The Heath Anthology of American Literature,* http://college.hmco.com (May 2004).

GLORIA J. HICKS
UNIVERSITY OF WYOMING

Drudge, Matt (1966–)

MATT DRUDGE, a popular and controversial internet journalist, grew up in the suburbs of Washington, D.C.,residing in the town of Takoma Park, Maryland. During his youth, Drudge was a relative loner and spent a lot of his time listening to talk radio, which is in abundance in the capital region. He specialized in current events and embraced the information and news-heavy culture of the nation's political center. In school, Drudge only succeeded in subjects that he could relate to current events, graduating 325th out of a class of 350 students.

Drudge held an array of jobs before succeeding as an internet journalist, including doing the night shift at a 7-11 convenience store, selling Time Life books over the phone, and working in a CBS gift shop. While working at the gift shop, Drudge overheard a variety of gossip from the news studio, where he thought of the premise for his overwhelmingly popular *Drudge Report* website. When he heard gossip, Drudge wondered what success he would have if he relayed it on the internet.

Acting upon his ideas, Drudge moved to Los Angeles and established his website in 1994. Gathering news stories from across the internet and working from his small apartment, he originally started it as a low-cost and low-income venture created on an old 486-based computer, but the website and Drudge quickly gained notoriety due to its right-wing slant.

Drudge's website is a collection of links to stories about entertainment, politics, current events, and daily columns by popular journalists. Occasionally, he authors his own articles, often when he is writing about a rumor or unconfirmed story. In 2004, Drudge lived in a lavish condominium in Miami, Florida, evidence of his website's quick rise to fame and continued advertising income.

Conversing with connections within the news industry and political realm, Drudge is often able to break big stories before they are released in the mainstream media. His website first received national attention in 1996 as a result of one of Drudge's breaking stories; he reported Senator Robert Dole's selection of running mate Jack Kemp in the presidential election before the story ran on the major news channels, and before it was announced by Dole himself. His largest "exclusive" which made an impact nationwide was the *Drudge Report*'s announcement of the occurrence of an inappropriate relationship between President Bill Clinton and a White House intern, launching the Monica Lewinsky scandal, which was subsequently reported by *Newsweek*. Throughout the scandal, Drudge remained on the forefront, reporting developments or other rumors before other media sources.

Drudge faces harsh criticism for his questionable contributions to journalism since many fellow reporters accuse him of publishing stories that are discovered or researched by other journalists. His treatment of the Monica Lewinsky scandal made him a hated target of some Clinton supporters, including well-known celebrities and politicians. In 1997, Drudge was sued for libel and defamation by one of Clinton's lawyers, Sidney Blumenthal, following a story in the *Drudge Report* that claimed that Blumenthal beat his wife. Drudge immediately apologized and removed the story, later reaching a settlement in the case in his favor. In response to Drudge's success, singer and actress Barbara Streisand even began to publish replies to his articles on her personal website.

Regardless of his questionable journalism, Drudge has been a runaway success. Income from his website exceeds $1 million. Some have tried to copy his success, while political pundits try to label him as the leader of online conservative thought, even though Drudge claims to promote libertarian values. With the success of his website, Drudge has changed the rules of journalism and the future of news on the internet.

SEE ALSO

Volume 1 Left: Media Bias, Left.
Volume 2 Right: Media Bias, Right.

BIBLIOGRAPHY

"Biography: Matt Drudge," vikingphoenix.com (May 2004); "Matt Drudge," wikipedia.com. (May 2004); Tim McDonald, "Online Matt Drudge Libel Case Comes to 'Wimpy Conclusion,'" www.newsfactor.com (May 2004); Matt Drudge with Julia Phillips, *Drudge Manifesto* (Penguin, 2000).

ARTHUR HOLST, PH.D.
WIDENER UNIVERSITY

The Right

E

Education

AMERICAN PUBLIC education has been a battle-ground for opposing political viewpoints since the mid-1950s, and became more intense in the 1980s. Although mainstream views have prevailed for the most part, conservatives have made significant progress in instituting their educational agendas. All conservatives are not religious. Nor are all liberals anti-religious. Nevertheless, educational battle lines have been drawn with the right supporting religious education in both private and public schools, and the left insisting on separation of church and state.

Ronald Reagan entered the White House in 1981 with the intention of restoring prayers to public schools and obtaining funding for private Christian schools. Despite Supreme Court decisions that ban prayer in public schools, conservatives have continued to work toward reinstating student-led prayers, if not those led by school officials. Advocates of school prayer offer polling data to support their position. They contend that large majorities are in favor of prayer in the schools, displaying the Ten Commandments, and teaching creationism. However, only 40 percent of the American public believe that creation should replace evolution in science classes. Conservatives have rallied behind a proposed constitutional amendment that would permit voluntary prayers in all public schools.

Just what goes in America's school textbooks is a matter of debate between conservatives and liberals.

Liberals point out that ultraconservatives are not concerned with putting religion back in the public school. Rather, they are determined to restore Christianity to public education. According to liberals, ultraconservatives have little tolerance for other religions. They find it hard to accept the fact that the religious freedom granted by the First Amendment encompasses the right to protect Christian children from exposure to other religious beliefs, just as it shields Muslim, Buddhist, and Hindu children from being exposed to Christian beliefs in government-supported public schools.

The Supreme Court's position on using public funds for religious schools has been somewhat confus-

Proponents of school choice want parents to be able to shop for the school that will best suit the interests of their children.

ing. For instance, public funds may be used to purchase textbooks, mandated services, and standardized tests. Government funds may not pay for teacher-prepared tests, charts, and maps. Since 1997, public school teachers have been allowed to offer remedial help to students in religious schools. Decisions on what public funds can and cannot be used for in religious schools are grounded in the Establishment Clause of the First Amendment. Laws that allow government involvement in religious schools must pass the three-tier test established in *Lemon v. Kurtzman* (403 U.S. 602, 1971). Such laws must have a secular rather than a religious purpose, may neither advance nor inhibit religion, and must avoid "excessive entanglement" of church and state.

Those who disagree with the court's position on using public funds in religious schools claim that such laws should be dealt with under the Free Exercise Clause rather than the Establishment Clause.

Religious groups have continued to be a constant presence in many public schools. Because of the Freedom of Access Act, which requires public schools to allow religious groups to meet on school campuses outside of school hours, religious groups have the backing of Congress and the Supreme Court. The National Network of Youth Ministries estimates that approximately 37,000 secondary schools around the country have voluntary, student-led youth ministries. Members of the religious right also regularly distribute copies of the Bible and the Ten Commandments.

Some conservative parents have grown so determined to protect their children from anything that even hints at "secular humanism" that they have engaged in campaigns to keep certain materials out of the public schools. Such a situation occurred in several states when conservatives demanded that *Impressions*, a Holt, Rinehart, Winston reader containing material written by A.A. Milne, Laura Ingalls Wilder, C.S. Lewis, Alice Walker, and Lewis Carroll, be withdrawn because they deemed it inappropriate for conservative children. Some parents objected to the fantasy in the reader, while others found fault with the reality. Parents also objected to environmentalist material because it was seen as anti-capitalism.

In the 1950s and 1960s, large numbers of white parents joined in the "white flight" movement, putting their children into private academies and religious schools to avoid integration of the public schools. By the 1980s, a number of black students were attending those same schools to avoid what many critics have defined as the debacle of public education. The National Center for Educational Statistics reports that 62 percent of children in private schools today live in homes where the total income is less than $20,000. The total of parental incomes for children in religious schools is $15,000. Many social conservatives who do not consider themselves part of the religious right have chosen to send their children to private and religious schools to avoid school violence and what they see as a lack of morals, respect, and discipline in public schools. Many parents are also attracted to the smaller student-teacher ratio and greater parental involvement in private and religious schools.

In response to the parents who reject public education, conservatives have been the loudest voices behind the movement for government-subsidized school vouchers, which would give each parent a certain amount for children to attend private or religious schools. Opponents to school vouchers argue that using tax funds to subsidize private and religious schools is a violation of separation of church and state. Many educators also oppose the use of vouchers because they believe it would cut desperately needed funding from public schools.

Proponents, on the other hand, maintain that the voucher system is not unconstitutional. They point to the fact that most Western democracies subsidize denominational and alternative schools. In June 2002, voucher advocates won a victory when the Supreme Court upheld Ohio's pilot voucher program in *Zelman v. Simmons-Harris*. The program allotted vouchers in amounts up to $2,250 to parents of children in grades kindergarten through 8. Of the 56 private schools covered under the voucher program, 46 were affiliated with churches.

Originally, the concept of school choice referred to the process of allowing parents to selectively choose among various educational alternatives. In practice, school choice has come to describe the right of parents to shop for schools and teachers that best fit the needs of their children without violating their own value systems. Since public schools are financed in large part according to tax dollars generated at the local level, many parents with the right to choose opt for schools in more affluent neighborhoods. This is the major reason that some African American parents have come out in favor of school choice, even though they tend to be liberal rather than conservative. Ironically, conservatives led the effort to take desegregation plans out of the hands of federal judges and back under the control of local school boards. They were successful in great part because of conservative judges who backed away from enforcing federal guidelines. As a result, many schools continued to be heavily segregated.

In 2004, one out of every 25 students in America was home schooled. Parents choose to home school for a number of reasons, and all parents who opt to personally educate their children are not conservative. However, the bulk of the home school movement is made up of conservative parents who do not want their children exposed to the "liberalism" of public education. Home schooling is now legal in all 50 states. Twenty-eight states require that students pass official evaluations, while 13 states simply require that parents notify officials of their intent to home school. Texas has no restrictions at all on home schooling. The George W. Bush administration has encouraged home schooling

because it works to Republican advantage. Seventy-six percent of 18-to-24 year olds who were home schooled vote in presidential elections, as opposed to 29 percent of the general population in that age group. Most of the ballots cast by those who were home schooled vote Republican.

While criticizing public schools is not limited to conservatives, they have been the most articulate in arguing that public schools do not work. Myron Lieberman, a vocal opponent of public education, recommends that schools be run for profit. In Lieber-

Conservatives have proposed a constitutional amendment to allow prayer in public schools.

man's view, competition, not government involvement, is the key to solving the education dilemma. His more radical suggestions include "load shedding," which would mandate government withdrawal from public education, the privatization of all educational services, and the sale of government educational assets.

Education scholar Joel Spring contends that much of the criticism of public education, which motivates the conservative education agenda, originated with conservative think tanks and not conservative parents. Spring cites such examples as the Heritage Foundation, the Olen Foundation, and the American Enterprise Institute. Conservative think tanks were closely involved in forming the educational policies of Ronald Reagan and George W. Bush.

In the late 1990s, thousands of American public schools introduced the concept of values education in the belief that students would act more responsibly if they were taught traditional American values. Both conservatives and civil libertarians have criticized the program. Conservative parents argue that the values being taught are not necessarily those in which they believe. Multiculturalism, political correctness, and religious tolerance are particularly abhorrent to many conservative parents. They also refuse to endorse any curriculum, including sex education, that mentions abortion and homosexuality. Liberals have been concerned with the potential for imposing conservative values on the children of liberal parents.

Rather than implementing reforms suggested by educators who know the problems with public education firsthand, many conservatives want to "throw the baby out with the bathwater." One of the programs most in jeopardy from conservative cuts is Head Start, which originated in 1965 as part of Lyndon Johnson's War on Poverty. The program was designed to improve school readiness for disadvantaged children. Through expanded programs, Head Start now serves low-income children from birth to five years of age, as well as pregnant women, by promoting parental involvement in education and offering healthcare screening, vaccinations, dental care, and assistance with special-needs children.

Republicans have traditionally been critical of Head Start. Reagan tried to eliminate it. In the Reagan tradition, Bush proposed $177 million in cuts to Head Start in fiscal year 2006. The losses are predicted to be greater if Bush follows through on his plan to fund Head Start through block grants to individual states. The Bush administration insists that Head Start is not needed because states already offer enough help for disadvantaged families.

The main plank of the Bush administration's educational reform package was the No Child Left Behind program, which received bipartisan support. The program also received bipartisan criticism. Democratic Senator Ted Kennedy, a major architect of the plan, suggests that the Senate will likely reconsider parts of the program. Most of the criticism centers on the fact that funding is insufficient to meet the requirements of the program. Critics also object to the increased testing and paperwork, and to the growth of bureaucracy generated in the course of implementing the program. Many educators would prefer to spend educational funds where they might be of more use, namely on limiting class sizes, hiring and retaining qualified teachers, funding salaries for support professionals, and providing up-to-date books and materials for classroom use.

SEE ALSO

Volume 1 Left: Church and State Separation; Johnson, Lyndon B.; Constitutional Amendments.
Volume 2 Right: Religion; Christian Coalition; Reagan, Ronald.

BIBLIOGRAPHY

"Bush's Budget Includes 756 M for Vouchers," *USA Today* (February 4, 2003); Joan Delfattore, *What Johnny Shouldn't Read: Textbook Censorship in America* (Yale University Press, 1992); "George Bush's Secret Army," *Economist* (February 28, 2004); Sarah Glazer, "Do School-Based Programs Violate Parents' Beliefs?" *CQ Researcher* (June 21, 1996); Myron Lieberman, *Privatization and Educational Choice* (St. Martin's, 1989); Myron Lieberman, *Public Education: An Autopsy* (Harvard University Press, 1993); Patrick Marshall, "Should the Court Allow More Spiritual Expression?" *CQ Researcher* (January 12, 2001); David Masci, "School Choice Debate: *CQ Researcher* (July 18, 1997); National Head Start Association, "Special Report: Funding and Enrollment Cuts in Fiscal 2006," www.nhsa.org (July 2004); Jennifer Niesslein, "Spanking Head Start," *The Nation* (October 20, 2003); "No Child Left Behind Act," www.ed.gov (July 2004); Joel Spring, "Choice," *Knowledge and Power in the Global Economy: Politics and the Rhetoric of School Reform*, David A. Gabbard, ed. (Lawrence Erlbaum, 2000); Joel Spring, *Conflict of Interests: The Politics of American Education* (McGraw-Hill, 2002); Joel Spring, *Political Agendas for Education from the Religious Right to the Green Party* (Lawrence Erlbaum, 2002); Reg Weaver, "Reforms Rightly Criticized," *USA Today* (January 13, 2004); Alan Wolfe, *School Choice: The Moral Debate* (Oxford University Press, 2003).

ELIZABETH PURDY, PH.D.
INDEPENDENT SCHOLAR

Egypt

THE MODERN HISTORY of Egypt dates from September 13, 1882, when the British army under General Sir Garnet Wolseley defeated an Egyptian force under Colonel Arabi Pasha at Tel-el-Kebir. Great Britain had been keenly interested in the fate of Egypt since it had purchased the controlling interest in the Suez Canal

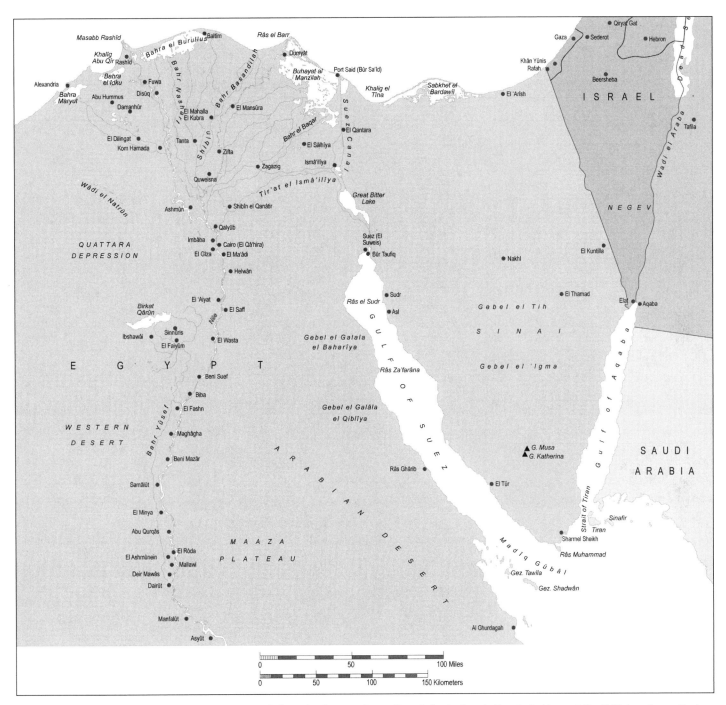

The right in Egypt's modern history has been especially active in pursuing nationalistic goals, whether trying to oust the British or fomenting Islamic extremism to topple the secular government and replace it with a theocracy.

under Prime Minister Benjamin Disraeli in November 1875. The canal provided the shortest maritime route to India, which had formally become part of the British Empire after the defeat of the Indian Mutiny of 1858. When Arabi roused extreme nationalists against foreigners and undermined the role of the modernizing Khedive Tewfik, the British forces were sent in to restore order. As M.J. Williams wrote in *Victorian Military Campaigns*, after Tel-el-Kebir, the Egyptian forces either "disarmed or simply demobilized themselves." In fact, as Lord Kinross had written in *Between Two Seas: The Creation of the Suez Canal*, "Disraeli's purchase of the canal shares was generally assumed to be a prelude to some form of British control over Egypt." Evelyn Baring, the future Lord Cromer, came to rule Egypt in what would be called the "Veiled Protectorate." Rather than depose the *khedive* (ruler) and govern directly, as was the case in India, Baring established the model of the British proconsul remaining in the background and allowing the *khedive* to actually rule.

No sooner had the British become de facto rulers of Egypt than they became embroiled in a massive revolt in Egypt's southern colony of the Sudan, which Mohammed Ali had seized in 1820. The Sudan erupted in the first modern Islamic extremist revolt under Mohammed Ahmed, the Mahdi, "the Expected One" of Allah, when the Egyptian army under General William Hicks was annihilated at El Obeid in November 1883. An effort to evacuate Egyptians and British from the Sudanese capital of Khartoum ended in disaster. It would not be until September 1898 that Anglo-Egyptian forces under Sir Horatio Kitchener would free the Sudanese from the benighted Mahdist regime. The Mahdi's successor, Khalifa Abdullah, would be killed in 1899.

During the first years of British rule in Egypt, the main problem was to control what was called "brigandage," the widespread epidemic of criminal gangs in the country. While reforming the Egyptian system of justice, much effort was applied to abolishing the use of torture, specifically flogging, to gain information from suspects in criminal cases. However, although Lord Cromer attempted to end the practice of *baksheesh*, or "bribes" for government bureaucracy officials, *baksheesh* may still continue to the present day. At the same time, the British attempted to reform the educational system in Egypt and contributed greatly to the country through projects like the first Aswan dam on the Nile River.

EGYPTIAN NATIONALISM

Nationalism did not end with the defeat of Arabi in 1882, but under British tutelage it developed in the parliamentary system. The Wafd Party later became the spokesman of those who wished Egyptians would once more freely govern themselves; unlike Arabi, Wafd Party spokesmen tended to be conservative and modeled their party after political parties in England. Yet, extremism continued as both a political and religious threat in Egypt. In 1910, Boutros Ghali, a long-time public servant, was assassinated by extremists for being perceived as betraying Egyptian nationalism.

World War I, beginning in August 1914, thrust Egypt into prominence again as the defender of the vital Suez Canal. Any attempts at furthering Egyptian self-government were put on hold in the interests of British imperial defense. The Ottoman Turks, the allies of imperial Germany, nearly captured the Suez Canal. It was not until 1917 that British General Sir Edmund Allenby would be able to mount the counterattack that would carry the British army into Palestine, Syria, and beyond, thoroughly routing the Turkish forces. T.E. Lawrence, the celebrated Lawrence of Arabia, served with British intelligence in the Arab Bureau in the Egyptian capital of Cairo before he joined the Arab Revolt in 1916.

After World War I, Egypt retained its imperial importance, a fact demonstrated by the speed with which England put down an uprising there in 1919. The uprising was the real birth of the Wafd Party under Zaghlul Pasha, who later became a prime minister, as did two other nationalist leaders: Ismail Sidky Pasha and Mohammed Mahmoud Pasha. The first party they formed was the Liberal Constitutional Party. As when Arabi was exiled after his rising instead of being executed, the nationalist leaders were simply bundled off the stage rather than dramatically put before a firing squad. Once again, the British channeled Egyptian nationalism in a conservative and parliamentary direction. Allenby was installed as the new proconsul and followed an enlightened approach toward Egyptian nationalism. The monarchy was established: Fuad, the son of Khedive Ismail, became the first king. Peter Mansfield observed in *The British in Egypt* that "British dominance in Egypt was sharply reduced."

In 1936, a treaty was signed that formed a step toward true independence for Egypt. However, as the occupying power, Great Britain weighted the treaty in its behalf. Peter Mansfield remarked that "the inequality implicit in the treaty could hardly have been tolerated by Egypt indefinitely. [But] the question remains academic because within three years of the treaty's ratification the outbreak of war with Germany [in September 1939] caused Britain to invoke Article VIII which, in placing all Egypt's facilities at its disposal, implied the virtual re-occupation of the country." The result was that when World War II broke out, King Farouk declared Egyptian neutrality, although Egypt remained the center of British warfare in the Middle East. Extreme nationalists formed groups like the Organization of Green Shirts, which patterned itself after the fascist Brown Shirts of Adolf Hitler and the Black Shirts of Benito Mussolini. The Green Shirts was the offshoot of the Misr al-Fatat, the "Young Egypt" movement, which had been founded by the nationalist lawyer Ahmad Hussein in 1933. Young Egypt was a close political ally of the religious extremists of the Muslim Brotherhood, which had been established by Hassan al-Banna in 1928. After the war, Farouk was toppled from his throne in the Free Officers Association coup of 1952. Many members of the new regime, like Gamal Abdel Nasser and Anwar Sadat, had membership in the Green Shirts. Nasser, who fought in the 1948 war against Israel, became leader of the country, although General Mohammed Naguib was titular head of state.

From 1954 on, Nasser ruled in name as well. In 1956, he caused the Suez Crisis when he nationalized the Suez Canal Company, precipitating invasion by England and Israel. Nine years later, his determination to have United Nations peacekeeping forces removed from the Sinai region led to the Israeli attack and victory in the June 1967 war. Throughout his tenure, Nasser also attempted to spread his influence by initiating the short-lived United Arab Republic in 1958 with Syria and waging a campaign in Yemen.

Upon Nasser's death, Anwar Sadat became president of Egypt. Being concerned about the growing Soviet presence in Egypt, he removed Soviet advisers from Egypt, who had helped Nasser in his plan for the Aswan High Dam. In October 1973, Sadat launched a surprise attack against Israel in the Yom Kippur War. Although defeated, he achieved his goal of proving Egyptian military prowess after the humiliating defeats under Nasser in 1956 and 1967. In retrospect, it appears he may have launched the attack as a prelude to making peace with Israel from a position of strength. In September 1978, at the Camp David accords, Sadat negotiated with Israeli Prime Minister Menachem Begin the first peace treaty between Israel and an Arab state. However, Sadat's peace with Israel marked him for death by the Islamic extremists linked to the Muslim Brotherhood. In October 1981, he was killed while watching a military parade ironically celebrating his 1973 war with Israel. As Ahron Bregman and Jihan El-Tabari noted in *Israel and the Arabs*, "Sadat's peacemaking had dramatically reduced the probability of war between Israel and the Arabs."

Beginning with Sadat's death, Egypt became increasingly involved in a civil war with the Islamic extremists. Hosni Mubarak, who succeeded Sadat, missed assassination at their hands in June 1995. In spite of the struggle against extremism, Mubarak's Egypt has been a country that has followed a pro-Western foreign policy and has been a supporter of the War on Terror.

SEE ALSO

Volume 1 Left: Egypt; Socialism; Third-Worldism.
Volume 2 Right: Middle East.

BIBLIOGRAPHY

Lord Kinross, *Between Two Seas: The Creation of the Suez Canal* (Morrow, 1969); Neil Macfarquhar, "Who After Mubarak?" *The Hindu* (December 26, 2003); M.J. Williams, "The Egyptian Campaign, 1882," *Victorian Military Campaigns*, Brian Bond, ed. (Praeger, 1967); "President Mohamed Hosni Mubarak, President of the Arab Republic of Egypt," www.sis.gov.eg (July 2004); Peter Mansfield, *The British in Egypt* (Holt, Rinehart, and Winston, 1971); Anthony Nutting, *Gordon of Khartoum* (Clarkson Potter, 1966); Winston S. Churchill, *The River War* (Award Books, 1964).

JOHN F. MURPHY, JR.
AMERICAN MILITARY UNIVERSITY

Eisenhower, Dwight D. (1890–1969)

DWIGHT EISENHOWER was an American military commander and president. Born on October 14, 1890, in Denison, Texas, and reared in Kansas, Eisenhower attended the U.S. Military Academy. There he first developed a love of poker and created a "poker face" that would serve him well in later years. During his long military career before World War II, he served under distinguished generals such as John J. Pershing and Douglas MacArthur. Eisenhower studied MacArthur's flair for drama during a long stint with him in the Philippines; in his later career he would develop into an even more capable politico-military commander than MacArthur, but with a far less egotistical way of operating.

Serving as a staff officer on the eve of World War II, Eisenhower was promoted above more senior officers to command Operation Torch, the Allied invasion of North Africa. The following July, he commanded the invasion of Sicily. In December 1943, Eisenhower was made supreme commander of the Allied Expeditionary Force. He moved to the United Kingdom from where he oversaw planning of the Allied invasion of Western Europe.

In that role, he would handle the most difficult coalition of Allies, and the most complicated diplomatic mission of any coalition commander since John Churchill, first Duke of Marlborough, waged war against Louis XIV in the early 18th century. Eisenhower faced the bewildering task of dealing with such a difficult array of personalities as Winston Churchill,

Bernard Montgomery, Charles de Gaulle, Omar Bradley, and George Patton and keeping them working together toward the goal of the destruction of Nazi Germany. That Eisenhower could work with such a difficult group of men and prevent any major splits in his coalition or his command testifies to his diplomacy.

Though Eisenhower would be famous as an anticommunist while president, during World War II he focused almost exclusively on harnessing the power of the Allies on the destruction of Nazi Germany. In the final months of the war in Europe, Eisenhower and the American high command trusted Soviet goodwill and did not conduct their military operations with an eye to a postwar power struggle. After the war, Eisenhower served as president of Columbia University and also as commander of the North Atlantic Treaty Organization. He published his military memoir, *Crusade in Europe*, in 1948.

In 1952, he ran for president as a Republican and defeated Democratic challenger Adlai Stevenson. Four years later, Eisenhower and his vice president, Richard Nixon, would be elected to a second term, once again defeating Democratic challenger Adlai Stevenson. Eisenhower inherited the Korean War from his predecessor, Harry Truman, and ended the war with an armistice in 1953, but only after threatening to use nuclear weapons against North Korean and Chinese targets. The cease-fire ended open warfare but left North and South Korea facing each other over a demilitarized zone in a standoff that continues to this day.

Eisenhower supported the development of the hydrogen bomb, an exponentially more powerful nuclear weapon than that used at Hiroshima and Nagasaki, Japan. He launched the Atoms for Peace program to foster the spread of nuclear technology for peaceful purposes, such as the generation of electricity and medical research, leading to the export of American-designed nuclear power reactors over the next decades. During his presidency, Eisenhower also fought the Cold War covertly. In 1953, the newly formed Central Intelligence Agency thwarted a communist coup in Iran and reinstalled the pro-United States shah. The following year, the CIA helped thwart a communist takeover of Guatemala. Communism did have two notable successes during the Eisenhower years: communist forces drove the French from Indochina and took control of North Vietnam, and communists also took control of Cuba. Both of these events would challenge American policies for years to come.

At home, Eisenhower served as president during the waning days of the power of Wisconsin Senator Joe McCarthy. His tenure as president also saw the first implementation of forced desegregation of American schools, as ordered by federal courts. He ordered troops to Little Rock, Arkansas, to execute a court order to desegregate schools.

Often underestimated, Eisenhower was a very gifted man with almost two decades of experience in positions of grave national responsibility by the time that he retired from public life in 1961. Eisenhower did not become a conservative icon after his retirement in the way Ronald Reagan did. Nevertheless, his practical contributions to human freedom by defeating Nazi Germany and standing fast against global communism earned him a place in history as the leader against the two great 20th-century totalitarian regimes, from both the right and the left. In his last years, Eisenhower retired to a farm in Gettysburg, Pennsylvania, near America's most famous battlefield. He died on March 28, 1969.

SEE ALSO

Volume 1 Left: Stevenson, Adlai E.; Democratic Party; Truman, Harry.
Volume 2 Right: Republican Party; Corporatism.

BIBLIOGRAPHY

Stephen E. Ambrose, *Eisenhower: Soldier and President* (Simon and Schuster, 1990); H. W. Brands, *Cold Warriors: Eisenhower's Generation and American Foreign Policy* (Columbia University Press, 1988); Dwight D. Eisenhower, *Crusade in Europe* (Doubleday, 1948); Dwight D. Eisenhower, *Peace with Justice: Selected Addresses* (Popular Library, 1961); Dwight D. Eisenhower, *Waging Peace, 1956–61: The White House Years* (Doubleday, 1965); Fred I. Greenstein, *The Hidden-Hand Presidency: Eisenhower as Leader* (Basic Books, 1982); Dwight D. Eisenhower Library and Museum, www.eisenhower.utexas.edu (July 2004).

MITCHELL MCNAYLOR
OUR LADY OF THE LAKE COLLEGE

Electorate, U.S.

THE ELECTORATE is the voter en masse. The electorate is as fickle and predictable as the population is, and for political strategists and organizers, elusive to quantify as well. The electorate in the United States has, since 1947 and 1948, been sending mixed signals by sending split tickets of elected officials to the White House, Senate, and Congress. Harry Truman had to deal with a Republican Congress, just as Dwight Eisenhower had to deal with a Congress that had increased Democratic majorities in it. Since Eisenhower's 1956 election, the electorate has been sending something other than a cohesive Congress and White House to Washington, D.C.

This split has caused both political strategists and theorists to wonder whether a divided government makes a difference in policy making, and whether this is a demonstration by the electorate that they cannot be labeled too easily as to what they want in a representative in the White House or Congress. By sending a divided group to Congress and the White House, the electorate may just be sending the checks and balances that were promised in the U.S. Constitution.

Even when Democratic presidents have had the electorate send them a Democratic Congress to deal with, such as Bill Clinton and Jimmy Carter, they have not had the same productive relationship as their counterparts like John Kennedy and Lyndon Johnson. In fact, Clinton was at his most productive when dealing with the electorate that sent him a Republican Congress. In the 2000 presidential election, a total of $3 billion was spent on trying to find, talk to, persuade, and attract the electorate of the United States to one party or another, mostly coming from groups that had very specific interests to advance.

To win, President George W. Bush and his campaign strategists needed to recognize and compartmentalize the electorates into their appropriate clusters in order to communicate with them and prompt them to react in the way the communicator or source of the message wanted them to. Political scientists can label two of the constituencies that Bush mobilized to win, one being those who did not think highly of politics or politicians, the other being the "indignant moralizers," as Norman Birnbaum calls them, who were generally antagonistic toward the Democratic Party and belonged to the fundamentalist Protestant churches. This was one of the groups of the electorate the Bush campaign targeted for their success in the election by identifying and locating where these voters were: generally centered in the south and west of the country. To get this vote, Bush's team relied on mobilizing the people of this group at the local level, and addressed their issues on the rights of the local and state government.

The Bush team based their message on research techniques that told them they could get the vote if that message was about gun control, race relations, and abortion in terms that agreed with the indignant moralizers. The message included, as well, promising deregulation along with large tax cuts to the upper income categories and elimination of taxes on inherited property. Although Bush won 500,000 fewer votes than Democratic candidate Al Gore, Bush won enough votes in the districts that would provide him with the highest return in the U.S. Electoral College, the institution that the founders of the republic conceived to protect the country against direct democracy.

Ralph Nader is often blamed for the failure of Gore's presidential campaign, as he won 98,488 votes in Florida, purely based on the assumption from research that says the votes that Nader got would have gone to Gore. It is a dangerous assumption that the electorate who voted for Nader nationally, about 2.7 million, would have voted for Gore. One has to look at why the electorate voted for Nader, and if they would have shown up at the polls at all without Nader on the ballot. Then one must look at why Nader attracted them from their electorate armchair, and could that attraction be copied or was it unique to the message of Nader? Other questions abound when looking at the electorate's voting habits and attitudes, to find out whether they will even show up to vote in the right states to make a difference on election night.

Other also-rans of note in the recent past include Pat Buchanan who garnered 448,868 votes in the 2000 presidential race, and Ross Perot's 1992 presidential campaign. Perot attracted 19 percent of the vote in the 1992 race, and fell to 8.4 percent of the vote in the following 1996 presidential race.

A revolution in how American politicians look at the electorate took place almost three decades ago. The election industry has been at the leading edge of the development of the most sophisticated marketing and demographic research tools. In fact, much of the research and development has been commercialized and stretched to encompass the needs of the large retailers and businesses looking for the all-elusive consumer.

Alexis de Tocqueville provides perhaps the best and simplest portrait of the American electorate, in his *Democracy in America*. The electorate is the citizen who belongs to an association, or club, or attends a town hall meeting or other forms of interpersonal interactions. It is this electorate that gives the theory of democracy its reality and it is this electorate that every campaigner wants to connect with. It is the job of the campaign worker to find the common links between the electorate and their communities, associations, and political activities and beliefs. In today's elections, pollsters want to record the real, solid opinions of the electorate and provide the campaigners with the location of the electorate, to help provide a composite picture of the electorate to the campaigner.

The electorate is a consumer. Voters are, in fact, the consumers of political stimuli, and the result wanted by the stimulator is an X in the right box on election day, or at the very least a positive response to a public survey poll. Politics has changed. The voters have changed, as have their public opinions and political behaviors. In the postindustrial stage that American society has entered, the average electorate has achieved a level of affluence, advanced technological development, levels of knowledge, and levels of cultural independence along with new lifestyles and expectations.

It can be argued that the electorate has not changed much, but that politics has changed and may have missed the fact that there are still basic needs of all voters to be met. The American electorate in the early 1960s was widely depicted as trustful, supported the political system, and felt that supporting one of the national political parties was important, that voters could have some difference with their votes. That same American electorate no longer feels as politically efficacious as it once did.

Several studies in the past have shown that the electorate has become more tolerant and wants more support given to groups that might hold unpopular or nonconforming democratic principles. Political parties no longer hold the same position in the minds of the American electorate, which can be seen by the number of independents participating in elections as well as ticket splitting. This has led to the finding that the support of the traditional parties in elections has slipped considerably and no longer can the party machinery count on the support of the people who voted for them in the last election.

In the past, the electorate may have found, or thought they had found, little control over the political agenda, but increasingly have now discovered what is called the New Politics: conflicts and political coalitions being formed on differences over issues that are new to the political agenda. It is now theorized that the electorate has developed a single-issue mentality that will make it even harder for the traditional political party organizer to marshal the electorate into one happy group to carry the candidates into office.

The influence of the mass media on the electorate has been the subject of many studies over the years. The research can be separated into two generations. With one generation, research tells of the hypodermic

effect of mass media communications on the electorate and how this has some automatic effect on the voting patterns and habits at the time. The second generation of research attempts to play down the direct impact of the media on the opinion leaders and their ability to lead followers to the voting booth and put an X where it is needed. But there is a third generation of research, yet to come out fully in the democratic system, that indeed finds there is a great deal of importance put on the messages in the media by the electorate on which to base voting decisions. It is for this very reason, political scientists suggest, that there has been a precipitous drop in voter turnout at all levels. The research may find that the traditional media have tried to set an agenda that they feel the electorate wants, only to find the electorate is finding political information not just from the mass media, but also from personal sources, whether that is by word of mouth, or by silicon chip.

VOTER TURNOUT

In *The New American Voter*, Warren E. Miller and J. Merrill Shanks divide the electorate into three generational categories: pre-New Deal, New Deal, and post-New Deal. They demonstrate that the decline in voter turnout is not due to a decline in the rate of voting. Miller and Shanks speculate that the generational differences in voter turnout are due to different political experiences during each generation's formative years. In *The Disappearing American Voter*, Ruy A. Teixeira attributes "about one-third of the gap between actual and potential turnout to the high costs of voting in the United States relative to other democracies. The most significant cost results from the burden of voluntary, personal voter registration versus the automatic registration systems generally found elsewhere. The remaining two-thirds of the gap is a consequence of a low estimation of the benefits of voting. A 'disconnect' has developed between people and politics, and the act of voting has become less meaningful to the citizenry."

Politics has always been about satisfying the electorate's personal values. The electorate in the United States is attempting to achieve implementation of its values somewhat through political preferences and policies, and, in turn, political choices are changing. Hence, there is an increasing need for the political industry to be able to sense this and to change to match the new landscape of the electorate. The trick is to find out the personal values held by the electorate, quantify them, and locate a cluster of either like-minded people, or people who could become like-minded, and target that group for communications efforts. A perfect example of how the New Politics has used marketing and public opinion research to identify their chosen electorate for victory is the debates between presidential candidates. When Gore and Bush debated on national television, for example, on October 2, 2000, with over 46.6 million people watching, the desired outcome was a vote for either of the two candidates. Presidential debates are designed specifically to win over the undecided voter and to reinforce choices among the electorate who have already made up their minds. This goal is at the heart of the messages delivered at the debate and the lead-up to the debate in all of the campaign messages. The electorate is being marketed to by the campaigns in the same way the soft drink or fast food companies do: Buy our candidate. But as marketers of mass-market goods are finding, the customer for their products and services is becoming a difficult target. So are the political campaigners and strategists finding the electorate difficult to locate, motivate, and placate with the right message to get the voter into the voting booth and vote in a predictable and logical fashion.

In the 1990s and 2000s, the political right in the United States has had more success than the left in identifying, segmenting, and marketing to the U.S. electorate. Solidly counting the Christian fundamentalist, conservative, and Republican factions in their ranks, the right has also been able to reach out to undecided groups. The left, meanwhile, has had more problems galvanizing liberal factions and Democrats with a cohesive message that stands against the right. The election of 2004 especially showed the left's unsuccessful scramble to organize its forces in opposition to George W. Bush's "compassionate conservatism."

SEE ALSO

Volume 1 Left: Democratic Party; Clinton, William J.
Volume 2 Right: Republican Party; Eisenhower, Dwight D.; Bush, George W.

BIBLIOGRAPHY

Richard S. Conley, *The Presidency, Congress and Divided Government: A Postwar Assessment* (Texas A&M University Press, 2003); Norman Birnbaum, "After the Debacle," *Political Quarterly* (v.72/2, April–June 2001); Warren E. Miller and J. Merrill Shanks, *The New American Voter* (Harvard University Press, 1996); Ruy A. Teixeira, *The Disappearing American Voter* (Brookings Institution, 1992).

NORMAN GREENFIELD
INDEPENDENT SCHOLAR

Elitism

ELITISM, IN ITS POLITICAL SENSE, expresses the attitude that society should be governed by a group of selected persons, elites, who are believed to have distinct and superior qualities. This definition refers to a set of political and cultural beliefs that excludes the views of the majority of people from the process of decision-making and concentrates power in the hands of a small minority. Here lies the distinction between the elite group, which is supposed to monopolize (social, cultural, and political) knowledge, and ordinary people, who are considered ignorant and uneducated. This may be explained in terms of an elitist position reflecting members' views in a favored group.

Historically, the development of the term *elitism* has come with the evolution of the word *elite*. *Elite* was used in 17th-century France to name groups of unique goods and, later, to refer to superior social groups. It began to be commonly used in social and political thought by the late 19th century. Although elitism was inherent to the 19th century's modern political perspectives, including republicanism, conservatism, and romanticism, in the early 20th century Vilfredo Pareto and Gaetano Mosca provided a comprehensive elite theory and a widespread explanation of elitism for social and political thought.

Defining the elite as having distinct capabilities and thus being the only group to govern society, they made the distinction between the rulers and the ruled. In this regard, their argument was based on the belief that society is made up of two classes: elites and masses.

This elitist position challenged socialist and Marxist egalitarianism (which foresaw a classless society), liberal individualism (empowering each individual as valuable and powerful), and democracy (at least in the sense of "rule by the people"). Max Weber (1918) and later his followers, J.A. Schumpeter (1942) and C. Wright Mills (1956), saw democracy as a game of competition of elites for political leadership and so denied the idea of rule by the people. Related to the question of how to govern society, in the views of these social and political theorists, it is obvious that there was emphasis on elitism and belief in the virtue of an elite group of individuals who deserve to be leaders.

In the elite theories, elitism achieved its hegemonic position and status by possessing some sources, values, or knowledge. Social and educational background and elite recruitment processes determined the ways to elite control of political and cultural status, economic wealth, and advantages. Among these elite groups were state (civil and military) officials, businesspersons, intellectuals, religious or social leaders, and politicians. The ability and capacity of elites to organize, communicate among, and mobilize their members was regarded as the main determining factor behind their hegemony and control.

The analysis of the role of elites in social and political life has been integrated in political science. This elite analysis examines the scope of the role elites play in society and politics, and to what extent politically influential elites affect decision-making processes and policy formation. At the heart of this perspective is the countertype of elite unity or the possibility of emergence of a counterelite movement. The argument for the emergence of a counterelite group is that the conflict between elite values and the masses results in the weakness or absence of links between elite groups and the rest of society. The result is the appearance of a new elite group voicing new social demands.

Although elitism is widely expressed in pejorative terms because of its anti-democratic rule of the minority in culture, politics, etc., it is inescapable in contemporary society. Contemporary society needs experts and this is possible through a selective process, functioning on the basis of limited access to some position. A limited number of people can become deputies, professors, professional artists, etc. Thus, one may say that elitism is one of the outcomes of a division of labor in modern society. But in this respect, what is the important issue is the way in which elitism is defined in political circles.

When we define elitism as a necessary human condition for the functioning of society, it comes to the fore as a necessary part of modern social life. However, when it is seen as a mere political position, arguing elitism versus democracy, it might become a threat to the principle of equality in contemporary democracies.

In this sense, elites' relation to democracy has been problematic. This is indeed about whether or not there is an incompatibility between elitism and democratic mechanisms. Here, liberal and pluralist democratic positions challenge the elite theories; contemporary society is politically, culturally, and economically diversified where a group of cohesive elites cannot achieve full dominance. Competition of groups to influence decision-making processes occurs through the efforts of leaders who are accountable to their own groups.

In the United States, in recent decades elites have emerged in the mass media, entertainment, and journalistic professions, as well as in institutions of higher learning, centered in several East and West Coast cities, reflecting liberal values. These elites have been criticized by conservative spokespeople, focusing on the disproportionate voice of the liberal elites.

Further, conservatives argue, liberal elites are out of touch with the values of "middle America," both the geographic heartland of the nation and the working middle class. Although liberal on numerous social and moral issues, for the most part liberal elites have not been identified with criticism of the American capitalist system itself.

SEE ALSO

Volume 1 Left: Democracy; Ideology; Political Economy; Liberalism.
Volume 2 Right: Education; Monarchism; Balance of Power; Coulter, Ann H.; Conservatism.

BIBLIOGRAPHY

Peter Bachrach, *Theory of Democratic Elitism: A Critique* (University Press of America, 2002); Tom Bottomore, "Elite Theory," *Twentieth- Century Social Thought*, W. Outhwaite and T. Bottomore, eds. (Blackwell Publishers, 1993); George Lowel Field, *Elitism* (Routledge, 1980); William A. Henry, *In Defense of Elitism* (Anchor, 1995); Robert Hollinger, *The Dark Side of Liberalism: Elitism vs. Democracy* (Praeger Publishers, 1996).

YILMAZ ÇOLAK, PH.D.
EASTERN MEDITERRANEAN UNIVERSITY, TURKEY

Ethnic Cleansing

THE IDEA OF ETHNIC CLEANSING, of physically removing a targeted human population group either by genocide or forced migration, has existed since the dawn of recorded history. Though the United Nations debated in the early 2000s definitions of genocide and ethnic cleansing, the concept of removing an undesired population has been used by both leftist and rightist rulers, as evidenced by the policies of Josef Stalin and Adolf Hitler. However, ethnic cleansing has been most apparent on the right side of politics, as it has been an extreme facet of fascism, nationalism, and totalitarianism.

The roots of ethnic cleansing can be seen as early as 586 B.C.E.: In the second siege of Jerusalem, Nebuchadnezzar of Babylon ended the problem of continued Hebrew resistance to Babylonian rule by effectively transplanting the entire city population to his capital city. This was the period of Hebrew history known as the Babylonian captivity. In 538 B.C.E., after his capture of the city, Cyrus the Great of the Persians permitted the Hebrews to leave the "waters of Babylon" to depart for their ancestral home again.

However, not all such examples of ethnic cleansing were so benign. In the 1580s, during the British conquest of southwest Ireland, Munster, a purposeful campaign seems to have been undertaken to remove the native Irish population and make room for the "Plantation" of the country by English adventurers. Richard Berleth writes in *The Twilight Lords: An Irish Chronicle* of how the English commander William Pelham admitted that "we consumed with fire all inhabitants and executed the people wherever we found them." These depredations made the region a traditional hotbed against British authority in Ireland.

In modern times, ethnic cleansing was seen in a stark way during World War II in the Soviet Union. When faced with the massive German invasion of June 1941, Soviet Premier Josef Stalin reverted to the harsh tactics of Tzar Ivan the Terrible in the 15th century. Entire populations were deported east to Siberia from homelands where they had lived for centuries, including Germans who had come to Russia to help modernize the country in the reign of Peter the Great (1689–1725), Crimean Tartars, and other ethnic groups deemed disloyal in the Great Patriotic War. It was not until Nikita Khrushchev consolidated his power following the death of Stalin in March 1953 that many of these people were allowed to return home. But thousands died in Stalin's ethnic cleansing campaign. Indeed, the insurrection in Chechnya in the 2000s has its roots in the sufferings of the Muslim Chechens in World War II at the hands of Stalin's brutal NKVD secret police and his Red Army.

Undoubtedly, the most horrific example of ethnic cleansing in modern times was the concerted attempt by Adolf Hitler and the German Nazis to erase the Jewish population in the "Final Solution to the Jewish Question." In what became known as the Holocaust, nearly 6 million Jews were uprooted in Europe by the Nazis and regimes of collaborators in countries like Romania, Hungary, France, and the Netherlands and sent to concentration camps or outright extermination camps, according to Edward Cranshaw in *Gestapo: Instrument of Tyranny*. (Genocide may be the more applicable term for the Holocaust, though the Nazi mission was to cleanse the ethnicity of the Aryan race via genocide of the Jews and other "undesirables.") In the Nazi SS, as Cranshaw wrote, Reinhard Heydrich "was for-

mally in charge of the 'final solution,' and [it was Adolf] Eichmann and his subordinates who rounded up the Jews and arranged for their delivery to the gas chambers." The Nuremberg War Crimes Tribunal after the war was the first instance in which perpetrators of such war crimes were tried, according to the 1945 Charter of the International Military Tribunal, for "violations of war or the customs of war."

Severe bloodletting has taken place in internecine strife in Africa in the years since World War II and during the partition of the British Empire of India into India and Pakistan in 1947. However, perhaps the most stark example of purposeful ethnic cleansing has taken place in the Balkans since the breakup of Yugoslavia in 1991. According to Roger Cohen in *Crimes of War: What the Public Should Know*, "between April and August 1992, [Serbs expelled] more than 700,000 Muslims from an area covering 70 percent of Bosnia." In July 1995, the Serbian Army of Yugoslav President Slobodan Milosevic took over the spa of Srebrenica in Bosnia and systematically killed some 7,000 people. Once again, the ghosts of the past hung over the charnel house. During World War II, Bosnian Muslims of the German SS "Handschar (Scimitar)" Division had slaughtered unknown numbers of Serbs for supporting the communist partisans of Josip Broz Tito.

Although a peace accord was reached in late 1995 at Wright-Patterson Air Force Base in Dayton, Ohio, fighting broke out again in 1999 when Milosevic attempted to apply ethnic cleansing to the Muslim population in Kosovo province. Defeated in the war, Milosevic was subsequently arrested for war crimes and prosecuted before an international tribunal.

SEE ALSO

Volume 1 Left: Titoism; Germany; Stalin and Stalinism.
Volume 2 Right: Ustashe; Fascism; Hitler, Adolf.

BIBLIOGRAPHY

"Newsmaker Profiles: Slobodan Milosevic," www.cnn.com (May 2004); "Srebrenica: A Cry from the Grave," WNET Channel 13, New York, www.pbs.org (May 2004); "The Trial of Slobodan Milosevic," www.un.org (May 2004); Richard Berleth, *The Twilight Lords: An Irish Chronicle* (Knopf, 1978); John F. Murphy Jr., Roy Guttman, and David Rieff, eds., *Crimes of War: What the Public Should Know* (W.W. Norton, 1999); Edward Cranshaw, *Gestapo: Instrument of Tyranny* (Da Capo, 1994).

JOHN F. MURPHY, JR.
AMERICAN MILITARY UNIVERSITY

The Right

Falangism

SPANIARD JOSE Antonio Primo de Rivera founded the fascistic Falange Española (Spanish Falange) in 1933. The Falange was pro-Catholic, anti-liberal, anti-communist, and nationalistic; its name is derived from the Macedonian unit of battle responsible for the destruction of democracy in Greece in the 4th century B.C.E. Primo de Rivera admired fascists Adolf Hitler in Germany and Benito Mussolini in Italy. Like them, he favored a strong state and opposed class struggle. As he wrote in 1933, "The State is founded on two principles—service to the united nation and the co-operation of classes."

The Falange emerged following the resignation of General Miguel Primo de Rivera, Jose Antonio's aristocratic father, who had ruled Spain from 1923 to 1930. The monarchy, which had ruled Spain since the 1400s, fell shortly thereafter and in 1931 popular elections established the Second Republic in power. The Second Republic issued a new constitution that gave women the vote, "separated Church and State, and abolished aristocratic title," Judith Keene points out. It then initiated reforms, most especially land reform, that undercut the centuries-long power and privilege of the church and the nobility. The Republican government also supported workers' rights and attempted to streamline the military by reducing the number of officers. These re-

forms antagonized the aristocracy, the church, and the military, all of which actively opposed the republic. It was in this tense political climate that the Falange developed and came to play such a powerful role in the ensuing civil war that engulfed Spain from 1936 to 1939.

The civil war began in July 1936 when the army, under the command of General Francisco Franco, revolted against the republic. From inside his prison cell where the Republicans had jailed him, Primo de Rivera exhorted the military to overthrow the republic and pledged Falangist support for an anti-government coup. However, Primo did not participate in the fighting; in November 1936 he was tried in a Republican court, found guilty of the illegal possession of firearms, and executed.

Reflecting its anti-republican politics, the Falange preached conservative ideas about women and maintained rigid gender roles. In 1934, Pilar Primo de Rivera, Jose Antonio's sister, started the Sección Femenina (Women's Branch) of the Falange. From a beginning membership of seven, the organization grew to include 400,000 women in 1938. Many of these women worked in *auxilio social*, (social welfare) and "provided food, clothing, and shelter to [Falange] widows, orphans, and the destitute, and taught them to 'love God and understand the Falange,'" explains Victoria Enders. These women accepted a patriarchal view of the world and their place in it; they counseled women that their primary duty in life was to be a loving mother and a submissive wife. Nevertheless, they dedicated much of their younger lives to public activity, first in support of the Falange and in opposition to the republic and then, after the defeat of the republic, to the dictatorship of Franco.

During the civil war, the Falangist forces formed battalions and fought in the Franco-led Nationalist Army against the republic. In 1937, Franco merged the Falange with other right-wing forces in Spain to form "the official political organization of the Spanish Nationalist state," Stanley Payne reports. The republic fell in 1939 and Franco assumed power and held it until his death in 1975. Although Spain was neutral during World War II, the Falangists formed the Blue Division, consisting of 47,000 volunteers, to fight on the side of Germany. Throughout his long rule, Franco relied on the Falange, along with the Catholic Church and the military, to provide him with a firm base of support.

SEE ALSO

Volume 1 Left: Spain; Socialism; Suffragists; Feminism.
Volume 2 Right: Fascism; Spain; Feminism.

BIBLIOGRAPHY

Victoria Enders, "And We Ate up the World: Memories of the Sección Femenina," Right-Wing Women: From Conservatives to Extremists, Paola Bacchetta and Margaret Power, eds. (Routledge, 2002); Judith Keene, Fighting for Franco (Leicester University Press, 2001); Stanley Payne, Falange: A History of Spanish Fascism (Stanford University Press, 1961); Stanley Payne, Politics and the Military in Modern Spain (Stanford University Press, 1967).

MARGARET POWER
ILLINOIS INSTITUTE OF TECHNOLOGY

Family First

FAMILY FIRST IS A CONSERVATIVE Christian organization based in Tampa, Florida. Its stated mission is to strengthen the institution of the family by making it a priority in people's lives, particularly through promoting traditional Christian principles for marriage and childraising. It has provided expert speakers for numerous media outlets, and runs a sizable site on the internet with advice and information on family life. Family First was founded in 1991 by Mark Merrill, a Tampa lawyer whose practice had brought him into contact with many troubled people. He had become convinced that almost all people in trouble with the law shared a common characteristic—a weak or disconnected family that failed to provide an upbringing strong in moral direction. Instead of merely reacting to the results of this failure, Merrill decided it was time to actively work to turn around this problem. From this determination came Family First.

Although Family First promotes conservative Christian values of a traditional family structure, it is not connected with or supported by any denomination. Its board of directors and staff include members of many churches, from Roman Catholics to Evangelical Protestants. As a result, they do not base their work on any particular sect's theology, but on general principles that conservative Christian denominations generally agree upon. They support the principle that a strong traditional family, with conventional gender and generational roles, is the best environment for bringing up healthy children who will be an asset to society. They have backed this assertion with sociological research linking such social ills as poverty, juvenile delinquency, and mental illness with absent fathers, divorce, and other breaches of the traditional family structure of father, mother, and children.

However, Family First does not limit its work to researching the sources of social ills. It also has an extensive outreach program to spread the values of traditional family structure that its members believe are critical to stemming and reversing social decay. One of the major means of reaching others used by Family First is its site on the internet, which includes an extensive collection of articles on various topics related to families, as well as interactive quizzes, brochures, and even a collection of free recipes for encouraging families to eat together. (Family First argues that shared family meals are one of the critical components of family cohesion, and that allowing family members to eat alone at random times and places instead of around a shared table contributes to the dissolution of the family.) Family First has also created some seminars to take to Christian groups, and has taped them for people who cannot attend an appearance by one of their guest speakers in person.

Family First divides its program into four major areas—marriage, parenting, fatherhood, and family life. It is significant that the group makes a distinction between fatherhood and parenting in general. This reflects a philosophy, common in conservative Christian thinking on family structure, that the father has a special leadership role not only over the children, but over his wife as well. This leadership concept is often referred to as "headship," referring to the metaphor used in the Bible, particularly in the various Pauline epistles, of the man being the head of the household as Christ is the head of the church (church here being used as a collective for all believers in Christ, rather than any particular denomination or congregation).

As part of this emphasis on fatherhood, Family First has also launched a subsidiary program known as All Pro Dad. This endeavor uses a football theme and has recruited a number of professional football players and coaches as spokesmen. All of these professional football spokesmen are themselves married and have children, and are able to use their own lives as good examples. The program includes the Play of the Day, a daily e-mail with advice on being a better father, free tutorials on improving one's fathering skills, and other resources for fathers. The organization has also developed local "teams" that meet monthly with their children for All Pro Dad's Day.

In addition to the free information available on the website, Family First offers materials for sale through its eStore. These range from commercial books and audio discs on various family-related subjects by such well-known Christian writers on the family as Dr. James Dobson and Tim LaHaye to booklets produced by Family First. Unlike most e-stores, the prices are stated in terms of a "suggested donation," emphasizing the nonprofit nature of Family First. People who cannot afford the stated prices are encouraged to contact Family First and work out a price and payment program they can manage.

In January, 2000 Family First launched *The Family Minute*, a radio program offering brief, punchy advice and commentary related to family life. When *The Family Minute* was first produced, it was carried by only two stations in two states. By 2004 it was broadcast nationwide, with 80 stations in 25 states. *The Family Minute* had a radio audience of 778,000, with an additional 35,000 receiving a transcript via e-mail. *The Family Minute* had become so popular that a number of transcripts were compiled and published as a book.

Family First generally focuses on the positive ways in which parents can strengthen their family relationships with one another and with their children, and minimizes such controversial subjects as wifely submission and corporal punishment that have attracted criticism to several denominations. By avoiding such doctrinal flashpoints, Family First can reach people of a wide spectrum of Christian beliefs.

SEE ALSO
Volume 1 Left: Feminism; Civil Liberties; Church and State Separation; United States.
Volume 2 Right: Christian Coalition; Christian Identity; Religion; United States; New Right.

BIBLIOGRAPHY
Michael Cromartie, ed., *No Longer Exiles: The Religious New Right in American Politics* (Ethics and Public Policy Center, 1993); Mark Merril, *Family Minutes* (Family First, 2003); Glenn H. Utter and John W. Storey, *The Religious Right: A Reference Handbook* (ABC-CLIO, 2001)

LEIGH KIMMEL, PH.D.
INDEPENDENT SCHOLAR

Fascism

IT IS A SUPREME IRONY that, according to American President Woodrow Wilson, World War I was fought to make "the world safe for democracy." Yet the war, which the greatest liberal statesmen of their generation were unable to prevent, ended in the birth of fascism, with communism one of the two most anti-democratic forces of modern times. Fascism or, as it was known in Germany, Nazism, was in a real sense the response of many front-line soldiers who survived the war against the political beliefs of the "donkeys" at home who had sent them to fight.

The two most visible human personifications of European fascism were Benito Mussolini of Italy and Adolf Hitler of Germany, who had both seen military service in the war. Hitler, who would go on to lead Germany in 1933, had won the Iron Cross for bravery in the trenches on the Western Front. According to Roger Eatwell in *Fascism: A History*, "Mussolini joined the [Italian] Army, serving with enthusiasm if not with great distinction, until injured when a shell exploded in a mortar during firing practice."

The militarism that was the hallmark of fascism had been evident even earlier in the writings of the Italian Filippo Marinetti, who rhapsodized in *The Futurist Manifesto* of 1909 of "war—the world's only hygiene—militarism, patriotism, the destructive gesture of the anarchists, beautiful ideas worth dying for." Indeed, the joyful way in which the nations of Europe had marched to war in August 1914 might serve to pinpoint fascism as a part of militarism, as one of the real causes—and

Two of the greatest fascists in history, Benito Mussolini (left) and Adolf Hitler smile at the height of their power in 1941. Each leader delved deep into his nation's conservative past to evoke the glory of its fascist movements.

not results—of the world conflict. However, it was in the aftermath of World War I that the movements historically classified as fascism made their appearance.

All such movements were inherently conservative in their appeal, traditionally making an obeisance to "king and country," even if in countries like Italy Mussolini would be the real power, not King Victor Emmanuel II, and in Spain it would be General Primo de Rivera who would hold tight the reins of power, not King Alphonso XIII. Also, the fascist movements were marked by a fanatic belief in the end justifying the means, of might justifying everything. Friedrich Nietzsche, wrote of such bemedaled elites, "we can imagine them returning from an orgy of murder, arson, rape, and torture, jubilant and at peace with themselves as though they had committed a fraternity prank," as

Christopher Simpson translates the German philosopher in *The Splendid Blonde Beast.*

In 1919, as the Great Powers tried to make sense of the shambles of a collapsed Europe at the Paris Peace Conference, Gabriele D'Annunzio emerged as the first recognized fascist leader in Europe. A true war hero from World War I and the role model for Mussolini, D'Annunzio made his mark in September 1919 when, like a medieval Italian *condottiere*, he carved out a city state in Fiume, which Italy's obliging Western Allies (Great Britain, France, and the United States) were going to give to Yugoslavia. The new state of Yugoslavia was being made with diplomatic glue out of the wreckage of the empire of Austria-Hungary and prewar Balkan countries like Serbia. Indeed, as David Frumkin wrote in *A Peace to End All Peace,* Italy was falling out quickly with its wartime comrades. Lord Curzon, the ultimate British imperialist, reproached Count Carlo Sforza, who would become Italian foreign minister in 1920, for having an "unloyal attitude" toward Allied plans for the dividing of the spoils of the conquered Ottoman Turkish Empire in the Middle East. Italy, however, was compelled to abide by the Treaty of Rapallo of 1922 that made D'Annunzio's Fiume into a "free city," thus sending the poet-activist into exile. The Rapallo Treaty, however, became for Italy what the Versailles Treaty would be for the Nazis in Germany, a diplomatic "stab in the back." Opposition to the treaty was strenuously voiced by Mussolini, then the sulphurous editor of the newspaper *Popolo d'Italia*.

Although still the recognized voice of Italian nationalism, D'Annunzio relinquished leadership of the movement to Mussolini, who, after his celebrated March on Rome with his Black Shirts, became prime minister of Italy in October 1922. While harkening back to the glories of ancient Rome—the very term *fascist* refers to the bundles of sticks, the *fasces*, that Roman officials carried with them as a symbol of authority—modern-day fascism was very much linked with the idea of the corporate state.

In the corporate state, the people were expected to robustly serve not only the state but the large corporations, which, as with Hitler in Germany, were the main supporters of the fascist party in power. The best definition of the corporate state may come from John Kenneth Galbraith. Galbraith wrote in *The New Industrial State* that "it is the genius of the industrial state that it makes the goals that reflect its needs—efficient production of goods, a steady expansion in their output, a steady expansion in their consumption ... coordinated with social virtue and enlightenment."

HITLER'S FASCISM

While Mussolini may have been the most operatic of fascist dictators, Adolf Hitler would prove to be the most ruthless when he took power in Germany. The Nazi Party, the National German Socialist Workers Party, had begun as the Committee of Independent Workmen, established by Anton Drexler in Munich in March 1918, at the time of the last great German offensive on the Western Front. Hitler joined the party in September 1919, according to William L. Shirer in *The Rise and Fall of the Third Reich*. Hitler, as he would later remember in his *Mein Kampf*, found in the philosophy of the party something that struck in his psyche a highly responsive (if not fanatic) chord. It was, as Hitler

wrote, "the longing for a new movement which should be more than a [political] party in the previous sense of the word." By April 1920, Hitler had emerged as the leader of the group: it was then that the name became "the National German Socialist Workers Party," the NSDAP, or the Nazi Party.

Much like Mussolini and D'Annunzio, Hitler would provide a pseudo-historical foundation by mining the past of his nation. Hitler and the Nazis, building on the work of earlier German ideologues like Lanz von Liebenfels, sought their inspiration in the days of the ancient German tribes. It was these tribes that Hitler and his later propaganda minister, Joseph Goebbels, held up as the source of the spirit of the German people, or *volk*. It was in 9 C.E. that the Germans under Arminius (Hermann) slaughtered three Roman legions under Quinctilius Varus in the Teutoberg Forest, as Michael Grant records in *The Twelve Caesars*. Those Romans who were not killed on the battlefield were later sacrificed to the Germanic gods.

By January 1933, through intricate deals made with the military and financiers of the conservative postwar German Weimar Republic, Hitler had made himself master, or *fuehrer*, of Germany. As Shirer wrote, "on this wintry morning of January 30, 1933, the tragedy of the Weimar Republic, of the bungling attempt for 14 years of the Germans to make democracy work, had come to an end." The 1930s, indeed, were the decade when fascism seemed like the wave of the future, especially to those who feared the communism of the Soviet Union. The Comintern, or Communist International, was the organization that Soviet Premier Josef Stalin used to propagate communist ideology worldwide, and was in full operation around this time.

BRITISH AND IRISH FASCISM

In the United Kingdom, fascism was represented by Sir Oswald Mosley, who launched his New Party in 1931. Mosley then created the British Union of Fascists (BUF) a year later. However, by 1936, with the face of Nazism beginning to show its true colors in Germany with persecution of the Jews, homosexuals, and any opponents of Hitler's self-styled Third Reich, the political climate froze in England for Mosley. In 1936, the government of Prime Minister Stanley Baldwin passed the Public Order Act, which severely restricted the increasingly thuggish tactics of the BUF.

Within the British Isles, there was also a fascist movement in Ireland, formed largely from veterans of the years of conflict with Great Britain and the grim civil war that came in its wake from 1922 to 1923. The Army Comrades' Association (ACA) officially re-formed itself in March 1932 with a National Executive, as Tim Pat Coogan wrote in *Eamon De Valera: The Man Who Was Ireland*. In the spring of 1933, following the triumph of Hitler in Germany, Coogan wrote that "the ACA also developed the habit of the one-armed Hitler salute. Its leader was former Irish Army General Eoin O'Duffy. Both salute [and a distinctive blue shirt] were adopted officially by the movement after July 20, 1933." However, De Valera, who had been the last leader of the IRA, the Irish Republican Army, in the civil war, was undeterred. Eventually, after forcing the ACA to disband in August 1933, De Valera was able to remove the Blue Shirt movement from Irish politics by eroding its popular support.

PORTUGUESE, FRENCH, AND SPANISH FASCISM

In 1932, Professor Antonio Salazar took power in Portugal as prime minister. As with Hitler in Germany, in 1933 he made his bid for power. Salazar developed the Estado Novo, or new state. The basis of his dictatorship was a platform of stability. Salazar's reforms greatly privileged the upper classes at the expense of the poor. Education was not seen as a priority and therefore not expanded. Salazar had a version of the secret police named PIDE who repressed dissent. However, unlike many of his contemporary dictators, Salazar's regime was less bloody due to Portugal's lack of a death penalty. Although Salazar would support Franco in the Spanish Civil War, like Franco he would avoid alliance with Mussolini and Hitler during World War II. Indeed, he would permit Great Britain and the United States to use the Portuguese Azores islands as bases against the Germans in the Battle of the Atlantic.

Fascism also figured in France between the wars, in the person of Charles Maurras's Action Francaise. Indeed, founded in 1894, Action Francaise may lay claim to being the true precursor of later fascist movements in Europe, a protofascist mass movement. According to the Shoah Research Center, "members advocated the removal of the republic and return to monarchy." As Shoah notes, "for nearly 50 years, Maurras's movement was a frontrunner of French Antisemitism." Another prominent group, drawn from the ranks of French veterans of World War I, was the Croix de Feu, or Cross of Fire.

In 1936, the Spanish Civil War broke out, bringing the third most important fascist dictator to the Euro-

pean stage. The civil war broke out initially as a mutiny of the Spanish troops in Morocco, including the elite Spanish Foreign Legion, against the Spanish Republic of the Popular Front government. The leader of the revolt was Francisco Franco, whose forces would soon be called the Nationalists. The Republican cause was seen as a crusade against fascism by many in Europe and the United States. International brigades were formed to help fight alongside the forces of the republic; the Abraham Lincoln Brigade was formed by Americans. However, behind the lines, Josef Stalin used the republic as a Trojan Horse to attempt to build a communist state in Spain. (Indeed, the gold reserves of the Spanish Republic were shipped to Moscow for "safekeeping," but never returned.) Franco's Nationalists received substantial help from Mussolini and Hitler, who viewed the civil war as a proving ground for their weaponry. On March 28, 1939, the Nationalists entered Madrid, and on April 1, Franco officially declared the war at an end.

When Hitler invaded Poland in September 1939, World War II erupted in Europe. In June 1940, when Hitler invaded France, Mussolini joined him half-heartedly in the attack. However, when Hitler met Franco at Hendaye in October 1940, Franco declined to enter the war on the side of Germany and Italy, although he would temporarily later commit his Blue Division to the fighting in Russia after Hitler invaded the Soviet Union in June 1941. By largely maintaining his neutrality, Franco thus became the only one of the Big Three of the fascist dictators in Europe to survive the end of the war in May 1945. Hitler would commit suicide, and Mussolini would be shot by Italian partisans, or resistance fighters.

While fascism, now called neo-Nazism, has remained a political force in Europe up until today, including the Pamyat movement in the former Soviet Union, it has ceased to be a political movement able to disturb the peace of a stable Europe.

SEE ALSO

BIBLIOGRAPHY

Christopher Simpson, *The Splendid Blonde Beast: Money, Law, and Genocide in the Twentieth Century* (Common Courage Press, 1995); "Action Francaise," Shoah Resource Center, www.yadvashem.org.il (July 2004); "The Spanish Civil War," www.sispain.org (July 2004); Roger Eatwell, *Fascism: A History* (Penguin, 1995); John Kenneth Galbraith, *The New Industrial State* (Houghton Mifflin, 1978); David Frumkin, *A Peace* to End All Peace (Avon Books, 1989); Tim Pat Coogan, *Eamon De Valera: The Man Who Was Ireland* (Harper, 1995).

JOHN F. MURPHY, JR.
AMERICAN MILITARY UNIVERSITY

Feminism

ALTHOUGH THE HISTORY of American feminism, understood as women's desire to achieve sexual equality, is as old as the United States itself, it was not until the 1960s that the modern movement took shape. Despite whatever inroads feminists claim to have made for women in recent decades, political and social critics on the right argue that, in reality, the feminist movement has exacerbated women's discontent by its devaluation of traditional gender roles and its division of women across the political spectrum.

Though the term *feminism* would not exist until the 20th century, as early as the 18th century, some women called for an improvement of women's status in society. Likely inspired by the egalitarian, revolutionary rhetoric, Abigail Adams, wife of future president of the United States John Adams, in 1776 reminded her husband to "Remember the ladies" as he and his fellow gentlemen developed plans for the new nation. In the years after the American Revolution, Englishwoman Mary Wollstonecraft and Judith Sargent Murray wrote essays urging greater independence for women through access to education. Generally referring to white, privileged, married women, these authors nevertheless inspired some 19th-century women to change their social identity.

During the 1830s and 1840s, a period of widespread reform across the United States, thousands of women became involved in moral reform societies in attempts to curb the abuses of alcohol. Their collective experiences and increased educational opportunities—made possible through the inception of female academies and seminaries—propelled the issue of women's rights to the social and political foreground alongside the question of abolition and the rights of African Americans.

Indeed, the earliest women's movement emerged in tandem with the anti-slavery movement. Finding parallels between slavery and women's loss of legal rights and social status upon their marriage, women used the skills they had learned as abolitionists to launch women's activism. But even these earliest activities divided women over the issues of sexual equality and women's appropriate role in society. When women gathered in Seneca Falls (New York) in 1848 for the first women's rights meeting, they produced the Declaration of Sentiments, which, in the language of the Declaration of Independence, condemned men for denying women their equal rights. Although most of the women's grievances met unanimous approval, the call for the right to vote earned far less support; its direct challenge to the traditional male-dominated social structure seemed too far-reaching to some women.

In the post-Civil War era, the granting of suffrage to African American males through the Fifteenth Amendment propelled the creation of the women's suffrage movement but divided women over whether to support or oppose the granting of suffrage to newly freed black men. The suffrage movement would remain fractured into the 20th century and during the Progressive era, a period of heightened reform. White, middle-class women's reform activities brought them into the public arena and seemed to better justify their need for the vote. Yet, the contrasting justifications for women's suffrage—sexual equality, women deserve the vote as equal citizens, versus sexual difference, women would bring unique qualities into the political arena—foreshadowed future divisions. By 1919, years of women's organized efforts in club movements and World War I pushed Congress to approve woman suffrage. The Nineteenth Amendment, granting women the right to vote, was ratified by the states in 1920.

The term *feminism* made its debut during the later years of the suffrage movement. It represented the break between the campaign for suffrage and the contemporary feminist movement. While some women activists saw the vote as the pinnacle of their efforts, other women saw the achievement of suffrage as a springboard to greater equality and independence from men. Though the years immediately after the passage of the Nineteenth Amendment saw a great deal of feminist-organized activism, the various women's groups that had united to win the vote splintered according to their arguments for gender equality or embracing sexual difference.

In particular, when in 1923 the National Women's Party proposed the Equal Rights Amendment (ERA), it was the source of great debate. Many women feared that its passage would invalidate legislation that protected women and would thus lead to a deterioration of conditions for women in the workplace. That the ERA caused internal strife and failed to gain widespread support in the 1920s foreshadowed some of the later problems and misunderstandings within the feminist movement in the late 20th century.

During the Great Depression and World War II era, women's activism subsided under the national war effort. When the war ended, families longed for a return to normalcy. Though the retreat to the suburbs obstructed women's organized efforts, many women embraced their traditional gender roles and looked forward to nurturing their families during the postwar recovery and the early stages of the Cold War. Over the course of the 1950s and early 1960s, however, historical factors such as the emergent civil rights movement in the south and women's greater access to higher education, to the workplace, and to birth control created an environment suitable for a revival of the feminist movement in the mid-1960s. Yet, the millions of American women whose lives were affected by the feminist movement in the 1960s and 1970s would not universally agree on all issues. Nor would the movement represent women across lines of race, class, and ethnicity. In particular, African American and Latino American women had to balance their identities as women with their identities as minorities; working-class women were more dedicated to issues common to all working people.

Yet, with the publication of Betty Friedan's 1963 *The Feminine Mystique*, which called attention to white, middle-class women's discontent in their roles as wives and mothers, the contemporary feminist movement was born. The mainstream movement was primarily made up of women like Friedan—middle-class, educated white women. Older, moderate professionals joined the National Organization of Women (NOW), founded in 1966 in response to the government's failure to impose anti-sex discrimination laws. Committed to the passage of a revitalized ERA, NOW devoted itself to helping women gain equal access to the public arena, particularly the workplace. Though the organization's tactics were less radical, over the years its members and its goals became more overtly political and controversial, including the support of gay and lesbian rights.

But it was the battle over the ERA in the late 1970s that both built NOW into a large organization and drew a strong backlash from conservative critics on the right. The ERA of the 1970s stated, "Equality of rights under the law shall not be denied or abridged by the United States or any State on account of sex." That many men opposed the ERA was hardly surprising; however, the proposed amendment also met resistance from certain women, particularly those who had cultivated their identities around their roles as wives and mothers and fiercely defended that convention.

Most famously, Phyllis Schlafly, a conservative Illinois lawyer, presided over the defeat of the ERA. Her organization, Stop ERA, benefited from the conservative opposition that gained force and energy in the 1970s. Right opponents to feminism sought to uphold the traditional family structure to which gay rights, abortion, and day care—causes supported by the left feminist movement and liberal social policies—posed a threat. Female anti-feminists also worried about the effects that women's entry into the workplace would have on their children. They believed the amendment would allow men to shy away from supporting their wives and would also free divorced men from paying alimony. Specifically, Schlafly argued that the ERA would undermine women, destroy the family, and increase homosexuality. ERA opponents also opposed "unisex" facilities and the drafting of women into military combat.

Despite harsh criticism from the right, the amendment was approved by the required two-thirds vote of the House of Representatives in October 1971 and by the Senate in March 1972. The ERA earned early support as 30 states ratified it, but despite a deadline extension to June 30, 1982, it ultimately failed to be ratified by the requisite 38 states. In addition to the defeat of the ERA, anti-feminists praised the 1976 passage of the Hyde Amendment, which prohibited the use of Medicaid monies for abortions.

NOW's focus on the ERA shifted its attention away from other causes such as childcare, abortion rights, and women living in poverty. And by the late 1970s, other groups of feminists who opposed NOW's more moderate liberal feminism came together with the goal of dramatically restructuring society's gender conventions. One of these groups of women's liberationists, who called themselves radical feminists, offered the most controversial analyses of male supremacy. These radicals attacked marriage, the nuclear family, heterosexuality, violence against women (especially rape), and sexist public policies such as healthcare.

Besides the conservative attacks, the feminist movement was plagued by its own internal contradictions and inequities. NOW's liberal feminist emphasis on integrating women into the public arena discounted the realities of the jobs that most women held. Radical feminists' argument that women must ally according to their sex made it difficult to unite women across lines of race and class. Socialist-feminists, who believed that socialism would facilitate women's liberation, did not appeal to enough women to build a strong movement. And by the 1980s, the issue of pornography emerged as a divisive issue for feminists, one group calling it degrading while another called it free expression. The hypocrisy and fractures within feminism only made the strong opposition from the right more potent.

By the 1980s, the feminist movement had made important inroads into gender discrimination, though some forms of inequality remained. But a younger generation of women, who were more certain that they enjoyed fair treatment under the law, rejected the politically charged term *feminism*, given its radical underpinnings and its anti-male rhetoric. Though anti-feminists fundamentally resented the disrespect for motherhood and traditional gender roles that feminism seemed to undermine, both feminists and anti-feminists agreed that American women, particularly poor American women, should not be entirely dependent on men. At the center of the divide over feminism, then, is the matter of how best to protect women's interests.

SEE ALSO

Volume 1 Left: Feminism; Friedan, Betty; Steinem, Gloria; Civil Rights.
Volume 2 Right: Conservatism.

BIBLIOGRAPHY

Nancy Cott, *The Grounding of Modern Feminism* (Yale University Press, 1987); Susan J. Douglas, *Where the Girls Are: Growing up Female with the Mass Media* (Three Rivers Press, 1994); Alice Echols, *Daring to Be Bad: Radical Feminism in America, 1967–75* (University of Minnesota Press, 1989); Carolyn F. Graglia, *Domestic Tranquility: A Brief against Feminism* (Spence Publishing Company, 1998); Rhonda Hammer, *Antifeminism and Family Terrorism: A Critical Feminist Perspective* (Rowman and Littlefield, 2002); Ruth Rosen, *The World Split Open: How the Modern Women's Movement Changed America* (Penguin Putnam, 2000); Phyllis Schlafly, *Feminist Fantasies* (Spence Publishing Company, 2003).

LINDSAY SILVER
BRANDEIS UNIVERSITY

Feudalism

FEUDALISM IS A TERM generally used to describe the political, economic, and social life of Europe from the fall of the western Roman Empire in 476 C.E. up to the rise of the modern nation-states in the 15th century. Feudalism can roughly be defined as a social system in which a strong warlord was able to provide protection for weaker citizens in his region. In return for providing protection from roving bandits, the warlord would receive military service, or agricultural or other economic support. Given this definition, feudalism actually first emerged in England after the Roman legions were withdrawn in 410 C.E. to defend Rome and the continental empire from the onslaught of the Germanic tribes and later the Huns.

According to the *Anglo-Saxon Chronicle*, the Romanized Britons were dealt a severe defeat at Crayford in 457 by the Germanic Angles, Saxons, and Jutes. Yet, according to the historians Gildas and Geoffrey of Monmouth, Ambrosius Aurelianus, a *dux bellorum*, literally a "warlord," rose up to lead the Britons against the enemy. Because of his martial prowess, the Britons assembled around Aurelianus to seek his leadership. Therefore, Aurelianus has a fair historical claim to being the first feudal leader in Western Europe. However, Aurelianus did not live to see his counterattack against the Germans completed. According to the Welsh monk Nennius, the *dux bellorum* who succeeded him was Arthur, who served later as the model for the celebrated King Arthur of the Round Table.

Throughout England and Western Europe, the invading Germanic tribes were becoming influenced by the Christian church and gradually established more formal political identities. Chiefs of the tribes became seen as kings, and the model for their realms was feudalism. Indeed, the only way for lesser warriors to gain property soon became to swear allegiance to their overlords in return for military service. Such a solemn act was called giving fealty, in which the new landowner became the vassal of his lord. Michael Howard, in *War in European History*, marks this military relationship as the heart of the feudal system.

By the 8th to 9th centuries, the "barbarian" tribes had evolved from tribal societies into kingdoms. In order to cope with the new responsibilities, the kings of the new states had to rely on the assistance of the Christian church and the pope in Rome. While the political structure of Western Europe had been devastated in the 5th century, the church had survived, and with it five centuries of administrative experience. Christopher Dawson, in *The Making of Europe*, notes the role of the church in helping to create new political institutions in Europe out of the wreckage of the western Roman Empire in the Middle Ages.

By the 9th century, the new feudal kingdoms were defending Christian Europe from a new wave of invaders. In 732, Charles Martel, commander of the Franks under Clovis, who had earlier invaded Gaul

(France), turned back the Muslim invaders at Tours, France. Alfred of Wessex, the only English monarch to earn the sobriquet of "The Great," confronted the Danish invasion under Guthrum in 878, and defeated the Danes at Ethandun. Guthrum made peace and accepted baptism into Christianity. The future Holy Roman Emperor Otto the Great crushed the Magyars at the Lechfeld, near Augsburg in modern Germany, in 955. Indeed, the climax of the feudal system could be seen in 800, when Charlemagne, descended from the Frankish invaders, was crowned the new Holy Roman Emperor. In Ireland, which existed without the traditional European feudal system, the High King Brian Boru defeated the Viking invaders at Clontarf in 1014, and was killed at the hour of victory.

While the new kingdoms were developing, they sought legitimacy by appealing to the Christian church and its ancient symbols. When William, Duke of Normandy, invaded England in 1066, he used as justification an oath he said that King Harold Godwineson had made while earlier in Normandy to accept William as king of England. Under the table upon which Harold made his oath, according to Winston Churchill, "was concealed a sacred relic, said by some later writers to have been the bones of St. Edmund."

THE DOWNFALL OF FEUDALISM

However, the system of vassalage that underlay the feudal system proved to be its Achilles heel. Some of the feudal lords, or barons, became actually more powerful than their liege lord, the king. Rodrigo Diaz, the famed Spanish "El Cid," was a vassal of King Alfonso VI of Leon-Castille. However, he became ruler himself of the principality of Valencia.

But such an alteration in the feudal balance of power could also evoke positive results. It was the barons of England who, in 1215, made King John sign the Magna Carta, the first document of human rights in English history.

A combustible event was when the monarch of one country was the vassal of the monarch of another. This was one cause of the Hundred Years' War between France and England. In Scotland, John Balliol was enthroned as king in 1292, and then swore fealty to Edward I of England as his vassal. This led to the Scottish War of Independence, with the great William Wallace and Robert the Bruce as champions in the fight for Scottish freedom. It would not end until Robert the Bruce's victory over Edward's son, Edward II, at Bannockburn in June 1314.

Feudalism would, nevertheless, serve as the unifying force for Western society until monarchs like Henry VIII in England and Francis I in France, in the 16th century, could afford to hire mercenary standing armies to overawe the "feudal arrays" of their mighty lords and thus raise up the modern nation-states. Although subordinated to the monarchies, the feudal aristocrats continued to play an important role in national affairs in their respective countries. Indeed, high officialdom in the church, the government, and especially the armed forces served as the preserve of the landed nobility.

Politically and economically, the period from the Industrial Revolution on was difficult on the landed nobility because it saw the balance of real power shifting to the mercantile and manufacturing classes, who usually supported, in England for example, the Liberal Party. The feudal aristocracy still based its position of power upon the ownership of their land, which in England, for example, did not produce the wealth of the factories of Birmingham or Manchester. Thus, the feudal nobles allied themselves with the more conservative political parties, like the Conservative, or Tory, Party, in England, and the Conservatives and Free Conservatives in imperial Germany, created after the defeat of France in the Franco-Prussian War.

REACTIONARY CONSERVATISM

During the years before World War I, the issues between right and left, such as widening the voting franchise to include more working-class people who had a decidedly liberal (or even leftist) agenda, met with growing resistance from the more reactionary elements of the landed lords. In 1908, when British Prime Minister Henry Asquith attempted limited social welfare legislation, the House of Lords, allied to the Tories, fought a bitter battle with Asquith's Chancellor of the Exchequer David Lloyd George, who would later serve as prime minister in his own right.

The majority of the landed aristocracy would continue to stand resolutely against change, fighting a rear guard action "for king and country," or "*fur koenig und vaterland.*" Indeed, in the 1930s, much of the landed *junker* aristocracy of Germany would stand with the Nazis of Adolf Hitler, as the Spanish landed nobility would support General Francisco Franco and his Nationalists, or Falangists, in Spain. However, through the 19th and 20th centuries, landed aristocrats also numbered among the era's leading progressives. For example, one of the guiding spirits behind the liberalization of Russia during the reign of Tzar Alexander II

(1856–81) was Count M.T. Loris-Melikov, who was guiding Russia toward a conservative constitutional monarchy. The last prominent Russian reformer before the revolution was Count Sergei Witte, who had been raised to the nobility for his role in ending the Russo-Japanese War of 1904–05. During the revolution of 1905 that followed the war, he was the one who proposed the Duma, the Russian parliamentary assembly. When Tzar Nicholas II refused to support Witte against the reactionaries, he resigned and the last hope for a "conservative revolution" in Russia left with him.

SEE ALSO

Volume 1 Left: Despotism; United Kingdom; France.
Volume 2 Right: Royalty; United Kingdom; Colonialism.

BIBLIOGRAPHY

Michael Howard, *War in European History* (Oxford University Press, 2001); Richard Fletcher, *The Quest for El Cid* (Knopf, 1986); Eric Linklater, *The Conquest of England* (Doubleday, 1966); Winston S. Churchill, *The Birth of Britain* (Bantam Books, 1958); Christopher Dawson, *The Making of Europe: An Introduction to the History of European Unity* (Catholic University of America Press, 2002); Edward Gibbon, *The Decline and Fall of the Roman Empire* (Modern Library, n.d.); Marc Bloch, *Feudal Society: The Growth of the Dependence*, L.A. Manyon, trans. (University of Chicago Press, 1961); J. Huizinga, *The Waning of the Middle Ages* (Anchor Books, 1954); Henri Daniel-Rops, *The Church of Apostles and Martyrs*, Audrey Butler, trans. (Anchor Books, 1962); Miklos Jankovich, *They Rode into Europe: The Fruitful Exchange in the Arts of Horsemanship between East and West*, Anthony Dent, trans. (Harrap, 1971).

JOHN F. MURPHY, JR.
AMERICAN MILITARY UNIVERSITY

Ford, Gerald R. (1913–)

GERALD RUDOLPH FORD, the 38th president of the United States, was born on July 14, 1913, in Omaha, Nebraska. He was the only child of Leslie Lynch King and Dorothy Gardner King, and was originally named Leslie Lynch King, Jr. When his parents divorced, Ford, who was only two years old, and his mother moved to Grand Rapids, Michigan, where she married Gerald Rudolph Ford and renamed her child, giving him the same name as her new husband. Ford went to local grade school and South High School in Grand Rapids, where he participated in a wide range of sports. Athletic and extremely competitive, Ford loved being outdoors and became an accomplished Eagle Scout.

After completing high school, Ford studied law at the University of Michigan, entering in 1931. His love of sports continued and Ford competed on Michigan's football team, which won national championships in 1932 and 1933. Although he was offered opportunities with several professional football teams following his graduation in 1935, Ford decided to accept a position as an assistant football coach at Yale University. While there, Ford continued his study of law and even found time to coach a freshman boxing team. In 1941, Ford graduated from Yale, receiving his law degree.

Next, Ford passed the bar examination and returned to Grand Rapids, opening his own law office with a business partner and friend from college. His new practice was put on hold, however, following the entrance of the United States into World War II. Ford joined the navy, going on to serve for over four years, of which he spent almost 18 months in the Pacific theater. Entering the navy with the rank of ensign, Ford retired with the rank of lieutenant commander after having accumulated 10 battle stars. Following the conclusion of the war, he returned to his law practice.

Shortly thereafter, Ford started to become more and more active in local politics and established a friendship with Arthur Vandenberg, a U.S. senator from Michigan. With Vandenberg's help and encouragement, Ford was able to secure a seat in the U.S. House of Representatives, as a member of the Republican Party.

Winning election after election every two years, Ford remained in the House of Representatives until 1973, when he became vice president. During his tenure in the House, he advocated strict money management and strong national defense programs. He quickly gained bipartisan recognition of his political skill, integrity, and openness. Instead of authoring landmark legislation, Ford preferred to drum up support for bills that he favored. His attendance throughout his tenure was over 90 percent, which is and was a remarkable number considering all the time constraints and requirements facing a member of Congress.

His strength and longevity in Congress made him an excellent candidate for executive office. In 1960, Michigan's Republican Party endorsed Ford as a potential vice presidential candidate, but he was not selected by presidential candidate Richard M. Nixon. By 1964,

President Gerald Ford addresses the nation in a televised speech announcing the pardon of Richard Nixon.

Ford attained the powerful post of House Minority Leader, in response to congressional Republicans' concern over a lack of strong leadership. Catapulted into the spotlight, Ford soon gained national recognition as one of his party's main public spokesmen. Ford's career took a drastic turn following Vice President Spiro Agnew's resignation on October 10, 1973. President Nixon, empowered to nominate a vice president by the Twenty-Fifth Amendment of the Constitution, selected Ford, who was subsequently confirmed by a majority vote in Congress. Consequently, Ford became the first vice president to be appointed to his position.

Ford began to travel the country and fight for Nixon's proposals, but the president soon proved unable to escape from the effects of the Watergate scandal. In the face of certain impeachment, Nixon resigned on August 8, 1974, and Ford was sworn in as president the next day. Inheriting a troubled and upset country, Ford's history of integrity and openness in Congress helped to calm citizens in the face of Watergate.

As president, Ford first selected Nelson A. Rockefeller, governor of New York, as vice president and then pardoned Nixon, acting in favor of "compassion," even though it proved controversial. In the aftermath of the Vietnam War, Ford established a conditional amnesty for those who had fled conscription into the military, simply requiring that war resisters perform civilian service that would not exceed two years.

Economically, the country was in recession and had high unemployment, but Ford was not in favor of public-works programs to put people back to work. Instead he favored tax cuts and spending reductions, but his programs and his veto were overridden by Congress, which passed spending projects without his support. Inflation decreased, but the unemployment problems remained unsolved.

Ford received the Republican presidential nomination in 1976, beating out Ronald Reagan, former governor of California. He was defeated by Jimmy Carter in the election because many citizens believed that he did not do enough to fight unemployment during his brief term in office. Disappointed, Ford returned to private life and has served on management boards for different U.S. corporations. He published his autobiography, *A Time to Heal*, in 1979.

Ford's service in Congress and his brief term as president established him as a middle-of-the-road conservative, loyal to the party and if anything, a shade more conservative in his positions than Nixon. Although completely free of any of the political baggage that burdened Nixon and the corruption that tainted Spiro Agnew, Ford's pardon of the former president allowed opponents to leave the impression that there had been a corrupt bargain in his selection to replace Agnew.

SEE ALSO

Volume 1 Left: Democratic Party; Carter, James E.
Volume 2 Right: Nixon, Richard M.; Republican Party.

BIBLIOGRAPHY

"Biography of Gerald R. Ford," www.whitehouse.gov (May 2004); Stephen C. Flanders, "Ford, Gerald Rudolph," American Presidency, www.grolier.com (May 2004); John Robert Greene, *The Presidency of Gerald R. Ford* (University of Kansas Press, 1995).

ARTHUR HOLST, PH.D.
WIDENER UNIVERSITY

Foreign Policy, U.S.

FROM THE BIRTH of the United States in July 1776 during the American Revolution, certain imperative goals have underlined U.S. foreign policy. The primary objective has always been to defend the United States, its citizens, and its territory from hostile attack. Perhaps only secondary has come the preservation of America's widespread overseas interests and maritime trade, which often have been synonymous.

America's foreign policy has its own left and right spectrum, and on balance it often reflects the ideology in power or office at a given time. This article traces the history of U.S. foreign policy over 200 years, a breadth of policies that more often veer to the conservative side than the liberal. Overall, the United States is a conservative country on the international stage. Its history of foreign policy cites more efforts at maintaining American hegemony and power than in pursuing liberal foreign engagements. As American foreign policy is retraced in this article, left and especially right shifts in political agendas are identified.

GLOBAL REVOLUTIONARY INTERESTS

Less than a year after the Treaty of Paris in September 1783 officially recognized American independence, the ship *Empress of China* left Philadelphia in 1784 to begin American trade with China. From then on, with an efficient U.S. Navy to offer protection and transportation, American foreign policy interests became global within years of the end of the Revolution. A significant fact is that these foreign policy goals have been remarkably adhered to by presidents from all political parties.

After the war, it was essential to American security to try to actually lay claim to the land promised the United States by the Treaty of Paris, which officially ended the war in September 1783. Essential to this was to claim the western boundaries given by the Treaty of Paris as "a line to be drawn along the middle of the said river Mississippi." However, the British in Canada were still abetting attacks on the western settlements by the Indian tribes. Two disastrous expeditions were led by Arthur St. Clair and Josiah Harmar in the old Northwest Territory. It was not until General Anthony Wayne's victory over the Indian Confederacy of Chief Little Turtle at Fallen Timbers in August 1794 that the Americans could feel relatively secure to the west. As Walter Millis wrote in *Arms and Men*, "this soon spelled the end for the small British garrisons" that had been supplying the hostile warriors.

While Great Britain had attempted to bar the United States from expanding to the Mississippi in the north, Spain had attempted to control access to the mouth of the river at New Orleans in the south. However, the American success against the Indian coalition at Fallen Timbers enabled American diplomat Thomas Pinckney to negotiate the favorable Treaty of San Lorenzo in October 1995. The treaty made clear that "the navigation of the said river shall be free to the citizens of the United States."

At the same time, American freedom of the seas was handicapped by British warships stopping American vessels to search for alleged British deserters. Also, the feared Barbary Pirates of North Africa raided American ships plying the trade routes of the Mediterranean Sea. During the administration of President George Washington in 1794, Congress authorized the building of six advanced naval frigates to guard American interests at sea. By the time that Vice President John Adams became the Federalist Party's president in 1796, the United States was embroiled in a naval war with Revolutionary France. France, which had gone to war with England in 1792, had been angered by the United States' not supporting it—as it had supported the United States during the Revolutionary War against England. However, the new "super frigates" of the American Navy, among them the *United States*, *Constitution*, and *Constellation*, soon proved more than a match for the French ships sent against them. In September 1800, Napoleon, who had seized power in 1799, ended hostilities with a treaty of friendship with the United States.

Thus, by the time Thomas Jefferson of the Democratic-Republican Party was elected the third president in 1800, American foreign policy had formed around two strong pillars that have been steadily used to promote it: military and naval might, coincidentally echoing the historical experience of the Mother Country, Great Britain.

Within three decades of independence, the United States was able to mount a simultaneous demonstration of national power which would have taxed nations possessed of far larger military establishments. Robert Leckie noted in the first volume of *The Wars of America* that "by 1801 the United States had paid Morocco, Algiers, Tunis, and Tripoli—the Moslem states of the Barbary coast—$2 million in ransom for captured American seamen and in tribute to allow American ships to sail the Mediterranean unharmed."

In April 1805, after marching 600 miles across a Libyan desert, diplomat William Eaton and Marine Lieutenant Presley O'Bannon, with American Marines and Arab allies, were able to strike at the stronghold of the Barbary Pirates at Derna on the North African coast. An American naval squadron provided gunfire support for this historic example of "power from the sea," the American ability to use naval power not to only land on hostile shores, but to move inland far enough at will to enforce U.S. foreign policy goals.

On April 30, 1803, the Louisiana Purchase, pressed by President Thomas Jefferson, greatly added to the size of the United States. Indeed, some, including Jefferson, believed it opened a path across the continent to the far Pacific Ocean. In order to explore and lay American title to the vast wilderness, Jefferson called on the only body of men trained in both rigorous operations and accurate observation: the U.S. Army. In spite of the victory at Fallen Timbers in 1794 and Pinckney's Treaty, both Great Britain from Canada and Spain to the south wished to keep the United States hemmed in by the Mississippi River. Even more, they constantly encouraged secessionist movements along the American east bank of the river to weaken the United States. As late as 1795, Spanish warships patrolled the Mississippi River from their base at New Orleans. Therefore, Jefferson felt that the bold adventures of Lewis and Clark and Zebulon Pike, were needed to demonstrate to the British and Spanish that the United States was to be the master in its own house. He assigned Meriwether Lewis and William Clark to lead a Corps of Discovery to the Pacific—and hopefully back again. At the same time, he dispatched Zebulon Pike on a much more mysterious journey.

Setting out on May 13, 1804, Lewis and Clark would make their epic trek to the Pacific and back with the loss of only one man, truly a dramatic demonstration of the effectiveness of any military establishment, especially one so young. As Clark had written on November 7, 1805, they finally were in view of "this great Pacific Ocean which we have been so long anxious to see." In September 1806, the Brave Rifles were back home in St. Louis. Wrote Clark on September 21, 1806, "every person, both French and American, seemed to express great pleasure at our return."

Zebulon Pike's explorations were fraught with more secrecy than the Corps of Discovery, although he too played a vital role in expanding America's military presence in the heartland of the country. Pike began a trek north on August 1805, while Lewis and Clark were exploring to the west. In a telling demonstration of America's intention to project its military might, at a post of the British North-West Fur Company on American soil, Pike forcibly took down the British Union Jack and had the Stars and Stripes raised proudly in its place at Hugh McGillis' Leech Lake Post. Pike began his second voyage of exploration—and likely espionage—in July 1806. Only this time he was captured by the Spanish from New Spain (Mexico), who suspected the real intention of his mission. Although captured by the Spanish, he was returned to American Louisiana on July 1, 1807. During his sojourn on his second trip, through the American West, and Mexico after his capture, he proved that espionage—the gathering of intelligence—was now an important "third force" to employ along with military and naval might to further American foreign policy interests.

WAR OF 1812

On June 18, 1812, the second war with Great Britain began, sometimes referred to as the Second War of Independence. While the War of 1812 began inauspiciously enough for the American forces, it demonstrated the wisdom of employing the army and the navy to protect American interests. In the beginning of the war, as Leckie noted, "there were less than 7,000 men in the regular Army." Nevertheless, the years of maturation since the Revolution had brought forth a generation of fighters on land and sea who would turn the tide in the war. Between August and October, the Americans restored the northern flank against Canada, with Oliver Hazard Perry's naval victory at the Battle of Lake Erie on September 10, and William Henry Harrison's triumph on October 4 on the banks of the River Thames in Canada. Killed with the British was one of America's great warriors, the Shawnee chief Tecumseh.

In December 1814 and January 1815, Andrew Jackson had stopped a major British invasion of the south, culminating in his victory at New Orleans on January 8, 1815. Although peace had been formally signed between the United States and Great Britain on December 24, 1814, at Ghent in Belgium, the slow pace of sailing ship communications had kept word of the treaty from arriving before the battle was fought.

The War of 1812 had witnessed the embarrassing burning of the American capital at Washington, D.C., in August 1814, when President James Monroe's White House had been set afire. But it had ended at New Orleans with the crushing of an army of British regulars that had succeeded in only recently defeating Napoleon. Furthermore, the war had seen the final realization of American control of the land east of the Mississippi River while at the same time opening the lands of the west to further exploration and settlement, and had established forever American rights to freedom of the seas.

During the nearly half century after the "peace of Christmas Eve" brought an end to the War of 1812, the United States, through successive changes in presidential administrations, continued to follow the developing foreign policy of earlier years. Within months of the victory of New Orleans, the U.S. Navy returned to its prewar campaign against the marauding Barbary Pirates. As John H. Schröeder wrote in *Command under Sail*, "In 1815, the dramatic success of Stephen Decatur's naval squadron in the Mediterranean further enhanced the Republic's confidence in the months after the War of 1812." In a pursuit of liberal foreign policy, the United States began naval patrols against the African slave trade, although slavery would not begin to be abolished in the United States until the Emancipation Proclamation of January 1863. (By sad contrast, the British had already ended slavery in their empire in 1833.)

On land, the American Army moved with deliberation to remove any enemy threat that might endanger the growing settlements west of the Mississippi. The Black Hawk War of 1832 was the last Native American struggle fought on the eastern shores of the "Father of Waters."

MONROE DOCTRINE

With the assurance of American freedom of the seas in the War of 1812, American interests now effectively reached out to South and Central America as well. When the Mexicans won their freedom from Spain in 1820, the United States supported the goal of national independence in the wave of revolutions that now swept Spain's former grand American empire. However, as the U.S. State Department notes, "In 1823, France invited Spain to restore the Bourbon power, and there was talk of France and Spain warring upon the new republics with the backing of the Holy Alliance (Russia, Prussia and Austria)." The result was the unique collaboration of the United States with Great Britain to keep the Western Hemisphere free from the power of the autocratic nations of Europe. (Napoleon had been overthrown in 1815 and the decrepit Bourbon monarchy restored.)

President James Monroe, acting in advance of the British, issued his famous Doctrine in December 1823. Speaking to Congress, he declared that any European attempt at recolonization would be viewed by the United States as "dangerous to our peace and safety." Backed up by the power of the British Navy, the European powers complied. The Americas were now included as part of the protection of the United States. Thus, the Monroe Doctrine can be viewed as a leftist policy that was anti-monarchal and pro-republican; it

laid claim to the concept of republican-type democracy in the New World.

When Antonio Lopez de Santa Anna became dictator in Mexico and abrogated the constitution of 1824, the American colonists in Texas, then a part of Mexico, revolted. However, at the same time, the national defense was still endangered because the British supported Santa Anna in 1836, still hoping to confine the United States to the east bank of the Mississippi River. Although the Texans were defeated at the Alamo in March 1836, President Andrew Jackson's apparently covert aid to Texan leader Sam Houston helped him defeat Santa Anna in April 1836 at San Jacinto. Although the United States recognized Texan independence, a disputed strip existed between Mexico and Texas. In May 1846 the United States went to war with Mexico; the war ended with the Treaty of Guadalupe Hidalgo in February 1848. The prime motive was to bring Texas into the American Union and gain the territory that later became the states of Arizona, New Mexico, and California.

MANIFEST DESTINY AND CIVIL WAR

It was the time of Manifest Destiny, a rightist foreign policy that declared it was America's future to populate the North American continent from "sea to shining sea." North in the Oregon Territory to the south of Canada, Great Britain tried to hem in the United States as well. In June 1846, the United States and Great Britain agreed to divide the disputed Oregon Territory between them along the 49th parallel east to the Lake of the Woods. The treaty gave both maritime nations the right of free passage on the Columbia River and the Strait of San Juan de Fuca. Thus, by 1848, the United States was finally secure within its continental borders.

The coming of the tragic Civil War in April 1861 did not make any real change in foreign policy, except that it moved the United States to the left, at least in the eyes of the anti-slavery groups in Britain and France. By the end of the war, the Union Navy of the national government had become a world-class fleet. During the war, it had frustrated both British and French intentions to possibly enter the war on the side of the Southern Confederacy. Indeed, after the war, American naval might was instrumental in causing Great Britain to pay a staggering $15.5 million indemnity in gold for having helped the South by building the sleek ships that had "run" the Northern blockade and commerce raiders like the CSS *Alabama*, which had devastated the Northern merchant marine.

France had taken advantage of American distraction by intervening in Mexico. In 1864, Napoleon III had placed the Austrian Archduke Maximilian on the throne in Mexico City, driving out the Mexican President Benito Juarez. However, after the war, both a heavy American military presence on the border under General Philip Sheridan and the U.S. Navy caused Napoleon to withdraw his support of Maximilian. A French garrison of some 50,000, including the famed Foreign Legion, was evacuated. Forsaken by the French, Maximilian was shot by a Mexican firing squad in 1867. Also in the same year, Secretary of State William H. Seward bought Alaska from Imperial Russia for $7.2 million. Thus, by 1867, the U.S. national defense policy of securing the country's territorial integrity—and keeping the seas free from hostile nations—had again been established.

With the Industrial Revolution introducing steam propulsion as an effective means of powering ships, the navy, as a way to protect the widening American interests, began to seek out coaling stations to power its ships. In 1867, the island of Midway was occupied in the Pacific. Throughout this era, the ability to project American power onto hostile shores and beyond remained an important and rightist part of defending national interests. In May 1871, an operation was mounted against Korea after the crews of several ships had been massacred. The expedition was inconclusive; 10 years later, a more pacific attempt secured a treaty, proving that peaceful means of securing the national defense could be successful. In 1876, a coaling station was also secured at Pago Pago in Samoa.

IMPERIALISM

Within 20 years, American foreign policy would truly become global, imperialist, and rightist in scope. The American battleship *Maine* blew up on February 15, 1898, in the harbor of Havana, Cuba, then a colony in rebellion against Spain. While the real cause of the catastrophe may never be known, the United States declared war on Spain on April 20. Within 10 days, future Admiral George Dewey was able to defeat the Spanish naval squadron at Manila Bay, Philippines, on May 1, 1898, adding the first colony to the new American empire. When the Treaty of Paris in February 1899 brought the war to an end, the United States was suddenly the heir of Spain's global empire.

With the assassination of President William McKinley in September 1901, Theodore Roosevelt, who had become vice president due to his heroism in

Theodore Roosevelt famously summarized American foreign policy as "speaking softly and carrying a big stick."

the Spanish War, assumed the presidency. However, by becoming a two-ocean power, the United States immediately thrust itself into the path of the Japanese, who had no conservative qualms about extending their Pacific realm.

Although Roosevelt brought the war between Japan and Russia to an end in in September 1905, the Japanese government saw the treaty as robbing them of the spoils of victory. Roosevelt was concerned about Japan achieving naval mastery in the Pacific. He wrote that Japan could "take the Philippines and Hawaii from us, if she obtained the upper hand on the seas."

It was not only in the Philippines and Hawaii that Roosevelt felt concern over Japan's future ambitions, but in China as well. After the Boxer Rebellion of 1900, the United States was forced to keep permanent naval and ground forces present to protect American interests and citizens, particularly the missionaries who had been a primary target of the Boxers' xenophobic rage. As part of the altruism that had infused American diplomatic policy since the Declaration of Independence, Roosevelt and his secretary of state, John Hay, advocated the Open Door policy for China, to prevent greedy nations from completely carving up the country. But to do so required the continuing presence of American naval and military power. In 1903, Roosevelt declared, "we infinitely desire peace, and the surest way of obtaining it is to show that we are not afraid of war."

As well as Japan, imperial Germany, united after the Franco-Prussian War of 1870–71, emerged as a new power in the world. German foreign and defense policy had remained under the careful care of Chancellor Otto von Bismarck until 1890, when the vainglorious (and possibly unstable) Kaiser Wilhelm II decided on becoming the commander of all German forces. Now, for the first time since the Civil War, the United States was faced with the possibility of hostilities with a European nation. Between 1908 and 1911, Germany became embroiled in two diplomatic crises in Morocco, which France regarded as in its sphere of influence. Gradually, Europe had become barricaded into two great alliances, the Central Powers of Austria-Hungary, Germany, and (until 1915) Italy, and the Entente Powers of Russia, France, and increasingly England.

WORLD WAR I

Faced with what they perceived as a growing threat to the United States and its freedom of the seas, modernization of the armed forces began under Roosevelt, and continued under his successor, President William Howard Taft. Although Europe was plunged into war on August 4, 1914, the United States, under President Woodrow Wilson, did not enter the conflict until April 1916. In his speech asking for a declaration of war, Wilson, a liberal, said America would fight "for the principles that gave her birth and happiness." During the previous two years, Germany's policy of unrestricted submarine warfare had been a constant provocation to the peace-loving Wilson—and a mortal threat to America's traditional freedom of the seas.

However, an even graver threat had arisen when the telegram from German Foreign Minister Arthur Zimmermann secretly promised Mexico the return of the territories it had lost in the Mexican War if it intervened on Germany's side. Congress declared war on April 6, 1916.

When war was declared, the regular army numbered some 200,000 men, including National Guardsmen on duty at the Mexican border, but, as R. Ernest Dupuy and Trevor N. Dupuy observed in *Military Heritage of America*, it "increased to four million men, or 20 times its original size." When Germany surrendered in November 1918, truly the New World had come to redress the balance of the Old.

After the war, traditional American isolationism worked against the efforts to export Wilsonian internationalism (a form of liberalism). Wilson's idea, realized through the League of Nations, was to create a world order conducive to the free association of nations—and to freedom of the seas for all. However, such ideas were beyond the vision of isolationist right-wing politicians. Senator William E. Borah of Idaho compared the League of Nations to becoming involved with "that level of debauchery and shame." Wilson's campaign to bring America into the League of Nations destroyed his health. In the end, in November 1919, the Treaty of Versailles ending the war was voted down in the Senate and with it the League of Nations.

With the refusal of the United States to enter the League, isolationism became the unofficial foreign policy of the United States and foreign policy shifted back to the right. In the Congress, the need for rearming the defense establishment incurred the same ire from the radical isolationists who had sunk the League of Nations. Borah would chair the Senate Foreign Relations Committee from 1924 to his death in 1940. Yet the armed forces still had to defend the homeland. In an attempt to reconcile both, the Washington Disarmament Conference of 1921–22 attempted to control the growth in naval power. Another conference was held in London in 1930. But in years to come, Nazi Germany under Adolf Hitler would rearm by deceitfully circumventing just such covenants. Hitler would become leader of Germany in January 1933.

WORLD WAR II

On December 7, 1941, the Japanese launched a surprise attack on the U.S. Pacific Fleet at Pearl Harbor in Hawaii. For the second time in 20 years, a global war caused the United States to turn aside from isolationism. When the United States declared war on Germany and Japan after the attack on Pearl Harbor, isolationists like the 1920s aviation hero Charles Lindbergh and the America First lobbyists were silenced. Even before the United States entered the war, President Franklin Roosevelt met with the British prime minister to announce the principles for which the "Great Democracies," to use Winston Churchill's phrase, stood. The document was the historic Atlantic Charter of August 1941. One of the goals was for "all peoples to choose the form of government under which they shall live." Another, harkening back to older times, was for "all men to traverse the high seas and oceans without hindrance." Thus, Roosevelt aligned U.S. interests with democracies against totalitarianism, a liberal leftist move that continued through the Cold War.

During the world war, the major Western allies, Great Britain, the United States, and France, formed an alliance with the Soviet Union. Earlier, the Soviet Union had turned away Great Britain and France when they had capitulated to Nazi Germany at the Munich Crisis in September 1938. A brief period of Soviet alliance with Germany had ended with the surprise German invasion of the Soviet Union in June 1941. In Western Europe, the Allies launched Operation Overlord on June 6, 1944, the long-awaited attack from the West on Germany's Fortress Europe. Some 7,000 naval vessels formed an armada that irrefutably represented the major goals of America's continuing foreign policy: defense of the United States and its interests, freedom of the seas, and a determination to preserve fundamental human liberty. At the same time, the Soviet Union attacked fiercely in Eastern Europe. Finally, in May 1945, with Hitler a suicide, Nazi Germany capitulated.

Yet, the wartime alliance with the Soviet Union did not endure much past the end of the war. Roosevelt died in April 1945 and was succeeded by Vice President Harry Truman. By January 1946, the Truman administration was already suspicious of the actions of the Soviets in newly conquered Eastern Europe. The Soviet Red Army appeared to be the stalking horse for the foundation of communist regimes throughout Eastern Europe, giving the lie to Stalin's support of the principles of the Atlantic Charter.

COLD WAR

Then, in June 1948, U.S. foreign policy was tested in Berlin, deep within the Soviet sector of a divided Germany. Cutting off the Western sector of Berlin from all communication and commerce, Russia attempted to lay economic siege to West Berlin. Through a masterful effort, the Western Allies kept West Berlin supplied from the air until the Soviets reopened ground access. While West Berlin was saved, the Cold War had begun.

In March 1949, Dean Acheson explained to the Soviets the purpose of the U.S.-led North Atlantic Treaty Organization (NATO), which was being formed to conserve traditional Western ideals of liberty in Western Europe. Premier Josef Stalin, speaking of America's core principles, stated: "The very basis of Western civilization is the ingrained spirit of restraint and tolerance." Yet in 1955, the Soviet Union militarized Eastern Europe with the Warsaw Pact, a Soviet-led alliance to counteract NATO.

American foreign policy, enunciated by Secretary of State John Foster Dulles during the administration of President Dwight D. Eisenhower (1952–60), became one of attempting to "contain" the spread of communist aggression through a global series of alliances. For over 30 years, the world divided itself into two armed camps, either in favor of the traditional values or supporting the despotic statist philosophy of the communist world. (Mainland China had been conquered by the communists of Mao Zedong in October 1949.)

The world was threatened by the specter of MAD, (Mutually Assured Destruction) through nuclear war. In October 1962, the aggressive policy of Soviet Premier Nikita Khrushchev brought the world perilously close to nuclear war when he clandestinely brought missiles to Cuba. Faced with President John F. Kennedy's resolute opposition, the Soviets withdrew their missiles in return for American reassurances that missiles would be withdrawn from Turkey. In 1965, President Lyndon B. Johnson committed American ground troops to South Vietnam in an effort to stem the tide of communist aggression in Southeast Asia. The thrust of U.S. foreign policy was thoroughly anti-communist, thus rightist, and came to a climax in the 1980s.

In January 1981, President Ronald Reagan, of the Republican Party, became president with a traditional, conservative belief in the values of American foreign policy. Indeed, he stated his belief that the United States should be for the world "a city upon a hill," echoing the earliest thoughts of the old Massachusetts Bay Colony in the 17th century. Reagan, supported in his administration by Secretary of the Navy John Lehman, decided on a policy of economically crushing the Soviet Union with the same massive defense spending that had made the United States the "arsenal of democracy" against Germany in World Wars I and II under Democratic Presidents Wilson and Roosevelt. In testimony before the House Appropriations Committee, Lehman showed the Reagan administration's commitment to a cornerstone of foreign policy. He said, "clear maritime superiority is a national objective, a security imperative." At the same time, Reagan pressed for an end to the fear of mass destruction that had hung over the Soviet Union and the United States throughout the Cold War by negotiating arms reduction agreements.

Simultaneously, Soviet Premier Mikhail Gorbachev wished to open up Soviet society after years of claustrophobic state control in his program of perestroika. Gorbachev also shared Reagan's hope of ending the Cold War. Much as Kennedy and Khrushchev had done, the two men found common ground. The Cold War ended symbolically in 1989, with the tearing down of the Berlin Wall that communist East Germany had erected in 1961 to keep its citizens from fleeing to the democratic West.

PREEMPTIVE POLICY

Although the Cold War ended the threat of thermonuclear war, still threats of another kind remained to imperil the traditional foreign policy of the United States. On September 11, 2001, Islamic extremists of Osama bin Laden's al-Qaeda group struck at targets at the World Trade Center in New York City and at the Pentagon in Washington, D.C., using hijacked commercial airplanes.

Not since Pearl Harbor had the United States been struck at home such a devastating blow. However, speaking from the same Oval Office from which Kennedy had addressed the nation during the Cuban Missile Crisis, President George W. Bush rallied the American people in defense of their traditional foreign policy and its roots in their heritage of liberty. In October 2001, in what was aptly called Operation Enduring Freedom, American ground, air, and sea forces attacked Afghanistan, the stronghold of al-Qaeda and its allies, the Taliban. Once again, in a dramatic projection of "power from the sea," Americans proved their commitment to their traditional foreign policy of defense of the nation and its citizens. However, in early 2003, Bush took foreign policy a large, rightist step further by declaring a policy of preemptive war and invading the sovereign nation of Iraq. Under Saddam Hussein, Iraq was seen as a threat due to suspicions of weapons of mass destruction being produced in Iraq that could possibly fall into terrorists' hands. For a country that prided itself on only attacking if first attacked, the policy of preemptive war was an uncomfortable strategy, especially for Americans on the left.

SEE ALSO
Volume 1 Left: United States; Soviet Union; Liberalism; Socialism; Communism; Democratic Party.
Volume 2 Right: United States; Republican Party; Reagan, Ronald; Conservatism; Isolationism.

BIBLIOGRAPHY
James C. Bradford, ed., *Command under Sail: Makers of the American Naval Tradition* (U.S. Naval Institute, 1985); John Lehman, *Command of the Seas: Building the 600 Ship Navy* (Scribners, 1988); John Lewis Gaddis, *The United States and the Origins of the Cold War* (Columbia University Press, 1972); Richard H. Kohn, *Eagle and Sword: The Beginnings of the Military Establishment in America* (The Free Press, 1975); Harry L. Coles, *The War of 1812* (University of Chicago Press, 1965); R. Ernest Dupuy and Trevor N. Dupuy, *Military Heritage of America* (HERO Books, 1984); Wilbur Cross, *Naval Battles and Heroes* (Harper and Row, 1960); John Winton, *An Illustrated History of the Royal Navy* (Thunder Bay Press, 2000); Kenneth Wimmel, *Theodore Roosevelt and the Great White Fleet: American Sea Power Comes of Age* (Brassey's, 2000); Richard Hofstadter, ed., *Great Issues in American History from Reconstruction to the Present Day* (Vintage Books, 1969); Chester G. Hearn, *The Illustrated Directory of the United States Navy* (MBI Publishing Company, 2003); Jack Murphy, *History of the U.S. Marines* (World, 2002); John Bakeless, *The Journals of Lewis and Clark* (Mentor, 1964); John F. Murphy Jr., Articles on Lewis and Clark and Zebulon Pike, *Wild West* (1990–92); Thomas Harbottle and George Bruce, *Dictionary of Battles from 743 BC to the Present* (Stein and Day, 1971); Edward L. Beach, *The United States Navy: 200 Years* (Henry Holt, 1986); "The Monroe Doctrine, 1823," www.usinfo.state.gov (July 2004); "The Lewis and Clark Journal of Discovery," www.nps.gov (July 2004); Hans Kohn, *American Nationalism: An Interpretive Essay* (Collins Books, 1962); Walter Millis, *Arms and Men: A Study of American Military History* (Mentor Books, 1956); T. Harry Williams, *Americans at War: The Development of the American Military System* (Collins Books, 1962); Frederic Austin Ogg, *The Opening of the Mississippi* (Cooper Square, 1963).

JOHN F. MURPHY, JR.
AMERICAN MILITARY UNIVERSITY

France

IN THE YEARS before the French Revolution, the right in France, the monarchy and its allied nobles, was in trouble. When Louis XV died and was interred in the cathedral of St. Denis, burial place of French kings, no public mourning accompanied his passing. There were too many French households with empty seats from his reckless pursuit of military glory. While Louis XV had been at least a capable king and a wily diplomat, any productive genes in his son and heir, Louis XVI, remained distinctly, as Abbot Gregor Mendel would have said, recessive. The depletion of the treasury continued, with an archaic system of finances that never repaired the deficit. In January 1772, only 20 years before the fall of the monarchy, the comptroller-general, Abbe Terry, would plead with Necker, "we beg you to help us before the day is over."

The internal taxation of France hinged on the activities of the *fermier-generaux*, "the tax farmers," who paid more attention to fattening their fortunes than to raising funds for the country. The entire burden of the taxes rested on the third estate, ultimately on the backs of the French peasants—those who could afford taxes the least. The first estate, the nobility, was exempt, while the priesthood of the second estate escaped with paying the *don gratuit*, a voluntary contribution that could be avoided if so wished.

In March 1778, Louis XVI performed perhaps the most altruistic act of his reign, yet one that would have disastrous consequences. He entered into a formal alliance with the infant United States against France's traditional enemy, England. While the war ended in victory and vengeance for France, triumph was bought at a high price. France groaned under a debt of some two million livres. Efforts to solve the problem finally led the king to summon the Etats-Generaux, the Estates-General, to a convention in Paris for May 1789.

Although the third estate had come to prominence economically during the long wars that France had fought since Louis XIV had invaded the Netherlands in 1672, the nobility had, unlike in England, conspired to keep them frozen out of the higher ranks of French government and society. As Crane Brinton noted in *The Anatomy of Revolution*, "the French nobility of the 18th century [made] access to the top difficult for ambitious non-nobles."

The third estate had always been outnumbered by the other two at such meetings, as the first and second estates would vote against it for the interests they held in common. This is what had led to the dissolution of the last convocation of the Estates-General in 1614. The third estate insisted on a more democratic, proportional representation, in which their topics of concern would be given a fair hearing. Finally, when their efforts met with no response, one of their leaders, the Abbe Sieyes, demanded in June that the third estate should reconstitute itself as a National Assembly. On June 20, as George Havens wrote in *The Age of Ideas*, the third estate met on an unused tennis court and, in what became known as the Oath of the Tennis Court, vowed "a solemn oath never to separate until the Constitution of the Kingdom shall be laid and established on secure foundations." The left in France was established and soon moved forward toward revolution, leaving the rightists, the monarchists, shocked and dismayed.

Liberal nobles, some of whom had served in the American Revolution, chose to sit with the third estate. Among these was the Marquis de Lafayette, who had fought with the Americans in some of the major battles of the war. Lafayette would become leader of the new National Guard. On July 11, inspired by the American Declaration of Independence (and the fact that its author, Thomas Jefferson, was then American ambassador to France), Lafayette proposed the Declaration of the Rights of Man and of the Citizen.

On July 14, the Paris mob, incited by street orators like Desmoulins, stormed the ancient prison of the Bastille in Paris, beheading its governor, de Launay, and impaling his head on a pike. It was on this grim day that the Duc de Liancourt pronounced to the dim Louis XVI that "sire, this is no riot, but a revolution." One month to the day after the fall of the Bastille, the clergy and nobility gave up their privileges, fearing the unleashed hostility of the common people. On October 10, a mob would force the king and queen to give up Versailles and move to the Tuileries Palace in Paris where they were kept virtually as prisoners.

Power had moved swiftly from the hands of moderates like the Comte de Mirabeau, who had urged Louis, "sire, the very idea of monarchy is not incompatible with revolution." But the perspicacious Mirabeau would die on April 2, 1791, leaving the constitutional forces without their best leader against the radicals. Jean-Paul Marat, the self-styled *ami du peuple*, "friend of the people," denounced the king as "a weakling without a soul, unworthy to sit on a throne." Sensing their fate, the king and his queen, escorted by her loyal paramour, the Swedish Count Axel von Fersen, attempted to escape on June 20, 1791, but were discovered at Varennes near the French border. They were taken to the Tuileries Palace in Paris.

A month later, the radicals attempted a coup under Marat on July 17, but their attempt to form a republic was crushed by Lafayette's National Guard. (Apparently, throughout the period, Lafayette was reluctant—

or unable to—assert the power he had as the living representative of both American and French Revolutions in an attempt to steer the revolution into yet a constructive liberal course.) The National Assembly, or convention, was now split between the moderate Girondins and the Jacobin radical faction. A month after Marat's aborted coup, the radicals reasserted their power in the streets when the Parisian *canaille*, the mob, stormed the Tuileries Palace on August 10, 1792, and massacred the Swiss Guards defending it.

An allied army raised under the Prussian Duke of Brunswick met with defeat at the hands of the new citizen army at Valmy on September 20, 1792, under General Kellermann. Louis gave up the crown on September 21, 1792. The French First Republic was proclaimed—any hope of a conservatively guided nation ended with the monarchy.

As the revolution progressed, its next conservative phases, after a left-wing Reign of Terror, was the five-man Directory, which still had to fight the wars unleashed by the revolution. One of its most promising generals to fight these wars was Napoleon Bonaparte, who had been born in Corsica. On October 5, 1795, with his famous "whiff of grapeshot," Napoleon crushed the final uprising of leftist mobs. Coming from an Italian noble family, he hated the excesses of la *canaille*. In 1796–97, aided by the Director Paul Barras, Bonaparte became the leader of the Army of Italy, and crushed the Austrian armies sent against him. Within a year, Napoleon would lead a French army to invade Egypt.

NAPOLEON BONAPARTE

However, the threat from the extreme left reasserted itself in 1799. The frightened Directors turned to Bonaparte for help. On November 10, they, with the help of Napoleon's soldiers, staged a coup. Napoleon, the Abbe Sieyes, and Roger Ducos would rule as three consuls. Soon Napoleon dominated France as the first consul. Within five years of his coup, in December 1804, Napoleon crowned himself emperor of the French. France would continue on the road of constitutional growth, which the excesses of the French Revolution had retarded.

Napoleon at once combined an autocratic approach (right-wing) with a great many modernizing reforms of administration, legal code, accounting, military organization, and technology. The modernizing tendency bears a strong resemblance to what is usually thought of as liberal reform, associated with the left. However,

Napoleon's rule was rightist and nationalist as a whole. He suppressed both the Jacobins and Monarchists, the latter still looking to return a Bourbon (Louis's family) to the throne. Napoleon introduced the Code Napoleon, a code of law that is still used in modified form today.

Napoleon's efforts to stabilize France along conservative lines were frustrated by conspiracies hatched by royalists within France who were in league with foreign powers like the Holy Roman Empire, England, Prussia, and Russia, all sworn to bring down the French leader. Unlike Louis XVI, Napoleon possessed a ruthlessness to maintain the sovereignty of the state by force. In March 1804, the Duc d'Enghein, an agent of England and possible candidate for the throne, was kidnapped in Germany. He was brought to France and shot. Eight other conspirators were sent to the guillotine. To lay an even more secure claim to France, Napoleon crowned himself emperor of the French on December 2, 1804, in front of an amazed Pope Pius VII.

It was the fate of Napoleon to spend most of his reign confronting the enemies of France on the battlefield. While on October 21, 1805, his hopes of defeating England were dashed by the British fleet under Lord Horatio Nelson at Trafalgar, Napoleon marched his invasion army across Europe to destroy the Holy Roman Empire and Russian army at Austerlitz on December 2, 1805, the anniversary of his coronation. However, in a desire to extend the Continental System to Spain and Portugal, Napoleon's invasion of the Iberian Peninsula in 1808 led to the direct intervention of England on behalf of Portugal. The miring of French troops in guerrilla warfare in Spain, what Napoleon referred to as his "Spanish ulcer," emboldened the Austrians to fight again. Although Napoleon ultimately crushed the Austrians under Archduke Charles at Wagram on July 6, 1809, it was a victory purchased with difficulty since his enemies had now learned his own military tactics and were beginning to use them against him. On June 24, 1812, Napoleon crossed the Niemen River to invade Moscow. He had with him over 700,000 men, the Grande Armee. It was the largest military force ever seen in Europe. After costly campaigns, Napoleon entered Moscow in a Pyrrhic triumph on September 14, 1812. With the approach of the Russian winter, Napoleon had to evacuate a month later, on October 24, 1812, and quickly discovered he was leaving too late in the season. By the time the Grande Armee arrived at Vilna in today's Lithuania, Napoleon had lost 400,000 men to the elements and disease, and had also lost 100,000 prisoners.

With the collapse of Napoleon's Russian campaign, Prussia again joined the war against Napoleon. As he tried desperately to regroup his forces, the armies of Austria, Prussia, and Russia moved against him. In spite of the ravages of the Russian campaign, Napoleon was able to crush all three armies at Dresden on August 26–27, 1813. However, in what was called the Battle of the Nations, Napoleon, in large part due to the defection of his Saxon contingent, was defeated in the Battle at Leipzig (October 16–18, 1813).

With the defeat at Leipzig, the Allied armies invaded France itself. In the campaign of 1814, Napoleon showed his old military greatness, but his forces were simply outnumbered; eventually behind his back, Paris was surrendered to the enemy on March 31, 1814. On April 6, 1814, Napoleon agreed to abdicate his throne. He was exiled to the island of Elba, which now was his kingdom. But Europe had not seen the last of him.

The former Comte de Provence, uncle of the dead Louis XVII, entered to rule in Paris as Louis XVIII. Conscious that he had come in, as it were, with an invading army, Louis XVIII nevertheless began a right-wing destabilizing purge of those who had fought with Napoleon. Moreover, the middle class, and the new nobility Napoleon had created, found their interests threatened by the return of the Bourbon emigres to France, who unwisely acted as if the clock had been turned back to 1787. Napoleon now began to be considered the one who had preserved the constitutional advances of 1789. On February 26, 1815, Napoleon embarked on the adventure of The Hundred Days. Returning to France, the army and many of the people flocked again to his imperial eagles. Louis XVIII was forced into hasty exile in Belgium at Ghent. Nevertheless, Napoleon's return was to be short-lived. On June 18, 1815, the British under the Duke of Wellington and the Prussians would defeat him at Waterloo. This time, he would be banished to St. Helena, an island in the South Atlantic, where he would die, apparently of natural causes, on May 5, 1821.

BOURBON RESTORATION

On the second abdication of Napoleon, Louis XVIII returned to France. He became active in the movement of the monarchs of Europe to contain the revolutionary movement that had crossed the continent with France's revolutionary armies. The fruit of their cooperation would be the Holy Alliance, which had its origin in the Congress of Vienna of 1814. The congress had convened to chart for Europe a future free of the revolutionary upsurges of the previous 20 years. As part of the Holy Alliance, or the Quadruple Alliance, Louis would send French troops to Spain in 1823 to put down a rebellion against King Ferdinand VII. In 1824, Louis died, and was succeeded as king by the Comte d'Artois, who would reign as Charles X.

The Bourbon Restoration, as it was called, would bring material prosperity to France but increased trading in a free-market economy did not evenly distribute the benefits of the French economic boom to all the population. Because of this, by 1830, the common people were inspired by a new sense of Jacobinism. The intellectuals and students, who had been educated in the system of schools organized by Napoleon, felt themselves harshly repressed by the monarchy, instead of being able to constitutionally express their liberal opinions. The result was the July Revolution of 1830. During the brief rebellion, the army refused to fire on the Paris crowds, who had hurled out the challenge of 1789, *"aux barricades,"* "to the barricades." Charles X, who as the Comte d'Artois, had been one of the first nobles to flee in 1789, did so again in 1830. He was succeeded by Louis-Philippe, who intelligently ruled as the citizen-king, thus enjoying a reign of peace and prosperity. However, in spite of his best efforts, Louis-Philippe found himself caught up in a "revolution of rising expectations" in France. Within France, the new aspirations of the people erupted again in violence in 1848, as a year of revolution swept over Europe.

The urban working class had been the one to suffer most from the growing industrialization since the 18th century. With no eye to preserving civil order, neither monarchy, aristocracy, nor the now-powerful bourgeoisie (the old third estate) had attempted to share the benefits with the workers, not even to the limited extent found in England. The result was the bloody July Days, when nearly 10,000 workers were slain by regular army troops in Paris.

With such bloody anarchy, the French of all classes began to yearn for a return to order. On December 10, 1848, Louis Napoleon, the nephew of the dead emperor, was elected president. However, he seized power in a coup d'etat in December 1851, as his uncle had done in November 1799. Now as Napoleon III, Louis Napoleon attempted to symbolize the return to imperial glory by his masterful rebuilding of Paris under Baron Haussmann. However, the lure of glory became too much for him and rather than address the serious needs of French society, he turned for glory in the East as had his uncle, the first Napoleon. In 1854, he joined in the Crimean War against Russia, in league with the old enemy, England. Although the French and English were victorious, and France regained some influence in the Middle East, particularly in today's Lebanon and Syria, it had little impact at home. Napoleon also became involved in the Italian Wars of Liberation, where he defeated the Austrians at Solferino on June 24, 1859. However, in 1870, he let himself be maneuvered into war against Prussia, whose Chancellor Otto von Bismarck realized that a victory over France would enable him to unite all Germany under Prussia's King William I. Napoleon went to war against the superior Prussian army and their allies from the different German states. On September 3, 1870, Napoleon III was captured when the fortress city of Sedan fell to the Germans.

However, the war would continue under a government of national defense, much similar, although middle class in origin, to the one of 1792. Finally, an armistice was made on January 25, 1871, between Jules Favre, a representative of the Committee of National Defense, and Bismarck. In the meanwhile, the working class of Paris, its grievances long unmet, erupted in the Jacobin violence of the Paris Commune. Bismarck had stood by and let the troops of the newly elected National Assembly at Versailles defeat the Paris *communards* themselves.

The new, self-proclaimed Third Republic continued to feel hostility toward Germany for the war, which resulted in the loss of the two provinces of Alsace and Lorraine. However, Bismarck had left open the door for French expansion overseas as a safety valve for the desire to regain the lost territories. Under imperialists like Jules Ferry, the French empire spread throughout Africa, the Pacific, and into Indochina, where a Chinese attempt to defeat French colonization was beaten back in the 1880s. However, French imperialism also carried with it the danger of a new European war. In 1898, Jean Baptiste Marchand's advance to Fashoda on the Nile River almost set off a war between France and England, which also claimed the Sudan after reconquering it from the extremist Muslim Mahdist movement at the Battle of Omdurman on September 2, 1898.

However, events in Europe had changed for the worse in 1890, when the stable European system designed by Bismarck was destroyed as the new Emperor Wilhelm II forced his chancellor into retirement. By 1894, France and Russia had come to an agreement, an alliance attempting to control the uncertain behavior of the kaiser. Ten years later, in 1904, England and France buried 30 years of colonial rivalry in an agreement also aimed at containing the threat of Germany. In 1905 and 1911, the kaiser provoked serious international crises

by attempting to assert German influence in Morocco, which France considered a legitimate colonial protectorate.

WORLD WAR I

Finally, on August 4, 1914, the growing European tensions exploded into World War I. France, supported by Great Britain and Russia, went to war against imperial Germany and Austria-Hungary. By the beginning of 1915, France was split by a vast network of trenches which would define war on what would be called the Western Front until 1918. In 1917, a wave of mutinies would rock the French army, virtually paralyzing it. It was only with the entrance of the United States in the war on the side of the British and French that the ascendancy was gained by the Allies again. On November 11, 1918, with the Allied armies near the German frontier and the kaiser overthrown in a revolution, the new German civilian government sued for peace. In May 1919, the Treaty of Versailles brought the long war officially to an end.

However, while the Congress of Vienna had opened the way to an era of peace in Europe, the punitive Treaty of Versailles led only to a long period of international uncertainty. The huge war reparations laid upon the German Weimar Republic, largely at the insistence of France's Premier Georges Clemenceau, only served to make the Weimar government seem the slave of Allies to the right-wing militarists in Germany who had violently opposed the peace accords. France would be governed for much of the 1920s by conservative coalitions, and for a brief period by radical socialists. However, neither group seemed able to fully come to grips with the massive reconstruction needed by France after the war. Moreover, an entire generation had been scarred by the war, and would be totally unprepared for the rearming of Germany, which would commence almost immediately after the war. When Adolf Hitler came to power in January 1933, France was singularly unprepared to face another round of German aggression, the third in slightly more than 60 years.

WORLD WAR II

In September 1938, Premier Edouard Daladier represented France at the Munich Conference. There, five years of appeasement led to the dismemberment of Czechoslovakia, giving Hitler some 6 million more Germans in the Czech Sudetenland for his Nazi Third Reich. After Munich, both France and England slowly

Philippe Petain (left) meets with Adolf Hitler, submitting the French government to the Third Reich.

awoke to the dangers of appeasement, but too late. In September 1939, Hitler invaded Poland and England, and France, which had given the Polish guarantees of support, went to war with Germany again. In May 1940, Germany launched its swift invasion of France and the Low Countries, once again rupturing the fragile European order. By June 1940, France capitulated to German aggression and Marshal Philippe Petain took charge of a French government in Vichy, which openly collaborated with the conquerors of Paris.

CHARLES DE GAULLE

Petain and collaborationist leader Pierre Laval were clearly allies of the Nazi regime and thus their government was extremely right-wing. However, French independence would be saved by Charles de Gaulle, who escaped to London to form a French government-in-exile. World War II would also be a civil war between France's Vichy regime and de Gaulle's Free French in London. In 1914, with British help, de Gaulle was able to wrest control of Lebanon and Syria from their Vichy garrisons. In November 1942, the Vichy garrisons opposed Operation Torch, the Allied invasion of North Africa.

When the Allies invaded France on June 6, 1944, the French responded with a heroic rising in Paris led by de Gaulle's French Forces of the Interior (FFI). On August 26, Paris was liberated by the Free French Army of Marshal Pierre Koenig and American forces.

Although victory came in May 1945, France was left with a divided heritage from the war, in which those who had collaborated sometimes met with savage retribution from those who had served in the Resistance movement, either leftist Gaullist or communist. Indeed, during the war, Jean Moulin, de Gaulle's leader of the Resistance, had been betrayed to the Germans by one of his own men. After the war, the Fourth Republic, instead of attempting to consolidate its position in Europe, tried, as the Third Republic had done after the Franco-Prussian War, to find renewed glory in the colonies.

During the war, the communist Ho Chi Minh would lead the resistance against the Japanese in French Indochina, today's Vietnam. He would be aided by the American OSS (Office of Strategic Services) Deer Team, with Archimedes Patti. When the Japanese surrendered on September 2, 1945, Ho had declared the Democratic Republic of Vietnam. In March 1946, Ho reached an interim agreement with the French, but the French were more interested in retaking the country. Open hostilities broke out when the French shelled Hanoi and would continue for eight years until the French were decisively defeated at Dien Bien Phu in May 1954.

No sooner had the French surrendered in Indochina than rebellion broke out in Algeria, which had been invaded by France in 1831. So close had Algeria become to France that it was considered part of Metropolitan France. The rebellion, which broke out in November 1954, ultimately became too much for the fragile Fourth Republic to bear—France seemed to some on the verge of anarchy. In 1958, de Gaulle was called back to power to lead the Fifth Republic.

De Gaulle moved quickly to bring an end to the Algerian war. In 1962, at Evian, an agreement was made with the revolutionary FLN, the Algerian National Liberation Front, and Algeria became independent. De Gaulle, in Europe, followed a uniquely French foreign policy much in keeping with traditional French politics. In 1965, he removed France from NATO, the North Atlantic Treaty Organization, causing NATO to relocate its headquarters from outside Paris to Brussels in Belgium.

His policy was aimed at building a peculiarly French nuclear deterrent, called the *force de frappe*. Underlining the traditional independent policy of France, he directed that the nuclear force would be ready for use *a tout azimuths*, "in all directions," implying that France could defend itself from all aggressors, even its former NATO allies. French foreign policy under de Gaulle re-

Rightist Charles de Gaulle led France on an independent path in the 1960s, away from the NATO and U.S. influence.

tained a rightist individuality that severely hampered concerted Western efforts against the Soviet Union. De Gaulle finally left the center stage of French politics in 1968.

Modern French politics follow logical rules about what party belongs on the left and right. In summary, a right coalition was dominant from 1958 to 1981. It consisted of the Rassemblement ["Rally"] pour la Republique (RFR), led by Jacques Chirac, a follow-on to de Gaulle's Union for the New Republic (UNR), together with the Union for Democratic France (UDF), headed by Giscard D'Estaing, Raymond Barre, and Jean Lecannet, which was formed in 1978.

While the left was dominated by the Moscow-oriented French Communist Party (CPF) and the Socialists (PS), there was an extreme right-wing National Front. It stood for capital punishment and immigration restriction, and tended not to be in the governing coalitions.

In 1988, Francois Mitterand defeated the Jacques Chirac government, bringing in a socialist-center coalition. With the decline of the CPF, the socialists made more alliances with center parties. Mitterand died in 1996; into the 2000s, Chirac was a right-wing president who appointed some left-wing prime ministers as a means of maintaining balance. In general, the president controls military and foreign policy and the prime minister runs the domestic side in recent years.

SEE ALSO

Volume 1 Left: France; French Revolution; Liberalism; Socialism; Communism; Third International (Comintern).
Volume 2 Right: Conservatism; Monarchism.

BIBLIOGRAPHY

Michael Howard, *The Franco-Prussian War* (Collier, 1961); John Steward Ambler, *The French Army and Politics* (Ohio State University Press, 1966); Douglas Porch, *The French Foreign Legion: A Complete History of the Legendary Fighting Force* (Harper, 1991); Thomas Carlyle, *The French Revolution: A History* (Penguin, 2002); Alexis de Tocqueville, *The Old Regime and the French Revolution* (Anchor, 1955); Edmund Burke, *Reflections on the Revolution in France* (Penguin, 1984); George R. Havens, *The Age of Ideas* (The Free Press, 1955); Georges Lefebvre, *Napoleon from 18 Brumaire to Tilsit* (Columbia University Press, 1969); Crane Brinton, *The Anatomy of Revolution* (Vintage, 1965); Richard Deacon, *The French Secret Service* (Grafton, 1990); Andre Maurois, *A History of France* (Ballantine, 1960).

JOHN F. MURPHY, JR.
AMERICAN MILITARY UNIVERSITY

Fundamentalism

FUNDAMENTALISM IS the belief that a given religious group has absolute historical foundations and was chosen by a divinity to become a holy nation, so that its radical political views are dogmatically justified and need to be defended in a militant and belligerent way, especially against modern and foreign worldviews. Although *fundamentalist* has been used as a secular adjective characterizing any person or group holding dogmatically to a given position, the origins of the term are related to three traditional monotheistic religions.

Fundamentalist attitudes were first ascribed to Pentecostals in the United States. But the same phenomenon was observed in the reaction of conservative sectors of the Catholic Church to modernism. Moreover, orthodox Judaism developed similar characteristics based on Zionism. In the same way, some radical political actions by Muslims brought about the development of fundamentalism within Islam. The understanding of fundamentalism requires the consideration of what is common and what is different between these and other religious views.

Fundamentalism has its origins in the 18th-century United States, when the so-called Covenant Theology interpreted the Bible, defined America as a chosen land, and oriented the missionary expansion toward the west and the "Great Awakening." In this process, a Protestant coalition was created between 1880 and 1890 in order to react to urbanization, the workers' movement, and foreign immigration to the United States. This led to the rise of evangelical fundamentalism in the 20th century.

Some Pentecostal groups proposed a literal reading of the Bible, developing doctrines such as biblical inerrancy, dispensationalism, and millennarianism, believing in the divine revelation of these ideas. In an attempt to convince others through proselytistic means, a series of publications called *The Fundamentals* was launched between 1909 and 1915, criticizing modernism and liberalism and confirming the biblical accounts by appealing to scientific theories.

CHRISTIAN FUNDAMENTALISM

Although *The Fundamentals* was launched within Pentecostalism, fundamentalism was by no means limited to this group. Similar ideas appeared in other denominations, articulating religion, dogmatism, and reactionary politics. One of the first impacts of Protestant fundamentalism occurred in 1925, in the trials against Dar-winism and evolutionary theory in the United States. Fundamentalists argued that evolutionary theory contradicted the doctrine of creation as told in the holy scripture. Although they lost this cause to liberals and their evangelical impetus became more restricted, they took this occasion to establish new institutions, schools, seminaries, publishing houses, and journals, using the mass media to express their ideas and to combat mainline Protestantism.

Different from the first Pentecostal fundamentalists, the generation after World War II criticized the sectarianism, separatism, and anti-intellectualism of their antecessors. However, they did not question biblical inerrancy, the emphasis on mass conversion, and the use of mass media. As part of their political strategy, they founded the National Association of Evangelicals (NAE) to congregate small denominations, Pentecostal and "neo-evangelical" groups, as well as to oppose the mainline Federal Council of Churches, which later became the National Council of Churches (NCC).

The impact of modernism was felt also within Catholicism. Modernism had already been criticized by Pope Pius IX in 1864 and by Leon XIII in the document *Testem Benevolentiae* from 1899. But after 1920, the conservative reaction included a radical critique of Catholic liberal movements that supported the New Deal. At this point, despite the Protestant majority, there was already a peculiar form of Catholicism within the American tradition. Father Francis Talbot, one of its conservative leaders, had even declared that true Catholics were the bastion of resistance to non-American progressivism and called for an adhesion to the "Constitution and traditional Americanism" that made the country what it was before 1914. During the 1960s, the term *fundamentalist* was used to identify those who wanted to return to traditional liturgies and rejected the changes approved during the Vatican II Council.

By that time, Protestant and Catholic forms of fundamentalism were appropriated by conservative politics and became part of the political strategies of McCarthyism, the "new conservatism," and the radical right.

JEWISH FUNDAMENTALISM

During the Jewish Diaspora, conservative groups gave emphasis to establishing synagogues and organizations that maintained the Talmudic traditions. In the United States, the Jewish Theological Seminar was founded in New York in 1886 in order to foster traditional education. This emphasis on tradition became stronger in the face of widespread anti-Semitism. It was also due to anti-Semitism that Jewish leaders left the Republican Party to join the Democratic Party. After World War II and the revelation of the Holocaust (Shoa), the attempt to secure traditional institutions of Jewish culture became even more important, leading to the search for the origins of Israel and the foundation of a new state in 1948.

However, the Jewish movements for settlement in Israel already had a long tradition and gained more force with the creation of the World Zionist Organization in 1896. The official recognition of the right to a Jewish nation in Palestine in 1917 and the foundation of Israel in 1948 brought several traditions together, such as the orthodox Sephardim and reformed and modernist Ashkenazim of East European origin, who came to represent different parties and institutions in Israeli politics. Jewish fundamentalism had its origins when political conservatism came closer to religious orthodoxy and insisted not only on the old Zionist hope in the complete restoration of Israel, but also on a return to the Talmudic literature, its liturgies and literal interpretations of sacred texts. Accordingly, a key point for understanding Jewish fundamentalism is the thesis that they are a chosen people, stemming from Abraham, who are entitled to conquer the promised land.

Fundamentalism became even stronger with the Gush Emunim movement, which was formed in 1974 in Israel, having Rav Tzvi Yehuda Kook as its inspiration. During the conservative government of Menachem Begin, political groups established connections with this movement, but its most important political ally has been the Likud Party. With the growth of the conservative position and the rise of the political right to power in Israel, fundamentalists established stronger associations with the Likud Party. They have provided historical and religious arguments for controversial initiatives such as the settlement in the Gaza Strip and the scaling up of the conflicts with Palestinians. Moreover, they questioned the views of liberal, socialist, assimilated, or reformed Jews and gained more popularity and visibility in Israel's contemporary politics.

ISLAMIC FUNDAMENTALISM

A similar attitude arose within Islam. According to Bassam Tibi, Islamic fundamentalism is a modern phenomenon with roots in a movement found in Egypt in 1928: the Muslim Brotherhood. This movement was founded by Hassan al Banna, but Sayyid Qutb was its most important leader, until his death in 1966. He was responsible for changing the understanding of jihad as a religious "holy war" to define it as a belligerent political opposition to modern Western culture and its influence on countries of the Muslim Ummah (community).

Islam is a traditional monotheistic religion based on the teachings of Muhammad, as registered in the Qur'an. However, there are internal differences and debates between moderate and radical Muslims that have clear sociological and political reasons. During the 1920s and until the 1940s, many regions influenced by Arab culture were passing through a major social and political transition, under the power of the British Empire. Many religious leaders saw the interference of foreign institutions as a threat to their religion and advocated a return to tradition, in a movement later defined as Islamism. During the 1960s, transformation of many urban settings—which absorbed the contingents from rural areas—brought about poverty, unemployment, and cultural shock, which were then aggravated by the conflicts between Arabs and Israelis. The reaction to this phenomenon gained more visibility in the international arena and became known as Islamic fundamentalism.

Some first examples of fundamentalism in action were seen in Islamic nations. The most famous example was the Islamic Revolution in Iran, in 1979, by which the Shiites took power and the Ayatollah Khomeini became their spiritual leader. Some countries started to impose Islamic Law (Sharia), while others experienced the growth of radical groups and parties, such as the Jemaah Islamiah in Indonesia, the Turabi in Sudan, the Jama'at Islami in Pakistan, and the GIA in Algeria, as well as the Taliban regime in Afghanistan. There was a return to tradition and a vehement opposition to any trace of Western culture. The most controversial issues are related to the role of women and the lack of human rights (especially in Iran, Sudan, and Afghanistan), as international humanitarian agencies have documented.

Other nations not necessarily defined as Islamic, but with a significant Islamic population, have also felt the impact of fundamentalists. In Turkey, pro-Islamist movements supported by the Refah Party opposed secularist groups and were successful in the elections during the 1990s. Even Western societies have felt the impact of Islamic fundamentalism, especially in Europe where there are tensions between religious traditions and modern law.

The impact of Islamic fundamentalism has been felt in other countries, such as Japan, the United Kingdom, and France. This also affected the United States: First by the growth of radical Islamic groups, especially the

Nation of Islam, led by Louis Farrakhan, among African Americans. And then later, by the religious-motivated terrorist attacks on New York City and the Pentagon on September 11, 2001. These latter events showed a form of religious violence based on the concept of jihad, which focused attention upon several extremist groups related to Islam, such as Hezbollah, al Qaeda, Islamic Jihad, and others.

As a result of these violent actions beyond its original borders, Islamic fundamentalism became equated with terrorism. However, as Bassam Tibi remarks, there is a need to differentiate among Islam, Islamic fundamentalism, radical belligerent positions based on a given political interpretation of Islam, and the extreme characterized by terrorism.

COMMON TRAITS OF FUNDAMENTALISM

The origins of fundamentalism are to be found in evangelical Pentecostals, who developed a form of revivalist theology. Based on this belief and in the consideration of the impurity of the secular world, they took over the belligerent mission of propagating their views against liberals and modernists. They considered themselves guardians of the original culture of the country, and demanded that Christian faith be translated into political action. As Martin Marty has argued, the several forms of fundamentalism reflect the same process, which is the radical encounter with modernity and the desperate attempt to avoid secularist changes in a traditional culture. The difference between these forms lies on the different contexts in which they faced the threat of modernity. As a modern worldview becomes global, as occurred during the 20th century, more and more religious groups are confronted with this challenge and react to it in a violent way.

There are common aspects among these different expressions of fundamentalism, including their origin at the beginning of the 20th century and their view of themselves as a "chosen people." Christian fundamentalism was the first phenomenon, because it was confronted first with modernity and liberalism. But after the popularization of fundamentalism in Jewish and Muslim contexts, there have been different expressions of the same phenomenon in other religions, in movements such as Hindu fundamentalism, Sikh fundamentalism, and others.

SEE ALSO

Volume 1 Left: Church and State Separation; United States. *Volume 2 Right:* Religion; Christian Coalition; Israel.

BIBLIOGRAPHY

Said Arjomand, *The Turban for the Crown: The Islamic Revolution in Iran* (Oxford University Press, 1988). Jeffrey Hadden and Anson Shuppe, eds., *Secularization and Fundamentalism Reconsidered III* (Paragon House, 1989); G. Marsden, *Fundamentalism and American Culture* (Oxford University Press, 1980); Martin E. Marty and R. Scott Appleby, *Fundamentalism Observed* (University of Chicago Press, 1994); Olivier Roy, *The Failure of Political Islam* (Harvard University Press, 1994); Israel Shahak and Norton Mezvinsky, *Jewish Fundamentalism in Israel* (Pluto Press, 1999); Bassam Tibi, *The Challenge of Fundamentalism* (University of California Press, 1998).

AMOS NASCIMENTO
METHODIST UNIVERSITY OF PIRACICABA, BRAZIL

The Right

Garvey, Marcus (1887–1940)

MARCUS GARVEY WAS born at St. Ann's Bay, Jamaica, the youngest of 11 children. Garvey left school at age 14 and moved to Kingston to work in a print shop. In Kingston, he learned firsthand about the dismal lot of his country's working class, his peers. He became a nationalist and reformer. When the members of the printers' union went on strike for the first time in 1907, he struck with them. He also edited *The Watchman*.

Garvey had ambitions; what he lacked was resources. He went to Central and South America, collecting information about discrimination against black people and seeking funding for his ambitions. Garvey traveled in the Panama Canal Zone to Ecuador, Nicaragua, Colombia, Venezuela, and Honduras. Everywhere, Garvey encountered his struggling expatriate West Indian countrymen. Still in need of resources, in 1912 Garvey went to England. He met Duse Mohammed Ali and got a job on Ali's *African Times* and *Oriental Review*. He began studying about colonial exploitation in Africa. He read Booker T. Washington's *Up from Slavery*, which advocated black self-help and accommodation to the dominant white society.

When he returned to Jamaica, after his government ignored his pleas for help for overseas West Indians, he established a training school based on his reading of Washington and the model of the Tuskegee Institute.

He began planning the Universal Negro Improvement Association (UNIA). His school attracted the attention of Washington, who invited Garvey to America. Garvey arrived late, after Washington had died. By then the American black leadership was split. Black veterans returning from World War I were unwilling to give way without resistance to the racists in white American society. Already Washington's accommodationist views were unacceptable to many black Americans. Refusing to accept second-class status as Washington had, new black leaders such as W.E.B. Du Bois took pride in themselves and argued that they deserved to be treated as all other citizens, regardless of the racism of the white power structure.

Settling in Harlem, New York City, Garvey began developing his movement. Garvey incorporated accommodation and equal rights as the two elements of his unique third-way black nationalist self-help organization. He advocated a return of African Americans to Africa as a means of restraining European colonialism. As part of his Back to Africa movement, Garvey organized the Universal Negro Improvement Association (UNIA) under the auspices of the African Communities League. The first UNIA convention, in New York in 1920, featured a parade down Lenox Avenue in Harlem and an evening address by Garvey to 25,000 people. He told of his plans to establish a nation-state in Africa. The UNIA grew quickly. Garvey published *The*

Negro World and spoke on a national tour. Quickly, the UNIA had more than 1,100 branches in 40 countries. Most branches were in the United States, but some were in the Caribbean, Latin America, and Africa.

The success of the UNIA brought millions of supporters and the resources for a migration to Africa. But the UNIA overextended itself and soon encountered financial difficulties. Among the other businesses was the Black Star Line. Initially three ships, the line was Garvey's dream method of transporting several millions to Liberia and Tanzania. The dream crumbled in 1922 when the United States charged Garvey with mail fraud in the sale of stock, Garvey's desperate measure to save his financially troubled transatlantic line. Garvey also established the African Communities League and the Negro Factories Corporation, and tried to get the League of Nations to give the UNIA former German colonies newly in play due to Germany's defeat in World War I. Garvey was convicted of fraud, sentenced to five years, imprisoned, and was effectively finished. In 1927, after commutation of his sentence, he was deported to Jamaica by President Calvin Coolidge.

In Jamaica, Garvey reentered politics, advocating minimum wages, land reform, legal reform, and self-government. He lost badly because his backers were not qualified to vote. He reestablished the UNIA, holding conventions in Jamaica and in Canada. In 1935, he moved to London, England, where he died in 1940.

Garvey believed in the black nationalism of Du Bois as well as the self-help philosophy of Washington. He did not want blacks to run away from America, but he did want them to go to Africa in large enough numbers to halt further European imperialism. He intended a strong Africa as a counter to white power throughout the world. He shared Du Bois's elitism, wanting only the best to colonize his African seat of power.

Garvey's projects failed. The closest success for his Back to Africa movement is Rasta, otherwise known as Rastafarianism. Followers of this movement believed the black homeland should be in Ethiopia. In 1920, Garvey stated that when Africa should have a black king, then deliverance would be near. In 1930, Ras Tafari became Emperor Haile Selassie I of Ethiopia. Yet, Garvey's black nationalism remained in the African American consciousness into the next century.

Garvey's nationalism was right wing because he defined it narrowly, restricting it to one race and excluding others. His conflict with Du Bois was in part because Garvey also valued the self-made man of middle-class capitalism while Du Bois's "talented tenth" was patrician elitism.

SEE ALSO

Volume 1 Left: Du Bois, W.E.B.; Douglass, Frederick.
Volume 2 Right: Black Separatism; Black Nationalism; Africa; Washington, Booker T.

BIBLIOGRAPHY

Edmund Cronon, *Black Moses* (University of Wisconsin Press, 1987); Ronald L.F. Davis, "Resisting Jim Crow: In-Depth Essay," www.jimcrowhistory.org (January 2004); Rupert Lewis and Patrick Bryan, eds., *Garvey: His Work and Impact* (Institute of Social and Economic Research, 1988); The Marcus Garvey and UNIA Papers Project, www.isop.ucla.edu (January 2004); Kevin Stokes, "Marcus Garvey: The Universal Negro Improvement Association and African Communities League" (2001) http://etext.lib.virginia.edu (January 2004); "The Afrocentric Experience: Marcus Garvey," www.swagga.com (January 2004).

JOHN BARNHILL, PH.D.
INDEPENDENT SCHOLAR

Germany

THE POLITICS OF THE RIGHT in Germany is a modern phenomenon related to the rise of conservative thinking in the 18th century. It received newer impulses during the 20th century, especially through the dictatorship of National-Socialism (Nazi Party), and the later division of the country into the communist East and the capitalistic West. Right-wing groups active in contemporary Germany have continued these traditions, developed new ways to influence cultural debates, and induced the participation particularly of the youth of the country.

ORIGINS OF THE RIGHT IN CONSERVATISM

Whereas aspects of the political right can be found in the nationalism of Herder and in the conservatism of Adam Müller and Justus Möser in the 18th century, it was Leopold von Ranke who established history as a science that would back conservative claims. Another distinguished thinker in this line was Friedrich Karl von Savigny, the founder of the historical critique of law, who was able to combine Friedrich W. Hegel's philosophy with new juridical and political doctrines in the 19th century. Another important but diffuse source for the political right in Germany is romanticism. Although

Germany has had its share of rightist regimes, from imperial Prussia to Adolf Hitler's Third Reich. It is in southern Germany, in the area of Bavaria surrounding Munich (München), that the country has its conservative core.

Wolfgang von Goethe was a vehement defender of the French Revolution, he later changed his opinion when Napoleon invaded Jena, thereby providing a basis to criticize liberal thought. Since many German writers and philosophers were acquainted with British writings, they emphasized the fundamental role of history and tradition. These ideas can be observed in many writers and artists who turned to Germanic mythical traditions, from the initiatives of restoration of folk tales by the brothers Grimm, through Novalis's religiosity, to Wagner's epopee of the Nibelungen. The conservative methodology of trying to find unchangeable and essential elements of society within history served to maintain traditional social hierarchy, monarchism, and traditional religion and to oppose the revolutions of 1848.

By the end of the 19th century, these different and disperse aspects combined, especially with traditional romantic aesthetics, and gave shape to conservatism as a whole. The existence of these various tenets created a conservative movement with different expressions and applications.

TO NATIONAL SOCIALISM

At the beginning of the 20th century, the articulation of a new social impetus led to the Weimar Republic. In view of this new situation, there was an attempt to pursue a "conservative revolution" at the time, aiming at a return to tradition. In the end the attempt failed, but the experience was important not only in preparing the ground for the dictatorship of National Socialism in Germany, but also for bringing to the surface a series of thinkers who remained influential during the 20th century well beyond their country of origin. Among the most influential conservative thinkers were Moeller van den Bruck, Oswald Spengler, Ernst Jünger, and others who became influential worldwide. At the same time, there was the impact of the dictatorship of National Socialism.

One of the most important and influential authors to provide theoretical tools for the constitution of conservative ideology in the 20th century was Carl Schmitt, who was notorious for his investigations of the philosophy of law. His definitions of law, state, and popular class, as well as his discussions on sovereignty and territory, influenced the ideological conception of conservatism and provided the foundations for National Socialism in Germany, since they justified an "enemy" and the conquering of new territories. One of his most famous distinctions was that of enemy, a conception

that is fundamental for the establishment of sovereignty and the decision for a specific policy. One of his basic ideas was that this political decision should be established in conformity with the social hierarchy, with representation of distinct orders within the community, and in accord with popular demand (*volksbegehren*). For this reason, Schmitt arrived at the conclusion in 1933 that popular claims should be the normative basis for the constitutional state, that is, that the people, in a populist sense, should constitute the political legitimization of the state.

POSTWAR GERMAN POLITICS

Between 1945 and 1989, the country was divided into two blocks representing both sides of the ideological divisions during the Cold War. Accordingly, the tension between left and right represented the tension between countries aligned with the United States and those with the Soviet Union. Thus, the Sozialdemokratische Partei of West Germany—Federal Republic of Germany (BRD)—withdrew the socialist content of its political program and approximated itself to the Christliche demokratische Partei, which was the most important conservative party opposing communism. In East Germany—Democratic Republic of Germany (DDR)—the party represented the Soviet orientation and opposed any dissidents, even though it would later accept perestroika. The reunification was welcomed by both the right and the left, bringing about the consensus that Germany should not remain divided. With the support of the foreign policy of the United States and the Soviet Union, led by Ronald Reagan and Mikhail Gorbachev, the whole process was accelerated and unification became an inevitable result.

The euphoria of bringing down the Berlin Wall in Germany in October 1989 set the rhythm for events in central and eastern Europe, which led to a series of rapid transformations. However, the lingering question of the "Vaterland" in Germany was raised again by conservative intellectuals and groups related to the extreme right (*rechtsextremismus*) who rearticulated traditional themes in politics, economics, religion, and culture. Revelations about the communist governments paralyzed the German left and allowed for the consolidation of the German right.

THE GERMAN RIGHT AFTER 1989

National politics was dominated by the Christliche-demokratische Partei (CDU) and personified by Prime

Minister Helmut Kohl, who led the coalition governing Germany between 1982 and 1996 and was responsible for the process of reunification. Behind the CDU was the traditional image of Schmitt—who died in 1976—and the work of intellectuals who justified nationalism and reinforced the traditional link among the CDU, German Catholicism, and conservative culture. Based on Schmitt's views of the foreign as enemy, political debates emerged on the right to asylum in Germany and the issue concerning a German identity. The focal point of the discussions was a proposal to change article number 16 of the constitution, which granted the right of asylum to refugees, since conservative politicians argued that the growing number of refugees in Germany was a threat to the project of a nationally homogeneous country. They also argued that foreigners were the root of many cultural and "socioeconomic problems" such as drugs, criminality, violence, and lack of civilization.

At the theoretical level, the historian Ernst Nolte defended a "cleansing" of the German cultural tradition, not only by the nonacceptance of multiculturalism but also through a process of forgetting episodes of recent German history. According to him, these moments, that is, World War II and the Holocaust, were not relevant to the definition of a German culture, since they were already over and did not need any further investigation. These views were defended by conservative authors such as Hermann Lübbe, Bernard Willms, and others, who provided arguments for radical-right groups that questioned negative interpretations of the Third Reich.

Lübbe not only defended a reinterpretation of German history, but also affirmed that the rights of the individual should be protected from any "foreign determination." According to him, this could be practically implemented through control of the borders, alteration of the constitution in this regard, and justification of anger toward foreigners. Willms also backed nationalism and a strong state that should defend the interests of its citizens. According to him, Germany should be understood and defined as a "German nation." In his book, *Idealismus und Nation*, he stresses this point repeatedly, arguing for categories to define what it really means to belong to such a nation and culture. This is put into practice through his association with the far-right Republicans.

At the practical level, these views were complemented by journalists and ideologues, who went as far as to defend extremist actions: Armin Mohler, Günther Maschke, Günther Rohrmoser, Gerd-Klaus Kaltenbrunner, Franz Schonhüber—the leader of the Republikaner.

The role of these intellectuals was to prepare a newer version of the so-called Conservative Revolution in Germany by bringing it to the public sphere. Many other exponents of this line of thought can be found in publications and think tanks. However, the responsibility for the connection between theory and praxis is found in the smaller parties: The National-demokrastiche Partei Deutschland (NPD) founded in 1964 and led by Günther Deckert; the Freiheitliche Deutsche Arbeitspartei (FAP), led by Friedhelm Busse; and the Republikaner, led by Schonhüber.

THE CULTURE OF THE RADICAL RIGHT

In the cultural realm, the above ideas were advanced by far-right organizations, by parties such as the NPD, and by the neo-Nazi movement, involving actions of youth, expressing xenophobia with violence against foreigners. Neo-Nazism was identified with musical groups such as Störkraft, Stuka, Endsieg, Böhsen Onkelz, and others, as well as with the publications *NS Kampruf, White Power, Proißens Gloria, Skinhead-Zeitung, Frontal*, and others, and slogans such as "Order, Discipline and Efficiency," "Foreigners Out!" (Ausländer raus!), "More work for Germans" during the 1990s.

Sensationalist publications and programs on the radio and TV explored the themes of neo-Nazi xenophobic violence, bringing them to public attention. Beyond this general view passed to the public, there is a network of activities that is not well perceived or pictured by the media. The Nationale-Offensive, for example, despite being characterized as radical-right, neo-Nazi, or fascist, was defined by its own members as national-socialist or national youth.

The mention of certain groups' names is enough to show their connection to ideas of the Third Reich: Nationale Liste, Neue Front, Volkssozialistische Bewegung Deutschlands, Deutsche Aktionsgruppe, Nationalistiche Front, etc. Specific movements for women, such as the Deutschen Frauen Front, as well as a branch of the Ku Klux Klan and paramilitary groups, such as the Wehrsportgruppe Hoffmann, are to be found among them. Different from conservatism, these are action groups much less interested in historical or conceptual debates.

Finally, there were also a religious dimension at play, since these groups expressed a "fascination for rituals." For instance, the Republikaner has used the image and works of Martin Luther to justify beliefs and actions of the radical right; a religious arm of conservative nationalism was established, represented by the German new religious right—the German evangelicals. They created the Evangelical Alliance in the 1990s, in order to criticize ecumenical relation and justify the Persian Gulf War; accepted the theology of evangelicalism and fundamentalism; and defended nationalism against the so-called invasion of Muslims.

Based on all these developments, the right has had a firm constituency and constant support in Germany. It maintains a long tradition of conservative thinking, is represented by political parties, has had a diffuse and widespread influence on culture, and has received its justification from religious discourses.

SEE ALSO

Volume 1 Left: Socialism; Germany; Fromm, Erich.
Volume 2 Right: Fascism; Hitler, Adolf; Nationalism.

BIBLIOGRAPHY

Jürgen Habermas, *The New Conservatism: Cultural Criticism and the Historian's Debate* (MIT Press, 1989); Sozialistische Studiengruppen (SOS), *Zwischen Neokonservatismus und Rechtsradikalismus. Politische und populistische Rechtstendenzen in der Bundesrepublik* (Hamburg, VSA-Verlag, 1986); R. Woods, *The Conservative Revolution in the Weimar Republic* (Macmillan, 1996).

AMOS NASCIMENTO
METHODIST UNIVERSITY OF PIRACICABA, BRAZIL

Gingrich, Newt (1943–)

DR. NEWTON LEROY Gingrich, more well-known as Newt Gingrich, was born on June 17, 1943, in Harrisburg, Pennsylvania. Originally named Newton McPherson, Gingrich was renamed after his new father, Robert Gingrich, following his parents' separation soon after his birth. During his youth, Gingrich quickly developed a love of reading. His lobbying career began at the very young age of 10 when he joined a group of schoolchildren who went to the mayor's office in Harrisburg to ask for the establishment of a town zoo. In 1956, his family moved to Europe as a result of his father's military career; he went to school at U.S. military institutions in Orleans, France, and Stuttgart, Germany. In 1960, Gingrich and his family returned to Fort Benning, in Columbus, Georgia, where he graduated from Baker High School in 1961. During his time there, Gingrich successfully ran his friend's student body president

campaign, was a National Merit Scholarship semifinalist, and was voted "most intellectual" by his classmates.

After graduating from high school, Gingrich continued to have a secret relationship with one of his math teachers, Jackie Battley, whom he married on June 19, 1962, while he was a freshman at Emory University in Atlanta, Georgia. Their first child was born only a year later, before Gingrich graduated from college. Even though his young family occupied much of his time, Gingrich was able to start a Young Republican Club at Emory, where he debated politics and the future of the United States with other interested students. In December 1965, he graduated with a degree in history.

From 1966 to 1970, Gingrich studied at Tulane University in New Orleans, Louisiana. While there, Gingrich was able to receive a draft deferment for the Vietnam War as a result of his family situation, although he was also flat-footed and nearsighted. Politically, he ran an on-campus campaign to drum up support for Nelson Rockefeller's presidential bid in 1968. In the beginning of 1971, Gingrich graduated with a Ph.D. in history, although his professors noted that his thesis on the status of education in the Belgian Congo wasn't exceptional and has never been published.

At the age of 27, Gingrich used his teaching career, which began with a professorship at West Georgia College, as a springboard for his political career, but he failed in his first two bids for the U.S. House of Representatives in 1974 and 1976. Accruing debts and losing his chance to gain tenure at the college, Gingrich obtained some financing from friends to write a novel and briefly moved his family to Europe.

He never finished the novel, but finally succeeded in his campaign to represent the citizens of Georgia's sixth congressional district in 1978 as a member of the Republican Party. Going on to serve 10 terms in Congress, Gingrich constructed a range of programs, known as New Age Reaganism, which included a balanced budget; the line-item veto; attacks on drugs, crime, and welfare; and evocation of supply-side economics. Serving as minority whip from 1989 to 1994, Gingrich became the speaker of the house following the rampant success of the Republican Party in the 1994 elections.

During his time as speaker, which lasted from 1995 to 1998, Gingrich engineered the Contract with America, which was based upon his and his fellow Republicans' campaign promises and his principles of New Age Reaganism. Conflicting and contrasting with President Bill Clinton, Gingrich was still able to pass nine of the 10 items in his contract, establishing term limits in the

House, better auditing of Congress, balancing the budget, cutting taxes, and increasing military spending.

Even though Gingrich was a constant critic of Clinton's ethics and morals, Gingrich was fined $300,000 by the Congressional Ethics Committee for his use of tax-exempt foundations for political funds, in violation of House rules. The scandal ultimately resulted in Gingrich's resignation from the speakership and from his congressional seat in 1998, especially after the relatively poor performance of the Republican Party in the 1998 elections.

In 2004, Gingrich was a senior fellow at the American Enterprise Institute, a conservative think tank based in Washington, D.C., where he focused on healthcare, information technology, and the military.

SEE ALSO

Volume 1 Left: Clinton, William J.; Democratic Party.
Volume 2 Right: Conservatism; Republican Party; Reagan, Ronald.

BIBLIOGRAPHY

"About Newt," www.newt.org (June 2004); Public Broadcasting System, "Frontline: The Long March of Newt Gingrich," www.pbs.org (June 2004); New Gingrich, *Reclaiming the Republican Revolution: A New Contract with America* (Regnery, 2004).

JOHN BARNHILL, PH.D.
INDEPENDENT SCHOLAR

Globalization

GLOBALIZATION refers to the spread of new forms of nonterritorial social activity. Since the vast majority of human activities is still tied to a concrete geographical location, the more decisive facet of globalization concerns the manner in which distant events and forces impact on local and regional endeavors. In popular discourse, globalization often functions as little more than a synonym for one or more of the following phenomena: the pursuit of classical liberal or free-market policies in the world economy; the growing dominance of Western forms of political, economic, and cultural life; the proliferation of new information technologies; as well as the notion that humanity stands at the threshold of realizing one single unified community in which major sources of social conflict have vanished.

Globalization is the result of advances in communication, transportation, and information technologies. The impact of recent technological innovations is profound, and even those who do not have a job directly affected by the new technology are shaped by it in innumerable ways as citizens and consumers.

Globalization, in its rightist sense, also involves the growth of multinational corporations or transnational corporations, and international institutions that oversee world trade and finance play an increasingly important role in this era of globalization. Globalization shares a number of characteristics with internationalization and is used interchangeably with it, although some prefer to use globalization to emphasize the erosion of the nation-state or national boundaries. Globalization has become identified with a number of trends, most of which have developed since World War II. These include greater international movement of commodities, money, information, and people, and the development of technology, organizations, legal systems, and infrastructures to allow this movement.

HISTORY OF GLOBALIZATION

The period of the gold standard and liberalization of the 19th century is often called the first era of globalization. Based on the *Pax Britannia* and the exchange of goods in currencies pegged to specie, this era grew along with industrialization. The theoretical basis was Ricardo's work on comparative advantage and Say's Law of general equilibrium. In essence, it was argued that nations would trade effectively, and that any temporary disruptions in supply or demand would correct themselves automatically. The institution of the gold standard came in steps in major industrialized nations between approximately 1850 and 1880, though exactly when various nations were truly on the gold standard is a matter of a great deal of contentious debate. The first era of globalization is said to have broken down in stages beginning with World War I, and then collapsed with the crisis of the gold standard in the late 1920s and early 1930s.

The second era of globalization accompanies a movement in economic thought called neoliberalism, which argues that in a world of floating exchange rates, it is economically ineffective for nations to use regulation to protect their internal markets, and that it is impossible to maintain economic autonomy and monetary policy autonomy. This period is generally referred to by the word *globalization* in the present form. Globalization in this era has been driven by trade negotiation rounds, which led to a series of agreements to remove restrictions on "free trade." The Uruguay Round led to a treaty to create the World Trade Organization (WTO), to mediate trade disputes. Other bilateral trade agreements, including sections of Europe's Maastricht Treaty and the North American Free Trade Agreement, have also been signed in pursuit of the goal of reducing tariffs and barriers to trade.

THE DEBATE OVER GLOBALIZATION

Very few people, groups, or governments oppose globalization in its entirety. Instead, critics of globalization believe the way globalization operates should be changed. The debate over globalization is about what the best rules are for governing the global economy so that its advantages can grow while its problems can be solved. On one side of this debate are those who stress the benefits of removing barriers to international trade and investment, allowing capital to be allocated more efficiently and giving consumers greater freedom of choice. With free-market globalization, investment funds can move unimpeded from where they are plentiful to where they are most needed. Consumers can benefit from cheaper products because reduced tariffs make goods produced at low cost from faraway places. Producers of goods gain by selling to a wider market. More competition keeps sellers on their toes and allows ideas and new technology to spread and benefit others.

On the other side of the debate are critics who see neoliberal policies as producing greater poverty, inequality, social conflict, cultural destruction, and environmental damage. They say that the most developed nations—the United States, Germany, and Japan—succeeded not because of free trade but because of protectionism and subsidies. They argue that the more recently successful economies of South Korea, Taiwan, and China all had strong state-led development strategies that did not follow neoliberalism. These critics think that government encouragement of "infant industries"—that is, industries that are just beginning to develop—enables a country to become internationally competitive.

Furthermore, those who criticize the Washington consensus suggest that the inflow and outflow of money from speculative investors must be limited to prevent bubbles. These bubbles are characterized by the rapid inflow of foreign funds that bid up domestic stock markets and property values. When the economy cannot sustain such expectations, the bubbles burst as investors panic and pull their money out of the country.

These bubbles appeared in Indonesia, Malaysia, and Thailand in 1997 and since then in Argentina, Russia, and Turkey. According to critics, a strong active government is needed to ensure stability and development.

Protests by what is called the anti-globalization movement are seldom directed against globalization itself but rather against abuses that harm the rights of workers and the environment. The question raised by nongovernmental organizations and protestors at WTO and IMF (World Trade Organization and International Monetary Fund) gatherings is whether globalization will result in a rise of living standards or a "race to the bottom" as competition takes the form of lowering living standards and undermining environmental regulations. One of the key problems of the 21st century will be determining to what extent markets should be regulated to promote fair competition, honest dealing, and fair distribution of public goods on a global scale.

A THREAT TO DEMOCRATIZATION

The process of globalization presents significant challenges to the democratization of the states. It should be noted that the interplay of democratizing institutions, democratic legitimations of power, and social movements was born out of an epochal redeployment of power from local to national. Once again, the end of the 20th century maybe another such epochal moment of redeployment of power, from national states to a variety of transnational structures, which are probably still only in embryonic form, is under way. Hence, globalization is not only a challenge to the democratization of the states but raises the issue of whether the democratization of the states is even going to continue to be meaningful in a world of transnational connection.

Although distant places have often had significant economic linkages, the volume and diversity of these linkages have enormously expanded as capital investments, goods and services, and labor have become mobile as never before. Giant corporate actors and otherwise atomized individuals alike can enter into nearly instantaneous contact with distant interlocutors through fax and e-mail. Governments, partly as a consequence, have been losing their capacity to control the economic and cultural life of the territories vulnerable to their authority, but additionally now often seem eager to shed some of their traditional responsibilities in the name of the allegedly superior efficiencies of the global marketplace. The impulse for transnational structures for decision making is rooted in various forms of cross-border connection that generate threats from which even powerful elites may be unable to protect themselves without new global structures of governance.

Threats emanating from the high-speed globalization process can be broadly categorized as follows: diminishing national policy autonomy, states' retreat from welfare commitments, and reinvigoration of exclusionary politics.

DIMINISHING NATIONAL AUTONOMY

In this emerging world of transnational connection, the abilities of national governments to manage many important things are diminishing. Control over flows of capital is proving especially elusive, but the movement of goods and even of the relatively less mobile individual workers has proven hard to control as well. Effective decision-making power over parts of the transnationalized economies is becoming established elsewhere than the states, and in several forms.

There are formally constituted transnational quasi-governments, of which the European Union is the most powerful within its formal jurisdiction and the United Nations the geographically broadest in its scope. There are also formally constituted agreements for regulating the levels and nature of economic integration without other quasi-governmental trappings, of which we might take the North American Free Trade Agreement (NAFTA) among Canada, the United States, and Mexico or South America's Mercosur as models. And then there are agreements among financial interests to make major decisions about the geography of capital flows, of which the International Monetary Fund and the World Bank are by far the most consequential.

At this historical moment when more citizens of more states than ever before in human history have been acquiring some control over the incumbents in office of the national states, the capacity of those incumbents to function as autonomous national policymakers has been seriously eroding. Few governments in the world today risk a serious confrontation with the economic policies dear to the IMF and World Bank. In short, states are weaker in the global marketplace. This particular challenge to democracy is very profound: The public can choose incumbents but it hardly follows from that fact that they thereby can choose policy, especially in central matters of economic life.

An important aspect of these diminished state capacities is the degree to which states are doing it to themselves. Students of contemporary politics, for ex-ample, speak of a hollowing-out of the state, as all sorts of functions pass upward to transnational bodies, downward to reinvigorated local or regional organs of government, and outward in the form of privatization by contracting out to private agencies. There is an ideological dimension to restricting the sphere of state action, in which even holders of state power are participating. It originates from the belief in the superiority of "the market" over "the state." What is striking about the current moment, however, is how issues of welfare and poverty have become marginal in political debates in some of the richer countries. In the new economic order, lifetime careers may be giving way to part-time, temporary jobs. Enhanced freedom from state regulation for owners of capital means downsizing, flexible specialization, outsourcing, capital mobility across interstate frontiers, and rapid technological change, which threaten economic security for many and drastically reduce welfare.

EXCLUSIONARY POLITICS

Part of what gives anti-welfare positions their special force today is a fragmentation of political identities. To the extent that poorer people are identifiable as ethnically distinctive, including an identity as recent immigrants, some political parties are able to denounce welfare as taking from "us" to give to "them." With millions of North African Moslems in France, Turks in Germany, and Albanians and Africans moving to Italy, the mobilization of xenophobic sentiment is readily linked to an attack on welfare. When Surinamese or Indonesians show up on Dutch welfare rolls, the Dutch rethink their generous unemployment insurance. Moreover, the weakening of labor in the transnational marketplace reduces the likelihood that a collective identity as workers will effectively override this fragmentation. The shift among a portion of France's workers from voting for the communists to voting for the anti-immigrant National Front is an important sign of the power of anti-immigrant politics in an age of globalized economics.

In the absence of policies directed at their inclusion, in the absence of notions of minimal acceptable standards of life guaranteed by a national community, will large numbers of poorer people feel materially or symbolically excluded from national life and simply opt out of support for a democratic practice that no longer aspires at both their inclusion and material advance? Such a possibility may be more profoundly corrosive of democracy than the direct exclusionary notions of xenophobic parties. But xenophobic politics is by no means insignificant.

The increased role of denationalized technocrats in positions of visible political power, and the openness of national economies to the transnational economy that those technocrats tend to promote, help sustain a communally oriented embrace of traditions. Religious fundamentalisms, xenophobic political parties, and ethnic violence are all energized. In the wealthier countries today, we see as a consequence some interesting divisions among those who identify with the political right, as some embrace reviving supposed communal traditions and the moral virtues under challenge in an individualistic age, while others champion the global capitalist marketplace and proclaim the individual will to be the sole repository of moral authority.

This is a globalizing economy in which wealthier countries have large numbers of immigrants, permanent, semipermanent, and temporary, and in various degrees of legality; in which transnational political institutions deploy armed force; and in which cultural hybridity is as close as the omnipresent TV. Such an economy generates political movements of the threatened and countermovements of those threatened by these movements. Some of these movements and counter-movements focus on the incursions of transnational capital and the semitreasonous actions of national governments that fail to protect the national essence. Others address the cultural challenge posed by the sacralization of the market.

Therefore, the present moment in the history of democracy is not an occasion for triumphal celebration but for concern. To summarize: the remarkable and radical geographic extension of democratic practices coincides with a number of serious threats. The leaching of power out of the national states, in part toward a variety of transnational institutions, raises the specter of a trivialization of the very real democratization of the states. On the edge of the 21st century, the unrivaled democratization of the states is now challenged by a new redeployment of power.

The actions of people in rural villages and urban workshops played a major role in the history of early modern states; the emerging social movements of the 19th century played a major role in the democratization of some of them. It remains to be seen whether the construction of the world order of the 21st century continues as a nearly exclusively elite project or whether social and political movements can inject a more democratic element into the emerging structures of global governance.

SEE ALSO

Volume 1 Left: Anti-Globalization; Protests. *Volume 2 Right:* Capitalism; *Laissez Faire.*

BIBLIOGRAPHY

John Gerrad Ruggie, "Territoriality and Beyond: Problematizing Modernity in International Relations," *International Organization* (v.47, 1993); Jan Art Scholte, *Globalization: A Critical Introduction* (St. Martin's, 2000); John Tomlinson, *Globalization and Culture* (Polity Press, 1999); Thomas Hylland Eriksen, *Tyranny of the Moment: Fast and Slow Time in the Information Age* (Pluto Press, 2001); Jagdish N. Bhagwati, *In Defense of Globalization* (Oxford University Press, 2004).

JITENDRA UTTAM
JAWAHARLAL NEHRU UNIVERSITY, INDIA

Goldwater, Barry (1909–1998)

BARRY GOLDWATER, born in Phoenix, Arizona Territory, served five terms as Republican senator for Arizona (1953–64 and 1969–86). In 1964, he was the Republican Party's presidential candidate, losing in a landslide against the incumbent president, Democrat Lyndon B. Johnson, with only 39 percent of the popular vote. His winning of five states in the deep south, plus his home state, however, foreshadowed the realignment of southern whites to the Republican Party. After a period of "me-too-Republicanism," Goldwater's anti-government conservatism and fierce anti-communism signaled the rebirth of the Republican Party as America's conservative voice.

Coming from a very assimilated Jewish background, Goldwater converted to Episcopalianism when he got married. As a businessman, he grew up to be a free-market conservative, celebrating the "rugged individualism" of the west even in the context of the Great Depression and the New Deal. A paternalistic sense of fairness toward his employees softened his anti-union and anti-government stance. Before and after World War II, in which he served as a pilot, Goldwater built his reputation in Phoenix and Arizona as a businessman and photographer. He involved himself in the so-called right-to-work campaign against union organizing activities and, upon assignment from the governor, established the Arizona Air National Guard, which became the first in the nation to be open to African Americans. Goldwater, despite having experienced some prejudice against Jews, was largely oblivious to the structural causes and features of racism and segregation. For him, these were problems of personal behavior that could not be rectified by government action. Thus, he did not see a problem with his strong insistence on states' rights, despite the fact that it provided a rationale for racially motivated segregationists. Similarly, Goldwater did not see a contradiction between his acceptance of the large role federal funds were playing in building infrastructure and defense facilities in Arizona and the west and his general opposition to the Democratic New Deal, which he viewed as encroaching on economic freedoms. His support of a strong military provides one explanation for this ambivalent position.

After serving as vice mayor in Phoenix and working on the gubernatorial campaign of Ernie Pyle in 1950, Goldwater was ready himself to take advantage of the temporary backlash against the New Deal. He ran for the U.S. Senate in 1952 and won against a Democratic incumbent on Dwight D. Eisenhower's coattails. He fiercely attacked the New Deal and Harry Truman's Fair Deal, which he likened to socialism, and the Democratic appeasement in foreign policy. Goldwater's anticommunist credentials were strengthened by an endorsement of Senator Joseph McCarthy.

Once in office, Goldwater continued to stress states' rights, for example, in arguing that the states, and not the federal government, should have responsibility for Native Americans and work to assimilate them. To critics, this would have meant to destroy Native American culture. Goldwater became disenchanted with Eisenhower's modern Republicanism, which accepted or at least did not attack many elements of the New Deal. He considered this as tantamount to accepting socialism. Eisenhower's timid foreign policy and his refusal to support Goldwater's friend, McCarthy, further alienated Goldwater from the president, but he still loyally supported Eisenhower's reelection.

Elected as chairman of the Senate Republican Campaign Committee (serving three terms, 1955–56, 1959–60, and 1961–62), Goldwater was able to build credibility and gain influence with the media and the Republican base while traveling throughout the country to raise funds. Both liked this new type of western conservative who was not afraid to speak his mind, especially after his reelection in 1958. The same was true for the growing circle of conservative intellectuals, for example William F. Buckley's *National Review* magazine, who wanted to join the free-market libertarians and the social conservatives to challenge liberalism. In his second term as senator, Goldwater began to seriously con-

front Eisenhower's policies, particularly the ever-growing federal budget, offering a conservative alternative to modern Republicanism in the mold of Robert Taft. He became a national figure, especially through participation in the highly public bipartisan investigation of illegal activities of labor unions, involving the Teamsters' Jimmy Hoffa and the United Auto Workers' Walter Reuther, which he used for the red-baiting of union officials and Democrats. Goldwater also voted against civil rights and anti-poverty legislation.

The evolving conservative Goldwater wing of the Republican Party challenged the centrist Vice-President Richard Nixon in 1960. Upon the recommendation of Robert Welch, founder of the fiercely right-wing John Birch Society, Goldwater wrote his *The Conscience of a Conservative* in 1960, together with the *National Review*'s Brent Bozell, stressing his familiar themes of freedom versus collectivism, states' rights, reduction of the government's size, and rolling back communism. Nixon angered conservatives when he sought a deal with progressive Republican Nelson Rockefeller, who represented the dominance of the Eastern establishment in the party and was resented by the GOP's right wing. While Goldwater eventually called for party unity in support of Nixon, he also started the process of "taking the party back," winning the heart of conservatives like Pat Buchanan. Goldwater's book became a bestseller and laid the groundwork for his campaign for the Republican presidential nomination in 1964.

Goldwater, however, never became an intellectual *National Review* Republican, preferring instead to use the networks he built as Campaign Committee chair. His appeal resulted from his conservative populism and frankness, and also from his western origins. The west had become a growth area and also engendered American folk images of individualism and the frontier. He seized the nomination against a weakened Rockefeller. In his acceptance speech, Goldwater declared: "Extremism in the defense of liberty is no vice. Moderation in the pursuit of justice is no virtue."

His opponent, Johnson, attacked Goldwater as an extremist, possibly starting the practice of negative campaigning with the "Daisy Girl" television commercial, which featured a little girl in a field, a military voice counting down, and a nuclear blast at the end. The ad made no reference to Goldwater, but people understood that it was a warning against Goldwater's aggressive foreign policy proposals.

Goldwater continued the new Republican focus on the south, where Eisenhower and Nixon had done surprisingly well, but departed from the original intent of

"Operation Dixie," which was designed to attract whites and African Americans alike. Instead, Goldwater stressed states' rights, which black Americans correctly read as a way to keep segregation in place. His campaign greatly accelerated the migration of southern whites to the Republican Party and mobilized the conservative base of the party. Ronald Reagan was to capitalize on both developments in 1980.

Goldwater returned to the Senate in 1969, retired in 1986, and died in Arizona May 29, 1998. Even though he moderated some of his position later in his career, his name and 1964 campaign stand for the white backlash against the New Deal and the anti-government right turn of the Republican Party and the country.

SEE ALSO

Volume 1 Left: Johnson, Lyndon B.; Democratic Party.
Volume 2 Right: Republican Party; Nixon, Richard M.

BIBLIOGRAPHY

Robert Alan Goldberg, *Barry Goldwater* (Yale University Press, 1995); Barry Goldwater with Brent Bozell, *The Conscience of a Conservative* (Victor, 1960); Rick Perlstein, *Before the Storm: Barry Goldwater and the Unmaking of the American Consensus* (Hill and Wang, 2001).

THOMAS GREVEN
FREIE UNIVERSITÄT, GERMANY

Greece

THE MODERN HISTORY of Greece can be said to have begun with the revolution of 1821 against the Ottoman Turkish Empire. The Turks had ruled what is now called Greece since 1453, when their Sultan Mohammed II conquered Constantinople, now called Istanbul. The centuries of Ottoman rule in the Balkans, the heritage of which continues today in the friction between Muslim and Christian in Kosovo and Bosnia, had been harsh. Families had been compelled to convert from their native Greek Orthodoxy or Roman Catholicism (especially among the Croats) to Islam. For those who remained Christian, the Ottomans imposed the hated *devshirme* system. Young Christian boys would be taken from their homes forcibly to join the elite Janissary (*yeni cheri*) army corps of the sultans, being raised as Muslims. Other less fortunate Christian youths would be castrated to serve as palace eunuchs. All Christians were subjected to a heavy tax as well to support the Ottoman State. According to Ira M. Lapidus in *A History of Islamic Societies*, this was called the *jizya*.

The revolution of 1821 had its origins in the Philhellene movement, or "the friends of Greece," which began in the Napoleonic Wars in 1814. A great supporter was the British port George Gordon, Lord Byron, who would die in Greece while fighting for Greek independence in April 1824. The decisive battle of the Greek war for independence was the battle at Navarino Bay, on October 20, 1827. On that day a largely British fleet under Vice Admiral Sir Edward Codrington engaged the Turkish fleet, which was aided by ships sent by the ruler of Egypt, Mohammed Ali. As Andrew Lambert wrote, the issue of the battle was not long in doubt. "The Muslim fleets were more numerous, they had only four battleships and some frigates to face an allied fleet with ten battleships."

According to the Greek Embassy in Washington, D.C., "In 1828, a small, independent Greek state was formed with 800,000 inhabitants. It was a penniless state of extremely size, consisting of the Peloponnese, Central Greece and the Cyclades." A more concrete foundation was laid at the Treaty of London in 1832 when Otho, the son of King Ludwig I of Bavaria, instituted a rightist hereditary monarchy for the Hellenes, as the Greeks called themselves. Otho, however, went against the spirit of conservative liberalism of the times and refused to abide by the constitution of 1844 that was forced upon him. During his autocratic rule, Great Britain intervened again in Greek affairs.

In 1864, a new constitution was promulgated for Greece, while a royal scion of Denmark became the new king as George I. A veteran officer of the Danish Navy, George had been called to rule by a Greek National Assembly. He would reign until his tragic assassination in 1913. During this period, Greece was affected by the growing pan-Slav movement, in which Tzarist Russia, seeing itself as heir to the Byzantine Empire crushed by the Muslims in 1453 and as protector of all Greek Orthodox peoples and Slavs in the Balkans. While this was directed against the Turks, it inevitably led to clashes with the British as well. In fact, in the Crimean War (1854–56), the British had joined the Turks in their battle against Russia's Nicholas I.

It was Greece's fate to be drawn into the struggle over the crumbling Ottoman Empire and its domains in the Balkans. In 1877–78, Russia seemed on the verge of conquering all of the Balkans and threatening Greece, until, once again, the British fleet intervened to keep the balance of power. Under the conservative Prime Minister Benjamin Disraeli, the British Mediterranean Fleet under Admiral Hornby appeared near Constantinople as a warning against Russian imperial ambitions. The Balkan situation was later resolved at the Congress of Berlin in 1878, but as R.R. Palmer and Joel Colton wrote in *A History of the Modern World*, "it left many continuing problems for later statesmanship to deal with." The Greek army of George I also moved to gain lands that had been historically been part of ancient Greece. In 1881, taking advantage of the weakness of Turkey, the Greeks annexed Thessaly.

In 1909, and not for the last time, the military intervened in Greek affairs, staging a coup that brought to power the Cretan Eleftherios Venizelos, who would dominate Greek affairs until 1935. A final solution to the problem of Turkish power in the Balkans did not come until the Balkan Wars of 1912–13, which effectively limited Turkish control to an area around Constantinople, which the Young Turks after their revolt of 1908 would rename Istanbul. According to the Greek Embassy, Greece gained "Thessaloniki, Yannina, Samos, Chios and Lesbos became Greek as well as all the land west of the Evros river, thanks mainly to Greece's powerful fleet. Also, the government had admitted deputies from Crete in the Greek Chamber before they had started."

Greece entered World War I in 1917 on the side of the Allies (England, France, and Russia), for no small reason because the Greeks' hereditary enemy, Turkey, had joined imperial Germany and Austria-Hungary. Although the Turkish empire was destroyed in the war, the Greek population of Turkey, which had lived there for nearly 3,000 years, was driven out in the aftermath. The Turks, under their nationalist leader Kemal Attaturk, carried out atrocities against the Greeks, and the ancient city of Smyrna was burned by the Turks in 1922.

Conservative democracy had little real success in the rocky soil of Greece. In 1923, a republic was declared, but in 1935, the son of King Constantine, George II, came to power in a rigged plebiscite. He turned to General Ioannis Metaxas in 1936 to reinforce his rule, making Metaxas in effect the royal protector of Greece. Despite militarism at home, the Greeks still considered themselves part of the Western democracies; after all, their country had given democracy to the world. When Italy issued an ultimatum to Greece on October 28, 1940, the Greeks defeated the subsequent Italian attack so badly that Nazi Germany invaded Greece in April 1941 in an attempt to salvage the glory of Italian dictator Benito Mussolini's tarnished impe-

rial eagles. The Greeks fought back with determination, backed by a British expeditionary force sent by Prime Minister Winston S. Churchill. However, both Greeks and British were defeated, and the remnants of the British force evacuated to Egypt after a stubborn, but doomed, final defense of the island of Crete. During the war, Greece suffered from German occupation, which also involved persecution of Greek Jews. A strong Greek resistance movement, aided by the British Special Operations Executive (SOE), continued the fight during the war against the German invaders until Greece was liberated in October 1944.

However, the defeat of Germany in 1944 did not mean peace for Greece. The communists had formed a major part of the Greek resistance, and backed by the Soviet Union began a revolt to gain power. British and American aid flowed into Greece, which became the first real battleground of the Cold War. Finally, as the Greek Embassy notes, "in 1946 the tragedy began of a war that cost thousands of lives, with Greek fighting Greek in the mountains and in the cities. It ended in 1949 with the defeat of the armed force of the Greek Communist Party (KKE)."

KING CONSTANTINE

The aftermath of the civil war did not bring with it any stability to constitutional Greece. A series of governments, both liberal and conservative, attempted to bring order to the country, the last being the government of George Papandreou, from 1963 to 1965. However, interference by King Constantine led to his dismissal in 1965 and, again, in 1967, a military coup took place in Athens, which ushered in the rule of the colonels. Any attempt at legitimacy was overthrown by the colonels, according to the interview of Constantin Costa-Gavras, who made his film, Z, about the coup. In 1973, militarists brutally put down a student revolt at the Athens Polytechnic Institute to oppose their dictatorship. A year later, the colonels were forced to surrender power, further disgraced by the virtually unopposed Turkish invasion and occupation of part of the island of Cyprus.

King Constantine, who had been forced to leave Greece, was not invited to return. A constitutional republic was proclaimed for Greece and a president was chosen, Constantine Tsatsos, a university professor and academician. Although the country was now constitutionally sound, it was threatened by the leftist terror group November 17. The November 17 movement carried on a long campaign of bombings until it was largely broken up in August 15, 2002, in the wake of the international crackdown on terrorism after the attack on America on September 11, 2001. With the opening of the Olympic Games in Athens in August 2004, security against terrorist attack was the primary concern.

SEE ALSO

Volume 1 Left: Greece; Democracy; Liberalism.
Volume 2 Right: Conservatism.

BIBLIOGRAPHY

Ira M. Lapidus, *A History of Islamic Societies* (Cambridge University Press, 1991); The Literature Network, "Lord George Gordon Byron," www.online-literature.com (July 2004); Andrew Lambert, "The Shield of Empire," *The Oxford Illustrated History of the Royal Navy,* J.R. Hill, ed. (Oxford University Press, 1995); R.R. Palmer and Joel Colton, *A History of the Modern World* (Knopf, 1971); Constantin Costa-Gavras, www.bfi.org.uk (July 2004); Embassy of Greece, "History of Greece," www.greekembassy.org (July 2004).

JOHN F. MURPHY, JR.
AMERICAN MILITARY UNIVERSITY

The Right

H

Harding, Warren G. (1865–1923)

WARREN GAMALIEL HARDING, 29th president of the United States, was born on November 2, 1865, in Corsica, Ohio, now known as Blooming Grove, Ohio. His father was a farmer and a doctor, while his mother dedicated herself to the eight children, of which Harding was the oldest. During his childhood, Harding helped out on the family's farm, worked in a local sawmill making brooms, and drove a team of horses for the Toledo and Ohio Railroad Company. In addition, he worked as an apprentice at a local newspaper, the *Caledonia Argus*.

In 1879, Harding was admitted to Ohio Central College, located in Iberia, Ohio, at the age of 14. Upon graduation in 1882, he became a schoolteacher, although he soon gave up teaching and moved to Marion, Ohio. Once there, he began to study law, but once again, soon decided that he didn't like it. Next, he tried selling insurance, but quit soon after starting. In 1884, Harding finally decided to pursue a career in newspapers, convincing his father and two of his friends to help him finance the purchase of the local newspaper in Marion, the *Star*. Soon after acquiring the paper, Harding's two friends dropped out of the partnership and Harding retained sole control of the paper, which had poor circulation and a bad reputation at the time of the takeover. In order to get the paper up and running successfully again, Harding courted local manufacturers and industries, persuading them to pay some of the costs in return for advertising space.

While working to make the *Star* more successful and profitable, Harding met Mrs. Florence Kling De-Wolfe, a prominent widow in Marion, who was notably industrious and ambitious. In spite of opposition from the widow's father, Harding married Florence in 1891. With his new wife's help, Harding's career began to take off and they worked together to bring the *Star* into prosperity.

Riding on the success of the newspaper, Harding became one of the leading citizens of Marion, becoming director of the county bank and a trustee at the local Baptist church. He translated his local popularity into a seat in Ohio's Senate in 1898, as a member of the Republican Party. By 1902, he was Ohio's lieutenant governor. After leaving politics for a short period of time in 1906 to work on his newspaper business again, Harding lost in his bid to become governor of Ohio in 1910, but soon after he was elected to the U.S. Senate in 1914.

In the U.S. Senate, Harding was a loyal member of the Republican Party. In addition, he and his wife enjoyed living in Washington, D.C., attending the various social events, where they soon developed a reputation as modest and kind individuals. This positive reputation may have been one of the main reasons that Harding,

Conservative President Warren G. Harding advocated a "return to normalcy," though many questioned what that meant.

who had only a modest list of credentials, was nominated by the Republican Party for the presidency in 1920 after political controversy and disagreement had blocked other stronger candidates from obtaining the nomination.

Harding and his advisers based his campaign on the slogan "A Return to Normalcy," even though many of his supporters did not know what the phrase exactly meant. He pursued a "front-porch" campaign similar to former President William McKinley, while his opponent, James A. Cox, campaigned in favor of U.S. acceptance of the League of Nations, primarily in the major cities. Following World War I, many citizens were drawn to Harding's vision, albeit vague, of "normalcy" and they elected him to the presidency with 61 percent of the vote.

From the start, Harding hoped to gain the appreciation of the people, opening the White House to the public. He formed his cabinet from what he called the "best minds" of the country, but some of his selections proved unfit for their positions, such as Secretary of the Interior Albert Fall and Attorney General Harry M. Daugherty.

In response to his election results, Harding believed that the American public wanted to remain isolated from Europe, staying out of the League of Nations and other European security collectives. Instead of collective security, Harding pursued disarmament treaties, which led to the Washington Conference of 1921. The resulting treaty, signed in 1922, required the United States, Britain, and Japan to follow quotas for the allowable number of warships.

Conservative Republicans in Congress were able to pass tax cuts and to create a new federal budget system, all with Harding's approval. In addition, they established high tariffs and restricted immigration significantly for the first time in the history of the United States.

THE HARDING LEGACY

In June 1923, Harding and his wife went on a trip across the country, but Harding became drastically ill during their return from Alaska, complaining of fatigue and food poisoning. Upon arrival in San Francisco, California, he developed pneumonia and died soon after on August 2, 1923, and the nation mourned his death. Vice President Calvin Coolidge assumed the presidency. One of Harding's greatest successes came to pass after his death as leaders of the steel industry agreed to cut the workday from 12 to eight hours.

However, Harding's presidential reputation was destroyed shortly after his death, when news of the scandal involving Secretary of the Interior Fall and his acceptance of bribes in exchange for private corporate development of oil deposits in Teapot Dome, Wyoming, appeared in the nation's leading newspapers. Later, Attorney General Daugherty was implicated in a major scandal as well, further damaging Harding's legacy and reputation.

SEE ALSO

Volume 1 Left: Democratic Party; Wilson, Woodrow.
Volume 2 Right: Republican Party; Coolidge, Calvin.

BIBLIOGRAPHY

"Biography of Warren G. Harding," www.whitehouse.gov (May 2004); Ellis W. Hawley, "Warren G. Harding," *Reader's Companion to American History* (Houghton Mifflin, 2004); John W. Dean and Arthur M. Schleslinger, *Warren Harding* (Henry Holt, 2004).

ARTHUR HOLST, PH.D.
WIDENER UNIVERSITY

Healthcare

HEALTHCARE IN THE United States encompasses myriad activities, from basic research performed under the National Institutes of Health to Medicaid, which provides medical care to the very poor. Even though the federal government does not provide Americans with actual health insurance, it nonetheless funds over half of the nation's overall health expenditures. Because the United States does not have national health insurance, however, the discussion of healthcare in America tends to revolve around that issue. The fragmented nature of the U.S. healthcare system reflects the dominance of conservative, right-wing views that oppose government financing of medical care.

Until the 20th century, government influence over healthcare was minimal. In 1798, the state began a program of health insurance for mariners, but that was the extent of its involvement. At the turn of the century, during the Progressive era, a noticeable shift occurred in government toward healthcare. Theodore Roosevelt enacted the Pure Food and Drug Act, which governed the contents of food and drug products for the entire country. By 1914, most states had enacted workmen's compensation laws to handle injuries and illnesses related to employment. Following on the heels of this development and the enactment of the British program of national health insurance for workers, Progressive reformers initiated a call for compulsory health insurance for low-income American workers. Such action occurred at a time when American medicine was undergoing considerable reform as well, calling on the state to regulate medical education and licensing requirements. It was in that atmosphere that reformers commenced their campaign for compulsory health insurance and alliances began to form right and left.

Health insurance was a new concept at the turn of the 20th century. Only since the late 19th century had medicine begun to exhibit curative powers with the new discoveries of antisepsis and anesthesia. Hospitals had traditionally served as refuges for the poor until new technology, such as the X ray, forced patients to come to a central location for treatment. Doctors prided themselves on the sliding scale they used to charge patients based on the patient's ability to pay. Likewise, the American Medical Association (AMA), founded in 1846, began to renew itself into a powerful professional and political force determined to preserve the autonomy of the profession. Alarmed by the threat of state control, healthcare came into the political arena and forces took sides on the right and left. From the perspective of the right, which included organized medicine, the most desirable situation for the nation's health would be to preserve the sacred trust of the doctor-patient relationship while funneling funds through complementary channels such as research and infrastructure.

The doctors allied themselves with powerful business interests in the legislative battles that followed. Leaders of big business were particularly helpful against compulsory insurance because they opposed provisions that would force them to pay part of the cost for their employees' medical care. The Progressive movement coincided with a surge in the labor movement, and so conservative business leaders, fearful of socialism, took steps to stem the tide of worker discontent with welfare capitalism. Under this system, employers provided various "welfare" benefits to workers, including limited medical care. Eventually, employers looked to new group-health insurance policies that were being offered by large insurers, again to stymie the efforts of reformers. In the legislatures and in Congress, the insurance industry and organized medicine elevated lobbying efforts to new heights as they struggled to maintain their autonomy from government interference. In 1920, the AMA declared the issue of compulsory health insurance dead.

THE NEW DEAL

The Great Depression brought a new wave of concern about the rising costs of medical care, but the AMA and conservative congressional forces dissuaded President Franklin D. Roosevelt from including national health insurance in the New Deal. Roosevelt proposed national health insurance shortly before his death, leaving the issue for his vice president, Harry Truman, to pursue. Truman made the issue the center of his Fair Deal. His proposal for a cradle-to-grave program, again inspired by the newly revised British system, became the hallmark of Democratic liberalism.

Again the AMA joined with right-wing Republicans and launched an extensive advertising campaign to "educate" the public about the evils of socialized medicine. *Socialism* became the buzzword for the right wing in the fight against national health insurance. Drawing on powerful Red Scare propaganda, conservative forces echoed the fears of the Progressive campaign. These tactics successfully defeated the Truman campaign for compulsory health insurance and ushered in a new era of national conservatism. What remained from the healthcare debate was the enactment of the Hill-Burton Hospital Construction Act of 1946, which gave funding for infrastructure rather than for the actual provision of medical care.

MEDICARE AND MEDICAID

Republican President Dwight D. Eisenhower embodied the right-wing doctrine against social insurance by maintaining a firm stance against national health insurance. A new proposal, Medicare, gained considerable popularity throughout the 1950s, however. John F. Kennedy, the new Democratic president, openly endorsed the program for medical care for the elderly, and Lyndon B. Johnson pushed the measure through Congress in 1965. The right won notable concessions, though, even as the leftist majority prevailed. Doctors were to set their own fee schedules, and hospitals based their payments on their own costs. Medicaid, medical assistance for the poor, relied on state operation.

The enactment of Medicare was a watershed moment in healthcare legislation. Many right-wing politicians voted for the measure believing that if they provided coverage for the most sympathetic groups—the poor and the elderly—universal coverage would be unnecessary. By the 1960s, many workers, particularly union members, received health insurance coverage from their employers, further reducing the need for a government-mandated system.

REPUBLICAN SHIFT

A fundamental shift occurred in the 1970s regarding the division of left and right. Partly as a result of the lax controls on Medicare reimbursement, healthcare costs soared astronomically. As the general economy began to suffer as well, concerns over medical care moved from access to controlling costs. With that in mind, Republican President Richard M. Nixon proposed a national health insurance plan that he believed would curb medical spending while at the same time providing coverage for those who fell in the gap between Medicaid and welfare capitalism. Nixon's plan rested on the employer mandate, by which employers would pay a significant portion of their employees' healthcare. Private insurers would serve as fiscal intermediaries. Nixon's move, although somewhat motivated by the Watergate scandal, signaled a new attitude from the right, that some form of government intervention was necessary in order to control healthcare inflation. The president also had instituted wage and price controls on the medical industry, the repeal of which led to even more inflation.

Nixon's plan came to naught, largely due to intransigence on the left. Led by Democratic Senator Edward M. Kennedy of Massachusetts, organized labor and other left-wing groups stuck to the Democratic dream of cradle-to-grave coverage, now spurred by such a system in neighboring Canada. Although Kennedy worked closely with Nixon's administration to come to a compromise, the lack of labor support for such an effort doomed the alliance. A testament to Nixon's devotion to the healthcare issue was the expansion of Medicare benefits to cover sufferers of kidney disease who relied on dialysis for treatment. Many supporters of this 1972 legislation saw it as another precursor to universal health insurance. Nixon's successor, Gerald R. Ford, continued Nixon's effort early in his administration but was soon distracted by the worsening economy. Attention turned to attempts to provide health insurance to the newly unemployed, but the same ideological divide that stymied action on universal health insurance prevented action for the unemployed.

DEMOCRATIC SHIFT

In 1977, new Democratic President Jimmy Carter appeared to bring some unity to the left and right concerning healthcare. Pressured by organized labor, Carter pledged support for national health insurance, but first pushed for controls on hospital costs. The cost control legislation was not successful and Carter introduced his insurance package late in his term. The plan, which considerably blurred the lines between left and right, closely resembled Nixon's proposal. This version had the backing of organized labor but was still unable to produce enough support to work through Congress.

In 1980, Republican Ronald Reagan ushered in a new wave of conservatism in the United States. Showing the same pragmatism that marked the Nixon administration, he threw his support behind a 1988 effort to add benefits to Medicare. Although the staunch conservative's approval was surprising, the backlash from the Medicare beneficiaries was even more startling. George H. W. Bush repealed the law in 1989, and showed no interest in expanding the government's role in healthcare until challenged by Democrat Bill Clinton in 1992.

A southern Democrat, Clinton was relatively conservative. Although committed to reform, he was wary of challenging the fiscal constraints that marked the efforts of his predecessor, Jimmy Carter. Clinton's Health Security Act aimed to provide universal health coverage through managed competition, a fairly new concept that played to the right's belief in the power of the free market. The plan proved unwieldy, however, and caused strain within the Democratic ranks, especially among those still committed to the cradle-to-grave ideal of national health insurance. Right-wing conservatism resurged again in the mid-1990s, and only piecemeal expansion of federal healthcare policies succeeded.

President George W. Bush signed another extension of Medicare in 2003 that brought back the prescription drug coverage of the 1988 law. Combined with the Medicare benefits was a provision to encourage health savings accounts, interest-bearing savings accounts that could be used for medical expenses. The accounts could be rolled over year after year and earnings would be tax-deductible. This move further illustrated the less-than-rigid delineations between right and left that characterized the late 20th century, although the tilt was clearly to the right. As the 2004 presidential election drew near, cries for full-fledged national health insurance continued to come from the left.

SEE ALSO

Volume 1 Left: Healthcare; Carter, James E.; Clinton, William J.; Roosevelt, Franklin D.; Democratic Party.
Volume 2 Right: Conservatism; Reagan, Ronald; Nixon, Richard M.; Eisenhower, Dwight D.; Republican Party.

BIBLIOGRAPHY

Jonathan Engel, *Doctors and Reformers: Discussion and Debate over Health Policy, 1925–50* (University of South Carolina Press, 2002); Beatrix Hoffman, *The Wages of Sickness: The Politics of Health Insurance in Progressive America* (University of North Carolina Press, 2001); Jonas Morris, *Searching for a Cure: National Health Policy Considered* (Berkeley Morgan, 1984); Paul Starr, *The Social Transformation of American Medicine* (Basic Books, 1982); Kimberley Green Weathers, *Fitting an Elephant through a Keyhole: America's Struggle with National Health Insurance in the Twentieth Century* (Ph.D. dissertation, University of Houston, 2004)

KIMBERLEY GREEN WEATHERS, PH.D.
UNIVERSITY OF HOUSTON

Hearst, William Randolph (1863–1951)

WILLIAM RANDOLPH HEARST was born on April 29, 1863, in San Francisco, California, the only child of George Hearst, a self-made multimillionaire, and Phoebe Apperson Hearst. He attended Harvard University but never graduated. He became "proprietor" of the *San Francisco Examiner* in 1887, which was owned by his father. William acquired the *New York Morning Journal* in 1895 but shortened the title to *New York Journal* in 1901. Inspired by Joseph Pulitzer, owner of the *New York World*, Hearst transformed the personality of his newspapers by combining investigative reporting and sensationalism. He believed in creating the news rather than simply reporting it. He built a journalistic powerhouse by expanding his empire horizontally into syndicated features; photograph wire services; magazines; newsreels; serial, feature, and animated films; and radio. At its peak, his media kingdom included 28 major newspapers and 18 magazines, in addition to several radio stations and movie companies. His national chain of publications included the *Chicago Examiner, Boston American, Cosmopolitan,* and *Harper's Bazaar.* The Great Depression seriously weakened his financial position. By 1940, he had lost substantial control over his considerable media holdings.

Hearst modernized journalism by introducing banner headlines and lavish illustrations in order to present exciting stories and increase his newspaper sales. Many believed Hearst initiated the Spanish-American War of 1898 to promote his newspaper by offering readers sensationalized versions of activities in Cuba. Though the phrase "yellow journalism" originally described the journalistic practices of Joseph Pulitzer, Hearst proved himself worthy of the title as the two New York newspapers used events in Cuba to compete for readers. While the two men shared an interest in sensationalizing the news, Pulitzer relied on the written word while Hearst depended on the power of illustrations to tell a story.

When an explosion sank the *Maine* and killed hundreds of sailors in Havana, Cuba, on February 15, 1898, journalists, including those from the *Journal,* recommended prudence rather than speculation regarding the tragedy. When Hearst learned of the explosion, however, he called the *Journal* editor on duty and asked what stories would appear on the front page. When the editor replied, "just the other big news," Hearst declared that there was no other big news and explained that the sinking of the *Maine* meant war. When *Journal* illustrator Frederic Remington requested return from Havana, indicating that all was calm, Hearst replied, "Please remain. You furnish the pictures and I'll furnish the war." Coverage of the Spanish-American War, often called "the *Journal*'s war," established a precedent of how journalists presented news in the 20th century. Hearst justified his approach to journalism by stating, "News is something somebody doesn't want printed; all else is advertising."

Hearst began his political life aligned with the Democratic Party largely due to his father's support of Grover Cleveland. In reality, Hearst had political aspirations of his own and spent many years of his life with an eye toward the White House. Strategizing his own presidential run, he became an outspoken supporter of the Progressive Era. He advocated reforms in public education and spoke out in favor of the alleviation, if not elimination, of the economic, political, and social abuses of capitalism. He hoped to win the White House in 1904 but came in second in the balloting for the Democratic presidential nomination. Bitter defeats in New York mayoral and gubernatorial races did not deter him from politics, and he served two terms in the U.S. House of Representatives. Among other progressive causes, Hearst supported municipal ownership of utilities, and he tended to support labor unions until the organization of the American Newspaper Guild. Then he feared that unionization of reporters would prevent him from dismissing writers whose spin on the news varied from his own perspective.

During World War I, Hearst criticized Woodrow Wilson's administration for not doing enough to keep the United States out of war. When his newspapers printed editorials encouraging Americans to remain neutral, Hearst was attacked for being pro-German and anti-England, a characterization that he reinforced during World War II when he spoke favorably of Hitler. Hearst helped Franklin Delano Roosevelt become president in 1932 but soon turned against the New Deal because he viewed its programs as latent socialism. Hearst used his newspapers to condemn the administration and printed numerous editorials criticizing programs such as the National Recovery Act and the Wealth Tax, calling the latter "essentially communism." In 1936, Hearst supported Republican Alfred M. Landon's presidential campaign, but Hearst's status in the United States was declining. In 1940, when Hearst supported Wendell L. Willkie's bid against Roosevelt, the Republican Party asked him not to contribute to the campaign.

As Hearst aged, he became more conservative simply because he had more and more to protect. Regardless of his refusal to denounce Hitler before the U.S. entry into World War II, Hearst was a virulent opponent of communism and the Soviet Union in that period. Initially, he championed Joseph McCarthy's effort to expose communists in the United States, calling it

one of the most important events of our time, but warned his newspapers to be cautious in their editorials on the matter.

Hearst's life was so sensational and controversial that it inspired one of the greatest movies of all time. Orson Welles's *Citizen Kane*, a technically brilliant piece of filmmaking, was released in 1941 and met with great success. Hearst's supporters viewed the movie as a vicious attack on a great man. When Hearst learned of Welles's film, he set out to protect his reputation by shutting the film down. Hollywood executives, led by Louis B. Mayer, rallied around Hearst, attempting to buy the movie in order to burn the negative. Hearst's defenders tried to intimidate theaters into refusing to show the movie. Threats of blackmail, smears in the newspapers, and federal investigations were used in this effort.

Hearst's evolution from turn-of-the-century Progressive to bitter reactionary by the 1930s came about not because he changed his ideological position, but because he had lived into a different political era without altering his early ideas. In addition to the personal challenges represented by the growing movement to unionize newspapers and the development of a highly progressive "Wealth Tax" in the New Deal, he found the New Deal and the Marxist ideas of the Communist Party in the 1930s, as well as Franklin Roosevelt's internationalism, threatening to his view of American society. His support for an America First isolationist position in the period 1939–41 was shared by many former Progressives.

In his personal life, Hearst married Millicent Wilson in New York City in 1903. The couple had five sons together: George, William Randolph Jr., John, and twins Randolph and David. In the 1920s, Hearst built a castle on a 240,000-acre ranch in San Simeon, California. After acting as a major political and journalistic force in the United States for over half a century, Hearst died at the age of 88 on August 14, 1951, in Beverly Hills, California.

SEE ALSO

Volume 1 Left: Progressive Party; Liberalism; United States; Roosevelt, Franklin D.
Volume 2 Right: Conservatism; Republican Party.

BIBLIOGRAPHY

David Nasaw, *The Chief: The Life of William Randolph Hearst* (Houghton Mifflin, 2000); Ben Procter, *William Randolph Hearst: The Early Years* (Oxford University Press, 1998); Louis Pizzitola, *Hearst over Hollywood: Power, Passion, and Propa-*

ganda in the Movies (Columbia University Press, 2002); E.F. Tompkins, *Selections from the Writings and Speeches of William Randolph Hearst* (San Francisco, published privately, 1948).

DANA MAGILL
TEXAS CHRISTIAN UNIVERSITY

Hegemony

FIRST DEVELOPED by the Italian Marxist theorist Antonio Gramsci during the late 1920s and 1930s while he was in prison as an opponent to fascism, the concept of hegemony has enjoyed vast popularity throughout the 20th century. Gramsci used the term in his *Prison Notebooks* where he explored the reasons that had led the Italian working-class to desert democracy and embrace fascism. The concept of hegemony has not remained restricted to political theory but has been widely applied to a number of cultural fields and disciplines from history to literary studies, from media to film theory.

Gramsci's hegemony is synonymous with social control and defines the winning of consent to unequal class relations, which it instead makes appear as natural and fair. Dominant elites in society, who are not limited to the ruling class, maintain their dominance by securing the consent of subordinate groups, such as the working class, through two means: hegemony and direct domination. Gramsci describes hegemony as "the 'spontaneous' consent given by the great masses of the population to the general direction imposed on social life by the dominant fundamental group; this consent is 'historically' caused by the prestige (and consequent confidence) which the dominant group enjoys because of its position and function in the world of production." Such general direction is mapped by intellectuals and by institutions such as schools, trade unions, and the church. Gramsci then contrasts hegemony with direct domination, "the apparatus of state coercive power which 'legally' enforces discipline on those groups who do not 'consent' either actively or passively." Administered by instruments of political domination, such as the police, direct domination stands in when hegemony fails.

This produces a split consciousness in the members of a subordinate group. In Gramsci's words, the worker in the modern mass society has one consciousness, "which is implicit in his activity and which in reality unites him with all his fellow-workers in the practical transformation of the real world. " Yet, at the same time, he holds another consciousness, which "he has inherited from the past and uncritically absorbed." The process of hegemony "holds together a specific social group, it influences moral conduct and the direction of will, with varying efficacy but often powerfully enough to produce a situation in which the contradictory state of consciousness does not permit of any action, any decision, or any choice, and produces a condition of moral and political passivity." Hegemony, therefore, does not function mainly by coercion: subordinate groups are dominated through their consensus and collusion thanks to their desire to belong to a social, political, and cultural system.

The central focus of hegemony is not the individual subject but the formation of social movements and their leadership. As Michael Denning has explained, the construction of hegemony is a matter "of participation, as people are mobilized in cultural institutions—schools, churches, sporting events, and in long-term historic projects—waging wars, establishing colonies, gentrifying a city, developing a regional economy." The participation in such a movement depends on how the patterns of loyalty and allegiance are organized, conveying specific cultural practices in a new historical bloc: by offering new values and world visions, such a historical bloc "creates the conditions for a political use or reading of cultural performances and artifacts, the conditions for symbolizing class conflict."

In theorizing the concept of hegemony, Gramsci was clearly concerned to modify the economic determinism typical of Marxist social theory, hence the success of the term. Rather than the totalizing and monolithic model of social control devised by the Marxists of the Frankfurt School, Gramscian hegemony allows a more complex and nuanced approach to the production and consumption of culture. Raymond Williams has tellingly described it as a process rather than a structure: "It is a realized complex of experiences, relationships, and activities, with specific and changing pressures and limits. In practice, … hegemony can never be singular … It has continually to be renewed, recreated, defended, and modified. It is also continually resisted, limited, altered, challenged by pressures not at all its own."

Hegemony does not work in a unilateral way. The working class can develop its own hegemony as a strategy to control the state by combining the interests of other oppressed groups and social forces with its own.

Working for the formation of a counterhegemonic discourse implies considering structural change and ideological change as part of the same struggle. The labor process may well be central for the class struggle, but it is no less crucial to address the ideological struggle if the masses of the people are to reject their internalized "false consciousness" and come to a consciousness allowing them to question the political and economic assumptions of the ruling elites.

However, this process of consciousness formation requires time and intellectual strengths, as people have internalized the assumptions of ideological hegemony: what is happening in society is common sense or the only way of running society. The basic beliefs and value system at the base of capitalist society are seen as either neutral or of general applicability in relation to the class structure of society.

Gramsci's concept of hegemony crucially advanced Marxist theory by showing that Marx was inaccurate in assuming that social development always originates from the economic structure and that the revolution could be the result of the spontaneous outburst of revolutionary consciousness among the working class. The usefulness of hegemony, however, is not limited to Marxist theory, alerting us, as it does, to the routine structures of everyday "common sense," which work to sustain class domination and tyranny.

SEE ALSO

Volume 1 Left: United States; Soviet Union; Cominform; Socialism; Anti-Globalization.
Volume 2 Right: United States; Soviet Union; Cold War; Globalization.

BIBLIOGRAPHY

Michael Denning, *The Cultural Front: The Laboring of American Culture in the Twentieth Century* (Verso, 1997); Joseph V. Femia, *Gramsci's Political Thought: Hegemony, Consciousness, and the Revolutionary Process* (Clarendon Press, 1993); Benedetto Fontana, *Hegemony and Power: On the Relation between Gramsci and Machiavelli* (University of Minnesota Press, 1993); Antonio Gramsci, *Selections from the Prison Notebooks* (International Publishers, 1971); Jackson Lears, "The Concept of Cultural Hegemony: Problems and Possibilities," *American Historical Review* (v.90, June 1985); Roger Simon, *Gramsci's Political Thought: An Introduction* (Lawrence and Wishart, 1991); Raymond Williams, *Marxism and Literature* (Oxford University Press, 1977).

Luca Prono, Ph.D.
University of Nottingham, England

Hitler, Adolf (1889–1945)

ADOLF HITLER WAS the key figure of National Socialism (German Nazi fascism) beginning in 1920, *fuehrer* (leader, guide), and Reich chancellor of Germany from 1933 to 1945. He was responsible for the Holocaust and instigator of World War II in Europe. Being one of the most charismatic and murderous dictators, Hitler hoped to conquer the world and, for several years, dominated most of Europe and much of North Africa.

In spite of mediocre capabilities and a sickly nature, the young Hitler undoubtedly was an artistically minded person and was trained as a painter for a while. His theatricality was revealed later in the staginess of his political activities. His outlook was a blend of intentionally politicized reading of ancient German-Scandinavian legends, anti-Semitism, extravagant cultural exceptionism, social Darwinism, and messianism. A fan of Richard Wagner's operas and German mythology, he acquired the belief in the superiority of an imprecise Aryan race. Germans were seen by him as the core of that master race who should build a superstate and conquer *lebensraum* (living space) by wiping out "wastrel peoples" (Jews, Gypsies, Slavs, etc.) in the struggle for survival among races, the struggle that he regarded as the essence of existence.

Historians may stress Hitler as a political phenomenon causality. Germany lost World War I and the imposed restrictions on Germany by the Versailles Treaty seemed ignominious. Voluntarily taking part in World War I as private first class (corporal), Hitler hardened to extreme nationalism and hatred of civilian politicians and Jews, whom he blamed for "stabbing in the back" the German army.

In the spring of 1919, he joined a small, violently nationalistic group in Munich, Germany, named the German Workers' Party, later renamed by him the National Sozialistische Deutsche Arbeitspartei, NSDAP or Nazi Party. The democracy of the Weimar Republic appeared to him to be the child of disgrace and betrayal. Germany seemed to be in anticipation of a dictator. Hitler accumulated and eventually mastered these sentiments, profoundly grasping mass psychology and paving the road to absolute power. He had two remarkable talents: public oratory and inspiring personal loyalty. A key element of his appeal was the sense of offended national pride caused by the Treaty of Versailles imposed on the defeated Germany by the Allies. The Nazi ranks grew rapidly. On July 29, 1921, Hitler became the party's absolute leader, or *fuehrer*. The disaster of the 1923 hyperinflation, in the course of which the rich became richer at the expense of the rest of the population, was organized by the corrupt liberal upper crust, but was explained as the consequence of Versailles reparations. Hitler thought the hour of national revolution had struck. On November 8, 1923, he attempted to defy both the government of Bavaria and the Reich government in Berlin by starting riots in Munich known as the Beer Hall Putsch. Its failure committed Hitler to a mild detention in Landsberg Prison. There he dictated the text of *Mein Kampf* (*My Struggle*)—the bible of National Socialism.

The Great Depression of 1929 to 1933 offered Hitler another chance. Step by step, his crew took command of Germany, combining violent propaganda with provocations, parliamentary jobbing with brute force, bullyboy tactics with intuitive skill. On January 30, 1933, Hitler was officially sworn in as chancellor. He quickly turned Germany into the most extreme fascist totalitarian state, which murdered millions of objectors and national minorities. He conducted punch foreign policy, openly threatening the Treaty of Versailles. He contracted an alliance with fascist Italy and supported fascist Francisco Franco in Spain. Hitler incorporated Austria into his new empire in 1938 and induced France and Britain to bargain away at the Munich Conference the Sudetenland of Czechoslovakia, inhabited by ethnic Germans; his Third Reich occupied the whole of Czechoslovakia the next year. By invading Poland on September 1, 1939, he launched World War II, which brought about 40 million human deaths and innumerable suffering for the whole world. He was eventually defeated chiefly by the Soviet and American armies and committed suicide in his bunker on April 30, 1945.

Considering the negative image of Hitler and hostile opinions of him today, it seems very difficult to feel sympathy toward this figure of evil. Yet, nevertheless, it happens. There is a curious term for the phenomenon of inclination to Hitler in Europe: *philofascism*. One can see this empathy as morbidly intuitive, illicitly and instinctively seeking a *fuehrer* and a willing acceptance of self-subordination and absolute submission to his will, rather than rational estimation of the real historical character. Philofascists tend to shift the focus of analysis from concrete political crimes against humanity to a philosophical and mysterious realm, the inner condition of acolytes who make a spiritual unity and organic whole with the tyrant.

Other commentators will point to the xenophobic, neofascist sentiments of a certain part of the present-day European electorate as flare-ups of nationalism from those fearing the dissolution of their nation in the influx of immigrants. People lacking individual merits but wanting to feel superiority because of the community of nation/race they believe is the "master race" also tend to prejudice in favor of Hitler.

In rightist conservatism, there exist two main approaches in qualifying Hitler as an ideological and political figure. One tendency, represented by Stephen Berry, Paul Johnson, Dan Branch, and others, characterizes him as Napoleon of the 20th century and creator of the analogical empire in Europe. The counterpoints of this sect condemn Hitler for millions of innocent victims and the incoherence of his nationalism, in which racism and social Darwinism overruled the better instincts of the German nation. Other exponents, such as James Gregor, Edward Feser, John J. Ray, and Ramsay Steele, are conscious of the odiousness of Hitler's image and the fact that staying in the right part of the political spectrum embodies the worst crimes of history and compromises the right 50 years later. Therefore, they fallaciously aspire to present him as a leftist. In contemporary politics, *Hitler* is the dirty word frequently used to label and discredit a political opponent, to tar somebody as a reactionary and/or extremist aspiring to absolute power.

SEE ALSO

BIBLIOGRAPHY

Adolf Hitler, "Mein Kampf and Other Writings of Adolf Hitler," www.hitler.org/writings (July 2004); Alan Bullock, *Hitler: A Study in Tyranny* (Harper and Row, 1962); Gordon A. Craig, *Germany 1866–1945* (Oxford University Press, 1981); Stephen Berry, "No Tears for the Fuehrer," www.la-articles.org.uk (July 2004); A. James Gregor, *The Faces of Janus* (Yale University Press, 2000); Gerhard L. Weinberg, *Germany, Hitler, and World War II* (Cambridge University Press, 1995).

IGOR CHARSKYKH
DONETSK NATIONAL UNIVERSITY, UKRAINE

Hoover, Herbert (1874–1964)

HERBERT HOOVER WAS born on a farm outside of West Branch, Iowa, in 1874, raised by his uncle in New-berg, Oregon, and in 1891 he enrolled in the pioneer class of Stanford University as a geology student. In 1899, he married Lou Henry. Before he became the 31st president, Hoover made his name as a mining engineer initially with the British firm Bewick, Moreing and Co., working in China and then establishing his own consultancy firm in 1908 as a so-called doctor of sick mines.

Hoover's international reputation developed when he was asked by the American Consul General to aid American citizens stranded in London (where he was living) at the outbreak of World War I. His prowess as an administrator was ably demonstrated as his committee assisted 120,000 Americans in returning home within six weeks. Later in 1914, Hoover headed the Commission for Relief in Belgium, whose task it was to feed and clothe hundreds of thousands of displaced Belgians. His first foray into political life occurred when in 1917, President Woodrow Wilson appointed him as U.S. food administrator to coordinate the production of food for American and allied forces as well as civilians during World War I.

With such international humanitarian credentials, the millionaire engineer and administrator focused his attention on running for political office. In 1920, Hoover declared his Republicanism and unsuccessfully sought the GOP's nomination for president. However, a degree of political consolation came when President Warren Harding appointed Hoover secretary of commerce in 1921. When President Coolidge announced that he would not seek renomination by the Republican Party to contend the 1928 presidential election, Hoover was urged to run for the presidency. Hoover obliged and was elected as the Republican Party presidential candidate, and he named Charles Curtis as his running mate.

By most accounts, Hoover was a progressive. The term *progressive* in 1920s and 1930s American politics is significantly different from what it implies today. The progressive movement preceding and during Hoover's time in public office was, ideologically speaking, a mixed bag of policy issues and principles and encompassed both Republicans and Democrats. In some sense, the movement contained both conservative and liberal tendencies. For example, progressives or those who may term themselves progressives included individuals who believed in prohibition, immigration restriction, and "Americanization" of aliens, which would appear to be associated with variants of conservative political thought. However, progressive policy commitments at the time also included urban housing projects, federal regulation of business, labor laws protecting the

rights of children, and improvements in industrial conditions such as factory regulation, issues that are underpinned by conceptions of social justice that we associate with political liberalism today.

Joan Hoff Wilson describes progressivism "a well-intentioned, if frantic, uncoordinated, and sometimes counterproductive movement … intended to produce both more democracy and more efficiency while preserving individualism and increasing cooperation." In addition to the disparate characteristics of progressivism, there existed some uniform features, such as a desire for efficiency as an antidote to human and economic waste; a rationalist focus on the betterment of society; an emphasis on social responsibility; an anti-corruption standpoint; and a desire to curb personal selfishness.

But what did it mean for Hoover to be a progressive? Hoover's political philosophy can be interpreted as "progressivism"; certainly as the term was understood at the time. His 1922 publication, *American Individualism*, was his attempt to communicate his brand of progressivism. His main philosophical concern was to reconcile individualism and cooperation through voluntarism. Decentralization of power and participatory democracy were also prominent themes. Although the book's title implies traditional *laissez-faire* individualism, Hoover's political philosophy was more progressive. For example, he advocated equality of opportunity; individualism; both liberty to be free from undue state interference and "ordered liberty" as a social responsibility; cooperation within local communities; and voluntary cooperation among private enterprise, labor and government rather than widespread federal regulation of business.

The defining event of Hoover's presidency was the Wall Street crash of October 1929 and the Great Depression that followed and lasted through his presidency and Roosevelt's first term. There are many theories that suggest reasons why the stock market crashed and why America suffered its most severe economic depression. Much of the traditional scholarship has attributed the blame to the policies of the Hoover administration; another view cites structural problems within the international economic system after World War I; and yet another suggests that it was an unusually large cyclical crisis that occurs habitually throughout American economic history. What is unequivocal is that the stock market crash of 1929 and the Depression changed people's attitudes toward government intervention in the economy, business regulation, and government welfare provision. In essence, the Depression

Herbert Hoover was a conservative progressive, what would be called a very moderate Republican today.

challenged the *laissez-faire* doctrine of old guard Republicans and some Democrats and even the voluntary corporatism of Hoover and other progressives who were ambivalent about the power and influence of the federal government in economic and social affairs.

Hoover's presidency was notable for other reasons as well. The passing of the Agricultural Marketing Act and the establishment of the Federal Farm Board attempted to help farmers form voluntary associations where they could arrange storage for produce and form marketing associations to sell their produce. This in turn would stabilize market conditions, as surplus goods would not be placed on sale, thus securing better prices for the goods on the market. The Hoover-Stimson doctrine on international relations stated that America would not renegotiate any territories gained through the use of force. It was a document that espoused Hoover's ideals of cooperation and ordered liberty between the United States and members of the international community. Hoover authored the Children's Charter, which called for the protection of the rights of all children irrespective of their race or class.

In addition, he reorganized the FBI with J. Edgar Hoover and appointed Chief Justice Charles Evans Hughes and Justices Owen Roberts and Benjamin Cardozo to the Supreme Court.

Therefore, Hoover can be seen as a philosophical liberal because he gave primacy to what he called "ordered liberty," preferred voluntarism to state intervention, was concerned with the centralizing tendency of the federal government and spoke many times on the importance of decentralized governance and local organizations, and advocated equality of opportunity. In American politics today, Hoover would be a very moderate Republican, a politician whose principles uncomfortably straddled both American liberalism and conservatism. Hoover is perhaps best understood as part of the progressive movement of the 1920s and 1930s, which was principled yet ideologically diverse.

SEE ALSO
Volume 1 Left: Progressive Party; Roosevelt, Franklin D. *Volume 2 Right:* Coolidge, Calvin; United States.

BIBLIOGRAPHY
Joan Hoff Wilson, *Herbert Hoover: Forgotten Progressive* (Little, Brown, 1975); Harris Gaylord Warren, *Herbert Hoover and the Great Depression* (Greenwood Press, 1980); Martin L. Fausold, *The Presidency of Herbert Hoover* (University Press of Kansas, 1985); William J. Barber, *From New Era to New Deal* (Cambridge University Press, 1985); William Starr Myers and Walter H. Newton, *The Hoover Administration* (Charles Scribner's Sons, 1936); Hoover Presidential Library and Museum, www.hoover. archives.gov (July 2004).

MATT BEECH, PH.D.
UNIVERSITY OF SOUTHAMPTON, ENGLAND

Hoover, J. Edgar (1895–1972)

J. EDGAR HOOVER, a long-term director of the Federal Bureau of Investigation (FBI), was born on January 1, 1895, in Washington, D.C. During Hoover's youth, his father had a mental breakdown, significantly reducing his family's income. As a result, Hoover was forced to leave school and search for employment. Soon after, despite the bad economic times, he found a job as a messenger at the Library of Congress. While working at the library, Hoover studied law at night at George Washington University. He earned a bachelor of laws degree in 1916 and followed it up with a master of laws in 1917.

Upon graduation, Hoover became an assistant in the alien registration section of the Department of Justice, where he served during World War I. During his time there, Hoover developed what would become one of his lifelong work pursuits: tracking and monitoring alien radicals within the borders of the United States. A dedicated worker, Hoover was rewarded with an appointment to head the General Intelligence Division in 1919, where he continued to monitor illegal activities by immigrants and aliens in the United States. His work led to a series of raids, labeled the Red Scare of 1919 and 1920 by the media. Even though Hoover was a determining factor in conducting the raids, having developed the list of suspected communists and aliens, his reputation remained untarnished while Attorney General A. Mitchell Palmer became the scapegoat.

Following the election of Warren G. Harding to the presidency, Hoover's continued hard work and administrative skill were rewarded again with his appointment to assistant director of the Bureau of Investigation, which later evolved into the FBI. In 1924, Hoover was appointed director by Attorney General Harlan Stone, which was a position that Hoover would to hold until his death in 1972.

During the first few years, he devoted himself to improving the quality of the bureau's employees and reorganizing the internal structure. He took great care in recruiting new employees and agents. Then, in 1926, Hoover established the bureau's fingerprint file, which has evolved to this day into the largest fingerprint file in the world. Next, Hoover began to lobby Congress to give the bureau more powers, such as the right to carry guns or to arrest suspects. In 1935, Congress responded by establishing the Federal Bureau of Investigation, which invested Hoover's agents and employees with greater powers and responsibilities.

With the newly established FBI, Hoover hoped to create a strong, centralized, and elite crime-fighting organization. He formed a scientific crime-detention laboratory and the FBI National Academy to allow for further research and training. Soon after, he searched for assistance in directing the bureau, which led to his appointment of Clyde Tolson as assistant director of the FBI. During the years of the Spanish Civil War, Hoover set up indexes of U.S. citizens who fought in Spain, as he continued his quest to root out communism in the United States. He organized the collection of information on Soviet sympathizers and became convinced in 1945 that there was a communist plot

brewing to overthrow the U.S. federal government. With the FBI, Hoover worked overtly and covertly to ensure that no such overthrow occurred. Throughout his 48 years as FBI director, Hoover was able to mold a powerful group of supporters, made up of presidents, members of Congress, journalists, and civic leaders. His ability to cooperate with the different interests and policies of the presidents, from Franklin D. Roosevelt to Richard Nixon, allowed for the formation of a strong and positive relationship between the executive and the FBI. As a result of Hoover's work, the FBI received expanded authorities and responsibilities and grew in size rapidly from 890 employees in 1940 to 10,000 employees in 1970. Still, Hoover was not without critics, many of whom decried his power, his authoritarian approach, and his accused violations of the Bill of Rights.

In addition, Hoover was able to dissuade Congress from pursuing independent investigations of FBI activity, but upon the end of Hoover's tenure, Congress moved to set boundaries on the powers of FBI directors and establish a 10-year term limit for the post. After Hoover, Congress began to exert much more influence over the FBI and even went on to criticize his harassment of political dissidents within the United States in a Senate report in 1976. Though well-known for his pursuit of radicals on the extreme left, Hoover did not hesitate to investigate those on the far right as well. Hoover died in Washington, D.C., on May 2, 1972.

SEE ALSO

Volume 1 Left: Civil Liberties; Civil Rights; King, Martin Luther, Jr.; Hayden, Tom; Communism.
Volume 2 Right: McCarthyism; Conservatism; Cold War.

BIBLIOGRAPHY

Curt Gentry, *J. Edgar Hoover: The Man and the Secrets* (W.W. Norton, 2001); "John Edgar Hoover," www.spartacus.schoolnet.co.uk (May 2004); Athan G. Theoharis, "Hoover, J. Edgar," *Reader's Companion to American History* (Houghton Mifflin, 2004).

ARTHUR HOLST, PH.D.
WIDENER UNIVERSITY

Hungary

FOR MOST OF THE LAST 60 years, until the 1990s, Hungary was a state-socialist country more or less under the domination of the Soviet Union. Hungary in the mid- to late 1940s was a country that the Soviet Union insisted be part of its sphere of influence.

Until the end of World War I, Hungary was part of the Austro-Hungarian Empire, which fought with Germany and the Ottomans against the Triple Entente of the United Kingdom, Russia, France, and their allies. Before World War I, Hungary was controlled by conservative governments that tried to stem the impact of the revolutions sweeping Europe in this period. However, the experience of the Great War, including death, hunger, and poverty, was more than the old regime could accommodate. By 1917, the Austro-Hungarian army was disintegrating, and there was a growing tendency toward desertion among the ranks of the navy and army. The Russian Revolution of 1917 provided an example for others to follow. In June 1918, there was a nine-day general strike, centered in Budapest. To preserve the old system, conservatives joined with liberals in supporting a new Social Democratic government under Count Mihály Károly, which formed a National Council on October 25, 1918, and a coalition government on October 31.

On November 16, 1918, just days after the Armistice ending the war, the monarchy was swept away and a People's Republic was declared, under the leadership of Károly. In that same month, Hungary's first Communist Party was formed, based in part on revolutionary ideas brought back by repatriated Hungarian prisoners of war, with Soviet-trained Béla Kun as leader. The Social Democratic government had a mildly reformist agenda, but progress on important issues, such as land reform, was slow. In January 1919, the Károly government decided to attack its opponents on both the left and the right, but by March the government could not maintain power and fell. On March 21, 1919, Béla Kun took power as head of a Revolutionary Governing Council and began to implement Soviet-style policies. The Western countries, particularly France and the United Kingdom, took notice of this and encouraged Rumanian and Czech forces to attack Hungary as part of their anti-Soviet policies. By August 1, 1919, Kun had fallen and a new trade union government was sworn in and reversed Kun's policies.

This was the beginning of over 20 years of right-wing authoritarian and eventually fascist and pro-Nazi government. The real power in Hungarian politics for most of this era was Admiral Miklós Horthy, who, in March 1920, became regent of the country. This also began the brief period known as the White Terror, in which one source reports that 5,000 opponents of the new regime, mainly communists, were killed while as many as 70,000 were jailed.

By the 1930s, Hungarian politics moved increasingly toward fascism and pro-Hitler policies. A pro-Nazi organization called the Arrow Cross Party was formed in the 1930s, and late in that decade Hungarian policy tilted increasingly toward Berlin, Germany. Its ideology was Hungarism, developed by Arrow Cross leader Ferenc Szálasi, defined as the idea that Greater Hungary could be created based on Christian, socialist, and Hungarian nationalist principles. As for the Jewish population, Szálasi said they would be required to leave this proposed entity.

In the spring of 1939, the Hungarian army participated in the liquidation of Czechoslovakia. Hungary's goal was to increase its territory, a long-term effort to reverse its territorial losses as a result of World War I. In 1941, Hungary agreed to attack Yugoslavia in concert with Nazi Germany, and it also attacked the Soviet Union, bringing the full weight of the Allies against it. In 1943, Hungary lost much of its army in the winter retreat from Stalingrad, in the failed Nazi invasion of the Soviet Union, and in March 1944, after Horthy tried to negotiate peace with the Allies, Germany occupied the country, ousted Horthy, and installed Szálasi, of the Arrow Cross, as supreme leader. By September 1944, after the successful opening of a second front in the west (D-Day), the Soviet Red Army entered Hungary and took over the country. By 1950, the Soviet Union had engineered a political monopoly for the Hungarian Socialist Workers Party, which ruled the country for the next 40 years. Under Soviet influence, fascism would not be allowed to rise again in central Europe.

SEE ALSO

Volume 1 Left: Soviet Union; Stalin and Stalinism.
Volume 2 Right: Fascism; Germany.

BIBLIOGRAPHY

George P. Blum, *The Rise of Fascism in Europe* (Greenwood Press, 1998); Paul Ignotus, *Hungary* (Ernest Benn Limited, 1972); Stephen J. Lee, *The European Dictatorships 1918–45* (Routledge, 1987); Barta István et al., *A History of Hungary*, Ervin Pamlényi, ed. (Collett's, 1975).

GEOFFREY R. MARTIN
MOUNT ALLISON UNIVERSITY, CANADA

The Right

I

Ideology

THE ORIGIN OF THE TERM *ideology* can be traced back to the European Enlightenment and especially to Destutt de Tracy, who is thought to be the first to use this term in print. There were, of course, earlier forms of the notion, for instance in Francis Bacon's concept of "idola." Further development of the term in the 18th century is closely linked to the French Encyclopedists' struggle against all forms of religious and traditional thought. Even the modern origin of the term *ideology* is European; nonetheless, the concept has ancient roots as well. It appears, for example, in the 15th-century Greek equivalent of the struggle between the ancients and the moderns, when representatives of the latter, champions of science and civilization, attacked the old traditions and religion, in some cases attempting to explain scientifically the origin of ancient religious beliefs.

The concept of ideology reached its heyday in the great philosophical and social-scientific systems of the 19th century. French philosopher and founder of positivism Auguste Comte criticized the negativism of the enlightenment ideologists' attack on tradition and metaphysics, and argued that the forerunners of science had an important ordering function in society. What is reserved for the domain of purely intellectual activity in Comte is generalized to the entirety of mental produc-

tion in society in Karl Marx. Marx stressed the historicity of the so-called material basis of ideology as well as the notion that human nature is itself a historical product just as much as its ideological correlatives. He further argued that the estranged or alienated forms of consciousness were not merely intellectual reflections but forms of human practice that play an active role in the functioning and transformation of society itself. The practical aspects of ideology were seen to be directly associated with the structure of class domination. Marx and Friedrich Engels generalized the question of ideology from the realm of science versus tradition to that of real versus mystified social processes, thus encompassing questions of theory and questions of political control within the same framework.

During the entire 19th century and early 20th century, the two aspects of the concept of ideology were elaborated upon. A broad array of terms seems to have been used in similar fashion. In the works of Georg Lukacs and Karl Mannheim, there emerged a tradition of the sociology that has been developed throughout the century, its most recent advocate being Jurgen Habermas, a prominent member of the Frankfurt School.

This approach, heavily represented in the Frankfurt School of German Sociology, has concentrated much of its effort on understanding the ideological basis of all forms of social knowledge, including the natural sciences. In France, Emile Durkheim (1965) elaborated the analysis of the relation between social structure and the organization of collective representations that are meant to reflect the former. Their wide-ranging ethnological ambitions had important influences on the development of anthropology in France and Holland and more recently among British symbolists. In the work of British functionalists, there has been a concentration on the way in which ideology maintains social solidarity, provides a "character" for the social order, or otherwise prevents social disintegration.

In the more recent work of structural Marxists, a more extreme functionalism is evident, one in which ideological "apparatuses" are conceived as instruments that exist to maintain the coherence of a mode of production, a system of economic exploitation that itself generates its own self-maintenance by way of the production of appropriate mentalities, political structures, and socialized subjects who are no more than the agents of the system.

Among both materialist and social determinist theoreticians, ideology has usually been assumed to be a locus in social structure corresponding to patterns of thought and cognition systems of values, religious organization, and so on, whose content is supposed in some way to reflect or, at the very least, to be a discourse upon a logically prior social structure. Also, among cultural determinists and value determinists, often referred to as idealists, the system of cultural categories or value orientation is said to determine or in some way provide the foundation for social action and organization.

In the classical social sciences, the discussions of ideology have been characterized by a pervasive dualism of idea versus reality, ideology versus practice, idealism versus materialism. This dualism, which has systematically conflated ideology and ideas, thought and meaning, has more recently been criticized. Theories of symbolic action, praxis theory, and theories of imaginary construction of reality have all in different ways tried to overcome the dualism inherent in sociological and anthropological discourse. These approaches elaborate on the recognition that the organization of material praxis is symbolically constituted, just as the structure of meaning is the product of social practice. Works on the symbolism of power, the social functions of knowledge, and the relation between culture and class have focused on the way in which symbolic practice organizes material realities.

Thus, it can be said that the ideology is one variant or form of these comprehensive patterns of cognitive and moral beliefs about man, society, and the universe in relation to man and society, which flourish in human society. Ideologies are characterized by a high degree of explicitness of formulation over a wide range of the objects with which they deal; for their adherents there is an authoritative and explicit promulgation. As compared with other patterns of beliefs, ideologies are relatively highly systematized or integrated around one or a few preeminent values, such as salvation, equality, and ethnic purity. They are more insistent on their distinctiveness from, and unconnectedness with, the outlooks, creeds, and other ideologies existing in the same society; they are more resistant to innovations in their beliefs and deny the existence or significance of those that do occur. Their acceptance and promulgation are accompanied by highly effective overtones. Complete individual subservience to the ideology is demanded of those who accept it, and it is regarded as essential and imperative that their conduct be completely permeated by it. Consensus among all those who affirm their adherence is likewise demanded; all adherents of the ideology are urgently expected to be in complete agreement with each other.

In social studies, a political ideology is a doctrine that explains how the society should work and offers the blueprint for a certain social order. A political ideology largely concerns itself with how to allocate power and to what ends it should be used. For example, one of the most influential and well-defined political ideologies of the 20th century was communism, based on the original formulations of Marx and Engels. Other examples of ideologies include: anarchism, capitalism, communitarianism, corporate liberalism, Christian democracy, fascism, liberalism, monarchism, falangism, nationalism, Nazism, neo-Nazism or neofascism, socialism, and social democracy.

IDEOLOGICAL POLITICS

Ideologies are always concerned with authority, and therefore they cannot avoid being political except by the extreme reaction-formation of complete withdrawal from society. Even in periods that saw no public politics permitted, ideological groups forced themselves into the political arena. Since the 17th century, every ideology has had its views on politics. Indeed, since the 19th century, most ideologies have come to be preponderantly political. Ideologies that concentrate on politics do so because for them politics embraces everything else. The evaluation of authority is the center of ideological outlook, and around it are integrated all other objects and their evaluations. Thus, no sphere has any intrinsic value of its own. There is no privacy, no autonomous sphere of art, religion, economic activity, or science. Each, in this view, is to be understood politically. This is true of Marxism, despite the fact that it is reputed to have made everything dependent on economic relationships. In Marxist ideology, the relations of production are property relations, that is, relationships of authority supported by the power of state.

Ideology, whether nominally religious or anti-religious, is concerned with the sacred. Ideology seeks to sanctify existence by bringing every part of it under the domination of the ultimately right principles. The sacred and the sacrilegious reside in authority, the former in the authority acknowledged by ideology, the latter in that which prevails in the "wicked world," against which ideology contends. From the viewpoint of an ideology, ordinary politics is the kingdom of darkness, whereas ideological politics is the struggle of light against darkness.

Participation in the routine life of the civil-political order is alien to the ideological spirit. In fact, however, there are many adulterations of this ideological purity, and purely ideological politics is marginal and exceptional. The need to build a movement strong enough to acquire power in the state, even by conspiracy and subversion, enforces compromises with, and concessions to, the existing political order. Failure, too, damages the purity of ideological politics. The pressure of competition enforces alliances and the adoption of procedures that are alien to their nature. Nonetheless, ideological politics, in splinters of implacable purity or in attenuation, often penetrate into civil politics, and conversely, civil politics often forces its way into ideological politics.

Among intellectuals, there are many who have inherited an ideological tradition and to whom ideological politics appeals as the only right politics. Even when intellectuals often appear to be convinced of the inefficacy of ideological politics, the categories in which ideologies view the world, as well as techniques and the heroes of the ideological politics, often stir and master their imagination.

Vilfredo Pareto, a positivist by tradition, once suggested that ideologies actually operate at three levels: one, the highest or "hermetic" levels involves a tiny circle of highly trained specialists who relish the subtle nuances of philosophical disputation; two, "esoteric" levels were intellectuals with the proper education to understand and care about the broad philosophical issues involved; and three, in the "exoteric" level, the need to appeal to a mass audience demands deemphasis

and crude simplification of philosophical schemata almost to the point of virtual. The masses, who figure so prominently in modern ideologies, simply lack the intellectual tools to fathom the doctrinal disputes characteristic of the politics of the intelligentsia. Thus, the abstruseness and complexity of the esoteric level of ideology give way to more concrete and visceral symbolizations at the exoteric level.

Still, the reference to philosophical issues cannot wholly disappear. At their deepest structural level, therefore, ideologies contend over such things as spiritualism versus mercantilism; theism, deism, pantheism, or atheism; idealism or empiricism; rationalism or romanticism; fatalism, determinism, or voluntarism; holism or individualism; realism or nominalism; dialectic or evolution; logic or intuition; absolutism or relativism; progress or decadence; and so on. Classic Marxism, for instance, stresses mercantilism, atheism, empiricism, determinism, holism, progress, and dialectic. Fascism displayed currents that suggest spiritualism, idealism, romanticism, voluntarism, holism, intuition, and decadence.

A further complication enters the picture because over time the same broad ideology can embrace several distinct philosophical currents. For example, in the three centuries of the history of liberalism, liberal thinkers have grounded the key liberal ideas of individualism, limited and representative government, historical progress and reform, separation of church and state, and equality of opportunity upon a wide variety of philosophical positions. These include classical rationalism, Lockean or Hobbesian empiricism, human skepticism, Hegelian or Kantian idealism, Darwinism, pragmatism, and more recently currents of logical positivism and linguistic philosophy.

As ideologies move from abstractions of philosophy to the greater concreteness of programs, they become more political and thus have greater accessibility to the masses. In the broadest sense, "program" refers to the stance an ideology takes toward the immediate status quo. A reactionary or right-wing ideology demands a halt to change or even restoration of a past "golden age," whereas reformist ideologies want selective, generally gradual, and moderate change in the current distribution of wealth, status, or power. Radical ideologies clearly tend toward revolution and want total restructuring of the social, political, and economic pyramids.

Since an ideology has a program, it needs the support of masses of people to implement it. Whether the core converts are a small sect of conspirators or a traditional mass party, still more members must be drawn to the movement inspired by the ideology. In other words, voters, supporters, activists, and intermediate and top leaders must be recruited and motivated to take the requisite political action. Depending on both the nature of the ideology and its historical circumstances, the targets for recruitment are the mass public; the much smaller "attentive" public of better-educated, better-off people; or perhaps still smaller groups of intellectuals. Often the hope is to have the ideology ripple out from the smaller to the larger groups.

At any rate, promoters of an ideology must act to reach and mobilize these groups for action. This is where the classic devices of rhetoric and propaganda come into play. Since virtually all ideologies employ propaganda techniques, to consider all propaganda pure and simple falsehood would beg the question. Many propagandists are convinced that the message they seek to convey is some ultimate truth. There are three central goals for propaganda. The first is to ensure the message reaches the designated group. The second is to mobilize favorable preexisting attitudes. Mobilizing preexisting favorable attitudes is easier than changing attitudes because the propagandist works with a structure that is already in place. The propagandist merely tries to refashion his message such that it strikes the positive responsive chord in the minds of its recipients. The third and most difficult is to change attitudes. According to Walter Lippmann (1889–1974), firmly entrenched attitudes constitute "stereotypes," which necessarily help us impose a measure of order and coherence upon our mental universe. Attitude change disturbs this and triggers certain defense mechanisms that act like antibodies in the physical system. One such is the "perceptual screen," which more or less unconsciously screens out messages and information alien to our pre-established mental framework.

In order to accurately reach the target group and manipulate or change attitudes with a view toward political action, propagandists and ideologists employ some standard techniques. First, attention-catching symbols are used to attract the target group. Symbols often refer to basic cultural or even mythical themes. If the message pierces the perceptual screen, the propagandist attempts to wear down any further resistance by repetition. Social psychology suggests that this may be more successful than thought. The second technique of propaganda involves gross oversimplification, whereby the propagandist strategically omits certain qualifying aspects of his message and purposely exaggerates others. The traditional question marks before a historical narrative are shelved in favor of starker and more dra-

matic contrasts. Thus, the favored groups of a particular ideology—the aristocracy, the middle class, the peasants, religious believers, the workers, the superior race, the "people"—will be depicted in more colorful and glamorous words than reality warrants. Similarly, the enemy or out groups will be depicted with highly negative terminology. Thus, it can be said that ideological politics is generally a distorting medium.

CRITIQUE OF IDEOLOGY

Thinkers through the ages have seen some primordial force at work that employs ideologies as convenient tools for rationalization and camouflage; nevertheless, various schools of thought dispute the real nature of that primordial force. The political critique, known as "political realism," finds its theorists in the ancient civilizations. It subordinates political ideas, ideals, and ideologies to the struggle of political power. With attaining, retaining, and expanding political power as the true content of politics, ideologies used to cover up the basic reality and misled the naïve and gullible. The doctrine of political realism has been put forward by Thucydides, Ibn Khaldun, Thomas Hobbes, Niccolo Machiavelli, Carl von Clausewitz, Friedrich Nietzche, and Henry Kissinger.

The economic critique of ideology derives largely from Marx. Marx employed an excessively broad notion of ideology embracing law, religion, ethics, philosophy, art, and literature. This is roughly equivalent to what modern social scientists would call "culture." Marx's "materialistic conception of history was a form of economic determinism, in which the basic economic facts of life—who owned the means of production and exchange, the basic mode of production, and technology—tended to shape the structure and dynamics of the rest of society.

Marx thus saw ideology as a form of "false consciousness" that functions to defend the domination of the ruling class by making the existing order seem right, just, divinely ordained, natural, immutable, inevitable, or otherwise beyond challenge. This system of illusions not only subjugated the ruled or exploited classes by preventing true insight into the inequalities of the present order, it actually afflicted members of the ruling class itself. In *The German Ideology*, Marx and Engels refer to a subgroup of the ruling class—ideologists in the narrow sense who make "perfecting the illusion about the class their chief source of livelihood."

Regarding the sociological critique of ideology, Karl Mannheim, in his book *Ideology and Utopia* (1936), views "ideology" and "utopia" as dichotomous and conflicting forms of social thought, though, many social scientists would consider both mentalities to be ideologies. A form of thought is an ideology in Mannheim's sense when it justifies and legitimizes the existing order and its upper-class beneficiaries. A utopia emerges when lower classes challenging the status quo require an intellectual weapon with which to attack the existing order. By contrasting the iniquitous present with an idealized image of the bountiful future, a utopia undermines the status quo and dramatizes the need for social change.

The psychological critique of ideology was advanced by Harold Lasswell (1929), whose three-stage model argues that political activists and leaders start out with a set of "private motives" of the standard Freudian sort, including personality traits, complexes, neuroses, and possibly psychoses, all originating from the famous Oedipus complex. In the second stage, political actors have "displaced" the private motives into "public objects." In the third and final stage, these displaced or politicized private motives undergo what Lasswell calls "rationalization in terms of public interest." In other words, leaders and activists need an ideology to justify their behavior and cover up the personal motives beneath it.

The various critiques of ideology provide vital insight about political life in general and the origin and function of political ideologies in particular. In many ways, they tend to focus on the underlying function of ideology at the cost of its obvious function of appealing directly to the normal and intellectual consciousness of the political actors.

IDEOLOGY OF LEFT-RIGHT

Originating in the politics of the French Revolution, the left-right ideological spectrum corresponded to the seating arrangements of the succession of legislative assemblies at that time and afterward. It so happened that extreme revolutionists congregated on the left side of the chamber. These were ardent advocates of democracy, equality, social change, anti-clericalism, and export of the revolution itself. As if to avoid contagion, their most extreme opponents, who were favorable to monarchy, aristocracy, stability, the church, and the traditional balance of power, ended up sitting on the right side of the chamber. Moderates had little choice but to occupy the center aisles. Over time, egalitarianism, radicalism, and the rest came to be associated with the French and then European "left," while hierarchy, tradition, cleri-

calism, and so on were tenets of the 19th-century "right." Over that century and into the 21st century, the left extended to include anarchists and communists while the right came to embrace fascists and Nazis. By the middle of the 20th century, social democrats, Christian democrats, liberals, and moderate conservatives had been squeezed into the "vital center" of Western and world politics.

In the United States, the terms *conservative* and *liberal* are often used to denote rightist and leftist views, respectively. Both types of descriptions exist on a continuum. Hitler was a rightist, but he was not conservative, Stalin was a leftist, but he was not liberal. The terms *rightist* and *leftist* should be used as ideological indicators. "Liberal" and "conservative" are not ideological indicators. An extreme liberal is willing to tolerate any change. An extreme conservative is unwilling to tolerate any change. When ideologues of any persuasion acquire power, they become increasingly conservative. When they have no power, they are liberal to the point of being revolutionary. An extreme leftist is someone who believes that the behavioral differences between persons are totally a product of their environment and that heredity plays no differential role in shaping what they become. An extreme rightist believes that environmental differences are unimportant and that only heredity, not environment, shapes people's behavior. There do not appear to be any persons at the boundary of the extreme right. But there are some people at the boundary of the extreme left. Most people fall somewhere along the continuum between the boundaries in a distribution that is continuously being skewed to the left.

OLD-NEW RIGHT AND FAR RIGHT

In the United States, the Old Right was a group of conservative Republicans of the interwar years, led by Robert Taft, who opposed American membership in the League of Nations and the New Deal. They successfully fought to cut down immigration in the 1920s. They were called the "Old Right" to distinguish them from their New Right successors of the Cold War, who were more friendly to both foreign and economic intervention.

New Right describes a form of conservatism in Britain carrying on from the Old Right, through the likes of Margaret Thatcher. They are ideologically committed to neoliberalism as well as being socially neoconservative. *New Right* has also been used as a term to describe a modern think tank of French political philosophers and intellectuals led by Alain de Benoist. Although accused by some critics as being far-right in their beliefs, they are nonetheless adamant that their ideas go beyond the normal left/right divide and actively encourage free debate.

The term *far right* is usually used to describe persons or groups who hold extreme nationalist, xenophobic, racist, religious fundamentalist, or other reactionary views. Typically the term is applied to fascists and neo-Nazis, although subscribers to left-wing views sometimes use the term very liberally to describe any group on the right of the political spectrum whom they disagree with.

SEE ALSO

Volume 1 Left: Liberalism; Communism; Socialism; Hobbes, Thomas; Locke, John; Ideology.
Volume 2 Right: Capitalism; Fascism; Conservatism.

BIBLIOGRAPHY

K. Marx and F. Engels, *Selected Works* (Progress Publishers, 1970); E. Durkheim, *Elementary Forms of Religious Life* (Macmillan, 1915); V. Turner, *The Forest of Symbols: Aspects of Nolembu Ritual* (Cornell University Press, 1967); P. Berger and T. Luckmann, *The Social Construction of Reality: A Treatise in the Sociology of Knowledge* (Doubleday, 1966); K. Marx and F. Engels, *The German Ideology* (International Publishers, 1964); K. Mannheim, *Ideology and Utopia* (Harcourt Brace, 1936); H. Lasswell, *Psychology and Politics* (Viking Press, 1929); N. Abercrombie, S. Hill, and B. Turner, *The Dominant Ideology Thesis* (Allen and Unwin, 1980).

JITENDRA UTTAM
JAWAHARLAL NEHRU UNIVERSITY, INDIA

Immigration Restriction

THE FIRST IMMIGRATION law in the United States was the Alien Act of 1798, which dealt with deportation and whose intent was less to deal with immigrants than to suppress the Jeffersonian opposition party. After Jefferson repealed the Alien and Sedition Acts, aside from the Naturalization Act of 1790 that limited citizenship to "free white persons," immigration restriction was a nonissue for 80 years. Between 1820 and 1930, the United States received approximately 60 percent of all the world's immigrants. America was growing and in need of workers. Anti-immigrant impulses in

the 1840s and 1850s resided in the Know-Nothing movement and the American Party, neither of which managed to effect restriction. Immigration control was regarded as a state power, not a federal one. And most states recruited immigrants rather than restricting them.

The exception was the west, where states from the 1870s began restricting Asian property ownership and citizenship. Westerners demanded national legislation; in 1875, Congress restricted citizenship to black and white people. The Chinese Exclusion Act of 1882, law until 1943, forbade Chinese immigration. Under the Cable Act of 1922, repealed in 1936, women who married Asian men lost their American citizenship. From the 1890s to the 1920s, eugenicists, restrictionists, and advocates of Americanism wanted to overturn the changes brought by new immigrants with different values, ways of life, and religions. Laws barred entry by the poor, diseased, criminal, and mentally deficient. After World War I, the Ku Klux Klan joined the anti-immigrant chorus. The 1924 National Origins Act established quotas based on percentages of immigration numbers prior to the new immigration. Then came the Great Depression and World War II. By 1945, the United States was more homogeneous than at any time prior to 1890.

World War II made Americans view Chinese Americans more sympathetically. A war against racism was indefensible while the United States exercised racist policies itself. The exclusionist phase waned. Latin Americans won the right to citizenship in 1940. Jews found refuge from Adolf Hitler's Holocaust. A half-million Mexican Braceros worked in 21 states. In 1942, Filipinos became eligible for military service and citizenship. Asian Indians got the right in 1944. The 1940 Alien Registration Act required registration and fingerprinting of all aliens over the age of 15. Koreans, confused with Japanese, remained under immigration restrictions, as did the interned Japanese. In the 1940s and 1950s, war brides were allowed to immigrate.

The McCarran-Walter Immigration and Naturalization Act of 1952 replaced the National Origins Act of 1924, allowing citizenship regardless of place of origin but keeping quotas. Loosened immigration led to a backlash from the American Legion and the Daughters of the American Revolution, which asked for a moratorium. The answer was no and the door was left half open. The Immigration Reform Act of 1965 eliminated quotas for Asians and set quotas for the Western Hemisphere at 120,000, with the rest of the world getting 170,000. The assumption was that the new immigrants would be from the same countries as the old new immigrants and that they would easily blend into a European-American United States. Surprisingly, the influx proved to be Asian, African, and Latin American. Also, Haitians, Vietnamese, Laotians, and Cubans came in the 1970s under various refugee asylum programs. And a massive surge in illegal immigration, especially through Mexico, overwhelmed the southwest and moved slowly north.

As in the Gilded Age, the new immigrants seemed to be unassimilable, leading to calls for restriction. In the 1980s, California led the U.S. backlash, which included English-only efforts, opposition to bilingual education and education of immigrant children, and restrictions on social entitlements. Organizations sprang up on both sides of the issue. The American Patrol was a vigilante group. More law-abiding groups included the Americans for Responsible Immigration, the Bay Area Coalition for Immigration Reform, the Border Solution Task Force, the California Coalition for Immigration Reform, and the Federation for American Immigration Reform. Even the environmentalist group Sierra Club seemed to be moving toward pro-restriction. In the 1980s and 1990s, immigration law changed almost annually, but neither amnesty nor tightened legal penalties could slow the migration. The face of the American population seemed destined to change, no matter how much conservatives wanted the status quo.

SEE ALSO

Volume 1 Left: United States; Immigration; Liberalism.
Volume 2 Right: Ku Klux Klan; White Citizens Councils; Christian Identity.

BIBLIOGRAPHY

Diane Alden, "States of Disunion: Stop the Invasion," www.stoptheinvasion.com (March 2004); Border Solution Task Force, "Goals and Objectives," http://thorin.adnc.com (March 2004); Ellis Cose, *A Nation of Strangers* (Morrow, 1992); James Crawford, *Hold Your Tongue* (Addison-Wesley, 1992); Roger Daniels, *Asian America* (University of Washington Press, 1988); Federation for American Immigration Reform, www.fairus.org (March 2004); John Higham, *Strangers in the Land* (Rutgers University Press, 1988); Ben Johnson, "The 1965 Immigration Act: Anatomy of a Disaster," www.frontpagemag.com (December 10, 2002); Maldwyn Allen Jones, *American Immigration* (University of Chicago Press, 1992); Barbara M. Solomon, *Ancestors and Immigrants* (University of Chicago Press, 1972).

JOHN BARNHILL, PH.D.
INDEPENDENT SCHOLAR

Imperialism

WHILE THE FIRST modern age of empires could be said to have ended with the British defeat in the American Revolution in 1783, the modern age of imperialism can arbitrarily be dated from the same historic event. Having lost its main overseas market in the infant United States, Great Britain in effect retaliated with a trade war that did not really draw to a close until the "Second American War of Independence" in the War of 1812. When that conflict ended with the Treaty of Ghent in December 1814, the new United States and Great Britain entered a historic friendship that has never seriously been dimmed to this day.

When the French Revolution overthrew the ancient Bourbon monarchy in 1792 and later executed King Louis XVI and his wife Marie-Antoinette, conservative thought in Great Britain naturally allied itself with the monarchies of Europe against the revolutionaries in Paris. Indeed, the Briton Edmund Burke's *Reflections on the Revolution in France* is still considered one of the best early expositions of conservative political thought. When Napoleon overthrew the French Revolutionary Directory in November 1799 to become the real power in France, the French revolutionary wars rapidly took on the character of the old mercantile wars of the 18th century. Except for the transitory Peace of Amiens in 1802, France and England were locked in a mortal struggle until Napoleon was defeated by the British Duke of Wellington and his Prussian allies at Waterloo on June 18, 1815. In 1806, Napoleon established what he called his Continental System, which attempted to shut out British goods from Europe. It would be to enforce this continental embargo that Napoleon would launch his two most disastrous invasions: Spain in 1808 and Russia in 1812. England retaliated with its Orders in Council, which attempted to bar French trade from virtually the rest of the world. Although France was rendered impotent at sea by its defeat at Trafalgar in October 1805, continued British efforts at enforcement led to the War of 1812 with the United States, as the new nation felt the British were severely threatening the freedom of the seas.

Indeed, rather than bring to a close any mercantile struggle over world trade, the Napoleonic Wars can be said to have inaugurated the second modern age of empires: the age of imperialism. While the first modern age of empires, colonialism, had been almost completely an economic struggle, the nationalism brought forth by the Napoleonic Wars, as with the fervent German war of liberation from Napoleon in 1813, imbued the mercantile contest with a new zeal, which can conveniently be called the imperial spirit. Each country gradually felt a call that empire was its destiny. Great Britain, in fact, obtained perhaps its first major new colonial possession, the Cape Colony, in 1806 in South Africa from the Dutch. The Duke of Wellington's earlier victory at Assaye in India in 1803 sealed the British dominance as the major European power in the Indian subcontinent, thus confirming the victory of Robert Clive at Plassey in 1755.

At the same time that England embarked on its colonization of India, France began its imperial adventure in Africa with the invasion of Algeria in 1830. This was partly undertaken by the French "citizen-king," Louis-Philippe, who had come to power in the revolution of 1830 to rid France of unemployed veterans who might oppose his rule. The conquest also marked the birth of the French Foreign Legion. From 1837 to 1847, Algerian resistance to French imperialism was led by Abd el-Kader, the emir of Mascara. When he was defeated, effective resistance to French penetration of North Africa ended. With it, the depredations of the Barbary pirates came to a close as well, because the French conquered their bases like Tripoli and Algiers from which they had raided Mediterranean commerce for centuries. By the end of the 19th century, except for the Belgian conquest of the Congo, France stood almost unequaled in North and equatorial Africa.

Yet, at the same time, the imperial expansion of France in Africa brought about the first major clash between France and Great Britain since the Napoleonic Wars. In 1875, British Conservative Party Prime Minister Benjamin Disraeli had acquired British control of the Suez Canal, the vital water artery to the British Empire in India. Inevitably, as foes of imperialism like the Liberal Party stalwart William Gladstone foresaw, this acquisition drew England into the affairs of Egypt. When an anti-foreign rebellion was led by Arabi Pasha in 1881 to 1882, the British became the de facto rulers of the ancient Land of the Pharaohs. In 1883 to 1884, disgust with Egyptian misrule in the Sudan contributed to perhaps the first Muslim extremist rising of modern times, the rebellion of Mohammed Ahmed, known as the Mahdi, "The Expected One" of Allah.

The Victorian hero Charles "Chinese" Gordon was sent to the Sudan to stabilize the situation and withdraw the Egyptians. His refusal to leave—and the seemingly desultory efforts of then Liberal Prime Minister Gladstone to relieve him—led to his death in the Sudanese capital of Khartoum in January 1885. When Conservative Party Prime Minister Lord Salisbury took office,

efforts in 1896 were under way to retake the Sudan. In 1898, the Anglo-Sudanese army under General Horatio Kitchener conquered Khartoum and reestablished Anglo-Sudanese control in September 1898. However, at the same time, French African troops under Major Jean-Baptiste Marchand arrived in the Sudan to establish French influence. Immediately, Kitchener moved to meet Marchand at Fashoda, and it appeared that a new Anglo-French war might erupt in the middle of Africa. However, a settlement was peaceably made and Marchand evacuated Fashoda by December 1898.

The United States, as well, became swept up in the imperial movement. In the Spanish-American War of 1898, the United States acquired an empire through the destruction of the old Spanish one and emerged as a world power. The American acquisition of the Philippines brought it into eventual disastrous confrontation with the only growing Asian empire, that of Japan.

Meanwhile, emerging from the Napoleonic Wars, Russia had been steadily conquering both the Caucasus region and the independent Muslim emirates of Central Asia. Concern over Russian penetration of Central Asia led to the "Great Game" of espionage between Russian agents and British agents from India. In 1885, a brief Russian occupation of western Afghanistan almost led to war between the two powers; a similar tense situation had already occurred in 1878. The British had fought two Afghan wars, in 1839 to 1842 and in 1878 to 1880, to prevent the country from falling under Russian influence.

Unlike the empires of colonialism, those of the age of imperialism embodied the growing social conscience of the 19th century. Englishmen like Gladstone and Joseph Chamberlain believed that the common people of England deserved a better share of the benefits of empire, and Gladstone tried unsuccessfully to extend Home Rule, a measure of self-government, to Ireland, arguably England's first colony. Strong anti-imperialist movements developed in the United States and England. And even among the most hardy of imperialists, like England's poet Rudyard Kipling, a feeling emerged that the imperial rulers owed their subjects overseas a better life and more opportunity and education than they had previously enjoyed. The French referred to the same responsibility as their *mission civilisatrice*, their "civilizing mission."

However, by the turn of the 20th century, concern over the growing power of imperial Germany began to eclipse imperial issues in France, England, and the United States. Germany was already building an empire in Africa and the Pacific, as well as extending ties in the

The concept of imperialism, once associated with territorial acquisition, now has connotations of cultural influences in globalization. A McDonald's restaurant in Japan (above) underscores how American culture has been infused into different world regions.

Middle East with the Ottoman Turkish Empire. The growing power of Germany brought together the three former imperial rivals, France, England, and Russia.

On June 28, 1914, the heir to the Austrian Empire, the Archduke Franz Ferdinand, was shot by Serb gunmen led by Gavrilo Princip in Sarajevo, in Bosnia-Herzegovina, recently joined to the empire. Germany supported Austria, and Russia came to the aid of Serbia. France, as Russia's ally, was drawn in. Great Britain supported France and stood against German invasion of neutral Belgium as a way of attacking France. When Germany did so, Great Britain declared war on Germany.

On August 4, 1914, World War I began. Almost inevitably, the struggle spread to their far-flung colonies. By the time the war ended, the empires of Austria, Germany, and Russia had been swept away and those of England and France irreparably weakened. The empires of the age of imperialism had passed, like those of the age of colonialism, victims of the great power rivalries of Europe.

The decline of the modern empires in the 20th century was accompanied by the rise of movements for national liberation. Although nationalistic in their aspirations, such movements often used the rhetoric and some of the social ideas of the radical left, while the defenders of the imperial presence took on aspects of the right. Such a contrast was particularly notable between left national liberation and right resistance in colonies such as French Indochina and Algeria, and British Kenya and Rhodesia, where European settlers and their local allies sought to preserve their position with a conservative loyalty to the metropolitan power.

SEE ALSO

Volume 1 Left: United Kingdom; France.
Volume 2 Right: Colonialism; United Kingdom; France.

BIBLIOGRAPHY

Barbara Tuchman, *The Guns of August* (Dell, 1962); Barbara Tuchman, *The Proud Tower* (Bantam, 1970); Winston S. Churchill, *The River War* (Award Books, 1964); Philip Magnus, *Gladstone: A Biography* (Dutton, 1964); A.P. Thornton, *The Imperial Idea and Its Enemies: A Study in British Power* (Anchor Books, 1968); Bernard Semmel, *Imperialism and Social Reform: English Social-Imperial Thought* (Ashgate, 1993); Edgar O'Ballance, *Afghan Wars: Battles in a Hostile Land, 1839 to the Present* (Brassey's, 2002); Douglas Porch, *The French Foreign Legion: A Complete History of the Legendary Fighting Force* (HarperCollins, 1992); Frank Freidel, *The Splendid Little War* (Dell, 1964).

JOHN F. MURPHY, JR.
AMERICAN MILITARY UNIVERSITY

India

ON AUGUST 15, 1947, the countries of India and Pakistan were formed from the partition of the British empire of India, which had formally become part of the British Empire, or Raj, in 1858, following the collapse of the Great Indian Mutiny. The empire had benefited from a period of enlightened rulers like Lord Curzon, who had permitted the development of political parties like the Indian Congress Party.

The British imperialists, unlike the Romans before them or the Soviet Russians after, always intended at one time in the future to grant independence to their colonies. The British Empire, in other words, was an *imperium* with a self-imposed expiration date, although affixing the exact date was something inevitably put off to the future. With this goal in mind, an entire class of *babus*, or Indian bureaucrats, was trained to rule the raj, serving with the Indian Civil Service (ICS) under the viceroy, who was the direct representative of the king or queen of England. Queen Victoria in 1858 was the first sovereign to rule India, and was from 1858 known as the queen-empress.

Thus, the right in India began with those concerned with maintaining the establishment structures that were built during the colonial period. Farther right, religion came into play as fundamentalist Hindu and Muslim factions battled for political power after independence.

Jawaharlal Nehru became India's first prime minister, beginning a tradition of democratic rule that has largely governed India in the past half century. This is in sharp distinction to the militarism that has shaped the political history of Pakistan. India became a republic within the commonwealth after adopting its constitution on January 26, 1950. From independence, the Republic of India's history was shaped greatly by its stormy relations with Pakistan, which had been traumatically severed from India in the partition that came upon independence, and subsequently as East Pakistan became Bangladesh.

However, India, with a Hindu minority, inherited its own political instability from religious forces which the British had vigorously handled during their rule. Hindu nationalism had been strong since the 1930s, with an extremist, neo-Nazi coloring. The movement had intended to inherit all of the former British Empire upon independence. It viewed the celebrated Mahatma Gandhi as a traitor for agreeing on partition with Mohammed Ali Jinnah, the leader of the subcontinent's Muslim population. On June 30, Hindu extremists killed Gandhi. As John F. Burns wrote in "Hindu Nationalist Still Proud of Role in Killing Father of India" in the *New York Times* on March 2, 1998, "Gandhi was killed with three pistol shots to the chest as he walked to an evening prayer meeting at an industrialist's house where he stayed during his sojourns in New Delhi."

Because of this horrific act, Burns continues, "For more than a decade after Gandhi's assassination, Hindu nationalist organizations were banned, and for at least 20 years after that the creed remained so tainted that Hindu nationalist parties were virtual pariahs. During this period, the family of Nehru would politically dominate Indian politics and, except under Indira Gandhi, would do so in a totally democratic manner."

Even before independence, it was evident that Kashmir would be an area of contention between the future India and Pakistan. Its ruler, Maharajah Hari Singh, was a Hindu, while most Kashmiris were Muslim, many of whom were interested in uniting with Pakistan. After independence, Hari Singh walked a tightrope as an independent ruler for two months. Then, in October 1947, with what India alleges was full Pakistani cooperation, tribesmen from Pakistan's Northwest Frontier Province invaded Kashmir. In order to save his princely state, the maharajah turned to India for assistance. As Victoria Schofield writes in *Kashmir in Crisis: India, Pakistan, and the Unfinished War*, "Indian accounts maintain that the whole operation into Kashmir was instigated at the highest level in Pakistan"—meaning the new leader Mohammed, Ali Jinnah.

The fighting would continue until the United Nations imposed a cease-fire on January 1, 1949. But, for 50 years to come, the situation along the LOC, the Line of Control separating Pakistanis and Indians in Kashmir, would serve as a flashpoint for war. In September 1965, war would erupt again between India and Pakistan over Kashmir, and a third time in 1971. As both nations became nuclear powers by the end of the 1990s, this confrontation took on immense global significance.

India faced another threat on the Northeast Frontier. Tibet, under its priest-king, the Dalai Lama, had been virtually independent from Chinese rule since the Chinese Revolution of 1912. However, upon the rise to power of Mao Zedong and the communists in 1949, Tibet had been brought back within the Chinese orbit. This brought Chinese and Indian forces close together in the Ladakh region. Both sides stood intransigent; Nehru declared, "we would prefer to be reduced to dust than submit to dishonor of any kind." Finally, open hostilities began in October 1962. As Dorothy Woodman wrote in *Himalayan Frontiers: A Political Review of British, Chinese, Indian, and Russian Rivalries*, "a massive attack began on October 20. The Chinese claim that India had opened the offensive was obviously nonsense."

Off India's southeast coast, in December 1962, the government of Ceylon, now Sri Lanka, negotiated an end to hostilities, another flashpoint for the emerging Indian nation.

THE GANDHI DYNASTY

When Nehru died in 1964, he was followed in 1966 by his daughter, Indira Gandhi, who became prime minister and would rule until 1977. In 1971, war began again between India and Pakistan, which would result in the Indian conquest of East Pakistan, soon to be known as Bangladesh. The pro-Indian guerrillas, the Mukhti Bahini, perpetrated atrocities against Pakistanis there or Bengali natives who supported Pakistan. In 1975, facing deepening political and economic problems, Gandhi declared a state of emergency and suspended many civil liberties. Seeking a mandate at the polls for her policies, she called for elections in 1977, only to be defeated by Moraji Desai, who headed the Janata Party, an amalgam of five opposition parties.

Gandhi returned to power in 1980. However, she became embroiled in a heated dispute with the large Sikh population in India, which historically furnished India with some of its best troops. Finally, she destroyed their Golden Temple in Amristsar. Then, on October 1, 1984, she was assassinated by her own Sikh bodyguards. Fatally, she trusted more their loyalty to India than loyalty to their religion. She was succeeded by her son, Rajiv.

However, extremism seemed to haunt the Gandhis, India's equivalent of the dynastic Kennedy family in the United States. In May 1991, Rajiv was assassinated by a Tamil nationalist from Sri Lanka (Ceylon), who set off a bomb while embracing him.

The murder of Rajiv Gandhi ended the Gandhi-Nehru political dynasty, which had ruled India virtually since independence in 1947. However, he died campaigning for the Congress-I Party (I for Indira), and the party rode to power on the vital sympathy vote. This Congress Party-led government served a full five-year term and initiated a gradual process of economic liberalization and reform.

After this, however, the Hindu nationalists made their first open bid for political power, emerging from the cloud they had been under since the murder of Mahatma Gandhi in 1948. The "History of India" internet reference notes that "The Hindu-nationalist Bharatiya Janata Party (BJP) emerged from the May 1996 national elections as the single-largest party in the Lok Sabha but without enough strength to prove a majority on the floor of that Parliament. Under Prime Minister Atal Bihari Vajpayee, the BJP coalition lasted in power 13 days." Nevertheless, Vajpayee remained the pivotal political figure in India, and in March 1998 became prime minister again. Part of the BJP's platform was a vigorous Indian nationalism. Soon after, Vajpayee carried Hindu nationalism into larger stakes as first India and then Pakistan conducted nuclear weapons tests in remote desert regions of each country. At the same time, tensions abruptly rose between the two regional powers. Hostilities erupted along the disputed Line of Control in Kashmir. Indian Defense Minister George Fernandes said in August 1999, "I don't think the situation is spiraling out of control," attempting to calm world concern. He argued that other nations should not be concerned about a nuclear clash, stating, "India has taken some self-imposed obligations not to use the nuclear weapon and purely looks at it as a deterrent." Then, in December 2001, a bloody raid on the Indian Parliament was blamed on Kashmiri extremists, who India claimed were backed by Pakistan. The specter of thermonuclear destruction chilled the usual fierce mutual responses over troubles in Kashmir. The *Holland Sentinel* reported on January 7, 2004, that "Two years after nuclear-armed India and Pakistan nearly went to war, their leaders agreed to hold landmark peace talks next month on all topics, including the issue of Kashmir."

SEE ALSO

Volume 1 Left: India; Third Worldism.
Volume 2 Right: Pakistan.

BIBLIOGRAPHY

John F. Burns, "Hindu Nationalist Still Proud of Role in Killing Father of India," *New York Times* (March 2, 1998); BBC On This Date, "1991: Bomb Kills India's Former Leader Rajiv Gandhi," (May 21, 1991); "India and Pakistan to Begin Peace Dialogue in February," *Holland Sentinel* (January 7, 2004); Dorothy Woodman, *Himalayan Frontiers: A Political Review of British, Chinese, Indian, and Russian Rivalries* (Barrie and Rockliff, 1969); Robert Fox, *A Story of War* (Barnes and Noble, 2002); Eric S. Margolis, *War at the Top of the World: The Struggle for Afghanistan, Kashmir, and Tibet* (Routledge, 2001); Paul Bracken, *Fire in the East: The Rise of Asian Military Power and the Second Nuclear Age* (Harper, 1999); Victoria Schofield, *Kashmir in Crisis* (Tauris, 2000).

JOHN F. MURPHY, JR.
AMERICAN MILITARY UNIVERSITY

Iran

THE MODERN HISTORY of Persia, as Iran was once called, began when it was recognized as one of the main oil sources in the Middle East. In May 1901, the British adventurer William D'Arcy Knox signed the first British oil concession, or agreement, with Persia's Shah Muzaffar al-Din. From the beginning, Great Britain guarded its oil supply with Iran jealously, realizing the critical importance of oil to its modernizing armed forces, especially its Royal Navy. Within seven years, the need for oil had ended one of the greatest power rivalries of the 19th century, the "Great Game" between England and the Russia of Tsar Nicholas II. In 1908, Great Britain signed an agreement with Tsarist Russia, basically dividing the country into Russian and British spheres of influence.

The mutual need for Iranian oil, in the face of the mounting power of imperial Germany, had forced them to come to an agreement. Knox had indeed found oil in Persia, in 1903 and 1904, but not in quantities to make it a successful commercial venture. In 1905, Knox traveled to France to try to sell his oil concessions to the wealthy Rothschild family. Realizing the desperate situation, the British Admiralty and British intelligence sent Sidney Reilly to France to stop the proposed negotiations. Reilly convinced him to sell out to the British. The British historian Robin Bruce Lockhart, whose father, Robert Bruce Lockhart, later worked with Reilly during the Russian Revolution, related what happened

next: "D'Arcy came home [to England] and on May 5th, 1905, as a result of Admiralty initiative, a Concession Syndicate was formed with the necessary finance and with the assistance of the Burmah Oil Company to continue exploration for oil in Persia. D'Arcy's interests in the event of oil being found were protected." In 1914, the Concession Syndicate would become known as the British Petroleum Company—the famous "BP." Thus, from the beginning of the 20th century, the industrial need for oil made the Middle East the most strategic area of the world—and one that the world's powerful nations would permanently continue to attempt to dominate.

However, a casualty of the move to divide Persia into British and Russian spheres was the constitution of 1906, which had been promulgated under political pressure by Shah Mazaffar ad-Din on the December 30. The constitution had called for an elected parliament, or Majlis. Muzaffar ad-Din (who died only a few days after signing the constitution) was denounced by his successor, Mohammed Ali Shah. Mohammed Ali Shah used Russian support and his Russian-officered Persian Cossack Brigade to crush the democratic opposition.

During the First World War, Persia became part of the hostilities against its will. Although desiring neutrality, Tehran, the capital, became the scene of intrigue by all the warring Great Powers. The German agent Wilhelm Wassmuss did much to stir up tribesmen to harass the British. Soon, the British formed the colonial South Persia Rifles as a defense force and, as in Iraq, the Assyrian population joined the war as well. Russia was forced to withdraw as a result of its November 1917 Revolution, and Great Britain became the dominant power. After the war, however, the Russian communists under V.I. Lenin, using subversion, made an effort to regain influence in Persia.

When the Anglo-Persian Agreement was signed in 1919, it was viewed as a capitulation to Great Britain by Persian nationalists. Taking advantage of the political crisis in Tehran, the Persian Cossacks Brigadier Reza Khan staged a successful coup in February 1921. In October 1925, the Majlis, which Reza Khan dominated, officially deposed the old Qajar Dynasty, and in April 1926, Reza was crowned shah. He chose "Pahlavi" for the name of his new dynasty, from the Farsi word meaning "heroic." Much like Mustafa Kemal in Turkey, who also came to power in the wake of the First World War, Reza attempted to modernize Persia, and chose the new name of Iran as a symbol of his intentions. The Persian Cossack ushered in an impressive series of nation-building reforms. Rather than rely on what sometimes seemed a hodgepodge of tribal levies, he had the Majlis authorize universal military conscription in 1926. Roads were built and factories were established. The Trans-Iranian Railroad was opened. He lay great emphasis on education as a way of preparing Iran for future progress, and in 1935 the first Western-oriented university was established. Under the guidance of his innovative justice minister, Ali Akhbar Davar, a new code of law based on Western models, not the Islamic Law, or Sharia, was promulgated between 1927 and 1932. Reza Khan also pushed through a General Accounting Act in 1934 and 1935, which was designed to put Iran on a more progressive financial footing.

The choice of a Western model for his legal code was part of an assault Reza Khan waged on the Islamic clergy, which he felt was an obstacle—as did Kemal in Turkey—to modernization. Among other reforms he instigated were taking away from the clerical ayatollahs (a rough Shiite equivalent to the Sunni imam) the administration of the *waqfs*, or charitable (and lucrative) religious endowments. He also forbade the wearing of the veil, a significant reform for Muslim women.

Eventually, Reza came afoul of Great Britain through attempting to gain more Iranian control of its oil reserves. The British accepted with bitterness the new deal the Shah made in 1932. However, the British continued to do business with the Shah, believing stability in the country was to their advantage. However, in the late 1930s, as with Rashid Ali al-Gailani in Iraq, Reza began to listen to pro-German advisors. The great British war correspondent of World War II, Alan Moorehead, would later recall in his *The March to Tunis: The North African War, 1940–43*, how the head of the Nazi penetration was the German ambassador, Count von Ettel.

When the Soviet Union was invaded by Nazi Germany in June 1941, the Soviet government put pressure on the Shah to oust the German agents. Rather than joining the Allied side, Reza committed the ultimate blunder of his career. Ignoring the advice of American President Franklin D. Roosevelt, who was already heavily committed to the Allied cause, the Shah took a suicidal step and barred shipments of supplies through Iran from British India to the Soviet Union. Therefore, from north and south, the Russians and British rapidly launched attacking columns into the heart of the Shah's Iran. Unable to face the strong Allied onslaught, the Iranians surrendered. On September 16, 1941, Reza wisely abdicated the ancient Peacock Throne of Iran in favor of his son, who became Shah Mohamed Reza Pahlavi.

The flow of war material from British India, across Iran, and into embattled Russia quickly resumed.

Under the new Shah's rule, Iran joined the Allies against the Axis (germany, Italy, and Japan) forces in the war. As a sign of the importance of Iran, the Tehran Conference was held in September 1943, which brought together U.S. President Franklin D. Roosevelt, British Prime Minister Winston S. Churchill, and Soviet Premier Josef Stalin. However, after the war, Iran became the first test of power in the Cold War. In December 1945, Jafar Pishevari, a politician linked with the communist Tudeh Party, attempted to create an autonomous Azerbaijan state in order for the Soviet Union to preserve the oil control that the tzarist regime had had in northern Iran. Only strenuous American and United Nations pressure caused the Soviets to remove backing from Pishevari, who fled to Moscow. A military aid agreement was signed in 1947 between the Iranian government and the United States.

After the war, the Shah, desiring to continue the reforms of his father, proclaimed the First Development Plan, from 1948 to 1955. However, continued nationalist feeling—highlighted by leftist, pro-Soviet forces—caused the parliamentary Majlis to nationalize the oil industry on March 15, 1951. The Shah was compelled to call the leftist Mohammed Mossadeq to power as prime minister. Mossadeq was backed by the Tudeh Party. The economy, already in serious condition, grew worse. In August 1953, in Operation Ajax, coordinated between the United States and the United Kingdom, Mossadeq was overthrown, and the Shah, who had fled, was restored to power. Operation Ajax was skillfully orchestrated in Tehran by CIA officer Kermit Roosevelt.

Rising revenues from oil allowed the Shah to continue his "White Revolution," aimed at modernizing his ancient monarchy along Western, secular lines. Two more development plans followed in 1955–62 and 1962–68. When martial law was ended after the Mossadeq Crisis, two political parties were formed, the Melliyun and the Mardom. In January 1962, a land distribution law was passed, under the urging of President John F. Kennedy. Other part of the White Revolution included profit-sharing for factory employees, nationalization of forests and pasture land, and a Literacy Corps, according to the U.S. State Department's "Iran: A Country Study." In February 1963, the Shah extended the voting franchise to women. However, the continuing secularization caused alarm among the extremists in the Iranian Muslim community, who saw their control eroding. One of those who gained notoriety for opposing the Shah was the Ayatollah Ruhollah

Khomeini, who was arrested in June 1963 for attacking the Shah.

However, domestic concerns began to take second place in Iran by 1965, when the United States under President Lyndon Johnson became involved in the Vietnam War on a large scale. The further escalation in the Cold War caused by the Soviet invasion of Czechoslovakia caused the United States to see Iran as an anti-communist bastion in Central Asia, next to the largely neutralist Afghanistan. President Richard Nixon made the Shah a keystone of American foreign policy in the region, and the refusal of the Shah to wholeheartedly support OPEC's (Organization of Oil Exporting Countries) oil embargo against the United States in 1973 was seen as his gratitude. The Shah also supported the sultan of Oman against the communist rebellion in Dhofar in the 1970s, to which the British sent soldiers of the elite SAS Regiment to give vital assistance.

However, internally Iran entered a period of crisis. After 1973, the shah's grandiose White Revolution began to outstrip the country's oil revenues, and political discontent grew. Increasingly, he began to rely on the military and the hated secret police, the SAVAK. At the same time, the religious extremists who opposed his modernization plan saw this as the time to strike. Their leader was the Ayatollah Khomeini, who from his French exile smuggled into Iran videocassette tapes urging the Shi'ites (Iran's religious Muslim majority) to defy the Westernizing Shah. On September 7-8, 1978, the Shah declared martial law and his troops fired on demonstrators. On the eve of the Shi'ite religious celebration of the month of Moharram, on December 1, 1978, the Ayatollah issued a call to his disciples. According to Gary Sick in *All Fall Down: America's Tragic Encounter with Iran*, Khomeini declared that Moharram would be the month that the Shah's "satanic government will be abolished." On January 16, 1979, the Shah left the country as a National Front government under Shapour Bakhtiar became the sole ruler of the country. On February 1, 1979, the Ayatollah returned in triumph to Tehran. On April 1, 1979, Khomeini proclaimed Iran an Islamic republic.

However, rather than accept the Bakhtiar government, the Ayatollah's followers worked behind the scenes to sow discontent in the government and armed forces. Amazingly, U.S. Ambassador William Sullivan supported the extremists' actions, believing only Khomeini could rule Tehran. Khomeini extremists worked to undermine any attempts to construct a constitutional government, and many students, following Khomeini's call against the United States as the "Great

Satan" who had backed the Shah, took over the American embassy in Tehran on November 1, 1979. Left-wing groups, including the communist Tudeh Party, supported the takeover. The hostages from the embassy would not be released until January 20, 1980, when Ronald Reagan succeeded Jimmy Carter as president.

Increasingly, the Khomeini regime began to attempt to export its Islamic revolution beyond Iran's borders. Within Iran, the moderate, secular government of Mehdi Bazargan fell from power. In September 1980, war broke out between Iran and Iraq, with Iraq covertly supported by Saudi Arabia and the United States in an attempt to stem the spread of the Islamic Revolution. Finally, after nearly one and a half million died, the war was brought to an end with a United Nations cease-fire on August 20, 1988. Meanwhile, the Islamic extremists in Tehran became a center of gravity for acts of terrorism. Terrorist attacks attributed to those following Tehran were committed on American soil. When the Ayatollah Khomeini died on June 3, 1989, the Iranian people, exhausted by the war, had grown tired of the excesses of the Pasdaran, the Revolutionary Guard. After eight years, the moderate Ayatollah Mohammad Khatami became president in 1997. Relations with conservative Muslim Saudi Arabia were restored after bloodshed occurred during the 1987 Hajj pilgrimage to Mecca, fomented by Khomeini stalwarts. In his drive to restore Iran to a position of international prestige, Khatami visited Pope John Paul II in the Vatican. Reelected to a second term in spite of opposition from the Khomeini stalwarts, Khatami committed Iran reservedly to the War on Terrorism after the attack on America on September 11, 2001. According to the *Philadelphia Inquirer* of January 25, 2004, Iranian Foreign Minister Kamal Kharrazi announced that the country planned to put on trial 12 suspected members of an al-Qaeda cell. Yet, also within the country, followers of Khatami and adherents of Khomeini's old regime are now locked in a struggle over elections which, might still chill the prospects for a continued moderation of the Islamic republic.

SEE ALSO

Volume 1 Left: Iran; Church and State.
Volume 2 Right: Iraq; Religion; Imperialism; Colonialism; Nationalism.

BIBLIOGRAPHY

Daniel Yergin, *The Prize: The Epic Quest for Oil, Money, and Power* (Simon and Schuster, 1991); Alan Moorehead, *The March to Tunis: The North African War* (Dell, 1968); Gary

Sick, *All Fall Down: America's Tragic Encounter with Iran* (Penguin Books, 1986); Anwar Faruqi, "As Throngs Gather for Hajj, the List of Saudi Worries Grows," *Philadelphia Inquirer* (January 23, 2004); Associated Press, "Iran to Try 12 al-Qaeda Suspects," *Philadelphia Inquirer* (January 25, 2004); Ken Moritsugu, "Europe Urged to Strike at Terror," *Philadelphia Inquirer* (January 25, 2004); Robin Bruce Lockhart, *Reilly: Ace of Spies* (Penguin Books, 1984); Michael B. Stoff, *Oil, War, and American Security: The Search for a National Policy on Foreign Oil* (Yale University Press, 1980).

JOHN F. MURPHY, JR.
AMERICAN MILITARY UNIVERSITY

Iraq

IN NOVEMBER 1914, the Ottoman Empire threw in its lot with that of imperial Germany and the Austrian Empire in World War I. Consequently, when the Western Allies were victorious, the Muslim Ottoman Empire, which had once posed a mortal threat to Christian Europe, was swept away. The words of the Iranian poet Firdawsi, which Ottoman Emperor Mehmet II spoke as he entered vanquished Constantinople in 1453, now stood as an epitaph for his empire. Firdawsi wrote, "the spider serves as gate-keeper in Khusrau's [Cyrus the Persian's] hall; the owl plays his music in the palace of Afraisiyab."

With the fall of Damascus, Syria, in 1918 to the British Empire forces of General Edmund Allenby, the future of what would be Irak—later Iraq—entered the spotlight. Captain T E. Lawrence, the future Lawrence of Arabia, had joined the Arab Revolt in December 1916, after having served British military intelligence in the Arab Bureau in Cairo. The revolt was led by Sharif Hussein, the keeper of the great Muslim holy places of Mecca and Medina. However, operational control was invested in his son, Prince Faisal, and it was to Faisal that Lawrence traveled with promises of British support and shipments of British gold. Even then, Lawrence saw future promise in Hussein and his sons. (Another son, Abdullah, served as his father's astute political advisor.) In February 1917, Lawrence wrote, "the Arab Movement has the capacity for expansion over a very wide area." While a guerrilla force, and thus unable to face the Ottoman Turks and their German advisers in open battle, Lawrence, Faisal, and the Arabs pinned down a significant number of Turks with their hit-and-run desert war. Peter Mansfield wrote in *A History of the Middle East* that the Arab Revolt "immobilized some 30,000 Turkish troops along the Hejaz Railway from Amman to Medina and prevented the Turco-German forces in Syria from linking up with the Turkish garrison in Yemen." When Allenby launched his Big Push with his attacks on Gaza and Beersheba on October 31, 1917, the Arabs played a vital role in harassing the Turkish Fourth Army. Lawrence and Faisal continued to make a signal contribution up to the ultimate triumph at the fall of Damascus in September 1918.

However, while Lawrence was urging Faisal and the Arabs to carry on against the Turks, at the same time he was cognizant of the Sykes-Picot Agreement of 1916, which had divided up the Middle East possessions of the Turks between the French and English. Roughly speaking, Great Britain would fall heir to Palestine, today's Israel, the West Bank, and Jordan, and France would receive modern Syria and Lebanon.

Feeling guilt at his duplicity, Lawrence nevertheless backed Faisal to be king of Syria and Lebanon. France responded with a military invasion that defeated Faisal and his followers. A French League of Nations mandate was proclaimed by the French for Greater Syria (Lebanon and Syria) on September 1, 1920. Faced with this patent betrayal of the promises of freedom that Lawrence and the British had given during the war, the entire Arab world simmered on the brink of a massive jihad, or holy war. British Colonial Secretary Winston S. Churchill, faced with the possibility of a situation England might not be able to contain (the rebellion in Ireland was raging at the same time) called a conference in Cairo in March 1921 to address the fulminating Middle East. Churchill, later a conservative luminary in London, as was his father Randolph Churchill, sought the advice of Lawrence, Allenby, and Gertrude Bell, perhaps the most influential woman in British foreign relations.

A League of Nations mandate was established for Iraq in July 1922, and Faisal, largely through the influence of Lawrence, eventually became the ruler of Iraq. His brother Abduallah become the emir, later the king, of Iraq. In 1923, however, the Treaty of Lausanne promised an independent state to the Kurdish population that inhabits Iraq, Syria, and Turkey. Although basically rescinded diplomatically, this promise still promotes dreams of an independent Kurdistan today, a possibility that would disrupt the entire Middle East. In 1930, a 25-year treaty was concluded between Faisal of Iraq and Great Britain. During this period, after the

Cairo Conference, Churchill began an innovative program of policing the Iraqis with Royal Air Force Rolls-Royce armored cars and plans, to save money on an army garrison.

When Faisal died in 1933, his son and successor as king was Ghazi, reputed to be a playboy monarch (he would later be killed in an automobile crash). Real power devolved upon the conservative Arab nationalist Nuri al-Said, whose extensive political service had begun under the Ottomans. While political democracy was ephemeral at best, still Iraq did not become a dictatorship under the rule of Faisal and his heirs, as later it would. With the discovery of oil in 1927, Iraq was on its way to becoming one of the major suppliers of oil in the world. As the 1930s wore on, the growing crisis of fascism in Europe spread to the Middle East. Germans, who had lived in the region since Kaiser Wilhelm's dream of the Berlin to Baghdad Railway before the First World War, began to form Nazi Party cells. They cultivated a pro-German clique within Iraqi politics and the armed forces known as the Golden Circle.

In March 1941, the pro-Nazi Rashid Ali al-Gailani seized power in Baghdad, the ancient capital of Iraq, with the Golden Square putsch. Nuri had to flee, as did the infant King Faisal II, who had become king when Ghazi died in an auto wreck in 1939. The British, faced with the power of German Field Marshal Erwin Rommel and the German Afrika Korps in North Africa, were now confronted by a dire threat to their vital supplies of oil.

The British responded with an invasion of Iraq, with the main fighting done by expeditions led by Brigadier Joe Kingstone and John Bagot Glubb Pasha, leader of the legendary Arab Legion. By the end of May 1941, Nuri al-Said was restored to power, and Rashid Ali in flight. The military leaders of the Golden Square were later executed. Under Nuri, Iraq joined the Second World War against Germany in January 1943, and stalwartly supported the war effort. As World War II was drawing to a close, Iraq joined the new Arab League in March 1945. Later, in December 1945, Iraq was admitted into the United Nations.

In 1956, Nuri and the Iraqi government helped establish the Baghdad Pact, which was designed to help curb the growth of Soviet communist influence in the Middle East. President Gamal Abdel Nasser of Egypt, who had first emerged in the Egyptian Free Officer's coup of 1952, which had toppled King Farouk was incensed. Nasser, a major recipient of Soviet military and economic aid, urged a military putsch in Baghdad in retaliation. Responding to Nasser's call, Iraqi General

Saddam Hussein as he looked upon being captured by American forces, thus ending a two-decade-long extreme-right dictatorship.

Abd al Karim Qasim led a bloody insurrection on July 14, 1958, which led to the killing of Nuri al-Said, the Prince Regent, and the young King Faisal II. Qasim's tenure in office was characterized by a leftist policy that caused CIA Director Allen Dulles in April 1959 to characterize Iraq as "the most dangerous [country] in the world."

In 1959–60, the Ba'ath Party launched a military coup and took power as the National Council of Revolutionary Command. One of the early Ba'ath plotters was Saddam Hussein. While temporarily in eclipse, the Ba'athists returned to full power in 1968, and Hussein emerged even stronger within the military Ba'ath command. President Ahmad Hassan al-Bakr resigned as president on July 16, 1979. Hussein emerged as the unchallenged ruler of Iraq, a position he would hold for two decades.

In foreign policy, Hussein carried out an aggressive war with Iran from 1980 to 1988, which began over disputed rights to islands and the strategic Shatt-al-Arab water artery to the Persian Gulf. The war raged unabated until a United Nations cease-fire brought it to an end in 1988. During the war, Hussein employed poison gas against the numerically superior Iranian Army of the theocratic Islamic extremist regime of the Ayatollah Ruhollah Khomeini. The first record use was, according to the United Nations, at Majnoon in March 1984. After peace came, the U.S. State Department estimated that "20,000 Iranian soldiers were killed in Iraqi chemical attacks from 1983–88."

Domestically, Saddam Hussein followed no less a brutal career. Chemical weapons were employed also against the Kurdish population, who still sought the independence that had been promised them by the Treaty of Lausanne in 1923. Hussein used chemical weapons on the Kurdish village of Halabja in 1988. His reign of terror embraced any potential dissidents in Iraq; untold thousands were killed in a campaign in which his homicidal sons, Oudai and Qusai, served as willing lieutenants. After his fall from power in the spring of 2003, the *New Yorker* magazine and *Time* documented countless incidents of his brutal rule. An article in the *New Yorker* documented how when a Baghdad butcher had been arrested for talking against the regime, he was arrested, ground up into ground beef—and then returned to his family.

In August 1990, Hussein resumed his foreign aggression with an invasion of the neighboring emirate of Kuwait. Responding to the occupation of Kuwait and the threat to Saudi Arabia and the vital supply of oil, President George H.W. Bush led a coalition in Operation Desert Shield (later Desert Storm) that effectively drove Hussein out of Kuwait by February 1991. However, in spite of the terms of the peace agreement, Saddam returned to his purge of the Kurds and Shi'ite Arabs, which forced the United States to establish a protected zone for the Kurds in northern Iraq. During the next decade, Hussein kept up his defiance of the United States and the United Nations, especially over concern that he was continuing the program to develop weapons of mass destruction (WMD), chemical, biological, and nuclear weapons, a program he had instituted before the war of 1990–91. He persisted in his recalcitrance in spite of an economic embargo that inflicted unspeakable hardship upon his own people. Following the expiration of a March 17, 2003, United Nations deadline to disarm and permit inspection of all possible WMD sites, the United States and Great Britain initiated the invasion of Iraq, Operation Iraqi Freedom, on March 20. On April 16, with the war ef-

fectively over, U.S. General Tommy Franks entered Baghdad. After an extensive manhunt, Hussein was captured near his native village of Tikrit on December 13, 2003.

SEE ALSO

Volume 1 Left: Middle East.
Volume 2 Right: Middle East; Totalitarianism.

BIBLIOGRAPHY

U.S. Library of Congress, "Iraq: A Country Study," www.memory.loc.gov (July 2004); "Operation Iraqi Freedom: Chronology," www.army.mil (July 2004); Robert Harris and Jeremy Paxman, *A Higher Form of Killing* (Random House, 2002); Desmond Stewart, *T. E. Lawrence: A New Biography* (Harper and Row, 1977); Georgiana G. Stevens, ed., *The United States and the Middle East* (Prentice-Hall, 1964); Andrew and Patrick Cockburn, *Out of the Ashes: The Resurrection of Saddam Hussein* (HarperCollins, 1999); Peter Mansfield, *A History of the Middle East* (Viking, 1991); Mort Rosenblum, *Mission to Civilize: The French Way* (Harcourt Brace, Jovanovich, 1986); Somerset de Chair, *The Golden Carpet* (Bantam Books, 1992).

JOHN F. MURPHY, JR.
AMERICAN MILITARY UNIVERSITY

Ireland

THE MODERN POLITICAL history of Ireland dates from the British Glorious Revolution of 1688, in which the Catholic Irish supported King James II against William of Orange. When James's army in Ireland was defeated in 1691, and the Treaty of Limerick signed, British rule in Ireland became complete. However, thousands of Catholic Irish would leave Ireland to carry on the fight against Protestant William of Orange in the armies of the Holy Roman Empire and France. Catholics who remained behind were subjected to the heavy penal laws if they did not abjure (disavow) their ancestral religion.

The 18th century saw a period of formative peace in Ireland, a fact noted by the repeal of many of the penal laws against Irish Catholics in 1778, 1782, and 1792, as the BBC noted in *Prosperity, Revolution, and Famine.* A growing crisis continued between Catholic groups, known as Defenders, and Protestants who called themselves the Peep O'Day Boys, and earned their sobriquet

Irish leader Eamon de Valera crushed a fascist, far-right movement that wanted Ireland to adopt Hitlerian policies.

by striking at dawn. This guerrilla war merged into the Rebellion of 1798, "The Rising of the Moon." However, in 1798, both Irish Catholics and Protestants, inspired by the ideals of the French Revolution, rose up as the United Irishmen, led by Theobald Wolfe Tone and Lord Edward Fitzgerald. The rebellion was put down with singular brutality by Lord Charles Cornwallis, anxious to redeem his ragged reputation suffered at his defeat in the Battle of Yorktown in the American Revolution in 1781.

Then, in 1845, the potato crop, the staple of the Irish diet, was struck by a blight, a new disease, as the BBC explained, "*Phytophthora infestans*, a microscopic fungus for which there was then no remedy, and which struck again with virulent force in 1846." Persistent English governance and the simultaneous shipping out of the country of valued food stock for sale led to a massive famine. Noted the BBC, "It is estimated that about a million people died during the Famine and that another million emigrated, the vast majority to Britain and North America. The government declared in 1848 that the Famine was over, but it continued to rage in 1849 and to a lesser extent until 1852." The Irish famine, *An Gorta Mor*, killed any hopes for a further reconciliation between the Irish people and the English government. Within 20 years, the first modern Irish revolutionary group, the Fenians, was active in Ireland. All future Irish "rebel" groups would look to the Fenians as their spiritual progenitors.

In 1916, the Easter Rebellion signaled the beginning of the final struggle for Irish independence, which would not end until a treaty with England in 1922 led to the evacuation of the 26 southern counties. However, a faction of the Irish Republican Army (IRA) refused to accept the treaty and a brutal civil war ensued in the south. Before it ended in 1923, more Irish had died than in the war against the British.

However, an unforeseen legacy of the civil war was that the anti-treaty faction of the IRA would be the latter-day breeding ground for rightist parties in Ireland, much like the German *freikorps* after World War I provided the seed of the later Nazi movement. Although with Eamon de Valera, the last commander of the IRA in the civil war, most veterans would constructively enter Irish politics, some would remain dangerously perched on the right-wing fringe. Under the banner of his Fianna Fail Party, the Warriors of Destiny Party, de Valera became the dominant figure in Irish politics.

With the rise of fascism in Europe after World War I, the movement spread to Ireland, Europe's most western outpost. In the summer of 1933, the Army Comrades Association (ACA), led by General Eoin O'Duffy, formally adopted the "heil Hitler" salute of the German Nazi Party (Hitler had come to power in Germany in January 1933). The ACA was more popularly known as the Blueshirt movement. At the same time, O'Duffy helped launch the Fine Gael, or United Ireland Party.

In fact, O'Duffy grew to personify fascism in Ireland. In June 1933, on a visit to Italy, then ruled by the fascist Benito Mussolini, the *Irish Times* quoted Duffy as saying that he "spoke of his great admiration for fascism." At the same time, the National Centre Party joined what was rapidly growing into a far-right coalition on the Irish political scene. William Cosgrave, who had been president of the provisional government during the civil war, became a parliamentary leader of the burgeoning Irish far right.

However, de Valera, then the undisputed political leader of Ireland, moved to quash the threat from the far right, as he did from those in the IRA who challenged his government. Unlike in Germany, where the fascists triumphed under the Nazis, in Ireland, through a Gaelic mixture of forceful suppression and politic negotiation, the rightist threat to Ireland evaporated by 1935.

SEE ALSO

Volume 1 Left: Irish Republican Army; United Kingdom.
Volume 2 Right: Fascism; United Kingdom.

BIBLIOGRAPHY

Brendan Kennelly, *The Penguin Book of Irish Verse* (Penguin, 1981); G.A. Hayes-McCoy, *Irish Battles: A Military History of*

Ireland (Barnes and Noble, 1997); British Broadcasting Company, *Prosperity, Revolution and Famine: The Battle of Clontarf 1014*, www.bbc.co.uk (July 2004); Robert Schaeffer, *Warpaths: The Politics of Partition* (Hill and Wang, 1990); Tim Pat Coogan, *Eamon de Valera: The Man Who Was Ireland* (Harper, 1993).

JOHN F. MURPHY, JR.
AMERICAN MILITARY UNIVERSITY

Irish Republican Army

THE ORIGINS OF the Irish Republican Army (IRA) lay in the struggle for Home Rule in Ireland in the 19th century. In a desire to ameliorate the aftermath of the brutal Great Famine of the 1840s, British Liberal Prime Minister William Gladstone introduced into the British Parliament the first Home Rule Bill, which was intended to give the Irish a say in their own affairs for the first time since the union with Great Britain in 1801 had dissolved the last Irish Parliament. However, the Protestant Ascendancy (particularly in the North of Ireland, the old Province of Ulster), those land magnates and members of Parliament who wished to preserve their peculiar position in a land of a Roman Catholic majority, frustrated all of Gladstone's efforts at the passage of Home Rule. In 1893, Parliament's House of Lords frustrated his last attempt.

In 1912, Herbert Asquith, the new liberal prime minister, submitted his Home Rule Bill to Parliament. This time, the Protestant response threatened violence. Edward Carson, a member of Parliament, threatened armed resistance if Home Rule passed. As David Fitzpatrick wrote in *The Oxford Illustrated History of Ireland*, "confrontation in Ireland developed with alarming rapidity after the initial parliamentary skirmishes of 1912." From 1912 to 1914, Protestants, especially in Ulster, signed a Solemn League and Covenant to fight Home Rule, and formed the Ulster Volunteer Force. Thanks to widespread support in Northern Ireland and in the Conservative (Tory) Party in England, this paramilitary force became extremely well armed, including a motorcycle detachment.

Unionist (those who wished to preserve the current union with Great Britain) army officers declared that they would not enforce Home Rule in Ireland, the so-called Curragh Mutiny, thus directly defying government authority. Asquith's Home Rule Bill in fact did pass in May 1914 in Parliament, but the coming of World War I in August caused its implementation to be tabled for the duration of the war—a major victory for the forces of the Protestant Ascendancy.

As a response to the establishment of the Ulster Volunteer Force (UVF), Professor Eoin MacNeill of the University College in Dublin felt compelled to organize the Irish Volunteers in November 1913, as James Mackay wrote in *Michael Collins: A Life*. Almost from the beginning, the actual control of the Volunteers, woefully undergunned by the standards of the Ulster force, was in the hands of the Irish Republican Brotherhood (IRB). The IRB was in the tradition of the Fenians of the 19th century and other militant groups that felt that armed resistance was the only recourse that Irishmen had after centuries of British oppression.

By spring 1916, a major split had developed in the Ulster Volunteers over both the lack of implementation over Home Rule and the concern over the extension of military conscription to Ireland. The sentiment was expressed in a play, *Under Which Flag*, which had been written by the famed Marxist labor organizer James Connolly. One of the characters in the play raised a Green Flag, the emblem of Irish nationalism, and declared, "under this flag only will I serve. Under this flag, if need be, I will die." Connolly had also helped form the Citizen's Army in response to the brutality with which the authorities had suppressed the strike of 1913.

In spite of the opposition of MacNeill, Patrick Pearse, Connolly, and members of the IRB like Tom Clarke, the Irish Volunteers planned for a rebellion in Dublin on Easter Monday, April 24, 1916. The Citizen's Army and the Irish Volunteers achieved complete surprise and seized the General Post Office and other strategic sites throughout a stunned Dublin. In front of the General Post Office, Pearse read to the onlookers the proclamation of the Irish Republic. On that date, the Irish Republican Army, formed from Connolly's Citizen's Army and the Irish Volunteers, could be said to have had its birthday.

After a bitter week of fighting, Pearse and the other commandants, including Eamon de Valera, who was an American citizen, were forced to surrender. In what would be a disastrous move, British commander General Sir John Maxwell had Pearse and 14 other leaders executed: de Valera alone escaped because of his American citizenship. The spectacle of the executions only galvanized Irish resistance to British rule. Among those survivors of the Easter Rebellion was Michael Collins, a native of County Cork, who had joined the

Irish Republican Brotherhood while working before the war in London.

When an amnesty was announced in December 1916 for the prisoners taken in April, Collins began immediately to reorganize the IRA into an effective tool for fighting the British. Other veterans of the Eastern Rebellion, like Cathal Brugha (born Charles Burgess), joined in the crusade for Irish independence. Soon, the fight spread from Dublin throughout Ireland, especially in the 26 southern counties where there was a clear Catholic majority.

While Collins organized an effective guerrilla struggle under urban conditions in Dublin, commandants like Tom Barry in Cork and Dan Breen in Tipperary fought a highly effective struggle against the British Army and its hated allies, the Black and Tans and the Auxiliary Forces. Finally, peace was made in December 1922 between the government of British Prime Minister David Lloyd George and the political representative of Irish Nationalism, the Sinn Fein Party. Michael Collins led the Irish peace delegations to the talks, which had been held in London. Ominously, when the instrument of peace was signed, Collins declared, "I may have signed my actual death warrant."

A peace treaty was ratified in the 26 southern counties (later the Irish Republic) in the new Irish Parliament, or Dail, on January 7, 1922. Eamon de Valera, who opposed the treaty as a capitulation to the English for surrendering the six northern counties of Ulster, resigned as the first minister of the infant Irish state. He and other former IRA commandants, now opposed to the treaty, soon were in open rebellion against what was soon called the Irish Provisional government. Now, the "flying columns" of IRA leaders like Dan Breen fought their former colleagues in the Dublin government in an effort to remain true to Irish nationalism. As Robert Kee wrote in *The Green Flag: Ourselves Alone*, "for many of the most idealistic IRA leaders—men like Liam Lynch and Ernie O'Malley—the [ideal of the Irish] Republic ... was a symbol which was solemn and very real." By the time the strife ended in 1923, more Irish had been killed in the civil war than in the six years of war with England. Among those killed were the veterans of the Easter Rebellion, on opposing sides, Michael Collins, commanding the Free State forces, and Cathal Brugha, fighting with the IRA.

In 1927, abandoning the IRA stand of not participating in the government, de Valera took a seat in the Dublin Dail. Five years later, Eamon de Valera and his Fianna Fail Party were elected to lead the Free State government against which he had rebelled a decade ago.

From that point on, the IRA was politically on the sidelines in Ireland. De Valera, the political pragmatist, had defeated de Valera the Republican idealist. In February 1933, according to Tim Pat Coogan in *Eamon de Valera: the Man Who Was Ireland*, a secret IRA document stated "the Fianna Fail government is not directed towards the achievement of our aims." From then on, a cold war was waged between the Irish government and the IRA. Indeed, de Valera would use the death penalty against those who had still kept up the dream of a united Ireland.

During World War II, de Valera would keep the Irish Free State neutral, although providing apparently secret support to Allied intelligence against the Germans. The IRA, however, gave support to the Germans as the enemies of England, as it had done in the First World War. With German support, an IRA bombing campaign against England was carried out: several of those arrested were executed by the British. IRA support for the Germans only continued to marginalize the IRA in Irish society, although a large number still believed in its ultimate goal of Irish unification.

Nevertheless, the IRA attempted to keep up the nationalist tradition of "a rising every generation"—until unification of the island was achieved. On January 1, 1957, Sean South was killed in a raid against a barracks of the Royal Ulster Constabulary in Brookeborough, giving rise to one of the best-known of Irish nationalist (or Republican) songs, "Sean South of Garryowen."

The IRA, disregarding political disputes within its own ranks, did not play a major role in Irish affairs until 1968-9, when Roman Catholic civil rights marchers in Northern Ireland were set upon by the Protestant thugs of the Unionist extremist the Reverend Ian Paisley. But so unprepared was the IRA to resume its old role as protector of the Catholic minority in the North that slogans were written saying, "IRA—I Ran Away." To meet the growing struggle, the Provisional IRA broke away from the traditional wing in December 1969. The entire Roman Catholic community and the Provisional IRA were electrified when, in January 1972, on "Bloody Sunday," soldiers of the British Parachute Regiment killed 13 people in a civil rights protest march. From then on, the IRA was effectively at war with the British government.

The 1981 hunger strikes, led by Bobby Sands, focused international attention and media on the problem in Northern Ireland, which had been exacerbated by conservative Prime Minister Margaret Thatcher's campaign to block all reference to the IRA from the British media. (However, peace talks did progress during her tenure in 1986–87.) After a party crisis forced her resignation, repeated attempts at reaching some type of peace settlement came when John Major succeeded her as prime minister, and undertook secret negotiations with Gerry Adams, president of Sinn Fein. The Downing Street Declaration in December 1993, by the governments of the Republic of Ireland and the United Kingdom, sought to open the way for negotiations between the Unionists and Sinn Fein. A cease-fire begun by the IRA in September 1994, and subsequently adhered to by the Protestant militants, broke apart in February 1996. The IRA agreed to yet another cease-fire on July 19, 1997, and the Protestant paramilitary groups observed it as well. However, a permanent end did not come to the violence until the Good Friday Peace Agreement of April 10, 1998. The agreement, which was ratified in Northern Ireland on May 22, 1998, for the first time provided for the representation of Sinn Fein in the political executive that would govern Northern Ireland.

The politics of Home Rule and Irish nationalism tend to cut across the lines of left and right. In general, in the late 19th century and early 20th century, those politicians in Britain advocating Home Rule for Ireland were found among the Liberals, while those supporting the continuation of Ireland under British rule were found among British Conservatives. The Protestant politicians of the Ulster region who fought against Home Rule for Ireland, which would result in a Catholic-dominated nation, found allies among British Conservatives who opposed Home Rule.

In the 26 counties that sought independence, some supporters of a more radical and revolutionary approach were drawn from Marxist ranks, similar in their political orientation to radical advocates of national liberation movements in non-European areas colonized by the European powers. However, the Irish Republican Army also drew upon nationalist sentiments and to that extent, it resembled rightist nationalism in other nations of the world.

It could be said that Irish nationalism has often represented a mixture of a politically radical movement and a culturally conservative one. The fact that during World War II elements of the IRA supported the Axis powers gave further evidence of the essentially rightwing nature of extreme Irish nationalism. However, in Northern Ireland, where the extremists of both the IRA and the Ulster Protestants continued to clash into the 1990s, the conflict took the shape of two nationalisms hostile to each other.

SEE ALSO

Volume 1 Left: Ireland; United Kingdom.
Volume 2 Right: United Kingdom.

BIBLIOGRAPHY

David Fitzpatrick, "Protestant Unionism," *The Oxford Illustrated History of Ireland,* R.F. Foster, ed. (Oxford University Press, 1986); James Mackay, *Michael Collins: A Life* (Mainstream, 1996); "Britain Irish Easter Rebellion, 1916," www.onwar.com (July 2004); Ed Moloney, *A Secret History of the IRA* (Norton, 2003); Brendan O'Brien, *The Long War: The IRA and Sinn Fein, 1985 to Today* (The O'Brien Press, 1993); Richard English, *The History of the IRA* (Oxford University Press, 2003).

JOHN F. MURPHY, JR.
AMERICAN MILITARY UNIVERSITY

Isolationism

ISOLATIONISM IS THE 20th-century term used to describe America's traditional noninvolvement in political and military affairs, particularly in Europe, as well as America's avoidance of entangling alliances, collective security commitments, and international organizations such as the League of Nations. Isolationists, those advocating unconditionally for a policy of isolationism, did not wish to alienate the United States from the rest of the world, nor did they oppose all American activity abroad. Rather, isolationists believed that the United States could lead the world much more effectively by building and sustaining democracy, freedom, and prosperity at home as opposed to diplomatic and military involvement in Europe. Moreover, isolationists favored building and maintaining military forces for the defense of the United States and opposed any attempt to police or rebuild the world in an American image.

Although it is a 20th-century term, the roots of isolationism can be traced back to the colonial period. Beginning with Massachusetts Governor John Winthrop's declaration that Americans dwelt in a "city upon a hill" and Thomas Paine's famous pamphlet *Common Sense* (1776) urging America to "avoid political connections with any European state," the American people were inculcated very early on with the belief that they could choose whether and when to participate in world affairs. President George Washington expressed similar beliefs in his farewell address of 1796, in which he urged his countrymen "to steer clear of permanent alliances with any portion of the foreign world." President Thomas Jefferson further reinforced the isolationist sentiment in America during his first inaugural address of 1801, in which he sought "peace, commerce, and honest friendship with all nations, entangling alliances with none." In 1823, President James Monroe further sought to limit America's political and military commitments to Europe while protecting its predominance in the Western Hemisphere, in what later became known as the Monroe Doctrine.

The isolationist sentiment displayed during the early 19th century fostered an intense belief that America was "a favorite child of God, Nature, and History." This consequently contributed to the development of American nationalism during the second half of the 19th century, further solidifying the isolationist sentiment. During this period, Americans believed "that the United States was so strong, so vigorous, so dynamic— so morally superior—that it could ignore all other countries." In 1863 during the American Civil War, for example, President Abraham Lincoln's secretary of state, William Henry Seward, rejected France's request for American assistance to pressure Russia to deal leniently with revolutionaries in Poland. Seward asserted, "our policy of nonintervention, straight, absolute, and peculiar as it may seem to other nations has become a traditional one, which could not be abandoned without the most urgent occasion, amounting to a manifest necessity."

Moreover, in the midst of the Civil War, Americans began focusing on Reconstruction, industrialization, the settlement of the west, and the development of the new south. Consequently, Americans established a greater sense of security, superiority, and power, which in turn made events in the rest of the world appear even less important than before. According to President Andrew Johnson, America's geographic location, territorial size, and growing industry made America "singularly independent of the varying policy of foreign powers" and protected Americans "against every temptation to enter entangling alliances."

By the end of the 19th century, however, the United States had become an industrial giant with worldwide economic interests, causing American imperialists to look favorably upon the possibility of overseas expansion. Isolationists, however, criticized the views of the imperialists. According to Carl Schurz, the Republican senator from Missouri, imperialism "would violate the isolationist tradition, embroil the United States in foreign wars that did not directly affect its interests, and

give cause for European intervention in the Western Hemisphere."

Nevertheless, the United States annexed Puerto Rico, the Philippines, and Hawaii; established a protectorate over Cuba; assisted Panama in gaining its independence from Colombia; and expanded its trade and investments all over the world. Consequently, the United States found it increasingly difficult to remain isolated from the political affairs of other nations.

The United States entered the 20th century by refusing to abandon its historic policy of isolationism. President Theodore Roosevelt, however, believed that the United States must play a major role in world affairs. He recognized that a major European conflict would affect the United States. Moreover, Roosevelt believed that if England failed to preserve the European balance of power, the United States would be required to do so. According to Roosevelt, "isolationism may have been a wise course for an infant United States"; however, "it was no longer possible in the twentieth century." Roosevelt, however, lacked the support of the American people and Congress. Consequently, Roosevelt used his executive powers to do what he could to maintain the European balance of power by permitting American representatives to participate in the Algerciras Conference in 1906. Although Roosevelt's efforts settled a Franco-German dispute over Morocco, Congress and the American people viewed his actions as an unnecessary abandonment of the isolationist tradition. The Senate, in ratifying the Algerciras agreement, declared that the United States was under no obligation to enforce its provisions.

President Woodrow Wilson shared Roosevelt's belief that America must play a major role in world affairs. At the beginning of World War I in 1914, however, Wilson declared an isolationist policy. According to Wilson, "World War I was a war with which we have nothing to do, whose cause can not touch us," and appealed to his "fellow countrymen to remain impartial in thought as well as in action." Nevertheless, events beyond Wilson's control, such as unrestricted submarine warfare and Zimmermann's telegram, forced the United States to enter the European conflict in April 1917 alongside England and France as an "associated power," further displaying America's continuing desire to remain out of Europe's political and military conflicts.

American isolationists denounced the decision to enter the war. According to Robert La Follette, the Republican senator from Wisconsin, "intervention was a violation of everything for which the Founding Fathers had stood in warning the nation to avoid Europe's squabbles."

At the conclusion of World War I, America was unable to distinguish any demonstrable gain from its involvement in the war, and millions of Americans were determined to prevent its recurrence. As a result, America reverted to its historic policy of isolationism. Isolationists recognized no danger to the nation's interest by detaching the country from the political and military affairs of Europe. Europe's peace, they argued, was not the responsibility of the United States. Consequently, the American people refused to honor the French security treaty promised at Versailles, refused to forgive France's and Britain's wartime loans, and refused to enter the League of Nations. Those most opposed to the League included Republican Senators Henry Cabot Lodge from Massachusetts, William Borah of Idaho, and Hiram Johnson of California.

The full force of the isolationists was not revealed, however, until the 1930s, when President Franklin Roosevelt sought discretionary power to aid victims of aggression. Isolationists fought back so successfully that the years 1934 through 1937 represented the culminating point of isolationist legislation. In 1934, Congress adopted the Johnson Act, which prohibited loans to nations that were in default on their existing obligations to the United States Treasury. In 1935, the Senate refused Roosevelt's request for American participation in the World Court. From 1934 to 1936, the Senate sponsored a Special Committee Investigating the Munitions Industry, chaired by the Republican senator from North Dakota, Gerald Nye. Following its formation in April 1934, the Nye Committee served for two years and became the "principal platform for isolationists preachments." Beginning in 1935, however, American isolationism transformed from mere indifference to the outside world into an active repudiation of anything resembling political, military, and in some cases, economic engagement. Consequently, Congress codified a series of formal neutrality laws seeking to protect the United States from the wars erupting in Europe by outlawing the kinds of contacts that had compromised U.S. neutrality two decades earlier.

The first Neutrality Act, passed in 1935, prohibited the shipment of munitions to nations once the president established the existence of belligerency. In February 1936, Congress extended the Neutrality Act for 14 additional months and also prohibited loans and credits to belligerent nations. In January 1937, given the increasingly unsettled state of the world, Congress resolved to enact permanent neutrality legislation,

Charles Lindbergh, through the America First Committee, was a vocal proponent of America's isolation from European affairs.

which reaffirmed the mandatory ban on arms and loans to countries at war, prohibited Americans from traveling on passenger ships of belligerent nations, and introduced the cash-and-carry principle, requiring warring nations wishing to conduct business with the United States to pay cash for raw materials and other nonmilitary items and carry the goods away on their own ships.

The following year, isolationists encountered their first failure. In January 1938, congressmen voted 209 to 188 against a resolution that would have allowed members of the House of Representatives to consider, debate, and vote on the Ludlow amendment. The proposed amendment, sponsored by Democrat Louis Ludlow of Indiana, would have prohibited Congress from declaring war until confirmed by a majority vote in a national referendum. In 1939, the isolationists began to weaken and Roosevelt increasingly aided the Allies through legislative and executive action. In November 1939, Roosevelt signed the revised Neutrality Act, which lifted the arms embargo, allowing allies France and Britain to purchase arms, ammunition, and combat aircraft from the United States on a cash-and-carry basis. In September 1940, the Burke-Wadsworth selective service bill was passed, invoking the first peacetime draft in American history. Furthermore, Roosevelt transferred 50 World War I destroyers to Britain in exchange for 99-year leases on British air and naval bases in the Western Hemisphere, which was known as the Destroyers-for-Bases deal. In September 1940, in response to Roosevelt's actions, isolationists announced the formation of the America First Committee, which became the leading isolationist mass pressure group battling the foreign policies of the Roosevelt administration. With its national headquarters in Chicago, the America First Committee grew out of an earlier student organization at Yale University founded by R. Douglas Stuart. Stuart served as its national director and General Robert Wood, chairman of the board of Sears Roebuck and Company, served as its national chairman.

The most prominent speakers of the America First Committee included Democratic Senator Burton Wheeler of Montana, Republican Senator Gerald Nye of North Dakota, and Colonel Charles Lindbergh. At its peak, the America First Committee had 450 chapters, a membership of 850,000, and an income of $370,000 donated by 25,000 members. The America First Committee, however, was unable to defeat any of Roosevelt's policies. Consequently, in March 1941, Congress passed and Roosevelt signed the Lend-Lease bill, which permitted the president to "sell, transfer title to, exchange, lease, lend, or otherwise dispose of defense articles to any country whose defense the President deemed vital to the defense of the United States." In July 1941, Roosevelt froze all Japanese assets in the United States. Last, in November 1941, Roosevelt authorized the arming of American merchant ships and permitted them to transport war-materiel cargo to belligerent ports.

The Japanese attack on Pearl Harbor on December 7, 1941, forced the United States into World War II as an active belligerent, disbanded the America First Committee, and ended isolationism. Furthermore, it led the United States to alter its foreign policy fundamentally, assume global political and economic commitments, and accept responsibility for the maintenance of world peace. In 1945, for example, the United States became a charter member of the United Nations, occupying a seat on the Security Council.

In 1949, the United States entered its first binding military alliance, the North Atlantic Treaty Organization (NATO). By the second half of the 20th century, isolationism became a discredited legacy of America's past surfacing in the wake of the Vietnam War.

SEE ALSO

Volume 1 Left: Cominform; Socialism; United States.
Volume 2 Right: Globalization.

BIBLIOGRAPHY

John Whiteclay Chambers II, *Oxford Companion to American Military History* (Oxford University Press, 1999); Wayne S. Cole, *Roosevelt and the Isolationists* (University of Nebraska Press, 1983); Federal Communications Commission-Job Corps, *Dictionary of American History* (Charles Scribner's Sons, 1976); Norman A. Graebner, *America as a World Power: A Realist Appraisal from Wilson to Reagan* (Scholarly Resources, Inc., 1984); Henry F. Graff, *The Presidents: A Reference History* (Charles Scribner's Sons, 1996); Leonard W. Levy and Louis Fisher, *Encyclopedia of the American Presidency* (Simon & Schuster, 1996); Manfred Jonas, *Isolationism in America* (Cornell University Press, 1966); Mary Beth Norton, David M. Katzman, Paul D. Escott, Howard P. Chudacoff, Thomas G. Paterson, William M. Tuttle, Jr., and William J. Brophy, *A People and a Nation: A History of the United States* (Houghton Mifflin, 1996); Ronald E. Powaski, *Toward an Entangling Alliance: American Isolationism, Internationalism, and Europe* (Greenwood Press, 1991).

RONALD C. DESNOYERS, JR.
ROGER WILLIAMS UNIVERSITY

Israel

THE STATE OF ISRAEL HAS long been an important aspect of American politics. The United States has provided Israel with unprecedented aid and support, almost single-handedly ensuring that Israel continues to prosper in the Middle East. Much controversy arises from this relationship, and American politicians have long felt international criticism about why they give so much support to the Jewish state. One contention is that because of the global importance of the Middle East, America's support for Israel gives it a viable partner in the region. The other contention is that America's support for Israel is based on domestic political goals of gaining important Jewish American votes and, equally as important, donations from pro-Israel government lobbyists.

Zionist leaders declared the state of Israel on May 14, 1948, thus creating a Jewish state in the heart of Palestine and the Middle East. Since its beginning, the state of Israel has remained at odds with the Palestinians and its neighboring Arab countries, including Egypt, Iraq, and Syria. The current crisis between Israel and the Palestinians remains one of the most volatile in the world. However, Israel continues to be the dominant Middle East country due to its close relationship with the United States, which grants Israel over $2 billion in aid every year.

While, for the most part, American Jews tend to support the Democratic Party, there has always been a close association between the state of Israel and the Republican Party. This relationship began even before Jewish leaders declared a state in 1948. This close relationship began in the aftermath of World War II, when over 250,000 Jewish refugees remained in former concentration camps. The question of what to do with the displaced persons became a pivotal issue in American politics beginning with the congressional elections in 1946 and the presidential election of 1948, and has continued since.

Thomas Dewey was the Republican governor of New York from 1943 to 1955, and one of the first Republican politicians to identify the importance of the Jewish vote in American politics. Traditionally, American Jewish voters have supported the Democratic Party, largely due to Franklin Roosevelt's concerted effort to win over Jewish voters. Dewey tried to break this trend and thus supported the Zionist policy of allowing the displaced persons to relocate to Palestine, where they would be free from anti-Semitism and able to establish their own private state. Dewey was also the Republican presidential candidate in 1948, although he lost to the incumbent, Harry Truman. Dewey nonetheless advocated for the prospect of a future Jewish state in Palestine, making it a major issue of the election that both parties would subsequently support, setting a standard for Republican politicians ever since.

Dwight Eisenhower was one of the few Republican presidents who believed that a strong American relationship with Israel would hurt American interests with the Arab Middle East. While not every Republican politician supports Israel, very few will be openly critical of the state for fear of domestic political backlash. Eisenhower would openly lessen America's relationship with Israel.

Most significantly, following the Suez Crisis in 1956, in which Eisenhower openly opposed British, French, and Israeli military actions against Egypt, he ordered the Israelis out of the Sinai Peninsula. However, while he placed less emphasis on the Israeli-American relationship, Eisenhower always made sure that he continued America's support of the Jewish state.

Israel's right-wing Ariel Sharon met with a receptive ideology in George W. Bush's White House.

Current events in Israel have caused controversy over America's unprecedented support of the country. While Israel remains in a violent struggle with Hamas, a radical Islamic organization opposed to the Zionist state, it has become susceptible to criticisms of its military actions against Palestinians by other countries. Both Israel and Hamas resort to violence, claiming retribution from the other's latest attack, both sides claiming to be the victims. America's support of Israel and lack of condemnation for its role in the current fighting have been viewed by other nations as biased, and have often divided the United States with members of the United Nations.

In addition, in his support of Israel, George W. Bush continued to refer to the Palestinians as terrorists, and in 2002 openly endorsed Israel's military strikes on Palestinians as being an appropriate defense against terrorism. However, Bush has opposed Israeli plans to build a defensive wall to keep the Palestinians out of the West Bank, and has urged Israeli Prime Minister Ariel Sharon to take steps of good faith toward the Palestinians. The contention of the United Nations Security Council is that Israel has used excessive force in its attacks on the Palestinians. In addition, further criticism claims that Israel illegally occupies territories in the West Bank and Gaza, and that the United States continues to supply Israel with the necessary financial and military aid needed to control its lands. Many nations feel that the U.S. pro-Israel stance is based more on domestic concerns to appeal to wealthy pro-Israel lobbyists as well as an well-organized Jewish-American voting bloc.

However, Bush's support for Sharon received support in America. This is not surprising considering how American and Israeli history has common links. In each country's quest for statehood, they share similar stories of David versus Goliath, and with the early 2000s' War on Terrorism, another common ground is reached as Bush battles al-Qaeda while Sharon confronts Hamas. Americans can identify with Israelis, and continue to support their cause. Bush's pro-Israel policy has been well received by Jewish Americans, who view him much more favorably than they did his father, George H.W. Bush, and could help secure the Republican Party stronger Jewish support.

SEE ALSO

BIBLIOGRAPHY

Isaac Alteras, *Eisenhower and Israel: U.S.-Israeli Relations, 1953–60* (University Press of Florida, 1993); John Bright, *A History of Israel* (S.C.M. Press, 1981); Alan M. Dershowitz, *The Case for Israel* (John Wiley & Sons, 2003); Baruch Kimmerling, *Politicide: Ariel Sharon's War against the Palestinians* (Verso, 2003); Steven L. Spiegel, *The Other Arab-Israeli Conflict: making America's Middle East Policy, from Truman to Reagan* (University of Chicago Press, 1985).

DAVID W. MCBRIDE
UNIVERSITY OF NOTTINGHAM, ENGLAND

Italy

THE POLITICAL HISTORY of the Italian right in the 20th century and into the 21st has been dominated by the figure of the fascist dictator Benito Mussolini and his regime, which repressed political opposition for 20 years and led Italy into the catastrophe of World War II. Since the final fall of Mussolini in 1945, Italian right-

wing parties have had to deal with his and the Fascist Party's (FNP) problematic legacy.

The term *fascism* comes from the Italian *fascio*, derived from the ancient Latin *fasces*, which referred to the bundle of lictors, or axe-headed rods, that stood for the sovereignty of the Roman Republic. The movement, of which Mussolini, a former Socialist Party member, became the leader, or duce, combined strong nationalism with an aggressive new style of activism that prized violence, colonialism, idealism, and anti-materialism.

Mussolini's rise to power started after the general election held in May 1921, which witnessed the election of a conspicuous number of fascist deputies and a surprising success for the FNP leaders. Together with the liberal democrats headed by Giovanni Giolitti, the political force that governed Italy in the first two decades of the 20th century, the fascists had formed the National Blocks. Under the intentions of Giolitti, the National Blocks were to put a stop to the growth of the Fascist Party, whose candidates would be placed on the same list with more experienced and respected liberal politicians, thus standing little chance to be elected.

Yet, the elected deputies for the Blocks were extremely heterogeneous and thus difficult for Giolitti to control, and the fascists managed to elect 45 deputies. The coalition governments that followed the election were unable to govern the country effectively and to put a stop to fascist violence, which started to push Italy toward a totalitarian regime. The fascist March on Rome, which took place in October 1922, signified the end of democracy.

Despite the many Jews who were members of the FNP, Mussolini became Adolf Hitler's main ally in 1937, passing racist and anti-Semitic legislation in Italy and entering World War II in support of Hitler. The disaster of the world conflict led to Mussolini's downfall in 1943, but in German-occupied northern Italy, the Duce was installed as leader of a new puppet fascist-based Italian Social Republic, which waged a savage civil war against Italian anti-fascists in 1944–45. Although the new democratic government officially condemned fascists, the effective repression carried out by the Allied forces and the Italian governing party after the war, the Christian Democrats, was much weaker, allowing a disturbing continuum between the regime and the republic to function as a dam to communism.

The MSI (Movimento Sociale Italiano, Italian Social Movement), the party created in 1947 by former fascists after democracy was restored and the Fascist Party was declared illegal, enthusiastically endorsed the political values that were at the base of the fascist dictatorship. The party drew most of its electoral strength in the southern regions and initially refused to consider anti-fascism a foundational value of the Italian republic. It quickly rose from 2.8 percent in 1948 to 5.8 percent in 1953. In 1954, under the leadership of Arturo Michelini, the party started to accept more moderate positions. In 1960, the MSI gave its external support to the Christian Democratic government led by Fernando Tambroni. As the support of the neofascists was vital for the government's existence, widespread popular demonstrations started throughout Italy, leading to Tambroni's resignation.

The most charismatic leader of the MSI, however, was Giorgio Almirante, who became secretary in 1968 and led the party to its best result in 1972 under the new name of MSI-Destra Nazionale (MSI-National Right), totalling 8.7 percent of the national vote.

The 1980s saw alternate results for the party, which was badly affected by the death of Almirante in 1988 and by judicial inquiries that linked some of its members to cruel terrorist attacks. The ensuing battle between the two main internal currents of the party, led by Gianfranco Fini and Pino Rauti, climaxed at the 1995 Fiuggi Conference, when the MSI was dissolved and the AN (National Alliance) was created with Fini as its leader. Fini progressively moved the party to positions typical of modern conservative parties (economic liberalism, defense of traditional values, opposition to high taxation) and was one of the founders of the Casa delle Libertà (House of Freedoms), the center-right coalition led by media mogul Silvio Berlusconi. Thanks to this alliance, neofascists were able to widen their electoral strength well above the 10 percent of the national vote and covered key government roles in 1994.

Fini became deputy prime minister following the 2001 general election and, in an official visit to Israel in 2003, paid homage to the victims of the Holocaust, retracting his claim that Mussolini was the best statesman of the 20th century. So far, the small groups that split from AN because of disagreements over Fini's moderate line have been unable to seriously damage the party's electoral base.

SEE ALSO

Volume 1 Left: Socialism; Communism; Italy.
Volume 2 Right: Fascism; Germany.

BIBLIOGRAPHY

Noberto Bobbio, *Ideological Profile of Twentieth-Century Italy* (Princeton University Press, 1995); Noberto Bobbio, *Left and Right: The Significance of a Political Distinction* (University of Chicago Press, 1997); Renzo De Felice, *Interpretations of Fascism* (Harvard University Press, 1977); John Pollard, *The Fascist Experience in Italy* (Routledge, 1998).

LUCA PRONO, PH.D.
UNIVERSITY OF NOTTINGHAM, ENGLAND

The Right

J

Japan

POLITICALLY, Japan was an empire ruled by an emperor who claimed direct descent, through an unbroken line of illustrious predecessors, from Amaterasu-Omikami, goddess of the sun. Since 1603, Japan had actually been governed by a delicately balanced system, often described as centralized feudalism, in which prime authority rested with a shogun, the head of the great house of Tokugawa, who ruled from his family's historical capital of Edo (modern Tokyo). In this Japan, politics, like social organization, was carefully stratified along hereditary class lines, and only a small elite was privileged to participate in the making or administering of political decisions. In short, prehistoric Japan was a specie of traditional Asian society, being predominantly rural, agrarian, immobile, stratified, authoritarian, and oligarchic in its primary sociopolitical characteristics.

However, the Meiji Restoration, when Emperor Meiji assumed formal power, marked an end of the long rule of Tokugawa Shogunate (1603–1867). Most of the leaders of the "Restoration Movement" were members of the privileged military or samurai class, operating with the approval of their particular feudal lords and a section of the imperial court nobility. Restoration effectively established a new oligarchy, originally military in nature and regional in its political loyalties, with the Sat-

suma and Chosu clans as primary powers and Tosa and Hizen fiefs as secondary ones. The new oligarchy continued to fear domestic as well as foreign enemies. Thus, for years the Meiji oligarchy was preoccupied with plans to strengthen and modernize the country to prevent political and economic intervention by the imperialist powers of the West. Some argue that the fear of the West spurred the development of Japanese nationalism, which greatly affected the politics of Japan.

Seeing the political change between the enactment of the Meiji constitution in 1890 and the assassination of Prime Minister Inukai, it can reasonably be concluded that the Japanese political system was slowly "evolving" along relatively liberal and democratic lines. During all these years, Japanese politics was largely a product of two major streams of domestic development: one authoritarian and the other parliamentary and at least protoliberal. Nonetheless, under the surface, actually authoritarianism was in the ascendancy.

The social background of the Meiji oligarchy created favorable conditions for the rise of *zaibatsu*, a collective term for the great cartels that controlled major sectors of the nation's economy. The growing weight of *zaibatsu* in the national economy greatly increased their role in domestic politics. Their size and wealth made it inevitable that they would maintain close association with the government. Though their political affiliations varied but all had active bureaucratic connections, they usually cooperated with both the civilian and military oligarchy. Nevertheless, it was not until World War I that some of the largest *zaibatsu* began to ally themselves closely with the major conservative political parties. Political campaigns and elections were very expensive, especially after the introduction of male suffrage in 1925, and *zaibatsu* contributed large sums to campaign funds, which enabled them to extract a substantial amount of political funds.

The period 1932–45 marked a reversion to authoritarian and militaristic ways that were certainly far more in the mainstream of Japan's political traditions than the brief years of "liberalism." The resurgent forces of Japanese militarism and ultranationalism felt threatened by the increasing power of political parties and the attendant development of a parliamentary system. The militarists and the ultranationalists also believed that these were years of unique opportunity for Japan. With intelligence and courage, they held, Japan could become a world power and create an empire that would ultimately dominate all Eastern Asia. If this opportunity were to be missed, however, Japan would have to resign itself to a slow process of national attrition, leading inevitably downward to an insecure and second-class status among the powers.

The shattering defeat in 1945 was a stunning blow to Japan. Although the political consequences of the war and defeat are hard to precisely specify, it does seem probable that the experience significantly increased people's general involvement in and concern about government and politics. The greater political awareness resulting from the postwar years provided a substantial foundation for the ambitious political reform of the Allied Occupation (1945–52). There were two prominent goals for the Allied Occupation: demilitarization and democratization. Demilitarization was a relatively simple problem, but democratization of a nation that had a long history of authoritarianism, militarism, and feudalism was really a complex task.

The basic occupation strategy, therefore, was to involve large section of Japanese people in supporting and implementing the reform programs. These include: 1) the purging of ultranationalist officials from designated public and private offices; 2) expansion of the franchise; 3) granting to labor the right to organize and bargain collectively; 4) land reform; 5) legal reform of the traditional family system; 6) decentralization of the powers of government; and 7) educational reform. These reforms, of course, brought democracy. However, the seeds of right-wing political ideology in Japan were dormant but not destroyed.

World War II General Hideki Tojo, though convicted as a war criminal, is hailed as a Japanese hero by modern right-wing factions.

The reappearance of postwar rightist forces is the subdued continuation of the prewar militarist and ultranationalist forces in Japan. Under the new circumstances, rightist forces backed long Liberal Democratic Party (LDP) rule in Japan. At present, Japan is again at a crossroads where right-wing people see General Hideki Tojo, the World War II war criminal, as a national hero. Harvard-educated commentator and historian, Hideaki Kase's film *Pride*, which glorifies Tojo, has been a smash hit in Japan. Kase is just one of the increasingly influential nationalist voices dominating the verbal civil war over the country's public memory of World War II. Their ranks include the hugely popular Shintaro Ishihara, the governor of Tokyo and the author of the book *Japan That Can Say No*, who is viewed as a possible prime minister, and famed cartoonist Yoshinori Kobayashi, a media favorite with a significant following.

Unapologetic about the war, these neoconservatives have written their own history textbooks to omit unpalatable accounts of the war. They have successfully lobbied to have the rising-sun flag and the national anthem—both closely linked to the war—declared as national symbols. And they have pushed to revise Japan's "Peace" constitution, which they say robs Japan of its sovereignty. "Look at the politics of Japan, and you will see an inclination to the right," said Yoshifumi Tawara, secretary general of the Children and Textbooks Japan Network 21.

SEE ALSO

Volume 1 Left: Japan; Asia.
Volume 2 Right: Asia; Monarchism.

BIBLIOGRAPHY

Ivan I. Morris, *Nationalism and the Right Wing in Japan: A Study of Post-War Trends* (Oxford University Press, 1960); Hayashi Masayuki, "The Emperor's Legions: A History of Japan's Right Wing," AMPO *Japan-Asia Quarterly Review* (v.23/2, 1988); Takagi Masayuki, "The Japanese Right Wing," *Japan Quarterly* (July-September 1989); Brian McVeigh, "Japan's 'Soft' and 'Hard' Nationalism," Japan Policy Research Institute (JPRI) *Working Paper No. 73* (January 2001); Kenneth Szymkowiak and Patricia G. Steinhoff, "Wrapping up in Something Long: Intimidation and Violence by Right-Wing Groups in Postwar Japan," *Terrorism and Political Violence* (v.7/1, 1995); Karel Van Wolferen, *The Enigma of Japanese Power: People and Politics in a Stateless Nation* (Tuttle, 1993).

JITENDRA UTTAM
JAWAHARLAL NEHRU UNIVERSITY, INDIA

John Birch Society

THE JOHN BIRCH Society is a secretive, strongly anticommunist league formed in 1958. Founded by Robert H.W. Welch, Jr., the society was dedicated to the principles—as interpreted by Welch—of the life of John M. Birch, a captain in the U.S. Army who died on August 25, 1945, while on a military mission in China. The society was groundbreaking not only for its extremely conservative principles, but for its political organization as well.

Because of his fluency in speaking Chinese, Birch had been picked to head a mission into China just 10 days after Japan surrendered in World War II. As he moved across China with his party, they were stopped by Chinese soldiers. They took him and another leader of the group to a nearby village, leaving the rest of the group alone. Birch and the other leader were shot and stabbed by the soldiers and left for dead. A village peasant found the other leader barely alive, and managed to get him to safety. Birch, however, did not survive the soldiers' treatment. When the other leader returned to the United States, he testified at a congressional hearing about what had happened.

In the mid-1950s, Welch came across a transcript of this hearing and was taken by the story, both by the seemingly heroic figure of Birch, a modest army captain killed while carrying out his orders, and by the apparent treachery of the soldiers, because China was supposed to have been a U.S. ally at the time. These two points fit into Welch's overriding worldview, that two things were working together to cause chaos in the United States: 1) the actions of the U.S. government helped communism to flourish in places such as Korea and China, and 2) it did not take actions that would have helped stop communism's successes. Either way, clearly only one conclusion could be drawn, at least for Welch: America was under the control of a communist conspiracy. Therefore, there was only one course of action: patriotic Americans must act immediately.

Welch communicated his ideas routinely through publishing lengthy letters, which were privately distributed to the conservative-minded people he had met. Eventually, these letters were bound together, becoming known as *The Black Book*, and then later as *The Politician*. Admittedly, not all conservatives accepted Welch's views. Many were skeptical and believed the decline in America came from a decline in moral values rather than from communist infiltration. However, Welch and his ideas received enough acceptance that he decided to form the John Birch Society.

Welch identified 11 businessmen to attend the founding meeting of the John Birch Society on December 8, 1958. At this meeting, Welch argued that specific actions were needed to fight communism. What happened at this meeting was recorded and distributed through *The Blue Book*, therefore allowing Welch's ideas to circulate nationally. As a result, many people contacted Welch, asking for guidance in setting up their own chapters. The John Birch Society chapters met in people's homes to discuss politics.

The society grew very quickly, claiming tens of thousands of members within just a few years. More important than its official membership numbers, though, was its organization. Welch single-handedly led the society, but gave the impression that the ideas of other people, about where the society should go, were regularly considered. For example, the society publication *American Opinion* provided a channel—the Member's Monthly Messages (MMMs) Page—for individual chapters to regularly submit ideas to Welch. Each idea was acknowledged by paid headquarters staff members who simply responded with the appropriate society stance on the topic, but the acknowledgements invigorated the membership and thereby encouraged the first real grassroots conservative activism in America.

Above all, the John Birch Society defined itself as a group for action, and the people who joined committed themselves to active, public labors for its purpose. The members were expected to participate in the fight against communism by organizing local action on a national society priority, gathering petition signatures, writing letters to local newspapers, and telling friends about the society, for example. These activities helped maintain a sense of urgency and activity among the membership and developed a tight sense of identity among them. These activities also brought the membership a lot of attention, both from other citizens and from groups such as the Federal Bureau of Investigation (FBI), which found the group to be nonthreatening.

While the John Birch Society was not explicitly politically active—Welch was firm about wanting it to remain nonpartisan—their activities helped redefine what was meant by "conservative" in the late 1950s and early 1960s. The society helped give voice to the fears of communism still present in American society, even after the McCarthy hearings. Furthermore, the society enabled radical conservatives to give voice to their concerns, thus demonstrating them as a force in the nation's political discussions. In turn, this forced liberals and moderates of all parties to listen to the society's concerns. Finally, the society was organized so that it generated an incredible amount of attention, so much so that it could not be ignored by the media, politicians, or even society at large. Therefore, it modeled a way to transform average citizens from passive, occasional donors into mobilized and vocal political participants. Though still present today with a website and publications, the society is much less active.

SEE ALSO

Volume 1 Left: Communism; Third International (Comintern); Communist Party, Soviet.
Volume 2 Right: Ideology; McCarthyism; United States; Conservatism.

BIBLIOGRAPHY
Jonathan Schoenwald, *A Time for Choosing: The Rise of Modern American Conservatism* (Oxford University Press, 2001); Benjamin R. Epstein and Arnold Forster, *Report on the John Birch Society* (Random House, 1966); Robert H.W. Welch, Jr., *The Life of John Birch: In the Story of One American Boy, the Ordeal of His Age* (Western Islands Publishers, 1954).

CLARE CALLAGHAN
INDEPENDENT SCHOLAR

Justice

JUSTICE IS THE SET of principles that regulates the process of distribution of goods, rights and duties, benefits and burdens, opportunities, and property in society. It is necessary to distribute scarce goods like wealth, praise, power, and love because there is greater demand for than supply of them. Scarcity leads to debates about the just distribution, for example, of income or political power. What kinds of institutions or organizations should deal with distributions? And which rules should govern their activities?

Justice is divided into distributive, retributive, and corrective branches. Theories of distributive justice stipulate who should get what and how. They also explain, adduce reasons, for the distribution or process of distribution they advocate. Retributive justice, principles of punishment, and corrective justice, principles of compensation, are dependent on distributive justice. When a person violates just distribution, for example by misappropriating something (theft), the violator deserves retribution commensurate with the violation. When persons lose rights or goods that are due them according to distributive justice, they deserve corrective justice, compensation, commensurate with the degree of loss.

The determination of distribution, retribution, and correction by consistent general universal principles (laws) laws should ensure impartiality. Universal laws that govern the behavior of types of individuals who share abstract properties cannot be used to single out particular individuals to settle personal scores. For example, unpleasant people who happen to be innocent should not be subjected to retributive justice, whereas charming crooks who are personal friends of the presiding judge should. Unjust regimes, for example tyrannies, are incapable of being impartial because they are founded on personal patronage and loyalty. In tyrannies, goods and sanctions are distributed according to changing political alliances and distributions of power, and so cannot be submitted to any general principles of justice.

The actual application of principles of justice to real life is not always accurate; it has margins of error. Attempts to limit inaccuracy include better methods of adjudication by trained legal personnel and judges and shifts in the margins of error in one direction through the principle of presumption of innocence, which reduces the margins of judicial error in conviction at the price of increasing them in the direction of acquittal.

The above concept of justice is shared by all, right and left. The right and the left, and various thinkers and schools within each political camp, advocate different conceptions of justice, different principles that should govern distribution. There are many possible ways to distinguish what the political right would characteristically consider as just. Today, most people would associate right-wing conceptions of justice with individual rights, personal autonomy, and responsibility. The political right would consider a just distribution to be less egalitarian than would the left. But this is a difference of degree rather than kind. No currently credible theory, right or left, holds that nothing should be distributed equally or that everything should be distributed equally: A right-wing libertarian like Friedrich von Hayek considered equality before the law a necessary basic condition for a just society. A left-wing theorist like John Rawls accepted that inequalities may be just, as long as they benefit those least favored by them. Still, within these limits right-wing justice tends to be less egalitarian and more individualistic.

In classical Greek and Roman philosophy, there is little emphasis on individual rights and autonomy. Still, ancient philosophers presented plenty of reasons for inegalitarian distributive justice. The ancients considered people to be born different, endowed with different levels of virtues such as wisdom, courage or good character. Therefore, goods such as political power, wealth, and liberty in general should be distributed in accordance with these natural distinctions. The Greeks and the Romans considered some people to be naturally, innately, slaves, and others to be born masters. In the *Republic*, Plato identified justice with a political structure that reflects the differences among three types of people, wise philosophers, loyal and disciplined guardians, and workers, who should respectively rule, fight, and labor. Aristotle also distinguished among three classes of people according to their merit: Pru-

dent masters who deserve to lead and manage states and estates, slaves who have no merit and deserve to be dominated by their masters, and artisans who have technical skills, should be free, but are devoid of political power. Aristotle's theory of distributive justice considers transfers within each class virtuous, but transfers from the masters to others as charity, a vice because it violates the just distributive model.

The introduction of the universal religions, Judaism, Christianity, and Islam, created a prima-facie case against unequal distribution to people who were considered to have been created in the image of the same God. Yet, universal religion preached equality before God, not among men. Natural and divine law was used to legitimize inequality in power and wealth.

JUSTICE AND RIGHTS

The modern right-wing association of justice with individual rights, liberty, and personal autonomy appeared only in the 17th century, with conflicts between European monarchies and their subjects in the presence of budding free-market economies. Citizens who did well economically in industry and trade had a vested interest in protecting their rights to hold on to what they gained and to practice the businesses and professions that brought them that wealth against state interference and taxation.

In the course of debating the contentious distribution of political power and wealth between the state and its citizens, the concept of right gained pivotal significance. Accordingly, justice began to be understood as the total distribution of rights in society. The monarchy and the middle classes each claimed that these rights supported their own position. The same issues of justice and rights were raised again later in the context of the conflict between liberalism and socialism since the early 19th century. This debate leads directly to the contemporary debate on justice between the political right and left.

There are natural, historical, and consequential conceptions of rights, and accordingly of justice. Natural theories of rights and justice claim that people are endowed from birth with certain rights, such as the right to be free economic agents who enjoy the fruits of their labor, and the state is charged with protecting these rights. When the state fulfills these duties, it is just. Historical theories suggest that peoples, families, and societies accumulate rights and duties through their actions in the past. The present distribution of rights is just if it was historically derived according to just rules. Consequentialist, sometimes called utilitarian, conceptions of rights consider a distribution of rights to be just if it is likely to maximize or increase some desired consequence, such as wealth or happiness. Natural, historical, and consequentialist theories of justices have been used separately or in combination with each other by a variety of right-wing thinkers to justify an unequal distribution of scarce goods. Three contemporary thinkers have been particularly influential in this context. The Austrian-born economist Hayek, who taught at the London School of Economics and the University of Chicago, influenced the reforms of the Margaret Thatcher conservative government in Britain and the Reagan Republican administration in the United States during the 1980s. The Harvard philosopher Robert Nozick introduced in his 1974 *Anarchy, State, and Utopia* the most celebrated retort to the academically dominant left-of-center theory of justice of his colleague John Rawls. U.S. Judge Richard Posner is the chief advocate of the economic interpretation of law and justice. Posner, who is a leading public intellectual in the United States, considers just laws to maximize wealth.

HAYEK'S RULES

In the classical liberal tradition, Hayek considered goals and purposes private and personal, neither just nor unjust. The actions people take in pursuit of their goals may be just or unjust since they may affect the actions of others. Justice is rules of conduct that may affect only the "abstract properties," not "concrete content," of the outcomes of individual actions, since "spontaneous order" is the unpredictable result of myriad interactions. Just rules usually protect negative rights, rights "not to" be harmed, interfered with, taxed, etc. Such rules protect "domains of action," where people are free to act without hindrance; these domains constitute rights.

According to Hayek, just rules set the fair rules of the social "game," not who "wins" it. To be impartial, just rules of conduct must be universal, and must conform to Kant's categorical imperative: Act as if the rule that governs your behavior is a law of nature! Hayek thought that these just rules are the rules of and regulations of the free market, most notably respect for private property and enforcement of contracts. Hayek thought that independent historical processes of moral evolution tend to converge in the regulations of the free market. Therefore, these rules of justice are naturally human, independent of history or culture. For Hayek, justice is rules that improve the chances of people to

have their wants satisfied, at the price of risk of unmerited failure. Hayek did not consider income and prices as rewards for past action, but as signals that let people know what they ought to do in the future. Prices are subjective values that people put on each other's labor. For example, surgeons do not earn more than garbage collectors because they are rewarded for their important hard work in the past, but as a signal to young people who choose a profession that there is greater demand in our society for surgeons than for garbage collectors. If too many people become surgeons, and not enough become garbage collectors, the signal may change. The connection among hard work, merit, and success is a tall tale told to children to encourage them to work harder; a tale told again and again by successful business people.

Just rules should encourage the greatest accumulation of wealth through the direction of wealth to where it is most productive, where it most increases the productivity of labor. For example, a privatized factory should be sold to the highest bidder, because that bidder probably bids the highest because of expectations for future returns. The precise rules of the economic game may be improved upon through trial and error, through a natural evolutionary process, as the economy evolves and becomes more sophisticated.

Hayek opposed what he considered "distributive justice," any fixed model of distribution of goods in society. Any fixed distribution requires continuous "correction" of the results of voluntary interactions and exchanges of the exercise of rights. These corrections, usually by a large and overbearing state, necessitate the violation of rights and therefore are unjust. Hayek considered just distributions to be the unintended, unplanned results of myriad interactions between people who follow just rules of conduct. Hayek rejected the idea that justice is distribution commensurate with merit or need. When virtuous people are unsuccessful, it is nobody's fault and it is absurd to blame "society" for it. For example, the just distribution of grades should not correspond with the degree of need of different students to get good grades. Nor does this distribution correspond with how much work each student put into preparing. Some smart students need no preparation, while some students whose aptitudes lie elsewhere may work quite hard with very meager results showing for it.

Hayek retracted from his rules when he accepted certain welfare measures such as education to minors that is paid, though not managed, by the state, a minimal income, and welfare insurance, as long as they do not interfere with the free operation of the market. Like most philosophers who analyzed the concept of rights, Hayek connected them conceptually with duties of people or organizations. Duties are the other side of the coin of rights. A person with a right may demand the government to fulfill or enforce the duty that comes with it. Hayek rejected claims for rights that either "hang" without any duty holder or are held vaguely against "society." For example, Hayek criticized the 1948 Universal Declaration of Human Rights for not specifying the duty holders for these rights. It was an attempt to combine liberal Western political rights with Marxist economic ones, without specifying the duty holder in either case. The wordings are too declarative and vague to be enforceable. For example, it is ridiculous to claim a universal right to holiday with pay that then would have to be applied to the Eskimos, for example. Hayek claimed that economic rights are inconsistent with political rights because their realization necessitates a command economy.

Hayek based his conception of justice on natural rights, further supported by their consequences on maximizing wish fulfillment. He attempted to combine Kantian deontology with Humean utilitarianism. Robert Nozick, by contrast, considered just distribution to follow exclusively from historical rights; he was indifferent to the economic effects of his system of social justice.

NOZICK'S THEORIES

According to Nozick, justice is reducible to individual rights, punishing their violators, and compensating those whose rights were violated. According to Nozick, people have presocial rights to property, life, and liberty. People have these absolute inviolable rights whether or not others recognize them. Rights create negative duties of noninterference, that is, not to infringe upon one's person or property, not to hinder access to exit from a country, and so on. Positive duties are voluntary, they require contractual agreement to do something for another. For example, the right to receive remuneration in exchange for the duty to write an encyclopedic entry, and vice versa, the right to receive an encyclopedic entry in return for the duty to pay for it. Rights are alienable; they can be given up. For example, an owner of a plot of land may alienate that property right and allow others to live on the land. The state cannot violate and must protect these rights.

Nozick's theory of property rights follows John Locke in considering a distribution of holdings just if it

follows just acquisition and just transfer. For example, if one bought a house from its previous owner through voluntary exchange of money for property, and the previous owner had the right to the property by voluntary exchange back to the first owner of the property, the present owner has the right to the property. In his famous *Proviso*, Locke stipulated the conditions of just acquisition: appropriation from nature creates entitlement by the mixture of labor with natural resources if the appropriation leaves as much and as good for others to appropriate. For example, the first settler on an uninhabited land may appropriate it for a homestead by laboring on it, if as much and as good land is left for the next settler. Nozick, however, did not specify the conditions of just acquisition.

Since the redistribution of wealth, for example through transfer payments, taxes for welfare, is involuntary, Nozick considered it theft. The state should limit its role to the protection of rights and enforcement of contracts (voluntary transfers). Nozick supported the classical liberal "night-watchman" conception of the state.

Unlike his main rival to the left, John Rawls, Nozick was indifferent to the outcome of his theory of justice. From Nozick's perspective, it does not matter whether or not justice results in desired consequences such as the maximization of wealth. However, many right-wing thinkers and supporters have come to favor social and economic inequalities not because of their histories, but because they have beneficial effects on the economy as a whole. The comparison between the economic failure of communist command economies and the innovation-generated success of freer economies to the West, and the crisis of the welfare state in the United Kingdom and the United States in the late 1970s led many to endorse right-wing conceptions of justice for their beneficial economic effects for most if not all members of society. These historical developments led to the growing popularity of consequentialist or utilitarian right-wing theories of justice. Unlike the previous types of theories of justice, utilitarians can only justify a model of distribution, not the assignment of a particular right or good to a particular person. For example, a utilitarian may advocate inequality of wealth because the wealthier members of society tend to save more and provide necessary capital for the economy. But the theory would not be useful for identifying who should be wealthy.

Richard Posner considered justice to be conducive to economic efficiency and wealth maximization. Posner supported the same individual rights as Nozick, but for consequentialist reasons, such as wealth maximization and measured willingness to pay for satisfactions. In an efficient, just society, goods are in the hands of the people who are most willing and able to pay for them because they gain the most utility from owning them. This is done by voluntary exchange, when the buyers obviously value a commodity more than the sellers. The more free exchanges, the more wealth utility is generated. With a free market, low transaction costs, and no monopolies, the market tends to reach maximal utility.

Just laws should reduce transaction costs and compensate for market failures such as externalities (costs that are not borne by buyers or owners, such as air pollution), information shortages (when buyers cannot make rational choices because they do not possess sufficient information about market conditions), and monopolies. Posner denied that there is a problem of distributive justice in an efficient market. As long as transaction costs are low, properties end up owned by those ready to pay the most for them. Posner believed that this is an improvement over previous versions of utilitarianism because wealth, unlike happiness, is more easily quantified empirically as the end of justice.

All right-wing theorists of justice criticize left-wing, egalitarian conceptions of justice for being internally inconsistent. If justice encompasses all rights, and rights for some people necessarily entail duties for other people, there are only so many rights that may be fulfilled. More rights entail more duties that in turn curtail other rights. The failure of communism and the crisis of the welfare state again strengthened the hand of right-wing theories of justice. On the other hand, the claims for restitution for past injustice in the form of theft of property (in colonialism) and labor (slavery) have led the political right to further concentrate on utilitarian arguments. The new, post-1990 emphasis in international politics on universal human rights as the basic component of justice divided the political right into those who call for a universal enforcement of human rights by military intervention, and those who favor a more limited role for the state, not just in distributive justice within its own society but also in the export of justice to other societies.

SEE ALSO

Volume 1 Left: Liberalism; Human Rights; Civil Rights. *Volume 2 Right:* Elitism; Colonialism; Monarchism.

BIBLIOGRAPHY

Aristotle, *Politics*, Benjamin Jowett, trans. (Dover, 2000); Tom Campbell, *Justice* (St. Martin's Press, 2001); F.A. Hayek, *Law, Legislation and Liberty: A New Statement of the Liberal Principle of Justice and Political Economy* (University of Chicago Press, 1976); John Locke, *Two Essays on Government* (Cambridge University Press, 1988); Robert Nozick, *Anarchy, State, and Utopia* (Basic Books, 1974); Richard Posner, *The Economics of Justice* (Harvard University Press, 1981).

AVIEZER TUCKER
AUSTRALIAN NATIONAL UNIVERSITY

The Right

Khomeini, Ruhollah (1900–1989)

AYATOLLAH RUHOLLAH Khomeini was the spiritual head (imam) of the Iranian Shia Muslims and leader of the Islamic Revolution of 1979 that overthrew Mohammad Reza Pahlavi, the Shah of Iran. Historians lay the blame on the shah or monarch himself for his Western-leaning social engineering using petrodollars in the previous decades. There was no popular demand for the shah's "white revolution" from above when, according to his words, "the whole structure was being turned upset down" through the attempt of rapid modernization.

In the 1960s, one of the country's leading ayatollahs, Khomeini, deploring the "moral degradation" he saw around him in women's emancipation and national secularization, pledged his opposition "as long as there was blood in my veins." Khomeini preached that the Shia doctrine of quietism, *taguiyya*, was a negation of Islam, and that Muslims were obliged to struggle for an Islamic state. The shah, who despised the religious establishment as bearded parasites living in the dark ages, paid little heed to the homilies of Khomeini, who in turn branded him as Genghis Khan's successor, who would have to go. But first, it was the ayatollah who had to spend 15 emigrant years in Turkey, Iraq, and France, tirelessly campaigning against the Pahlavi dynasty and handily making use of its faults. Everything worked

well against the shah: his pro-Western sympathies, economic errors, too-fast transformation of everyday life, and ignoring the servants of Islam. Khomeini got the Holy Banner into his hands. Maybe, in other cases, it would not be so dangerous if one recollects Ataturk, who dared to challenge Islam in Turkey 50 years earlier and won the battle. But it was quite different with Iran. There wasn't a revolutionary upsurge of lower classes to support the modernization; the mullahs' (religious leaders') reputation was sacrosanct. Instead, there was the hated tyrant who, according to the Shiite canon, had no formal right to reign over the faithful. The educated spoke for securing Islamic traditions too. Yeoman farmers, turned by the shah into a rural proletariat, were accruing grudges against being resettled to "model towns"; meanwhile their sons went into the cities and formed the ayatollah's mob of anti-government protestors. Their brothers in the army were reluctant to shoot at them when the time came.

The shah, faced with persistent insurgencies, lost the will for power and fled the country on January 16, 1979, to die in exile a year later. Khomeini returned to Iran triumphantly on February 1, 1979. Different elements of society created a strange alliance around him. This coalition of nationalists, liberal Islamists, secularists, and leftists soon decayed as the clerics began to rule the state as Khomeini seized ultimate power on February 11, 1979. After the referendum, an Islamic republic was declared in which a president was elected every four years. Only the candidates approved by the top clergy could run for the office. Khomeini himself became head of state as leader of the revolution, and later supreme spiritual leader, being vested with both political and religious primacy and implementing *velayaet-e faquih* (the guardianship of the jurisconsult). The Islamic revolution was true to conservative type because its leader's goal was to reestablish Sharia or Islamic Law and traditions.

Khomeini proclaimed his intention to spread the Islamic Revolution to neighboring countries and further on to the whole world. The major obstacle and main power hostile to this project was sure to be the United States, which was stigmatized by Khomeini as "Big Satan." His storm-troopers, mostly students, named Guards of Islamic Revolution, captured the American embassy in Tehran, holding diplomats hostage for 444 days. "It's almost impossible to deal with a crazy man, except that he does have religious beliefs, and the world of Islam will be damaged if a fanatic like him should commit murder in the name of religion against 60 innocent people," wrote President Jimmy Carter, who unsuccessfully attempted to rescue the captives militarily; America was obliged to ransom them at a heavy price.

Being a political and religious zealot, Khomeini turned Iran into a militant, intolerant theocracy. In the first two years of its existence, it executed over 8,000 people, convicted in Islamic courts of being "enemies of Allah." It dispatched the minorities' leaders and wrecked churches and synagogues. Tens of thousands of Iran's professional and middle classes were expelled or forced to flee the country. Khomeini's harassment generated great sociopolitical tension in Iran. The neighboring dictator of Iraq, Saddam Hussein, decided to take advantage of the situation and occupied a set of disputable bordering Iranian territories. Khomeini saw Allah's gift in the bloody war of 1980 to 1988, which was necessary in order for him to unite the people and effectively rule the country.

In 1988, an established Anglo-Indian writer, Salman Rushdie, published a controversial book of fiction, *The Satanic Verses*, which drew Khomeini's attention, who pontificated: "I inform the proud Muslim people of the world that the author of *The Satanic Verses* book, which is against Islam, the Prophet and Koran, and all those involved in its publication who were aware of its content, are sentenced to death." In this case, Khomeini's intolerant action formed a strange conjunction of the right and the left, who became as hostile to Khomeini as the White House was. Rushdie became a Noble Prize winner and multimillionaire, but he also had to live incognito, being concealed from paid and voluntarily committed murderers who were eager to accomplish the imam's fatwa (proclamation).

Strengthening of the Islam factor in world politics is firmly associated with Khomeini's name. His teaching and policy provided enormous impetus to the Islamic revival, politicization of Islam, and Islamization of politics in Eurasia. The vocabulary of jihad (holy war) and martyrdom was vindicated. His choice was the absolute denial of the West as the incarnation of evil. The most extremist militant anti-Western and anti-Israeli groups in the Middle East and worldwide were sponsored by him or regarded him as their patron. "Our politics is our religion and our religion is our politics," his followers declared. His authority remained beyond question up to his death. The regime he created remains largely in place in the early 2000s, out of step with its neighbors and at odds with much of the rest of the world.

SEE ALSO

Volume 1 Left: Iran; Church and State Separation; Carter, James E.
Volume 2 Right: Iran; Iraq; Religion.

BIBLIOGRAPHY

Imam Sayyid Ruhollah al-Musavi al-Khomeini, "The Last Will," www.wandea.org.pl (July 2004); Kazem Ghazi Zadeh, "General Principles of Imam Khumayni's Political Thought," www.wandea.org.pl (July 2004); R.A. Khumaynei, ed., *Sayings of the Ayatollah Khomeini: Political, Philosophical, Social, & Religious* (Bantam Books, 1985); H.E. Chehabi, *Iranian Politics and Religious Modernism: The Liberation Movement of Iran under the Shah and Khomeini* (Cornell University Press, 1990); William Forbis, *Fall of the Peacock Throne* (McGraw-Hill, 1981); Vanessa Martin, *Creating an Islamic State: Khomeini and the Making of New Iran* (Tauris, 2000); Baqer Moin, *Khomeini: Life of the Ayatollah* (Tauris, 1999).

IGOR CHARSKYKH
DONETSK NATIONAL UNIVERSITY, UKRAINE

Korea, South

THE REPUBLIC OF KOREA (ROK), or South Korea, was established August 15, 1948. Syngman Rhee was chosen as the first president through elections supervised by the United Nations. The period of Rhee's rule is the First Republic. From the end of the Korean War (1950–53) until 1960, Rhee, who was a graduate of several American universities, grew increasingly autocratic. He was supported by the Liberal Party and by the Democratic Party. He lost Democratic Party support over his autocratic rule. Rhee's government was marked by enough corruption that it eventually sparked riots. Repression evoked more civil disturbances, forcing his resignation.

From April 1960 until May 1961, there was a brief period of democratic rule in the Second Republic. The constitution was revised and Chang Myon, head of the Democratic Party, was elected prime minister. However, factions in the Democratic Party fought bitterly for power. The military, fearing chaos, took control on May 16, 1961.

Major General Park Chung Hee, along with other officers, created the Supreme Council for National Reconstruction. The National Assembly was abolished. Military officers were put in charge of the government's agencies. In June 1961, General Park established the Korean Central Intelligence Agency (KCIA), headed by Colonel Kim Jong-pil. After Park organized the Democratic Republic Party, he retired from the military. He ran as president in October 1963, winning only narrowly. He won elections in 1967 and 1971 during a time of great economic development. However, he moved the regime ever closer to dictatorship until in October 1972 he dissolved the National Assembly and offered the country a new constitution, the *yushin* ("renewal") reform. The Yushin Constitution made the president the head of the military and the civil administration, and the chairman of the National Conference for Unification. This body was an electoral college for electing the president.

In 1975, Park enacted Emergency Measure Number 9 to meet increasing opposition. This law made it a crime to criticize the Yushin Constitution. On October 26, 1979, Kim Jae Gyu, head of the KCIA, assassinated Park. The Yushin government collapsed and civilian rule was restored. In December 1979, Choi Kyu Ha, head of the interim civilian government, released numerous political prisoners. The Democratic Republic Party, headed by Kim Jong-pil, and the New Democratic Party, headed by Kim Young Sam began to compete vigorously for votes in the coming election. In the absence of repression, wage strikes, student protests, and factional struggles within the parties occurred To stop student protests aimed at removing the military from politics, Major General Chun Doo-hwan declared martial law on May 17, 1980. Basic civil rights were suspended and opponents were jailed. Revolts broke out in several locations with fighting that killed several thousand people. Four top generals created a Special Committee for National Security Measures. They closed publications, abolished political parties, and repressed dissent. In 1980 the Fifth Republic was established. Retired General Chun Doo Hwan was elected president. In 1987, protests led to the "democratic opening" and the end of autocratic and military rule and the Sixth Republic.

Until 1988, autocrats or military dictators usually governed. In 1989, the right wing was divided between the Peace and Democracy Party and the Reunification Democratic Party, along with several splinter parties. Party mergers and splits have continued to occur since then. They were able to exclude the left for several more years. For most of its history Korea was the "Hermit Kingdom" and a protectorate of China. Now Korean nationalism is divided between those on the right who look to the United States and those on the left who look to China.

SEE ALSO
Volume 1 Left: Korea, South; Korea, North; Asia.
Volume 2 Right: Asia.

BIBLIOGRAPHY
Michael Breen, *The Koreans: Who They Are, What They Want, Where Their Future Lies* (St. Martin's Press, 2004); Donald Stone MacDonald, *The Koreans: Contemporary Politics and Society* (Westview Press, 1996); Jongryn Mo and Chung-in Moon, eds., *Democracy and the Korean Economy* (Hoover Institution Press).

ANDREW J. WASKEY
DALTON STATE COLLEGE

Ku Klux Klan

THE KU KLUX KLAN (KKK) is a nativist and racist organization that first appeared in the American South during radical Reconstruction. The KKK has waxed and waned over time as its potential followers have perceived challenges to their extremely conservative view of what is truly American. Although the first Klan leadership came from leading Confederates, with each revival it has tended to attract lower-class individuals while middle-class "respectable" nativists and racists have preferred to work through such organizations as White Citizens Councils and the Council of Conservative Citizens.

The American Civil War was a struggle to define the Union, with the Confederacy seeking to sever it and the Lincoln Republicans seeking to preserve it. For radical Republicans the war was more than simply an attempt to coerce the seceded states back into the Union. For the radicals, the war's end was an opportunity to destroy the old power structure and establish a new one more compatible with radical tastes. They legislated measures to provide for black rights and to establish federal dominance over the states.

President Andrew Johnson and many southerners disliked the Freedmen's Bureau, established by Congress in March 1865. The bureau worked to help former slaves make the transition to free status. It found jobs and helped create health and educational facilities. In its first year, it established over 4,000 schools and 100 hospitals as well as food and shelter. Congress attempted to expand the bureau in February 1866. Johnson vetoed this bill as well as the Civil Rights Bill that countered the southern Black Codes, which some states had enacted to control the newly freed blacks by limiting their voting rights, their rights to serve on juries, their right to testify, and more important in the short run, their rights to carry weapons or to work in certain jobs. The radicals increased their majority in the elections of 1866. The Reconstruction Act of 1867 established five military districts that covered the South. It mandated new elections with suffrage for male freedmen. It required the Southern states to guarantee adult suffrage and ratify the Fourteenth Amendment before they could be readmitted to the Union. This time, Congress had the radical votes to override Johnson's veto.

THE FIRST KLAN

While Congress was fighting the executive branch, in Pulaski, Tennessee, in May 1866, the first Ku Klux Klan organization was forming. The KKK uniform included masks, white cardboard hats, and sheets. The KKK tortured and killed blacks, white sympathizers, and immigrants (the KKK blamed immigrants for electing radicals).

In April 1867 in Nashville, Tennessee, the local Klans came together to form a broader umbrella group. The leaders were mostly former Confederate soldiers. The reputed first Grand Wizard, Nathan Bedford Forrest, had had a distinguished military career as a Confederate soldier, rising from private to lieutenant

general. The war destroyed him financially, and he struggled to rebuild as a planter and insurance salesman in postwar Tennessee before becoming in the 1870s a railroad president in Alabama. Forrest left the Klan when it became too violent for him. The Klan peaked was between 1868 and 1870. Forrest attempted to disband the KKK in 1869, but local klaverns persisted even after the overall organization disappeared. The KKK was important in reestablishing white rule in Tennessee, Georgia, and North Carolina from 1868 to 1870.

KKK-like groups included the White Brotherhood, the Knights of the White Camellia, and others. Their initial purpose was to intimidate the freedmen from voting. Even after whites had reestablished control of state and local governments, the KKK and other groups continued to threaten blacks who dared to increase their influence or independence by unionizing, becoming financial successes, organizing against oppression, or otherwise seeming to forget their place in the stratified society.

Congress, still dominated by radical Republicans such as Benjamin Butler, asked President Ulysses S. Grant to investigate the KKK, which he did in 1870. In 1871, a grand jury reported that the KKK was an organized and strong force with a sizeable membership, arms, and a willingness to resort to night riding and terrorism against the Republican Party in the South, white or black. The Force Act of 1870 and Ku Klux KLan Act of 1871 gave Grant the power to suspend habeas corpus in counties where the KKK was active. He also had authority to use force to suppress disturbances and to impose severe financial penalties on terrorist organizations. He used the legislation several times—sending troops to South Carolina, sending troops to some other areas, arresting hundreds of Southerners for conspiracy—but as the Radical commitment waned and conservatives recaptured control of areas where blacks enjoyed a temporary feeling of equality, social and political arrangements became more satisfactory to the Klan. With blacks relegated to second- or third-class status and whites back in control, the KKK had won its fight for white supremacy. In an environment compatible with its interests, the KKK faded away. By the time the Supreme Court ruled the Ku Klux Klan Act unconstitutional in 1882, the point was moot.

The years between Reconstruction and World War I were again turbulent as the United States closed its frontier and industrialized rapidly and ruthlessly. The closing of the frontier and the opening of industrial jobs to unskilled labor were factors in the shift from traditional immigration patterns. New immigrants from southern and eastern Europe—Jews and Catholics as well—revived the nativist impulse. While elite and middle class reformers battled in the press and the courts to control the new immigration, there was no need for violence. The KKK slumbered until 1915.

Then, the United States was wallowing in a resurgent racism that had begun in the 1890s, formalized by *Plessy v. Ferguson*. William J. Simmons, who had read Thomas Dixon's *The Ku Klux Klan* (1905) and watched D.W. Griffith's *Birth of a Nation* reformed the Klan in that year. Simmons's main opponent was the National Association for the Advancement of Colored People (NAACP), which rejected the accommodationist philosophy of Booker T. Washington, which had dominated years of the nadir of race relations. World War I brought out a decline in lynching. The end of the war saw a massive increase, with more than 70 black lynching victims, including 10 in uniform. World War I produced a "New Negro," less subservient and disinclined to accommodate to racism. From 1919 to 1922, another 239 lynchings occurred, and unpunished white-on-black violence increased.

The KKK after World War I incorporated a strong nativist animosity toward foreigners as well as socialists, communists, Jews, and Catholics. In the 1920s, the KKK was strong. It held its 1920 convention in Atlanta, Georgia, reputedly the area of strongest Klan support. Quickly the KKK moved out of the South. The leadership of Hiram W. Evans after 1922 led the organization to sufficient political strength in the 1920s that Klansmen served in state office in Maine, Indiana, Oregon, Texas, and Oklahoma. Membership in 1925 was estimated at 4 million. The Klan was conviction-proof in the South, facing generally sympathetic white juries.

Excess brought the KKK down—temporarily. In Indiana, finally, a Klan leader, David C. Stephenson, was convicted of second-degree murder. Other Klansmen, including the governor and the mayor of Indianapolis, were revealed as corrupt, and the membership plummeted to 30,000. Through the 1930s and 1940s, the organization declined, disbanding in 1944. The end of World War II and the black demands for equality that sparked the civil rights movement of the 1950s brought the Klan back to life. Robert Shelton led the White Knights of the Ku Klux Klan, but there were many other Klans in the 1950s South. Klan intimidation in Mississippi was such that in 1960, only 2 percent of the African American population was registered to vote; yet blacks were 42 percent of the Mississippi population. Lynching went through a resurgence too.

The 1963 bombing of the Sixteenth Street Baptist Church in Alabama killed four girls and injured 23. Identified by a witness, Robert Chambliss was arrested and charged with placing the bomb and committing murder as well as possessing dynamite without a permit. He was convicted on the lesser charge. The NAACP and other organizations began the Freedom Summer in 1964. White mobs often targeted the "freedom schools" in Mississippi. Methods of intimidation included firebombing of homes and churches as well as the beating of volunteers. In 1964, the KKK murdered three men. Although the violence garnered national publicity, the tide was with the Klan as the civil rights movement faded and bigotry went underground in the 1970s and 1980s.

In 1981 in Mobile, Alabama, KKK members, upset at a jury verdict clearing a black man in a policeman's murder, decided to lynch a black as a lesson. They lynched 19-year-old Michael Donald. A token police investigation produced a whitewash and a protest march led by Jesse Jackson. The FBI took over the case and got an easy confession. The case was the springboard for the demise of the Klan. The mother of the victim contacted the Southern Poverty Law Center, which helped her file a civil suit against the Klan. In 1987, a white jury ordered the Klan to pay Donald's mother $7 million. The Klan lost all assets, including its Tuscaloosa headquarters. The execution of the killer in 1997 was the first instance since 1913 that a white man had gone to his legal death for a crime against a black man.

By 2002, there was no national Klan. Would-be members had other outlets, such as the Aryan Nations and militias. In 1977, Bill Baxley became attorney general of Alabama. He reopened the Chambliss case, using evidence ignored in the first trial. Convicted, Chambliss was sentenced to life. The Federal Bureau of Investigation announced in 2000 that four Klansmen, including Chambliss, had bombed the Sixteenth Street Baptist Church in 1963. One was dead, but the FBI arrested the other two. One was convicted in 2002.

The Klan, in its first incarnation, represented a form of resistance by terror to the perceived threat of black political power during Reconstruction. In its second incarnation, from the 1920s into the modern era, it has taken on a broader form of reactionary resistance to a variety of changes in American life, including not only changes in white-black relations but also the impact of immigration and urbanization. In this regard, local remnants of the Klan in the early 21st century represent examples of extreme reactionary and sometimes violent organizations.

BIBLIOGRAPHY

Anti-Defamation League, "Extremism in America: Ku Klux Klan, 2004," www.adl.org (January 2004); Kathleen M. Blee, *Women of the Klan: Racism and Gender in the 1920s* (University of California Press, 1991); David Mark Chalmers, *Hooded Americanism: History of the Ku Klux Klan* (New Viewpoints, 1981); Nancy MacLean, *Behind the Mask of Chivalry: The Making of the Second Ku Klux Klan* (Oxford University Press, 1955); Southern Poverty Law Center, "The Intelligence Project: Tracking the Threat of Hate," www.splcenter.org (January 2004); Spartacus Schoolnet, "Ku Klux Klan," www.spartacus.schoolnet.co.uk (January 2004).

JOHN BARNHILL, PH.D.
INDEPENDENT SCHOLAR

Kuomintang

THE KUOMINTANG had its origins in the Chinese Revolution of 1912. In that year, the Ching (Manchu) Dynasty had been overthrown, after ruling China since 1644. The revolt had been instigated by those who wished to see the decrepit, Mandarin-governed kingdom replaced by a modern state. This desire had received renewed impetus by the humbling of China by foreign powers, who had divided the once proud land into spheres of influence. Also, the military weakness of the Chings had been shown by their inability to protect China during the 1894–95 war with Japan and the foreign expeditions during the Boxer Rebellion of 1900.

Perhaps the most important agent for change in China came from the overseas Chinese, the community that had sought avenues for prosperity closed to them at home. The overseas Chinese have been portrayed, with varying degrees of understanding, by fiction writers as diverse as the Englishman Joseph Conrad in Typhoon, and by Americans such as Ambrose Bierce and Mark Twain.

By the opening years of the 20th century, the outspoken leader for a new China among the overseas community was Doctor Sun Yat-sen, who had been born in 1866 in Choyhung, China. After spending some years in still-independent Hawaii, he received his medical degree in the British colony of Hong Kong in 1892. He opened his first office in Portuguese Macao. In Hong Kong, he was exposed to Western ideals of democracy, as he would be in later residence in the United States. Surprisingly, he later abandoned his Western political beliefs in emulation of the communist regime in Russia, imposed by the Bolshevik Revolution of November 1917. Faced with the unique problems of still-feudal China, Sun felt the communist model provided the better avenue for Chinese modernization. Like many modernizing Chinese of the revolutionary generation, he had embraced Protestantism as his religion. Among those whom Sun would later consider his "sworn brothers" in conspiracy was Charles Jones Soong, whose family would make a lasting impression on modern China. Charles Soong had converted to Methodism in 1880 in Wilmington, North Carolina.

In his search for allies to unseat the Manchus, Sun allied himself with the Chinese secret societies, whose descendants include the Triads, which play an influential role in global organized crime. However, historically, they had been founded as resistance groups against the Manchu invaders. They had been guerrilla fighters defending the last native Chinese dynasty, the Ming, against the Manchu invaders, as Martin Booth writes in *The Dragon Syndicates*. The groups had unified under the battle cry of "fan ching—fuk ming" ("overthrow the Ching—bring back the Ming"). At the same time, Sun sought the support of Japan, which was attempting to capitalize on its ascendant role in East Asia following the humbling of Russia in the 1904–05 war. Japanese influence was not in itself inimical. The Emperor Meiji-Mutsohito was attempting to lay the foundations of a liberal parliamentary system in Japan in this period.

With the support of the secret societies, the overseas community, and Meiji Japan, Sun founded the Tung Meng Hui, or Revolutionary Brotherhood, in Japan in 1905, shortly after the struggle with Tzarist Russia. The seeds of the future Kuomintang, or Nationalist Party, were in Sun's Revolutionary Brotherhood, and its philosophy foreshadowed that of the later organization. From the first enunciation of his Three Principles, Sun felt the Chinese people should have an integral state of their own, with their own self-rule, and opportunity for economic growth. When revolution broke out, Sun returned to China and was elected president of the new republic at Nanking on New Year's Day, 1912. Yet surprisingly, he would abdicate power to General Yuan Shih-kai, a holdover from the Manchus, in March 1912. At the same time, the chief organizer of

Chiang Kai-shek (above) led the rightist Kuomintang Party and was defeated by Mao Zedong's leftist communists.

purge of the communists in Shanghai designed to destroy their influence within the Kuomintang and China. The adviser Borodin hastily fled north to the safety of the Soviet Union. Chiang became the paramount ruler of China in 1928 with the success of his Northern Expedition. But the feud with the Chinese communists, although temporarily buried during the fighting with Japan, endured for 20 years. In 1937, in a forced meeting at Sian with communist emissary Chou En-lai, Chiang would agree to a wartime Popular Front movement against the Japanese invaders. However, after the war, the internecine civil war erupted again, and Chiang and the Kuomintang were forced to retreat to the island of Taiwan in October 1949, protected by battle squadrons of the U.S. Navy. Mao Zedong, although not an early leader of the Chinese Communist Party, had emerged as its chairman during the long battle with Chiang.

In Taiwan, Chiang established the Kuomintang in power again. Protected by anti-communist administrations in Washington, D.C., Taiwan under the nationalists became one of the first economic successes of post-World War II Asia. Politically, Chiang very much still dominated the scene. In 1972, Chiang felt betrayed when American President Richard M. Nixon visited the communist People's Republic to establish normal relations between the two countries in an historic meeting in Shanghai. However, the American guarantee of protection for the Kuomintang regime in Taiwan, should the mainland Chinese attempt to unify Taiwan with the rest of China by force, remained tacitly intact. When Chiang died in April 1975, his son, Chiang Ching-kuo, bowing to growing demands for democracy, began a necessary liberalization of the Kuomintang and the Taiwanese government. In March 2000, nearly 90 years of Kuomintang rule ended with the free election in Taiwan of Chen Shui-bian's Democratic Progressive Party. However, the threat of mainland Chinese invasion should Taiwan declare independence remains frightening and real.

SEE ALSO

Volume 1 Left: China; Communism; Soviet Union; Maoism.
Volume 2 Right: McCarthyism; United States; China.

BIBLIOGRAPHY

Don Lawson, *The Eagle and the Dragon: The History of U.S.-China Relations* (Crowell, 1985); A. Whitney Griswold, *The Far Eastern Policy of the United States* (Yale University Press, 1938); Martin Booth, *The Dragon Syndicates: The Global Phenomenon of the Triads* (Carroll and Graf, 1999); Lyon Sharman, *Sun Yat-sen: A Critical Biography* (Stanford University

the Kuomintang, Sung Chiao-jen, was assassinated. The entry of Yuan Shih-kai began the devastating era of the *tuchuns,* the Chinese warlords, usually provincial military governors, who devastated China with their wars.

Meanwhile, in 1923, Sun began to allow communists to join the Kuomintang, which opened up for him funds from the communist regime in Moscow, Russia. Soviet advisers followed, notably Mikhail Borodin. Chiang Kai-shek, a leading Kuomintang military light, studied in the Soviet Union.

However, on March 12, 1925, Sun died. Immediately, a rift developed between the communists in the Kuomintang and Chiang Kai-shek, who was militantly anti-communist. In 1927, Chiang backed a bloody

Press, 1934); Lloyd E. Eastman, ed., *Chiang Kai-shek's Secret Past: The Memoir of His Second Wife, Ch'en Chieh-ju* (Westview Press, 1993); Edgar Snow, *Red Star over China* (Bantam Books, 1978), Jonathan D. Spence, *The Gate of Heavenly Peace: The Chinese and Their Revolution, 1895–1980* (Viking Press, 1981); Jerry Israel, *Progressivism and the Open Door: America and China* (University of Pittsburgh Press, 1971).

JOHN F. MURPHY, JR.
AMERICAN MILITARY UNIVERSITY

The Right

L

La Guardia, Fiorello H. (1882–1947)

FIORELLO H. LA GUARDIA was a maverick politician who was instrumental in bringing about a series of reforms during 12 years as mayor of New York City, and whose popularity sparked New York's unusual multiparty political system. Fiorello Raffaele Enrico La Guardia was born at 7 Varick Place near Manhattan's Washington Square, the second of three children of Achille La Guardia and Irene Luzzato (Coen) La Guardia. Achille, a musician, was unable to find work in the depressed early 1880s and enlisted in the U.S. Army. The family relocated to Dakota Territory (now North Dakota) in 1885. La Guardia spent his formative years in Prescott, Arizona Territory, and always regarded it as his hometown. Although neither parent was active in their respective religions, they sent their children to the Episcopal church because it was the best in Prescott. Fiorello changed his middle name to Henry.

At age 15, he enlisted in the Spanish-American War as a correspondent for the *St. Louis Post-Dispatch* and was sent to Cuba. After the war, the family returned to Irene's hometown of Trieste, then part of Austria. La Guardia joined the U.S. consular staff in Budapest, Hungary, at age 18 and served in various postings in southeastern Europe for six years before returning to New York to study law. La Guardia became involved in the Republican Party in these days, when it was the more progressive of the two major parties, and because it was not the machine party that governed New York City. He graduated from New York University in 1910 and opened an office on William Street. He made his first run for Congress in 1914 but lost to a candidate of the Tammany Hall (Democratic) machine. He never stopped running and won the seat in 1916, making him the first Italian American to serve in Congress. He served as an aviator in World War I while a Congressman.

He was reelected in 1918 but ran instead for president of the New York City Board of Aldermen in 1919. It was unusual for a congressman to run for local office, but La Guardia was the first Republican to win citywide. La Guardia chose to return to Washington, D.C., in 1922, running from a New York Upper East Side district. Tammany Hall smeared La Guardia, whose mother was Jewish, as an anti-Semite. La Guardia bested the Jewish Democratic candidate (who didn't speak a word of Yiddish) in a Yiddish debate and won the election. La Guardia was reelected until his defeat in the Democratic landslide of 1932. His greatest legislative achievement was the Norris-La Guardia Act of 1932, which guaranteed rights to striking workers.

La Guardia considered joining the Franklin Roosevelt administration, but chose to return to New York and run for mayor. The Tammany machine was in chaos over the mid-campaign resignation of incumbent James Walker in a scandal. La Guardia easily won as a fusion candidate. His mayoralty was marked by his sweeping reorganization of the city government, which led to the death of the Democratic machine. La Guardia's electoral success prompted the creation of a third party, the American Labor Party, so traditional Democratic voters could vote for Republican La Guardia at the top of the ticket and then bring in the rest of the Democratic ticket.

This helped La Guardia win as both the Republican and Labor candidate in 1937. Although the party was supplanted by the Liberal Party eventually, it was the origin of New York's unique system whereby multiple parties run the same candidates (and third-party candidates sometimes win). La Guardia was also a major player, along with New York state official Robert Moses, in making New York City a modern metropolis by securing state and federal funds for public works projects in the city. He was elected to an unprecedented third term in 1941.

Always a colorful and blunt personality, he is perhaps best remembered by New Yorkers for his reading of comic strips on the radio during a 1945 newspaper strike. A major legacy of his was replacing the Tammany Hall machine with a large bureaucracy that continued to grow until New York City's bankruptcy in the 1970s.

La Guardia married Thea Almerigotti in 1919. They had a daughter, Fioretta, who died in infancy from tuberculosis, which claimed her mother the same year. La Guardia married his longtime legal secretary, Marie Fisher, in 1929. They adopted two children, a son, Eric, and a daughter, Jean, who was Thea's niece. La Guardia died in New York on September 20, 1947, and is buried at Woodlawn Cemetery in the Bronx.

SEE ALSO

Volume 1 Left: Democratic Party.
Volume 2 Right: Republican Party.

BIBLIOGRAPHY

Ernest Cuneo, *Life with Fiorello* (Macmillan, 1955); Lawrence Elliott, *Little Flower: The Life and Times of Fiorello La Guardia* (William Morrow, 1983); Thomas Kessner, *Fiorello La Guardia and the Making of Modern New York* (Penguin, 1989); Fiorello H. La Guardia, *The Making of an Insurgent, 1882–1919* (Lippincott, 1948).

TONY L. HILL
MASSACHUSETTS INSTITUTE OF TECHNOLOGY

Laissez-Faire

LAISSEZ-FAIRE describes an economic doctrine that allows for a free-enterprise system to operate according to its own economic laws and opposes governmental regulation of commerce beyond the minimum necessary. The term translates from the French as "to let alone." In the 18th century, *laissez-faire* enjoyed influence in many different areas of everyday life as early European economic thought overlapped with political, philosophical, and religious ideology. More frequently, *laissez-faire* has been associated with the general prescriptions of the classical economists and, in particular, a belief in the efficiency of a free-market economy.

In economics and politics, the *laissez-faire* policy functions best as an economic system in which there is no interference by government. *Laissez-faire* is based on the belief that a natural economic order, in the absence of deliberate influences or adjustments, secures the maximum welfare for individual citizens and the entire community. While *laissez-faire* occasionally functioned in the 17th and 18th centuries in formulating social policy, the influence of the ideology was most powerful in the economic sphere.

Historically, *laissez-faire* was a theoretical reaction against mercantilism. The aim of mercantilism was to maximize foreign trade as well as internal reserves of bullion, the gold and silver necessary for making war. Such commercial controls sought to strengthen the state. Navigation laws, trade monopolies, taxes, and strict economic regulations oppressed the growing class of merchants during the period of European colonial expansion in the 17th and 18th centuries. As a result, a group of pioneer economists banded together in the 1700s to oppose such harsh economic measures. Known as the French physiocrats, this group first devised the principles of *laissez-faire*. The physiocrats challenged state interference in economic affairs and opposed the taxation of commercial activities.

Many European intellectuals and scholars wrote about economic progress and the role of individuals in a successful marketplace. The most important economic work of the 18th century was *Inquiry into the Nature and Causes of the Wealth of Nations* by Adam Smith. Published in 1776, the book claimed that economic autonomy was the basis of a natural economic system. Accordingly, he advised that the mercantile system of England—including the navigation acts, bounties, many tariffs, special trading monopolies, and domestic regulation of labor and manufacturing—be terminated. The government intended these regulations to preserve the wealth of the nation, to acquire wealth from other nations, and to increase available labor for its working citizens. Smith argued that such policies actually stalled the expansion of wealth, development of industry, and increases in trade. He maintained that the best way to promote economic growth was to allow individuals to pursue their own economic benefit. As individuals sought to improve their own prosperity by meeting the needs of others through a free market, Smith insisted, the economy naturally would expand. Consumers would find their needs met as producers and merchants engaged in free competition for business.

During the 18th century, mercantilism assumed that the Earth's resources were limited; hence, one nation could only acquire resources and wealth at the expense of others. Smith's book challenged this belief. He considered the resources of nature, such as water, air, soil, and minerals, as unlimited. To him, they necessitated exploitation for the progress of the human race. In fact, Smith asserted that neither nations nor peoples should remain deprived.

The concept that individuals should exploit nature's infinite bounty for their benefit stemmed from Smith's radical notions. In the 18th century, the world's population was smaller and its citizens poorer. In Smith's view, the magnitude of undeveloped resources held great potential. For people of his time, true improvement of the human condition seemed to lie in the uninhibited exploitation of natural resources. This idea dominated Western economic policies until recently.

Smith is generally considered the founder of *laissez-faire* economics. His book, commonly referred to as *Wealth of Nations*, was a complex tome. For instance, Smith did not contest all government activity in the economy, but reasoned that the government should provide armies, navies, roads, and schools for its citizens. He maintained that the government should assume specific commercial ventures, such as the opening of hazardous new trade routes. Such endeavors were economically advantageous but too costly for a private undertaking.

Economists who followed Smith's teachings dominated private and public discussions of industrial and commercial policy in European intellectual circles. Although classical economists thought that the government was responsible for tasks essential to the public good, they also believed that economic growth was best achieved through a competitive free enterprise system. According to *laissez-faire*, which allowed consumers to make personal economic decisions in the marketplace,

competitive efforts by individuals in society would meet market demands; thus, a natural economic balance was achieved that benefited society as well as the individual. Classical economists saw any government action in the economy as malicious meddling. While insisting that the government should sustain a sound currency, enforce contracts, protect property, and impose low tariffs and taxes, *laissez-faire* dictated that economic cycles be left to the efforts of private enterprise. These economists assumed that the government would maintain enough armed forces and naval strength to defend the nation's economic structure and foreign trade. The middle classes were drawn to *laissez-faire* due to its emphasis on thrift, competition, and personal diligence.

Smith famously alleged that an "invisible hand" in free-market competition would provide for fair pricing. He considered governmental trade restrictions, minimum wage laws, and product regulation as detrimental to a nation's economic well-being. Smith's concept of government nonintervention remained vastly popular throughout the Victorian era (1819–1901) and continues to play an important part in contemporary economic policy. At times, however, governmental leaders have manipulated his words to rationalize poor working conditions by suggesting that child labor laws, maximum working hours, and factory health codes act as a violation of their workers' rights and, thereby, of Smith's ideology. Nevertheless, the doctrine of *laissez-faire* functioned as an integral part of 19th-century European liberalism (liberalizing or liberating the economy). In general, capitalists still defend Smith's policies.

As the system of capitalist enterprise developed in the 19th century, an increasing number of businesses began merging with competitors to form huge trusts in order to manipulate prices and production. Merchants had expected competition to regulate the market. Instead, it seemed to facilitate the establishment of monopolies. As a result, governments discarded the tenet of absolute state noninterference and banned contracts restraining trade and excessive competition procedures. Consequently, the practice of *laissez-faire* was modified, but not abandoned. In its place, a revised form of *laissez-faire* eliminated the high costs of competition and received credit for lowering consumer prices. In this way, the emphasis within *laissez-faire* economics shifted from unfair competition to encouragement of production based on the individual as a means of economic progress.

Surprisingly, Smith was not a champion for the capitalist class. One of his least-known beliefs warned that capitalists seldom gather together without conspiring

Adam Smith is considered the father of free-market principles, but was not a champion of the capitalist class.

against the public. In specific situations, Smith supported anti-monopoly laws. His defense of competition remained contingent on the fact that it encouraged economic growth, something Smith felt would benefit all members of society. He anticipated that as markets grew, increased demand for labor would thwart businesses from abusing their employees. Nevertheless, Smith could not have predicted the future in terms of urbanization, nor could he have foreseen future problems in the labor market. His confidence in future economic growth failed to consider the prospect that capitalists might disproportionately consume the benefits of economic expansion. The failure of free-market competition to significantly improve living conditions of individuals became a primary concern of Smith's scholarly descendants.

Subsequent intellectuals, such as British economists David Ricardo and Thomas Robert Malthus, hypothesized that overpopulation, low wages, and starvation would forever plague society. In 1798, Malthus published his "Essay on the Principle of Population." In this work, Malthus contended that population would eventually outpace the food supply, as the human population would grow geometrically and the food supply arithmetically. Ricardo followed this grim account with

his *Principles of Political Economy* in 1817. He proposed his theory of the Iron Law of Wages, which hypothesized the future of wage labor based on child labor and reproduction. He avowed that, in the long term, wages would always lean toward a minimum level. His argument only verified employers' desire to keep wages low and provided a theoretical defense for opposition to labor unions. Thus, economics as an academic discipline began with Smith's guarded optimism. Due to dreary theses by scholars such as Ricardo and Malthus, the field became known as "the dismal science."

British and French teachings of this classical political economy influenced American ideas about the role of government in the economy. Significant economic publications by Jean Baptiste Say and Harriet Martineau were particularly important as the ideas of *laissez-faire* influenced American economic ideology. The doctrine strongly influenced American economic thinking during the Jeffersonian and Jacksonian eras prior to the American Civil War. Despite prevalent federal economic regulations before the war's end in 1865, the government generally intervened less in the economic sphere afterward.

SEE ALSO

Volume 1 Left: Political Economy; Socialism; Liberalism.
Volume 2 Right: Capitalism; Libertarianism.

BIBLIOGRAPHY

Stuart Bruchey, *Enterprise: The Dynamic Economy of a Free People* (Harvard University Press, 1990); A.W. Coats, ed., *The Classical Economists and Economic Policy* (Routledge, 1971); Sidney Fine, *Laissez-faire and the General-Welfare State: A Study of Conflict in American Thought, 1865–1901* (University of Michigan Press, 1956); F.W. Hirst, ed., *Free Trade and Other Fundamental Doctrines of the Manchester School* (1903); Richard Holt, *The Reluctant Superpower: A History of America's Global Economic Reach* (Kodansha International, 1995); Emma Rothschild, *Economic Sentiments* (Harvard University Press, 2001).

DANA MAGILL
TEXAS CHRISTIAN UNIVERSITY

Landon, Alfred M. (1887–1987)

ALFRED M. LANDON was the Republican presidential nominee of 1936, and he served two terms as the governor of Kansas. Alfred Mossman Landon was born in his grandfather's parsonage in West Middlesex, Pennsylvania, the son of John M. and Anne (Mossman) Landon. His father was an oil prospector, and the family lived in Pennsylvania and Ohio. He graduated from Marietta Academy in Marietta, Ohio, in 1904. He went on to the University of Kansas, where his father was, by that time, working oil fields there. He quickly became a leader in student organizations, and as a result of his adeptness at campus politics, he was nicknamed "The Fox." Landon received a law degree from the university in 1908, but he never practiced law. He soon went into the oil business himself.

Landon made his first foray into politics in 1912, accompanying his father, who was a delegate to the Progressive (Bull Moose) Party convention that ran Theodore Roosevelt for president. Landon was successful at organizing his county for Roosevelt; the Progressive ticket carried the county. In 1915, he married Margaret Fleming, and to this union was born a daughter, Margaret Anne (Peggy) Landon. The elder Margaret Landon died soon thereafter. Landon left the child in her grandparents' custody while he entered service in World War I. The war ended before Landon had a chance to see duty. He returned to his daughter and petroleum business. Landon served briefly as the secretary to his political mentor, Henry J. Allen, when the latter served as governor of Kansas. He became chairman of the Kansas Republicans in 1928.

In 1930, Landon married the former Theo Cobb, to whom he was introduced by his daughter Peggy. To this marriage was born a daughter, Nancy, and a son, John Landon. Landon was elected governor of Kansas in 1932 and reelected in 1934. These were both good years for Democrats, and Landon was the only Republican in the west to win a governorship in 1932, and the only Republican in the country to win one in 1934. Landon maintained fiscal austerity during his two terms as governor, but Democrats charged that this was because his administration was unwilling to help the needy at the depths of the Depression. Nevertheless, maintaining a balanced budget and being one of the few prominent Republicans helped him win the Republican presidential nomination in 1936. The election was an overwhelming landslide for President Franklin D. Roosevelt, who was reelected with the electoral votes of all but two states. Indeed, prior to this election, Maine had been regarded as a bellwether in presidential elections, from whence came the saying "as Maine goes, so goes the nation." After the 1936 Republican debacle, Landon lampooned his loss by saying, "as Maine goes, so goes

Vermont." Although both Richard M. Nixon and Ronald Reagan were reelected with greater proportions of the electoral vote than Roosevelt's margin over Landon, Roosevelt's popular-vote margin over Landon remains a record.

The calamitous defeat spelled the end of Landon's political career. He remained a respected figure in Republican circles, but was quick to preempt any suggestion that he be the party's nominee in 1940. He returned to Kansas and his oil fortune. During World War II, he assumed the role of an elder statesman, speaking out frequently on foreign policy. He was circumspect about his life, describing himself as "an oilman who never made a million, a lawyer who never tried a case, and a politician who carried only Maine and Vermont."

Landon's career reflected his progressive or left-of-center Republicanism, although by 1936 in the midst of the New Deal, he was regarded as a representative of fiscal conservative Republicanism. Landon lived to celebrate his 100th birthday on September 9, 1987. He died at his Topeka, Kansas, home five weeks later, on October 12, 1987, and is buried in Mt. Hope Cemetery in Topeka.

SEE ALSO

Volume 1 Left: Roosevelt, Franklin D.; Democratic Party; New Deal
Volume 2 Right: Republican Party; Conservatism.

BIBLIOGRAPHY

Richard B. Fowler, *Alfred M. Landon* (L.C. Page Publishers, 1936); Donald R. McCoy, *Landon of Kansas* (University of Nebraska Press, 1966).

TONY L. HILL
MASSACHUSETTS INSTITUTE OF TECHNOLOGY

Libertarianism

A POLITICAL IDEOLOGY, libertarianism values and promotes personal liberty and responsibility, small government, and a free-market economy. Libertarianism is also known as classical or 19th-century liberalism. During the 20th century, the "liberal" label was appropriated in the United States, though not in Europe, by those who value personal liberty and a state that intervenes extensively in the economy. Hence, the "libertarian" label was created in 1950 to distinguish between the two ideologies.

Libertarian analysis locates political regimes between statist and libertarian poles according to their size of government. At the statist pole are totalitarian regimes that expand the state to occupy all the social space between the family and the state, abolishing civil society, for example, communism and Nazism. At the other pole, Libertarians would keep the state as small as possible, concerned with defense and law enforcement. Only anarchists would suggest doing away with the state altogether. While conventional political analysis of ideologies considers communism and fascism to be at opposite ends, libertarians consider them to be two heads of the same totalitarian monster.

Libertarians may be divided into a right-wing majority and a left-wing minority. Left-wing libertarians also value individual rights and free association. However, they believe that liberty and small government should result in associations that foster greater economic equality. Right-wing libertarianism is the prevalent interpretation of the philosophy.

Libertarians consider the state to be often the source of social problems rather than their solution. The concentration of power in any single institution is bound to lead, given human nature, to inefficiency, waste, and corruption at best and tyranny at worst. At its totalitarian extreme, the state sets to have complete control of the economy, a command economy, an attempt to run society like an army. Libertarians like Ludwig von Mises and Friedrich von Hayek highlighted the inefficiencies of command economies, the absence of incentives to innovate or work harder, and the absence of a price mechanism that indicates to producers that there is more or less demand through higher or lower prices, respectively. Consequently, command economies are marked by waste, overproduction of what nobody wants, and shortages, underproduction of what people need.

Libertarians construct the political system on the basis of inviolable individual rights. The government cannot violate these rights, even by popular democratic consent, and must protect them against popular intolerance. The right to private property is particularly important for libertarians. Private property guarantees personal independence and creates incentives for long-term planning and care of the property as well as for its optimal economic use.

A free market emerges when independent property owners exchange goods voluntarily. The distribution of ownership that emerges as a result of countless individ-

ual transactions is a spontaneous, unplanned order. Universal laws that do not benefit any particular special interest should regulate voluntary interactions between individuals. Some libertarians believe that the best laws emerge spontaneously, for example common law. When laws are planned, imposed from the top down, they are subjected to unforeseen consequences at best and service to special interests at worst.

Historically, libertarian ideas emerged as a result of the economic and political struggles in Europe between the industrious and trading middle classes and the aristocratically controlled central government that attempted to tax them and control their economic activities. John Locke introduced in the late 17th century the theory that the state is founded on a social contract with its citizens that should ensure the protection of their rights, mainly to life, liberty, and property. These ideas influenced many of the founders of the United States, most notably Thomas Jefferson. The Industrial Revolution and the globalization of free trade and migration during the 19th century created, despite colonialism and lingering monarchic regimes in Europe, conditions that resembled the kind of world libertarians would like to live in. The outbreak of World War I led to decline in global trade and the Russian totalitarian revolution. After the war, the introduction of immigration restrictions in the United States further damaged the global economy. The rise of totalitarianism in Russia, Italy, and Germany; the economic Depression of the 1930s; and the ensuing expansion of the state even in democratic countries (the New Deal in America) seemed have sealed the fate of libertarianism.

Economic stagnation in welfare economies led to a crisis in the 1970s and the rehabilitation of libertarian ideas. Though neither Margaret Thatcher's Conservatives nor Ronald Reagan's Republicans actually reduced the size of the state substantially, they did reduce taxes, and emphasized the values of enterprise, personal responsibility, and privatization. These policies have not been reversed by subsequent administrations. Libertarians, who founded their own party in the United States, struggle today for a reduction in taxation and the size of government, free trade, the lifting of tariffs and immigration restrictions, greater civil rights, a private or voucher-based education system, and a strictly defensive use of the military.

The implosion of communism, a global wave of privatization, and globalization followed not just the failure of command economies but the idea that such economies can ever fulfill their promise. However, there remains a gap between libertarian theory and political reality. Apparent privatization and libertarian rhetoric have been used in postcommunist Europe and parts of Latin America to attract investors and conceal crony capitalism and other types of political corruption. In Western Europe, social-democratic tax-and-spend policies are still entrenched.

SEE ALSO

Volume 1 Left: Socialism; Communism; Liberalism; United States.
Volume 2 Right: Rand, Ayn; Buckley, William F., Jr.

BIBLIOGRAPHY

David Boaz, *Libertarianism: A Primer* (The Free Press, 1997); David Boaz, ed., *The Libertarian Reader: Classic and Contemporary Readings from Lao-Tzu to Milton Friedman* (The Free Press, 1997); David Friedman, *The Machinery of Freedom: Guide to Radical Capitalism* (Harper & Row, 1973); Jan Narveson, *The Libertarian Idea* (Temple University Press, 1988); Murray N. Rothbard, *For a New Liberty: The Libertarian Manifesto* (Fox & Wilkes, 1996).

AVIEZER TUCKER
AUSTRALIAN NATIONAL UNIVERSITY

Limbaugh, Rush (1951–)

RUSH HUDSON Limbaugh III, an undisputed "king" of conservative talk radio, was born on January 12, 1951, in Cape Girardeau, Missouri. During his youth, Limbaugh became interested in radio and even was a deejay known as Rusty Limbaugh at a local radio station while still in high school in the late 1960s. Limbaugh's father, a conservative judge and influential member of the local community, had actually owned the station before Rush began his deejay career there.

Following his graduation from high school, Limbaugh was accepted and admitted to Southeast Missouri State College. After only one year at college, Limbaugh dropped out in order to pursue radio. He held a variety of positions across the country at small radio stations until he took a more permanent position as a public relations assistant for the Kansas City Royals baseball team. He stayed with the Royals for five years, then returned to radio in 1983, working at a Kansas City, Kansas, station as a talk show host and commentator. In this position, Limbaugh began to develop his controversial conservative commentary style, but it did not prove to be too appealing to the Kansas City area and his show was canceled after only 10 months on air.

Soon after, however, Limbaugh found a radio station, KFBK in San Diego, California, that was in the middle of a financial mess and in need of something new. He was hired in 1984 and was given a three-hour morning show without constraints on content from the owners. This time, Limbaugh's signature style, which was a mixture of conservative political commentary and harsh satire directed at liberals, took hold and was much more successful than in Kansas City. Shortly thereafter, Limbaugh's show became one of the most popular radio shows in San Diego, quickly becoming a dominant force in market share.

Limbaugh's reputation and ratings began to gain national attention. In 1988, Limbaugh's success was recognized by Edward McLaughlin, founder of the Excellence in Broadcasting Network, also known as Premiere Broadcasting, who offered Limbaugh a radio show in New York City with a national audience. His first few weeks with a national audience were overwhelmingly successful, and Limbaugh was well received by his listeners who were mostly conservative Caucasian males. His listeners loved Limbaugh's approach, which entailed characterizing liberal groups as "feminazis," "environmental wackos," and "hustlers for the homeless." In addition, he soon developed a nickname for his listeners, "dittoheads," because they always called in to the radio show to "ditto" or approve what he was saying on air.

Only after four years on the national level, Limbaugh became the most popular radio talk show host in the United States. With every show, he continued his quest to reveal the liberal "fallacies" within politics and the media and also continued to use his sharp and what his critics label "unkind" satire. On many of his shows, Limbaugh prefaced his news segments on the AIDS outbreak by playing Dionne Warwick's "I'll Never Love This Way Again" and his stories on homelessness with Clarence Henry's "Ain't Got No Home."

Limbaugh's influence in the realm of politics was believed to play a major part in the Republican Party's widespread success in the 1994 elections, in which the Republicans recaptured the House of Representatives. In addition to his on-air support of Republican candidates, he made many personal appearances at conservative fundraising and campaign events.

His influence went beyond elections, exemplified by Bill Clinton's lobby reform package, which originally had bipartisan support until Limbaugh's on-air comments spurred many listeners to call their representatives and senators in opposition to the proposed reforms.

During the mid-1990s, Limbaugh translated his radio power into success in other media. In addition to the radio show, Limbaugh had a nationally syndicated television show, which ran for four years. and published a bestselling book titled *The Way Things Ought to Be*. His success didn't go without recognition, as Limbaugh received the National Association of Broadcasters' Marconi Radio Award for Syndicated Personality of the Year in 1992, 1995, and 2000.

By 2001, however, Limbaugh's overwhelming influence and success began to wane. His television show had been cancelled and his next book, *See, I Told You So*, sold significantly worse than his first bestseller. Some radio stations even began syndicating other talk show hosts around the same time that comedian Al Franken released his bestselling book, *Rush Limbaugh Is a Big Fat Idiot*.

The problems continued and in October 2001, Limbaugh admitted to his listeners that he was completely deaf in his left ear and had substantial hearing loss in his right ear, resulting in changes in his voice and delays in the call-and-response portion of the radio show. In December 2001, Limbaugh underwent cochlear implant surgery, which remedied some of his hearing difficulties.

His problems did not end there, however, as Limbaugh became embroiled in controversy in September 2003 concerning the media, sports, and African Americans, and in a prescription drug abuse scandal in October 2003. As a result of the ESPN scandal, he lost his commentating position there and the drug scandal resulted in Limbaugh's admission to prescription drug addiction and the need for treatment.

SEE ALSO

Volume 1 Left: Media Bias, Left; Liberalism; Feminism; Clinton, William J.
Volume 2 Right: Media Bias, Right; Conservatism; Feminism; New Right.

BIBLIOGRAPHY

Rush Limbaugh, *The Way Things Ought to Be* (Simon & Schuster, 1993); "Rush Limbaugh," www.wikipedia.com (May 2004); Michael Janofsky, "Drug Fighters Turn to Rising Tide of Prescription Abuse," *New York Times* (March 18, 2004).

ARTHUR HOLST, PH.D.
WIDENER UNIVERSITY

Lincoln, Abraham (1809–1865)

ABRAHAM LINCOLN is often associated with saving the Union and freeing the slaves, actions that seem to easily describe a liberal statesman. Though Lincoln took liberties in exercising his executive power in the midst of the Civil War, it is important to remember that he served his presidential terms during the most extraordinary of circumstances. Examining his actions during the war (the suspension of habeas corpus, the issuing of the Emancipation Proclamation, the suppression of the northern press) fails to reveal Lincoln's core conservatism, an ideology to which he held fast throughout his career.

Lincoln based his political ideology on a strict adherence to the Constitution's provisions and restrictions. He did not look to the Constitution as a suggestive guide, but as a rulebook of what may and may not be done to carry out effective republican government. He looked to both the Constitution and the Declaration of Independence to discern the political ideologies of the founding fathers so that he could remain as close as possible, in his own beliefs, to their expectations for republican government. The founding fathers often wrote of the dangers of self-interest in maintaining a strong republic. Self-interest, they believed, must be sacrificed for the public good in order for government to work. As long as issues such as slavery so fiercely divided Americans, no common ground could be reached and despotism would result. As long as southerners believed that slavery was a positive good and northerners believed it was morally wrong, the two regions would remain hopelessly at odds with one another, pursuing separate, conflicting interests. Lincoln's desire to strive for unity between the regions on the issue rested in the restriction of slavery to the places in which it already existed. This containment policy, he believed, would lead to slavery's natural dissolution and remove the issue that created such virulent self-interest among Americans.

Lincoln believed in the strength of the Constitution because it allowed Americans the freedom to draw their own lines, which, in turn, kept the Constitution strong. He had no problem with the existence of both wage and slave labor in the United States as long as the line between the two remained clear. Issues such as the Dred Scott decision and the Kansas-Nebraska Act troubled him greatly because they allowed for the unchecked growth of slavery.

He was, however, firmly committed to preserving the institution of slavery where it already existed because the Constitution gave Congress no express power to abolish it.

Lincoln may be considered no less than a committed conservative when contrasted with the revolutionary actions of the South in its attempt to separate itself from the Union. His opposition to secession rested entirely upon the idea that the Constitution did not allow it. The South's decision to leave the Union rather than accept the election of a man whom it opposed was indeed revolutionary in its rebellion against constitutional provisions. In his first inaugural address, Lincoln addressed this very issue, stating, "continuing the Government is acquiescence on one side or the other. If a minority in such case will secede rather than acquiesce, they make a precedent which in time will divide and ruin them … Unanimity is impossible. The rule of a minority, as a permanent arrangement, is wholly inadmissible; so that, rejecting the majority principle, anarchy or despotism in some form is all that is left."

Lincoln's belief that, constitutionally, no state could leave the Union led him to treat the seceding states as rebellious children rather than enemies. He asserted on many occasions that since the southern states remained part of the Union, they maintained their constitutional rights, including the right to keep their slaves. Even the Emancipation Proclamation exempted those states that had held legitimate elections to "reenter" the Union. He preferred reunion of the states through the constitutional electoral process rather than through civil war.

Much of Lincoln's conservatism also rested on his need to appeal to a national electorate. This fact was especially true as the election of 1864 approached and the war continued. Congressional Republicans could quite easily run their campaigns on an anti-southern platform since they appealed to only northern voters. They often supported the harshest of measures to win the war, including immediate emancipation. Lincoln did not have such a luxury. He needed the votes of the slaveholding border states that had not joined the Confederacy and continued to provide the Democrats with political support.

Though many of Lincoln's core principles may be considered conservative, the outbreak of war required that he set many of them aside in order to preserve the Union. As the war continued, Lincoln realized that the South had to be absolutely conquered in order to maintain the ideologies upon which the founding fathers established the nation. In other words, Lincoln set his conservative beliefs aside for the moment, for the purpose of saving them in the future.

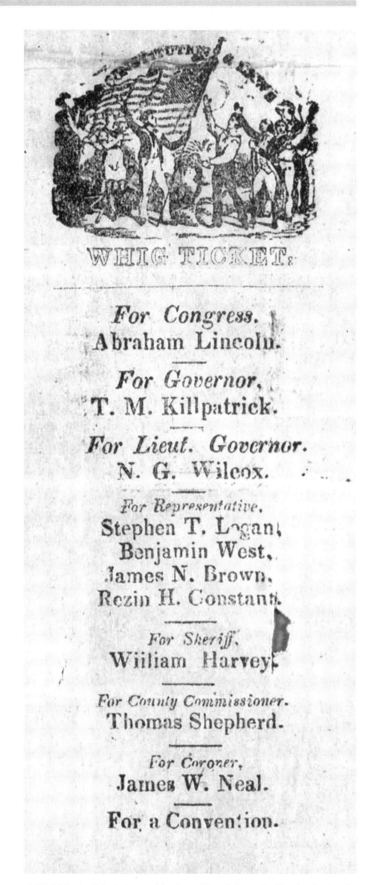

A Whig Party ticket shows Abraham Lincoln's early Illinois electoral aspirations, as he heads the congressional candidacy.

SEE ALSO

Volume 1 Left: Lincoln, Abraham; American Civil War; United States; Abolitionism.
Volume 2 Right: Conservatism; Republican Party.

BIBLIOGRAPHY

Christopher Dell, *Lincoln and the War Democrats: The Grand Erosion of Conservative Tradition* (Fairleigh Dickinson University Press, 1975); David F. Ericson, *The Shaping of American Liberalism: The Debates over Ratification, Nullification and Slavery* (University of Chicago Press, 1993); Michael F. Holt, "The Politics of Union," *Abraham Lincoln and the American Political Tradition* (University of Massachusetts Press, 1986); Abraham Lincoln, "First Inaugural Address," http://showcase.netins.net (June 2004); James M. McPherson, "Abraham Lincoln and the Second American Revolution," Stephen B. Oates, "Abraham Lincoln: Republican in the White House," and John L. Thomas, "Lincoln's Fraternal Democracy" *Abraham Lincoln and the American Political Tradition* (University of Massachusetts Press, 1986).

STEPHANIE R. ROLPH
MISSISSIPPI STATE UNIVERSITY

Lind, Michael (1962–)

A PROLIFIC WRITER and the Whitehead Senior Fellow at the New American Foundation, Michael Lind serves as co-director of the American Strategy Project. Lind's articles have been published in such prestigious publications as the *New Yorker*, *Harper's*, and *New Republic*. Identifying himself as a fifth-generation Texan, Lind spent most of his early life, including his undergraduate years, in the Lone Star State. He first left Texas in the 1980s to study foreign policy at Yale University.

In 1996, Lind received national attention for his scathing attack on multiculturalism and its opponents in *The Next American Nation: The New Nationalism and the Fourth American Revolution*. Lind's attack on conservatism was expanded that same year with the publication of *Up from Conservatism: Why The Right Is Wrong for America*. As a protégé of ultraconservative William F. Buckley, Jr., Lind had been viewed as a rising young Republican who would serve the interests of conservatism with fierce loyalty. He continued to endorse the ideologies of neoconservatism until 1998, when he rejected the right in favor of what be called the "radical center." Denying that he had changed his ideology, Lind insisted that it was the Republican Party that had swung to the extreme right, blaming the shift on radical conservatives such as Pat Robertson and Patrick Buchanan. Lind announced that he was pro-choice (in regard to abortion), a supporter of the right of homosexuals to join the military, and an advocate for social welfare programs initiated by Franklin Roosevelt's New Deal.

By calling himself a centrist, Lind placed himself in an ideal position to hurl criticisms at both liberals and conservatives, contending that both the Democrats and Republicans had lost touch with reality. Lind's favorite target became George W. Bush, who Lind believed (along with millions of other Americans) stole the 2000 election from Democrat Al Gore, with the connivance of his brother, Florida Governor Jeb Bush, Republicans in Congress, and conservatives on the Supreme Court.

In *Made in Texas*, Lind used his first-hand knowledge of Texas politics to vilify Bush and his Texas cronies, who included Vice President Dick Cheney. Lind maintained that the Bush gang succeeded in reshaping national politics to suit the interests of the Texas oil industry and southern conservatives. Lind became an outspoken opponent of Bush's handling of the war in Iraq and pointed out that few of the president's advisers guiding military strategy had actual military experience. Lind also abhorred the fact that conservative think tanks became instrumental in shaping Bush's foreign policy. Lind insisted that Bush had been chosen as the designated heir to the party of Jefferson Davis, the president of the Confederacy.

While many of his opponents insisted that he had become a liberal, Lind rejected the label. Indeed, a number of political writers admitted that Lind's ideology was difficult to identify since he endorsed elements of both liberalism and conservatism. For instance, Lind agreed with the conservative view that the Vietnam conflict was a "just, constitutional, and necessary" engagement. He contended that the United States was justified in protecting its interest in inhibiting the growth of communism, even though American strategy could often be immoral and counterproductive. On the other hand, Lind's affinity with the far-left was obvious in his proposals for redistributing American land and wealth.

SEE ALSO

Volume 1 Left: Liberalism; Democratic Party.
Volume 2 Right: Bush, George W.; Buckley, William F., Jr..

BIBLIOGRAPHY

Ted Halstead and Michael Lind, *The Radical Center: The Future of American Politics* (Doubleday, 2001); Theodore Hamm,

"The Crawford Conundrum," *The Nation* (March 17, 2003); John Kampfner, "Forever Free," *New Statesman* (April 7, 2003); Michael Lind, *Made in Texas: George W. Bush and the Southern Takeover of American Politics* (Basic Books, 2003); Michael Lind, *The Next American Nation: The New Nationalism and the Fourth American Revolution* (Free Press, 1995); Michael Lind, *Up from Conservatism: Why the Right Is Wrong for America* (Free Press, 1996); Michael Lind, *Vietnam: The Necessary War: A Reinterpretation of America's Most Disastrous Military Conflict* (Free Press, 1999); Michael Lind, "The Weird Men Behind George W. Bush's War," *New Statesman* (April 7, 2003); "Michael Lind, Whitehead Senior Fellow," www.newamerica.net (September 2004).

ELIZABETH PURDY, PH.D.
INDEPENDENT SCHOLAR

Lindbergh, Charles A. (1902–1974)

CHARLES A. LINDBERGH was a pioneer of aviation who was the most famous man in the world at age 25 but parlayed that into only small political success. Charles Augustus Lindbergh was born in his grandparents' home in Detroit, Michigan, on February 4, 1902, the son of Charles A. Lindbergh, Sr., and Evangeline Lodge (Land) Lindbergh.

Lindbergh was raised on a farm outside Little Falls, Minnesota, on the Mississippi River, where his father, a Swedish immigrant, had settled fresh from law school. Charles, Sr., served 10 years in the U.S. House of Representatives as a Republican. (He ended his political career in opposition to World War I, a paradigm his son would follow.) Lindbergh graduated from Little Falls High School in 1918. He attended the University of Wisconsin from 1920 to 1922 but left to attend flying school. He bought his first plane, a Curtiss Jenny, in 1923. Lindbergh joined the army in 1924 and trained to be a pilot. He finished top in his class the next year and went to work as a pilot in St. Louis, Missouri.

Lindbergh enlisted a group of St. Louis businesspeople to underwrite his ambition of flying solo across the Atlantic Ocean. The tie to St. Louis gave the plane its name, *The Spirit of St. Louis*. Lindbergh set a cross-country record, making the maiden voyage of the *The Spirit of St. Louis* from San Diego, California, to New York City.

Soon thereafter, he set off on his groundbreaking nonstop solo flight to Paris, which he accomplished in 33.5 hours, arriving in Paris, France, on May 21, 1927. This was an achievement celebrated around the world. Lindbergh was awarded the Congressional Medal of Honor. He made a flying tour of the country, visiting all 48 states. Irving Berlin wrote a song in Lindy's honor called "Why Should He Fly for So Much a Week When He Could Be Sheik of Paree?"

Later that year, while on a goodwill tour of Latin America, Lindbergh met the U.S. ambassador to Mexico, Dwight W. Morrow, and his daughter, Anne Spencer Morrow. Lindbergh and Anne were married on May 27, 1929. They had six children, Charles, Jr., John, Land, Anne, Scott, and Reeve.

Tragedy struck the young couple on March 1, 1932, when Charles, Jr., not yet two years old, was kidnapped from their home in Hopewell, New Jersey. The baby's body was found on May 12. An investigation of unprecedented scope, which involved the Federal Bureau of Investigation despite its lack of jurisdiction, eventually led to Bruno Richard Hauptmann, a carpenter and German immigrant. Hauptmann was convicted of the kidnapping, murder, and extortion in 1935 and executed on April 3, 1936. As a result of this crime, interstate kidnapping was made a federal offense. The Lindberghs moved to England in 1935 to escape the publicity over the trial. They remained abroad until 1939, when rumblings of war, and then war, came to Europe.

Lindbergh was instrumental in establishing the America First Committee in 1940. Although the group was in existence little more than a year, it had 800,000 members who supported the group's aim of keeping the United States out of World War II. However, the war had broad popular support, and Lindbergh's isolationism put him somewhat outside the mainstream of American politics.

Lindbergh conceived of the various European nations as different elements of a single Western civilization rather than as natural warring parties, presaging the later thesis of Samuel Huntington. His view was that the United States should stay out of what he believed would necessarily be a struggle inherently destructive to Western civilization. America First's central values were:

The United States must build an impregnable defense for America.

No foreign power, nor group of powers, can successfully attack a prepared America.

American democracy can be preserved only by keeping out of the European war.

"Aid short of war" weakens national defense at home and threatens to involve America in war abroad.

Lindbergh testified before Congress in 1941 and urged a neutrality pact with Germany. He resigned from the army air corps under public pressure afterward. Lindbergh made a remarkable speech in Des Moines, Iowa, on September 11, 1941, in which he blamed the agitation for war on the British, the Jews, and the Franklin Roosevelt administration. Lindbergh's speech was roundly condemned, and he was attacked as an anti-Semite and Nazi sympathizer. Following the Japanese attack on Hawaii later that year, there was no keeping the United States out of the war. Moreover, the conflict was then expanded beyond Lindbergh's conception of a fratricidal Western conflict to an intercivilizational war. The America First Committee was disbanded four days after the Pearl Harbor attack. Lindbergh himself offered to go to war, but he was rebuffed. Toward the end of the war, Lindbergh managed to become an aviator once again, and he flew over two dozen sorties.

Lindbergh's anti-war agitation had cooled the public's interest in him as a speaker and celebrated American, and he and his wife went into near-seclusion for many years after the war ended. He received a number of awards and honors. President Dwight D. Eisenhower made him a brigadier general in the air force in 1954. James Stewart played him in the acclaimed film *The Spirit of St. Louis*. Lindbergh gradually developed conservation as his main interest. In 1968, he addressed the Alaska legislature on the subject. It was his first speech since the fiasco in Des Moines. Lindbergh fathered three children with a German mistress between 1958 and 1967. This was kept secret until 2003.

On August 26, 1974, Lindbergh died of lymphatic cancer at his home in Maui, Hawaii.

SEE ALSO

Volume 1 Left: United States; Roosevelt, Franklin D.
Volume 2 Right: Isolationism; Conservatism.

BIBLIOGRAPHY

Wayne S. Cole, *Charles A. Lindbergh and the Battle against American Intervention in World War II* (Harcourt Brace Jovanovich, 1974); Kenneth S. Davis, *The Hero: Charles A. Lindbergh and the American Dream* (Doubleday, 1959); Charles A. Lindbergh, *Autobiography of Values*, William Jovanovich and Judith A. Schiff, eds. (Harcourt Brace Jovanovich, 1978); Joyce Milton, *Loss of Eden: A Biography of Charles and Anne Morrow Lindbergh* (HarperCollins, 1993); P.J. O'Brien, *The Lindberghs: The Story of a Distinguished Family* (Philadelphia: International Press, 1935); Walter S. Ross, *The Last Hero: Charles A. Lindbergh* (Harper and Row, 1967).

TONY L. HILL
MASSACHUSETTS INSTITUTE OF TECHNOLOGY

Lobbying

PUBLIC OPINION, and how to curry it, is the lifeblood of the political machine in any capital, and nowhere more so than in Washington, D.C. Lobbyists can be described as political persuaders, trying to influence the public opinion as well as the opinions and actions of people in positions who make and carry out public policy. They are paid to do this by the interests that have a direct connection to the results that come from the making and carrying out of public policy.

In the United States, there are a dozen or so foundations that provide the lion's share of conservative funding. To name a few, the John M. Olin Foundation, the Lynde and Harry Bradley Foundation, the Scaife Family Foundations, and the Smith Richardson Foundation give so much in aggregate terms to lobbyists that they have become known as the "four sisters." Others are the Adolph Coors Foundation, which led the launch of the Heritage Foundation, a conservative think tank; the Charles G. and David H. Koch Foundations; the J.M., Phillip M. McKenna, Earhart, and Carthage Foundations; and the Claude R. Lambe charitable foundations.

These conservative funders have helped a new generation of right-wing activist intellectuals, though the conservative think tank world is not entirely funder-driven. A picture has emerged that U.S. institutions have been influential, by shopping ideas to politicians and officials at all levels of government and to the various candidates in the presidential campaigns from these think tanks. A very real and recent instance of this can be found in the George W. Bush administration with Donald Rumsfeld and Condoleezza Rice, both of whom are Hoover Institution alumni. The conservative think tanks, of which many are lobbyist groups, organizations, or individuals, grew from the recent period in world history that has seen the United States withdrawing from the momentous economic and political changes across the world, a retreat from Keynesian economic policies. The generally accepted purpose of think tanks is to promote ideas, and they have flourished since their start, to a point that there are some 3,500 think tanks worldwide. The Brookings Institution was instrumental in lobbying and advocating for the Jimmy Carter administration to start down the path of deregulation with initiatives that had their seeds in the Brookings think tank. The Heritage Foundation saw its influence in the Ronald Reagan administration grow through the successful adoption of the Strategic Defense Initiative and tax reforms. These well-funded think tanks promote their political agenda, which is set primarily by corporate and/or commercial interests.

Some of these lobbyist groups include groups or organizations that portray themselves as grassroots organizations, although those are fabrications of the pharmaceutical, manufacturing, financial, and insurance lobbies. They come dressed looking like citizens' groups, but in fact are just the offshoot public relations arms of corporate lobbyists. They are there to act as the lobbyists or political persuaders who frame a picture of populist sentiment for advocating measures that are, in many instances, not in alignment with the American public's wishes.

The lobbyists or political persuaders are good at framing issues to affect the balance of competing ideas or values. By rearranging these public values, or the values of the bureaucrats or elected officials, an effect on public opinions and policies can be made through effective and persuasive political communications. Arthur Lupia and Mathew D. McCubbins (1998) suggest that the function of political communications is enlightenment, and by extension that is also the role of the lobbyist or think tank organization, and works well when the recipients of the message or lobbying have values that are well ordered and consistent with respect to the issue or policy.

To help bring these values into being as well ordered and consistent on a policy or issue that is related to the lobbying efforts, framing the issue or policy properly in the communications of the message is important. This will lead to issues or policies that are in fact shaped from the social problems or policy solutions wanted by the lobbyist. Framing has been portrayed in the literature as endemic to the objective of good-news media coverage, which in turn helps to build public opinion in favor of a policy or issue, which in turn is felt by the political or bureaucratic machines involved in the crafting, changing, or elimination of policy. Framing is the basis for the lobbyists' or political persuaders' rhetoric arsenal, which guides all understanding of the problems' origins and suggestions for solutions. Issues

or policies can be framed in a narrow way, to highlight or emphasize only a narrow piece of the puzzle or the broader picture. The effect is deliberate on the part of the lobbyists or political persuaders so that the receivers of the messages have their judgements and opinions affected by these targeted ideas and rhetoric.

As an example of lobbyists or political persuaders that actually "live" in the government is an internal government organization such as the Food and Drug Administration (FDA) during the Bill Clinton presidency. The FDA sought to classify nicotine as a drug, thus labeling cigarettes as a drug delivery system. This would then allow them more control over regulation and elimination of the sale of cigarettes without special restrictions.

Conservative funders identify talented strategic thinkers and give them financial support and broad latitude, funding work by such strategists as Paul Weyrich, Ralph Reed, C. Boyden Grey, Grover Norquist, Irving Kristol, Reed Irvine, Ed Feulner, Gary Bauer, William Bennett, Howard Phillips, and others. Conservative philanthropists operate as movement strategists first, and funders second. The few hundred politicians who govern America have an estimated 60,000 lobbyists dedicated to making them vote for laws in favor of the lobbyists' programs.

Right-wing lobbyists, and in fact lobbyists from both sides of the political spectrum, do not consider the halls of Congress to be the only arena in which to practice their profession. Hollywood has always been considered fair game for the purposes of both left- and right-wing lobbyists or political persuaders. A case in point is the pulling of a television mini-series on the life and times of Ronald and Nancy Reagan by CBS. It is suggested by many that it was not broadcast because the production deeply disturbed right-wing lobbyists who did not want Reagan's reputation sullied. This can be cited as an example of lobbyists' needing to manage the message.

Lobbyists do not necessarily operate only at the national level. For example, in Texas, the business lobby has taken unprecedented control of state government. As Andrew Wheat said in the *Texas Observer*, "rather than having corporations pay lobbyists millions of dollars to influence government, the state's new leaders recruited some of Texas' most powerful lobbyists to run the government directly." Tommy Craddick, a veteran right-wing Republican backbencher who was poised to become the speaker of the state house when the legislature convened, was reported in the same article to have appointed three business lobbyists to manage his transition team: Bill Miller, Bill Messer, and Bill Ceverha. They represent clients from the pharmaceutical, property insurance, and health insurance industries.

Another situation that amply illustrates the effect a right-wing lobbying effort can have was the work of some 475 paid lobbyists, who in July 2003, strove to push a bill through the Senate that could severely restrict class-action lawsuits. The lobbying army was made up of nearly five corporate lobbyists for each U.S. senator. The insurance industry alone had 139 lobbyists promoting the bill, with health maintenance organizations counting 59 lobbyists, banks and consumer credit corporations having 39, automobile corporations with 32, the U.S. chemical industry with 20, and the oil corporations another 19, all pressing their case. Essentially, the proposed law and the lobbyists' goals would move all class-action lawsuits out of state courts and into already clogged federal courts, where corporate interests are less likely to be attacked.

In an article in the *Atlantic Monthly*, Christopher Caldwell makes the point that, "The United States, after all, has high immigration, widening class differences, and two parties that are united, some say, by nothing so much as their tendency to put the wishes of lobbyists over the wishes of voters." This, in an article that talks about the entry of Jörg Haider's Freedom Party into Austria's government, albeit with only 27 percent of the vote, and how the lobbyists led 14 other European Union countries to sever official diplomatic contacts with Austria. The point being made is that lobbying is becoming an export industry for the United States, as American lobbyists are showing their counterparts in other countries how to get the message across.

Since there are lobbyists in almost all state or provincial, county, and city or town governments, one can only assume they will represent both sides of the spectrum for the issues and concerns of their employers. Lobbyists or political persuaders can work on issues based on the highest bidder or for some moral or ethical cause. What stays the same are the methods they must employ to get their jobs done, and their issues and policies adopted into public policy.

SEE ALSO

BIBLIOGRAPHY

Karen Paget, "Lessons of Right-Wing Philanthropy," *American Prospect* (September 1, 1998); Thomas E. Nelson, "Policy Goals, Public Rhetoric, and Political Attitudes," *Journal of Politics* (v.68/2, May 2004); Arthur Lulpia and Mathew D. McCubbins, *The Democratic Dilemma: Can Citizens Learn What They Need to Know?* (Cambridge University Press, 1998).

NORMAN GREENFIELD
REGISTERED GOVERNMENT LOBBYIST, CANADA

Luce, Henry R. (1898–1967)

JOURNALIST AND OWNER of Time, Incorporated, Henry Luce was born in Tengchow, China, of missionary parents and educated at Hotchkiss School, and Yale and Oxford universities. Luce served in the U.S. Army during the World War I, but the armistice came before he could leave for the front. After the war, he worked at various newspapers, until he and a friend founded *Time* magazine in 1923. During his career, he published *Fortune*, *Life*, *Sports Illustrated*, and the documentary series *The March of Time* that aired on radio and newsreels.

Luce did not believe in striving for objectivity, and as a result, the line between reporting and opinion often blurred. In keeping with his journalistic philosophy, in the late 1930s, he warned of the coming crisis in Europe due to the rise of the fascists and grew concerned about their anti-Semitism. He worked tirelessly to convince Americans of the need to fight the forces of evil in the world, and he castigated the Franklin Roosevelt administration for its tardiness in getting directly involved in World War II.

His classic statement of prewar policy, entitled "The American Century," appeared in his photo magazine, *Life*, in the winter of 1941, and in his essay, he urged Americans to get involved in the conflict or Germany's Adolf Hitler would only grow in strength, and defeating him would prove more difficult. Luce, ever the internationalist, believed the United States bore the responsibility of leading in world affairs.

Beginning in 1940, he became directly involved in politics. Luce loaned his managing editor at *Fortune* to Republican presidential candidate and internationalist, Wendell Willkie, to serve as both campaign manager and speechwriter. Despite his efforts, Luce failed to keep Roosevelt from winning a third term.

Luce loved the China of his youth, and as a result, he mourned the loss of the nation to the communists led by Mao Zedong. Despite warnings from his correspondents about Nationalist Party leader Chiang Kaishek's corruption, he believed Russia's Josef Stalin sabotaged China. In addition, Luce believed President Harry Truman's administration's lack of resolve to rescue the Nationalist leader resulted in China's fall to communism. As the journalistic voice of the "China lobby," Luce, and his wife, Congresswoman Clare Booth Luce, succeeded in getting aid for the Nationalist government of Chiang on Taiwan island and thwarting the official recognition of communist China.

Although a loyal Republican, Luce loathed Senator Joseph R. McCarthy because he felt he hurt both the party and the anti-communist cause. After meeting Dwight Eisenhower at his North Atlantic Treaty Organization (NATO) headquarters, Luce came away convinced that Eisenhower should run for president in 1952 on the Republican ticket. After receiving extremely positive campaign coverage from *Time*, Eisenhower crushed Democrat Adlai Stevenson in the campaign, and the grateful president appointed Luce's wife ambassador to Italy. Luce so identified with Ike that, during the Eisenhower era, foreign leaders and journalists often assumed that Luce served, as biographer James Baughman noted, as the "minister of information" for the Eisenhower administration.

In the 1960 presidential election, though Luce voted for Richard Nixon, Time, Inc., granted remarkably fair and even-handed coverage to Senator John Kennedy, the Democratic nominee. Luce wrote the introduction to Kennedy's book *Why England Slept* in 1940, and was a friend of the ambitious family patriarch, Joseph P. Kennedy. Despite their official party affiliation, the Luces sat in the presidential box during Kennedy's inaugural ball. Luce agreed with Kennedy's anti-communism and his inaugural pledge to fight communism around the world. He supported both Kennedy and Lyndon Johnson's efforts to rescue South Vietnam from communist domination. Though Luce's wife seconded Senator Barry Goldwater's nomination at the 1964 Republican convention, Luce was cool to Goldwater's candidacy. Despite American attitudes to the contrary, Luce continued to support Johnson's effort to stem the tide of Bolshevism in Southeast Asia.

Luce did not possess direct political power, but he did have the ability to influence public opinion. Though often controversial, there is no doubt that he was one of the 20th century's most powerful journalists. He died in Phoenix, Arizona, in 1967.

SEE ALSO

Volume 1 Left: Media Bias; Kennedy, John F.
Volume 2 Right: McCarthyism; Eisenhower, Dwight D,; Media Bias; Hearst, William Randolph.

BIBLIOGRAPHY

James L. Baughman, *Henry R. Luce and the Rise of the American News Media* (Macmillan, 1987); John K. Jessup, *The Ideas of Henry Luce* (Atheneum, 1969); W.A. Swanberg, *Luce and His Empire* (Scribner's, 1972); Robert E. Herzstein, *Henry R. Luce: A Political Portrait of the Man Who Created the American Century* (University of Chicago Press, 1994).

James S. Baugess
Columbia State Community College

The Right

M

Manifest Destiny

IN 1845, JOHN L. O'SULLIVAN argued persuasively for the acquisition of the Oregon Territory under the right of what he termed "our Manifest Destiny." Invoking predominant legacies of American religious providence and secular expansionism, O'Sullivan's phrase has resonated for some 150 years in the national spirit of continental expansionism and global influence. Although explicit political invocation has ebbed and waned throughout times of crisis and conflict, Manifest Destiny cannot be understood merely as a political doctrine. Rather the ideological, cultural, and social values embedded in the belief of American providence and territorial expansion comprise an important and central narrative regarding the origins, history, and purpose of America as a nation. These values, if not the doctrine itself, remain constant today, as they have throughout much of America's history.

The religious overtones of O'Sullivan's phrase are unmistakable and stand as a central theme in the American Anglo-Saxon narrative of divine providence. Drawing from colonial beliefs of America as the "New Israel" and "New Eden," early Americans and particularly Puritans envisioned their new world as an extension of God's promise or covenant to his chosen people. As O'Sullivan himself noted, the Manifest Destiny of America lay not merely in the right to land, but rather in the entire "revelation of right" through which the "magnificent domain of time and space" becomes the domain of God's promise. Thus, the posturing of America as the "New Israel" had at its core not merely the historical break from Europe but also the theological break from the Old World and its failures and corruptions.

While many nations throughout history have had similar divine providence myths, equally important to O'Sullivan's notion of Manifest Destiny was the growing technological and industrial power of the United States in the middle of the 19th century. America's role as an emerging world power, premised upon industrial growth and the belief of America as a "stage" for the rights and liberties of man, was the secular counterpart to the religious underpinnings of Manifest Destiny. This divine imperative of Manifest Destiny was thus coupled with industrial strength and Enlightenment ideals prevalent at the time to argue for the imperative of mass land acquisition, not only from indigenous people who left the land "fallow" but also from European nations and especially Britain, which (it was argued) sought to counter the ideals of Jeffersonian democracy and the providence of American power.

In terms of continental expansion, Manifest Destiny was perhaps most visible as a political doctrine in the mid-18th century annexations of Texas, Oregon, and California. Between 1824 and 1853, approximately

A painting titled "American Progress" or "Westward the Course of Destiny" by George A. Crofutt, 1873, features an allegorical female figure leading pioneers and railroads westward, and captures the spirit of Manifest Destiny.

1.7 million square miles of land were appropriated or conquered from Mexico alone. Under James Polk, the Oregon Territory was usurped from British control in 1846. In the ensuing war with Mexico, ending in 1848, the United States wrested control of Texas from Mexico, as well as California north of the Rio Grande. By the middle of the century, the American continent stretched from coast to coast.

The annexation and conquest of land from Mexico were important for reasons beyond the political and economic benefits such land provided to the United States. For while the doctrine or belief of Manifest Destiny demanded the acquisition of land from both the British and Mexico in the 1840s, the rationale and effects of such acquisitions varied greatly between the two and highlight the racism and Anglocentrism inher-

ent in the narrative of Manifest Destiny itself. In the case of Oregon, it was enough for Polk to speciously call for the "reannexation" of this territory. In the case of Texas, and later California, the discourse of Manifest Destiny took on more insidious and racial overtones. Opinion pieces and news stories of the day highlighted the achievements of pioneers and settlers, lauding the American history of conquest over indigenous peoples, extolling the virtues of Christianizing "savages" and Catholics.

In this regard, the national narrative of Manifest Destiny was a narrative for a small but powerful group of Americans who stood to profit enormously from the settlement and expropriation of land and labor. Other Americans, immigrants and slaves, were largely exempted from this "destiny."

The relative economic and political isolation that followed the Civil War saw a marked decrease in overt proclamations of Manifest Destiny. In one sense, the goal of coast-to-coast settlement and conquest had been achieved, and while European nations put massive effort into imperialistic enterprises, the United States concerned itself more with the reconstruction of the South as well as maintaining its growing industrial power and quelling labor unrest in the Northeast. With the rise of the 1893 depression and the subsequent war with Spain in 1898, however, the nationalistic imperative of Manifest Destiny again became political, albeit with a slightly different focus on global as opposed to continental aspirations. In 1898, the United States seized control of Cuba, Puerto Rico, Guam, Wake Island, and Manila. These territorial expansions were coupled with a growing belief in social Darwinism, eugenics, and various political theories that extolled the "burden" of the white man and the duty to press forth with "civilization" not only nationally but to all corners of the Earth. Such beliefs were hardly fringe, and the central focus on race cannot be underestimated.

Although critics of American expansionism were not remiss in comparing the actions of the United States to the imperialism and colonialism of Europe, such criticism was equally countered with the logic that Manifest Destiny was "God's plan" for all people, and that through American and Anglo-Saxon intervention, this plan would eventually be bestowed upon all nations.

By the beginning of the 20th century, the explicit invocation of Manifest Destiny as a serious political doctrine had already begun to wane, however. As a political doctrine it is now all but dead. What has remained, and what remains to this day, as Anders Stephanson notes, is the "millenarian commitment to the prophetic role of the United States." This was clear in the case of Wilson's Fourteen Points, as in the case of the Marshall Plan and subsequent American involvement in Southeast Asia, Central America, and the Middle East. Indeed, the logic and impetus for the most current war on terrorism and the war in Iraq bear striking parallels to earlier narratives of Manifest Destiny, where in the words of George W. Bush, America once again has been "called into a unique role in human events."

SEE ALSO

Volume 1 Left: Anti-Globalization; United States; Church and State Separation.
Volume 2 Right: Hegemony; Imperialism; United States; Bush, George W.

BIBLIOGRAPHY

Roberta Coles, "Manifest Destiny Adopted for 1990s War Discourse: Mission and Destiny Intertwined," *Sociology of Religion* (v.62/4, 2002); Julius Pratt, "The Origin of 'Manifest Destiny'," *American Historical Review* (v.32/4, July 1927); Anders Stephanson, *Manifest Destiny* (Hill and Wang, 1995); Albert K. Weinberg, *Manifest Destiny: A Study of Nationalist Expansionism in American History* (Johns Hopkins Press 1935).

WILLIAM R. WOOD
BOSTON COLLEGE

Martial Law

MARTIAL LAW CAN BE defined as the imposition of rule over civilians by military authorities during an emergency. A broader definition comes from the British Wikipdia reference: "Martial law is instituted most often when it becomes necessary to favor the activity of military authorities and organs, usually for urgent unforeseen needs, and when the normal institutions of justice either cannot function or could be deemed too slow or too weak for the new situation, i.e. due to war or civil disorder, in occupied territory, or after a coup d'etat. The need to preserve the public order during an emergency is the essential goal of martial law. Usually martial law reduces some of the personal rights ordinarily granted to the citizen, limits the length of the trial processes, and prescribes more severe penalties than ordinary law. In many countries martial law prescribes the death penalty for certain crimes, even if ordinary law doesn't contain that crime in its system."

As a militaristic form of government that often curtails if not outright eliminates civil liberties, it is on the hard-right, autocratic side of the political spectrum. The best course for discussing this controversial subject is within the British and American experiences from which the concept of martial law derived.

By the reign of Queen Elizabeth I (1558–1603), the use of armed force by the monarch had become severely circumscribed to times of armed rebellion or in the case of foreign invasion, as with the Spanish Armada in 1588. Indeed, during this period, except for bodies of mercenaries, the trained bands of militia, and the royal bodyguards wearing the red rose of Elizabeth's Tudor family, there really was no armed force in England. Henry VIII, her father, who had died in 1547, had completed the subjugation of the mighty feudal lords begun by his father, Henry VII (Tudor), when he became king in 1485.

During Elizabeth's reign, she had come to accept ruling in conjunction with the emerging parliament, which represented the growing middle class in the prosperous Tudor age. However, at her death in 1603, the crown passed to James I, who, as previous ruler of Scotland, had been used to a more autocratic rule. With Scotland generally a poorer country than England, no assertive middle class had really arisen to serve as a counter to excessive royal authority. This led to a continuing controversy in James's reign, with Sir Edward Coke becoming the leading parliamentarian opponent of James's autocratic conception of kingship. James, however, was astute enough to govern (if grudgingly) with Parliament rather than lose his new throne.

RIGHT TO RULE BY LAW

James I's son, Charles I, was even more autocratic, and unfortunately less astute. In January 1642, Charles I committed an unthinkable act. He entered the House of Commons to attempt to arrest Henry Pym and four other members who were vocal critics of his policies. Warned in advance, the five were able to flee. The result was the English Civil War, which would come to a grim close when Charles I was beheaded for treason in January 1649. While the Civil War established Parliament's right to rule by law over Charles's arbitrary kingship, the rule of Parliament dissolved into the more detested "rule of the major generals" of the army, who were commanded by the Lord Protector, Oliver Cromwell. With a thoroughness that would have done credit to totalitarian regimes of the 20th century, the ancient civil liberties of England were crushed by the booted and spurred dragoons of Cromwell's new model army. (Although Sir Thomas Fairfax had always been the titular commander, the dour Cromwell was the real force in the command.)

Two years after Cromwell's death in 1658, Charles I's son succeeded him as Charles II in 1660. Learning from his father's example, and not wishing to return to exile (or worse), Charles II ruled with Parliament until his death in 1685. However, his brother, James, Duke of York, had the autocratic disposition of his father rather than the dissipated political wisdom of his wily brother. James had reinforced his autocratic views with a lifetime of military service, having captured New York from the Dutch in 1664. When he became king in 1685, his concept of a militant monarchy came disastrously in conflict with the ideas of an increasingly assertive Parliament.

The result was that James was overthrown in the Bloodless Revolution of December 1688, when James's daughter Mary and her husband William of Orange were brought from the Netherlands to rule England in his place. Significantly, the new royal couple were first compelled to submit to the Declaration of Rights of February 13, 1689, which stated in part that the House of Lords and the House of Commons in Parliament did "claim, demand, and insist upon ... their undoubted rights and liberties." In April 1689, Governor Edmund Andros, whom James had appointed to rule most of New England, New Jersey, and New York, was cast out of office for the same absolutist rule of his royal master when news of the revolution spread to English North America.

Therefore, the constitutional growth of English liberties that was taking place in the home country was effectively carried to the New World. Significant in the growth of the concept of English law and self-government was the work of John Locke. Locke's *Two Treatises on Government*, which appeared in 1690, discussed the very nature of the contract that existed between ruler and ruled, in which those who ruled agreed to do so for the prosperity—and for the good—of the ruled. Locke stated in his Second Treatise that people agree "together mutually to enter into one Community, and make one body politic." He noted clearly, looking back to the Bloodless, or Glorious, Revolution, that if the ruling power is "made use of to impoverish, harass, or subdue [the people] to the arbitrary and irregular commands of those who have it: there it presently becomes Tyranny." Over the next decades in the British colonies, Locke's words would be remembered.

After the French and Indian War ended in a British victory, the reigning sovereign, George III, attempted to enforce payment for the war on the 13 colonies, in spite of the fact that they had made splendid voluntary contributions during the war. His autocratic methods evoked widespread dissent. When in 1767, his sycophants in Parliament enacted the Townshend Acts, which put duties on certain commodities without the consent of the colonists, John Dickinson wrote his seminal *Letters from a Farmer in Pennsylvania* attacking the laws as unconstitutional, echoing Locke's vision that excessive government action led to tyranny.

As the 1760s wore on, colonial indignation grew at the arbitrary efforts of the king and his ministers, especially Lord North, to bend the colonies to their will. Increasingly, George III began to employ the militaristic methods of James II, who had in England used his troops to brutally suppress the rebellion of his own nephew, James, Duke of Monmouth, in 1685. On March 5, 1770, British soldiers in Boston fired into a mob of demonstrators who were harassing them, killing some five and injuring six, although Boston attorney John Adams, using the Massachusetts legal system, succeeded in getting the soldiers acquitted on only charges of minor offenses. However, the first blood had been shed in the American Revolution.

By doing so, George III began what was virtually a military occupation of Boston, later to be treated as a virtually occupied city: the first major use of martial law in the soon-to-be United States. The founding fathers, experienced in the effects of what a government's standing army could do under martial law, carefully considered the proposition in declaring independence from Britain and setting up the new nation.

THE STANDING ARMY

When the American Revolution was won and American independence was recognized in the Treaty of Paris in September 1783, a key point for the founding fathers was to regulate the use—and very existence—of any American standing army. This issue virtually split the Constitutional Convention, which met in Philadelphia in May 1787. The Federalist camp, with leaders like Alexander Hamilton, advocated a strong central government, and the anti-Federalists, with the spirit of men like George Mason, wanted more power given to the states. A main concern of the anti-Federalists was that a strong central government, supported by a regular standing army, would only lead to an American version of the despotism of George III.

It was not until the Bill of Rights, the first 10 amendments to the Constitution, was ratified in December 1791 that Americans were free from a government relying on overt military rule. The fact that the president could in effect nationalize the state militias did not necessarily provoke fear in the delegates. As members of the revolutionary generation, they felt that, if they had overthrown an autocratic king, then so too could they depose an arbitrary president.

Yet, almost immediately, there was indeed the need for armed force to keep civil order. In 1794, efforts to place an excise tax on whiskey, a commodity that even served as currency on the frontier, provoked a rebellion. To quell it, President George Washington amassed an army of some 15,000 men. Although armed resistance was limited, the army behaved at times brutally. As Catherine McNichol Stock wrote, the soldiers "treated their captives cruelly and in a few cases fatally [and

were] looting, plundering, and disrupting life in general." Once again, a lesson had been learned about the use of armed force in a civilian crisis. From then on, the use of troops in domestic American affairs became more limited. And the imposition of martial law—the suspension of civil law—was something that was looked at with awe and suspicion.

During the American Civil War, beginning in April 1861, President Abraham Lincoln would come the closest of any president to date to declaring a national state of martial law. Indeed, his suspension of the writ of habeas corpus, especially in the case of the former Ohio Congressman Clement L. Vallandigham in May 1861 for supporting the South, was in fact a step on the road to rule by presidential decree, or fiat.

Moreover, Vallandigham had been arrested by Union (Northern) Army troops, not police or sheriffs. In writing to Erastus Corning in June 1863, Lincoln in effect redefined the provision of habeas corpus in the Constitution. He wrote, "arrests by process of courts, and arrests in cases of rebellion, do not proceed altogether from the same basis … In the latter case, arrests are made, not so much for what has been done, as for what probably would be done." Lincoln, in other words, was saying that a man would be presumed as guilty unless proven otherwise.

POSSE COMITATUS

In order to redress the situation that Lincoln had unconstitutionally exploited, the Posse Comitatus Act was passed soon after in 1878, which defined the limits and use of the military in governing civilian populations in America. Since the Civil War, there have been instances when martial law has come to be enforced, but only for brief periods of time. In 1892, at Coeur d'Alene, Idaho, rebellious mine workers blew up a mill and shot at strikebreaking workers. The explosion leveled a four-story building and killed one person. Mine owners asked the governor to declare martial law, which he did. At the same time, a request was made for federal troops to back guardsmen. Over 600 people were arrested. The list was whittled down to two dozen ringleaders who were tried in civil court.

In 1914, imposition of martial law climaxed the so-called Coal Field Wars in Colorado. Dating back decades, the conflicts came to a head in Ludlow in 1913. The Colorado National Guard was called in to quell the strikers. For a time, the peace was kept, but it is reported that the makeup of the guard stationed at the mines began to shift from impartial normal troops to companies of loyal mine guards. Clashes increased and the proclamation of martial law was made by the governor. President Wilson sent in federal troops, eventually ending the violence.

In 1934, California Governor Frank Merriam placed the docks of San Francisco under martial law, citing "riots and tumult" resulting from a dockworkers' strike. The governor threatened to place the entire city under martial law. The National Guard was called in to open the docks, and a citywide institution of martial law was averted when goods began to flow. The guardsmen were empowered to make arrests and to then try detainees or turn them over to the civil courts.

Martial law and San Francisco were no strangers: following the earthquake of 1906, the troops stationed in the Presidio were pressed into service. Guards were posted throughout the city, and all dynamite was confiscated. The dynamite was used to destroy buildings in the path of fires to prevent the fires from spreading. Troops were ordered to shoot looters. Though there was never an official declaration of martial law, the event is often cited as such. However, at all times it appears the troops took their orders indirectly from the civil authority.

MODERN USE OF MARTIAL LAW

Though not a state at the time, Hawaii was placed under martial law in 1941, following the Japanese attack on Pearl Harbor. Many of the residents of Hawaii were, and are, of Asian descent, and the loyalty of these people was called into question. After the war, the federal judge for the islands condemned the conduct of martial law, saying, "Governor Poindexter declared lawfully martial law but the Army went beyond the governor and set up that which was lawful only in conquered enemy territory namely, military government which is not bound by the Constitution. And they ... threw the Constitution into the discard and set up a military dictatorship."

Three other more recent events saw presidents use extraordinary powers. In 1952, President Harry Truman ordered the government to seize the nation's steel mills. These were held for seven weeks until, as Richard E. Neustadt explained in *Presidential Power*, "the Supreme Court held that he had exceeded his authority." On September 2, 1957, the segregationist governor of Arkansas, Orville Faubus, called out the National Guard to prevent integration of the Central High School in Little Rock, Arkansas. On September 23, however, President Dwight D. Eisenhower "called the

Arkansas National Guard into federal service, thus removing it from Faubus's hands, and ordered regular army troops to Little Rock. Order was restored and the Negro [African American] children," Neustadt recorded, "returned to school." In October 1962, the same scenario was enacted when James Meredith, an African American air force veteran, attempted to enroll at the University of Mississippi. As the BBC noted, "Hundreds of extra troops have been brought in to join Federal forces already stationed in the nearby town of Oxford as the violence spread to its streets." Earlier, President John F. Kennedy had called the Mississippi National Guard into federal service, as had President Eisenhower at Little Rock.

Since the 1990s, with terror attacks like the Oklahoma City bombing of the Murrah Federal Building in April 1995, and the terrorist attacks of September 2001, calls have come from the right for the invocation of martial law. Thomas R. Lujan expressed a prescient opinion: "the U.S. Army has participated in an arguably unprecedented number and type of domestic employments. These include disaster relief operations, military support to law enforcement in the war against drugs, and discrete cases of military support to federal law enforcement agencies."

It is a premise that the rule of martial law will be employed again in the United States given a national emergency. The critical element of success is strict conformance with the legal framework established by the Constitution and federal law. The *Washington University Law Quarterly* noted in "The Posse Comitatus Act: A Principle in Need of Renewal" that "The Act embodies the traditional American principle of separating civilian and military authority and currently forbids the use of the Army and Air Force to enforce civilian laws. In the last 15 years, Congress has deliberately eroded this principle by involving the military in drug interdiction at our borders. This erosion will continue unless Congress renews the PCA's [Posse Comitatus Act] principle to preserve the necessary and traditional separation of civilian and military authority. The need for reaffirmation of the PCA's principle is increasing because in recent years, Congress and the public have seen the military as a panacea for domestic problems."

Indeed, alarmists have seen the Patriot Act of 2001 as an overture to the introduction of martial law throughout the United States. However, given the constitutional history of the United States, beginning indeed before its independence in 1776, it would be extremely unusual for the American view of martial law, based on its British precedent, to change. Martial law exists, and in extreme situations may in fact be required. However, with past experience as a guide, it is a legal last resort to forestall anarchy, a legal breathing space that only exists until civilian law is able to function once more.

SEE ALSO

Volume 1 Left: Liberalism; United States; United Kingdom; Anarchism; Locke, John.
Volume 2 Right: Conservatism; United States; United Kingdom; Posse Comitatus.

BIBLIOGRAPHY

"Martial law," http://en.wikipedia.org (June 2004); Stuart Prall, *The Bloodless Revolution: England, 1688* (Anchor Books, 1972); Peter Laslet, ed., *John Locke's Two Treatises of Government* (Mentor Books, 1965); Walter Mills, *Arms and Men: A Study of American Military History* (Mentor Books, 1956); "The Posse Comitatus Act: A Principle in Need of Renewal," *Washington University Law Quarterly* (Summer 1997); Thomas R. Lujan, "Legal Aspects of Domestic Employment of the Army," *Parameters* (Autumn 1997); Mario Cuomo and Harold Holzer, *Lincoln on Democracy* (Harper, 1990); Ernest R. May, ed., *The Ultimate Decision: The President as Commander In Chief* (George Braziller, 1960); Richard E. Neustadt, *Presidential Power* (Mentor Books, 1964); BBC, "On This Day, October 1, 1962," www.bbc.com (June 2004).

JOHN F. MURPHY, JR.
AMERICAN MILITARY UNIVERSITY

McCarthyism

BY THE TIME IGOR Gouzenko announced in September 1945 that the Soviets were operating a spy ring in Canada, the uneasy world war alliance between the Soviet Union and the United States, rivals since the late 19th century, enemies since the Bolshevik revolution of 1917, was done. Soviet expansionism and American anti-communism began the clash of the Cold War.

During World War II, the United States and the Soviet Union were joined in the common struggle against fascism despite their long-standing philosophical disagreements. With the war won, the differences overwhelmed the common interest, and the one-time allies split into opposing camps. The Soviet Union pursued an aggressive policy of establishing satellites in the countries its troops occupied, a buffer against the threat from central Europe. The United States and Great Britain read the expansion as an attempt by "monolithic communism" to spread through the world. The "Iron Curtain" fell between east and west. The conflict grew when the enemy, defined by many Americans as an atheistic anti-democratic monolith, spread its tentacles into China. In 1949, the forces of America's ally Chiang Kai-shek fell to the communists under Mao Zedong. The promises of victory and peace after World War II seemed to be in ashes. Americans felt overwhelmed by the spreading tide of communism.

For five years after the war, the threat of communism seemed to grow with each revelation. The culmination of the second Red Scare was the product of a young Wisconsin senator's need for a campaign issue. When Senator Joseph McCarthy alleged that 200 card-carrying communists were in the U.S. government, the era of McCarthyism was begun.

McCarthy did not spring from nowhere. His anti-communism was consistent with government anti-communism. Even the governments of the United States and Canada seemed to be filled with communist infiltrators and sympathizers. The Harry Truman administration began a serious investigation of the bureaucracy, rooting out communists and former communists and demanding loyalty oaths.

The Congress took on the communists too, especially in the House Un-American Activities Committee (HUAC), established in 1938 to investigate persons suspected of being unpatriotic. HUAC used the Alien Registration Act of 1940 as its authority. The Alien Registration Act outlawed the advocacy or abetting of any effort to overthrow the U.S. government, and it required all alien residents over age 14 to register and file a statement of occupational status and political beliefs. Almost half a million registered under this law, which had as its primary purpose the identification and undermining of the American Communist Party and other left-wing political organizations. The House of Representatives authorized HUAC to take on the task of finding out who, if anyone, was trying to overthrow the government.

Under Chairman J. Parnell Thomas (R-NJ), HUAC began investigating in 1947 the motion picture industry. Interviews with 41 friendly witnesses identified 19 Hollywood left-wingers. Bertolt Brecht testified and then departed for East Germany. Ten others refused to testify, citing their constitutional right to remain silent. The committee cited them for contempt, the courts upheld the decision, and the Hollywood Ten served sentences of six to 12 months. The 10 were: Alvah Bessie,

Herbert Biberman, Lester Cole, Edward Dmytryk, Ring Lardner, Jr., John Howard Lawson, Albert Maltz, Samuel Ornitz, Adrian Scott, and Dalton Trumbo.

One of the liberals was the actor Larry Parks. He admitted that he was a Communist Party member during the period from 1941 to 1945. He was reluctant to do so, but in a private session he named associates. Later witnesses, former members of left-wing groups, added names under duress and fear of imprisonment. Among these witnesses were Lee J. Cobb, Richard Collins, Roy Huggins, Elia Kazan, Isobel Lennart, and Budd Schulberg.

Three former FBI agents and the right-wing television producer Vince Harnett published *Red Channels* in 1950. This pamphlet named 151 movie industry workers (writers, directors, performers) who had belonged to "subversive" organizations prior to the war but had not yet been uncovered by HUAC or blacklisted. The authors sent copies of *Red Channels* to potential employers in the industry, which blacklisted all the named persons until they agreed to appear before HUAC and convince the committee that they had repudiated their pasts. One of the Hollywood Ten, Edward Dmytryk, was having financial problems,so he testified, naming 26 people. Dmytryk also claimed that he had been under pressure to make films supporting the Communist Party line. The lists continued to grow until over 320 people were blacklisted. Most of these people's careers never recovered.

While the investigations of Hollywood were in full swing, the government was also using the Alien Registration Act directly against party leaders. In October 1949, after a nine-month trial, 11 were convicted of violation of the act. Another 46 were arrested over the next two years. And espionage cases were occurring at the same time, most notably those of Alger Hiss and Julius and Ethel Rosenberg. With so many communists everywhere, there seemed to be a conspiracy. The mood was set.

OVERREACTION

In this environment, on February 9, 1950, McCarthy found the issue he needed to revitalize his re-election campaign. McCarthy claimed that he had a list of 205 known members of the American Communist Party in the State Department. Actually, the list was an old one, a public record at that, published by the secretary of state in 1946 as part of the preliminary screening of 3,000 federal workers. The list included communists, but it also included sexual deviants, alcoholics, and fas-cists. McCarthy would use the "list" on other occasions, letting the number vary and not actually showing its contents to anyone. McCarthy had an ally in the FBI. Long-time anti-communist J. Edgar Hoover fed information from his massive FBI collection of dossiers to the Wisconsin senator. Neither Hoover nor McCarthy spent much time validating information in the dossiers. McCarthy continued to make allegations, and political tensions increased.

By then the war in Korea had begun, and it was going badly in the early stages. Coming on top of the loss of China and eastern Europe, the risk that North Korea might overrun the South fueled the fear already vivid after five years of Red-hunting and Cold War rhetoric. McCarthy used the environment to his advantage. He focused initially on New Deal Democrats and members of the Truman administration, including George Marshall and Dean Acheson, whom he accused of being "soft on communism." He painted Truman as a dangerous liberal.

McCarthy used his position as chairman of the Government Committee on Operations of the Senate as his forum for a two-year investigation of government agencies. His interrogations did result in the firing of some government workers who admitted past ties to the American Communist Party. McCarthy demanded that they name other members as a sign that they had repented. The witch hunt led artists and intellectuals into exile. James Baldwin, Herbert Biberman, Lester Cole, Chester Himes, Joseph Losey, Ollie Harrington, and Richard Wright were among those who went to Europe.

McCarthyism was a factor in the victory of Republican Dwight Eisenhower in the 1952 election, and McCarthy seemed able to sway congressional elections as well. When William Benton of Connecticut spoke against McCarthyism, McCarthy and his allies accused Benton of having protected known communists and of having bought and displayed "lewd art" while assistant secretary of state. McCarthy also accused Benton of disloyalty for having his *Encyclopedia Britannica* printed in England. Benton lost his reelection bid in 1952.

Roy Cohn became chief counsel to McCarthy's committee in 1952. Cohn came with the recommendation of Hoover, impressed by Cohn's efforts in the prosecution of the Rosenbergs. Cohn brought in his friend, David Schine, as chief consultant. McCarthy began targeting libraries. His staff found 30,000 anti-American, pro-communist books in overseas libraries. Librarians removed the offending volumes.

McCarthy's opponents had been busily looking for evidence that he had engaged in homosexual activities.

They also investigated a rumored sexual relationship between Cohn and Schine. The first to break the story of McCarthy's homosexuality was Hank Greenspun of the *Las Vegas Sun*, in an October 1952 article. McCarthy considered but rejected a libel suit against Greenspun. He didn't want to have to testify about his sexual activities. He married his secretary and the couple adopted a baby.

McCarthy continued investigating communist infiltration. When he started an investigation of the U.S. Army in 1953, his attempt to discredit Army Secretary Robert Stevens infuriated Eisenhower, who began working to bring McCarthy down. The army began leaking anti-McCarthy information to journalists who opposed him. One leak pertained to McCarthy and Cohn's efforts to keep Schine from being drafted and Cohn's efforts to get Schine special privileges. The story broke in the column of Drew Pearson on December 15, 1953.

The media had not been totally quiet. I.F. Stone, George Seldes, Herb Block, Daniel Fitzpatrick, and Freda Kirchway were among the writers and cartoonists who had opposed McCarthyism. The administration's change emboldened others, such as Edward R. Murrow, Walter Lippmann, and Jack Anderson.

Eisenhower unleashed Vice President Richard Nixon, who spoke on March 4, 1954, about "Men who have in the past done effective work exposing communists in this country have, by reckless talk and questionable methods, made themselves the issue rather than the cause they believe in so deeply."

Finally, the Senate held hearings on the army and McCarthy entanglement. On December 2, 1954, the Senate censured McCarthy by 67 to 22. McCarthy lost his chairmanship, his power base, and his forum, and the media lost interest in him. Some of those blacklisted did manage to return to work, but the stain of McCarthyism remained, and the impulse that fed it remained through the end of the century.

The United States in the postwar years had communists and former communists in government. The Truman administration's purges demonstrated that. What remained were the lists of "subversive" organizations, the loyalty oaths, and a lessened right to dissent. There is no way to know what might have been without McCarthyism and the second Red Scare. No one will ever know how many ideas never entered the public forum because of the blacklists and the anti-communist conformity. There is no question that the loss of so many talents affected the intellectual life of the nation. Even without McCarthy, though, the U.S. government con-

Senator Joseph McCarthy of Wisconsin unleashed an anti-communist witch hunt that came to be known as McCarthyism.

tinued to pursue alleged communists. The FBI under Hoover continued to be extremely active, especially when the postwar conformism of the 1950s gave way to the activist 1960s. FBI "anti-communist" activities included the COINTELPRO program against political dissent in the 1960s and 1970s. Anti-communism allowed the CIA to intervene in the Middle East and Latin America. Government secrecy grew as the Cold War progressed and some people saw the United States as a national security state, running roughshod over law in the name of national security. The McCarthyite hysteria promoted the growth of government intrusion on formerly private matters. And the habit of public and private suppression of communism through loyalty oaths, blacklisting, and other measures reduced the efficacy of any challenge to the Cold War state.

The extreme American left had been struggling since long before World War II because of its overly close ties to Soviet communism. After McCarthy, it was practically dead. The move of the public mood to the right weakened not only communists but socialists and radical unionists as well. Internationally, U.S. foreign policy became bipartisan, but the consensus of the cold warriors reduced the amount of debate about the role of the United States in the world. There was no challenge from the left, radical or moderate. Without challenge, the United States often put aside its historical commitment to liberty and justice and supported repressive right-wing governments because they professed to be anti-communist.

SEE ALSO

Volume 1 Left: Communism; Socialism; Third International (Comintern).
Volume 2 Right: Capitalism; Conservatism; Republican Party; Hoover, J. Edgar.

BIBLIOGRAPHY

American Masters. "McCarthyism," www.pbs.org (Janary 2004); Michael Barson and Steven Heller, *Red Scared! The Commie Menace in Propaganda and Popular Culture* (Chronicle Books, 2001); Jesse G. Cunningham and Laura K. Egendorf, eds., *The McCarthy Hearings* (Greenhaven Press, 2003); M.J. Heale, *McCarthy's Americans: Red Scare Politics in State and Nation* (University of Georgia Press, 1998); Ellen Schrecker, *The Age of McCarthyism* (St. Martin's Press, 1994).

JOHN BARNHILL, PH.D.
INDEPENDENT SCHOLAR

Media Bias, Right

THE CONCEPT OF MEDIA objectivity, and even media balance, has been widely criticized by observers on both the left and right sides of the political spectrum. Those who accuse the modern media (primarily the news press, radio, and television) of having a right-wing bias focus on the issue of media ownership, the pressure of advertising, the relations among media, business, and government, and the process of news production.

Critical media scholars take issue with the cornerstone of traditional journalism, which claims that the modern news media produce an objective, truthful and neutral account of events where journalist and the news media are detached observers, separable from the social reality on which they report. Robert Hackett and Yuezhi Zhao discuss the "regime of objectivity" as a "walking corpse, kept in motion only by the interests vested in it and the absence of a stronger alternative." Other scholars' work on newsworthiness illustrates the problems with objectivity. Newsworthiness is deter-

mined by themes, continuity, and consonance. For a story to be newsworthy it must be comprehensible, and it becomes comprehensible when it fits into a "frame" that arises from past news stories. A story will also be considered of greater interest if it can be covered the same way as past, similar stories, and if it lends itself to coverage through familiar themes.

POLITICAL ECONOMY

Those who identify right-wing media bias examine ownership and economic pressures on the media, based on a theoretical position that looks for the economic dimension underlying social and political life. When applied to the media, political economy seeks to highlight the fact that it is the business of newspapers to make money. A political economy perspective emphasizes the need to examine the ownership of the press and the economic influence on the press by its for-profit nature. The political economy perspective argues that the media is directly or indirectly affected by the social forces of our society—social forces that frequently are the expression of dominant economic power.

Media ownership is important because it addresses the adage that "freedom of the press is for those who own one." Researchers in this area explore how much influence a media owner exerts on the content of the news, either directly through edict or indirectly through the creation of an ideological climate that shapes the presentation of journalists' work. In the case of direct impact by owners, we have seen examples of this in Canada where a corporate tycoon, such as Conrad Black, bought media outlets in a conscious effort to disseminate his worldview through his newspaper chain. Australian-born Rupert Murdoch, president and CEO of News Corporation, is also frequently cited in the same regard.

Ben Bagdikian (1992) notes that the lack of competition has resulted in a homogenous media product that serves the interests of a small number of owners. He argues that in the United States, the national news media have been remarkably inattentive to the growing economic and social failures induced by government policies benefiting large corporations and other powerful segments of society at the expense of the general population. Bagdikian maintains that owners have always wielded enough influence that stories involving their own interests are reported in their favor. But now when a large corporate owner intervenes, alterations in coverage and analysis affect reports reaching millions. He points to the example of Lawrence Grossman, the former president of NBC News, who when speaking at Brandeis University, said that when the stock market crashed in 1987, he received a phone call from Jack Welch, chairman of General Electric, owner of NBC, telling him not to use words in NBC news reports that might adversely affect GE stock.

Some media scholars focus on the general pro-capitalist climate of profit-oriented media. Todd Gitlin (1985) and Herbert Gans (1980) have examined the decision-making processes of large media organizations and have found that there are a number of economic factors that serve to shape the news product and direct it to a status quo orientation. "The imperatives of keeping costs down and profits up affect the news-gathering procedures, content, and form of daily newspapers in every market," Robert Entman explains. These factors include the cost-cutting measures, so familiar to many journalists and media watchers, in which journalists are laid off. To replace the work of these people, the media rely instead on wire services. The use of wire services has the effect of reducing the amount of local news and importing coverage and perspectives from centralized news clearinghouses. The cutback in journalists usually means a reduction in investigative reporting, pursuit of nontraditional sources, and reliance on press releases, easy-to-locate officials, and media handlers. Focus is restricted to the same institutions and sources and coverage tends to privilege preplanned media events as opposed to spontaneous social problems.

The for-profit orientation of media corporations also tends to result in a situation where the media try to aid their supporters—namely their advertisers and the wider business community. This orientation can affect news content directly and indirectly. In terms of direct influence, we see journalists and editors bowing to advertisers' requirements for a hospitable climate for their ads. Media scholars note that such events are rare because the rules of the game are generally known within the industry. In terms of a more indirect effect on media content, observers have noted a rise in upbeat, personality-based news stories. It is argued that these stories, particularly those on television news placed prior to going to commercial break, are intended to keep the public in the "buying mood" where a story of poverty or war may cause the audience to react negatively to an advertisement for unnecessary purchases.

PROPAGANDA MODEL

The propaganda model of the media comes out of the work of noted intellectual Noam Chomsky and his col-

laborator, Edward Herman. At root, Chomsky contends that "violence, deceit and lawlessness are natural functions of the state, any state." Yet in "liberal democracies," like the United States and Canada, such a realization on the part of the majority must be discouraged, since it might lead to efforts to transform politics, the economy, and society. The "manufacture of consent," achieved through the media and education systems, is the means through which a false, alternative framework is imposed on the population. For Chomsky and Herman, the "propaganda model" points to the subordination of most private and public media to the interests of the dominant elite.

Chomsky argues that key decisions over what happens in an industrial capitalist state are in the hands of a small elite, which controls major corporations, media and government. This group dominates the way the society is run in economics, law, and government, and imposes its interests through ideological and legitimation systems—one of which is the media. Chomsky argues that this anti-democratic approach is justified in the eyes of the power holders because they subscribe to a philosophy that holds that the people who own the country ought to govern it. He points to Walter Lippmann's comments in 1921 that the concept of the manufacture of consent would revolutionize the practice of democracy.

Lippmann argued that the ruling elite needed this form of social control because the public wasn't up to dealing with the burdens of democracy. Lippmann favored the use of "necessary illusions" to keep the masses in line so that they wouldn't become so arrogant that they wouldn't submit to civil rule. Thus propaganda was seen as an appropriate tool for these purposes.

For Chomsky, the media are essentially involved in the manufacturing of consent. The elite that owns the economy and controls politics is probably the most class-conscious group, and its members are likely to read the *Wall Street Journal*. In the Chomskyan theory, the business press provides a more frank account of the reality of political and, in particular, economic news since managers are regarded as needing an accurate understanding of reality in order to make decisions. This is not to say that the *Wall Street Journal* is "objective," since there is no such thing. Rather, the press that serves elites can include ideas that the more popular press must avoid. For example, this "know-thy-enemy" principle would explain why the *Wall Street Journal* would run a weekly column by left-wing journalist Alexander Cockburn, who normally writes for publications like

The Nation, while more centrist papers that appeal to a mass audience will not.

Most journalists, opinion leaders, and mainstream academics are both victims and villains, however, since they believe the false framework and also propagate it throughout society. Material presented in the media will affect the opinions of attentive readers or provide distraction for the inattentive, according to Chomsky. The majority of the population follow orders and pay the costs of the decisions made by the elites. They just need to be distracted from political and economic developments, to focus on sports, entertainment, and circuses instead.

The manufacture of consent is facilitated by the media's role in gatekeeping and agenda setting. Gatekeepers let in stories that conform to acceptable themes played out in the daily news. As Herman notes, "Gatekeeper biases are reinforced by the preferences and biases of advertisers, their natural gravitation to convenient and official sources, and their fear of negative feedback (flak) from bodies and groups that might threaten their position." Elite media set the agenda for all other media by determining what is newsworthy. Chomsky notes that the *New York Times* is the most important newspaper in the United States, if not the English-speaking world. The *Times* creates history, since history is defined as what is in the newspaper of record's back issues and archives. Every evening, the top stories from tomorrow's *Times* are transmitted around the country to regional dailies to tell them what the news and issues are. News media affect public opinion about social and political issues by selecting which stories to use and what priority to give them. Thus some media theorists believe that the media do not necessarily tell people what to think, but they do tell them what they should think about.

THE NEWS CONSTRUCTION PERSPECTIVE

The news construction perspective is another alternative to the objectivity school. Arguing that no account of events is "reality written down" but only a specific story about reality, the news construction approach focuses on the mechanics of news production and professional practices as the source of the shape and structure of news content. Theorists in the news construction tradition have taken this conception of ideology and developed a number of sophisticated theories that attempt to analyze the process by which the news is ideologically formed. Stuart Hall (1974) argues that the basic principles of objective reporting, such as consensus,

balance, impartiality, and sticking to professional practices, are themselves not ideologically neutral. These elements of contemporary journalism are, he argues, a set of crucial intervening concepts that direct and guide the journalist in handling the minefield of political and ideological conflict in a particular way, and in generating a standard kind of news perspective.

SEE ALSO

BIBLIOGRAPHY

Ben Bagdikian, *The Media Monopoly* (Beacon Press, 1992); Noam Chomsky, *The Chomsky Reader* (Pantheon Books, 1987); Robert M. Entman, *Democracy without Citizens: Media and the Decay of American Politics* (Oxford University Press, 1989); R. Ericson, P.M. Baranek, and J.B.L. Chen, *Visualizing Deviance: A Study of News Organizations* (University of Toronto Press, 1987); Herbert Gans, *Deciding What's News: A Study of CBS Evening News, NBC Nightly News, Newsweek and Time* (Vintage Press, 1980); Todd Gitlin, *Inside Prime Time* (Pantheon, 1985); Robert A. Hackett and Yuezhi Zhao, *Sustaining Democracy? Journalism and the Politics of Objectivity* (Garamond Press, 1998); Stuart Hall, "Media Power: The Double Bind," *Journal of Communications* (v.3, 1974); Edward S. Herman, *Beyond Hypocrisy: Decoding the News in an Age of Propaganda* (Black Rose, 1992); Justin Lewis, *The Myth of the Liberal Media: The Propaganda Model of News* (Film, Media Education Foundation).

GEOFFREY R. MARTIN
MOUNT ALLISON UNIVERSITY, CANADA

Messianic Cults

IN MODERN TIMES, the story of Messianic cults embraces both Christian and Jewish faiths, since the coming of the Messiah stands at the *kerigma*, or essential truths, of both faiths.

Perhaps the first known modern Messianic thought came fittingly in 1492, when in fact the modern age began with the discovery of the New World by Christopher Columbus. Tragically, 1492 also marked the expulsion of the Jews from Spain, who had contributed so much to Hispanic culture. Gershom Scholem, in *Major*

Trends in Jewish Mysticism, chronicled the devastating effect the Expulsion had on students of the esoteric Kabbalah. Wrote Scholem, "the birthpangs of the Messianic era, with which history is to 'end,' or (as the apocalyptics would have it) to 'collapse,' were therefore assumed to have set in with the Expulsion." According to Scholem, perhaps the best known of the Expulsion-era Kabbalists was Abraham ben Eliezer Ha-Levi in Jerusalem, who was "an untiring agitator and interpreter of events 'pregnant' with redemption."

Considerably more controversy surrounded David Reuveni (Reubeni), an Italian Jewish dwarf who, as Leo Rosten wrote in *The Joys of Yiddish*, "in the year 1524 announced in Venice that he was the brother of the King of one of the Lost Tribes [of Israel], the tribe of Reuben." At a time when the Turks under Suleiman the Magnificent were mounting a great invasion of Christian Europe, David announced to Pope Clement VII that his brother commanded—to quote Rosten—"thousands of splendid Jewish soldiers behind the Turkish lines." It was indeed a critical time for Christian Europe because in December 1522, the island of Rhodes was lost to the Turks after a heroic defense by the Knights of St. John of Jerusalem, known popularly from their later bastion as the Knights of Malta. In 1526, the Turks would destroy the army of King Louis II of Hungary at Mohacs.

The pope believed Reuveni and sent him on to Portugal where he was well-received. One Portuguese became so enamored of this false Messiah's cause that he was circumcised and took the name of Solomon Molko. Molko, in fact, accurately foresaw an earthquake in Portugal and a flood of the Tiber River in Rome, which naturally impressed the pope. Reuveni was so convincing in this hour of crisis for Christianity that he even gained an audience with the Holy Roman Emperor Charles V. The Holy Roman Emperor garnered a great victory at Vienna in 1529 when Suleiman was frustrated in his attempt to seize the city. There seems then to have been no more need for Reuveni's phantom legions. In 1532, Molko was burned at the stake at an auto da fe, an "act of Faith," by the Holy Inquisition, and Reuveni would follow his faithful disciple in 1552 in Portugal.

The experience of Reuveni and Molko shows that while under stress, governments and people may accept fanciful, even dangerous leaders and movements but once calm is restored, they are rejected. Sometimes, in the case of Reuveni and Molko, they are put to death. In May 1498, Girolamo Savonarola, a Dominican monk, was hanged at Florence, Italy, for defying the Roman Catholic Church. Earlier, he had gained respect for his preaching aimed at reform of the religious life of the church. Later, however, he went on to preach for the intervention of the French King Charles VIII in both church and Italian affairs. Refusing to be silent, he was excommunicated from the church in May 1497. When he defied his excommunication and continued to preach, his execution became a foregone conclusion.

Born two years after Molko's execution, Isaac ben Solomon Luria continued the Kabbalistic study of the Messiah that had begun with the Expulsion from Spain. Although not a cult in the modern sense, Kabbalistic students represented an enduring strain of mysticism in Judaism that would even survive the Holocaust of World War II. Luria's dedicated follower, Hayim Vital, is the main source of what we know of his teachings; indeed so profoundly did he impress his students that he was considered a *tzaddik*, a truly "holy man." As with many Kabbalists, Luria, working in Safed in Palestine, brought a type of conservatism to his religious thought, which helped it to survive in the basically Orthodox Jewish society in which he lived and worked. Vital's best-known document is the *Shemonah Shearim*, the *Eight Gates*. Concerning Luria's thought, Scholem commented, Luria was "decidedly conservative in his persistent attempts to relate what he had to say to older authorities, especially to the *Zofar* [one of the principal books of Kabbalistic learning]." The *Zofar*, or *Book of Splendor*, was a product of 13th-century Jewish mysticism in Spain. After Luria's untimely death in Safed in 1572, his teachings were carried on by his disciples Vital and Joseph ibn Tabul.

PROTESTANT REFORMATION

At the time of the Protestant Reformation, perhaps the first example in modern times of a Messianic following arose with the Anabaptist movement, which was focused largely in Germany. Challenging both Catholic and Protestant ideas on baptism, the Anabaptists found themselves hounded by both the guardians of the old order, the Roman Catholic Church, and the protectors of the new, Protestant leaders like Martin Luther. Their belief in total equality of all men and an equable distribution of wealth sent tremors through the contemporary civil establishment as well. Under the preacher Melchior Hoffmann, the Anabaptists in Munster in Westphalia, Germany, carried on a virtual reign of terror against those who defied their zealotry. They claimed that Munster had been chosen to be the New Jerusalem, and chose the adolescent John of Leyden to rule as "king of Zion." When the government of the Holy Roman Emperor Charles V took Munster on June 24, 1535, John of Leyden was executed and his body hung in a cage as a warning against such social chaos.

Another example of the discovery of a false Messiah dates from a similar period of persecution to the Expulsion from Spain. In 1648, Europe was still in the agony of the Thirty Years War, which the Treaty of Westphalia would in that year put to a merciful end. However, in what is now Ukraine and Poland, a savage uprising was in progress among the Cossacks led by Bohdan Khmelnitsky. The Ukrainian, or Zaporozhe, Cossacks, slaughtered between 100,000 and 300,000 innocent Jews. Amid the slaughter yard of the Ukraine, Jews looked for a Messiah to save them from this hell on earth. Sabbatai Zevi, in this time of mass disruption, answered the call. His family had arrived in Salonika in the Ottoman Empire, part of the vast diaspora of Sephardic Jews from Spain.

From Smyrna in Turkey, where he had been born in 1626, Sabbatai's movement spread through the Jewry of the Middle East, in spite of the opposition of the religious authorities in the Holy Land, where Sabbatai Zevi visited unproductively in 1662. With all Europe now entering a period of anti-Semitism, Jews from Europe also began to clutch at the hope that Sabbatai was, as his fervent disciples claimed, "the King of the Jews." However, the Turkish authorities took him as a threat to the civil order, much as the Romans had done to Jesus Christ centuries before. Unwisely, as Chaim Potok wrote in *Wanderings*, in December 1665, the name of the Sultan Mehmed IV was dropped from the morning prayers in the Smyrna synagogue and "in its place was inserted the name of Shabbatai Zevi [sic] as king of the Jews." The government of Mehmed IV gave this false Messiah the option of converting to Islam or facing execution in 1666. Sabbatai opted for conversion, and ended his life as Mehemet Effendi in 1676, wisely taking a form of the sultan's name as his own. Once again, while social unrest caused a false savior to rise up, more conservative forces, seeing the pressure such movements caused on the social fabric, moved to "damage control," whether the authorities were Catholic or Muslim.

During the same era, England was torn asunder by the Civil War (1642–49), in which King Charles I was ultimately tried and executed by the parliamentary forces led, militarily, by Sir Thomas Fairfax and Oliver Cromwell. While John Lilburne and his Levellers preached the full equality of men (as had the earlier An-

abaptists), the Fifth Monarchy men saw in these tumultuous years the "End Times" of the Bible. They characterized themselves as the Fifth Monarchy Men from the passage in the Old Testament Book of Daniel (2:44) in which a fifth monarchy would inaugurate a new age on earth. Indeed, the Levellers and Fifth Monarchy Men were part of the more extremist movement that arose during the unrest of the Civil War years. One of their main tracts was Henry Archer's *The Personal Reign of Christ upon Earth* (1642).

MILLENARIANS

This Christian group, like others before and after them, were called "millenarians," because they hoped for the coming of the End Times, and most of them for the Second Coming of Christ. For them, the beheading of the king signaled the beginning of their fifth monarchy, but in 1653 with his instrument of government, Oliver Cromwell established his Protectorate. Unwilling to antagonize the Fifth Monarchy Men, the Protectorate went easily against them, largely because of sympathy for them and the Levellers in the rank and file of the parliamentary army. One of the leaders was Major-General Thomas Harrison. Although imprisoned under the Protectorate, Cromwell took no further steps against his comrade in arms. However, in 1660, Charles II became monarch, the son of the executed Charles I. With parliament now supporting him, and owing no debt to the Fifth Monarchy Men or Levellers, he had Harrison executed as one of the regicides who had sought the death of his father. Thus again, when society became more conservative in outlook, steps were taken to suppress the radical groups that had arisen in times of social stress.

GREAT AWAKENING

Within the United States, currents of religious ecstasy from Great Britain found a ready home. While not as extreme as those like the Anabaptists in Reformation Germany, religious fervor was self-evident in the "Great Awakening," the movement that swept over the Middle Atlantic colonies in the 18th century. Among the first spokesmen was William Tennent, who arrived in Pennsylvania in 1718. Tennent represented a clear link with the Presbyterians of England, among whose congregations were found the Fifth Monarchy Men and Levellers of the English Civil War. Tennent founded the Log College, whose successor is considered to be Princeton University. In 1734, Jonathan Edwards ignited the Great Awakening in New England with sermons on themes that highlighted the sulphurous dangers of hell and the need for immediate penance before an "angry God." The movement became a background theme in the colonies until the time of the American Revolution, when again a time of great social upheaval made "true believers" of even more.

In 19th-century America, the themes of war and social unrest played a similar role in the rise of cults. After the War of 1812, according to Sean Wilentz in his article "Religious Cults Have Become a Great American Tradition" in the *Los Angeles Times*, "a band of religious seekers who called themselves the Pilgrims migrated from Woodstock, New York, until they reached the promised land of Missouri and faded into obscurity." In the 1830s, a man who called himself Matthias founded a "kingdom" near Sing Sing, New York. "Matthias," as Paul E. Johnson and Sean Wilentz wrote in *The Kingdom of Matthias*, had earlier visited with the Mormon prophet and founder Joseph Smith in Kirtland, Missouri. Some of his ideas, like the Sword of Laban and the Priesthood of Melchizedek, he grafted from the Book of Mormon. However, the sexual debauchery that characterized the reign of the "king" was far removed from the practices of the Mormons—the Church of Jesus Christ of Latter-Day Saints—which would perform such a valuable role in bringing civilization to the western frontier.

In 1839, a Baptist preacher named William Miller announced in Low Hampton, New York, that Jesus Christ would appear on earth again in 1843. When the Second Coming did not materialize, the Millerites were naturally disappointed. However, in the 1860s, some of Miller's followers were founders of the Seventh Day Adventist Movement. Aside from Matthias and his frenzied followers, the Messianic, or millenarian, groups or cults in the America of the 19th century reflected the stability of the times. There was none of the violence or religious extremism that had characterized the earlier Anabaptists.

The early 20th century saw little remarkable in the development of Messianic cults, at least when compared with the latter years of the century. Then, faced with a new millennium approaching, apostles of fear again preyed upon the unsuspecting. In the late 1970s, the paradigm appeared for the new wave of dangerous Messianic cults: the People's Temple of Jim Jones. Jones and his followers reflected the growing rootlessness of society in the world after World War II, what the 19th-century French sociologist Emile Durkheim referred to as "anomie."

Jim Jones was born James Warren Jones in Lynn, Indiana, in 1931. Brian Lane wrote that Jones's "first sermon was preached to a group of children when Jones was just 12 years old." In 1951, he opened his People's Temple in Indianapolis, Indiana, and catered to the poor and those distant from their families. He affiliated himself with the Disciples of Christ, and thus could be ordained a minister by an accepted Protestant denomination. In 1964, Jones declared that he had a revelation that the earth would be consumed by a thermonuclear explosion on July 15, 1967, and began a move of his growing People's Temple to Ukiah in northern California, presumably because of its remoteness from known nuclear targets. Once again, his apparent prophecy was triggered by a period of distress. The issue of thermonuclear war was a key point in the 1964 U.S. presidential election, with Democratic candidate Lyndon B. Johnson portraying his Republican rival, Senator Barry Goldwater, as one who would hastily graduate to atomic weapons in a confrontation with the Soviet Union. By the 1970s, Jones had become a political force in San Francisco, capitalizing on its reputation as a New Age nexus for diverse and often bizarre beliefs. However, in August 1977, *New West* magazine published a damaging report on Jones, his alleged sex orgies among his followers, alleged extortion and child abuse.

Fearing prosecution, the self-anointed Messiah fled with his followers to the country of Guyana in South America beginning in 1977. There, Jones, with the support of the Marxist regime, founded a settlement that soon became known simply as Jonestown. By early 1978, the *San Francisco Chronicle*, which had once lauded Jones's involvement in civic affairs, now damned him. The *Chronicle* warned that "the Rev. Jim Jones has involved his 1,100 followers in a threat of mass suicide." Indeed, Jones often had his followers practice for mass death in his "White Nights" drills. Since many of the People's Temple devotees were from California, Congressman Leo Ryan from San Mateo County in California flew to Guyana to investigate; he arrived on November 15, 1978.

As with earlier cults, the People's Temple had been tolerated—even encouraged—while it posed no perceived harm to society. With the allegations left behind in San Francisco, a call had come from an organization of former Temple members and relatives of current ones known as the Concerned Relatives to press for an investigation of the People'ss Temple. Ryan had gone to Guyana on their request. The threat of government intervention—in the form of Ryan's visit—caused the unstable Jones to order the mass suicide of the cult. On

November 18, 1978, some 913 members, including 260 children, were given cyanide with Kool-Aid. Jones's armed guards forced those who were reluctant to partake of the lethal concoction. Earlier that day, Ryan himself had been shot and killed. Jones died of a gunshot wound. Now, whenever new Messianic cults would emerge, the specter of the mass deaths at Jonestown would always emerge with them.

DAVID KORESH

Vernon Wayne Howell will always be remembered as David Koresh, the charismatic leader of the Branch Davidian movement in Waco, Texas. The Davidians were a group that had severed themselves from the Seventh Day Adventists, who themselves had begun among the adherents of the "prophet" William Miller. In 1991, Howell underwent an apparent ecstatic religious conversion in which he became convinced he was the "Lamb" mentioned in the Book of Revelation, also fittingly called the Book of the Apocalypse. In the book, the Lamb opens the book, which unleashes fire and pestilence upon all creation. It was at this time that Howell took the name of David Koresh. Stories began to circulate, as with the earlier Jonestown, of child abuse and the possession of large stores of arms and ammunition at the Branch Davidians' home, which ominously was called Rancho Apocalypse. On February 28, 1993, agents of the Bureau of Alcohol, Tobacco, and Firearms stormed the compound with loss of life. Such an assault only reinforced the beliefs of Koresh and the hold he apparently had upon his hapless brethren.

Then, after a prolonged siege, federal and local authorities struck again. A conflagration erupted, perhaps caused unexpectedly by the CS gas used ironically to peacefully subdue the heavily armed cultists. Before the flames died away, Brian Lane estimated in *Killer Cults: Murderous Messiahs and Their Fanatical Followers* that out of some 90 Branch Davidians in the compound, only perhaps nine survived. Once again, when the forces of law and stability moved against a cult, as at Jonestown, mass tragedy was the result. However, as before in the history of such Messianic movements, the need for the reestablishment of order had been tragically set in train by the cult itself.

As the millennium year of 2000 neared, law enforcement authorities around the world became acutely aware of the danger of millennial cults seeking to bring on the End Times—which they believed would bring the Second Coming of Christ—through acts of violence they would commit. Furthermore, fears of the millennium were aggravated by the Year 2000 crisis, in which people were frightened that all computers, which presumably had not been programmed to date beyond 1999, would crash throughout the world. This, believers felt, would lead to universal anarchy and suffering. It was for this concern that the American Federal Bureau of Investigation (FBI) issued its "Project Megiddo" Report and the Canadian Security Intelligence Service its "Doomsday Religious Movements" alert in 1999. "Project Megiddo" records the story of the Concerned Christians of Monte Kim Miller, who traveled to Jerusalem in 1998 in the belief that Miller would "be killed in a violent confrontation in the streets of Jerusalem in December 1999." His death would lead to "an apocalyptic end to the millennium, at which time all of Miller's followers will be sent to heaven." Fortunately, Israeli security authorities moved in to round up the 14 Concerned Christians who had moved to Jerusalem in January 1999 and deported them. However, although the millennium year passed without any cult violence, the crisis showed again how in times of stress, people turn to even the most extreme movements if they offer them the hope of comfort and salvation.

SEE ALSO

Volume 1 Left: United States; Church and State Separation.
Volume 2 Right: Religion.

BIBLIOGRAPHY

Paul Fregosi, *Jihad* (Prometheus, 1998); Leo Rosten, *The Joys of Yiddish* (Pocket Books, 1968); Paul E. Johnson and Sean Wilentz, *The Kingdom of Matthias: A Story of Sex and Salvation in 19th Century America* (Oxford University Press, 1994); "Girolamo Savonarola 1452–1498," www.historyguide.org (July 2004); Perle Epstein, *Kabbalah: The Way of the Jewish Mystic* (Shambhala, 1978); Gershom Scholem, *Major Trends in Jewish Mysticism* (Schocken Books, 1995); Chaim Potok, *Wanderings* (Fawcett, 1978); Ernle Bradford, *The Shield and the Sword: The Knights of Malta* (Fontana, 1972); "Anabaptists," *Catholic Encyclopedia*, www.newadvent.org; (July 2004); "English Dissenters: Fifth Monarchists or Fifth Monarchy Men," www.xlibris.org (July 2004); C.V. Wedgwood, *The King's Peace, 1637–41, The King's War, 1641–47* (Fontana, 1977); "The Great Awakening," *Columbia Encyclopedia* (Columbia University Press, 2001); "Full Text of the FBI Report Project Megiddo," www.cesnur.org (July 2004); James J. Boyle, *Killer Cults* (St. Martin's, 1995); Brian Lane, *Killer Cults: Murderous Messiahs and Their Fanatical Followers* (Trafalgar Square, 1997); Richard Hofstadter and Michael

Wallace, eds., *American Violence: A Documentary History* (Vintage Books, 1970); Canadian Security Intelligence Service, "Doomsday Religious Movements" (July 2004); Gershom Gorenberg, *The End of Days: Fundamentalism and the Struggle for the Temple Mount* (The Free Press, 2000); Mark Juergensmeyer, *Terror in the Mind of God: The Global Rise of Religious Violence* (University of California Press, 2000); Philip Lamy, *Millennium Rage: Survivalists, White Supremacists, and the Doomsday Prophecy* (Plenum, 1996).

JOHN F. MURPHY, JR.
AMERICAN MILITARY UNIVERSITY

Mexico

POLITICS IN MEXICO is unique because the country has operated mostly under a state-controlled, one-party system since 1929, even though that party has been pitted against a number of other parties in popular elections.

While the governing party has been authoritarian, it has never been totalitarian. This unique one-party system has flourished, because Mexicans tend to be more interested in practicalities like jobs and contracts than in ideology. Thus, Mexico has become known for its stability and continued economic growth. This stability has made Mexico the only Latin American country that has never experienced a military coup. Instead, Mexican presidents have peacefully yielded power at the end of their six-year terms.

While the Party of the Institutional Revolution (PRI), Mexico's ruling party, began as a revolutionary party, espousing secularism, nationalism, and populism, the party has encompassed all branches of Mexican political ideology. Scholars have identified the "pendulum effect" in Mexican politics, which means that control of the ruling party has consistently swung from left to right and back again, making PRI's ideology difficult to pinpoint. Overall, the party has been conservative in domestic policies but liberal on foreign policy issues.

The emphasis on liberalism or conservatism has generally been dependent on particular presidential administrations, with the extreme left represented by Lazaro Cardenas during the revolutionary period (1934–40), and the extreme right personified by Gustavo Diaz Ordaz (1964–70). PRI's rightward shift began in 1940 with the election of Manuel Avila Camacho.

The Cardenas regime, with its policies of land reform, support for the *ejidos*, its nationalization of petroleum, as well as its foreign policy of supporting the Loyalists in the Spanish Civil War, came closest to the social-democratic model of European states.

Because PRI has operated on a patronage system, the party has historically amassed enormous political loyalty. It has further enhanced its popularity by working in tandem with the Catholic Church, the Mexican military, and the academic community. PRI has sometimes retained its power through what many consider to be fraudulent means. In 1988, for example, President Carlos Salinas de Gortari was awarded 50 percent of the vote despite numerous challenges to the official vote count. Subsequent electoral reforms included counter-forgery features on paper ballots and guarding privacy inside the voting booth.

PRI's major opposition, the National Action Party (PAN) was founded in 1939 but was unable to win a presidential election until 2000 when Vicente Fox became Mexico's first non-PRI president in seven decades. As a center-right party, PAN is consistently pro-business. On social issues, most members of PAN are opposed to abortion and homosexuality. Some more conservative members of PAN also believe in art censorship and hope to wipe out profanity and miniskirts.

Despite PAN's win in 2000, the PRI was not totally defeated. The party won 209 of 500 lower house seats and 60 of the 128 senate seats. PRI has splintered over possible strategies for a return to power in 2006. Because they control only 30 percent of house seats and 38 percent of senate seats, Fox and PAN have been prevented from following through on many campaign promises.

While political power in Mexico is normally concentrated in the hands of the president, there are no constitutional measures for presidential control of a recalcitrant legislature. Many Mexicans have particularly been upset over PAN's inability to call members of PRI to task for alleged incidences of abuses of governmental power and fraudulent activities.

SEE ALSO

Volume 1 Left: Mexico; PRI (Mexico).
Volume 2 Right: Conservatism.

BIBLIOGRAPHY

M. Delal Baer, "Mexico at An Impasse," (January/February 2004); Patrick Ai Camp, *Politics in Mexico* (Oxford, 1996); James W. Dow, "The Mexican Political System and the

Promise of Reform," http://personalwebs.oakland.edu (November 2004); Brian Hammett, "Mexican Conservatives, Clericals, and Soldiers," *Bulletin of Latin American Research* (April 2001); Daniel Levy and Gabriel Székely, *Mexico: Paradoxes of Stability and Change* (Westview, 1983); James D. Lockcroft, *Mexico: Class Formation, Capital Accumulation, and the State* (Monthly Review Press, 1983); "Mexico Enjoys a Real Election Campaign," *Economist* (April 29, 2000); Dale Story, *The Mexican Ruling Party: Stability and Authority* (Praeger 1986).

ELIZABETH PURDY, PH.D.
INDEPENDENT SCHOLAR

Middle East

THE MODERN HISTORY of the Middle East began with the opening of the Suez Canal in November 1869, creating a dramatic shortcut from the Mediterranean Sea to the Red Sea, the Persian Gulf, and the Indian Ocean beyond. With that one event, the Middle East was brought into cultural, economic, and political contact with the developing world of Europe and the United States, after languishing for centuries under the rule of the ailing Ottoman Turkish Empire, the "Sick Man of Europe." As Philip K. Hitti wrote in *History of the Arabs*, after the Turks had failed to seize Vienna, Austria, in 1683, "to the internal forces of corruption and decay were added external forces in the 18th century" when the European Great Powers began to cast envious eyes at the spacious Ottoman lands.

As a direct result of the increased commerce in goods and ideas, the Middle Eastern lands were exposed to the forces of modernity. This was especially true in Egypt, where the *khedive*, or ruler, Ismail, had been carrying on a program of modernization aimed at creating a stable society in a country where too much loyalty still remained with anarchic clans and tribes. Ismail owned significant shares in the Suez Canal Company.

The Suez Canal project had been the brainchild of the Frenchman Ferdinand de Lesseps, who would go on to attempt the first Panama Canal. Great Britain had also sponsored it as a shortcut to its imperial "crown jewel," India. The British already had a close commercial relationship in Egypt, and thus an interest in ensuring stability, since Egyptian cotton had become a necessary import after American cotton exports stopped during the American Civil War (1861–65). Since the Albanian mercenary Mohammed Ali had ruled Egypt (1805–49), his descendants had given the country perhaps the most enduring, conservative rule in the Middle East.

In spite of growing anarchy in parts of the Ottoman lands, American and European interests began to filter into the region. What is now known as the American University in Beirut was founded in 1866, three years before the opening of the Suez Canal, by Dr. Daniel Bliss. The university became a significant site for educating the local population, in opposition to the languishing education system of the Ottoman Turks. At the same time, the Roman Catholic Church and its teaching orders, particularly the French, worked to expand their educational systems in the Levant, the general term then used for Palestine (today's Israel, Jordan, and West Bank), Lebanon, and Syria. The French had enjoyed close ties with the Levant since the time of the Crusades.

In the 1880s, traditional Muslim institutions, particularly the *ulama*, or learned men of Islam, began to feel their positions threatened by modernization. One of the leading Islamist thinkers of the time was Jamal al-Din al-Afghani (1839–97), who, Wilfred Cantwell Smith said in *Islam in Modern World*, "advocated both local nationalisms and pan-Islam," the movement that viewed all Muslim countries as the traditionally unified Dar al Islam, or "Land of Islam." Religious leadership led to mob violence.

In order to be more sensitive to the desires of Egyptian nationalists, the British under Evelyn Baring, Lord Cromer, established what was discreetly called the "Veiled Protectorate." With the threat of political extremism temporarily halted, the nationalists were able to take their case to the legislature through parliamentary means.

In Palestine, new influences were being felt as well. After the Russian pogroms, or anti-Semitic rioting, in 1881, socialist societies began to organize to return to the Jews' traditional homeland of Palestine. As Charles D. Smith wrote in *Palestine and the Arab-Israeli Conflict* of movements like the BILU group: "their vision of agricultural communes led ultimately to the forming of the *kibbutzim* [collective farms], which many saw as the embodiment of Zionist principles." The agricultural villages preceded the more familiar collective farms, or *kibbutzim*. Beginning in 1890, modernization was made more feasible in Palestine when the French were granted concessions by the Ottomans to run the railways. By 1900, Jewish settlement in Palestine had become more

The construction of the Suez Canal, linking the Mediterranean Sea with the Red Sea and the Indian Ocean, marked the beginning of the modern era in the Middle East when European powers took a strong interest in national developments.

organized under the aegis of the Jewish Colonization Society (JCA). This era in Jewish settlement is usually called the First Aliyah, or "rising up" to the Jews' ancestral home. This political movement was known as Zionism. Under the leadership of the visionary Theodore Herzl, the first world congress of the Zionist movement was opened in August 1897. As Herzl stated in his opening address, the movement's goal was to "lay the foundation stone of the house that is to shelter the Jewish nation."

A year later, the British in Egypt were able to reestablish order in the Egyptian Sudan, where the first Islamic extremist movement of modern times, led by Mohammed Ahmed, the "Mahdi," or "the Expected One of Allah," had seized power in 1885. On September 2, 1898, at Omdurman, an Anglo-Egyptian army led by Commander in Chief General Horatio Herbert Kitchener decisively defeated the Mahdist Army. When the battle was over, as Philip Ziegler wrote in *Omdurman,* one British officer rejoiced, "our spirits soared at

the thought of a square meal and, better still, a long, hot drink." Thirty years earlier, during the Crimean War, the British and the French had established themselves as forces for constructive reform in the Ottoman Empire, when they had supported the Turks against the Russians. With the reconquest of the Sudan, that commitment was reemphasized.

However, in the same year, a destabilizing factor was injected into the Middle East when Kaiser Wilhelm II visited Jerusalem in 1898, where he would meet Herzl in November. After Wilhelm had accepted the resignation of Chancellor Otto von Bismarck in March 1890, he had conducted German foreign policy himself, with no great success. He fancied himself the heir of the German Emperor Frederick Barbarossa, who had died on his way to the Third Crusade (1188–92). Determining to make Germany paramount in the Ottoman Empire, he set out to undermine England and France with a militaristic policy. In 1905, he would declare that "our final trump card will be Islam and the Muslim World." As part of his policy, in 1902 construction began in Iraq on what would later be called the Berlin to Baghdad railway.

The Ottoman Empire, although in political decline, had a history of toleration for its multiethnic population. Constantinople, later Istanbul, was a model city for the industrious coming together of many peoples, who tended to congregate in their own ethnic enclaves. Indeed, as Nicole and Hugh Pope wrote in *Turkey Unveiled: A History of Modern Turkey*, "a French-style constitution and parliament was promulgated shortly after the accession of Sultan Abdulhamit [Abdul Hamid] II (1876–1909)." In 1913, Turkish Army officers of the Young Turk movement seized effective power in the empire. While promising electoral progress, they followed a pan-Turkish party line that boded ill for minority groups in the empire, notably the Jews and Armenians. Not even the Arabs were safe from them. The Young Turks looked with disfavor on the Jewish immigrants of the Second Aliyah, roughly 1904–14, because they were more politically conscious Zionists. Among them was the future first prime minister of Israel, David Ben-Gurion. The Zionists faced increased suspicion and opposition to settlement from the Turkish regime.

NATIONALIST EGYPT

Meanwhile, nationalism continued to be a force in Egypt. Bruce B. Lawrence wrote in *Shattering the Myth: Islam beyond Violence*, "the nationalist movement coalesced around Sa'd Zaghlul [who] founded the opposition Wafd Party that reflected an elision of political independence with dedication to Islam." Yet, extremism continued as both a political and religious threat in Egypt. In 1910, Boutros Ghali, a long-time public servant, was assassinated by extremists for being perceived as betraying Egyptian nationalism. A further destabilizing element in the 1910 killing was that the Boutros Ghali family belonged to Egypt's Coptic Christian minority.

A sense of nationalism also gripped the Arab community, where a conservative society sought productive change in the modern world. George E. Kirk, in *A Short History of the Middle East*, quotes a nationalist manifesto from Cairo written before World War I. It declared, "the reform of which we speak is [based] on the complete independence and the formation of a decentralized Arab state which will revive our ancient glories and rule the country on autonomous lines, according to the needs of each province." The leadership of the new Arab nationalism centered on Sharif Hussein, who was the protector of the Muslim holy places of Mecca and Medina, and a direct descendant of the Prophet Mohammed.

Careful preparations were made between Hussein's son Abdullah and the British in Cairo, where the Arab Bureau served British military intelligence. On its staff was a young officer, T.E. Lawrence, Lawrence of Arabia. On June 5, 1916, Sharif Hussein declared the beginning of the Arab Revolt. On October 12, Lawrence left for the Arabian port of Jiddah on the Red Sea for a fact-finding trip to see what the British could do to promote the Sharif's uprising. Desiring a closer view of the Arab Revolt, Lawrence undertook a 100-mile journey to the Hejaz region to meet with Prince Faisal, the son of the Sharif who was in active command of his father's tribesmen. The meeting took place on October 23, 1916. Lawrence's report was the first one ever received in Cairo from the front lines of the Arab Revolt. By the beginning of December 1916, Lawrence was back to advise the troops of Prince Faisal.

During World War I, the Arabs played a significant role as guerrillas, severely hampering the ability of the Turkish Fourth Army to defend itself against the main offensive of British General Sir Edmund Allenby. Peter Mansfield wrote in *A History of the Middle East* that the Arabs "immobilized some 30,000 Turkish troops along the Hejaz Railway from Amman to Medina and prevented the Turco-German forces in Syria from linking up with the Turkish garrison in Yemen."

The war also affected the Yishuv, or the Jewish community in Palestine. News had reached them of the Young Turks' attacks on the Armenians, in which they perished in the hetacombs after being driven into the Syrian desert. Jeremy Wilson wrote that in 1915, the Turks "had displaced entire Armenians populations from their homelands, committing terrible massacres and leaving thousands to die of starvation in the deserts." Word of the genocide of the Armenians reached the Jews; they feared they would be the next victims.

Aaron Aaronsohn was a pioneer of scientific agriculture in Palestine, indeed perhaps one of the founders of the idea of the *kibbutzim*; ironically, he was also the agricultural adviser to the Turk Jemal Pasha. In the fall of 1916, he contacted the British and formed the NILI spy organization, what British military intelligence referred to as the "A" organization. What the NILI group provided was vital to General Allenby's campaign against the Turks in Palestine. During the war, however, secretive diplomacy had sown the seeds for a tumultuous postwar era. In early January 1916, six months before the start of the Arab Revolt, Mark Sykes and George Picot had begun work on an agreement that would effectively nullify the hope of Arab independence that was now unifying the Arab population. Then, on October 31, 1917, Arthur Balfour wrote in what would become known as the Balfour Declaration: "His Majesty's government views with favor the establishment in Palestine of a national home for the Jewish people."

Statecraft, while needed in the light of the wartime emergency, did not necessarily prepare the way for a peaceful future. In fact, Arab nationalists, seeing a betrayal by France and England, took to the streets. In Egypt, widespread upheaval required a dramatic show of force by Allenby, now the imperial proconsul, to prevent a national insurgency from breaking out. The leading nationalists, like Zaghlul Pasha, Ismail Sidky Pasha, and Mohammed Mahmoud Pasha, were temporarily detained. In handling the crisis, Allenby showed a perceptive understanding of Arab nationalism that underscored the close working relationship he had had with Lawrence during the war. In fact, in 1922, Egypt would be granted its independence, although defense and foreign policy would largely remain under British influence due to the vital necessity of the Suez Canal.

In Palestine, any wartime sense of community against the Turks quickly evaporated. Severe rioting broke out in Jerusalem on April 4, 1920. The situation was so tense that Allenby would have to send Royal Navy warships from Egypt to provide support for the British authorities. Author Benny Morris commented in *Righteous Victims: A History of Zionist-Arab Conflict, 1881–1999*, that "more than a dozen other Haganah [Jewish settler militia] members were each given three years' hard labor. On the other hand, most of the Arab rioters arrested were given light sentences. Jewish commentators compared the British behavior toward the rioters and the defenders with that of the Russians during the pogroms," the vicious anti-Semitic riots that the tzarist authorities incited against the Jews living in Russia and Russian-occupied areas of Poland.

In Syria, Arab aspirations faced their worst check at the hands of the French. Prince Faisal led an Arab government and in March 1920, the Second Syrian Congress proclaimed the full independence of Syria. Like Palestine with the British, Syria and Lebanon—then called "Greater Lebanon"—had been given to the French as a mandate state by the League of Nations. This was done with the intention of guiding the peoples toward a more productive future. Alarmed at the motion of the Syrian Congress, the French invaded Syria and defeated Faisal's forces in July. After a brutal rule by General Maurice Sarrail, he was fired. In his place, the French Republic dispatched Henri de Jouvenel to become the new high commissioner. While Jouvenel was unsuccessful in stopping the nationalist agitation, he is considered the most liberal of the high commissioners to have ruled Greater Lebanon during the French mandate. Jouvenel proclaimed Lebanon a republic and made it known that France's policy envisaged the conclusion of a Franco-Syrian treaty of alliance to replace the mandate, on the basis of the British precedent in Iraq; and he tried to open negotiations to that end with the Arab nationalist leaders. Although nationalist feeling remained high in Lebanon and Syria, Jouvenel, as with Allenby in Egypt, ensured that it took a parliamentary form instead of mob action in the streets.

CAIRO CONFERENCE

During the same postwar period, the British took decisive steps to attempt a definitive political settlement of the Middle East. The Cairo Conference convened on March 12, 1921. The leading figures were Winston S. Churchill, then the British colonial secretary; Lawrence of Arabia; Allenby; Gertrude Bell, one of the most distinguished of British Middle East experts; and Sir Percy Cox, the British high commissioner in what was then Mesopotamia. The conference created the land of Trans-Jordan, on the east bank of the Jordan River, for Abdullah, the son of Sharif Hussein, who had been defeated in a power struggle with Abdul Aziz Ibn Saud, who would go on to rule what is now called Saudi Arabia.

Ibn Saud had played a modest role in the war compared with Sharif Hussein, but had helped thousands of Turkish troops stay on the defensive so as to render them incapable of joining in the fighting against the Arab Revolt. In 1921, the grateful British rewarded him by recognizing Ibn Saud as the Sultan of Nejd, as Madawi al-Rasheed wrote in *A History of Saudi Arabia*. With British support declining for Hussein, in 1926 Ibn Saud made himself master of all that is now known as Saudi Arabia.

Although rivals with the Hashemites, the family of Sharif Hussein, Saudi Arabia and the kingdoms of Transjordan and Iraq, which would be provided respectively for Hussein's sons Abdullah and Faisal, did represent a conservative axis of moderate Arab states in the volatile Middle East.

Mesopotamia, now called Iraq, would become a kingdom for Faisal, whom the French had exiled from Lebanon. Amazingly, by March 15, Churchill could cable London: "all authorities have reached agreement on all the points, political and military." However, a permanent solution was not found to the quest for independence for the Kurdish people, in what is now Syria, Turkey, and Iraq.

ISLAMIC EXTREMISM

During the 1920s, Islamic extremism took a firm hold on Islam, beginning with the foundation of the Muslim Brotherhood in Egypt in 1928. Hassan al-Bana was the founder, with the assistance of Sayyid Qutb. The Muslim Brotherhood was hostile toward all secular attempts to rationalize the Middle East. It held that, as a thousand years earlier, only the *sha'ria*, the Islamic law, should govern in the Dar al Islam, "The Land of Islam." Qutb wrote, "Islam is people's freeing themselves from servitude to God's servants." The Muslim Brotherhood would be banned. Both Qutb and al-Bana would be killed by conservative modernizing regimes in Egypt. Agents of King Farouk most likely killed al-Bana in 1949, and Qutb was hanged under Gamal Abdel Nasser in 1966. In the 1920s as well in Palestine, Haj Amin, the Grand Mufti of Jerusalem, contributed to fomenting unrest between Arabs and Jews, gravely weakening the area's potential for economic growth. Major rioting occurred again in 1929.

The Cossack adventurer Reza Khan had become the new shah of Persia in April 1926. He created what would be the last dynasty to rule Persia, calling it the Pahlavi dynasty, from the Farsi word meaning "heroic." During his reign, he pursued a vigorous policy of modernization. Nine years later, in 1935, the first Westernized university was opened in Tehran, the capital. From 1927 to 1932, a Western-style code of laws—not based on the ancient Islamic *sha'ria*—was introduced in the country. Symbolic of the forward turn in events, he changed the name of the country from the antique Persia to the more modern Iran. For much of his reign, the revenues from the oil trade became a necessary source of funds for his modernization policy. At the end of April 1933, the tough new shah negotiated a new oil agreement with the British, with terms much more favorable to Iran.

In the 1930s, the affairs of the Middle East were overshadowed by the rise of Adolf Hitler and the Nazis to power in Germany. The central movement in Egypt was the Organization of Green Shirts, which patterned itself after the Brown Shirts of Hitler and the Black Shirts of Benito Mussolini's Fascist Party in Italy. The Green Shirts was the offshoot of the Misr al-Fatat, "the Young Egypt" movement, which had been founded by the nationalist lawyer Ahmad Hussein in 1933. Young Egypt was a close political ally of the religious extremists of the Muslim Brotherhood. Hussein made clear his call to arms to the younger Egyptian generation, of which Nasser and Anwar Sadat were members. The organization had fascist overtones and openly admired Nazi achievements.

Because of the growing Nazi persecution, some "60,000 German Jewish refugees arrived in Palestine in the 1930s," according to Yigael Allon in *Shield of David: The Story of Israel's Armed Forces*. "Among them," Allon noted, "were eloquent advocates of Arab-Jewish cooperation and amity." In spite of these overtures, Haj Amin fomented what would become known as the Great Arab Revolt of 1936. For three years, until British force won out in 1939, a virtual civil war crippled Palestine under the Haj's baneful influence. An important role was played in suppressing the Haj's armed gangs by the Special Night Squads. These were formed by the British Captain Orde Wingate, who relied on men drawn largely from the Haganah, the militia of the Jewish settlements. He became known to the Jews of the Yishuv as *Hayedid*, or "our friend."

WORLD WAR II

When World War II broke out, it sent a vast shock wave into the Middle East. Although still guarded by a British garrison, Egypt's King Farouk declared neutrality. In 1936, Great Britain had signed in effect a treaty giving Egypt independence, but when the war began virtually took control again because of the war emergency. Farouk's declaration of neutrality was his response.

However, not only was Farouk personally pro-fascist, a great admirer of Benito Mussolini, but many in the Egyptian Army agitated for a German victory. This was especially true after German Field Marshal Erwin Rommel arrived in North Africa in February 1941 and began his triumphal march toward Egypt. Finally, British Ambassador Miles Lampson acted drastically in February 1942. In a show of force, he compelled Farouk to accept as his new prime minister, Nahas Pasha, of the Wafd Party, who placed Egypt firmly on the British side.

Meanwhile, restriction on immigration to Palestine set by the British to placate the Arabs during the revolt severely limited the number of Jews who could escape the Nazi death camps. The Yishuv put into effect a massive program during the war of bringing in refugees by illegal means. The organization given this daunting task was the Mossad, later the Israeli intelligence service. Paradoxically, the British at the same time looked on the Jews as their only allies in the Holy Land, given the Arabs' enthusiasm for the Germans. Unlike the Arabs, some 130,000 Jews volunteered for service. Under Yizhak Sadeh, the Haganah developed the elite Palmach companies. Future leaders of the Israeli Army, like Moshe Dayan and Yigael Allon, served in the Palmach companies, which supported the British in the conquest of Syria and Lebanon. (When France was defeated in June 1940, the French collaborating regime at Vichy had taken over the Middle East possessions.)

At the height of the fighting against Rommel's vaunted Afrika Korps, the British forces were surprised by a pro-Nazi coup in Iraq. Led by Rashid Ali al-Gaylani, the regent for the six-year-old King Faisal II, the fascist Golden Square society in April 1941 had overthrown the legitimate government of Prime Minister Nuri Said, and was determined to bring Iraq, and with it the gate to the oil fields of Persia (Iran), into the Axis orbit. The Golden Square putsch was the culmination of neo-Nazi agitation within Iraq.

The outbreak of the war rapidly healed any rifts between Great Britain and France over colonial affairs in the Middle East, which were now so trifling when faced with war with Hitler's Germany. Two British expeditionary forces were hastily drawn from the front against Rommel to face the dangerous situation in the East. One was known as "Kingcol," after its commander, Brigadier Joe Kingstone. The other column was known as "Habforce," because its goal was to seize the important air base at Habbaniya, on the Euphrates River west of Baghdad. Both attack forces were composed of regular British Army troops and the famed Jordanian Arab Legion, then under the command of Sir John Bagot Glubb, the celebrated "Glubb Pasha." The need to reconquer Iraq was imperative. Already, German Luftwaffe planes based in Vichy French Syria were planning to use the Royal Air Force base at Habbaniya. Somerset de Chair wrote *The Golden Carpet*, perhaps the only known source on the progress of "Kingcol." The trek of the two British columns, over nearly 500 miles of desert, must stand with the greatest exploits of military history. With Habforce and Kingstone's forces closing in, Baghdad surrendered on May 31, 1941. With the surrender of his government, Rashid Ali fled. The four generals who had comprised the Golden Square, Salah al-Din Sabbagh, Fahmi Aid, Kamil Shahib, and Mahmud Salman, were court-martialed for treason and all were executed. However, the real danger of the Nazis lay in oil-rich Iran, next to Iraq. Somerset de Chair, who acted as the intelligence officer for Kingcol, noted in *The Golden Carpet* that "we examined closely the set-up of the German Fifth Column [underground movement] in Persia, where 4,000 Germans in commercial occupations were organized under Gaulieters [Nazi Party leaders] and could be mobilized on the telephone."

IRANIAN MISCALCULATION

The same fatal attraction for German Nazism that had infected Iraq also spread to oil-blessed Iran. Somerset de Chair's intelligence estimate of the depth of German penetration into Reza Shah's Iran was accurate. Peter Mansfield observed in *A History of the Middle East* that Iranian "nationalist sentiment, especially among the ruling class and senior army officers, tended to be pro-German. The Nazi regime had begun seizing the advantage before the war. German companies played a leading role in Iranian industrialization, German propaganda was vigorous and Nazi agents were active throughout the country." One of those who heeded the words of the Nazi propagandists appeared to be Reza Shah himself.

When the Soviet Union was invaded by Nazi Germany in June 1941, the Soviet government put pressure on the shah to oust the German agents. Rather than joining the Allied side, Reza committed the ultimate blunder of his career. Ignoring the advice of American President Franklin D. Roosevelt, who was already heavily committed to the Allied cause, the shah stopped all passage of aid to Russia through Iran. August 1941 could not have been a worse time for Shah Reza to take his stand. On the Eastern Front, the German Second Army and the Second Panzer (Tank) Group were in the process of a massive offensive against the Russian troops in the Ukraine, making a secure source of oil for the Russians a matter of national survival. On the contrary, for the British the month of August 1941 presented a lull in the battle with Rommel's Afrika Korps, and troops could be spared for any operation against Iran.

Therefore, from north and south, the Russians and British rapidly launched attacking columns into the heart of the shah's Iran. Unable to face the strong Allied onslaught, the Iranians surrendered. On September 16, 1941, Reza wisely abdicated the ancient Peacock Throne of Iran in favor of his son, who became Shah Mohamed Reza Pahlavi. The flow of war materiel from

British India, across Iran, and into embattled Russia quickly resumed. The turn of the tide took place in the Middle East when the British defeated the Desert Fox (Rommel) at El Alamein on the Egyptian frontier in October 1942. Although the war in North Africa would not end until the Germans surrendered in Tunisia in May 1943, the threat to the Middle East had passed.

THE FOUNDING OF ISRAEL

After the surrender of Germany in May 1945, the Middle East—particularly Palestine—became the goal of the surviving remnant of Hitler's barbaric *Endlosung*: "The Final Solution to the Jewish Question." The survivors of this Holocaust were helped in their flight to Palestine by the Jewish Brigade, which served with the British Army in Italy in 1944–45. Agents of the Mossad established close relations with the brigade and, in some ways, acted as a shadow administration with cooperative British officers. However, the British elections in 1945 saw the departure of the Zionist Winston Churchill as the British prime minister and the arrival of Clement Atlee at 10 Downing Street as his replacement. Atlee and his foreign secretary took a decidedly dim view of Jewish settlement in Palestine, which would have served to lift the country out of the turmoil of the years of the Arab Revolt and the world war. However, the Jewish Agency, the de facto government of the Yishuv under David Ben Gurion, was determined to bring in those who had survived the death camps of the Third Reich. Rather than negotiate with the Jewish Agency, the British government only hardened its stance against immigration.

A virtual insurrection broke out in Palestine until in 1947, the British announced that they would leave Palestine. The final decision on the future of Palestine was left in the hands of the new United Nations (UN), which on November 29, 1947, voted to create the Jewish homeland promised in the Balfour Declaration. On May 14, 1948, David Ben-Gurion proclaimed the birth of the sovereign state of Israel. Immediately, five Arab nations, Egypt, Iraq, Lebanon, Jordan, and Egypt, declared war, as they had threatened to do should the Jews declare independence. In the end, hostilities continued, even after the United Nations threatened to cite the Arab governments for aggression under the UN Charter on July 15, 1948. Finally, by January 1949, the fighting drew to a close. A major Egyptian offensive into the Negev Desert in the south of Israel had been turned back. Only the Arab Legion remained undefeated among the Arab forces. Israel signed an armistice with

Egypt on February 24, 1949. Similar agreements were made with Lebanon on March 23, Jordan on April 3, and Syria on July 29, 1949. Of the five Arab belligerent countries, only Iraq, which contributed the least to the fighting, did not sign an armistice with the new state of Israel.

The refusal of the Arab states to recognize what Arab militants still in the 2000s call the "Zionist entity" in their midst guaranteed a continued state of tension in the Middle East. The future economic development of the region has perhaps been given a permanently crippling blow by the lack of any inclusive peace settlement. In a sense, the lack of agreement by most Arab states on Israel's "right to exist" has kept the region in almost a perpetual state of tension, making the mirror image of Karl von Clausewitz's view that war is the continuation of politics by other means the basic fact of life in the Middle East. Further wars were to follow in 1956, 1967, and 1973.

Within Egypt, the end of the war issued in a period of constitutional turmoil. The nationalists lost all respect for Farouk after his capitulation in 1942. Ten years later, Farouk was toppled from the throne by the Free Officers movement and moved to Italy, where he became known as the most prominent sybarite in exile there. Gamal Abdel Nasser emerged as the leading member of the Free Officers group, after gaining a reputation as a brave frontline soldier in the 1948 War with Israel. Unfortunately, he spent too much of Egypt's limited wealth on prosecuting a bloody "cold war" with Israel after the 1949 negotiations. Much of the funds he could have given to help the oppressed Egyptian *fellahin*, or farmers, was devoted to war. As the son of a peasant himself, Nasser did take genuine concern in their well-being. While of limited actual effect, the land reforms he and the Free Officers instituted served as a template for land reform in other Arab nations. In 1961–62, Nasser reaffirmed his convictions with his Charter of National Action. As a result of his need for funds, Nasser turned to the Soviet Union for assistance. In fact, Egypt became the main client state of the Soviet Union in the Middle East. According to Walter Laqueur in *The Struggle for the Middle East: The Soviet Union in the Mediterranean*, "advanced Soviet missiles had been used in the sinking of the Israeli destroyer Eilat in October 1967."

In July 1956, Nasser capitalized on his growing popularity by nationalizing the Suez Canal Company. In October, Israel, England, and France attacked to open the canal and restore its ownership to the company. Although militarily thrashed, Nasser profited from the invading countries' being compelled to withdraw under a November United Nations cease-fire agreement. Indeed, he used his enhanced status to dabble in the affairs of other Arab countries. In Iraq, ruled by the young Faisal II, the government of Prime Minister Nuri al-Said took a decidedly Western view in supporting the Arab world against Soviet subversion; in 1955, the Iraqi government hosted the formation of the Baghdad Pact coalition.

As now the Soviets' main agent in the Arab world, Nasser took harsh measures against the pro-Western Iraqi government. In a grim coup, he is believed by some intelligence sources to have backed the Iraqi Free Officers movement, which in 1958 overthrew the monarchy, killing both the young king and his prime minister. Brigadier Abdul Karem Kassim became the military strongman in Baghdad, supported by Colonel Aref. Yet, within the year, Nasser's plot unraveled, as Kassim deposed Aref before the year was out. Blaming an uprising in 1959 on Nasser, he became his former backer's most vitriolic foe.

Nasser's plans for a United Arab Republic began in 1958 with a constitutional union with Syria. Although such a union potentially posed a threat to Israel, had moderate Arab views prevailed, the United Arab Republic (UAR) would have provided a meaningful epiphany for the spirit of Arab nationalism As such, the UAR would have helped heal the aggravating situation in the Middle East between Arab and Jew and not worsened it. Granted independence by the Free French forces of General Charles de Gaulle in 1941, Syria was dominated by the Arab socialist Ba'ath Party, which had been founded by Michel Aflaq, one of the leading spirits of the resurgent Arab nationalism. However, over time, the Syrians began to feel that they were definitely the junior partners in the UAR. However, the conservative landowners who formed the most solid political faction in Syria ultimately compelled Syria to secede from the political union with dominant Egypt in September 1961.

Nasser's attempt to influence the civil war that raged in Yemen met with little success as well. In September 1962, he intervened in the Yemeni civil war, with the main distinguishing event that he became the first Arab head of state to authorize the use of poison gas against another Arab people. By 1967, all Egyptian troops, many of whom were combat engineers, were withdrawn. In June 1967, Nasser compelled the equivocal secretary general of the United Nations (UN), U Thant, to remove the UN peacekeeping force, which had been in the Sinai since the conclusion of the 1956 War. Is-

rael, seeing this as a prelude to an Egyptian onslaught, launched a preemptive strike on June 5, 1967. By the time hostilities ended through UN intercession on June 10, the armed forces of Egypt, Jordan, and Syria were devastated.

The Six-Day War of June 1967 put the Arab-Israeli conflict at the center of Middle Eastern events more than any political event since the Arab Revolt of 1916. With the Soviet Union backing confrontational states like Egypt and Syria, and the United States Israel, the solution to the Arab-Israeli dispute became—and still is—the key to any real stability in the region. The end of the war saw the rise of Palestinian terror groups like the Palestine Liberation Organization (PLO) and the Popular Front for the Liberation of Palestine (PFLP). Although Ahmad al-Shuqayri was the founder of the PLO, power soon passed to Yassir Arafat, believed to be the nephew of the Grand Mufti of Jerusalem. The Popular Front for the Liberation of Palestine was the brainchild of Dr. George Habash, a Marxist physician, in 1967. The two organizations, rather than becoming effective pressure groups for Palestinians—including the wide Palestinian community outside the Middle East—devoted themselves to terror attacks against Israel.

More than that, they effectively allied themselves with similar groups in Europe, the Irish Republican Army, the Basque separatist ETA in Spain, the Brigati Rossi in Italy, and the Baader-Meinhof gang in West Germany. Using freelance terrorists like Carlos "The Jackal" Ramirez Sanchez and Abu Nidal as well, they carried on a reign of true political terror throughout the 1970s. Thus, much potential international support for the Palestinian cause evaporated under the constant drumbeat of terror assaults. One of the most flagrant was the attack by the Black September faction of the PLO on the Israeli Olympic team in Munich, Germany, in September 1972, when the attackers were most likely aided by the East European intelligence service, the STASI. Indeed, this first terror war would continue unabated into the 1980s.

The serious situation in the Middle East was underscored by the October 1973 war, where Israeli intelligence was caught unprepared in detecting a surprise Egyptian attack by President Anwar Sadat, who had succeeded Nasser on the latter's death in 1970. The war began on October 6, 1973, catching the Israelis unprepared on Yom Kippur, the Day of Atonement. The surprise attack, coming especially on a major holy day when many of Israel's reservist soldiers were at home with their families, was a devastating blow to the state of Israel. For the first few days, the actual fate of the country hung in the balance. In desperation, Prime Minister Golda Meir appealed directly to the American president to help counterbalance the massive Soviet war material that both Sadat and Assad were able to fling at the country. The American response was the largest aerial resupply effort in the history of warfare.

Yet, in the middle of the war, suddenly a nuclear pillar of fire loomed over all. Discussions began over an appeal from Sadat for a joint American-Soviet force that would be sent to the theater of war to help keep the peace if a cease-fire could somehow be reached between the belligerents. Premier Leonid Brezhnev, who was gradually winning his Kremlin power struggle against Alexei Kosygin, sent a message to this effect to President Richard Nixon on October 24. The message contained a passage that raised the risk of thermonuclear war. Wrote Brezhnev, "I will say it straight that if you find it impossible to act jointly with us in this manner, we should be faced with the necessity urgently to consider the question of taking appropriate steps unilaterally." The implied threat of unilateral Soviet action in the Middle East struck like a bolt of lightning at the Nixon administration, already under siege at home because of the Watergate crisis.

Immediately, the Brezhnev ultimatum galvanized Henry Kissinger, who was acting as both the secretary of state and the national security adviser to Nixon. The United States raised its condition of military readiness from Defense Readiness Condition (DEFCON) IV to DEFCON III, implying the seriousness with which Washington took the Brezhnev letter. When the Soviet leadership met again the next day, the news of the massive American preparations greeted a shocked Brezhnev and his advisers. Brezhnev had never intended the threat of war with the United States, but the incredibly high importance that the United States put on maintaining the security of Israel, and its own strategic position in the Middle East, had left no room for taking chances. Fortunately, for the United States and the Soviet Union, and the rest of the world, the crisis passed as quickly as it had arisen.

On the ground, with the help of the American airlift, the Israelis had recovered from their initial shock. The Syrian, Iraqi, and Jordanian armed forces had been quickly crushed. On the southern front with Egypt, by October 22, the Egyptian Third Army had disintegrated. The Israeli tanks of General Avraham Adan reached the bank of the Suez Canal before that evening. By the next morning, the Third Army was completely surrounded by Israeli forces. Moreover, having crossed the canal into Egypt, the Israelis occupied some 1,000

square miles of Egyptian territory, the first time perhaps in history that a Jewish army had conquered part of the land of the pharaohs. On October 24, the Israelis accepted the United Nations cease-fire and allowed supplies to reach the beleaguered Egyptian Third Army.

The end of the 1973 War was to have unexpected consequences. The oil-rich nations of the world had formed OPEC, the Organization of Petroleum Exporting Countries, whose membership was largely among the Arab states. Reacting to the Arab defeat, as Mansfield wrote, "the Arab states declared an oil boycott of countries supporting Israel [including the United States]. By the end of 1974 the price [of oil] had quadrupled, from about $3.50 a barrel to $15.00."

It was only later that the real reason for Sadat's launching the war appeared to arise. Within Egypt, he had already ended dependence on the Soviet Union, to allow greater freedom of action in international affairs. He showed this when in September 1978, he entered into political talks with Israel's Prime Minister Menachem Begin, under the guidance of American President Jimmy Carter. The talks were supposed to address both the question of peace between Egypt and Israel, as well as the problem of the Palestinians, according to Charles D. Smith in *Palestine and the Arab-Israeli Conflict*. The Camp David agreements led to the Egyptian-Israeli peace treaty of March 1979, the first treaty of peace between an Arab state and Israel. However, the question of the Palestinians, and the Israeli settlements on the West Bank that had been built, remained a source of unrest and tension.

In the same year, 1979, the Islamic Revolution under the Ayatollah Khomeini broke out in Iran. In the early 1970s, Reza Shah Pahlavi, using increased oil revenues, had attempted to continue the modernization of his father. But the religious extremists who opposed his modernization plan saw this as the time to strike. Their leader was Khomeini, who from his French Parisian exile smuggled into Iran videotapes urging the Shi'ites (Iran's religious Muslim majority) to defy the Westernizing shah.

On September 7 and 8, 1978, the shah declared martial law and his troops fired on demonstrators. On the eve of the Shi'ite religious celebration of the month of Moharram, December 1, 1978, the Ayatollah issued a call to his disciples. According to Gary Sick in *All Fall Down: America's Tragic Encounter with Iran*, Khomeini declared that Moharram would be the month that the shah's "satanic government will be abolished." On January 16, 1979, the shah left the country as a National Front government under Shapour Bakhtiar became sole

For more than seven decades, the drilling and refining of Middle Eastern oil has been at the crux of regional and world conflict. Above, an oil rig set ablaze by Saddam Hussein forces after his invasion of Kuwait is brought under control by U.S. contractors.

ruler of the country. On February 1, 1979, the Ayatollah returned in triumph to Tehran. On April 1, 1979, Khomeini proclaimed Iran an Islamic Republic. Increasingly, the Khomeini regime began to attempt to export its "Islamic Revolution" beyond Iran's borders. Within Iran, the moderate, secular government of Mehdi Bazargan fell from power. In September 1980, war broke out between Iran and Iraq, with Iraq covertly supported by Saudi Arabia and the United States in an attempt to stem the spread of the Islamic Revolution. American support of the Iraqis turned to revulsion when Iraqi dictator Saddam Hussein employed chemical weapons against the Iranians, first at Majnoon in March 1984, according to Robert Harris and Jeremy Paxman in A *Higher Form of Killing.* Finally, after nearly one and a half million died, the war was brought to an end with a United Nations cease-fire on August 20, 1988.

THE 1980s AND 1990s

Within two years, Iraq would be at war again, as Saddam Hussein began a decade of destabilization in the Persian Gulf. In a move to steal the oil reserves of Kuwait to pay the debt for the war, Saddam invaded the Gulf sheikhdom in August 1990. The United Nations in November 1990 passed Resolution 678, which empowered member nations to employ all means necessary to end Iraqi occupation of Kuwait. When Saddam defied the UN, the coalition mustered by the senior President George Bush launched a devastating air attack, followed by a massive ground assault. After 100 hours of fierce ground combat, Bush could proclaim to the American people on February 27, 1991, "Kuwait is liberated. The Iraqi army is defeated." However, completely deceiving the American negotiators under General Norman Schwarzkopf, the coalition's chief, Saddam turned on his Kurdish and Shi'ite Muslim populations a true reign of terror.

In December 1987, Palestinians, long restive under Israeli rule, began their intifada, or uprising, in the territories occupied by Israel in 1967. In the same year, the Islamic extremist group Hamas, led by Shaikh Ahmed Yassin, launched its first suicide bombings against civilian targets in Lebanon. In January 1993, secret negotiations began in Oslo, Norway, to open a dialogue between Palestinians and Israelis. The talks were fruitful, and what would later be called a "road map" to a final, constructive solution to the problem of the Palestinian people was initiated. A Palestinian Authority was established with Yassir Arafat as its chairman. The land in the West Bank and the Gaza Strip was to become a de jure Palestinian state. Since then, however, real progress has been disappointing. A main part of the Palestinian-Israeli rapprochement was that Arafat would reign in the terror groups like Hamas that operated from the territory of the Palestinian Authority. This Arafat has been unable—or unwilling—to do. In 2000, when minister Ariel Sharon visited the Temple Mount in Jerusalem, near the revered Muslim shrine of the Dome of the Rock, Palestinians, most likely at Arafat's instigation, began a second intifada.

In the wake of widespread disillusion with Arafat's failure to curtail terror attacks, in the aftermath of the assassination of Hamas's founder Shaikh Ahmed Yassin in March 2004, Sharon, now prime minister, said an attack on Arafat was now possible. However, after President George W. Bush objected to such an attack as unnecessarily destabilizing an already shaky situation, Josef Federman wrote in the *Philadelphia Inquirer* on April 26, 2004, that "Israeli leaders yesterday backed away from Prime Minister Ariel Sharon's latest threats against Yassir Arafat, saying there were no immediate plans to kill the Palestinian leader."

Yet, while no action was yet taken on Chairman Arafat, serious events had taken place in the struggle with terrorism. After bombing the American embassies in East Africa, in Tanzania and Kenya, in the summer of 1998, Osama bin Laden and his al Qaeda extremist organization launched the attacks on America on September 11, 2001.

After being deprived of his Saudi Arabian citizenship in 1994, bin Laden had made his headquarters in Afghanistan, where he had forged close ties with the extremist Taliban of Mullah Mohammed Omar. The Taliban ruled most of Afghanistan from 1996. When Afghanistan refused to surrender bin Laden, an American and British coalition attacked in October 2001. However, after severe fighting in December, it is believed that bin Laden and his senior lieutenants, like the Egyptian Dr. Ayman al-Zawahiri, were able to make their escape to the lawless tribal territories of Pakistan, thanks to the connivance of Afghan warlords. In March 2004, the Pakistani Army made an attack on the territory of the Waziri tribe, but gave enough advance warning so that the fugitives may have made a second escape from justice.

At the same time, Saddam Hussein's Iraq still remained a source for concern, especially with suspicions that he was amassing again his arsenal of weapons of mass destruction (WMD): nuclear, biological, and chemical weapons. On March 6, 2003, President George W. Bush announced dissatisfaction with the imperious way in which Hussein was refusing full compliance with UN efforts to ascertain if he had rebuilt his WMD arsenal. Finally, in Operation Iraqi Freedom, on March 20, the British and American coalition forces under American General Tommy Franks struck. As the PBS *Frontline* show described the final attack on Baghdad, "U.S. forces secure Baghdad after final desperate resistance by Fedayeen and Ba'ath Party militias who are fighting almost alone. The regular Iraqi Army soldiers don't fight or even surrender en masse, as the Americans hoped; they simply go home. Late in the afternoon of April 9, in Baghdad's Firdos Square, the statue of Saddam Hussein is pulled down."

While the initial aftermath of the conquest of Iraq proved almost an anticlimax, within a year of the end of the war, the coalition forces faced heavy renewed resistance from Shi'ite militants, Iraqi insurgents, and foreign fighters linked with al-Qaeda who are determined to thwart the reconstruction plans for Iraq taking shape under the civilian administration.

SEE ALSO

Volume 1 Left: Iran; Middle East; Saudi Arabia; Egypt; Israel. *Volume 2 Right:* Iran; Iraq; Saudi Arabia; Egypt.

BIBLIOGRAPHY

Ahmad Gross, "Kaiser Wilhelm II: Deutschland und der Islam," www.enfal.de/grund44htm (July 2004); Wilfred Cantwell Smith, *Islam in the Modern World* (Mentor Books, 1957); Nicole and Hugh Pope, *Turkey Unveiled: A History of Modern Turkey* (Overlook, 1998); Philip Ziegler, *Omdurman* (Knopf, 1974); Samir Raafat, "The Boutros Ghali We All Don't Know," *Jordan Star* (September 26, 1996); John F. Murphy Jr., *Sword of Islam: Muslim Extremism from the Arab Conquests to the Attack on America* (Prometheus Books, 2002); Albert Hourani, *A History of the Arab Peoples* (Harvard University Press, 1991); Peter Mansfield, *A History of the Middle East* (Viking, 1991).

JOHN F. MURPHY, JR.
AMERICAN MILITARY UNIVERSITY

Militia Movements

HISTORICALLY, the American militia was the first permanent armed force in the original 13 British colonies of the future United States. As Howard L. Peterson wrote in his *History of American Artillery, Round Shot and Rammers in Virginia*, "the Lost Colony of 1587 on Roanoke Island boasted falcons, sakers, and small breechloaders," which were types of 16th-century British cannon. Under the command of soldier of fortune John Smith, Jamestown, Virginia, the first permanent English settlement in the United States, established a militia company as a protection from Virginia's Native Americans.

PREREVOLUTIONARY MILITIA

In *Arms and Armor in Colonial America*, Peterson documented the continual shipments of arms which London sent out to the militia companies, set up as quickly as the new colonies or plantations were established. The Pilgrims of Plymouth Rock, who settled Massachusetts in 1620, as Peterson recorded, had only "small guns of the minion and saker class" to defend against Indians and possible attacks from the French north in New France, modern-day Canada. The militia movement grew in sophistication as the colonies developed. Douglas Edward Leach noted, "as early as 1639, the colony of Massachusetts had been able to hold a training session for two regiments lasting the whole day." With the beginning of the wars with France, King William's War in 1689, the colonial militias faced another direct threat as the French from New France sought to eradicate the English colonies with the aid of the Iroquois tribe and the tribes from the Great Lakes. During the same time, the Spanish in the south did the same with their allies among the southern tribes. James Oglethorpe settled Georgia with districts and towns in 1732 to provide a buffer for the more prosperous Carolina colonies. The nexus of Spanish power in the south at this time was Castillo de San Marcos at St. Augustine in Florida, dating from 1565 as the oldest permanent European city in the present United States.

As the long struggle with the French continued, the colonial regiments, with so little manpower coming from England, began to evolve into professional regiments. Indeed, as American historian Francis Parkman wrote in *Montcalm and Wolfe*, it was the Virginia troops under Colonel George Washington who began the last of the French wars, the French and Indian War (1756–63). In May 1754, in what is now western Pennsylvania, Washington fought a skirmish with the French and Native Americans under Ensign Coulon de Jumonville, who was killed. As Parkman commented, "this obscure skirmish began the war that would set the

world on fire." In July of the following year, Washington and his colonial Virginia troops helped cover the retreat of the regular British battalions under General Edward Braddock, formerly of King George II's Second Regiment of Foot Guards, the Coldstream Guards. Another famous figure in the history of the American militia movement, Daniel Boone, made his first appearance in the Braddock campaign in Pennsylvania. (Philadelphia's Benjamin Franklin organized the transportation for the campaign.)

It is from the French and Indian War that the rift between the regular soldiers from Great Britain and the colonial, or provincial, troops can be dated. However, throughout the war, the British regulars were desperately dependent on the troops that the colonies could furnish in the struggle with the French. The colonial troops proved themselves at the Battle of Lake George (New York) in September 1755 when New York troops under Sir William Johnson, the superintendent for Indian Affairs (with his Native American allies), decimated regular French troops under Major General Ludwig Augustus, Baron von Dieskau, and French Canadian militia, and allied natives. The fact that, two months after Braddock's defeat, a force made up entirely of American militia had turned back a major French invasion was not lost on the English colonists. At the same time, it established the belief that militia, well trained and led, could stand against any regulars.

MILITIA EFFORTS

Throughout the remainder of the French and Indian War, colonial militia regiments grew in campaign experience. In the major British attack on Fort Ticonderoga, New York, in July 1758, militia from New England as well as New Jersey were well represented. The colonies made a massive effort. Parkman writes that "New Hampshire put one in three of her able-bodied men into the field." But underscoring it all was the political feeling among the colonists that they were acting with what they deeply believed was their heritage as freeborn Englishmen. Parkman said of Massachusetts, "her contributions of money and men were not ordained by an absolute king, but made by the voluntary act of a free people." Any future attempts at an exercise of arbitrary power by England would clearly have unforeseen and unpleasant consequences. Ironically, among the British officers who would fall at Ticonderoga was Lord George Howe, who was beloved by the Americans. Had Lord Howe survived, the entire future of colonial relations with England may have been dramatically different. The attack launched on July 8 by General James Abercromby against the French under Major-General Louis-Joseph, the Marquis de Montcalm, led to a brutal slaughter of the attacking British and colonial troops. Any American respect for the "superior" military abilities of regular army officers—and British in particular—died on the bloody field outside the French Fort Carillon, later called Ticonderoga.

REVOLUTIONARY MILITIA

By the time of the Boston Massacre in 1770, precursor to the American Revolution, the 13 colonies were able to rely on a drilled body of men, in general equivalent in size to the general (white) male population. The years following the massacre saw great growth in the militias of the colonies. When the Port of Boston was closed, following the Boston Tea Party, Committees of Correspondence were formed in all the colonies, thus permitting a limited coordination of action among the colonial militias—perhaps the first American experience of a joint military command. When the British under General Gage marched out of Boston to seize the gunpowder stores of the militia companies, it was the militia companies of Massachusetts at Lexington and Concord (April 19, 1775) whose musketry began the Revolution.

The performance of the militia was mixed, and the state militias took second place to the regular American army under Washington, who assumed command at Boston under congressional orders in June 1775. In many ways, the American Revolution repeated the story of the French and Indian War, but in totally American terms.

At times, the American regular army officers became exasperated by militia leaving camp when their enlistments were expired, and on the battlefield they could not be totally relied upon. But, for home defense, they were the only force against British raids and those launched by the pro-British Indians and Tories (Loyalists). However, under the overall command of American Brigadier-General Daniel Morgan, the southern militia played an important role in the victories in South Carolina at King's Mountain (October 7, 1780), and under Morgan directly at Hannah's Cowpens (January 17, 1781).

At the same time, a vigorous guerrilla war was waged by the noted "Swamp Fox" Francis Marion and Andrew Pickens. When the war ended with the Treaty of Paris in September 1783, the militia emerged even more strongly as the iconic emblem of Americans at war: the citizen soldier who would drop his plow and take up his musket to fight for his family and land.

During the debates surrounding the adoption of the U.S. Constitution in 1787, the militia issue inflamed the arguments about the new national government. Members of the Federalist group under Alexander Hamilton of New York believed that a strong national army was necessary to preserve American independence from foreign powers like Spain, France, and England, and at the same time to preserve national unity. But at the same time, the anti-Federalists, such as George Mason of Virginia, remembering the heavy hand of the British regulars, felt that the militia ought to be the main defender of the new nation.

Finally, a Solomonic compromise was arrived at: while the new regular army would be created, the militias would remain. Indeed, they would benefit from contact with the regular forces in uniformity of training and equipment. As Mason phrased it, "the militia ought therefore to be the more effectively prepared for the public defense."

In the major American wars of the 19th century, the War of 1812, the Mexican War (1846–48), the Civil War (1861–65), and the Spanish-American War of 1898, the militias and other volunteer units continued to play an important role. During the Mexican War, for example, on May 13, 1846, Congress authorized volunteers "not exceeding 50,000 men." At Buena Vista, on February 23, 1847, Mississippi Volunteers under Jefferson Davis distinguished themselves under General Zachary Taylor. In the Civil War, after the firing on Fort Sumter by the Confederates in April 1861, Union President Abraham Lincoln immediately called for 75,000 volunteers. Even now, according to R. Ernest Dupuy and Trevor N. Dupuy in Military Heritage of America, "the militia of the various states could only be called to the Federal colors only with the consent of the governors." With the entire regular army at some 16,000 when Civil War hostilities began—and with many of them leaving to join the South—volunteers and regular militia units became a much needed resource on both sides. During the Spanish-American War of 1898, the Rough Riders of future President Theodore Roosevelt captured the American imagination when the cowboy volunteers stormed San Juan Hill in Cuba with the regulars of the U.S. 10th Cavalry Regiment.

With the coming of World War I in August 1914, American army officers such as Leonard Wood, and other Americans including former President Theodore Roosevelt, foresaw an inevitable future American entry into the war. As part of this preparation, the National

Defense Act of 1916 was passed allowing, according to *Military Heritage of America*, "over a period of five years the Regular Army to be increased to 220,000 men, the National Guard to be raised to 450,000." Finally, Washington's goal had been achieved: a militia that would be "well-organized ... upon a plan that would pervade all the States." Throughout the two world wars, the Korean War, and the Vietnam War, the Act of 1916 provided for the general governance of the state national guards, as the militias now were usually called. However, in the 1990s, during the administration of President Bill Clinton (1992–2000), a new development emerged in the history of America's militia movement: the right-wing militia.

MODERN RIGHT-WING MILITIA

In August 1992, the wife and son of white supremacist Randy Weaver, who had ties to the Aryan Nations movement, were gunned down in a battle with federal and state law enforcement authorities at Ruby Ridge in Idaho. Then, in April 1993, the siege of the Branch Davidian compound at Waco, Texas, by federal agents and local law enforcement authorities ended in a tragic fire. A large number of people on the American right began to be concerned that the liberal Clinton administration was beginning a full-scale attack on traditional American freedoms. Clinton administration efforts to limit the selling and possession of assault rifles also galvanized the National Rifle Association, a staunch pro-gun-ownership organization.

The modern American militia movement arose out of the pressures of the time. The philosophy behind much of the movement was that of Christian Identity, a belief whose origin could be traced to the "White Israelite" school of John Wilson in England in the 1840s. Wilson believed that the races of northern Europe were descended from the Twelve Lost Tribes of Israel and that they, not the Jews, were the true Chosen People of God. American preachers of Christian Identity in the 20th century believed that the nonwhite races of the world are in fact "the mud people" and that the Jews, far from being chosen by God, are actually the Children of Satan. Many militia members identified with the Aryan Nations movement of Reverend Richard Butler and John Trochmann, founder of the influential Militia of Montana.

The militia movement spread rapidly throughout the country in the wake of Waco and Ruby Ridge. One of the ideological founders of the movement was Christian Identity spokesman John Potter Gale, who be-

The Anti-Defamation League alerts its members to right-wing militia by posting notices on its website as above in 1998.

lieved in the "unorganized militia." The term *unorganized militia* stems from the constitutional debates of the Continental Congress; one of the speakers, the anti-Federalist Mason, said, "I ask, sir, what is the militia? It is the whole people, except for a few public officials." The constitutional precedent claimed by the modern militia movement may be the reason that so little federal authority has been set against it. As of 2004, the only real federal force has been used against the Montana Freemen in a siege that lasted 81 days, beginning in March 1996, which was coordinated by the Federal Bureau of Investigation (FBI).

The sophisticated tactics used by Director Louis Freeh's FBI showed a high degree of evolution from when the bureau was first faced with such confrontations at Ruby Ridge and Waco. In Michigan, a group ousted from the state militia movement for radicalism, later called the North American Militia, was dissolved when leaders Brad Metcalf and Randy Graham received severe prison sentences for plotting to bomb targets, including an Internal Revenue Service building. With the advent in 2000 of the more conservative administration of President George W. Bush, the militia movement, by far composed of law-abiding citizens, appeared to have become more reconciled again with federal power in Washington, D.C.

SEE ALSO
Volume 1 Left: American Revolution; United States.
Volume 2 Right: Bruder Schweigen; Christian Identity; Aryan Nations.

BIBLIOGRAPHY
"The Unorganized Militia," www.city-net.com (May 2004); Anti-Defamation League, "The Militia Movement: Extremism in America," www.adl.org (May 2004); R. Ernest Dupuy

and Trevor N. Dupuy, *Military Heritage of America* (HERO Books, 1984); Robert Leckie, *The Wars of America* (Bantam Books, 1968); Donald R. Hickey, *The War of 1812: A Forgotten Conflict* (University of Illinois Press, 1989); Francis Parkman, *Montcalm and Wolfe* (Collier Books, 1962); John F. Murphy Jr., "Report on Early American Army" (U.S. National Park Service, 1992); W.M. Wallace, *Appeal to Arms: A Military History of the American Revolution* (Crown, 1964); Douglas Edward Leach, *Arms for Empire: A Military History of the British Colonies in North America, 1607–1763* (Macmillan Publishers, 1973); T. Harry Williams, *Americans in Arms* (Collier Books, 1962).

JOHN F. MURPHY, JR.
AMERICAN MILITARY UNIVERSITY

Mises, Ludwig von (1881–1973)

ECONOMIST, PHILOSOPHER, and social scientist Ludwig von Mises is considered among the most original and influential libertarian thinkers of the 20th century. Mises was the chief advocate of the subjective theory of value: Philosophers and economists have attempted to understand why different things have different values for different people, why different commodities have different prices, and why the same commodities have different prices at different times.

Classical economics, as well as Karl Marx, adopted the labor theory of value, according to which prices represent the amount of labor put into producing a product. Mises and his Austrian School of economics argued that values cannot be reduced to any "objective" quantifiable empirical property. Instead, values reflect myriad, constantly changing individual subjective preferences.

The subjective theory of value implies that society and the state cannot be dedicated to the promotion of any value or set of values, but for the creation of conditions where individuals may pursue myriad radically different values and goals without interfering unnecessarily with each other's activities. This environment is a free market where exchanges ensure that goods are distributed to those who value them the most.

Another implication of the subjective theory of value is that it is impossible to adjust supply to demand without a free-market mechanism that determines the price, and also conveys information to producers to produce more of a product, concentrate innovation ef-

forts in that sector of the market, or import more of it if the price rises, or reduce production if the price falls. Consequently, socialist command economies where bureaucrats or politicians determine prices are subjected to waste when they overproduce what nobody wants, and shortages when they do not produce enough of what people like. Central planning is further complicated by the inability to evaluate the values of state-owned production units that are not bought or sold and do not have to compete for profits in markets where they have monopoly status.

The inefficiency of socialist economies forces them to close themselves off from external competition through protectionism and severe restrictions on emigration and immigration. The ideology that legitimizes these measures is nationalism, the main cause of war and destruction in the 20th century. Eventually, demographic growth and economic stagnation and failures force nationalist states to adopt an expansionist aggressive policy—wars to gain more resources through territorial expansion—the nationalist wars of the 20th century.

Mises, who lived through the inflation of the 1920s, the Depression of the 1930s, and exile and war in the 1940s, blamed economic failures on excessive government intervention in the market. Government monetary policy, the central determination of interest rates, led, in Mises's opinion, to imbalances in capital markets that exacerbated the extreme imbalances of economic cycles. Mises sought to limit the tendency of governments to print paper money irresponsibly by linking the quantity of money in the market to gold reserves.

Mises applied his criticism of socialism not just to command economies of the totalitarian variety, but also to interventionist social-democratic policies. Mises attempted to prove that any intervention leads inevitably "on a slippery slope" to more intervention to correct the undesired effects of the first intervention, which leads before long to totalitarian government that should correct everything. Eventually, Mises thought, there is only a bivalent choice between liberty and totalitarianism and no middle way. Developments since the period when Mises formulated his arguments vindicated his arguments against command economies more than his slippery slope argument against welfare states.

Mises used "subjectivism" in a broader sense to argue for a methodological distinction between the natural and human sciences in the tradition of neo-Kantian philosophers. Any science that deals with humans as a subject matter (psychology, the social sciences, and economics) cannot be an empirical science like physics or

Ludwig von Mises is considered to be among the most original libertarian thinkers of the 20th century.

most of this period he had an unpaid position at New York University. Despite the failure of academic institutions to hire Mises, he was influential through his publications and personal contacts both on general economic theory and the Austrian School of economics, including, most notably, Friedrich von Hayek and Murray Rothbard. Mises's rejection of the quantitative-mathematical turn in economics that followed Keynesian economics as shallow and inapplicable to real economic situations that unfold over long periods of time and are not necessarily in a state of equilibrium separated the Austrian School from mainstream economics. Within mainstream economics, Milton Friedman combined Mises's criticism of command economy and monetary policy with mathematical modeling.

SEE ALSO

Volume 1 Left: Socialism; Political Economy; Marx, Karl.
Volume 2 Right: Capitalism; Libertarianism.

BIBLIOGRAPHY

Eamonn Butler, *Ludwig von Mises: Fountainhead of the Modern Microeconomics Revolution* (Gower, 1988); J. Patrick Gunning, *The New Subjectivist Revolution: An Elucidation and Extension of Ludwig von Mises Contributions to Economic Theory* (Rowman & Littlefield, 1991); Jeffrey M. Herbener, ed., *The Meaning of Ludwig von Mises: Contributions in Economics, Sociology, Epistemology, and Political Philosophy* (Kluwer, 1993).

AVIEZER TUCKER
AUSTRALIAN NATIONAL UNIVERSITY

chemistry because its subject matter cannot be directly observable, is unpredictable due to free choice, and is not subject to universal laws. Mises rejected, on methodological grounds, the claim of some Marxists that Marxism is the science of society or history that discovered the laws that govern historical change and predict future historical developments. Instead, Mises suggested that economics is a deductive science that deduces from a small number of axiomatic assumptions descriptions of human behavior that are valid so long as the assumptions are true, but do not necessarily describe an actual state of affairs in the world.

Mises was born in a provincial capital in the multiethnic and tolerant, yet authoritarian Austro-Hungarian Empire. He grew up and was educated in the intellectually vibrant capital of Vienna at the closing years of the empire, where he came under the influence of the economist Carl Menger. Apart from military service during World War I, Mises worked until 1934 at the Austrian Chamber of Commerce. He moved then to take a teaching position at the University of Geneva in Switzerland, before emigrating to the United States in 1940. For

Monarchism

EARLY KINGDOMS in Europe seem to have existed from almost the beginning of oral history, the accounts of which were put into writing only centuries later. Perhaps the first known history of a European monarchy is found in pre-Christian Ireland. Padraic Colum noted in his *A Treasury of Irish Folklore* that "more than any other European [epic poetic] cycle outside the Greek, the stories of the early Iron Age in Ireland have epical character and epical scope," especially the *Tain Bo Cualgne, The Cattle Raid of Cooley.* The Tain chronicle the adventures of the son of the King of Cooley, Cu Chulainn, in Ulster, today's Northern Ireland. Colum estimates that "the stories were formed into an epic tale probably 1,300 years ago."

The Roman historian Livy, in his history of Rome, talks about the king of the Aborigines, Latinius, who led his army out to defend his kingdom from Aeneas, who had survived the fall of Troy in the Trojan War. While in good part considered myth, Livy's early accounts of Rome detail the existence of a monarchy before the establishment of the Roman Republic. The last king of Rome was Tarquin, who was deposed when the republic was founded in 509 B.C.E.

THE ROMAN LEGACY

The idea of monarchism, or kingship, as it is perceived today was perhaps the strongest legacy bequeathed by the western Roman Empire, which fell when Emperor Romulus Augustulus was deposed by the warlord Odacer in 476 C.E. When Theodoric the Ostrogoth had Odacer killed, he quickly took on the trappings of the empire as the first true European king. Edward Gibbon wrote in *The Decline and Fall of the Roman Empire* about "the visible peace and prosperity of a reign of thirty-three years, the unanimous esteem of his own times." While the political institutions of western Europe were largely in shambles, the Christian Church, led by the pope in Rome, carried on an institutional and administrative heritage that dated, according to the New Testament Acts of the Apostles, from the time of Christ. For the new Germanic kings—many tribes like the Goths (Visigoths and Ostrogoths) could no longer be accurately typed as "barbarian"—the church was the only place they could seek that would give them legitimacy in their rule. This was needed not only against their rivals but also against the other tribes pressing upon them, such as the Vandals.

The new kings like Theodoric came from a warrior society that had raised its rulers up by acclamation of their warrior deeds. Julius Caesar wrote of one of these German tribes, the Suebi, in his *Gallic Wars*: "they draw every year a thousand men to be used as warriors fighting outside their frontiers." However, such basic ideas of kingship relied upon the ruler's ability to keep his warlords and warriors happy with booty and plunder. Such a wealthy king was Hrothgar the Dane, whom the hero Beowulf helped to kill the monster Grendel. Norma Lorre Goodrich wrote of Hrothgar's palace, Heorot Hall, in *The Medieval Myths*: "the lofty gables and gleaming roof of Heorot Hall came into sight." If such a king as Hrothgar grew unlucky in battle, he could easily be deposed and slain. The notion of a warlike king ruling through the strength of his sword endured in the story of the youthful Arthur, who proved himself

worthy of the right to rule by being the only one who could withdraw the sword Excalibur from the stone at the village fair.

In western Europe, only the church could confer on the new kings the legitimacy and protection from being overthrown that they desperately needed as they built the new European political institution: the kingdom. In doing so, the church worked to create the ideal of monarchy, the kingship. In the act of coronation, the king would be crowned by a high representative of the church, usually a bishop. On September 3, 1189, Richard the Lionheart, the great English Crusader king, was crowned at Westminster in London by Baldwin of Exeter, the Archbishop of Canterbury, leader of the Church in England.

By being crowned by a church official, the king was invested with authority by the church itself, whose pope claimed temporal authority on Earth as the vicar of Christ. Thus began the theory, intrinsic to monarchism, of the divine right of kings—that kings ruled not only by their legitimacy on earth, but also by right of divine approbation from heaven. So any upstart baron or feudal lord who challenged the king also contested the "Will of Providence." In extreme cases, such a lord could be excommunicated by "bell, book, and candle" and cut off from the community of the faithful. This not only condemned his soul (unless penance, or sincere contrition, was made) but also absolved his vassals from obedience to him. In practice, however, if a lord was strong enough to overthrow his king, then the temporal authority of the church would usually be compelled to make peace with him.

However, the support of the church for the monarchy also implied that the church expected the king to rule his people by Christian precepts. When a king transgressed against the church or its representatives, punishment would follow. On December 29, 1170, four knights, inflamed by the anger of King Henry II, Richard's father, killed the Archbishop of Canterbury, Thomas Becket. In penance, the king made pilgrimages to the shrine of Becket, who was made a saint, and had to negotiate a new settlement with the church at Avranches, France, in 1172, according to Winston S. Churchill in *The Birth of Britain*. When King John, Richard's brother, refused to accept Stephen Langton as Archbishop of Canterbury in 1206, Pope Innocent III placed all England in 1208 under interdict, allowing no Christian sacraments to be performed. He excommunicated John in 1209. After a French invasion, and facing rebellious barons, John was forced to make his peace with the church in 1213.

Indeed, at times, the representatives of the church championed political liberty as well when it was threatened by a king. William Lamberton, Bishop of St. Andrews, stoutly defended Scottish freedom when it was buffeted by the invasions of Kings Edward I and II of England. He supported both William Wallace and then Robert Bruce, who decisively defeated Edward II at Bannockburn in 1314.

However, the institution of monarchy was not a magic talisman to protect the lives of kings. The British King Henry V, the victor over the French at Agincourt in 1415, died in 1422. He left behind as king his feeble son, Henry VI. This led to the dynastic feud between the Houses of York and Lancaster, both descended from King Edward III. Henry VI was killed in 1471 on the orders of King Edward IV, of the House of York. Edward was succeeded in 1483 by his brother, Richard III. Richard in turn was killed at the Battle of Bosworth in 1485 in battle with Henry Tudor of the House of Lancaster. Justification for Richard III's killing was in part supplied by the fact that he was widely believed to have violated the institution of monarchy by conniving in the death of Edward's sons, the young Edward V and his brother Richard, Duke of York, after he had them imprisoned in the Tower of London in 1483.

In spite of political upheaval, the institution of monarchism has survived intact until modern times. Even in the 20th century, persistent monarchies reigned until violently overthrown. For example, in July 1918, while they were prisoners of the revolutionary Bolshevik regime, Tzar Nicholas Romanov II of Russia and his family, it is believed, were executed at Ekaterinburg. Modern forensic evidence has risen to dispute which members of the Tzar's imperial family were actually killed. In 1991, the bones of the slain royal family were exhumed, the year when the rule of the Russian Bolshevik, or Communist Party, ended.

The remains were given a religious funeral by the Russian Orthodox Church in July 1998, with all the trappings of the Romanov dynasty of which Nicholas was the last ruler. Many Russians of all backgrounds and in the church believe him and his family to be martyrs. Thus, even in Russia, a country that had officially eradicated monarchy as a form of government, the spirit of monarchism still served as a unifying force around which people from all classes of society could unite.

Through the late 19th century and most of the 20th, monarchism coexisted peacefully with various forms of secular government. However, the power of the monarchy steadily decreased as parliamentary structures relegated monarchies to more symbolic and less powerful roles. This trend was most evident in the United Kingdom, but also continues today in countries such as Sweden and the Netherlands, where the monarchy works with the socialist-leaning governments and still provide a nationalistic unifying force.

SEE ALSO

Volume 1 Left: Despotism; French Revolution; Russian Revolution.
Volume 2 Right: Feudalism; United Kingdom; France; Austria.

BIBLIOGRAPHY

Julius Caesar, *War Commentaries of Caesar*, Rex Warner, trans. (Mentor Books, 1960); Norma Lorre Goodrich, *The Medieval Myths* (Mentor Books, 1961); Burton Raffel, ed., *Beowulf* (Mentor Books, 1963); Aubrey de Selincourt, ed., *The Early History of Rome* (Penguin, 2002); David Willis McCullough, ed., *Wars of the Irish Kings* (Crown, 2000); "Archbishops of Canterbury," www.britannia.com (May 2004); S.T. Bindoff, *Tudor England* (Penguin, 1950); Alfred Duggan, *My Life for My Sheep* (Anchor Books, 1957); James Reston, Jr., *Warriors of God: Richard The Lionheart and Saladin in the Third Crusade* (Anchor Books, 2001); Padraic Colum, ed., *A Treasury of Irish Folklore* (Wings Books, 1967); Evan Macleod Barron, *The Scottish War of Independence* (Barnes and Noble, 1997); Mark D. Steinberg and Vladimir M. Khrustalev, *The Fall of the Romanovs* (Yale University Press, 1995); "Russia's Last Tsar," *St. Petersburg [Russia] Times*, www.sptimes.ru (May 2004).

JOHN F. MURPHY, JR.
AMERICAN MILITARY UNIVERSITY

Muslim Brotherhood

OF ALL ISLAMIC MOVEMENTS in the 20th century, none has had the impact of the Muslim Brotherhood (al-Ikhwan al-Muslimin) of Egypt. It was founded by Hassan al-Bana in 1928. The Muslim Brotherhood was a reaction to what was seen as the modernization—Westernization—that was sweeping Egypt since the British annexation in September 1882. It was also perceived as a reaction against the corruption of the Egyptian state, even though every British proconsul had carried on a campaign to make the Egyptian administration more honest and responsible to the people.

Moreover, philosophically from the beginning, the Ikhwan was against what would be considered democratic thought or representational government. On a Muslim Brotherhood internet site, an unidentified spokesman states clearly that "This depends on your definition of democracy, if democracy means that people decide who leads them then Ikhwan accepts it, if it means that people can change the laws of Allah and follow what they wish to follow then it is not acceptable. … About personal freedom, Ikhwan accepts personal freedom within the limits of Islam. However, if personal freedom to you means that Muslim women can wear shorts or Muslim men can do *Haram* [forbidden] actions, then Ikhwan does not approve of that."

Within Egypt, the Muslim Brotherhood in the 1930s formed a political alliance with the organization of Green Shirts, which patterned itself after the Brown Shirts of Adolf Hitler and the Black Shirts of Benito Mussolini's Fascist Party. The Green Shirts was the offshoot of the Misr al-Fatat, the Young Egypt movement, which had been founded by the nationalist lawyer Ahmad Hussein in 1933. "Young Egypt" was a close political ally of the religious extremists of the Muslim Brotherhood, which had been established by Hassan al-Bana in 1928. Hussein made clear his call to arms to the younger Egyptian generation, of which Gamal Abdel Nasser and Anwar Sadat were members "the task requires those who are prepared to die, suffer hardship and welcome sacrifice. These qualities cannot be found among the older generation. It is the youth, the new, generation, soldiers of Young Egypt, upon whose shoulders falls the task of resurrecting our glory." The Brotherhood, through its political alliance, thus put it with a group far removed from its Islamic tenets in its quest for political power. The Library of Congress Country Studies Program for Egypt observed that Young Egypt was "also a militaristic organization whose young members were organized in a paramilitary movement called the Green Shirts. The organization had fascist overtones and openly admired Nazi achievements. As German power grew, Young Egypt's anti-British tone increased."

After the war, they began a terror campaign in Egypt against secular power. As Daniel Benjamin and Steven Simon wrote in *The Age of Sacred Terror*, "beginning in 1948, they attacked British and Jewish businesses … in an effort to accelerate Britain's withdrawal from Egypt and protest Jewish settlement in Palestine." In 1951, Sayyid Qutb became the leading ideologist of the Brotherhood. In 1948, he had visited the United States as a representative of the Egyptian Ministry of Education. What he saw there filled him with revulsion for Western culture: "Humanity today is living in a large brothel!"

Three years after the shooting of al-Bana, the Brotherhood had its revenge on Farouk when its allies in the Free Officers movement, the modern form of the Young Egypt organization, toppled the king in a July 1952 coup. As Peter Mansfield wrote in *A History of the Middle East*, "On the night of 22–23 July, army units loyal to Free Officers seized all the key points in the capital, against only token resistance." The Free Officers formed the Revolutionary Command Council (RCC) to govern Egypt. Although Major-General Mohammed Neguib was the leader of the RCC, the power was held by Colonel Gamal Abdel Nasser. In circumstances not entirely clear, Nasser entered into a power struggle with Neguib, who apparently was supported by the Ikhwan. Neguib was ousted and Nasser emerged as sole ruler of Egypt. In October 1954, the Brotherhood staged an assassination attempt on Nasser, by Abdul Munim Abdul Rauf, which led to the Ikhwan being outlawed.

When Nasser died of a heart attack in 1970, his successor, Anwar Sadat, attempted to make peace with the Ikhwan. With the enhanced showing of Egyptian military forces in the October 1973 war against Israel, Sadat was popularly strong enough to negotiate with them. However, in March 1979, Sadat signed the peace treaty with Israel's Prime Minister Menachem Begin, earning himself the hatred of the brotherhood and all groups allied to it. At a military parade on October 6, 1981, the anniversary of his attack on Israel, Sadat was attacked in his presidential reviewing stand by army militants led by Khaled Islambouli. Sadat was mortally wounded; later in April 1982, Islambouli and four confederates were executed. While Islambouli and his mutinous troops apparently could not be linked to the Ikhwan, certainly the Brotherhood would have viewed as the killing of one who betrayed Islam. Justification for the shooting came from Shaikh Omar Ahmed Rahman, later one of the main plotters in the first World Trade Center bombing in New York City in February 1993.

In an attempt to make peace with the brotherhood, Sadat's successor, Hosni Mubarak, attempted to make peace again with the Ikhwan. In 1984, the Muslim Brotherhood was legalized. However, its violent methods passed to Islamic groups who followed its heritage. They caused Mubarak to launch a campaign against them for—in truth—the control of Egypt. Some 40,000 may have died in the fighting. An attempt was made on Mubarak's life as well in June 1995 during a visit to the Ethiopian capital of Addis Ababa. In 1997, some 40 foreign tourists were massacred by an offshoot of the Brotherhood, the Gamaat al-Islamiyya. By 1998, the Egyptian Army and the security forces, perhaps with clandestine American support, had virtually brought the Islamic insurrection to a close.

Throughout the Muslim world, the Brotherhood established branches. As in Egypt, violence was often the path it followed to achieve its goals. On June 25, 1980, the Syrian branch attempted to assassinate President Hafez al-Assad. In retaliation, he unleashed the Syrian Army on the brotherhood stronghold of Hama; some 15,000 to 25,000 people were killed in an assault that began in February 1982. During the Russian invasion of Afghanistan (1979–89), the Ikhwan was responsible for raising "Arab-Afghan" units to go and fight in the jihad against the Russian *kufr*, or "unbelievers." Among these were Saudi Arabians with Osama bin Laden.

One of the most influential disciples of the Brotherhood was Ahmed Yassin, who fled with his family to Gaza during the 1948 war of Israeli independence; the United Nations estimated some 480,000 Arabs were displaced during the fighting. Having studied in Egypt, Yassin returned to Gaza, where he established a branch of the Ikhwan. In 1987, Yassin would establish Hamas, or "zeal," in Arabic. With Hizbollah, the Party of God, Hamas became the most intransigent foe of Israel and its continued existence. After a *shahid*, or suicide bomber, killed 10 Israelis in Ashdod on March 14, 2004, the Israeli government targeted him for assassination. On March 22, 2004, missiles from an Israeli attack helicopter ended his life.

Yet, perhaps the most powerful man in the history of the brotherhood still remains at large. The year Qutb was hanged in 1966, the Egyptian physician Ayman al-Zawahiri wrote in his memoirs that there was "an immediate interaction with Sayyid Qutb's ideas and the formation of the nucleus of the modern Islamic Jihad in Egypt." Ayman al-Zawahiri would go on to be the number two figure in the al-Qaeda group of Osama bin Laden. In September 2001, he would be regarded as the chief planner behind the attack on America. In April 2004, al-Zawahiri appeared to be in hiding with Osama bin Laden in the anarchic tribal lands of Pakistan.

SEE ALSO

Volume 1 Left: Middle East; Egypt.
Volume 2 Right: Middle East; Egypt; Religion.

BIBLIOGRAPHY

"Muslim Brotherhood Movement," www.ummah.org.uk (July 2004); Guy Stair Sainty, "The Spanish Military Orders," www.chivalricorders.org (July 2004); John F. Murphy Jr. *Sword of Islam: Muslim Extremism from the Arab Conquests to the Attack on America* (Prometheus, 2002); Daniel Benjamin and Steven Simon, *The Age of Sacred Terror* (Random House, 2003); Judith Miller, *God Has 99 Names* (Touchstone, 1996); Mark Huband, *Warriors of the Prophet: The Struggle for Islam* (Westview, 1998); Dilip Hiro, *Holy Wars: the Rise of Islamic Fundamentalism* (Routledge, 1989); Philip Mansfield, *A History of the Middle East* (Viking, 1991); Richard Fletcher, *The Quest for El Cid* (Knopf, 1990); Madawi al-Rasheed, *A History of Saudi Arabia* (Cambridge University Press, 2002); Ahron Bergman and Jihan El-Tabiri, *Israel and the Arabs: An Eyewitness Account of the War and Peace in the Middle East* (TV-Books, 2000;) Lawrence Wright, "The Man behind Bin Laden," *New Yorker* (September 16, 2002).

JOHN F. MURPHY, JR.
AMERICAN MILITARY UNIVERSITY

The Right

National Review

THE *NATIONAL REVIEW* is a weekly magazine of conservative opinion, considered one of the most influential conservative magazines in the United States. The *National Review* features the writing of many of the nation's leading conservative thinkers and makers of opinion. Writers who have been published in the magazine include John Derbyshire, David Frum, Russell Kirk, James Burnham, L. Brent Bozell, Larry Kudlow, Rich Lowry, Kate O'Beirne, Whittaker Chambers, and George Will, among others.

William F. Buckley, Jr., founded the *National Review* in 1955. Buckley was born into a wealthy family, graduated from Yale University in 1950, served in the Central Intelligence Agency, and was an editor for the *American Mercury* before he started the *National Review*. Buckley's term as editor of the magazine ran from 1955 to 1990. He still owned the publication in 2004. His columns, syndicated by Universal Press Syndicate, are carried by more than 300 newspapers in the United States.

In its early days, the *National Review* was the herald of anti-communism, and supported one of the most prominent conservatives in the United States, Senator Joseph McCarthy. The magazine is largely known today for its position against "big government" and the "liberal establishment." The magazine is credited with rallying conservatives to the call to organize and transforming them into a dominant political movement. Conservative Republican candidates like Barry Goldwater and Ronald Reagan benefited from the political movement inspired by the *National Review*.

Though conservatives today dominate many media and political arenas, at its beginnings, the *National Review* was alone in the belief that there was a need or a market for a magazine featuring conservative thought. Today, there are other publications that share the field such as the *Weekly Standard*, *National Interest*, *Policy Review*, and *Public Interest*. In the 2000s, conservatives have criticized the *National Review* for moving away from its historical roots of conservatism. Liberals accuse the magazine of everything from spreading disinformation to right-wing demagoguery. Despite its critics, the magazine continues to publish successfully and has made the move to the internet with *National Review Magazine Online*.

SEE ALSO

Volume 1 Left: Liberalism; New Left; Clinton, William J.
Volume 2 Right: Buckley, William F., Jr.; New Right; Reagan, Ronald; Conservatism.

BIBLIOGRAPHY

American Conservative Union Foundation, "The Problem of *National Review*," acuf.org/issues (April 2004); "American

Writers: Russell Kirk, William F. Buckley, and the Conservative Movement," www.americanwriters.org (April 2004); John B. Judis, *William F. Buckley, Jr.: Patron Saint of the Conservatives* (Simon & Schuster, 1988).

ARTHUR HOLST, PH.D.
WIDENER UNIVERSITY

National Rifle Association

THE NATIONAL RIFLE Association of America (NRA), founded in 1871, is the oldest civil rights organization in the United States from the perspective of the right wing in America. It is the brainchild of Colonel William Church and General George Wingate, who were troubled by the inadequate marksmanship of their Union troops during the Civil War. The initial impetus of the NRA, then, was the need to "encourage rifle shooting on a scientific basis." NRA membership rolls reached 4 million by 2004.

Although the NRA is widely considered to be among the nation's most effectual special interest groups, its first 100 years were devoted primarily to promoting the shooting sports and to firearms education, including the governance of national shooting matches since 1872 and the certification of police and civilian instructors. The NRA currently trains more than a million citizens each year in the safe use of firearms.

Countering leftist critics who contend the NRA promotes gun violence, the organization began the "Eddie Eagle" gun safety program in 1988. Endorsed by the National Safety Council, the program is aimed at prekindergarten to sixth-grade children, more than 17 million through 2004. Other NRA programs, since the late 1990s, include "Refuse to Be a Victim" seminars that have helped thousands of women and men develop a personal safety plan.

The NRA is the preeminent defender of "America's First Freedom"—Article II of the U.S. Constitution's Bill of Rights: "A well-regulated Militia being necessary to the security of a free State, the right of the people to keep and bear Arms shall not be infringed." Forty-three state constitutions also have provisions for the right to keep and bear arms. The NRA, based on *U.S. v. Cruickshank* [92 U.S. 542 (1875)], declares that Article II does not create the right to keep and bear arms; rather it, along with others in the Constitution, merely protects preexisting rights from encroachment—rights that are basic to a free civilization. The NRA asserts the law-abiding individual's right to own firearms because "the people" in Article II means the same thing everywhere in the Constitution.

To help preserve Article II, the NRA established its Legal Affairs Division in 1934, replaced in 1975 by the powerful NRA Institute for Legislative Action. The NRA supports the enforcement of existing laws against illegal gun use rather than the passage of new laws restricting firearm ownership. The clear link between citizen gun ownership and criminal deterrence is another message priority for the NRA. The organization opposes any attempt to register firearms to their owners. It has fought hard to defeat required waiting periods to obtain firearms, instead reluctantly agreeing to an "instant check at point of purchase" system (NICS) in the mid-1990s. "Instant check" for the NRA means that the records should be instant for the purpose of purchase and then destroyed, an interpretation supported by federal law.

The NRA fights for fundamental rights aside from those that threaten Article II. For instance, it has vehemently opposed the abridgement of free speech created by the McCain-Feingold campaign finance reform law. It has also supported George W. Bush's rejection of the United Nations' attempt to control small arms in America—but most fundamentally because it violates America's sovereignty.

There are at least five major issues at the forefront of the NRA's fight to preserve Article II. They are: 1) stopping the Clinton gun ban (which expired in September 2004) or any other gun ban (the government has no authority to illogically declare cosmetic features of firearms to be "assault weapons" because features of all firearms can be so declared); 2) promoting the right to carry concealed weapons for self-preservation against predatory people and animals (allowed in 38 states as of 2004); 3) the myth of ballistic imaging (guns are scientifically proven not to have individual "fingerprints" and any attempt to fingerprint them is a de facto registration system); 4) the promotion of state laws that forbid localities from infringing on citizens' rights to own guns; and 5) passage of state and federal laws that disallow suing gun manufacturers for the criminal misuse of their lawful products (such lawsuits are seen by the NRA as an attempt to bankrupt gun manufacturers through expensive court battles, thereby circumventing legislatures' control of the gun issue).

The NRA has suffused a realistic and powerful presence into the American political scene. As former Clinton administration spokesman George Stephanopoulos said about the NRA membership, "They're good citizens. They call their Congressmen. They write. They vote. They contribute. And they get what they want over time."

SEE ALSO
Volume 1 Left: Gun Control; Constitutional Amendments; Bill of Rights.
Volume 2 Right: Second Amendment.

BIBLIOGRAPHY
National Rifle Association, www.nra.org (August 2004); Stephen Halbrook, *That Every Man Be Armed* (University of New Mexico Press, 1984); David Kopel, Stephen Halbrook, and Alan Korwin, *Supreme Court Gun Cases* (Bloomfield Press, 2004); Don Kates, "The Second Amendment: A Dialogue," *Law and Contemporary Problems* (v.49, 1986).

GARY S. GREEN
CHRISTOPHER NEWPORT UNIVERSITY

National Wilderness Institute

THE NATIONAL WILDERNESS Institute (NWI) was founded in 1989 by Rob Gordon and Ben Patton in order to provide a conservative counterpoint to the liberal environmental and conservationist groups of the late 20th century. Since then, the institute has provided a "voice of reason on the environment," and "uses science to guide the wise management of natural resources for the benefit and enjoyment of people." NWI places most of its emphasis on a philosophy that includes economic growth and individual freedom as intrinsically connected to the Earth's resources, with a strong conviction that private stewardship, and not government regulation, will best serve to conserve and restore natural resources.

As dedicated outdoorsmen and proclaimed conservatives, Gordon and Patton have combined their love for nature and outdoor activities with a definitive philosophy based on right-wing politics. Concerned about government interference through legislation, the possible loss of property, and possible loss of the individual's civil rights and even livelihood, Gordon and Patton created a "preeminent" organization dedicated to nongovernmental intervention, property rights, and the individual's civil liberties. They have used scientific research, political influence, and widespread media coverage to promote a more conservative approach to current environmental problems.

The National Wilderness Institute wants to persuade those conservatives who are suspicious of all environmentalists that private management of the environment is important to all people, conservative or liberal. To this end, the institute includes in its mission statement a direct appeal to those conservatives: "NWI supports site and situation specific practices which unleash the creative forces of the free market, protect or extend private property rights, and reduce the inefficient and counter-productive effect of government regulations." One method used by the institute includes educating the American public through a variety of venues. Television interviews, radio shows, contributing to textbooks, press releases, testifying before Congress, writing and publishing journal articles, and supporting environmental studies—all help NWI disseminate its environmental policies.

In keeping with its mission, in 1996, NWI published its statement on conservation in the United States: "Individuals, Liberty and the Environment: A Distinctly American Conservation Ethic." Using the organization's mission as a foundation, the document explicates NWI's belief in the interdependence between man and nature and between Americans' unalienable rights and their responsibilities toward the environment.

NOT AS GREEN AS IT SEEMS

However, the institute may not be as "green" as it seems. According to the Science & Environmental Policy Project, NWI has received funds from several corporations whose environmental record makes them suspect as strong advocates for environmental protection. Mobil, Chevron, and Exxon all made respectable contributions to the National Wildlife Institute in 1994. In 1997, the Hardwood Manufacturers Association funded the NWI lobbying organization. Many left-wing publications and organizations have even accused the institute of trying to overturn the Endangered Species Act (ESA).

In 1997, the institute published a study based on a year-long research project entitled "Conservation Under the Endangered Species Act: A Promise Broken." Based upon their research, many of the claims of the success of the ESA were erroneous. NWI claimed that no species were "saved" as a result of the ESA, and that many of the species listed as endangered were never really in danger of becoming extinct. Basically, the study claimed that very little that the ESA espoused as successes resulting from their actions or initiatives really were based upon the ESA.

Many of the institute's publications, testimonies to Congress, and scientific reports accuse the Environmental Protection Agency (EPA) and other government and nongovernment agencies of skewing facts to promote public hysteria and of using their influence to shut down small businesses. Granted, many of the initiatives and research of the NWI attack the EPA or refute the claims of the agency, but when the EPA passes a ruling that happens to support the institute's ideology, NWI has no problem in commending the agency. When in January 2004 the EPA proposed a ruling that provided consistency in its pesticide reviews, the institute issued a press release: "National Wilderness Institute: Proposed EPA Rule Would Make Pesticide Reviews More Consistent, Help Endangered Species."

REFUTING LEFTIST CLAIMS

In working toward its goals of combining the conservative ideals of the sanctity of individual liberty, limited governmental interference, and the protection of property rights with the environmental ideals of resource management and the self-renewal aspects of the environment, NWI challenges the decisions of the EPA, hires scientists to refute various leftist groups' findings, and lobbies against public policies that might endanger its supporters' and members' property or liberty. Once the brainchild of two young sportsmen who love nature and belong to the political right wing, the National Wilderness Institute continues to support conservative ideals for environmental conservation through scientific research, lobbying, and education.

SEE ALSO

Volume 1 Left: Environmentalism; United States; Greenpeace; Nader, Ralph.
Volume 2 Right: Capitalism; *Laissez-Faire.*

BIBLIOGRAPHY

National Wilderness Institute, www.nwi.org (May 2004); "New-Style Conservation," *Policy Review* (September-October 1996); www.sepp.org/indenvir (May 2004); *Mother Jones* magazine, www.motherjones.com/news/feature/1997 (May 2004); Michael J. Catanzaro, "National Wilderness Institute," *Human Events* (April 3, 1998).

GLORIA J. HICKS
UNIVERSITY OF WYOMING

Nationalism

NATIONALISM, ONE OF THE modern ideologies, expresses the state of being national, national affection, and nationality. This definition explains nationalism as a set of ideas that members of a particular state, nation, society, or region may collectively feel. Nationalists who advocate national unity and independence try to form or build a nation on the basis of different notions of political legitimacy and sovereignty. One can talk about various forms of nationalism because it is a multifaceted political, social, and cultural phenomenon that can be found to some extent in all types of ideologies, from extreme right to extreme left. Thus, there have been several forms and versions of nationalism. Its main characteristic is that it provides a legitimizing ethos for a group of elites by implying that groups of similar people should have their own government or autonomy.

Nationalism has constituted one of the main ideological bases for all modern political and social movements for more than 200 years. It is commonly agreed that nationalism as a political, social, and ideological school of thought came to the fore by the French Revolution. The anti-Jacobin French priest Augustin Barruel first used the term *nationalism* in print in 1789. The Jacobins effectively put into practice nationalist projects. When the French Revolution made the idea of the rule of the people popular, they sought to define the people as the "French nation." The Jacobins put a strong emphasis on the creeds of French nationalism—French language and race, national festivals and ceremonies, emotions toward the flag and homeland, and popular self-government—to achieve political and social unity.

The idea of nationalism began to spread after the revolution throughout much of continental Europe. Especially during the Napoleonic wars (1792–1815), nationalist feelings and ideas began to dominate intellectual activities. France's invasions in Italy and Germany caused resentment and a desire for independence particularly among elite groups. It was the idea of achieving national unity imitated from France. During the early 19th century, nationalism also spread to South and Central America when, under the leadership of Simon Bolivar and Jose Martin, the colonies of Spain and Portugal declared their independence.

Nationalist movements in 19th-century Europe became the sole political movement. During that century, Thomas Jefferson and Thomas Paine had set up the foundations for American nationalism, and Jeremy Bentham and William Gladstone for British nationalism. Italian and German cases in Europe signify two nation-building efforts in the 19th century: Italy became a united state in 1861 and Germany in 1871. To attain national unity via self-determination, German nationalists and others strove to mobilize the people by stressing cultural values more than political ones. Nationalism gradually spread as an intellectual movement and school in the whole of central and Western Europe, when European multinational empires, namely Ottoman-Turkish, Austria-Hungarian, and Russian-Tzarist, started to disintegrate in the face of nationalist and separatist forces. As a result, new nation-states began to appear in Central and Eastern Europe and the Balkans. Greece and Serbia in the first half of the 19th century and Romania and Bulgaria in the second half of the 19th century achieved independence from Ottoman Turkey. Nationalist uprisings occurred among the Czechs and the Hungarians against the Austrian Empire.

By the late 19th century, nationalism had become a widespread popular movement in Europe and the rest of the world. It became the basic legitimizing force in the hands of the state elite and politicians, the basic motto for education and intellectual life, which was accelerated especially by the spread of print capitalism, including newspapers, journals, and books. However, during that time, there emerged a radical shift in the understanding and nature of nationalism.

It gradually turned into a tool of repressive and reactionary movements that negated to a greater extent the search for its progressive and liberal ideals. So patriotism, chauvinism, and xenophobia became the codes of nationalism, which were also associated with the quest for colonialism.

One can say that both World War I and World War II broke out because of nationalism. Nationalist ambitions formed the basis for leaders to expand their territory and influence areas. By the end of the First World War, Europe became the continent of nation-states with the breakup of the Austro-Hungarian and Ottoman empires.

It was an era of new movements called "national self-determination," according to which each nation or ethnicity has its own state within the geographical region in which it lives. Eight new states came to the fore, including Finland, Hungary, Czechoslovakia, Poland, and Yugoslavia. However, in the post-World War I period, national tensions continued to exist and, coupled with the frustrations of defeats, especially in Germany, and the unsatisfied ambitions of Italy and Japan, led to World War II.

Nationalism during the 20th century spread throughout the rest of the world. Its effect became tremendous in the colonized world as a force to revolt against colonial rule. It was anti-colonial nationalism making a different synthesis with the goals to achieve political and cultural independence from colonizers. Nationalist uprisings spread throughout the colonized world. By 1945, the British, French, Dutch, and Portuguese empires disintegrated in the face of anti-colonial nationalist movements. After the mid-20th century, Middle Eastern, African, and Asian countries achieved independence (1947: India and Pakistan from Britain; 1948: Indonesia from Holland; 1960: Nigeria from Britain; 1962: Algeria from France).

By the 1970s, the rise of ethno-nationalism occurred within nation-states all over the world. Simply, it has been a reaction to homogenizing affect of nation-building. This new form of nationalism came as a form of separatist movements, such as nationalist tensions in Northern Ireland and Scottish nationalism, Quebec separatism in Canada, the rise of Basque separatism in Spain, East Timor in Indonesia, the Arab-Israeli conflict, and so on. In recent times, the collapse of the communist Eastern Bloc led to the revival of nationalism again. The Soviet Union, Czechoslovakia, and Yugoslavia disintegrated and new nation-states were created in Eastern Europe, the Balkans, Caucasus, and Central Asia.

VERSIONS OF NATIONALISM

In the literature there are several versions of nationalism. But it has been largely analyzed in terms of two common forms, namely civic and ethnic nationalism. Such analysis works through a duality of categories, civic/Western/liberal/individualistic versus ethnic/Eastern/cultural/collectivistic. The first category is usually deemed as good, and the second, bad. This dichotomous model has recently attracted many criticisms that reject the idealization of the civic model as only a political entity free from any exclusionary and chauvinistic content.

In this distinction, culture has a peculiar position generally tied with the ethnic/Eastern type of nationalism, so it is exclusionary in the definition of membership for different ethnic and cultural groups. Nevertheless, all aspects considered within the frame of culture are in fact deep-seated in both conceptions, and so all that is collected under the name of "civic" may also be bound up with a movement for exclusion, cultural assimilation, and suppression.

To overcome confusion, classifying nationalism as "top-down" or "state-led" and "bottom-up" or "state-seeking" seems to be more explanatory. According to top-down nationalism, the sovereign state seeks to have a nation through describing and determining its nature and boundaries. Its pioneers have two functions—reforming the existing state and modernizing/nationalizing the people believed to be "backward"—which are closely interrelated with the formation of the nation. This stand makes the pioneers think of themselves as the only group that can interpret the collective interest of the nation. Thus, it is subject to the logic of nation-building seeking to turn its more or less heterogeneous people into a homogenous nation. According to that logic, membership in a political and cultural community is defined more or less in political terms rather than racial and ethnic.

It is therefore not exclusive in accepting outsiders as members, but they must give up their old ways of life and culturally integrate with the imagined cultural community. That community signifies a way of life surrounded by cultural memories, myths, and symbols. French and Turkish nationalisms are two good examples of this type of nationalism.

Contrary to the state-led one, bottom-up nationalism is about a movement to form a state. By struggling and organizing on the basis of nationalism, the leaders of a national or ethnic group strive to form their own independent political entity. They claim a separate state on the basis of the emergence of a unique national community. It is the quest for turning the existing people into fellow citizens.

So it appeared to be a unifying force by collecting separate power centers under the canopy of a unified, centralized state, as in Germany, and self-conscious nationalist groups setting up the state, as in Israel. In that nationalist understanding, ethnic and cultural features taken for granted as the identity of people are regarded as the identifying aspects of membership in both nation and state. In other words, it is exclusive in defining the criteria of citizenship.

Both types manifest in two different ways in the process of establishing unity; between the state and culture and between the state and its citizens. In fact, the "direction" of this process has a central place in the production of culture that is realized through memories, myths, rituals, and common ancestry. In this sense, the role of nationalism in culture production becomes much clearer by situating it in the two types of process of establishing the ties between state and citizens. Thus, here it seems necessary to shed some light on national-

ism's relationship with statehood, culture, and citizenship to understand what kinds of narratives leaders use to forge a sense of membership in both state and nation.

The relation between nationalism and the modern state comes with the claim that those who assume to be a coherent nation have their own independent state or vice versa. It is a nationalist ideology of the nation-state, which standardizes and subjugates all perceived qualities of life under a national culture. To the extent that culture provides a sense of identity for this community, the state tries to provide a link between state and society, between individual and community, between past and future. Here, as an ideology of common culture, nationalism is prone to the process of identification evolving around symbolic attachments and a sense of collectivity.

In this respect, citizenship status seeks to be determined by providing a link between membership in the political community (state) and belonging to the cultural community (nation). All leaders of modern states use several mechanisms to foster such membership. Among them is a narrative that dwells mainly on ethnicity, religion, nationality, and common ancestry. In fact, it is true for all modern states, including liberal, multicultural, federal, or even presocialist states.

The politics of citizenship formation itself includes inescapable exclusions, exclusion of those who are deemed as either internal and external "outsiders," or "others" by those in power. Nationalist narratives seem necessary to help individuals belong to a political and cultural community. At the same time, sometimes they pave the way for restrictive and repressive policies for the "others."

Globalization has challenged the conventional nature of nationalism through two well-known simultaneous processes: universalization (changing the existing notion of sovereignty) and revival of micro- or ethno-nationalisms (questioning the homogenizing account of nation-states). In the former, it reflects processes of development of new international, regional bodies leading to the cooperation of two or more states in which geographical proximity plays an ultimate role. Discussions turning on the latter one signify, in dealing with rising diversity, a form of multicultural nationalism that makes it possible for minorities or the excluded to be represented as "they are" at the national level, but at the same time implies a certain level of disintegration in national politics.

In conclusion, since the late 18th century, nationalism has been the dominant doctrine and ideology for most political, social, and cultural movements. It is still evolving into new forms. But, in the face of a rapidly globalizing world, it is very difficult to speculate what will happen in the future to the nature and role of nationalism.

SEE ALSO

BIBLIOGRAPHY

Benedict Anderson, *Imagined Communities: Reflections on the Origin and Spread of Nationalism* (Verso, 1991); David Brown, *Contemporary Nationalism: Civic, Ethnic & Multicultural Politics* (Routledge, 2000); Ernest Gellner, *Nations and Nationalism* (Cornell University Press, 1983); Montserrat Guibernau and John Hutchinson, *Understanding Nationalism* (Polity Press, 2001); Eric Hobsbawm, *Nations and Nationalism since 1780* (Cambridge University Press, 1990); Anthony D. Smith, *Nationalism and Modernism: A Critical Survey of Recent Theories of Nations and Nationalism* (Routledge, 1998); Charles Tilly, "The State of Nationalism," *Critical Review* (v.10/2, 1996).

YILMAZ ÇOLAK, PH.D.
EASTERN MEDITERRANEAN UNIVERSITY, TURKEY

New Right

THE NEW RIGHT is a form of radical activism in culture, which continues the tradition of the Old Right of the 1920s, has its roots in the radical right of the 1950s, and emerged in the 1980s in the United States during the administration of Ronald Reagan. It has connections to new conservative tendencies in Europe, such as those that supported Margaret Thatcher in England; a series of movements and their politicians in France, identified as the Nouvelle Droite; and a new form of conservatism in Germany. The most important characteristic of the New Right is the use of popular culture to spread its message. Its most visible political element is the appropriation of religion as a cultural issue, especially in its interface with mass media and its articulation with partisan politics.

In the United States, the New Right has been characterized primarily by the New Christian Right. The New Right and the New Christian Right became popular due to their reaction to the impact of the New Left during the 1960s and part of the 1970s. As conservatism discovered new popular movements aligned to the right and established strong partnerships with them, it was able to have much more influence on American and European cultures.

RADICAL ACTIVISM IN THE 1950s

After 1945, conservatives were concerned with their identity in the postwar United States. The definition of their position was discussed in terms of the difference between the prewar Old Right of the 1920s and the need for a new right more akin to current events. The result, however, was the rise of radical activism by the extreme right in the United States, which was unleashed primarily by McCarthyism. After 1950, anti-communism and the Cold War between the United States and the Soviet Union were the common ideology that was able to shape a new form of consensus among conservatives. Joseph McCarthy, a junior senator from Wisconsin, became notorious for his controversial views and initiatives against minority groups expressed through the radio and newspapers. Charges of being sympathetic to communist tendencies were brought against not only professed communists, but also liberals, homosexuals, African Americans, and others who were identified as being anti-American. Based on this articulation, the Republican Party tried to elect Douglas MacArthur for the presidency in 1944, 1948, and 1952, in an attempt to profit from his initiatives.

In 1955, the *National Review*, a journal of new conservatives, was first released and became a factor of unification, expansion, diffusion, and legitimization of both conservatism and the right in the United States, giving support to McCarthyism as well. This initiative of William F. Buckley, Jr., was, in a certain way, an answer to Albert Jay Nock's article written in 1937 and entitled "Isaiah's Job," which affirmed that the masses were looking for a prophet without success.

Buckley had previously published *God and Man at Yale* in 1952, in which he argued that his alma mater should return to its religious tradition and banish liberalism. In 1954, in a joint venture with his brother-in-law Brent Bozell, he wrote *McCarthy and His Enemies*, defending the senator against liberals and supporting the moral concerns he had raised. Buckley received the support of his father—William Buckley, a millionaire who gave him $100,000 to initiate the publication project—and raised another $300,000 to start publishing the *National Review*.

Others acknowledged the resurgence of conservatism as a political force and responded by supporting or opposing it. Also in 1955, Louis Hartz published *The Liberal Tradition* and received an attack by Clinton Rossiter, who published *Conservatism in America*. A series of articles appeared under the title "The New American Right," edited by Daniel Bell and featuring articles by Richard Hofstadter, David Riesman, Nathan Glazer, Peter Viereck, Talcott Parsons, H.H. Hyman, and S.M. Lipset. The collection dealt with McCarthyism, going back to its origins in the debates around fundamentalism during the 1920s and analyzing its cultural impact, especially the broad feelings of resentment toward liberalism that were then present in some popular movements and among blue-collar workers in general.

From this moment on, the tensions between popular culture and liberalism began to gain the form of a cultural war. Nothing shows this resentment of conservatives better than the book Buckley wrote in 1959, *Up from Liberalism*. In the first part, the book aimed at pointing out the failure of liberalism and its political avoidance of conflicts, and in the second part it acknowledged the self-criticism of conservatism for not being able to address or persuade the masses. Buckley observed the failure of conservative discourse, but at the same time foresaw its rehabilitation if it would abandon eloquent and extravagant jargon in favor of a more concrete and elaborated political philosophy. "Freedom, order, community and justice in the age of technology" was the formula he stressed as the condition for a conservatism more in tune with reality.

The rise of the right had also been promoted through associations with the Ku Klux Klan, the American Liberty League, the John Birch Society, and other groups whose connections to conservatism were assumed when common issues were at the forefront. However, such ties are hard to establish and are usually rejected by the right due to the extreme nature of these associations.

On the other hand, social science tools have been used to explain and measure their impact. Daniel Bell dedicated two books (*The New Right* in 1955 and *The Radical Right* in 1964) to the study of these movements, while Allen Broyles published *The John Birch Society: Anatomy of a Protest* in that same year and David Chalmers presented statistics about the Ku Klux Klan in *Hooded Americanism: The History of the Ku Klux Klan* in 1965. In *The Politics of Unreason: Right-Wing Extremism in America* of 1970, Seymour Martin Lipset attempted to show how the radical right was a form of extremism similar to the radical left, with belligerent and irrational

strategies that soon separated the right wing from traditional conservatism.

There is no doubt that conservative leaders were clearly connected to grassroots associations and movements once involved in actions against communist and civil rights groups in the 1950s, as well as groups campaigning for Barry Goldwater in the 1960s and the Christian right in the 1970s. Among the books dedicated to these issues are Louis Gasper's *The Fundamentalism Movement* (1963) and Clifton White's *Suite 3505: The Story of the Draft Goldwater Movement* (1967). At the beginning of the 1970s, less attention was given to such groups due to the major impact of the counterculture from the left, even though a series of publications presented new data on the right wing. It was only with the greater impact of the Christian right on American politics and the election of Ronald Reagan as president of the United States that a new interest arose in the area. The book *American Evangelicalism: Conservative Religion and the Quandary of Modernity* (1983), by James Davidson Hunter, is a good example of this trend. In 1995, Sara Diamond presented a very detailed sociological account of right-wing movements in the United States in her *Roads to Dominion: Right-Wing Movements and Political Power in the United States*, ranging from the period right after World War II up to the times of the Reagan presidential administration. The very title of her book reveals the implicit dialogue with Friedrich von Hayek's *Road to Serfdom*, thus indicating a connecting line among the several initiatives: the new conservatism after 1945 and the belligerent right of the 1950s.

NEW CONSERVATISM AND THE NEW RIGHT

The New Right in the United States has updated the strategies of the traditional right and the radical right. After all the problems associated with the radical right, the new conservatives and members of the right realized that there was need for a political method that would bring consensus among the various conservative tendencies of American society.

Following this realization, other publications appeared: Barry Goldwater wrote *Conscience of a Conservative* in 1960 and Milton Friedman, following the leitmotif of traditional conservative economics inspired in Hayek, published *Capitalism and Freedom*. However, it was in the elections that this new ideological system was more transparent. One of the first initiatives in this regard was the New York Conservative Party—founded by conservative leaders such as Daniel Mahoney, Henry Paolucci, Thomas Molnar, Frank

Meyer, and others—whose "Declaration of Principles," issued in February 1962, combined libertarianism, anti-communism, and anti-liberalism.

The Republican Party, through a committee led by F. Clifton White and William Rusher, articulated a coalition for a conservative political majority, which was to be led by a conservative president. A short while after the rise and fall of Senator Joseph McCarthy, all conservative forces were once again reunited to support Arizona's Senator Barry Goldwater as the Republican Party's candidate in the campaign for the presidency in 1964 and Ronald Reagan's run for governor in California. This was the climax of their political action, which was frustrated, however, by the loss of Goldwater by a margin of 16 million votes to Democratic Party candidate Lyndon Johnson.

The New Right can be seen as an attempt by the Republican Party to change its electoral strategies. Although it was successful in electing Richard Nixon, the problems with the Vietnam War and the scandal of Watergate had left its marks on the right. Moreover, there was the issue of government corruption, which affected the perception that voters had of the federal administration. It was only with the greater impact of the religious groups in American politics, as they joined to elect the Democrat Jimmy Carter as president in 1976, that conservatives and the right realized that a strategy was necessary to obtain the support of these groups for the Republican candidate. This led to an association in order to elect Reagan president of the United States in 1980.

It was with this perspective and the support of the New Christian Right that Reagan was elected president and a new interest arose in the study of the relationship between conservatism and religion. The book *American Evangelicalism: Conservative Religion and the Quandary of Modernity* (1983), by James Davidson Hunter, is an example of this trend.

THE NEW RIGHT IN EUROPE

The same trends that characterize the New Right in the United States influenced other countries as well. England was influenced by the conservative politics of Margaret Thatcher, a period also called Thatcherism. Thatcher was elected first in 1979, and again in 1983 and 1987, and was responsible for a series of liberalization measures, such as the privatization of public services and cuts in social programs. It is important to note, as Hayek had already done in 1944, that "liberalism" in Europe means a form of conservatism, so that these liberalizing changes in England must be seen as initiatives toward the right.

This explains the application of the term *New Right* in the British context. While this term applies mostly to economic aspects, especially to a new doctrine within economic liberalism, it was also identified as New Right. Also, there were several cultural and religious elements at play, such as the return of xenophobia and nationalism, tensions with foreigners and with non-Christian religious groups, as well as a resurgence of moralism that led to proposals for the state's regulation of sexuality.

In Germany, national politics during the 1980s was also dominated by the right, represented by the prime minister and the Christliche-demokratische Partei (CDU). Under his leadership, the conservatives governed Germany between 1982 and 1996, and were also considered as representing the New Right in its European sense, although in Germany its popular expression was identified as radical right (Rechtsradikalismus). This meant a turn to radical liberalization in the economy, allied with the inclusion of moral issues in the political agenda, not necessarily to moralize politics but to control private life. Also there arose a controversial discussion related to the possible participation of Germany in wars as an ally of the United States. In all these aspects, there were similarities with England. In Germany, however, there were two specific issues at play: the historical processing of the heritage of National-Socialism and the process of reunification between East Germany and the West.

In both cases, the issue concerning a German identity was at stake, and this is the point upon which the New Right based its arguments in the public sphere. To affirm German identity, the right went back to Carl Schmitt's views on the foreign as enemy, and became involved in discussions on the right to asylum in Germany, arguing that foreigners were the reason for the cultural and economic problems. They also indirectly supported many radical right initiatives. Historians such as Ernst Nolte, politicians such as Gerd-Klaus Kaltenbrunner and Franz Schonhüber—leader of the neo-Nazi party Republikaner—and several groups, including neo-Nazis and skinheads, were part of this scenario. Finally, this also included religion, as evangelicals turned to Billy Graham and created the Evangelische Allianz in Germany.

In France, the New Right (Nouvelle Droite) was represented by young politicians who embraced conservative ideas that had become taboo in the country after World War II. Moreover, during the 1980s France had been governed by the socialists led by François Mitterrand. Nevertheless, French thinkers and politicians began to search for the roots of conservatism and the right. The most important among them was Alain de Benoist, who published the book *Vu de droite* in 1977 and received much publicity in newspapers such as *Le Monde* and *Nouvel Observateur* in 1979, when the label "Nouvelle Droite" became popular. One of their aims was to fight communism, another to restore the real European roots of civilization, and also to influence politics. One important element in achieving these ends was to influence education, and therefore, journals such as *Nouvelle Education*, *Nouvelle École*, and *Elements*—which was officially "the journal of the New Right"—were published. One of the results of this action was the controversial discussion about religious education in public schools in France and the religious rights of

Muslims. On the political front, two parties of the extreme right became notorious: the Action Française and the Partie de la Front Nationale (PFN), led by Jean-Marie Le Pen. As Marieluise Christadler has shown, the French New Right was engaged in a "culture war," supported by think tanks such as the group GRECE. This involved more extreme initiatives, such as the neo-Nazi publication of the *Féderation d'Action Nationale et Européene* (FANE). One of the results of these initiatives was the return of anti-Semitism and the search for a pure European identity.

RELIGION AND CULTURE WARS

The cultural aspect of the New Right became evident as different movements turned their attention to religion and what they defined as moral issues. However, it is primarily in relation to the United States that the articulation between politics and religion as a basic operating modus of the New Right can be seen most clearly. One reason for this is cultural. In his essay opening a series of studies on the radical right of the 1950s, Daniel Bell quoted Gunnar Myrdal affirming that it was natural for the ordinary American "when he sees something that is wrong to feel not only that there should be a law against it, but also that an organization should be formed to combat it." If this was true for the 1950s, it was even more so for the 1980s.

The emerging New Christian Right was a coalition of religious interest groups that asserted that they were expressing the fundamental but latent religious concerns of most people in the United States. They organized around such associations as the Moral Majority, the Christian Voice, and the Religious Roundtable in the 1980s. Modeling themselves on the success of the television evangelist Billy Graham, such leaders as Jerry Falwell, Pat Robertson, and others started television programs and created the Christian Broadcasting Network (CBN), and later the Divinity Broadcasting Network produced by Freddie Stone. Television programming became the major way of raising funds, and also the primary means of delivering their message.

The New Christian Right had a largely political character and took up issues that were considered to be eroding the moral fabric of the nation. Stances supported by the New Christian Right and the New Right were the pro-life movement against abortion and the traditional family role for women. Phyllis Schlafly for instance, successfully led a campaign against the Equal Rights Amendment arguing that it would corrode family values. Other issues included the censorship of

Republican Ronald Reagan became an icon of the New Right after coalescing conservative and Christian electoral groups behind him.

Margaret Thatcher (at a NATO meeting) was leader of the Conservative Party and the first woman prime minister of the United Kingdom, and earned the nickname "the Iron Lady" for her sometimes ruthless application of New Right conservative principles to British politics.

pornography, opposition to divorce, and extramarital relations. This latter question was particularly significant during the Bill Clinton administration in the 1990s when these groups were able to bring to the public sphere and debate a major issue relating to the president's sexual mores.

However, long before the Clinton administration, the New Christian Right had made links with the New Right in the political arena. By incorporating high-technology innovations, utilizing magazines, books, radio, music recordings, and primarily television to reach a large population, the New Christian Right and New Right were able to successfully diffuse their message, raise considerable funds, and sway elections. They both joined forces to elect Ronald Reagan, and in fact, Falwell was indicated by Reagan to be the liaison between the White House and the religious community.

The coalition of the New Right with the New Christian Right and the neoconservative movements helped to mold a foreign policy under Reagan that articulated human rights in terms of religious freedom, especially in opposition to Muslim and communist countries unwavering support for the state of Israel (which some Christians believe to be the condition for the Second

Coming of Christ); the fusion of Christianity, capitalism, and democracy into interchangeable terms; and a general attitude of uniquely American moral supremacy. In terms of domestic affairs, they opposed programs that they interpreted as corroding the stability of the family, such as welfare programs, high taxes, and abortion clinics.

However, by 1987 sexual and financial scandals involving the religious leadership of the New Christian Right, as well as organized reactions by the left, caused the Moral Majority and other conservative organizations to disband. New Right politicians became unsure of whether they wanted to be associated with the New Christian Right. The poor showing of Robertson in the 1988 presidential elections seemed to reinforce the decline of the New Christian Right, as did the 1992 election and subsequent reelection of Clinton, a Democrat and liberal. Also, Robertson's and Falwell's interpretation of the September 11, 2001, attacks as the wrath of God on a liberal and pro-gay nation did not sit well with the general public or the Republican president.

However, the New Christian Right turned its substantial energies to local politics. Robertson formed the new Christian Coalition in 1989 to work on issues in neighborhoods, city councils, school boards, and state legislatures. For instance, by gaining seats on local school boards they brought up the debate of allowing prayer in public schools, including creationism as an alternative to evolution, and censoring books that supported racial diversity and homosexuality or that were considered to question traditional family values. In the view of the right, the liberals predominated in the academic community and were adversely influencing basic education with "secular humanism."

The Christian Coalition also concentrated on voter registration and on training potential candidates for office. Ralph Reed, executive director of the Christian Coalition until 1997, who outlined his theology and politics in his book *Active Faith* (1996), urged a less belligerent form of born-again Christianity that would have lasting effects on mainstream America.

Jerry Falwell, one of the leaders of the Moral Majority, negated the separation of church and state in America.

For the New Right, the support or ire of the New Christian Right has become a serious consideration for candidates. Despite their ups and downs, the New Christian Right organizations continue to maintain grassroots support and have demonstrated their power to turn an election. James Dobson's *Focus on the Family* radio program, Gary Bauer's Campaign for Working Families, and the Concerned Women for America and Traditional Values Coalition are a few of the programs, people, and organizations of the New Christian Right acting politically for their beliefs.

It is clear that this form of politics is distinct from the religious and political conservatism of before. However, there was a common trend in both tendencies, which allows their articulation around a wider movement. For example, anti-communism reunited religious people, politicians, and the conservative intelligentsia along common ranks. It was also responsible for the connection between the positions of an old aristocratic conservatism and the more radical political and communicative strategy of the New Right. It is at this point that a clearer picture emerged of the political, partisan, and religious aspects of conservatism in the United States.

But as society was constantly changing, a new trend would appear, criticizing and at the same time complementing the radical politics of the New Right. While new conservatives were spending most of their energies pointing out the failures of the liberal welfare state, for people in the streets these arguments were too abstract and too weak to be taken seriously. It was, however, with the support of mass diffusion among newspaper editors, radio commentators, and television evangelists that the New Right found a practical application, gained a new impetus, and received radical support, leading to the foundation of several organizations that would spread its word.

SEE ALSO

Volume 1 Left: New Left; Media Bias, Left; Liberalism; United States; Church and State Separation.
Volume 2 Right: Reagan, Ronald; Christian Coalition; Media Bias, Right; Religion; Republican Party.

BIBLIOGRAPHY

Daniel Bell, ed., *The Radical Right* (Anchor Books, 1964); Julien Brun, *La Nouvelle Droite* (Nouvelles Editions Osvald, 1979); L. Medcalg and Karel Dolbeare, *Neopolitics: Political Ideas in the 1980s* (Random House, 1985); Herfried Münkler and Richard Saage, *Kultur und Politik: Brechungen der Fortschrittsperspektive heute* (Westdeutscher Verlag, 1989); George Nash, *The Conservative Intellectual Movement in America since 1945* (Basic Books, 1979); Ralph Reed, *Active Faith: How Christians Are Changing the Soul of American Politics* (The Free Press, 1996).

AMOS NASCIMENTO
METHODIST UNIVERSITY OF PIRACICABA, BRAZIL

Nietzsche, Friedrich (1844–1900)

BORN IN 1844 in the small Prussian town of Röcken and named after Friedrich Wilhelm IV, Friedrich Nietzsche came from a family in which his father and his two grandfathers were Lutheran ministers, and as a child he was pious. At the university, he was strongly influenced by philosopher Arthur Schopenhauer, and composer Richard Wagner took the place of a father to the young student, his own father having died when he was four. Nietzsche attained early academic success and was elected a professor of classical philology at the University of Basel at 24. He retired at 34 due to his health, and composed most of his major works in the following nine years while leading a wandering existence. His health collapsed shortly after his completion of *Ecce Homo* in 1889, and he died after 11 years of senelescence in 1900, though the early diagnosis of syphilis has been challenged by recent research.

Nietzsche's thought progressed through three periods. His earliest, corresponding to *The Birth of Tragedy* (1872) and *Untimely Meditations* (1873–76), was characterized by hope in the revival of German culture through the romanticism represented by the music of Wagner. In a second, positivist period, beginning with *Human, All-Too-Human* (1878) and lasting until *The Gay Science* (1882), he grew disillusioned with German romanticism, extolling instead reason and science, and drawing from the French aphoristic tradition. Nietzsche's mature thought is developed in *Thus Spoke Zarathustra* (1883–85) and subsequent books, which are preoccupied with the origin and function of values.

Nietzsche's mature writings expound the doctrines of "will to power" (*Wille zur Macht*), perspectivism, the master and slave moralities, and the Superman (*Übermensch*). His presentation of these themes is dominated by unresolved tensions, a characteristic stylistic predilection that draws upon both Hegelian dialectic and his own themes of transvaluation and the rejection of ascetic binaries. The will to power rests at the core of causation and is, for Nietzsche, a validation of life (the ability to "say yes! to life"). The concept is adapted from Schopenhauer's "will to live." It is from the will to power that the human motivations toward domination, love, violence, and search for truth derive, as well as nonhuman teleologies.

Western philosophy and religion were motivated by the assumption that existence requires explanation, which arises alongside the experience-deprecating "slave morality." Slaves converted the attributes of their masters into vices; the meek would then inherit the earth, and charity, humility and obedience replaced competition, great-spiritedness, and autonomy. With the modern dissolution of religious absolutes in the solvent of positivism (the "death of God"), the absoluteness of slave morality would lead to the experiences of nihilism and purposelessness, caused by the ascetic ideal outliving belief in God. The Superman is capable not of reverting to the ancient master morality, but rather of transvaluing Christian values into a response to nihilism drawing upon affirmation of life, creation, and will. The Superman, though recognizing mortality, could endure the prospect of infinite repetition of life (the myth of "eternal recurrence") without self-deception or evasion and with only pleasure. Nietzsche's philosophy thus embraces both a description of life that is at root pessimistic and a normative response that is affirmative, joyful, and capable of heroism.

His work was unfortunately edited during his dementia by his sister Elizabeth, who attached to it an interpretation consonant with her own attachment to Nazism.

Nietzsche does not fall easily into categories represented by the political left or right, though uses made of his work have cycled between them. The left is to Nietzsche a symptom of crisis, with socialist and democratic egalitarianism representing the heirs of Christian slave morality; the right, represented by Otto von Bismarck, is nationalist, allied with Christianity, and rests upon a decrepit nobility. He preferred a transvaluation of politics to accompany the transvaluation of values, with right and left being subsumed by a great politics of the future.

Nietzsche was nonetheless inventor of an atheism of the political right, and his apocalyptic politics of the "last man" is an implicit response to the last state of history foreseen by Marxism. He provoked a conservatism based upon neither religion nor the restoration of a Christian *ancien regime*, but upon order and natural aristocracy (as explained in Georges Sorel's *Reflections on Violence*, 1908), as well as a revitalized Catholic response. The Wilhemite and Nazi uses of Nietzsche, as well as his own rejection of Hegel, made him marginal to the left in France, and except for the leftist Georges Bataille, uses made of Nietzsche during the first half of the 20th century were principally on the right. H.L. Mencken, for example, saw Nietzsche as attempting to reconcile Darwinian selection with ethics, a project that continues in sociobiology. From 1950 onward, Nietzsche's translator, Walter Kaufmann, successfully brought out liberal aspects of his work and thought, and subsequently postmodernists, existentialists, and poststructuralists would draw, respectively, from his perspectivalism, stress on creative will, and anti-Marxism and genealogical approach to the origin of values.

While Nietzsche's influence is not universal—Hans Georg Gadamer, for instance, studiously avoided reading his works—it is nonetheless pervasive, with Martin Heidegger, Theodor Adorno, Michel Foucault, and Jacques Derrida inhabiting his tradition of anti-modernism, and that tradition setting the terms for Jurgen Habermas's defense of Enlightenment and modernity. Nietzsche thus principally appears for contemporary conservatives as an influence to be counteracted—or at minimum, reinterpreted.

Allan Bloom illustrates the first response in *The Closing of the American Mind*. Bloom refers to Nietzsche as the father of contemporary America, and traces to his influence the concepts of lifestyle, identity, charisma, and the construal of values as a projection of creative will upon an inherently meaning-deprived world. For Bloom's Nietzsche, as for Plato's Euthyphro, "we do not love a thing because it is good, it is good because we love it"; thus, commitment endues value on what is valued; intellectual honesty and authenticity of will, rather than love of truth, characterize proper state of mind. Similarly, Gertrude Himmelfarb attributes to Nietzsche the rerendering of universal "virtues" as instrumental and local "values." Bloom betrays Nietzsche's influence even while diagnosing the pathologies of modernity to it; in declaring that television had replaced the newspaper, he echoes Nietzsche's own assertion that the newspaper had replaced prayer in modern bourgeois life. Both reflect a concern with the progressive usurpation by the busy, cheap, and ephemeral of the eternal, and the rise of a popular culture that alters, subverts, and degrades tastes.

Peter Berkowitz conversely finds Nietzsche's concern with the best life and "right making based on right knowing" strongly within the moral philosophical tradition. Berkowitz's reading of Nietzsche sought to restore to prominence the "unresolved antagonism" and "contest of extremes" between Nietzsche's assumption that morality is an artifact of human will and his conviction that there is a rank-ordering of desires and forms of life.

Similar ambiguity is found in Leo Strauss's apparent denunciation in "Note on the Plan of Nietzsche's *Beyond Good and Evil*" (1973) of Nietzsche as at odds with the Platonic tradition and a purveyor of relativism, though Nietzsche scholar Laurence Lambert argues that the work reveals a neglected affinity and debt to Nietzsche. Strauss follows Nietzsche and Heidegger as viewing modernity's crisis of nihilism as creating the possibility of return, through rediscovery of the ancients, to principles modernity has forgotten or neglected. For Strauss, the return is to Plato and Aristotle, to "dehistoricise" morality and ground it in nature; for Nietzsche, as for Heidegger, the return is to the pre-Socratics instead, before the architects of metaphysics had set western civilization on a course which preordained modern nihilism.

SEE ALSO
Volume 1 Left: Liberalism; Hume, David; Locke, John.
Volume 2 Right: Hitler, Adolf; Fascism; Conservatism

BIBLIOGRAPHY
Peter Berkowitz, *Nietzsche: The Ethics of an Immoralist* (Harvard University Press, 1996); Alan Bloom, *The Closing of the American Mind* (Simon & Schuster, 1988); Gertrude Himmelfarb, *The De-Moralization of Society: From Victorian Virtues to Modern Values* (Vintage Books, 1996); Laurence Lambert, *Leo Strauss and Nietzsche* (University of Chicago Press, 1996); Friedrich Nietzsche, *Collected Works*, Giorgio Coli and Mazzino Montinari, eds., Walter Kaufmann, trans. (30 vols., Cambridge University Press, 1967–).

PATRICK BELTON
OXFORD UNIVERSITY

Nigeria

OIL-RICH NIGERIA is Africa's most populous country with an estimated 133 to 137 million residents from more than 250 ethnic and tribal groups. No census has been taken since 1960, some would say because of the decentralized, right-wing nature of the national government, which under a 1999 constitution has delegated political power away from the capital, giving extensive local authority and autonomy to its 36 states.

In 2003, 28 political parties registered with the Independent National Electoral Commission to participate in the next election, and 22 of the parties were new to the political scene. Nigeria had not held successful elections under civilian rulers since independence from Britain in 1960, with attempts in the mid-1960s and in 1983 ending in violence and army coups. Following nearly 16 years of military rule, a new constitution was adopted in 1999. A peaceful transition to civilian government was completed with right-centrist and retired

Olusegun Obasanjo, president of Nigeria, addresses the Millennium Summit of the United Nations.

Army General Olusegun Obasanjo as president. In 2003's national balloting, Obasanjo was reaffirmed as president with almost 62 percent of the vote.

What makes Nigeria unique is its almost even population split between Muslim and Christian, and what some would say is the army's role in ensuring that the poorer Muslim north has dominated the oil-rich Christian south. This was done by decentralizing power and giving ultimate authority to the outlying states.

Muslims make up a significant majority in the north, as opposed to a mostly Christian population in the south. The predominantly Christian Ibo tribe of the oil-rich Biafra region in southeast Nigeria tried unsuccessfully in the 1960s to secede, and was forced into submission during a brutal civil war by Nigeria's predominantly Muslim military. The forced starvation of at least 1 million Ibo men, women, and children is listed among history's worst genocides, ranking in the top 10 after Hitler's decimation of European civilians, Mao's purges during the Cultural Revolution, Pol Pot's forced evacuation of Cambodia's cities, and Menghitsu's starvation of an estimated 1.5 million Ethiopians. The result was that Nigeria retained its major source of foreign revenue, oil and gas, which provide 20 percent of the country's gross domestic product, 95 percent of its foreign exchange earnings, and about 65 percent of the government budget.

The Ibos are Christian and have a strong entrepreneurial spirit. They are predominantly right-leaning, supporting a free-market economy and autonomous local government. They dominate Nigerian commerce and finance. However, Muslims have historically controlled the military. That power has been used to ensure the dominance of the north. Ibo support of strong local government instead of centralized power has protected their interests, but has also promulgated a growing and aggressive Islamist radicalism in the north. Local governors were given a free hand to institute state religion.

In 2004, 12 Nigerian northern states had officially instituted the official enforcement of Shari'a or Islamic religious law. This is permitted under the 1999 national constitution, which grants unusual autonomy to each state. Shari'a provides stern penalties for moral offenses, such as the cutting off of hands for theft and the stoning of "adulterous" women, which has occurred in Kaduna, Kano, Katsina, Sokoto, and Zamfara. It is also used to enforce respect for Islam with severe penalties for conversion to Christianity, speaking against the authority of the Koran holy book, or making comments disparaging of the Prophet Mohammed. Another outgrowth has been the spread of Islamist terrorism.

In 2004 when a unit of a group called Jamiyy'a Salafiyya li'l-Daw'a wa-'l Jihad was subdued in neighboring Chad, a large number of its members were Nigerians. The most immediate threat posed by the rise of Islamist radicalism in northern Nigeria was to the unity and very existence of Nigeria itself. Clashes between the dominant Muslims and the minority Christians in the north have been bloody.

Critics of Nigeria's central government say that President Obasanjo could intervene, asserting federal authority. However, he cites the constitutional guarantees of state rights. The result is a potentially explosive situation, which could be ignited by a major decline in oil revenues. Nigeria's oil riches have not solved the country's woes.

In 2000, Nigeria received a debt-restructuring deal from the Paris Club and a $1 billion credit from the International Monetary Fund, both contingent on market-oriented reforms such as limiting government spending, modernizing the banking system, curbing inflation, and resolving inequities in the regional distribution of oil earnings. During 2003, the Nigerian government deregulated fuel prices and announced the privatization of the country's four state-owned oil refineries.

SEE ALSO

Volume 1 Left: Africa; Nigeria.
Volume 2 Right: Africa; Globalization.

BIBLIOGRAPHY

Michael Radu, "The Nigerian Threat," *Front Page Magazine* (June 11, 2004); *National Geographic Atlas of the World* (National Geographic Society, 1999); Banjo Odutola, "2003: Our Checkmating Politics," www.lagosforum.com (July 2004); *The World Almanac and Book of Facts* (World Almanac, 2004); *The World Factbook* (CIA, 2003); William Tordoff, *Government and Politics in Africa* (Indiana University Press, 1997).

ROB KERBY
INDEPENDENT SCHOLAR

Nixon, Richard M. (1913–1994)

RICHARD MILHOUS NIXON was one of only two Americans to hold all four federal elective offices: U.S. representative, senator, vice president, and president. He was also the only president ever to resign the office. Nixon was born in the house his father built in Yorba Linda, California, on January 9, 1913, second of the five sons of Francis A. (Frank) Nixon and Hannah (Milhous) Nixon. Nixon graduated from Whittier College in 1934 and Duke University Law School in 1937. He was rejected by the Federal Bureau of Investigation (FBI) and unable to find work at any eastern law firm, returned to Los Angeles County and went to work in a small law firm. On June 21, 1940, Nixon married Thelma Catherine (Patricia) Ryan. They had two daughters, Patricia (Tricia) and Julie. Julie married Dwight David Eisenhower II, grandson of the former president. Nixon served in the navy as a lieutenant commander in the South Pacific during World War II.

Upon his return, he answered an ad seeking a candidate for Congress in the 12th Congressional District of California. Nixon won the election. In the House, he was outspoken as a member of the House Un-American Activities Committee, and his aggressive questioning of former communist Alger Hiss led to Hiss's conviction for perjury. (In the 1990s, it was proven that Hiss had indeed spied for the Soviet Union.) This brought Nixon national fame and great respect within Republican circles. In 1950, Nixon ran for the U.S. Senate in an extremely bitter and divided race against Democratic Congresswoman Helen Gahagan Douglas. Nixon attacked Douglas as "the Pink Lady," and she referred to him as "Tricky Dick," an epithet that would stick to him for the rest of his life. Republicans were successful in attaching Nixon to the coattails of the popular Republican Governor Earl Warren. Although Warren had tried to stay neutral on the Senate race, Republicans were successful in baiting his Democratic opponent to endorse Douglas, and Warren had no choice but to endorse Nixon. Nixon won in a landslide and took his seat early, on December 1, 1950, to fill a vacancy.

In 1952, Nixon was chosen to run for vice president on the Republican ticket headed by Dwight D. Eisenhower. It is believed this was offered as a reward for Nixon's infiltration and sabotage of Warren's campaign at the convention. Nixon was able to swing the California delegation (pledged to Warren as a "favorite son") to Eisenhower, preventing Warren from swinging his delegates to some other candidate, especially Senator Robert A. Taft of Ohio, who was Eisenhower's principal opponent. (Warren became chief justice of the U.S. Supreme Court the next year for his role in the convention.) The main job of a vice presidential nominee is to campaign and draw as little attention as possible away from the presidential nominee. Nixon failed at the latter part.

His campaign was soon dominated by allegations of financial improprieties. His solution was to go on live television (then a novelty) and lay bare all of his personal finances, claiming that the only gift he had ever accepted from a supporter was a dog named Checkers. Nixon's remarkable television appearance came to be called the "Checkers" speech. The speech had the intended effect of ending the controversy, and the Eisenhower-Nixon ticket swept to victory. Nixon's eight years as vice president were largely unremarkable. When asked in 1960 to name an idea of Nixon's he had used, Eisenhower said, "If you give me a week, I might think of one. I don't remember." Eisenhower seriously considered dropping Nixon from the ticket in 1956, but in the end decided such a move would cause unnecessary controversy for his reelection effort and focus undue attention on the vice presidential nominee. Nixon was already in the spotlight due to Eisenhower's suffering a serious heart attack the year before. Despite the concern about the commander-in-chief's health, Eisenhower and Nixon were reelected in a landslide.

Nixon was able to position himself successfully to be the Republican nominee in 1960. The key to his besting the field was his meeting in 1959 with Soviet leader Nikita Khrushchev. Nixon and Khrushchev toured an American home exhibit in Moscow, Soviet Union, and got into a heated exchange at the model kitchen in the exhibit. This came to be known as the "kitchen debate."

Nixon was nominated almost by acclamation at the 1960 Republican National Convention in Chicago. He chose as his running mate Senator Henry Cabot Lodge of New York. Nixon lost to Democratic Senator John F. Kennedy of Massachusetts. It was the closest popular vote in history to that time. There is considerable consensus that the televised debates, the first in history, were pivotal in the election. Nixon was ill-prepared for the debates and didn't make the most of his appearance. Kennedy came across looking much better, and those who saw the debates on television tended to believe that Kennedy had won. Those who only listened on the radio, on the other hand, tended to believe that Nixon was the winner.

Nixon was also hamstrung by a promise to visit all 50 states during the campaign, and spent parts of the final week in such unlikely spots as Cheyenne, Wyoming, and Anchorage, Alaska. There was substantial speculation that the Democratic machine in Chicago had stolen the election and narrowly tilted Illinois to Kennedy. A partial recount showed that the machine had stolen votes to defeat a local prosecutor, but only a small number of votes in the presidential race were questioned. Illinois's 27 electoral votes would not have made the difference anyway, and Nixon abandoned the idea of a large-scale recount.

Nixon ran for governor of California in 1962. He lost to Democrat Edmund G. "Pat" Brown by a respectable margin. In his concession speech the day after the election, Nixon took out his fury on Brown and the reporters themselves, and announced that he was leaving politics: "You won't have Nixon to kick around anymore, because, gentlemen, this is my last press conference." Nixon moved to New York and joined a law firm. He spent most of the decade raising money for Republicans and serving on corporate boards.

Nixon entered the presidential field in 1968 and defeated New York Governor Nelson Rockefeller and California Governor Ronald Reagan to win on the first ballot. Internal polling showed that Nixon would be better off without a running mate—none of the likely candidates helped the ticket—so he chose the closest thing available to a cipher, Maryland Governor Spiro T. Agnew. The Democratic nominee, Vice President Hubert H. Humphrey, was at a disadvantage due to the increasing unpopularity of the Vietnam War, the failure of the party to unify following a Chicago convention that was marred by violence in the streets, and the presence of a third-party candidate, Alabama Governor George Wallace, who would deprive the Democrats of some of their most reliable states. Nixon tapped into

Republican Richard Nixon made his early political mark as an anti-communist, only to later open relations with communist China.

the Chicago violence to tarnish Humphrey and the Democrats as the party of youth unrest while painting the Republicans as the party of law and order. It was once again a razor-thin margin in the popular vote, but Nixon won the electoral college handily.

Nixon's first term was dominated by the Vietnam War. He covertly increased the scope of the war, but also reduced the size of the war overall, and a cease-fire was announced only days into his second term. Nixon also made four appointments to the Supreme Court in his first term, setting in motion a conservative judicial revolution that is still salient today. Nixon made overtures to the Soviet Union and China that are seen as the hallmark of his presidency. During his reelection campaign in 1972, burglars with ties to the Central Intelligence Agency (CIA) and the Nixon campaign broke into the Democratic headquarters at the Watergate complex in Washington, D.C. Nixon's second term was dominated by the investigation into this break-in and subsequent cover-up and related scandals. Nixon had been secretly taping his conversations for nearly two years.

The Supreme Court ruled that Nixon must turn the tapes over to investigators, and he resigned on August 9, 1974, after being advised by congressional supporters that he was facing certain impeachment and removal from office. Gerald R. Ford, who had been appointed vice president the year before after Agnew resigned due to a scandal of his own, became the first appointed president. He issued Nixon a full pardon for all alleged activities a month later. Nixon went into a self-imposed exile at his home in San Clemente, California, emerging only in 1977. He wrote a series of books in his later years and eventually regained respect as an elder political statesman.

Nixon died in New York City on April 22, 1994, and is buried alongside his wife at his birthplace in Yorba Linda, California.

Because of the fact that he built his earliest successes on criticisms of Alger Hiss, who spied for the Soviet Union, and of Helen Gahagan Douglas, who had received support from Communist Party membership in California, Nixon was often classed as a right-wing Republican of the Red-baiting type. However, his voting record and his positions and policies as president tended to align him with the moderate, internationalist wing of the Republican Party rather than with its extreme right wing.

SEE ALSO

Volume 1 Left: Vietnam War; Civil Rights; Kennedy, John F.; Johnson, Lyndon B.
Volume 2 Right: Republican Party; Eisenhower, Dwight D.; Taft, Robert A..

BIBLIOGRAPHY

Jonathan Aitken, *Nixon: A Life* (Regnery, 1994); Stephen E. Ambrose, *Nixon: The Education of a Politician, 1913–62* (Simon and Schuster, 1991); *Nixon: The Triumph of a Politician, 1962–72* (Simon and Schuster, 1989); Stephen E. Ambrose, *Nixon: Ruin and Recovery, 1973–90* (Simon and Schuster, 1991); Richard M. Nixon, *RN: The Memoirs of Richard Nixon* (Grosset & Dunlap, 1978); Richard Reeves, *President Nixon: Alone in the White House* (Simon and Schuster, 2001); Garry Wills, *Nixon Agonistes: The Crisis of the Self-Made Man* (Houghton Mifflin, 1970).

TONY L. HILL
MASSACHUSETTS INSTITUTE OF TECHNOLOGY

The Right

Opus Dei

THE ROMAN CATHOLIC religious organization known as Opus Dei was founded by Josemaria Escriva in Spain in October 1928. In the words of Opus Dei's official literature, "during a spiritual retreat, Father Josemaria saw what it was that God was asking of him: to found Opus Dei, a way of sanctification in daily work and in the fulfillment of the Christian's ordinary duties."

Opus Dei was founded in the tradition of the religious brotherhoods, the *santos hermanidades*, which had played such a distinguished role in the history of Spain. Their origin had been in the wars of the Reconquista. However, after the Reconquista was completed with the conquest of Moorish (Muslim) Grenada in 1492, the nature of the brotherhoods became less martial and more of a service type, like the Society of Jesus, or Jesuits, founded by Ignatius of Loyola. What distinguished Opus Dei—(literally, the "Work of God")—is that it was intended for lay people, those who did not wish to enter the religious life. Another such Roman Catholic group is the Third Order of St. Francis.

When the Spanish Civil War broke out in 1936, the communists on the side of the republic used the war to launch a purge of all religious members they could shoot. When Francisco Franco and the Nationalists won in 1939, many Spanish communists would flee the country, as did Escriva, who eventually returned to Madrid to study for a doctorate in law. In 1946, when travel was once again safe after World War II, Father Escriva went to Vatican City where he obtained a doctorate of theology at the Lateran University. Escriva traveled through Europe spreading his ideas of Opus Dei, finding a rewarding climate especially in Mexico and Latin America in 1974 and 1975. There, Spanish traditions of mysticism and El Fe—the Roman Catholic Church—still remained strong. This was even true in Mexico in spite of the fact that the government was officially anti-clerical since the triumph of Alvaro Obregon in 1920. Not long after his last trip to Latin America, Escriva died in June 1975. Yet the effect he had had on so many prompted an early canonization as a saint in the Roman Catholic Church. Opus Dei notes that "on October 6, 2002, John Paul II canonized the founder of Opus Dei in St. Peter's Square before a multitude of people from more than 80 countries."

Opus Dei strives to promote what Spanish mystics would have called the "inner life," that is, the development of the soul. However, since it is primarily an organization of lay people, Opus Dei's main emphasis is on the outer life of society, not the inner one of contemplation. The organization notes: "These are always not-for-profit ventures that provide an educational, charitable or similar social service, and include conference centers, schools and universities, student residences, youth clubs, farm schools and medical clinics." Opus Dei has sometimes been presented as a sinister "fifth column"—determined to spread the tentacles of Catholic power throughout society. However, it has established a reputation for good works; its productive members are found in all walks of life. At a time when the greatest threat to the West is found in the dedicated zealots of Islam, an organization like Opus Dei promotes the religious values of the West that gave rise to the ideas of democracy that are anathema to Islamic extremists like al-Qaeda and the Muslim Brotherhood.

SECRET ALLEGATIONS

Regardless of its stated position, allegations continue to swirl around the Opus Dei organization. These were only enhanced when it was revealed that the long time Soviet "mole" in the Federal Bureau of Investigation (FBI), Robert Hanssen, was a member of Opus Dei. Following Hannsen's charges for espionage, ABC News broadcast a special investigation of Opus Dei. Wrote reporter David Ruppe, "Opus Dei's rise is perhaps best symbolized by the recent relocation of the group's headquarters from suburban New Rochelle, New York, to a new $54 million brick complex in midtown Manhattan. A chapel in the building is expected to be blessed by Cardinal Edward Egan, the archbishop of New York.

Opus Dei's strength can also be marked by the $17 million it says was collected last year by its largest U.S. fundraising organ, the Woodlawn Foundation. Members are increasingly found in prominent church positions. The pope's own spokesman, Joaquin Navarro-Valls, is a member. Still, much remains to be known about the group, which declines to provide specifics on the composition of its membership and its sources of income. "I think they really fly under everybody's radar screen and that they're a lot more powerful than a lot of people think," says the Reverend James Martin, a Jesuit priest and associate editor of the respected Jesuit magazine *America*, who has written critically of the group.

Concerns over Opus Dei becoming an increasingly powerful conservative group continue, regardless of official Opus Dei declarations to the contrary. The organization refuses as a rule to comment on who is a member of Opus Dei. It is interesting to note that some of the strongest criticism of the movement comes from within the church itself, especially from the Society of Jesus, the Jesuits. Perhaps the strongest attacks have come in Peru against Cardinal Juan Luis Cipriani

Thorne, 61, who is a member of Opus Dei. Opposition toward Cipriani and Opus Dei extends into the hierarchy of the church in Peru. With concern about the ultimate objectives of Opus Dei strong within the Roman Catholic Church itself, the allegations of secretive political goals held by Opus Dei will only continue. Sources on Opus Dei are few, yet it should be noted that according to the British Wikipedia reference on the internet, "The Italian parliament investigated Opus Dei in 1986 and cleared it of being a secret society." Considering the Vatican's influence in the Italian parliament, this conclusion is hardly enlightening.

According to the Opus Dei website, here is their self-description: "Opus Dei is a personal prelature of the Catholic Church. It was founded in Madrid on October 2, 1928, by St. Josemaría Escrivá. Currently over 80,000 people from every continent belong to the prelature. Its headquarters, together with its prelatic church, are in Rome."

SEE ALSO
Volume 1 Left: Spain; Church and State Separation.
Volume 2 Right: Spain; Religion.

BIBLIOGRAPHY
David Ruppe, "Opus Dei on the Rise, Conservative Catholic Group Grows Quietly," ABCNews.com (June 18, 2001); Sandro Magister, "Watergate in Lima: Opus Dei Cardinal Accuses Bishops and the Vatican Curia," www.chiesa.com (July 2004); "Opus Dei," Wikipedia, www.en.wikipedia.org (July 2004); Guy Stair Sainty, "The Spanish Military Orders," www.chivalricorders.org (May 2004); Richard Fletcher, *The Quest for El Cid* (Knopf, 1990); Daniel Benjamin and Steven Simon, *The Age of Sacred Terror* (Random House, 2003); Judith Miller, *God Has 99 Names* (Touchstone, 1996).

JOHN F. MURPHY, JR.
AMERICAN MILITARY UNIVERSITY

Orientalism

EDWARD SAID's *Orientalism* (1979) is a remarkable turning point in the genealogy of this term. Before the publication of his book, Orientalism generally referred either to an artistic genre or to the scholarly discipline, which concerns itself with the study of the languages, literatures, and cultures of the Orient. Said pointed out two other definitions: a style of thought that establishes

Redefining Orientalism, Edward Said revolutionized the understanding of how the West looked at the East.

epistemological and ontological distinctions between the Occident and the Orient and a corporate institution that defines, authorizes views about, and rules over the Orient.

Said did not dispute the existence of idiosyncratic differences between the geopolitical categories. Instead, he criticized the way in which the differences are hierarchically organized in order to justify ahistorical, culture-centric judgments about self and the other. Specifically, for Said, Orientalism involves the creation and perpetuation of discourses and practices that endorse political as well as cultural superiority of the Occident over the Orient. Moreover, it represents the Orient as an exotic, mysterious, and dangerous space upon which the Occident is justified to inscribe its technologies of governance and self.

Orientalism, as a worldview, operates through rigid, mutually exclusive binary oppositions such as rational/irrational, normal/different, dynamic/stagnant, self/other, and Occident/Orient. The qualifiers on the same side of each binary are grouped together and identified as the irreconcilable opposites of the qualifiers on the other side of the binary. These juxtapositions are then articulated through prevalent political and cultural paradigms so that they refer to a tangible social group, ideology, or belief system.

It is, however, necessary to note that Orient and Occident do not refer to fixed categories but to time-bound discursive constructs. In other words, their geographical and substantial scopes vary across time on the basis of shifting power relations. Yet, the transformation does not eradicate the inequalities and incongruities that binaries imply for political, cultural, and subjective identity-formation in the newly designated geopolitical categories.

The Orientalist categorization of social reality has particularly served to legitimize colonial administrations, political mandates, and racist and sexist practices. If a group is associated with the undesirable side of binary oppositions, it calls forth the assistance and/or the guidance of supposedly superior groups. An interesting example is the mainstream Western feminism's treatment of Oriental women as always oppressed individuals who are presumed to have neither the resources nor the capacity to break away from their patriarchal bondage.

Another example is the association of Islam with religious fundamentalism, political extremism, terrorism, and a backward social structure. Besides suppressing the genuine voices of supposedly inferior groups, Orientalism therefore provides the allegedly superior groups with a positive image, self-reliance, and cultural resources of power.

Orientalist perspective has been an influential undercurrent in the social sciences as well. The three major theories, that is, classical Marxism, classical liberalism, and structural functionalism, view Occidental societies as the ultimate apex of modern civilization and Oriental societies as units in the process of development. In a similar vein, modernization theory explains the un(der)development of Oriental societies with their adherence to obscure traditions and beliefs. Said's critique refuted the validity of such analytical reductionisms. It reinforced the cultural/textual turn in the social sciences, motivated the emergence of postcolonial studies, and strengthened the currency of poststructuralism and the Foucauldian paradigm.

Said's followers criticized his inadequate attention to gender dynamics, reductionist focus on the Middle East, and underestimation of Oriental agency vis-à-vis the Occident. Some of them particularly investigated how Oriental groups use Orientalist discourses against themselves (self-Orientalization) and against other non-Occidental groups. Their reexamination of Orientalism brought about a more comprehensive analysis of how movies, travelogues, and popular media create and perpetuate power inequalities between as well as within the presumed geopolitical categories.

In conclusion, Orientalism, as it is defined by Said and elaborated by his followers, can be associated with a rightist worldview. It categorizes social phenomena into rigid, ahistorical binaries that help maintain and justify the existing dynamics of domination and subordination. Instead of evaluating a culture in and of itself, it dictates ethnocentric presuppositions about truth. The critique of Orientalism, on the other, hand supports a leftist perspective. It encourages a re-examination of taken-for-granted truths and points out how knowledge is imbued with temporally and spatially specific power struggles. In this respect, it highlights the possibilities of a dialogue among different communities.

SEE ALSO

Volume 1 Left: Socialism; Cold War; Anti-Globalization.
Volume 2 Right: Capitalism; Globalization.

BIBLIOGRAPHY

Fred Y.L. Chiu, "Sub-orientalism and the Subimperialist Predicament: Aboriginal Discourse and the Poverty of State-Nation Imagery," *Positions* (v.8/1, 2000); Edward Said, *Orientalism* (Vintage Books, 1979); Edward Said, *Covering Islam: How the Media and the Experts Determine How We See the Rest of the World* (Vintage, 1981); Gyan Prakash, "Orientalism Now," *History and Theory* (v.34/3, October 1995); Leti Vollp, "The Citizen and the terrorist," Mary L. Dudziak, ed., *September 11 in History: A Watershed Moment?* (Duke University Press, 2003); Meyda Yecenoclu, *Colonial Fantasies: Towards a Feminist Reading of Orientalism* (Cambridge University Press, 1998).

BURÇAK KESKIN-KOZAT
UNIVERSITY OF MICHIGAN

The Right

P

Pakistan

PRIOR TO INDEPENDENCE in August 1947, Pakistan was the western provinces of the British Empire, or Raj, of India. Because of its geographic proximity to Afghanistan and the wild tribes of the Northwest Frontier, it always formed more of a military enclave than the rest of the country. This became the Republic of India when the great Indian Empire was partitioned into the two nations. Indeed, future Pakistani cities like Quetta began life more as garrison towns than as civilian settlements like the cities of Bombay and Calcutta in what would be India. This military factor, as far as the pervasive influence of Islam, would contribute to the more conservative, rightist mien of Pakistan after independence.

The man who justly deserves the name given to him, the "Father of the Country," Quaid-i-Azam, was Mohammed Ali Jinnah. He was born in 1876, 18 years after the British Indian dominion passed from the rule of the British East India Company to the direct rule of the British Empire. Queen Victoria from then on was known as the "Queen Empress." A Muslim, Jinnah benefited from the same culture of democracy that England brought to the Indian subcontinent, even though it contained the embryo of future opposition to British rule. Although a believer in Muslim-Hindu cooperation, like his great contemporary, Mohandas K.

Gandhi, Jinnah eventually became conscious of what he perceived to be an overwhelming Hindu element in the growing Indian movement for independence. In 1928, Pandit Motilal Nehru wrote what became known as the "Nehru Report," which outlined the form that a future independent India would take. According to the "Political History of Pakistan," "The recommendations of the Nehru Report went against the interests of the Muslim community. It was an attempt to serve Hindu predominance over Muslims." Henceforth, Jinnah would bend his efforts to form a homeland for the Muslim people of the empire. In 1940, he issued a formal call for a Muslim homeland.

On June 3, Lord Louis Mountbatten, the last viceroy of British India, announced formal plans for the partition of the subcontinent. On August 15, India emerged with what was then West Pakistan with the Northwest Frontier, and East Pakistan near the old Indian province of Bengal. The birth of the two nations unleashed one of the bloodiest episodes in modern history. Unknown tens of thousands were killed and perhaps 15 million people became refugees. The barbarity committed by fanatics on both sides poisoned the relations of India and Pakistan for years to come. Immediately, the partition led to the first armed confrontation between the two countries.

The problem lay in the princely state of Kashmir. Its ruler was the Maharajah Hari Singh, a Hindu, but its population was greatly Muslim. After independence in August 1947, Pashtuns from (now) Pakistan's Northwest Frontier province invaded it. With no effective armed forces, the maharajah turned to India for help. As Tipu Salman Makhdoom wrote in *Historical Perspective on the Kashmir Crisis,* "With the Maharaja losing control over his state, he signed an Instrument of Accession to the Indian Union in October 1947. On October 27, the Indian army entered Kashmir. Pakistan responded, and localized warfare between India and Pakistan continued during 1948. India took the Kashmir issue to the United Nations Security Council, and the war ended in a cease-fire, which took effect in January 1949."

However, Kashmir would remain for 50 years a combustible issue between India and Pakistan, with a Muslim insurgency (most likely having been supported by Pakistan) keeping Kashmir broiling with civil unrest. War would erupt between India and Pakistan twice more, in 1965 and in 1971. During the 1971 war, East Pakistan was lost to an Indian thrust from the old center of British power—in Bengal. As the Library of Congress Country Studies history of Bangladesh notes, "The independent, sovereign republic of Bangladesh was first proclaimed in a radio message broadcast from a captured station in Chittagong on March 26, 1971. Two days later, the Voice of Independent Bangladesh announced that a Major Zia (actually Ziaur Rahman, later president of Bangladesh) would form a new government with himself occupying the presidency." East Pakistan thus became Bangladesh—doomed after over 30 years to still being one of the poorest countries in the world.

Internally, the political development of the country suffered with the premature death of Jinnah on September 11, 1948. Politically, representative government seemed in Pakistan to continue to remain an election away. In October 1958, President Iskander Mirza would abrogate the constitution of 1956, permitting the establishment of martial law. The administrator designated under martial law, General Mohammed Ayub Khan, would oust Mirza as president himself on October 27, 1958. The political heritage of the military garrisons from the days of British rule in what became Pakistan proved stronger than any incipient parliamentary system. Caesarism became the governing norm in the nation. Martial law, as an example, would be proclaimed again under General Yahya Khan from 1969 to 1971, around the time of the third war with India. Indeed, if anything, the loss of East Pakistan only solidified the hold of militarism on the country, for West Pakistan—now the entire country—was composed of the provinces that had seen most of the military activity of the British Raj since the First Afghan War of 1842. These were the provinces of Sind, Punjab, Baluchistan, and the always tumultuous tribal NWFP, the Northwest Frontier Province.

Military rule in Pakistan, at least for the time being, was discredited with the army's defeat in the 1971 war with India. Zulfikar Ali Bhutto became the nation's first civilian martial law administrator in December 1971, but later under a new constitution was elected the civilian prime minister in August 1973. The founder of the socialist Pakistan Peoples Party in 1967, he followed a reformist program while prime minister that angered conservatives in the country. But, by doing so in areas like land reform, he may have also served to avert any concerted communist effort to seriously destabilize the country, although localized insurgencies continue today. After a controversy over alleged rigged elections, the army once again took power in July 1975, under Army General Chief of Staff Mohammed Zia-ul-Haq.

However, four years later, Pakistan's internal political crisis was overshadowed by a greater threat: in December 1979, the Soviet Union invaded neighboring Afghanistan. The United States viewed the Soviet invasion as a dangerous heightening of Cold War tensions. In June 1981, President Ronald Reagan, as Edgar O'Ballance writes, "needing a strong viable ally in the southern Asia dimension of the superpower conflict, offered more generous military aid to President Zia." From then on, Pakistan became America's prime ally in the war in Afghanistan. Peshawar became the main point of entry into Afghanistan for those Muslim mujahideen, or "holy warriors," who wished to fight the kufr, the infidel Russians and their puppet regime in power in Kabul, the capital of Afghanistan. The Pakistani intelligence service, the ISI, became the main conduit for covert U.S. armed shipments to the mujahideen. However, at the same time, Zia built up Islamist parties to serve as a cat's paw to pave the way for making Afghanistan a nation in the Pakistani sphere of influence.

In November 1988, Benazir Bhutto succeeded her father as prime minister of Pakistan, the first woman to head a Muslim state. However, President Ghulam Ishaq replaced her in power in an internal political conflict. Mian Muhammad Nawaz Sharif was elected prime minister on November 1, 1990. Nawaz Sharif's government remained in power until April 19, 1993. With growing concern about Islamist influence within Pakistan, Sharif, who was seen to favor the radicals, served a short term in office. In July 1993, both Khan and Sharif resigned, and Benazir Bhutto came back to power, only to be dismissed from power again in November 1996. The continuing political feud caused the army to enter politics again in October 1999; in June 2001, former Army Chief of Staff General Pervez Musharraf became president.

In September 2001, Musharraf, at the strong insistence of American President George W. Bush and Secretary of State Colin Powell, became a reluctant ally in the new War on Terror. While castigated for not being vigorous enough in the campaign, which led to the invasion of Afghanistan in October 2001, he faced a very real threat from the Islamists within Pakistan. Indeed, as CNN reported on December 14, 2003, "Pakistan President Pervez Musharraf narrowly escaped an assassination attempt when a bomb exploded just after his motorcade had passed by. 'It was certainly a terrorist act and, certainly, it was me who was targeted,' the military leader told reporters shortly after the attack." In spite of the attempt on his life, Musharraf pursued the attack on suspected al-Qaeda terrorists and the Taliban, which had been ousted from Afghanistan in the October 2001 American-led invasion. With its continuing history of strong military rule, Pakistan remains in the rightist camp, yet not so far to the right as to become an Islamic theocracy.

SEE ALSO

Volume 1 Left: Asia; Communism; Soviet Union.
Volume 2 Right: Religion; Asia; Bush, George W.

BIBLIOGRAPHY

Edgar O'Ballance, *Afghan Wars: Battles in a Hostile Land, 1839 to the Present* (Brassey's, 2002); Stephen Tanner, *Afghanistan* (Perseus, 2002); Victoria Schofield, *Afghan Frontier: Feuding and Fighting in Central Asia* (Tauris, 2003); CNN, "Musharraf Eludes Assassination Bid" (December 14, 2003); "Comprehensive Reference on the Political History of Pakistan," ww.storyofpakistan.com (June 2004).

JOHN F. MURPHY, JR.
AMERICAN MILITARY UNIVERSITY

Pan-Africanism

PAN-AFRICANISM refers to a multifaceted international movement that involves the intellectual, emotional, and physical connection of people of African descent to the continent of their forebears. It is a form of Black Nationalism, a term that refers to the belief that black people have a common experience based on cultural factors stemming from the African Diaspora (the forced dispersion of people of Africa to other lands) with the resulting issues of slavery and other forms of exploitation. Pan-Africanism, the highest form of Black Nationalism, reflects the idea that people of African descent have similar experiences, interests, and a collective worldview, and that a return to Africa is one way to escape the control of the oppression of other nations. It focuses on the idea that solidarity will enable black people to control their own destiny. The slogan for the movements associated with pan-Africanism was "Africa for the Africans."

BACK TO AFRICA

There have been many times throughout history that attempts were made to return people of African descent to the mother continent, especially efforts in the United States. In spite of these attempts, there was a very low emigration rate, due to a number of factors, including the abject poverty that made it difficult to leave America, poor organization, and resistance by white capitalists who desired to maintain a cheap labor pool.

In the early 1800s, some notable whites, including Thomas Jefferson, believed that a return of blacks to Africa was a worthy goal; the foundation of the American Colonization Society and the establishment of the west African township of Liberia occurred during this period. Physician and journalist Martin R. Delany, who is credited with the pan-African slogan "Africa for the Africans," was another advocate of mass emigration attempts just prior to the American Civil War. Although the slaves were freed after the war, conditions were far from favorable for blacks. Other attempts were made to promote the emigration, such as a venture by Delany to return blacks to Africa through a private shipping company, but they all failed to produce the desired results.

In the later part of the 19th century, other movements attempted to return African Americans to Africa. A missionary named Joseph Booth who was working in Nyasaland in the latter part of the 19th century became a staunch advocate for pan-Africanism. He wrote *Africa for the African*, in which he argued against the common perception that Africans were intellectually inferior and recommended that the oppression against them and their descendants cease. He also suggested that Africans should be in charge of their own continent and not under the control of Europe or other foreign governments; this government by Africans would appear in the form of a united Christian nation. This new nation did not materialize, however, due to a strong distrust by blacks of the whites who were trying to orchestrate the change. Years of oppression and war by the Europeans contributed to this heightened level of distrust.

DU BOIS AND GARVEY

In the early 1900s, two key figures continued to promote the ideal of pan-Africanism. Black sociologist W.E.B. Du Bois and Marcus Garvey had differing perspectives on the subject, and in fact, the two had much contempt for each other. Du Bois was a professor of sociology at Atlanta University in the United States. He was of African, Dutch, and French ancestry, though he fully accepted the label "Negro," not in a negative, but a positive, light. Du Bois was an intellectual, being the first person of African descent to obtain a Ph.D. from Harvard University. He was a professor, a prolific and eloquent writer, race reformer, and one of the most powerful black people in America in the 1900s.

Du Bois founded the Niagara Movement, a black activist group that was the precursor to the National Association for the Advancement of Colored People (NAACP), in which Du Bois also served as office holder and editor of the organization's journal, The Crisis. Du Bois constantly worked for racial equality in America but began to question whether the nation would ever be truly egalitarian. He began to consider other options for African Americans. Du Bois was probably one of the first people to actually use the term pan-Africanism and he planned to make the term a commonly used one.

In 1900, Du Bois attended the First Pan-African Congress, held in London, England. Some of his ideas of black pride were communicated in 1903 with the publication of Souls of Black Folk. His disillusionment after World War I, which he initially supported, grew when black soldiers who were sent to war still returned to an oppressive nation. In addition, lynching and other forms of violence as well as discrimination increased to a new intensity in 1919. It was in that year that Du Bois formed the Second Pan-African Congress, which met in Paris, France. At this conference, a proclamation was made for legal protection from violence and abuse, protection from foreign exploitation, the abolition of slavery, the removal of the death penalty, the right to industrial and educational training, and the right to par-

ticipate in governmental affairs. Du Bois attended the Third and Fourth Pan-African Congresses held in London in 1922 and 1923, and the fifth convention held in New York City in 1927.

Du Bois made his first trip to Africa in 1924, a pilgrimage that he considered to be the "great event" of his life. Eventually, Du Bois became discouraged by the lack of support by white and black Americans for racial equality and moved to Ghana, where he died in 1961.

Garvey was quite different in his approach to pan-Africanism. Garvey, a, Jamaican-born, dark-complexioned, rotund, and highly charismatic individual, moved to America in 1916 and started the Universal Negro Improvement Association in 1917. Soon, he would become one of the world's leading African American voices for pan-Africanism. Very much the showman, he and his immediate followers would dress in colorful uniforms as they marched through Harlem, New York City, and other venues. His following of "Garveyites" grew to one of the largest Black Nationalist organizations in the world. His newspaper, Negro World, enjoyed wide circulation and many black people sent Garvey money to promote his plans to return black people to Africa to be free of oppression. He established the Black Star Line shipping establishment with the intent to use the fleet to have Africans returned to Africa. Garvey made many enemies, including Du Bois, and he gained a reputation as a troublemaker, especially to government officials. His arrest for mail fraud led to a prison sentence in 1923 and subsequent deportation to Jamaica.

Du Bois and Garvey were key figures in the pan-African movement of the early 20th century but there were a number of other advocates. There were others, such as historians G. Carter Woodson and George Padmore, who promoted black pride in academia. In the 1920s, there was also a resurgence of African interest in the arts as cultural nationalism was promoted through paintings, poetry, songs, and novels; Langston Hughes and other writers became popular for providing a romanticized connection between American blacks and Africa. Harlem, in New York City, was especially recognized as a cultural center for African pride and entertainment during this period.

In the middle part of the century, there were several international conferences involving black nationalism, not only in Africa but in Arab nations as well. Groups such as the All African People's Organization promoted these conferences. A more inclusive approach brought in many nations but spurred much infighting as well. The movement, however, continued to grow and evolve.

The 1960s in America was a time of much racial conflict between blacks and whites. Black leader Malcolm X became a key figure among separationists and called for African Americans to actively fight white oppression, which was in contrast to Martin Luther King, Jr.'s advocacy of nonviolent resistance, and to return to Africa. In the later part of the decade, the Black Power movement revived the issue of black nationalism and pan-Africanism in the United States through organizations such as the Black Panthers Party, the most prominent of these groups. The Black Panthers, founded in California in 1966, and its key figures, Huey Newton, Bobby Seal, and Eldridge Cleaver, adopted a Marxist-Leninist stance and were quickly seen by the government as dangerous. The Black Panthers' radical ideas bore the influence of Du Bois's notion of the implausibility of racial harmony and the notion of "self-segregation" from the white race. There were other key figures promoting Black Nationalism during this period as well, exemplified by activist Stokely Carmichael.

Carmichael was elected chairman of the Student Non-violent Coordinating Committee (SNCC) to found the Black United Front and later the All-African People's Revolutionary Party. He was also at one time the honorary prime minister of the Black Panthers. Carmichael issued a call for black people all over the world to return to Africa and purchase land there. He believed that only by a return to the homeland and the removal of whites from Africa, through violent means if necessary, would people of African descent be able to eliminate the oppression of blacks. After a few visits to Africa in the late 1960s, Carmichael moved to Africa, changed his name to Kwame Ture, and continued to push for black separatism until his death in 1998. African American artistic endeavors also flourished during the 1960s as poetry, books, movies, art, and music projected even more of an emphasis on black solidarity than in the 1920s.

Pan-Africanism continues but doesn't have the revolutionary zeal of earlier times, at least in the United States. It has become concentrated in Africa rather than Europe or America. As a broad set of movements over more than a century, pan-Africanism has drawn both on right-wing concepts of nationalism and on left-wing ideas of socialism and social justice.

SEE ALSO

Volume 1 Left: King, Martin Luther, Jr.; Du Bois, W.E.B.; Carmichael, Stokely; Black Panthers.
Volume 2 Right: Capitalism; Colonialism; Black Separatism; Black Nationalism; Garvey, Marcus.

BIBLIOGRAPHY

Mary Frances Berry and John W. Blassingame, *Long Memory: The Black Experience in America* (Oxford University Press, 1982); P. Olisanwuche Esedebe, *Pan-Africanism: The Idea and Movement 1776–1963* (Harvard University Press, 1982); Colin Legum, *Pan-Africanism: A Short Political Guide* (Praeger, 1965); Tony Martin, *The Pan-African Connection: From Slavery to Garvey and Beyond* (Majority Press, 1983); Walter Rucker, *A Negro Nation within the Nation: W.E.B. Du Bois and the Creation of a Revolutionary Pan-Africanist Tradition, 1903–47* (Black Scholar, 2002); William M. Tuttle Jr., ed., *W.E.B. Du Bois* (Prentice-Hall, 1973).

LEONARD A. STEVERSON, PH.D.
SOUTH GEORGIA COLLEGE

Patriotism

PATRIOTISM IS LOVE of country, devotion to its welfare, and willingness to sacrifice for it. Because patriotic loyalty is to the nation, a patriot can support or criticize the current government. Leftist patriots generally are more willing to criticize in times of crisis. Because conservatives often equate the government with the nation, especially if the government is conservative, the right can sometimes come to confuse criticism of the current government and its policies with treason, a crime against the state. From the rightist perspective legitimate patriotism requires a virtually unquestioning support that may or may not approach jingoism and chauvinism.

Conservative patriotism is heavily nationalist and tradition-bound. Its advocates reject multiculturalism and religious heterodoxy. They advocate the establishment of English as the national language and promote a Christian nation. They reject criticism of national myth and heritage, especially criticism from those who note that the myth disagrees with the historical record. Patriotism resting on narrow and intense nationalism is prideful, and pride dislikes scars and marring of the perfect.

Taken to the extreme, right-wing patriotism degenerates into chauvinism, best expressed in the phrase "my country, right or wrong." It can also become jingoism, an aggressive attempt to give the rest of the world, or some part of it, the blessings that the rightist patriot enjoys. Some jingoist patriots forget that other parts of the world have their own patriotic feelings, their own

Patriotism can take on jingoistic characteristics, especially in times of war or national crisis. Uncle Sam, normally a somewhat benign symbol of the United States, took on a decidedly more aggressive physique after the terrorist attacks of 9/11.

nationalism, their own definition of what is good and appropriate. And rightist patriotism wraps itself in Christianity, emphasizing God's blessing of America and the phrase "under God" in the Pledge of Allegiance.

Historically, right-wing patriots have rallied around the flag and suppressed criticism in times of crisis. World War I's American Protective League and other vigilante organizations enforced conformity and attacked those who declined to buy government bonds, minorities, socialists, and anti-war critics. In the 1950s, right-wing patriotism fueled McCarthyism. In the 1960s, conservative patriots attacked flag-burning anti-war activists. Federal Bureau of Investigation Director J. Edgar Hoover's surveillance of anti-war dissidents and

civil rights leaders flourished under the guise of right-wing patriotism.

The terrorist attacks of September 11, 2001, evoked an outpouring of patriotic expression. Much of it was common to both right and left, for example the wearing of lapel pins and the display of American flags on cars and homes. The rightist response also became strongly nationalistic and jingoistic. Politicians charged treason when leftist patriots questioned some government policies: mass detention without due process, loosening of legal protections, the Patriot Act, and other radical measures, up to and including the war against Iraq—all questioned by leftist patriots, but for the most part accepted by rightists. When President Bush stated, "If you're not with us, you're against us," it was rightist patriotism. When Senator Tom Daschle questioned an administration request of the Senate, Senator Trent Lott, in an example of labeling patriotic criticism as unpatriotic, said, "How dare Senator Daschle criticize President Bush while we are fighting our war on terrorism?" The issue was irrelevant. Loyalty required unquestioning support of the administration.

LACK OF DEBATE

Patriotic loyalty by citizens and representatives gave the administration the opportunity to move the nation to the right. The Patriot Act passed with token debate and little dissent as Congress rallied loyally around the administration. The same lack of debate characterized the unfolding of wars against Afghanistan and Iraq. The wars united the nation in support of the administration and against the critics, who were again sometimes regarded as "giving aid and comfort to the enemy," committing treason. The patriot became angry—whether left or right—as the charges flew.

Patriotism approaching jingoism blinds Americans to the way the world sees them. Flag-waving media fuel misconceptions by portraying the world as more supportive than polling data show it to be, and by labeling the foreign critics, as it sometimes does domestic ones, as weak and cowardly and near-traitors. Blind patriotic acceptance of the government means that significant percentages of the people believe uncorroborated claims, such as a link between Saddam Hussein and al-Qaeda. Right-wing patriots are sometimes blindsided when reality disrupts their beliefs, as was the case when no weapons of mass destruction were found in Iraq—a primary pretext for the U.S. preemptive war. Some rightist patriots grant the right of dissent—grudgingly—but they expect the dissenters to be willing to accept the unfavorable reaction they evoke.

Nationalistic patriotism has positives: it promotes unity in times of crisis. Critics note that it also degenerates to flag waving, clichés, and conformity. The Pledge of Allegiance in itself is a positive statement of patriotism; sometimes the crisis atmosphere leads to pressure to recite even when the desire is not there. Nationalist patriotism also promotes conformity, racism or xenophobia, aggressiveness to the point of jingoism, and suppression of civil liberties.

SEE ALSO

Volume 1 Left: Liberalism; Civil Rights; United States.
Volume 2 Right: Republican Party; Bush, George W.

BIBLIOGRAPHY

Charlie Daniels, *Ain't No Rag: Freedom, Family, and the Flag* (Regnery, 2003); Geobopological Survey, "Patriotism: What Is It, and Does It Matter? (2001)," www.geobop.com (June 2004); Mark Gerzon, *A House Divided* (G.P. Putnam's Sons, 1997); David Limbaugh, "Dissent Does Not Equal Patriotism," *WorldNet Daily* (March 14, 2003); Christopher L. McCargar, "History Professor Debates Meaning of Patriotism," *University of Nevada Zephyr* (April 18, 2002); William Pierce, "The Nature of Patriotism: What Factors Control Whether People Are Loyal to Their Country?" *Free Speech* (April 1997); Brian Yates, "Why Liberals Hate America," www.bushcountry.org (June 2004).

JOHN BARNHILL, PH.D.
INDEPENDENT SCHOLAR

Peronism

PERONISM IS AN ARGENTINE political movement and ideology named after Juan Peron. Peron was president of Argentina from 1946 to 1955 and from 1973 to 1974. He, along with Eva Peron, his wife, defined Peronism, one of the most important political movements in 20th-century Argentine history.

Peronism reflected and built upon the nationalist sentiment that surged in the 1930s and 1940s, particularly among the military. It opposed foreign economic control (in the 1930s, 50 percent of capital investments in Argentina were foreign-owned) and the landed oligarchy that had ruled the nation since the late 1800s. Peronism was against liberalism, both because of its association with the oligarchy and the British and, more importantly, because Peron believed liberal ideology was unable to defeat communism, which he strongly disliked. Instead, Peronism advocated nationalism, an end to Argentine economic and political dependency, industrialization, and a better standard of living for the workers. Peronism is also called Justicialism, which Peron defined as socialism without Marxism.

Peronism largely mirrored the political beliefs of Peron. He rose to prominence following the 1943 coup that brought the military to power. In 1945, he held the positions of secretary of labor and welfare, war minister, and vice president. He used these powerful positions to sponsor legislation that improved conditions for the workers and to build his base of support among the working class and in the military. The economic

Under the leadership of Evita (Eva Peron), Peronism incorporated women into the national political discussion.

windfall that Argentina reaped from selling its products in World War II allowed Peron to distribute higher wages to the working class. In October 1945, Peron secured his place as the undisputed national leader when, following his ouster from power, masses of Argentine workers crowded the Plaza de Mayo and demanded that he be reinstated. In February 1946, he won the presidential election.

Although Peron admired Mussolini and Peronism drew on certain aspects of fascist ideology, it was not a fascist movement. The tremendous loss of human life Peron witnessed in Spain as a result of the civil war horrified him, and, unlike fascists, he was Catholic. He was democratically elected president and he maintained the republican institutions of the country; during his presidency, both the Congress and the judiciary functioned. However, Peron was an authoritarian figure who persecuted his political opponents and restricted their freedom of expression.

Peronism was anti-communist because Marxism promoted class conflict whereas Peronism advocated national unity. However, Peronism sponsored rights for workers, who were among its prime supporters and beneficiaries. Peron created new unions and increased wages; in 1948, workers received 40 percent more than they had in 1943.

Under the leadership of Eva Peron (Evita), Peronism also incorporated women into the movement and national political life. Breaking with the past figurehead role of the first lady, Eva Peron was a major force in securing the vote for women (1947), the establishment of the Fundacion Eva Peron (1948), and the creation of the Partido Peronista Femenino (Female Peronist Party) (1949). Although Eva always attributed her thoughts and activities to her husband and never appeared to challenge Argentine gender roles that defined women as wives and mothers, she did develop a new image for women as public figures and political activists. Women responded favorably; in the 1951 presidential elections, the majority of women gave their votes to Peron.

Peronism entered into a crisis in the 1950s due to the 1952 death of Evita and the drop in prices for Argentine products sold internationally. Peron lost the support of the Catholic Church, the industrialists, and much of the military, which overthrew him in 1955. The church turned against Peron because, among other things, he legalized divorce (1954) and removed religious instruction from the schools (1955). Peron went into exile and the Peronist movement split into left and right factions. On the left, the Montoneros claimed Catholicism, Peron, and Eva Peron as their inspiration, adopted guerrilla warfare, and kidnapped wealthy Argentines to finance their movement. In an attempt to simultaneously establish their legitimacy and draw on the positive image of Evita and her concern for the people, one well-known Montonero slogan was "If Evita were alive she would be a Montonero."

Despite years of exile and military repression, Peron and Peronism continued to evoke passionate support among workers and other Argentines. In 1973, Peron returned to Argentina and the presidency, only to die in office in 1974. A brutal military dictatorship ruled Argentina from 1976 to 1983, but, like previous ones, it was unable to defeat Peronism. In 1989, Carlos Saúl Menem, a Peronist, was elected president and in 2003 Néstor Kirchner, also a Peronist, became president of Argentina.

SEE ALSO

Volume 1 Left: Argentina; Populism; Communism; Liberalism; South America.
Volume 2 Right: Fascism; Argentina; Spain.

BIBLIOGRAPHY

Ben Plotkin Mariano, *Mañana es San Peron: A Cultural History of Perón's Argentina* (Scholarly Resources, 2003); Donald C. Hodges, *Argentina 1943–87: The National Revolution and Resistance* (University of New Mexico Press, 1988); Benjamin Keen and Keith Haynes, *A History of Latin America* (Houghton Mifflin, 2004); Juan Peron and Juan Domingo, *Peron Expounds His Doctrine* (AMS Press, 1973); David Rock, *Authoritarian Argentina: The Nationalist Movement, Its History and Impact* (University of California Press, 1993).

MARGARET POWER
ILLINOIS INSTITUTE OF TECHNOLOGY

Peru

THE RIGHT IN THE Andean nation of Peru played a crucial role in the social and political development of the nation. Among all the South American nations, Peru's political and social development is the most intertwined with its historical development. From its inception as a Spanish colony through its tardiness in gaining independence to the export-oriented growth of the 19th century, Peruvian conservatism has assumed a staunch and strict sense of moral nationalism. In the 20th century, the Peruvian right, those in the military, members of the middle class, as well as the landowning oligarchy sponsored a seemingly contradictory notion of traditionalism and nationalistic modernity. Most conservatives believed in the inherent necessity of modernity. However, most conservatives were unable to handle the ramifications or consequences of that modernity. As a result, when modern ideologies emerged, especially on the left, the conservative right wing reacted harshly, mostly through creating an alliance with the defender of the status quo—the military.

Armed with the ideology of traditional conservative politics and modern economic policies, the right wing surfaced in the mid-20th century as a viable political force. In 1948, General Manuel Odría, a prominent leader in the military, assumed political power. He assumed power to please the oligarchy and the conservative landowning policies of the landed elite. Odría, with the consent of the conservative oligarchy, ruled Peru as a dictator from 1948 to 1956. In this period, Odría ruled without a legislative branch or a judicial branch. Along with a repressive political system, Odría initiated numerous economic reforms, which did improve the Peruvian economy. He promised tax reform, educational reform, and a school-building program. Despite his plans for reform, however, the conservative rich were called upon to contribute their fair share. Moreover, by the end of Odría's term, 49 percent of schoolchildren in Peru did not even have a desk in their classrooms.

The conservative alliance of the military and the oligarchy, with its ideology of traditionalism and nationalism, reached its major roadblock in the 1960s. In 1963, a military junta gained power over the democratically elected government. Over the next few years, the military junta gave power to the conservative-based Popular Action Party (AP). The AP appealed to the landowning oligarchy's traditional and conservative viewpoints. Thus, the conservative right had found a powerful ally.

On July 18, 1963, a military coup toppled the liberal government of Fernando Balaunde. At the head of an odd coalition, the conservatives feared the nationalistic policies of the incoming president as well as his seeming flirtation with foreign ideologies. The army suspended the constitution and acted as a caretaker regime. The conservatives clung to power until 1968. In the five-year period, the junta had persecuted organized labor and hunted violent guerrilla groups, which had emerged since the coup. The conservatives' traditionalism had once again taken root.

This traditionalism, over the next 30 years, was challenged to a tremendous degree. In 1968, a group of army officers, hostile to Balaunde and angry over a dispute with Standard Oil, toppled the regime. The conservatives had hoped that this new military regime would be nationalistic and uphold traditional values. However, the officers involved in the coup had been trained abroad and many returned with Marxist political leanings. At the least, many had become favorable to the notion of social justice in the Peruvian political system. The military junta had essentially duped the conservatives. Over the next 20 years, the right in Peru suffered as the military became increasingly politicized and part of the leftist movement.

In recent political developments, the conservatives have tended to act within the confines of the existent political system. Many have opted to join political parties and negotiate their political disagreements through political routes rather than through direct military intervention. Specifically, the conservative right has become increasingly part of the political process through party channels, like Popular Action and Unidad Nacional (UN), which in the election of 2001 received 4.2 percent and 13.8 percent of the popular vote, respectively.

In 1990, the right in Peru received a political boost and a sense of legitimacy when Peruvians elected Alberto Fujimori to the presidency. Until his election, few political pundits knew who this politician was. He was an agricultural engineer who was born to Japanese parents. In the election of 1990, he ran against a center-right coalition led by the famed Peruvian writer Mario Vargas Llosa. In the midst of an economic collapse, Fujimori's message of political reform appealed to many of the lower sectors.

Once elected, he implemented his political and economic reforms. He implemented radical free-market reforms, removed long-standing government subsidies, and essentially reduced the role of the state in all areas of Peruvian life. Fujimori's economic policies proved successful as hyperinflation ended in Peru and the economy was in an upswing throughout the remainder of the 1990s.

President Fujimori also acted quickly to attack the 10-year-old guerrilla insurgency that plagued the nation. In 1992, in reaction to the guerrilla attacks and his perception that the legislative branch hindered any true policy toward the guerrillas, Fujimori, with the aid and support of the military, dissolved Congress and ruled the nation. He seized dictatorial power in the midst of a chaotic political situation.

Within a few years, the main guerrilla group, the Shining Path, had been defeated and it seemed that Fujimori's policies had proven successful. In 1995, he successfully won reelection to the presidency. In his second term, however, Fujimori turned to repressive tactics to curtail political opposition. He increasingly relied on the Peruvian intelligence service, led by Vladimir Montesinos, to repress freedom of expression, both in the legal sphere and the political arena.

In 2000, Fujimori decided to run for an unprecedented third term. Under the Peruvian constitution, there was a two-term limitation. With increasing criticism and accusations of voter fraud, Fujimori defeated a former World Bank adviser, Alejandro Toledo. Fujimori's victory was short-lived, however, as the fraud accusations and international pressure forced Fujimori to resign, essentially curtailing the influence of the right wing in Peru.

SEE ALSO

Volume 1 Left: Peru; South America.
Volume 2 Right: South America; Globalization.

BIBLIOGRAPHY

Arnold Payne, *The Peruvian Coup d'Etat of 1962: The Overthrow of Manuel Prado* (Institute for the Comparative Study of Political Systems); Tad Szulc, *Twilight of the Tyrants* (Henry Holt and Company, 1959); United States Congress, House Committee on International Relations, Subcommittee on the Western Hemisphere, "Prospects for Free and Fair elections in Peru: Hearing before the Subcommittee on the Western Hemisphere of the Committee on International Relations" (March 14, 2001).

JAIME RAMÓN OLIVARES, PH.D.
HOUSTON COMMUNITY COLLEGE, CENTRAL

Poland

IN THE YEARS following World War II and the establishment of a communist regime in Poland, all center and right-wing parties were banned and declared illegal. Many right-wing activists were arrested and some were executed. No rightist organization could function legally in Poland until the Velvet Revolution of 1989. Small independent groups that tried to organize various activities were broken up, their members arrested, beaten up, and often thrown out of their jobs (or studies).

The changes in Poland (and in the former Soviet Bloc in general) in 1989 opened the possibility to organize and register all types of political parties, with the exception of those that had racist and fascist elements in their programs. In effect, a large number of parties were registered on a local and a national scale. Many claimed to be right-wing. Since there was no right-wing tradition, many of the newly formed parties saw their anti-communism as being their "rightness," certainly duly opposite to communism. On the other hand, some politicians looked for conservative ideas abroad, and many of them copied the right-wing party programs from before World War II. Historians agree that not all of this was adequate for Poland in the 1990s.

The characteristic features of the Polish right wing are lack of tradition, lack of stable programs, and lack of stability of the parties themselves. Of the four or five parties that can be considered right-wing or center-right-wing, only one has existed since the fall of communism in 1989 and paradoxically was not represented in parliament by 2004. The programs of these parties vary greatly and it is very hard to show more than one or two common elements. These are Christian values, national values, and the observance of relatively strict law enforcement. They differ on economic concepts as well as on Poland's role in the European Union (EU).

The oldest and decidedly the most right-wing party is Unia Polityki Realnej—UPR (Union of Realistic Politics). UPR is a party with the most market-oriented program of all Polish parties. It strongly opposes bureaucracy, and postulates low taxes, free trade, and privatization of all sectors of the Polish economy. UPR strongly backs Polish alliance with the United States and is anti-EU, considering the latter to be a cumbersome, bureaucratic machine. Its most well known politician is Janusz Korwin-Mikke. UPR is not represented in the 2004 parliament; since 1993 it has not passed the necessary threshold.

Liga Polskich Rodzin—LPR (League of Polish Families)—was formed just before the elections in 2001. Its program is conservative, anti-EU, stressing national values and the social teaching of the Catholic Church. LPR often pronounces extremely populist slogans. The leader of the party, Marek Kotlinowski, remains in the shadow of Roman Giertych, who is the party's most quoted and visible spokesman. In this way, Giertych continues a long family tradition of nationalistic, Catholic politics dating back to the 19th century. LPR has a small representation in the parliament and backing from about 8 percent of the electorate.

Prawo i Sprawiedliwosc—PiS (Law and Justice)—is another right-wing party, which was established by the Kaczynski brothers (Jaroslaw and Lech) just before the 2001 elections. Unlike members of LPR, both brothers were engaged in politics since 1989, changing parties several times. PiS is a Christian-Democratic party with a very conservative program based on the concept of a well-ordered legal state. To achieve this, PiS mentions the need to rediscuss the death sentence in Poland. PiS is represented in the parliament and can count on about 10 percent backing.

Platforma Obywatelska—PO (Citizens' Platform)—is yet another party formed just before the 2001 elections. It was formed by a group of experienced politicians who have been members of numerous parties in the past, some of which vanished in the meantime. PO should be placed somewhere between the right wing and the center. Within the party, there are two clearly visible streams: conservative and liberal. PO, which led in public opinion polls in 2004, has a very strong liberal economic program. Special stress is put on diminishing state bureaucracy, introducing tax reforms (low linear tax), and introducing a well-ordered state. PO is decidedly for Polish membership in the EU.

Donald Tusk heads this party, with Jan Rokita and Zyta Gilowska being the most known politicians.

There are three more right-wing parties represented in the parliament: Ruch Odbudowy Polski—ROP (Movement for Poland's Reconstruction), Stronnictwo Konserwatywno-Ludowe—SKL (Conservative Peasant Party), and Ruch Katolicko-Narodowy—RKN (Catholic-National Movement). They were formed as various politicians left other parties and set up their own. All three are conservative, stressing the role of the Catholic Church and Polish national tradition. Yet none of them play any important role on the political scene. They might not survive beyond the next elections.

Poland's political right wing is extremely diversified. It is broken up into many small parties and factions, which often disappear after a short period of time. None of the parties currently in the parliament have a long tradition and thus a stable political, economic, and social program. They stress the national, conservative, and Catholic values, but often interpret them in a different way. In effect, the forming of one right-wing party or coalition appears to be impossible at present, while any changes, shifts, and reshuffles among the existing parties are very likely.

SEE ALSO

Volume 1 Left: Poland; Solidarity; Communism; Soviet Union; Socialism.
Volume 2 Right: Soviet Union; Religion.

BIBLIOGRAPHY

M.B. Biskupski, *The History of Poland* (Greenwood Press, 2000); *Polityka* (v16, April 17, 2004); Jakub Basista, "Poland," G.T .Kurian, ed., *Encyclopedia of World Nations* (Facts on File, 2002); Polish political party internet websites: www.upr.org.pl; www.lpr.pl; www.pis.org.pl; www.po.org.pl (April 2004).

JAKUB BASISTA, PH.D.
JAGIELLONIAN UNIVERSIT, POLAND

Polls and Pollsters

PUBLIC OPINION polls have become an accepted part of everyday life in the 21st century. Political pollsters announce what the public thinks about a candidate or issue after surveying a few hundred randomly selected individuals, sometimes using controls to develop subgroups based on characteristics such as sex, race, age, education, and level of partisanship. Presidents of both parties monitor their approval ratings religiously, despite the fact that the public is notoriously fickle. For instance, George H.W. Bush's approval ratings, which soared to 83 percent during and immediately after the Gulf War, were so high that few Democrats were willing to challenge him in the 1992 election. However, Democrat Bill Clinton defeated him 370 to 168 in the electoral vote and 42.93 percent to 37.38 percent in the popular vote.

Since all presidential candidates except Harry Truman have used private pollsters to conduct polls since the early 1930s, pollsters have become adept at gathering polling information that furthers the interests of candidates and political parties. Liberals claim that right-wing pollsters slant polls to produce data that are distributed to conservative media, making it seem as if public opinion supports extremist views on certain issues such as abortion, religion in public schools, affirmative action, and gay marriage.

Republican pollsters have been particularly gifted at identifying and exploiting weaknesses in the background, character, and policies of Democratic candidates. For example, Republican pollsters/strategists developed the notorious Willie Horton ad used against Michael Dukakis in the 1988 election. The ad, based on polling results, purported to inform voters that Dukakis was weak on crime, unlike Bush who was depicted as strong on law and order. The Bush team also made *liberal* an ugly word by presenting Dukakis as a "card-carrying member of the American Civil Liberties Union (ACLU)," falsely identifying Dukakis as an extreme left-winger who was out of touch with mainstream America. When Republicans tried similar tactics against Bill Clinton in the following election, Clinton's savvy team refused to buckle as Dukakis had done. When Clinton was accused of adultery, he and Hillary appeared on television to face the issue head-on.

Pollsters have become amazingly accurate at identifying groups that hold the key to swing votes in a particular election. Such was the case in the 1994 election when "angry white men," who were apparently furious at advantages given to women and minorities, wrested control of Congress from the Democratic Party. The 1994 election led to the Republican Party's Contract with America, which established a far-right agenda for the next two years. Other pollsters have leveled heavy criticism at Republican pollster Frank Luitz, who allegedly conducted polls suggesting that 70 percent of

Americans supported the conservative position spelled out in the Contract with America. In 1995, the *Miami Herald* broke the story that Luitz had only dealt with focus groups, which had only been asked to respond to slick Republican slogans.

Scandal over Republican polling methods also surfaced in February 1996 when several campaign advisers told talk-show host Larry King that they had used "push polls" to discredit Democrats during the Iowa caucuses. Beginning with Nixon's campaigns in the 1940s, push polls were conducted by feeding potential voters negative information under cover of conducting public opinion polls. Nixon's push polls involved telling potential voters that his Democratic opponents were communists.

President Herbert Hoover was not a fan of opinion polls, which were primitive by today's standards. In the late 1920s, pollsters depended on such methods as mailed-in newspaper ballots, straw votes, and man-on-the-street interviews. Rather than using polls, Hoover ordered his staff to gather data from newspaper editorials around the country. The data were then analyzed to discover what the public thought about certain issues and whether or not they approved of Hoover's policies. After defeating Hoover in 1932, Democrat Franklin Roosevelt became the first president to use polling as a major tool for campaigning and governing. Roosevelt's immediate successors, Democrat Harry Truman and Republican Dwight Eisenhower, were not convinced of the need for private polling and paid less attention to public opinion polls.

Richard Nixon made polling an integral part of his strategy both as candidate and as president. In 1968, Nixon pollsters conducted surveys on Vietnam, key issues, political attitudes and preferences, and socioeconomic data. These were used to develop the "Silent Majority" strategy that paved the way for the Ronald Reagan conservatism of the 1980s. In 1969, journalist Joe McGinniss published *The Selling of the President 1968*, revealing that Nixon had been packaged and sold just as commercial products were sold. Nixon critics contended that he used polling as a means of increasing presidential power and gathering ammunition to be used against Congress. Nixon was notorious for allowing only a selected few access to poll data and for hiding the source of his poll funding from members of Congress. Nixon was not above changing poll data to keep the Republican National Committee from learning what the public really thought about him. Unlike Democratic presidents who have used a number of pollsters, most Republican candidates from the 1970s to the

1990s employed either Robert Teeter or Richard Wirthlin to head up polling teams. Teeter, Gerald Ford's chief pollster, admitted that Ford was the ideal candidate because he followed advice to the letter. Teeter convinced Ford to limit his personal appearances because polls indicated they were followed by a drop in support for Ford. Teeter developed the multidimensional scaling method used to measure candidate ideology as perceived by voters.

Political candidates often blame pollsters for feeding them the wrong information when they lose elections. After Republican Robert Dole lost the 1998 presidential nomination to George H.W. Bush, he called pollster Richard Wirthlin "Dr. Worthless." Undaunted by Dole's criticism, Wirthlin became a key adviser to Ronald Reagan. As might be expected of a former actor, Reagan was particularly interested in approval ratings, seeking approval from all quarters. Whenever his approval ratings dropped, Reagan suffered. Even though he was known as the "Great Communicator," Reagan refused to give press interviews during periods of declining support.

Wirthlin began conducting polls for Reagan during the 1976 primary. He used tracking or rolling polls to measure public opinion on a daily basis. Wirthlin founded the Public Information System (PINS), which allowed him to store and analyze data from polls conducted between 1976 and 1980 to provide essential data used by the Reagan team to win the White House in 1980. Wirthlin developed what became known as the "hierarchical values map," designed to illustrate how strongly the public felt about key issues. Responding to poll data, Wirthlin advised Reagan that his best strategy was to exhibit strong leadership characteristics to remind voters that President Jimmy Carter was not viewed as a successful leader. Following Wirthlin's advice, Reagan asked voters, "Are you better off today than you were four years ago?" The strategy worked, as did the political packaging designed by Wirthlin and his colleagues.

Teeter served as director of research for Nixon and as chief pollster/strategist for Ford. Teeter also worked in both Reagan campaigns. Teeter, who used daily interviewing and rotating samples to gather information, also employed dial tuning to measure audience reaction during debates. He had a gift for identifying key groups of swing voters. In 1992, Teeter led the polling team for George H.W. Bush. Many analysts see the Bush campaign of 1992 as the epitome of successful packaging. Bush handlers successfully erased the "wimp" image with which Reagan had tarred Bush during the 1988 primaries and led him to a resounding victory over Democrat Michael Dukakis. They accomplished this through negative campaigns and labeling, partly because the Dukakis team refused to aggressively attack the Republican portrayal of Dukakis and the Democratic Party.

During the 2000 presidential election, George W. Bush admitted that he depended on polls and focus groups for information on public opinion before he announced his stand on key issues. During that campaign, the Republican National Committee paid for polling conducted by Republican pollster Matthew Dowd. Bush added pollster Jan van Lohuitzen to his polling team in 2001. In the 2004 election, the president's pollsters and strategists were kept on their toes, attempting to deal with fluctuating support that resulted from diminishing public support for the war in Iraq and public outrage over intelligence and prison abuse scandals that erupted during the campaign.

SEE ALSO

Volume 1 Left: Pollsters and Polls; Democratic Party; Clinton, William J.
Volume 2 Right: Reagan, Ronald; Bush, George H.W.; Bush, George W.

BIBLIOGRAPHY

Bruce E. Altschuler, *Keeping a Finger on the Public Pulse: Private Polling and Presidential Elections* (Greenwood, 1982); Adam J. Berinsky, *Silent Voters: Public Opinion and Political Participation in America* (Princeton University Press, 2004); Albert H. Cantril, *The Opinion Connection: Polling, Politics, and the Press* (Congressional Quarterly, 1991); Charles S. Clark, "Are Advisers and Handlers Harming Society?" *CQ Researcher* (October 4, 1996); Robert M. Eisinger, *The Evolution of Presidential Polling* (Cambridge University Press, 2003); Richard Feldstein, *Political Correctness: A Response from the Cultural Left* (University of Minnesota Press, 1997); Jack W. Germond and Jules Witcover, *Blue Smoke and Mirrors: How Reagan Won and Why Carter Lost the Election of 1980* (Viking, 1981); Diane J. Heith, "One for All: Using Focus Groups and Opinion Polls in the George H.W. Bush White House," *Congress and the President* (Spring 2003); Nick Moon, *Opinion Polls: History, Theory, and Practice* (University of Manchester Press, 1999); David W. Moore, *The Superpollsters: How They Measure and Manipulate Public Opinion in America* (Four Walls Eight Windows, 1995); Larry J. Sabato and Glenn R. Simpson, *Dirty Little Secrets: The Persistence of Corruption in American Politics* (Random House, 1996).

ELIZABETH PURDY, PH.D.
INDEPENDENT SCHOLAR

Posse Comitatus

THE POSSE COMITATUS, also known as the Sheriff's Posse Comitatus, is a conservative movement that holds that the local county is the basic, and only truly legitimate, governing unit in the United States. It traces its beliefs back to English Common Law in the Middle Ages when the shire was the core political unit and the sheriff the main law enforcement authority. The Posse Comitatus Handbook states: "in the formation of this constitutional republic, the county has always been and remains to this day, the true seat of the government for the citizens who are the inhabitants thereof. The County Sheriff is the only legal law enforcement officer in these United States." *Posse Comitatus* can be translated as "the posse [armed assembly] of the county." It receives reinforcement for its beliefs from the Posse Comitatus Act of 1878, which states in part: "It shall not be lawful to employ any part of the Army of the United States, as a posse comitatus, or otherwise, for the purpose of executing the laws." This was after the South had just endured military occupation during Reconstruction after the Civil War and the troops had been called out to enforce federal order during the strikes of 1877.

According to the Federal Bureau of Investigation (FBI), it is a "loose knit, nationwide organization founded in 1973." This current incarnation of the Posse Comitatus is interested in "limiting the capability of federal, state, and local law enforcement officers; and limiting access of all law enforcement representatives in trespassing on individual property." From 1972 to 1977, the FBI conducted an "extremist matter/white hate investigation" of the Posse Comitatus. During the 1980s, many members of the Posse reflected the growing western animosity toward "Big Government" regulation of their lives and the role that large banking institutions were having in the disappearance of the traditional midwestern family farm. Ronald Reagan capitalized on this "Sagebrush Rebellion," which helped elect him to the White House in 1980. The economic concerns of the midwestern farmer led some members of the Posse into active support of the tax resistance movement as a way of fighting back against the federal bureaucracy, which they believed was imperiling not only their homes but their way of life.

The Posse has received notoriety through the conflicts some of its members have had with law enforcement authorities, although these members in no way represent the group itself. In 1974, Thomas Stockheimer, head of the Wisconsin State Posse, was con-victed for the assault of an Internal Revenue Service officer. Fleeing the authorities, he was captured three years later in West Virginia. In 1975, the FBI reported a threat on Vice President Nelson Rockefeller, which generated the investigation of the Posse Comitatus.

In the 1980s, many midwesterners felt betrayed because their economic situation grew worse—not better—during the Reagan administration (1980–88). As a result, increasing numbers of Posse Comitatus members turned toward extremist solutions. The FBI estimated 12,000 to 50,000 Posse members in 1976, and many thousands more sympathizers. James Ridgeway notes in his *Blood in the Face* that, in 1981, some 300 Posse members attended a paramilitary training camp, while in 1982, some 40 people, led by Posse members, stopped a Wallace, Kansas, sheriff from repossessing farm equipment. In 1983, Ridgeway noted, "Springfield, Colorado was the scene of a near-riot led by Posse members trying to block an auction of a local member's farm."

In February 1983, Gordon Kahl, decorated for heroism in World War II, was leader of a Posse group in a skirmish in which two federal marshals were killed. In his own account, Kahl reported how his son Yorie had been shot by men from two cars. He wrote how he took his Mini-14 rifle out and "I shot .... until the man on the passenger side [of one car] fell, and I was able to tell he was out of the fight." Two months later, federal authorities tracked Kahl to Arkansas, where he was killed in a gun battle. It was such incidents as these that caused the FBI to mount a second investigation of the Posse "in 1980 throughout 1986 on possible domestic security/terrorism activities."

The leader of the Posse, James Wickstrom, gained 16,000 votes when he ran for Wisconsin state senator in 1980. In 1981, he served as the Posse's self-styled "National Director of Counter-Insurgency." Under Wickstrom, the Posse Comitatus has fully embraced the Christian Identity movement as its creed. The official Posse Internet site states: "this website is dedicated to the Children of YHVH (pronounced "Yahweh"); the Anglo-Saxon, Germanic, Teutonic, Scandinavian, Lombardic, Celtic peoples of the earth."

SEE ALSO

Volume 1 Left: Cultural Diversity; United States.
Volume 2 Right: Christian Identity; Xenophobia.

BIBLIOGRAPHY

"Posse Comitatus," www.foia.fbi.gov (May 2004); "Sheriff's Posse Comitatus," www.posse-comitatus.org (May 2004);

Howard L. Bushart, John R. Craig and Myra Barnes, *Soldiers of God: White Supremacists and Their Holy War for America* (Pinnacle Books, 1998); Joel Dyer, *Harvest of Rage: How Oklahoma City Is Only the Beginning* (Westview Press, 1998); Alan M. Schwartz, ed., *Danger: Extremism: The Major Vehicles and Voices on America's Far-Right Fringe* (Anti-Defamation League, 1996); James Ridgeway, *Blood in the Face: The Ku Klux Klan, Aryan Nations, and the Rise of a New White Culture* (Thunder's Mouth Press, 1995).

JOHN F. MURPHY, JR.
AMERICAN MILITARY UNIVERSITY

Prohibitionism

THE PROHIBITION movement works to outlaw the manufacture, sale, and consumption of alcoholic beverages. In the United States, the movement was responsible for the actual prohibition of alcohol by constitutional amendment from 1919 to 1933. Although Prohibition was repealed by a second constitutional amendment in the latter year, the prohibition movement has never completely ceased, and the Prohibition Party continues to field candidates for president and vice president.

The movement drew its impetus from the 19th-century liberation movements, which also included abolitionism and women's suffrage. Many people, especially women, were active in all three causes. The Women's Christian Temperance Union (WCTU) was founded in 1874 and continues to exist. Originally, the WCTU crusaded for temperance rather than prohibition. The WCTU defines temperance as moderation in all things healthful and total abstinence from all things harmful. Those who choose total abstinence are called teetotalers because when they signed the WCTU pledge, a large "T" was placed next to their name on the roster. The WCTU pledge, which people can still take today, is as follows:

> I hereby solemnly promise, God helping me, to abstain from all distilled, fermented and malt liquors, including wine, beer and hard cider, and to employ all proper means to discourage the use of and traffic in the same.

Alcohol consumption was very different before the Industrial Revolution. Before fresh, pure water was readily available, alcoholic beverages were consumed in its stead, meaning that most people were heavy drinkers by today's standards. As pure water became more prominent in everyday consumption (to the point that it is piped into every home), alcohol took on less of a role in everyday consumption and became more of an end in itself for the people who continued to drink it regularly. This was contrary to the Puritan ideals upon which colonial America was based. Although the colonists, including the Puritans themselves, drank a great deal, drunkenness was greatly frowned upon. As other beverages (besides water, also milk and modern commercial concoctions such as soft drinks) supplanted the need for daily consumption of alcohol, the argument went, alcohol was superfluous and destructive to the American way of life, because its use was by that time heavily connected with drunkenness.

The venues of drinking had also changed. One thinks of the taverns of England transplanted to colonial America. Michie Tavern, near Charlottesville, Virginia, where Thomas Jefferson and James Monroe imbibed, still stands. It was a monument for the "drys," showing the stark difference between colonial American drinking places and practices, where Alexis de Tocqueville might have observed Americans drinking in moderation and discussing the great issues of the new republic, and contemporary saloons, which were dens of vice, iniquity, drunkenness, and lawlessness. The Anti-Saloon League, in fact, had to use no exaggeration or hyperbole to attract members, because all of its members were aware of the problems of saloons created across America and in their own communities.

Twenty-six states had prohibition either through their state constitutions or by statute or referendum. Maine had been dry as early as 1858. North Dakota and Oklahoma had been dry since their respective admissions to the United States in 1889 and 1907. The problem with state-level prohibition or county-level prohibition (which still exists in many rural counties) is that it creates a traffic, if not in illegal sales and importation, at least in individual consumers traveling to "wet" states or counties to purchase or consume; it is practically a mandate to drink and drive. This was a major argument in favor of national Prohibition.

National Prohibition passed through Congress mostly because the alcohol industry did not take the Prohibition movement seriously and assumed that Prohibition would never pass. Indeed, through the largely successful efforts of the drys, through the WCTU and the Anti-Saloon League, to pass state-level prohibition and generally give liquor a bad name, the alcohol indus-

Cases of liquor from the Blue Valley Distillery Company are opened during a Prohibition arrest in Colorado.

In another bust, officials dump wine from barrels into a hole in the ground to keep it out of the public's hands.

try had a sordid reputation in the 1910s and probably could not have led an anti-Prohibition effort anyway. The industry could have been a backer of a successful semi-independent lobbying force, however. It might still have been no match for the legislative savvy of Wayne Wheeler of the Anti-Saloon League, particularly on the state level.

The movement gained the impetus it needed to succeed due to wartime conservation efforts. Maximum quantities of grains, it was argued, were needed for the war effort (World War I), and this made it all the more sensible to outlaw alcoholic beverages. It also helped the drys achieve ratification since there was little press coverage of the movement in the cities, which were the key base of wets. Indeed, the city press was quite preoccupied with the war in the 1917 to 1918 period. On December 17, 1917, the House passed the amendment by a vote of 282 to 128. It had previously been approved by the Senate by a vote of 65 to 20. Mississippi became the first state to ratify the amendment, on January 8, 1918. Nebraska became the 36th state to ratify, on January 16, 1919, making the requisite three-fourths of states to ratify the amendment. Pursuant to the text of the amendment, it took effect one year later. In six state legislatures—South Dakota, Wyoming, Utah, Idaho, Washington, and Kansas—there was not a single negative vote in either house. In the 46 state upper chambers that adopted the amendment, there were 1,310 votes in favor and 237 against. In the lower chambers, there were 3,782 votes in favor and 1,035 against. This illustrates

the broad bipartisan support for the amendment and the near-absence of organized opposition. Some have noted that rural areas (generally dry) had an advantage in state legislatures over cities (generally wet) in the era before the "reapportionment revolution" mandated that all legislative districts be of roughly equal population. (For example, in 1918, Minneapolis had eight seats in the Minnesota Senate when it deserved 11 according to a strict population allocation.) Thus, rural drys might have had a small advantage, but it was very small compared with the large margins by which Prohibition passed in the states (12 to 2 and 33 to 24 in New Jersey, then as now a very urban state).

The alcohol industry attempted an 11th-hour move to clean up saloons, to pledge they would be temples not of drunkenness but of moderation. This was an attempt to restore the tavern of the 18th century. It was too little too late. That kind of move, one author noted, might have had an effect had the industry attempted it in 1909 rather than in 1916. Congress soon passed the Volstead Act (named after its sponsor, Minnesota Congressman Andrew Volstead) to enforce Prohibition. President Woodrow Wilson vetoed the bill, citing problems with the enforcement provisions, but the veto was overridden quickly in both houses, and Prohibition took effect as scheduled on January 16, 1920.

The main problem of Prohibition was a lack of enforcement. The Volstead Act provided for the appointment of special enforcement agents but did not adequately compensate them. Many writers have noted that the low compensation for agents virtually dictated that they take bribes from violators in order to survive. The administration of President Warren G. Harding was notoriously venal, right to the top, and graft and corruption were tolerated, if not outright encouraged. Following Harding's death in 1923, the passive leadership of Calvin Coolidge provided no solution to the enforcement problem. By the time Herbert Hoover became president in 1929, the liquor wars had escalated beyond the point where a mere increase in enforcement activity would have made a difference. President Herbert Hoover coined the term *noble experiment* to describe Prohibition in 1928, but this was more an epitaph than praise for Prohibition. There was a sense in the country that Prohibition would end when the political will could be amassed to do so.

An unintended consequence of Prohibition was the removal of control of what had been a legal industry from legitimate owners and their replacement by organized crime. This affected the spirits (hard liquor) distillers more than it did breweries and vintners, because those companies were able to stay in business during Prohibition. Breweries produced near-beer (less than 0.5 percent alcohol) and vintners switched to producing grape juice and table grapes.

The alcohol industry maintains that Prohibition was repealed because it was a failure at controlling drinking and drunkenness, and it uses this argument to counter modern alcohol prohibitions. Contemporary and historical data do not bear this conclusion out. There is no question that alcohol consumption declined to a fraction of what it had been before Prohibition. Despite the many legends of speakeasies and home distilleries and international smuggling, it is clear that few people participated in these activities and their consumption under those circumstances was reasonably uncommon.

Other than the wealthy in major cities, who had greater access to alcohol, anecdotal evidence suggests that those who were heavy drinkers before 1920 managed to have only a few drinks a year during Prohibition. In fact, it was not until 1984 that per-capita alcoholic beverage consumption in the United States rose to the level it had been before Prohibition. Most alcoholism treatment facilities in the United States simply shut down during Prohibition due to a lack of business. Neighboring Canada, meanwhile, continues to have much higher levels of alcohol consumption, partly because Prohibition there effectively only took place during World War I. (Most provinces had bans on legal sale of alcohol into the 1920s, but the ban on manufac-

ture was lifted by the national government at the end of the war.)

The reason Prohibition was repealed was not that it was ineffective at restricting alcohol consumption but that people, demoralized by the Depression, were so desperate to find a way to revive the economy that they responded to the movement to repeal Prohibition as a means to provide this needed boost. (Subsequent to the election of Franklin D. Roosevelt as president, a series of economic initiatives collectively known as the New Deal were implemented, so it is uncertain what effect, if any, the repeal of Prohibition had on the economy.) One interesting facet of the repeal of Prohibition was that the 21st Amendment was ratified not by state legislatures but rather by conventions in the various states. This meant that a veritable referendum had to be held in each state, with voters choosing between a wet and a dry delegate to the state ratifying convention. Repeal was accomplished nearly as swiftly as enactment had been 15 years earlier. The 21st Amendment has had an impact beyond merely repealing Prohibition; the amendment contains a clause giving the states special jurisdiction over commerce and consumption of liquor. The Supreme Court has held that this provision of the amendment supersedes the Commerce Clause of the Constitution, which gives Congress jurisdiction over interstate commerce. (A few states tried to use the amendment in the 1980s to keep Congress from imposing a national 21-year-old drinking age, but the Court held that withholding highway funds to states that did not raise their drinking age was within the purview of Congress.)

The Prohibition Party has fielded candidates in every presidential election since 1872. Its platform for the 2004 election declares, "Alcohol is still America's number one drug problem. It is a leading cause of poverty, crime, broken homes, automobile and boating accidents, physical and sexual abuse, political corruption, mental illness, wasted manpower, disability and premature death. At least 200,000 Americans die each year because of alcohol." In addition to urging a return to Prohibition, the platform calls for the blood alcohol standard for drunk driving to be lowered to 0.05 percent from the 0.08 percent that most states now have. For the fifth consecutive election, the party's candidate was Earl Dodge of Colorado. In 2000, the party was on the ballot only in that state.

SEE ALSO

Volume 1 Left: Civil Rights; Wilson, Woodrow.
Volume 2 Right: United States; Conservatism.

BIBLIOGRAPHY
Jack S. Blocker, Jr., ed., *Alcohol, Reform and Society: The Liquor Issue in Social Context* (Greenwood Press, 1979); John Kobler, *Ardent Spirits: The Rise and Fall of Prohibition* (Putnam, 1973); David E. Kyvig, ed., *Law, Alcohol, and Order: Perspectives on National Prohibition* (Greenwood Press, 1985); Charles Merz, *The Dry Decade* (University of Washington Press, 1969).

Tony L. Hill
Massachusetts Institute of Technology

Protests

TRADITIONALLY, organized right-wing movements and protests are regarded as inherent threats to democracy due to the strong legacy of European fascism. Yet, within the larger canvas of right-wing movements, fascism is only one of the prominent themes. This suggestion even applies to Jörg Haider's Freedom Party in Austria and Gianfranco Fini's National Alliance in Italy. These are radical-right parties rather than self-acclaimed fascist ones. Fascist ideology has a specific intellectual and sociopolitical pedigree, and it is based on an integrated set of concepts combined with anti-liberalism, corporatist-statist politics, militant nationalism, and xenophobia. Therefore, it is not advisable to equate all right-wing movements, particularly those that lead to political protests and action, with fascism.

It is the more radical arm of right-wing protest movements—commonly known as right-wing extremists or radicals—that constitutes the majority of groups involved in active political protests. This group of movements, in turn, does show some commonalities with fascism, whether they are involved in direct acts of an extremist nature and political violence or not. This is due to the fact that their extremism relates to their ideological claims rather than their strategies of protest. It should also be noted that right- and left-wing protest movements exhibit many similarities.

Their tactics, organizational hierarchies, and the nature of their ultimate political objectives vis-à-vis the state apparatus and society at large can often be defined in similar terms. The main dividing line between the two tends to be the association between right-wing movements and conservatism, religiousness, patriotism, nationalism, reactionary responses to economic and political change, and racism on the one hand, and left-wing movements and liberalism, secularism, internationalism, egalitarianism, and revolutionary visions, on the other.

These differences in terms of ideological affinities most often manifest themselves in the themes that protest movements embrace as their cause. Issues such as protestation of the right to abortion, of taxes, of extended minority rights, as well as outcries for further freedom in terms of property rights or increased curtailment of immigration, are some of the typical themes that occupy right-wing protest movements, particularly in Western and industrialized or postindustrial countries. In the non-Western world, right-wing protest movements also tend to stand close to defensive nationalism, patriotism, nativism, economic Darwinism, and rigid religiosity.

However, the particular issues ailing non-Western societies have a lot to do with perceived or real Western dominance over them, and hence the actual issues guiding political action require a different reading of their ideologies. In the absence of well-functioning legal systems or uncertain political processes, the chances of radical right-wing movements seizing the state apparatus and leading to anti-democratic forms of governance are greater. The same dictum, of course, applies to radical left-wing movements. In this context, for instance, whether to include radical Islamic movements in non-Western contexts among right-wing or left-wing movements and how to deal with their political consequences are a matter of ongoing controversy.

At the extreme end, right-wing protest movements have a history of operating in such a way that overtly or covertly leads to the harassment, intimidation, or harming of select individuals, groups, or communities. Motivation by hatred is the most common cause that underlines the collective mentality characteristic of these movements. They also tend to entertain well-developed narratives of conspiracy theories that portray the participants of the group as victims, and hence call for defensive action as a means of self-protection. In general, right-wing movements of protest use populist politics as their platform of justification, and extreme or radical right-wing movements constitute no exception to this trend. Their actions aim at uniting a select group against another select, or more appropriately put, target group. Hence, right-wing protests can pose the possibility of widening social and political differences and divisions, as well as fostering cultural and political warfare.

Still, on a global scale, it is possible to identify some main trends that can lead to the categorical identification of right-wing political action. The United States functions as a template for such purposes as it has a markedly long history of right-wing politics and protest movements. The most blatant manifestations of right-wing action in the American context are centered upon the race issue. Organized violence against African American communities and individuals is a typical example of racist hatred commonly coloring the repertoire of the American radical right. Many of these activities were led by the Ku Klux Klan (KKK), which was originally formed in the 1860s in the American South in the wake of the Civil War. During the First World War years, the Klan members began to target Catholics and Jews as well as others who looked like newly arriving immigrants, in addition to blacks. Current reincarnations of the Klan and its several chapters date back to the 1960s civil rights disturbances, exhibiting a combined distaste for African Americans and Jews and organizing themselves under the banner of white supremacists. Since the 1980s, the Klan is often cited in the same breath with neo-Nazi groups. During its long history, the Klan and its affiliate groups are believed to be responsible for at least 5,000 documented lynchings across the United States.

Interestingly, when the House Un-American Activities Committee was determined to go after presumed communists during the 1950s, it refused to look at the case of the KKK. This action is highly suggestive of linkages between racism and punitive anti-communism in American politics. Another theme that binds many right-wing extremist movements together in the American as well as other contexts is that of anti-Semitism, which was eminently present during the McCarthy hearings. Many of the right-wing movements with an anti-Semitic conviction cite a document of dubious origin titled *The Protocols of the Learned Elders of Zion*, which has been in circulation since the early 1900s. The *Protocols*, first published in tzarist Russia, are a full-blown Jewish conspiracy theory, suggesting that the Jews have a well-developed plan to destroy the white, Gentile races and seize power over the world. They consist of the minutes of 24 purported meetings of anonymous Jewish leaders in their suggested quest for world domination. The currency of the *Protocols* is at such a degree that some members of the current American right-wing movements claim that the United Nations is indeed a key organ of the Jewish plans for one-world government to subject all non-Jews to servitude.

At least in America, political causes such as gun control—or rather freedom to hold firearms—make strange bedfellows. Although there is a marked tendency among right-wing groups to disparage Jews and attribute societal problems to assumed Jewish control of finances, trade, and media, during the 1990s, conservative groups such as Jews for the Preservation of Firearms Ownership (JPFO) did join forces with the gun lobby. This was due to the belief prevalent among the group members that governments have always been the most marked killers of their citizenry, and thus the ordinary citizen should be entitled to self-protection. Oddly, the JPFO takes an oppositional stance regarding the Anti-Defamation League of B'nai B'rith, which has traditionally been the most recognized defender of the Jewish faith and rights in North America.

STRATEGIES AND TACTICS

Openly racist organizations, such as the KKK, exhibit a semi-organizational structure and coordinate their actions at a nationwide spectrum. Right-wing groups like the Skinheads, on the other hand, are gang-type movements, which preach an entire lifestyle bordering on regular engagement with criminal activities without necessarily endorsing it through organizational activities. They do, however, hold national and international conventions. Their origins can be traced back to groups such as the Silver Shirts in the 1930s and the Christian Defense League of the 1970s in the North American context. They target identifiable minorities, and unlike the KKK, their appeal is veritably international. In effect, their presence is felt particularly strongly across Western Europe. Furthermore, despite their small numbers, they account for a very large number of violent and deadly incidences.

In the American context, Skinhead leaders such as Tom Metzger and Richard Butler are effective ideologues and preachers of the supremacist cause in terms of providing clear directions for action for the new recruits. Skinheads operate in a manner similar to Nazi Storm Troopers (known as the SS) and use some of their insignia and dress codes. They entertain territorial imperatives in the sense that they desire to create all-white enclaves in preparation for an Armageddon-like total war.

A common characteristic of the majority of right-wing protest movements in the United States and elsewhere is the self-identification of their participants as "minutemen." The term suggests that the participants of the protests can be ready at a moment's notice, as they claim to act out of inner belief and conviction rather than following a politically organized cause. A typical example laying this claim is that of Christian Identity groups particularly active in the area of anti-abortion protests and anti-homosexual protests in the name of preservation of family values. Many of these groups are non-specific in terms of their denominational alliances, and yet they all claim a superior religious ethics related to Christianity. There are hundreds of such small groupings scattered across the geography of North America. The formal origins of at least some of them go back to the writings of Edward Hine, in particular his *Identification of the British Nation with Lost Israel* (1871). Hine theorized contemporary white Christian populations as descendants of the Anglo-Saxon-Teuton whites, pointing out that these are the true people of the Covenant. Accordingly, Anglo-Saxons (in particular Nordic, Aryan, and British), and not the Jews, are the real chosen people of God.

CITIZEN MILITIAS

Since the mid-1990s, a new type of right-wing movement emerged on the North American scene: citizen militias. The central tenet of this movement is patriotism. However, similar to that of Christian Identity groups, the militia movement in general tends to avoid appropriation of particular stigmas or a centralized organizational structure.

The movement tends to table open-ended and yet alarming questions such as "Do you know what really is happening to your country? Who's causing it? Can you do something about it?" Composed loosely of organized paramilitary groups of mostly young to middle-aged white men, this movement definitely has a military edge, as they are preparing for the worst. They feel wronged by their own government, haunted by the economy, and mistrust the people in power to a heightened degree. They wish to reclaim their inalienable rights and to stand against the official misuse of power. In their survivalist call, they are known to organize paramilitary training camps, stockpile food and arms, excel in security systems, and have their own intelligence networks.

Canada, compared with the United States, at first appears to be a "peaceful kingdom," as Stephen Scheinberg put it (1997). At least since the 1970s, it has been characterized by pluralism and multiculturalism. Yet, it has its own fair share of right-wing politics and action. Canadian neo-Nazi groups are well-known for their steady engagement in violent protests. Furthermore, they have been singularly and internationally successful in their large-scale propaganda efforts for the denial of the Holocaust. In addition, the Quebec separatism issue brought to the surface many of the silenced prejudices

of majority populations: when the separatists lost the vote in the 1995 referendum, the blame was put on the shoulders of the ethnic minorities in the francophone province.

The minorities issue is indeed the one that constitutes the determining color of European right-wing movements, France and United Kingdom being the prime cases. Both countries have established democratic traditions and have been hosting growing minority communities as their empires shrunk and finally became defunct after World War II. Both states have been facing large-scale and populist reactionary movements that voice resentment of at least some sections of their populace regarding the issue of multi-ethnicity, religious and linguistic diversity, economic-resource limitations, and unemployment. Similar concerns also plague Dutch, Scandinavian, and to a certain degree Mediterranean polities within the larger context of the European Union. With the latest enlargement of the Union (2004), there are also issues related to the tensions between Europeans, who live east and west of the proverbial Elbe River. Eastern Europeans, as they enter the Union, bring their own problems related to racism, xenophobia, anti-Semitism, as well as unrealistic expectations from liberalism into Europe. In addition, they face discrimination and fear themselves as the presumably backward people of the continent. The resultant tensions are expected to lead to further protests with protectionist, nativist, and racial undertones.

INTELLECTUAL TRADITIONS

In conclusion, the phenomenon of right-wing politics and protest must be regarded as a movement with international reach and global trends. Although the groups espousing radical right-wing ideologies and putting them into action do so within the boundaries of nation-states, there is a wide array of international and historical links that create parallel movements. Right-wing protests do not develop in isolation from each other, at least on the ideological platform. The assorted representatives of the movements' leaders, such as David Duke, Ernst Zundel, Tom Metzger, and Vladimir Zhirinovsky, all draw inspiration from similar intellectual traditions. Each society's right-wing protestors and ideologues are likely to find sympathizers of their cause among their neighbors. French ideologue Jean-Marie Le Pen's success in the 1983 local elections was followed by a similar success story in the 1994 Euro-elections when the Front National won 10 of the 81 French seats. Subsequently, in Germany, the Republikaners fashioned their party politics following the Le Pen model of gradual electoral success. In the 1990s, in turn, the Republic Czechoslovak Republican Party claimed to follow the German model for republicanism. In the American context, Duke also openly referred to Le Pen's success as a key inspiration for the formation of the Populist Party, which then laid the way for his election as a Louisiana state legislator.

In addition to the influence of political strategies across the national borders, there is now a recognized international trade of racist, anti-Semitic, supremacist, and anti-abortionist material facilitated by organized or semi-organized groups engaged in right-wing politics. Gary Lauck, operating out of Germany, is the largest international supplier of neo-Nazi propaganda, and he provides publications in 10 different languages. There are telephone "hotlines" that provide recorded messages of heavy ideological content. In British Columbia, Tom Metzger's White Aryan Resistance runs one of Vancouver's most used hotlines for right-wing propaganda. There are also international workshops, consortia, and conventions that bring leaders of the radical right together, in addition to the electronic media and the vast array of communication and information sources offered by it.

In this context, the widespread upsurge of protest movements and political action from the right is of little surprise to the students of the field. Right-wing movements traditionally had a strong populist agenda, and flourished among groups who felt they were wrong or left out by the system, or who felt they were the true owners of the land, culture, and society that are then invaded and forced to change by strangers and foreigners.

The internationalization of such worries and fears added a new dimension to these protest movements and provided a common arsenal of strategies, tactics, and ideological turning points.

Globalization, with all its uneven results, further added to the misery of disgruntled groups as well as those who do not wish to share or give up their privileges. The result is an increasingly dynamic and rich global geography of right-wing political action, which cannot be treated as the total sum of odd outbursts of self-righteousness or radical flair.

SEE ALSO

Volume 1 Left: Protests; Liberalism; France; Germany; United Kingdom.
Volume 2 Right: Immigration Restriction; Conservatism; France; Germany; United Kingdom; Ku Klux Klan.

BIBLIOGRAPHY

J. Coates, *Armed and Dangerous: The Rise of the Survivalist Right* (Hill and Wang, 1987); Fred Cook, *Ku Klux Klan: America's Recurring Nightmare* (Julian Messmer, 1981); Kathy Marks, *Faces of Right-Wing Extremism* (Branden Publishing, 1996); Stephen Scheinberg, "Canada: Right-Wing Extremism in the Peaceable Kingdom," *The Extreme Right: Freedom and Security at Risk*, Aurel Brown and Stephen Scheinberg, eds. (Westview Press, 1997); Michi Ebata, "The Internationalization of the Extreme Right," *The Extreme Right: Freedom and Security at Risk* (Westview Press, 1997); R. Ginzburg, *100 Years of Lynchings* (Black Classics Press, 1998).

NERGIS CANEFE
YORK UNIVERSITY, CANADA

The Right

R

Rand, Ayn (1905–1982)

BORN ALISSA ROSENBAUM into a middle-class family in St. Petersburg, Russia, in 1925 she immigrated to the United States, where she achieved success and fame. She is best known for objectivism, which rests on reason and fact and emphasizes individualism, limited government, and classical liberal protection of life, liberty, and property. She wrote both fiction and nonfiction works.

The communist Russian Revolution of 1917 and the subsequent civil war destroyed middle-class life in Russia and forced the family to the Crimea for a time, but Rand returned to Petrograd (the new Soviet name for St. Petersburg) to attend the University of Petrograd, where she studied history, philosophy, and literature. Her studies of American history and politics and the excesses of communism led her to admire American individualism, energy, and optimism as contrasts to collectivism, gloom, and decay. After graduation from Petrograd in 1924 and a year in the State Institute for Cinema Arts studying screenwriting, she left for America in 1925, ostensibly to visit relatives. In the United States, she would be free to write what she chose. She studied English in Chicago, Illinois, then moved to Hollywood, California, where she met movie director Cecil B. DeMille, who gave her a job as extra on *King of Kings*, and writer Frank O'Connor, whom she married

in 1929. Rand and O'Connor remained married until his death in 1979.

Working for DeMille helped Rand finance her writing. She also worked nonwriting jobs. Finally, in 1932, she sold her first screenplay, *Red Pawn*, to Universal Studios. That year her first stage play also debuted, *Night of January 16th*. She was also working on *We the Living* (1936), which was rejected for several years because its theme was the brutality of Soviet life, and the 1930s was a time when many American intellectuals, including her reviewers, were either communists or admirers of the Soviet experiment.

While *We the Living* was being rejected, in 1935, Rand began work on *The Fountainhead* (1943), which focused on individualist ethics—independence and integrity. Howard Roark, the hero, embodies heroic and principled living. Again the publishers were reluctant, with 12 rejecting the manuscript, and reviewers and intellectuals were negative. The novel became a bestseller despite reviewer opinion. It made Rand famous and financially independent. In 1949, Rand wrote the screenplay for a Gary Cooper and Patricia Neal movie for Warner Brothers.

Her magnum opus, *Atlas Shrugged*, began taking form in 1946, while Rand was working part-time as a screenwriter. In 1951, she moved to New York and worked on the novel full-time. The novel appeared in 1957. It is a well-developed expression of her political and ethical philosophy, objectivism, which defines "man as a heroic being, with his own happiness as the moral purpose of his life, with productive achievement as his noblest activity, and reason as his only absolute," expresssed one commentator. The book was a bestseller, and Rand wrote no more fiction although, she regarded herself as a novelist rather than a philosopher.

The two novels attracted a following more for their philosophy than for their artistic qualities. Psychologist Nathaniel Branden and economist Alan Greenspan and other early followers convinced Rand to turn to nonfiction as a way of developing her philosophy systematically. She wrote and lectured between 1962 and 1976 on what became known as objectivism. Her articles appeared in *The Objectivist Newsletter* (1962 to 1965), *The Objectivist* (1966 to 1971), and *The Ayn Rand Letter* (1971 to 1976). The essays were the basis for nine nonfiction books that developed the philosophy and applied it to social issues. Book titles include: *The Virtue of Selfishness*; *Capitalism: The Unknown Ideal*; *Introduction to Objectivist Epistemology*; and *The Romantic Manifesto*.

Her most important professional relationship was with Branden, later to achieve fame as leader of the self-esteem movement. His Nathaniel Branden Institute was a major objectivist institution in the 1960s. He wrote and lectured on objectivism until 1968, when he and Rand had a professional and personal disagreement that severed the relationship and halted the growth of both his institute and the objectivist movement. Rand remained active until 1976; from that point on she reduced her workload as her husband's health deteriorated. She died in 1982 in New York City.

Rand advocated rational self-interest and self-responsibility rather than selflessness, the traditional ethical virtue, as the basis for a successful society. She espoused classical liberalism, which emphasized that freedom to define oneself free of government intervention or obligation toward others was a virtue. Her objectivist liberalism is better known currently as libertarianism.

All of Rand's books are still in print, with 20 million copies sold and hundreds of thousands selling each year. A survey in the 1990s by the Book of the Month Club and Library of Congress found *Atlas Shrugged* second only to the Bible in influencing respondents. Objectivism remains alive in the Cato Institute, the Ayn Rand Institute, and the Objectivist Center.

SEE ALSO

Volume 1 Left: Socialism; Russian Revolution; Communism. *Volume 2 Right:* Libertarianism; Capitalism; United States.

BIBLIOGRAPHY

The Atlas Society, "Rand and Her Work, 2001" www.atlassociety.com (June 2004); Nathaniel Branden, *Judgment Day: My Life with Ayn Rand* (Houghton Mifflin, 1989); Jon Dorbolo, "Great Philosophers: Ayn Rand," http://oregonstate.edu (June 2004); Objectivist Center, "All about Ayn Rand," and "What is Objectivism?" www.ayn-rand.com (June 2004); Michael Paxton, *Ayn Rand: A Sense of Life* (Gibbs Smith, 1998).

JOHN BARNHILL, PH.D.
INDEPENDENT SCHOLAR

Reagan, Ronald (1911–2004)

RONALD REAGAN ENTERED politics after a long and successful career as a film and television actor. He would be a famous man even if he had never been elected president. Ronald Wilson Reagan was born in Tampico, Illinois, on February 6, 1911, the younger of the two sons of John E. Reagan and Nelle Clyde (Wilson) Reagan. Reagan graduated from Dixon (Illinois) High School in 1928 and went to Eureka College, putting himself through by washing dishes at the women's dormitory, and graduating in 1932 with a degree in sociology and economics. He went to work as a sports announcer for an Iowa radio station, and it was at this time that he honed the storytelling skills that earned him as president the nickname "the great communicator." Instead of seeing the game, Reagan only got the play-by-play as it came over the ticker tape, and he had to take a telegraphic report and add description so that, for example, "Ruth flies to short" became "Babe Ruth steps up to the plate. The crowd roars its approval. Here's the pitch. Strike one. The crowd is hissing and booing. Here's the pitch. He hits. Ott is under it. Out!"

In 1937, Reagan became a contract player for Warner Brothers and shortly made his debut in *Love Is on the Air*. He became a notable star with his performance in *Knute Rockne: All-American*, which added the phrase "Win one for the Gipper" to the lexicon of Reaganisms. His most notable film was *Kings Row*, where he played a surgery patient who became paralyzed. This led him to utter the line "Where's the rest of me?" which became the title of his first autobiography. In 1942, he entered the army cavalry, reportedly aided in part by cheating on the eye test. He spent the war making movies for the U.S. Army. One of the most notable, and far more than a mere training film, was Irving Berlin's all-soldier show *This Is the Army*. After the war, Reagan continued to make pictures commercially, and he was also active in the Screen Actors Guild and served five terms as its president. He was the only U.S. president to have led a labor union. He worked for General Electric Company as a spokesperson and the host of the company-sponsored television series *G.E. Theatre*.

The General Electric association was a conservatizing force on Reagan, putting him into close association with the moneyed Republican elite, something missing in most of his Hollywood associations. (The entertainment industry remains primarily a left-leaning culture.) In 1962, Reagan switched from the Democratic to the Republican Party. His first major foray into politics was making a TV commercial for Barry Goldwater's 1964 Republican presidential campaign. *Where's the Rest of Me?* was published the next year. Reagan also ended his acting career, wrapping up a three-year run as host of the long-running *Death Valley Days*; his final film, *The Killers*, was supposed to have been the first made-for-TV movie, but it was deemed too violent for the small screen and was released in theatres instead. It was Reagan's only bad-guy role.

Reagan was elected governor of California in 1966, defeating Democratic incumbent Edmund G. "Pat" Brown, who had defeated Richard Nixon four years earlier. Reagan tested the waters for the presidential nomination in 1968, but he was clearly not ready for the national stage and won no primaries. He took a hard line against his state's share of civil unrest during the civil rights, women's, and anti-war protest movements in the late 1960s and early 1970s, and was reelected governor in 1970.

Reagan declined to seek gubernatorial reelection in 1974. He was succeeded by Edmund G. "Jerry" Brown, Jr. He sought the presidential nomination again in 1976, challenging the incumbent Republican, President Gerald R. Ford, who had become president upon Richard Nixon's resignation two years earlier. It was a hard-fought contest, although Ford maintained momentum throughout the nomination campaign. Reagan was forced to announce his running mate in advance of the convention. This is generally regarded as a sign of weakness. The running mate, U.S. Senator Richard S. Schweiker of Pennsylvania, then part of the liberal wing of the Republican Party, probably did not make a large difference in the nomination battle. Ford was nominated on the first ballot but went on to lose a narrow election to Democrat Jimmy Carter in which Ford's pardon of Nixon and handling of the economy were much at issue.

Reagan never stopped running after 1976, spending time helping Republicans all over the country raise money for their races. When the 1980 nomination race came, Reagan was ready to cash in his many markers, and he had broad national support for the nomination, while his little-known and underfunded challengers (including George H.W. Bush) had much narrower bases of support. Reagan easily won the nomination. He chose Bush as his running mate. It was a bad year to be Jimmy Carter running for reelection. The economy was in even worse shape than when Carter had beat Ford, and 53 Americans were being held hostage in Iran and Carter had been unable to free them—having suffered the embarrassment of a failed covert hostage rescue mission.

If Carter had any chance of winning, he forfeited it by debating Reagan on television the week before the election. Carter was no match for Reagan's oratory, well polished by decades as a performer. Reagan won handily, although it was no landslide. Carter was further hindered by the presence on the ballot of a former Republican, John Anderson, who ran as an independent and won a critical slice of the usually Democratic vote in major urban areas. While Carter worked furiously to have the hostages released before Reagan took office, their release was delayed until only minutes after Reagan was sworn in. At 69, Reagan became the oldest president at inauguration and a few months later became the oldest president in history.

Reagan and his ideological allies, who wanted less government intrusion into people's lives, at least in the economic sphere, took Washington, D.C., by storm. Although the House of Representatives was still under Democratic control, Reagan was able to prevail and secure passage of broad tax and spending cuts. But the honeymoon was brief. Reagan and three others were wounded by gunfire while Reagan and his entourage were leaving a hotel on March 30, 1981. An armor-piercing bullet lodged within inches of Reagan's heart, but emergency surgery was successful, and Reagan was released less than two weeks later. He was the only president to survive being shot while in office. The assailant, John W. Hinckley, Jr., who apparently acted to impress a film actress, was unexpectedly found not guilty by reason of insanity the next year and committed to a mental institution. Also that year, Reagan appointed the first woman to the Supreme Court and squared off against the air traffic controllers' union during an unauthorized strike.

Chief Justice Warren E. Burger (center, right) administers the oath of office to Ronald Reagan (center, left) in the rotunda of the U.S. Capitol for Reagan's second presidential term, beginning January 21, 1985.

The economy soured in Reagan's second year as president, and Republicans suffered losses in the midterm elections. By 1983, the economy had recovered, and Reagan was able to capitalize on such issues as the Soviet Union's downing of a Korean airliner and an invasion of Grenada to repel a communist regime. In the 1984 election, the Democrats were divided, and even when the Democratic nominee, former Vice President Walter F. Mondale, picked the first woman to run for vice president, Geraldine A. Ferraro, it provided only a short-term boost. Mondale's campaign was soon mired in issues related to Ferraro's personal finances. Reagan, meanwhile, had an excellent campaign, and faltered only briefly after his first debate with Mondale, where he provided a few rambling and incoherent answers. This raised the "age" issue, where the specter of a 73-year-old chief executive suddenly seemed troubling. Reagan defused the issue in the second debate with a well-timed one-liner. He remarked that he would not try to score political points on the age issue by raising his opponent's "youth and inexperience." (The point was

better as a one-liner than the subject of serious discussion: Mondale had served 20 years as an elected official to Reagan's 12, and at 57 was older than the average new president.) Reagan won the biggest landslide in the electoral college in history, carrying every state except Mondale's home state of Minnesota and the District of Columbia.

Reagan was frequently hindered as a lame duck in his second term. He made little progress on his agenda in 1985–86, and Democrats regained control of the Senate in the 1986 election. The year was also one of great tragedy, with the explosion of the space shuttle *Challenger*, several terrorist attacks in the Middle East, and the crash of a U.S. troop transport plane in Newfoundland and Labrador. That year had opened badly for Reagan personally with a diagnosis of colon cancer, prompting invocation of the 25th Amendment for the first time.

Reagan fared better in the area of arms control, when he and new Soviet leader Mikhail Gorbachev practically decided to do away with nuclear weapons. In late 1986, a major scandal erupted when it was disclosed that the administration had made secret arms sales to Iran, whose proceeds were directed to rebel fighters in Nicaragua. For once, it seemed, the "Teflon" president finally had something that would stick to him, although the inquiry failed to implicate Reagan personally. In 1987, Reagan saw two Supreme Court nominations go down to defeat as the Senate rejected Robert Bork as too conservative, and the nomination of Douglas Ginsberg was withdrawn after the nominee revealed he had been a habitual marijuana user.

Reagan took a hard conservative line with the Soviet Union, first famously calling it the "Evil Empire," and vastly increasing the U.S. defense budget. Then, when the Soviet economy couldn't keep up with a renewed arms race, Reagan encouraged Gorbachev in his liberalization policies, which eventually led to the dissolution of the Soviet Union. He was often accorded the credit for "winning the Cold War," but other commentators point to a host of factors that also were responsible for communism's defeat after 70 years.

Reagan's presidency was best encapsulated by the buoyant feeling he provided for many after too many years of gloom and bad news. Reagan exuded a carefree approach to office, not caring if anyone faulted him for working eight-hour days and taking month-long vacations at his ranch near Santa Barbara, California. (His predecessor was known for working 16 hours a day, six days a week.) Despite his many political failures and the second term being full of setbacks, Reagan left office personally more popular than any president since modern polling began. Reagan was always more popular with the general public than with elites. To some extent, Reagan's career as an entertainer and as a passive person whose role had usually been reading someone else's words colored the public perception of him, at least as told through the voice of the news media. Many of the popular biographies published during and soon after his presidency highlighted this aspect of the man in their titles, among them, *The Reagan Presidency: An Actor's Finest Performance*; *The Acting President*; *President Reagan: The Role of a Lifetime*; *Make Believe*; and *Sleepwalking Through History*.

Reagan married Sarah Jane Fulks, an actor whose stage name was Jane Wyman, in Glendale, California, on January 24, 1940. Reagan is the only president to have been divorced. He married Nancy Davis, who was born Anne Frances Robbins, on March 4, 1952, in Los Angeles, California. Reagan retired to the wealthy and exclusive Bel-Air neighborhood of Los Angeles. He did some speaking when he first left office. A tour of Japan was particularly profitable. Reagan pocketed $2 million in speaking fees, compared with $1.6 million salary for eight years as president. His last public appearance was at the funeral of Richard Nixon in April 1994.

In November 1994, it was revealed that Reagan was suffering from Alzheimer's disease and went into seclusion as his health deteriorated for the next 10 years. Reagan technically died from pneumonia at his Los Angeles home on June 5, 2004. He had lived longer than any other president. June 10, 2004, was a national day of mourning, on which all federal offices (including post offices) and many banks were closed. This was an unprecedented honor for a former president, although some presidents who died in office were so honored. Reagan was buried at his presidential library in Simi Valley, California.

SEE ALSO

Volume 1 Left: Carter, James E.; Democratic Party; United States.
Volume 2 Right: Bush, George H.W.; Thatcher, Margaret; New Right; Nixon, Richard M.

BIBLIOGRAPHY

Lou Cannon, *President Reagan: The Role of a Lifetime* (Simon and Schuster, 1991); Jane Mayer and Doyle McManus, *Landslide: The Unmaking of the President, 1984–88* (Houghton Mifflin, 1988); Edmund Morris, *Dutch: A Memoir of Ronald Reagan* (Random House, 1999); Ronald Reagan with Richard G. Hubler, *Where's the Rest of Me?* (Duell, Sloan, and Pierce, 1965); Ronald Reagan, *An American Life: The Autobiography* (Simon and Schuster, 1990); Bob Schieffer and Gary Paul Gates, *The Acting President* (Dutton, 1989); Tony Thomas, *The Films of Ronald Reagan* (Citadel Press, 1980);

TONY L. HILL
MASSACHUSETTS INSTITUTE OF TECHNOLOGY

Realpolitik

REALISM OR REALPOLITIK is the school of thought that posits that international relations are governed by power and national interest, not morality. The personal relationships of politicians and diplomats are irrelevant in the realist view, for nations base their decisions on the demands of national interest, not on the basis of friendship. The goal of international relations, from a realist perspective, is to seek a balance of power rather than the triumph of ideals. One of the most famous and earliest examples of a consciously realist diplomacy is presented in the fifth book of the Greek historian Thucydides' *The History of the Peloponnesian War*. In the so-called Melian Dialogue, presented by Thucydides, the Athenians memorably told the Melians that the strong would do what they wished and the weak would have to endure. In 416 B.C.E., the Athenians invaded Melos, massacred the adult male population, and enslaved the rest of the population. *The Prince*, written in 16th-century Italy by Niccolò Machiavelli, offers another blueprint for anyone seeking to practice Realpolitik. Machiavelli advocated ruthlessness in the pursuit of power and advised that rulers are better off if feared by their citizens rather than loved. He also advised readers that a prince should devote himself above all else to preparing for war. In the early 19th century, Prussian general and military scholar Carl von Clausewitz wrote his treatise *On War*, which offered another famous realist proscription. For Clausewitz, war was an instrument of statecraft, or, as he phrased it, "a continuation of policy by other means."

European leaders have often employed realism when conducting their diplomacy. During the Thirty Years' War, French leader Cardinal Richelieu subsidized the army of Protestant King Gustavus Adolphus of Sweden, and later made an alliance with Sweden in order to achieve a balance of power in Europe. In the 20th century, a superb example of cynical Realpolitik was the Nazi-Soviet Pact. By that 1939 nonaggression agreement, Nazi Germany and the Soviet Union agreed not to attack each other but to invade and absorb Poland.

Realism has enjoyed a checkered history in the United States. As American policymakers discovered during the Vietnam War, it is difficult for America to sustain a strong moral commitment to a war to maintain a balance of power or for reasons of national interest. In both the 1991 and 2003 invasions of Iraq, large numbers of Americans vocally opposed conflicts waged in America's national interest.

The Persian Gulf War of 1990–91 offers superb insight into America's difficult relationship with realism. American dependence on Middle Eastern oil meant that Saddam Hussein's invasion of Kuwait was intolerable to America. Nevertheless, President George H.W. Bush conceived of the war as a struggle against aggression rather than one waged in defense of America's national interest. Even in defense of so valuable a commodity as oil, America would not tolerate a conflict waged along realist lines. Few American politicians

clearly identify themselves as realists. Theodore Roosevelt employed a kind of modified realist view. He acted ruthlessly to foment revolution in Panama in order to be able to build the Panama Canal; building a canal that would allow the American ships to move rapidly from the Atlantic Ocean to the Pacific Ocean without sailing around South America was clearly in America's national interest. Yet Roosevelt's strong ideals and moral sense leavened his pursuit of the balance of power.

Only during the presidency of Richard M. Nixon would realism enjoy a brief heyday in American foreign policy. Nixon and Henry Kissinger, who served as national security adviser and, later, as secretary of state, pursued a policy known as détente. That approach to foreign policy sought to treat the Soviet Union as a permanent member of the international scene and to seek peaceful cooperation and accommodation with the Soviets, rather than confrontation. Nixon's dramatic opening to China in 1972 was also clearly part of a strategy aimed at a balance of power.

Both the left and the right criticize realism for its amorality. During the 1980s, Ronald Reagan abandoned the realism of previous Republican Presidents Nixon and Gerald R. Ford, and pursued a foreign policy based on pressing for the exportation of American ideals and on condemning the Soviet Union as "the face of evil in the modern world." Rather than seeking to balance Soviet power around the globe, Reagan modified the approach, backing American ideals with military and economic power and pushing the Soviet Union to collapse. This American combination of realism and idealism proved successful for the United States in the Cold War.

SEE ALSO

Volume 1 Left: United States; Kennedy, John F.
Volume 2 Right: Reagan, Ronald; Nixon, Richard M.; Bush, George H.W.

BIBLIOGRAPHY

Carl von Clausewitz, *On War*, Michael Howard and Peter Paret, eds., trans. (Princeton University Press, 1976); Jonathan Haslam, *No Virtue Like Necessity: Realist Thought in International Relations since Machiavelli* (Yale University Press, 2002); Henry Kissinger, *Diplomacy* (Simon & Schuster, 1994); Niccolò Machiavelli, *The Prince: A New Translation*, Harvey C. Mansfield, Jr., trans. (University of Chicago Press, 1985); John J. Mearsheimer, *The Tragedy of Great Power Politics* (Norton, 2001); Hans Morgenthau, *Politics among Nations: The Struggle for Power and Peace* (Knopf, 1948); Thucydides, *The*

Landmark Thucydides: A Comprehensive Guide to the Peloponnesian War, Robert B. Strassler, trans. (The Free Press, 1996).

MITCHELL MCNAYLOR
OUR LADY OF THE LAKE COLLEGE

Religion

RELIGION CAN BE DEFINED very generally as a set of metaphysical beliefs and ritualistic practices shared by members of a given community regarding one or more deities or supernatural forces. The general philosophical function of religion lies in its ability to provide meaning to existence and explain the origins and mysteries of life and death. To expand on this definition would require some metaphysical considerations. However, another way to view religion is from the sociological and anthropological perspective, since from these areas of study, religion is seen as an empirical experience with its rituals, institutions, locations, symbols, creeds, and visual forms, which can be more directly accessed. From a political perspective, however, religion becomes interesting due to its ideological character, since it is a set of beliefs that do not remain abstract but are immersed in historical and cultural contexts.

All things considered, religion is a set of beliefs that has motivated social action thus it has been shown to be an important ideological tool in politics, which can be used in several forms to promote given partisan or political views. Therefore, religion can be an instrument for both the political left and right. There is a long history of religious involvement in what could be considered leftist issues. However, attention will be given here to the interface between religion and the right, especially in the United States.

EARLY RELIGIOSITY

The United States was initially settled by religious groups seeking to organize a pure society, untouched by what they considered the perversity of the Church of England. Strongly influenced by John Calvin, the Puritans saw themselves as a chosen people, and their covenant theology defined the Puritan settlements as a chosen land—in reference to the promised land in the Old Testament. However, due to a series of contradictions within their theology, the need to prioritize survival strategies in a harsh new land, and the fact that

people lived on farms far from one another, less theological fervor was found after the second and third generations, although most people still attended church.

The first Great Awakening of the 18th century revitalized the churches and brought the belief that religious experience was a "new birth" inspired by the preaching of the word. George Whitefield and other religious men preached emotionally charged sermons as they went through the colonies. This evangelical spirit was opposed by some churches and split others who criticized the anti-rationalism and overt emotionalism of the movement. The antithesis to evangelicalism was deism, which embraced enlightenment rationality, rejected the divinity of Christ, and emphasized morality. Some of the prominent Founding Fathers were deists, such as Thomas Jefferson, Benjamin Franklin, and John Adams, who carefully worded the Constitution and the Bill of Rights to reflect a rational separation of church and state. Both deism and evangelicalism helped to provide justification for the American Revolution by considering the American design of civil and religious liberties to be a "light to the nations" against oppression and ignorance. However, deism eventually fell under the increasing and widespread popularity of the evangelical movement.

With the advent of civil religion, patriotism and religious beliefs were merged. As Alexis de Tocqueville, in his travels through the United States in the early 1830s, expressed, religion in the United States was "indispensable to the maintenance of republican institutions." A second wave of revivalist movements called the second Great Awakening in the 19th century occurred as the United States was expanding west. While the revivals of the western frontier were marked by emotional preaching, the eastern revivals were more subdued and had a definite social character. Out of the second Great Awakening, numerous mission societies arose, such as the American Bible Society, as well as those aimed at social concerns including abolition and temperance. The idea of Manifest Destiny further emphasized the idea of a chosen people and provided justification for westward expansion of the United States by revitalizing the sense of national purpose and mission. Extending democracy and freedom was closely linked to religious views, which held the United States up as a nation chosen by God.

In general, this sense of mission, mixed with patriotism and immersed in the particular context of the period, provided the necessary background for a number of political actions, such as the Civil War (for both the North and the South), abolition, the temperance movement, the women's movements, as well as the later civil rights movement. However, the early Puritan and the revivalist legacies are particularly important to understanding the way in which religion in the United States became involved with the politics of the right. These early moments and experiences paved the way for the rise and influence of fundamentalism and evangelicalism in the beginning of the 20th century.

As conservatism and the right gained force in the United States during the 20th century, religion also played a significant role. The traditional character of the church as a social institution with a pragmatic nature became indispensable for the conservative movement.

PROTESTANTISM

The Protestant tenets that hold that the Bible is the sole source of God's word and that the individual conscience is a valid interpreter of the scripture, as well as the idea of a priesthood of believers that gives autonomy to each person unlike the rigid hierarchies of the Catholic Church, have resulted in differing interpretations of the Bible and the fragmentation of Protestantism into numerous denominations. However, in the United States, fundamentalism and evangelicalism represent theological trends, which have been appropriated by right-wing politics.

Fundamentalism has its roots in the revivalism of the 18th and 19th centuries and is a term used to denote a religious doctrine based on the fundamentals of the Old Testament and the Ten Commandments. Fundamentalism emerged in opposition to liberal theology and as a critique to modernism. When liberal Christian scholars began to study the Bible as a historical document in an attempt to understand the context in which it was written, fundamentalists charged that this tendency questioned divine inspiration and biblical inerrancy, which they held as basic truths. Between 1909 and 1915, *The Fundamentals* was published to spell out the basics to which Christians should adhere. One of the principal issues of fundamentalism has been its opposition to the teaching of evolution and its millenarianism or the hope for the immanent Second Coming of Jesus Christ—after which there would be 1,000 years of peace.

Fundamentalism first became part of a political movement in 1925 when William Jennings Bryan who had campaigned against evolutionary theory throughout the country, participated as prosecutor in a trial against John Scopes for teaching evolution. The media fiercely ridiculed the trial and the movement was largely

discredited. However, fundamentalism later emerged in the 20th century in a far more sophisticated way. It was in this period that it established new institutions, schools, seminaries, publishing houses, journals, and missionary boards, using the mass media for the expression of their ideas. Its rhetoric has been progressively appropriated by conservative politicians who also consider themselves the guardians of cultural values, religion, and tradition in the country.

In turn, evangelicalism developed a form of revivalist theology that gave more value to the intensely personal accounts of the Gospel passages, emphasizing that true religious knowledge could be acquired only through faith and personal salvation. Based on this belief and in the consideration of the impurity of the secular world, evangelicals took over the radical mission of propagating piety and public morality. They considered themselves the moral keepers of the original culture of the country, as they started campaigns against corruption, lack of hygiene in public facilities, prostitution, and alcoholism in the late 19th and early 20th centuries.

This shows already the necessary link between Christian faith and social action, but it should be noted that this action had different consequences according to the different theoretical and political bases upon which it rests. Thus, the orientation for evangelical social action was a conservative radical approach opposed to liberal social gospel, which was influenced by socialist thought, labor movements, and a community, rather than strictly individual ethics.

The evangelical confessional action had its basis in an educational and ethical system, which was internalized in axioms, and this explains the initiative of many churches and confessions in founding schools or maintaining colleges. With their emphasis on missionary expansion and conversion of new national and ethnic groups that had immigrated to the United States, evangelicals experienced extraordinary growth. Different from fundamentalists, evangelicals were open to religious and political tolerance, advocating civil obedience and giving value to the "American way of life." But both movements, fundamentalism and evangelicalism, were related to the strategy of conservatism against liberalism. As a result, they strongly opposed liberal "mainline Protestantism" and other religious systems, including Catholicism and Judaism.

THE NEW CHRISTIAN RIGHT

The New Christian Right began as a coalition of religious interest groups organized around such associations as the Moral Majority, the Christian Voice, and the Religious Roundtable in the 1980s. Jerry Falwell, Pat Robertson, and others started television programs and created the Christian Broadcasting Network (CBN) and later the Divinity Broadcasting Network.

The New Christian Right had a largely political character and took up issues that were considered to be eroding the moral fabric of the nation. They supported the pro-life movement against abortion and a traditional family role for women. Other issues included the censorship of pornography and opposition to divorce and extramarital relations.

The New Christian Right joined forces with the political New Right to elect Ronald Reagan, and Falwell was tapped by Reagan to be the liaison between the White House and the religious community. The coalition of New Right with the New Christian Right and the neoconservative movements helped to mold a foreign policy under Reagan that articulated human rights in terms of religious freedom, especially in opposition to Muslim and communist countries; unwavering support for the state of Israel, which some Christians believe to be the condition for the Second Coming of Christ; the fusion of Christianity, capitalism, and democracy into interchangeable terms; and a general attitude of U.S. moral supremacy. In terms of domestic affairs, they opposed programs that they interpreted as corroding the stability of the family, such as welfare programs, high taxes, abortion clinics, and so on.

However, by 1987, sexual and financial scandals involving the religious leadership of the New Christian Right, as well as organized reactions by the left, caused the Moral Majority and other conservative organizations to disband. New Right politicians became unsure of whether they wanted to be associated with the New Christian Right. However, the New Christian Right turned its energies to local politics. Pat Robertson formed the new Christian Coalition in 1989 to work on issues in neighborhoods, city councils, school boards, and state legislatures. In the view of the right, the liberals predominated in the academic community and were adversely influencing basic education with "secular humanism." Ralph Reed, executive director of the Christian Coalition until 1997, who outlined his theology and politics in his book *Active Faith* of 1996, urged a less belligerent form of born-again Christianity that would have lasting effects on mainstream America.

Despite their ups and downs, New Christian Right organizations continue to maintain grassroots support and have demonstrated their power to turn an election. James Dobson's Focus on the Family radio program,

Gary Bauer's Campaign for Working Families, Concerned Women for America, and the Traditional Values Coalition are a few of the programs and organizations of the New Christian Right acting politically for their beliefs.

CATHOLICISM

Liberalism and modernism were also seen as a threat within Catholicism, and many conservative tendencies arose against it. In fact, modernism within the Catholic Church had already been criticized by Pope Pius IX (1835–1914) in 1864, and by Leon XIII (1810–1903) in the document *Testem Benevolentiae* of 1899. After 1920, there was again a conservative reaction opposing modernism and supporting the pope.

In the United States, such a reaction included a radical critique of Catholic liberal movements for their support of the New Deal. At this point, despite the Protestant majority, there was already a Catholicism peculiar and closer to the American tradition. Father Francis Talbot, one of the conservative leaders, had even declared that true Catholics were the last to resist a non-American progressivism, and called for an adhesion to the "Constitution and traditional Americanism" that had made the country what it was before 1914.

Within Catholicism there has been controversy surrounding Vatican II, which some traditional Catholics hold has been wrongly interpreted by modernists while others promote the return to a pre-Vatican II period. This has come out in some more conservative groups.

Conservative Catholics were historically involved with such right-wing movements as the John Birch Society, and many Catholics supported Father Coughlin, an anti-Semitic radio-priest whose program became very popular during the 1930s. One of the most ultraconservative Catholic groups, Opus Dei, works in a way quite different from the evangelical or fundamental Protestants, since rather than broadly announce its goals through the mass media, it works in almost cult-like secrecy through manipulation. In 1982, Pope John Paul granted the unique status of "personal prelature," meaning that the groups could operate juridically without geographic boundaries.

Opus Dei began its activities in the United States in 1949 and promotes traditional Catholic values, especially concerning women's role and opposes liberalism and what it identifies as immorality. It has made a noted effort to recruit young college students, government officials, professionals, intellectuals, and business executives. Historically, Opus Dei has had more influence in

Europe and Latin America, with associations with the Franco regime in Spain.

Other conservative Catholic groups working in a more open way within the political arena are the American Catholic Alliance, which is a voter education organization, and the Catholic League for Religious and Civil Rights led by William Donohue, a former Heritage Foundation scholar. Some prominent conservative Catholics have used Catholic categories to support their views concerning free-market capitalism, anticommunism, and traditional roles for women. They include William F. Buckley, Jr., Michael Novak, Pat Buchanan, and Phylis Schlaffly. Conservative Catholics have been wooed by the Christian Coalition to form a Catholic alliance and are supportive of their fight against abortion.

However, many right-wing Catholics differ from their Protestant counterparts on such issues as welfare, the death penalty, nuclear weapons, and economic inequalities and are cautious of the anti-Catholic rhetoric of some of the Protestant groups. Just the same, many conservative evangelical and Catholic Church leaders signed in 1994 a statement entitled "The Christian Mission in the Third Millennium."

JUDAISM

Jewish conservatism was closely related to orthodoxy and its claim to a return to the old liturgy and the Zionist hope in the restoration of Israel. The Orthodox movement has consistently resisted the influence of the Enlightenment and consequent modernity. They hold to a literal interpretation of the Torah as representing the divine word of God. Orthodox supporters of Zionism have organized into the Mizrachi movement, which upholds nationalism based on religious beliefs that the world will recognize the restoration of their homeland and that the Jews will lead an international spiritual revival toward redemption.

The Jewish immigration to the United States started with the traditional Sephardim, and then, in the second half of the 19th century, received the influence of reformed and modernist Ashkenazim. The great emphasis in the conservative synagogues was on education, and as a result the Jewish Theological Seminary was founded in New York in 1886. This emphasis on tradition and education became stronger in the face of anti-Semitism, which was a growing issue from the end of the 19th century to the end of World War II. At that time, for their economic relations, Jews were thought to be strictly related to liberalism, an idea that was rein-forced by the fact that many Jews left the Republican Party to join the Democrat Party due to Catholic anti-Semitism. With the Holocaust, World War II, and its many consequences, the question and the role of Jewish culture in the United States became more important, especially with the foundation of Israel in 1948. These events gave more power to the conservative position within Judaism and the Jewish community, at the same time that it became a fundamental issue in the foreign and internal policy of the United States.

ISLAMISM

Islam is a traditional monotheistic religion based on the teachings of Muhammad, as registered in the Qur'an. However, there are internal differences and debates between moderate and radical Muslims that have clear sociological and political reasons. While modernist Muslims do not feel threatened by the ideas of modernity and accommodate their faith to include scientific and social ideas such as evolution, democracy, and women's emancipation, revivalist Muslims, or fundamentalists, refute modernism and hold to traditional ideas. Of the fundamentalist Muslims, there are groups who believe that Islam should be spread to the entire world, and of these, some are willing to use terrorist means to do so.

Discontent with modernism emerged as the Arab nations, unable to form a pan-Arabism, turned to Islam. Liberal Islamic regimes, which embraced modernism, failed to provide benefits to the general population and discontent arose. During the 1920s and until the 1940s, many regions influenced by Arab culture were passing through a major social and political transition to modernity. One of the results was the creation of several groups of fundamentalists, such as the Muslim Brotherhood, a movement founded in Egypt in 1928. Also, the volatile geopolitical context of oil-rich Arab states between the forces of the Cold War saw the rise of Islamic groups to counter Western influence.

Islamic fundamentalism is present also in the United States, particularly through African American movements. This process became notorious after the conversion of Malcolm X and his militancy in Islamic groups, as well as by the conversion of important public figures, such as Muhammad Ali. The closer interaction between religion and politics led to the growth of other Islamic groups as well. Among them, the Nation of Islam, led by Louis Farrakhan, is the most important, having organized marches in Washington, D.C., in order to demonstrate force and support.

After the Islamic Revolution in Iran in 1979, much more attention was given to Islam in the United States, also with the concern that the articulation between religion and politics in Islam might lead to belligerent or terrorist actions. The terrorist attacks in New York City and Washington, D.C., on September 11, 2001, which were motivated by a mixture of religious and political beliefs, brought new attention to this issue. They provoked not only further studies on the politics of Islam and its impact in the United States, but also a widespread popular reaction and suspicion toward Islam.

RELIGION AND POLITICS

There are many other religions in the United States, but the above groups are the most traditional and represent the majority. In all cases of fundamentalism, we can find adherence to a supposedly literal interpretation of the holy scriptures, the belief in being a chosen people, and an opposition to modernism and the Enlightenment with a certain nostalgia for an earlier tradition or homeland. In the United States, Protestantism is the largest—despite the importance of Catholicism, Judaism, and even Islamism for conservatism and the right—and has played a crucial role in the resurgence of conservative politics. These religious traditions have been appropriated by several groups that have found the strategic connection between religion and politics.

SEE ALSO

Volume 1 Left: Church and State Separation; Civil Liberties; Liberalism; Malcolm X; United States.
Volume 2 Right: Christian Coalition; Fundamentalism; Muslim Brotherhood; Manifest Destiny; Bush, George W.

BIBLIOGRAPHY
S. Ahlstrom, *A Religious History of the American People* (Yale University Press, 1972); R. Bellah, *The Broken Covenant* (Seabury, 1975), R. Pierard, *Evangelical Christianity and Political Conservatism: The Unequal Yoke* (J.P. Lippincott, 1978); G. Daly, *Transcendence and Immanence: A Study in Catholic Modernism and Integralism* (Oxford University Press, 1980); P. Gleason, ed., *Catholicism in America* (Harper & Row, 1970); J. Hunter, *American Evangelicalism: Conservative Religion and the Quandary of Modernity* (Rutgers University Press, 1983); G. Marsden, *Fundamentalism and American Culture* (Oxford University Press, 1980); Martin E. Marty and R. Scott Appleby, *Fundamentalism Observed* (University of Chicago Press, 1994); R. Niebuhr, *The Kingdom of God in America* (Harper & Row, 1959); R. Quebedeaux, "Conservative Protestants in Modern American Society: Who's Influencing Whom?" W.

Garret, *Social Consequences of Religious Belief* (Paragon House, 1989); Israel Shahak and Norton Mezvinsky, *Jewish Fundamentalism in Israel* (Pluto Press, 1999); Bassam Tibi, *The Challenge of Fundamentalism: Political Islam and the New World Disorder* (University of California Press, 1998).

AMOS NASCIMENTO
METHODIST UNIVERSITY OF PIRACICABA, BRAZIL

Republican Party

THE REPUBLICAN PARTY is the only third party in American history to become a major party. It dominated politics in the United States from 1860 to 1932, and in the early 2000s, it seemed on the threshold of becoming the dominant party again. The party was founded in Ripon, Wisconsin, on February 28, 1854, the outgrowth of a series of meetings held in the North in opposition to the concept of letting popular referenda in Nebraska and Kansas decide the slavery question there. The Republicans believed the question of slavery needed a definite answer from the national government, and that slavery should be prohibited throughout the United States. (Strangely enough, the same bill led to the fracture of the Democratic Party, because those from the South believed it gave too much power to the territorialists to settle the slavery question.) The party formally adopted its name on July 6 of that year, in Jackson, Michigan.

The party's first presidential candidate, John Charles Fremont, "the Pathfinder," in 1856 managed to win all of New England, New York, and four midwestern states. This displaced the Whig Party, which had won in that region previously. The Democratic Party fractured over the slavery question in 1860, and this allowed the new party and its candidate, Abraham Lincoln, to win. Before Lincoln had even taken office, several Southern states voted to secede from the United States. The party was thus established on clear North-South lines, and these dominated for 104 years.

From Lincoln until Franklin D. Roosevelt in 1932, only two Democrats were elected: Grover Cleveland to nonconsecutive terms in 1884 and 1892, and Woodrow Wilson in 1912 and 1916. During the era that Republicans dominated, the Republican Party was the more progressive of the two. It was Republicans who freed the slaves and saved the Union, took a hard line with the states on Reconstruction, and instituted the Progressive-era reforms. The Republicans lost in 1912 due to a fracture within the party, when former Republican President Theodore Roosevelt returned to challenge the incumbent, Republican William H. Taft, by running under the banner of the "Bull Moose" Progressive Party. The progressivism of the Republicans waned with the venality of Warren G. Harding and the passivity of Calvin Coolidge. Although more progressive than either of his predecessors, Herbert Hoover was an ineffective president and his failure to end the Great Depression early led to his ouster in 1932. This led the Republicans into the wilderness for 20 years, during which time they were reduced to a rump of upper-class business people and others who were discontented with Democratic rule.

The Republicans nominated Dwight D. Eisenhower on the second ballot in 1952. This was the last presidential nomination to take more than one ballot. Eisenhower was very popular throughout his tenure, and he had no trouble defeating Democrat Adlai E. Stevenson II twice, but Ike did not attract large numbers of Americans to the Republican Party permanently. The 1960 election between Republican Vice President Richard M. Nixon and Democratic Senator John F. Kennedy was very close in terms of the popular vote. Many Republicans believe that the Democratic machine in Chicago, Illinois, had stolen the election for Kennedy. A preliminary recount revealed that the machine had indeed tampered with the election for Cook County state's attorney, but there were only a handful of questionable votes taken from Nixon. Nixon decided not to pursue a recount.

BARRY GOLDWATER

The Republican nadir in recent history was the 1964 election, but in this election were the seeds of the future Republican revival. Many Republicans believed Democratic President Lyndon B. Johnson to be unbeatable, if nothing else due to sympathy for the recently assassinated Kennedy. So the stars within the Republican Party let the conservative wing of the party pick Senator Barry M. Goldwater of Arizona as the presidential candidate. Goldwater's fierce conservatism became an issue both within the party and in the larger campaign. Goldwater had frequently been part of a small group of senators who opposed progressive legislation, including some that had passed with broad bipartisan support. (This illustrates the inherent danger of being one of a handful in opposition.) He had opposed passage of the

Civil Rights Act of 1964, a landmark of the postwar period. To Goldwater and his ilk, liberty meant not the ability of a person to rent a room regardless of his race, but the ability of a landlord to rent to whomever he wished, including race as a factor. Goldwater responded, "extremism in the defense of liberty is no vice. Moderation in the defense of liberty is no virtue." It was widely acknowledged that the ticket had no chance. Goldwater carried only his home state and a small number of states in the Deep South. This was significant because it marked the shattering of the Democrats' lock on what had been their most loyal territory. On this new Republican South the party would build its victories in the decades to come. Also noteworthy in the 1964 campaign was the enlisting of former Democrat Ronald Reagan, an actor and corporate spokesperson, as a campaigner for Goldwater. Reagan narrated an extended-length television commercial for the campaign. This marked Reagan's entry into partisan politics, and in 1966, he was elected governor of California.

RICHARD NIXON

The Republicans captured the presidency again in 1968 largely on the basis of popular dissatisfaction with the social upheaval in America that started with the Kennedy assassination. The Democrats were deeply divided over the Vietnam War, and Johnson declined to seek reelection as a result. The emergence of youth protest over the war at the same time as the sexual revolution and the civil rights revolution were at their peak led many to seek the more sedate Republican ticket of Nixon and Maryland Governor Spiro T. Agnew. Nixon also engaged widespread dissatisfaction with the activism of the U.S. Supreme Court under Chief Justice Earl Warren. The court, in recent years, had outlawed apportionment of state legislatures by less than strict population measures; banned prayer in schools; extended the national Bill of Rights to state criminal prosecutions, including the exclusion of evidence obtained in illegal searches; mandated the instruction of rights to criminal suspects before questioning; and required the provision of free lawyers to indigent defendants. Given Nixon's history as a staunch and aggressive anti-communist, it was unlikely that he would be less resolved than Johnson in winning the war, but his Democratic opponent, Hubert H. Humphrey, was not in a position to do anything about it, being hamstrung by his loyalty to Johnson. It was another extremely close election in terms of the popular vote, but Nixon won easily in the electoral college, aided in part by the third-party candidacy of George Wallace, who deprived the Democrats of their formerly "Solid South." (Although Nixon escalated the Vietnam War, partly in secret, the war was in fact phased out during his presidency.)

Political scientist Kevin Phillips, then a Republican, predicted in the seminal 1969 book *The Emerging Republican Majority* that as Americans increasingly became suburbanites, they would adopt the political values of suburban Republicanism. This trend was delayed due to the emergence of Watergate and its related scandals in the 1970s, but by the 1980s, it was clear that most of suburbia would be as strongly Republican as the remaining inner cities became sharply Democratic.

Nixon had no trouble flattening his Democratic opponent, Senator George McGovern of South Dakota, in 1972, whose campaign was centered on ending the Vietnam War. Despite the magnitude of this victory—McGovern carried only Massachusetts and the District of Columbia—Nixon was haunted by the prospect of losing another close election. His administration and presidential campaign used a variety of illegal, unethical, and even downright criminal means to ensure his reelection and the embarrassment of his opponents. This included breaking into the psychiatric records of antiwar protestors, blackmailing Democratic presidential candidates with unflattering personal data, and most significantly, a burglary at the Democratic National Committee headquarters at the Watergate complex. On the night of June 17, 1972, a botched burglary there gave birth to what is known as the Watergate scandal. Reporters for the *Washington Post* eventually connected the Watergate burglars to the CIA and the president's closest advisers. During the congressional investigations that followed, it was revealed that Nixon had secretly taped his office and telephone conversations in the White House for nearly two years. Although the president fiercely fought the subpoenaing of these tapes, going all the way to the U.S. Supreme Court (which unanimously ruled that he must turn them over to House investigators), their release proved that Nixon had known about the burglary shortly afterward and had ordered the cover-up that consumed his presidency. Nixon resigned on August 9, 1974.

GERALD FORD

Nixon's successor, Gerald R. Ford, who had replaced Agnew the year before after Agnew, too, was embroiled in a scandal, became the country's first unelected president. His chances of winning an election began to unravel in the first month of his presidency, when he pardoned Nixon for any crimes he may have committed while in office. Although he maintained this was a move calculated to heal the nation (avoiding what certainly would have been a bitter criminal prosecution and trial of Nixon), cynics suggested Nixon had made a deal to ensure his pardon. In reality, some believe Ford was simply too honest and too politically naïve to realize the implications his pardon would have on the 1976 election. Ford faced a challenge within the Republican Party from Reagan. It is rare that an incumbent Republican president faces an intraparty challenge.

Apparently Reagan recognized Ford's vulnerability and felt he did not deserve the deference normally shown to elected incumbent presidents. Although the outcome of the convention was too close to call right up to the balloting, Ford was nominated on the first ballot. He lost another close election in terms of the popular vote to Democrat Jimmy Carter, the former governor of Georgia. Three issues weakened Ford and ensured his defeat: pardoning Nixon, having to fight a prolonged nomination battle, and denying federal aid to New York City. Ford lost New York only narrowly, and undoubtedly his refusal to help the country's largest city in the time of its fiscal crisis a year earlier (which inspired the headline, "Ford to City: Drop Dead," words the president never spoke) was sufficient to move the 2,000 votes by which Carter carried the state. Carter had also pilloried Ford on the poor performance of the economy, but this was a strategy that would come back to bite Carter in 1980.

Carter had been at best a moderately successful president, and he had been dealt the bad hand of a worldwide oil crisis that fueled inflation at home, and Iranian militants had seized American hostages in the wake of the revolution in Iran. Carter's move to rescue the hostages resulted in the deaths of American military personnel in a crash. A crowded field entered the Republican nomination race, but by late March, it was obvious Reagan would be the nominee. The Republican nomination was truly a coronation, with even the staunchest supporters of Reagan's opponents being pressured to vote for Reagan. Those who didn't were humiliated publicly. An absurd rumor swept the convention,\ that Reagan had chosen Ford as his running mate and that they would have a "co-presidency." Reagan had to appear in person at the convention a day early to quash the rumor.

Reagan ran a fairly solid election campaign, and Carter was hampered by the presence of Representative John Anderson of Illinois, one of Reagan's challengers from the nomination, as a third-party candidate. Anderson was the first minor candidate to appear on the ballot in all 50 states, and he drained votes from Carter en masse. Carter, who decided to sit out a debate between Reagan and Anderson, made the fatal mistake of debating Reagan. Carter was no match for Reagan's superior television skills, honed in more than 30 years as a broadcaster and actor.

By election time, the same economic indicators that Carter had skewered Ford with four years earlier were even worse, and Reagan turned to the audience and asked, "Are you better off now than you were four years ago?" While it was a close race at the time of the debate, polls showed that many people made up their minds between the debate and the election and most chose to vote for Reagan. Reagan thus won by a much larger margin than had there been no debate. Reagan also led the Republicans to capture the Senate, which resulted in

A local Republican campaign poster shows a focus on attracting African American voters to the Grand Old Party.

the defeat of 11 Democratic incumbents. Reagan's first year in office was a watershed time for the party. Reagan managed to get even the Democratic House of Representatives and its recalcitrant speaker, Thomas P. O'Neill, on board for his economic recovery program.

Although the Republicans suffered huge losses in the 1982 House elections, they retained the Senate, and the country remained largely committed to "Reaganomics." With the economy doing so well by 1984, Reagan's Democratic opponent, former Vice President Walter F. Mondale, was unable to gain a foothold, and once again Reagan asked the debate question, "Are you better off now than you were four years ago?," this time expecting a positive response. Some questioned Reagan's capability as the oldest president (then 73), given his wild and woolly performance in the first debate, but Reagan managed to quiet this with a successful oneliner in the second debate, and he was re-elected with the biggest electoral margin in history, Mondale carrying only his home state of Minnesota and the District of Columbia.

Although the "Reagan Revolution" largely fell by the wayside in the second term, as the Democrats regained control of the Senate in 1986 and Republican senators and members of Congress were harder to keep in line knowing Reagan would not be running again, the Republican Party remained steadfastly loyal to the course Reagan had set. Indeed, since the silencing and ouster of the moderate wing of the Republican Party at the 1980 convention, there has been no resurgence of such forces within the party, and the party continues to represent an ideological spectrum from somewhat conservative to extremely conservative. The veneration shown Reagan at his death in 2004 reveals the depth of gratitude among Republicans for his reshaping of their party.

Vice President George H. W. Bush, one of Reagan's opponents in the 1980 nomination battle, succeeded Reagan as the nominee in 1988, albeit without much help from the incumbent president. Polls showed the Democrats as poised to win the White House back, but the party was paralyzed by the poor campaign abilities of its nominee, Massachusetts Governor Michael S. Dukakis. Although it was no landslide, Bush won comfortably. Bush was faulted for his passive governance and his indifference at the fall of the Soviet bloc in the first year of his presidency. Bush greatly alienated Republicans in the summer of 1990 by agreeing to a tax increase, after he had made the phrase "Read my lips: No new taxes" a mantra in his presidential campaign. After these missteps, many Republicans were indifferent to his reelection, and more than a few openly supported the third-party bid of Texas billionaire H. Ross Perot. With the Republicans hopelessly divided, Democrat Bill Clinton, governor of Arkansas, won the 1992 election easily.

Clinton made many missteps too, and Republicans built up an enormous body of anger and even hatred for Clinton and his wife, Hillary. By crafty manipulation of the media and constant caressing of Clinton-haters through talk radio, the Republicans, led by House Minority Whip Newt Gingrich of Georgia, were able to capture both houses of Congress in the 1994 election and set their sights on retaking the presidency in 1996. The Republicans were more aggressive in their takeover than was warranted. They forced an unnecessary showdown over the budget with Clinton in 1995 that led to the shutdown of the federal government. As the gates were closed at the Grand Canyon and other national parks, the Republicans realized they had overplayed their hand, as the public largely took the side of Clinton. Deals were quickly made to reopen the government. Senate Majority Leader Robert Dole became the presidential nominee in 1996, but it was believed all along that Clinton would win, and the 1996 campaign proved an anti-climax.

Years of aggressive Clinton hating were primed for the explosion of a sex scandal surrounding the president in January 1998, when it was revealed that Clinton had engaged in sexual relations with a 24-year-old White House intern. Republicans called for Clinton's resignation or impeachment, but once again the Republicans had overplayed their hand because polls continued to show strong support for the president. The Republicans came perilously close to losing their House majority in 1998 (something of an anomaly, since an election six years into a president's tenure is usually a disaster for his party), and Gingrich was forced to resign. The Republicans nevertheless went ahead with their impeachment of Clinton, although polls showed the vast majority of Americans were against it. It is believed this was an effort to placate the Clinton-haters among the party's core constituency. Neither article of impeachment received the votes of conviction from even a majority of senators.

If the impeachment effort accomplished only one thing, it kept Vice President Albert A. Gore, the Democratic nominee in 2000, from running on the Clinton-Gore record. The economy had produced the greatest growth in history during those years, but the vice president basically ignored this achievement. The 2000 election was the longest in history to that time, with both

Republican Senator Robert Dole of Kansas ran unsuccessfully against President Bill Clinton in 1996.

Gore and Republican George W. Bush, son of the former president, sealing their respective nominations in March. By the end of the campaign, it was shaping up as the closest election in 40 years. The Senate tied 50-50 in the election, including the landmark election of Hillary R. Clinton, sitting First Lady, and also the election of a dead man in Missouri. The House broke nearly as closely. The identity of the true winner of the presidential contest may never be known. Although Gore won the popular vote, Bush only won the electoral college after a series of recounts in Florida were halted by the U.S. Supreme Court and that state's electoral votes were awarded to him.

Despite the imbroglio in Florida, Republicans believed they were better poised to govern the United States than the still numerically larger Democrats. This is because the Republicans are much more united as a party than the perennially fractious Democrats, hampered by identity politics and a proportional representation process that ensures they will perpetually be a divided party. Indeed, the Republicans are on the verge of becoming the majority party in the country. The Democrats face a bias in the electoral college that has Republicans winning small states with a disproportionate number of electoral votes and amassing narrow victories in competitive states, while the Democratic plurality in the popular vote is fueled by their large margins in what are by this time noncompetitive states like California, New York, Illinois, and Massachusetts.

So the paradigm was followed in the 2004 election with George W. Bush's Republicans closely allied with the Christian Right, tightly focused on moral values, and victorious over the Democratic effort. The Republican Party thus gained a stronger mandate in 2004.

SEE ALSO

Volume 1 Left: Democratic Party; United States; Clinton, William J.; Johnson, Lyndon B.

Volume 2 Right: Conservatism; Gingrich, Newt; Reagan, Ronald; Eisenhower, Dwight D.

BIBLIOGRAPHY

Niels Bjerre-Pouslen, Right Face: Organizing the American Conservative Movement, 1945–65 (Museum Tusculanum, 2002); Mary C. Brennan, Turning Right in the Sixties: The Conservative Capture of the GOP (University of North Carolina Press, 1995); Thomas Byrne Edsall, Chain Reaction: The Impact of Race, Rights, and Taxes on American Politics (Norton, 1991); Lewis L. Gould, Grand Old Party: A History of the Republicans (Random House, 2003); John B. Judis and Ruy Texeira, The Emerging Democratic Majority (Scribner's, 2002); Kevin P. Phillips, The Emerging Republican Majority (Arlington House, 1969); Nicol C. Rae, The Decline and Fall of Liberal Republicans: From 1952 to the Present (Oxford University Press, 1989); Robert A. Rutland, The Republicans: From Lincoln to Bush (University of Missouri Press, 1996).

TONY L. HILL
MASSACHUSETTS INSTITUTE OF TECHNOLOGY

Roosevelt, Theodore (1858–1919)

THEODORE ROOSEVELT, the 25th president of the United States, clearly represented a departure from the pattern of previous presidents, particularly those who had served in the last decades of the 19th century. Roosevelt was younger at age 42 when he took office than any of his predecessors had been. He understood that the position of president gave him an important forum, a "bully pulpit," as he called it, with which to affect policy and the public mood. He took a strong stand in in-

ternational affairs, and was intensely proud of his role in securing the independence of Panama from Colombia and the subsequent Panama Canal Treaty. Elected as vice president to William McKinley on the Republican Party ticket, he succeeded to the office on the assassination of McKinley on September 14, 1901. He was reelected to the presidency for a full term in 1904 and served until March 1909, when his handpicked nominee, William Howard Taft, followed him in office.

Even though Roosevelt's personality was colorful and his policies often direct and forthright, he has presented a problem to historians and biographers alike when they seek to categorize his ideological positions. Some have simply accepted the contemporary assessment of Roosevelt as a progressive, while others have seen in him a Bismarck-like conservative whose reforms were intended only to forestall the danger of revolution. At least one biographer attributed his rise to prominence as well as his policies to a simple lust for power. Still others, plumbing his psychological background, have offered a much less flattering assessment that suggests that his aggressive foreign policy and his domestic reforms were based on a patronizing form of racism and class-consciousness, as well as a deep-seated fear of being seen as weak or indecisive, which produced an exaggerated and larger-than-life appearance of toughness and decisiveness. Recently, the latter view has been amplified by an analysis that reflects on Roosevelt's attempt to establish his masculinity.

Roosevelt was born into a wealthy family in New York City, but was troubled by ill health in the form of severe asthma and nearsightedness. He undertook a program of physical exercise in a home gym, including boxing, that he dubbed "the strenuous life" to compensate for these disabilities. As a child, he traveled in Europe, learning both French and German. He was educated at Harvard and briefly attended Columbia University Law School. He ran for the New York State Assembly and served from 1881 to 1883, and was elected speaker of the assembly, the youngest to serve in that post. He married, but both his wife and his mother died on the same day in 1884. Grief-stricken, he moved to the Dakota Territory, where he took up ranching and participated in the capture of an outlaw who had stolen a boat from him. He returned to New York City in 1886 and remarried. In 1888, he served on the U.S. Civil Service Commission as a reward for political work in the campaign of President Benjamin Harrison. In 1895, he was appointed New York City police commissioner, and then resigned the position to raise a regiment to serve in the brief Spanish-American War in the spring and summer of 1898. Later in 1898, the Republican Party machine, seeking an attractive candidate for governor to offset a reputation for scandal, selected him as the nominee, and he won the office, to serve for two years. To balance the ticket with McKinley, he was selected to run as vice president in 1900, and he had only served in that post six months when McKinley's sudden death propelled him into the presidency.

As president, he endorsed a program of conservation of natural resources that led to the establishment of national parks and a system of national forest management. However, his style of conservation for use was quite different from the concept of natural preservation of wilderness advocated by more radical conservationists like John Muir, whose ideas served as the forerunner of later environmental protection approaches.

Roosevelt was a dedicated hunter and even as a child had combined birdwatching with the shooting and preservation of birds. Thus, even this most notable form of Roosevelt's progressive legacy has tended to be conflated in the public mind with views to which he did not adhere. Nevertheless, he added a great body of land to that under federal protection: he designated 150 national forests, five national parks, the first 18 national monuments, the first four national game preserves, and other projects for a total of almost 230 million acres. That area equaled in coverage about that of all the East Coast states from Florida to Maine.

His policies regarding big business have been popularly remembered as a form of "trust-busting," since legislation extending the Sherman Antitrust Act and the Food and Drug Act was enacted during his administration. In this regard, the Justice Department during his more than seven years in office actually undertook fewer anti-trust suits than under the immediately following four-year administration of William Howard Taft, who somewhat ironically is remembered as a more traditional and conservative Republican.

One interesting assessment of Roosevelt's ideology suggested by Richard Hofstadter shows that Roosevelt's policies and actions tapped into the discontent of the so-called status revolution of his era. That status-revolution argument asserts that middle-class white Americans at the turn of the century, including salaried professionals like ministers, teachers, journalists, and lawyers, particularly those in small cities and towns, believed that their natural position of leadership had been usurped by the rise of large corporations, labor unions, boss-run political machines, and newly arrived immigrants. Thus their support of reform, so this argument runs, was in fact a reactionary attempt to restore a government operated by their own class, in the form of efficiency experts and a qualified and educated elite. Roosevelt, with his anti-trust rhetoric, his energetic style, his own elite background, and his support for the regulation of large corporations in the public interest by commissions of experts, fits rather well into this model of progressive-as-reactionary.

In his own time, he was much admired by many (but not all) progressive Republicans, and indeed, his followers led a walkout from the Republican convention in 1912, to create a separate third party, the Progressive Party, which selected him as its standard-bearer for the presidency in that year. When questioned by a reporter about his health and readiness for office in this campaign, he asserted that he felt as "fit as a bull moose in the rutting season," thereby creating the "Bull Moose" image for that third party. His unsuccessful run for the presidency so divided the Republican vote that Woodrow Wilson, the Democratic nominee, with some 42 percent of the popular vote, won a clear victory in the electoral college. Roosevelt got about 28 percent of the vote; Taft, about 23 percent. In the electoral college, however, Wilson received 435 of the 531 electors. Within two years after Wilson took office, he instituted some of the very reforms that Roosevelt had advocated during the campaign, such as the establishment of the Federal Trade Commission and the Federal Reserve banking system.

Despite Roosevelt's rhetoric of opposition to the excesses of large corporations and his advocacy of a program that he dubbed "The New Nationalism" in 1912, which captured much of the progressive aspiration for a reformed and regulated economy, most of his programs and ideas represented a means of preserving the basic capitalist structure of American society rather than altering it in a radical direction. The fact that in the 1912 election, Eugene Debs, the Socialist candidate for the presidency, polled almost 900,000 votes (about six percent of those cast) suggests that Roosevelt was not perceived by the more radical left in the period as a viable alternative to the establishment, but rather as part of it.

SEE ALSO

Volume 1 Left: Progressive Party; United States.
Volume Right: Republican Party; Taft, William H.

BIBLIOGRAPHY

John Morton Blum, *The Republican Roosevelt* (Harvard University Press, 1954); James MacGregor Burns, *The Three Roosevelts: Patrician Leaders who Transformed America* (Atlantic

Monthly Press, 2001); James Chace, *1912: Wilson, Roosevelt, Taft & Debs—The Election That Changed the Country* (Simon & Schuster, 2004); Herbert Croly, *The Promise of American Life* (Macmillan, 1909); Richard Hofstadter, *The Age of Reform* (Knopf, 1955); Richard Hofstadter, *The American Political Tradition and the Men Who Made It* (Knopf, 1948); Edmund Morris, *The Rise of Theodore Roosevelt* (Modern Library, 2001); George E. Mowry, *Theodore Roosevelt and the Progressive Movement* (University of Wisconsin, 1946); Henry Pringle, *Theodore Roosevelt, a Biography* (Harcourt Brace, 1931); Sarah Lyons Watts, *Rough Rider in the White House: Theodore Roosevelt and the Politics of Desire* (University of Chicago Press, 2003).

RODNEY P. CARLISLE
GENERAL EDITOR

Royalty

ROYALTY OR NOBILITY consists of people within a state possessing various special hereditary privileges, rights, and honors, including titles. In other words, it is a conservative, usually right-wing aristocratic or patrician class. The nobilities of the various modern states of Europe came into existence when feudalism, a social system based on land tenure, succeeded the imperial government of Rome after the Germanic invasions. During the unsettled social and economic conditions that followed the fall of the Roman Empire in the 5th and 6th centuries, some men acquired land, usually by conquest.

These men then granted parts of their holdings to others, over whom they thereafter exercised certain rights, including taxation and the administration of justice, and from whom they were entitled to various services. Those who granted the land were known as lords and those who accepted it were known as vassals. The lords of a nation formed its nobility, their rank depending on the extent of their possessions. The prepositions *de* in the names of French nobles and *von* in the names of German nobles (both meaning "of" or "from") express the idea of landownership that is fundamental to the feudal concept of royalty.

Since the French Revolution (1789–99), the tendency in European countries has been strongly toward the abolition of hereditary titles. In France the royalty was first deprived of its special rights and privileges, and then, in 1790, all hereditary titles were abolished by

decree. Napoleon I, however, created a new royalty, granting titles and estates to those who had served him well, especially in military affairs. After Napoleon's downfall, Louis XVIII, King of France, restored to the pre-revolutionary royalty many of its former privileges, rights, and honors. The Second Republic (1848–52) once more abolished the royalty in France, but Napoleon III restored the aristocratic class. Under the Third Republic (1871–1945), the royalty was once more abolished. In contemporary France, persons who have inherited titles may use them as part of their family name, but they possess none of the special rights or honors of the former royalty.

In Germany, titles of royalty existed from early Medieval times until they were abolished when the region became a republic in 1918. After 1918, members of the former nobility were permitted to use titles only as part of a name. In Russia, titles of royalty similar to those of the nations of Western Europe were instituted by Emperor Peter I. All such titles were abolished by the Revolution of 1917. In Spain, titles of royalty still exist. Members of the higher nobility bear the title of grandee; the lesser nobles are known as *los titulados de Castilla*. In Italy, Belgium, and Portugal, only courtesy titles exist.

In the United Kingdom, the sovereign still grants titles of royalty. The British royalty is divided into upper royalty and lower royalty. The upper consists of all those who hold a hereditary rank above that of baronet; it includes those with titles of duke, marquis, earl, viscount, and baron.

Among the lower royalty are those holding the rank of baronet, knight, and esquire. The upper royalty makes up the British peerage, and its members have the right to hereditary seats in the House of Lords. Life peers can also be created. They hold the rank for their own lives only; the title does not descend to their children. The Appellate Jurisdiction Act of 1876 gave the Crown the right to give judges the rank of lord of appeal and grant them life peerages. The Life Peerages Act of 1958 gave the Crown the right to create other life peers besides judges, and about 10 are now created each year. All life peers are appointed to the House of Lords, where members review legislation passed by the House of Commons and serve as Britain's highest court of appeals.

No royalty exists in the United States. Article I, Section 9, of the Constitution of the United States specifies that no title of royalty will be granted by the United States, and in addition it forbids any person holding government office from accepting any such title from a foreign ruler without the express consent of Congress. A private American citizen who accepts a title of royalty automatically resigns his or her citizenship.

The former royalty in different countries forms the core of conservative, right-wing political structures as they quickly moved in the democratic political processes. These royal families reestablished themselves in the capitalist economic system and in many cases effectively defended their inherited mobile and immobile properties.

Emperors and empresses had the style of Imperial Majesty (HIM, His or Her Imperial Majesty). Members of imperial families, generally had the style of Imperial Highness (HIH). In Austria, the members of the imperial family, due to their status as also members of the royal family of Hungary, held the style of Imperial and Royal Highness (HIRH). In Russia, while the more senior grand dukes and grand duchesses held the style of Imperial Highness, more junior princes and princesses of Russia held the style of His or Her Highness (HH).

Kings and queens have the style of Majesty (HM). Members of royal families (princes and princesses) generally have the style of Royal Highness (HRH), although in some royal families (for instance, Denmark), more junior princes and princesses only bear the style of His or Her Highness (HH).

Reigning grand dukes and grand duchesses hold the style of Royal Highness (HRH). The styles of members of grand ducal families has been inconsistent. In Luxembourg, more senior members of the family have also been Royal Highnesses, but only due to their status as princes of Bourbon of Parma. In Baden and Hesse and the Rhine, junior members held the style of Grand Ducal Highness (HGDH). Members of other grand ducal families generally held the style of Highness (HH). Reigning dukes and duchesses bore the style of Highness (HH), as did other members of ducal families.

The elector of Hesse-Kassel also bore the style of Highness, as did other members of the Hesse-Kassel family. Mediatized dukes and reigning and mediatized *Fürsten* and *Fürstinnen* bear the style of Serene Highness (HSH, German *Durlaucht*), as do other members of princely families. Mediatized counts and countesses bear the style of Illustrious Highness (German *Erlaucht*).

Dukes and duchesses in the peerages of England, Scotland, Great Britain, Ireland, and the United Kingdom bear the style of Grace, "Your Grace." They are also known as Most Noble, although this style is largely archaic except in the most formal situations. Marquesses and marchionesses bear the styles of The Most

Honourable and Lordship, "His Lordship," "Her Ladyship." Earls, countesses, viscounts, viscountesses, barons, and baronesses bear the styles of The Right Honourable and Lordship.

Nonmediatized noble dukes in Germany bear the style of Serene Highness (HSH) or High Born (*Hochgeboren*). Nonmediatized noble *Fürsten* in Germany bear the styles of Serene Highness, Princely Grace (*fürstliche Gnaden*), or High Born. Other nonmediatized German nobles of the rank of count or higher bear the style of High Born German nobles, and below the rank of count bear the style of High Well Born (*Hochwohlgeboren*).

SEE ALSO

Volume 1 Left: United Kingdom; France; Germany. *Volume 2 Right:* Monarchism.

BIBLIOGRAPHY

T.F. Thiselton-Dyer, *Royalty in All Ages: The Amusements, Eccentricities, Accomplishments, Superstitions, and Frolics of the Kings and Queens of Europe* (John C. Nimmo, 1903); E. Shils and M. Young, *The Meaning of Coronation, Sociological Review* (v.1, 1953).

JITENDRA UTTAM
JAWAHARLAL NEHRU UNIVERSITY, INDIA

Russia, Post-Soviet

The collapse of the communist regime of the Soviet Union in 1991 created an unusual political situation, in which it was often difficult to apply traditional terms of "left" and "right." "Leftists" often sought to inhibit or prevent change, since the left had been the establishment in the previous system. Traditional leftist and rightist stances were sometimes fused, as in various "left-patriotic" or "national Bolshevik" organizations.

At the end of the Soviet era, people were unaccustomed to discussing alternative policies or institutions, even among acquaintances, and had little understanding of each other's preferences or even of what innovations they themselves would eventually advocate, tolerate, or seek to stifle. The earliest political organizations were therefore large, amorphous, and subject to internecine fighting. Political platforms were incoherent if they existed at all. Many parties became personalistic vehicles for specific leaders. Mergers, splits, and recombinations were numerous. An early "rightist" example was

Pamiat' (Memory), a "historical-patriotic association" that emerged in 1987 and was tied together by a concern over Jews, Masons, and CIA agents and a nostalgia for Josef Stalin (a "strong boss"), old monuments, and the tzarist-era spelling of words.

The state introduced certain rules to stabilize the party system and weed out the less viable contenders, with mixed results. Half the seats of the State Duma, the lower house of the Federal Assembly, are elected from single-delegate districts and half from party lists allocated by proportional representation. (Each voter casts two ballots, one for an individual candidate and another for a party.) Since 1993, no party can receive any of the party-list seats unless it wins 5 percent of the party-list vote (rising to 7 percent in 2007).

In the parliamentary elections of 1995, four parties passed the 5 percent threshold, whereas the other 39 contending parties, together representing 49 percent of the votes cast, failed to get in. That contributed to a reduction in the effective number of parties, yet the process of party formation and re-formation continued. Under a 2001 law, parties must have at least 10,000 members, with no fewer than 100 members in each of 50 of Russia's 89 constituent jurisdictions. This law spurred another round of mergers, and within two years the number of parties had been reduced from nearly 200 to about 50.

Depending on one's definition, the "right" may include: 1) parties oriented toward nostalgic or nationalistic sentiments, or 2) parties seeking to "impose" a liberal, market-oriented economic system.

In broad terms, the major concerns of the nostalgic/nationalistic right in Russia have included law and order; the maintenance of an adequate military defense; the loss of "empire" and international status associated with the collapse of the Soviet Union; the loss of tradition (including, in some cases, Cossack tradition) associated with the pre-Soviet Russian empire; and the fate of the 24.3 million Russians left at the time of the Soviet collapse in the "near abroad," that is, in the 14 non-Russian successor states of the Soviet Union. Many rightists oppose the presence of "foreigners" in Russia, often including Jews and the minority nationalities that comprise 20 percent of the country's population, who are often identified with crime in the Russian popular mind. These rightists tend to view the outside world, especially the United States, as taking advantage of Russia's weakened condition, and they are sensitive to the existence of U.S. air bases in former Soviet Central Asia and the expansion of the European Union and NATO into former Warsaw Pact countries and even the former

Baltic republics of the Soviet Union. The latter have left the Russian exclave of Kaliningrad surrounded by EU/NATO territory.

Parties of the liberal right take their model from the market-oriented economies of the West. They also prefer a Western-style democratic government but are confronted by a dilemma in that they attract relatively few votes in fair elections. While sincere advocates of economic reform, they have had limited impact in the legislature because their "intellectual integrity" often forbids them to endorse compromises, even with each other.

Conceivably, a third category of rightist party is the "party of power," created by the president to support the state and government. It derives its electoral strength from its presumed connection to the real center of power. Thus, in 1995 Yeltsin created Our Home Is Russia. Unity was created to replace it in 1999, and in 2001 Putin transformed that into United Russia by absorbing Unity's former rivals, parties led by Moscow's mayor and prominent governors. Our Home Is Russia tended to win about 10 percent of the vote; United Russia in 2003 became the first party to win an outright majority in the Duma (226 seats). Neither party offered much of a program, but both tolerated moderate reforms. The Kremlin has encouraged communist individual dissidents to found new parties, such as Motherland and the Party of the Rebirth of Russia, allegedly to undermine the vote for the Communist Party of the Russian Federation.

LIBERAL DEMOCRATIC PARTY OF RUSSIA

The most famous and resilient force on the right is the (inappropriately named) Liberal Democratic Party of Russia, led by Vladimir V. Zhirinovsky. The party began operating as early as 1988 and was officially registered in 1992. The Liberal Democrats attracted international attention in December 1993, when they received the largest share (22.92 percent) of the party-list vote in parliamentary elections. (They fell to 6 percent by 1999 but rebounded to more than 11 percent in 2003.) Zhirinovsky, who was once described as a "dangerous buffoon," has promoted nationalism, anti-Semitism, and xenophobia. He excoriates both the communists and the West and has promised to establish hegemony over South Asia. He has advocated the restoration of the Russian empire, including the former Soviet republics, Finland, and Alaska. The practice, however, bears little resemblance to the rhetoric. In key Duma votes, the Liberal Democrats have been among the more reliable supporters of the government, whether Boris Yeltsin or Vladimir Putin.

CONGRESS OF RUSSIAN COMMUNITIES

The Congress of Russian Communities championed the rights of Russians living in the "near abroad," but it was primarily identified with its leader, retired General Alexander Lebed, who had a notable and curious career. As deputy commander of paratroopers, Lebed played a key role in thwarting the attempted coup of August 1991. While commander of the 14th Army, in 1992, he defied orders to remain neutral and imposed an end to a brief ethnic war between Slavs and Romanians in the successor state of Moldavia (Moldova), preserving a would-be Slavic state (the Trans-Dniester Republic) within Moldavia. Lebed openly admired General Augusto Pinochet of Chile, who had transformed his country's economy while killing "no more than three thousand people." He dropped that analogy in favor of Charles de Gaulle, however, when he ran for president in 1996, calling for an end to the (first) war in Chechnya. He came in third in the first round of the election and backed Yeltsin in the second round. Then, during his three months as Yeltsin's national security adviser, he negotiated a settlement with the Chechens. Lebed's influence waned after he assumed the governorship of the Siberian territory of Krasnoyarsk. In 2002, he died in a helicopter accident. The party has faded from the scene.

UNION OF RIGHTIST FORCES

The Union of Rightist Forces, the successor to Russia's Choice and Russia's Democratic Choice, was formed in 1998 as an alliance of movements and registered as a political party in 2002. It advocates a liberal, market-oriented economy, and several of its leaders were prominent officials in the Yeltsin government in the early years of economic reform. The party is popular among business leaders but few others. In the Putin era, some of its leaders began taking more statist positions to improve their standing with the government. It received 8.7 percent of the party-list vote in 1999; it failed to pass the 5 percent threshold in 2003 but won three individual seats.

In September 2004, seeking to centralize authority in the face of continued Chechen terrorist attacks, President Vladimir Putin proposed the elimination of single-delegate elections to the State Duma, leaving only election by party lists. Some observers commented at

Russian President Putin veered strongly right by accumulating personal power after terrorist attacks in September 2004.

the time that the national parties, all based in Moscow, would be easier to control than individual regional candidates. Putin also proposed ending the direct election of governors.

SEE ALSO

Volume 1 Left: Russia; Soviet Union.
Volume 2 Right: Soviet Union.

BIBLIOGRAPHY

Harold Elletson, *The General against the Kremlin: Alexander Lebed—Power and Illusion* (Little, Brown, 1998); Vladimir Kartsev, *Zhirinovsky!* (Columbia University Press, 1995); Michael McFaul et al., *Between Dictatorship and Democracy: Russian Post-Communist Political Reform* (Carnegie Endowment for International Peace, 2004); Lilia Shevtsova, *Putin's Russia* (Carnegie Endowment for International Peace, 2003).

SCOTT C. MONJE, PH.D.
INDEPENDENT SCHOLAR

The Right

S

Sabbatarianism

SABBATARIANISM IS the view that insists that one day of each week must be reserved for religious observance as prescribed by the Old Testament Sabbath Law. The sabbatarians' main thesis is simple: The Sabbath is one of the Ten Commandments, and the Ten Commandments do not correspond to a temporary ceremonial law but are to be regarded as eternally significant moral law. However, a distinction is to be made between strict or literal sabbatarianism and semi-sabbatarianism. Strict or literal sabbatarianism contends that God's directive concerning the Sabbath Law is natural, universal, and moral.

Consequently, the Sabbath requires humankind to abstain from all labor except for those tasks necessary for the welfare of the society. In this view, the seventh day, the literal Sabbath, is the only day on which the requirements of this law can be met. Historically, we see a trend toward sabbatarianism in the Eastern Church during the 4th century and the Irish church during the 6th century when in effect a dual recognition of both Sabbath and Sunday was stressed. It was not until the Reformation, however, that sabbatarianism found a more profound and semi-institutionalized form. This is despite the fact that in his "Letter against the Sabbatarians," Luther openly opposed the doctrine, pointing out the legalistic pitfalls inherent in the view. John Calvin also agreed with Luther's stance on the meaning and observance of Sabbath.

The development of Judaizing the Sabbath day as done by strict sabbatarianism is first illustrated in the history of a sect of sabbatarians: Socinians, founded in Transylvania in Hungary toward the end of the 16th century. Their first principle, which led them to separate from the rest of the Unitarian body, was their belief that the day of rest must be observed along with the Jews on the seventh day of the week and not on the Christian Sunday. The greater part of this particular sabbatarian sect joined the Orthodox Jews in 1874, thus carrying out in practice the Judaizing principle of their founders to its full extent.

Although there does not seem to be any immediate or obvious connection between the observance of the seventh day and the rejection of infant baptism, these two practices are often found together. Thus, sabbatarianism made many recruits among the Mennonite Anabaptists in Holland and among the English Baptists who, much as they differ on other points of doctrine, agreed in the rejection of paedo-baptism. It is presumably a result of the contact with Anabaptism that sabbatarianism also developed an association with heavily dissenting views on political or social questions.

The most conspicuous of English Sabbatarian Baptists was Francis Bampfield (d. 1683), brother of a Devonshire baronet and originally a clergyman of the

English Church. He was the author of several works and ministered to a congregation of Sabbatarian Baptists in London, England. In the British Isles, although the greater number of sabbatarians have originated from the Baptists, one of the most notable of them was associated with the Wesleyan Methodists. This was the prophetess Joanna Southcott (1750–1814), like Bampfield a native of Devonshire, who composed many spiritual poems and prophetical writings and became the mother of a sect of sabbatarians, also known as Southcottians or Joannas. Southcott's disciples confidently awaited the birth of the promised Messiah whom the prophetess of 64 was to bring into the world, despite the fact that she eventually died of the disease, which had given a false appearance of pregnancy.

In the New World, on the other hand, the Seventh Day Baptists originated in 1631, with the bringing of sabbatarianism from England to Rhode Island and New York. The most notable proponent of strict sabbatarianism in the United States is the Seventh Day Adventist Church, although several smaller adventist groups hold similar views. Their arguments for the universally binding character of the Sabbath law are the following: 1) it is part of the moral law and therefore should be treated as eternal; 2) it was given at the creation; and 3) it was not abrogated in the New Testament.

Semi-sabbatarianism holds essentially the same view as strict sabbatarianism in terms of observing the Sabbath, but the day of observance is moved from Saturday, the seventh day, to Sunday, the first day of the week. It was Albertus Magnus who first suggested a structured semi-sabbatarianism by dividing the Sabbath command into 1) the moral command to observe a day of rest after six days of labor, and 2) the ceremonial symbol that applied only to the Jews in a literal sense. Thomas Aquinas lifted this formulation to the status of official doctrine, a view later held by a large number of reformed theologians as well. Semi-sabbatarianism also reached its zenith in English Puritanism, finding its way to the New World through the early colonists. Sunday restrictions and so-called blue laws in various U.S. states are a constant reminder of the influence of this view. Organizations such as the Lord's Day Observance Society (est. 1831) and the Imperial Alliance for the Defense of Sunday (England) have sought to preserve the principles of semi-sabbatarianism, albeit with decreasing success since World War II.

Among the list of sabbatarian communities, those who stand closest to Judaism are the Jewish sect of sabbatarians. However, they derive their name not from the Sabbath Law but from their founder, Sabbatai Zebi or Zevi. His teachings were not exclusively concerned with the special observance of the Sabbath, either. Rather they constituted a form of Messianism within the Jewish Kabbala tradition.

Sabbatrianism has influenced the politics of the right by infusing religious doctrine into government. Several of the United States still have "blue laws" that dictate what business can be conducted on Sundays. According to the *Christian Science Monitor*, "Whippings, fines, burnt tongues, severed ears: such were the Puritans' penalties for breaches of the Sabbath. Under the 'blue laws' of the 1700s, the punishments could be invoked for simple misdeeds ranging from shuffleboard to skipping church. Most colonial edicts have gone the way of scarlet letters. But one has remained intact in states from Connecticut to Texas: the ban on Sunday sales of alcohol. Now, a stubborn seam of Puritanical America is coming undone … Supporters of the repeal call this trend the natural confluence of flagging state economies and a steady erosion of antiquated blue laws. Critics decry it as an attack on the Sabbath—and on leisure itself. And both sides agree it's a further indication that Sunday is becoming just an ordinary day."

SEE ALSO
Volume 1 Left: Church and State Separation; United States. *Volume 2 Right:* Religion; Christian Identity; United States.

BIBLIOGRAPHY
Sara B. Miller, "In Battle for Sunday, the 'Blue Laws' Are Falling," *Christian Science Monitor* (December 5, 2003); Kenneth L. Parker, *The English Sabbath: A Study of Doctrine and Discipline from the Reformation to the Civil War* (Cambridge University Press, 2002).

NERGIS CANEFE
YORK UNIVERSITY, CANADA

Saudi Arabia

SAUDI ARABIA WAS founded through an alliance of the Al-Saud and Al-Wahhab families. The former has been the temporal power and the latter the spiritual power. Wahhabism, or Muwahhidun, as it is called in Saudi Arabia, is a puritanical version of Islam. The theology of Muhammad Abd al-Wahhab (1703–92) presented in his book *Tawhid* stresses the oneness of Allah. His teachings were partly derived from ibn

Taymiyah (1263–1303). He taught that Islamic theology could develop but rejected many practices that could be viewed as human. These included celebrating the Prophet Muhammad's birthday, Sufi practices such as pilgrimages to the tombs of saints, performing or listening to music, and dancing.

Abdul Al-Aziz ibn Saud (1880–1953), the founder of the modern state of Saudi Arabia, used Wahhabism to break tribal loyalties. He settled its extreme followers, the Wahhabi Ikhwan (Brotherhood), into villages. Their beliefs were like those of the the Khariji of early Islam who taught that those who opposed their view of Islam were apostates. The zeal of the Ikhwan for Islamic conquests beyond the kingdom led them to revolt (1927–30). They accused ibn Saud of apostasy because he was not as extreme as they, thus constituting the first religious opposition of the right to the Al-Saud. Although suppressed, the children and grandchildren of the Ikhwan now constitute a major source of the religious opposition of the right.

In 1965, a group of Muslim zealots led by Prince Khaled bin Musa'id, a grandson of King Abdul Aziz ibn Saud, fought with the police while attempting to take control of a radio station. The prince and several others were killed. This was followed in 1966 by bombings in Riyadh and elsewhere. It culminated on March 25, 1975, when Prince Faisal bin Musa'id assassinated his uncle, King Faisal, in revenge for his brother's death. He was executed soon afterward. On November 20, 1979, a group led by Juhaiman bin Muhammed Al-Utaibi seized the Grand Mosque in Mecca. They were inspired by the Islamic Revolution in Iran, by the beginning of a new Islamic century, and by the teachings of Shaikh Abdul Aziz bin Baz, head of the Prophet's Mosque in Medina. While only about 300 in number, it took weeks and a special French unit to root them out. The survivors were executed. Among those killed were some non-Saudi citizens, which demonstrated a linking of opposition in different social groups.

Religious opposition has continued to grow with increasingly sophisticated means used by leaders educated in the West. Many clerics in Saudi Arabia put their sermons onto cassette tapes. These are sold like books-on-tape. Web sites are also used as media for preaching against the Al-Sauds. This includes the Shiite movement led by Sheikh Hasan al-Saffar. The basic problem that the Al-Sauds are facing is the definition of the Islamic creed (*da'wa*). Who is in charge of defining "true" Islam? Saudi Arabia is already, because of Wahhabism, based on a fundamentalist Islamic belief system. The opposition that has been growing claims that they are

Abdul Al-Aziz ibn Saud, founder of modern Saudi Arabia, used religion to break tribal loyalties.

not Islamic enough. The opposition can be called extreme fundamentalism. It is led by members of the Saudi religious establishment, or *ulama*, that is, Islamic religious scholars. The great increase in graduates from Saudi universities with degrees in Islamic studies has led to an increase in those who are educated and yet oppose the regime. Some may be paid members of the state, while others are independent. A combination of these has engaged in criticism of the Al-Saud regime.

Opposition is growing from radical Islamic movements inspired by extreme doctrines of Islamic purity. In the 1980s, thousands of Arabs, including many Saudi Arabians, went to Afghanistan to fight the Soviets. Wealthy Saudis also provided great sums of money for the war. Among the Saudis who went was Osama bin Laden. Born in Saudi Arabia to a Yemeni family, he and many others learned of the radical teachings of the Egyptians while in Afghanistan. Already immersed in Wahhabism's view of pure Islam, they were taught the doctrines of Sayyid Qutb, the Islamic Group movement, and others with similar views of the purity of Islamic practice, but with a revolutionary interpretation of jihad.

Bin Laden was outraged in 1990 when the Saudi government allowed thousands of foreign troops to enter Saudi Arabia during the Gulf War. Bin Laden saw this as a violation of Muhammad's teaching that Arabia was for Muslims only. To bin Laden, the Saudi royal family is apostate because it has allied itself with the

West rather than prosecuting jihad against it. Bin Laden, along with Dr. Ayman al-Zawahiri and others, formed al-Qaeda (the Base). By 2004, its attacks against foreigners and the Saudi government had become frequent.

SEE ALSO
Volume 1 Left: Saudi Arabia; Middle East.
Volume 2 Right: Middle East.

BIBLIOGRAPHY
Mamoun Fandy, *Saudi Arabia and the Politics of Dissent* (Palgrave, 1999); Joshua Teitelbaum, *Holier Than Thou: Saudi Arabia's Islamic Opposition* (The Institute for Near East Policy, 2000); Stephen Schwartz, *The Two Faces of Islam: The House of Sa'ud from Tradition to Terror* (Doubleday, 2002).

ANDREW J. WASKEY
DALTON STATE COLLEGE

Second Amendment

"A WELL REGULATED Militia, being necessary to the security of a free State, the right of the people to keep and bear Arms, shall not be infringed." The Second Amendment of the U.S. Constitution is part of the Bill of Rights proposed by the First Congress. Congress passed 10 constitutional amendments in 1789 and sent them to the states for ratification. The Bill of Rights emerged out of anti-Federalist objections to the Constitution of 1787; it was ratified by the states in 1791.

Orphaned by constitutional scholars and variously embraced and despised by partisans on either side of the debate over the role of firearms in American life, the Second Amendment remains a very contentious issue into the 21st century. Scholars, politicians, and activists continue to debate whether the Second Amendment guarantees an individual the right to firearms ownership or if it refers to an 18th-century aspect of national defense that has long since faded into anachronistic obscurity.

The Second Amendment has roots in the military history of England. During the 17th century, England underwent a series of developments that were part of what historians term the "military revolution." In that revolution, armies of Europe expanded in size and developed tactics to integrate gunpowder weapons fully into tactical systems of the day. Those tactics stressed fighting in large linear formations that required great

discipline from soldiers. On the European continent, armies grew in size and professionalism, and helped to reinforce a growing trend toward centralization of power seen in many states at that time. In France, the development of a large army went hand in hand with the development of the absolutist state.

England, with a heritage of liberty, resisted the development of a permanent standing army. In the early 17th century, England did not maintain a standing army, preferring forces created ad hoc to expensive permanent armies. Parliamentary victory in the English Civil War had replaced the arbitrary rule of Charles I with the Cromwellian dictatorship resting on the power of the New Model Army. Suspicion of a standing army increased in the 1680s with James II's suppression of Monmouth's Rebellion and his increasing penchant for absolutism. When England created its own Bill of Rights in 1689, it included the provision, "that the subjects which are Protestants may have arms suitable for their defense suitable to their conditions and as allowed by law."

During the War for American Independence, Americans preferred to rely on the militia and an army with short-term enlistments to fight the British. Unfortunately for the Patriots' ideas on defense, the exigencies of the war required that America have a well-trained professional army in order to achieve final victory. While colonial militias enjoyed early successes in the fighting around Boston, Massachusetts, in 1775, later encounters between the untrained Americans and British regulars resulted in British successes. Only after George Washington developed the Continental Army into a disciplined, well-trained force could American troops succeed in open battle against the British.

Perhaps because they were militarily effective, standing armies were seen as instruments of arbitrary power, as corrupt, violent forces to abuse and oppress innocent civilians. The militia, by contrast, was viewed as a virtuous body of free men fighting in defense of their liberties. In colonial America, fear of standing armies, and specifically the outrages committed by British troops on American soil, helped to fuel the movement that became the American Revolution. Thomas Jefferson, in his pamphlet "A Summary View of the Rights of British America," stated:

> That in order to enforce the arbitrary measures before complained of, his majesty has from time to time sent among us large bodies of armed forces, not made up of the people here, nor raised by the authority of our laws: Did his majesty possess such a

right as this, it might swallow up all our other rights whenever he should think proper. But his majesty has no right to land a single armed man on our shores, and those whom he sends here are liable to our laws made for the suppression and punishment of riots, routs, and unlawful assemblies; or are hostile bodies, invading us in defiance of law.

These words offer a clear view of the link in the minds of many American colonists between standing armies and arbitrary rule. In *Federalist 46*, James Madison would echo those sentiments, arguing that the militia would protect against even the attempt of a tyrannical federal government to impose arbitrary rule upon America. Madison also noted that subjects of arbitrary regimes are often unarmed and that an armed populace is a necessary but not sufficient condition to the overthrow of tyranny.

The Second Amendment does not address hunting; rather it affirms an 18th-century tension seen between standing armies as instruments of tyranny and the militia as the sole defense of republican government. To an 18th-century reader, standing armies were composed of the dregs of society, of mercenaries. Such armies could be used by a tyrant to destroy free government. Indeed, to a nation of men who came of age reading the histories of ancient Rome, the examples of Marius, Sulla, and Julius Caesar would have been familiar: tyrants who used a professional military to usurp the power of the Roman Republic and finally to destroy it. This view is consistent with classical republican ideas that were popularized by Niccolo Machiavelli: only virtuous citizens, with a stake in society, could be counted on in defense of their country. These ideas on defense, armies, and the militia enjoyed favor with the anti-Federalist faction in America in the 1780s and 1790s, and found their expression in the Bill of Rights.

Eighteenth-century jurists also stressed a right to self-defense. In the first volume of his *Commentaries on the Laws of England*, eminent English law professor Sir William Blackstone listed three basic rights of Englishmen: "the right to personal security, the right of personal liberty, and the right of private property." Blackstone entitled the chapter in which that right is discussed "On the Absolute Rights of Individuals." Early commentator on the U.S. Constitution, editor of Blackstone's *Commentaries*, and professor of law at the College of William and Mary, St. George Tucker also described the right to bear arms in absolute terms. Tucker railed against any attempt to abridge the right to bear arms and clearly viewed any such attempts as an abomination on the order of an abridgement of free speech or free assembly. Befitting a student of liberty and of Blackstone, Tucker asserted that the right of self defense was the first right of mankind.

Debate still rages over several parts of the amendment. First, scholars argue over the meaning of the word *militia*. They seek to answer the following question: does the word *militia* refer to a specific military organization, like today's police forces or National Guard? Or does it refer to all of the sovereign citizenry in the republic? If the former is true, then individuals have no right to weapons; if the latter is true, then individuals do have the right to keep and bear arms. This dilemma leads to the second major point of debate over the amendment, namely, does it offer an individual or a collective right to weapons ownership? The fact that this amendment has a preamble, the section that refers to the militia, further complicates interpretation.

Scholars display a wide range of opinions regarding the Second Amendment. Yale University law professor Akhil Reed Amar notes in *The Bill of Rights* that it is possible to view *militia* and *people* as similar in meaning, for in the 18th century the militia would be composed of all males of age. Amar also argues that the Fourteenth Amendment alters the meaning of the Second Amendment and that it applies the right to keep and bear arms to individuals. Scholars H. Richard Uviller and William G. Merkel contend that the amendment refers specifically to the militia as a particular kind of military unit. They also argue that since the 18th-century militia no longer exists, even in modified form, the Second Amendment is silent on whether or not citizens have a right to keep and bear arms.

Yet Leonard W. Levy, author of *Origins of the Bill of Rights*, argues that such a notion is mistaken and that the amendment does, in fact, guarantee an individual right to bear arms. Levy finds precedent for his opinion in both English and colonial history, although he also argues that the 18th-century view of a militia as a counterweight to a national army is no longer practical, and that arms should be kept for the purposes of self-defense.

The Second Amendment also sits at the crossroads of the national debate in America over gun control. Many on the left advocate gun control, which is ironic, since they are often vociferous in the support of anything else that might be labeled a civil right. They apparently hope that if firearms are banned or severely restricted, then rates of violent crime will decrease. Such arguments do not address the fact that murder and other violent crimes have a far longer history than firearms. Conservatives, by contrast, claim an unrestricted right to own firearms, guaranteed by the Second Amendment, although, as discussed above, scholars debate whether or not the text of the amendment supports that argument.

The gun control debate, therefore, falls into a comfortable and well-known, liberal and conservative split. Liberals prefer the restriction or removal of a fundamental right, especially one so out of fashion and avowedly Anglo-Saxon, preferring that the state hold a monopoly of violence and a responsibility for the protection of its citizens. In their view, the government should shoulder that burden, just as it should the burden of healthcare. Such a view emphasizes the "militia" clause and advocates the position that individuals have no right to arms, which are themselves the cause of needless violence and death.

Conservatives, by contrast, emphasize that Americans have an unabridged right to own firearms, as guaranteed in the Second Amendment. Individual rights are placed above the ephemeral goal of achieving safety through disarmament.

SEE ALSO

Volume 1 Left: Bill of Rights; Gun Control; Constitutional Amendments.
Volume 2 Right: Constitutional Amendments.

BIBLIOGRAPHY

Akhil Reed Amar, The Bill of Rights: Construction and Reconstruction (Yale University Press, 1998); Carl T. Bogus, ed., The Second Amendment in Law and History: Historians and Constitutional Scholars on the Right to Bear Arms (New Press, 2000); Stephen P. Halbrook, That Every Man Be Armed: The Evolution of a Constitutional Right (University of New Mexico Press, 1984); Gary Kleck and Don B. Kates, Armed: New Perspectives on Gun Control (Prometheus Books, 2001); Leonard Williams Levy, Origins of the Bill of Rights: Politics and Ideas in the Making of the Constitution (Yale University Press, 1999); Joyce Lee Malcolm, To Keep and Bear Arms: The Origins of an Anglo-American Right (Harvard University Press, 1994); John Phillip Reid, In Defiance of the Law: The Standing-Army Controversy, the Two Constitutions, and the Coming of the American Revolution (University of North Carolina Press, 1981); Lois G. Schwoerer, "No Standing Armies!": The Antiarmy Ideology in Seventeenth-Century England (Johns Hopkins University Press, 1974); St. George Tucker, View of the Constitution of the United States with Selected Writings (Liberty Fund, 1999).

MITCHELL MCNAYLOR
OUR LADY OF THE LAKE COLLEGE

Segregation

SEGREGATION IN the United States could rightly be considered a conservative sociopolitical practice. Since white racial supremacy had been the norm in both black-white relations and white interaction with Native Americans and Asian Americans as well, any racial ideology initiated by whites without the consent of the other race or races involved would be a manifestation of conservatism. Segregation certainly meets that definitional criterion.

There are two kinds of segregation, de jure and de facto. The former means segregation by law; this type of segregation was once sanctioned by either local or state law and upheld by the courts, even the U.S. Supreme Court. This kind of segregation is no longer allowed. The latter means racial separation that occurs by individual choice, not by law; it generally occurs in social situations, and it is practiced routinely in America today.

There had been a long history of various kinds of racial and ethnic segregation throughout the centuries around the world. Jews had been singled out in many European countries at least as far back as the 1500s, and Gypsies became targets of similar segregation ordinances in Europe in more modern times. Many examples of segregation throughout history came as a result of class warfare; slaves and masters could not live or work side by side in most cultures where slavery was practiced. The feudal system, although a step above a slave-labor system, likewise allowed little interaction and no equality between serfs and lords. Even in industrialized nations since the 1700s, poor workers and their bosses, despite occupying common ground physically, existed in separate spheres psychologically, resulting in a primitive, undefined form of segregation. The most notable case of pure racial segregation in modern times outside of the United States was South Africa's apartheid system, which ran concurrently with American segregation of the black race, although outlasting it by some two decades. Even now, there arises in the world from time to time attempts at "ethnic cleansing," which turns mere segregation into mass murder and/or genocide.

Thus, the United States did not invent segregation, and it certainly never practiced the most extreme, notorious forms of it. American segregation is commonly considered a black-white racial phenomenon, but in fact segregation of Native Americans by whites was the first manifestation of de jure segregation in the United States, beginning with the creation of the Bureau of Indian Affairs and the development of the reservation system in the 1820s. In a sense, segregation of Native Americans is still practiced today, although it is now merely de facto segregation, since anyone wanting to escape the reservation on which he or she was born is free to do so.

Similarly, on the Pacific coast, the state of California enacted laws segregating Chinese immigrants in the 1850s, and by 1900 it did the same to Japanese immigrants, much to the displeasure of the government of Japan. A diplomatic crisis even erupted in 1906 between the United States and Japan over California's law segregating Japanese schoolchildren. Laws requiring separate schools for various Asian ethnic groups stayed on the books in California until the 1940s.

Laws requiring black-white separation were more widespread and noticeable because virtually every state had some type of de jure segregation of the races at one point or another. In the northern states prior to the Civil War, blacks were routinely proscribed to a lesser social status both legally and by custom. The first challenge to northern segregation came in 1849 in Boston, Massachusetts, when a black Bostonian sued the city for the right to send his daughter to the nearest public school rather than across town to the all-black school.

Although this case was not successful, it stirred the cauldron of change, and by 1855, Massachusetts had passed a law desegregating the state's public schools. Lesser types of segregation in the North continued, however, including in Massachusetts, until the Civil War. Blacks could not join the army, navy, or militia of any state; they could not vote or hold office in most states; and their options for residences and jobs were severely limited as well.

The Civil War was the great watershed event in the history of the United States and African Americans especially. Congress, under extremely liberal "radical" Republican leadership, took steps during and after the war to break down the racial divide in America, eliminating the laws against black service in the military forces, and trying to do away with voting restrictions and other racist proscriptions. Passing the Thirteenth, Fourteenth, and Fifteenth Amendments to the U.S. Constitution and several "enforcement bills" and civil rights bills, including the monumentally important Civil Rights Act of 1875, Congress sought to impose racial equality upon the defeated South when parts of the victorious Union had not embraced that idea themselves.

A host of problems mitigated against the success of such a plan. First, ultraconservative white southern for-mer Confederate Democrats refused to cooperate with this liberal northern Republican agenda for their Reconstruction and fought the plan all the way, through the creation of Black Codes, then the Ku Klux Klan and similar terrorist groups, and ultimately the "redemption" of their states. Second was the weak leadership of President Ulysses S. Grant, who would not use federal troops to enforce the laws passed by his own party. Third, the disputed election of 1876, which resulted in the Compromise of 1877, placed new President Rutherford B. Hayes in an anti-civil rights position from his first day on the job. Fourth, the U.S. Supreme Court ruled in the collective civil rights Cases of 1883 that the Civil Rights Act of 1875 was unconstitutional. Subsequent Supreme Court rulings would reiterate and strengthen that point of view. Finally, a vast majority of white Americans simply opposed granting equality to blacks during those pivotal years of the late 1800s.

It is impossible to distinguish laws requiring physical separation of blacks and whites from the overall systematic process of white Americans and their governments depriving blacks of civil rights and equality in other forms. Disfranchisement, lynching, economic and educational proscription, and segregation in public facilities and designated neighborhoods are all part-and-parcel of the same "race problem" that came to be commonplace in the United States between about 1877 and 1955. The total system of racial discrimination, in all its many forms, during this post-Reconstruction/pre-civil rights movement period was called "Jim Crow."

Although such abuses of black citizenship were most noticeable and numerous in the South, they were in fact nationwide. They seemed more pronounced in the South because that is where about 90 percent of blacks lived prior to World War I. Upon the great migration of blacks leaving the southern sharecropping fields for the industrial cities of the North during and after the war, the problems of segregated neighborhoods, workplaces, and schools, followed as did a new version of the lynching problem:race rioting. In St. Louis in 1917, a race riot erupted when white workers on strike reacted violently toward black scab workers who sought to take their jobs. In Chicago, Illinois, in 1919, one of the worst race riots in American history broke out when a black swimmer crossed the imaginary line in Lake Michigan and floated into the white swimming area. Detroit, Michigan, experienced a similarly bizarre and deadly race riot in 1943, caused by blacks and whites crossing imaginary territorial lines in the city.

JIM CROW, OR SEGREGATIONIST LAWS

During the heyday of Jim Crow in the South, each state made its own segregation laws. They went from the fairly standard, such as segregated cars on trains, to the unique and strange, such as segregated telephone booths in Oklahoma and segregated checkers matches in Alabama. Although all segregation laws were declared null and void by the Civil Rights Act of 1964, in custom and practice, some were still observed in isolated towns around the South as late as the 1980s. Basically, it required the pre-civil rights movement generation's dying off and a new generation taking control of the social and political machinery in the South to see the final destruction of American segregation.

Attempts to end Jim Crow laws were few and mostly unsuccessful prior to the 1950s. One of the most important reasons for this failure to challenge and defeat segregation was that civil rights organizations such as the NAACP chose to focus their efforts on violations of black citizenship rights that seemed more disturbing by comparison: lynching, disfranchisement, and unequal educational opportunities. Another reason lay in the fact that prior to the second wave of the Great Migration, which occurred during World War II, there was not yet a large enough black middle class or urban presence in the North to take on the fight against southern segregation. Once that sizeable urban middle class came into existence, it first had to break down the color barriers in its own new northern cities and states before embarking on the southern crusade. The Congress of Racial Equality (CORE) stood in the vanguard of civil rights organizations that fought segregation in the North, waging successful battles against the practice in Chicago by staging sit-ins as early as the 1940s.

Other nonpolitical methods were also introduced in the 1940s to remove the color barrier. The hiring of black superstar athlete Jackie Robinson by the all-white Brooklyn Dodgers baseball franchise in 1945 became an important catalyst for ending segregation in sports. The blurring of the lines between black music and white music with the rise of Elvis Presley and other white rhythm-and-blues performers in the mid-1950s likewise pushed the idea of integration in entertainment upon the masses long before the masses would have otherwise been ready for it.

Presidential leadership in ending segregation was almost nonexistent before the Harry Truman administration from 1945 to 1952. After the compromise of 1877, the next attempt by a president to do anything positive for African Americans came with Benjamin Harrison's single term from 1888 to 1892. He supported the Federal Elections Bill, which would have enforced the Fifteenth Amendment. Had it passed Congress, the voting power of blacks would have undoubtedly short-circuited the whole Jim Crow system in its infancy; but it did not pass, due to an extremely violent white conservative backlash. In 1901, new President Theodore Roosevelt tried symbolically to erase the color line by inviting Booker T. Washington to the White House for dinner, but again the conservative backlash was so intense that even the independent-minded Roosevelt dared not disrupt the status quo again. With the advent of Woodrow Wilson's presidency, the White House actually put a presidential seal of approval upon the practice of segregation, ordering all federal facilities in Washington, D.C., segregated.

President Franklin Roosevelt took the first small steps toward undoing the Jim Crow system. He created a "black cabinet" of advisors, and he supported his wife Eleanor's embracing of the National Council of Negro Women and the concert of black opera star Marian Anderson on the steps of the Lincoln Memorial in 1939, which was arranged by Eleanor and his secretary of the interior, Harold Ickes. He also ordered the integration of American military bases during World War II. President Truman went much further, desegregating the entire U.S. Armed Forces across the board by executive order. He also put his personal stamp of approval on "To Secure These Rights," a document issued by a special advisory committee on racial issues that he created, which basically said the federal government must take the responsibility for correcting the civil rights abuses against black Americans or they would never be corrected.

Eisenhower was a moderately conservative Republican. He did not approve of the civil rights movement that ensued in earnest under his watch, but neither did he openly oppose the *Brown v. Board of Education* decision, the Montgomery bus boycott, the forced integration of the public schools of Little Rock, Arkansas, or the two civil rights acts passed by Congress during his second term. Thus, he did nothing to quell the spirit of the liberal racial reform movement of the 1950s. Presidents John F. Kennedy and Lyndon B. Johnson guided the most sweeping racial reform measures through Congress and/or against the southern states since Reconstruction. The Civil Rights Act of 1964, the Voting Rights Act of 1965, and the Civil Rights Act of 1968 all combined to produce something resembling a revolution in American race relations. From the end of the Johnson administration to the present, there have been

A poll tax receipt for a "colored female" in Smith County, Texas, is evidence of one kind of Jim Crow law that tried to control African American voting. In this case, the woman had to pay a $1.75 fee to vote.

occasional executive attempts to alter the racial status quo, but more important measures have come through the courts. Awash with cases of affirmative action and reverse discrimination, federal courts have in no way achieved a final verdict on the subject of American race relations. Nevertheless, the issue of segregation per se has surfaced in recent years, and seems unlikely at this point ever to arise again as a major problem in the United States.

SEE ALSO

Volume 1 Left: Desegregation; Kennedy, John F.; Johnson, Lyndon B.; Affirmative Action.
Volume 2 Right: Apartheid; Supreme Court; Republican Party; American Civil War.

BIBLIOGRAPHY

Dee Brown, *Bury My Heart at Wounded Knee: An Indian History of the American West* (Henry Holt, 1970); Leonard Dinnerstein et al., *Natives and Strangers: A Multicultural History of Americans* (Oxford University Press, 1996); John Hope Franklin and Alfred E. Moss, Jr., *From Slavery to Freedom: A History of African Americans* (McGraw-Hill, 2000); Grace Elizabeth Hale, *Making Whiteness: The Culture of Segregation in the South* (Pantheon Books, 1998); John David Smith, ed., *When Did Southern Segregation Begin?* (St. Martin's Press, 2002); Thomas Adams Upchurch, *Legislating Racism: The Billion Dollar Congress and the Birth of Jim Crow* (University Press of Kentucky, 2004); C. Vann Woodward, *The Strange Career of Jim Crow* (Oxford University Press, 1974).

THOMAS ADAMS UPCHURCH, PH.D.
EAST GEORGIA COLLEGE

Shockley, William B. (1910–1989)

WILLIAM SHOCKLEY WON the Nobel Prize in physics in 1956. His research on transistor circuits remains instrumental in modern technological advances. During the later years of his life, however, Shockley became an advocate of eugenics, the study of the relationship between race and intelligence, which tarnished his scientific legacy.

Shockley was born in London, England, to American parents. At age three, the Shockley family returned to their home in California, where Shockley was home-schooled until he was eight years old. Shockley attended high school at the Palo Alto Military Academy before transferring to the Los Angeles Coaching School to study physics. Later, Shockley transferred to Hollywood High, where he graduated in 1927.

In the fall of 1927, he enrolled at the University of California at Los Angeles (UCLA). He attended UCLA for one year and, in 1928, transferred to the California Institute of Technology (Cal Tech) in Pasadena, where he was awarded a Bachelor of Science degree in physics in 1932. Later in 1932, Shockley entered the Massachusetts Institute of Technology (MIT) on a teaching fellowship. He earned his Ph.D. in physics from MIT in 1936.

From 1940 to 1955, Shockley gained recognition as a scientist with Bell Laboratories. When the United States entered World War II, Shockley took a leave of absence from Bell Labs to conduct military research for the War Department. From 1942 to 1944, Shockley served as the research director of the Anti-Submarine Warfare Operations Group, which was set up by the Navy Department at Columbia University in New York City. In 1944, Shockley acted as consultant to the Office of the Secretary of War until the war ended, when he returned to Bell Labs, in 1945.

Upon his return to Bell Labs, Shockley and two colleagues, John Bardeen and Walter Brattain, began research on semiconductors and transistors, which revolutionized modern electronic technology. The publication of Shockley's *Electrons and Holes in Semiconductors* in 1950 quickly became essential reading for students and research scientists. Shockley left Bell Labs in 1955 to operate his own research laboratory, Shockley Research Laboratories, in what is now known as Silicon Valley. In 1956, Shockley, with Bardeen and Brattain, was awarded the Nobel Prize for the transistor research conducted at Bell Labs. During his tenure at Bell Labs, Shockley also lectured at Princeton University and Cal Tech, and continued to counsel the U.S. government on scientific matters. He served as the scientific adviser to the Joint Research and Development Board from 1947 to 1949 and as the deputy director of the Department of Defense's Weapons Systems Evaluation Group from 1954 to 1955. In 1962, Shockley was appointed to the President's Science Advisory Committee on Scientific and Technical Manpower.

In the mid-1960s, Shockley's research turned away from physics and toward theories of eugenics, the study of the relationship between race and intelligence. He believed that differences in standardized IQ test scores among whites, Asians, and African Americans signaled that intelligence could be gauged by skin color. Shockley theorized that IQ test scores proved that Asians possessed genetic superiority over whites and that whites possessed an inherent genetic superiority over African Americans. He further believed that IQ test scores among African Americans could be raised 10 points for every 1 percent of Caucasian genes that was in their heritage.

Shockley's theories drew great criticism from anthropologists and biologists, among others, because of his inexperience in those fields. But, because of his notoriety as a Nobel laureate, Shockley and his theories gained widespread attention in the national press. The politically and racially charged nature of his claims provoked criticism from many. In 1980, Shockley sued the *Atlanta Constitution* for $1.25 million for comparing his theories to Nazi genetic experiments during World War II. The court agreed that the report was libelous, but awarded Shockley only $1 in damages.

The later years of Shockley's life were consumed with discussions of his belief in the link between race and intelligence rather than his earlier contributions to science and invention. In 1982, Shockley ran for the Republican nomination for California's U.S. Senate seat and discussion of eugenics consumed his campaign. He finished eighth in California's Republican primary. William Shockley died in 1989 at age 79.

SEE ALSO

Volume 1 Left: Cultural Diversity; Desegregation.
Volume 2 Right: Segregation; Black Separatism.

BIBLIOGRAPHY

J.L. Moll, *Biographical Memoirs* (National Academy Press, 1996); T. Wasson, ed., *Nobel Prize Winners* (H.W. Wilson, 1987); A. Alland, Jr., *Race in Mind: Race, IQ, and Other Racisms* (Palgrave Macmillan, 2002).

JAMES WERTZ
AMERICAN UNIVERSITY

Singapore

THE REPUBLIC of Singapore is a technically modern, economically prosperous 646-square-kilometer city-state of 4.7 million people (2003). It is a tightly regulated society with limited political freedoms and strict social and cultural order offering an attractive alternative of "soft" or paternalistic authoritarianism to the Western liberal democratic model. In the 14th century, Chinese merchants described Singapore, known in

Singapore is a strict, conservative city-state society that enjoys significant wealth.

those times under the name of Temasek, as a greenless island inhabited by pirates. According to a Malayan legend, a Sumatran prince met a lion on the island, and that good meeting inspired him to found the city of Singapore (The City of the Lion), which became a strategic trade state. The neighboring powers were competing for control over it when the Europeans joined the competition, beginning in the 15th century. The most successful were the British, who in 1921 constructed a great naval and air base in Singapore, and in 1924 incorporated Singapore into their empire. In the course of World War II, the Japanese invaded Singapore on February 8, 1941. The English made a courageous resistance; nevertheless, a week later, the fortress fell. It was almost destroyed during the years of the war.

Along with stressing the key significance of the Singapore battle, the conservative historian Paul Johnson explains the defeat of the English by the necessity of the Anglo-American alliance aiding Soviet Russia against Hitler. For Johnson, the capitulation of the Singapore garrison does not mean that Japanese turned out to be stronger than the English.

Britain surrendered in February 15, 1942 with 91,000 men. When General Itagaki handed his sword to Admiral Mountbatten in 1945, he had 656,000 men in the Singapore command. "Elsewhere the British received the capitulation of more than a million," asserts Johnson in *Modern Times: A History of the World from 1920s to the 1990s*, forgetting to add that it happened after Japan had been defeated by America in the Pacific war theater.

From 1946 to 1948, mass strikes began in Singapore and a state of siege was declared. The guerrilla war under the communist leadership was waged for 12 years. Singapore became self-governing in 1959 and the People's Action Party (PAP) took power through parliamentary elections. The stable government was led from 1959 to 1990 by Prime Minister Lee Kuan Yew. Industrialists attracted ever more investments, changing the visage of the city-state, which has become a not less prosperous Asian country than Japan.

Singapore received independence on August 9, 1965. The corporatized structure of a one-party system, absorbing talented youth into political management, coupled with a consumerist, apathetic citizenry has made competitive politics irrelevant.

Successful industrialization was accompanied by the Employment Act and the Industrial Relations (Amendment) Act, created to promote industrial peace and discipline among the workforce. Engaging business in policymaking was a distinctive feature of the Singaporean regime. But it aggressively tackled bureaucratic corruption before undertaking an economic dash as a way to establish the credibility of authorities in the eyes of citizens.

After the shock of two oil crises in the 1970s, the government started a program of economic restructuring. This was achieved by modifying education policies, expanding technology and computer education, offering financial incentives to industrial enterprises, and launching a productivity campaign. Public housing was given top priority. Singapore runs a modern, effective health system, the heart of which is the government control of inputs and outputs and strict rationing of health services according to wealth.

Today, few nations rival Singapore in economic connections to the world. Singapore's total trade is valued at 341.5 percent of its gross domestic product (GDP), more than 13 times higher than the proportion in the United States. Although Singapore has a GDP of only about one-tenth that of Italy, it receives approximately the same amount of foreign direct investment inflows. Internet access in Singapore is more common than in the United Kingdom or Germany. On average, Singaporeans spent 707 minutes on international telephone calls in 2000, more time than the citizens of any other nation. Seven million people visited Singapore in 2000, almost twice its population, and more people than visited Japan.

In the Corruption Index published by Transparency International, Singapore regularly has the lowest level of perceived corruption, beating the developed Western countries. The success story of Singapore shows that corruption has been reduced by creating specialized administrative offices supporting the courts in matters related to court notifications, budget and personnel management, cash, and case flows.

To liberate the system, as Western critics insist on, means to raise the capacity for individual autonomy and, in consequence, fuel the demands for more personal liberty. This trend, as Singaporean officials warn, will presage an unraveling of community and social responsibility. There is no need for a risk. The cultural and social superiority of the Singaporean model is dramatically illustrated by a comparison of Singapore and Los Angeles, California, cities of roughly the same size: In 1993, Los Angeles had 1,058 murders and 1,781 rapes, whereas Singapore had 58 murders and 80 rapes.

Lee Kwan Yew, the former long-term prime minister of Singapore and the chief architect of the country's political and social system, believes that the social and cultural prosperity of Singapore is due to the strict communitarian order advancing "the greatest good to the greatest number." Radical Western individualism and competition among self-seeking individuals will breed social dislocation and social pathology among members of society.

Immigration statistics indicate that lots of people are eager to move to Singapore which has 20,000 to 30,000 new permanent residents a year. So in the final analysis, rightist authorities argue, Singapore is a place where people are happy to live. Singaporean authorities reject accusations of inhumanity, arguing that the rights of criminals have not been given precedence over the rights of victims. They keep chiefly to a traditional alternative to the liberalist concept of political society and human rights. What is considered cruel treatment in the West is regarded as the necessary punishment to protect social and political life in Asia. With such an approach, moral values are assumed to be valid only in their particular cultural contexts.

Prime Minister Goh Chok Tong (2004) believes that Singapore has a more stable and secure social order precisely because it prizes the ability to meet complex technocratic challenges more than contending with a freewheeling press and strong opposition, and because it emphasizes social and community obligations rather than celebrating individual rights. Being a small state, Singapore has no international ambitions and is seeking friends and partners all over the globe.

SEE ALSO

Volume 1 Left: Singapore; Communitarianism; Human Rights. *Volume 2 Right:* Conservatism.

BIBLIOGRAPHY

"Singapore's Constitution," www.oefre.unibe.ch (July 2004); Bilahari Kausikan, "Governance That Works," *Journal of Democracy* (v.8/2, April 1997); Raymond Callahan, "Singapore 1942: Britain's Greatest Defeat," *The Journal of Military History* (v.67/1, January 2003); "Singapore's Big Gamble," *Foreign Policy* (May 2002); Michael Elliott, "The Caning Debate: Should America Be More Like Singapore?" *Newsweek* (April 18, 1994).

IGOR CHARSKYKH
DONETSK NATIONAL UNIVERSITY, UKRAINE

South Africa

THE REPUBLIC OF SOUTH AFRICA, which occupies the southern tip of the African continent, has been of interest to Europeans for centuries, for both strategic and economic reasons. In the last century, the right-wing policies of successive governments in South Africa have been based on racial exclusion and were for many decades enshrined in the country's laws. South Africa before the 1990s is remembered for its policy of apartheid, its official policy of racial separation and inequality. Interestingly, South African government policies were implemented through the passage and rule of law, made by white minority legislatures.

Southern Africa has long been known as rich in natural resources, including food and later gold and diamonds. Militarily, southern Africa was important because it guarded the major sea routes to Asia, including India and China. The Dutch were the first Europeans to establish a permanent settlement, in the southern Cape, in 1652, which was the period of Dutch hegemony in Europe. Because of a shortage of local labor, and plentiful land, South Africa in the 18th century imported Africans, mainly from Angola and Dahomey, as slave labor.

During this time, both British and Dutch colonists emigrated to the area. From the 1790s to the 1810s, South Africa flipped back and forth from Britain and the Netherlands during the era of the Napoleonic Wars, but by 1815 the British received the Cape Colony by treaty. In 1834, the British emancipated slaves throughout the empire, including in South Africa, and this is also the decade of the Great Trek, in which the descendants of the Dutch colonists, who called themselves Afrikaners, left the Cape Colony to establish new settlements in the interior, in competition with the indigenous African people, and ultimately to create what would be known as the Boer republics, such as the Transvaal. It is also interesting to note that in the 1860s, indigenous Africans, people of mixed race, and people from India all had some political rights in the British-controlled Cape Colony.

The question of who would control South Africa—the British or the Afrikaners—came to a head in the 1890s, and led to the Anglo-Boer War, from 1899 to 1902. The British won this war, but the peace settlement was generous to the Afrikaners. It should be noted that little consideration was given to the interests of the indigenous Africans. In 1910, the Union of South Africa was established as a dominion of the United Kingdom, with powers and status similar to those of Canada, Australia, and New Zealand.

While the apartheid policy is associated with the post-World War II era, it can be seen as an intensification and continuation of policies established in the first half of the 20th century. In these early governments of this new Union, power was shared by descendants of both the British and Afrikaner settlers. Significant pieces of legislation were passed, such as the Mines and Works Act, Defence Act, Native Land Act, Native Affairs Act, Natives (Urban Areas) Act, and Industrial Conciliations Act, all of which worked against the interests of indigenous Africans. Certain jobs were restricted to whites only, blacks were denied the right to strike, and there were restrictions on where blacks could live.

In the 1930s, it was affirmed that Africans would elect only a token number of representatives and that they must be white. Further, before World War II, South African governments established a reserve system, similar to those found in other British dominions, including Canada, where the indigenous populations would live. This policy was a forerunner of the apartheid-era Bantustan policy.

The major change in 1948 came with the election to power the National Party, which was exclusively an Afrikaner movement. Over the preceding decades, the Dutch descendants came to outnumber the British and they felt increasingly alienated from the British and other Europeans, who were increasingly critical of the government's race policies. The National Party government, led by Dr. D.F. Malan, proceeded over the next couple of decades to bring in strong laws to entrench the white minority's superiority and control of the country. Legislation such as the Population Registration Act, Group Areas Act, Prohibition of Mixed Marriages Act, Immorality Act, Suppression of Communism Act, Unlawful Organisations Act, and Internal Security Act regulated every aspect of the lives of Asians and indigenous Africans. The official policy of the government was that there was a hierarchy of races, and that whites were superior to Indians and those of mixed race, while these were superior to indigenous Africans. South Africa was also accused of being an international aggressor, based on attacks against its neighbors and continuing occupation of South West Africa, which would later become Namibia.

A steady stream of legislation implemented this ideology. In 1951, the Pass Laws were updated to require that all Africans carry identification papers. The Bantu Education Act gave the central government authority over separate and inferior education of indigenous Africans. Protests, of which there were many, were often met with force. The year 1960 saw the Sharpeville massacre, in which 69 Africans were killed and 180 were injured when police opened fire on a demonstration against the Pass Laws. Shortly after, the African National Congress was banned under the Unlawful Organizations Act, and the Sabotage Act was passed in 1962. In 1963, the Rivonia trials began, leading to the convictions of Nelson Mandela and others. Mandela would be held in the notorious Robben Island prison for almost 30 years.

In 1967, the Terrorism Act introduced unlimited detention without trial, and in 1968 the Political Interference Act banned people from joining forces with people of another racial group. Under the homeland policy, Transkei became the first Bantustan to achieve nominal "independence," though it was not recognized by the world community. In 1976, police again fired on protestors, mainly children this time, in Soweto, who were protesting against inferior education. Activist Steve Biko died in police custody in 1977. In the same period, the government passed a new constitution, which provided three separate legislatures, one each for whites, coloreds, and blacks, but this did nothing to reduce international and domestic resistance.

The 1980s was a period of unremitting pressure on the apartheid regime, both domestic and international. In 1985, the government declared a state of emergency, but by 1989 a new leader, F.W. de Klerk, took office as president. He proposed to dismantle the apartheid system, which happened in the 1990s. Walter Sisulu, Mandela, and the rest of the political prisoners were released; the apartheid-era laws were repealed; the bans on people and organizations were lifted, along with the state of emergency; and the country moved to elections on a one-person, one-vote basis.

By 2004, the African National Congress (ANC) had been in power for 10 years. One of the remaining issues is whether the ANC has been able to live up to its socialist and egalitarian commitments. There are some observers, such as Patrick Bond, who argue that post-apartheid South Africa has paid a high price in accommodating itself to both the mainly white domestic economic power holders and to the global capitalist economic system.

SEE ALSO

Volume 1 Left: Socialism; United Kingdom.
Volume 2 Right: South Africa; Apartheid; United Kingdom.

BIBLIOGRAPHY

Patrick Bond, Elite Transition: From Apartheid to Neoliberalism in South Africa (Pluto Press, 2000); R. Davenport and C. Saunders, South Africa: A Modern History (Macmillan, 2000); R. Hyam and P. Henshaw, The Lion and the Springbok: Britain and South Africa since the Boer War (Cambridge University Press, 2003); Gerhard Schutte, What Racists Believe: Race Relations in South Africa and the United States (Sage Publications, 1995); Erik A. Walker, A History of Southern Africa (Longmans, Green and Company, 1957).

GEOFFREY R. MARTIN
MOUNT ALLISON UNIVERSITY, CANADA

South America

THE SOUTH AMERICAN right is a political group that has evolved by incorporating various ideologies of strong traditional institutions, such as the economical and political systems of colonialism, agrarian oligarchism, conservatism, and militarism. These institutions were also complemented by other positions that are not necessarily characteristic of the right, but were often adapted to its interests: Catholicism, positivism, nationalism, populism, and neoliberalism.

The combination of these characteristics resulted in the application of a series of adjectives for South America and Latin America in general: the continent of popular Catholicism, the land of caudillos, of totalitarian populist regimes and old agrarian "feudal" systems under corrupt governments. Especially during antidemocratic governments, these characteristics have been combined with the interests of the right. For this reason, the right in South America has often been equated with military dictatorships, which have, in turn, often received the reaction of leftist movements, which have historically upheld republican, socialist, or democratic ideals. As a result, South America has experienced a high degree of conflict between left and right during the 20th century.

This, however, is intrinsic not only to the internal political structures of the continent, but also to foreign relations, particularly those with the United States. Already in 1823, U.S. President James Monroe affirmed that any foreign—especially European—intervention in any country of the Americas would be considered a threat to the security of the United States, justifying later interventions in countries such as Panama, Cuba, and the Dominican Republic in the 19th century. During a good part of the 20th century, the tension between left and right in South America was also interpreted in terms of the Cold War conflict. After the 1980s, with the beginning of the democratization process in South America, these views have continued to influence politics, and the right has remained influential, but mainly through the action of various political parties, organizations, and institutions.

THE POWER OF COLONIALISM

South America was colonized primarily by the Spanish and the Portuguese, beginning in 1492 and lasting more than three centuries. The origins of the South American right emerged from the agrarian structures of oligarchism, slavery, and mercantilism, as well as from the Catholic Church and the juridical elite, which were used by Europeans to serve their interests as colonizers.

While the Spanish colonization of Latin American countries included the creation of independent dioceses, universities, printing houses, and political jurisdic-

The major countries of South America, including Brazil, Argentina, Chile, and others have all experienced right-wing regimes. When anti-communist, these regimes usually enjoyed the strong support of the United States.

tions, which were kept united and loyal by a strong military, the Portuguese ruled by means of ideological tools. Education was centralized at the University of Coimbra, Portugal, which trained bureaucrats to serve the Portuguese colonies in America, Africa, and Asia. Together with a local elite and the religious leadership, they created structures to dominate workers, slaves, and native groups.

From the beginning, the military was an important institution for control and order in the colonies. The first examples of military violence were the incursions of Francisco Pizarro and the *colonizadores* against the natives in the 16th century. A similar modus operandi could be seen in several other regions, in acts that led to the destruction of pre-Columbian empires and numerous native tribes. The church and its missionary efforts have been considered "the right arm of colonialism." The church promoted and benefited financially from the slavery of Africans and induced the natives to accept evangelization along with the system of colonization. Religious imagery and icons functioned to make the domination of the crown and the landholders appear as natural and sacred. Enrique Dussel, Eduardo Hoornaert, Hans-Jürgen Prien, and others have analyzed these aspects in the multivolume collection *Historia General de la Iglesia en América Latina* (CEHILA).

There was also the institution of bureaucracy, based on the legal framework that had already existed in Spain and Portugal. Those responsible for this area were trained in the law schools of Portugal and Spain—especially Coimbra and Salamanca (Spain)—in order to perform the administrative duties in the colony. They had the function of collecting taxes, running the courts, supervising the commercial activities, and supporting the policies implemented by the crown. In a study about the courts in colonial Brazil, *Sovereignty and Society in Colonial Brazil: The High Court of Bahia and Its Judges*, Stuart Schwartz affirms that lawyers and judges rather than the military were responsible for reinforcing royal decisions in the colony.

Finally, there was the agrarian system. Although it has been compared to European feudalism, the agrarian structure was an important part of the "modern worldsystem" as defined by Immanuel Wallerstein. Large portions of land were given to certain families, who had the power and responsibility of exploiting those areas and creating the basic infrastructure for economic activities. Timber extraction, mining of gold and silver, and agriculture crops of cotton, coffee, cacao, sugarcane, and others for export became the most important economic activities in South America. At the local level,

the landlord and his property were the central structure around which others would orbit: bureaucrats would collect taxes, priests would do their missionary work among natives and administer the sacraments, the military would cooperate with security. While these complementary relations were developed to maintain the power of the crown, the distance from the controlling power facilitated the creation of particular types of colonial culture and forms of conservatism, whose remnants are still visible today

CONSERVATISM AFTER INDEPENDENCE

The 19th century witnessed a series of movements for independence in South America. These movements included not only those groups that organized rebellions and attempted revolutions, but also the economic elite who were paying heavy taxes to Spain and Portugal to finance wars in Europe. The independence of South American countries cannot be seen only as the result of intellectual and popular movements based on the ideals of the Enlightenment, for the involvement of the elite in negotiating new forms of economic trade with Europe was also influential.

After a series of declarations of independence and the writing of constitutions in new South American republics during the 1800s, European conservatism, which had had an impact in the former colonies, was institutionalized. The party politics generally followed the conservative-liberal scheme, whereas conservatives were seen as the right and liberals were understood as representing the left. Conservatives in Mexico supported the wars of independence from Spain, but then tried to establish a monarchy of the Bourbon family in Mexico City, while in Brazil, conservatism arrived later, directly from France, as both countries had their own *Partido Conservador*. The role of conservatism in Argentina during the 19th century was defined by José Luis Romero in his book *El orden conservador*. He argued that conservatism could take different positions according to the needs of the moment. Thus, conservatives could be provincial caudillos who aimed at maintaining the old colonial order, or also liberal conservatives, who were influenced by the so-called generation from the 1880s and incorporated modern and positivist ideas into their political thinking.

POSITIVISM, NATIONALISM, POPULISM

Positivism was the main ideology at the end of the 19th century in Latin America. At first, it emerged as a liberal position, opposed to clericalism and to the aristocracies, defending the interests of new liberal professional classes. Soon thereafter, the association between positivism and militarism led to a new form of politics by the right as traditional institutions were modernized.

Mexico and Brazil are good examples of this change, as both countries adopted the same motto: "order and progress." This motto represented the emergence of positivism and its association with a mitigated form of conservatism, for while the idea of "progress" referred to the scientific and developmentalist beliefs of positivistic militarism, the idea of "order" referred to the traditional conservative assumption of maintaining the order of the status quo ante.

Nationalism can be seen as a second wave in the politics of the right. In Argentina, the 1920s witnessed the emergence of an extreme right, which was associated with nationalism, Catholicism, and fascism. The authoritarian right was led by intellectuals such as Carlos Ibarguren, Leopoldo Lugones, and Manuel Gálvez with publications such as *La nueva república* and *Nueva orden*. The right was also represented by Catholic nationalism in the Catholic Action movement and the *Criterio* journal. In Brazil, the "nationalist Brazilian right" during the 1930s was represented by integralism, a movement founded by Plinio Salgado in 1932, which emphasized the ideas of "homeland" and "nation." This movement favored authoritarianism and organized associations and paramilitary groups according to the fascist model in vogue in Europe at that time.

The turn to a nationalistic right also marked the rise of military dictatorships during the 1930s, with the coming to power of the first dictators in South America. In Argentina, General Uriburu took Yrigoyen's office in 1930 by means of a coup d'etat, as did President Getulio Vargas in Brazil. Since South American countries supported the United States and the alliance against European fascists during World War II, many military dictatorships had to adapt themselves to new times under the pressure of the United States, which demanded the adoption of social and democratic government measures.

Populism was also a particular South American phenomenon, which brought together elements that belong to both the right and the left. The most characteristic examples of populism were Getulio Vargas in Brazil and Juan Peron in Argentina. Peron cannot be completely reduced to the authoritarianism of the right, due to the complexity of his populism—especially due to the social policies he implemented, which made him the "father of the poor." The same is valid for Vargas in Brazil. However, both turned to the right as they showed fascist sympathies, adopted militarism, and questioned democracy in order to retain power.

THE POLITICAL RIGHT AND MILITARISM

In 1959, Fidel Castro and Ernesto "Che" Guevara led a successful revolution in Cuba, as they ousted the dictator Fulgencio Batista, despite the support he was receiving from the United States. The triumph of the Cuban Revolution had a great impact in South America because several movements began to work toward similar revolutions in their respective countries. During the 1960s, there was a series of attempted rebellions in the continent and growing opposition to the United States. The reaction against these groups led to a new wave of military governments, which consistently supported the right.

In Argentina, President Arturo Frondizi was elected as a candidate of the Radical Party in 1961, but later turned to the right, as he adopted repressive measures and issued the Law in Defense of Democracy against members of the left. In 1966, the military took over and placed General Onganía as president. After the extreme left—the Montoneros—assassinated former President Uriburu in 1970, the military reacted violently, promoting a "Dirty War" from the 1970s until 1982, when they experienced a humiliating defeat by the British in a war over the possession of the Falkland/Malvinas Islands. This led to a new democratization process in modern Argentina.

In Brazil, the military overthrew a leftist government in 1964. During this time, General Goulbery do Couto e Silva became the leader of a group of officers at the War College, which was responsible for drawing a policy of "national security" and selecting the military who would act as presidents. To impose military rule, the government created several centers, such as the Department of Political and Social Orders (DOPS) and the Center for Internal Defense Operations (CODI), which were responsible for the repression of citizens and organizations that opposed the military dictatorship. The military ruled until 1984, when a process of "opening toward democracy" began to take place.

In Uruguay, a similar process occurred especially after 1969, when the economic situation of the country worsened and the population showed sympathies toward leftist groups, especially the Tupamaros. As a reaction, legal measures were taken by the government in order to repress guerrillas and popular manifestations. At the same time, groups of the right, such as the Tradition, Family and Property movement, and members of the military began to gain more power in the government with the enactment of security measures. President José María Bordaberry from the liberal party headed a repressive regime but was ousted by the military, and Aparicio Méndez became president. Only in 1985 would a civilian, Julio María Sanguinetti, be elected president.

In Colombia, the experience of violence against civilians continued through the 20th century. Opposition between the conservative and liberal parties often resulted in violent battles. In the late 1950s, the liberals and conservatives formed an alliance, the National Front, in order to avoid violence and share power. Unable to incorporate other organizations, the National Front was confronted by groups who were dissatisfied with the economic and political situation.

The Liberal and Conservative Parties worked in alliance for the 1970 elections to counter a common enemy, former dictator General Rojas. After his narrow defeat, members of his group formed a guerrilla movement (April 19 Movement, M-19) against the government.

They were joined by leftist movements: the National Liberation Army (ELN), created in 1962, and the Colombian Revolutionary Armed Forces (FARCs). Organized drug trafficking, known as cartels, have gained considerable political power. Paramilitary right-wing groups associated with drug trafficking and/or the military have also arisen. The American "war on drugs" has invested considerable military aide to stop primarily the FARC group. Unable to control the fighting, the liberals, who had won the presidency for 12 straight years, lost to the right in 1998. As of 2002, the right-wing independent Alvaro Iribe has favored outright fighting with the FARC and has imposed security measures.

In Chile, despite the fact that the country was relatively calm during the 1960s, when many other South American countries were experiencing turmoil, the election of socialist candidate Salvador Allende in 1970 altered the situation. Due to the several initiatives of Allende's government, which brought him closer to Cuba and further from the United States, several movements from the right and the military opposed his government.

On September 11, 1973, a military coup led by General Augusto Pinochet provoked the death of Allende and initiated a violent period in Chilean history, with the arresting and killing of thousands of civilians, while millions fled the country. Pinochet ruled as military dictator until 1989.

POLITICAL PARTIES IN DEMOCRATIC STATES

Since the democratization process in the 1980s and 1990s, the politics of the right have been anchored in political parties that adopted the values of a long conservative tradition, now modernized and adapted to newer situations. The right has been represented mainly by several political parties, which receive the support of church sectors, remnants of the old oligarchies, movements of landowners, and others. The right has been able to find its niche within party politics under a democratic regime, electing presidents at the beginning of the 21st century.

In Argentina, the political right had already formed groups such as the Argentinean Civic Union, the Alliance of the Nationalist Youth, the Argentinean Anti-Communist Alliance, and the Center Democratic Union (UCD) to defend its specific interests. Even during the 1990s, fascist groups were still active. But the rightist side of the Peronist movement was most influential. Under the neo-Peronist President Carlos Menem, elected in 1989, many groups of the right regained power, and Menem pardoned the military officers who had been convicted of human rights violations during the military period.

The examples of right-wing parties in Brazil were not as radical as in Argentina. During the military period, only two parties were allowed: the National Renovation Alliance (ARENA) on the right and the Brazilian Democratic Movement (MDB) on the left. With the democratization process, a series of other parties were created out of ARENA. Among the most important parties, which disguised their position through the traditional politics of conciliation, was the Social Democratic Party (PDS), to which many of the old traditional members of ARENA migrated. Later on, the Liberal Front (PFL) organized to maintain the same conservative and oligarchic basis, despite its elusive name.

In Peru, there was a mixture of neoliberalism and conservatism, not only after Fujimori's coup to become president, but also with politicians such as Mario Vargas Llosa, the award-winning writer who later turned to politics, adopting a conservative position. In Colombia, President Uribe represented a turn to the right, as he expressed the interests of Colombian oligarchies and the politics of the United States. In Bolivia, President Sanchez de Losada expressed nostalgia for military rule, while in Chile a new and clearer approximation to the United States served to question the possibility of a stronger South American Common Market (MERCOSUR).

For all these reasons, it can be said that the right has deep roots in Latin America, strong traditions reinforced by authoritarian groups and military power, and a continuous impact through newly adapted and invigorated party politics.

SEE ALSO

Volume 1 Left: South America; Chile; Brazil; Argentina.
Volume 2 Right: United States; Chile; Brazil; Argentina.

BIBLIOGRAPHY

José Luis B. Beired, Sob o signo da nova ordem. Intelectuais autoritários no Brasil e na Argentina (São Paulo, Ed. Loyola, 1999); Sandra McGee Deutsch, Counterrevolution in Argentina: The Argentine Patriotic League (University of Nebraska Press, 1986); Gérard Debrun, A Conciliação (São Paulo, Brasiliense, 1982); Raymundo Faoro, Os donos do poder: Formação do patronato político Brasileiro (São Paulo, EDUSP, 1975); Clara Nieto, Masters of War: Latin America and U.S. Aggression: From the Cuban Revolution through the Clinton Years (Seven Stories, 2003); Alain Rouquié, The Military and the State in Latin America (University of California Press, 1985); Nelson W. Sodré, A ideologia do colonialismo (Petrópolis, Vozes, 1981).

Amos Nascimento
Methodist University of Piracicaba, Brazil

Soviet Union

THE RUSSIAN REVOLUTION of October 1917, which brought the leftist Bolshevik (or Communist) Party of Vladimir I. Lenin into power, had its origins in World War I, a war driven by monarchical alliances on the right. In August, fulfilling its alliance obligations to France, the Russia of Tzar Nicholas II entered the war on the side of France. By August 4, Great Britain would join them. These countries were opposed by imperial Germany and Austria-Hungary, sometimes called the Austrian Empire. At first, the entry of Russia into the war was felt to be a great blessing to beleaguered England and France. Yet, the immense size of the country was its own downfall. As Barbara Tuchman wrote in The Guns of August, "as the Grand Duke [Nicholas] confessed to [Raymond] Poincaré [the president of France], the problem was that in an empire as vast as Russia, when an order was given no one was ever sure whether it had been delivered."

In August 1914, the high command, the STAVKA, was totally unprepared for modern war. By 1916, war weariness had begun to spread through the Russian people. Orlando Figes, in A People's Tragedy, quotes a soldier writing to his wife in November 1916, "they have suffered so much, that it's all they can do to stop their hearts from breaking and to keep themselves from losing their mind."

On February 23, 1917 (March 8 in our modern calendar), workers began to demonstrate against the suffering from the cost of the war on the Eastern Front (a term used to distinguish the fighting in Eastern Europe from that in France, the Western Front). At the time, Nicholas was fatefully out of the capital at his military headquarters at Mogilev. Before he could return to the capital of St. Petersburg, changed to Petrograd because it seemed too German, a provisional government under Prince Georgi Lvov was installed in the former tzarist Winter Palace. However, the new provisional government was unable to stop the rioting in the aroused capital. By February 28 (March 12, new style), as Figes notes, the casualties of the near anarchy were "up to 1,500 people killed and about 6,000 wounded." Nicholas abdicated, ending over three centuries of rule by the House of Romanov in Russia.

However, even with Nicholas dethroned, Lvov was unable to govern because a parallel regime already existed, with roots in the revolution of 1905. Workers, peasants, soldiers, and sailors formed soviets, or councils, throughout Russia. During the months to come, the provisional government, under Lvov and then his minister for war, Alexander Kerensky, fought a losing battle against the soviets. In April, Lenin returned from exile in Zurich and immediately sought an alliance with the soviets, and ultimately won their support for his Bolshevik Party. The death knell for the provisional government came in August 1917. At that time, Kerensky had sought General Lavr Kornilov to restore order in the capital. Instead, Kornilov saw an opening to make himself military dictator. To Kerensky's chagrin, he had to turn to the Bolsheviks and the soviets for enough fighting men to defeat Kornilov, who was arrested on September 1, 1917. When a Democratic Conference ended on September 14, with no decision on how to share power between middle-class parties like the Kadets and the soviets, Lenin saw a wedge in which to make his bid for supremacy. On October 7, Lenin secretly returned to Petrograd from Finland, where he had fled from arrest during the summer.

By October 15, although all Petrograd papers were discussing the possibility of a Bolshevik coup, Kerensky still would take no action against them. On October 25, while Kerensky was back at Pskov, the navy cruiser *Aurora*, supporting the Bolsheviks, fired blank rounds at the Winter Palace, home of the provisional government. Lenin issued a proclamation decreeing the end of the provisional government, and the Winter Palace was stormed by troops loyal to him and the Bolsheviks. As Leon Trotsky, Lenin's lieutenant in the seizure of power, wrote about the attack, "The palace did not surrender but was taken by storm—this, however, at a moment when the power of resistance of the besieged had already completely evaporated." The next day, supported by the Council of Soviets, Lenin took power. The Bolshevik Revolution, which Kerensky, the last true Russian liberal, had done virtually nothing to oppose, had taken place.

RIGHTIST COUNTERREVOLUTION

However, the Bolsheviks' hold on power was tenuous. It not only inherited the war with Austria-Hungary and Germany, it also faced a growing rightist counterrevolution within Russia. Kerensky, who had fled, and the tzar, who would be killed with his family in July 1918, were now totally out of the political equation. When Germany showed every sign of continuing the war, Lenin was forced to make a peace at Brest-Litovsk in March 1918. There was an Allied intervention, beginning with the British at Murmansk, to prevent the huge amount of war supplies being surrendered to the Germans. However, the foreign intervention would remain peripheral to the struggle against the anti-Bolshevik Russians, who called themselves the "White Armies," as opposed to the "Red" Bolsheviks. Throughout the civil war, the Allies and the Whites showed little or no coordination of efforts. Indeed, at Vladivostok, the Americans were as concerned with the Japanese military presence as they were with the Bolsheviks.

When Kornilov was killed in April 1918, leadership of the Whites passed to a loose coalition led by General Anton Denikin, who would later be succeeded by General Baron Peter Wrangel. From November 1918, the "supreme leader" of the Whites was Alexander V. Kolchak of the Black Sea Fleet. From the beginning, the Whites were handicapped by competing ambitions and a dreadful lack of coordination of their offensives.

On the other hand, Lenin was favored in having the talents of Leon Trotsky, who served him as commissar for Military and Naval Affairs. But as the civil war worsened, Lenin turned a policy of pitiless terror toward anyone he and the party deemed an "enemy of the peo-

ple." The civil war ground to a grim end. In November 1920, as W. Bruce Lincoln writes in *Red Victory: A History of the Russian Civil War*, the White armies of Baron Peter Wrangel evacuated the Crimea in the face of the attacks of Trotsky's best general, Mikhail Frunze. Frunze exulted: "our triumphant Red standards are now firmly planted on the shores of the Crimea." By March 1921, all enemies of the revolution had been crushed in the former Russian empire by Trotsky's Red Army. Lenin, speaking at the Tenth Congress of the Communist Party on March 8, 1921, could say, "The last of the hostile armies has been driven from our territories."

With the danger of the Whites and foreign intervention passed, Lenin now had to face the reconstruction of a ravaged country. Indeed, his authority was challenged at the Ninth Communist Party Congress in March and April 1920, where party members challenged the centralization of authority that had taken place during Lenin's war rule. One ominous sign was that the sailors at the Kronstadt naval base, which protected the capital, revolted at the same time. They had been among the first adherents of the revolution. Their rebellion was crushed with extreme brutality by Lenin.

The New Economic Policy (NEP) was introduced, which began to bring capitalism back to the new socialist state and veering Lenin to the right. However, at the same period, Lenin's health entered a critical state of decline in December 1921 and continued to deteriorate. While still alive, he saw the power struggle begin that almost ripped his new state apart, between Trotsky and Josef Stalin. Trotsky, as Lincoln points out, had never taken time to build a secure power base within the Communist (Bolshevik) Party; his time had been spent with the army. However, Stalin had spent the revolution and civil war years cultivating allies within the party.

Gradually, Lenin turned against Stalin but before he could act, in March 1923, he suffered another stroke. On January 1, 1924, Lenin died, apparently from a massive heart attack.

TOTALITARIAN STALIN

By 1927, Stalin had succeeded in removing his main rival, Trotsky, from any hope of succeeding Lenin. From then on, his tenure in power—he would rule until his death in March 1953—would be marked by a ruthless extermination of all real (or perceived) rivals for power. Stalin, a leftist by way of communistic philosophy, was a rightist in his totalitarian rule. He used the triumph over Trotsky, who increasingly had urged less centralized party leadership, to force upon Russia his drive for "collectivization" of agriculture. Forced modernization was brought to the people by a ruthless secret police. Pursued with no regard for the human cost, the collective farm movement, breaking up centuries of Russian agricultural practice, helped produce a hideous famine, notably in the "bread basket" of Russia, the Ukraine. Some 5 to 10 million people perished.

The use of terror that Stalin unleashed in the murder, on December 1, 1934, of S.M. Kirov, secretary of the party's Central Committee, was more than a continuation of the policy of Lenin. While Lenin saw violence as the classic "means to an end," Stalin institutionalized it as state policy. Indeed, in a real way, it was here that Stalinism, as opposed to Lenin's idea of communism, began. With the beginning of the purge trials after the death of Kirov, Stalin turned against the "revolutionaries" and began to seek a new type of "party man" who had no memory of the past before Stalin's most recent radio speech.

In June 1941, disregarding information from many sources, Stalin's Soviet Union was massively attacked by the Nazi Germany of Adolf Hitler, who had signed a Non-Aggression Pact with the Russians in August 1939. The purge had wrecked the Russian armed forces, causing the country to lose the services of leaders like Marshal Mikhail Tukhachevsy and Vasili Blyukher. Hitler's main thrust at Moscow would eventually be stopped in December 1941. In doing so, Stalin forged alliances with the "bourgeois" countries like the United States and Great Britain, led by President Franklin D. Roosevelt and Prime Minister Winston S. Churchill. At wartime conferences, such as at Tehran, Iran, in 1943, they decided upon the strategy to defeat the common German menace. On April 30, 1945, Russian Marshal Georgi Zhukov began the final offensive on the German capital of Berlin. Within Berlin on the same day, Hitler committed suicide.

As with Lenin 25 years earlier, the main task facing Stalin was to rebuild a devastated Soviet Union. Philip G. Roeder wrote in *Soviet Political Dynamics: Development of the First Leninist Polity* that "Stalin committed the Soviet Union to reconstruct the system he had built earlier. The Fourth Five Year Plan (1946–50) placed primary emphasis upon rebuilding heavy industry, with particular emphasis to those strategic sectors of the economy essential to Soviet military power." The program of Five Year Plans had been the centralized planning effort that Stalin had followed since he had become supreme in Russia. Outside Russia, he would look, with the aid of the communists who had fled the Germans before and during the war, to build a block of pro-Soviet client states out of what once had been the free countries of East Europe.

KHRUSHCHEV ERA

When Stalin died on March 1, 1953, a troika, or ruling triumvirate, now ruled Russia collectively. It was formed of Lavrenti Beria, the surviving head of Stalin's secret police, Nikita Khrushchev, and Georgi M. Malenkov. In December 1953, convicted under the law passed at the time of Kirov's murder in 1934, Beria was executed, allegedly by Khrushchev himself. By 1956, Khrushchev, who had served his "boss" so well, was now supreme in Russia. It was in that year that Khrushchev took the extraordinary step of denouncing "The Boss" at the 20th Party Congress in February 1956. With that speech, some scholars see Khrushchev v moving solidly to the right, away from Stalin's socialist state.

It was under Khrushchev that Soviet foreign policy began to dominate Russian planning, putting increasing strains on the Soviet economy. Khrushchev engaged the Soviet Union in the Cold War against the United States. In October 1962, he brought the world perilously close to thermonuclear war when he introduced ballistic missiles into Russia's satellite in the Western Hemisphere, the Cuba of Fidel Castro. It was only the common understanding of the terror they faced that enabled Khrushchev and American President John F. Kennedy to retreat from the abyss of an atomic war. The Soviet Union would withdraw the missiles from Cuba, while the United States would do the same with its Jupiter missiles then in Turkey.

In July 1963, Khrushchev failed in another area of foreign policy. Stalin had supported Mao Zedong when the Chinese communist had seized power in China in October 1949. Stalin had supported Mao in the Korean War from 1950 to1953 against the United States as a way of tying American forces down in the Orient. A division between Russia and China over who was the legitimate heir of Lenin and Stalin had begun in 1955. By the summer of 1963, it had become an ideological schism that would not heal. During the same period, Khrushchev had heavily invested in supporting the Arab nations against Israel in the Middle East, although the Soviet Union and the United States had acted together in championing Israel's creation in 1948. The only real result of the massive Soviet investment had been to see Khrushchev's main client, Egypt, decisively defeated in the Middle East war of 1956.

By 1964, the Soviet party leadership had become disaffected with Khrushchev. Not only had his foreign policy become a costly luxury, but his domestic economic Seven Year Plan had been a failure. On October 15, 1964, the Central Committee of the Communist Party announced that he had been "relieved of his duties" in the communist leadership "in view of his advanced age and deterioration of his health"—of course, at his own request.

However, Khrushchev had demonstrated the learning curve of a true statesman. Only months after the Cuban Missile Crisis, he agreed to a partial Nuclear Test Ban Treaty in July 1963. In April 1964, both he and American President Lyndon B. Johnson agreed on a "substantial reduction" in the production of enriched uranium, a vital element in nuclear weapons.

BREZHNEV DOCTRINE

Leonid Brezhnev succeeded Khrushchev as the first secretary of the Communist Party. Surprising those who had seen a liberalization of Russia during Khrushchev's tenure, Brezhnev praised Stalin instead. Indeed, he reassumed in the 23rd Party Congress (March–April 1966) the title of general secretary of the party, which Stalin had held. In foreign affairs, in his Brezhnev Doctrine, he would follow an aggressive "party line" that Khrushchev had abandoned after the vicious foreign criticism of his invasion of Hungary in October 1956. In August 1968, Brezhnev would smash the brief liberal "Prague Spring" with an invasion of Czechoslovakia by Soviet troops and those of his Warsaw Pact allies, the Soviet equivalent of the North Atlantic Treaty Organization (NATO) in Western Europe. Yet, while committed to holding together the Soviet hegemony in Eastern Europe, Brezhnev was committed to continuing the dialogue on nuclear weapons with the United States—a far cry from the frosty 1950s in the Cold War when both nations lived under the specter of MAD, "mutual assured destruction." In May 1972, in spite of Soviet support of North Vietnam in the Vietnam War, President Richard M. Nixon made a historic journey to Moscow, the capital since the Russian Revolution. There, in the new spirit of relaxation of tensions between the Soviet Union and the United States, he and Brezhnev signed two agreements, generally referred to as SALT I that substantially reduced the risk of nuclear weapon confrontation between the two Cold War superpowers.

However, in December 1979, Brezhnev took a step to enforce his doctrine that would ultimately bring the Soviet Union to its knees. Soviet forces attacked Afghanistan on December 27, 1979. The Afghan president, the communist Hafizullah Amin, was killed in the capital of Kabul, most likely by Soviet KGB or Spetsnaz (special forces) troops. In his place, the Soviets put Babrak Kamal, who was considered more dependable for Soviet interests.

The invasion set off an immediate Cold War crisis with the United States, which had been caught completely off guard. An American strategy was formulated, which included plans for assistance to the Afghan resistance, soon to be known as the mujahideen, or "warriors of the faith."

Under President Ronald Reagan, American policy became more demonstrative. The United States, in effect, was determined to "roll back" the Soviet occupation of Afghanistan as part of an overall strategy to win the Cold War. Reagan greatly increased aid to the mujahideen in Afghanistan. At the worst time for the continued survival of the Soviet system, it entered a period of grave instability.

Brezhnev died in November 1982, by which time the full impression was gaining that Afghanistan was becoming the "Soviet Vietnam." The Soviet regime was now suffering from the grim prospects. Yuri Andropov, who had crushed the brief "Prague Spring" of Czech Premier Alexander Dubcek with the KGB, took over as general secretary at a time when he was already dying from a kidney condition. Konstantin Chernenko, dying from emphysema, became the leader in December 1984. A senior KGB analyst, Nikolai Leonov, was quoted by Stephen Kotkin as saying "we were ashamed of our state, of its half-dead leaders, of the encroaching senility." Chernenko died in March 1985, with his urn joining those of Brezhnev and Andropov in the Kremlin Wall.

GORBACHEV'S MOVE TO THE RIGHT

Within days of Chernenko's death on March 10, 1985, Mikhail Gorbachev succeeded him as general secretary. For the first time since Lenin, the Soviet Union was led by a party figure who had the iniative to try to reform the system. Gorbachev tried to move the Soviet Union to a path on the right and in so doing contributed to the downfall of the state. In 1986, Gorbachev began a massive attempt to reconstruct the Soviet economy. One of the facts that emerged was that defense expenditures amounted to a stunning 20 to 30 percent of the Soviet annual budget. This was at a time when, increasingly exposed to the Western economy, Soviet citizens wanted a more consumer-based economy. Indeed, Gorbachev opened the era of perestroika, the attempt to radically reform Russia's economy, and of glasnost, when the government would mount an "open door" campaign to open up the dark past of the Soviet Union.

At the same time, the different nationalities of the Soviet Union were becoming restive, as they saw the Russian population of Leningrad (as Petrograd had become) and Moscow seeking a more open society. Nationalism and rightist movements were awakened throughout the Soviet Union. In the Ukraine, where the last anti-Soviet guerrillas had been crushed in 1956 (the same year as the Soviet invasion of Hungary), the new nationalism caused the defection from Soviet allegiance of, as Dominic Lieven observed in *The Russian Empire and Its Rivals*, "crucial elements of the republic's communist elite, headed by First Secretary Leonid Kravchuk."

Central, however, to Gorbachev's new policy was the end of Cold War differences with the United States. Reagan, whose career had been inspired by anti-communism, showed true intellectual courage in reaching out to Gorbachev, in view of the fact that in his first term of office he had denounced the Soviet Union as "an evil empire." Amid continued efforts to lessen the danger of nuclear war, a real relationship grew between the two heads of state. Then, on February 8, 1988, Gorbachev announced plans for a unilateral withdrawal of all Soviet forces from Afghanistan during a 10-month period.

Yet, Gorbachev's main battle was still to be fought in the Soviet Union. Fearing that the Communist Party would not be able to carry out his perestroika, at the July 1988 Party Congress, Gorbachev unveiled a plan to bring back the soviets. In effect, Gorbachev was now hoping for support for his new revolution "from the bottom up." However, by attempting to marginalize the Party Central Committee and bureaucracy, he was also undermining the government that kept the Soviet Union together. In 1989, he attempted to open a Congress of People's Deputies, another step away from the centralism of the old Soviet Union.

By 1990, the Soviet Union was also affected by the growing nationalist movements in Eastern Europe. The republics that made up the Union of Soviet Socialist Republics began to secede when Gorbachev refused to use force to retain them. In March 1990, the Baltic republics of Latvia, Lithuania, and Estonia were the first to leave.

Then Russia, under Boris Yeltsin, who had been elected to the Congress of People's Deputies in 1989,

also seceded. Yeltsin would emerge as Gorbachev's main rival for power in the state simply because the new Russia was the largest and most industrially advanced of the republics. But, if the Soviet system was in the throes of crisis, Gorbachev's refusal to use the old Soviet methods to control it was recognized by the awarding of the 1990 Nobel Peace Prize.

In January 1991, Gorbachev attempted once to use the old Stalinist methods to hold the Union together. In that month, internal OMON security troops raided a television station in the Lithuanian capital of Vilnius, killing at least 14 protestors, according to *Faces of a Nation*. It was the last time Gorbachev would resort to force to hold the Soviet Union together.

However, the "old guard," which desired a reversal of course, attempted a coup on August 19, 1991, when Gorbachev and his wife, Raisa, were on holiday in the Crimea. On the same day, the old guard military officers and KGB set in motion a plan to seize power from Boris Yeltsin in Moscow. After two days of near chaos, the planned putsch collapsed, and its ringleaders, especially KGB Chief Vladimir Kryuchkov and Defense Minister Marshal Dmitri Yazhov, were arrested on August 21.

However, after the coup, Gorbachev was eclipsed by Yeltsin, whose brave stand against the coup in Moscow had marked him as the leader of the evolving Soviet state. At the end of August, Gorbachev resigned as general secretary of the Communist Party. By the end of the year, the Union of Soviet Socialist Republics was officially dissolved.

SEE ALSO

Volume 1 Left: Russia, Post-Soviet; Asia; Communism; Lenin, Vladimir; Stalin and Stalinism.
Volume 2 Right: Russia, Post-Soviet.

BIBLIOGRAPHY

David Remnick, *Lenin's Tomb: The Last Days of the Soviet Empire* (Vintage, 1994); "Soviet Union," Library of Congress, www.loc.gov (July 2004); John Lehman, Jr., *Command of the Seas: Building the 600 Ship Navy* (Scribner's, 1988); Robert Service, *Lenin: A Biography* (Harvard University Press, 2000); Giulio Douhet, quoted in *War in the Modern World* (Collier, 1962); Thedore H. von Laue and Angela von Laue, *Faces of a Nation: The Rise and Fall of the Soviet Union, 1917–91* (Fulcrum, 1996); Nikolai Gogol, *Dead Souls* (Airmont, 1965); Erik Durschmied, *Blood of Revolution* (Arcade, 2002); Dominic Lieven, *The Russian Empire and Its Rivals* (Yale University Press, 2000); Stephen Kotkin, *Armageddon Averted: The Soviet Collapse, 1970–2000* (Oxford University Press, 2001);

Gorbachev Mikhail Sergeevich Biography, www.nns.ru/e-elects/e-persons/gorbach.html (April 2004); Orlando Figes, *A People's Tragedy: The Russian Revolution, 1891–1924* (Penguin, 1996); Christopher Andrew and Oleg Gordievsky, *KGB: The Inside Story* (Harper, 1990).

JOHN F. MURPHY, JR.
AMERICAN MILITARY UNIVERSITY

Sowell, Thomas (1930–)

ECONOMIST, LECTURER, researcher, and author Thomas Sowell was born in Gastonia, North Carolina, during the depths of the Great Depression, but moved to Harlem, New York City, as a child and attended public schools. Sowell entered Howard University, an African American university in Washington, D.C., but after a year and a half, he transferred to Harvard University where he majored in economics. Sowell received his bachelor's degree in economics from Harvard in 1958, his master's degree in economics from Columbia University in 1959, and his Ph.D. in economics from the University of Chicago in 1968. Throughout his career, Sowell's writing demonstrates academic rigor, lucid prose, and powerful arguments. He is a libertarian in economics and a conservative on most social issues, but he has registered as an independent in politics since 1972.

Sowell's greatest exposure is his regularly syndicated columns, which appear as part of *Jewish World Review*, and the internet site *Townhall*. His columns appear in over 150 newspapers. Many Americans know Sowell through his appearances on the *Rush Limbaugh Show*, when fellow black economist Walter Williams of George Washington University serves as substitute host for Limbaugh. Limbaugh's listeners enjoy listening in as Williams and Sowell discuss the free market and traditional social values. The conversations aired between Williams and Sowell are enlightening, educational, and informative. Despite his prodigious work for academics and government officials, he communicates successfully with those who are not economists or professors. Recent publications written for a nonacademic audience include *Basic Economics* (2000) and *Applied Economics* (2003), in which Sowell demonstrates his ability to make difficult subject matter understandable and practical.

A prolific writer, he has written works on economics, history, social policy, ethnicity, and the history of ideas. His specialty is economic history, a discipline close to his heart. Yet, since finishing his formal education and leaving the university for a think tank, he is much more interdisciplinary in his approach to his writing and research. He has authored 26 books, compiled seven collections of his syndicated columns, written two monographs, and written several scholarly articles in both academic and popular publications. He is also a contributor to several anthologies.

Sowell brings varied experience to his work. He has served as labor analyst for the Department of Labor, lecturer, professor, project director for the Urban Institute, and since 1980, he has worked as a Rose and Milton Friedman Senior Fellow in Public Policy at the Hoover Institution in War, Revolution, and Peace, located on the campus of Stanford University in California. His work at the Hoover Institution is the most productive of his career.

SKEPTICISM

Because Sowell witnessed so many of the economic failures of the last century firsthand, and through a myriad of experiences, he is skeptical of government intrusion into the economy. His skepticism makes him a controversial figure amid the traditional liberal orthodoxy of American academia. He opposes most federal regulation, racial quotas, rent controls, racial preferences, judicial activism, and other issues of concern dear to the liberal establishment and intelligentsia. Most of the conclusions set forth in his writings are in direct opposition to the assumptions held by the white liberal academy and black activists.

An example of his forthrightness occurred June 10, 1990, in appearance on C-Span's *Booknotes*, to discuss his book, *Preferential Politics: An International Perspective*, where he referred to the current civil rights leadership as "hustlers." In another interview, he recounted the negative response he received after he submitted a glowing report of a predominately black school in Washington, D.C., an overwhelmingly African American city. The black community responded with hostility because "it didn't justify new government programs, and it didn't show how the evils of white people were fatal to blacks."

Simply stated, Sowell believes the hustlers are those who take advantage of the system in the name of an oppressed race for personal gain.

His rejection of race-based preferences is most strident in his attacks on the American educational system. He laments what he sees as constant pandering to special interest groups such as minorities and athletes, policies he witnessed firsthand—and opposed, much to his detriment during his teaching career. Sowell vehemently opposes lowering the standards of education and dumbing down curriculum in the name of social justice and equality, a practice that he believes hurts all students—regardless of their race.

In his autobiography, *A Personal Odyssey*, Sowell wrote a stirring account of his academic career in which he detailed some discrimination, but lamented that most of what offended and angered him came from paternalistic white liberals. Sowell declared that the reason he did not radicalize leftward was that his academic career began two years before the passage of the Civil Rights Act of 1964 and he received tenure a year before the implementation of affirmative action policies. These facts, he asserts, "spared me the hang-ups afflicting many black intellectuals who were haunted by the idea that they owed their careers to affirmative action or to the fact that writings on race had become fashionable." Yet, he also admits that timing helped his career advance in that, as he wrote, "I happened to come along right after the worst of the old discrimination was no longer there to impede me and just before old racial quotas made the achievements of blacks look suspect."

His friends and colleagues have urged him to cease writing about race and "return to the things in which I did my best professional work—books on economics like *Knowledge and Decisions*, or books on ideas like *A Conflict of Visions* and *The Quest for Cosmic Justice*."

Sowell is the intellectual guru of many on the right of the political spectrum. Often read and quoted by other right-leaning intellectuals, as well as conservative radio talk show hosts, his impact on libertarian and conservative thought is incalculable.

SEE ALSO

Volume 1 Left: Affirmative Action.
Volume 2 Right: Libertarianism; *Laissez-Faire*.

BIBLIOGRAPHY

Thomas Sowell, *A Personal Odyssey* (The Free Press, 2000); *Contemporary Authors, New Revision Series* (Gale Group, 2001); Ray Sawhill, "Black and Right," www.salon.com (November 10, 1999), Thomas Sowell, www.tsowell.com (April 2004); Thomas Sowell, "Preferential Policies: An International Perspective," *Booknotes*, Brian Lamb, interviewer, www.booknotes.org (June 10, 1999).

JAMES S. BAUGESS
COLUMBIA STATE COMMUNITY COLLEGE

Spain

IN 1492, TWO EVENTS took place that shaped modern history in Spain. In January 1492, King Ferdinand and Queen Isabella captured Grenada, the last Moorish (Muslim) city in Spain. In October 1492, Christopher Columbus, sailing for Ferdinand and Isabella, discovered the New World and claimed it for Spain. By freeing Spain from Islamic dominion, Ferdinand and Isabella liberated Western Europe from the last danger of Muslim conquest, a landmark that would not take place in Eastern Europe until the Austrian conquests of the 17th century. By supporting Columbus in his first voyage of discovery, they (mostly Isabella) opened the New World to Western trade and enterprise. Thus, the story of the right in Spain was the story of growing imperialism and colonialism.

Francisco Pizarro conquered the Inca Empire in South America and extended Spain's colonial empire.

Only 12 years after Columbus's first voyage of discovery, in 1504 Hernando Cortés arrived for the first time on the Spanish island of Hispaniola, now the Dominican Republic and Haiti. In 1519, Cortés would sail again for the New World, with an army to conquer the wealth of the Aztec Empire, which, he had been told by those on Hispaniola, existed in Mexico to the west. Landing at Vera Cruz, he began a historic voyage inland to meet the Emperor Montezuma II and wrest control of his realm. After Cortés captured Montezuma, the emperor was killed in a confrontation with his own people—or by order of Cortés. Aztec resistance was carried on by Cuauhtemoc, who finally surrendered to Cortés after a major Spanish attack, aided by Cortés's native allies. As Cortés himself wrote, the war ended on "Tuesday, the feast of Saint Hippolytus, the thirteenth of August, in the year 1521."

In June 1534, Francisco Pizarro conquered the Inca Empire in South America by executing the emperor, Atahualpa. However, jealous other *conquistadores*, or conquerors, killed Pizarro in his palace at Lima in June 1541. In spite of such incidents, as C.H. Haring wrote in *The Spanish Empire in America*, "before the middle of the 16th century [Spain was able] to erect two vast political entities in the New World, the viceroyalty of New Spain, established in 1535, and that of Peru, organized in 1544." In 1540, Francisco de Coronado would lead an expedition north from Mexico as far as Kansas, and in 1565 Pedro de Menendez would found the first permanent European city in the United States at Saint Augustine in Florida.

The great riches from its New World empire would enable Spain to dominate Europe. Charles V, who was king of Spain in the time of Cortés, was also the Holy Roman Emperor. Indeed, the next century would be referred to by the Spanish as *el siglo de oro*, "the golden century." In 1556, the great empire would be divided between Spain and the Holy Roman Empire. Earlier, in 1571, the empire would defeat the last major Muslim attempt to conquer Western Europe by sea in the decisive Battle of Lepanto. However, Spanish imperial ambitions began to empty the vast Spanish treasury. In 1588, Philip II, the son of Charles V, suffered the first main Spanish reverse in his failure to capture England with the Spanish Armada, the so-called Enterprise of England. Still, the Spanish *tercios*, the great battalions of infantry, would dominate European warfare. However, almost exactly a century after the foundation of the viceroyalty of Peru (so named because a viceroy ruled in the name of the king), Spanish dominance ended in 1643. On May 19, 1643, Louis, the Grand Conde, would achieve a great French victory over the Spanish army of Don Francisco de Melo.

Nevertheless, although its hegemony was broken, Spain would continue to play a major role in European, and American, affairs. It was the death of Charles II in 1700 that ignited the War of the Spanish Succession in Europe, to see who would sit on the throne of Spain. The conquest of Gibraltar from the Spanish in the war in 1704 firmly sealed England's role as a maritime power in both the Old and New Worlds. When the grandson of King Louis XIV of France, the "Sun King," became king of Spain as Philip V, Spain entered a second age of power through its alliance with France, the Bourbon Family Compact. During the American Revolution under Charles III, after France became an ally of the United States in March 1778, Spain followed. The viceroy of New Spain, Bernardo de Galvez, became one of the "Founding Fathers" of the United States through his conquest of the southern British outposts of Mobile in present-day Alabama (1780) and Pensacola in Florida (1781).

By the reign of Charles III, the notorious Inquisition of the 16th and 17th centuries in Spain was ending in the era of the Enlightenment, when the eye of conservative reason began to debunk the fears and hate of an earlier age.

When the French Revolution saw the execution of France's Louis XVI in January 1793, Spain entered the alliance against revolutionary France. However, in 1795, the paramour of Spain's Queen Maria Louisa succeeded in extricating Spain from the alliance against Napoleon, an act that gave him the title "The Prince of the Peace." In 1808, Godoy's hopes of influencing Spanish politics ended when Napoleon occupied Spain on his way to invading Portugal, England's only remaining European ally. Charles IV, the rightful king, was forced to abdicate in favor of Ferdinand VII. Spain would enter history as "the Spanish Ulcer," and Napoleon's campaign in Spain would lead to the advent of Arthur Wellesley, the future Duke of Wellington. On June 18, 1815, Wellington would decisively defeat Napoleon at Waterloo in Belgium.

However, the Bourbon Family Compact held: in 1823, King Louis XVIII of France sent an army to support the new king of Spain, Ferdinand VII, when the latter was threatened by an armed rising. Within 10 years, in 1833, Spanish unrest again threatened the peace of Europe. In that year, a rebellion took place against Queen Isabella II, fomented by the brother of the then-dead Ferdinand VII, Don Carlos. The conflict, prefiguring the bloody Spanish civil war of a century later, was known as the Carlist War. King Charles X of France offered the new French Foreign Legion, which had been founded in 1831, to Isabella to crush the Carlist rebellion. By 1840, Don Carlos had fled and the revolt had been brought to an end.

Yet, within a year, Spain fell under the control of General Espartero, who would rule as regent of Spain, although Isabella II would be queen until 1868, when she abdicated. She would be officially deposed in 1870. Beginning with Espartero, Spain's history was a depressing chronicle of caudillismo, the supremacy of military "men on horseback" who stifled the conservative reformism that had been the legacy of Spain's Enlightenment under Charles III. It would not be until 1874 that General Campos would bring back a stable monarchy under Alphonso XII, but again the king owed his throne, much like the Roman emperors of old, to swords, not ballots. A constitution would be introduced in Spain in 1876.

In 1898, Spain would enter the disastrous war with the United States, which would signal the end of the empire begun by Christopher Columbus in 1492. The United States gained Cuba, Puerto Rico, and the Philippine Islands, as Spain reluctantly shed the last mantle of imperial grandeur. In the wake of Spain's defeat, caudillismo returned to Spanish politics when Miguel Primo de Rivero seized power in 1823, according to the *Columbia Encyclopedia* for 2001, "dissolving the Cortes [the Spanish Parliament] and then establishing, with the full approval of King Alfonso XIII, a military directory."

When Rivero was exiled in 1930, the stage was set for the ultimate Spanish constitutional crisis during the second Spanish Republic (a first had briefly existed from 1873 to 1874). Alfonso XIII was forced to go into exile after popular elections introduced the Second Republic. However, the conservative CEDA party remained at odds with the Socialist Party, and the republic remained in a precarious political situation.

FRANCISCO FRANCO

Finally, in 1936, fearing growing communist interference, General Francisco Franco, supported by the Spanish Foreign Legion and native troops from Spanish Morocco, crossed into Spain to begin an open rebellion against the government of the republic. Styling themselves the Nationalists, Franco and his supporters received open support from conservative elements. Extremists supporting the Republican Popular Front government soon gave themselves over to communist-

King Juan Carlos and Queen Sofia of Spain witnessed the transfer of power from fascism to democracy in Spain.

supported reprisals against the Catholic Church, including the wholesale massacre of priests and nuns in their convents. Armed force was added to the Republican forces by the anarchist trade union movement (a labor oxymoron) the CNT, which could call on some million members. The war soon brought Germany and Italy into the struggle on the side of the Nationalists, with England and France's Third Republic, also led by a Popular Front government, aiding the republic. But the republic was the chief beneficiary of aid from Soviet Russia, whose Premier Josef Stalin would attempt to create a communist Spain in the Iberian Peninsula, using his NKVD secret police to reinforce the army of the Republicans. In March 1939, the Nationalists entered Madrid, and Franco proclaimed the end of the civil war.

However, when World War II erupted in September 1939, Franco surprised Adolf Hitler, the German *Fuehrer*, by proclaiming his neutrality. Unlike Hitler,

Franco's fascism was political, not ideologic, and he remained a Spanish patriot at heart. A meeting between the two dictators at Hendaye in October 1940 produced little except robust martial music. Besides, with some 500,000 Spanish dead, the country was hardly in any condition to enter what promised to be a much larger war.

Later, however, Franco, to assuage Hitler, would commit his Blue Division to fight alongside the Germans in the war against Russia. The Blue Division would be recalled in October 1943 to Spain. When Germany surrendered in May 1945, many former Germans like Otto Skorzeny, Hitler's leading commando, found welcome exile in Madrid, but Spain escaped any sanctions from the West because Franco had observed his neutrality (other than the commitment of the Blue Division) carefully.

After a bloody reckoning with the forces of the republic, Franco at home began a program of attempting to rebuild a shattered society and economy. During the 1950s and 1960s, every effort was made to improve international relations, and the country's economy recovered. In 1969, Franco proclaimed Juan Carlos de Borbon, the grandson of Alphonse XIII, his successor with the title of king. Franco died in 1975, and a constitutional monarchy was established. President Adolfo Suarez introduced important political reforms. Upon Franco's death, Juan Carlos had become king. Spain joined NATO in 1985, and the European Community in 1986. The year 1992 formally marked Spain's reentry into the family of nations, as the Olympic Games were held in Barcelona that year. The year 1992 also was the 500th anniversary of the first voyage of Columbus to the New World and a cause for the renewal of ties between Spain and the New World including a symbolic re-creation of the voyage of Columbus with reconstructed sailing ships bearing the names of his *Nina*, *Pinta*, and *Santa Maria*.

Tragically, 12 years later, events would focus on Spain's other old role, that of the frontier of Western Europe against the forces of Islamic extremism. In March 2004, Madrid was rocked by a series of bombing attacks attributed to Islamic groups linked with the terrorist organization of Osama bin Laden, al-Qaeda. The BBC noted, "The devastating terror attacks in Madrid saw 10 bombs explode on four trains in three stations during the busy morning rush hour. Four bombs exploded on a train just outside Atocha station. Each of the trains was laden with commuters; office workers, students and schoolchildren." With the large Spanish coastline on the Mediterranean the goal of thousands of refugees from poverty in North Africa, it only remained to be seen which terrorists might attempt to enter Spain among them.

SEE ALSO
Volume 1 Left: Spain.
Volume 2 Right: Fascism; Monarchism; Colonialism; Imperialism.

BIBLIOGRAPHY
"The Spanish Civil War," www.spartacus.schoolnet.co.uk (July 2004); "Primo de Rivera, Miguel," www.bartleby.com (July 2004); William Weber Johnson, *Cortes: Conquering the New World* (Paragon, 1975); C.H. Haring, *The Spanish Empire in America* (Harcourt Brace, 1975); Manuel Godoy, "Spanish Prince of Peace," www.napoleonguide.com (July 2004).

JOHN F. MURPHY, JR.
AMERICAN MILITARY UNIVERSITY

States' Rights

STATES' RIGHTS HAVE been an important element of the American federal political system. While major areas of policymaking responsibility, such as the treaty power and the power to coin money, have been delegated to the federal government, others arguably have been reserved to the states. When the federal government has attempted to legislate in reserved areas, states have at various times raised claims to their rights in order to negate the federal initiative, with various degrees of success.

The idea of states' rights resulted naturally from the multiplicity of societies that participated in the American Revolution. In addition, many of the grievances against the British government that drove the American colonists to rebellion centered on British rejection of the Americans' understanding concerning their colonial assemblies' (soon to be their states') rights. Most famously, the Americans insisted that only their local assemblies could tax them, but they also complained that the royal government had dissolved the New York assembly, reorganized the Massachusetts assembly, refused to approve bills passed by the Virginia assembly, and in many other ways denied American colonists the self-government to which they believed themselves entitled. Although the Imperial Crisis of the 1760s and 1770s imbued a sense of shared dangers and common interests in the leaders of the American Revolution, it was to 13 separate colonial-cum-state governments that they looked for a substitute for discredited royal authority. While coordinating American efforts in the War for Independence, members of Congress also persisted in seeking the interests of their own respective states in lieu of the common good where feasible.

The most significant conflict over states' rights during the American Revolution arose over the question of the original 13 states' western land claims. While some states, such as Rhode Island, Delaware, and Maryland, were confined to small areas on the Atlantic Coast, others (particularly Virginia) pointed to their charters in claiming extensive western lands. (Virginia's claims, for example, extended all the way northwest to what is now Wisconsin.)

ARTICLES OF CONFEDERATION

These claims led to serious dissension within the revolutionary congresses. When the Articles of Confederation were sent to the states for ratification by the Second Continental Congress, for example, Maryland announced that it would not ratify the Articles until Virginia surrendered its trans-Ohio River land claims.

In the interim, delegations from other states periodically raised questions concerning governance of the western lands and adjudication of Virginia's western claims. Virginia congressmen, led by George Mason, James Madison, and James Monroe, responded by enunciating a doctrine of states' rights and reserved powers: Congress, they said, had been delegated no power to adjudicate Virginia's claims, so they would not even discuss the matter in Congress. Vindicating its land claims was their state's right.

Ultimately, Virginia ceded its trans-Ohio River lands on its own terms and Maryland joined the other 12 states in ratifying the Articles. Still, the question of states' rights remained a live one. In form, the Confederation government was a league of sovereigns, and Article II announced that the states would remain sovereign. The Articles left virtually all power, including the power to tax and the power to raise armies, in the hands of the states, to whom congressmen remained beholden for their offices.

Reformers, calling themselves Federalists, insisted even before the Articles' ratification that the central, or federal, government needed more power. Prominent politicians who thought the Confederation too weak included George Mason, Patrick Henry, and others who later would oppose the Constitution of 1788, along with virtually all of that constitution's eventual supporters.

The types of power that reformers such as George Washington, James Madison, and Alexander Hamilton thought the federal government should be given spanned the gamut. While the revolutionary congresses were, in the apt description of John Adams, really assemblages of ambassadors, these men hoped to erect a real government in the Confederation's (and, to some degree, the states') place.

CONSTITUTIONAL CONVENTION

At the Philadelphia Convention of 1787, debate was shaped by the Virginia Plan, James Madison's template for a new government, as modified by his fellow Virginia delegates before presentation to the full Convention. The most significant opposition to the Virginia Plan took the form of concern for the place of the states within the federal system. Thus, some delegates, such as the majority of those from New York and Luther Martin of Maryland, withdrew from the Convention entirely.

Other delegates, mainly from the less populous states, joined in presenting the New Jersey Plan as an alternative to Virginia's. Whereas Virginia had called for granting taxing and war powers in the federal government and for removing the states from the process of selecting members of Congress, as well as for apportioning both houses of the new Congress by population and otherwise undercutting or eliminating various of the states' rights, small-state delegates resisted all of these ideas.

The New Jersey Plan's proposal for equal apportionment of a unicameral legislature chosen by state legislatures ultimately found its place in the Constitution's Senate, which featured equal representation for states and senators selected by state legislatures. In addition, as Maryland's Martin suggested before his withdrawal from the Convention, chief executives were to be selected by an Electoral College in which small states were overrepresented. Since the president would nominate all other high-ranking executive and judicial officials and the Senate would confirm them, small states' rights had manifold protections.

Article I, Section 8, of the Constitution included a careful listing of the powers of Congress, which implicitly reserved other powers to the states. Ultimately, this implicit recognition of states' rights was rendered explicit by the ratification of the Tenth Amendment. In fact, the entire Bill of Rights was understood as a limitation on federal powers, thus a recognition of states' rights. Even the nationalist Chief Justice John Marshall agreed with this interpretation in his epochal opinion for the Supreme Court in *Barron v. Baltimore* (1833).

Among the significant devices for ensuring ongoing recognition of states' rights was the constitutional enshrinement of their role in controlling America's armed forces. Not only did the unamended Constitution say that the officers of the militia would continue to be chosen by the state governments, which would retain responsibility for training them, but the Second Amendment guarded against federal efforts to disarm individuals, just as George Mason had desired. Advocates and opponents of the Constitution alike saw the militia as a significant hedge against federal oppression.

ONGOING SOVEREIGNTY

The amendment process provided by the Constitution, too, recognized the ongoing sovereignty of the states. The Constitution, it said, would take effect among the ratifying states as soon as nine of them ratified; those that did not choose to ratify would remain outside the Union. In the end, North Carolina did not join the Union until well after the Constitution took effect and the first Congress met, and Rhode Island, which had been more concerned about threats to liberty and to local self-government posed by attempts to strengthen the federal government than any other state, spent years as, in effect, a foreign country.

Early in the life of the new government, the program of Secretary of the Treasury Alexander Hamilton spurred opposition to the Washington administration. Among the concerns voiced by congressional opponents, ironically led by Representative James Madison, was that Hamilton was ignoring the distinction between the powers delegated to the federal government and those reserved to the states.

Thus, when Hamilton's proposal to charter a bank came before the House of Representatives, Madison insisted that it was unconstitutional. In the cabinet, President Washington asked for formal opinions on this question. Secretary of State Thomas Jefferson said that since there was nothing in the Constitution expressly granting Congress power to charter a corporation, let alone a bank corporation, and since the guiding principle of constitutional interpretation must be that all the powers not delegated by the Constitution to the federal government were reserved to the states respectively or to the people, chartering a bank must be understood as a state's right, not as the federal government's; thus, he

concluded, the charter bill was unconstitutional. Hamilton responded to this argument by saying that since Article I, Section 8, included grants to Congress of several specific powers related to regulation of the economy, the general responsibility to regulate the national economy lay with Congress. Chartering a bank, he said, could help fulfill that task. If the end were legitimate, he opined, and the means not prohibited, the bill must be considered constitutional. Finding no express prohibition of the charter bill in the Constitution, Hamilton judged it constitutional. President Washington, siding with Hamilton, signed the law.

While they divided on the social implications of Hamilton's larger fiscal system and on foreign policy, constitutional interpretation was perhaps the hottest flash point of disagreement in the First Party system of Hamiltonian Federalists and Jeffersonian Republicans. It came to a head in 1798.

Then, Congress passed and President John Adams signed the Alien and Sedition Acts, measures intended to give the Executive greater control over foreigners and to tamp down domestic dissent in the midst of a diplomatic emergency. Republicans countered with the Virginia and Kentucky Resolutions of 1798–99 and the Virginia Report of 1800. In those four documents, two of which were penned by Madison and one by Jefferson, the Republican opposition laid out the entire constitutional case against 1790s federalism. The states, they said, in sovereign conventions had given the Constitution effect by ratifying it; as the parties to the Constitution, the states had the ultimate right to decide whether federal measures were unconstitutional; in case a federal policy was unconstitutional and dangerous, states had the right "and [were] in duty bound to interpose" to prevent the unconstitutional policy from taking effect within their respective borders.

This theory of interposition/nullification would be the centerpiece of states' rights thinking down to the Civil War. It was not put to trial in the age of Jefferson, however, because the Republicans finally won a presidential election in 1800, and the Alien and Sedition Acts passed into history.

States' rights were not solely a southern notion. By the time he left office in 1809, President Jefferson had imposed a draconian trade embargo that had wrenching effects, and met with massive resistance, in New England. When his secretary of state and presidential successor, James Madison, followed the embargo with a war against Great Britain, New Englanders pondered, and arguably committed, outright treason. Governors refused to lend their militias to the defense of the nation, despite constitutional provisions; northern militiamen refused to leave their states, despite officers' orders; prominent citizens discussed taking New England out of the Union. All of these measures arguably were states' rights.

South Carolina politicians pushed assertion of states' rights to the brink of armed conflict from 1828 to 1833 with their formal theory of nullification. Arguing that the protective tariffs of 1824, 1828, and 1832 were unconstitutional and dangerous, they called a sovereign convention to nullify them within South Carolina's borders. It did so, and President Andrew Jackson's Nullification Proclamation made clear that he rejected their constitutional arguments. Nullification, he said, was treason and would be treated as such. Henry Clay offered compromise measures in Congress satisfactory to both sides, so the nullification ordinance was repealed; still, states' rights extremists believed that their measure had wrung concession from the federal government, and they would not forget this example.

Of course, the ultimate contest over states' rights was the Civil War of 1861–65. With the election of Abraham Lincoln in 1860 on an avowedly sectionalist platform, the seven Deep South states seceded from the Union. Fire-eaters said this was a peaceful solution to the growing sectional antagonism. In fact, northern abolitionists had called for northern secession for years, and many of them counseled letting the Deep South go in peace; secession, they said, was a state's right.

ABRAHAM LINCOLN

The most significant dissent came from Abraham Lincoln. According to him, the Constitution had been ratified not by the states separately, but by one American people. (This surely would have surprised North Carolina and Rhode Island in 1789.) Since one people had ratified the Constitution, no state could leave the Union without the others' consent. He vowed to enforce the tariff, long a source of sectional strife, despite the Deep South's supposed secession.

Deep South leaders, meanwhile, including a number of former U.S. cabinet members and congressmen, drafted a new Confederate States Constitution and selected Mississippi's Jefferson Davis as their new nation's president. To Davis, as to the majority (but by no means all) of the white South, the American Revolution was being vindicated by their attempts to create a separate American nation.

The Civil War's outcome put an end to secession as a live constitutional option. Lincoln's Emancipation Proclamation and the subsequent adoption of the Thirteenth Amendment also abolished slavery, at once freeing four million slaves and depriving slave owners of an enormous amount of property. For the first time, a constitutional amendment limited the powers of the states in an enormous area formerly reserved to them. It would be followed by the Fourteenth Amendment, intended to guarantee freedmen and their descendants citizenship and equal basic rights, and the Fifteenth Amendment, supposed to protect blacks' voting rights.

By the end of the 19th century, the Fourteenth and Fifteenth Amendments were essentially unfulfilled promises. The Democratic Party in the South became the white man's party, and white supremacy meant depriving blacks of social, economic, and political rights. Northerners turned their backs on the southerners who had helped them win the Civil War, and states' control over race relations was nearly complete.

With the coming of the Depression, Franklin Roosevelt, who had run for president on a traditional limited-government Democratic platform, became an advocate of a very activist federal government. His opponents, such as Georgia's Democratic Governor Eugene Talmadge, insisted that New Deal measures to regulate the economy and provide for the poor overstepped the line between federal and state responsibility, thus violating states' rights. In 1937, the Supreme Court shifted from agreeing with New Deal opponents to accepting the New Deal's constitutionality.

World War II worked a change in racial attitudes, and the Cold War contest for the hearts and minds of third world peoples pressured American policymakers to change the South's racial system. At the 1948 Democratic Convention, Minneapolis Mayor Hubert Humphrey called for the Democratic Party to abandon its Jeffersonian devotion to states' rights in the name of a new advocacy of civil rights, and President Harry Truman agreed. Despite the third-party effort of disgruntled southern Democrats, Truman's platform committed the national Democratic Party to resuscitating blacks' rights.

BARRY GOLDWATER

In the 1960s, a series of three major congressional laws passed by bipartisan majorities over nearly unanimous southern Democratic opposition restored blacks' civil rights. The lone significant Republican opponent of these measures, libertarian Arizona Senator Barry Goldwater, objected to the Civil Rights Act's possible wholesale violation of states' rights, but the Supreme

Court ultimately decided that the Fourteenth Amendment had reallocated powers between the states and the federal government in such a way as to empower Congress to intervene to help blacks achieve an equal place in American society.

It is because states' rights have been a rallying cry of the opponents of the New Deal and of federal intervention to vindicate blacks' rights that they are now seen as primarily a concern of the right in recent American history. However, this is not an accurate perception. Rather, states' rights tend to be asserted by whichever faction or party finds itself in a federal minority and a state majority, and they tend to be opposed by the party that controls the federal government. Thus, for example, Massachusetts Governor Michael Dukakis, later the 1988 Democratic presidential nominee, sued the presidential administration of Ronald Reagan in the 1980s to prevent deployment of the Massachusetts National Guard to Honduras. Dukakis, like other liberals, opposed American policy in Nicaragua at the time, and he rightly understood that the reason for the deployment was to intimidate Nicaragua's Marxist government. His state, he insisted, had a constitutional right to control training of its National Guard. Ultimately, however, Dukakis lost his suit, which was won by a conservative federal administration generally committed to states' rights.

On the other hand, conservatives, including both Presidents George Bush and Ronald Reagan, have pointed to states' rights in opposing the abortion decision *Roe v. Wade* (1973). Chief Justice William Rehnquist and others on the Supreme Court have taken this position from the beginning, and Rehnquist's career shows steady devotion to the idea of states' rights, as does that of Justice Clarence Thomas. Despite a number of Republican Supreme Court appointments, they have never commanded a majority.

The major change in American politics regarding states' rights in the past seven decades is that there no longer is a large interest group or sectional minority particularly concerned with the issue. Thus, neither party cares about it overmuch in practice, though some conservative Republicans, especially those determined to overturn *Roe v. Wade*, continue to adhere to it in principle.

SEE ALSO

Volume 1 Left: Liberalism; Democratic Party; Jefferson, Thomas.
Volume 2 Right: United States; Republican Party; Lincoln, Abraham.

BIBLIOGRAPHY

Charles A. Ambler, *Thomas Ritchie: A Study in Virginia Politics* (Bell Book & Stationery, 1913); Lance Banning, *The Jeffersonian Persuasion: Evolution of a Party Ideology* (Cornell University Press, 1978); Raoul Berger, *Federalism: The Founders' Design* (University of Oklahoma Press, 1987); Raoul Berger, *Government By Judiciary: The Transformation of the Fourteenth Amendment* (Liberty Fund, 1997); H. Lee Cheek, *Calhoun and Popular Rule: The Political Theory of the Disquisition and Discourse* (University of Missouri Press, 2004); Thomas J. DiLorenzo, *The Real Lincoln: A New Look at Abraham Lincoln, His Agenda, and an Unnecessary War* (Prima Publishing, 2002); Richard E. Ellis, *The Union at Risk: Jacksonian Democracy, States' Rights, and the Nullification Crisis* (Oxford University Press, 1987); Daniel Farber, *Lincoln's Constitution* (University of Chicago Press, 2003); Ronald M. Labbé and Jonathan Lurie, *The Slaughterhouse Cases: Regulation, Reconstruction, and the Fourteenth Amendment* (University Press of Kansas, 2003); Andrew Lenner, *The Federal Principle in American Politics* (Rowman & Littlefield Publishers, 2001); Forrest McDonald, *States' Rights and the Union: Imperium in Imperio* (University Press of Kansas, 2000); William W. Freehling, ed., *The Nullification Era: A Documentary Record* (Harper & Row, 1967); William J. Watkins, Jr., *Reclaiming the American Revolution: The Kentucky and Virginia Resolutions and Their Legacy* (Palgrave Macmillan, 2004); Herman Belz, ed., *The Webster-Hayne Debate on the Nature of the Union* (Liberty Fund, 2000).

KEVIN R.C. GUTZMAN, J.D., PH.D.
WESTERN CONNECTICUT STATE UNIVERSITY

Supreme Court

THE U.S. SUPREME COURT was created on September 24, 1789, by Article III, Paragraph 1, of the U.S. Constitution. Article III, Paragraph 1, simply provides that "the judicial Power of the United States shall be vested in one supreme Court, and in such inferior Courts as the Congress may from time to time ordain and establish." The Supreme Court is the highest tribunal in the nation for all cases and controversies arising under the Constitution or laws of the United States, serves as final arbiter of the law, and functions as guardian and interpreter of the U.S. Constitution.

The Supreme Court consists of one chief justice and a number of associate justices predetermined by Congress, and is currently fixed at eight. Justices are nominated by the president, require confirmation by the Senate, and serve for life. Consequently, when vacancies on the court have become available, virtually all presidents have attempted to "pack" the court with justices whose political ideology is consistent with their administration's political agenda, thereby influencing the court in either a liberal or conservative direction. When the Republican Party endorsed a constitutional amendment limiting abortion, for example, President Ronald Reagan sought to appoint conservative justices who respected "traditional family values and the sanctity of innocent human life."

Typically, an entire court era is described in terms of its political preferences, whether conservative or liberal. Historically, conservative courts have been primarily concerned with preserving existing institutions against the threat of radical change, view affirmative action policies skeptically, and are generally reluctant to expand the fundamental rights of equal protection law. Liberal courts, however, have tended to rule in favor of individuals claiming a denial of civil liberties such as the right to privacy; freedom of speech, religion, and press; and illegal discrimination. Furthermore, liberal courts have favored expanding the rights of the criminally accused.

The Warren Court (1953–69), for example, has been labeled liberal for its transformation of constitutional law and American society by giving minorities victories they had been unable to obtain from reluctant legislatures and obstinate executives. Consequently, the Warren Court significantly altered the legal system by departing from the earlier courts' conservative decisions, implementing the largest expansion of civil rights and civil liberties in the nation's history.

Earl Warren assumed the position of chief justice at the opening of the October 1953 term with the court confronting one of the most significant issues in American history, the constitutionality of racial segregation. In *Brown v. Board of Education* (1954), the court invalidated racial segregation within the public school system. Warren, delivering the opinion of the court, emphasized the impact that racial segregation had on children and thus triggered the civil rights revolution of the 1950s and 1960s. The Warren Court captured national attention with its highly controversial decision in *Brown*, which served as a preview to the court's commitment to social justice and protection of the individual against the state. The Warren Court's greatest controversy, however, emerged when it adopted a series of broad rulings protecting criminal defendants. In 1961, the Supreme Court began to exert strict control over

criminal justice policy by applying specific requirements of the Bill of Rights to the states by means of the Due Process Clause of the Fourteenth Amendment. In *Mapp v. Ohio* (1961), the court declared that the exclusionary rule, which prohibits evidence obtained in violation of the Fourth Amendment as inadmissible in federal proceedings, is applicable to state courts. In *Gideon v. Wainwright* (1963), the most famous of the Warren Court cases, the court extended the Sixth Amendment right to counsel to state proceedings. In *Miranda v. Arizona* (1966), the court declared that at a minimum, a person accused of a criminal offense must be informed of his right to remain silent and to the presence of either a retained or appointed attorney prior to a police interrogation.

The liberal trend of the Warren Court did not go unnoticed. Conservatives criticized the court for its expansive interpretation of the Bill of Rights and accused the court of "coddling criminals and handcuffing the police." During the 1968 presidential campaign, Republican candidate Richard M. Nixon criticized the court's activism. Focusing on the court's prior decisions involving criminal procedure, Nixon proclaimed that the liberal Warren Court had gone too far and denounced the court's decision in *Miranda v. Arizona* (1966). If elected, Nixon promised to appoint "strict constructionists" to the court who viewed themselves as "caretakers of the Constitution and servants of the American people."

Following the election, Nixon fulfilled his promise and subsequently changed the composition of the court in his own more conservative image. He named Warren Burger chief justice and Harry Blackmun, Lewis Powell, and William Rehnquist associate justices. Burger was chosen because of his opposition to the Warren Court's decisions involving criminal procedure and for his criticism of judicial activism. Rehnquist, the most conservative member of the Burger Court, was chosen for his views on criminal justice and for his endorsement of a more moderate role for the court. The newly appointed conservatives seemed intent on rewriting much of the constitutional law that was decided during the Warren Court.

When Warren Burger assumed the position of chief justice in 1969, many feared that the Burger Court (1969–86) would overturn both *Mapp* and *Miranda*. Although the Burger Court was more conservative than its predecessor, *Mapp* and *Miranda* were not overturned but rather modified and narrowed. In *Harris v. New York* (1971), for example, the court held that a statement obtained in violation of *Miranda* could be used for the

The Supreme Court building housed a conservative court in 2004, including Justices Clarence Thomas, Anthony M. Kennedy, David H. Souter, Ruth B. Ginsburg, Sandra D. O'Connor, Stephen G. Breyer, Chief Justice William H. Rehnquist, John P. Stevens, Antonin Scalia.

purpose of counteracting perjury at trial. In *New York v. Quarles* (1985), the court adopted the "public safety" exception to *Miranda*. The court, with Rehnquist writing for the majority, held that when there is a danger to public safety, *Miranda* should not "be applied in all its rigor to a situation in which police officers ask questions reasonably prompted by a concern for public safety." The court's ruling in *Oregon v. Elstad* (1985) was more comprehensive in its implications for Miranda. The court held that a voluntary confession obtained in violation of *Miranda* did not exclude a later confession secured after proper *Miranda* warnings had been given.

From 1969 to 1974, however, the Burger Court made no significant attempt to alter the applicability of the exclusionary rule, although Burger despised it. According to Burger, in his dissenting opinion in *Bivens v. Six Unknown Named Agents of Federal Bureau of Narcotics* (1971), "the only reasonable justification for the rule was that it might deter law enforcement authorities from using improper methods to obtain evidence." The

court began narrowing the reach of *Mapp* in *United States v. Calandra* (1974), in which the court held that the exclusionary rule does not apply to grand jury hearings. The court's ruling in *United States v. Leon* (1984) created the "good faith" exception to the exclusionary rule. Under the "good faith" exception, illegally seized evidence "may be admitted where the police officer conducting the investigation acted in objectively reasonable reliance on a warrant issued by a detached and neutral magistrate that subsequently is determined to be invalid." Justice Byron White, delivering the majority opinion of the court, stated, "Suppression is appropriate only if the officers were dishonest or reckless in preparing their affidavit."

President Ronald Reagan continued the Republican policy of appointing conservatives to the U.S. Supreme Court. In 1986, following the retirement of Burger, Reagan elevated Associate Justice William Rehnquist to the court's center chair and named Antonin Scalia as associate justice. Following his appointment, Rehnquist began moving the court further to the right because, for the first time in 50 years, the court had a conservative majority. The following year, conservative Anthony Kennedy was appointed associate justice. Consequently, the Rehnquist Court (1986–) now had a five-justice conservative core or foundation, consisting of Rehnquist and Associate Justices White, O'Connor, Scalia, and Kennedy.

Although composed of a conservative majority, the court often saw defections by one or more of its members. President George H. W. Bush, however, was able to select replacements for Justices Brennan and Marshall, the last remaining liberal justices from the Warren Court era. In 1990, Bush nominated David Souter, who succeeded Justice Brennan, and the following year, he nominated Clarence Thomas, who succeeded Justice Marshall. Consequently, the court divided into two distinct conservative blocs, one composed of Rehnquist and Associate Justices Scalia and Thomas, and the other composed of Associate Justices O'Connor, Kennedy, and Souter.

With the retirement of White in 1993, President Bill Clinton became the first Democratic president in 26 years to make an appointment to the Supreme Court, choosing Ruth Bader Ginsburg as White's successor. The following year, Clinton elevated Stephen Bryer to associate justice. The changing political dynamics of the court, including the appointments of Ginsburg and Bryer, have led to three ideological blocs on the Rehnquist Court: A conservative bloc consisting of Rehnquist, Scalia, and Thomas; a center-right bloc consisting of O'Connor, Kennedy, and Souter; and a center-left bloc consisting of Stevens, Ginsburg, and Bryer. When the members of the court's conservative bloc vote together in a divided decision, they always support the more conservative position. Typically, the outcome depends upon the votes of O'Connor and Kennedy. Although they lean toward the conservative side on some issues, one of them is more than likely to move toward the liberal side on many others. Consequently, the conservative bloc only prevails if O'Connor and Kennedy both join it on any given issue.

Nevertheless, the conservative bloc of the Rehnquist Court has ultimately prevailed as victorious on issues involving racial preferences and federalism. In *Adarand Constructors, Inc. v. Pena* (1995), for example, the court held that all race-conscious programs sponsored by the government, whether disadvantaging whites or blacks, are presumed to be unconstitutional and subject to "strict scrutiny." In *United States v. Morrison* (2000), the court ruled that Congress has no au-

thority under the Constitution's Commerce Clause to regulate gender-motivated violence against women.

Although the Rehnquist Court's decisions regarding federalism, including its decision in *Morrison*, are considered its most remarkable conservative achievements, it is doubtful that the decisions will have any significant long-term effect.

SEE ALSO

Volume 1 Left: Supreme Court; Liberalism; Democratic Party. *Volume 2 Right:* Republican Party; Conservatism.

BIBLIOGRAPHY

Richard A. Brisbin, Jr. *Justice Antonin Scalia and the Conservative Revival* (Johns Hopkins University Press, 1997); Lee Epstein and Thomas G. Walker, *Constitutional Law for a Changing America* (CQ Press, 2001); Howard Gillman and Cornell Clayton, *The Supreme Court in American Politics* (University Press of Kansas, 1999); Lino A. Graglia, "The Myth of a Conservative Supreme Court: The October 2000 Term," *Harvard Journal of Law & Public Policy* (v.26, 2003); Kermit L. Hall, *The Oxford Companion to American Law* (Oxford University Press, 2002); Kermit L. Hall, *The Oxford Companion to the Supreme Court of the United States* (Oxford University Press, 1992); Donald E. Lively, "The Supreme Court Appointment Process: In Search of Constitutional Roles and Responsibilities," *Southern California Law Review* (v.59, 1986); William P. Marshal, "Conservatives and the Seven Sins of Judicial Activism," *University of Colorado Law Review* (v. 73, 2002); David W. Neubauer, *America's Courts and the Criminal Justice System* (Wadsworth Publishing, 1999); William G. Ross, "The Role of Judicial Issues in Presidential Campaigns," *Santa Clara Law Review* (v.42, 2002); William G. Ross, "The Supreme Court Appointment Process: A Search for a Synthesis," *Albany Law Review* (v.57, 1994); Bernard Schwartz, *A History of the Supreme Court* (Oxford University Press, 1993); Herman Schwartz, *Packing the Courts* (Charles Scribner's Sons, 1988); Ernest A. Young, "Judicial Activism and Conservative Politics," *University of Colorado Law Review* (v.73, 2002).

RONALD C. DESNOYERS, JR.
ROGER WILLIAMS UNIVERSITY

Survivalists

THE SURVIVALIST MOVEMENT dates from the years of the Cold War, circa 1948 to 1989, when Americans lived in fear of nuclear attack from the Soviet Union. The main impetus for survivalism came in fact from the federal government, when the Civil Defense office urged all Americans to build fallout shelters in the event of a thermonuclear war with the Soviets. It was the hope that by building the shelters, and provisioning them, citizens could survive until the federal, state, and local governments could rebuild enough to aid them, and for the fallout from nuclear explosions to decrease enough for outside living again.

The nuclear shelter movement from the outset attracted the vehement support of those committed to extreme anti-communist groups like the John Birch Society, whose belief in a subversive "Red" takeover of the country exceeded the known subversive elements in the country that were being watched carefully by the Federal Bureau of Investigation (FBI) under its director, J. Edgar Hoover. Indeed, extreme survivalists armed themselves to fight off any other people—including neighbors—who would attempt to storm their nuclear refuges. However, in fact, the publication by the National Security Agency (NSA) in the 1990s of the VENONA transcripts from Soviet agents in the United States did portray Russian infiltration of the country on a scale much larger than had been realized within the general public or the press.

EXTREMIST LINKS

The threat from nuclear war receded with the beginning of the SALT (Strategic Arms Limitation Talks) agreements between the Soviet Union and the United States in 1972, the Anti-Ballistic Missile Treaty. However, ironically, the survivalist movement continued to grow in disproportion to the arms threat. Mistrust of government, which had been at the heart of the movement since the "Red Scare" of the 1950s, continued to grow. Survivalists also began to forge links with the Aryan Nations, founded in the 1970s by Richard Butler in Hayden Lake, Idaho.

Reverend Butler's philosophy was strongly influenced by the Christian Identity movement, which views the White Aryan Nation as the true "Chosen People" of the Old Testament, not the Jews. According to Christian Identity, the Jewish people are in reality the "Children of Satan," and nonwhite races like blacks, Mexicans, and Asian peoples are the "mud people." A primary tenet of Aryan Nations belief is that the United States was now ruled by a largely hostile Zionist Occupation Government (ZOG), which perpetuates the alleged financial control of world Jewry, whose pur-

ported design for world control was the subject of the 19th-century Protocols of the Elders of Zion. Thus, as the 1970s ended, the survivalists had fused to a certain degree with the more extreme right of the American political spectrum.

By the 1980s, fueled by the western American reaction to the concerns of big government and the deepening farm crisis, some identified with the survivalist movement and other rightist groups began to take up arms against the federal government. One such group was the Posse Comitatus, in the midwest heart of the country. James Ridgeway notes in *Blood in the Face* that in 1981, some 300 Posse members attended a paramilitary training camp, while in 1982, 40-odd people, led by Posse members, stopped a Wallace, Kansas, sheriff from repossessing farm equipment. In February 1983, Gordon Kahl, decorated for heroism in World War II, was leader of a Posse group in a skirmish in which two federal marshals were killed. Kahl was later shot and killed.

RUBY RIDGE

In 1992, the focus of concern was at Ruby Ridge in Idaho, where Christian survivalist Randy Weaver was besieged at his home by local and state law enforcement authorities and the Hostage Rescue Team (HRT) of the FBI. FBI sniper Lon Horiuchi, a graduate of the U.S. Naval Academy, shot to death Weaver's wife, Vicki. Weaver's son Sam and a U.S. marshal also died. At the same time, the militia movement rose up within the United States. Patterning themselves after the colonial militias that fought the British in the American Revolution, the militias saw themselves as defending against an assault on their liberties by the Clinton administration in Washington, D.C. One of the leaders of the militia movement is John Trochmann, who founded the large Militia of Montana (MOM). In 1990, Trochmann, who has testified before the U.S. Congress, was a featured speaker at the Aryan Nations annual congress at Hayden Lake.

When the year 2000 approached, many computer experts feared that 2000, the year Y2K on computers, would cause universal computer failure. This was based on the concern that many of the early computer programmers, using obsolete computer languages like COBOL and PASCAL, had not programmed past the year 1999. Survivalists began to prepare for a severe crash in the nation, as given publicity in radio shows like Art Bell's *Coast to Coast*. Fortunately, the computer problem was fixed, with minimal known disruptions.

Nevertheless, the fear only strengthened the survivalists' mistrust of big government and big business, and ensured the movement would survive into the new millennium.

SEE ALSO

Volume 1 Left: United States; American Revolution.
Volume 2 Right: Christian Identity; Posse Comitatus.

BIBLIOGRAPHY

Igor Ivanov, "The Missile Defense Mistake Undermining Strategic Stability and the ABM Treaty," *Foreign Affairs* (September/October 2000); "Posse Comitatus," FBI, www.foia.fbi.gov/posse (July 2004); "Sheriff's Posse Comitatus," www.posse-comitatus.org (July 2004); John F. Murphy Jr., *Day of Reckoning: The Massacre at Columbine High School* (Xlibris, 2001); Howard L. Bushart, John R. Craig and Myra Barnes, *Soldiers of God: White Supremacists and Their Holy War for America* (Pinnacle Books, 1998); Jess Walker, *Every Knee Shall Bow: The Truth and Tragedy of the Randy Weaver Family* (Harper, 1995); Alphonso Pinckney, *The American Way of Violence* (Vintage, 1972).

JOHN F. MURPHY, JR.
AMERICAN MILITARY UNIVERSITY

Sweden

THE POPULAR GOVERNMENT in Sweden rests upon an ancient political tradition. The Swedish unicameral parliament, Riksdag, stems from the ancient court system used by all Germanic peoples—the Ting (tribal courts)—and the election of kings in the Viking age. It became a permanent institution in the 15th century. The government of Sweden is a limited constitutional monarchy with a parliamentary system. King Carl XVI Gustav of the House of Bernadotte became king of Sweden in 1973. His authority is formal, symbolic, and representational. Crown Princess Victoria, legitimate daughter of the monarch, born in July 14, 1977, is heir apparent, though a constitutional amendment is required to allow a female succession. The executive authority of the government is vested in the cabinet, which consists of a prime minister and roughly 20 ministers who run the government departments.

Sweden is a country that leans heavily to the left. Internationally, the Swedish model has been recognized as socialism in the capitalist marketplace. There is a major governmental influence. However, rightist and right-leaning political discourse has ways to assert power. For instance, the Moderate Coalition Party, or Moderata samlingspartiet (commonly referred to as Moderaterna), is a liberal-conservative political party in Sweden. It is a member of the International Democrat Union and European Peoples Party/European Democrats. The party was founded as a coalition of conservative members of parliament in the Swedish Riksdag during the second half of the 19th century. In elections, it was known under the name "Allmanna valmansforbundet" or the "Public Election Alliance." During the first half of the 20th century, the loose coalition was organized into a proper party and in the late 1960s the present name was adopted, replacing "Hogerpartiet," or the "Right-wing Party," which had been in use for a number of decades.

In the 1970s, under party leader Gosta Bohman, the traditional conservative policies had to give way to more liberal policies, especially in the economics field. This resulted in a successive upswing in the elections and Gosta Bohman became minister of the economy in 1976. Roughly a decade later in 1991, a Moderate-led government under Carl Bildt as prime minister had made its way to power. The party emphasizes personal freedom, free enterprise, and reduction of the public-sector growth rate, while still supporting most of the social benefits introduced since the 1930s. The party also supports a strong defense and Sweden's membership in the European Union. Its voter base is urban businesspeople and professionals, but the party also attracts young voters, main-street shop owners, and, to a modest extent, blue-collar workers.

Another party, the Christian Democrats, or Kristdemokraterna, was founded in the 1960s but did not enter parliament until 1985, in an electoral alliance with the Center Party and on its own accord in 1991. The leader since April 3, 2004, is Goran Hagglund. He succeeded Alf Svensson, who had been the party's leader since 1973. Ideologically, it is a Nordic Christian Democrat party, having a big part of its voter base among those who belong to free churches, Methodists, Baptists, etc. They seek better ethical practices in government and the teaching of traditional values in the schools. They also want to improve care for the elderly and have an extensive family policy program.

Furthermore, Sweden has witnessed the rise of right-wing extremism and neo-Nazism. The Swedish Nazi groups, or NS groups as they prefer to call themselves, have emerged as political projects out of the music scene. In peaceful Sweden, neo-Nazis in 1999

The Swedish Riksdag, or parliament, has been dominated by leftist parties in coalition with conservative interests.

SEE ALSO
Volume 1 Left: Sweden; Socialism.
Volume 2 Right: Conservatism.

BIBLIOGRAPHY
Jeffrey Kaplan and Leonard Weinberg, *The Emergence of a Euro-American Radical Right* (Rutgers University Press, 1999); Tore Bjorgo, "Militant Neo-Nazism in Sweden," *Terrorism and Political Violence* (v.5/3, 1993); Jeffrey Kaplan and Tore Bjorgo, *Nation and Race: The Developing Euro-American Racist Subculture* (Northeastern University Press, 1998); Tore Bjorgo, *Racist and Right-Wing Violence in Scandinavia: Patterns, Perpetrators, and Responses* (Tano Aschehoug, 1997).

JITENDRA UTTAM
JAWAHARLAL NEHRU UNIVERSITY, INDIA

murdered two police officers, assassinated a labor union activist, bombed a journalist and his son in their car, and in 1998, Nazis also sent a letterbomb to the Swedish minister of justice.

A survey conducted jointly by Sweden's four largest newspapers showed that in a number of cases, threats caused police officers, prosecutors, jurors, and witnesses to withdraw from investigations and court cases. As a result, criminal cases against extremists sometimes had to be dropped. Several journalists and politicians were intimidated into silence. Although the threats from the neo-Nazis and other xenophobic gangs do not represent a threat to the stability of democracy in Sweden, these threats are certainly undermining several important aspects of the democratic process in the country.

In recent years, many right-wing extremist organizations have lost their appeal. There are several different explanations of why the Nazi and extreme right movements have collapsed during the last few years. One of the most important factors is that the Swedish state answered the menace with increasing repression against public nazi meetings, and it has now become "illegal" to wear Nazi symbols or to salute in the "Heil Hitler" manner ("heila") in public. Both Nordland and Ragnarock Records have three legal trials pending for their racist song lyrics. With the use of direct actions and demonstrations, several Nazi boutiques or stores have been closed and it is very difficult for the Nazis to hold demonstrations, concerts, or public meetings.

Switzerland

TRADITIONALLY PEACEFUL and compromising, Swiss political debate at the beginning of the 21st century is marked by a dramatic challenge from the increasingly popular far right. Capturing the largest share of the vote in Switzerland's October 2003 parliamentary elections, the radicalized right now openly questions the decades-old model of consensus politics for which Switzerland is widely known. As is often the case, contemporary controversies such as this one have deep historical roots.

The political right in Switzerland dates from the country's modern inception in 1848. Liberals and conservatives formed the basis of an early two-party system, in which the Liberal Party (today's Radical Democratic Party, or FDP) dominated and the Conservatives (today's Christian Democratic Party, or CVP) provided the usually loyal opposition. The Conservatives laid claim to Switzerland's heavily Catholic cantons and first gained a share of Swiss governing authority in 1891.

At the turn of the 20th century, a schism within the liberal FDP produced two new splinter parties—the left-wing Social-Democratic Party (SP) and the agrarian Swiss People's Party (SVP). The FDP evolved to constitute a classic center-right party, embracing open markets and minimal state intervention in the economy while seeking to protect individual rights and liberties. The SP drifted far left of its FDP origins to become an avowedly socialist party. It was, however, the People's

Party that over time emerged to torment the more moderate Swiss political establishment.

Through an arrangement that became known as the "Magic Formula," the Radicals, Christian Democrats, Social Democrats, and the People's Party agreed in 1959 to share power in the country's governing Federal Council. In what amounted to a permanent coalition, the formula worked its magic quite convincingly for 44 years, with the FDP, CVP, and SP each holding two seats on the Council and the SVP consistently having just one. That formula came to an abrupt end when the SVP, led by billionaire industrialist Christoph Blocher, rocked the Swiss political establishment on October 19, 2003, by capturing almost 27 percent of the national vote to become the country's largest parliamentary party.

Capitalizing on popular anxieties over immigrants, rising unemployment, and closer relations with the European Union, Blocher's SVP joined a growing trend among Europe's xenophobic, nationalist parties by securing impressive electoral gains. By portraying immigrants and asylum seekers as drug addicts and criminals, the radicalized SVP doubled its support among Swiss voters in just a decade. Buoyed by their success in 2003, the German-speaking Blocher and his SVP overturned the 2:2:2:1 formula in the seven-seat Federal Council by demanding and securing their own second seat. Switzerland's mainstream right, in the form of the conservative Christian Democrats, became the big loser, relinquishing their second seat in the cabinet and trading places with the once-junior SVP. Blocher, who had been roundly condemned by human rights organizations and by the United Nations for fomenting intolerance during the 2003 campaign, became minister for justice and police. The radical right and the more mainstream, conservative right are clearly distinguishable. While the radical right in the guise of the SVP promotes a populist nationalism (similar in tone and message to those of Jean-Marie le Pen's Front National in France or Jörg Haider's Freedom Party in Austria), the center-right FDP and Catholic CVP continue to regard themselves as the natural, moderate parties of government in Switzerland. While the SVP is staunchly opposed to closer institutional ties with either the United Nations (UN) or the European Union (EU) on grounds that membership would entail unacceptable costs in lost sovereignty, the Christian Democrats and Radicals adamantly favor membership. Swiss voters rejected UN membership in 1986 but reversed their position in 2002. The SVP's opposition to the EU finds considerable support, especially among German speakers; conversely, the parties on the mainstream right contend that Switzerland's future by necessity lies within the EU.

A number of much smaller and less consequential parties also compete for popular support on the Swiss right. Chief among these are the Protestant People's Party, the Federal Democratic Union, and the Freedom Party of Switzerland (formerly the Auto Party). It is, however, the unprecedented success of the SVP that suggests that a more confrontational style has emerged on the Swiss political scene.

SEE ALSO

Volume 1 Left: Social Democracy; Christian Democracy; Switzerland.
Volume 2 Right: France.

BIBLIOGRAPHY

H.-G. Betz and S. Immerfall, *The New Politics of the Right: Neo-Populist Parties and Movements in Established Democracies* (Macmillan, 1998); Jurg Martin Gabriel and Thomas Fischer, eds., *Swiss Foreign Policy, 1945–2002* (Palgrave Macmillan, 2003); Harold Glass, "Consensus and Opposition in Switzerland: A Neglected Consideration," *Comparative Politics* (v.10/3, 1978); Christopher T. Husbands, "Switzerland: Right-Wing and Xenophobic Parties, from Margin to Mainstream?" *Parliamentary Affairs* (v.53/3, 2000); Martin Schain, ed., *Shadows over Europe: The Development and Impact of the Extreme Right in Western Europe* (Palgrave Macmillan, 2002).

WILLIAM M. DOWNS, PH.D.
GEORGIA STATE UNIVERSITY

The Right

T

Taft, Robert A. (1889–1953)

ROBERT A. TAFT was the son of President William H. Taft, a major figure within the Republican Party and a presidential contender in 1952. Robert Alphonso Taft was born in Cincinnati, Ohio, the firstborn of the three children of William Howard Taft and Helen (Nellie) (Herron) Taft. Will Taft was then a judge, and Robert's maternal grandfather was U.S. attorney. Young Robert accompanied his father to the Philippines when the senior Taft was governor general. While his father was president, Taft graduated first in his class at Yale University in 1910, and he was also first in his class at Harvard Law School in 1913. Taft married Martha Wheaton Bowers, daughter of the solicitor general in his father's administration, on October 17, 1914. The couple settled in Cincinnati. They had four sons, William Howard III, Robert, Jr., Lloyd, and Horace. Taft tried to enlist in World War I but was rejected due to his eyesight. He served as a lawyer under Herbert Hoover in the predecessor to the Food and Drug Administration (FDA). He also worked as a lawyer for a relief organization in Europe and was decorated by the governments of Belgium, Finland, and Poland. Hoover functioned as a mentor to Taft for the rest of his life.

Taft was elected to the Ohio House of Representatives in 1920 and was reelected in 1922 and 1924. He served as majority leader and speaker of the house in

Robert A. Taft's isolationist stance drew Dwight Eisenhower into the Republican 1952 presidential nomination race.

his last term. Taft followed Hoover's lead in embracing initiatives for modernizing state government and fostering efficiency in the economic arena. He was elected to the Ohio Senate in 1930 but lost in the Democratic landslide of 1932 along with his mentor. In defeat, Taft returned to the law but was outspoken in the national arena in opposition to Franklin Roosevelt's New Deal program. Taft was the leader of many economic conservatives who viewed the New Deal's economic centralization as anathema to free-enterprise capitalism.

He was elected a U.S. senator from Ohio in 1938, defeating a Democratic incumbent, and was reelected in 1944 and 1950. He acquired a reputation as an isolationist for opposing U.S. entry into World War II. Taft is best known as the Senate sponsor of the Taft-Hartley Labor Relations Act of 1947, which prohibits jurisdictional strikes and secondary boycotts and closed shops, and allows states to pass "right-to-work" laws. The act was passed only by overriding the veto of President Harry S Truman. He entered the Republican presidential race in 1948 after serving as Ohio's favorite son in 1936 and 1940. (A favorite son is a local leader whom the state's delegates agree to support on the first ballot so the state and its leader may have leverage in subsequent ballots.) He came in second to New York Governor Thomas E. Dewey, who was nominated on the second ballot. Taft's central message was "Peace at any cost, except at the threat to the country's freedom." Taft, by this time known as "Mr. Republican," again ran for the nomination in 1952. According to some sources, Dwight D. Eisenhower, who had been either apolitical or a Democrat before then, chose to run for president as a Republican expressly to defeat Taft's isolationist stance. Technically, there was only one ballot, but Eisenhower won the nomination as a result of a substantial number of vote changes only after the preliminary results had been announced. Taft became majority leader of the Senate in January 1953.

Taft died suddenly in New York City on July 31, 1953, and was buried in Indian Hill Episcopal Church cemetery in Cincinnati. The carillon and its hundred-foot tower on Capitol Hill are dedicated to his memory. His son Robert A. Taft, Jr., served a term in the U.S. Senate from Ohio in the 1970s, and his grandson, Robert III, was elected governor of Ohio in 1998 and reelected in 2002.

SEE ALSO

Volume 1 Left: Roosevelt, Franklin D.; Truman, Harry; Democratic Party.
Volume 2 Right: Taft, William H.; Eisenhower, Dwight D.

BIBLIOGRAPHY

Caroline T. Harnsberger, *Man of Courage: Robert A. Taft* (Wilcox and Follett, 1952); James T. Patterson, *Mr. Republican: A Biography of Robert A. Taft* (Houghton Mifflin, 1972); William S. White, *The Taft Story* (Harper, 1954).

TONY L. HILL
MASSACHUSETTS INSTITUTE OF TECHNOLOGY

Taft, William H. (1857–1930)

WILLIAM H. TAFT is the only person to have headed two branches of the U.S. government, as president from 1909 to 1913 and as chief justice from 1921 to 1930. Taft was born in Cincinnati, Ohio, the second of five children born to Alphonso Taft and Louise Maria (Torrey) Taft. (Alphonso Taft had five children from his first marriage as well.) Alphonso Taft was a lawyer who had served as secretary of war under President U.S. Grant and as attorney general under Grant and President Rutherford B. Hayes. His father had been a judge in Vermont. Taft, who was known as Will, graduated as salutatorian from Yale University in 1878 and the Cincinnati Law School in 1880 and became a lawyer. He served as a law reporter for the newspapers and then became a prosecutor. In 1882, he was named a revenue collector by President Chester A. Arthur, but Taft soon left the job because he was appalled by the highly partisan nature of his assignment. He went into private practice.

He married Helen (Nellie) Herron in Cincinnati on June 19, 1886. They had two sons, Robert (who became a U.S. senator and presidential candidate) and Charles (who became mayor of Cincinnati), and a daughter, Helen (who served as dean of Bryn Mawr College). In 1887, when he was not yet 30, he became a judge on the superior court of Cincinnati, where he served until 1890, when he became solicitor general of the United States. He won 15 of the 18 cases he argued in his first year as the government's chief lawyer before the Supreme Court. In 1892, he returned to Cincinnati to serve as a judge on the U.S. Circuit Court of Appeals. From 1896, he also served as dean of the University of Cincinnati law school.

Both these appointments ended in 1900 when he became president of the Philippines Commission. He became governor-general of the Philippines the next year. He declined an appointment to the Supreme Court in

1902, a position he had long wanted, because he did not want to leave the work he was doing in the Philippines. In 1904, he followed in his father's footsteps, becoming secretary of war under President Theodore Roosevelt. Although it was a time of peace, the department was charged with construction of the Panama Canal, and Taft was also a negotiator in ending a war between Russia and Japan.

Taft initially rejected the idea of succeeding Roosevelt, preferring to wait for a Supreme Court nomination, but Roosevelt was adamant and his wife convinced him to run. Taft's only elective experience before he ran for president had been one judicial election in Cincinnati. Taft was nominated on the first ballot at the Republican National Convention in Chicago. He was the first cabinet member other than secretary of state to become president.

Taft's inauguration was held during a late-winter blizzard in 1913. His inaugural parade was abandoned, and Taft's wife became the first to ride to the White House with the president. Despite his being brought up through the ranks, as it were, by Roosevelt, during Taft's presidency, the Republican Party fractured, leading Roosevelt to run as a third-party candidate in 1912. Part of the impetus for this was the administration's tariff bill, the Payne-Aldrich Act of 1909, which managed to alienate people in both wings of the party. Taft wanted to veto the bill, but grudgingly signed it.

The most noteworthy achievement of his administration was the admission of New Mexico and Arizona as the 47th and 48th states. The Interstate Commerce Commission was expanded during Taft's administration. The first campaign finance disclosure bill was also passed. Taft was the first president to open a baseball season with a ceremonial pitch. His wife, Helen, led the effort to plant the first Japanese cherry trees in Washington, D.C., now a hallmark of the capital. Taft found Roosevelt a difficult president to follow. It is rumored that Taft once said that whenever he was addressed as Mr. President, he felt like looking behind him to see if Roosevelt were standing there. Taft was the heaviest president. He weighed 300 pounds at one point. According to legend, after getting stuck in a bathtub in the White House, a special tub was built to accommodate him. It is still used in the White House residence.

Buoyed by the many liberal Republicans Taft had alienated, Roosevelt returned to challenge Taft for the Republican nomination in 1912. (The Republican Party then had a large and vibrant liberal wing.) Taft won the nomination on the first ballot, but Roosevelt charged that Taft had cheated by seating slates of delegates committed to the incumbent rather than Roosevelt delegates who had been legitimately elected. Roosevelt quickly formed a third party, the Progressive "Bull Moose" Party. Roosevelt's third party candidacy eclipsed Taft's and let Democrat Woodrow Wilson win the presidency with only 42 percent of the popular vote. Roosevelt carried six states and left the incumbent with only Utah and Vermont. Taft told his successor, "I'm glad to be going. This is the lonesomest place in the world."

Taft became a law professor at Yale after his defeat. He also served as president of the American Bar Association. Wilson made him chairman of the National War Labor Board. In 1921, he was appointed chief justice of the United States by President Warren G. Harding. Taft functioned as a leader within the judiciary, serving as a spokesperson on legislative matters pertaining to the judiciary as no chief justice had done before. Under Taft's leadership, Congress created the Conference of Senior Circuit Judges (now the Judicial Conference of the United States) in 1922, the principal policymaking body concerned with the administration of the federal judiciary.

He lobbied successfully for passage of the Judges' Bill of 1925, which eliminated nearly all of the mandatory jurisdiction of the court, meaning the court became free to pick and choose the cases it wanted to hear via the granting of *certiorari*. During his tenure, plans were laid for the court to have its own building, which was completed only after his death. Taft was a judicial activist of a conservative bent, not unlike a modern chief justice, and he shepherded the conservative wing of the court, which went on to unmake the New Deal. "Under Taft's leadership the judiciary wielded the authority of a super-legislature," wrote judicial scholar Alpheus Thomas Mason.

Taft continued to advise presidents privately while he was chief justice. Taft, who walked three miles to and from the court most days, retired from the court on February 3, 1930, and died on March 8 of that year. He was the first president buried at Arlington National Cemetery in Virginia.

SEE ALSO

Volume 1 Left: Democratic Party; Progressive Party; Supreme Court.
Volume 1 Right: Republican Party; Roosevelt, Theodore.

BIBLIOGRAPHY

Donald F. Anderson, *William Howard Taft: A Conservative's Conception of the Presidency* (Cornell University Press, 1973);

Judith I. Anderson, *William Howard Taft: An Intimate History* (Norton, 1981).

TONY L. HILL
MASSACHUSETTS INSTITUTE OF TECHNOLOGY

Taxes

"NOTHING," said Benjamin Franklin, "is certain in life but death and taxes." Over the years, since taxes have become so manifest, many have come to believe that death may be more evenhanded. However reluctantly, most people agree that taxes are necessary to finance the operation of governments and to regulate an economy for the public good. Governments on the right see taxes as a necessary evil to provide essential services to society. In these political systems, the government that taxes least governs best. Governments on the left, however, see taxes as necessary means to fund a wide social network of public services, such that tax expenditures reach all levels of society.

Former Supreme Court Justice Oliver Wendell Holmes once said, "Taxes are what we pay for a civilized society." Holmes believed that social benefits would result from the imposition of taxes. For him, although people work to meet individual needs and the needs of their families, there are some services, such as police, fire protection, and national defense that they cannot provide or purchase for themselves.

Taxes are levied on citizens to bear the cost of these kinds of government services in the general public interest. No government policy affects as many of us as does tax policy. Thus the question is not whether citizens should be taxed, but rather how and by how much. Taxation has always maintained a controversial character. It is difficult for many individuals to understand the nature of the public good and to immediately see the benefits taxes provide to them. Thomas Paine wrote of "the greedy hand of government, thrusting itself into every corner and crevice of industry."

Using their extensive powers to raise money, governments can tax people for money to spend on what they regard as the public good. What constitutes the public good at any particular time and place depends on the values present in society and, to a very important extent, on the scale of priorities governments place on spending tax dollars. Public goods such as the protection of the environment are funded through the general tax system rather than on the user-pay principle that is characteristic of private goods, such as buying a car or going to a movie. Public goods benefit all citizens and thus are derived by means of taxation because they are not likely to be produced by the voluntary acts of individuals.

Taxes go to the heart of public debates on politics, as political scientist Harold Lasswell once remarked: "who gets what, when, and how." What will be taxed? Will certain taxes be imposed temporarily or permanently? How is the burden of taxes to be distributed between individuals and corporations? How are taxes to be imposed—on sales, property, income, wealth, and on death? At what rates are taxes to be levied? Should deductions and exemptions from taxation be permitted? Who should be spared from certain taxes and for what reasons?

CENTURIES OF TAXATION

Taxes have been imposed by governments for thousands of years. The oldest tax system, recorded on clay tablets, was established 6,000 years ago in a place called Lagash. Tax collectors armed with the power of seizure traveled the land to amass heavy war taxes.

Egyptian hieroglyphics depict ancient tax agents known as scribes, getting tough on delinquent taxpayers, confiscating personal property, and even forcing them to pay their taxes through involuntary labor. Exempt from their own taxes, scribes collected taxes on beer, fish, fruit, honey, and wine. Many of the people who constructed the Great Wall of China were paying their taxes with their labor. Chinese tax collectors were powerful bureaucrats who conducted audits, prosecuted delinquent tax collectors, and testified at court.

The Romans enabled their empire to grow by means of an efficient tax system imposed in all parts of their domain. But as time went on, the system became corrupt and unjust, contributing to the demise of the Roman Empire. Roman tax agents were so resented that soldiers had to accompany them when collecting taxes in order to act as bodyguards.

Even the Catholic Church found ways, with the blessing of the state, to extract resources from parishioners. The Church tithe, for example, under which parishioners would pay a tenth of their income to the clergy, long predates the emergence of the modern state. What distinguished these early forms of extraction was that they were occasional, sometimes random, and often justified by little more than brute force or the right of conquest.

In the Middle Ages, taxes were levied on everything from commercial activities to personal property. Popular legend made heroes out of tax resistors like 13th-century William Tell, who was forced to shoot an apple off his son's head by angry government tax collectors. Lady Godiva gained the reputation of a heroine when she took the dare of her husband to ride naked through town in protest of high taxes. By the 1600s, taxes were imposed on people in Europe to pay for extravagant bureaucratic lifestyles and for wars waged by monarchs.

At about this time in history, the incremental role of the state was instituted by many European governments, creating ever-increasing revenue demands placed upon ordinary citizens. As important as the sheer rise in revenue demands from emergency wartime situations was the gradual expansion of public indebtedness after wars ended. Wars meant not just increased costs to be met in the present but also an increase in public debt, and this had to be serviced by taxation payments when wars were not being waged. Under Henry VIII's otherwise controversial reign, one important and permanent administrative development occurred for raising state revenues: peacetime taxation.

Taxes spawned popular resistance: "The art of taxation," said Jean-Batiste Colbert (1619–1683), France's chief minister to Louis XIV, "consists in so plucking the goose as to obtain the largest possible amount of feathers with the smallest amount of hissing." Few people enjoyed paying taxes—"to tax and to please," so Edmund Burke argued, "is not given to men"—and resistance against extraction has been an ancient pastime. History before the rise of the modern state is littered with tax revolts and peasants' rebellions against unreasonable forms and levels of taxation. With the rise of the modern state in the 18th century, both the imposition and resentment against taxation became more popular and systematic.

In America, the British colonies launched a revolution against King George III, protesting sugar, tea, and stamp taxes. In 1773, anger over taxation reached a powerful climax at the Boston Tea Party, in which colonists dressed as Mohawk Indians dumped about 350 chests of British tea into Boston Harbor as a gesture of tax protest. This series of tax revolts was powerful incentives taken by the colonists that eventually gave birth to the United States of America.

At the start of its unique experience with individual freedom and limited government, "taxation without representation is tyranny" was the mantra of the American Revolution. Later, to finance the Civil War, President Abraham Lincoln introduced the first U.S. income tax, lasting for only a brief period of time because wealthy Americans resisted it so strongly.

For both the rulers and the ruled, it seemed that taxation might be more bearable if, at least formally, it could be construed as chosen by the people. Taxation required a perceived legitimacy. Thus it became systematic, continuous, legal, rational, extensive, regularized, and bureaucratized. In the 19th century, one theory about why governments would have to raise public revenues by means of various forms of taxation was proposed by a German economist, Adolph Wagner, in 1883. Wagner's law of increasing state activity postulated that government expenditures would grow at a faster rate than the total output of goods and services in industrialized economies, thus requiring a wider range of taxation than had been previously envisioned.

In North America, Canada and the United States maintained a small tax structure well into the 20th century. Customs and excise taxes—indirect forms of taxation—had accounted for over 50 percent of colonial revenues in Canada and the United States. Tariffs were used in both countries to protect and subsidize nascent industries. Not until 1913 did Americans pay income taxes, eventually becoming the largest source of federal government revenues. Canada followed suit in 1916 with the establishment of a business profits tax, and in 1917 imposed its income tax on all citizens who earned more than $2,000 per year.

MANY KINDS OF TAXES

There is a vast assortment of taxes. Some, such as income taxes, are highly visible to taxpayers. Others, such as value-added taxes, are sometimes all but invisible because they are included in the purchase price of products at the wholesale and retail levels. Taxes are imposed and collected by various levels of government around the world, national governments, subnational governments in federal systems, and municipal governments. Revenue taxes are levied in order to fund government services and programs. These represent the majority of taxes at all levels of government in the developed economies of the world. Restrictive taxes are levied in order to control certain activities that legislatures believe should be controlled.

Governments raise revenues from a variety of sources. There are direct taxes on earnings of individuals and corporations, known as individual income taxes and corporate income taxes. Personal income taxes are paid directly to the government by individuals. Corporate taxes are taxes on company profits as defined by

The Internal Revenue Service's Form 1040 is a standard income tax form that most Americans get to know only too well. For conservatives, such taxes, especially income taxes, should be lowered on a permanent basis.

taxing authorities. A direct tax is a tax imposed on a person who it is intended should pay the tax. However, an indirect tax is one that is levied against one person in the expectation that it will be paid by another person. An excise tax is an example of an indirect tax. An excise tax levied on a supplier of a product will be passed on to the consumer.

Great Britain introduced the first general personal income tax with the passage of the Act of 1799. The Act imposed a comprehensive income tax on all residents of Great Britain and included exemptions and abatements for dependents. Austria adopted an income tax in 1849, as did Italy in 1864. Australia, New Zealand, and Japan instituted one by the mid-1880s. Germany and the Netherlands legislated their income tax in the 1890s. Other states took longer to use an income tax to raise government revenues. The United States used it for a brief period of time during the Civil War. In 1913, the income tax was permanently enacted following the ratification of the Sixteenth Amendment

to the U.S. Constitution. Canada instituted the income tax in 1919 as a temporary measure to pay for World War I. But the tax has remained a permanent revenue regime since that time.

There are also indirect taxes on income gained when goods and services are purchased. These include a general tax, sometimes referred to as a value-added tax (VAT) or a goods and services tax (GST). The VAT is collected at each stage of the production process from raw material extraction through manufacturing to retail sales. The GST is a national sales tax on consumption imposed on most purchases.

There can also be taxes on specific goods and services, known as excise taxes and duties. Normally the heaviest excise taxes fall on alcohol and tobacco, sometimes referred to as "sin taxes." Property taxes, based on the value of taxable property, are an important source of revenue for municipal governments such as towns and cities. The property tax is based on wealth. Taxing the value of existing property creates two problems. First, the property must be assessed to determine what the property is worth. Because the assessment is only an estimate, it is subject to challenge. Second, sometimes owners with low incomes of property that is assessed as valuable have difficulty paying the tax.

Wealth taxation is one of the oldest methods of government revenue collection, having been used since ancient times. Ancient Greece levied a general property tax not only on land and dwellings, but also on cattle, furniture, money, and slaves. When a government taxes one group in society more heavily than it taxes another, it influences the distribution of income throughout the economy. The effects of taxes on the distribution of income may be summarized in terms of progressivity, higher tax rates for higher incomes.

A progressive tax system takes a larger share of income from people the higher their income is so as to yield more equal distribution of net income. A proportional tax system takes amounts of money from people in direct proportion to their income. The government takes the same shares from everyone, rich and poor alike. A regressive tax system takes a larger percentage of income from people the lower their income is. A regressive tax causes poorer people to pay a higher percentage of their income than richer people pay. Rarely are taxes obviously regressive. No nation-state deliberately charges a higher rate of taxes for poor families and a lower rate for rich ones. Thus a tax system is said to be progressive if it decreases the inequality of income distribution and regressive if it increases the inequality of income distribution, other things being equal.

Taxes, therefore, can have an impact on the distribution of income in three ways: 1) progressive taxes can make the poor richer and the rich poorer; 2) proportional taxes can have no net effect on income; 3) regressive taxes can make the rich richer and the poor poorer.

Sometimes taxes are used in ways that resemble government spending programs. For example, one of the ways of dealing with polluted lakes is to spend public funds to regenerate them. Taxes may be used to penalize polluters who persist in an undesirable activity or to provide concessions to companies that install pollution-abating devices. Tax concessions that seek to induce desirable market responses are called tax expenditures—tax revenues foregone in order to achieve purposes that the government believes are desirable.

There are those who advocate abolishing tax systems based on progressivity and proportionality. They want to replace the traditional tax systems with a simple flat tax. The flat tax would eliminate all or most exemptions, exclusions, deductions, and special treatments. It would be based on applying the same percentage (say 20 percent) on all forms of income. For those promoting this kind of tax the benefits are simplicity and efficiency. A flat tax could be filed on a postcard, thus eliminating the need for tax accountants, lawyers and lobbyists. It would eliminate the current incentives of taxpayers to underreport income, overstate exemptions and thereby evade taxation.

EVALUATING A TAX SYSTEM

Evaluating a tax system involves how the public perceives the operation of the system and the benefits they receive from it. For a tax system to work positively requires that taxpayers perceive the system to be fair, efficient, and progressive. Fairness is evaluated by the perception of the tax burden and by observing who benefits from the system. From a global perspective, overall tax burdens in the United States are relatively low. They are low when compared with the tax burdens imposed by Sweden, Denmark, and Norway with their highly developed welfare systems. Generally, among the most advanced economies in Europe, Asia, and North America, the top and middle marginal tax rates are gradually being reduced so as to compete in the global economy.

In the global economy, there is a widely held view that high tax rates discourage work, savings, and investment. There is the belief that economic growth in many developed economies can be stunted by high tax rates. Because there is an increased mobility of individuals and firms, there are external pressures for governments to keep their top tax rates down so as to attract the best professionals, corporations and workers. The politics of taxation centers on the question of who actually bears the heaviest burden of a tax. Which income groups must devote the largest proportion of their income to taxes? The argument of progressivity is generally defended on the principle of ability to pay: The belief is that high-income groups can afford to pay a larger percentage of their income in taxes at no more of a sacrifice than that required of lower-income groups to devote a smaller proportion of their income to taxes.

This assumption is based on what economists call marginal utility theory. The word *marginal* is used regularly in the field of taxation and it means "extra" or "additional." The marginal tax rate is the extra income tax paid in relation to an increase in income. According to marginal utility theory, each additional dollar of income is slightly less valuable to an individual than preceding dollars. For example, a $5,000 increase in the income of an individual already earning $100,000 is much less valuable than a $5,000 increase to an individual earning only $10,000 or no income at all. Therefore, the marginal utility theory argues that added dollars of income can be taxed at higher rates without violating equitable principles.

Others argue for proportionality. They say that equity can only be achieved by taxing everyone at the same percentage of their income. By using the rule of proportionality, personal and corporate initiative as well as enterprise is not penalized by the tax system. According to the advocates of proportionality, whenever incomes are taxed at different rates, people will figure out ways to take advantage of the differential. They will hire lawyers, accountants, and lobbyists to find or create exemptions, exclusions, deductions, and preferential treatment for their own sources of income.

These loopholes are regarded by governments as tax expenditures. These are revenues lost to the government because of various exemptions made available to taxpayers in the tax system. Government revenues from individual and corporate taxes would be substantially higher were it not for special provisions in tax laws that enable taxpayers to avoid paying taxes on portions of their income.

Taxation is often used in more subtle ways to stimulate or restrain various aspects of the economy or the whole economy. This is called fiscal policy. This kind of policy involves the linkages among the taxing, spending, borrowing, budget, and debt reduction practices of a government in order to achieve economic stability in a competitive world. A budget is a document that announces how much the government will collect in taxes and spend in revenues and how those revenues will be allocated among various programs.

Taxes are evaluated on the basis of their effects directly on the economy and society. The fiscal effect may increase or decrease unemployment or inflation as money is taken out of the hands of consumers. Tax policies may also put money back into the hands of taxpayers, which can stimulate consumption or investment. The distributional effect results from government policies about who should carry the tax burden more or less. Whether a tax is progressive or regressive depends on what percentage of income governments decide to take from various income groups.

The regulatory effect of taxes may either discourage or promote a certain activity, for example, a heavier tax on gas-guzzling vehicles. While taxes have the primary purpose of raising money to finance government operations, programs, and services, they are also used for social control.

Thus the imposition of taxes is evaluated on economic consequences. Tax increases can be used to control price increases and unemployment. Tax increases tend to reduce spending and are used to lower price increases. By doing this, tax policy has to be consistent with economic objectives. If it is desirable to encourage the expansion of the petroleum industry, it is consistent with economic objectives to give a tax break to that industry and not necessarily give it simultaneously to other sectors. If a government does not want consumers to purchase air conditioners for automobiles, then it can levy an excise tax on this product. If a government wants consumers to drink wine produced in the national market as opposed to imported wine, the tax policy could reflect this objective. The tax on imported wine could be increased, while the tax on domestic wine could be decreased.

Another factor that can affect the system of taxation is failure on the part of individuals and groups to report income. Sometimes referred to as the "underground economy," this unreported economic activity is not measured as a contribution to the gross domestic product (GDP). The transactions that occur in the underground economy may be legal or illegal activities. The illegality involved can be that such transactions are not reported for tax purposes. Or it can be that the activities violate the law and still constitute part of the underground economy.

When people avoid paying taxes, they are indeed evaluating the system of taxation. The growth of the underground economy is often a reaction to rising rates of taxation and is a form of tax resistance as well as tax evasion. The higher the taxes, the greater the incentive to avoid paying them and the more there is to be gained by going underground. Estimates of the size of the underground economy in the United States are as low as 2 to 5 percent of the gross domestic product to as high as 15 percent by some economists. They are estimated as higher in other economies, such as in Argentina, Italy, and Russia.

In the final analysis, tax policies are those public policies that attempt to collect revenues for government use so as to stabilize the economy and provide benefits and opportunities among different groups in society. Every government has a panoply of tax policies, whether it be a federal or unitary state. The use of taxation as a tool for the achievement of the goals of government flows from the political orientation of those in power.

Political conservatives want to use the tax system so as to provide opportunity in society with minimal government regulation, spending, and assistance to the poor. Political liberals see taxation as a means to support social programs that assist the disadvantaged while encouraging economic growth and prosperity for all.

SEE ALSO

Volume 1 Left: Socialism; Social Security; Welfare and Poverty; Democratic Party; Conservatism.
Volume 2 Right: Capitalism; Conservatism; Libertarianism; Republican Party.

BIBLIOGRAPHY

Todd Buchholz, *New Ideas from Dead Economists* (Penguin, 2003); Liam Murphy and Thomas Nagel, *The Myth of Ownership: Taxes and Justice* (Oxford University Press, 2002); Eva Piroska Soos, *The Origins of Taxation at Source in England* (International Bureau of Fiscal Documentation, 1998); Joel Slemroad and Jon Bakija, *Taxing Ourselves: A Citizen's Guide to the Great Debate over Tax Reform* (MIT Press, 1998).

JAMES JOHN GUY, PH.D.
UNIVERSITY COLLEGE OF CAPE BRETON, CANADA

Technocracy, Inc.

THE TERM *technocrats* has been applied to government officials, usually civil servants with no specific ideological background but with expertise in their technical area, who have been raised to cabinet or other senior posts. The term implies an expert, without party affiliation, often selected to serve during an interim or transitional government. However, Technocracy, Inc., is a specific organization, founded in 1933, with branches in the United States and Canada, that has advocated the transformation of the political structure into an apolitical system using technical and scientific principles to organize society. It continues to exist in the 21st century, if only in the form of a few adherents and a website giving access to some of its literature.

The ideology of Technocracy, Inc., represents a non-Marxist critique of capitalist society. Although it resembles Marxism in that it claims to be based on a scientific analysis of society and history, Technocracy, Inc., bears more resemblance to the essentially elitist and conservative concept of a Platonic republic, governed by philosopher-kings and relying on a faith in science as the solution of social issues. With its essentially apolitical character, the literature of the organization explicitly denied any precedent in existing political ideas of either the left or right.

The organization and the philosophy derive from its founder, Howard Scott, a West Virginia-born consulting electrical engineer. A brilliant child prodigy, Scott's education as an engineer was abruptly terminated on the death of his father, who had earned a fortune in the logging business. Despite the setback, Scott made a successful career as an independent consultant. While studying national electrical problems, he developed the notion that the concepts of vector analysis and finding the optimum energy solution to complex systems problems held the key to economic prosperity.

Scott briefly toyed with the idea of forming an alliance with the remnants of the Industrial Workers of the World at the end of World War I, but after submitting a couple of articles to the union's publication, the cooperation ended. He organized a group called the Technical Alliance in 1918–19 with several other engineers, architects, and scientists, but it was dissolved in 1921.

In 1933, he revived his ideas and founded the nonprofit corporation Technocracy, Inc. The organization adopted the yin and yang symbol of a circle bisected by a serpentine curve, half chromium and half vermillion in color (which the organization defined as a "monad"). With no specific political agenda, and with no attempt to utilize labor or other existing organizations as a base, it appeared to grow very gradually through a program of inexpensively printed and distributed pamphlets mostly authored by Scott, with scattered membership discussion groups known as "chartered sections" requiring a minimum of 50 members, many in rural sections of Canada and the United States. Politicians holding elective office were declared ineligible for membership. The peculiar emblem of the organization was soon posted on rural highways across North America, found along with such Americana as Burma-Shave signs through the 1950s.

Scott's writings reflected and tapped into the popular disillusionment with the capitalist system that appeared on the verge of collapse following the stock crash of 1929 and the onset of the Great Depression. Scott argued that the natural resources and industrial capacity of the United States and Canada were more than sufficient to provide a decent living for all residents in North America.

The collapse of the system, he argued, derived from the failure to apply a strictly scientific approach to the management of industry and society and to the distribution of goods.

Scott specifically rejected not only Marxism but fascism and all "political methods" of making social decisions, claiming instead that an engineering approach based on the measurement of energy units would represent the ideal system for North America. Instead of a price and market system, Technocracy, Inc., visualized a system in which work and products would be measured by units of energy expended or required for their production and distribution. Among the few prior social commentators cited by Scott and other adherents of Technocracy, Inc., was Thorstein Veblen, the social critic, most famous for his *The Theory of the Leisure Class*, published in 1899.

Scott used his own version of vector analysis to calculate efficient structures that he dubbed "machines for living" and wider systems, including a new waterway transportation system for the United States, fully automated factories, continent-wide integrated communications and electrical transmission networks, and product life-cycle planning. He also visualized a system of automated control for automobile transportation. What later engineers would recognize as a systems approach was at the core of his thinking in the 1920s, about four or five decades ahead of its time.

Technocracy attracted some degree of attention in the 1930s with its promise of prosperity for all, but Scott's apolitical agenda as well as his apparently elitist approach caused its following to wane. Although the organization outlived Scott, who died in 1970 at the age of 77, it retained only a smattering of adherents. Many of Scott's ideas persisted, but the organization always had the appearance of a personality cult or a group of admirers of Scott's often cryptic descriptions of how to apply engineering concepts to socioeconomic problems. Although some prior utopian schemes had relied upon a Messianic view that science and technology would generate a social system free of politics, Technocracy, Inc., reflected a unique set of proposals that bore little resemblance to any other ideology. Although essentially a radical and utopian critique of capitalism, Scott's elitism helps place the movement on the right.

SEE ALSO

Volume 1 Left: Liberalism; Socialism.
Volume 2 Right: Fascism; Totalitarianism.

BIBLIOGRAPHY

Ralph Chaplin, *Wobbly: The Rough-and-Tumble Story of an American Radical* (University of Chicago Press, 1948); Henry Elsner, Jr., *The Technocrats: Prophets of Automation* (Syracuse University Press, 1966); Howard Scott, "The Scourge of Politics in the Land of Manna," *One Big Union Monthly* (1920); Howard Scott, *A Thermodynamic Interpretation of Social Phenomena* (Technocracy, Inc., 1933); www.technocracyinc.org (December 2004).

RODNEY P. CARLISLE
GENERAL EDITOR

Thailand

THE KINGDOM OF THAILAND is a Buddhist country in Southeast Asia that was known as Siam through most of its long national existence. The population exceeded 62 million in 2002. The capital of the country is Bangkok (6 million). Thai statehood comes from the ancient states of Sukhothai, founded in 1238, and its successor, Ayutthaya, established in the mid-14th century. They had close trade and cultural contacts with China and India. The right in Thailand historically has been with the monarchy. Siam's kings took the strongest points of Chinese experience and used them successfully. Thailand was the only Southeast Asian country that avoided European colonial domination.

Strong central authorities thrust French, English, and other traders and missionaries out of the country on the eve of the 18th century. In the 19th century, the Siamese monarchy found itself under constant French and English pressure. It was seeking the Russian Empire's patronage and got it. So Siam preserved its customs and conception of governmental authority, though Western influence in the middle of the 19th century led to royally sponsored reforms.

In 1932, Thailand became a constitutional monarchy. During World War II, it was in a loose alliance with Japan, and since 1945, Thailand has opened its markets to foreign capital, especially American. Soon the country became an ally of the United States in the Cold War in Asia. Up to the end of the 1970s, the political situation in the country was unstable. Thailand saw a series of military coups d'etat. The numerous abuses on the part of the military bureaucracy caused grandiose scandals from time to time. When a new coup at the end of the 1970s led to the restoration of the 1932 constitution, the situation noticeably changed. Further challenges to the parliamentary multiparty system failed in 1991 and 1992. Thailand experienced a period of rapid successful development in 1990s when all macroeconomic indicators increased markedly.

Thailand's economy consisted not only of industrial and agricultural export (rubber, rice) but also an energetic focus on developing a number of high-tech electronics and petrochemical industries. However, following years of speculation in the real estate market and growing corruption in the government, the country's currency plummeted in July 1997, setting off a crisis in Asian financial markets and plunging the country into a deep recession, which was not overcome until 2001.

Today, the king of Thailand has little direct power but is a symbol of national identity and unity. King Bhumibol, who has been on the throne since 1946, enjoys popularity and moral authority. Thailand is illustrative of the need for traditional institutions to have a wider base of social support in the age of widening political democracy.

Thailand is governed under the constitution of 1997, its 17th since 1932. Thailand's legal system blends principles of traditional Thai and Western laws and includes the constitutional court, the administrative courts, and the courts of justice, organized in three tiers. In Thailand's southern border provinces, where Muslims constitute the majority of the population, Provincial Islamic Committees have limited jurisdiction over probate, family, marriage, and divorce cases. Violence in the south of Thailand has for years been blamed on a group of separatists who vowed to turn the region into a Muslim state, launching attacks on police and government-operated schools.

The Thai bicameral parliament, the National Assembly, consists of the senate and the house of representatives. The senate is a nonpartisan body with limited legislative powers, composed of 200 directly elected members from constituent districts, with every province (of 76) having at least one senator. The house of representatives has 500 members, 400 of whom are directly elected from constituent districts, and the remainder drawn proportionally from party lists. The heads of provinces are career civil servants appointed by the minister of interior with the exception of Bangkok's governor, who is popularly elected.

Thailand progressed toward democracy from the 1980s onward. But it is a specific democracy adapted by local Buddhist tradition. The concept of democracy has been used by the Thai elite as an instrument for maintaining order and securing hegemony over the population. In this perspective, the ideas of civil society, civic virtue, social capital, and democracy itself are all part of the weaponry deployed in an effort to create "good cit-

King Bhumibol of Thailand has little direct authority, but is the nominal head of a constitutional monarchy.

izens" who act as guardians of the elite-defined common good.

As Peter Poole argues, "Military as well as civilian leaders sought support from two major institutions: the Thai monarchy and the elite civilian bureaucracy. The bureaucracy tended to side with the military, hoping to use the strength and discipline of the armed forces to implement its own goals of national development. King Bhumibol on the other hand tried to draw the best qualities of both leadership groups, the strength and modernizing zeal of the military and the civilian politicians' commitment to democracy and traditional values."

A growing popular rejection of violence in politics, as widely used by the military in the previous decades, brought the Democratic Party, led by Chuan Leekpai, to power in September 1992. Since then, the coups, as the method of updating interior politics, were superseded by parliamentary elections. The Thai Nation Party led by Banharn Silpa-archa carried an election of 1995. The next two years brought the coalition governments of Chavalit Youngchaiyudh and Chuan Leekpai to power. In the January 2001 elections, telecommunications ty-

Modernization has come to Bangkok, Thailand's capital, under a succession of conservative governments.

coon Thaksin Shinawatra and his Thai Rak Thai party swept in on the populist platform of economic growth and development.

Being a fast-growing economy and a mecca for foreign investments, Thailand became a case for discussion of the sweatshop problem after the worst industrial fire in the history of capitalism occurred at the Kader toy factory in Bangkok in 1993. Liberals condemned profit-seeking owners for the barbaric exploitation of the youth workers, and shamed the customers. In reply, conservative writers argue that sweatshops are a normal step in economic development, and that a worker chooses a job there because she thinks herself better off in that job than at her next-best alternative.

SEE ALSO

Volume 1 Left: Asia; Anti-Globalization.
Volume 2 Right: Globalization; Asia.

BIBLIOGRAPHY

Michael Connors, *Democracy and National Identity in Thailand* (Routledge/Curzon, 2003); Craig J. Reynolds, ed., *National Identity and Its Defenders: Thailand Today* (Silkworm Books, 2003); David K. Wyatt, *Thailand: A Short History* (Yale University Press, 2003); Peter A. Poole, *The Vietnamese in Thailand: A Historical Perspective* (Cornell University Press, 1970).

IGOR CHARSKYKH
DONETSK NATIONAL UNIVERSITY, UKRAINE

Thatcher, Margaret (1925–)

BORN OCTOBER 13, 1925, Margaret Thatcher, née Roberts, grew up in the small British town of Grantham. Her father owned a grocery store there and early on inculcated her with the Victorian virtues of hard work and thrift, along with a strong Methodist faith. Her childhood in the store and her father would both be major influences on Thatcher and would help to shape her intense dislike of borrowing and of the welfare state. Her father, Alfred, was an autodidact and a passionate conservative. Thatcher performed well in school and went to Oxford during World War II to study chemistry. In 1951, she married businessman Denis Thatcher. She later read law and became a tax attorney, a job that offered a thorough grounding in how the government could deprive its citizens of their property in order to fund various socialist schemes.

During the 1940s, Thatcher read a book that would have a lasting influence on her outlook: Friedrich von Hayek's *The Road to Serfdom*. Hayek's polemic argued that socialist government controls of the economy inevitably led to the kind of despotic states of the Soviet Union or Nazi Germany. This intellectual grounding in free-market economics and anti-communism would complement the shopkeeper's values that she absorbed in her childhood and help turn her into one of the most vociferous and successful critics of the welfare state in history. For one who made her way in the world through discipline and hard work, the free rides offered by British socialism were an abomination.

Thatcher was first elected to Parliament in 1959 and received her first ministerial job as secretary of state for education 11 years later in the cabinet of conservative Prime Minister Ted Heath. Heath and his party lost the 1974 general election; the following year, Thatcher seized control of the leadership of the Conservative Party. Four years later, on May 4, 1979, Thatcher and the Conservative Party won a general election with a 44-seat majority, making Thatcher prime minister. Thatcher sought to introduce free-market reforms to Britain's socialist economy. Her government sought to reduce taxes and government spending as well. In the introduction to her memoir, *The Downing Street Years*, Thatcher listed three points that she emphasized as she took power: to reverse the economic decline of Britain, to keep government spending within planned limits, and to remain resolute in the implementation of conservative reforms.

When Thatcher took over as prime minister, Britain was in the midst of severe economic difficulties after suffering through decades of socialist mismanagement. Trade unions crippled the country with strikes. Abroad, the Soviet menace expanded unchecked, spreading into Afghanistan and extending its power into Latin America, unhindered by the malaise-stricken America of the Jimmy Carter years. While her American counterpart sought peace at almost any price, Thatcher, because of her tough rhetoric, anti-communism, and resolute assertion of Britain's place in the world, earned the nickname "The Iron Lady" from the Soviets.

Thatcher repudiated détente, the approach to the Soviet Union pioneered by the administration of U.S. President Richard Nixon, which sought peaceful coexistence with the Soviets. By contrast, Thatcher believed that the nations of the West could only deal with the Soviet threat from a position of strength. Likewise, she also opposed many ideas popular in Europe, such as unilateral nuclear disarmament. Considering the vast disparity in numbers of conventional forces between the West and the Soviet Union, such disarmament would be an invitation for a communist invasion of Western Europe. Instead, Thatcher preferred to maintain a credible deterrent to aggression.

In 1981, America inaugurated a president more to Thatcher's taste. Ronald Reagan was an ideological ally of Thatcher's, and the two got along well together, with a friendship grounded in similar ideas on economics and foreign policy. In particular, Reagan and Thatcher stood together with the goal of maintaining a Western nuclear force to deter Soviet aggression, even though many in Europe advocated unilateral nuclear disarmament. Because the Soviet Union possessed vastly larger numbers of conventional forces than Western Europe and the United States, only a nuclear force could halt a possible Soviet invasion of Western Europe.

On April 2, 1982, Argentina invaded the British dependency of the Falkland Islands (known as the Malvinas to Argentines), prompting a ferocious response from Thatcher's government. Three days later, a British task force left for the Falklands with the mission of evicting the Argentine invaders. On May 2, Thatcher ordered the HMS *Conqueror* to destroy the Argentine cruiser *Belgrano*, which potentially threatened the invasion force. May 20 saw the first landing of British troops on the islands and the beginning of the reconquest. British forces finally compelled the Argentine troops to surrender on June 14. Although few in the world knew where the Falklands were at the beginning of the conflict and Britain had lost much of its empire by the 1980s, Thatcher established the precedent that Britain would not tolerate aggression. She also established her own reputation as a very tough statesman and restored her popularity at home. In the 1983 general election, the Conservative Party would retain power and earn a 144-seat majority in the House of Commons.

During her tenure as prime minister, Thatcher made significant strides in restoring the British economy. In order to do so, she focused on several major goals. She began a program of privatization, or the returning of national industries to private control. She also sought to curb the power of Britain's trade unions. Above all, she sought to limit government expenditures and to lower British taxes.

From March 1984 to March 1985, Britain endured a major strike by the National Union of Miners (NUM). In previous years, trade unions had wielded enormous power and even brought down Heath's government in the prior decade. At the heart of the strike was the miners' desire that unprofitable coal pits remain open at government expense, providing miners with jobs, despite their inability to turn a profit. Thatcher wanted to eliminate inefficient nationalized industries that relied on government subsidies and were immune to forces of the free market. These industries were expensive and provided lesser-quality products than those industries that could compete in a free economy. The miners' union remained one of the most redoubtable socialist strongholds in Britain, and the coal pits in which they worked remained open only at enormous public expense. Nationalized coal production guaranteed jobs to coal miners at taxpayers' expense, ensuring a steady base of support for nationalized industries and for the Labour Party. During this year-long strike, picketers engaged in all manner of hooliganism, prompting confrontations with the police. For the strike, the NUM was able to draw financial support from two foreign sources: Libya and the Soviet Union. Eventually, the strike collapsed. The collapse was an enormous victory for Thatcher and the government over the power of Britain's most powerful union. By the end of her time as prime minister, almost two-thirds of government-controlled industries would be returned to private control.

On October 12, 1984, the Irish Republican Army (IRA) bombed the hotel in which Thatcher was staying in Brighton. Although the blast detonated near her hotel room, she narrowly escaped death or serious injury. Despite the assassination attempt and continuing IRA terrorism, the following year Thatcher did negotiate the Anglo-Irish Agreement with the Republic of Ireland, signed at Hillsborough Castle, allowing the Republic of Ireland to consult in the affairs of Northern Ireland.

Her third term as prime minister began with a Conservative Party electoral victory in 1987, in which the party retained a 101-seat majority. She continued to cause controversy, introducing a poll tax to help pay for local government and opposing Britain's closer integration with Europe. In November 1990, Thatcher finally lost power as a result of a challenge to her leadership. Although she initially received a majority of votes to retain control of her party, she did not win by a large enough margin; before the second ballot, several of her cabinet members abandoned her. On November 28, 1990, Thatcher resigned as prime minister. She was succeeded by John Major. After losing her position as prime minister, Thatcher turned to writing her memoirs, The Downing Street Years and The Path to Power, and later produced a volume of her collected speeches and a book on international relations. In 1992, she was named Baroness Thatcher and moved from the House of Commons to the House of Lords. From 1993 to 2000, Lady Thatcher served as chancellor of the College of William and Mary in Williamsburg, Virginia.

On June 11, 2004, she made a rare public appearance to attend the funeral of her great friend, Ronald Reagan. Against the advice of her doctors, Thatcher journeyed to Washington, D.C., and later to Simi Valley, California, to pay her respects to the former president. In her eulogy, she compared Reagan to Mr. Valiant-for-Truth from Bunyan's Pilgrim's Progress.

SEE ALSO

Volume 1 Left: Labour Party, UK; Liberal Party, UK; Liberalism; Socialism; United Kingdom.
Volume 2 Right: Conservatism; Conservative Party, UK; United Kingdom; Reagan, Ronald.

BIBLIOGRAPHY

John Campbell, Margaret Thatcher (Jonathan Cape, 2000–2003); Peter Jenkins, Mrs. Thatcher's Revolution: The Ending of the Socialist Era (Harvard University Press, 1988); Margaret Thatcher Foundation, www.margaretthatcher.org (June 2004); Chris Ogden, Maggie: An Intimate Portrait of a Woman in Power (Simon and Schuster, 1990); Geoffrey Smith, Reagan and Thatcher (W.W. Norton, 1991); Margaret Thatcher, The Collected Speeches of Margaret Thatcher, Robin Harris, ed. (HarperCollins, 1997); Margaret Thatcher, The Downing Street Years (HarperCollins, 1993); Margaret Thatcher, The Path to Power (HarperCollins, 1995); Margaret Thatcher, Statecraft: Strategies for a Changing World (Harper Collins, 2002); Hugo Young, The Iron Lady: A Biography of Margaret Thatcher (Farrar, Straus and Giroux, 1989).

MITCHELL MCNAYLOR
OUR LADY OF THE LAKE COLLEGE

Theocracy

THE CONTINUED EFFECT of theocracies during the 20th century until today can be illustrated by the experiences of Russia, Spain, and Iran. In Russia, until the Russian Revolution, although the primate of the Russian Orthodox Church was the spiritual ruler of the congregation, Tzar Nicholas was considered to be the leader of the church on earth, its temporal authority. This had always been the theological foundation for the Russian monarchy since the time of the fall of the Byzantine Empire to the Ottoman Turks in 1453. The theory behind this was that Russia was "the Third Rome."

Following the fall of Rome in 476 and then of the Byzantine capital of Constantinople in 1453, Russia (then Muscovy) was the inheritor of the spiritual and temporal power of the early Christian state established by Emperor Constantine. Tzar Ivan IV "the Terrible" in the 16th century made this virtually a state policy, and the Romanovs who took the throne in 1613 kept it so until Nicholas II was forced to abdicate in 1917.

When what were believed to be the remains of the tzar and his family were given a state burial in July 1998, the tradition of the old Russian theocracy was still so strong that a movement began in the Russian Orthodox Church to have the tzar canonized (made a saint) as a martyr dying for his religion. Most experts believe the tzar and his family were murdered in July 1918 at the instigation of Vladimir Lenin and his Bolsheviks, who had seized power in October 1917.

Russian Orthodoxy continues to gain in influence in Russia. Indeed, in August 2004, the internet site, *Russia Religious News,* reported that study of the Russian Orthodox Church would be incorporated in the curriculum of the secular municipal school in the city of Tambov.

Following the collapse of the Romanov dynasty, the idea of a theocratic government was perpetuated in Spain. Indeed, since Spanish unification in 1492 under Ferdinand and Isabella, church and state were so closely knit that it could be said that Spain was always a "theological monarchy."

Indeed, during the days of the Spanish Inquisition, church and state worked closely together in the interrogation and execution of so-called heretics. Disloyalty to the church was seen as treason to the state. This was apparent when the Jews were evicted from Spain in 1492 for being not only un-Christian but sympathetic to the Muslims, who had just lost under Sultan Boabdil their last Spanish city at Grenada.

Although Spain's Alfonso XIII fled Spain for France before the Spanish republic was challenged in the civil war in 1936, the institution of the church remained strong. Indeed, the suffering of the Roman Catholic clergy and nuns at the hands of Spanish Republican extremists during the civil war remains one of the blackest chapters of the history of the war. The excesses of the Republicans made the war seem like a religious crusade to some who supported the rightist Falangists, or Nationalists, of General Francisco Franco, who battled the Republicans. Philip Knightley wrote in *The First Casualty* that "the old order, the Nationalists, fought to purge their country of the Reds [Communists who were the Republic's strongest supporters and most grim executioners], to resurrect their idea of a pure, Christian Spain."

After Franco won the Spanish Civil War in 1939, the church rallied around him as he assumed the position of *caudillo,* the undisputed ruler of Spain. In effect, the triumph of the Falange represented a reassertion of the old alliance of cross and crown seen during the days of the monarchy. In the early years of the Franco regime, church and state had a close and mutually beneficial association. The loyalty of the Roman Catholic Church to the Franco state lent legitimacy to the dictatorship, which in turn restored and enhanced the church's traditional privileges.

However, the Church liberalization that followed the Second Vatican Council, which ended in 1965, led to a split between Franco and the Spanish Church. By the end of his rule (he died in 1975), the church had become one of his strongest critics. Extremist Catholics like the Warriors of Christ the King, in a tragic turnaround from the days of the Spanish Civil War, began to attack and kill progressive Spanish priests. However, the majority of Spanish Catholics maintained a common ground between loyalty to the church and to the state. Indeed, it could be said that the overall role of the Church—as the main critic of the Falangist state—paradoxically helped pave the way for the triumph of Franco's ultimate goal. Following his death in 1975, Juan Carlos II restored the Spanish monarchy with no serious civil unrest, and with the support of the Catholic Church.

Within four years, in 1979, theocracy became the de facto government in Iran when the Ayatollah Ruhollah Khomeini became the ruler of a new Islamist state in Iran, following the overthrow of Shah Reza Pahlavi. The ayatollah, who received his title for achieving superior spiritual learning in the Shi'ite sect of Islam, established a rigid theological governing structure in Iran based upon the Islamic Law, the Sharia. Although civilian authorities ran a state government, there was never any doubt that the ayatollahs, in the spiritual center of Qum, were the real rulers of the state. Khomeini pursued a rigid Islamic orthodoxy, best shown in his issuing of the *fatwa,* the sentence of death, on novelist Salman Rushdie for his *The Satanic Verses,* which was published in 1988.

Attacking Rushdie for more than just blaspheming Mohammed the Prophet as the dissolute "Mahound," Khomeini did so because the book was an assault on a passage in the Koran. According to Brent Sleeper of Carleton College, Muslims believe the passage occurred when "Satan is supposed to have interfered here with the transmission of the holy words to Muhammad and tricked the prophet into interjecting an additional verse which allowed for a mixture of Islam and the indigenous polytheistic faith" of the Arabs before the time of Mohammed. Khomeini, ruling as the leader of a theocratic Iran, used his power to declare death for Rushdie for drawing great attention to an idolatrous part of the Koran that still really defies all textual explanation.

Although Khomeini died in 1989, the ayatollahs still kept a firm hold on the government of Iran. The population grew tired of the religious right's control of policy and responded with the overwhelming election of the moderate Ayatollah Mohammed Khatami as the fifth president of the Islamic Republic of Iran in the May 1997 elections by gaining almost 70 percent of the votes cast. He was reelected president in 2001 by an even greater mandate of the Iranian people (almost 78 percent of the vote cast). Nevertheless, today some 25 years after the revolution, the all-important offices of state security are still controlled by the rightists followers of Khomeini, and the real freedom that most Iranians dreamed of when they overthrew the shah still remains an elusive dream.

In August 2004, Khatami openly warned of the spread of "fascism" in Iran, in a strongly worded attack against detractors of his reformist policies, newspapers reported. "The goal of the Islamic revolution is not to establish a fascist vision in society in the name of religion and the [1979 Islamic] revolution," Khatami told a joint meeting of the cabinet and parliament. "Nor is it to attack and put pressure on those who do not share this vision," the Iranian president said. "The disaster today is that we are trying, through a fascist vision of religion and the revolution, to push out the competitor" from the political arena. According to Khatami, "the only way to defend Islam, independence and freedom is to twin religion with liberty."

SEE ALSO

BIBLIOGRAPHY

"Spain: Roman Catholic Church," www.exploitz.com (July 2004); Brent Sleeper, "Satanic Verses and Last Temptations," 1992, Carleton College, www.flightpath.com (July 2004); "Mohammad Khatami," www.iranchamber.com (July 2004); "Khatami Voices Concern over Future of Iran," www.iranexpert.com (July 2004); Russian Archives Online, "The Last Tzar,"www.russianarchives.com (July 2004); Ivo J. Lederer, ed., *Russian Foreign Policy: Essays in Historical Perspective* (Yale University Press, 1962); Philip Knightley, *The First Casualty* (Harcourt Brace, 1975); "Russia Religion News," www.stetson.edu (August 2004).

JOHN F. MURPHY, JR.
AMERICAN MILITARY UNIVERSITY

Think Tanks

AMERICAN RIGHT-WING think tanks are nonprofit corporations that develop ideas for conservatives to use in the policy process. They are one form of the several right-wing organizations that are furthering conservative visions of a society organized by conservative rather than liberal or socialist principles.

Backed by conservative foundations, think tanks support conservative and libertarian scholars who write books or articles on specific current and long-range public policy issues. The issues cover the spectrum of American politics. The use of think tanks is due to the belief of conservatives that most of the print, television, and radio media are controlled by liberals. In addition colleges; universities; law schools; many religious institutions including the boards of mainline Protestant churches; and most professional organizations are also controlled by liberals who continually push their own political agenda.

Historically, conservatism has been anti-intellectual, unlike its opponent, liberalism. Developing idea centers is a new phenomenon in the history of conservatism. In many ways, ironically, it is a return to classical liberalism. There are a number of right-wing think tanks. Among the most important are the American Enterprise Institute; Capital Research Center, Cato Institute; Claremont Institute; Competitive Enterprise Institute, Ethics and Public Policy Center; Free Congress Foundation; Galen Institute; Goldwater Institute; The Heritage Foundation; Hoover Institution; Hudson Institute; Intercollegiate Studies Institute; Ludwig von Mises Institute; and National Center for Policy Analysis.

The American Enterprise Institute (AEI) was founded in 1943. Its headquarters is in Washington, D.C. and is one of the largest and most respected think tanks. The Cato Institute is headquartered in Washington, D.C. It is named for *Cato's Letters*, written at the time of the American Revolution. Founded by Edward H. Crane in 1977, it conducts public policy research in order to put traditional American political philosophy into public policies. The Claremont Institute is located in Claremont, California. It began in 1979. Its mission is to change the political direction of America in order to restore the principles of the American founding fathers to their rightful place in national life. It has a summer program for young conservatives.

The Ethics and Public Policy Center was founded in 1976 in order to promote the Judeo-Christian moral tradition as a source of ideas in both domestic and foreign policy debates. The Free Congress Foundation is based in Washington, D.C. It promotes cultural and political conservatism. Its main interest is the "culture war." It is directed by Robert Spencer. The Galen Institute is a nonprofit free-market research think tank. It focuses on the area of public health policy. It seeks to promote conservative positions on health issues that include freedom of choice, competition, and an informed public in matters of health choices. It was founded in 1995 by Grace-Marie Turner. It promotes discussions on health issues through the Health Policy Consensus Group. It also publishes papers on the issues. In 2003, the Galen Institute created the Center for Consumer Driven Health Care as a center for conservative ideas on health issues.

The Heritage Foundation is one of the most important and visible of the conservative think tanks. According to conservative radio talk-show host Rush Limbaugh, it is where some of the finest conservative minds in America work. The Heritage Foundation started in 1976 as a research and educational institute. Its mission is to develop and promote conservative public policies that are based on the principles of capitalism, constitutionalism, traditional Americanism, and a strong national defense. It has been very successful in influencing American politicians.

Specifically, the Heritage Foundation had a tremendous influence on the presidency of Ronald Reagan. Many conservative changes promoted and gained by Reagan were first proposed by its policy analysts. The ideas of enterprise zones, the tax cuts of the 1980s, the High Frontier of missile defense satellites, the Strategic Defense Initiative, and other ideas originated with its scholars. During the 1986 summit meetings that Reagan held with Soviet General Secretary Mikhail Gorbachev, the latter complained that Reagan was too influenced by the Heritage Foundation.

The Hoover Institution on War, Revolution and Peace is located at Stanford University in California. It is a public policy research center. Its studies are on both domestic and foreign issues involving politics and economics. It was founded by former President Herbert Hoover. It has gathered an internationally known group of scholars to promote a "conservative" society.

The Hudson Institute is a public policy think tank that studies long-term trends for government, business, and nonprofit organizations. It is free-enterprise oriented. It encourages technology, individual responsibility, free markets, and strengthening America's national security. Herman Kahn is an important scholar who, along with Max Singer and Oscar Ruebhausen, founded the Institute in 1961 in New York. After Kahn's death in 1984, the institute moved to Indianapolis, Indiana. In the beginning, many of its studies were in the area of the military. In recent decades, its focus has been more on education and trends of the American workforce. In

2004, the Institute moved to Washington, D.C., in order to concentrate on issues of national security and foreign policy.

The Intercollegiate Studies Institute (ISI) is a think tank that promotes conservatism to college students. It has developed a program to nurture future leaders as conservatives. It uses an extensive educational program to encourage the conservative education of both students and faculty.

The Ludwig von Mises Institute was founded to develop and promote the ideas of Ludwig von Mises (1881–1973). He was part of the Austrian School of economics and is very popular with conservative economists. The von Mises Institute has issued a great number of publications. It uses fellowships to encourage conservative scholars and to promote its classical liberalism (that is, now conservative individualism). The von Mises Institute was founded in 1981 in Auburn, Alabama, by Llewellyn H. Rockwell, Jr. Von Mises's widow, Margit von Mises, chaired the board until she died in 1993. A number of important conservative economists such as F.A. Hayek and Henry Hazlitt have been involved with this institute. Over 200 scholars research for it and aid in 500 annual teaching events.

The National Center of Policy Analysis (NCPA) was founded in 1983 at the University of Dallas by John C. Goodman. It seeks to promote private enterprise and to oppose government regulations.

Right-wing think tanks are part of the effort of conservatives to win the "war of ideas" in America and elsewhere. In the last three decades of the 20th century, they have had considerable success in reshaping policies and public policy debates at the national, state, and local levels.

SEE ALSO

Volume 1 Left: Think Tanks; Liberalism.
Volume 2 Right: Conservatism.

BIBLIOGRAPHY

Donald E. Abelson, *Do Think Tanks Matter? Assessing the Impact of Public Policy Institutes* (McGill-Queens University Press, 2002); David Brock, *The Republican Noise Machine: Right-Wing Media and How It Corrupts Democracy* (Crown Publishing Group, 2004); Philip H. Burch, *Reagan, Bush and Right-Wing Politics: Elites, Think Tanks, Power and Policies: The American Right-Wing, at Court and in Action: Supreme Court Nominations and Major Policy Making* (Elsevier Science & Technology Books, 1999); Andrew Denham, *Think-Tanks of the New Right* (Ashgate Publishing, 1996); Andrew Denham and Mark Garnett, *British Think Tanks and the Climate of*

Opinion (UCL Press, 1998); Matt Innis and Justin Johnson, *Directory of Think Tank Publications* (Politico's Publishing, 2001).

ANDREW J. WASKEY
DALTON STATE COLLEGE

Totalitarianism

THE TERM *totalitarian* was first used in Italy, where Fascist Party thinkers suggested that the total nation should be devoted to the same political goal. That principle lay behind the effort common in all of the totalitarian regimes to dominate youth organizations, the educational establishment, news and entertainment media, labor unions, and other organizations to institute party control. Although some such measures reflected the leftist concept of state socialism, the resultant regimes were authoritarian and ruthlessly suppressed individual liberty and ideological deviation from the official line.

Totalitarianism is the form of dictatorship that emphasizes total control of the lives of the people it abuses. It is one of the ironies of history that the very technological progress of the past 140 years, since Samuel F.B. Morse first used electromagnetic energy to send messages over the telegraph, also made possible a degree of social and political control unimagined by the despots of ancient Greece and Rome.

Totalitarianism is to be seen through the historical experiences of Nazi Germany and Soviet (communist) Russia. This is because, of all the countries considered totalitarian, these two have had the greatest impact on history and had the earliest technologies for such cradle-to-grave despotism.

The main engine that drove these 20th-century despotisms was a highly centralized political party. In Germany, it was the National Socialist Workers Party (NSDAP), or Nazi Party. It was the Bolshevik Party, later referred to as communist, that took control of Soviet Russia, or the Soviet Union.

Adolf Hitler joined the Nazi Party in September 1919, where, he later recalled, he soon became board member number 7. As Joachim C. Fest noted in *Hitler*, "his growing reputation as a speaker solidified his position within the party." From the beginning, Hitler showed the talent for centralization that would later take the party to its *Machtergreifung*, its seizure of power in Germany. Fest said, "his 'talent for combination' seized upon the most disparate elements and fitted them together into compact formulas." In November 28, Hitler and his Nazi Party attempted a coup in Munich in the Beer Hall Putsch. The putsch failed and Hitler was arrested and served time in Landsberg Prison. On January 30, 1933, Hitler became chancellor of Germany, however, and moved quickly to consolidate his power. On March 23, a law giving Hitler the legislative right to rule by decree was overwhelmingly voted in by the German parliament, or Reichstag. William L. Shirer observed in *The Rise and Fall of the Third Reich*, "the one party totalitarian State had been achieved with scarcely a ripple of opposition or defiance." With the ability to rule by decree, executive fiat, Hitler was now the effective ruler of the German people.

The German Nazi Party had taken over in a period of great turbulence, when street battles with the German communists were frequent and bloody. By appealing to the national desire for order, Hitler became chancellor. The centralized control of his party, and the willingness to use his storm troopers, the SA of Ernst Roehm, had bulldozed all opposition.

It was during similar chaos in Russia following the abdication of Tzar Nicholas II in February (new calendar March) 1917, that Vladimir Lenin was able to strike with his Bolsheviks.

The provisional government of Prime Minister Georgi Lvov proved unable to control the anarchy in the streets or the soldiers on the Eastern Front, who were weary of fighting in World War I. Troops from the front set off the rioting in the capital of Petrograd on July 3, which became known as the "July Days." Lvov was replaced by his minister of defense Alexander Kerensky, who called on General Lavr Kornilov to restore order. However, Kornilov opted to stage a military coup himself. On August 29, Kerensky declared himself commander in chief and appealed to the Russian people for help. As Leon Trotsky, Lenin's second in command in the Bolshevik Party in this period, wrote in *The History of the Russian Revolution*, Kornilov's "military insurrection was thus firmly set in motion. This must be understood literally: three cavalry divisions, in railroad echelons, were advancing on the capital." Kerensky's order to the soldiers of Petrograd read: "General Kornilov, having announced his patriotism and loyalty to the people has withdrawn regiments from the front and sent them against Petrograd." Kornilov's rebellion collapsed and troops loyal to the provisional government imprisoned him on September 1, 1917. However, as Robert Service wrote in *Lenin: A Biography*,

Kerensky had "turned in panic to the parties of the soviets, including the Bolsheviks, to support him by sending out agitators to persuade Kornilov's troops to obey the Provisional Government and allow Kornilov to be detained in custody." Seeing the uncertainty that governed Russian political affairs, Lenin used the centralism of his Bolsheviks to press for power. They had effectively become the main spokesmen for the *soviets*, or councils, of workers, soldiers, sailors, and peasants that now effectively governed the capital Petrograd, which had been changed from St. Petersburg in 1914 when World War I began. To Russian ears, the name sounded too German.

Although technically part of the old Social Democratic Party, from the Social Democratic Party Congress, which began on July 30, 1903, in Brussels, Belgium, Lenin had begun to forge his majority, or Bolshevik wing, into a highly centralized political machine. He would look back in 1920 to write, "classes are led by parties, and parties are led by individuals who are called leaders. ... This is the ABC. The will of a class is sometimes fulfilled by a dictator."

However, even by the middle of October, Kerensky and his provisional government could not decide on a decisive course against the Bolsheviks, who were commonly thought to be planning a seizure of power. By then, all the troops of the critical Petrograd Military District had been infiltrated by the Bolshevik agitators. On October 25, Lenin issued a proclamation decreeing the end of the provisional government, and the Winter Palace was stormed by troops loyal to him and the Bolsheviks. The next day, supported by the Council of Soviets, Lenin took power.

What George Orwell wrote in his essay "Looking Back on the Spanish [Civil] War" about fascist dictators like Hitler was aptly applied to communist ones like Lenin and Josef Stalin. Wrote Orwell, "if the Leader says of such and such an event, 'it never happened'—well, it never happened. If he says that two and two are five—well, two and two are five."

Once in control, a totalitarian party turns to its "organs" of repression in order to defend itself not only from enemies against the party—but also against members thought to be disloyal. Lenin's means of repression was the Vecheka, the All-Russian Commission for Combating Counterrevolution and Sabotage, under "Iron Feliks," Feliks Dzerzhinsky. From the beginning, Lenin's brief was to rule by terror any who opposed the "dictatorship of the proletariat," which, according to the Bolsheviks, they represented. The state secret police would endure until the collapse of the Soviet system in 1991. Even to the end, members of the last incarnation, the KGB, would call themselves "Chekists."

Hitler's secret police, which would attract such fear and hate in occupied Europe in World War II, was the Gestapo, the secret state police. Shirer recalled, "it originally was established for Prussia [then a state in Germany] by [Hermann] Goering on April 26, 1933, to replace Department 1A of the old Prussian political police." Edmund L. Blandford opined in SS *Intelligence: The Nazi Secret Service* that "the sanctioning of police terror across Germany was the Nazis' way of rooting out not only the Reds [Communists] and Jews, but all who doubted the new regime. From a few dozen personnel, it expanded to employ some 40,000 men and women, including clerks, but not including the huge number of unpaid informers across the Reich."

One cannot overemphasize the role of the informers in these totalitarian societies, informers both paid and unpaid. They not only represented the "eyes and ears" of Nazis and Bolshevik regimes in the general population. Their very existence was meant to sow fear among the people that whoever they spoke to might turn them in to the authorities, with nothing needed in the way of evidence. This in itself served to chill any real hope of opposition. Informers also functioned to serve base personal motives. Nobody will ever know how many people were imprisoned or perished because of the words of a hostile or jealous family member, neighbor, coworker, or friend.

Central to the totalitarian party was complete control of the life of the individual: idle time was freedom's temptation. Both Hitler and Lenin realized the essential need to grasp young minds and mold them for the service of the state. As Alfred Vagts stated in *A History of Militarism: Civilian and Military*, "the militaristic education of youth in fascist [as in Italy and Germany] and communist countries commenced almost as soon as the child could walk." "The mobilization of German youth," observed Klaus P. Fischer in *Nazi Germany*, "was one of the most important goals of National Socialism," Nazism. To do this, the Nazis mobilized German young people in the Hitler Jugend, the Hitler Youth. Founded officially in December 1936, Fischer noted, "membership in the Hitler Youth rose to 8,870,000 at the beginning of 1939." Youth sports were also highly regimented in the "Joy Through Strength" movement, an outgrowth of the German emphasis on physical culture from the 19th century. When the war came, the Hitler Youth, led by Baldur von Schirach, would form one of the most fanatic units of Hitler's elite SS: the 12 SS (Hitler Jugend) Division, which fought in the Normandy Campaign in July 1944. For others, as Willi Frischauer observed in *The Rise and Fall of Hermann Goering*, "the Air-Sports Association had become a National Socialist Flying Corps," where the future ground crews and pilots of the German air force, the Luftwaffe, would be trained.

In Soviet Russia, the Komsomol, the Communist Youth Organization, was established in the People's Commissariat for Education. Basil Dmytryshyn noted that "each [of the Commissariat's agencies] had the same objective [to] strengthen the belief in the economic system of socialism and their faith in the leadership of the Communist Party." As with Nazi Germany, youthful sports were highly controlled by the party. The OSSOVIAKIM movement, as it later was called, helped train the future snipers of the Red Army in World War II. Complete control of education was the cornerstone of both systems in indoctrinating the young, and textbooks and teachers were under equally strong supervision in both countries. Klaus Fischer noted that in the Nazis' desire to form a new generation of dutiful soldiers, even young children's reading books were changed, "especially in the lower grades, where war stories and heroic exploits displaced fairy tales or animal stories."

Ever cognizant of the need of a culture of captivation, Nazis and communists took full advantage of modern communications. In the age before television was widespread, the radio and motion pictures were wholly put at the service of states. Newspapers were too, of course, but their impact on the psychology of the people was less potent and immediate. A free media in a dictatorship is, after all, an electronic oxymoron.

Joseph Goebbels was the twisted genius who orchestrated the propaganda phenomenon of the Third Reich like the 1934 Nuremberg Party Rally. Goebbels made it into a visual symphony of the triumphant Nazi state. To aid him, he could call on Leni Riefenstahl, the most inventive—and slavishly National Socialist—of Germany's filmmakers. Her film *Triumph of the Will*, about the rally, is a triumph of the filmmaker's art—and a prostitution of the cinema art in the service of dictatorship.

Hitler, the main star of the film, was known to spend hours practicing the tones of voice and the gestures that enthralled the German people to do his will. To help project the proper image, in a party where anti-Semitism was a prime doctrine, all Jews had been driven out of communications and entertainment. Many others fled for fear of persecution for anti-Nazi views. In Soviet Russia, as in Nazi Germany, all media came

under the control of the state. The Bolsheviks, especially Lenin, understood the value of motion pictures in binding the people to their proletarian regime. Lenin is supposed to have said, according to Orlando Figes in *Natasha's Dance: A Cultural History of Russia*, "for us the most important of all arts is the cinema."

Sergei Eisenstein served as a soldier in the Red Army fighting near Petrograd, the capital, during the civil war. His film *October* (1928), made under Lenin's successor Josef Stalin, immortalized the Bolshevik Revolution, depicting the storming of the Winter Palace, home of the conservative provisional government, with more enthusiasm than historical accuracy.

While communications was essential to the totalitarian regimes, industry and labor were more important, since they represented the backbone of any modern society. When Hitler gained power, it was in many ways due to the support of German industrialists like Gustav Krupp, who saw in the Nazis a guardian against a communist takeover of Germany. Peter Batty noted in *The House of Krupp* that "Gustav lived for profitable production, whereas Hitler dreamed of glory and grandeur, which could only be based on the profitable production of industrialists like Gustav." Therefore, ruthless state planning, such as would happen when Lenin took power in Russia, was impossible for the Nazis in Germany. On February 20, 1933, as James Pool recorded, a meeting took place with the senior industrialists and bankers of Germany, where they pledged their financial support to the Nazis. Among those present were Krupp and the banker Hjalmar Schacht, who was Hitler's main financial adviser. Impressed with the state planning of the communists in Russia, Hermann Goering, already head of the Gestapo and the German air force, plunged ahead with his idea of the Four Year Plans, copying like an acolyte Stalin's Five Year Plans then in Russia. Later, as Shirer noted, Goering would also be put in charge of the plundering of Russia, and the rest of occupied Europe.

In Soviet Russia, state planning of the economy was almost obsessive. Indeed, the rigidity of the system imposed by Lenin and hammered into place by Stalin would ultimately help to undo the communist system. An incipient—but interesting—experiment in the return to capitalism under Lenin's New Economic Policy (NEP) was ended by Stalin. A series of Five Year Plans was introduced to push Russia into an industrialized future. This included the forced collectivization of farming as well as the rapid growth of industry. Stalin would announce in 1929 that Russia was "advancing full steam along the path of industrialization to Socialism, leaving behind the agelong 'Russian backwardness.'" However, both Nazis and communists saw that the absolute control of labor was essential to control of the state. It had been the workers of Petrograd who had helped the (then) Bolsheviks to conquer their adversaries in the great October Revolution. While the Nazis owed less to the workers—and to the German Army more—still they knew that labor was an essential stone in the foundation of their Thousand-Year Reich. Trade unions were eliminated in Germany, and all workers became members of the German Labor Front (DAF), under Robert Ley. In Fischer's words, the DAF, too, fulfilled the party's goal of "immersing all Germans in the Nazi experience." Shirer reported that the law that created it on October 24, 1934, said the DAF was "the organization of creative Germans of brain and fist."

In communist Russia, the party resorted to clever sophistry to eliminate the need for trade unions. As the party was that of the workers' soviets, it was the embodiment of the laboring "masses." Therefore, when it took power in 1917, the need for unions—which had come into being for the purpose of defending workers against grasping capitalists—had "withered away," to use a communist phrase. Much of the industrial work was done by slave labor forces, composed of either political prisoners, Jews, and gypsies in Germany, or later prisoners of war.

In the Soviet Union, the forced labor camps were controlled by the GULAG, the Main Administration for Camps of the secret police. The *zeks*, prisoners, were, if needed, worked to death for the benefit of the state. The system was very important in the modernization of the Russian economy.

The human cost in both systems was horrific: some six million Jews and non-Jews are believed to have perished in the German camp system. From the forced collectivization of Soviet agriculture, the famine that followed, and the toll of the gulag, up to 20 million lives are believed to have been lost.

Nazi Germany fell in May 1945 at the end of World War II in Europe. The Soviet system slowly collapsed between 1989 and 1991. But the worst of it had died with Stalin in March 1953.

SEE ALSO

Volume 1 Left: Soviet Union; Stalin and Stalinism; Germany. *Volume 2 Right:* Germany; Hitler, Adolf.

BIBLIOGRAPHY

Anne Appebaum, *The Gulag: A History* (Doubleday, 2004); Eugen Kogon, *The Theory and Practice of Hell: The German Concentration Camps and the System behind Them* (Berkley, 1971); George Orwell, "Looking Back on the Spanish War," *A Collection of Essays* (Anchor Books, 1954); Peter Batty, *The House of Krupp: The Steel Dynasty That Armed the Nazis* (Cooper Square, 2001); Maria Riva, *Marlene Dietrich* (Ballantine, 1992); Basil Dmytryshyn, *USSR: A Concise History* (Scribners, 1978); William L. Shirer, *The Rise and Fall of the Third Reich* (Crest, 1960); Alfred Vagts, *A History of Militarism: Civilian and Military* (The Free Press, 1959); Orlando Figes, *Natasha's Dance: A Cultural History of Russia* (Picador, 2002); Robert Service, *Lenin: A Biography* (Harvard University Press, 2000; Klaus P. Fischer, *Nazi Germany: A New History* (Continuum, 1996); Joachim C. Fest, *Hitler* (Harcourt Brace, 1974); Willi Frischauer, *The Rise and Fall of Hermann Goering* (Ballantine, 1951); James Pool, *Hitler and His Secret Allies: Contributions, Loot, and Rewards* (Pocket Books, 1997).

JOHN F. MURPHY, JR.
AMERICAN MILITARY UNIVERSITY

Turkey

THE TURKISH RIGHT has been dominant in Turkish politics since the first free elections were held in 1950. The center-right parties have ruled Turkey since then, except during periods of military rule and some short-term coalitions led by center-left parties. The distinction between right-wing and left-wing in Turkish politics began with the leadership of the Republican People's Party (RPP, 1923–present) in 1965 when it declared its position at the left of center. Then, its counterparty, the Justice Party (JP, 1961–80), called itself a center-right party. The Democrat Party (DP, 1946–60), the Motherland Party (MP, 1983–present), the True Path Party (TPP, 1983–present), and the Justice and Development Party (JDP, 2000–present) became the major center-right parties. Besides these, there are some religious right-wing parties represented by the National Salvation Party (NSP, 1971–80), the Welfare Party (WP, 1983–98), the Virtue Party (VP, 1998–2001), and the Happiness Party (2001–present) line. The nationalist right wing has been represented by the National Action Party (NAP) since the 1970s.

The DP was founded by a group of liberal-conservative elite as a splitting party from the RPP, came to power in 1950 with an overwhelming majority, and, winning the 1954 and 1957 elections, remained in power until the 1960 military intervention. The DP, as a coalition of various social groups, put forward a synthesis between liberal-democratic principles and local values, and claimed to defend the interests of the masses against the rule of the centralist bureaucratic elite represented by the RPP leadership. However, during its rule, its leader failed to implement promises for a more democratic regime, and followed a majoritarian view of democracy marginalizing all oppositions. Then, being accused of deviating from the official ideology, Kemalism, it was ousted by the military in 1960 and its three leaders were executed.

Its main successor was the JP, which ruled the country from 1965 to 1971 as a one-party government and returned to power as a series of JP-led coalition governments after the short-lived RPP-NSP coalition of 1973–74 until the 1980 military intervention. Like the DP, the JP maintained liberal and pro-private enterprise policies and nationalist-conservative discourse. The coalition on the right wing, based on peripheral forces, broke down by the late 1960s. This fragmentation led to the emergence of religious right (represented by the pro-Islamist NSP in the 1970s) and nationalist right (represented by the NAP) parties. The NSP, the NAP, and the JP played a pivotal role in 1970s ideological polarization and conflict.

The military intervention in 1980 outlawed all political parties and ruled the country from 1980 to 1983. In the 1983 elections, the MP, under the leadership of Turgut Ozal, won the majority and remained in power until 1991. Initiating neoliberal policies, it challenged the bureaucratic establishment with a motto of change and modernization. The MP helped to integrate some of the conservative majority into the center on the basis of a wide ideological spectrum. By the rise of the TPP (the real heir of the JP) in the 1991 elections, it started to lose ground. The TPP represented a more conservative, populist, and egalitarian ideology. Their struggle, under new young leaders, continued to dominate Turkish politics throughout the 1990s, and at the end of the decade, both remained under the national threshold in the 2002 elections.

The 1990s was the turning point for right-wing politics in Turkey. During that time, when center-right politics began to dissolve as a result of global and national transformations, the religious and nationalist right dominated Turkish politics. The Islamist WP became the leading party in the 1995 elections and became a coalition partner that resulted in Turkey's fourth "indirect" military intervention in 1997. The nationalist NAP gained a significant amount of votes in the 1999 elections and became a coalition partner. Another turning point for the Turkish right occurred with the 2002 elections, regarded as a true "popular revolution from below," according to political analysts.

The JDP, one of the successors of the religious right VP, gained an overwhelming majority with 363 seats in the 550-member parliament. Its victory was partly the result of past failures of all center-right and center-left political parties to cope with Turkey's major economic and political problems. JDP leaders see the JDP as a "conservative democratic" party like the Christian Democratic parties of Western Europe. In this respect, they claim to have the mission of combining Islamic values with both democracy and modernity. In the JDP program, democratization, economic liberalization, and Turkey's European Union membership are therefore given priority. The Turkish right has a different tradition from Western right-wing politics, which usually seeks to preserve the status quo. But, as left-wing parties have done in the West, the Turkish center-right has attempted to transform the establishment to represent those who have been excluded from power. Although Turkey's center-right represents such progressive will, its extreme wing, represented by reactionary and nationalist groups, has hindered Turkish democratization.

SEE ALSO

Volume 1 Left: Christian Democracy; Church and State Separation; Turkey; Asia.
Volume 2 Right: Conservatism; Asia.

BIBLIOGRAPHY

Metin Heper and Barry Rubin, eds., *Turkish Political Parties* (Frank Cass, 2002); Ergun Ozbudun, *Contemporary Turkish Politics* (Lynne Rienner, 2000); Hugh Poulton, *Top Hat, Grey Wolf and Crescent: Turkish Nationalism and the Turkish Republic* (Hurst & Company, 1997); David Shakland, *Islam and Society in Turkey* (Eothen Press, 1999); Erik J. Zürcher, *Turkey: A Modern History* (I.B. Tauris, 2001).

YILMAZ ÇOLAK, PH.D.
EASTERN MEDITERRANEAN UNIVERSITY, TURKEY

Uganda

UGANDA IS A landlocked African nation that has been victimized by civil war, tribal conflict, and, according to some observers, ill-conceived leftist philosophies that have crippled its economy and political system. At the beginning of the 1900s, British colonists introduced cultivation of cotton, coffee, and sugar for export. An influx of nonnative peoples began in the 1920s, Asians primarily from Indian subcontinent countries, who established themselves as entrepreneurs, traders, and bankers.

In 1962, Uganda became independent with Milton Obote as head of state. He was deposed in 1971 by Idi Amin, who ordered all Asians with British passports to leave, some 60,000 business leaders. Since they were the backbone of Ugandan commerce, industry, and finance, their expulsion crippled Uganda's economy, particularly when their businesses were handed over to Amin's political cronies, many of whom had no business acumen or management experience. The result was devastating. By way of comparison, in 1965, Uganda and South Korea were equals economically and in terms of industrial development. By 2004, South Korea was a strong, exporting nation, while Uganda remained an impoverished third world nation, worse off than in 1965. Amin's rule was eccentric in other ways, including the seemingly random taking of life, with an esti-

mated 300,000 Ugandans killed during the 1970s. When he was deposed and sent into exile, Obote returned to power, but civil turmoil followed, with approximately 200,000 Ugandans seeking refuge in neighboring Rwanda, Congo, and Sudan and a reported 100,000 Ugandans killed.

In 1985, a military coup deposed Obote. The National Resistance Army (NRA), an anti-Obote group led by Yoweri Kaguta Museveni, kept fighting after it was excluded from the new government. It seized control of the country on January 29, 1986, and Museveni was declared president. The new Ugandan constitution imposed by Museveni required the suspension of political parties, but an active, minority Conservative Party continued to exist, although it and all other political parties were banned from nominating candidates for office. In 2000, a referendum was held regarding a return to a multiparty system. Support for the no-party system received 90 percent of the vote; however, the Conservative Party noted in the international press that less than 50 percent of eligible voters cast ballots, in essence boycotting the process and protesting the lack of political competition.

Advocates of multiparty politics remain defiant and say they will not be stopped. Conservative Party leaders detained by police for organizing a public meeting have vowed to continue doing so. Although officially banned, opposition parties gained significantly in local 2002 elections. Although Museveni had refused to approve the Political Organization Bill in 2001, which would have allowed parties to organize at grassroots levels, defiance seems to be growing. Breaches within the NRA ranks have also emerged with dissent and are expressed by such politicians as First Deputy Prime Minister and Internal Affairs Minister Eriya Kategaya, Foreign Affairs Minister James Wapakhabulo, and Bidandi Sali, a local government minister. In 2004, Museveni remained defiant but showed signs of relenting, such as forming a task force to explore opening up Ugandan politics.

Even though Museveni has been able to stabilize Uganda politically and economically, and to control its borders, areas of conflict continue.

Northern Uganda has long been plagued by the right-leaning Lord's Resistance Army (LRA), a Christian religious movement that operates out of southern Sudan. That movement emerged in 1986, and fighting was intense with about 5,000 LRA fighters killed. By December 1987, it had been suppressed, but leaders fled to Kenya, where surviving members regrouped. The LRA claims to be a Christian fundamentalist organization with a right-wing ideology and is led by Joseph Kony. In December 1999, after a peace agreement was struck between Uganda and Sudan, LRA activities diminished. Along the border of the Democratic Republic of Congo (DRC), the Allied Democratic Force (ADF) presents another threat. It is made up of Islamic groups, Hutu guerrillas from the DRC and Rwanda. The president of the ADF is Sheikh Jamil Mukulu. It tends to be neither right- nor left-wing in ideology, but instead has a goal of establishing an Islamic theocracy based on Muslim Sharia religious law.

One reason why the international community has not applied more pressure on Uganda and Museveni to reform and liberalize its political system may be because of the dramatic progress being made in the economic realm. This has resulted in conservative Western governments looking the other way in the face of anti-democratic activity and leftist, liberation rhetoric.

SEE ALSO

Volume 1 Left: Uganda; Africa; Liberalism.
Volume 2 Right: Africa; Conservatism; Totalitarianism.

BIBLIOGRAPHY

"Country Profile 2000: Uganda" (The Economist Intelligence Unit, 1999); Keesing's Record of World Events 2000 (Keesing's Limited, 2000); National Geographic Atlas of the World (National Geographic Society, 1999); Roger Tangri and Andrew Mwenda, "Military Corruption and Uganda Politics since the Late 1990s," Review of African Political Economy (v.30/98, 2004); The World Almanac and Book of Facts (World Almanac, 2004); The World Factbook (CIA, 2003); William Tordoff, Government and Politics in Africa (Indiana University Press, 1997).

ROB KERBY
INDEPENDENT SCHOLAR

Ukraine

THE MODERN HISTORY of Ukraine began with the efforts of the Ukrainian people to throw off Russian Bolshevik rule in the Revolution of 1917. Conquered by Russia in the 17th and 18th centuries, the Ukrainians had never lost their zest for freedom. One of their heroes had been the Cossack Bohdan Kmehlnitsky, who had fought for Ukrainian freedom in the 17th century. Tragically, his Cossacks, in fighting for their own rights, savagely murdered thousands of innocent Jews in one of the first pogroms in East European or Russian history. The greatest account of the Ukrainian Cossack struggle for freedom was Taras Bulba, written by one of Russia's greatest writers, Nikolai Gogol. Coincidentally, Gogol was born in the Ukraine in March 1809.

When Tzar Nicholas II was forced to abdicate in March 1917, the Ukrainians took this as the end of their allegiance to Russia. As Basil Dmytryshyn wrote in USSR: A Concise History, "there had been developing and maturing for some time a national movement." Ukrainian nationalism took form in the establishment of the Rada, or central Executive Council, soon after the fall of the tzar. Premier Alexander Kerensky, head of the Russian provisional government since he replaced Prince Georgi Lvov on July 7, was anxious to come to an agreement with the Ukrainians. Not only would the secession of the Ukraine bring Russia's enemies in World War I, Germany and Austria-Hungary, almost within striking distance of Moscow, it would severely deprive Kerensky of the vital Ukrainian coal and grain reserves that Russia needed for survival.

At first, the Ukrainians simply wished for more autonomy within the empire, and an end to "Russification" the policy followed during the time of the tzars in occupied regions like parts of Poland, Estonia, Latvia, and Lithuania, which attempted to erase national culture and language to help cement the peoples to the authority of Russia and its tzars. When there was no immediate response, on June 23, Ukrainians announced in the First Universal Document their intention to begin controlling their own affairs. On July 12, 1917, Kerensky visited the ancient capital of the Ukraine, Kiev, and gave general acceptance of Ukrainian demands. In a time of war, Kerensky simply had no other alternative.

After Vladimir I. Lenin and the Bolsheviks gained power in the October (new calendar, November) 1917 Revolution, they moved quickly to reincorporate the Ukraine within the bounds of the old Russian Empire. But, as Robert Service noted in *Lenin: A Biography*, he was "an ideologue, but he was also a sinuous politician in pursuit of his ideological goals. In order to govern Ukraine it was crucial, as Lenin discerned, to attract political groups that had once been hostile to the Bolsheviks." In January 1918, Russian Red Army troops occupied Kiev.

However, Lenin would die prematurely in January 1924. Josef Stalin, who had become general secretary of the Bolshevik (Communist) Party in 1922, did not possess any of the political tact of Lenin. And, although he was the party's resource on "nationalities questions" in the new Soviet Union, he showed no understanding of the dialectics of Ukrainian national development. Under Stalin, the Ukraine was forcibly incorporated into the Soviet Union. And, as the "wheat basket" for much of the country, it suffered acutely under the movement to collective agriculture that took place after Stalin consolidated his power with the fall of Leon Trotsky in 1927. (Trotsky, as opposed to the ruthless centralism of Stalin, had countenanced—-at least a measure of—democracy within the party ranks.)

THE UKRAINE SOVIET

The full brunt of the farm collectivization movement struck the Ukraine in 1931 and 1932, as part of Stalin's First Five Year Plan to modernize the Soviet economy. The impact of the forced movement, enforced by the political purges of the internal security troops and the secret police, then the OGPU (later the NKVD), had a catastrophic effect upon the Ukrainian people. Basil Dmytryshyn noted that "in the Ukraine alone, some 27,000 party members and candidates" were removed from the Communist Party. In terms of life and death, the toll was horrific. According to the internet site, *The Artificial Famine/Genocide in Ukraine in 1932 and 1933*, "This resulted in the death of between 7 to 10 million people, mainly Ukrainians. This was instigated by Joseph Stalin and his henchman Lazar Kaganovich."

When Nazi Germany invaded the Soviet Union in June 1941, Ukrainians welcomed the Germans as liberators and many joined what they thought was the common fight. When the Ukrainians realized that the Germans considered them as subhumans, many joined the Soviet resistance against the Germans in the Partisan units, which were trained and supplied by the Red Army. "The first attempt," Otto Heilbron wrote in *Partisan Warfare*, "at organizing the Partisan Movement was made by the Main Administration of Political Propaganda of the Red Army," after Stalin made a patriotic appeal to the people of the Soviet Union on July 3, 1941. Heilbron noted that "by 1943, the Partisans were now organized almost like a regular army." However, many Ukrainians continued to fight on the opposing side—not so much in favor of the Germans as against the Soviets who had so ravaged their people.

Indeed, even after the German defeat in May 1945, Ukrainian guerrillas continued to fight against the Russian Army. The Peter J. Potichnyj Collection on Insurgency and Counter-Insurgency in Ukraine at the University of Toronto, Canada, contains extensive archives on the Ukrainian resistance. These include "A group of documents from the Archive of Misiia UPA in Germany. These documents cover the period 1943-1951 and were brought by couriers from Ukraine. They were in possession of Dr. Lev Rebet, a noted Ukrainian revolutionary, who was assassinated by a Soviet agent." The Ukrainians were organized into the Ukrainian Insurgent Army, which had a Foreign Representative Office in New York City.

After the war, both Josef Stalin and his eventual successor, Nikita Khrushchev, carried out a campaign of assassination of leaders of the Ukrainian resistance overseas. Lev Rebet, leader of the NTS (National Labor Alliance), would be killed in October 1957 and Stepan Bandera of the OUN (Organization of Ukrainian Nationalists) would die in October 1959. Tragically, Bandera had besmirched the Ukrainian fight for resistance by collaborating with the SS in the Holocaust, the attempt by the Nazis to exterminate the Jews of Europe. Bandera was involved with one of the Einsatzgruppe, the special action squads, which were responsible for the taking of tens of thousands of Jewish lives.

The most symbolic event of the breaking apart of the Soviet Union in the 1980s took place in the Ukraine. At Chernobyl, in April 1986, Ukrainians witnessed the worst nuclear plant accident in history. According to the World Nuclear Association, "The Chernobyl accident in 1986 was the result of a flawed reactor design that was operated with inadequately

The nuclear accident at Chernobyl (being inspected above), in Ukraine, contributed to the downfall of the Soviet state.

trained personnel and without proper regard for safety." Taking advantage of the implosion of the Soviet Union, the Ukraine once again declared its independence on August 24, 1991.

The document "Political Developments since 1989" noted that "only two-and-a-half years after Ukraine's independence the first free parliamentary elections took place on March 27, 1994." Ex-prime minister and leader of the Interregional Bloc for Reforms, Leonid Kuchma was elected president." In December 2004, Kuchma left office after a bitter and divisive election that brought a more Western-leaning government to power.

SEE ALSO

Volume 1 Left: Ukraine; Soviet Union.
Volume 2 Right: Soviet Union.

BIBLIOGRAPHY

Otto Heilbron, *Partisan Warfare* (Praeger, 1962); "Political Developments since 1989," www.europeanforum.bot-consult.se (July 2004); World Nuclear Association, "Chernobyl," March 2001, www.world-nuclear.org (July 2004); Heinz Hoehne, *Order of the Death's Head*, Richard Barry, trans. (Ballantine, 1971); Stephen Kotkin, *Armageddon Averted: The Soviet Collapse* (Oxford University Press, 2001); "President of the Ukraine," www.president.gov.ua (July 2004); Basil Dmytryshyn, *USSR: A Concise History* (Scribners, 1978); Orlando Figes, *A People's Tragedy: The Russian Revolution* (Penguin, 1996); Christopher Andrew and Oleg Gordievsky, *KGB: The Inside Story* (Harper, 1990); David Remnick, *Lenin's Tomb: The Last Days of the Soviet Empire* (Vintage, 1994).

JOHN F. MURPHY, JR.
AMERICAN MILITARY UNIVERSITY

Ultramontanism

ULTRAMONTANISM IS derived from *ultra montes*, which means "beyond the mountains." It is a term used to designate traditional Catholicism that recognizes the pope as the ultimate authority and spiritual leader, and has traditionally advocated the doctrine of papal infallibility. The term reflects the fact that for most of the Catholic world, the pope is physically located on the other side of the Alps. Ultramontanism reflects the position of Roman Catholics who have historically privileged centralized papal authority over national leaders and local ecclesiastical structures. Historically, it was opposed by such nationalist movements as Gallicanism in France, which defended the special rights of the French monarch in the French Church, and ecclesiastical Gallicanism, which tried to claim an administrative independence from Rome for the French clergy, Josephinism in Austria, and the radical Febronianism in Germany—all ideologies promoting strong national churches, as well as Conciliarism, which subordinated papal authority to the ultimate jurisdiction of a council of bishops.

These countermovements arose during the crisis of the Great Schism, a division in the Roman Catholic Church that lasted from 1378 to 1417, during which time the relationship between papal authority and general councils was negotiated. Ultramontanism is divided into old ultramontanism and new ultramontanism. Old ultramontanism was a Medieval doctrine, and the term was frequently found in 13th-century texts and continued to be used until the Babylonian Captivity, a period from 1304 to 1377, when the pope was based in Avignon (France) and the papal authority was seen by some as being in the captivity of the French monarchy.

The tenets of ultramontanism were largely adopted by the Society of Jesus in the 17th century, and were promoted by theologians such as Francisco Suarez, an opponent of such diffusion of the papal authority as the divine right of kings doctrine.

During the post-Napoleonic era, new ultramontanism was resurrected in France, as a French Catholic project aimed to reverse the influence of Enlightenment rationalism and secular humanism on Church affairs and to revivify papal authority. A similar neo-ultramontanism emerged in Germany, where it resulted in a political struggle between the German Chancellor Otto von Bismarck and the papal authority. The rift between Germany and the Vatican lasted approximately 30 years, but diplomatic relations were restored by the end of the 19th century and the anti-Catholic laws passed during that period were repealed.

The revival of ultramontanism was supportive of such unilateral papal acts as the declaration of the immaculate conception in 1854 and the promulgation of the *Syllabus of Errors* in 1864. The 1870 proclamation of papal primacy and infallibility was a triumph and an apex of the ultramontanist agenda. Even though the Second Vatican Council (1965) reaffirmed papal infallibility, its approval of an increased role for the college of bishops and a greater voice for the laymen in congregational issues weakened the doctrine of ultramontanism. John Paul II, the Pope (from 1978), has favored the ultramontane principles of strong papal authority and centralization of the power of the Catholic Church in the Vatican.

The critics of ultramontanism view it as an authoritarian and reactionary ideology that seeks a return to a Medieval social cosmology, when the position of the Catholic Church was centralized, unambiguous, and undisputed, and that ignores the relationship between the religious and the civic spheres that has evolved.

SEE ALSO

Volume 1 Left: Communism; Church and State Separation. *Volume 2 Right:* Religion; Theocracy.

BIBLIOGRAPHY

Patricia Byrne, "American Ultramontanism," *Theological Studies* (June 1, 1995); Marvin O'Connell, "Ultramontanism and Dupanloup: The Compromise of 1865," *Church History* (v.53/2, 1984); Jonathan Sperber, *Popular Catholicism in Nineteenth-Century Germany* (Princeton University Press, 1984); Thoms Bokenkotter, *A Concise History of the Catholic Church* (Doubleday Books, 2004).

VERONICA DAVIDOV
NEW YORK UNIVERSITY

Unilateralism

THE HISTORY OF UNILATERALISM in the United States is often traced to a speech given by future president John Quincy Adams on July 4, 1821, in which he announced that "America goes not abroad in search of monsters to destroy." Adams was echoing the policy established by first president George Washington who insisted that the United States remain neutral in the face of European wars. Even Thomas Jefferson, the founder of the Democratic party, advocated avoiding excessive entanglements with other nations.

American unilateralism remained entrenched, and formed the basis for American neutrality in World War I. However, after the United States entered the war as an "associated power" with the Allies, Woodrow Wilson became an advocate of an international League of Nations to enforce peace. The League and the Treaty of Versailles were defeated in the U.S. Senate, and the official doctrine of the United States remained unilateralist over the period 1920 to 1941. During this period, the doctrine became known as isolationism, and neutrality legislation passed during the 1930s was designed to prohibit the United States from becoming engaged in another European war.

The "Cash and Carry" Neutrality Act of 1939, passed within a few weeks after the outbreak of World War II, was intended to prevent the United States from becoming either a creditor to the Allies or to become engaged through its shipping as a target for German submarines. The law, based on the experience of World War I, was calculated to prevent the recurrence of the issues that had drawn the United States into that earlier conflict. However, unilateralism came to an end with the Japanese attack on Pearl Harbor, and the entry of the United States into the war as an ally of Britain and the Soviet Union. Roosevelt developed a vision of a war-free world where all nations could live in peace, and the concept of the League of Nations was revived with the creation of the United Nations.

In contemporary times, particularly since the resurgence of conservatism in the 1980s, American unilateralism has come to signify action taken in international affairs without benefit of consultation with significant allies or with international bodies.

Scholars contend that this contemporary view of unilateralism evolved from the influence of the Christian Right on Ronald Reagan in the 1980s. Because Reagan was determined to prove the military might of the United States, he never hesitated to initiate unilateral military action around the globe. Reagan justified attacks, such as those in Afghanistan, Angola, and Nicaragua, as necessary to American interests. Reagan maintained that his unilateral decision to build up nuclear weapons was a necessary result of the liberal call for "unilateral disarmament" in the 1970s.

At the beginning of the twenty-first century, Republican George W. Bush established American unilateralism with policies that included refusing to ratify treaties prohibiting the use of land mines and nuclear testing, withdrawing from compliance with the Kyoto Protocol designed to prevent global warming, initiating the war in Iraq, decreasing support for the United Nations, and America's pro-Israel stance despite increasing support for Palestinian rights around the world.

In the months before the 2004 election that propelled the Republicans to victory, *Business Week* warned that a second George W. Bush administration should seriously reconsider its policy of unilateralism because of the enormous costs associated with the policy, not only in a fiscal sense and in the number of American lives lost in Iraq, but also in the damage that unilateralism has done to America's reputation with allies. Critics are particularly harsh in vilifying Bush for failing to follow through on the opportunity for global cooperation in the aftermath of the attacks of September 11, 2001.

A number of George W. Bush's critics have maintained that the initiative for his brand of conservative unilateralism can be traced to Vice President Dick Cheney who has advocated the policy since the early 1990s and to far-right members of Congress who won their seats during the "Conservative Revolution" of 1994.

SEE ALSO

Volume 1 Left: Democratic Party; Wilson, Woodrow; Roosevelt, Franklin D.
Volume 2 Right: Republican Party; Bush, George W.

BIBLIOGRAPHY

Tom Barry and Jim Lobe, "The Men Who Stole the Show," www.fpif.org/papers (December 2004); Pascal Boniface, "The Specter of Unilateralism," *Washington Quarterly* (Summer 2001); "Making a Better Foreign Policy," *Business Week* (September 13, 2004); Walter A. McDougall, *Promised Land, Crusader State* (Houghton Mifflin, 1997); Duane Oldfield, "The Evangelical Roots of American Unilateralism: The Christian Right's Influence And How to Counter It," www.fpif.org/papers (December 2004); Clyde Prestowitz, *Rogue Nation: American Unilateralism and the Failure of Good Intentions* (Basic Books, 2003); Jed Rubenfeld, "The Two World Orders," *Wilson Quarterly* (Autumn 2003); J. Tirman, *Sovereign Acts, American Unilateralism and Global Security* (Harper and Row, 1989).

ELIZABETH PURDY, PH.D.
INDEPENDENT SCHOLAR

United Kingdom

THE UNITED KINGDOM claims to be the birthplace of the terms left wing and right wing based on the working class House of Commons' chambers being in the Parliament Building's left wing with the aristocracy's House of Lords' chambers being in the right wing. Historically, demands for reform tended to originate in the Commons (the left wing) and were resisted by the Lords (the right wing). Most scholars today, however, agree that the terms *left* and *right* originated in revolutionary France.

Of course, conservatism is as old as human politics, emerging the first time a change was proposed in some prehistoric council and was opposed by defenders of tradition, precedent, stability, past success, and/or principle. In general, British right-wing conservatism has aspired to the preservation of that which is best in society and with a skepticism toward radical change.

In the modern United Kingdom, a number of right-wing splinter groups are politically active, including the British National Party, best known for its demands for toughened immigration restrictions; the Christian People's Alliance, which calls for a return to Christian principles in government; the United Kingdom Independence Party, which seeks to withdraw Great Britain from the European Union; and Pro-Life, which, when it was projecting a higher profile, sought an official ban to abortion.

However, a glance at parliament puts such minority parties' influence into perspective. After the 2001 elections, three parties comprised 93.6 percent of the membership of the House of Commons: the Labor Party with 412 seats or 42.1 percent, the Conservative Party with 166 seats or 32.7 percent, and the Liberal Democrats with 52 seats or 18.8 percent. All other parties, left, right, or centrist, made up 6.4 percent of the total House with 29 members.

What do modern British conservatives believe? The party emerged between 1750 and 1850 as a negative response to the abrupt changes convulsing European societies, particularly in France where the aristocracy was being guillotined daily to the cheers of the working class. At the same time, the beginnings of industrialization had brought substantial changes to British society, including demands for universal, although male-only, suffrage. It was in the debates over the Reform Act of 1832 that the term *conservative* began to be used in describing the Tory position, resisting the changes the populace demanded.

BRITISH CONSERVATISM

And so it was that the perception emerged that "conservative" is synonymous with defense of the status quo and resistance to change. Conservatives began to be regarded as protectors of a model of society they considered appropriate for everyone. However, "conservative" and "conservatism" have evolved dramatically. Some political figures might be properly described as conservatives, but would not describe themselves as such.

Outsiders looking in tend to offer flawed definitions, asserting that conservatives live in perpetual pessimism or that they are automatically aligned with everyone else identified with the extreme right, such as defenders of the conviction that the British monarchy's rule by divine right, or anarchists of the libertarian persuasion who hold that government regulation is repugnant in any form. Often, conservatives are tarred with the same brush as fascists, neo-Nazis, and fundamentalist Islamists. J.S. Mill commented that the Conservative Party was, "by the law of their existence the stupidest party." But British conservatives such as Edmund Burke, Benjamin Disraeli, Lord Salisbury, Michael Oakeshott, and Margaret Thatcher might instead offer that the conservative worldview tends to be skeptical reductionism, demanding of grand proposals and principles close examination with the question: "Is this radical proposal for change really a good idea, given local conditions?"

In the 18th century, British conservatism seemed to focus on preservation of the rule of the aristocracy, with wariness toward the type of revolution occurring in France. In the 19th century, British conservatism seemed preoccupied with the question of how much reform to tolerate. In the 20th century, it tended to struggle against Marxism at home and abroad, so that it was an easy mistake to perceive 20th-century British conservatism purely as anti-communist/anti-socialist. If that were the only basis of conservatism, however, in the 21st century with the decline of communism, conservatism should have disappeared, lacking a reason to exist. The collapse of the Soviet Union and the privatization of key British industries would have resolved conservatism's goals. This, however, was not the case. Instead, conservatism has tended to conform to the skeptical reductionism model, continuing to have an important role as it questions such concepts as feminism, ecologism, radical democratic theory, libertarianism, unrestricted immigration, separation of church and state, and the wisdom of Britain being homogenized into the European Community.

Although modern British conservatism has a variety of voices, the Tories are the most influential; indeed the Tories are the only conservative party to have formed governments, under such giants as Winston Churchill and Margaret Thatcher.

CONSERVATIVE ORIGINS

The Tories are said to have origins that are "lost in the mist of history," perhaps tracing their lineage back to the supporters of the Tudor court in the 16th century. In the 17th century, the Tories' defining belief was the legitimacy of Stuart claims to the throne, but evolved into an opposition to the ruling Whigs. Only in the 19th century did Tories embrace the title of "Conservatives," particularly in their resistance to the Reform Act of 1832. "Conservative" was a self-description used by one of the most prominent Tories, Sir Robert Peel, in his speech, known as the Tamworth Manifesto, in 1834. That period also spawned what is said to be the first nongovernmental British conservative institution, the Carlton Club, founded in 1831.

No other British era is comparable to the 1830s and early 1840s, when both the working class and the middle class demanded fundamental changes. From 1829 to 1832 they focused on demands for parliamentary reform, resulting in mass riots and economic boycotts.

The Reform Acts of 1832, 1867, and 1884 awarded voting privileges to British subjects who previously had no voice in politics. The first act was the most controversial. Despite conservative resistance, it reapportioned representation in Parliament in a way that gave the industrialized cities better representation. It also gave the vote to the lower social and economic classes, extending the right to cast a ballot to any male who owned a household worth 10 pounds sterling. That added 217,000 voters to an electorate of 435,000. Overnight, one man in five could vote.

For many conservatives, the effect was troublesome, for it allowed the middle classes to share power with the upper classes. A case can be made that the Reform Act of 1832 accomplished peacefully in England what the French Revolution gained through considerable bloodshed.

A key political issue during that time was poverty. Britain's population had boomed during Queen Victoria's reign, and social reformers called on the government to take a role in helping "less well-off" people. However, the conservatives were philosophically opposed to spending tax revenues on charitable services. Conservatives expounded on principles of self-help. The attitude was "If you are poor, do something about it and stop feeling sorry for yourself."

The Reform Act of 1867 extended the vote still further down the class ladder, adding almost a million new voters. Stunned, some conservatives debated whether this power shift would create a democracy run amok that would, in turn, destroy England's very culture. In response, the National Union of Conservative Associations was founded and began to establish local party associations across the nation, embracing the new electorate and welcoming them into the political process. In 1870, the Conservative Central Office was founded to coordinate what had become a volunteer army of grassroots conservatives.

One key to British conservatives' modern-day success is these local constituency associations, which enjoy considerable local autonomy and have historically been quite inclusive of disagreeing factions, such as during the 1980s when conservative "dries" supported Thatcher's plan to "roll back the state" and get the government out of ownership of key industries—which was opposed by conservative "wets," who espoused a less dramatic approach with selective state participation in the economy. Keeping both groups inside the conservative tent under the Conservative Party slogan of "One Nation" was much wiser than replicating the destructive split of the Tories in the 1840s over the Corn Law, in which one faction supported high tariffs on imported farm products to protect British farmers and another faction demanded dropping the tariffs so as to allow consumer grocery prices to drop.

The Reform Act of 1884 and the 1885 Redistribution Act tripled the electorate again, giving the vote even to farmworkers. Voting began to be regarded as a right rather than a privilege granted to property owners. It would be 1928 before suffrage was extended finally to all adult women.

WINSTON CHURCHILL

From 1929 to 1939, the years of the Great Depression, a liberal young Labour Party member of Parliament, Winston Churchill, the son of Parliament veteran Randolph Churchill, turned conservative, voicing opposition to self-government for India, making no secret his distrust of Hitler, and energetically urging Britain to prepare for eventual war. When Poland was invaded by the Nazis, a mutual protection treaty pulled Britain into the war in 1939 on the side of the Poles. Churchill was exonerated and public opinion supported his succession of the disgraced Neville Chamberlain as prime minister in 1940.

The darkest days of World War II followed. The British Army was almost lost when the Nazi advance across France pushed the Allies into the sea, forcing the dramatic evacuation of British forces at Dunkirk. The fall of France followed, then the Battle of Britain in the air, basically an aerial terrorist campaign against predominantly civilian targets designed to destroy the morale of the nation. Churchill's pugnacity and rousing speeches rallied the British to "never, never give up," urging his compatriots to fight on the beaches, to fight in the streets, to fight in the countryside, refusing to surrender so that, "if the British Empire and its Commonwealth last for a thousand years, men will still say, 'This was their finest hour.'"

Churchill was able to secure military aid and moral support from the United States. After the Soviet Union and the United States entered the war in 1941, Churchill established close ties with leaders of what he called the "Grand Alliance." Traveling ceaselessly throughout the war, he did much to coordinate military strategy and to ensure Hitler's defeat. His conferences with Roosevelt and Stalin also shaped postwar Europe.

However, after the war, he was unresponsive to popular demands for social change and was defeated in the 1945 elections. As opposition leader, Churchill criticized the "welfare state" reforms of Labour Prime Minister Clement Attlee and warned of the dangers of Soviet ambitions in his famous 1946 speech in Fulton, Missouri, which declared that "an Iron Curtain" had fallen across Europe.

But what followed were difficult days in terms of conservative power and ideology. Anthony Eden suc-

control inflation or contain the trade unions through legislation, then two defeats at the hands of striking coal miners led to Heath's defeat.

THATCHERISM

After the Conservatives' election losses in February and October 1974, Heath was defeated in 1975 party elections by one of his cabinet ministers, Margaret Thatcher, who had already distinguished herself by calling for dramatic nationwide changes. Commentator Stuart Hall was perhaps the first to coin the term *Thatcherism* when describing Thatcher's calls for dramatic reforms, back when they were still coming from the minority side of the aisle. In 1979, the Conservative Party won the general election and it was Mrs. Thatcher who rose to the position of the United Kingdom's first woman prime minister. Her first two years in office were not easy. As a result of her policies, unemployment was high, but the economy gradually showed improvement. Her economic and social policies from 1979 to 1990 centered on her vision of the restoration of Great Britain as a world power, the deregulation and privatization of the economy, and a tough social policy geared to restore incentives for achievement and get the able-bodied off welfare rolls.

After her election victory in 1979, *Thatcherism* saw regular usage in the news media. It was considered a derisive term in some conservative circles because of the implication that the party was dominated by the prime minister, when, in fact, Thatcher, like all British leaders in her office, had to skillfully maintain responsiveness to her constituencies. Without such, a prime minister can expect to be replaced virtually overnight, unlike American presidents, who stay in power for four-year terms regardless of mid-term unpopularity.

One theme of Thatcherism was that the Conservative Party had failed to raise a loud enough voice of dissent as Great Britain became increasingly socialist. The Tories' seeming postwar ambivalence to creeping Marxism was just as responsible as the Labour Party for the nation's decline, Thatcher declared. She was quoted as blaming her own party for failing to live up to its own convictions. "Tories loosened the corset of socialism, but they never removed it," she remarked, declaring that socialism had to be cast aside altogether. Her conservative point of view was that the United Kingdom had become a welfare "nanny state" with diminished international influence. Socialist policies had removed any incentive for excellence, hard work, or initiative, she preached. One result was a burgeoning national

Conservative Winston Churchill rallied nationalism in the United Kingdom to fight Germany in World War II.

ceeded Churchill in April 1955, but retired after Britain was humiliated internationally in Egypt's seizure of the Suez Canal and Britain's failed invasion of the canal zone in January 1957. The aristocratic Sir Alec Douglas-Home and Harold Macmillan led the conservatives next, but into a period of economic stagnation. In 1970, conservative Edward Heath, who was from a lower-middle-class background, became prime minister. By then, British conservatives had accepted a variety of policies that ran counter to conservative tradition, such as the emergence of the welfare state, government acquisition of key industries, socialist intervention in economic affairs, and partnership in industry between trade unions and employers. Such compromises enabled the Conservative Party to regain power in 1951 and then to remain in office until 1964, but little differentiated them from the Labour Party. Despite Heath's personal achievements in taking Britain into the Common Market, his failures between 1970 and 1974 to

debt and inflation, severely eroding the formerly high status of the British pound sterling. Thatcher called for a more competitive economy with free-market rewards for productivity, and set about to accomplish a sea change in the mindset of the British people as to the role of a centralized government in their lives.

When Heath was voted out as prime minister, his defeated Conservative Party turned to Thatcher, but many assumed she was merely a caretaker, filling the role until a permanent candidate was found. As leader of the loyal opposition, with the conservatives in the minority in Parliament, she promoted turning back the Labour clock on the welfare state and getting the government out of key industries. Concern over Britain's serious economic decline and the vast power wielded by the trade unions created a receptive public mood among voters.

When she first stepped into the prime minister's shoes at the close of the 1970s, Britain was considered the "sick man of Europe," handicapped industrially by unwieldy union power, hampered domestically by governmental social welfare programs, and suffering from a general national sense of defeatism. The Conservative Party had compromised for years with Labour, in Thatcher's estimation, resulting in the United Kingdom's humiliating need for an International Monetary Fund bailout like some faltering, third world, banana republic. Thatcher espoused a plan for free trade and privatization, a vision to rebuild Britain by harnessing the strength of its people. She fanned basic British resolve and virtue, in the tradition and legacies of such British heroes as Lord Nelson and Winston Churchill, undertaking the challenge not because it was easy, but because it was right.

Thatcher has said her personal views of morality were transformed by World War II, which she says taught her "the failure of appeasement and the lesson that aggression must always be firmly resisted." A key challenge that would symbolize her impact on the nation was the Argentine invasion of the seemingly inconsequential Falkland Islands, an archaic British colonial outpost off the coast of South America, several desolate, rocky, and almost Antarctic islands inhabited primarily by English-speaking shepherds descended from British stock.

The Falklanders had voted repeatedly to remain a part of the United Kingdom and appealed for Great Britain's help when in 1982 they were attacked and occupied by armed forces from the Spanish-speaking republic of Argentina, which annexed the islands and renamed them the Islas Malvinas.

The Argentines had thought the weakened United Kingdom, led by a woman, would just surrender the islands. Instead, Thatcher mobilized her nation, rushed aircraft carriers, bombers, and troops aboard famous Cunard Line luxury liners to the South Atlantic; sank the Argentine navy in a matter of days; defeated the Argentine army within weeks; and blew the Argentine air force out of the sky. The Argentine government collapsed, its military leaders deposed by civilian leadership that sued for peace.

THE REAGAN CONNECTION

Caspar Weinberger, defense secretary for Ronald Reagan, regarded Thatcher's decision to recapture the Falkland Islands as one of the toughest tests of her resolve. She heard expert advice that warned Britain couldn't support a war 7,000 miles away, particularly after the United States took a position of neutrality in the conflict. "But she was determined to go ahead and do it because she thought it was the right thing to do," Weinberger said. "And she acted as if the possibility of military defeat did not exist."

Nor did she hesitate when deciding whether to deploy cruise missiles in England in response to moves by the Soviet Union. Although the move was opposed by huge peace rallies, Weinberger says Thatcher "felt it had to occur to demonstrate to the Soviets that they could not deploy their missiles without some kind of responsive deployment."

Thatcher gained the respect of Reagan. During a state visit, he shared with her that he was convinced that it was possible to undermine the Soviet empire. Former CIA Director Robert Gates says that "Reagan, nearly alone, truly believed in 1981 that the Soviet system was vulnerable … right then." Thatcher listened. She signed on. In his famous speech to the British House of Commons in 1982, Reagan stood with Thatcher and declared, "It is the Soviet Union that runs against the tide of history by denying human freedom and human dignity to its citizens. The march of freedom and democracy will leave Marxism-Leninism on the ash heap of history." Thatcher would write later that the West was "slowly but surely losing" the Cold War. She eagerly embraced Reagan's strategy to win it. She became, in her own words, "his principal cheerleader" in the North Atlantic Treaty Organization.

That strategy rested on six pillars agreed upon by the two leaders: supporting internal disruption in Soviet satellite nations, especially Poland; drying up the Soviets' sources of hard currency; overloading the So-

The New Right, formed by Ronald Reagan (left) and Margaret Thatcher, promulgated conservative values in the West.

viet economy with a technology-based arms race; slowing the flow of Western technology to Moscow; raising the cost of the wars the Soviet Union was fighting; and demoralizing the Soviet populace by generating pressure for change. The Reagan-Thatcher arms buildup impacted the Kremlin. Their call for a high-tech defense system against nuclear weapons in 1983 helped convince the Politburo to select Mikhail Gorbachev as a less hard-line Soviet leader in 1985. The "Strategic Defense Initiative was a very successful blackmail," says Gennady Gerasimov, the Soviet Foreign Ministry's top spokesman during the 1980s. "The Soviet economy couldn't endure such competition." Gorbachev himself agrees that the Reagan-Thatcher plan exhausted his country economically. "Reagan's truth-telling, together with the examples of Mrs. Thatcher's economic success and Pope John Paul's moral strength, gave millions of people courage to rise up when the opportunity for change came," says President Vaclav Klaus of the Czech Republic. According to Jeffrey Archer, the British political insider and novelist, the political marriage of Reagan and Thatcher "had a lot to do with not necessarily the end of the Soviet Union, but the speeding up of the whole process."

Attempting to take advantage of Thatcher's distraction with the Cold War, a group of IRA convicted terrorists in British prisons undertook a hunger strike. But Thatcher held fast to her conviction that Britain should never negotiate with terrorists. "Again she came right back and was not in any way deterred from her actions," Weinberger reflects. She did not falter even when she became the target of an Irish Republican Army bomb during a Conservative Party conference in Brighton, England. John Lukacs, a conservative historian, admires the strength of Thatcher's character "unreservedly and especially when it had come to the Falklands' War." Yet, he believes she represents a "curious" English Conservative Party mix: half Churchill and half Neville Chamberlain. Her response to the "brutality of the Argentines was excellent," he says. "She acted Churchillian." At the same time, he thinks that her Midlands shopkeeper mentality, her suspicion of Europe and of Europeans, and her belief in economic materialism were reminiscent of Chamberlain.

French Prime Minister Francois Mitterand once said, "She has the lips of Marilyn Monroe and the eyes of Caligula." But when the Soviet Union fell, it was the end of the Thatcher era, much as Churchill fell from grace at the end of World War II. "Historically, her style of politics flourished, as did Reagan's in the Cold War," Young says. "But once the Cold War came to an end, she lost one of her most important reasons to exist."

One great difficulty during her time in office was the issue of Europe. Her long-serving Foreign Secretary Sir Geoffrey Howe resigned in November 1990 in protest at Thatcher's attitude toward the European Union. Michael Heseltine challenged Thatcher for the leadership, and while he failed to win, he gained 152 votes, enough to make it evident that change was needed. Thatcher resigned and a prominent member of her cabinet, John Major, won the next national elections. She left the House of Commons in 1992, and now sits in the House of Lords as Baroness Thatcher, an honorary role bestowed by the Queen.

Detractors today reject claims that Thatcher proved for all time the validity of key British conservative principles. They claim her economic successes were short term and won at a huge cost of mass unemployment and deindustrialization. As for boasts that she won the Cold War, they say the Soviet Union was collapsing under its own weight anyway. Her dramatic reductions in the welfare state and privatizations of state-owned industries only netted vast profits for party cronies, they allege. Her policies inflicted great suffering on key elements of British democracy, such as the trade unions, the civil service, and local government authority.

"Thatcherism" was merely Reagan's America and alienated the United Kingdom from the European Community. The charge is that Thatcher hijacked the Conservative Party and rejected its "One Nation" inclusive traditions.

SEE ALSO

Volume 1 Left: United Kingdom; United States; Socialism; Labour Party, UK; Liberal Party, UK.
Volume 2 Right: Conservatism; New Right; Reagan, Ronald; Thatcher, Margaret; Conservative Party, UK.

BIBLIOGRAPHY

Anushka Asthana and Gaby Hinsliff, "Equality Chief Banded as 'Right Wing,'" *London Observer* (April 4, 2004); Stuart Ball, "A Brief History of the Conservative Party," www.conservatives.com (July 2004); Susan Crabtree and Tiffany Danitz, "The Legacy of Margaret Thatcher," *Insight on the News* (v.12, 1996); Hellen Dale, "Signs of Life: Credo from New Tory Leader Inspires Trust," *Washington Times* (January 7, 2004); "Did President Reagan Really Win the Cold War?" *Christian Crusade Newspaper* (v.52/6, 2004); Eric Hobsbawm, *Industry and Empire: The Birth of the Industrial Revolution* (New Press, 1999); Quintin Hogg, *The Case for Conservatism* (Penguin Books, 1947); Giles Marshall, "We Tories Must Change, or Face Eternal Oblivion," *New Statesman* (v.130, 2001); Lain McLean, "Conservatism," *The Concise Oxford Dictionary of Politics* (Oxford University, 1996); *National Geographic Atlas of the World* (National Geographic Society, 1999); *World Almanac and Book of Facts* (World Almanac, 2004); *World Factbook* (World Fact Book, 2003).

ROB KERBY
INDEPENDENT SCHOLAR

United States

IN THE UNITED STATES, both liberalism and conservatism stem from the classical liberal theories that gained prominence in Europe and America with the writings of Thomas Hobbes, John Locke, Jean-Jacques Rousseau, Adam Smith, and John Stuart Mill. Classical liberalism was adopted and refined for American use by Thomas Jefferson and the supporters of the Declaration of Independence in 1776. Under the guidance of James Madison, classical liberalism provided the foundation for the U.S. Constitution in 1787. As classical liberals, the Founding Fathers believed that rational human beings have the right to create governments that are designed to protect individuals from internal as well as external harm without trampling on basic human rights, such as the right to "life, liberty, and the pursuit of happiness."

During the early days of constitutional government, ideological divisions concerning the role of government caused classical liberals to split into the left (liberals) and the right (conservatives). Despite this split, classical liberalism remained integral to the process of governance in America, with both conservatives and liberals accepting its basic tenets. This commonality has historically resulted in a similarity of the two major political parties that is unique to the United States. American conservatism, as it is understood in contemporary terms, developed during the mid-20th century in response to the liberal policies of President Franklin Roosevelt during the Depression and World War II. Conservative Republicans represent the right end of the political spectrum, while liberal Democrats represent the left wing of American politics.

CONSERVATIVE THEORY

In Western political theory, conservatism traces its roots to British political and social philosopher and activist Edmund Burke, who presented his conservatives theories in *Reflections on the Revolution in France* in 1790. While Burke recognized the legitimacy of the American Revolution wherein Americans were fighting to reclaim traditional English rights, he argued that the French were not justified in overthrowing the monarchy to establish popular sovereignty.

Drawing on the theories of Greek philosopher Aristotle to explain his views on equality/inequality, Burke rejected the views of Enlightenment thinkers, who tended to be classical liberals. Aristotle believed in a natural inequality that allowed masters to rule over slaves, men to dominate women, and parents to control their children. Equality was possible, in Aristotle's view, only among equals. Burke accepted this "natural" inequality, maintaining that good government was composed of a descending hierarchy of monarchy, aristocracy, and the people. The latter group was made up of property owners, merchants, nobles, and the landed gentry. According to Burke, inherited prejudices form an acceptable element of respected tradition to which all conservatives owe allegiance.

Burke rejected the classical liberal explanation that civil societies formed as individuals left the state of nature for the security of government. Burke argued that civil society was the natural state of man. Rather than the natural rights philosophy espoused by John Locke and Thomas Jefferson, Burke insisted that rights were only relevant when they existed in a given society. Burkean conservatism espoused the belief that order is the main function of any government, with liberty playing a secondary role. Burke contended that conservatives should be guided by a dependence on religious tenets, a strong love of kindred, and a healthy respect for equality and justice.

Aristotle's philosophy was also evident in Burke's explanation of virtues, which depended heavily on the continued acceptance of organized institutions. Burke's most prized virtues were religiosity, patriotism, loyalty, and moderation. However, Burke departed from Aristotelian thought to argue in his *Appeal from the Old to the New Whigs* in 1791 that human nature derived from convention and habit. Burke declared that human beings were shaped by the political institutions that existed in any given society. Deviating from the established policies of these institutions was likely to be dangerous in Burke's view. Reform rather than innovation was necessary to serve the interests of society. Religion and morals were irrevocably intertwined in Burkean thought, leading to the conservative claim that prevailing morals were "right" and all deviations from the norm were "wrong." Burke's most articulate opponents were Thomas Paine in America and Rousseau and Mary Wollstonecraft in Europe. These liberals staunchly rejected conservatism, which they saw as the antithesis of liberalism, arguing that it promoted the interests of elitist property owners.

At its core, conservatism is anti-intellectual, which places it at odds with much of established American political thought. Indeed, some liberals claim that there is no conservative political thought, simply reactions to and rejections of liberal political thought. Despite this claim, certain principles are associated with rightist philosophies. The true conservative believes that God is the center of all things, which leads to respect for the existing moral order, adherence to tradition and customs, an inclination toward prudence of action, a distrust of change, acceptance of class divisions, a belief in the perfectibility of humans beings, acceptance of a natural inclination to amass property, and a preference for private and community rather than governmental solutions to problems.

Conservative and liberal definitions of liberty tend to vary. While liberals see liberty as government noninterference in individual rights, conservatives often equate liberty with individuality. Liberals claim that this view of liberty is more economic than political and that it leads to a rejection of the principles of equality inherent in the American political system. The conservative tends to distrust government and prefers government intervention at the lowest level possible. The liberal, on the other hand, frequently looks to the national government for protection from denial of rights by state and local governments.

18th-CENTURY CONSERVATISM

When the Federalists who supported the ratification of the Constitution set out in late 1787 to convince the 13 states that they had more to gain than lose by accepting the need for a strong central government, no organized political parties existed. In *Federalist Number 10*, James Madison warned against factions, which he believed promoted self-interest and threatened the foundations of liberty. To Madison, political parties were exaggerated factions that advanced the interests of elites while ignoring the needs of the people as a whole. The Federalists, who were the liberals of their day, triumphed over the conservative anti-Federalists, who clung to the tradition of strong state governments joined to a weak national government by a loose confederation. Their victory turned the Federalists into an organized political party. With George Washington's election as president and Federalists in place throughout all levels of government, Federalist policies became the status quo, and the Federalist Party became a conservative rather than a liberal party.

When the Founding Fathers created the office of the presidency in Philadelphia, Pennsylvania, in 1787, they already knew that George Washington was likely to become the first president. As the only political party, the Federalists under Washington were relatively united. By the time that Vice President John Adams succeeded Washington in 1797, cleavages had already appeared. The Democratic-Republicans, or Jeffersonians as they were also called, offered alternatives to the rightist policies of the Adams administration. The Jeffersonians were particularly appalled at the conservative use of the Sedition Act of 1798 to attempt to silence all opponents. When Thomas Jefferson and James Madison campaigned against the Federalists in 1796 and 1800, rightist newspapers launched an anti-liberal attack, calling Jefferson an atheist because of his views on freedom of religion and his insistence that a wall of separation should exist between church and state. Conservatives claimed that Jefferson would draw the new country into European wars. As president, Adams com-

As a conservative, John Adams believed in a strong executive and and court system, and issues of law and order.

mitted himself to building a navy to protect the United States from foreign invasion and announced that the country would remain neutral in order to maintain economic and domestic relations with both England and France. As a conservative, Adams was adamant about issues of law and order. He believed in a strong executive and had enormous respect for the authority of the American court system. Adams lost the 1800 election to the Jeffersonians, and the conservatives did not return to the White House until 1825 when Adams's son, John Quincy Adams, who later achieved national attention for his fight against slavery as a member of the House of Representatives, became president. The House of Representatives chose Adams as president, even though Democrat Andrew Jackson had won the popular vote. Conservative infighting and the splintering of the Federalist Party helped to place Jackson in the White House in 1828, and his liberal polices ush-

ered in the period that became known as Jacksonian democracy.

19th-CENTURY CONSERVATISM

During the early to mid-1830s, the American right was represented by the Whig party, which advocated reforms aimed at helping the United States to prosper. Whigs supported building roads, canals, and railroads and were staunch advocates of westward expansion. The Whigs were unfortunate in their selection of presidential candidates. William Henry Harrison won the 1840 election, only to die two days after his inauguration. Although most Whigs believed that Vice President John Tyler would continue to promote their policies, as president, Tyler reverted to his Democratic roots and promoted liberal policies instead. Abraham Lincoln deserted the Whigs for the new Republican Party.

Historians believe that the Republican Party had its beginnings in Ripon, Wisconsin, on March 20, 1854, when a group of dissatisfied Democrats, Whigs, Free Soilers, and other individuals met to assert their opposition to the Kansas-Nebraska Act. As an effort to avert civil war, Congress was considering the repeal of the Missouri Compromise Act of 1820 and the Compromise of 1850. These acts had been designed to prohibit the expansion of slavery into the Northwestern Territory. The growing tensions over slavery resulted in a major split in the Democratic Party in 1860, with the southern Democrats backing John Breckenridge and the northern Democrats supporting Stephen Douglas. Lincoln won the election with less than 40 percent of the popular vote.

Lincoln was never a strong partisan, and he was fond of saying that his policy was to have no policy. Lincoln believed in both individualism and equal opportunity and was committed to preserving the Union at all costs. As the Civil War dragged on, Lincoln became convinced that the abolition of slavery was essential to winning the war and issued the Emancipation Proclamation, freeing all slaves in the seceded states. However, Lincoln did not believe that the abolition of slavery would bring about racial equality. He accepted separation of the races as a way to avoid further internal conflict.

After the Civil War ended, Lincoln met the radical Republicans in Congress head-on over the issue of Reconstruction. The Republicans wanted to hold the southern states accountable for their disloyalty, thereby ensuring that Republicans remained in power.

While Lincoln was often vilified by conservatives during his presidency, his death elevated him to the status of a martyr; and in 1887, Republicans began holding Lincoln Day rallies to remind Americans of their conservative heritage. Republican Presidents William Howard Taft, Teddy Roosevelt, and Herbert Hoover invoked Lincoln's name to justify their policies.

After Lincoln's death, Andrew Johnson had the unenviable task of reuniting the country. While Johnson agreed with Lincoln that the executive should manage Reconstruction, radical Republicans in Congress insisted that the constitutional power to declare war gave them the final voice in guiding the country through Reconstruction. A showdown occurred when Johnson was impeached for firing a cabinet member in violation of the Tenure of Office Act. Although Johnson was not removed from office, he became even more ineffective in fighting the strong-willed legislature.

Ulysses S. Grant, who won by using his fame from the Civil War, fared somewhat better with the Republican Congress. However, a plethora of scandals during his administration also weakened his effectiveness. The 1876 election effectively settled the battle when Republican Rutherford B. Hayes, who had lost the popular vote to Democrat Samuel Tilden, promised to end Reconstruction in exchange for southern support when the task of determining the winner of the election was given to a special commission because of alleged voting irregularities.

EARLY 20th-CENTURY CONSERVATISM

The succession of Theodore Roosevelt to the presidency after the 1901 assassination of William McKinley by an anarchist began a period of progressive reform in the United States. Though a loyal Republican, TR, as he was known, endorsed the progressive belief that government could effectively deal with many of the nation's problems by taking an active role. He worked out compromises between industry and workers, launched attacks against huge trusts, involved the United States in global politics, began construction of the Panama Canal to provide a gateway from the Atlantic to the Pacific, and took unprecedented actions in the field of conservation. After leaving the White House, TR lost a bid for a third term on the Bull Moose (Progressive) ticket to Democrat Woodrow Wilson. The Progressives, who included both liberals and conservatives, advocated direct democracy, progressive reform, conservation, the abolition of child labor, and women's suffrage.

In the United States, post-World War II conservatism evolved directly in response to the economic theories of John Maynard Keynes and the New Deal politics of Franklin D. Roosevelt. The twin crises of the Great Depression and World War II had allowed the national government to intrude in what had previously been considered the provinces of state and local governments, big business, and private charities. Dismayed over what they saw as out-of-control government, small groups of libertarians, agrarians, individualists, collectivists, nationalists, and other dissidents banded together and began to call themselves Conservatives. Business leaders were at the forefront of the conservative movement because they feared the labor movement that had been generated as the Industrial Revolution spread to the United States, creating an inevitable chasm between factory owners and workers.

Politicians and business leaders of the period were well aware that labor movements had been instrumental

Milton Friedman's libertarian views became especially popular during the Reagan era of the 1980s in the United States.

in the rise of extremist movements in a number of other countries. While such doctrines never achieved mainstream acceptance in the United States, they did attract large numbers during the 1930s in what became known as the Red Scare. Because the Great Depression had reached the United States in 1929, scores of people were without food, shelter, and jobs. Out of fear, Americans became more vulnerable to extremist ideologies from both the left (socialism/communism) and the right (fascism).

Republican President Herbert Hoover believed that state and local governments and private charities were responsible for helping those in need and continued to deny that the United States was in crisis. Democrat Franklin Roosevelt won the 1932 elections by assuring Americans that the only thing they had to fear was fear itself, and rapidly turned the United States into a social welfare state. Despite conservative attempts to undo all the vestiges of New Deal programs, such programs as welfare and social security have remained in place. While southerners tended to remain loyal to the Democratic Party in what became the solid South, conservative Democrats often sided with Republicans in Congress, giving Republicans a stronger voice even when Democrats controlled both houses of Congress.

MID-20th-CENTURY CONSERVATISM

The threat of leftist doctrines continued to drive American conservatives until the end of the 20th century, when the Cold War with the Soviet Union drew to a close. The McCarthy era of the 1950s, in which conservatives attempted to prove that the country had been infiltrated by communism, had begun an organized attack on American liberalism that resulted in the rise of the New Right in the mid-1960s.

Conservatives throughout the latter half of the 20th century cited the philosophies of economist Friedrich August von Hayek as a basis for conservative thought. However, Hayek refused to accept the conservative label, insisting that he remained a liberal. He accused conservatives of being unable to offer viable alternatives to liberalism, contending that conservatives were hampered by their inability to work with those who did not share their convictions. In "Why I Am Not a Conservative," Hayek stated that the most objectionable characteristic of conservatives was their readiness to reject new knowledge in the face of substantial documentation.

The conservative affinity for Hayek arose chiefly from his rejection of Keynesianism and socialism in *The Road to Serfdom* (1944). Hayek believed that socialism was inevitable if the role of the national government continued to expand. Hayek and a group of fellow dissidents formed the Mont Pelerin Society in 1947 to bring free-market advocates together.

The New Right was also stimulated by the work of Milton Friedman, who led the Chicago School of Economics in a move to the right in opposition to what they saw as unnecessary government controls on the economy. In *Capitalism and Freedom* (1962), Friedman argued that the promotion of individual freedom was the chief purpose of government, reiterating the traditional conservative argument that freedom and individuality were irrevocably bound. Friedman argued that the only other acceptable roles of government were preserving law and order, enforcing private contracts, and fostering a competitive market.

The founding of the *National Review* in 1955 by conservative William F. Buckley, Jr., gave the New Right a highly visible forum to proclaim its views. Making no bones about its rightist views, Buckley asserted that the only acceptable role of the national government was to protect lives, liberty, and property. The journal was also unashamedly anti-communist, anti-intellectual, anti-globalization, and anti-wage and price controls. The New Right movements that developed simultaneously during the 1970s and 1980s in the United States, Great Britain, New Zealand, and Australia encompassed two distinct strands of political thought. Neoliberals, who acted chiefly in response to their personal disillusionment with the left, promoted free-market economies and limited government interference, and had a strong preference for individualism over the leftist insistence on equality. Neoconservatives, also known as hawks, hardliners, and ultraconservatives, endorsed the New Right's views on patriotism, duty, family, and tradition. They accepted without question the need for social authoritarianism and natural, hierarchical societal structures.

In 1964, the New Right chose Arizona Senator Barry Goldwater to challenge Lyndon Johnson and his Great Society liberalism. Goldwater was considered too far to the right to appeal to mainstream Americans at a time when liberal politics ruled the day. While the Goldwater campaign failed, carrying only Arizona and five southern states, the election of 1964 is seen as a pivotal election in American politics.

The campaign articulated the concerns of the growing conservative movement over civil rights issues. Many southerners deserted the Democratic Party to vote for the Republicans, who promised to end government interference in what many saw as state and local affairs.

As a young member of Congress during the McCarthy era, Richard Nixon participated in the search for communists inside the U.S. government. Nixon brought this distrust of the left into the White House with him in 1968, adding such prominent liberals as future presidential hopeful John Kerry, entertainer Barbra Streisand, and television executive Norman Lear to his "enemies list" because he viewed them as anti-American.

Nixon won the 1968 election by promising to end the excesses of the Great Society. He also pledged to end hostilities in Vietnam, cut back on the government's intrusions into business, and promote law and order. Nixon's victory was facilitated by deep divisions in the Democratic Party, which was torn over the twin issues of race and Vietnam. During the campaign, Robert Kennedy, the leader among Democratic contenders, was assassinated. Two months later, the Democratic convention erupted in chaos amid violent protests on the streets outside the convention hall. Vice President Hubert Humphrey was chosen to head the ticket, even though he had not won a single primary. Large numbers of southern Democrats opted to vote for the third-party ticket of Alabama governor and white supremacist George Wallace.

Nixon failed to deliver on his campaign promises. Instead, this representative of the New Right expanded government's regulatory and bureaucratic powers. Rather than ending the war in Vietnam, the Nixon administration accelerated hostilities by bombing Laos and Cambodia. Conservatives were also dismayed when Nixon expanded the global role of the United States. Nixon's paranoia about liberal conspiracies led to the bugging of Democratic headquarters at the Watergate Hotel during his 1972 reelection campaign and to his eventual resignation in August 1974. Despite his failures as president, Nixon's recognition of the "silent majority" reenergized American conservatism.

LATE 20th-CENTURY CONSERVATISM

Anti-liberalism reached its peak with the election of ultraconservative Ronald Reagan in 1980. When the Reagan team spread out across the United States to identify hot-button issues to garner support for the Republican ticket, they found that many Americans wanted respect for their religious views on political issues. The Republicans were subsequently successful in winning the support of the Religious Right and in unfairly identifying the Democratic Party as anti-Christian, even though a self-avowed born-again Christian resided in the White House. Republicans also endorsed the idea of family values, arguing that a return to traditional values would solve the major problems in American society.

Democrats accused Republicans of being out of step with the changing social mores and of trampling on individual liberties in their rush to project their own values onto the rest of the country. Liberals cited Republican efforts to outlaw abortion, reactionary views on segregation, backlash against women's rights, and narrowing of rights of the accused as justification for their attacks. While liberals insisted that morality cannot be legislated, conservatives have consistently attempted to do so. Reagan's attempts included the appointment of conservative Supreme Court justices who were predicted to overturn *Roe v. Wade* (410 U.S. 113), the 1973 decision that legalized abortion.

In addition to religious and moral issues, the Reagan team promised to curb inflation by reining in government spending. But by the end of Reagan's second term, the national debt had surpassed $2 trillion, and the trade deficit had expanded to more than $15 billion a month. Reagan also promised to restore American confidence by expanding the military to meet the looming threat of communism. The right claimed that Reagan was instrumental in bringing about the end of communism, citing his refusal to meet with Soviet leaders and his support of anti-communist regimes in developing nations in South America and Africa. Liberals, however, pointed out that communism's demise could be attributed to economic and political factors within the Soviet Union.

They also noted that Reagan's military expansion had not only contributed to the astronomical deficit but had taken funds away from social programs, leaving the poorest Americans to bear a disproportionate share of the financial burden of Reaganomics, or "voodoo economics," as candidate George H. W. Bush called it in 1980. The Iran-Contra scandal and reports that Reagan was unaware of what was going on in the White House and of actions taken in his name diminished his reputation. However, his popularity rebounded in 1994 after his family announced that he was suffering from Alzheimer's disease, and he was eulogized as one of the greatest presidents in history when he died in 2004.

After failing to win the Republican nomination in 1980, moderate Republican Bush aligned himself with Reagan in order to use the vice presidency as a vehicle to the White House. He was successful in 1988, partly because he promised, "Read my lips, no new taxes." When Bush was forced to eat his words, many conservatives turned against him. He never found a comfortable fit with his far-right supporters. As a result of inconsistent policy decisions, Bush pleased neither wing of the Republican Party. This disharmony among the Republicans, coupled with a failing economy, returned the Democrats to the White House with the election of Bill Clinton in 1992 for the first time since the 1976 election of Carter.

The right won a resounding victory in the 1994 off-year elections, placing ultraconservative Newt Gingrich in position as speaker of the house. Gingrich announced that the right had been successful in negotiating a Contract with America, which was designed to undo all vestiges of liberalism in the United States, regardless of the fact that a Democrat sat in the White House. Liberals claimed that anti-liberalism was behind the impeachment of Clinton in 1999. The general public refused to buy the conservative attempt to oust the president, and Clinton's approval ratings remained around 70 percent throughout the process. Perhaps because of the fear of a backlash at the polls, the Senate acquitted Clinton of charges of perjury and obstruction of justice.

According to Gingrich, the Contract with America called for reforming Congress by removing congressional exemptions to public laws; auditing Congress for waste, fraud, and abuse; cutting the number of congressional committees and staff by one-third; limiting the terms of committee chairs; banning the use of proxy votes in committee proceedings; opening committee meetings to the public; requiring a three-fifths vote to raise taxes; and guaranteeing honest accounting reports and zero-base line budgeting.

Congressional Republicans also announced that in order to promote conservative causes, they would introduce a number of new bills. The Fiscal Responsibility Act was aimed at securing a balanced budget amendment and a legislative line-item veto. The Taking Back Our Streets Act called for stronger truth-in-sentencing guidelines, good-faith exemptions to the exclusionary rule, effective death penalty provisions for federal crimes, and further drastic cuts to liberal social programs. The Personal Responsibility Act tightened the availability of welfare by targeting teenage mothers and setting limits on welfare eligibility. The Family Reinforcement Act strengthened child support enforcement, provided tax incentive, for adoption, set up tax exemptions for elder care, and targeted child pornographers. The American Dream Restoration Act provided tax breaks for middle-class Americans, including a child-care tax credit, the repeal of the marriage tax

penalty, and the creation of the American Dream Savings program.

The National Security Restoration Act was aimed at removing all American troops from United Nations command and upgrading national security. The Senior Citizen Fairness Act repealed the 1993 tax increases on social security benefits and created tax incentives for private long-term elder care. The Job Creation and Wage Enhancement Act cut capital gains taxes, established incentives for small businesses, and called for the creation of new jobs and increased wages. The Common Sense Legal Reform Act was aimed at protecting business interests by limiting damage awards in product liability cases. The Citizen Legislature Act ostensibly established term limits on power-hungry career politicians, but liberals claimed that it was an attempt to remove powerful Democrats from their strongholds. The "conservative revolution" never completely recovered from Gingrich's resignation as speaker in 1998 amid accusations of adultery and campaign finance irregularities.

CONTEMPORARY CONSERVATISM

While some members of the right felt vindicated by the election of George W. Bush in the hotly contested election of 2000, the son was no more able to satisfy the divergent wings of the Republican Party than his father had been, leading many conservatives to question his conservative credentials. One leading conservative newspaper dubbed him a "flexible" conservative. Most of the criticism of the Bush II presidency came, as expected, from the left. Former Democratic Vice President Al Gore, who had opposed Bush in the 2000 election, insisted that the War on Terrorism had allowed Bush to perpetrate "the worst strategic fiasco in the history of the United States." In addition to partisan sniping, many Americans on both the right and left were concerned with the fact that Bush's unrestrained spending and the War on Terrorism and Iraq had resulted in a deficit of over $500 billion.

Some scholars and writers believe that the pull toward the far right in American politics has resulted in the rise of what they call "paleo-conservatives" who endorse the conservatism of the old rather than the new right, leading to the popularity of maverick presidential candidates such as Ross Perot, who in 1992 drew support from Americans who felt alienated from both the Republican and Democratic parties. The paleo-conservatives reject neoconservatism generally and free trade agreements and modern wars in particular.

Dissatisfaction with the two-party system also led to the growth of the Libertarian Party as a viable third party. While libertarians are conservative by nature, many are more in line with the Democratic Party on social issues because they reject governmental attempts to regulate individual choices. The true libertarian accepts no governmental authority over individuals at all and would like to abolish income tax, police departments, courts, and other established institutions. Libertarians believe that governments are more likely than individuals to interfere with liberties, and they contend that any kind of offensive violence is aggressive, unjust, and criminal.

The beginning of the 21st century saw the chasm between conservatives and liberals in the United States widening rapidly. The Republican Party maintained its preference for free trade, limited government, and law and order and continued its attacks on abortion, women, civil rights, criminal rights, and homosexual rights. However, many mainstream newspapers continued to insist that the right had lost sight of the realities of American politics.

In *The Right Nation: Conservative Power in America*, two British journalists suggested that the center in America has shifted toward the right as conservative think tanks, businesses, interest groups, and media outlets have successfully promoted arch-conservatism as mainstream political thought. Some critics of this arch-conservatism argue that the co-option of the right by self-interested billionaires has threatened democracy.

In a thought-provoking editorial on May 24, 2004, the liberal *New York Times* suggested that Senators John McCain (R-AZ), Susan Collins (R-ME), Olympia Snowe (R-ME), and Lincoln Chafee (R-RI) are the only moderate Republicans left in the Senate. Since each house of Congress has veto power over the other when passing legislation, the ideology of senatorial Republicans has far-reaching implications for the country as a whole as well as for the Republican Party. Contemporary liberals insist that because Americans tend to cluster around the middle of the political spectrum, efforts to pull the country too far to either the left or right have often backfired. They speak from experience, since they are well aware that the leftist policies of the New Deal and the Great Society paved the way for contemporary conservatism and the swing to the right.

SEE ALSO

Volume 1 Left: United States; Liberalism; Socialism; Roosevelt, Franklin D.; New Deal; Johnson, Lyndon B.; Democratic Party.

Volume 2 Right: Republican Party; Libertarianism; Reagan, Ronald; Roosevelt, Theodore; Lincoln, Abraham; New Right.

BIBLIOGRAPHY

Norman P. Barry, *The New Right* (Croom Helm, 1987); David Brock, *The Republican Noise Machine and How It Corrupts Democracy* (Crown, 2004); Ralph Adams Brown, *The Presidency of John Adams* (University of Kansas Press, 1975); Edmund Burke, *Reflections on the Revolution in France* (Stanford University Press, 2001); "Edmund Burke," http://cepa.newschool.edu (May 2004); George W. Carey, ed., *Freedom and Virtue: The Conservative/Libertarian Debate* (Intercollegiate Studies Institute, 1998); David Donald, *Lincoln Reconsidered: Essays on the Civil War Era* (Vintage, 2001); Samuel Francis, "Beautiful Losers: Why Conservatism Failed," Gregory Schneider, *Conservatism in America Since 1930: A Reader* (New York University Press, 2003); Milton Friedman, *Capitalism and Freedom* (University of Chicago Press, 1962); Bruce Frohner, "Burkean Virtue and the Conservative Good Life," *Perspectives on Political Science* (Winter 1994); Newt Gingrich, "Contract with America," Gregory Schneider, ed., *Conservatism in America Since 1930: A Reader* (New York University Press, 2003); Lewis L. Gould, *1968: The Election that Changed America* (Ivan R. Dee, 1968); David G. Green, *The New Right: The Counter-Revolution in Political, Economic, and Social Thought* (Wheat Sheaf Books, 1987); "The Greening of John McCain," *New York Times* (May 24, 2004); William R. Harbour, *The Foundations of Conservative Thought: An Anglo-American Tradition in Perspective* (University of Notre Dame Press, 1982); F.A. Hayek, "Why I Am Not a Conservative," Gregory Schneider, ed., *Conservatism in America Since 1930: A Reader* (New York University Press, 2003); F.A. Hayek, *Road to Serfdom* (University of Chicago Press, 1994); Bob Herbert, "A Speech That's No Joke," *New York Times* (May 28, 2004); Ted Honderich, *Conservatism* (Westview, 1991); Russell Kirk, *Ten Exemplary Conservatives* (Heritage Foundation, 1986); Isaac Kramnick, ed., *The Portable Edmund Burke* (Penguin, 1999); Irving Kristol, "What Is Neo-Conservatism?" David L. Bender and Bruno Leone, eds., *The Political Spectrum* (Greenhven, 1981); Andrew Loxley and Gary Thomas, "Neo-conservatives, Neo-liberals, the New Left and Inclusion: Stirring the Pot," *Cambridge Journal of Education* (v.31/3, 2001); James Madison, "Federalist Number 10," www.constitution.org (May 2004); B.J. McCormick, *Hayek and the Keynesian Avalanche* (St. Martin's Press, 1992); John Micklethwait and Adrian Wooldridge, *The Right Nation: Conservative Power in America* (Penguin, 2004); Malcolm Moos, *The Republicans: A History of Their Party* (Random House, 1956); Hall Morris, "The American Whig Party, 1834–56," http://odur.let.rug.nl (May 2004); Robert Nisbet,

Conservatism: Dream and Reality (Oxford University Press, 1986); Eric Rauchway, *Murdering McKinley: The Making of Theodore Roosevelt's America* (Hill and Wang, 2003); Murray N. Rothbard, "What Is Libertarianism," Gregory Schneider, ed., *Conservatism in America since 1930: A Reader* (New York University Press, 2003); Joseph Scotchie, *Revolt from the Heartland: The Struggle for an Authentic Conservatism* (Transaction Publishers, 2002); Dennis Wainstock, *The Turning Point: The 1968 United States Presidential Campaign* (McFarland Publishers, 1988).

ELIZABETH PURDY, PH.D.
INDEPENDENT SCHOLAR

Ustashe

THE USTASHE OR USTASHA, meaning "uprising" in the Croat language, was a movement in World War II that traced its origins back to the melting pot of the Austrian Empire (Austria-Hungary) in the 19th century. The decisive defeat of the Austrian armies of Emperor Franz Josef by the Prussians in 1866 gave a boost to the nationalities of the empire to seek their own destiny. The Magyars of Hungary had already rebelled in 1848 under Lajos Kossuth, but their aspirations were crushed by the Russian troops in 1849.

In 1867, the Austrian Empire officially became the dual monarchy of Austria-Hungary, thus giving the Magyars of Hungary parity with the largely German population of Austria. However, the other ethnic groups of the empire also desired recognition. Among these were the Croats, who formed the Party of Right, under Ante Starcevic. Other groups, usually linked together as the Yugoslavs, the South Slavs, also sought self-determination and eventually found common cause with the Party of Right.

While the dual monarchy lasted, the Party of Right endured as a splinter group, which did, however, gain one significant recruit: Ante Pavelic. Pavelic lived in the neighboring Balkan area known as Bosnia-Herzegovina. However, the beginning of World War I changed the entire political equation when the long-standing quarrel between the dual monarchy and the neighboring kingdom of Serbia led to the assassination of Franz Josef's heir, the Archduke Franz Ferdinand, on June 28, 1914, in Sarajevo. As with the German and Russian empires, Austria-Hungary did not survive the war. The last Hapsburg ruler, Emperor Karl, abdicated in 1918.

After the Treaty of Versailles in 1919 ending World War I, Croatia became part of the kingdom of Croats, Serbs, and Slovenes, to be better known as the kingdom of Yugoslavia—the South Slavs. However, the formation of the new state did not contain the growing nationalism of the ethnic groups. Indeed, according to John Lukacs, the later Yugoslav leader Josip Broz Tito would reminisce about the tranquil days of the dual monarchy. The Party of Right was eclipsed by the Croatian Peasant Party, the creation of the brothers Stjepan and Ante Radic. The hostility among the ethnic groups was shown on June 28, 1928—the 14th anniversary of the death of the Archduke Franz Ferdinand—when Ante Radic was shot and mortally wounded by a Montenegrin deputy on the floor of the Parliament in the Yugoslav capital of Belgrade.

On January 6, 1929, King Alexander took over personal rule of Yugoslavia, further alienating his kingdom's ethnic groups. Ante Pavelic sought refuge abroad, where he established links with the Macedonian terror group Internal Macedonian Revolutionary Organization (IMRO). It was at a time when rightists were becoming inflamed by the oratory of the Italian poet Gabriele D'Annunzio, whose September 1919 march with his black-shirted followers on the city of Fiume would later inspire Italy's Duce, Benito Mussolini. Once in power, Mussolini took a personal view of events in the Balkans; indeed, his precipitous attack on Albania would eventually lead to Adolf Hitler's invasion of Yugoslavia in April 1941. As part of his dream of reestablishing a Pax Romana (invoking a "Roman Peace") in the Balkans, he became patron of the movement that Pavelic founded, the Ustasha. Indeed, Mussolini is alleged to have been behind the Ustasha assassination of King Alexander on October 7, 1934, at Marseilles in France. The French Foreign Minister Louis Barthou was slain with the king. When French authorities demanded the extradition of Pavelic and his lieutenant, Eugen Kvaternik, from Italy, the Duce refused, as Cali Ruchala noted in the "The Pavelic Papers."

Pavelic and his Ustasha movement gained power in their native Croatia following the invasion of Yugoslavia by Hitler on April 6, 1941. The reigning King Peter II of Yugoslavia was toppled and on April 10, the independent state of Croatia was proclaimed by Eugen Kvaternik's father, Slavko. Ante Pavelic ruled the new state as its *poglavnik*, or "leader." During the German occupation of Yugoslavia in World War II, the Ustasha, like similar fascist groups in Romania and Hungary, supported the Germans. Concentration camps were founded and run by the Ustasha armed militia. Under Hitler's influence, Pavelic followed the same anti-Semitic policy of the German Nazi Party. According to the Simon Wiesenthal Center in Vienna, Austria, some 30,000 Jews, 29,000 gypsies, and 600,000 Serbs died in the camps.

Pavelic's militia also fought on the German side against the Red Partisans of Josip Broz Tito, once a sergeant in the Yugoslav Army. As such, they also fought, although to the north, on the same side as the Bosnian Muslims who were recruited into the German SS by the exiled Grand Mufti of Jerusalem, al-Hajj al-Husseini. In 1944, with Tito's Partisans on the offensive and the Russian Red Army entering the Balkans, Pavelic and his associates became some of the many who used the escape network out of the Balkans and into South America. As British Prime Minister Winston S. Churchill and others began to see that Soviet Premier Josef Stalin was bent on conquering—not liberating from the Germans—the countries of Eastern and Central Europe, political opinion in Washington, D.C.; London, England; and the Vatican in Rome, Italy, began to turn in favor of Pavelic. He was sheltered in the papal hideaway of Pope Pius XII at Castelgandolfo in Italy. Father Krunoslav Dragonovic was instrumental in orchestrating the escape of Pavelic to South America. There, he acted as security adviser to Argentine President Juan Domingo Peron, and survived an assassination attempt in Argentina in 1957. Afterward, he fled to Spain, where he died on December 28, 1959. During the second disintegration of Yugoslavia, after 1992, the blood feuds of the Serbs, Muslims, and Croats were a direct result of the savage fighting that had taken place in the Balkans during World War II. And once again, as in 1941, an independent state of Croatia was established.

SEE ALSO

Volume 1 Left: Hitler, Adolf; Germany; Titoism.
Volume 2 Right: Germany; Totalitarianism.

BIBLIOGRAPHY

Cali Ruchala, "The Pavelic Papers: From the Ratline to the Firing Line," www.pavelicpapers.com (May 2004); Mark Aarons and John Loftus, *Unholy Alliance: The Vaticans, The Nazis, and the Swiss Banks* (St. Martin's Press, 1998); John Loftus, *The Belarus Secret* (Knopf, 1982); Kenneth Macksey, *Military Errors of World War Two* (Castle Books, 2002); Tom Bower, *The Paperclip Conspiracy* (Michael Joseph Publishers, 1987).

JOHN F. MURPHY, JR.
AMERICAN MILITARY UNIVERSITY

The Right

Vietnam War

THE VIETNAM WAR WAS a protracted struggle between communist North Vietnam and noncommunist South Vietnam and an important aspect of the global struggle between the communist world and the free world, known as the Cold War. Direct involvement of the naval and military forces of the United States of America failed to stem the communist onslaught.

Before World War II, Vietnam had been a French colony. In 1945, the French attempted to regain control of their former colony of Vietnam. French efforts were opposed by a broad range of interests; particularly effective were the communists in the country, led by nationalist and communist leader Ho Chi Minh. Viet Minh and French forces fought a long war that resulted in French defeat at Dien Bien Phu in 1954. Shortly thereafter, the French withdrew and the Geneva Conference agreements partitioned Vietnam into a communist North and noncommunist South.

Communist efforts to gain control of all of Vietnam continued. In the early 1960s, the United States began to provide military aid to South Vietnam. U.S. policy makers hoped to stop the spread of communism in Southeast Asia, continuing the policy of containment employed by the United States since the early days of the Cold War. Also, conservatives in particular feared that if South Vietnam fell, then the rest of Indo-

china would come under communist dominion as well, a school of thought known as the Domino Theory. At first, aid came in the form of U.S. Special Forces advisors; after the passage of the Gulf of Tonkin resolution by the U.S. Senate, the United States deployed vastly larger numbers of troops to Vietnam. By 1969, the number of American troops in Vietnam would exceed half a million.

U.S. forces fought against both North Vietnamese regular army (NVA) units and communist guerrillas in the south, known as the Viet Cong. Despite overwhelming technological superiority U.S. forces rarely initiated contact with their opponents. Although U.S. forces managed to kill a relatively high number of their enemy for every soldier lost, the United States lacked both an overall strategy and the will to win the war. Bloody, indecisive fighting demoralized the home front and left soldiers with low morale. The replacement policy adopted by the U.S. military proved corrosive to soldiers' morale as well. Rather than deploy large units in which soldiers had long trained and served together, the United States transferred replacements individually into units already in theater, which all too often prevented the development of unit cohesion so necessary to success in battle.

Because of Cold War constraints, fearing that China or the Soviet Union might become directly involved in the war, U.S. troops did not invade and conquer North Vietnam, the most direct road to victory. Instead, most of the war on the ground was fought in the South. An air campaign known as "Rolling Thunder" did strike targets in North Vietnam, but as part of a strategy of graduated pressure, in which U.S. policymakers sought to "communicate" with their opponents rather than inflict upon North Vietnam the level of destruction visited upon Germany and Japan by U.S. air power in World War II. Conservatives decried this kind of approach as ineffective. In addition, America rejected conservative leadership at home and in the global struggle against communism, by choosing liberal Democrat Lyndon Johnson as president in 1964 rather than Republican Barry Goldwater.

The Tet Offensive, launched on the Vietnamese lunar new year in 1968, saw an all out attack on U.S. forces across South Vietnam, even briefly capturing the American embassy in Saigon, the capital of South Vietnam. Although American forces achieved a victory by destroying Viet Cong forces, the United States perceived the victory as a defeat, in part because of its treatment in the press.

With the election of Richard Nixon in 1968, the war began to change character. Nixon ordered the bombing of communist bases in Cambodia and then ordered the invasion of Cambodia in 1970. The Nixon administration implemented a policy known as "Vietnamization," which aimed to strengthen the South Vietnamese military and reduce the numbers of American troops in Vietnam. North Vietnam launched a massive invasion of the South in 1972, but its offensive failed. The following year, on January 27, 1973, the Paris Peace Accords provided for an end to the hostilities, and the preservation of a noncommunist South Vietnam. Because of President Nixon's resignation as a result of the Watergate scandal and congressional and national exhaustion and disgust with the war, the United States did not aggressively enforce the agreement, despite the sacrifice of over 50,000 Americans in defense of South Vietnam. South Vietnam fell to a North Vietnamese invasion in 1975.

American involvement in Vietnam spawned a massive anti-war movement at home. Organizations such as Students for a Democratic Society couched opposition to the war in anti-imperialist and revolutionary terms, and were allied with the rise of the New Left and the counterculture, two movements that specifically sought to undermine traditional American values. Whether intentional or not, a vigorous and vocal antiwar movement helped serve as a fifth column in the United States, undermining the war effort and helping to turn the people of South Vietnam into communist slaves. Conservative celebrities such as John Wayne spoke out in favor of fighting communism and defending the American way of life, but they were all too often marginalized in the contemporary media and in the historical record.

The Vietnam War caused fractures in American society that lasted long after the final American withdrawal from Vietnam in 1975. Although launched under the Democratic administrations of John Kennedy and Lyndon Johnson, support for the war became identified with conservatism and with the Republican Party. This was particularly true after the implementation of Nixon's "Southern Strategy," designed to pull traditionally Democratic southern white males away from the Democratic Party. American defeat in Vietnam caused lasting damage to American credibility in foreign policy and to the institutions of the American military; only during the administration of Ronald Reagan would the United States recover from that damage. The war also caused a rift in the country between those who thought the war was morally wrong and those who supported American efforts to save Southeast Asia from communism.

SEE ALSO

Volume 1 Left: United States; Kennedy, John F.; Johnson, Lyndon B.
Volume 2 Right: Nixon, Richard M.; United States.

BIBLIOGRAPHY

Stanley Karnow, *Vietnam: A History* (Viking, 1991); Henry Kissinger, *Ending the Vietnam War* (Simon & Schuster, 2003); H.R. McMaster, *Dereliction of Duty* (HarperCollins, 1997); Robert S. McNamara, *In Retrospect: The Tragedy and Lessons of Vietnam* (Times Books, 1995); Lewis Sorley, *A Better War* (Harcourt Brace, 1999); Harry G. Summers, *On Strategy: A Critical Analysis of the Vietnam War* (Presidio, 1982).

MITCHELL MCNAYLOR
OUR LADY OF THE LAKE COLLEGE

Washington, Booker T. (1856–1915)

BOOKER T. WASHINGTON WAS one of the most influential African-Americans of the late 19th and early

20th centuries. He was an educator, school administrator, orator, race spokesperson, author, and high-profile public figure. His driving desire was to help black Americans acquire better living conditions, which he attempted to do through appeasing powerful white elites. A masterful communicator, he was given rare positive attention for blacks of his era, but critics believed he was simply a pawn to white interests.

Washington's two autobiographies, the classic *Up from Slavery* and the lesser-known *The Story of My Life and Work*, tell of the hardships of his youth, although some critics think these might have been exaggerated to emphasize his personal success story. Washington was born in abject poverty in Virginia to a slave mother; he was, in fact, born into slavery. He never knew the identity of his father, but it is likely that this person was a white man from a nearby plantation. Since he was not given a last name, he picked the name Washington, a name also later adopted by his half brother. When the Civil War ended, Washington's mother and stepfather moved the family to Malden, West Virginia, where the youngster ended up working in the local salt mines. He managed to attend school despite long hours at work, and at age 16, he attended Hampton Normal and Agricultural Institute in Virginia. At Hampton, he became very influenced by the person who would become his mentor and father figure, General Samuel Chapman Armstrong, the institute's white headmaster. It was Armstrong's belief that the solution to black inequality was the provision of strict vocational education that included character-building principles. It was Armstrong's stringent training that Washington would emulate and promote throughout his career, and that would later culminate into the so-called Tuskegee idea.

After finishing his education, Washington taught for a few years at a West Virginia school and later attended a year in seminary. Shortly afterward, Armstrong offered his young protégé a teaching position at Hampton, a position he held for two years. He then moved to Alabama on Armstrong's recommendation to start the Tuskegee Normal and Industrial Institute. Washington was skillful in dealing with wealthy northern whites to obtain funding for the school and in placating those in the local positions of authority. Many whites saw his emphasis on agricultural and industrial vocational training as a way of keeping blacks in lower-level jobs; however, it was seen by many blacks as a way to gain some degree of financial independence.

At Tuskegee, the male students received vocational and industrial training in areas such as carpentry, masonry, blacksmithing, as well as agricultural training in livestock and crop production, and the females received instruction in cooking and sewing. For all students, Washington stressed character-building with an emphasis on hygiene and etiquette. He also required attendance at religious services, though these services were nondenominational in nature.

In 1895, Washington gained fame when he gave a powerful oration, referred to as the Atlanta Compromise. In this speech, he recommended that northern business owners, southern leaders, and African Americans enter into a situation that would benefit all groups. He suggested that blacks and whites should remain segregated and that blacks should embark on vocational careers, not challenging the powerful white power structure. Many people, especially whites, saw this as an acceptable agreement while blacks believed that for the present at least, they needed to assume a subservient role and not force radical change.

Critics, including the African American social reformer W.E.B. Du Bois, who believed in academic education for blacks and in radical social change, saw this strategy as unacceptable. The dispute between these two leaders became one of the preeminent theoretical dialogues of the early 20th century.

Washington continued to promote his ideas, and his power and influence increased substantially. He had numerous followers, both black and white, and many powerful business and political leaders, including the U.S. president, who requested his input on social and political matters. As his popularity grew, he came under fire from groups that were critical of the "Tuskegee machine." He was paranoid of groups such as Du Bois's small but energetic Niagara Movement, and even sent spies into these organizations to keep him abreast of their activities. He opposed the principles of the National Association for the Advancement of Colored People (NAACP) and the pan-African movement, a Black Nationalist movement that advocated racial segregation and a reinforcement of ties of black people to Africa, organizations that were also affiliated with Du Bois.

Despite the negative attention from critics, Washington's charismatic appeal made him a figure popular with many black and white Americans. He was awarded an honorary master's degree from Harvard University (the first such degree awarded to a black person), had a family dinner with President Theodore Roosevelt, and was even entertained by Britain's Queen Victoria. In time, his ideas of slow and nonradical change began to loose luster with many black Americans, and his power began to diminish in his last years. When, in 1915, the most powerful African American of his era passed away, there was no other person to fulfill the legacy of Booker T. Washington and the Tuskegee model of racial advancement.

In the context of African American opinion in the first decade of the 20th century, Washington's accommodationist philosophy was seen as conservative, while the doctrines of the Niagara Movement and the NAACP, which stood for civil rights and a racially egalitarian society, were viewed as radical or left. Washington recommended that African Americans seek to gradually build a place in capitalist society through hard work and acceptance of the status quo, classic values of 19th- and early 20th-century conservatism.

SEE ALSO

Volume 1 Left: Du Bois, W.E.B.; Niagara Movement.
Volume 2 Right: Black Separatism; Black Nationalism; Pan-Africanism.

BIBLIOGRAPHY

Louis R. Harland, Booker T. Washington: The Making of a Black Leader (Oxford University Press, 1972); Louis R. Harland, Booker T. Washington in Perspective: Essays of Louis R. Harland (University of Mississippi Press, 1988); E.L. Thornbrough, ed., Booker T. Washington (Prentice-Hall, 1969); Booker T. Washington, Up from Slavery (Penguin, 1986).

LEONARD A. STEVERSON, PH.D.
SOUTH GEORGIA COLLEGE

Welfare and Poverty

GOVERNMENTAL PUBLIC support programs are as old as the Babylonian Empire—when Hammurabi made protection of widows and orphans part of his celebrated code. In 1601, Queen Elizabeth I attempted to identify and assist England's needy. However, the first government-supported welfare program in modern times came in Germany in 1883 with legislation that introduced accident insurance for workers. The idea spread to surrounding countries, and soon laws required health insurance as well as retirement pensions. By the 1930s, state-supported welfare programs in some form existed in most of the world, spurred by socialist theory and the increasing power of labor unions.

Simultaneously with the advent of the Industrial Revolution, influential capitalists had opposed such

concepts, saying government assistance violates the concepts of laissez-faire economics—or state nonintervention—and that social programs financed by tax revenues are counterproductive. The debate continues. At one extreme is the left's Marx-Engels utopia, never quite accomplished, in which private ownership of property is abolished and all citizens are provided for according to their need, with everyone working diligently and energetically to the best of their ability for the good of a democratic and egalitarian society. At the other end of the spectrum is the right's philosophy that human nature precludes such a socialist ideal and that the resulting "nanny state" eliminates incentives for achievement. Without discomfort, says this argument, there is no need for innovation or even effort: "Necessity is the mother of invention."

In America, President Franklin D. Roosevelt's Social Security Act of 1935 extended federally funded pensions to the elderly as well as payments to help the blind and children without working parents. In 1965 during President Lyndon Johnson's ambitious War on Poverty, Medicare medical insurance was given to the aged. Medicaid was created for low-income families.

But not everyone believed the programs were effective or a good idea. "Here in California," then-Governor Ronald Reagan said in 1971, "nearly a million children are growing up in the stultifying atmosphere of programs that reward people for not working, programs that separate families and doom these children to repeat the cycle in their own adulthood." Reagan voiced disdain for bureaucrats whose job performance, he said, was gauged by how many new clients they had enrolled for the public dole: "They go out and actually recruit people to be on welfare."

"The irony is that misguided welfare programs instituted in the name of compassion have actually helped turn a shrinking problem into a national tragedy," Reagan said in a radio address to the nation on February 15, 1986, and continued:

> From the 1950s on, poverty in America was declining. American society, an opportunity society, was doing its wonders. Economic growth was providing a ladder for millions to climb up out of poverty and into prosperity. In 1964 the famous War on Poverty was declared and a funny thing happened. Poverty, as measured by dependency, stopped shrinking and then actually began to grow worse. I guess you could say, poverty won the war. Poverty won in part because instead of helping the poor, government programs ruptured the bonds holding poor families

together. Perhaps the most insidious effect of welfare is its usurpation of the role of provider. In states where payments are highest, for instance, public assistance for a single mother can amount to much more than the usable income of a minimum wage job. In other words, it can pay for her to quit work. Many families are eligible for substantially higher benefits when the father is not present. What must it do to a man to know that his own children will be better off if he is never legally recognized as their father?

Under existing welfare rules, a teenage girl who becomes pregnant can make herself eligible for welfare benefits that will set her up in an apartment of her own, provide medical care, and feed and clothe her. She only has to fulfill one condition—not marry or identify the father. Obviously something is desperately wrong with our welfare system. With only about half of what is now spent on welfare, we could give enough money to every impoverished man, woman, and child to lift them above the poverty line. Instead, we spend vast amounts on a system that perpetuates poverty.

Reagan and those who shared his views charged that such key programs as Aid to Families with Dependent Children discriminated against the destitute by encouraging their children to engage in sexual promiscuity—indeed, young unwed mothers' government checks increased every time they had another baby. "Welfare needs a purpose," Reagan said. "To provide for the needy, of course, but more than that, to salvage these, our fellow citizens, to make them self-sustaining and, as quickly as possible, independent of welfare. We should measure welfare's success by how many people leave welfare, not by how many are added."

His position was that engaging people in constructive work had to be the cornerstone of successful welfare reform. Work, Reagan believed, carries with it economic and social benefits for both the individual and the society; not only do employed citizens contribute resources to the economy rather than consume them, but they also enhance their own responsibility, independence, and freedom.

He and critics of federal programs in years since state that the federal bureaucracy continues to grow and the national deficit continues to rise, yet America's poverty rate in 2002 was higher than in 1965. Furthermore, the benefits have not been enjoyed by the poor, they say. Instead, the vast majority of the federal welfare budget went not to the poor, but to the bureaucrats—the department managers, clerks, lawyers, paper-shufflers, politicians, and consultants—all running a maze of overlapping and often redundant programs.

The entire welfare bureaucracy should be shut down, says Llewellyn H. Rockwell of the Mises Institute, a conservative think tank. "If it had the will," Rockwell writes, "Congress could kill the redistributionist monster, the Welfare State, that's consumed at least $5 trillion in wealth since the Great Society. How? Cut anywhere and everywhere, abolish whole agencies, and return the $350 billion saved from next year's spending to the taxpayers in the form of a tax cut of the same size."

Why would Rockwell propose such measures? "Americans hate welfare," he writes. "It violates cultural strictures against the free ride, taxes the productive to reward the unproductive, perpetuates poverty and makes the government strong and the people weak. If this destruction were ended immediately, masses of people would be reintroduced to the work ethic, taxpayers would have more money in their pockets and voluntary spending on private charity would go up. Until then, poverty, sloth, and bureaucracy will continue to be subsidized by you and me."

Indeed, welfare "cannot be reformed," agrees conservative author Michael Tanner. "Instead, it is time to end it and to finally realize that state-supported efforts to cope with poverty are doomed to failure." Private charities, Tanner says, "are far more effective than government welfare programs." They can individualize their approaches and "target the specific problems that are holding people in poverty. They are also much better at targeting assistance to those who need it most and at getting the most benefit out of every dollar."

Tanner continues:

The bureaucracy of the welfare state keeps millions in poverty," charges the Freedom Activist Network, one of many internet groups in which arguments against the Welfare State are exchanged. The welfare bureaucracy "crushes private charity, stifles the development of medicines and new forms of health care, and steals the opportunity for millions of America's poorest workers to invest their money. And it is growing every year, eating more and more of every person's income.

The welfare state is really a monopoly of the bureaucracy over everything it touches. By taking our money for aid to the poor, the bureaucracy makes it impossible for this money to be donated to a charity that may be more in line with our values. By taking money for social security it becomes impossible for the poorest members of society to invest this money themselves—with much higher returns.

But beyond that, the bureaucracy of the welfare state causes structural problems to society and economy that usually end up hurting the most disadvantaged members of society. Welfare to the poor has caused millions to be imprisoned in structural poverty and dependence on the state. It has also had a demonstrated negative effect on the development of the minority entrepreneurial economy. Social security has caused millions of dollars to be taken out of circulation from the economy where it would have bolstered the development of life-affirming technology. What's more, it,has caused national dependence on a bureaucracy that is going bankrupt. And the regulation associated with the health care industry and its entitlement programs have led to soaring medical costs for millions of people and a stifling of development of innovations in medical care.

Are such statements merely the mad ravings of right-wing fanatics who care nothing about the poor?

"In our generosity we have created a system of handouts, a second-rate set of social services which damages and demeans its recipients, and destroys any semblance of human dignity that they have managed to retain through their adversity. In the long run, welfare payments solve nothing, for the giver or receiver; free Americans deserve the chance to be fully self-supporting." Who said that? Senator Robert F. Kennedy, while campaigning for the Democratic presidential nomination. The welfare state, said Kennedy shortly before his assassination, has "largely failed as an anti-poverty weapon."

In the midst of the Great Depression, Franklin Roosevelt—whom conservatives consider the founder of the welfare state—issued a stern warning when he introduced the concept of Aid to Dependent Children: "Continued dependence on relief induces a spiritual and moral disintegration fundamentally destructive to the national fiber. To dole out relief in this way is to administer a narcotic, a subtle destroyer of the human spirit."

In stark contrast, Reagan resisted calls from fellow conservatives to end all welfare programs, saying that aid should not be taken from people who really need and deserve it, such as the truly impoverished elderly, blind, and disabled. What he sought, Reagan said, was to take people off the welfare rolls who didn't belong

there—and to interrupt the generational cycle that had made a monthly welfare check a way of life for millions.

Reagan said that Roosevelt's New Deal and Johnson's Great Society had the best of intentions but failed—that between 1965 and 1980, the federal budget jumped to roughly "five times what it had been," while the federal deficit grew to 53 times as much and the amount of money doled out under various federal entitlement programs quadrupled to almost $300 billion a year. Meanwhile, America's poverty rate in 2002 was higher than in 1965.

"Along the way," said Reagan, "a lot of the decision-making authority traditionally exercised at the grass-roots level of America was transported to Washington"—with decision-making taken away from the communities and states, to be centralized in Washington, D.C. Much worse than that, he said, was the narcotic of giveaway programs that "sapped the human spirit, diminished the incentive of people to work, destroyed families, and produced an increase in female and child poverty, deteriorating schools, and disintegrating neighborhoods."

According to Reagan, "the liberals had had their turn at bat in the 1960s and they had struck out." But the question of welfare and welfare reform is not always philosophically black and white, nor within the perceived boundaries of the right opposing welfare or the left promoting it.

In Toronto, Canada, in 1995, Liberal Party leader Lyn McLeod campaigned in Ontario's provincial elections with promises to cut 12,000 government jobs, get tough on welfare cheaters, and force welfare recipients to take training courses or face a reduction in benefits. She also called for the privatization of billions of dollars in government public works projects. The irony was that this was virtually the identical position of her Conservative opponent, Mike Harris, only a year earlier. He had released a plan for Ontario that would have cut 13,000 government jobs, toughened penalties for welfare cheaters, and forced welfare recipients to take job training courses. His plan had been panned by McLeod's Liberals as heartless and unworkable.

Such a blurring of right vs. left culminated in 1996 when U.S. President Bill Clinton, a Democrat on the left side of the aisle, signed into law massive welfare reforms pushed through by such conservatives as Newt Gingrich and Dick Armey. The new laws brought in the most sweeping changes in social policy since Roosevelt's New Deal.

The changes represented a dramatic reversal of U.S. welfare policy, including requirements that at least half of the population then on welfare would be working or training for work by 2002, the granting of lump sums to states to run their own welfare and work programs, an end to federal guaranteed cash assistance for poor children, a five-year limit per lifetime on most benefits, the requirement that the head of every welfare family get some sort of job or lose all benefits, and the establishment of stricter Supplemental Security Income eligibility standards.

SEE ALSO

Volume 1 Left: Liberalism; Democratic Party; Johnson, Lyndon B.; Roosevelt, Franklin D.; Welfare and Poverty.
Volume 2 Right: Conservatism; Republican Party; Reagan, Ronald.

BIBLIOGRAPHY

Gary Andres, "Counterfeit Compassion," *National Review* (June 4, 2004); Lou Cannon, *President Reagan: The Role of a Lifetime* (Simon and Schuster, 1991); Steven Hayward, "Welfare Reform: Another Win for the Gipper," Ashbrook Center for Public Affairs 1999, www.ashbrook.org (June 2004); Edmund Morris, *Dutch: A Memoir of Ronald Reagan* (Random House, 1999); Charles Murray, *Losing Ground: American Social Policy 1950–80* (Basic Books, 1984); Marvin Olasky, *The Tragedy of American Compassion* (Basic Books, 1992); Llewellyn H. Rockwell, Jr., "Welfare Reform: True and False," *The Free Market* (Mises Institute, December 1995); "Social Welfare," *The Columbia Encyclopedia* (Columbia University Press, 2004); Michael Tanner, *The End of Welfare: Fighting Poverty in the Civil Society* (Cato Institute, 1996); Walter I. Trattner, *From Poor Law to Welfare State: A History of Social Welfare in America* (Simon and Schuster, 1974); Catharine Tunnacliffe, ed., "Who's Tory Now? Everybody," *Toronto Weekly Eye* (April 6, 1995).

ROB KERBY
INDEPENDENT SCHOLAR

White Citizens' Councils

BY VARIOUS NAMES, this white supremacist organization persisted from the mid-1950s through the beginning of the 21st century. In the aftermath of the *Brown* decision of May 1954 (beginning desegregation in American schools), Robert B. Patterson of Indianola, Mississippi, formed the first Citizens' Council in Greenwood, Mississippi, on July 11, 1954. The council's primary goal was the preservation of segregation regardless of *Brown*. In 1956, Patterson wrote that to him integration was one with totalitarianism, communism, and darkness while segregation was American freedom of association, states' rights, and the survival of the white race. The councils were to be the more civilized alternative to the Ku Klux Klan (KKK), what the journalist Hodding Carter referred to as the "uptown KKK." The Mississippi legislature censured Carter in 1955 for his criticism of the councils.

During the year after the desegregation decision by the U.S. Supreme Court, hundreds of Citizens' Councils arose in the south. A November Citizens' Council pamphlet read in part, "The Citizens' Council is the South's answer to the mongrelizers. We will not be integrated! We are proud of our white blood and our white heritage of six centuries. ... If we are bigoted, prejudiced, un-American etc., so were George Washington, Thomas Jefferson, Abraham Lincoln, and other illustrious forebears who believed in segregation. We choose the old paths of our founding fathers and refuse to appease anyone, even the internationalists."

The council examined local candidates for elections to make sure they were correct on the issues of African American voting and integration. The local council also coordinated economic pressures brought to ensure conformity. The typical council had only one or two dozen regular members, and most of them came from the community's elite: businessmen, politicians, lawyers, and large-scale planters. They eschewed the titles and structure so popular with the Klans. There were no Klaverns and Kleagles in the Citizens' Councils. A council had four committees. Information and education set out to ensure that both white and black understood the virtues of segregation and the perils of integration. The other committees were membership and finance, legal, and political. The councils met briefly in informal settings. They established their plans and set the next meeting. They used no letterhead, no literature, no offices, nothing tangible to identify them.

The councils left the violence and the recruitment of lower-class whites to the Klans. The Citizens' Councils looked down on the KKK, but the KKK was convenient for handling the weightier tasks: cross burnings, demonstrations, and other racists actions. Within 13 months, in August 1955, there were over 60,000 members in 253 councils, not solely in the south. A year later, there were councils in 30 states. The state councils affiliated under the Citizens' Councils of America (CCA) were committed to racial separation and states' rights in matters of education, marriage, public morals, and general good order. The CCA was formed in New Orleans, Louisiana, in 1956 at a convention representing Alabama, Arkansas, Florida, Georgia, Louisiana, Mississippi, North Carolina, South Carolina, Tennessee, Texas (which had the Oklahoma proxy), and Virginia. The CCA was headquartered first at Greenwood and later at Jackson, Mississippi. The executive secretary was Robert B. Patterson.

The CCA maintained the same goals that the individual councils had. It was committed to Americanism, the preservation of segregation, and states' rights. It used organized protests and vigorous local intervention in federal attempts to desegregate. It also worked nationally against the influence of the National Association for the Advancement of Colored People (NAACP), which it frequently accused of being a communist front. It called for a stronger right to "freedom of personal association." It maintained its distinctiveness as a mainstream and modern urban organization in contrast to the rural and backward KKK. Still, its party line was that African Americans were mentally deficient. At its peak, the council had the power in Mississippi to elect a white supremacist governor, Ross Barnett, after he promised to maintain white supremacy. But the segregationist effort seemed only a rearguard action. The councils could not stem the civil rights movement.

As African Americans gained politically in the 1960s and 1970s, the politics of racism became impractical. Local politicians shifted to accommodate the new power base or found themselves involuntarily retired. The CCA faded. By the 1970s, it was ready to disband, having fallen from its peak of 250,000. Many of the unrepentant members moved into the ultraconservative John Birch Society and other right-wing organizations. Then, in the more conservative 1980s, racism and the CCA reemerged as the Council of Conservative Citizens (CCC), with Patterson editing *The Citizen Informer*.

The CCC couched its racism in code—complaining about "special preferences," "giveaway programs," and "third-generation welfare mothers." The CCC had affinities for other groups such as the Birchers, and was able to recruit workers in the names of old racists such as George Wallace and Lester Maddox. The CCC found a hospitable reception in the south by political leaders. A sometime visitor to CCC meetings was Republican Senator Trent Lott, former Senate majority leader, and the CCC claimed nearly three dozen state legislators and hosted at least two gubernatorial candidates. The CCC used the old CCA mailing lists. It took the mainstream conservative line on gun control, immigration, and affirmative action, but it also held the racist positions of the older white supremacist organization. By 1999, although strong in Mississippi, Alabama, and Georgia, the CCC had only 15,000 members in 20 states.

SEE ALSO

Volume 1 Left: Desegregation; Malcolm X; King, Martin Luther, Jr.; Electorate, African American.
Volume 2 Right: Klu Klux Klan; Shockley, William B.; Segregation.

BIBLIOGRAPHY

Anti-Defamation League, "Extremism in America; Council of Conservative Citizens," www.adl.org (March 2004); John Cannon, "Racism and the Republican Party," www.another-perspective.org (March 2004); Council of Conservative Citizens, "The True Voice of the American Right," www.cofcc.org (March 2004); "History of the Modern Civil Rights Movement," *Jackson Sun* (2003); Neil R. McMillen, *The Citizens' Council: Organized Resistance to the Second Reconstruction, 1954–64* (University of Illinois Press, 1971); Jared Taylor, *Paved with Good Intentions: The Failure of Race Relations in Contemporary America* (Carroll & Graf, 1992); George Thayer, *The Farther Shores of Politics: The American Political Fringe Today* (Simon & Schuster, 1967).

JOHN BARNHILL, PH.D.
INDEPENDENT SCHOLAR

Will, George F. (1941–)

GEORGE F. WILL, journalist, political analyst, and amateur baseball historian, was born in Champaign, Illinois. During his youth, Will developed his lifelong love of baseball and also became interested in American politics. First, he studied at Trinity College in Hartford, Connecticut, before attending Magdalene College, part of Oxford University, and then Princeton University, obtaining a master's and a doctorate degree. Upon completion of his extensive schooling, Will became a professor at Michigan State University, where he taught political philosophy. Soon after, he took a similar position at the University of Toronto. After some time, Will decided to delve into the political scene and worked as a staff member on the U.S. Senate.

Finally, his career path led him into the realm of political commentary and journalism, where he has become one of the most widely recognized and widely read writers and commentators in the United States. With publications appearing in more than 450 newspapers, a biweekly column for *Newsweek* magazine, and television appearances as a commentator on ABC News and ABC's *This Week*, Will has arguably become one of the most influential conservative political analysts on the pundit circuit.

In his analysis, Will is well-known for his conservative yet mainstream approach to American politics and culture. Due to his popularity, numerous collections of Will's columns have been combined and published, such as *The Morning After: American Successes and Excesses, 1981–1986*; *The Pursuit of Virtue and Other Tory Notions*; and *The Pursuit of Happiness and Other Sobering Thoughts*.

Excessive government spending and multiterm members of Congress are regular targets of criticism by Will, who advocates more moderate spending proposals and term limits, allowing for a government in which democracy is closer to the people and more reflective of their needs. With term limits, Will believes that more members of Congress will be interested less in their careers and more in fighting for the good of the U.S. citizenry.

Even though Will mostly advocates on behalf of these conservative positions, he does not seek to weaken the central government or the Republican Party. Instead, he advocates that conservatives move away from their emphasis on self-interest and individualism and start pursuing interests that have the good of all citizens in mind. Utilizing this approach, Will has composed powerful columns and writings against poor decisions in government spending, government inefficiency, and the gridlock that results from squabbles between political parties.

Will does not concentrate all of his writings or commentaries simply on the subject of politics and government, but also writes extensively about the environment, advertising, and ethics. Baseball is by far his passion. Will's works on baseball include *Bunts: Curt Flood, Camden Yards, Pete Rose, and Other Reflections on Baseball* and *Men at Work: The Craft of Baseball*, which topped the U.S. bestseller list for over two months in 1990.

Will's efforts have not gone without recognition. In 1976, he won the Pulitzer Prize for commentary as a result of his newspaper columns, and has won many other awards for his *Newsweek* columns. These awards include being a finalist in the 1979 National Magazine Awards, recipient of the 1978 National Headliners Award, winner of the 1980 Silurian Award for editorials, and recipient of the 1985 Best Writer Award given by the *Washington Journalism Review*. More recently, in 1997, the *National Journal* named Will one of the top 25 most influential journalists in Washington, D.C.

SEE ALSO
Volume 1 Left: Media Bias, Left; Democratic Party.
Volume 2 Right: Media Bias, Right; Republican Party.

BIBLIOGRAPHY
"George F. Will Biography," www.washingtonpost.com (March 2004); "George Will," www. townhall.com/columnists (March 2004); David Plotz, "George F. Will: He Can't Be Walter Lippmann; Maybe He Should Be Baseball Commissioner," slate.msn.com (March 2004).

ARTHUR HOLST, PH.D.
WIDENER UNIVERSITY

Willkie, Wendell (1892–1944)

WENDELL WILLKIE WAS the Republican candidate for president in 1940 and the only major-party candidate of the 20th century who never held elective office. He lost to President Franklin D. Roosevelt, who became the only person ever to win a third term. Lewis Wendell Willkie was born in Elwood, Indiana, fourth of the six children of German immigrants Herman and Henrietta (Trisch) Willkie. Henrietta Willkie was the first woman admitted to practice law in Indiana. The Willkies stressed education for their children; their personal library contained nearly 6,000 volumes. Willkie graduated from the Culver Military Academy and went on to the University of Indiana.

His political enemies later alleged that he was a rabble-rousing socialist in his college days, but in reality, he merely recruited students to attend an economics class on Marxism. He graduated in 1913 and received a law degree from the university in 1916. In breaks from his law study, he worked briefly as a high school teacher in Kansas and as a chemistry technician in Puerto Rico. He briefly joined his father's law practice, but in 1917, he entered the U.S. Army, and it was there that his first and middle names became reversed.

Willkie declined to correct this clerical error—probably because he had always gone by his middle name anyway—and went by Wendell L. Willkie for the rest of his life. In 1918, he married Edith Wilk, a librarian. Willkie was hired as a staff lawyer at Firestone & Co., the tire manufacturer. According to legend, the head of the company, Harvey Firestone, learned of Willkie's left-of-center politics (although by this time Willkie had eschewed socialism and was a mere Democrat) and wished him well, but told him that no Democrat would ever amount to anything.

He did pro bono work fighting the Ku Klux Klan in a series of prosecutions in the 1920s. Willkie went to New York in 1929 as senior counsel for Commonwealth & Southern, a utility holding company. He became president of the company in 1933. It was this connection and the New Deal that turned him into a Republican; Roosevelt's Tennessee Valley Authority (TVA) had condemned some of the company's assets in that state. This led to a long legal battle that went to the U.S. Supreme Court. Willkie voted Republican for the first time in 1936. Despite all his success in business, Willkie preferred to dress and maintain the lifestyle of an Indiana farmer.

Willkie left the company in 1940 to assume the Republican presidential nomination. He was a serious "dark horse" candidate, running an amateurish campaign composed of many unseasoned advisers. The Republicans nominated him on the sixth ballot. Willkie ran a campaign that was populist by the standards of the 1920s, but his populism was no match for the New Deal activism of Roosevelt. Roosevelt won a third term decisively. Willkie pledged to act as the "loyal opposition" over the next four years. That time span found the United States involved in war, and Roosevelt found a role for Willkie as an unofficial envoy on the international scene. Willkie started to build a 1944 presidential campaign on the theme of international cooperation, but his campaign was a failure. Nevertheless, his 1942 book, *One World*, was a bestseller and its ideas influenced the founding of the United Nations after the war.

Willkie died unexpectedly in New York on October 8, 1944, from coronary thrombosis. He was buried at East Hill Cemetery in Rushville, Indiana. His grave is marked by a huge cross inscribed with excerpts from his writing.

SEE ALSO

Volume 1 Left: Roosevelt, Franklin D.; New Deal; Democratic Party.
Volume 2 Right: Republican Party.

BIBLIOGRAPHY

Ellsworth Barnard, *Wendell Willkie: A Fighter for Freedom* (Northern Michigan University Press, 1966); Mary Earhart Dillon, *Wendell Willkie* (Lippincott, 1952); Steve Neal, *Dark Horse: A Biography of Wendell Willkie* (University Press of Kansas, 1989).

TONY L. HILL
MASSACHUSETTS INSTITUTE OF TECHNOLOGY

The Right

X-Z

Xenophobia

XENOPHOBIA IS the discrimination or hatred of foreigners, either defined as outsiders or as those who are in effect part of one's own society but perceived as incommensurably different from the majority. The most pointed, long-term, and widely documented case of xenophobia in history is that of anti-Semitism.

Cavalier explanations of the dynamics of anti-Semitism, in particular, and xenophobia, in general, that treat them as results of innate characteristics of a culture or as a consequence of economic malaise in the larger society are not only insufficient, but are also conducive to the normalization and perpetuation of the hatred and violence commonly associated with such exclusionary practices. Instead, the problem of hatred of foreigners and intolerance for ethnic, religious, racial, and cultural difference has to be put into the larger context of the dominant culture in a society.

There are, and historically have always been, observable links among migration, racism, discrimination, ethnoreligious stereotyping and xenophobia. Increased ethnoreligious and racial diversity in societies makes the reality of the heterogeneity of human communities ever more obvious. In the absence of political, legal, social, and economic mechanisms to ensure mutual respect and to mediate relations across differences, xenophobia and various related forms of racism become manifest. Interestingly, xenophobia has been a chronic problem that ailed and still ails many of the advanced Western societies rather than just the so-called third or developing world. Particularly among European societies that received substantial numbers of immigrants since World War II, both as workers and as asylum-seekers, migrants have become the very targets in internal disputes about national identity. This is indicative of the fact that with the mass elimination and departure of Jews from Europe, xenophobia did not necessarily loosen its grip across the continent.

In general, however, xenophobia is by no means an exclusively European phenomenon. In the age of nation-states as opposed to empires, as societies grapple with changing realities of their multiethnic, multireligious or multiracial makeup, there has been a marked increase in discrimination and violence directed against migrants, refugees, and others who are categorized as different in many parts of the world.

Although racism and xenophobia are distinct phenomena, they often overlap. While racism generally implies distinctions made based on difference in physical characteristics, such as skin coloration, hair type, facial features, etc., xenophobia denotes behavior-based discrimination arising from the perception that the other is foreign to, or originates from outside, a given community or nation. Racism is an ideological construct that assigns a certain race or ethnoreligious group to a position of power over others on the basis of physical and cultural attributes as well as economic wealth. Generally, it involves the establishment and sustenance of hierarchical relations where the self-appointed superior race exercises domination and control over others.

Xenophobia, on the other hand, refers to attitudes, prejudices, and behavior that reject, exclude, and often vilify its targets, based on the perception that they are outsiders or foreigners to the community, society, or nation. In many cases, it is difficult to distinguish between racism and xenophobia, as they exhibit similar motivations for exclusive and demeaning behavior and, in particular, violence. However, there is one element that may be missing in racism that is often manifest in xenophobia: religious identity. Manifestations of xenophobia occur not only against people with different physical characteristics, but also against those who look and act similar or even have shared ancestry but who are believed to be of a different and assumedly dangerous religious conviction.

Even in markedly racist societies with a history of legalized ethnoracial discrimination, it is possible to take measures to alleviate or at least curtail the culture of the hatred of the foreigner or those deemed as essentially unassimilable and different.

The Roll Back Xenophobia campaign, established in South Africa in 1998, is a succinct example of how political determination can produce such a widely visible and national effort to confront rising incidences of xenophobic hostility and violence. The campaign began as a joint initiative among national and international institutions: the South African Human Rights Commission, the National Consortium on Refugee Affairs, and the office of the United Nations High Commissioner for Refugees. It emphasized broad, multifaceted, and synchronized activities by government, civil society, and communications media, including information campaigns by national and local government, retraining of the police force, strengthening of labor rights protections for migrant workers, sensitization of trade union officials, awareness raising by religious organizations, reinstitution of codes of conduct for civil servants, as well as the inclusion of migration- and refugee-related concerns in primary, secondary, and tertiary education. These measures, in the larger context of the anti-apartheid movement in the country, are suggestive of a tidal wave of change in South African society in terms of how they try to deal with differences in their own midst.

Another example that points in a positive direction in terms of societal and state action for the elimination of xenophobia is the reforms made in Canadian immigration policies since the 1980s. Immigration and refugee policy discussions are rarely separable from general debates on racial, interethnic, and interreligious relations within host communities. Therefore, strong border controls are often advocated as necessary for the acceptance of racial, cultural, or ethnoreligious minorities by the dominant culture.

Still, while immigration historically discriminated among nationalities, ethnicities, and religions, it is possible to reform them to alleviate at least the overt marks of racism or xenophobia. Racism and xenophobia are clearly observable when procedures target particular ethnoreligious groups for exclusion, lack transparency, or when the immigration process itself is made so grueling for select groups that it can act as a deterrent. With regard to refugee applications, for instance, the systematic use of detention often singles out specific nationalities or ethnoreligious groups more than others. Meanwhile, many refugees have no choice other than to use irregular entry, increasingly at the hands of smugglers. Thus, they risk the fact that their irregular migration will be held against them in their asylum claim, and if they gain entry, they will be set apart from other minorities and mainstream society.

The establishment of the European Monitoring Centre on Racism and Xenophobia (EUMC) in Vienna, Austria, by the European Union in 1997 is an important initiative to develop a regional institutional mechanism to monitor and counter xenophobia. This organization not only keeps records of the growing amount of racial and xenophobic discrimination and violence directed toward migrants and other ethnoreligious minorities in Europe. It also attempts to identify and highlight examples of good practice in challenging and remedying these practices. While the center is funded by the European Union, it is an independent body and aims to be unbiased and transparent in its activities. Its mandate states that it gives no greater priority to European nationals than it does to migrants and refugees.

The global nature of violence and discrimination against migrants, refugees, and settled ethnoreligious minorities is increasingly acknowledged by the post-World War II international human rights regime, as well. There is not yet wide acceptance by signatory states of the basic rights and entitlements recognized for unauthorized migrants in the United Nations 1990 International Convention for the Protection of the Rights of All Migrant Workers and Members of Their Families. However, under the International Labor Organization conventions related to migrant workers, undocumented migrants are entitled to equal treatment in respect to rights arising out of present or past employment regarding remuneration, social security, and other benefits as well as trade union membership and exercise of trade union rights. Nonetheless, the undocumented remain especially vulnerable to abuse as they are generally unwilling or unable to seek protection from authorities when confronted with xenophobic violence.

SEE ALSO

Volume 1 Left: Immigration; Desegregation.
Volume 2 Right: Immigration Restriction.

BIBLIOGRAPHY

Hannah Arendt, The Origins of Totalitarianism: Part I: Anti-Semitism (Harcourt & Brace, 1951); Robert S. Wistrich, Demonizing the Other (Harwood Publishers, 1999); Stephen Castles and Mark Miller, The Age of Migration (Guildford Press, 1993).

NERGIS CANEFE
YORK UNIVERSITY, CANADA

Yahweh ben Yahweh (1935–)

YAHWEH BEN YAHWEH is the leader of an indigenous African American supremacy cult, the Nation of Yahweh, which has also been called the Yahwehists, Nation of Israel, Tribe of Judah, Temple of Love, and other names. The cult has been linked with numerous murders. Yahweh ben Yahweh ("God, son of God" in Hebrew) has taken his name from the sacred Tetragram of the Hebrew scriptures to combine theological elements of the "sacred name movements" with Black Hebrew Israeli movements. His teachings contain an emphasis on black nationalism and supremacy, resembling the views of Marcus Garvey and Elijah Muhammad. In the 1980s, Yahweh ben Yahweh wrote a number of books, You Are Not a Nigger!, Our True History, The World's Best Kept Secret, and Yahweh God of Gods. He taught that blacks were the true Jews and that God and Jesus were black. Claiming that he had been chosen to lead blacks to a new promised land of Israel, he urged his followers to give up their "slave names" and to adopt Hebrew names.

Yahweh ben Yahweh was born Hulon Mitchell, Jr., on October 27, 1935, at Kingfisher, Oklahoma, the son of a fundamentalist preacher and the eldest of 15 children. After high school, Mitchell served in the U.S. Air Force. He eventually earned a bachelor's degree from Philips University and a master's degree in economics from Atlanta University. After he joined the Black Muslims, Mitchell changed his name to Hulon X. He rose to a position of leadership. He ran a Black Muslim mosque in Atlanta, Georgia, but left the Black Muslims in the early 1970s under charges of misappropriating funds and sexual improprieties with underaged Muslim women. He then became a Christian radio evangelist before moving to Miami, Florida.

In 1979, Mitchell arrived in Miami, Florida, where he became the spiritual leader and founder of the Nation of Yahweh. Eventually his religious organization attracted followers in over 1,300 cities and towns, amassing assets in excess of $50 to $250 million, although the exact figures are not known and may be much lower.

In 1981, Yahweh opened his first Temple in Liberty City (Miami, Florida). Soon the Nation of Yahweh flourished attracting members and establishing numerous black-owned businesses. They were able to turn slums and drug neighborhoods into centers of production painted white and serviced by a fleet of vehicles, all white. They also established temples in most major American cities. For this they gained the praise of local political leaders.

However, in the late 1980s, Miami police traced the bodies of murdered whites, usually street people—the homeless, derelicts, and drug addicts—back to the Yahwehists. In addition, some blacks who had spoken against the religion were murdered. Many of the murders were very gruesome, involving mutilation and decapitation of the victims. In 1992, Yahweh ben Yahweh and 16 of his followers were tried in federal court on conspiracy and racketeering charges for murder, arson, and extortion. Yahweh and six followers were convicted of conspiracy but not murder, largely on the testimony of Robert Rozier, a former National Football League player and cult member. Trial in state court for murder led to an acquittal.

After Yahweh ben Yahweh's conviction, the Nation of Yahweh was nearly invisible until April and May 2001, when two Yahwehist conferences met in Montreal, Canada. A thousand followers, wearing white robes and turbans, gathered to hear that Yahweh ben Yahweh was a persecuted messiah wrongly hanged on a cross of judicial persecution. They also pledged loyalty to Yahweh ben Yahweh as "the son of God." On September 25, 2001, Yahweh ben Yahweh was released from Ray Brook federal prison in New York on parole, having served 11 years of his 18-year sentence. He then returned to Miami. The latest 2004 report on Yahweh ben Yahweh said he was creating a new ministry to protect the free-exercise rights of Black Muslims, African American Jehovah's Witnesses, Sikhs, Rastafarians, and other marginalized groups.

Because Yahweh and his followers established a reputation for rehabilitating many homeless individuals and providing aid to the poor, he received the public support of Miami Mayor Xavier Suarez. Partly because of his standing with the local Democratic party, state attorney general Janet Reno refused to bring state charges against Yahweh in some 15 or more gruesome murders and numerous allegations of sexual abuse of minors. As a consequence, federal authorities, using the Racketeer Influenced and Corrupt Organization (RICO) statute, conducted raids and brought the indictment against Yahweh and six of his followers, the first time the RICO statute had been used against a religious organization.

SEE ALSO

Volume 1 Left: Malcolm X; Civil Rights.
Volume 2 Right: Black Separatism; Black Nationalism.

BIBLIOGRAPHY

Sydney P. Freedberg, *Brother Love: Murder, Money and a Messiah Ben Yahweh* (Pantheon Books, 1994); Sydney P. Freedberg and Donna Gehrke, "Black 'Messiah' Leads Followers into Legal Trouble," *Washington Post* (July 2, 1991); Pete Hamill, "Mr. God Raises Hell," *Esquire* (v.115/34, 1991); Terry E. Johnson, "Yahweh Way," *Newsweek* (v.108/31, 1986); Charles Leerhsen, "Busting the Prince of Love," *Newsweek* (v.116/45, 1990); *United States v. Yahweh Ben Yahweh*, 792 Federal Supplement 104 (S.D. Fla. 1992); *United States v. Robert Louis Beasley, et al* (Yahweh ben Yahweh), Eleventh Circuit Court of Appeals (January 5, 1996).

ANDREW J. WASKEY, PH.D.
DALTON STATE UNIVERSITY

Zionism

ZIONISM IS THE political philosophy that follows the idea of a national homeland for the Jewish people. Eventually, Zionists believe that this should be in Palestine. Although in 70 C.E., the Roman General Titus, son of the Emperor Vespasian, had driven the Jews out of Jerusalem, many still remained in the country. Flavius Josephus, the historian of the Jewish war, wrote that "the army had no more people to slay or to plunder, because there remained none to be objects of their fury." Defying the Romans, Palestine remained throughout the Middle Ages and the Ottoman Empire (1453–1918) a vibrant center for Jewish religious thought. This was especially true in the region around Safed, which in the 17th century would become the center for study of the Kabala, Jewish mysticism.

However, the destruction of Jerusalem marked the great diaspora, or expansion of the Jews throughout the world: too many, it should be noted, first as Roman slaves. Over the centuries, in Germany, the Russian Empire, and Poland, the Jews would develop an extremely intense sense of themselves and their mission in the world as the Chosen People, who would prepare an unsanctified world for the coming of the Meshiach, the Messiah. The most zealous school in Germany and Eastern Europe was the Hasidim, who practiced an ecstatic Judaism that seemed out of place to their more conservative landsmen, or brethren. Gershom Sholem, in *Major Trends in Jewish Mysticism* notes that "the Hasidim were intimately connected with the whole of Jewish life and the religious interests of the common folk." As such, the Hasid community served a conserving interest by binding together the Jews they served in the face of sometimes barbaric persecution, the dreaded pogroms.

At the same time, the Jewish people developed a language of their own, Yiddish, which became a cultural bond among them against the oppressive outer society. Within the ghettoes to which they were confined, Yiddish led to a bountiful courage, whose most visible light was Sholom Aleichem, the origin of the famous musical about Teyve, *Fiddler on the Roof.* As Miriam Weinstein wrote in *Yiddish: A Nation of Words,* "Yiddish was accruing a consciousness of its past and a mission for its future."

While Yiddish was helping to develop a strong sense of community within East European Jewry with its spirit of *Yiddishkeit,* another movement grew up that was able to take advantage of the closely knit society that Hasidism and *Yiddishkeit* had created. This was Zionism, which to the history of Jewry was politically what the Hasids were to religion and Yiddish to culture. While Moses Hess had been writing along Zionist lines in the 1840s, it was the conservative Theodore Herzl who, in 1897, made Zionism a political force with an impact in both Europe and America. To pious Jews, Zionism represented the great *aliyah*, or "coming together" of the Jewish people in their ancestral home of Palestine centuries after Titus's barbaric diaspora.

Actual Jewish resettlement of the Holy Land began in 1855 with land purchases from Arab landowners by Sir Moses Montefiore. From Hess would come the socialism that would become the force that bound Zionism together—yet also enforced something of a rigidity into this philosophy. Walter Laqueur wrote in *A History of Zionism: From the French Revolution to the Establishment of the State of Israel* that "for Hess, a Jewish state was not anend in itself but a means toward the just social order to which all peoples aspired." Jewish settlement continued in the Holy Land throughout the end of the 19th century and early 20th, either with the backing of noted Zionists like the Rothschild family or individually as refugees from the pogroms that convulsed the traditional Jewish areas of settlement in Eastern Europe and Russia. While much land was purchased from the Arabs, other marauding Arabs, like Bedouin tribesmen, would attack the growing Jewish agricultural settlements.

From the 1880s, according to Yigael Allon in *The Making of Israel's Army*, "local 'cells' had begun to be formed for self-defense against robbery, theft, marauding, murder, and rape." Groups like the Bar Giora, which was founded in Jaffa in September 1907, attempted to organize the Jews into a Semitic version of the settlers on the old American frontier, who would plow their fields, a musket tied to their arm. These organized groups of Jewish militia were called *hashomer*, or "watchmen." In 1903, grave massacres in Kishinev in Russia had hastened the pace of Jewish immigration. According to Laqueur, a serious proposal was made at the Seventh Zionist Congress in 1905 about an alternative plan to establish a Jewish homeland in Uganda. However, "it was, not unexpected, abandoned."

When the Ottoman Empire, which ruled Palestine, entered World War I on the side of Germany in the fall of 1914, the Jews made a great effort to enlist the help of the Western Allies, especially Great Britain, in their hope for settlement in Palestine—the Holy Land. Their orderly settlements stood out in positive contrast to the Arab villages among them and the marauding Arab tribes who pillaged both. Vladimir Jabotinsky, one of the more militant Zionists, believed that it was necessary to demonstrate a Jewish commitment to the war effort by fighting on the British side. Chaim Weizmann, who had become the leading Zionist figure since the death of Herzl in 1904, also favored cooperating in the Allied cause. After much negotiation, John Patterson,

the famed killer of the man-eating lions of Tsavo in Kenya, agreed to lead the Zionist Mule Corps.

Although at first relegated to carrying out supply duties during the disastrous Gallipoli campaign against the Turks in 1915, the Mule Corps became the nucleus of the Jewish Legion, which Patterson led with British General Edmund Allenby in his conquest of the Holy Land in 1917 and 1918. Mounting diplomatic and military pressure caused the British government to issue the famed Balfour Declaration. After a cabinet meeting on October 31, 1917, Lord Balfour wrote would become known as the Balfour Declaration: "His Majesty's government views with favour the establishment in Palestine of a national home for the Jewish people."

After the war, Jewish settlement, the great *aliyah*, came to Palestine in far greater numbers. The Muslim Grand Mufti of Jerusalem, Haj Amin al-Husseini spread dissension among the Palestine Arabs. Resentment led to serious sporadic rioting between Arabs and Jews during the 1920s; two of the worst were in Jerusalem in 1920 and 1929.

Arab opposition to the organized and careful Jewish *aliya* became more acute in the 1930s, when Jewish immigration to Palestine was affected by the ruthless anti-Semitism of Adolf Hitler's Nazi dictatorship in Germany. This brought the Jewish problem of Nazi persecution into direct conflict with Lord Passfield's White Paper, which had in October 1930 criticized Jewish settlement. By 1936, the Grand Mufti had fanned Arab hostility in the great revolt, which would continue to the eve of the Second World War in 1939.

Once again, in World War II, the Jews sought to legitimize their claims to a Palestinian homeland through participation in the war against Nazi Germany and its allies. This was in great distinction to the Arabs, some of whom, like the Grand Mufti, openly supported Hitler. In 1944 and 1945, the Jewish Brigade fought bravely with the British in Italy. By this time, the Jewish Agency, led by David Ben-Gurion, a veteran of the old Jewish Legion in World War I, had become the de facto government for the Yishuv, the Jewish Community, in Palestine, which the British ruled as a mandate territory from the League of Nations since after World War I. The Holocaust of World War II, in which some 6 million European Jews died in the Nazi *Endlosung*, the Final Solution to the Jewish Question, swung world opinion behind Jewish aspirations. On November 29, 1947, the United Nations General Assembly voted, with the United States and the Soviet Union the main supporters, to partition Palestine to create the Jewish homeland promised 30 years earlier in the Balfour Declaration.

On May 14, 1948, David Ben-Gurion proclaimed the birth of the sovereign state of Israel.

SEE ALSO

Volume 1 Left: Zionism; Israel; Middle East.
Volume 2 Right: Israel; Middle East.

BIBLIOGRAPHY

The Works of Josephus, William Whiston, trans. (Hendrickson, 1987); Yigael Allon, *The Making of Israel's Army* (Bantam, 1970); Leo Rosten, *The New Joys of Yiddish* (Random House, 2001); Gershom Sholem, *Major Trends in Jewish Mysticism* (Schocken Books, 1974); Miriam Weinstein, *Yiddish: A Nation in Words* (Ballantine, 2001); Walter Laqueur, *A History of Zionism: From the French Revolution to the Establishment of the State of Israel* (MJF, 1972); Charles D. Smith, *Palestine and the Arab-Israeli Conflict* (St. Martin's Press, 1992); David J. Goldberg, *To the Promised Land: A History of Zionist Thought from Its Origins to the Modern State of Israel* (Penguin, 1996).

JOHN F. MURPHY, JR.
AMERICAN MILITARY UNIVERSITY

Resource Guide

These resources are provided for further study on left and right politics. For more resources by topic, please see each article's bibliography.

Books

Ahlstrom, S., *A Religious History of the American People* (Yale University Press, 1972)

Aitken, Jonathan, *Nixon: A Life* (Regnery, 1994)

Alteras, Isaac, *Eisenhower and Israel: U.S.-Israeli Relations* (University Press of Florida, 1993)

Andrain, Charles F., and Apter, David E., *Political Protest and Social Change* (New York University Press, 1995)

Appleby, Joyce, *Thomas Jefferson* (Henry Holt, 2003)

Aptheker, Herbert, *Abolitionism: A Revolutionary Movement* (Twayne Publishers, 1989)

Aristotle, *Politics*, Jowett, Benjamin trans. (Dover, 2000)

Arnold, Scott N., *The Philosophy and Economics of Market Socialism* (Oxford University Press, 1994)

Avrich, Paul, *Sacco and Vanzetti: The Anarchist Background* (Princeton University Press, 1991)

Barry, Norman P., *The New Right* (Croom Helm, 1987)

Baughman, James L., *Henry R. Luce and the Rise of the American News Media* (Macmillan, 1987)

Baum, Lawrence, *The Supreme Court* (Congressional Quarterly , 1995)

Bennett, David H., *Demagogues in the Depression: American Radicals and the Union Party* (Rutgers University Press, 1969)

Biles, Roger, *A New Deal for the American People* (Northern Illinois University Press, 1991)

Birch, Anthony H., *The British System of Government* (Routledge, 1998)

Biskupic, Joan, and Witt, Elder, *The Supreme Court and Individual Rights* (Congressional Quarterly, 1997)

Brands, H.W., *Woodrow Wilson* (Times Books, 2003)

Brimelow, Peter, *Alien Nation: Common Sense about America's Immigration Disaster* (Random House, 1995)

Bruchey, Stuart, *Enterprise: The Dynamic Economy of a Free People* (Harvard University Press, 1990)

Buchholz, Todd, *New Ideas from Dead Economists* (Penguin, 2003)

Bullock, Alan, *Hitler: A Study in Tyranny* (Harper and Row, 1962)

Caro, Robert A., *The Years of Lyndon Johnson* (Knopf, 1982–2002)

Chalmers, David Mark, *Hooded Americanism: The History of the Ku Klux Klan* (New Viewpoints, 1981)

Coakley, John, ed., *Politics in the Republic of Ireland* (Routledge, 1999)

Coicaud, Jean-Marc, *Globalization of Human Rights* (United Nations, 2003)

Collins, Rodnell, *Seventh Child: A Family Memoir of Malcolm X* (Carol Publishing Group, 1998)

Conley, Richard S., *The Presidency, Congress and Divided Government* (Texas A&M University Press, 2003)

Cook, Chris, and Taylor, Ian, *The Labour Party: An Introduction to Its History, Structure and Politics* (Longman, 1980)

Cope, Kevin L., *John Locke Revisited* (Twayne, 1999)

Dahl, Robert Alan, *On Democracy* (Yale University Press, 2000)

Dell, Christopher, *Lincoln and the War Democrat* (Fairleigh Dickinson University Press, 1975)

Douglass, Frederick, *My Bondage and My Freedom* (University of Illinois Press, 1987)

Dunkerley, James, *Power in the Isthmus: A Political History of Modern Central America* (Verso, 1988)

Engels, Friedrich, *The Principles of Communism* (Monthly Review Press, 1952 reprint)

Finch, Minnie, *The NAACP: Its Fight for Justice* (Scarecrow Press, 1981)

Fletcher, George P., *Our Secret Constitution: How Lincoln Redefined American Democracy* (Oxford University Press, 2001)

Foerstel, Herbert N., *Freedom of Information and the Right to Know* (Greenwood Press, 1999)

Freedberg, Sydney P., *Brother Love: Murder, Money and a Messiah Ben Yahweh* (Pantheon Books, 1994)

Freidel, Frank, *The Splendid Little War [Spanish-American War]* (Dell, 1964)

Friedan, Betty, *The Feminine Mystique* (W.W. Norton, 1963)

Fromkin, David, *A Peace to End All Peace* (Avon Books, 1989)

Gorbachev, Mikhail, *Perestroika: New Thinking for Our Country and the World* (Harper & Row, 1988)

Gordon, Ann D., ed., *The Selected Papers of Elizabeth Cady Stanton and Susan B. Anthony* (Rutgers University Press, 1998)

Habermas, Jürgen, *The New Conservatism: Cultural Criticism and the Historian's Debate* (MIT Press, 1989)

Hair, William Ivy, *The Kingfish and His Realm: Life and Times of Huey Long* (Louisiana State University Press, 1997)

Harding, Vincent, *Martin Luther King: The Inconvenient Hero* (Orbis, 1996)

Hart, David M., *Forged Consensus* (Princeton University Press, 1998)

Hatt, Christine, *Mahatma Gandhi* (World Almanac Library, 2004)

Hiro, Dilip, *Iraq: A Report from the Inside* (Granta Books, 2003)

Howard, Michael, *War in European History* (Oxford University Press, 2001)

Johnson, Jacqueline, *Stokely Carmichael: The Story of Black Power* (Silver Burdett, 1990)

Katz, Friedrich, *The Life and Times of Pancho Villa* (Stanford University Press, 1998)

Ketcham, Ralph, ed., *The Anti-Federalist Papers and the Constitutional Convention Debates* (Mentor Books, 1986)

Kyvig, David E., ed., *Unintended Consequences of Constitutional Amendments* (University of Georgia Press, 2000)

Leffler, Melvyn P., *A Preponderance of Power* (Stanford University Press, 1992)

Lichtenstein, Nelson, "Socialist Movement," *Dictionary of American History* (Thomson Gale, 2003)

Lowery, David, and Brasher, Holly, *Organized Interests and American Government* (Boston: McGraw Hill, 2004)

Macpherson, C.B., *The Political Theory of Possessive Individualism, Hobbes to Locke* (Oxford University Press, 1962)

Marx, Karl, *Wage-Labour and Capital and Value, Price and Profit* (International Publishers, 1976)

Moses, Wilson J., *The Golden Age of Black Nationalism* (Oxford University Press, 1988)

Odom, William E., *The Collapse of the Soviet Military* (Yale University Press, 1998)

Orwell, George, *1984* (New American Library, 1981)

Remnick, David, *Lenin's Tomb: The Last Days of the Soviet Empire* (Vintage, 1994)

Rittberger, Volker, ed., *Global Governance and the United Nations System* (United Nations University Press, 2001)

Schrecker, Ellen, *The Age of McCarthyism* (St. Martin's Press, 1994)

Schwartz, Barry, *George Washington: The Making of an American Symbol* (Temple University Press, 1976)

Service, Robert, *Lenin: A Biography* (Harvard University Press, 2002)

Sigerman, Harriet, *Elizabeth Cady Stanton: The Right Is Ours* (Oxford University Press, 2001)

Taggart, Paul, *Populism* (Maidenhead, 2000)

Tibi, Bassam, *The Challenge of Fundamentalism: Political Islam and the New World Disorder* (University of California Press, 1998)

Walker, Stanley, *Dewey: An American of This Century* (Whittlesey House, 1944)

Yarmolinsky, Avrahm, *Road to Revolution: A Century of Russian Radicalism* (Collier Books, 1962)

Journals, Magazines, and Newspapers

American Journal of Political Science
American Politics Journal
American Prospect
British Journal of Political Science
Chicago Tribune
Christian Science Monitor
Economist
Free Speech
International Feminist Journal of Politics
International Herald Tribune
International Journal of Politics
Journal of Political Economy
Journal of Politics
Los Angeles Times
Nation, The
National Review
New Republic
New York Times
Newsweek
Time
Wall Street Journal
Washington Post
Weekly Standard

Internet Sources

www.democrats.org, Democratic Party
www.greenparty.org, Green Party
www.uup.org, Ulster Unionists Party
www.lp.org, Libertarian Party
www.republicans.org, Republican Party
www.aicpa.org, American Independent Party
www.adl.org, Anti-Defamation League
www.socialistparty.org, Socialist Party
www.dsausa.org, Democratic Socialist Party
www.communist-party.org, Communist Party
www.cpgb.org, Communist Party of Great Britain
www.fda.gov, Food and Drug Administration
www.bushcountry.org, Republican Party
www.atf.gov, Bureau of Alcohol, Tobacco, Firearms and
    Explosives
www.pbs.org, Public Broadcasting Corporation
www.completecampaigns.com, Complete Campaigns
www.spd.de, German Socialist Party
www.europa.eu.int, European Union Website
www.politicalgraveyard.com, The Political Graveyard
www.ndi.org, National Democratic Institute
www.politicalresources.net, Directory of Politics
www.idu.net, Iraqi Democratic Union

Appendix: Glossary

A

abdication: voluntary resignation from office by a queen or king. The most famous abdication in recent history was in 1936, when Britain's Edward VIII abdicated the throne because the British establishment would not permit him to marry Wallis Simpson, an American divorcée.

abrogation: the repeal of a law, treaty, or contract, either by mutual agreement or unilaterally.

absolutism: theory of absolute government. Power can be vested in an individual (as a dictator), an office (as a monarchy), a party, or a government administration. The government is not restricted legally by any other government agency. Thus absolute government can lead to absolute power vested in one individual. e.g., a dictatorship.

academic freedom: the right of a professor at a university to pursue research and publish scholarly findings, whether popular or controversial, without political or any other kind of social pressure being put on him or her.

accord: a diplomatic agreement that does not have the same binding force as a treaty, but is often treated as such, e.g., the Camp David accord signed between Israel and Egypt at Camp David in 1978; the accord between Israel and Jordan in 1994. The term can also refer to any agreement reached by two conflicting parties.

accountability: the extent to which people are held responsible for their word and actions. For example, an employee is accountable to his boss; a congressperson to her constituents, and a U.S. president to the people as a whole.

acculturation: the process by which people adapt to or adopt a culture that is not their own.

Achilles' heel: a defect, weakness, or point of vulnerability. Based on the Greek myth of Achilles, a warrior in ancient Greece. While being dipped in the waters of immortality, he was held by his heel, thus making this the one part of his body that was mortal. He was eventually killed in the Trojan War by a wound in the heel.

acid test: a crucial test of the value of something or someone. A politician might face the acid test of his popularity in an election. The term is also used in accounting as a measure of a company's ability to pay immediate liabilities.

act of state: the action of a government for which no individual can be held accountable.

activism: getting involved in political affairs, by such actions as running for political office, taking part in demonstrations, getting support for issues. Often used to refer to the activities of grassroots protest movements, as in animal rights activists, etc.

adjournment: the suspension of business for a specified time.

adjudication: the hearing and deciding of a legal case in a court of law.

administration: the management of institutional or governmental affairs; a term for the government itself and its policy-makers; as in the Clinton administration; the period in which a government holds office; as in the Persian Gulf war took place during President George H. W. Bush's administration.

adversary system: the system of law in which a case is argued by two opposing sides: a prosecutor who tries to prove that the defendant is guilty and a defender, who argues for the defendant's innocence. The case is then decided by an impartial judge or a jury. The U.S. and Great Britain operate under the adversary system.

aegis: any power or influence that protects or shields, as when nations take part in peacekeeping operations under the aegis of the United Nations, or in humanitarian missions under the aegis of the Red Cross.

affidavit: a declaration in writing signed and sworn to under oath.

affirmative action: the giving of preferential treatment to women and minorities in business and education to redress the effects of past discrimination. Affirmative action began in the 1960s; it has benefited hundreds of thousands of minorities and helped in the creation of an African American middle class. The number of women in professional and managerial jobs has also increased considerably as a result of affirmative action. However, during the 1990s, affirmative action became a contentious issue.

  While the bulk of minorities and civil rights leaders still support it, many conservatives claim that it amounts to "reverse discrimination." Supreme Court decisions in 1995 limited the scope of affirmative action programs in business and education. In 1997, California banned preferential treatment for minorities or women in state hiring practices.

affluence: wealth or riches.

affluent: wealthy; an affluent society is one in which there is an abundance of material or consumer goods. The term *affluent society* was popularized by economist John Kenneth Galbraith in 1964, and it is often used to describe the United States and other flourishing Western societies.

agenda: things to be done. Often used to describe political platforms, as in the Republican (or Democratic) agenda, meaning the policies each party hopes to pursue and enact.

aggregate demand: the total demand for goods and services in an economy, including demands for consumer goods and investment goods, the demands of local and central government, and of other countries for exports.

aggregate supply: the total supply of goods and services in an economy, including imports and exports, that is available to meet aggregate demand.

aggression: applied to belligerent actions by one state against another; as in Iraq committed an act of aggression when it invaded Kuwait in 1990.

agitation: in a political sense, refers to keeping an issue or a debate constantly before the public; as in there was considerable agitation for political reform in China in the late 1980s. Usually used to refer to opposition to the status quo (in communist countries, those who campaigned for human rights would often be referred to as agitators by the government).

agitprop: originally set up as the Department of Agitation and Propaganda by the Central Committee of the Communist Party of the USSR. Later usage came to be more general, involving activities that encouraged acceptance of left-wing ideology.

agrarian: relating to land or agriculture.

ahistorical: unrelated to history.

aide-de-camp: an officer who serves as confidential assistant and secretary to a higher-ranking officer, such as a general.

alien: a visitor or resident in a nation of which he or she is not a citizen.

allegiance: loyalty to a principle, a leader, or a country, as in the Pledge of Allegiance.

alliance: joining together in pursuit of mutual interests; as in the alliance of the United States, Britain, and the Soviet Union that defeated the Nazis in World War II. The term can also refer to domestic politics, as an alliance of liberal interest groups is fighting to preserve affirmative action policies against conservative opposition.

altruism: unselfish concern for the welfare of others.

ambassador: the highest-ranking diplomatic officer, who acts as personal representative of one state to another.

amendment: a change in a document made by adding, substituting, or omitting a certain part. The U.S. Constitution has 26 amendments, adopted after the original ratification of the Constitution. Amendment can also refer to a change in a bill while it is being considered in a legislature.

amnesty: an act by which the state pardons political or other offenders, usually as a group. In 1977, for example, President Carter granted amnesty to all Vietnam draft evaders. Amnesties are often used as a gesture of political reconciliation. In 1990, the ruling Sandinistas in Nicaragua declared amnesty for over a thousand political prisoners as a prelude to a general election. Amnesties also sometimes occur after a change of government or regime.

anarchy: the absence of government; disorder, chaos in a society.

anarchism: a doctrine that advocates the abolition of organized authority. Anarchists believe that all government is corrupt and evil. Anarchism was a force in 19th century Russia, associated with Prince Peter Kropotkin and Mikhail Bakunin. Types of anarchism range from pacifism to violent revolution. President William McKinley was assassinated by anarchists in 1901.

annexation: the act by which one state takes possession of another state or territory, usually a smaller one, without the consent of the party being taken over. For example, in 1938, German troops invaded Austria and annexed it. The citizens of Austria thereby became subjects of Germany.

anthropology: the study of humankind; often used to refer only to the study of primitive peoples.

Anti-Ballistic Missile Treaty (ABM): a landmark arms control agreement signed in 1972 by the Soviet Union and the U.S., this treaty limited anti-ballistic missiles to two sites of 100 anti-ballistic missile launchers in each country. In 1974 this was reduced to one site.

anti-clericalism: opposition to the influence of organized religion in state affairs. The term was applied particularly to the influence of the Catholic religion in political affairs.

anti-communism: opposition to communism. Anti-communism was the defining mark of U.S. foreign policy during the Cold War, which sought to check Soviet expansion around the globe. In domestic politics, being seen as "tough on communism" was often a litmus test for American politicians; anything less was to court electoral disaster. Anti-communism reached an extreme during the McCarthy era in the early 1950s, when Senator Joseph McCarthy led an unscrupulous witch hunt to root out alleged communist sympathizers in U.S. government service.

anti-Semitism: hostility toward Jews. Anti-Semitism is as old as Christian civilization. Jews were despised because, according to Christian belief, they had rejected Christ and continued to practice a religion that was not the true one. During the 19th century anti-Semitism became racial rather than religious. Jews were persecuted for being Jews, not for practicing a particular religion. Anti-Semitism was found throughout 19th-century Europe, particularly in Russia, Germany, and France. Russian anti-Semitism reached a peak in the period 1905–09, with an estimated 50,000 victims. But anti-Semitism reached its peak in Nazi Germany in the 1930s and 1940s. Jews were held to be inferior to what Nazis described as the Aryan master race. Jews were held as the scapegoat for all the ills suffered by the Germans. They were deprived of all their civil rights, and banned from trades and professions; their property was confiscated. The persecution culminated in Adolf Hitler's "Final Solution," which was the attempted destruction of the entire Jewish race.

anti-trust laws: federal and state laws designed to restrict monopolistic business practices that interfere with free trade. These are thought necessary to protect the public interest (from price-fixing, for example).

apolitical: not concerned with politics. The term might be used to describe someone who does not care to vote, or a nonpartisan organization. *Fast Times* is an apolitical newsmagazine, in that it is not affiliated with any political party.

apologetics: a branch of theology that deals with the reasoned defense of Christianity.

apologist: someone who writes or speaks in defense of a belief, faith or doctrine. If someone wrote in defense of the Vietnam War, for example, he would be an apologist for that war.

appeasement: giving in to unreasonable demands or threats out of weakness or stupidity. In political discourse, appeasement has a very negative connotation. It harks back to the buildup to World War II, when Britain and France did nothing to check German rearmament and aggression, particularly the Nazi occupation of the Sudetenland in Czechoslovakia in 1938. Since World War II, Western politicians of all stripes have done everything possible to avoid having the term applied to their policies in the international arena.

appropriation: money used to pay for government-approved expenditures.

arbitrary: derived from opinion, random choice, or chance. When people speak of an arbitrary decision, they usually mean an unfair one, one that is not based on logic, standard rules, or accepted customs.

arbitration: settlement of labor disputes in which each side agrees to accept the decision of an arbitrator, who is a kind of judge appointed because of his acceptability to both sides. Sometimes the arbitrator may be a group or a panel rather than an individual.

archives: the place where public records and documents are kept, and also the documents themselves.

aristocracy: a government that is controlled by a small ruling class. Also refers to that class itself, sometimes called simply the upper class. The aristocracy may owe its position to wealth, social position, military power, or another form of influence or training. These attributes are usually inherited.

armistice: ending of hostilities; as in the armistice of November 1918 marked the end of World War I.

arms control: any international agreement that limits the type and number of weapons or armed forces. Arms control played a major role in superpower politics during the 1970s and 1980s, and a number of nuclear arms control agreements were signed by the United States and the Soviet Union. These were the Anti-Ballistic Missile Treaty (1972) the First Strategic Arms Limitation Treaty (1972), the Second Strategic Arms Limitation Treaty (1979), the Intermediate-Range Nuclear Forces Treaty (1987), the First Strategic Arms Reduction Treaty (1991), and the Second Strategic Arms Reduction Treaty (1993). In 1994, the United States had about 14,900 nuclear weapons, down from the record number of 30,000 in 1967, and the Russians had about 29,000. See also disarmament.

arraignment: a court hearing in a criminal case during which the defendant is informed of his or her rights and is required to plead guilty or not guilty.

Association of Southeast Asian Nations (ASEAN): promotes economic cooperation amongst member countries, which include Brunei, Indonesia, Malaysia, Philippines, Singapore, and Thailand. ASEAN also encourages cultural development, promotes peace and stability in Southeast Asia, and cooperates with other international organizations. Its headquarters is in Jakarta, Indonesia.

atavism: reversion to an earlier type; resemblance to remote ancestors.

Attorney General: the highest legal officer in the United States, who heads the Justice Department, and is chief legal advisor to the president. Each state also has an attorney general.

austerity: severity or harshness. Often used to describe economic conditions; as the Polish people are undergoing a period of austerity as the economy makes a transition from communism to capitalism.

autarchy: political self-rule; complete independence, particularly economic self-sufficiency, in which through government controls a nation's economy (or a group of nations) is isolated from the rest of the world. During the Cold War, the Soviet bloc practiced economic autarchy, trading only within itself.

authoritarian: a form of government in which a large amount of authority is invested in the state, at the expense of individual rights. Often power in authoritarian systems is centered in a small group of autocratic leaders. Usually used in a negative sense.

autocracy: a government in which almost all power rests with the ruler. The Soviet Union under Stalin and Iraq under Saddam Hussein are examples of autocracies.

automation: in industry, the performing of routine tasks by machines that were formerly done by humans; any manufacturing system in which many of the processes are performed automatically or controlled by machinery.

autonomy: a limited form of self-government. In the U.S., states have a certain autonomy, which allows them to make their own laws regarding local matters. In international affairs, the Palestinians have been promised autonomy in Gaza, formerly occupied by Israel. Autonomy does not usually extend to control over foreign affairs.

B

balance of payments: a statistical record of all the economic transactions between one country and all other countries over a given period. The transactions include goods, services (including investments) private and governmental capital, and gold movement.

balance of power: the concept that world peace is best served when no one power in any region gains sufficient military strength to dominate other states in that region. The term was first used to describe European statecraft in the 19th century. Keeping the balance of power on the European continent was a cornerstone of British diplomacy—the concept being that if one power or coalition of powers got too strong, the weaker states would make an alliance to combat it. Alliances therefore were not a matter of ideology but of simple pragmatism; they would continually shift to maintain the balance of power. In that way, an equilibrium was maintained that discouraged wars. After World War II, the idea of the balance of power was in some ways superseded by what was termed the "balance of terror," but balance-of-power diplomacy is always present in one form or another.

For example in the 1980s, the U.S. supported Iraq in its war against Iran because it did not want Iran to become the dominant power in the region. Strengthening Iraq maintained the regional balance of power. Balance-of-power politics is also a factor in the U.S. decision to

normalize relations with Vietnam. A strong Vietnam, it is believed, will act as a check on the hegemony of China in the region.

balance of terror: the phrase was coined by British prime minister Winston Churchill . It refers to the situation during the Cold War, when both the United States and the Soviet Union had the capacity to destroy each other with nuclear weapons. In the event of war, the destruction on both sides would have been so huge that neither side was prepared to risk starting such a conflict. A balance of terror existed. The doctrine of MAD (Mutual Assured Destruction) was a later variant of the idea of the balance of terror.

balance of trade: the balance between what a country spends on imports and what it earns by exports. A favorable balance of trade is when revenue from exports is greater than expenditure on imports.

balanced budget: a budget in which expenditure is equal to, or not greater than, income. In the 1990s, there was growing concern about the federal budget deficit, and a proposal for a constitutional amendment that required the federal government to balance its budget annually passed the House of Representatives in 1995. It was, however, defeated in the Senate. Some economists argue that an unbalanced budget may not always be detrimental or bad.

Sometimes it is necessary to go into debt to ensure a stable future. For example, almost all states have laws that require them to balance their budgets each year, but they will issue bonds to finance large projects that are not within their annual budgets.

balkanization: to break up into small, hostile units, as happened to the Balkan states (Yugoslavia, Bulgaria, Greece, Albania, Turkey, and Romania) after World War I. A more recent example occurred in Lebanon during the 1980s, when the country split up into many warring factions with no central authority. The term *Lebanonization* was for a while used as the equivalent of balkanization.

ballistic missiles: long-range missiles that are mechanically guided only on the first part of their flights, after which they move under the force of gravity only, i.e. they become free-falling objects as they approach their target. Ballistic missiles are accurate and fast. They can cross an entire continent in 30 minutes and have great destructive power.

ballot: a printed piece of paper on which a voter indicates his or her preference from a list of individual candidates or parties; the act of voting or the entire number of votes cast at an election.

barter: to exchange goods or commodities without the use of money.

belligerency: the term *belligerent* is used to refer to countries that are at war. International law grants to groups involved in an insurrection in their own country the status of belligerency, which means they are given the rights and obligations of a state to the extent that this is necessary for the prosecution of the civil war.

bias: an inclination or prejudice that prevents objective judgment of something, as in hiring practices showed a bias against minorities.

bicameral: two separate legislative chambers.

bicameral government: a government that consists of two legislative bodies rather than one. The United States has a bicameral system, since both the House of Representatives and the Senate have to approve a bill before it can become law. All U.S. states have bicameral legislatures, with the exception of Nebraska, which has a unicameral system.

big stick: to carry a big stick is when an individual, group, or nation backs up its demands with a credible threat of force or some other pressure that is sufficient to get the other party to accede to its wishes. The term was coined by President Theodore Roosevelt, who said that a nation, like a man, should "tread softly but carry a big stick."

bilateral: involving two parties, usually countries; as in a bilateral trade agreement between the United States and Japan.

bilateralism: joint economic or security policies between two nations. Bilateralism may refer to trade agreements or to military treaties and alliances. It also refers to cooperation between allies.

Bill of Rights: any bill that lays out the rights of individuals vis a vis the state. The Bill of Rights refers to the first 10 amendments to the U.S. Constitution, which lay out individual liberties. Thomas Jefferson wrote to James Madison in 1787 that "A bill of rights is what the people are entitled to against every government on earth, general or particular; and what no just government should refuse, or rest on inference."

bipartisan: in American political discourse, refers to policies that have the support of both Democrats and Republicans. Bipartisanship is often most apparent in foreign policy, in which it is considered advisable for the country to present a united front.

black consciousness: a movement that emerged in the United States in the 1960s, on the heels of the civil rights movement, which began in the 1950s. It refers to the cultivation among blacks of their own distinct cultural identity, and the realization that being black was something they could be proud of. Black consciousness tended to reject white liberal thinking about racial issues and set out to chart an independent course for black social and political progress. Black consciousness was linked to the movement sometimes known as "black power" that also emerged in the mid-1960s. Black consciousness was also a strong force in South Africa in the 1960s and 1970s, as part of the growing opposition to the system of apartheid.

blacklist: in the early 20th century, a list maintained by an employer of workers who had joined unions and thus should not be hired. Such blacklists were made illegal in 1935. Blacklist now refers to any list by any organization of individuals whom it disapproves of and whom it may take punitive measures against. In 1984, for example, it was disclosed that the United States Information Agency had maintained a blacklist since 1981 that contained the names of liberal Democrats and others deemed unsuitable by agency officials. The list was destroyed.

black market: illegal trading in goods at prices that are higher than the legal or usual prices. In many countries in which consumer goods are scarce, a black market forms a kind of underground economy through which people get what they want if they are prepared to pay the price.

bloc: a grouping of individuals, groups, or nations that work together to achieve common objectives. A bloc can be economic, military, or political in nature. For example, the countries of Eastern Europe under communism were referred to as the Eastern bloc; the 12 countries that make up the European Community form a trading bloc; a group of legislators from different parties might come together on a certain issue and form a bloc to vote on that issue.

block voting: when multiple votes are cast by one group on behalf of its members.

blockade: any military action by sea or air designed to isolate an enemy and cut off its supply and communication lines. In 1962, the United States instituted a naval blockade of Cuba (although it was called a "quarantine") in response to the presence of Soviet nuclear missiles in that country.

Bolshevism: synonymous with communism. The term comes from the Russian word *bolshevik*, which means majority, and referred to the party led by Lenin (leader of the communist revolution in 1917), after it won a majority of votes at the Russian Social-Democratic Party conference in 1903. Used in the West in a derogatory sense.

bourgeois: used by Marxist theorists to describe anything associated with capitalists, including manufacturers, merchants, and small-business owners such as shopkeepers. These groups were the opposite of the proletariat, or working people. Bourgeois has come to refer simply to the middle classes, those between the upper classes and the working classes on the social scale. The term is often used in a derogatory sense to refer to anything conventional, respectable, etc., as in "bourgeois values."

boycott: to refuse to do business with an organization or nation, as when the Soviet Union boycotted the 1984 Olympic Games in Los Angeles. Also refers to a refusal to buy or sell something, as when, consumers are urged by an interest group to boycott a particular manufacturer's goods.

breach of the peace: a violation of the public peace, as in a riot. Also refers to any disorderly conduct. See also secondary boycott.

brigandage: theft or robbery.

brinkmanship: in political diplomacy or negotiation, the art of taking big risks, even to the brink of war, in the hope that the adversary will back down. Brinkmanship can be a way of testing an adversary's resolve. In 1994, Iraq amassed troops on the Kuwaiti border, testing U.S. response—this was an act of brinkmanship on the part of Iraq's Saddam Hussein. Hussein backed down and withdrew the troops when it became clear that the United States would mobilize to repel a possible invasion of Kuwait. Much of brinkmanship consists of bluffing, but it can be a dangerous game to play if either side misinterprets the moves of the other.

budget: a statement of estimated income and expenditure over a given period for an individual, group, government, or organization. If revenues exceed expenditures, there is a budget surplus; if expenditure is greater than revenue, there will be a budget deficit.

bureaucracy: the administration of a government; all government offices taken together; all the officials of a government. The term is often used in a negative sense, when someone wants to point the finger at perceived inefficiencies or incompetence. Large bureaucracies are often seen as inflexible, with too many rules and red tape, making them unresponsive to the needs of people.

business cycle: the general pattern of expansion and contraction that businesses go through. In terms of the national economy, the existence of business cycles means that a period of growth is usually followed by a recession, which is followed by a recovery.

by-election: an election to fill an office that has become vacant before its scheduled expiration date. If a Congressperson dies in office, for example, a by-election would be held to fill the seat.

bylaws: laws made by local authorities; regulations made by social or professional associations.

C

cabinet: an advisory committee to a president or prime minister, formed by the heads of government departments.

cadre: the nucleus around which a permanent military unit can be built, such as a cadre of officers. Also refers to the most dedicated members of a political party.

caliphate: the office or rank of caliph (meaning "ruler") in a Moslem country. The term derives from the title taken by the successors of Mohammed, the founder of Islam.

canon law: the laws that govern a Christian church organization.

canvass: to solicit votes; to examine carefully, as in to canvass public opinion.

capital: a city that is the seat of government of a state or nation; money used in business, where it refers to the wealth or assets of a firm. Capital is one of the three main factors of production, the others being land and labor.

capitalism: an economic system in which the means of production, such as land and factories, is privately owned and operated for profit. Usually ownership is concentrated in the hands of a small number of people. Capitalism, which developed during the Industrial Revolution, is associated with free enterprise, although in practice even capitalist societies have government regulations for business, to prevent monopolies and to cushion domestic industries from foreign competition. Opponents of capitalism say that the economy should be organized to serve the public good, not private profit. Supporters say capitalism creates wealth, which creates jobs, which create prosperity for everyone.

capitulation: the act of surrendering or submitting to an enemy; a document containing terms of surrender. The term can also be used in a nonmilitaristic sense, as in the liberal members of the party felt that the president's policy was a capitulation to pressure from the right.

carpetbagger: an outsider. The term was originally applied to politicians from the northern United States who went to the south after the Civil War to try to exploit the unstable situation there for their own profit. (They often carried all their belongings in a carpetbag.) Now used to refer to a politician who runs for office in a state or other district that is not his home.

carte blanche: a signed paper, intentionally left blank so that the bearer can fill in whatever he pleases. To give someone carte blanche is to give her complete power to decide something, or to name her own conditions or terms.

Carter Doctrine: the doctrine enunciated by President Jimmy Carter in 1980, stating that "An attempt by any outside forces to gain control of the Persian Gulf region will be regarded as an assault on the vital interests of the United States, and such an assault will be repelled by any means necessary, including military force." The Carter Doctrine, although it was not formally invoked, was put to the test after Iraq invaded Kuwait in 1990. The resulting Persian Gulf war in 1991 showed that the United States did indeed regard the attempt by a belligerent country to gain control of more than its allocated share of the region to be an assault on the vital interests of the United States.

caste: an exclusive, often hereditary class or group. Hindus in India live in a caste system, with four distinct classes, or castes, who traditionally are not allowed to mix with each other.

casus belli: an act or a situation that justifies a declaration of war. The Japanese attack on Pearl Harbor in 1941 was the casus belli that brought the United States into World War 11.

caucus: a private meeting of members of a political party to plan action or to select delegates for a nominating convention; also refers to distinct groups, either official or unofficial, in Congress, as in the Black Caucus in the House of Representatives.

censorship: the prevention of publication, transmission, or exhibition of material considered undesirable for the general public to possess or be exposed to. This can include the censorship, in the national interest, of military secrets or of obscene material. One of the important public debates of 1995 was whether there should be censorship of material published on the Internet, the global network of computers.

census: an official count of the population of a district, state, or nation, including statistics such as age, sex, occupation, property owned, etc. In the United States, a census is held every 10 years.

centralization: the administration of a government by a central authority. Centralization, understood as the concentration of power or authority in the hands of the state, is often associated with socialist or communist systems.

(However, a statement that centralization is associated with socialist systems could be misleading. The Spanish socialists have been much more decentralist than the Spanish right. The French socialists decentralized during the 1980s; the Gaullists in contrast had been very centralist. The British conservatives centralize more than the British left does. And most far-right, very conservative or fascist such as Adolf Hitler's, Benito Mussolini's, or Francisco Franco's regimes have been very centralist.)

centrism: a political position that is neither left nor right but which occupies the middle ground.

chain of command: the order in which authority is wielded and passed down. A military chain of command would extend from the most senior officers in an unbroken link down to the ranks.

character assassination: an unrelenting series of attacks on a person's character, often employing exaggerated, distorted, or even false information. When used in political races, character assassination is a tactic designed to take attention away from issues and place it on the opposing candidate, who is portrayed as being unfit for office.

charisma: in political speech refers to a person's flair and personal magnetism, his or her ability to inspire voters. Charismatic candidates exude charm and power; they excite people and can persuade them to be devoted to their cause. To say a politician lacks charisma is virtually to say he is dull. Examples of charismatic leaders include President John F. Kennedy and Dr. Martin Luther King, Jr.

charter: the laws, including the powers and organization, granted to a city by the state legislature; the constitution of an international body, such as the United Nations.

chauvinism: an unreasoning and aggressive kind of patriotism. Also refers to any contemptuous attitude to another race, nation, or sex, as in male chauvinism.

cheap money: also called easy money, the term refers to economic conditions in which there are low interest rates and high credit availability. The opposite is tight money.

checks and balances: a mechanism that guards against absolute power in any governing body by providing for separate governing bodies having equal power. Power is equitably distributed or balanced amongst the various branches of government (e.g., legislative, judicial, executive) and provisions are made for checking or restricting too much power in any one office. The system of checks and balances is a major part of the American system of government provided by the Constitution to prevent any person or persons or sector of government from gaining too much power. The system emphasizes the interdependence of various forms of government.

It operates among the judicial, executive, and legislative branches of government as well as between state and national governments. Examples of how the system works are: the ability of Congress to impeach a public official; the interpretation by the Supreme court of a legislative action; and the presidential veto.

Christian Democrats: political parties in several countries in Europe, including Belgium, France, Germany, Italy, and the Netherlands. Christian Democrats are usually Roman Catholics, and have had considerable influence on political policies in the above countries since the end of World War II, particularly in the area of social reform.

church and state: the U.S. Constitution provides for the strict separation of church and state. The First Amendment states that "Congress shall make no law respecting an establishment of religion." The issue is still a live one today: Opponents of the movement to introduce prayer into public schools argue that such a provision would violate the constitutional separation of church and state.

citizen: a person who is a member of a state or nation, either by birth or naturalization. Anyone born in the United States is a U.S. citizen and is entitled to full civil rights.

civil disobedience: refusal to obey laws. This tactic is most effective when used by fairly large groups as a way of getting unjust laws changed. Mahatma Gandhi and his followers in India mounted many campaigns of mass civil disobedience in their campaign for independence from Britain. The American civil rights movement in the 1950s and 1960s, led by Martin Luther King, Jr., used the same tactic. Civil disobedience is usually passive and nonviolent, aimed at bringing injustices to the attention of lawmakers and the public at large.

civil liberties: the freedoms people have a right to in a society. They consist mostly of freedom of movement and association, freedom of religion, and freedom of expression. The idea of civil liberties is deeply embedded in the United States; it is enshrined in the Bill of Rights.

civil rights: rights granted by a state to all its citizens. In the U.S. this refers to the rights enshrined in the Constitution and Bill of Rights. Civil rights prevent the government from intruding on personal liberties.

civil service: all nonmilitary employees of the government.

civil war: a war between different factions, whether geographical or political, within one state or nation.

civilian: anyone who is not in military service.

civitas: a Latin term meaning "citizenship."

clan: a close-knit social group held together by ties of kinship (as in clans in the Scottish Highlands) or other common interests. Sometimes writers refer to large or well-known political families as clans, like the Kennedy clan, etc.

class: a number of people or things grouped together; a group of people that are linked together because of certain things held in common, such as occupation, social status, economic background: ruling class, middle class, working class, etc.

class struggle: conflict between different classes in a society. The idea of class struggle held an important place in Marxism. Karl Marx divided society into two broad groups: the capitalists, or bourgeoisie, and the proletariat, or workers. Their interests were inevitably opposed, according to Marx, because one group (the proletariat) was always being exploited by the other (the bourgeoisie), so that capitalist society was a constant struggle between them. Marx believed that eventually the proletariat would triumph and a new classless society would emerge. The idea of class struggle, as with other main tenets of Marxism, holds much less appeal worldwide now than it did for most of the 20th century, because of the general failure and collapse of Marxist systems around the globe.

classical economics: the dominant theory of economics from the 18th century until superseded by neoclassical economics in the 20th century. It is associated with Adam Smith's *Wealth of Nations* (1776), John Stuart Mill's *Principles of Political Economy* (1848), and the work of David Ricardo, who were the first to systematically establish a body of economic principles. The basic idea was that the economy functioned most efficiently if everyone was allowed to pursue their own self-interest.

Classical economics therefore favored *laissez-faire*; the primary economic law was that of competition. See also Keynesianism; neoclassical economics.

clemency: leniency or mercy to an offender or enemy.

closed shop: a business in which all the employees must be members of a labor union. The closed shop is most common in the printing, transportation, and construction industries. The Taft-Hartley Act of 1947 made the closed shop illegal for firms engaged in interstate commerce.

closure: also called cloture, the term refers to the process by which a filibuster can be ended in the Senate. A motion for closure requires the votes of three-fifths of the Senate, i.e. 60 votes.

coalition: a combination of parties or states. For example, in 1991 a U.S.-led international coalition defeated Iraq in the Persian Gulf war. Domestically, coalitions can be made up of many organizations that band together to pursue a particular cause, as for example the Christian Coalition is a coalition made up of many different Christian organizations for the purpose of influencing public debate on moral affairs. There can also be legislative coalitions, in which legislators team up with others to advance a particular issue or piece of legislation, even though they may not be of the same party or agree on any other issues.

code: a systematically organized set of laws, such as the criminal code, the civil code.

codification: the act of arranging laws in a code.

coercion: the use of force or other powerful means of persuasion to get someone to do something. Often used to refer to government by force.

coexistence: a tacit agreement between two or more groups, parties, nations, etc., that are in fundamental disagreement or conflict, that they will not go to war. Coexistence is not quite the same as peace, because the parties remain wary of each other and often hostile, but they accept that widely different ideologies and social systems can exist without those differences alone being a cause for war.

cohort: a group of soldiers. Also refers to an assistant or colleague.

Cold War: the struggle between the United States and Western Europe against the Soviet Union and its Eastern European allies. It involved confrontation but no actual "hot" warfare. The Cold War began in the 1940s when the United States believed it was imperative to check Soviet expansionist designs on Western Europe. It reached its height during the 1950s and 1960s, when the threat of nuclear annihilation hung over the world, particularly during the Cuban Missile Crisis in 1962. The Cold War made itself felt all over the globe; it was as if the entire world was divided into two units, East and West. No small regional third world conflict was insignificant.

The United States backed any regime that was anticommunist; while the Soviets tried to expand their influence anywhere they could, from Cuba and Central America to the Middle East and Africa. The Cold War eased slightly during the 1970s as a result of the U.S.-Soviet policy of détente. It finally began to wind down in the late 1980s. In 1985, Mikhail Gorbachev had come to power in the Soviet Union and had begun his policies of glasnost (openness) and perestroika (restructuring). The Soviet Union and the United States agreed to wide-ranging arms control measures. Then, when communism crumbled in Eastern Europe in 1989, without resistance from Moscow, U.S.-Soviet relations warmed dramatically. By 1990, the Cold War was virtually over. Many claim that the United States won the Cold War because of the massive U.S. arms buildup during the Ronald Reagan administrations of 1981–89. The Soviets knew they could not match this and so had to come to the bargaining table. Others say that the Soviet Union would have been forced to reform anyway because its economic system was so inefficient.

collaboration: working with another person, or with many others, on a project, such as a literary or scientific endeavor. Collaboration also refers to cooperating with an enemy.

collective: any enterprise in which people work collectively, such as collective farms in Russia and China.

collective bargaining: negotiations about terms of employment (wages, hours, etc.) conducted between an employer and the representatives of a group of workers, usually a labor union.

collective responsibility: the responsibility borne by everyone who participates in a decision to abide by that decision and be responsible for its consequences. Great Britain applies the doctrine to the prime minister's cabinet, which is collectively responsible to Parliament for its decisions.

collective security: an agreement by participating nations that they will take joint military action against any nation that attacks any one of them. NATO and the Warsaw Pact are examples of collective security agreements.

collectivism: refers to all economic and political systems that emphasize central planning and group, as opposed to individual, endeavor. Thus socialist and communist societies are collectivist. The theory of collectivism emphasizes the value of cooperation under, usually, authoritarian leadership. The efforts of the individual matter less than the goals of the group as a whole.

collectivization: the transfer of something from private to public ownership. For example, the establishment of communism involved the collectivization of land and private property.

collegialism: a theory that the church is an organization equal to and independent of the state, with authority resting in its members.

colonialism: the system whereby a state acquires and rules colonies.

colonization: the establishment of a colony. Sometimes this involves moving a group of people from the colonizing state into the area to be colonized, usually to solidify control and facilitate administration of the area.

colony: a territory that is ruled by another state. Hong Kong, for example, was a colony of Great Britain until 1997, when China took over responsibility for it. Many colonies have a limited amount of self-government.

Cominform: the Communist Information Bureau, set up in 1947 to coordinate the activities of communist parties in the Soviet Union, Eastern Europe, France, and Italy. It was dissolved in 1956, on the initiative of the Soviet Union, in an attempt to reassure the West about Soviet intentions.

Comintern: the Communist International, also known as the Third International. The Comintern was founded in Russia in 1919 with the purpose of promoting revolutionary Marxism. As such, it encouraged revolution in capitalist countries. It was dissolved in 1943, during World War II, to ease the fears of Russia's Western allies.

comity: rules of etiquette in international relations that do not have the force of law but make international relations smoother.

commercialism: the methods of commerce and business. Sometimes in social commentary, the term is used in a negative sense, as when a writer bemoans the commercialism of our society, which is said to squeeze out moral or spiritual values, or the conducting of business (i.e., the making of money) where it is not appropriate-such as the commercialism involved in the O. . Simpson trial, for example.

commissar: formerly the title of Soviet administrative officers, particularly the heads of government departments. The term was dropped in 1946 in favor of minister.

Committee on the Elimination of Racial Discrimination (CERD): a UN committee; created by the International Convention on the Elimination of All Forms of Racial Discrimination. CERD examines reports of racial discrimination; operates UN libraries in New York and Geneva; reports to the UN General Assembly. Headquarters is in Geneva, Switzerland.

common good: the welfare of all. See also commonwealth; national interest; public interest; social welfare.

common law: the legal system of most English-speaking countries, including the United States, based on custom, habit, and precedent. Common law is supplemented by statutory law, which is established by legislation. The distinction between common law and statutory law has become blurred in modern times, because much of common law has been converted into statutes.

Common Market: see European Union.

commonwealth: similar in meaning to common good. The term originated in 17th century political thought. The idea was that all members of a society had certain common interests that contributed to the good of all (originally called the "common weal") and which they should therefore pursue and protect.

commune: the smallest territorial district in some European countries. More commonly used to denote a small group of people living communally, working together and sharing proceeds, etc.

communism: the political system under which the economy, including capital, property, major industries, and public services, is controlled and directed by the state, and in that sense is "communal."

Communism also involves a social structure that restricts individual freedom of expression. Modern communism is based on Marxism, as interpreted by the Russian revolutionary leader Vladimir Ilyich Lenin (1870–1924). See bolshevism; Communist Manifesto; dialectical materialism; Leninism; Marxism; Marxist-Leninism.

Communist Manifesto: one of the most influential documents in modern history, the appearance of which marked the birth of modern socialist theory. Published by Karl Marx and Friedrich Engels in 1848, the manifesto began by declaring that the history of all societies was that of class struggle. It then described the history of the rise of the bourgeoisie, who had developed the system of production and distribution on which capitalism was based. But in doing so, they had created an entirely new class, the proletarians, who possessed no land, wealth, craft, or trade, and so were forced to labor in the factories of the bourgeoisie.

The proletarians were driven into a ceaseless struggle with their oppressors, who were always exploiting them because of capitalism's need for ever cheaper production. But the proletariat, or workers, were destined to win the struggle. The last passage of the manifesto became famous. "The workers have nothing to lose but their chains. They have a world to win. Workers of all lands, unite!"

competition: rivalry. In economics, it refers to a situation in which two or more companies vie for business; if, for example, there is competition between sellers for a limited number of buyers, this will tend to bring down the price of the commodity being sold. Buyers can also compete with each other; the result is usually that prices go up. Competition is a cornerstone of the free-enterprise system and extends itself into all areas of U.S. society: people vie for the best university places, the best jobs, etc. According to this idea, competition provides the spur for people to succeed and to excel.

competitiveness: in political speech, competitiveness often refers to the need to make sure that U.S. goods and services are on a par with or better than those of its foreign competitors. Commentators often point out in this respect that we live in an increasingly competitive world.

compromise: a settlement in which each party gives up something, or makes a concession, for the purpose of reaching an agreement. It also refers to something that is midway between two things. Someone once said that politics is the art of the possible; it might also be said that politics is the art of the compromise. Politicians constantly have to make compromises to keep the widely different groups that make up society, and who all have their own interests to defend, satisfied. Without compromise it is difficult to reach agreements and keep government running.

conciliation: the process of getting two sides in a dispute to agree to a compromise. The conciliator is a third party not involved in the dispute. The agreement has to be voluntary; the process of conciliation, unlike arbitration, does not compel the disputants to accept the proposed solution.

confederation: a group of states that join together to execute some government functions, such as the conduct of defense or foreign policy, but remain independent, sovereign states. The United States was a confederation from 1778 until 1787, after which it became a federation.

conflict of interest: a situation in which a person's private interests are in conflict with the public interest that he is entrusted with representing. For example, if a legislator has investments in a certain business, and that business stands to benefit or lose by a particular piece of legislation, he is involved in a conflict of interest. He may choose to declare this conflict and abstain from voting. If he does not, he runs the risk of later being accused of unethical conduct.

congress: a representative assembly, such as the U.S. Congress. In the United States, Congress consists of the House of Representatives and the Senate. Congress also refers to the two-year period that starts on January 3 each odd-numbered year, in which each particular Congress holds its meetings and debates. Thus one can speak of the achievements of, say, the 92nd Congress.

conscientious objector: someone who refuses to serve in the military for religious or moral reasons. He may believe, for example, that it is wrong to fight or kill under any circumstances.

conscription: compulsory enrollment in the armed services. Also called the draft. The draft was ended in the U.S. in 1973, due to its unpopularity during the Vietnam War.

consensus: agreement. In politics, consensus refers to occasions when there is broad agreement on specific issues and/or the overall direction of policy, either between political parties or in public opinion, as for example in 1993 there was a consensus among Democrats and Republicans about the need for healthcare reform. Consensus politics, the seeking for the middle ground on the assumption that society has shared values, is the opposite of politics driven by sharp ideological confrontation.

consent of the governed: the idea that a just government must be based on the consent of the people who live under its jurisdiction. Government must be an expression of the popular will. This concept is found in the writings of theorists from the 17th to the 19th centuries, especially John Locke, Jean-Jacques Rousseau, and John Stuart Mill. Locke's work influenced the Founding Fathers, and the Declaration of Independence states that "governments are instituted among men, deriving their just powers from the consent of the governed, that whenever any form of government becomes destructive of these ends, it is the right of the people to alter or abolish it."

conservatism: a political philosophy that tends to support the status quo and advocates change only in moderation. Conservatism upholds the value of tradition, and seeks to preserve all that is good about the past. The classic statement of conservatism was by the Irishman Edmund Burke, in his *Reflections on the Revolution in France* (1790), in which he attacked the French Revolution. He compared society to a living organism that has taken time to grow and mature, so it should not be violently uprooted. Innovation, when necessary, should be grafted onto the strong stem of traditional institutions and ways of doing things: "it is with infinite caution that any man ought to venture upon pulling down an edifice which has answered in any tolerable degree for ages the common purposes of society."

conservative parties: political parties that advocate conservatism. In the U.S., the Republican Party is more conservative than the Democratic Party, and although the Democrats have traditionally had a conservative wing (based in the south) in the last two decades, much of it has joined the Republicans. The current trend in the Republican Party is toward greater conservatism.

conservative: a person who supports conservatism. Naturally, those who are most conservative are usually those who have the most to conserve, such as those who own wealth and property, or who are otherwise privileged, and thus have a stake in the disposition of things as they are. A conservative tends to be for the free market in economic affairs, and against what he calls "big government"—an excessive federal bureaucracy that intervenes in a wide range of social and economic areas. Conservatives prefer a kind of individualistic self-sufficiency. On social issues, conservatives are pro-family, anti-abortion, and in general support traditional moral values and religion. Conservatives usually favor a strong military.

consortium: an association or partnership of states or companies. Often an association of bankers.

conspicuous consumption: refers to consumption of goods or services that is mainly designed to show off one's wealth. The term was coined by Thorstein Veblen in the 1890s, who said that all classes in society, indulged in conspicuous consumption, even the poor (who, like the wealthy, sometimes buy something that is not essential and which is beyond their means). According to Veblen, the way to decide whether a certain item belongs in the category of conspicuous consumption is to ask, "whether, aside from acquired tastes and from the canons of usage and conventional decency, its result is a net gain in comfort or in the fullness of life."

conspiracy: a planning and acting together in secret, especially for an unlawful purpose.

conspiracy theory: the idea that many important political events or economic and social trends are the products of conspiracies that are largely unknown by the public at large. Conspiracy theorists often assume that the political authorities are involved in massive deceptions and cover-ups to disguise their actions and intentions. Official versions of events are regarded with suspicion. Conspiracy theories are probably as old as human society itself. The one that has gripped the public imagination like no other claims that President John Kennedy was killed not by a sole assassin acting alone, but by a conspiracy involving (take your pick) the Mafia, the Cubans, the CIA, the military-industrial complex.

Conspiracy theories have also flourished around the assassinations of Robert Kennedy and Martin Luther King Jr, in 1968. Many members of the citizens' militias

that have received so much publicity since the the April 1995 bombing of the federal building in Oklahoma City harbor conspiracy theories. These theories claim that the U.S. government, in cooperation with the media, international bankers, and the United Nations, is somehow orchestrating a plot to establish a tyrannical New World Order that will enslave America.

constitution: a document that describes the fundamental legal and political structures of a state. A constitution may be written or unwritten.

constitutional government: a form of government in which a constitution details the powers available to each branch of government, and the rights of the individual in relation to the government. Any action by the government that is not in accord with the constitution is considered illegitimate.

constitutional law: the law that governs relations between the state and the citizens of a country.

constitutional monarchy: a system of government in which the head of state is a hereditary king or queen who rules through a constitution.

constitutionalism: government according to a constitution. The term also refers to the branch of political science that deals with the theory of constitutional government.

consul: an official appointed by one country who lives in another country and assists his country's nationals with their business dealings.

consumer: in economic terms, someone who consumes goods and uses services. Consumer is distinguished from producer, since a consumer uses the goods or services to fulfill needs, not to produce more goods.

consumer activists: people who are active in protecting the interests of consumers by pressing for higher standards of safety, healthfulness, truth in labeling, and customer service among producers of consumer goods.

consumption: in economics, the term refers to the using up of goods or services, as opposed to production. It also refers to the amount used up.

containment: refers to the policy of the U.S. that began in 1947 and continued throughout the Cold War. It aimed to contain communism within its existing limits. This could either be through military means, as in Korea and Vietnam, or through technical and economic assistance to noncommunist countries. See also Cold War.

contempt of court: obstructing the business of a court; disobeying a court order; acting in such a way as to undermine the dignity or authority of a court.

corporation: an organization of people bound together to form a business enterprise or any other stated function. A quarter of U.S. business firms are corporations, but over three-quarters of all sales are through corporations. Ownership shares of a corporation are sold to buyers, but shareholders do not get much direct say in how the corporation is run. Another distinguishing characteristic of a corporation is the principle of limited liability, under which owners of corporations are not liable for debts of the firm.

cosmopolitan: belonging to the whole world, not just one locality or nation. A cosmopolitan person would be at home in many countries; a cosmopolitan city would be one with many different nationalities congregated.

cost-benefit analysis: a comparison between the cost of a specific business activity and the value of it. A cost-benefit analysis is not limited to monetary calculations, but attempts to include intangible effects on the quality of life. For example, say there is a proposal to build a new factory in a town. The factory may bring economic benefits, but what if it also gives off toxic emissions? In a cost-benefit analysis, the increase in jobs and other economic activity that the factory would bring has to be measured against the possible damage to the health of the community.

Council for Mutual Economic Aid (Comecon): was set up in 1949 by Eastern European countries, as a counterpart to Western Europe's Organization for European Economic Co-operation. Comecon exists to co-ordinate the various national economies-to provide, for example, adequate raw materials, and also to facilitate cooperation in science and technology.

counterculture: the term given to the youth movement of the 1960s, which rejected many aspects of mainstream American culture. The counterculture had both a political and a personal dimension. Politically, it was left-wing. Counterculturalists loathed the concentration of power and resources in the military-industrial complex, opposed the Vietnam War; they espoused the causes of minorities, and tried to create a new social order based on cooperation, not competition. The counterculture was strongly anti-authoritarian. It also promoted ecological awareness, feminism, and utopianism.

In their search for personal fulfillment, counterculturalists tried to expand their minds through drugs and meditation; sex and rock music was added to the mix to create a personal ethos of abandonment to a kind of Dionysian freedom. The movement petered out in the early 1970s, and the term *counterculture* had fallen into disuse, until it was revived in 1994 by House Speaker Newt Gingrich, who accused the Clinton administration of embodying counter-culture values, implying that those values were at the root of America's social malaise.

counterrevolution: the overthrowing of a revolution and the return to the social order that preceded it. A famous series of counter-revolutions took place throughout Europe in 1848. After revolutions had overthrown monarchies and autocrats all over the continent, a conservative backlash restored the ousted monarchies and aristocrats to power.

coup d'état: a sudden revolution in which control of a government is seized by force. Also means a sudden stroke of policy.

court-martial: a military court convened for the trying of military personnel for military offenses.

covenant: a binding agreement. In law, a covenant is a writing, under seal, containing the terms of agreement between two parties. A covenant may also be a clause containing a subordinate agreement or stipulation in a deed. Another meaning of covenant, although not used often, is international treaty, such as the Covenant of the League of Nations in 1919.

credibility: believability. In political discourse, it sometimes refers to a politician's standing with the electorate. If he is perceived to have broken many promises, for example, his credibility will be low. He will have what is sometimes known as a "credibility gap." The same applies to international relations. If a country's policies are always changing, little credibility will be given to each new position adopted.

criminology: the study of crime and criminals.

criterion: a standard of judgment; any rule, principle, law, or fact by which a correct judgment may be formed. The plural is *criteria*. If someone wishes to apply for Medicaid, for example, she must meet certain criteria before she can be eligible.

cult of personality: the term refers to authoritarian regimes in which the enormous power of the leader is reinforced and enhanced by exaggerated propaganda centered on him personally. The leader's picture is everywhere, on billboards, in public squares and buildings; he is supposed to be the embodiment of wisdom, compassion, courage, and leadership—a true father of the country, possessing almost superhuman powers. The term was first used in 1956 by the Russian Communist Party when it denounced Josef Stalin for indulging in a personality cult when he was in power, from 1924 to his death in 1953.

Cultural Revolution: refers to the period of social and political upheaval in China from 1965 to 1968. The Cultural Revolution was a massive attempt to reassert the principles of revolutionary Maoism (the doctrine associated with the Chinese leader Mao Zedong) and teach them to a new generation of Chinese. Any elements in the Communist Party that were considered liberal or influenced by the model of Russian communism under its then leader, Nikita Khrushchev, were denounced. There were massive party purges.

A personality cult of Mao emerged. Revolutionary fervor was whipped up by groups known as Red Guards; writers, economists, and other intellectuals were criticized and denounced. Schools and colleges were closed as thousands of urban teenagers were sent to work in the countryside. The Cultural Revolution had run its course by 1968. In ensuing years, many of the measures promoted by the Cultural Revolution were gradually eased.

curfew: a time, usually in the evening, after which it is forbidden to appear in the streets or in public places. Curfews are sometimes imposed by an occupying army in a city in order to maintain its control, but in unstable countries in times of great upheaval, the legitimate authorities may impose a curfew as a way of maintaining public order.

currency: refers to legal tender that is "current," that is, it is in circulation as a medium of trade and exchange.

currency convertibility: the right to exchange the currency of one country, at the going rate of exchange, for that of another.

This enables a person to carry out a transaction in a foreign market while using the currency of his own country, which the seller can then convert to his own national currency. Currency convertibility is an essential element of world trade.

D

dark horse: someone in a race (including a political race) who is not well-known and whose chances of winning are considered slight, except by a few.

de facto: Latin phrase meaning "by the fact of"; in fact, whether right or not. For example, if a revolution has just taken place in a country, the new government will be the de facto authority, i.e. the actual, existing authority, regardless of whether it has any legal claim to the position. De facto is the opposite of de jure.

de jure: Latin phrase meaning "from the law"; by right. The opposite of de facto.

dead heat: a tie. When contestants in a race finish in exactly the same time. A political dead heat would be when, say, two candidates or parties show exactly the same level of support in an opinion poll, or when two parties in an election win the same number of seats or poll the same percentage of votes.

deadlock: when something comes to a standstill because of pressure from two equal but opposing forces, as when a jury is unable to reach a verdict.

decentralization: the breaking up of central authority, and the distribution of it over a broader field, such as local authorities.

Decentralization is an idea that is currently driving national politics: both parties are advocating a reduction in the powers of the central (i.e., federal) government and the distribution of many of those powers to the states.

default: failure to do something, such as pay money due (a country might default on its loan payments, for example), or appear in court when required to.

deficit financing: the practice of deliberately operating with a budget deficit, financed by borrowing. The purpose of deficit financing is to stimulate the economy by increasing government spending, which will increase purchasing power and create more jobs.

deflation: a reduction in economic activity in an economy, marked by falling prices and wages (or a slowing of the increase), less employment, and fewer imports. Deflation marks the downturn in a business cycle. It can be produced by raising taxes, increasing interest rates, or cutting government spending. Deflationary policies may be pursued to improve the balance of payments by reducing demand and so reducing imports.

defunct: no longer existing. The Soviet Union, for example, is a defunct organization.

delegate: a person authorized to act for others; a representative. To delegate means to give someone the authority to act as one's agent or representative.

delegation: a group of delegates, often representing a larger group.

demagogue: a person who tries to win political support by playing to people's fears and prejudices, trying to build up hatred for certain groups. Adolf Hitler, who stirred up the masses by telling them the Jews were responsible for German ills, was a demagogue. In the United States, Senator Joseph McCarthy, who led a witch hunt for communists in U.S. society during the 1950s, was also a demagogue.

democracy: government by the people; the rule of the majority. There is no precise definition of democracy on which all could agree. Even communist countries tend to call themselves democratic, and the mere fact that a government is elected by a majority of the popular vote does not of itself guarantee a democracy. A broad definition might include the following points (based on Thomas R. Dye and L. Harmon Ziegler's book *The Irony of Democracy*): Participation by the mass of people in the decisions that shape their lives; government by majority rule, with recognition of the rights of minorities; freedom of speech, press, and assembly; freedom to form opposition political parties and to run for office; commitment to individual dignity and to equal opportunities for people to develop their full potential.

demographics: pertaining to demography, which is the science of statistics such as births, deaths, marriages, racial composition, etc., in a population. Political scien-

tists study changing demographics in a community and analyze how that might affect voting behavior, etc. An example of such a change is the city of Los Angeles, which in the 1950s and early 1960s was almost exclusively white, but has now become one of the most multicultural cities in the country. Its demographics have changed dramatically.

deport: to send out of the country. An illegal immigrant, for example, may be deported if he cannot prove he has a right to stay in the country.

depression: in economics, the term refers to a prolonged slump in business activity, leading to low production, little capital investment, mass unemployment, and falling wages. The worst depression in American history lasted from 1929 to 1933.

desegregation: the elimination of segregation by race in schools and public places. In the United States, desegregation began in 1954, with the Supreme Court ruling in the *Brown v. Board of Education* case that "Separate educational facilities are inherently unequal." Although it faced plenty of opposition in the south, desegregation gathered strength through the civil rights movement that began in 1955 and reached its peak in the mid-1960s.

despot: a tyrant; a ruler with absolute power.

despotism: rule by a despot; the methods of a despot.

destabilize: to make unstable or insecure. Often used in a political sense about a government or a nation, especially when the destabilization is deliberately created by dissidents or rebels within a country, or by agents of a foreign power who want to disrupt or overthrow the government. The United States, like many governments, has done its share of destabilizing, notably in Chile in the early 1970s, when it engineered the fall of the Marxist government there.

détente: the easing of strained relations between states. In recent history, the term is applied to relations between the Soviet Union and the United States in the 1970s that led to increased trade and arms control agreements. Détente ended with the Soviet invasion of Afghanistan in 1979.

deterrence: a defense policy in which a country ensures that it has sufficient military power to deter a potential enemy from making an attack. Deterrence is fundamental to U.S. policy, and underlies all the arguments about the need to keep the military strong. The greatest deterrents are considered to be nuclear weapons. Although they have existed since 1945, they have not been used since the end of World War II. The mere possession of nuclear weapons is sufficient to deter an enemy, because, unless a country's entire nuclear arsenal could be wiped out by a first strike, the destruction caused by the inevitable retaliation would be too great a price to pay. The doctrine of deterrence through nuclear weapons is a paradox: such weapons have kept the peace.

devaluation: reduction in the value of a nation's currency in relation to other currencies. Devaluation usually takes place because of an emergency, such as a balance-of-payments deficit in which the value of a country's imports is far greater than the value of its exports. Devaluation has the effect of boosting exports (because they are cheaper in terms of foreign currencies) and reducing imports (because they are more expensive in terms of foreign currencies).

devolution: the redistribution or delegation of political power away from a centralized body to a lower, often regional, authority.

dialectic: originally meant the art of argument, a method of logical inquiry that proceeded by question and answer. The idea of dialectic was developed by the 19th-century German idealist philosopher Hegel into a way of understanding all natural and historical processes: everything conformed to a dialectical process of thesis, antithesis, and synthesis. One thing produces from within itself its own opposite or negation, and from the conflict between the two emerges a synthesis. Hegel's idea of dialectic was adapted by Karl Marx to form dialectical materialism, the foundation of Marxist doctrine.

dialectical materialism: the central theory of Marxism, which Karl Marx adapted from the idealist philosophy of Hegel. Marx applied Hegel's theory of dialectic to political and economic history. Capitalism (thesis), produced its opposite, socialism (antithesis), from within itself by means of the proletariat, out of which eventually emerged a communist society (synthesis). Marx believed this to be an inexorable law of history.

dictatorship: system of government in which power is concentrated in the hands of one person, the dictator.

Dictatorships are rarely benevolent and often have scant regard for human rights. The classic dictatorships in the 20th century were those of Adolf Hitler in Germany, Benito Mussolini in Italy, and Josef Stalin in the Soviet Union.

dictatorship of the proletariat: a Marxist concept that was in fact first formulated before Karl Marx by a Frenchman, Auguste Blanqui. It refers to an interim period immediately after the proletariat (the working class) has triumphed over the bourgeoisie (capitalists). The rule of the proletariat then gives way to the classless, or communist society.

diehard: someone who is extremely reluctant to relinquish his opinions or beliefs, even when they are outmoded. Today there are probably many diehard communists in Russia, or in the United States there are diehards who still believe in racial segregation.

diminishing returns: a principle of economics that states that if one factor of production is increased while others remain fixed, the resulting increase in output will level off after a time and then decrease. In other words, if a company decides to employ more workers but does not increase the amount of machinery, it will eventually reach the point of diminishing returns, where the addition of each new worker will add progressively less to output than did the previous additions. To avoid diminishing returns, the optimum relationship between all the factors of production at any given time must be evaluated.

diplomacy: the methods by which relations between nations are conducted.

diplomatic immunity: special rights given to diplomats, including immunity from the laws that operate in the country to which they are assigned.

direct action: when a group acts to achieve its goals without going through the accepted channels of communication or decision-making. If a group of workers, for example, goes on strike without the support of their union or commits acts of sabotage, they are taking direct action.

direct democracy: democracy in which the people as a whole make direct decisions, rather than having those decisions made for them by elected representatives. A referendum is a form of direct democracy, as is the practice of recall, by which an elected official may be voted out of office between elections if enough people sign a petition to remove him and then win the subsequent vote. A novel version of direct democracy was introduced onto the American political scene by Ross Perot, when he ran as an independent candidate for president in 1992. Perot proposed that some national decisions could be arrived at directly by the people through the use of electronic "town meetings." The idea arose because of widespread public dissatisfaction with the performance of Congress, which in the eyes of many was out of touch with the country as a whole.

directive: an executive order or general instruction.

dirty linen: in political speech, the term refers to secrets such as sordid infighting, or outright scandal, that political parties would sooner keep secret. Displaying dirty linen in public is to have the less savory aspects of one's life put on public view.

The British royal family, for example, has not had much success over the last few years in keeping its dirty linen private. (The marital woes of Prince Charles and Princess Diana, for example.)

disarmament: reduction of armaments. Attempts have been made to reduce arms ever since the end of World War I. A disarmament conference was held in Geneva from 1932 to 1934, but no agreement was reached. After World War II, the United Nations established committees on disarmament and formed a Disarmament Commission in 1952. Talks were held from 1955 to 1957 on banning nuclear weapons. From the 1960s there was limited success, including the Nuclear Test-Ban Treaty (1963) and the nuclear Non-proliferation Treaty (1968). In the 1970s, as a result of the policy of détente between the United States and the Soviet Union, more treaties were signed, limiting the increase of nuclear weapons (see arms control). Further treaties in 1987, 1991, and 1993 reduced the superpowers' stock of nuclear weapons.

However, they did nothing to alleviate the continuing danger of nuclear proliferation. And as far as conventional armaments are concerned, the idea of disarmament seems no more than a visionary dream. From 1988 to 1990 the arms trade was the world's biggest industry. Many developing countries, among them Brazil, India, Egypt, and both Koreas, were by 1990 among the world's top arms producers and exporters. In the third world, the concept of arms control or disarmament simply does not exist.

discrimination: treating a person differently and unequally because of race, gender, country of origin, color, age, physical handicap, or other factors. In the United States, equal opportunity laws aim to prevent or redress discrimination in the workplace.

displaced person: a person who has had to leave his own country as a result of war or persecution.

dissident: one who dissents or disagrees. In political speech, the term refers to a person who protests injustices or abuses perpetrated by the government of his country. Dissidents are common in totalitarian or communist countries. Many Chinese dissidents are imprisoned or persecuted for advocating democracy, as were Russian dissidents such as Andrei Sakharov in the Soviet Union under communism. Some dissidents, such as Lech Walesa of Poland and Vaclav Havel of the Czech Republic, eventually win their battles against the state and, in these two cases, became presidents of their countries.

divide and rule: the practice of keeping power by making sure that enemies are always kept divided and therefore too weak to mount an effective challenge. The Roman Empire perfected the strategy of divide and rule, and the British Empire employed the same tactic.

divine right: the term usually refers to the divine right of kings, a medieval belief that the king was appointed by God to rule, and this divine right was passed on by heredity alone. The belief had virtually died out by the end of the 19th century, except among a few die-hard groups.

division of labor: a method of production on which modern industrial economies are based. It relies on specialization. Each worker performs only one, often very narrow, task in the production process. The division of labor is considered to be more efficient than other methods, in that workers do not waste time changing tasks and can acquire more skill by specialization. The disadvantage of the division of labor is that work often becomes repetitive and boring, especially when the division of labor is carried to extremes, as in the modern auto plant, where tasks can be as narrow as the repeated tightening of nuts and bolts in a factory all day, every day.

doctrinaire: theoretical and impractical. A doctrinaire person may have many theories for the regeneration of society, but will attempt to apply them rigidly, without allowing them to bend to fit particular circumstances.

doctrine: something taught as the principles or creed of a religion or political party. Similar in meaning to dogma. Doctrine also refers to certain foreign policies, such as the Monroe Doctrine or the Carter Doctrine.

dogma: a doctrine or belief, as laid down by an authority such as a church. Also means an arrogant assertion of an opinion. When someone states his fixed beliefs and opinions and will not evaluate them objectively or listen to any counterargument, he is speaking dogma.

dogmatism: rigid adherence to dogma; arrogant assertion of opinion, whether facts or evidence support it or not.

domestic: pertaining to one's own country. Thus, a government will have a domestic policy dealing with policies within its own borders, and a foreign policy for everything outside those borders.

domino theory: an idea current during the Cold War that justified U.S. support of South Vietnam against invasion by communist North Vietnam. The theory was that if one Southeast Asian state went communist, others, such as Laos and Cambodia, would follow, giving the communists much greater influence. Sometimes used today to describe the spread of Islamic fundamentalism.

double jeopardy: the law that says a person cannot be tried twice for the same offense. It is part of the Fifth Amendment, which states that "No person shall ... be subject for the same offense to be twice put in jeopardy of life or limb."

draconian laws: severe or cruel laws. The phrase refers to Draco, a ruler of ancient Greece in the 7th century B.C.E., who imposed a severe code of laws on the city of Athens in 621. In political speech today, for example, a government that is facing social unrest or rebellion might take draconian measures to restore order.

drawback: money collected as customs duty on imported goods and then refunded when the goods are sent out as exports.

due process: legal procedures designed to protect the rights and liberties of individuals. In the United States,

due process refers to the constitutional requirement that "no person shall be deprived of life, liberty, or property without due process of law." In practice, it means that someone accused of a crime must be given a fair chance to present her own case.

dumping: in economics, a term that means selling a product in large quantities abroad for a lower price than it fetches in the domestic market. Usually this is done to dispose of a surplus and to gain a competitive advantage with foreign suppliers.

dyed-in-the-wool: unchangeable, from the process of having yarn dyed before being woven, which makes it retain its color better. One might refer to someone, for example, as a dyed-in-the-wool conservative, meaning that he is never likely to change his conservatism.

dynasty: a succession of political rulers who belong to the same family. Dynasties are less common now than they used to be in the days when hereditary monarchs held sway, but in some countries power is still passed on by a ruler to another member of his family. Sometimes even in a democracy, powerful political families seem almost to attain the status of a dynasty. Examples include the Kennedys in America, the Bhuttos in Pakistan, and the relatives and descendants of Mahatma Gandhi in India.

E

earmarked: set aside for a special purpose, as when in a budget, funds are earmarked for certain projects.

ecclesiastical: pertaining to church matters, as in ecclesiastical courts, ecclesiastical history, etc.

ecology: the branch of biology that deals with the relation between living things and their environment. Ecology is an important political issue today, although it is usually comes under the umbrella of "environmental" issues. These include the human destruction of the environment (cutting down of rain forests, thinning of the ozone layer, for example), which in the opinion of environmentalists constitutes a grave threat to life on earth. See environmental protection; greenhouse effect; ozone layer; toxic wastes.

economic growth: the increase in a nation's production of goods and services, often measured annually in the gross national product (GNP). In 1994, for example, the economic growth rate of the United States, in terms of the GNP, was 4 percent, which is considered a fairly high rate of growth.

economic warfare: conflict between nations over economic issues, which results in each side taking action against the other, to raise tariffs, restrict imports, or boycott the other's goods.

economics: the science of the allocation of limited resources for the satisfaction of human wants.

economy: the entire system of production, distribution, and consumption of goods and services in a country.

ecumenical: universal. Used in reference to cooperation, understanding, and unity among different churches, as in the ecumenical movement.

ecumenism: the ecumenical movement within Christian churches, which has been a notable feature of Christianity over the last 30 to 40 years. Also refers to the cultivation of greater understanding and tolerance among different religions.

egalitarianism: the doctrine that advocates equal political and social rights for all citizens. As such, egalitarianism is enshrined in the U.S. Constitution. It does not mean that all people should be equal, but that they should all have equal opportunity.

election: the process by which public or private officials are selected from a field of candidates by the marking of ballots in a vote.

electorate: all the people in a district that are eligible to vote in elections.

eleventh hour: the last moment; only moments before it would be too late, as in "the arrival of the U.S. cavalry at the eleventh hour saved the settlers from an Indian attack."

elite: an exclusive, carefully selected group or class, usually small, that possesses certain advantages of wealth, privilege, education, training, status, political power, etc. One might refer, for example, to the governing elite of a country, or to the U.S. Marines as an elite force.

elitism: the doctrine that advocates leadership by a select group or elite. Elitism is not something that any U.S. politician would openly advocate, since it runs counter to the democratic ideal. However, it often proves a useful term when one politician wants to snipe at another one. For example, if a politician appears to be advocating a policy that denies equal opportunity for all, he might be accused by his opponents of elitism.

emancipation: setting free from slavery or oppression, as in the Emancipation Proclamation, a declaration by President Abraham Lincoln that became effective in 1863, that all the slaves who were in the Confederate states, who were in rebellion against the United States, were free men.

embargo: a government-imposed ban on trade with a specific country. For example, the United States has a trade embargo on Cuba; a similar embargo imposed on trade with Vietnam was lifted in 1994. Sometimes an embargo can be imposed on a particular commodity only, as when the United States imposed a grain embargo on the Soviet Union as a protest against the Soviet invasion of Afghanistan in 1979.

embassy: the official residence and offices of an ambassador in a foreign country.

embezzlement: the act of fraudulently taking money or goods that have been entrusted to one's care.

emigration: going to live permanently in a country other than one's own.

eminent domain: the right of a government to take private property for public use, even if the owner refuses consent, provided that adequate compensation is paid. The right is described in the Fifth Amendment of the constitution, which says, "nor shall private property be taken for public use, without just compensation."

empire: a state that unites many different territories and peoples under one rule, as in the Roman Empire, the British Empire. Often the territories are spread widely apart across the globe, and do not possess the same constitutional status as the "mother" country.

enclave: an area that is surrounded or enclosed by territories that belong to another country. The area of Nagorno-Karabakh, for example, is an Armenian enclave within the state of Azerbaijan (and is the cause of a long-running war). The term can also be used when a country or territory is divided along sectarian grounds.

One might speak, for example, of a Roman Catholic enclave within largely Protestant Northern Ireland.

entente: an international agreement or alliance. A famous entente was the Entente Cordiale, signed between Britain and France in 1904; another was the Triple Entente, an alliance among Britain, France, and Russia, which grew out of the Entente Cordiale and lasted until 1917.

entrepreneur: someone who sets up a new business undertaking, raises the money necessary, organizes production, and appoints the management. The entrepreneur bears the financial risk involved, in the hope that the business will succeed and make a profit.

environmental protection: the preservation of natural resources. In 1969, the National Environment Policy Act stated that such protection is the responsibility of the federal government, and it was with this in mind that the Environmental Protection Agency (EPA) was formed in 1970. Since then, a network of environmental laws has been passed, covering such areas as the quality of air and water, toxic wastes, endangered species, and pesticides. See also greenhouse effect; ozone layer; toxic wastes.

envoy: a person sent by a government to a foreign country to conduct diplomatic business. An envoy ranks below an ambassador.

equal opportunity: the idea, which enjoys a broad consensus in the United States, that opportunities in education, employment, or any other field should be freely available to all citizens, regardless of race, gender, religion, country of origin, or any other factor that could be used to discriminate against someone. The Equal Employment Opportunity Commission (EEOC), which was created in 1964, promotes equal opportunity in hiring, promotion, wages, and employment.

equal pay: the principle that pay should be according to the work done, not according to who the worker is. In other words, women who perform the same tasks, demanding the same skill and level of responsibility as men, should receive the same pay. The Equal Pay Act of 1963 prohibits discrimination in the workplace regarding pay based on gender.

equilibrium: in economics, the term refers to a stable economic condition in which all significant variables remain constant over a period of time. For example, a market will be in equilibrium if the amount of goods that buyers wish to purchase at the prevailing price is exactly matched by the amount that the sellers wish to sell at that price. There is then no reason for the price to change, which it would do if either of the variables (supply or demand) were to change.

equity: the capital, or assets, of a firm, after the deduction of liabilities.

establishment: the group that holds power in any section of society, political, military, academic, or religious. The establishment is much broader than a political party or social class; it is usually conservative, upholding traditional ways of doing things; to outsiders, some establishments can seem like closed, secretive, elusive "clubs."

ethics: the study of standards of conduct and moral judgment.

ethnic: someone who is a member of an ethnic group (a group distinguished from others by race, customs, language, etc.), particularly a member of a minority group within a larger community. The United States is composed of a large number of ethnic groups. The extent to which an ethnic group should subordinate its heritage in order to become an "American" is a controversial issue.

ethnocentrism: belief in the inherent superiority of one's own cultural, ethnic, or political group.

ethos: the characteristic attitudes, beliefs, and habits of a group, as in, the conservative ethos of hard work and self-reliance.

exile: the banishing of someone from his homeland for a specified period or for life; the person who is so banished. Exile is not as common a punishment as it was before modern times.

But exile is still the frequent fate of deposed dictators, who would otherwise have to face charges in their own land. Sometimes they choose voluntary exile rather than face the consequences of their rule. In 1994, the military rulers of Haiti chose to go into exile rather than resist a U.S. invasion.

expansionism: the policy of expanding a nation's territory or sphere of influence. The term usually has a negative connotation, suggesting that a nation has its eyes on more than its fair share of things, as in Soviet expansionism.

export: the sending of goods or services to a foreign market for the purpose of selling.

extradition: the giving up by one nation of a person accused or convicted of a crime to another nation where the offender is to be tried or, if already convicted, punished.

Eurocommunism: communism in Western Europe, particularly in France and Italy; with the exception of Britain, it has gained more of a foothold than it has in the United States. Western European communist parties tend to be more democratic than their Eastern European or Russian counterparts, and have some measure of genuine public support. They have also tended to pursue policies that are independent of Moscow, particularly in the wake of the Russian invasion of Czechoslovakia in 1968. The term became current in the 1970s.

European Union (EU): In 2004, the EU had some 25 members, including Belgium, Denmark, France, Germany, Greece, Ireland, Italy, Luxembourg, the Netherlands, Portugal, Spain, and the United Kingdom. For over 40 years, member countries have been developing common policies on a wide range of issues, such as agriculture, environment, trade, labor practices, and research and development. In 1993, all barriers were removed to the free flow of trade, goods, services, and people among all member countries, which made the EU the largest trading bloc in the world. Another step toward European unity was taken in 1998, when the EU created a European Central Bank and single currency, the euro. Membership in the EU is open to any European democracy. The presidency of the EU rotates every six months among member nations; summit meetings are held every June and December in the host country. Headquarters for the EU is in Brussels, Belgium. The EU has many institutions, including the European Parliament, which has delegates from the member countries. It meets each month for one week in Strasbourg, France. It keeps watch over EU activities and supervises such organizations as the European Atomic Energy Commission (Euratom).

evangelical: strictly speaking, the term refers to anything that is contained in the four gospels in the New Testament, or to the Protestant churches that emphasize salvation by faith rather than good works. But nowadays the term is also used more loosely, often simply to describe a "born again," or fundamentalist, Christian.

evangelism: a zealous effort to spread the word of the gospel, i.e., the beliefs of Christianity.

ex officio: Latin term meaning "because of one's office." It means that if, for example, someone is on a committee as an ex officio member, he is on the committee because of the office he holds, rather than because he was elected or otherwise appointed to the committee.

executive privilege: the privilege extended to the executive branch to withhold certain information from Congress or the courts. The need to withhold may be to preserve the confidentiality of communications within the executive, or to serve the national interest. Throughout U.S. history, presidents have invoked executive privilege, although the concept is not explicitly stated in the Constitution.

The privilege was restricted by the Supreme Court in 1974 after President Richard Nixon invoked it in the Watergate scandal. The court ruled that executive privilege could not be applied to prevent evidence from being supplied in a criminal case. In 1998, President Bill Clinton invoked executive privilege in an attempt to prevent his aides from testifying before a grand jury in a criminal inquiry. As in 1974, the courts ruled that executive privilege must give way to a criminal case.

expatriate: someone who has renounced his citizenship of the country in which he was born and has become a citizen of another country.

exploitation: taking advantage of something for one's own use or benefit, especially in an unethical manner. Thus, an employer who pays unreasonably low wages or makes unreasonable demands on his employees is guilty of exploitation. In Marxist theory, exploitation refers to the making of profit (by capitalists) from the labor of others (the proletariat).

expropriation: the confiscation of private property by the state, often without adequate compensation. This was often done by communist regimes. Another example: when whites in South Africa in the 1990s realized that there would soon be a black government in power committed to land redistribution, many feared that this might lead to the expropriation of their property (a fear that has not proved justified).

F

Fabianism: the socialist ideas outline by the Fabian Society, a group founded in Britain in 1884. It rejected violent revolution, arguing that socialism would come about through the ballot box after a long period of political evolution.

faction: a group within an organization (often within a political party) that has different goals from those of the party as a whole, and seeks to promote those goals. James Madison warned against what he saw as the dangers of factions when he defined the term: "A number of citizens, whether amounting to a majority or minority of the whole, who are united and actuated by some common impulse or passion, or of interest, adverse to the rights of other citizens, or to the permanent and aggregate interest of the community." In modern political speech, faction does not necessarily have a negative connotation, however. It can mean simply "subgroup," as in the moderate (or liberal or conservative) faction in a political party.

fait accompli: a French phrase that means "an accomplished fact." A fait accompli refers to something that is already done, making any debate over it useless. In politics, an executive might simply go ahead and make a decision, perform an action, or initiate a policy as a way of bypassing potential opposition. He can then present his actions as a fait accompli, so wrong-footing his opponents.

fascism: a nationalistic, authoritarian, anti-communist movement founded by Benito Mussolini in Italy in 1919. Fascism was a response to the economic hardship and social disorder that ensued after the end of World War I. The main elements of fascism were pride in the nation, anti-Marxism, the complete rejection of parliamentary democracy, the cultivation of military virtues, strong government, and loyalty to a strong leader. Fascists wore a uniform of a black shirt and and used a greeting derived from ancient Rome: the outstretched arm. Mussolini's Black Shirts (as they were known) seized power in 1922. A movement modeled on fascism, Germany's National Socialism (Nazism) also began its rise in the 1920s.

In 1936 in Spain, General Francisco Franco's fascists seized power and precipitated a three-year civil war, with Franco victorious. Italian fascism collapsed with the death of Mussolini and the end of World War II. Although since then there have been South American military regimes that have adopted some of the terminology and concepts of fascism, fascism in its classic form is considered to have died with Mussolini. Sometimes the term is used now as a term of abuse, triggered by any real or imagined outbreak of authoritarian thought or behavior.

featherbedding: a labor union practice of limiting work or output in order to preserve jobs. Featherbedding may result in the employment of unnecessary workers.

federalism: the system of government that operates in a federation.

federation: a state made up of a number of subdivisions or individual states, which share power with the central government. Each of the smaller units retains control of many aspects of its own affairs, but grants to the larger political unit the power to conduct foreign policy. The relationship between the states and the central, or federal, government is laid down in a constitution, which cannot be changed without the consent of a specified number of states (in the United States, it is two-thirds). The United States is a federation, as are Australia and Canada.

fellow traveler: someone who goes along with a specific belief without openly endorsing it. Often used in respect to communism about those who are not members of a communist party but who support its cause. Fellow travelers may lie low because they do not want to risk the consequences of associating with dangerous or unpopular beliefs. The term is used in an accusatory way: calling someone a fellow traveler is a hostile comment.

feminist: one who supports the beliefs and goals of feminism. A feminist is usually a woman, but a man can be a feminist too.

feudalism: a medieval form of social, economic, and political organization. Feudalism had a pyramidal structure. At its head was the king; below the king was a hierarchical chain of nobles, down to the lords of individual manors, the manor being the basic social and economic unit. The lords leased land to tenants, offering them protection in exchange for military and other services. Society was thus knit together in a network of obligation and service. The lowest part of the pyramid was occupied by serfs, who were obliged to cultivate the land belonging to their lord. There was thus no mobile middle class in feudalism; social rank was fixed by inheritance and could not be changed. When, at the end of the Middle Ages, a middle class did begin to emerge, it marked the beginning of the end of feudalism.

fiat: an order or decree issued by a legal authority. A fiat may be of an arbitrary nature, as, for example, when it is used as an instrument of government by an authoritarian regime that is not compelled to have laws approved by a legislative body. Government by fiat may be the last resort of a regime that has no legitimate mandate to rule.

fifth column: a treasonous group or faction that gives support to an enemy. For example, a nation might be successfully fighting an external enemy, but then be undone by the appearance of a fifth column within its midst. The term dates from the Spanish Civil War (1936–39), in which four columns of rebels attacked Madrid, while rebel contingents within Madrid organized a campaign of sabotage and uprisings. They became known as the fifth column.

figurehead: someone who is nominally in a position of authority but who holds no real power.

filibuster: holding up legislation or other business in the U.S. Senate by organizing continuous speeches in opposition so that no vote can be taken. Sixty Senators are needed to vote to end a filibuster. In 1995, the nomination of Dr. Henry Foster for surgeon-general was defeated by a filibuster in the Senate. Filibusters are often used by minority groups to offset their numerical disadvantage.

fireside chat: the term has its origins in the radio addresses given by President Franklin D. Roosevelt in the 1930s. Roosevelt aimed for informality to convey the impression that he was speaking directly to all the American people, grouped around their own firesides. The term can be used today when a contemporary president or any politician attempts to do a similar thing.

fiscal policy: the use government makes of its taxing and spending powers to achieve particular ends, such as the rate of growth of the money supply or the amount of the budget deficit or surplus. Fiscal policy includes decisions about what level of taxation, and what type of taxation (direct, like income tax, and indirect, like sales tax), to impose.

foreign policy: the objectives pursued by a state in its dealings with other states, and the methods and course of action used to pursue them. P.A. Reynolds, in *An Introduction to International Relations*, defines foreign policy as "The range of actions taken by varying sections of the government of a state in its relations with other bodies similarly acting on the international stage ... in order to advance the national interest."

fourth estate: the press and other media. The term was first used in England in the 18th century. Estate means the same as class, the other three being nobility, commoners, and clergy.

franchise: a privilege granted to an individual or a corporation by a government to operate a business. The term also refers to a practice in the retail trade where a company (the franchisor) gives another company (the franchisee) the right to operate under the franchisor's name. The advantage for the franchisees is that they can have immediate name recognition for their business (particularly if the franchisor is nationally known). The franchisors gains by expanding their business with the minimum of capital.

free enterprise: the economic system that is fundamental to capitalism. The means of production are privately owned and decisions regarding producing and pricing are governed by market forces. i.e., prices are regulated only by free market competition. There is only minimal government intervention.

free market: economic transactions that are conducted under the conditions of a free enterprise, market economy, i.e. one that is controlled only by forces of supply and demand. See also supply and demand.

free trade: international exchange of goods without government regulation, such as tariffs, quotas, exchange controls, subsidies to domestic producers, etc. The principles of free trade hold that a country that is efficient at producing a given product will profit from exporting it to countries that are less efficient at producing it. In return, such a country can use the wealth it gains for exports to buy goods and services that are being more efficiently produced elsewhere. When each country focuses on what it does best, market forces of supply and demand organize distribution for maximum economic growth, and consumers benefit from lover prices. In 1995, the General Agreement on

Tariffs and Trade (GATT) marked a new leap towards worldwide free trade. Tariffs will be cut by an average of 40 percent in the 124 participating countries.

front organizations: organizations that provide respectable cover for subversive or criminal activities. The mafia, for example, conducts many of its operations under cover of apparently respectable businesses, which serve as front organizations.

fundamentalism: the term is usually applied to a certain kind of religious conservatism, whether Christian, Muslim, or other, that takes the words of the Bible, or other sacred text, as literal truth and advocates the adherence to biblical (or Koranic) prescriptions and values in social and political life as well as private life. Christian fundamentalists, for example, advocate the teaching in schools of what they call creation science, which asserts that the biblical account of the creation of the world in the Book of Genesis is literally true and can be read as real history and real science. Critics accuse fundamentalists of intolerance and censorship; fundamentalists reply that they merely wish to return the country to its roots in Christian civilization and Christian moral values.

G

gag rule: any order from a court, or other authority, not to discuss something. For example, the administration of President George H. W. Bush instituted a gag rule that disallowed federally financed family-planning clinics from informing their patients of the availability of abortion services. (The rule was lifted by the Clinton administration in 1993.)

general strike: a strike that is not limited to one trade or industry but involves several, and is sufficiently widespread to paralyze the economy. In U.S. history, general strikes occurred in the early days of unionism, but were generally short-lived and diminished as labor unions became more practiced and successful at negotiating with employers. The general strike has been a more effective weapon in Europe. In Britain in 1926, for example, a general strike involving miners and transportation workers brought the country to a standstill for nine days.

genocide: the systematic killing of a whole people. The term was first applied to the Nazi attempt to exterminate the Jews during World War II. It has been applied more recently to the war in Bosnia, where the Serbs were accused of practicing genocide against the Muslim population, and to ethnic conflict in Rwanda in 1994, which resulted in the killing of thousands of members of the Tutsi tribe by Hutus. Another example in history would be the killing of an estimated 600,000 Armenians by the Turks in 1915. See also Holocaust.

geopolitics: the influence of geographic factors on international politics. These include size, location, natural resources, topography, and terrain. To give just a few examples of geopolitical considerations: the Middle East, as a main route between East and West, has always been considered of great strategic importance, and since the discovery of oil in the region, it has become even more so. Topography has historically been important for Britain, because as an island it could not be conquered except by the sea. Therefore, it built up the biggest navy in the world, which also encouraged trading and the acquisition of overseas territories, which led to the development of the British Empire. Geographic influences on foreign policy-making tend to be stable over time and change only slowly.

gerontocracy: a government controlled by old men.

gerrymander: to deliberately and unfairly arrange voting districts to favor one party or group-usually by those who are in power and want to preserve it. However, the Voting Rights Act of 1965 encouraged a new kind of gerrymandering; it has been called "affirmative gerrymandering," the rearranging of electoral districts so that they contain a large percentage of minorities, and so greatly increase the chance that a minority candidate will be elected to office. This sometimes results in congressional districts of unusual shapes that have (so opponents of the practice argue) no justification, since they are spread wide geographically, and do not constitute a real community with common interests.

globalization: usually used to refer to the emergence in recent years of a global economy based on the principle of free trade. Trade agreements such as the North American Free Trade Agreement (NAFTA) and the Uruguay Round of the General Agreement on Tariffs and Trade (GATT) accelerated this process. Advocates of globalization say it ensures growing prosperity for everyone; doubters say that some groups and nations will be at a disadvantage, and also point to the downside of economic interdependence, as witnessed by the ripple effect created by the Asian economic crisis that began in 1997. Still other experts are concerned that economic globalization gives too much power to multinational corporations at the possible expense of human rights and democracy.

gold standard: refers to a monetary system in which the unit of currency is equivalent to a given amount of gold; currencies can be converted into gold at a fixed price; and gold is usable as a currency. The gold standard has not been in operation in any country since the 1930s, as a result of the worldwide disruption caused by the Great Depression. In other words, the value of the currency is not related to the value of gold on the free market.

good offices: the means by which a state that is not a party to a dispute may be a channel for suggestions by others for a settlement, but does not get otherwise involved.

Gordian knot: in Greek legend, an oracle revealed that a knot tied by King Gordius of Phrygia could only be undone by one who was destined to become the ruler of all of Asia. Alexander the Great tried to untie it but failed, after which he cut it with his sword. The phrase now refers to any perplexing or apparently insoluble problem, and to cut the Gordian knot refers to finding a quick solution. So the Republican proposals to balance the federal budget by 2002 might be described as attempts to cut the Gordian knot of the budget deficit.

graft: to use public office for private gain; to take advantage of one's position to make money. When House Speaker Newt Gingrich revealed that he had accepted a $4.5 million book advance shortly after becoming Speaker, he was accused in some quarters of graft. (He later rejected the advance.)

grandstanding: the term refers to a deliberate attempt to win applause from an audience. In political speech, a politician might be accused of grandstanding when he makes statements or speeches that are designed to win quick applause from the public, or certain sections of it, but which do not contribute substantially to the matter under discussion (although the politician will undoubtedly deny that he is grandstanding: he is, of course, making serious and constructive proposals.)

gross national product (GNP): the value of all the goods and services produced by a country in a one-year period. GNP is used as a means of assessing the condition of a nation's economy.

greenhouse effect: sometimes called global warming, it is caused by atmospheric pollutants, mostly from the burning of fossil fuels (like the gasoline in automobiles) that form a barrier in the upper atmosphere which traps the heat being radiated from the earth. Since the heat cannot escape, temperatures at the earth's surface begin to rise, creating changes in the earth's weather patterns.

guerrilla: a person who practices guerrilla warfare.

guerrilla warfare: the term *guerrilla* comes from the Spanish, meaning "skirmishing warfare." Guerrilla warfare is when a small band of irregular soldiers, which would be no match for the enemy in a conventional battle, wages war by making surprise attacks on enemy supply lines, etc.

guild: an association for the promotion of mutual interests or for mutual aid, as in a writers' guild, etc. Guilds arose in Medieval times when men of the same craft or trade would group together to uphold standards and protect each other.

H

habeas corpus: a right that safeguards a person against illegal imprisonment. *Habeas corpus* is a Latin phrase that means "you must have the body." It refers to a writ that requires a person to be brought before a court to establish whether he is being detained legally.

hack: a worker for a political party, usually at a fairly low level of the organization, who is unquestioning in his loyalty to the party. Also refers to someone hired to do writing, often of a routine or uninspired nature.

hard currency: currency that has a stable value in international exchange and is therefore freely convertible into currency of other countries. The opposite is soft currency, which is subject to exchange controls. Hard currency serves as an international currency.

head of state: in a presidential system, the head of state is the president, who is considered to be the symbolic embodiment of the nation. In parliamentary systems, the head of state is not the prime minister but a figure considered to be above politics and representing the nation as a whole. In these systems, the head of state may have mainly a ceremonial function, as in present-day Germany and Israel. In a constitutional monarchy, the king or queen is the head of state—real power may be limited but symbolic power may be great.

hegemony: authority or influence. Usually used to refer to international affairs, to describe the dominance of a specific country, as in the 19th century was the period of British hegemony; the post-World War II era was one of U.S. and Soviet hegemony.

hierarchy: an organization with people ranked in order of grade, rank, etc. An executive, for example, would be high in the company hierarchy; a sales clerk would be low in that hierarchy.

Holocaust: the systematic extermination of whole peoples conducted by the Nazis in World War II. The Holocaust was the most terrible example of genocide in modern history, perhaps in the entire history of the world. It marked the only time that the resources of a large industrial state have been dedicated to rounding up, transporting and killing so many people in such a short space of time, for no reason other than the victims' race. Jews were gathered from all over Europe for the slaughter; in one two-month period in 1944, 438,000 Jews were shipped to Auschwitz alone.

    This is what awaited them: "The victims, unsuspecting, walked to the gas chambers under the blank and baleful gaze of the SS, and then were turned into smoke that blackened the skies, and a stench so awful and pervasive that Lyon [a survivor, Gloria Lyon, who was taken to Auschwitz when she was 14] lost her sense of smell for nearly five decades after." (From *Newsweek*, on the 50th anniversary of the liberation of Auschwitz.)

hostage: someone who is held against his will as a bargaining chip or as security. For example, in the 1980s, terrorists in the Middle East took Westerners hostage frequently, hoping to use them as a bargaining chip to win the release of Arab prisoners in U.S. and Israeli jails. And in May 1995, when Serb forces in Bosnia took UN soldiers hostage, they tried to use them as security, hoping to prevent an attack by NATO forces.

human rights: human rights were defined in the Universal Declaration of Human Rights, which was adopted by the United Nations in 1948. It was a historic step brought about in response to the horrors of World War II. Article 1 of the declaration states, "All human beings are born free and equal in dignity and rights. They are endowed with reason and conscience and should act towards one another in a spirit of brotherhood."

    Article 2 states, "Everyone is entitled to all the rights and freedoms set forth in this Declaration, without distinction of any kind, such as race, color, sex, lan-

guage, religion, political or other opinion, national or social origin, property, birth or other status." President Jimmy Carter's administration made human rights an important aspect of American foreign policy; those countries that violated human rights were less likely to have good relations with the United States than those who observed these rights.

humanitarian: an individual or organization devoted to promoting the welfare of humanity, especially to relieve pain and suffering. Thus the Red Cross is a humanitarian organization; sending aid to starving people is a humanitarian act.

I

iconoclastic: literally refers to the breaking or destroying of images. Thus an iconoclastic person is one who attacks or ridicules society's traditions or traditional institutions and cherished beliefs when he feels they do not live up to their ideals, have become corrupt, or have outlived their usefulness. Martin Luther, who founded the Reformation by denouncing abuses in the Roman Catholic Church, was a classic iconoclast.

idealism: the belief that politics should be governed by high ideals, based on the perception of how things should be rather than how they actually are. The term usually suggests impracticality, something that does not take into account the inherent imperfections and limitations of human nature and society.

ideology: the political doctrine of a party or group, as in communist ideology.

immigration: the movement into a new country of a person who is not a citizen of that country, to live there permanently.

impeachment: an accusation of misconduct brought against a person holding public office. The House of Representatives has the sole power to bring charges of impeachment, and the Senate has sole authority to try the case. Conviction requires a two-thirds majority. President Richard Nixon resigned as president in 1974 rather than face impeachment over his part in the Watergate scandal. The only presidents to be impeached were Andrew Johnson and William Clinton.

imperialism: the policy that aims at building and maintaining an empire, in which many states and peoples, spread over a wide geographical area, are controlled by one dominant state. Imperialism is the opposite of the principle of self-determination, which is the more generally accepted creed today. As such, although imperialism has existed from the time of Alexander the Great, it is not currently fashionable. Much of the twentieth century history of the third world, for example, is of the dismantling of the legacy of 19th century European imperialism.

implied powers: powers that are not stated explicitly in the U.S. Constitution but can be inferred, based on the interpretation of the powers that are expressed.

import: to bring goods or services from a foreign country into one's own country for purposes of sale. The opposite of export.

import quota: a form of government control over the number of imported goods. It may apply to a specific nation only, or to all imports of a certain item. It is designed to protect domestic industries.

in vogue: fashionable. If a political idea is considered in vogue, it simply means that a lot of people are currently talking about it and advocating it.

inalienable right: a right that is derived from natural law, a God-given right that cannot be taken away. The Declaration of Independence states that "all men are created equal, that they are endowed by their Creator with certain unalienable rights, that among them are life, liberty, and the pursuit of happiness."

incentive: something that acts as a spur to action. In economics, for example, a system of incentive pay, in which wages are based on production, rather than a fixed rate per time, may improve output. Salespeople who work on commission are also on an incentive system.

income tax: a tax levied by the government, at federal and state level, on personal and corporate incomes. Its main purpose is to finance government operations.

income policy: any government policy that exerts some kind of control over wages and prices. This is usually done to keep inflation down, and can take various forms: a wage freeze; voluntary controls; voluntary controls where the government sets a norm; a wage norm backed up by extra taxes on companies that exceed it.

incorporation: the creating of a corporation by going through the legal formalities. Applicants must apply for a charter, which is issued by the state, and which sets forth the powers, rights, and privileges of the corporation. Also refers to the application of the protections of the Bill of Rights to the states, a process also known as absorption. See also corporation.

incrementalism: a cautious type of decision-making, often used in budgeting, in which a limited range of gradual changes to a given policy are discussed, and then tested by implementation one at a time. Incrementalism can be frustrating to those who want radical change, because it means that governments tend to carry on the policies of their predecessors, with only small deviations.

independent counsel: also known as special prosecutor. An independent counsel is appointed on the recommendation of the attorney general to investigate possible wrongdoing by senior officials in the executive branch, including the president. The appointment itself is made by a panel of three federal appellate court judges. A special prosecutor is considered necessary to avoid a conflict of interest that might otherwise occur if the case was investigated by Justice Department prosecutors.

indictment: a document submitted by a grand jury to a court, accusing an individual of a specific crime.

individualism: the idea that the individual should be allowed to shape his or her own destiny, without having governments interfering and deciding on his or her behalf what is in his or her interests. Individualism is the opposite of totalitarianism, in which individuals are subordinate to the state. Individualism developed in the 18th and 19th centuries: the Founding Fathers all believed in individualism, which is enshrined in the Bill of Rights. The free-enterprise economic system is also based on the idea of individualism: if everyone pursues his own interests, the community will flourish.

indoctrination: instruction in or teaching of dogma, doctrine, principles, or beliefs. The term is usually used in a negative sense, to imply a rigid absorption of ideas or theories without critical evaluation or intelligent thought or discussion.

Industrial Revolution: the industrial and technological changes that started in England around 1760 and spread rapidly to other countries. The Industrial Revolution laid the foundations of the modern industrial system. Its main features were the invention of new machinery, which led to large-scale factory production; the rise of industrialists who headed large enterprises; the rise of a wage-earning class; the expansion of trade; the growth of cities; and the depopulation of the countryside.

industrialization: being industrialized, that is, to establish or develop industrialism.

INF Treaty: Intermediate-Range Nuclear Forces Treaty. This was an arms control agreement signed by the United States and the Soviet Union in 1987. Both sides agreed to eliminate intermediate- and short-range nuclear missiles from Europe. The agreement was ratified by the U.S. Senate in 1988.

infidel: a person who does not believe in any religion; an unbeliever. Someone who adheres to a religion different from one's own, particularly if that religion is non-Christian (similar to pagan). Now almost always used in a derogatory sense.

infiltration: penetration, in the sense of troops penetrating enemy-occupied territory, or spies getting a foothold in a hostile organization, or, in an totalitarian society, the spreading of new political ideas that may be perceived as subversive by the authorities.

inflation: an economic situation characterized by steadily rising prices, and falling purchasing power. It is in part caused by wage rates increasing faster than productivity.

infrastructure: the structure that underlies and makes possible all economic activity in a country. Infrastructure includes utilities, and communications and transportation facilities. Sometimes the term is extended to include such assets as the level of education among a country's citizens, as well as their industrial and administrative experience and skills.

injunction: a legal order from a court that prevents an individual or group from carrying out a certain action.

insurgence: a revolt or uprising, as in there was an insurgence in Mexico at the beginning of 1994.

insurgent: rebelling against the government or other form of political authority.

insurrection: rebellion or revolt, similar to insurgence.

integration: the opposite of segregation, integration means encouraging the free and equal mixing of different races, in education and public places. Integration in education was ordered by the Supreme Court in the *Brown v. Board of Education* case in 1954.

intellectuals: similar to intelligentsia, those who are perceived by themselves and by others as forming an intellectual or learned class. Karl Marx thought that the support of at least some members of the intellectual class was necessary for a successful socialist revolution. It is sometimes claimed that American society is on the whole suspicious of intellectuals, because intellectualism smacks of elitism, which is contrary to the American democratic tradition. It is a rare politician who admits to having intellectual interests; the man-of-the-people image is considered a better vote-getter.

interest: a group of people with a common cause, as in business interest; extra money paid for the use of money that is lent; benefit or advantage, as in it is in his interest to go.

interest group: a group that lobbies for the interests of its members. This activity is protected by the First Amendment: "the right of the people peaceably to assemble and to petition the government for redress of grievances." Interest groups mediate between individuals and the state. They may promote their interests by working to elect officials who are sympathetic to their cause. They may make donations to election campaign funds, for example-a practice that has recently come under fire, as the public perception has grown that many elected officials are virtual prisoners of special interest groups.

Others say that the activities of many different interest groups that influence policy are a healthy sign of a pluralist system. See also lobby.

intermediate-range missiles: missiles that can carry nuclear warheads over a distance of 600–3,000 miles. These include U.S. cruise missiles (range of 1,600 miles) and Pershing II missiles (range of 1,100 miles). The numbers of these missiles was greatly reduced by the INF Treaty in 1987.

International Atomic Energy Agency (IAEA): UN agency that works for the acceleration of the peaceful use of atomic energy in order to create peace, health and prosperity throughout the world; it encourages research and development on the peaceful uses of atomic energy. Headquarters is in Vienna, Austria.

International Court of Justice (ICJ) of the United Nations: the principal judicial organ of the United Nations, sometimes known simply as the World Court. Its jurisdiction covers cases that are submitted to it by UN members; it gives advisory opinions and renders judgments. The court has 15 judges, elected by the General Assembly and the Security Council, for 9-year terms. It sits in The Hague, Netherlands.

international law: rules, principles, and conventions that govern the relations between states. International law has been built up piecemeal through agreements, tribunals, international conferences, long-established customs. There is no international lawmaking body, as such, and national governments themselves decide whether they will adhere to the principles and conventions of international law. The Statute of the International Court states the basis on which international law rests and on which it adjudicates in cases brought before it: "(a) international conventions, whether general or particular, establishing rules expressly recognized by the contesting states; (b) international custom, as evidence of a general practice accepted as law; (c) the general principles of law recognized by civilized nations."

International Monetary Fund (IMF): the IMF was established in 1946, with 39 members. Membership now stands at 182 countries, which includes all the major countries of the world. Each member contributes to a pool of funds that are made available, under certain conditions, to countries that need temporary help. The United States, with the world's largest economy, contributes most to the IMF, providing about 18 percent of total quotas (about $35 billion); Palau, which became a member in 1997, has the smallest quota, contributing about $3.8 million. Financial assistance is usually accompanied by requirements designed to get the recipients' economy onto a more secure footing. The goal of the IMF is to keep currencies stable so that financial weak spots do not unbalance the world economy or allow individual nations to go bankrupt.

internationalism: the belief that the greatest possible cooperation among nations in trade, culture, education, government, etc. is the best way to build peace. This is the opposite of isolationism and nationalism. In the 20th century the founding of the League of Nations (1919) and the United Nations (1945) was a great step forward for internationalism. See also isolationism; nationalism.

intervention: interference of one state in the affairs of another.

interventionism: the policy that advocates intervention in the affairs of other nations in specific instances or as a general principle. Intervention can be military or humanitarian.

investment: in terms of economics, investment is the spending of money on capital equipment, such as factories or machinery. In a more general sense, investment refers to purchasing an asset that can produce more money (buying shares, for example), or to any expenditure that involves a temporary loss in the hope of future benefit.

invisible hand: a term coined by Adam Smith in his classic text The Wealth of Nations (1776). The idea is that if everyone in a society is pursuing his own economic self-interest, an "invisible hand" ensures that he will also be serving the interests of society as a whole. Self-interest is equated with universal interest. Such a notion is at the heart of the free-enterprise system. Smith's phrase means that a person guided by self-interest will be "led by an invisible hand to promote an end which was no part of his intention."

Iron Curtain: a phrase made famous by British Prime Minister Sir Winston Churchill, in a speech at Westminster College, Fulton, Missouri, in 1946, when he said, "An iron curtain has descended across the continent." The Iron Curtain divided democratic Western Europe from the communist Eastern bloc, consisting of the Soviet Union and Eastern Europe.

Islamic fundamentalism: a movement designed to return Moslem countries, many of which are ruled by secular governments, to a system of government based on the principles of the Koran. Islamic fundamentalism made its first impact in recent history in 1979, when it was responsible for the overthrow of the Western-backed shah of Iran, replacing him with a virulently anti-Western government that was strongly influenced by conservative Islamic clerics.

Islamic fundamentalists oppose the Westernization of their countries because they believe it undermines the traditional religious values of their society. They want to install Islamic Law, Shari'a, under which, for example, alcohol would be outlawed, and sexes would be segregated in the workplace. Islamic law is also known for its harsh penal code, including the amputation of hands and feet of criminals. Islamic fundamentalists are currently waging a civil war against Algeria's secular government; fundamentalism is also a force in Egypt and amongst the Palestinians, where militant Islamic groups such as the Islamic Jihad and Hamas are dedicated to overthrowing the peace process between Israel and the Palestine Liberation Organization.

There is a widespread fear in the West that Islamic fundamentalism in its militant form could become a strong destabilizing force in Europe, North Africa and the Middle East. Some even suggest that now that the Cold War is over, Islamic fundamentalism has replaced the Soviet Union as the greatest danger to the West. This is an extreme view, and ignores the diversity amongst Muslim groups, not all of whom are a threat to Western interests.

isolationism: the policy of detaching one's country as much as possible from international affairs. American foreign policy in the 19th and early 20th centuries, and then again between the two world wars, was dominated by isolationism. It was made possible by America's relative physical isolation, with oceans on either side of it.

This policy was abandoned after World War II, in part because of the decline of British power, the rise of the Soviet Union, and the technological revolution in weaponry that rendered the United States vulnerable to attack as never before. In today's interdependent world, it would be hard to imagine America, or any major power, could pursue a pure isolationist policy.

ivory tower: used figuratively to refer to a place cut off from the real world. If a professor at a university, for example, comes up with a controversial idea to solve some social problem, people will be quick to say that he lives in an ivory tower and does not understand the nature of the real world.

J

Jacobinism: the political doctrines of the Jacobins, a society of revolutionary democrats in France during the time of the French Revolution (1789–94). The term can be used to refer to any political radicalism.

Jeffersonian democracy: refers to the principles held by President Thomas Jefferson, some of which, such as the

belief in the inalienable rights of the individual and the hatred of despotism, can be found in the Declaration of Independence, of which he was the principal author. Jefferson's ideal was an agrarian society, made up of self-sufficient farmers, under the leadership of natural aristocrats by means of republican institutions. Jefferson disliked industrialization and the growth of big cities. He also preferred a weak federal government, with authority vested in state and local governments, as a protection against government abuse of power.

jihad: an Arabic term meaning "striving" or "effort" in the service of God, which was applied to political conquest on behalf of Islam. Thus a jihad is a holy war.

jingoism: aggressive and warlike patriotism. Usually used in a derogatory sense. A politician might advocate a jingoistic foreign policy, but he would not call it that—a task hat would be left to his opponents.

judicial review: the power of the Supreme Court to decide whether a law is Constitutional or not.

judiciary: the branch of government and the system of courts that interpret the law.

junta: the term for a military government.

jurisdiction: the right of a political or legal authority to exercise that authority over a territory, subject, or person, as in the case came under the jurisdiction of the district court.

jurisdictional dispute: a dispute between government bodies over which one has authority over a particular area, for the providing of services, taxation, or prosecution in a criminal case.

just war: a war that is supported by the overwhelming majority of people in the country that is fighting the war, because they believe that they are in the right. World War II is considered a just war, because it was universally known amongst the United States and its allies that Nazi Germany was evil. The war in Vietnam in the 1960s and 1970s would not generally be referred to as a just war, because the lines between good and evil were not so easy to determine.

K

Keynesianism: the economic theories of John Maynard Keynes, and his followers. The Englishman Keynes's best known work was the *General Theory of Employment, Interest and Money*, published in 1936 at the height of the Great Depression. Keynes shifted the attention of economists from microeconomics to macroeconomics. Much of his book is on the causes of unemployment. Keynes stated that the economy had no self-balancing equilibrium that resulted in full employment, as classical economics insisted. On the contrary, it could be in equilibrium at less than full employment (the first time this theory had been proposed). Keynes believed it was therefore the job of government to stimulate spending through deficit financing to ensure full employment. Keynes's theory was vastly influential. Since then, governments have tended to accept a responsibility to provide full employment—although they have not always been successful in doing so. See also classical economics; neoclassical economics.

keynote: the main point in a lecture or discussion, as in the keynote of the president's address was the importance of moral values.

kitchen cabinet: the closet advisers of a president or prime minister. A kitchen cabinet may well consist of people who are not members of a formal cabinet. They may be close friends or cronies of the president, who trusts and values their advice.

L

labor movement: organized labor unions in the United States, and their history. At the turn of the century, only about 3 percent of the country's labor force belonged to unions. Up to the 1930s, unions were actively suppressed by employers. Workers inclined towards organizing were often fired and blacklisted, and sometimes even beaten up or locked out of the plant. The courts often ruled that union attempts to increase wages and influence working conditions through strikes and picketing were illegal.

But membership grew nonetheless, especially during the Great Depression of the 1930s. By the 1960s, over 30 percent of the labor force was unionized. Since then membership has declined, in part because of the decline of highly unionized industries such as railways and the clothing trade, and the increase in white-collar workers, who have less of a tendency to organize than blue-collar workers.

By 1990, the percentage of the labor force that was unionized dropped to about 18 percent. The political influence of the labor movement has declined accordingly.

labor union: an organization of workers that negotiates collectively with employers over wages, working conditions, etc.

laissez-faire: a guiding principle of free enterprise systems, laissez-faire is a French phrase which literally means "let do." It refers to the belief that government should not intervene in the conduct of trade and industry. Proponents of *laissez-faire* argue that the principle promotes freedom and economic growth.

lame duck: someone who is ineffectual or helpless. Sometimes used for an officeholder who is nearing the end of his term of office and either is not seeking, or is not eligible for another term. His authority is considered to be considerably eroded. For example, when President Lyndon Johnson announced in 1968 that he would not seek his party's nomination for president, he became a lame duck president for the remaining months of his term.

landlocked: encompassed by land, i.e., without a sea coast.

landslide: an overwhelming victory in an election. Of recent U.S. presidential elections, those in 1980, 1984, and 1988 can be considered landslides, because the Democratic candidates carried only a few states in each case, and were thus "buried" under a landslide.

law and order: the condition existing in a society when the vast majority of the population observes the generally established rules of conduct. Traditionally, "law and order" has been a rallying cry for conservatives, especially at election time, who want tougher measures to deal with crime and criminals.

layman: someone who is not a member of a profession, or who is not an expert on a specific topic, as in to the layman, the language of lawyers can be unintelligible.

leadership: those who hold the positions of power in a party, government, legislature, etc.; the ability to lead—not only to be able to manage people and institutions, but to show others a path and inspire them to want to follow it. Societies going through periods of uncertainty often bemoan the lack of leadership and long for a "strong leader," but in many cases they get more than they bargained for—dictators of all stripes may be "strong leaders" but that doesn't mean that they leave their societies better than they found them.

Former U.S. Secretary of State Henry Kissinger recently made a distinction between the modern political leader and those of a former generation, such as Sir Winston Churchill: "The political leaders with whom we are familiar generally aspire to be superstars rather than heroes. Superstars strive for approbation; heroes walk alone. Superstars crave consensus; heroes define themselves by the judgment of a future they see it as their task to bring about. Superstars seek success in a technique for eliciting support; heroes pursue success as the outgrowth of inner values." See also statesman.

League of Arab States (LAS): also known as the Arab League; member nations include: Algeria, Bahrain, Djibouti, Egypt, Iraq, Jordan, Kuwait, Lebanon, Libya, Mauritania, Morocco, Oman, Qatar, Republic of Yemen, Saudi Arabia, Somalia, Sudan, Syria, Tunisia, United Arab Emirates, and Yemen Arab Republic. The LAS works toward peace in the Arab region, promotes cooperation amongst members in military, health, communication, and cultural matters. The headquarters is in Tunisia.

lease: a contract in which one party gives to another the use of property, such as land or buildings, for a specified time for a specified payment.

leftist: a person or group that adheres to the left wing on political issues. Often used to describe insurgents, as in leftist guerrillas.

left-wing: on the left of the political spectrum. The term can include communism, socialism, or liberalism. It originated in the seating arrangements in 19th century European parliaments, where the conservatives would sit on the right side of a semicircle (as seen from the point of view of the presiding officer, often the king) and the socialists on the left. The more radical the group, the further to the left they sat.

left-wingers: people who advocate generous spending on the welfare state, vigorously promote the rights of women and minorities, are suspicious of high spending on defense, tend to be internationalist in outlook, favor government controls on the free-market system, and generally favor social welfare over business interests. In the United States, the left wing is not a major factor in national politics, as far as elections are concerned. The Democratic Party has some left-wing adherents, but it tries to minimize their influence when election time comes around. Left-wing groups, however, often form powerful interest groups that do exert influence on particular issues. See also communism; liberal; liberalism; Marxism; socialism.

legalism: strict adherence to the letter of the law, or to bureaucratic red tape, to the exclusion of all else, including common sense.

legalistic: the same as legalism.

legality: the condition of being legal; in conformity with the law.

legislation: laws enacted by a legislature; also the process of making laws.

legislator: a person who is a member of a legislative body, elected to represent the interests of her constituents.

legislature: the branch of government that is responsible for making laws. In the United States, as laid down by the Constitution, only Congress can make laws.

legitimacy: the attribute of a government that came to power through legal means; the state of being sanctioned by law.

leisure class: any group of people who do not have to work for a living, or who work very little and have time for leisure and recreation. Despite predictions in the 1950s and 1960s that new technology would mean that people would have to work fewer hours, this hasn't happened: Americans now spend more time working than they did several decades ago. The leisure class has not become any bigger.

Leninism: the modern form of Marxism as developed by Vladimir Ilyich Lenin. Lenin led the uprising that overthrew the Russian government in the October Revolution of 1917. He applied Marxism to the new kinds of capitalism that had developed since Marx's day, such as the increasing concentration of capital in larger organizations of producers. Lenin believed that the constant search for raw materials, driven by the need to make a profit, resulted in imperialist policies that led to recurrent wars. The state was merely a tool of the ruling class and therefore had to be destroyed.

One of the distinctive aspects of Leninism was the creation of the party, a disciplined group of revolutionaries who would act as the vanguard of the proletariat.

Lenin did not believe that capitalism would collapse merely through the weight of economic forces; there had to be a catalyst, and this was the party. Through the party, Lenin justified extreme measures for seizing and consolidating power, and laid the basis for the authoritarianism that transformed the Soviet Union into a dictatorship and kept all power in the hands of the Communist Party (where it remained until as recently as 1991). Thus, the original Marxist idea that the state would gradually wither away turned out to be the opposite of the truth-the power of the state continued to grow.

liaison: a linking up or connecting to, so as to coordinate activities, especially of a military nature.

liberal: in political speech now in the United States, a liberal is a person who believes it is the duty of government to ameliorate social conditions and create a more equitable society. Liberals favor generous spending on the welfare state; they exhibit a concern for minorities, the poor, and the disadvantaged and often see these conditions as a product of social injustice rather than individual failing. This also applies to crime and juvenile delinquency, where liberals are as concerned with removing the social causes of such behavior as they are with detection and punishment.

Liberals also tend to be concerned about environmental issues and the defense of civil liberties, and do not favor excessive military spending. The label of "liberal" is something that many politicians now seek to avoid, since it is out of keeping with the public mood. In the presidential campaign of 1988, George Bush used this to telling advantage, labeling his Democratic opponent Michael Dukakis a liberal, and making the term sound subversive and un-American. President Clinton tried to distance himself from traditional liberalism in his campaign of 1992, calling himself a New Democrat instead. See also liberalism.

liberalism: in 19th-century in Europe, the great age of liberalism, the term stood for freedom from church and state authority and the reduction of the power of royalty and aristocracy, free enterprise economics, and the free development of the individual. Liberalism advocated freedom of the press, religious toleration, self-determination for nations.

It was liberalism that established parliamentary democracy. The Founding Fathers might be termed liberals. In the 20th century, liberal parties were caught between conservatives and socialists and their influence

declined. Today, liberalism stands for something rather different than it did in the 19th century (more government rather than less government). See also liberal.

liberation: freedom, emancipation; often applied to the freeing of a people after enemy occupation (the liberation of France in 1944, for example). Revolutionary movements sometimes call themselves liberation movements—meaning liberation from an oppressive government. Liberation can also simply mean the gaining of equal social and economic rights, as in the women's liberation movement, now more usually called feminism.

libertarianism: the belief that government should not interfere in the lives of citizens, other than to provide police and military protection. Libertarianism cannot easily be placed on the left-right scale that is usually used to analyze political philosophies. Libertarians are strong supporters of capitalism and free trade and yet also tolerant on social and lifestyle issues, which are considered none of the government's business.

The basic philosophy is "live and let live." For example, libertarianism would remove the ban on consensual activities, often called "victimless crimes," such as drug use and prostitution, which do not harm the person or property of another. A Libertarian Party was formed in 1971 and regularly contests presidential elections, winning nearly half a million votes in 1996.

liberty: freedom, particularly from any unnecessary restraints imposed by governmental authority. Liberty was one of the slogans of the French Revolution ("Liberty, equality, fraternity") and it has proved a rallying cry ever since. It is central to America: liberty is one of the inalienable rights described in the Constitution ("life, liberty, and the pursuit of happiness"), and it has always been what America sees itself as standing for, as, for example, in President John F. Kennedy's inaugural address in 1961, when he said, "Let every nation know, whether it wishes us well or ill, that we shall pay any price, bear any burden, meet any hardship, support any friend, oppose any foe to assure the survival and the success of liberty."

lien: a legal term that refers to the claim a lender has on someone's property, as security in the event of nonpayment of a debt.

limited government: the clarion call of the mid-1990s in the United States, a limited government is one that does not have enormous power. Such a government is in fact provided for in the constitution, with its methods of checks and balances. However, many argue that over the last three decades, the federal government has become too big, taking on more responsibilities and powers than the Constitution intended, and created a huge bureaucracy that is unresponsive to public needs. It is this that has led to calls for a more limited, smaller, central government.

limited war: a war in which a nation does not use all the military or economic resources it possesses. The war in Vietnam was for the United States a limited war, with only gradual increases in force being applied, and the military being held back by political considerations. The Persian Gulf War in 1991, in which massive and overwhelming force was used, was still a limited war because at no point did the U.S. consider using nuclear weapons, nor, it seems, did the Iraqis use the chemical weapons they apparently possessed. Limited war is the opposite of total war. See also total war.

lobby: similar to an interest group, a lobby is any individual or group that attempts to exert an influence over legislation or other government action. Lobbyists come from all sectors of society: business, professional, labor, farm, education, church, consumer associations. The practice of lobbying, according to its advocates, gives ordinary people a voice in government; but those who argue that special interest groups are too powerful say that lobbying hinders democracy, because what is good for the special interest may not be good for the country as a whole.

local government: any government that is not state or federal, such as county, city, town, or village.

M

Machiavellian: one who adopts the principles of Niccolo Machiavelli (1469–1527), a Florentine political theorist who advocated the use of duplicity and cunning in political affairs. Machiavelli thought man was naturally evil and was best governed by the use of fear and force: "Whoever desires to found a state and give it laws, must start with assuming that all men are bad and ever ready to display their vicious nature." An unscrupulous and crafty strategy was acceptable because the ends justified the means.

macroeconomics: a branch of economics that is concerned with the overall picture of the economy, with aggregates rather than individual parts. Macroeconomics

deals with data such as the level of employment, gross national product, economic growth, balance of payments, inflation, etc., rather than with individual companies or markets, which is viewed as microeconomics.

magistrate: a judge of a minor court.

majority: more than half of a given thing, as when a political party has the largest share of seats in a legislature; also means being of full legal age, as in she reaches her majority on her next birthday.

Malthusian: refers to the theory of Thomas Malthus, an 18th-century British clergyman and professor of political economy, whose *Essay on the Principle of Population* (1798) developed the theory that the world's population tended to grow faster than its food supply. If the population continued to increase, there would be mass starvation. Malthus thought that famine, poverty, and war were natural checks against population growth and should not be alleviated by misguided compassion. Malthus also advocated restraint on the size of families. Although Malthus was proved incorrect as far as Western industrial society is concerned, the dramatic world population growth in the 20th century, and the fact that some third world nations cannot feed their rising populations, have led to a renewed interest in Malthusian theories in some circles.

mandate: an order or command; the wishes of constituents expressed to a representative. Politicians usually like to maintain that they have a mandate for the policies they pursue, which gives the policies the legitimacy that they need. When politicians win elections by big margins, they tend to assume they have a mandate, and are sometimes thereby more bold in pursuing their goals than they might otherwise be. Some of President Clinton's opponents questioned whether Clinton had a firm mandate from the people because he was elected president in 1992 with less than 50 percent of the vote (to which Clinton supporters might reply that he had more of a mandate than any other candidate in that election).

manifesto: a public statement of beliefs or plans by a government or other group, such as the Communist Manifesto.

maritime law: a collection of laws, built up by custom over centuries, that relate to shipping. Maritime law deals with such matters as registration, license, and inspection procedures and with contracts regarding insurance, carrying of goods and passengers, towage, and supplies.

market: the buying and selling of goods and commodities in a marketplace. This has nothing to do with a particular location—it refers only to the conditions where buyers and sellers can conduct business together. A market results whenever the forces of supply and demand operate.

market forces: refers to the mechanism by which basic questions of buying and selling are answered, such as the quantity of goods to be produced, the price they are to be sold at, etc., when this takes place without government intervention. If, for example, a supply of certain goods suddenly becomes scarce (say a fruit crop is badly affected by the weather), the law of supply and demand will ensure that the price for those goods goes up, and this is an example of market forces at work.

martial law: rule of a state by the military, usually as a temporary measure, caused by an emergency. The term can also refer to a period of harsh rule by a military regime that is not sanctioned by popular vote or the nation's constitution. For example, for much of the 1980s, Pakistan was placed under martial law by the military dictator, General Zia ul-Haq.

Marxism: the theory developed by Karl Marx and Friedrich Engels, which became the official doctrine of communism. According to Marxism, the key to how society operated was economics; all other aspects of society, such as politics and religion, were conditioned by the economic system. Under capitalism, society was divided into two classes: the capitalists, who owned the means of production and distribution, and the workers, or proletariat, whose labor was exploited by the ruling class. Marx saw history as a dialectical process in which two opposing forces (thesis and antithesis) generate a third, synthesizing force.

According to this view, capitalism would eventually break down because of its own contradictions, and this would lead to the proletarian revolution and the establishment of the classless society. In the later part of the 19th century, Marxism was adopted by labor and socialist movements in Europe. In the 20th century, Marxist governments came to power in Russia and Eastern Europe, and in varying guises in Asian countries such as China, North Korea, Vietnam, Cuba, and in some African countries. In none of these countries did the state eventually wither away and a classless society replace it.

On the contrary, Marxist societies were characterized by large and inefficient bureaucracies and had all the trappings of a police state. After the collapse of Soviet and Eastern European communism in 1989 and 1990, Marxism remained a viable system in only a few countries.

Marxism-Leninism: the term was first used by Josef Stalin in 1924: it referred to the interpretation of Marxism by Lenin, which became the official Soviet ideology during the rule of Stalin, and beyond. It included the doctrine, developed from Lenin, that the absolute power of the communist party had to be maintained during the interim period of the building of socialism.

However, much communist ideology was so adapted by Stalin that some of it bore little relation to Marx's or Lenin's original thoughts. For example, it was Stalin, not Marx or Lenin, who proclaimed "socialism in one country" (the idea that socialism could succeed in Russia without the assistance of worldwide revolution). See also Marxism; Leninism.

mass media: the media that reaches huge numbers of people: television (over 99 percent of American homes have one) and the press. Of the two, television is probably the most important, since over two-thirds of the public say that television provides most of their views on what is going on in the world. The same percentage say that television is their most trusted news source. This fact gives a lot of power to the major TV networks, regarding what they report and how they report it.

Marxist: a believer or expert in Marxism.

masses: the vast majority of people in a given population; the common people.

massive retaliation: part of the concept of deterrence during the Cold War. The policy of massive retaliation meant that any nuclear attack on the United States would be met by an overwhelming nuclear response. The belief was that knowledge of this policy would deter the Soviet Union from launching a first strike.

materialism: putting the highest value on the acquisition of wealth and consumer goods rather than on developing a spiritual or moral life. In philosophy, materialism is the doctrine that describes matter as the only reality—even mind and feelings can be explained in terms of matter.

matriarchy: a society that is dominated by women; the opposite of patriarchy. Also refers to a society or tribe where inheritance is passed down through the female line.

mayhem: in law, the offense of deliberately maiming a person.

McCarthyism: to accuse a person, or a number of persons, of subversive activities by the use of smears and half-truths, and without any supporting evidence. The term alludes to Senator Joseph McCarthy who claimed in 1950 that he had the names of 57 "card-carrying" communists in the State Department. He produced no evidence, but continued his witch hunt against alleged communists for several years, using it as a means of attacking leading Democrats and intellectuals. McCarthy was censured by the Senate in 1954, but not before his demagoguery had sent a wave of fear, known as the "Red Scare," through American society.

media: all the means by which news is disseminated in society: newspapers, magazines, television, radio. Conservatives often claim that the media is biased against them (a charge that would be hard to prove), and this dissatisfaction has in part led to the phenomenon in the last couple of years of "talk radio," call-in shows that are heavily dominated by right-wing hosts and contributors. The United States has been called the world's first "media state," in which the media dominates the political process. Because of the decline in political party organizations, politicians now take their message straight to the people via the media.

Elections can be won or lost by paid TV advertising campaigns; "media events," designed to showcase the candidate and his wares, are carefully orchestrated. But the media has imposed its own laws on political discourse. Speeches, instead of being full of carefully—argued substance, are geared to 10-second "sound bites" for the evening news; a politician's "image" is everything, and is carefully crafted by media-savvy experts. The result is often a media-packaged candidate whose real political convictions are hard to determine.

mediation: the use of an independent party to help settle a dispute between two other parties. Mediation is sometimes used in labor disputes or in international disputes. Unlike in arbitration, the disputants enter into no agreement to accept the suggestions of the mediator.

mercantilism: a school of economics in the 18th and 19th century that was directly opposite to the school of classical economics. Unlike the *laissez-faire* classicists, mercantilists believed in government action designed to encourage the flow of gold and other precious metals into the country.

mercenary: a person who offers his services for pay, and does not have any personal adherence to the cause he represents. Usually used of a mercenary soldier, but can apply in other fields as well.

meritocracy: a society in which power is wielded by those who deserve it, based on their talents, industry, and success in competition rather than through membership of a certain class or the possession of wealth, etc. America prides itself on being a meritocracy, an equal opportunity society; the ideal of a meritocracy is often cited by those who oppose affirmative action.

messianism: a doctrine that is inspired by the prospect of the imminent arrival of a messiah, a savior, who will lead his people to freedom.

methodology: the science of methods; a system of methods.

microeconomics: a branch of economics that deals with the individual parts of an economy, rather than the aggregate, which is the sphere of macroeconomics.

military-industrial complex: the extremely close political, economic, and bureaucratic relationship that exists between the Pentagon and its network of defense contractors. The phrase was coined by President Dwight Eisenhower in his farewell address in 1961, when he warned that "In the councils of government we must guard against the acquisition of unwarranted influence, whether sought or unsought, by the military-industrial complex. The potential for the disastrous rise of misplaced power exists and will persist." Because of the huge amounts of money (and large numbers of jobs) involved, the military-industrial complex has a profound influence on the nation's security policies.

militia: an armed force of citizen soldiers. Originally, militia systems were based on the idea that every citizen was obliged to serve his country; George Washington's army consisted of 41 percent militia. The other justification for a militia is that it safeguards the country against the possibility of gross abuse of power by a government or professional army. The Second Amendment of the U.S. Constitution states, "A well regulated Militia, being necessary to the security of a free State, the right of the people to keep and bear arms shall not be infringed," a clause that is hotly debated today by gun control advocates and their opponents. The state militia was replaced in 1916 by the National Guard. However, the 1990s saw a resurgence of interest in the idea of a citizen's militia, and many states now have such organizations.

Some of them are dominated by right-wing patriots and believers in conspiracy theories, who believe the U.S. government is becoming a tyranny and that they must take steps to defend themselves against it before it is too late.

millenarianism: the term originally referred to the Christian belief that Christ would return, and in this Second Coming would establish his thousand-year reign (the millennium), which would be followed by the Last Judgment of all humanity. The term is now used in a wider sense to describe a certain form that this belief has taken in Christian sects and movements. Norman Cohn, in his classic book *The Pursuit of the Millennium*, describes the following beliefs that millenarian movements profess: Salvation is thought to be collective (that is, to be enjoyed by the faithful as a group); it will be realized on this earth, not in an other-worldly heaven; it will come soon, probably within the lifetime of the believers; it will utterly transform all life on earth to perfection; and it will be miraculous, in that it will be accomplished by supernatural agencies.

Millenarian sects and movements flourished at various times in Europe from the 11th to 17th centuries. Elements of millenarian beliefs are found in many Christian churches and movements today, and some New Age groups profess similar beliefs.

minimum wage: the lowest hourly rate that an employer must pay an employee. Federal law mandating a minimum wage was first enacted in 1938, when the rate was set at 25 cents an hour. In 1995, President Clinton proposed an increase of 90 cents, to $5.15, to be phased in over two years. He pointed out that under the current minimum wage a full-time worker would still fall under the official poverty level. Republicans in general oppose a rise in the minimum wage, arguing that it would lead to job losses by prompting factories to move to countries with even lower wages, such as Mexico. Indepen-

dent analysts say that in 1995, the minimum wage hit a 40-year low in terms of real buying power.

minority: less than half. The Senate minority leader, for example, is the leader of the party that has less than 50 percent of the seats in the Senate. Minority also refers to ethnic or racial groups in a society, when they form part of a large society. A Native American, for example, is referred to as a minority, as are Native Americans collectively. The same applies to blacks, Hispanics, and other ethnic groups.

mixed economy: an economy in which elements from the free-enterprise system are combined with elements of socialism. Most industrial economies, now including those in the postcommunist world, are mixed economies. Even in the United States, that bastion of capitalism, some enterprises, such as the Post Office, are publicly owned, and business is subject to federal regulations.

mobilization: the process of calling up the armed forces in preparation for war.

moderate: not extreme. Moderate political policies are those that occupy the middle ground, between the right and the left, and that do not try to effect fundamental societal change. As such, moderate is the opposite of radical.

modus operandi: Latin phrase meaning "manner of working," as in the modus operandi of an army, an organization, a political system.

modus vivendi: Latin phrase meaning "manner of living," which is used to describe informal arrangements in political affairs, as in the two sides reached a modus vivendi regarding the disputed territories. They may not agree, but they have worked out a way of living with their differences.

momentum: the impetus of something that is already moving. In election campaigns, politicians always strive for momentum—a good performance in one presidential primary, for example, will give them momentum going into the next one.

monarchy: form of rulership whereby a queen or king, empress, or emperor holds absolute or limited power, usually inherited. By the 21st century, most European monarchies have become constitutional or limited, meaning political power is vested in elected officials and the monarch's duties are largely ceremonial. Such monarchies often represent a strong symbol of national identity in the people's minds. In some countries of Africa, the Middle East, and Asia, monarchs still continue to hold absolute power.

monetarism: the economic school that places growth in the money supply as central to economic planning.

money supply: the amount of money in an economy, made up of circulation currency and demand deposits (checking accounts) in commercial banks (the latter make up three-quarters of the money supply). It does not include U.S. government deposits. The total amount of money supply results from the interaction of banks, the Federal Reserve, business, government, and consumers.

monism: the doctrine that only one ultimate being exists. Thus Judaism, Christianity, and Islam are monistic religions.

monopoly: exclusive control of something. In economics, it refers to exclusive control of a commodity or service in a given market—which usually leads to higher prices for the consumer. Monopolies are not common in American industry, partly due to anti-trust laws. The term also refers to an exclusive privilege, granted by the state, of engaging in a particular business or providing a service.

Monroe Doctrine: a U.S. foreign policy that opposes European intervention in the political affairs of the Western Hemisphere. It was first laid down by President James Monroe in 1823, who stated that "the American continents, by the free and independent condition which they have assumed and maintained, are henceforth not to be considered as subjects for future colonization by any European powers. We should consider any attempt on their part to extend their system to any part of this hemisphere as dangerous to our peace and safety." In return, the United States agreed not to interfere in the internal affairs of Europe. The Monroe Doctrine was at the center of debate regarding U.S. involvement in World War I and World War II, and was also invoked during the Cuban Missile Crisis in 1962, when the Soviet Union installed nuclear missiles in Cuba—a violation of the Monroe Doctrine. However, analysts claim that the Monroe Doctrine is now declining in importance.

moralism: a doctrine that prescribes a code of ethics but does not link it to religion.

muckraker: a journalist who exposes conduct or practices that are against the public interest. Modern-day journalists who expose malpractices prefer to be called "investigative reporters." Referring to a character from *Pilgrim's Progress*, President Theodore Roosevelt first applied the term to early 20th-century reporting practices, calling them the "men with the muckrakes." He criticized them for focusing exclusively on corruption without providing a positive outlook for social problems.

mudslinging: the practice of trying to discredit political opponents by spreading lies, distortions, and innuendo about them. Mudslinging is part of what is today called "negative campaigning," and by many accounts has been on the rise in recent election campaigns, although it has existed as long as politics has.

multilateralism: pertaining to several sides. It can refer to international trade among more than two countries without discrimination among them, or to international diplomatic accords or treaties among more than two states. It is multilateralism, for example, when the U.S. consults with its European allies before making important foreign policy decisions, so that a unified position may emerge.

multinational corporations: corporations that have operations in more than one country. A United Nations report estimated that multinationals were responsible for 20 percent of industrial production in the non-communist world (this was before the fall of communism in Eastern Europe).

multiple warheads: several warheads (the part of the weapon that carries the explosive charge) on one strategic missile. Multiple warheads are also referred to as MIRVs, for multiple independently targetable reentry vehicles. Each warhead can be guided to a different target. The creation of multiple warheads in the 1980s made the nuclear balance between the superpowers more unstable because it made a first strike more attractive. Al Gore explained how the thinking went: "If the Soviet Union and the United States have three missiles apiece and that's their total arsenal, and each missile has six warheads, then the nation launching a first strike can launch one missile and put two warheads there, two there, and two there [Gore hits three paper cups on a table]. In the aftermath, the aggressor has two thirds of its forces remaining, and the victim has none." (Quoted in *The Power Game*, by Hedrick Smith.)

multipolar: having many poles. The term is often used to refer to the post-Cold War world, which is multipolar rather than bipolar, meaning that there are now many centers of global power rather than just two (the United States and the Soviet Union).

municipal law: local legislation; also refers to the national law of a country, as opposed to international law.

Muslim Brotherhood: a fundamentalist Islamic group that is a political force in several Arab countries. In Egypt, it is the largest opposition party in the National Assembly; in Jordan, the Muslim Brotherhood was brought into the government by King Hussein after it won 33 of 80 seats in parliament in 1990.

N
Napoleonic law: often considered the chief legacy of Napoleon Bonaparte, the Code Napoleon (Napoleonic law) came into effect in 1804 and remains the law of France. It is a collection of legal principles, in five sections: the civil code, the code of civil procedure, the code of criminal procedure and penal law, the penal code, and the commercial code. The Codes were based on common sense rather than any legal theory. According to the *Cambridge Modern History*, "the Codes preserve the essential conquests of the revolutionary spirit—civil equality, religious toleration, the emancipation of land, public trial, the jury of judgment. ... In a clear and compact shape, they presented to Europe the main rules which should govern a civilized society."

nation: a large group of people bound together by common tradition and culture and usually language. Sometimes used synonymously with state, but this can be misleading, since one state may contain many nations. For example, Great Britain is a state, but contains the English, Scottish, Welsh, and part of the Irish nations. Iraq is a state, but contains three distinct nations: the non-Arab Kurds, the Shi'te Muslims in the south and the Sunni Muslims who hold power in Baghdad. And single nations may be scattered across many states, as was the case with the Jewish nation which existed in many states before the creation of the state of Israel in 1948, and is now the case with the Kurds. See also nation state.

nation state: usually used to describe the modern state, but strictly speaking applies only when the whole population of a state feels itself to belong to the same nation. This is certainly more the case now than it was in the nineteenth century and earlier, when large empires, such as Austria-Hungary, were states but contained many nations. But many states today still contain many nations (partly because of the arbitrary way that the borders of states were redrawn after both world wars, and by the colonial powers as they withdrew from Asia and Africa), and with the rise of nationalism that has followed the fall of communism, this has been one of the main reasons for instability in states such as the Soviet Union and Yugoslavia.

national debt: the total amount that the national government owes.

national interest: the real interests of the country as a whole. To determine what is in the national interest a community needs common agreement on its goals and the extent to which any proposed action contributes to these goals. This is not always easy to obtain. As P.A. Reynolds states in *An Introduction to International Relations*: "The words, 'the national interest' are among those most frequently to be heard from the lips of politicians. Many of them, if pressed, might be hard put to say with precision what the words mean, still less to define the criteria by which the interest is to be determined."

national liberation: usually refers to the freeing of a country from colonial rule, or from oppressive rule of any kind. Wars to accomplish this end are often called wars of national liberation; guerrilla groups (usually leftist) that fight to overthrow their governments sometimes call themselves national liberation armies.

nationalism: excessive, narrow patriotism; the belief that the promotion of one's own nation as a culturally distinct and independent entity is more important than any international considerations. Nationalism flourished during the 19th century, which saw the rise of the nation-state, and the breakup of the Austro-Hungarian and Ottoman empires, which were composed of many nations. Since the demise of communism, nationalism has again become one of the chief driving forces in world affairs, and is at the root of many wars.

nationalization: the act by which government takes over a business enterprise or service that has formerly been privately owned. Opponents of nationalization say it is inefficient because it leads to overcentralization, and is costly. Supporters say that nationalized industries are easier to coordinate and can be expanded more easily and efficiently.

natural law: the eternal law that governs the entire universe, instituted by God, present in humans, and which should be the basis on which human society rests. Humans can deduce what natural law is through their reasoning power and their innate moral sense of what is right. Theorizing about natural law and its application in society goes back to Plato and Aristotle. Natural law is contrasted to statute law, which is those laws that are enacted by human authority.

natural rights: similar to what the framers of the U.S. Constitution called "unalienable rights," those rights that are given to humans by God or nature, such as life, liberty, and the pursuit of happiness. The Bill of Rights (the first 10 amendments to the Constitution) embody this concept of natural rights, which was given modern formulation by English, French, and American thinkers in the 17th and 18th centuries.

naturalization: the conferring of citizenship on a person who was formerly an alien, that is, a citizen of another country.

negotiation: discussion; bargaining to reach an agreement.

neoclassical economics: an economic theory that built on the foundation laid by the classical school of Adam Smith and David Ricardo. Neoclassical economics, developed in the 20th century, retained a belief in the value of a free market economy but also developed a theory of prices and markets that did not depend on the classical theory that the value of a good depended on how much labor it incorporated. Neoclassicists argued that price was dependent solely on the forces of supply and demand. See also classical economics.

nepotism: the practice of appointing relatives to positions for which others might be better qualified. In 1961 President John Kennedy feared that when he appointed his brother Robert Kennedy attorney general he would be accused of nepotism.

neutrality: legal neutrality under international law is granted to a country that has renounced all war in favor

of permanent neutrality. Switzerland, Sweden, Austria, and Ireland are examples of such countries, although they are permitted to defend their borders if attacked.

New Deal: the far-reaching social and economic programs enacted during the first and second terms of President Franklin Roosevelt. The New Deal was inaugurated in 1933 to overcome the Great Depression. Unemployment relief was increased, industry and agriculture were revitalized, and large public works and other programs that eventually gave employment to 10 million people were set up. Unemployment dropped from 17 million to 7 million. The banking system was also reformed, and in 1935 the Social Security Act was passed, giving security to the working population. The New Deal aroused opposition at the time as "creeping socialism," but its main provisions have endured.

New Left: a radical movement in American politics that began in the mid-1960s and had run its course by the early 1970s. The New Left grew out of dissatisfaction with Democratic liberalism, which was perceived as not fully embracing the civil rights movement or being fully committed to ending poverty. New Left theorists decided that liberals were no more in favor of change than conservatives. The escalation of the war in Vietnam was another factor that gave rise to the New Left, which supported the Vietnamese, as it did the Black Panther movement at home. Both were seen as allies in the global struggle against racist imperialism.

New Right: the term arose during the 1979s to describe a new type of conservatism that placed the highest values on social issues and pressed for constitutional amendments permitting prayer in schools and banning abortion. The New Right lost some momentum in the 1980s, but it is now a potent force once more, in the form of the Christian Coalition and its supporters. Opponents claim that the New Right, or radical right as it is sometimes called, is intolerant of all views but its own. Supporters say they are trying to guide a country that has lost its way back to its spiritual foundations.

nihilism: from the Latin word *nihil* meaning "nothing." Nihilism was an intellectual movement in Russia in the 19th century. Nihilists rejected everything in society, all authority, all accepted values, traditions, and social institutions. They wanted to destroy everything in order to build a new society in which the absolute freedom of the individual was paramount. Nihilists have been compared to the beatniks of America in the 1950s.

Nobel Prize: Royal Swedish Academy of Sciences awards Nobel prizes to individuals who make outstanding contributions in literature, economics, medicine, physiology, physics, and chemistry in Stockholm, Sweden. The Norwegian Nobel Committee awards the Nobel Peace Prize to an individual who has made an outstanding contribution to world peace in Oslo, Norway. The first prize was given in 1901; thereafter, Swedish scientist and inventor Alfred Nobel established a trust fund for the prizes. The Nobel Prizes are announced on October 21, the anniversary of Alfred Nobel's birthday; prizes are awarded on December 10, the anniversary of his death. Headquarters is in Stockholm, Sweden.

nobility: high social rank, especially that which is inherited, or that is conferred by title; the body of nobles in any society.

nomads: people who have no permanent home but who constantly move about in search of food and pasture. Nomadic tribes are found in parts of Asia and Africa.
nomination: the naming of a candidate by a party as their representative in an upcoming election; an appointment by the executive branch of the U.S. government of a person to fill a particular office, subject to the confirmation of the Senate.

nonaligned: nonaligned countries choose not to align themselves with any kind of military alliance or bloc. They hold to such ideals as expansion of freedom in the world, replacement of colonization by independent countries, and greater cooperation amongst nations. See also nonaligned movement.

nonaligned movement: an organization of over 100 different countries whose members do not belong to any military alliance (such as NATO or the Warsaw Pact). The movement was founded by Prime Minister Nehru of India, and Presidents Tito of Yugoslavia and Nasser of Egypt as a vehicle for nonaligned countries to come together to solve problems without benefit of military alliance.

Its members represent the full spectrum of political systems from democratic to one-party communist forms of government, including countries such as India, Pakistan, Singapore, Malaysia, Indonesia, Cuba, Egypt, most African and some Latin American countries. A summit is held every three years with the host country providing a chairman for the three-year period until the next summit meeting. The Coordinating Bu-reau of Foreign Ministers meets more often. The headquarters is the host country.

nonconformist: a person who does not act in accordance with established beliefs or practices, especially in connection with an established church.

nonintervention: the principle that a nation should not interfere in the internal affairs of another during peacetime. The principle is often little adhered to, especially in regions that a great power regards as its own sphere of influence. See also Monroe Doctrine.

nonpartisan: not affiliated with any political party.

nonproliferation: not multiplying. The term is used to refer to restrictions on the spread of nuclear weapons. There is a Non-Proliferation Treaty on nuclear weapons that was signed in 1968 by 115 nations and has now been signed by 140. However, India, Pakistan, and Israel, all states with nuclear capability, have not signed. India and Pakistan both conducted tests of their nuclear weapons in 1998, causing new fears of nuclear war. Also, since the breakup of the Soviet Union in 1991, there have been several incidents in which materials used to make nuclear weapons have been smuggled out of Russia and into Europe, leading to new concerns about proliferation.

nonviolence: the policy of pursuing political goals through peaceful protests involving large numbers of people. Nonviolence as a weapon of protest has been advocated by the great Russian writer Leo Tolstoy and was put into action by Mahatma Gandhi and his followers in India in their campaign for independence from Britain. Nonviolence, coupled with civil disobedience, was also a main plank of the American civil rights movement in the 1950s and 1960s, led by Martin Luther King, Jr. Nonviolence can be effective because it carries a moral authority that violence does not, and so can often win widespread sympathy for the protestors. See also civil disobedience.

normalization: return to a standard state or condition. In political speech, it refers to when a state brings its relations with another state back to normal after a period of rupture, as when the United States decided to normalize its relations with Vietnam in 1995.

North Atlantic Treaty Organization (NATO): a military alliance signed in 1949 by 16 countries: Iceland, Norway, Denmark, Spain, Portugal, Greece, Turkey, Italy, Belgium, the Netherlands, France, United Kingdom, Germany, Luxembourg, United States, and Canada. The purpose of NATO is the joint defense of all of its members and the peaceful coexistence with all nations; it regards an attack upon any one member as an attack upon all members. NATO organizes joint defense plans, and military training and exercises. The North Atlantic Council (NAC) is the principal organization of NATO and has permanent representatives from the 16 member countries; it has several committees such as the Defense Planning Committee (DPC), which meet on a regular basis. Headquarters is in Brussels, Belgium. In 1994, NATO agreed to accept new members, and in 1997, formal invitations were issued to Poland, Hungary, and the Czech Republic.

nuclear family: refers to the five countries that openly possess nuclear weapons. These are the United States, Russia, Britain, France, and China. Sometimes referred to as the nuclear club. However, other countries possess nuclear weapons but have not openly acknowledged the fact. These include India, Pakistan, and Israel. Some other countries, such as Libya, Iran and North Korea, are thought to have secret programs to develop nuclear weapons.

O

obscenity: something that is indecent and offensive. Obscene material is usually of an explicit sexual nature. A current national debate concerns the proliferation of obscene material over the Internet, and whether it should be censored. Those who oppose censorship often cite free speech, although in 1957 the Supreme Court ruled that obscenity was not protected under the First Amendment. However, one of the problems is that a workable definition of obscenity is hard to come by. Is something obscene, as some argue, if it violates "community standards"? But this begs the question of which community one is talking about, since standards are not uniform throughout the country, nor, perhaps, are they so within different segments of the same community.

obsolescence: in economics, a reduction of the life of capital assets, such as machinery, by improvements in technology or economic changes, rather than through natural wear-and-tear.

oligarchy: a political system that is controlled by a small group of individuals who govern in their own interests.

oligopoly: control of goods or services in a given market by a small number of companies. An example is the U.S. auto industry, in which three major manufacturers account for over ninety percent of the output of passenger cars.

olive branch: figurative expression referring to any peace offering from one person or group to another.

ombudsman: a public official who is appointed to investigate complaints by individuals about the activities of government agencies.

omnibus bill: from the Latin meaning "for all," an omnibus legislative bill contains many miscellaneous provisions, as in the omnibus budget bill that Republicans hope to push through Congress in the fall of 1995.

open society: a society, such as the United States and most European countries, in which individuals have freedom of movement and there are no restrictions on travel to and from other countries; public buildings and officials are relatively accessible, secrecy is at a minimum and there is a free flow of information. The opposite of a closed society, such as Albania and North Korea, which do not permit free travel or open intercourse with other countries.

opportunism: in politics, the practice of adapting one's actions to gain any short-term personal advantage that may be available, but without regard for principle or long-term consequences.

opposition: the party or parties in a legislative body that are against the party or parties that control the legislature.

oppression: severity, especially when practiced by a government that puts too heavy burden upon its citizens, in terms of taxes or unjust laws.

Organization of African Unity (OAU): membership consists of independent African states. OAU works to promote solidarity amongst members, improve the quality of life in Africa.

Organization of American States (OAS): created in 1948 to defend the sovereignty of the nations of South and North America; OAS also is involved in the settlement of disputes and promotion of economic and cultural cooperation in the region.

Organization for Economic Cooperation and Development (OECD): an international, intergovernmental organization with 24 member countries; promotes policies designed to achieve the rapid economic growth, employment, and standard of living in member countries, encourages sound economic expansion of world trade on a multilateral, nondiscriminatory basis in accordance with international obligations. Holds annual ministerial meeting every May in Paris, France where its headquarters is located.

Organization of Petroleum Exporting Countries (OPEC): Members are the oil-producing nations from the Middle East, Asia, and South America. OPEC coordinates the policies of members and determines the best means to safeguard their interests such as ensuring the stabilization of international oil prices.

orthodoxy: the generally, conventionally accepted principles or beliefs of a religion, or political party; the usual view.

ozone layer: ozone is a form of oxygen that is found in the earth's upper atmosphere. The ozone layer screens out harmful ultraviolet radiation from the sun. In recent years, hole have started to appear in the ozone layer, which are attributed to widespread use of chlorofluorocarbons (CFCs), commonly found in spray cans, refrigerators, and air-conditioning units. Damage to the ozone layer is expected to result in a variety of problems, among them an increase in skin cancer.

P

pacifism: the doctrine that holds that war is never justifiable and that all disputes between nations should be settled peacefully. Probably the most powerful statements in favor of pacifism this century were written by Russian novelist-turned-Christian anarchist, Leo Tolstoy, in tracts such as "Bethink Yourselves," written to protest the Russo-Japanese war of 1904–05.

pact: a broad term that refers to an international agreement, such as the Nazi-Soviet pact in 1939.

pan-African: the movement that aspires to the unification of all Africa, a federal arrangement that would result in a kind of United States of Africa, and which would be based on African traditions. Pan-Africanism began in earnest in the early 1900s and gathered momentum in the 1950s as African countries began to win their independence from colonial rule. In 1963, the Organization of African Unity (OAU) was founded, and it has since been the primary continent-wide African organization. But over the last 30 years, much of the steam has gone out of pan-Africanism. Ethnic, regional, and ideological barriers have been too great, and many of the newly independent African countries have been reluctant to contemplate surrendering their sovereignty to an all-African federation. In elections in South Africa in 1994, the Pan-African Congress performed poorly.

pan-Arab: the movement toward Arab unity, associated with the name of Gamal Abdel Nasser, who was president of Egypt from 1956 to 1970. Nasser made Egypt into the dominant Arab power and in 1958 he spearheaded a union between Egypt and Syria, hoping eventually to unite all the Arab nations under his leadership. But Iraq resisted and Syria withdrew from the union in 1961.

Although the Arab world is still divided, for decades the Arab nations have been trying to achieve the political unity among themselves envisioned by Nasser. In spite of the many differences among the 19 Arab nations, the Arabs feel themselves to be united by a common language, Arabic, and by their Islamic culture, which permeates all aspects of daily life.

pan-Islamism: a mainly 19th-century movement that aimed at uniting all Muslims. Pan-Islamism made some progress in India, but it failed in 1914 when the Indian Muslims failed to rise up in support of a proclamation by the Muslim Ottoman Empire of a holy war against the Christian British occupiers. However, in recent years, the idea of a pan-Islamic movement has found renewed vigor in Islamic fundamentalism, which is unified in its opposition to the Westernization of Islamic societies.

paramilitary: forces that work alongside of, or in place of, regular military forces. Often they do not have any official sanction and act in secret. Some of the citizens' militias that have recently sprung up in the United States are paramilitary organizations.

parity: equality. In political discourse, the term is employed in a variety of contexts: employment parity (when the makeup of a company's workforce is the same as the makeup of the population as a whole in its region); racial parity (when economic status of racial groups is equal); wage parity (the requirement that workers in certain occupations receive the same pay as workers in another, specified occupation).

parliament: the name was first given to the British legislature, which dates back to 1275, and has since been adopted in many other countries. Countries with parliaments operate under the parliamentary rather than presidential system.

The government is formed by the party that has a majority of seats in parliament. The government then controls the legislature, until such time as it loses its majority, usually in an election, but sometimes also by a vote of no-confidence.

participatory democracy: a system of government in which individuals and interest groups are involved directly in decision-making.

partisan: adhering to one party or another in a debate or on an issue, as in the debate was dominated by partisan politics.

partition: the division of a country into parts. This happened, for example, in Ireland in 1922, when the country was divided into the Republic of Ireland and Northern Ireland; and in Germany in 1945, when it was partitioned into West Germany and East Germany.

party line: the official doctrine or platform of a political party. The term is often used in a derogatory sense, implying a rigid adherence to party policy, as in communist bureaucrats always had to toe the party line.

party platform: the statement of beliefs and program of action that a political party proposes to take. It is issued at the party's national convention.

passive resistance: another term for nonviolent campaigns of civil disobedience. See nonviolence; civil disobedience.

passport: a document issued by a government to its citizens that grants an individual the right to travel abroad, confirms his identity, and that he or she is a citizen of the country that issued the passport. A passport is required for foreign travel; it entitles the bearer to the protection of his own country.

paternalism: governing or controlling a group, either employees or citizens of a state, in a way that suggests a father dealing with his children. In the United States, employees generally resent being subject to paternalism, because it smacks of charity and condescension. They would rather be treated like equals and negotiate

their own agreements. Other cultures, notably Japan, may feel differently about paternalism.

patriarchy: a society that is dominated by men. In anthropology, the term refers to a form of social organization in which the father is the head of the family or tribe, and descent and kinship is through the male line.

patrician: a person of high social rank; an aristocrat.

patrimony: something that is inherited, especially relating to property.

patriotism: love of one's country and loyalty to it, especially in relation to other countries.

patronage: jobs and other favors that an elected or appointed official is able to bestow on his political supporters.

peaceful coexistence: a phrase that was frequently used during the Cold War, to refer to the idea that even though the Soviet Union and the United States had differing social systems and were in an adversarial relationship, they could still exist together without resorting to war. The phrase could also be used for any situation in which rivals need to work out a "live and let live" arrangement.

peer: a member of the nobility, especially in Britain; an equal, as in being tried by a jury of one's peers.

people's democracy: the term used by communist governments to describe their political system, which does not resemble Western democratic systems.

per capita: for each person, as in per capita income increased last year.

persona non grata: Latin phrase meaning a person who is not acceptable or is unwelcome. If a diplomat is declared persona non grata, he must leave the host country.

philosopher king: the idea that the ruler of a country should also be the wisest person. This idea goes back to Plato's *Republic*. Plato's ideal ruler emerged from an elite group, formed out of the highest talent and given the most thorough training. This was training in the abstract disciplines of mathematics, science and philosophy, up to the age of 35.

There was no practical training in the administration of affairs. The philosopher ruler would prefer not to have to rule, since he was devoted to the study and cultivation of wisdom—he served the state out of a sense of duty. (Plato thought that anyone who wanted power was de facto unsuited for it.) Today we might see this as an elitist and undemocratic system of selecting a leader, and question whether such abstract training would fit a person for the task of practical politics.

pigeonhole: refers to the killing of a bill by a Congressional committee when it refuses to vote on whether the bill goes for consideration to the House of Representatives or the Senate. Pigeonholing is a frequent practice.

plank: any of the principles contained in a party political platform, as in welfare reform is a major plank of the Republican agenda.

planned economy: an economy that is controlled by the central government, which sets goals, priorities, production schedules, prices, etc.
    Planned economies are characteristic of socialist societies. Mistrusting the capitalist system of *laissez-faire*, which results in social injustices, they attempt to promote the public good by manipulation of economic forces. As the economies of the Soviet Union and Eastern Europe under communism revealed, however, planned economies are rarely as prosperous or as efficient as those that embrace free enterprise. Sometimes called a command economy.

plebiscite: a vote of all the people in a territory or country on an important issue, usually a matter of national sovereignty. Sometimes voters are presented with a choice between continuing to be ruled by the existing power, choosing independence, or some other course, such as annexation. In 1935, for example, the region of Saar chose to remain part of Germany rather than become part of France.

plenipotentiary: a person invested with full authority to act as a representative of a government.

pluralism: government carried out by a process of bargaining and compromise among a variety of competing leadership groups (business, labor, government, etc.). Advocates of pluralism claim that it best serves the democratic ideal in a complex modern society, in which individual participation in every act of decision-making is impractical.

According to pluralism, individual rights and interests are protected by a sort of extra-constitutional checks and balances: No single group holds the dominant power position, power is always shifting, and individuals can have influence on policy-making through being active in one of these power groups. Some claim that America is such a pluralistic society; other theories say that pluralism is in fact a myth and American society is elitist.

plutocracy: government by the wealthy; or a group of wealthy people who control or influence a government.

pocket veto: the process by which the U.S. president may veto a bill by not signing it. A bill normally becomes law 10 days (excluding Sundays) after it is submitted to the president for signature, if Congress is still in session. If Congress adjourns within that 10-day period, without the president having signed the bill, the bill is killed. A pocket veto cannot be overridden by a two-thirds vote in the Senate, as is the case with other presidential vetoes.

point of order: a question raised at a formal meeting about whether the action being taken is within agreed rules about how business is to be conducted.

polarization: showing two contrary directions and tendencies. In political speech, the term has come to refer to the process by which two sides in a dispute or a political issue move steadily further apart so that no rational solution or dialogue seems possible. One could say, for example, that American politics today is undergoing a sharp polarization due in part to the divisive and shrill tone of much public debate. When one side makes a provocative or extreme point, the other side finds itself responding in kind in order to be heard, so a polarization is set in motion.

police power: the power of a state to regulate the actions of individuals and society as a whole in order to protect and promote the general welfare, including public health, safety, and morals.

police state: a state in which the police, particularly the secret police, have wide and arbitrary power to survey, harass, and intimidate the citizenry, who are denied their civil rights and cannot protest their treatment or seek redress through the normal administrative or judicial channels of government. Such is the case in totalitarian societies, which rule by force rather than law.

political access: the ability to gain the attention of people in positions of influence in the political world. Gaining political access is the function of lobbyists.

political asylum: the granting of refuge by a state to an individual who has fled his country because of persecution.

political capital: the sum total of potential political influence that a politician builds up, by doing favors to others, supporting another lawmaker on a key issue, etc., so that when the time comes he can draw on this reservoir of capital because others are indebted to him.

political party: a political organization that puts up candidates at elections who support the party's policies and attempts to win power so that it can put its policies into operation.

political theory: the study of the philosophy of the state and of government, or of a particular idea relating to it.

politician: a person who participates directly in politics (usually party politics) as candidate for or holder of public office. Politicians often rate low in public esteem, as lacking integrity ("they'll promise anything to get elected"), but many politicians would say this is an unfair characterization of them. They would point out that many of them are motivated by a genuine desire for public service, and that they have to work in an imperfect system that demands flexibility and a willingness to compromise if anything is to be accomplished.

politicization: the giving of a political character to something. For example, if a debate over some previously nonpolitical issue becomes divided along party political lines, this would be a politicization of the debate.

politics: the process of government; the study of government.

populism: the term was originally used to describe political movements in Europe at the end of 19th century that appealed to the rural poor. In the United States, the Populist Party was formed in 1890 as a protest movement by farmers and laborers; it functioned until 1908. The term is now used to describe mass political movements, or a party platform that purports to represent a populist sentiment, usually understood as the collective

voice of the ordinary person on social and economic issues.

pork-barrel: a "pork-barrel" project is a publicly funded project promoted by a legislator to bring money and jobs to his or her own district. The "pork" is allocated not on the basis of need, merit, or entitlement; it is solely the result of political patronage, the desire of legislators to promote the interests of their own district, and thereby build up their local support. In 1998, Senator John McCain (R-AZ) claimed that $10 billion in pork-barrel projects was being allocated in that year's appropriations bills. Many of the projects McCain declared to have no valid national purpose were in the home states of senators who happened to sit on the Appropriations Committee.

possession: any territory belonging to an outside country.

postmortem: happening after death. Can be used figuratively, as in party leaders held a postmortem discussion about the reasons for their defeat.

pragmatic: dealing with things in a practical, "whatever works" manner, rather than relying on ideology or other theoretical considerations.

preamble: an introduction to a law or constitution that describes its purpose.

precedent: in law, a judicial decision that serves as a guide for future decisions in similar cases. Can also apply to administrative decisions made by the executive branch of government.

prejudice: a preconceived idea, usually unfavorable, about something, or an adverse judgment about someone or something, either in ignorance of the facts or in direct contradiction of them, as when a person exhibits a prejudice against a specific racial group.

prerogative: special exclusive powers, as for example, the powers that are vested only in the presidency and not in the legislature. The exclusive powers of a monarch are referred to as the royal prerogative.

president: the chief executive and head of state in a republic; an officer who presides over a legislative body. For example, the vice president of the United States is also the president of the Senate.

pressure group: the same as interest group: an organized lobby, not directly affiliated with a political party, that puts pressure on elected officials to further the interests of its members. See also interest group; lobby.

prestige: renown or reputation based on excellence of achievement, as in Nelson Mandela's prestige results from his lifelong dedication to justice in South Africa.

price controls: government control of prices to keep the cost of living down. It most usually happens in time of war, but there also instances in peacetime: in 1971 in the United States all prices were frozen for 90 days as a measure to fight inflation.

primary elections: elections held to nominate a candidate for a particular party at a forthcoming election for public office. Voters may only vote in the primary held by their own party (except in the case of a "crossover" primary). Primaries developed in the early 20th century as a way of making the selection of candidates more democratic, rather than relying on the judgments of party leaders.

prime minister: the leader of the government and head of the cabinet in parliamentary systems. The prime minister is also the leader of his or her political party.

prior restraint: the power to prevent publication of something, or to require approval of it before publication. In most cases, prior restraint is unconstitutional, prohibited under the First Amendment, which guarantees freedom of the press. There have been exceptions in cases of the publication of obscenity.

privacy: the U.S. Constitution guarantees the right to privacy, and the Privacy Act of 1974 contains measures that safeguard the individual against government misuse of personal information. The act also gives the individual the right to find out what personal information is stored by any federal agency.

private enterprise: a cornerstone of the free-market, capitalist system, the term refers to those businesses that are owned by individuals rather than some level of government.

private sector: that part of the economy that is made up of business enterprises owned by individuals or groups of individuals, and also includes consumer expenditure for goods and services. It is in contrast to the public sec-

tor. In the United States, the private sector accounts for about four-fifths of the economy.

privatization: the return of a publicly owned enterprise, whether a business or a service, to individual ownership. The opposite of nationalization. Supporters of privatization claim that private ownership in a competitive market promotes efficiency and improves service.

pro-choice: refers to those individuals and groups who support the idea that a pregnant woman has a right to choose whether she will give birth to the baby or have an abortion.

pro-life: the name given to the individuals, and the social movement that oppose abortion rights.

probe: an investigation by an appointed committee into alleged corruption or illegal activities.

productivity: output of goods and services. It can be measured in terms of labor productivity (output per worker, for example) or capital.

proletariat: the Marxist term for the working class, meaning in particular those workers who own nothing but their labor (unlike artisans, who may own their own machinery or tools).

propaganda: a Latin word that was first used by Pope Gregory XV in 1622, when he established the Sacred Congregation of Propaganda, a commission designed to spread the Catholic faith worldwide. Since then, propaganda has taken on a much broader meaning, and refers to any technique, whether in writing, speech, music, film ,or other means, that attempts to influence mass public opinion. Propaganda was used by both sides in World War I to demonize the enemy and so make the war more acceptable at home. It was refined by the totalitarian societies that emerged between the two world wars in Russia, Germany, and Italy. For example, Leni Riefenstahl's film, *Triumph of the Will*, which recorded Hitler's Nuremberg rallies, was a masterpiece of propaganda for the Nazi regime (and is still used for propagandist purposes by white supremacy groups). Propaganda is also used in democratic societies, although it is rarely called that, except by those who oppose its content or message. Any group that advocates its cause with the intent of influencing opinion might be said to be practicing propaganda, especially if its methods are blatantly biased or misrepresent facts.

proportional representation: an electoral system that awards seats in a legislature on the basis of percentages of the vote won, not on the "first past the post," winner-takes-all system that operates in the United States In other words, if a party polls a certain percentage of the vote, it is guaranteed the same percentage of seats in the legislature.

Advocates of proportional representation, which operates in some European countries, say it is a fairer system than winner-takes-all, because in the latter system a party can win a considerable number of votes and get only a paltry number of seats for its efforts. Opponents of proportional representation say it makes for weak, minority government. So many parties are represented that no single party has an overall majority, so governments tend to be made up of coalitions of many parties, which undermines their capacity for decisive, unified action and firm leadership.

protectionism: the practice of protecting domestic manufacturers from foreign competition by the imposition of tariffs and quotas on imported goods.

protectorate: a state that is not fully independent, and is under the protection of a larger state, which typically handles foreign affairs and defense.

Protestant work ethic: the concept developed by sociologist Max Weber that linked the growth of Protestantism to the rise of capitalism. Protestantism, particularly Calvinism and related Puritan doctrines, claimed that worldly success was a sure sign that a person belonged to those who were "saved." If a man prospered, it showed that he was divinely favored, so a "work ethic," emphasizing duty, hard work, and thrift, evolved. This individualistic ethic coincided with an economic phenomenon that was also individualistic: the growth of private capital, and the emergence of capitalism. Weber linked the two together as cause and effect.

protocol: a document that records the basic agreements reached in negotiations prior to the final form in which the agreements appear. Protocol also refers to the diplomatic manners that apply in ceremonial and formal business between states (seating arrangements at dinners, procedures at conferences, etc.)

providence: the beneficent operation of divine will in human affairs. Also means skill in management.

provocation: incitement; the cause of resentment.

proxy: someone who acts on behalf of another (in filling out an absentee ballot, for example).

public interest: the common good or welfare of all. In practice, it would be difficult to find complete agreement on what is in the "public interest." Once one gets beyond generalities and platitudes (it is not in the public interest to allow drunk drivers on the highway), one comes up against differences in the values people hold; sometimes by appealing to the public interest, politicians try to universalize what are merely personal beliefs and values (or the interests of a section of the community) that may not in fact find common assent. See also national interest.

public morals: commonly accepted standards of right and wrong in a community.

public opinion: a generally held attitude toward a particular issue in a community, as in public opinion favored a reform of the healthcare system. Public opinion, which can be evaluated through public opinion polls, acts as a check on what is possible for a government to do.

For example, public opinion was strongly opposed to sending American ground troops to Bosnia, which is one reason such an option was not been seriously considered during that conflict. The problem with public opinion is that on some issues, it can be easily manipulated by the mass media.

public opinion poll: a survey taken of a representative cross section of the general public to determine its views on a particular matter. Public opinion polls today are conducted for almost every conceivable topic. Although the statistical methodology that underlies polls has become increasingly sophisticated, they are of varying accuracy. Often, subtle changes in the wording of a question can produce very different results, and on some matters, people may be reluctant to be fully honest with the interviewer.

public ownership: ownership by some level of government of a business enterprise, as opposed to private ownership, in which an individual or individuals are the owners. When a government takes over the running of a business or industry, it is called nationalization.

public sector: that part of the economy that involves, or is controlled by, federal, state, or local government as opposed to the private sector. The public sector accounts for about one-fifth of the total economy of the United States.

public works: construction projects for public use, such as roads and bridges. Sometimes a government will make recourse to such measures in times of economic recession, as a form of "pump priming,"the belief that borrowing money and spending it on the wages and materials needed for public works will improve the economy. Public works were a major part of the New Deal in the 1930s, which pulled the United States out of the Great Depression.

puppet regime: a regime that is controlled by the government of another state. For example, Vichy France, which refers to the French government after France fell to the Germans in World War II, was a puppet regime, since it was subservient to Germany.

purge: to get rid of party members and other citizens who are not toeing the official party line or who are perceived as a potential or actual threat. Purges are usually associated with totalitarian societies: The Soviet Union under Josef Stalin had massive purges.

Q

quid pro quo: a Latin phrase meaning "one thing for another"; tit-for-tat. For example, during the Cuban Missile Crisis in 1962, President John Kennedy gave a personal (although not official) pledge that the crisis could be defused by a quid pro quo: If the Russians removed their missiles from Cuba, the United States would within a few months remove its own missiles from Turkey.

quisling: a traitor or collaborator, after Vidkun Quisling, a Norwegian who was a Nazi sympathizer and revealed state secrets about Norwegian defenses to German agents in 1940, six days before the German occupation of Norway began in World War II. Quisling served as a puppet prime minister during the war; he was executed in 1945.

quorum: the number of members of a legislature, or of any organization, who have to be present before official business may be conducted.

R

racism: the discrimination against a person or group solely because of their race. Any political doctrine that claims the superiority of one race over another.

radical: favoring fundamental change in society. Traditionally, radicalism has been identified with the left, but radicals can be on the right too. Some would argue that in America today, the radical agenda is that of the right rather than the left, although conservatives would say that special interest groups like feminists and gays are pushing a radical agenda. Radicalism has a long history in Europe from the 18th century on; in America it was advocated by Tom Paine.

raison d'état: French phrase meaning a "reason of state." A reason of state is something that is of vital importance to the state, which justifies the action that a state may perform in regard to it, but which usually cannot be made public at the time.

raison d'étre: a French phrase meaning the "reason for existence." The raison d'étre of the American civil rights movement was to secure equal rights for black people; the raison d'étre of the U.S. military is to defend the nation.

rank and file: in military usage, refers to the main body of soldiers in an army, excluding the officers. The term also applies to the ordinary people who form the main part of any group, as in the party rank and file supported the most conservative candidate.

ratification: the formal adoption of a treaty by a state, by a vote of its legislators. For example, the GATT treaty had to be ratified by the Senate before it became binding on the United States. The term also applies to approval by the states of constitutional amendments.

rationing: the control by a government of the right to purchase essential goods when those goods are scarce. Usually used as a wartime measure to ensure that everyone has at least a minimum supply of essentials.

raw materials: materials in their natural state that are used in manufacturing to create something else. Raw materials become of political importance when their supply is obstructed or threatened, as happened in 1990, when Iraq's invasion of Kuwait threatened to put a sizable portion of the world's oil supplies in unstable hands.

reactionary: resisting progress; wanting to go back to the old ways of doing things, even if those ways are no longer appropriate. Usually used in a derogatory sense. People rarely describe themselves as reactionaries. But someone who thinks of himself as a conservative may be a reactionary to his opponents.

Reagan Doctrine: The name given to a policy pursued by President Ronald Reagan, of American support for anti-communist revolutions. Reagan announced in his State of the Union address in 1985, "We must not break faith with those who are risking their lives on every continent ... to defy Soviet-supported aggression and secure rights which have been ours from birth. Support for freedom fighters is self-defense." The Reagan administration advocated this policy for three main reasons: Anti-communist rebels should be supported because they were fighting for an end to tyranny; if they were defeated their countries would fall under Soviet domination; and it was necessary to back anti-communist rebels because defending freedom was a long-established American tradition.

realism: that which deals with the facts, with things as they are, not with idealistic notions of what they might or should be. Practical rather than visionary or imaginative. In politics, realism is similar to realpolitik in meaning.

realpolitik: German term now used in English that means politics based on strictly practical rather than theoretical or idealistic notions, and practiced with a hard or cynical edge without any sentimental illusions. Realpolitik is power politics; the practitioner of realpolitik pursues the interests of his own group or country ruthlessly; he expects the other side to do the same.

rebellion: armed resistance to authority or government, similar to revolution.

recession: usually defined as a contraction in the gross national product that lasts six months or longer. A recession might be marked by job layoffs and high unemployment, stagnant wages, reduction in retail sales, and slowing of housing and car markets. A recession is much milder than a depression, and is often considered a normal part of the business cycle. The last recession experienced by the United States was in 1991 and 1992. Voter discontent with the economic recession was in part responsible for the defeat of George H.W. Bush in the presidential election of 1992.

redistribution: reallocation by a government of the wealth of a nation. This is usually done by taxes and welfare benefits—high taxes for the wealthy finance benefits for the poor. Redistribution is one of the central tenets of the welfare state and socialism.

referendum: a national or local vote on a single issue. Most U.S. states require referendums on amendments to the state constitution.

reform: a change or modification of that which exists.

refugee: a person who has been driven out of her homeland by war or natural disaster and who seeks safety in another country.

regime: refers to a method or system of government; is often used to refer to a military government, or to a government that lacks legitimacy.

regimentation: making people think and act in the same manner. Regimentation is a characteristic of totalitarian societies.

regionalism: policies that recognize the distinctive character of different regions in a country, and allow them some autonomy over their own affairs. Regions can be distinctive due to language, culture, and history.

rehabilitate: to restore the good name or reputation of, as in former President Richard Nixon spent many years after he resigned over the Watergate scandal trying to rehabilitate his reputation. In sociology, the term is used to refer to restoring a criminal to a condition in which he can return to society and refrain from committing further crimes.

rehabilitation: the act of rehabilitating or state of being rehabilitated. Rehabilitation is one stated purposes of the U.S. prison system, which is why in most states the system is run by the Department of Corrections. The tension between the need to punish and the need to rehabilitate has always been present in the prison system.

reparations: payments demanded of the losers in a war by the victors as compensation for damage suffered, usually to civilians and property. For example, heavy reparations were exacted by Britain, France, and the United States from Germany after World War I.

repatriation: the sending back of a person to his country of origin, as in the repatriation of prisoners of war.

representation: that which is performed by a representative, delegate, or agent, especially a representative in a legislature.

representative government: a system of government in which the people elect agents to represent them in a legislature.

repression: in politics, refers to crushing of dissent, crackdown on a rebellion, or similar, as in writers and intellectuals fought against government repression.

reprisals: retaliation taken in revenge for some injury suffered, as in, the government decided to take reprisals against the country responsible for terrorist acts.

reprieve: to delay the punishment of, particularly with reference to capital punishment; to give temporary relief to.

republic: the form of government in which ultimate power resides in the people, who elect representatives to participate in decision-making on their behalf. The head of state in a republic is usually an elected president-never a hereditary monarch. A republic is founded on the idea that every citizen has a right to participate, directly or indirectly, in affairs of state, and the general will of the people should be sovereign. The United States is a republic.

retaliation: revenge or reprisal, on a tit-for-tat basis. Retaliation is the repaying of an attack by an enemy with an second attack.

retroactive legislation: legislation that applies to a specified period before the legislation was passed, as well as to the present and future.

reverse discrimination: the term is used by those who oppose affirmative action programs, who say that the effect of such programs is no longer to end discrimination against blacks but to discriminate against whites.

revisionism: the drastic reevaluation of an accepted theory or doctrine, or historical event or person. A revisionist historian, for example, might offer a completely new view of a highly revered figure that shows her in a negative light, or vice versa. President John F. Kennedy and Sir Winston Churchill are two historical figures who have recently been subjected to revisionist treatment by historians.

revolution: a rebellion in which the government is overthrown, usually by force, and a new group of rulers takes over. Sometimes the whole social order is overthrown. Can also refer to any large-scale change in society, as in the Industrial Revolution.

revolutionary: a person who advocates or instigates a revolution; that which causes a drastic change in society.

rhetoric: the art of persuasive and impressive speaking or writing. Can also mean speech or writing that is elaborate or showy or insincere.

right to work: state laws that prohibit collective bargaining agreements between employers and unions from including the closed shop, or any clauses that mandate union membership for employees.

right-wing: on the far conservative side of the political spectrum, the opposite of left-wing. Right-wing politics usually favors: a free-enterprise system in which business is unfettered by government regulation; a strong military; does not favor much spending on social services, and is "tough on crime." The term can include authoritarians and reactionaries. See also conservative; reactionary.

riot: a violent public disturbance by (in law) three or more people.

royalty: kingship; the office of king or queen; a royal person or persons.

rubber stamp: to approve something in a routine way without giving the matter much thought.

rule of thumb: a rule about the performance of an action that is based on practical experience rather than theoretical or scientific knowledge. Any way of doing something that works, whether it is technically "correct" or not.

ruling class: the group of people, as a class, that holds power in any society.

S

sabotage: intentional obstruction or destruction of organized activity.

sacred cow: any principle or thing that is regarded as being beyond attack or untouchable. For example, in current political debate about balancing the federal budget, Social Security is considered a sacred cow, and no politician would dare risk proposing to cut it.

sanctions: punitive measures, usually taken by several countries in concert, designed to put pressure on a country to change its policy. The United Nations, for example, has put economic sanctions on Serbia in order to deter it from supporting the Bosnian Serbs in the war in Bosnia. Sanctions may be economic (banning trade, for example) or diplomatic (withdrawal of relations). They are usually imposed because a country is considered to be in violation of international law.

sanctuary: a place of refuge or protection, where a person is immune from punishment by the law.

satellite country: a country that is in effect, although not in name, controlled by another, usually larger country. Before the fall of communism, the countries of Eastern Europe were satellites of the Soviet Union, that is, they could not pursue any economic, social or foreign policies that the Soviet Union did not approve of.

scarcity: an axiom of economics is that there are not enough resources to go around. There is always a situation of scarcity in that there are fewer goods available than there are people who want them (even if there are plenty of goods, there are always people for whom the goods are too expensive). In this sense, economics is the science of the allocation of scarce resources.

secession: the act of seceding or withdrawing (from some organized entity such as a nation), as when Slovenia and Croatia decided to secede from Yugoslavia in 1991.

secondary boycott: a boycott in which one of the parties involved attempts to exert an influence over a third party. Usually this is when a labor union, in a labor dispute, attempts to put pressure on an employer who is not directly involved in the dispute, in the hope that this will eventually produce pressure on the employer directly involved. Most secondary boycotts are illegal under the Taft-Hartley Act of 1947. See also boycott.

secret ballot: a vote that takes place in secret, one where the voter does not have to disclose for whom she voted.

sect: a religious group that breaks away from a mainstream church. The Branch Davidians, for example, are

a sect. Can also refer to any group of people who have a common philosophy and common leadership.

sectarian: characteristic of a sect; devoted to a sect. The term is often used to refer to conflicts where religious allegiances play a large factor, as in sectarian violence in Northern Ireland.

secular: not connected with religion or the sacred, as, for example, a secular education would be one that is not based on religious teachings or principles.

security: something that gives protection or safety. National security, for example, relates to policies that provide for effective national defense against an external or internal threat.

sedition: plotting or rebelling against, or stirring up resistance to, a government.

segregation: the separation of people in society—in schools, the workplace, and public places—on the basis, usually, of race. The system of apartheid in South Africa was based on the principle of segregation, and segregation was the norm in the American south until the civil rights movement of the 1950s and 1960s brought it to an end.

self-determination: the principle that no nation should in peacetime interfere in the internal affairs of another nation. The principle is not always adhered to, particularly when a great power considers that a particular country falls within its sphere of influence. See also nonintervention.

separation of powers: a system of government in which the three branches of government executive, legislative, and judicial—are independent of each other. Each has powers that the others cannot impinge upon. The doctrine was first formulated in the 18th century by the French philosopher Montesquieu. The Founding Fathers thought that the separation of powers, which is the system of checks and balances that is enshrined in the constitution, was the best way to prevent tyranny.

separatism: a movement by a region or territory or ethnic group to break away from a country of which it is a part. Since the fall of communism, separatism has broken out in many regions in Europe, as groups of people with a distinct cultural identity have sought to free themselves from the larger nation that formerly contained them.

servitude: the state of being in slavery or bondage. It can also mean compulsory service or labor, such as a prisoner may undergo as punishment.

show trials: trials held in totalitarian societies that are a travesty of justice and a mockery of fair trials. The defendants are certain to be convicted, whether guilty or not, the trial merely serving as a pretext to dispose of them and a warning to others. The most notorious show trials were held in the Soviet Union under Stalin from 1935 to 1938, in which many of Stalin's fellow revolutionaries and Russian army leaders were charged with and convicted of treason. Historians doubt whether any of them were in fact guilty.

shuttle diplomacy: first used to describe former U.S. Secretary of State Henry Kissinger's personal role during the period following the 1973 Yom Kippur War when he was helping to negotiate a disengagement agreement between Israel and the defeated armies of Syria and Egypt. Shuttle diplomacy is now widely used to describe a process whereby a diplomat, envoy, or other negotiator from one nation personally travels back and forth (i.e. "shuttles") between different states that are in conflict and meets with the leaders of each side in an attempt to broker a ceasefire or forge some other diplomatic solution. Recent examples of U.S. shuttle diplomacy include the work of U.S. Middle East Coordinator Dennis Ross in 1995 and 1996, who "shuttled" many times between Israeli leaders and those in the PLO (Palestine Liberation Organization) in an attempt to further the Middle East peace process.

silk stocking district: an area where wealthy, aristocratic people live.

silver-tongued: eloquent and persuasive. Refers to politicians or others who have persuasive oratorical skills.

sit-down strike: a strike in which striking employees take possession of the employer's property (machinery, etc.) and prevent it from being used.

sitting on the fence: refusing to take a stand one way or another. Politicians are often accused of sitting on the fence when, nervous of offending powerful interests on both sides of an issue, they try to avoid stating a clear position one way or the other.

skinheads: skinheads, so called because of their shaven heads, originated in England, but are now found worldwide. Most of them are aged between 13 and 25. Many groups of skinheads espouse a crude form of nationalism, and have been responsible for thousands of incidents in Europe and North America of beatings, fire-bombings, and race-baiting. Many skinheads, who tend to hang around in small groups, are linked to other political right-wing groups, and to each other, through shared music (a form of rock called "oi," originating in England) and skinhead magazines.

social contract: the political theory that a state and its citizens have an unwritten agreement between them, a social contract into which they voluntarily enter. In the theory of Thomas Hobbes, such a social contract was necessary to lift mankind out of a primitive "state of nature" in which life was "nasty, brutish and short." Jean-Jacques Rousseau also postulated an original state of nature before there was organized government, but for him it was an idyllic, carefree condition. The state became necessary as individual inequalities developed, but the only social contract that would not corrupt mankind was one based on direct democracy in which the general will was the basis for law.

social Darwinism: the evolutionary theories of the natural historian Charles Darwin, especially the idea of the "survival of the fittest" and "natural selection," applied to the sphere of human society. Social Darwinists, who in America were associated with the British philosopher Herbert Spencer, advocated an extreme form of *laissez-faire* economics, and supported individualism to the extent of opposing compulsory free education.

social justice: a situation in which all individuals and groups in a society are treated fairly and equally, regardless of race, gender, or any other factor that could be used to create situations of injustice.

Social Security: the Social Security Act was passed in 1935; it established a national social security service, which included benefits for the elderly, unemployed, and aid to the states for the care of the old, dependent children, and the blind. At first, benefits were for private sector employees only, but in the 1950s Social Security was extended to self-employed, state, and local employees, household and farm workers, and members of the armed forces and clergy. Disability insurance was added in 1954. In 1965, Medicare, which provided health insurance for those over 65, and Medicaid, which provided healthcare for the poor, were added. In 1972, a law was enacted that linked Social Security benefits to the rise in the cost of living. The result has been that over the last two decades Social Security has taken up more and more of the federal budget, but current proposals to balance the budget leave Social Security mostly exempt from cuts, the exceptions being Medicare and Medicaid.

social services: services provided by the government to improve social welfare for those who need it, such as the elderly, the poor, the disabled, and children. Services might include insurance, subsidized housing, healthcare, family allowances, and food subsidies.

social stratification: the layering of a society, in the sense that some people will be above others in the social scale, in terms of class, income, education, etc. For example, societies in which a class system is strongly present can be said to be highly stratified.

social welfare: the well being of the community. Social welfare is an intangible; it is hard to quantify. It cannot be measured in terms to the quantity of goods and services available, because this is to equate welfare with material abundance. Social welfare is not the same as standard of living. The utility of something, the ability of a good or service to satisfy human want, will vary from person to person.

A more accurate evaluation of social welfare would have to be something like a quality of life index and include such things as environmental factors (quality of air and water), social indicators like levels of crime and drug abuse, availability of essential services like education and hospitals, and other nonmaterial factors like religious faith. The more diverse the community the harder it is to evaluate social welfare, since different groups may place widely varying values on different aspects of community life.

socialism: a political system in which the means of production, distribution, and exchange is mostly owned by the state, and used, at least in theory, on behalf of the people. The idea behind socialism is that the capitalist system is intrinsically unfair because it concentrates wealth in a few hands and does nothing to safeguard the overall welfare of the majority. Under socialism, the state redistributes the wealth of society in a more equitable way, with the ideal of social justice replacing the profit motive. Socialism as a system is anathema to most Americans, although many social welfare pro-

grams like Medicare and Medicaid (once derided by their opponents as "socialized medicine") and Social Security are socialistic in effect, since they are controlled by the government and effect a measure of income redistribution that could not happen if market forces were the sole factor in the economic life of society. See also communism; Leninism; Marxism.

socialization: the process by which individuals adapt themselves to the norms, values, and common needs of the society.

society: any group of people who collectively make up an interdependent community.

sovereignty: independent political authority, as in those who oppose their country joining the European Community fear the loss of national sovereignty to a central, European body. Also means the quality of being supreme in power or authority, as in sovereignty was vested in the National Assembly.

speculation: the practice of buying something (usually securities, commodities, or foreign exchange) at a fairly high risk for the purpose of selling the same thing later for an above-average return.

sphere of influence: areas in which another state wishes to exert its influence so that no hostile government or ideology can take root there. For example, the United States regards Central America as coming within its sphere of influence, which accounts for its attempt during the 1980s to overthrow the communist Sandinista regime in Nicaragua. Before its demise in 1991, the Soviet Union regarded Eastern Europe as its sphere of influence, which is why it felt justified in invading Czechoslovakia in 1968 when that country appeared to be adopting more liberal policies. By and large, each superpower accepted the validity of each other's clearly defined spheres of influence, although there were many areas where spheres of influence were disputed.

stagflation: in economics, high unemployment and inflation taking place at the same time.

standing orders: the rules for parliamentary procedures that apply to all sessions until changed or repealed.

stare decisis: a Latin phrase that means "let the decision stand." It refers to a legal doctrine that emphasizes the binding force of precedents. If there is a legal precedent, that precedent should be followed in all similar cases.

START: Strategic Arms Reduction Treaty I was signed in 1991 by the United States and the Soviet Union. It provided for a one-third reduction of nuclear missiles, over a seven-year period. It was the first treaty to mandate reductions in nuclear weapons by the superpowers. START II was signed by the United States and Russia in 1993. It called for both sides to reduce their long-range nuclear weapons to one-third of then current levels within 10 years, and to eliminate land-based multiple warhead missiles.

states' rights: in the U.S. system of government, the rights that are given to the states rather than the federal government.

Often the term is used by people who feel that federal policies are interfering with their own rights. Opponents of the civil rights movement in the 1950s and 1960s, for example, invoked the idea of states' rights to block federally mandated desegregation.

statesman: a person who shows great wisdom and skill in the handling of the affairs of government. Being a political leader does not of itself make a statesman, and few would attain to such a designation without internationally acknowledged wisdom in foreign affairs. Statesmen are often perceived as being above the partisan fray of politics, able to discern, and having the courage to articulate, what the real long-term interests of a country are. See also leadership.

status: condition or position with regard to law, as in his status was that of a legal alien; position or rank, as in his high status in the academic world was unchallenged.

status quo: the existing state of affairs, at any given time, as in people opposed to the proposed changes fought to maintain the status quo.

statute: in the broad sense, any law or rule. More specifically, a statute is a law enacted by legislation.

steering committee: a committee within a legislative body that facilitates the passage of legislation, by arranging the order of business, mobilizing votes, etc.

stimulus: an aspect of fiscal policy, in which a government creates more spending power in the economy by reducing taxes or increasing its spending.

straddle the fence: to adopt an ambiguous position on an issue, in the hope of winning support from both sides.

Strategic Defense Initiative: also known as SDI and Star Wars. SDI was announced by President Ronald Reagan in 1983. It was designed to create a completely new form of national defense through the creation of a defensive shield around the United States, which would allow incoming nuclear weapons to be destroyed by laser guns before they hit their target. Reagan believed that SDI could put an end to nuclear weapons by making them useless. However, many experts were certain that SDI could not possibly work at all; others said it could not protect the entire U.S. population and would merely force the Soviet Union to aim more nuclear warheads at the United States. But in spite of these concerns, the Reagan administration committed large resources to the development of SDI, and it was an important factor in negotiations with the Soviet Union during Reagan's two terms of office. (The Soviets opposed the development of SDI.) The administration of President George H. W. Bush was less enthusiastic about Star Wars, and the idea gradually was dropped, especially since the end of the Cold War made a nuclear attack on the United States less likely. It was revived in 1995 by Republican senators who say that the threat of nuclear proliferation is such that it warrants more research into the development of a land-based missile defense system.

strategy: the science of planning military operations, as in U.S. strategy during the Persian Gulf War. Also used more loosely to refer to any form of planning for action, as in the president's strategy for the election campaign.

straw vote: an unofficial vote that is used to either to predict the outcome of an official vote or to gauge the relative strength of candidates for office in a future election. For example, long before the Republican caucuses took place in 1996 for the selection of a nominee for president, straw votes had to be conducted in various states. A good showing in a straw vote can give a candidate a boost, but does not necessarily predict later success.

strawman: a weak argument or opposing point of view that is set up by a speaker so that he can knock it down easily and appear to win an argument or debate. Sometimes a strawman may represent an exaggerated position that none of the speaker's opponents is in fact advocating—but the speaker hopes that his listeners do not know this.

strike: the withdrawal of labor by a group of workers, acting collectively, in order to achieve some goal such as higher wages or better working conditions, or to resist management proposals for changes that they oppose.

structural unemployment: job losses caused by major shifts in the economic environment, and which are hard to alleviate. For example, if the coal mining industry in a country is in a long-term decline, it will create structural unemployment. A body of workers who are not easily retrained, centered in particular areas, where new industry cannot be quickly introduced. Structural unemployment is distinguished from short-term fluctuations in unemployment caused by workers moving between jobs.

subpoena: a writ ordering a person to appear in court.

subsidy: a grant made out of public funds to support some private enterprise that is considered to promote the public good. A current debate in the United States is whether the government should continue to subsidize the arts, through organizations such as the National Endowment for the Humanities.

subsistence: means of support or livelihood; means of living. People who have enough only to cover basic needs are considered to be living on a subsistence income.

subversive: tending to undermine, disrupt, or overthrow something already established, as in lawlessness and violence are subversive of public order. A subversive individual or group is one that tries to undermine the existing form of society or government.

succession: the assumption of an office, after the previous incumbent's period of authority expires, for whatever reason (incapacity, resignation, death). Also refers to the order in which persons will replace a king or president if those figures are no longer able to perform their functions.

For example, in the United States, the vice president is first in the line of succession to the presidency; the Speaker of the House of Representatives is second. In Britain, Prince Charles is first in the line of succession to the throne.

suffrage: the right to vote. Democratic societies are characterized by universal suffrage, which means that all adult citizens have the right to vote. The United States has had universal suffrage since 1920, when the Nineteenth Amendment was enacted, which extended the right to vote to women.

summit diplomacy: meetings between the heads of governments of major powers who discuss the relations between them. During the Cold War, summit diplomacy developed as a major means by which the United States and the Soviet Union tested each other and tried to reach a rapprochement, or at least understanding of each other's position, on a variety of issues. Summit meetings were dramatic and comparatively infrequent events, and the hopes and fears of the world often seemed to hang on the outcome. Since the end of the Cold War, the importance of such summit meetings have vastly decreased. When President Bill Clinton met with Russia's President Boris Yeltsin, for example, it seemed only a routine matter.

superpower: a superpower is a state that is powerful economically and militarily, that can act influentially over most of the globe, that can influence the behavior of other states and maintain that influence for an extended period of time, and that can also take effective action on its own without needing the consent of other nations. In the post-World War II era, there have been two superpowers, the United States and the Soviet Union. Since the demise of the Soviet Union in 1991, the United States is the only state that could be called a superpower. However, as the 1990s showed, even a superpower faces restrictions on what it can do to accomplish its goals. The United States felt compelled to assemble an international coalition to fight the Persian Gulf War in 1991, rather than go it alone. It has not even been able to impose its will on its own European allies. This is partly due to the end of the Cold War: now there is no longer a Soviet Union as a common enemy. More nations feel free to pursue their own course, without reference to Washington. And in spite of the fact that the United States is the sole standing superpower, the political world is now multipolar rather than bipolar: other powers are on the rise, such as Japan, China, and Germany, whose status as economic superpowers gives them an increasing influence in world affairs.

supply and demand: the economic mechanism that operates in a free-enterprise system and that is responsible for prices, based on the assumption that sellers want to sell at the highest price they can, and buyers want to buy at the lowest possible price. If something is in heavy demand but short supply, prices will go up, and vice versa. A rise in price will reduce demand and expand supply, and vice versa (i.e., a fall in price will expand demand and contract supply).

surplus value: the difference between a worker's wages and the value of the goods he produces. According to Karl Marx, surplus value was a measure of the exploitation of the worker by the capitalist, i.e., the worker contributed more than he received, and the profit went to the employer.

symposium: a conference organized for the discussion of a particular subject.

syndicalism: a form of socialism that aimed to combine public ownership of the means of production with the elimination of central government. This was to be accomplished through the labor movement, which would overthrow the government; labor unions would then become the fundamental element in the new society. Syndicalism originated in Europe during the 1890s and had some influence up to World War I; the movement petered out in the 1920s.

syndicate: an association between two or more companies to carry out a joint enterprise that requires large capital, often to establish control of a particular market.

synthesis: the putting of two or more things together to create a whole, as in the bill before Congress represented a synthesis of many different proposals.

T

tariff: a surcharge placed on imported goods and services. The purpose of a tariff is to protect domestic products from foreign competition.

taxation: a compulsory payment levied by a government on its citizens to finance its expenditure. It can be levied either on income or as a surcharge on prices (sales tax). Income tax is a direct tax (everyone who earns a certain amount has to pay it); a sales tax is an indirect tax (affects only those who buy the taxed goods).

territorial waters: waters over which the jurisdiction of the adjacent state is extended, including seas, bays, rivers, and lakes.

terrorism: the pursuit of a political aim by means of violence and intimidation applied to citizens rather than a military enemy. Modern terrorism emerged in 1968 with the hijacking of an Israeli El Al plane by Palestinians in Algeria. Terrorism has since become one of the most frequent and powerful means of waging war.

terrorist: a person who advocates or takes part in terrorist acts. However, the definition is not as simple as it looks. One man's terrorist is another man's freedom fighter, and yesterday's terrorists have a habit of becoming today's statesmen. Robert Mugabe, president of Zimbabwe, led a terrorist campaign to establish black majority rule in what was then white-ruled Rhodesia in the 1970s. Menachem Begin, prime minister of Israel from 1977 to 1983, had been a terrorist seeking to expel the British from Palestine in the late 1940s. Yassir Arafat, who was behind numerous acts of terrorism committed by the Palestine Liberation Organization in the 1970s and 1980s, was the recipient of a Nobel Peace Prize for his efforts in reaching a peace agreement with Israel.

theocracy: a state or government that is run by priests or clergy. A recent example of a theocracy is Iran immediately after the overthrow of the shah in 1979, when the Ayatollah Khomeini gained power. Theocracies are becoming more common as Islamic fundamentalism grows in strength.

third party: can refer either to a minor party, such as the Socialist Party or the Libertarian Party, whose support is so small that it has no significant effect on a national election, or to a party that presents a viable alternative to the Republicans or Democrats. During the late 18th and 19th centuries, there were a number of powerful third parties in American politics. The Greenback Party, the Union Labor Party, and the People's Party, for example, forced the major parties to pass significant anti-monopoly and labor legislation. In 1912, Theodore Roosevelt's Progressive Party split the Republican vote and helped the Democrats win back the White House. In 1996, Ross Perot's Reform Party won 7 percent of the vote in the presidential election. However, in modern times third parties have had no success in breaking the two-party system, and often complain that restrictive ballot access requirements in many states are designed by the major parties to keep them off the ballot.

third world: the impoverished or developing countries of the world, made up mostly of Asian, African, and South American countries.

torture: the deliberate infliction of extreme physical pain. For much of Western history, torture has been an accepted way of eliciting information or compelling a confession, or simply as punishment.

total war: a war that threatens the very existence of a nation, and in which every available weapon is used. Also means a war in which all the economic resources of the nation are mobilized as part of the war effort. This concept was developed in the 19th century; it applies to both world wars. Total war, in the sense of using all available weapons, has been virtually unthinkable in the nuclear age, as it would result in the destruction of both sides.

totalitarianism: a system of government where the ruling authority extends its power over all aspects of society and regulates every aspect of life. Totalitarian states maintain their existence by a combination of methods, including secret police, the banning of opposition, and control of the media. Everything in society is shaped to serve the ends of the totalitarian state. Education, for example, is rigidly controlled so as to socialize youth into the desired political attitudes. Nazi Germany and the Soviet Union were examples of totalitarian states.

toxic wastes: waste matter produced in industrial or technological processes that is harmful to humans and the environment.

trade union: an organization of workers who do similar jobs. A trade union exists to take collective action on behalf of its members in negotiations with employers over wages, working conditions, etc. Trade unions are usually composed of skilled or semiskilled workers who have learned a craft.

treason: betrayal of one's country. In the U.S. Constitution, treason is defined as making war against the United States (by a U.S. citizen) or as giving aid and comfort to the enemy.

treaty: a formal, binding international agreement that may cover issues including the regulation of trade, the making of peace, or the forming of military alliances. In the United States, all treaties proposed by the executive branch and negotiated with a foreign country must be approved by a two-thirds majority in the Senate.

tribunal: a court or other body that is empowered to hand down decisions.

truce: a temporary or short-term cessation of hostilities.

Truman Doctrine: a policy enunciated in March 1947 by President Harry Truman, when he pledged U.S. support for "free peoples who are resisting attempted subjugation by armed minorities or by outside pressures." If America failed to do this, said Truman, world peace would be endangered. The speech referred in particular to U.S. aid to Greece and Turkey.

trusteeship: a commission by the United Nations to a country to administer a region, which is known as the trust territory. The trust territory is not a colony—the idea is that it should be developed so that it can eventually assume complete independence. For example, the Trust Territory of the Pacific Islands, administered by the United States.

tyranny: despotism; unjust, oppressive rule. James Madison defined the recipe for tyranny as the accumulation of all power and authority, including executive, legislative. and judiciary in the same hands. The U.S. Constitution contains checks and balances to ensure that the conditions for the creation of a tyranny cannot appear.

U

underground: political or military opposition that cannot come out in the open. Often happens in times of war, when a country is occupied by an enemy, as in the French underground during World War II.

unemployment rate: the measure of how many unemployed people as a percentage of the workforce.

unilateral: involving one side only. Thus, when Zimbabwe (then known as Rhodesia) made a unilateral Declaration of Independence from Britain in 1965, it meant that the declaration was made by only one party out of the two parties involved, i.e., Britain was not part of the agreement.

united front: refers to a situation in which several groups or individuals who have some differences of opinion patch them up in order to deal with others, as in the union leaders put aside their differences and presented a united front to the employers.

United Nations (UN): The UN was established after World War II to solve international disputes that threaten world peace and security. The UN also works to protect human rights; promote the protection of the environment; help the advancement of women and the rights of children; and fight epidemics, famine, poverty. It assists refugees, delivers food aid, combats disease, and helps expand food production; makes loans to developing countries and helps stabilize financial markets. The UN has six main organs, all based in New York, except the International Court of Justice, which is located at The Hague, Netherlands. The General Assembly is the main deliberative body. All 185 member states are represented in it, and each has one vote. Decisions are usually taken by simple majority. Important questions require a two-thirds majority. The 15-member Security Council has primary responsibility for maintaining peace and security.

United Nations Children's Fund (UNICEF): provides aid and development assistance to children and mothers in developing countries. Headquarters is in New York.

United Nations Commission on Human Rights (UNCHR): established by the UN Economic and Social Council to promote human rights worldwide; tries to solve problems around such issues as the death penalty, freedom of religious beliefs, and racial discrimination. Headquarters is in Geneva, Switzerland.

United Nations Economic and Social Council (ECOSOC): aims to promote higher standards of living, full employment, and economic and social progress in member nations. It issues reports and makes recommendations on a wide range of economic, social and cultural matters.

United Nations Educational, Scientific and Cultural Organization (UNESCO): promotes collaboration among nations through education, science, and culture.

United Nations Secretariat: the office of the secretary-general of the United Nations, the chief administrative officer of the UN. He has the power to bring to the attention of the Security Council any matter that he considers a threat to world peace.

universalism: the theological doctrine that all people, rather than the selected few who belong to a particular faith, will eventually find salvation in God.

usurpation: the seizing of something, usually a position of power or authority, that is not rightfully one's own.

When, for example, the military in Haiti overthrew the democratically elected government of Jean-Bertrand Aristide in 1991, it was an act of usurpation.

usury: the loaning of money at an excessively high rate of interest.

utilitarianism: a political philosophy developed in England in the 19th century, by thinkers such as Jeremy Bentham and John Stuart Mill, which says that the duty of government is to promote "the greatest good for the greatest number." This could be accomplished by actions that promoted pleasure and avoided pain (these being the two things that human were ruled by). Pleasure was not defined in hedonistic terms; being of service to others, for example, could be classified as a "pleasure."

utility: in economics, the ability of a good or service to satisfy human want. It is therefore a psychological thing and cannot be measured in absolute terms. Goods that have utility for one person may not for another. And goods that have utility for one person at a certain time may not at another time.

utopia: an imaginary place in which the social and political system is perfect: all citizens have all their needs met in an ideal way. The term refers to a book, *Utopia*, by Thomas Moore, published in 1516, although other writers, from Plato on, have described the ideal society. Utopia can also refer to any scheme designed to create an ideal society, and it can sometimes be used to imply that something is well-intentioned but completely impractical.

V

vanguard: the foremost part of an advancing army. Used figuratively to refer to being opinion leaders. The Republicans might claim, for example, that since they captured the House and Senate in the elections of November 1994, they are in the vanguard of social policy and change.

Vatican Councils: major pronouncements of the Roman Catholic Church about the nature of the faith. The first Vatican Council was held in 1869 and 1870. it declared the personal infallibility of the pope when speaking *ex cathedra* to be a dogma of the church. The second Vatican Council, 1962 to 1965, was notable for its ecumenical and liberalizing spirit. It made a more positive evaluation of the value of other faiths: they could also be channels for God's grace; salvation could be attained by non-Christians.

vendetta: prolonged, bitter hostility.

veto: to cancel or make void (legislation, etc.) The president of the United States has a veto power over legislation that Congress passes to him for signing.

vicious circle: a situation in which the solution to one problem merely gives rise to another problem, and the solution to that problem leads back to the first problem, often in a more acute form.

vigilante: self-appointed individual or group that takes on the responsibility for maintaining law and order in a community, when the normal channels have become ineffective. Vigilante groups have been a feature of life in the troubled area of Northern Ireland, for example, for over 20 years.

visa: an endorsement on a passport that shows that the holder has a legal right to enter a specific country.

vox populi: a Latin expression meaning "voice of the people," with implications that popular sentiment is theoretically at one with the divine will. It was usually thought to have occurred during times of crisis when the voice or opinion of the people was made manifest or became evident; monarchs have been dethroned, governments toppled, and revolutions started in the name of vox populi.

W

war crime: a crime against humanity, such as deliberate killing of civilians or mistreatment of prisoners, committed during a war. The most notorious example of war crimes in recent history is those committed by Nazi Germany during World War II. In 1946, at the Nuremberg Tribunal in Nuremberg, Germany, 24 Nazis were tried by the allied powers for war crimes. Nineteen were found guilty and 12 were sentenced to death.

ward heeler: a low-level political functionary in a ward. A ward is a district of a city or town for administrative or voting purposes. "Heeler" is an allusion to a dog that obeys its master when called to heel. A ward heeler might solicit votes for his party or perform small tasks for his political bosses. The term is used contemptuously, implying that the ward heeler is a subservient hanger-on of politicians more important than himself.

warhead: the head, or front section, of a weapon such as a torpedo, rocket, or other projectile that contains the explosive charge, as in nuclear warhead.

Warsaw Pact: the military organization of Eastern Europe signed in Warsaw, Poland, in 1955, by Albania, Bulgaria, Czechoslovakia, East Germany, Hungary, Poland, Romania and the Soviet Union. It was a communist counterpart to the North Atlantic Treaty Organization (NATO). Warsaw Pact members were bound to assist each other in the event of an attack on any one of them. Albania withdrew in 1961. The Warsaw Pact collaborated in the invasion of Czechoslovakia in 1968—the only time it took military action. The pact was ended as a military alliance in 1991, when the demise of communism and the end of the Cold War made it superfluous.

ways and means: the financial resources of a government. For example, the Ways and Means Committee of the House of Representatives, which considers everything relating to the raising of revenues.

welfare: public financial or other assistance (food stamps, for example) given to people who meet certain standards of eligibility regarding income and assets.

welfare state: a state that supplies a large number of social services to its citizens, as a right, without requiring them to pay directly for them.

Westernization: the adoption of Western habits, customs, forms of government, and social organization, often applied to third world countries seeking to modernize and industrialize their economies. Westernization can have a backlash, however, if it is done too quickly or without respect for local culture. A classic example is Iran under the shah, who from 1953 to the 1970s, tried to Westernize the country but only succeeded in igniting Islamic traditionalists against him.

whip: the term is derived from fox-hunting in England. It was adopted by political parties in the British Parliament, and the United States borrowed the term from the British. A whip is the legislator responsible for enforcing party discipline or strategy; he assists the leadership in managing its legislative agenda. Part of the whip's responsibility is to keep track of legislation and try to ensure that all members are present when an important vote takes place, or if not, that a "pairing" arrangement is made with the opposing party. The majority whip is the whip of the party that controls the House or Senate; after the majority leader, he is the senior party figure in each house. The same applies to the minority whip.

women's movement: the modern women's movement began in the 1960s, when it was known as the women's liberation movement. It arose out of the civil rights movement, when women began to perceive that like an oppressed minority, they too needed to take radical action to secure their rights. The National Organization for Women (NOW) was created in 1966, and remains one of the spearheads of the women's movement, which attempts to promote the progress of women in all spheres of life.

working class: industrial workers, and others, skilled and unskilled, who work in manual occupations, as a class. In Marxist thought, the working class is referred to as the proletariat.

world government: the goal of some internationalists for centuries. William Penn, the founder of the Quakers, had a plan for a world government, as did the 18th-century German philosopher Immanuel Kant. The world rule of the proletariat also plays a part in Marxism.

But the idea of one world government has never been a serious possibility; the strength of nationalism and the rivalry of different economic and social systems would seem to make it impractical. In spite of this, conspiracy theorists today believe that a plot to create a world government, involving the United Nations, international bankers, and sections of the U.S. government, is well advanced.

white elephant: something that is of little use or profit, especially something that is maintained at great expense. Some in Britain argue that the Falkland Islands, which Britain retained possession of after a war with Argentina in 1982, are a white elephant, because they cost a huge amount of money to defend, and yet they are very small and have only a tiny population.

World Bank: formally known as the International Bank for Reconstruction and Development; its purpose is to promote economic and social progress in developing nations by raising productivity; it lends funds, provides advice, stimulates outside investments. World Bank funds come primarily from money raised in the world capital markets. Headquarters is in Washington, D.C.

World Health Organization (WHO): international health agency of the UN that promotes the highest level of healthcare for all peoples. WHO emphasizes healthcare for developing nations by helping them develop new technologies and utilize existing ones. Headquarters is in Geneva, Switzerland.

X, Y, Z
xenophobia: irrational dislike of foreign people and foreign things.

yardstick: standard of comparison. For example, in the debate over healthcare reform in 1993, the Canadian healthcare system was sometimes used as a yardstick to evaluate the American system and proposed reforms.

zealot: fanatic; a person who is extremely partisan. Adolf Hitler was a zealot, so also, by most people's reckoning, was the Ayatollah Khomeini of Iran.

zeitgeist: A German word now commonly used in English. It means literally spirit of the times, and refers to prevailing currents of thought and feeling in a society. For example, an aspect of the zeitgeist of America in the 1970s was disillusionment with and distrust of political institutions.

zero-sum: a situation in which a gain for one must result in a loss for another.

Zionism: a movement that began in the 19th century for the return of the Jews to Palestine. Started by a Hungarian Jew, Theodor Herzl, Zionism was, and is, held together by the belief that Jews worldwide are all descendants of the ancient Hebrews, and therefore share a common nationality by virtue of their link to the historical kingdom of Israel.

STEVE POSNER
IAMERICAN SPIRIT POLITICAL DICTIONARY
WWW.IAMERICANSPIRIT.COM

Index

PHOTO CREDITS

Page 9: Georgians For Choice 19: www.civil-war.net; 27: Library of Congress; 44: www.noelcollection.org; 50: www.alchemist-light.com; 62: www.acusd.edu; 69: Library of Congress; 71: wwww.sweetmarias.com; 78: www.aloveleyworld.com; 88: Library of Congress (2); 90: Lyndon B. Johnson Library; 99: www.vulturebooz.de/marx; 120: U.S. Department of Corrections; 129: News Guangdong; 132: Arkansas State University News; 138: Library of Congress; 155: Greenpeace; 158: www.mek.iif.hu/porta; 168: Massachusetts Institute of Technology; 179: Library of Congress; 184: World Peace Forum 2003; 188: University of Texas Library (2); 190: Kommunistische Partei Deutschlands Bildergallerie (2); 194: www.infoshop.org/portraits; 202, 203: Greenpeace; 211: Library of Congress; 214: White House Press Office; 219: www.modertimes.com; 222: United Nations; 241: www.4dw.net/royalark; 245: Partito Communista Rifondazione; 249: Library of Congress; 254: United States Senate; 259: Library of Congress; 270: European Union mediatheque; 274: Liberal Party of Canada; 281: Library of Congress; 287: www.constitution.org; 289: Social Security Administration; 295, 298: Library of Congress; 306: WCPO television studio; 314: Library of Congress; 326: www.irs.princeton.edu; 333: United States Senate; 343, 350: Library of Congress; www.aryanunity.com; 356, 359: Library of Congress; 361, 362: www.indymedia.org.uk; 372, 374: Library of Congress; 379: University of Nevada; 392: Library of Congress; 404: Socialist Party USA; 406:www.marxists.org; 420, 421: Library of Congress (4); 437: www.michaelariens.com; 439: www.uscourts.gov; 453: www.cbv.ns.ca; 481: www.nofear.org Copyright John Filo; 496: Library of Congress; 505: www.landscapedecor.com; 512: Library of Congress; 519: PROLIFE Minnesota Billboard Archives; 525;www.fernandez-gamio.de; 530: Photo Disc, Inc.; 537: www.joergl.at; 548: www2:sju.edu; 553 Library of Congress; 564: www.usofficepristina.rpo.at; 570: www.pomexport.com; www3:sympatico.ca; 582: www.worldhistory.com; 587: Churchill Portrait by Yousuf Karsh www.aristos.org; Washington, D.C. Museum; 599: Conservative Party, United Kingdom; 611: Library of Congress; 620: National Aeronaatics and Space Administration; 621: www.mlchapel.org; 636: National Archives and Records Administration; 644, 648: Library of Congress; 656: http://perso.club-internet.fr; 657: http://mairie.wanadoo.fr/mairie.montcarnet; 676, 685: Library of Congress; 697: www.cse.unl.edu; 704: www.globalsecurity.org (U.S. Department of Defense - Centcom); 706: www.ucd.ie/archives; 711: Library of Congress; 713: http://eree.hu; www.earthstation1.com; 731, 736: Library of Congress; 741: Chicago Historical Society; 750: Library of Congress; 757: National Archives and Records Administration; 767: www.cs.nott.ac.uk; 775: U.S. Army; 779: Anti-Defamation League; 781: http://chasholloway.com; 796: www.townhall.com; 797: North Atlantic Treaty Organization; 798: www.GoTricities.com; 801: United Nations; 803: www.politicallibrary.org; 807: www.frittogvil.no; 814: www.lazer-103.com; 816: http://galeon.hispavista.com; 824: Library of Congress (2); 834: Library of Congress; 844: www.harriscountygop.com; 845: Library of Congress; 851: avax.balthost.info/ promo_images; 855: Saudi Arabian Information Resource; 861: www.middlepassgemuseum.com; 863: Photo Disk, Inc.; 877:www.indianer-welt.de; 879: www.smu.edu; 886: Photo Disk. Inc.; 890: Peter Ericson; 893: U.S. Senate; 903: wwwsasin.chula.ac.th; 904: www.arrakeen.ch; 918: www.gla55pak.com; 923: Library of Congress; 925: www.reagan.dk; 928: Library of Congress; 929: University of Chicago.

SETON HALL UNIVERSITY

University Libraries So. Orange, NJ 07079-26